The Writer's
HANDBOOK
2005

The Writer's HANDBOOK 2005

Preface by **WILLIAM ZINSSER**

Edited by **ELFRIEDA ABBE**

The Writer Books

The Writer Books is an imprint of Kalmbach Trade Press, a division of Kalmbach Publishing Co. These books are distributed to the book trade by Watson-Guptill. For all other inquiries, including individual orders or details on special quantity discounts for groups or conferences, contact:

Kalmbach Publishing Co.
21027 Crossroads Circle
Waukesha, WI 53187
(800) 533-6644

Visit our website at www.writermag.com to learn more about *The Writer* magazine, view current articles, or order copies of *The Writer's Handbook*.
Secure online ordering available.

ISBN 0-87116-212-1
Printed in the United States of America
04 05 06 07 08 09 10 11 12 13   10 9 8 7 6 5 4 3 2 1

Publisher's Cataloging-in-Publication Data
(Prepared by The Donohue Group, Inc.)

The writer's handbook. -- [1936-

   v. ; cm.
   Annual
   Editors: 1936, S. G. Houghton, U. G. Olsen.--1941- A. S. Burack.--2001- E. Abbe.
   ISSN: 0084-2710

1. Authorship--Handbooks, manuals, etc.   2. Publishers and publishing. I. Houghton, Samuel G. (Samuel Gilbert), 1902-1975.   II. Olsen, Udia G. III. Burack, A. S. (Abraham Saul), 1908-   IV. Abbe, Elfrieda.

PN137 .W73
029.6
                                      36028596

Project Editor: Philip Martin
Assistant Editor: Amy Glander

Art Director: Lil Weber
Cover Design: Mike Soliday

Acknowledgments

Thanks to Philip Martin, project editor, for his assistance in assembling this volume. Thanks also to many others at Kalmbach Publishing Co. who helped with the preparation of this 69th edition, including Jeff Reich, Ron Kovach, and Beth Bakkum of *The Writer* magazine staff. Thanks also to Kristin Schneidler for her copy-editing—and especially to Lesley Weiss and Amy Glander, who worked long and hard to verify information in the market-listings section.

We all know that the publishing world is in a constant state of flux, and some information in the market listings may have changed since last updated. We would greatly appreciate any feedback from readers, with corrections or comments on how to improve the usefulness of the information presented. Kalmbach Publishing Co. has a tradition of outstanding customer service, and we look forward to continuing to improve and refine this long-standing resource to writers in coming years by incorporating your feedback.

If you know of new or overlooked markets of significance to aspiring writers that you wish to recommend for future volumes, please forward those ideas to Amy Glander, The Writer Books, 21027 Crossroads Circle, P.O. Box 1612, Waukesha, WI 53187-1612, or send an e-mail to the attention of aglander@kalmbach.com.

CONTENTS

ARTICLES

Success in Freelance Writing

Get Your Book Published

The Craft of Writing

MARKETS

Nonfiction Magazines

PREFACE

by William Zinsser

In the early 1990s I wrote a number of articles for *Travel Holiday* magazine. I liked the magazine partly because it sent me to interesting places all over the world. But mainly I liked to write for it because its standards were so high. Its editor, Maggie Simmons, not only hired good writers like Diane Ackerman and Saul Bellow. She also never forgot that she was running a school, and under her mentorship her young staff of editorial assistants, copy editors, researchers, photographers, and graphic designers grew steadily in the mastery of their craft and in the pride of doing it well. I always valued working with them as we shepherded my pieces into print.

One Monday in 1996 that small world came to an end. The morning newspapers announced that a media conglomerate had bought *Travel Holiday*. The new owners told most of the staff to clean out their desks and be gone by Friday. Thrown out on the street, the young men and women felt betrayed and bewildered. They were also a family in a state of bereavement, and Simmons invited them to meet in her apartment to sort out their feelings and start the healing process. She asked me if I would talk to them out of my longer experience in a profession that has never been accused of sentimentality in its treatment of the help.

I began by recalling that my boyhood dream had been to get a job on the *New York Herald Tribune*, which was then the best-written and best-edited paper in the country. That dream came true in 1946, when I came home from World War II. The older editors on the *Trib* who made us rewrite what we had already rewritten were custodians of the craft of journalism. Theirs were the values that I learned when I was young and that I've tried to apply to my work ever since. It was the best job in the world, and I expected to stay there forever.

But the paper began to lose money and to lose advertising and readers. To try to get new readers, the owners cheapened their paper with gimmicks—a process that only accelerated its long, slow decline. Eventually I realized that the *Trib*'s standards were no longer *my* standards, and one day in 1959 I just quit. The best job in the world lasted only 13 years.

When I called my wife, she asked, "What are you going to do now?" I thought it was a fair question; by then we had a one-year-old daughter. I said, "I guess I'm a freelance writer." And that's what I was for the next 11 years. At that time it was still possible for a writer in America to be a generalist; general-interest magazines hadn't yet lost their advertising to television. At first I wrote mainly for the *Saturday Evening Post*. Then the *Post* died. Then I wrote a column for *Look*, and *Look* died. (Meanwhile, the *Herald Tribune* also died.) Then I got a contract to write for *Life*, and a few years later *Life* died. My past is littered with the bones of dead publications. But all those deaths taught me a valuable lesson: writers should live in the expectation that they will wake up some morning and find that their bosses have left in the night.

I told the young men and women in Simmons' apartment that publishers and editors will come and go, but you have to live with your values forever. Don't ever lower those standards. Ultimately, they are your only security. Don't waste your energy resenting the buccaneers who buy and sell magazines. There will always be plenty of other magazines. Get on with your life.

And that's what they did. With grace and courage the orphans of the old *Travel Holiday* picked up the broken pieces of their careers and went about finding jobs at other publications. Often they found better jobs because they were now better at what they did.

This *Writer's Handbook* is a rich resource for anyone trying to survive as a writer—one of life's toughest gigs. "Thousands of markets for your work," it says on the cover, and that's a lot of markets. Somewhere in these encyclopedic pages you'll find plenty of help in matching your interests and your aptitudes to a like-minded publisher, editor, or agent.

But finally, your best resource will always be you. Only you can stave off the goblins of disappointment and self-pity. I've never wasted any time moping about rejection. When one of my articles comes back with a note saying, "I'm afraid it doesn't quite suit our needs at the moment," I don't rail at the editor for not appreciating the jewel he or she was offered. I write a new cover letter, put a new stamp on the envelope, and take it out to the mailbox—by noon. I want to be in charge of my own momentum.

Writing is hard and lonely work, and only you can keep yourself "up" for the daily running of the race. In 1988, I went to Florida to write a book called *Spring Training*, about the Pittsburgh Pirates. The Pirates manager, Jim Leyland, and his coaches kept reminding me that baseball is "a negative game."

A batter who hits .300, the game's standard of excellence, fails seven times out of 10. A pitcher who pitches well is often sabotaged by errors, bad bounces, and other factors he can't control.

As I listened to this litany of failure, it began to sound familiar, and suddenly I realized why. Initially, even the best writers are .300 hitters, struggling every day against terrible odds to say what they want to say. I wondered how the Pirates kept their young men motivated in the face of such adversity.

Positive thinking, I saw, was at the heart of everything they did. "If we're losing ten to nothing in the ninth inning with two outs, I just know that if we get two people on, we're going to win," said the pitching coach, Ray Miller, who told me he had been an optimist all his life. Since then I've often been grateful for how much I learned from those Pirate coaches about how to teach writing: matters of confidence and self-esteem.

All you can do, finally, is to practice your craft as honorably as you can, every day. Believe in yourself and in your life narrative. If you make an honest transaction with your experiences and your emotions you'll find the markets you deserve.

William Zinsser is a writer, editor, and teacher who has long been a freelance writer for leading magazines. He taught writing at Yale, where he was master of Branford College. He has written 17 books, including *On Writing Well*, which has sold more than one million copies, and the recently published *Writing About Your Life*.

INTRODUCTION

by Elfrieda Abbe

If you are like me, you knew you wanted to be a writer when you picked up your first book and read it. You may have carried this dream inside you through your school and university days, a dream encouraged by teachers who praised your poetry or prose.

Maybe while working at another job to support yourself, you've been keeping journals or writing stories or chapters for your book, but have never been published. Maybe you're working as an editor or reporter and yearn to break out on your own.

One of the most common questions we get at *The Writer* magazine is: how do I become a writer? Many of those who ask us this question are already *writing*, but they just haven't reached their dream of getting published, yet.

For 117 years, *The Writer* has been helping readers not only be the writers they've dreamed of being, but also to improve their craft, ride out the rejections and disappointments, and sustain lifelong relationships with writing.

In the magazine's pages, many of the best writers of our time regularly share what they've learned about creativity, inspiration, techniques, challenges, and rewards. We've collected the best of these articles from the past year for inclusion in this 69th edition of *The Writer's Handbook*. You'll find a collection of advice from writers such as Erica Jong, Dennis Lehane, Sara Paretsky, Donna Tartt, J.A. Jance, Anne Tyler, Evan Hunter (aka Ed McBain), Elizabeth Peters, and Dean Koontz. Many of these writers started out just like you—writing between job and family responsibilities, writing on lunch hours, early in the morning, or late at night.

In this book, you'll find a group of wise and seasoned mentors guiding you on your writing path with advice on everything from finding the courage to get started to developing characters, creating plot twists, dealing with the vagaries of the publishing business, and disciplining yourself to write.

You'll find a dazzling array of approaches. J. A. Jance, for example, lets the story lead her. She discusses how once, she neared the end of one of her mysteries to discover that the person she thought had done the deed was innocent. Gwendoline Butler, on the other hand, knows who did it before she begins.

If you dream of breaking into movies, Rick Reichman gives you nuts-and-bolts instructions for making your screenplay better, starting with the first scene. If you're ready to venture out as a freelancer, Kelly James-Enger's chapter on freelancing tells you what you need to do to succeed.

You'll find techniques for getting yourself out of a writing jam or your head out of a writing slump.

There are common threads in these essays. No one claims that writing is easy. You just have to put your seat in the chair and write, whether you think the words you're producing are good or not. What sustains you in your struggle is the love and joy of writing.

Erica Jong captures that spirit in her essay "A Writer's Notebook":

"To write," she says, "is to be reborn, to affirm the self, the soul, and the creative spirit."

I imagine that other writers represented in this book feel that way, too. Whether you're looking for a practical solution to a writing problem or an inspirational boost, their words will help you do the thing you love most: write.

SECTION ONE

Success in Freelance Writing

FREELANCE 101

Getting started as a professional writer

by Kelly James-Enger

When you're writing for your own satisfaction, there are no rules dictating what you can and can't do. You can scribble on the back of a legal pad, scratch a poem on a bar napkin, or hammer out your novel on a dusty old typewriter.

But perhaps you're ready to take the next step and get your work published. Or maybe you've already seen your work in print and want to explore new markets or different types of writing.

When you decide to write for publication, things change. You can't just toss your wonderful manuscript in the mail and hope that someone will buy it. You must first find the right potential markets for your work and determine what kind of material they're looking for at this time. That's rule number one: remember that you're now writing for someone other than yourself.

Rule number two: follow the standards for the proper way to approach editors and submit your work. While your essay may be wonderful, it's unlikely to be read or purchased if it's written in crayon—or, more common a problem, if it's three times too long for what a publication typically publishes. New writers sometimes ignore the basics when it comes to submitting their writing, assuming that it's only the writing itself that's important. The truth is that even the most stellar work is likely to be ignored if it's submitted to an inappropriate market or in an inappropriate format.

There are other aspects to writing for publication—what editors need and expect from writers—that new freelancers may be unaware of. This can be summed up by rule number three: be professional. Being professional involves acting in a helpful, reasonable, and appropriate manner, especially once you do manage to attract an editor's eye.

Assuming you already have basic writing skills, you don't need a journalism or English degree to succeed as a professional writer. But you do need to learn about the basics of freelancing. It's a time-consuming job that takes dedication, desire, and determination.

I made that commitment several years ago, when I quit my job as an attorney to become a full-time freelance writer. To help you on your freelance journey, I've put together some basic guidelines to keep you on track. If you dream of taking the next step—becoming a successful writer—read on.

Before you begin

Make the commitment. If you're writing for yourself, you can write whenever you feel like it—and skip it when you don't. But you've made the commitment to get published. Now you have to follow through. Begin by setting up a writing schedule, whether it's writing every day or three times a week. Can you carve out a half-hour each day before you go to work or every night after dinner? On your calendar or day planner, write down when you'll write—*in ink*. Treat your writing as you would any other obligation. Otherwise, it's likely to end up at the bottom of an already crowded to-do list.

Decide what you want to write. It's a given that you love to write. Otherwise, why would you take up such a challenging career? The question is, then, *what* should you write about? You have all these great ideas, but when it comes time to shape them into articles, they fly right out of your head.

The following exercise will help you narrow down what to begin writing about. Write down subjects in which you have an interest or specialized knowledge. For example: have you traveled the world? Lived in different parts of the United States? Raised children? Dealt with a chronic medical condition?

Are you an avid gardener? Do you run your own business? Do you have first-hand knowledge of a particular industry, trade, or profession?

Make your lists under the following headings:

- I have specialized knowledge about:
- My work background includes the following subjects:
- My hobbies and interests include:
- I know or have access to experts on the following topics:
- I'm interested in the following subjects:
- I'm currently dealing with these life issues:

Take a look at your lists, and choose the subjects that most appeal to you. It's fine to have more than one area you want to work on at a time. But if your time is limited, you will need to decide which one is most important to you and work on it first, prioritizing the rest.

Setting up your business

Before you start writing and submitting your work to editors, you'll need to set up a workspace and create or buy the basic professional materials, equipment, and supplies you will need.

You don't have to have a separate office when you start freelancing, but you do need a computer and printer (or access to them). Today's editors expect writers to have word-processing software and e-mail.

While the advent of e-mail has made owning a fax machine less important, fax access is still helpful. If you don't have a fax, make arrangements to use a friend's fax number. Or you can have faxes sent to you in care of the nearest Kinko's, UPS Store, or OfficeMax, for a small fee.

You may never meet any of your editors in person. That's the good news—you can toil away in pajamas or sweatpants and no one's the wiser! This means that the first impression you make will be through your stationery and business card. You need a straightforward professional letterhead that includes your address, phone number, e-mail address, and, if you have one, fax number. Stay away from cutesy drawings or cartoons—most writers want to present a more polished image. Your stationery needn't be fancy or expensive. With your word-processing software, you can create a letterhead design, which you also can use for your cards and envelopes.

Where to sell your work

The next step in your freelance career is to figure out where to sell your work. Which markets are right for you? You can start with this book, which lists thousands of markets for nonfiction books, novels, short stories, magazine articles, essays, and poetry, and provides contact information and a description of what each publication is looking for.

Here's a quick rundown of potential markets for freelancers.

Magazines. Thousands of magazines purchase freelance work. Consumer magazines are those you can find on the newsstands. Trade publications are aimed at people in a particular industry or profession and are often available by subscription only. For magazine articles, you usually send a query letter first and then write the piece after you receive an assignment. (Or an editor may offer to look at a piece on speculation—"on spec"—meaning that he's willing to read it with no guarantees of purchasing it.) The exceptions to the rule are essays, short fiction, and humorous pieces; for them, you send in the completed work, with a brief cover letter introducing it.

Newspapers. Newspapers are a great place for new writers to gather writing experience and gain clips. Most local publications pay modestly (ranging from $5 to $125 for features). They're often looking for freelancers, or "stringers," and it's a good way to hone your reporting and writing skills. Call your local newspaper with a list of story ideas and express your interest in freelancing for the publication. She may ask you to write about an idea you've pitched or send you out to cover another story. (As a courtesy, ask the editor if she's on deadline before you start your spiel.)

Online. For publication on websites, make your approach via e-mail. Depending on the site, you might send a query or the completed manuscript. Many websites don't pay anything for accepted submissions, and many more pay very little, so you may want to make online publishing your last resort.

Corporate/business writing. Writing for businesses gives you a chance to sell your writing and "publish" your work. Unless you have a copywriting background, though, you'll want to read up on sales-writing techniques. For example, you'll need to know the difference between a *feature* and a *benefit*—and how to write customer-oriented copy—before you take on your first gig.

The Copywriter's Handbook and *Secrets of a Freelance Writer: How to Make $85,000 a Year*, both by Robert Bly, cover the basics of writing pieces like brochures, ads, and sales letters, and include suggestions on marketing your services and running your freelance business. *The Well-Fed Writer: Financial Self-Sufficiency as a Freelance Writer in Six Months or Less*, by Peter Bowerman, is another excellent resource.

Analyzing and approaching markets

You'll find basic information about publishers in this handbook. But before submitting your work to a specific market, it pays to do more research. Pick up a copy of the magazine either at your local bookstore or library, or order a sample issue from the publisher, and study what type of articles it publishes and the tone. Is it literary, popular, intellectual, entertaining? Does it include long in-depth articles or short snappy ones?

Try to describe the typical reader. Often, you can find useful details on the publication's website. Look at the page intended for advertisers to find such demographics as gender, age, marital status, income, and education of the average reader. You can also tell a lot from the magazine's advertisements. Do they appeal to men or women? What age group do they target? Are the ads for upscale products? Use these details to write your own description of the typical reader. This will help you later when you write your query letter.

Many publishers provide writers' guidelines that spell out what the editors are looking for. Often, these are available online, or you can obtain a copy by sending a self-addressed stamped envelope (SASE) to the publication and requesting them.

With the magazine and guidelines in hand, consider these factors:

- What type of material do they accept?
- How many words do they want?
- Who is their audience? (Your research helps here.)
- How do they want you to submit material? For example, a magazine may

specifically request query letters first, not completed articles.
- What do they pay for material?
- What is their response time?

Keep all your market information in one place, so you'll have it to refer to when you're preparing your work for submission.

Once you've picked a market, you're ready to submit a query.

The all-important query letter

While some magazines will accept completed manuscripts, most prefer query letters first. A query introduces your idea, demonstrates why readers of the publication will be interested in the story, outlines how you'll approach the story, and convinces the editor that you're uniquely qualified to write the piece. It also allows an editor to give feedback and direction before you start writing.

Many magazines accept queries by e-mail. To e-mail a query, include the entire text in the body of the message, not as an attachment. And resist the temptation to be too casual or overly friendly. Your e-mail query should be in the same format as a letter that you'd mail.

A sample query appears below. Note how it:

- Catches the editor's attention with a first-person anecdotal lead in the first two paragraphs.
- Shows why the magazine's readers will be interested (paragraph #3).
- Describes the approach you propose to take with the story, the type of experts you will interview, and a possible sidebar (paragraph #4).
- Demonstrates familiarity with the market (by mentioning a specific section of the magazine) and highlights relevant writing qualifications (and how the writer's personal experience will bring a unique perspective to the piece).

Sample query letter for magazine article

February 12, 2002

Ms. Erin Eagan, Managing Editor
Bally Total Fitness
RB Publishing Inc.
2424 American Lane
Madison, WI 53704

Dear Ms. Eagan:

As a longtime runner, I compete in a half-dozen races every year. Last March, I signed up for one of the first 5Ks of the season. It was a perfect Sunday spring morning, clear, cool, and windless, and I was rested, fit, and

(continued)

(Sample magazine query, continued)

ready to race. Until I pinned on my race number, stretched, and bent over to tie my shoe just before the race—and felt a flash of pain streak up my back. I straightened up to discover that running was out of the question—I could barely walk, and even a slow jog brought tears to my eyes. My race was over before it had begun.

After spending the rest of the day alternating between ice packs and heating pads, I still hadn't improved. I made an appointment with a sports medicine specialist Monday morning and explained what had happened. "It's not fair!" I cried. "I could see if I was overweight or stressed or was lifting something wrong. But I didn't do anything!"

Yet my doc told me that this kind of injury isn't unusual, even in fit men and women. No matter how healthy you are, a back injury can occur at any time, and more than 80 percent of Americans will experience back pain at least once in their lives. I'm happy to report that, with the right drugs, rest, and gentle stretches—not to mention a few massages—my back is now on the mend. Now I'm determined not to let another back injury sideline me. I'm religiously performing my back exercises and am going to incorporate regular stretching into my routine as well.

"Back to Basics: Reduce your Risk of Injury" will explain why back injuries are so common and describe how readers can avoid them and maintain back flexibility and strength. I'll interview respected physicians and sports medicine experts about prevention and treatment options, including stress reduction techniques (stress appears to contribute to and aggravate back injuries). A possible sidebar might list simple back exercises to do as "preventive maintenance." While I estimate 1,200 words for this story, that's flexible, depending on your needs.

Interested in this topic for your "Physical Health" section? I'm a full-time freelancer who's written about health, fitness and nutrition for magazines including *Fitness, Shape, Self, Oxygen, Energy for Women, Redbook, Family Circle, Marie Claire*, and *Woman's Day*; clips are enclosed.

Let me know if you have any questions about this story idea; I look forward to hearing from you soon.

Very truly yours,
Kelly James-Enger

Submissions and payments

You can keep track of your submissions in a simple notebook. (There are software programs that do the same thing, if you prefer to do it on the computer.) Keep track of when, how (via e-mail or snail mail), and where you send your queries and manuscripts. You also should record the general topic of your query and the responses you receive.

When you get a positive response to a query or sell a manuscript, you can make a new entry that details the assignment, including the deadline, word count, and agreed payment.

When you receive an assignment, make a note in your assignment log, but also write the deadline on your calendar or in your daily planner. That way, you have the deadline noted in two places—a useful "double-diary" system.

If an editor notifies you that he or she wants to purchase rights to your piece, ask if you need to send an invoice. Some publications require these from the writer; others simply generate their own internal request for payment. While software programs such as Quickbooks include invoices, a short letter on your stationery serves the same purpose. Include the title of the piece, the agreed-upon fee, your Social Security number, and an invoice number for reference.

Working with editors

Once you get the assignment, editors will expect you to be professional, resourceful, and easy to work with. You'll have a leg up on other writers if you keep these tips in mind.

Be pleasant. Say you write an essay, and an editor buys it. Five months later, when you've practically forgotten about it, she calls and asks you to review the galleys ASAP. Don't whine about the short notice; do it immediately (and graciously) to help make her job easier. An editor trying to close an issue has plenty on her mind already; she wants to work with writers who won't give her a hard time.

Be able to disagree without making it personal. You can argue a point without getting nasty. Your editor's rewritten lead weakens the piece considerably? Remain calm and point out why you're not happy with the new version. You don't have to be a jellyfish, but you can disagree respectfully and thus maintain your relationship.

Deliver what you promise. This goes beyond meeting the deadline. It means that you turn in the story as the editor assigned it. If she wants 1,500 words and two sidebars, that's what you write—not 2,500 words, figuring that she will cut it down.

Treat deadlines seriously. If you discover that you're going to need more time to finish a piece (say, one of your critical sources is unavailable until after the piece is due), talk to your editor immediately. Ask for an extension so that she can plan for the late story. The worst thing you can do is to simply not turn it in—and then dodge your editor, who's wondering where the story is.

Survival tactics

Now you've been introduced to the basics of submitting work for publication. That's not all there is to it, though. As a freelancer, you'll need to know how to overcome rejection, stay motivated, meet deadlines, and overcome writer's anxiety, among other things. Here are my survival tips:

Set your own deadlines. You may not be used to working on anyone's schedule but your own. The time will come, however, when an editor gives you a deadline that you'll have to meet. Get used to writing on deadline by setting your own target dates for finishing your projects. If you're working on a big project, like a book, break it into smaller chunks—say, chapter by chapter—and set deadlines for each one, plus a deadline for completing the whole thing.

Become a sponge. In the same way you want to gather information about potential markets, you should gather information about the type of writing you're interested in. This handbook contains articles about varied writing styles, techniques, and genres, but you may find it helpful to read other books devoted to your specific craft. Also, reading *The Writer* or other magazines dedicated to writing and publishing will help you stay informed on developments in the field and expose you to diverse ideas from other working writers. You'll improve your own work—and your chances of getting published—in the process.

Overcome rejection. Trust me, you will get rejected. All writers do. The first step to coping with rejection is to expect it. That doesn't mean you shouldn't have faith in your work. It does mean that you realize your odds of having work turned down are high, especially if you're a new writer. By remembering that it's normal, you ease its sting.

Second, treat rejections as opportunities. If you have another idea that's right for that market, start your new query or cover letter with language like "Thank you very much for your response to (title of the essay or query). While I'm sorry you can't use it at this time, I have another idea for you to consider," and mail it to the market. In the meantime, tweak the original query if necessary and resubmit it to another publication. Your work won't sell sitting on your hard drive. You've got to get it out there.

Finally, don't take it personally. Any rejection you receive is only for that particular piece by that particular editor at that particular publisher. It's not a reflection on you or your abilities as a writer. The timing may be wrong, the editor may not care for the idea, or she may already have something similar in the works. A rejection can even be a positive sign if the editor took time to write a personal note like "Sorry, not quite right for us" or "Nice essay, but we're overstocked." Instead of stewing over why your work was turned down, find another market for it. Taking action is the best way to overcome rejection.

Calm writer's anxiety. Call it writer's block, performance anxiety, or plain, old-fashioned self-doubt—every writer suffers from it at one time or another. Anxiety is common, normal, and part of the writing process for all of us.

Perfectionism is a major source of writing-related anxiety. If you expect your first draft to be perfect, you're setting yourself up for disappointment. Good writing is rewriting—and sometimes rewriting again (and again).

Give these techniques a try next time you're feeling anxious, stuck, or blocked:

- Schedule your writing. Having a regular writing habit works for nearly everyone. You'll start training your brain to turn on and get creative every morning at 6 a.m. or each night at 9 p.m. Instead of worrying about when you'll write, you simply stick to the schedule.
- Switch gears. Do something different—vacuum, walk, read, do a crossword puzzle. Or write something else for a while.
- Break it up. When an assignment appears overwhelming, you're likely to feel anxious. Break the work up into smaller steps—conducting research, doing interviews, transcribing notes, writing a draft, and so on—and focus on one step at a time.
- Move your body. Nothing conquers a writer's anxiety like physical exercise. Take brief movement breaks away from the computer, even if it's only five minutes to get up, stretch, and take some deep breaths. You'll feel calmer and more able to focus on your work.
- Be gentle. Writers are often their own harshest critics. Be nice to yourself. If you picture an audience for your work, think of someone who gets it—your best friend, spouse, or someone who thinks like you do.

Stay connected. Writing is a solitary activity, but that doesn't mean you have to go it alone. In fact, hooking up with other writers can help you find new markets for your work, improve your chances of publication, and stay motivated through the tough times. If you have friends who write, you can ask for help with a particularly tricky lead or use them as a sounding board for story ideas. You also have someone to share the inevitable ups (you got the assignment!) and downs (after three months, the editor turned down your proposal) of freelancing.

Your freelancing friends can also introduce you to markets you may not have considered for your work. No matter how many hours you devote to market research, you can't keep up on all the magazines, newspapers, and websites that might be interested in your writing. Sharing information with other writers about possible markets can give you the inside track into netting assignments. So where do you find your fellow writers?

- Check with your local library or bookstore. Many have writers groups already in place; if not, offer to help create one.
- Go back to school. Community colleges and universities offer a variety of writing-related classes. Look for workshop-type classes that will give you a chance to get to know your fellow students.

• Go online. There are a number of e-mail lists, bulletin boards, and news-groups where you can meet other writers and share information. Do a Google search or go to http://freelancewrite.about.com/cs/newsgroupslists/ for a list of links.

• Join up. Consider joining a writers organization such as the National Writers' Union (www.nwu.org) or Society of Children's Book Writers & Illustrators (www.scbwi.org), or attend a writers conference (check out lists of writers groups and organizations at www.writermag.com). Shaw Guides has an extensive list of conferences and workshops at http://writing.shawguides.com. At conferences, you'll hone your skills, learn more about the publishing process and meet other writers.

Stay motivated. Writing well is a demanding job, and sending out work and getting published is even tougher. The writers who succeed are resilient, dedicated, and more than a bit stubborn. Those qualities will help you survive the ups and downs of freelancing.

One of the most effective ways to stay motivated is to set two types of goals for your writing. Set an outcome goal and then design production goals to get you there. An outcome goal is often what you're striving for in terms of publishing your work. It might be "I'll publish my work in a national magazine." A production goal, on the other hand, is a small, measurable, specific goal that will help you reach your outcome goal—like "I will send out three queries each month" or "I will write for 30 minutes every day."

When you're writing for publication, you need both. The production goals, although seemingly minor, will help keep you on target to reach your outcome goals. They also give you a way to track your progress. After six months of sending out queries, for example, you may not reach your goal of being published in a national magazine (yet), but you will have met your production goals of writing every day. That kind of success helps keep you on track—while making you a better writer and improving your chance of getting published in the process.

Take the next step. You may feel nervous, maybe even terrified, the first time you mail off an essay or hit "send" to e-mail an article query. That's normal. Remember, though, that to be a published writer, you have to take the first step and actually submit your work. Chances are slim that you'll run into an editor at the grocery store, who, after staring at you for several minutes, will approach you with the words, "You appear to be a writer of some talent. Would you like to write for me?" You might laugh at the idea, but many writers secretly hope that they won't have to make the effort to publish their work. They'll meet someone who knows someone (who knows someone) and magically be "discovered."

Hey, you *can* be discovered, but it won't be at the grocery, dry cleaners, or even the bookstore. You'll be discovered by making yourself visible—by honing your writing skills, researching the best markets for your work, and getting your work in front of editors. There's no mystery to how unpublished writers become published writers—it simply takes time, work, and a refusal to give up. But the reward of seeing your first byline (and your 10th, and your 50th) makes it well worth it.

Kelly James-Enger is a freelance journalist, speaker, writing instructor, and contributing editor at *The Writer*. She is author of *Ready, Aim, Specialize! Create Your Own Writing Speciality and Make More Money* (The Writer Books, 2003), which gives advice to freelance writers on how to increase their income by focusing on top niche markets. She is also author of two novels, *Did You Get the Vibe?* and *White Bikini Panties*. She can be reached at her Web site: www.kellyjamesenger.com.

10 EASY WAYS TO GET STORY IDEAS

Your next assignment could be right under your nose

by Debbe Geiger

If you're looking for a stream of marketable ideas that editors will snap up, your own backyard is fertile ground.

Most of my ideas come from everyday life. I pick them up as I'm picking up my daughter from elementary school, or from conversations I overhear at the gym. Something may spark my interest during a dinner conversation.

I've become a successful freelance writer and a regular contributor to *Newsday* by keeping my ears and eyes open to whatever is going on around me. Here is my top-ten list of resources for story ideas:

Friends and family. Don't just talk when conversing with your friends; listen to what they are saying. What are their concerns and interests? How are they enjoying themselves on the weekends?

My sister's divorce and her desire to remarry prompted a story on how to get back in the dating game after age 40.

Strangers. What drives the PTA leader to be so involved? How does the mayor juggle his responsibilities? Watch people when you're out. At McDonald's, a friendly grandmother in the role of hostess greeted my family. She gave the kids balloons and brought them ice cream for dessert. The unexpected down-home service at a fast-food restaurant hit me right away—a story!

Children. From hot new games to issues at school, children offer a never-ending bank of story ideas. Listen to what your kids are saying and track what interests them.

One day my daughter's friend jumped in our car and taught my daughter to roar like a lion. "It's yoga," she proudly announced. The encounter turned into a story on the yoga-for-kids class she was taking.

Yourself. What are your hobbies? No matter how you live—whether you're a single parent, pregnant, retired, disabled, or beset by a health problem—there are common threads that can be woven into saleable story ideas.

When I was diagnosed with high blood-pressure after taking birth-control pills, I pitched and placed a story in *Better Homes and Gardens* on how I had worked fitness into my life after the diagnosis.

Community. Check out bulletin boards. Read flyers. Be observant at local events. Be alert to new businesses and new offerings, whether at a fitness club or a craft store.

Civic and religious associations. What new programs are being offered at a nearby church or temple? Do civic groups in your town sponsor special projects?

Hobbies. How do you spend your downtime? I turned my love of gardening into a story on "whimsical ways to grow vines."

Newspapers and magazines. When you find a news item or feature that grabs you, don't be afraid to rework it. There is always an opportunity for writing about the same topic from a different angle or by giving it in-depth coverage.

My local newspaper reported an outbreak of Listeria, a type of food poisoning. I was pregnant, so I wrote about the danger the condition poses for a pregnant woman and her unborn child.

Vacation and travel plans. What made your trip special? What would you have done differently? My sister-in-law's decision to take her kids out of school for a vacation resulted in a piece on the pros and cons of this growing trend.

Holidays and seasons. Editors are always seeking fresh approaches to seasonal stories. Learn the lead times of your target publications. Watch for holiday ideas this year to write for publication next year.

Now, with these tips in mind, go forth and become an idea-generator. Editors will love you.

Debbe Geiger is a writer whose articles have appeared in *Newsday*, *Better Homes and Gardens*, *Cooking Light*, *First for Women*, and elsewhere. She lives in Massapequa, N.Y. This article appeared in *The Writer*, March 2004.

KNOW YOUR AUDIENCE

Seek demographic information for your target magazine markets

by Lynn Alfino

The editor's e-mail read: "Trim some of the details that may be interesting to scholars but not to Aunt Mary. Keep things that have more popular appeal since ours is a popular-level magazine." Such was my first lesson in considering who my readers were and writing to them. But with my academic-historian background, writing colloquially for consumer publications did not come naturally. This editor's advice made it clear that identifying with the magazine's readers would be a pivotal step in my making the jump from academia to popular media—a move that ultimately resulted in more sales to more magazines.

Discovering who your audience is, and writing to that group, doesn't start with the article. It begins before you write your initial query. Editors receive hundreds of queries every year, and you want yours to shine above the rest. A query that shows an awareness of the magazine's audience and its needs will receive more attention than a generic query sent willy-nilly.

Publications have target audiences and generally cater to their needs. As a writer, you should anticipate your audience's needs or expectations in order to convey information. The first question you should ask is, "Why am I writing this? What is my goal or purpose?" To communicate successfully to your audience, understanding your purpose for writing will make you a better writer.

The second question you need to ask is, "Who am I writing for? What segment of the population buys this publication?" Writing is infinitely easier if you have a specific audience in mind, and you will produce more focused queries and articles if you show editors that you have some idea of who buys their magazine each month. A young woman's magazine that routinely features articles on sex is unlikely to be enthused about your query on the latest trends in religion. Conversely, an established magazine that caters to home and family is unlikely to buy your idea on the joys of being single.

You'll be able to speak more clearly to your audience if you can sketch an accurate picture of who's in it. To identify and write to your audience, consider several factors:

Age. Determining your readers' age level will help define interests and goals. Teenagers might be eager to read about dating and the latest computer games, but adults may be more interested in family travel and money management.

Education. This point especially helps you determine your vocabulary. A highly educated audience may be more tolerant of controversy and have greater interest in global affairs. Magazines geared toward a specialized readership (*Canadian Geographic, Aviation History, Food Management*) often attract readers who already know much about the subjects and want to learn about new trends, discoveries, products, and services. Accept that there will be some people who already know more than you do, so check your facts to avoid embarrassment. If you need to wear the hat of an expert, rely on experts and reliable sources to lend that authoritative air. I wrote several historical articles for a religious publication that I knew was delivered to the Vatican every week, so chances were good that someone more knowledgeable than I was going to read it! I made triple-sure my facts were checked with those "in the know."

Occupation and economic status. People are accustomed to different vocabularies, value systems, and levels of understanding. Be careful not to include too much jargon, which may only be understandable to a few. The reader may not know what these terms are or how they pertain to what they want to know. For instance, an article on medical issues can be a difficult read for the general public if specialized terminology is used without explanations. Not everyone knows that Selective Serotonin Reuptake Inhibitators are synonymous with anti-depressants, unless you note this. Writing for consumer magazines assumes a different audience than a trade periodical, which may go deeply into a subject and assume a professional level of knowledge. Are your readers generally employed in white- or blue-collar jobs? Will they expect long explanations or definitions of key terms? Sometimes this information can be included in a sidebar. Are they novices, general readers, specialists, or experts? What is their level of information about your subject?

Leisure activities and income level. Do the magazine's ads feature luxury cruises and expensive trips to exotic locations, or create an image of readers who enjoy inexpensive family camping trips, crafts, and home renovation?

Sex and marital status. While men do read women's magazines, and women have been known

> You'll be able to speak more clearly to your audience if you can sketch an accurate picture of who's in it.

to thumb through *Playboy*, on the whole, magazines generally have a target audience, and knowing who it appeals to can sharpen your marketing strategies. Both sexes may be interested in health, career, travel, and money management, but from different slants.

Now that you know what demographic information to look for, obtaining it need not be a time-consuming effort. Lots of information about your audience is available in the "Writer's Guidelines" many magazines provide, marketing books such as *The Writer's Handbook*, a publication's website and, most obviously, the magazine itself.

Read and analyze the publication's content and don't forget to study the advertisements. Are the products and services geared toward a particular group? Education and travel ads bespeak a different audience than escort services and ads for fishing equipment. Use this information to slant your query and article.

Valuable information about your intended audience is often available on a publication's website under "Mission Statement," "About Us," "Writers' Guidelines," "Submissions," and "Contact Us." Links to information for advertisers can also sometimes provide a demographic profile of the audience.

Websites can save the day. I sold my first five-page feature article to an esteemed American magazine, *St. Anthony Messenger*, solely on the information I got from its website. My research had shown it was a prime market for my subject, a historical piece on a legend surrounding a tiny church in Rome I had visited. But the magazine was unavailable in my hometown of Toronto, and even theological libraries came up empty. Its website came to the rescue with a selection of articles published over the past year. I studied the articles until I noted their formula: they all began with personal anecdotes, included specialized vocabulary and terms, and were slanted toward middle-class adults of both sexes. This analysis proved invaluable in producing a manuscript that sold immediately, with minimal editing.

Inspirational author Anne Culbreath Watkins goes the whole nine yards and studies the "fine print" of publications. She looks at the number of subscribers and newsstand sales, and whether the publication is national, regional, or international. Often, this information can be found in the front pages of the magazine. By studying back issues, the website, and the guidelines, she determines what style is most frequently used, recently covered subjects, and who the regular writers are. "If a publication runs a lot of articles about kids, then I know the magazine is slanted toward parents," she says. "Inspirational pubs look for lots of personal stories, or interviews with people who have inspiring stories to tell." By studying the articles already published, she determines how info-rich and quote-heavy the piece needs to be.

> Valuable information about your intended audience is often available on a publication's website.

Entries in writers guides such as *The Writer's Handbook* often outline desired topics and discuss a publication's readers—for example, "women over 35 who are juggling family and career" or "18-35 interested in travel, fashion, and music." Don't be afraid to query on topics outside the blurbs, but realize they may be a harder sell and require a decided slant toward the publication's audience.

When writing for different audiences, be careful not to "dumb down." Stay humble and remember when you were "just a reader," before the days you read with an analytical eye. The best writing instructs, entertains, and inspires, without condescension. Many writers don't change their style when writing to different audiences, but they do adjust their message, how they say it, and what information they include. Children's author and equestrian expert Donna Campbell Smith keeps her audience firmly in mind, but doesn't "write down" to kids. "I don't really write differently for adult and youth readers," she says. "But the subject matter is usually different—for example, kids aren't interested in the technology used to make saddles, but they are interested in the newest style of riding helmet with the cool pictures on the side."

Knowing your target audience can help you connect emotionally. And when you slant your queries and articles toward your intended readers, your writing will come more easily and be more fun.

Lynn Alfino, of Whitehorse, Y.T., Canada, is a veteran freelance writer whose articles have been published in magazines and newspapers throughout North America. She is at work on a nonfiction book about last-place finishers in the Alaskan Iditerod dogsled race. This article appeared in *The Writer*, May 2003.

HOOKS
FOR MAGAZINE ARTICLES

The key to reeling in assignments

by Robert Bittner

I thought I had a great story for *Pages*, a bimonthly magazine about books. It was about the rise of "creative nonfiction" and the growing number of popular authors who were writing it. My editor was unconvinced. "It's an interesting idea," he said, "but I'd need to see more in order to see how this article would be distinguished from all the others."

In other words: "Yes, there might be a story here. But why should my readers be interested in it *now*? What's the hook?"

Hooks are exactly what editors want when they read queries. A hook can be a recent research statistic, a timely news peg, or a unique angle that says, "This is fresh, and it's worth your time." Ignore the hook that can grab editor—and reader—interest, and your query might sink to the bottom of the stack. Find a great hook, though, and you can reel in an assignment.

From hook to nuts

Good hooks tell readers why your story is relevant. Sure, you can grab attention with a dramatic scene or a provocative quote. But these elements are more like the bait. They create interest, but they aren't necessarily strong enough to keep readers hanging on through your last paragraph.

The best approach is to combine intriguing bait with a strong hook. For example, the title of Lisa Collier Cool's article "Why are we so big?" (*Good Housekeeping*, May 2002) may sound like just one more story about women and weight. But the hooks Cool uses make this piece stand out.

First, she opens the article with a sentence—"Nancy Hix, 47, fervently wishes she were thinner"—that immediately catches reader interest. That's the bait.

(After all, don't a lot of us wish we were thinner, too?)

She then follows up with two hook-laden paragraphs that explain the need to keep reading: "Right now, one in four of us fits the medical definition of obesity . . ." (surprising news) and "Being overweight or obese contributes to the deaths of 300,000 Americans per year—and may soon overtake smoking as the number-one cause of preventable death" (timely news).

Some writers call these "why should you care" paragraphs "nut graphs." They spell out the central idea of your article in a nutshell and tell readers what they'll gain by reading on. If you can't clearly state in a couple of sentences why readers should care about your story now, you may need to do more initial research to find the real hook.

Be surprising

The strongest hooks are not simply newsy or trendy. They are also surprising.

I bet there weren't many pitches to *Preservation Online*, the Web-based publication of the National Trust for Historic Preservation, that linked historic preservation with the movie *8 Mile*, starring rapper Eminem. But for Detroit-based freelance writer and publisher Jennie Phipps, that was the surprising hook that led to a sale.

In the movie, a house is burned because people suspect a young girl was raped there. It's a turning point in the life of Eminem's character.

"The house that was burned was in Highland Park, a troubled but independent city completely encompassed by the city of Detroit," Phipps explains. "Highland Park is on the National Historic Register for its collection of Arts and Crafts bungalows—the largest in the country. But the city is in receivership. The state has appointed an administrator, and it was her decision to allow Universal Pictures to film the house-burning scene in return for the removal of two other houses deemed 'unrestorable,' a couple of visits to the schools, and a $2,000 payment. She made this decision over the objections of the community. Community members pointed to the terrible arson problem the city has and insisted that burning a house under these circumstances could make the arsonists feel justified. The head of the city council said, 'Nothing good can come from making a spectacle out of torching a house.' "

Preservation Online purchased Phipps' story without knowing her or asking to see a single clip, she says.

Be strong

An article hook shouldn't be something we tack on at the end of the writing process because we've been told that every article has to have a hook. Instead, the best hooks are strong enough to support every idea that follows.

Freelancer Tim Harper found such a hook for a story that helped him break into one of his goal markets, *The Atlantic Monthly*. "I'm an aging-but-still-game recreational basketball player," he says, "and over the years, I've written a number of freelance stories about pickup hoops. At a writers conference a few years ago, I was talking to an editor from *The Atlantic Monthly*, and he happened to mention that he's a basketball junkie, too.

"I thought about what he and I and so many others love about the game and why we still play it. I came up with the idea of finding the 'best pickup basketball player in America.' Only it wasn't some young skywalker who should be in the pros. It was a 52-year-old real estate executive who lives for the game. The editor loved the hook because it offered both an evocative look at the game and a provocative challenge that would make readers think."

The power of a strong hook

Finally, if you've come up with a great hook, don't assume that it can be used in only one way, for only one query or article. There's power in a strong hook. Jim Morrison, past president of the American Society of Journalists and Authors, is a seasoned freelancer who has written for many top magazines, including *Southwest Spirit*, *Smithsonian*, and *Reader's Digest*. But even he admits he can underestimate the power of a great hook.

"Several years ago, my *American Way* editor called to say the magazine was going to start running short 400-word pieces. He wondered if I could help them out. I searched my slush pile, found a *Wall Street Journal* clip about a former medical examiner in Lawrence, Kan., who had stolen a portion of Albert Einstein's brain—and still had it. I suggested I interview the guy and write a witty piece. That, I figured, was all it was worth: 400 words, $500.

"Flash forward about three years and I open my *Harper's* to find about a 12,000-word story titled 'Driving Mr. Albert,' by a brilliant writer named Michael Paterniti. Now, I wasn't the first guy to write about Einstein's brain; there were at least half a dozen before me. But it took Paterniti to see the insanity of it and go pick up the medical examiner and take him on a wild cross-country ride. The story won a National Magazine Award, a six-figure book advance, and a seven-figure movie deal."

Well, I'm still waiting on that seven-figure movie deal. But I eventually found a hook that worked for my creative-nonfiction query to *Pages*. With a little research, I learned that one of the key proponents and teachers of creative nonfiction, Walt Harrington, had a new book coming out that combined his personal experience of learning to hunt with insight into his own writing process.

My editor replied with an attention-grabbing hook of his own: "Would you be willing to do an 800-word story . . . ?"

Robert Bittner of Charlotte, Mich., has written for *Pages*, *Preservation*, and other publications. His most recent book is *Your Perfect Job*, a career guide. Visit him on the Web at www.robertbittner.com. This article is from *The Writer*, August 2003.

KILLER QUERIES
FOR ARTICLES

How to write a pitch
that sells in record time

by Sharon McDonnell

Remember Sheherazade, the princess who told the sultan a story every night for 1,001 nights—stories so spellbinding that, instead of putting her to death, he married her?

That's how I feel when I query an editor. After all, as a full-time freelance writer for 11 years, I am writing queries to prolong my professional life.

Luckily, I've landed many assignments so rapidly that there's often no need to follow up. I've sold stories from a query within a few hours, an hour, and even minutes—and so many within a day or a few days that I've lost count. Often, I've gotten assignments without submitting clips—a no-no, supposedly—purely because an editor loved the query. My stories have run in *The New York Times*, *American Way, Robb Report, The Christian Science Monitor, American Profile, Islands Magazine, ARTnews, Specialty Travel Index, Newsday, Computerworld, American Journalism Review, New York Magazine*, and many other publications.

How did I learn to hone my query-writing skills? From "pitch letters" I wrote daily at a PR agency in New York City, where I once worked. We wrote pitch letters to persuade major media in newspapers, magazines, TV, and radio to run a story about a client. These were tightly written little gems that usually told an anecdote or two to humanize the story. They were penned with pizzazz and often custom-tailored to a particular section or columnist. Our clients seemed to expect press releases that were deadly dull, turgid pieces touting how wonderful they were, filled with corporate-speak. We were mum on how the pitch letters they never saw actually did the trick. Pitch letters turned out to be the perfect training ground for my future career selling my own stories for money—instead of merely "selling" the idea to another writer or news desk.

So, thank you to the hard-bitten TV news producer who told me deadpan: "Ya got 10 seconds. Make ya pitch." And to the *Crain's New York Business* editor who said, "Give me one good reason why I should run this piece." After I reeled off three, he said "stop"—then "sold." After printing a bunch of opinion pieces I wrote for clients and sold by pitch letters, he offered the ultimate accolade: "You could sell me anything."

Here is what I have learned about writing queries that sell in record time:

Never bore the editor. Editors are pitched all day long by PR people about companies, products, and services that claim to be the best, the biggest, and, God forbid, "unique"—the bane of an editor's existence. Yawn. Predisposed to hate boredom, editors are subjected to it day in, day out. Make their day: Try to sparkle, surprise, or jolt an editor out of his or her seat with a story well told, or something they haven't heard before. Humanize a story with at least one person; whether you're writing about health, business, art, food, public policy, or travel, chances are somebody has done something interesting, if not downright peculiar. Journalism veterans say look for the "man-bites-dog" story. They're not kidding. Strive for a "Well, I'll be damned" response, and tease an editor into wanting to hear the whole story.

Try to convey the tone of your future story in your query, whether it be dramatic, bizarre, funny, or moving. Your personality may be bursting with talent and wit, and your writing style may shine with brilliance and originality, but if your query is dull or mundane, why should an editor make the leap that your story will be any different? Sure, you probably enclosed clips with your query—but the editor may assume a hard-working editor colleague polished a rough stone into a jewel.

Write your query like you're telling a story in a bar. What I mean is be conversational and chatty when you query an editor, not pedantic. Cut to the chase—be snappy and spin your tale. When you confide riveting news to a friend or try to impress a stranger in a bar, you either get to the point immediately or tantalize a bit until the kicker, right? Usually, you punctuate it with some vivid dialogue. Surely you don't begin with how you awoke that morning, commuted, worked all day, and, then, you a) won a trip to Europe, b) got engaged, or c) told off the boss. Your companion's eyes would glaze over and he or she would start eyeing the door. Why should an editor be any different?

I once met a man in a bar who said he had been pursued by the police of three countries. Sought for 1960s antiwar activity, he married a woman who had defected from a European Communist country. Clearly, he knew the meaning of a lead—in fact, he was a journalist and author. Save all the details of your story until you've hooked your reader.

Query by e-mail. To get really swift replies from editors, you need to send queries by e-mail. I've snagged 15-minute response times from *The Christian Science Monitor, The New York Times, Toronto Star*, and Worth.com this way. The *Monitor's* response to my arts-related travel story: "Wonderful! We'll send you a contract. What's your fax number?"

How do you find editors' e-mail addresses? Easier than you think. Market listings in magazines like *The Writer*, books like *The Writer's Handbook*, free newsletters like *Writing for Dollars* and WritersWeekly.com, and paid newsletters like FreelanceSuccess.com and *Travelwriter Marketletter* include editors' e-mail addresses, plus pay rates and writers guidelines. Online discussion forums of writers organizations like the American Society of Journalists and Authors (ASJA), whose members include more than 1,000 professional freelance journalists and book authors, often share editors' e-mail addresses and those who don't like e-mail queries. (ASJA, by the way, considers queries so important that its Query Project, at www.asja.org, features samples of winning queries for *Smithsonian, Family Circle, The Atlantic, Fitness, Woman's Day*, and in-flight magazines, among others, for members on its website.)

Just about any publication has a website, so check for a "contact us," "staff directory," or similar link if you can't find e-mail addresses elsewhere. Newspapers often offer a long list of e-mail addresses for any imaginable editor. Obviously, sending an e-mail to the appropriate editor—health, business, arts—will speed a response; sending it to the wrong editor or a general mailbox slows the process. Some magazines online list only an e-mail address for "editorial." In this case, try to find the appropriate editor's name on the website, so your subject line will read "Query for Edith James" or "Health query" and be forwarded to the right person. Or call for the e-mail address.

As for clips, I either paste a few in the body of my e-mail—because many editors don't open attached files from strangers—or, after my list of credits, ask how the editor prefers to see clips, in hopes my query alone will suffice.

Make it easy for an editor to contact you. It's good sales advice to make it easy for your customer to buy. Yet many writers don't query by e-mail; they send snail-mail queries without including an e-mail address or even a telephone number. This forces an overworked editor to waste time and compose a letter on, heaven forbid, paper and mail it, which can take weeks to reach you. Editors yearn to just hit "reply" to an e-mail or pick up the phone. In the rare cases when I use snail-mail for editors who prefer it, my e-mail address is always at the top of my letter, right under my phone number. Rather than look for your phone number in a directory, an insanely busy editor will be sorely tempted to turn to a more accessible writer.

Diane Benson Harrington, managing editor of FreelanceSuccess.com, advised, "Work on getting queries to sound like magazine articles rather than sales letters—make them intriguing enough to draw the editor in. Provide a title for an article—one that really sings. Focus on making sure the idea is really nailed down and not at all vague. That's probably the biggest mistake writers make with queries—not taking time to make sure the idea is really honed and on target."

Reward yourself. I've figured out how to turn what many writers regard as a dreary chore into fun. Like most people, I find the lure of a reward irresistible, and my reward of choice for a query that snags an assignment is treating myself to a gourmet dinner at a restaurant in New York City. As a fan of ethnic cuisines, I practically salivate every time I sit down to draft a query, as I'm hell-bent on winning yet again. Of course, due to other commitments and slow payment, my prizes are often stacked like planes circling LaGuardia Airport—but it's a thrill to think a batch of dinners is just waiting to be claimed. Go ahead, laugh—this has worked like a charm for me for years. It's one heck of a motivator for the five to ten queries I write every week without fail.

Positive reinforcement is a powerful psychological tool that trains the mind. Obviously, likes and dislikes are very personal, so pick something that will work to motivate you to perform well.

Here, then, are five samples of queries that worked.

Sample query #1
(Sold to *The New York Times*)

Dear Mr. Madden:
Meet Win Baker of Wilton: a man obsessed by a portrait of a beautiful but mysterious dead artist.

No, it's not *Laura*, the 1944 movie starring Dana Andrews as a detective who falls in love with the portrait of a dead woman, but close.

When Baker purchased The Cliffside Inn, a charming Victorian-style inn in Newport, Rhode Island, in 1989, it came with one painting and a tape which spun an unusual tale. The inn was the summer cottage of Beatrice Turner, a reclusive Philadelphia socialite who painted it black, wore only Victorian garb until her death in 1948, and was a prolific but unknown artist of astonishing proportions.

After she died, over 3,000 paintings were found spilling from every corner of the house. Most were burned, by order of the executors of her estate, because she had no heirs and no one claimed the artworks. A few were rescued by a neighbor, an attorney who became Turner's posthumous impresario. He took them on a national tour, which resulted in a *Life* magazine photo spread in 1950, but the paintings disappeared again after his death.

A former TV executive and independent producer, Baker knew a story when he spotted one. After extensive detective work, he managed to locate over 70 artworks, which now adorn his inn, recreated as a shrine to Turner's memory. . . .

[Said Madden, editor of the Connecticut Weekly section of *The New York Times*, "That's a good yarn. We'll run it," and did—as a full-page story with a striking photograph of one painting. Now, perhaps I could have proposed a straight travel article, and written a query about a beautiful inn in Newport decorated with paintings. But it was the obsessive nature of Baker's quest to track down 70 paintings by a former owner of his inn—and his converting the inn to a museum venerating her memory—that intrigued me. So I proposed a profile—this, after all, was the story of the inn. It was a dramatic story—I could see it as a movie—so my query was written in a dramatic style. And the inn owner lived in Connecticut, so it was a natural to pitch to that section.]

Sample query #2
(Sold to Worth.com)

Dear Bruce:
After 26-year-old Amy Biehl, a white American anti-apartheid activist, was stabbed and stoned to death by a black South African mob in 1993, her parents went to the poverty-stricken township where it occurred with their three other children—not to seek vigilante-style revenge against her killers, but to understand.

Amy's parents, Linda and Peter Biehl, did more than understand. The California couple started a foundation with 15 programs to create jobs for thousands in Guguletu Township, and even employed two of Amy's repentant killers after their release from prison. One company is a bakery: its slogan, "Amy's bread: the bread of hope and peace."

"What they are doing sends electric chills down your spine," Archbishop Desmond Tutu reportedly said of the Amy Biehl Foundation.

[Talk about "man bites dog." If you were a parent, would you hire your child's killers, or launch a foundation to help solve the crime's root causes? Not to mention the irony of an apartheid-hater being killed by the people she sought to help. Bruce Trachtenberg, then philanthropy editor of Worth.com, assigned the story a few hours after my e-mail, which ran in 2000.]

Sample query #3
(Sold to *American Way*)

Dear Tracy:
Despite the stereotypes of Peace Corps volunteers helping natives in steamy African jungles and other Third World countries and joining right after college, more Americans are joining the Peace Corps and being sent to places like Russia, Romania, and Poland, where they serve as business advi-

sors so capitalism can start and flourish. More now join after retiring from business careers, or as a mid-career time-out.

Some entrepreneurs even credit their two-year Peace Corps stints as the inspiration for their businesses—as do the inventors of the Snugli, the baby-carrier with straps, who served in Africa, and a New Yorker whose high-end rug company was inspired after she helped form women's textile co-ops in Fiji.

After a 30-year career at the IRS, Steve Wolf retired to advise youth enterprises in Slovakia. A retired teacher and her retired executive husband served in Liberia. Paula Simpson, a twenty-something Merrill Lynch employee, served in Moscow, and Dina Siber, a tech employee, in Albania.

[Tough to get an airline-magazine assignment after Sept. 11, 2001? My query on the increased business focus of the Peace Corps, offering specific examples and describing how some entrepreneurs were inspired by their service, was assigned in November 2001. Wrote my editor: "This idea seems particularly appropriate in this post-Sept. 11 world. People seem to be more eager to help others, and the fact that this Peace Corps program has business benefits is even better." She added that it should have a prescriptive slant. "I'm wondering about the specific angle: We need to approach the story as either 'here's something you, the reader and an employee, might do for your career and yourself, maybe now that you're laid off' or as 'here's something you, the hiring manager, might do.'"

My May 2002 story showed how volunteers obtained valuable business experience from the Peace Corps, as well as taught artisans to sell crafts on the Web and business owners how to write business plans and improve computer skills.]

Sample query #4
(Sold to *Robb Report*)

Dear Laurie:

When Grace Kelly became Princess Grace of Monaco in 1956, she wore Fleurissimo, a perfume of tuberose, rose, violet, and iris commissioned especially for her wedding by the House of Creed in Paris. The scent remained exclusively hers for five years, before it was released to the general public.

Named the official parfumerie to the English royal family by Queen Victoria—that's the gold crest of the Prince of Wales on the bottles and packaging—Creed, founded in 1760, was also chosen by Empress Eugenie of France, Emperor Francis Joseph of Austria-Hungary, and Queen Dona-Maria Christina of Spain.

No wonder customers who appreciate the finest and the air of aristocratic exclusivity have included Jackie O, Cary Grant, Robert Redford, Audrey Hepburn, and Madonna.

Even if you don't look like these paragons of beauty or elegance . . .
you can smell like them.

[While Creed has an illustrious history, I personalized it with allusions to
Princess Grace and icons of glamour from Jackie Onassis to Audrey Hepburn.
Since wealthy Americans often fancy themselves as quasi-royalty, I felt the
mention of European royals would help. It did—and my story ran with my suggested title, "Heaven Scent."]

Sample query #5
(Sold to *USA Weekend*)

Dear Ms. Balog:
There's not a lot to laugh about these days—a dragging economy, high
unemployment, and world conflict can make many of us want to stay in bed
with the covers over our head. "When you feel least like laughing is when you
need it the most," states speaker and Certified Laughter Leader Donna
Cutting of St. Petersburg, Florida.
We'll all have a chance to practice on May 4, 2003, as World Laughter Day
is celebrated across the United States. Started in Bombay, India, in 1998 by
Dr. Maden Kataria, and brought to the United States by Steve Wilson,
"Cheerman of the Bored" of World Laughter Tour, Inc., in Columbus, Ohio,
the plans for this year's celebration are to "giggle and guffaw to reduce
stress and help pave the way to world peace by preventing hardening of the
attitudes."

[Denise O'Berry, a freelance writer in Tampa, Fla., landed an assignment in
a day from *USA Weekend*'s News & Views editor—her first story for this
Sunday section—from this e-mail query.]

Sharon McDonnell of Brooklyn, N.Y., is a freelance writer whose articles
have appeared in many publications, including *The New York Times* and
The Christian Science Monitor. She is also the author of *You're Hired! Secrets
to a Successful Job Search* and four other books. This article appeared in
The Writer, May 2004.

A NO-FRET, NO-SWEAT PLAN TO GET IT DONE

Write in blocks of time to overcome doubt and meet deadlines

by David Taylor

Other than an empty mailbox, the most frightening sight for a writer is the blank page. Sometimes I even hate finishing a page because I know another one awaits, its vastness daring me to fill it with my puny thoughts and meager vocabulary. How could I produce anything worthy of the writers who have gone before me? I used to make C's in high school English!

And so goes the constant babble of recrimination spewed by the monster of self-doubt.

The source of this monster's power is not merely the risk of humiliation every time we write. There's also the mystique surrounding creativity. Humans have explored deep space and the enigma of DNA, but we still know little about creativity—except that some of us have more of it than others, and that if we study our craft and work real hard, maybe, just maybe, the magic will happen, but maybe not.

It's that possibility of not measuring up, of Monster Doubt's voice drowning out our own, that makes some of us write not at all, others of us write less than we would like, and many of us write at a lower level than we want. But what if sitting down and doing it were not so anxiety-ridden?

When I first began to freelance full time, I was forced to deal seriously and quickly with issues of self-doubt and procrastination and their effect on my daily output. Out of necessity, I developed block writing, a technique that helps me overcome self-doubt, especially when it's time to create that crucial first draft. Here's how it works:

The block-writing regimen

To begin block writing you need a timer, preferably with an alarm, to divide your writing day into 45-minute or one-hour blocks, each followed by a short break.

The goal is simple: to put derriere in chair and not get up until the end of the block of time. Eventually, doing this will become automatic. You just do it—without the complaining, the hesitation, or the extra push of will.

And when things aren't going well and the demons of doubt snarl their loudest, you simply can tell yourself: "Well, I could sit down for at least *one* block."

There are three essential rules to follow while block writing:

Accept the "law of regularity." Tell yourself: "If I sit down for enough writing blocks, eventually the work *will* get done." Avoid goals like, "During each block, I will produce two pages of copy." It doesn't work that way. You never know what's going to happen once you sit down. You could produce 20 pages or two pages or none at all. Each outcome will have occurred for a legitimate reason. All you know is this: spend enough time in the chair and eventually it will get done.

Commit. Like any regimen, whether a weight-loss diet, exercise program, or good dental hygiene, block writing will work only if you give yourself to it and play by the rules. That means no matter how much you dread writing that day, no matter how unprepared you feel, no matter how frightened of failure you may be, no matter how sleepy you are, the simple act of putting your tush in a chair and starting the timer becomes the most important thing you can do to ensure your eventual success. It means you're acquiring a writer's discipline.

Trust. You must believe that during each session, something will get done. Even an hour of false starts is important. Sometimes you have to write stuff you won't use to clear the way for stuff you will, or say things the wrong way in order to find the right way. But most of all, you must trust that if you simply sit down for your time in the harness, eventually the work will get done.

Benefits

Imposing artificial structure on the creative act of writing seems counterproductive. I remind you, however, of the formula for classical Greek tragedies, from Sophocles to Euripides: the fall of a flawed protagonist in a high position and use of dramatic irony to evoke pity and fear. Structure and pattern have the power to free our creativity. Here are other benefits of block writing:

Defined limits. For writers plagued by doubt, simply sitting down isn't enough. Without a tight seat-belt, it's too easy to spring back up at the first itch of doubt, the first wretched paragraph or unyielding problem. By allowing yourself to get up in frustration, you reinforce failure—not success.

Artificial pressure. Full-time writers have no problem staying motivated. If they don't write, they don't pay the bills. Simple enough. But as a part-time freelancer with a full-time paycheck, you have little to lose besides pride. Sometimes we need the motivation that real-world pressure provides—whether it's making the mortgage payment or an editor's deadline. Writing blocks apply pressure that feels familiar, especially to the procrastinator in us, who depends on outside pressure to get things done.

Sharper focus. I used to watch college students make this mistake every day: "I'm going to the library to study for three hours." Well intended, but few students know how to break long study-periods into effective blocks with specific, achievable goals. The result is sadly predictable—wasted time despite honest effort, ending in frustration and disappointment.

But writing is like a construction project, and from foundation to rooftop we must constantly ask, "What comes next?" Writing in blocks of time encourages focus on one thing at a time: an effective lead, a main character's backstory, or a bridge section between main points.

Required rest. How long you can sustain concentration and remain efficient is an individual call. But one truth applies: Going beyond your productive limit eventually leads to frustration, which can become its own problem. I have found 45-minute to one-hour blocks to be the most comfortable work period for me. The key is to be disciplined and give up romantic notions of working furiously while in the breathless grip of inspiration, losing all sense of self and time, emerging with masterpiece in hand. On some days that may happen; when it does, feel blessed and know it was possible because you treated the other 364 days like a job, complete with coffee breaks.

Concrete goals. Vague dreams lack the juice to sustain us through the tough work that a writing project requires. You may "want to be published." Fine, but as a binding contract with yourself, that's a little soft around the edges. You need to set specific goals for each block. All of these things help bind us to the ultimate writing contract: to write our best, to grow from the challenges we've set, and to be proud that we're doing it—not merely dreaming about it.

Like any regimen, whether a weight-loss diet or good dental hygiene, block writing will work only if you completely give yourself to it.

Lessons

Over the years, block writing has taught me the following lessons, without which I don't think I could make a living doing this:

- To write, no matter my mood or level of fear.
- To keep my head down and butt in chair, ignoring the long, arduous road I must travel to produce final copy.
- To derive primary satisfaction from the actual process of creating, not its outcome.

While I always hope that the final product will be one of my best, I know that there will always be successes and failures and things in between, but the satisfaction and joy of my craft will never abandon me.

David Taylor of Savannah, Ga., is a former executive editor at Rodale Press and author of *The Freelance Success Book: Insider Secrets for Selling Every Word You Write*. This article appeared in *The Writer*, August 2003.

10 TIPS
FOR FREELANCE SUCCESS

Make your editor your biggest fan

by Robert Bittner

During a "Champions on Ice" show, Olympic figure-skating star Michelle Kwan was clearly the audience favorite. She skated beautifully, hitting all of her jumps and floating gracefully across the ice.

But the audience was cheering even before the music started. They applauded Kwan's landings before she left the ice. The reason? Time after time, Michelle Kwan has proved herself to be a true professional with a likable public persona. Because of the audience's past relationship with her, they wanted to see her succeed.

Ah, if only editors could be so supportive of their writers . . .

Well, they can. Put the following 10 tips to work in your own writing life, and you'll take a giant leap forward in generating editorial enthusiasm. You may not get applause, but you'll build relationships and probably get more assignments.

1. Show that you care about your target markets. "Showing that you care" means understanding the publication you're writing for—and demonstrating that understanding.

Freelancer and former magazine editor Judy Keene explains: "When I was an editor, the quality I valued most—and found least—was an almost perfectly honed sense of my magazine's voice: its tone and point of view, our readers' needs, knowledge of previously run material, etc. I had a couple of freelancers who knew the publication and our audience almost as well as I did. When I saw a query from one of them, I knew before even reading it that I was going to find something absolutely on target. Barring something similar in the works, their assignment rate was close to 100 percent."

2. Be a team player. "For editors who ask reasonable things, I am more than willing to help out," notes freelancer Margaret Littman. "That's what you do for your co-workers in an office setting—and that's the way I think of editor/writer relationships. If I learn a fact or see an item that I think may be of use to that editor, regardless of whether or not I think it will turn into an assignment for me, I'll pass it along, just as I would in an office. Being willing to be a team player makes editors more likely to call me with assignments."

3. Stay in touch during the down times. Writer Elizabeth Johnson makes it a point to contact one of her editors even when she's not working on an assignment. "Every few weeks, I drop her an e-mail letting her know that I'm available. Sometimes she'll call me back in a day or so with an assignment. Recently, she didn't have any assignments for me, but because she knew I was available, she passed my name on to another editor at the publication, who had a feature she needed to assign. It was a surprise story for which I wouldn't have been considered if I didn't keep in regular contact."

4. Follow up on your assignments. "When I e-mail a finished story to an editor, I always follow up a few days later just to make sure it was received, if I haven't heard anything," writer Dara Chadwick notes. "If I run into a potential problem on a story, I'll usually let the editor know way ahead of the deadline. Many times, I'm able to work around the problem and still meet the deadline. But I think most editors appreciate knowing."

5. Mind the details. Integrity and accuracy are the traits that keep many editors going back to the same freelancers. That means finding reliable, authoritative sources and checking facts.

"Notice the deadline," adds Meg Guroff, a feature editor at *AARP The Magazine*. "I know I'm supposed to say, 'Always meet the deadline,' but, frankly, most of the best writers I know have deadline problems. Writers who blow past the deadline without comment cannot be trusted with work in the future, but a chagrined phone call a day or two ahead saying the first draft will be a little late is not always a catastrophe."

6. Be patient. Many magazines receive hundreds of queries every week and don't always have staff available to review them. Holidays, sick days, vacations, office meetings, and overall work flow all play a part in how quickly an editor can respond to a new story idea or a completed assignment. As a result, it can sometimes take six to eight weeks for an editor to get back to a writer just to say "No thanks." Sometimes—thanks to the internal approval process—it can take even longer to get a go-ahead. In such cases, patience is a virtue. Even so . . .

7. Be persistent. Go-aheads also can take a while at *AARP The Magazine*. Guroff adds, however, "I'm much more likely to keep pushing [in-house on a writer's behalf] if the writer checks in periodically, without a hint of aggravation. Besides reminding me of their idea, this also demonstrates that the writer will be good at tracking down potentially reluctant sources. Same goes if you've turned in copy and haven't heard anything in a while." Don't be afraid to keep knocking, politely, until you get a response.

8. Be willing to revise. When writer Sal Caputo turned in his copy for a bridal magazine's new advice column for grooms, he learned he still had some work to do.

"Apparently, I was a little too irreverent," he says. "The editor wanted more *Everybody Loves Raymond* than *Saturday Night Live*. I took a deep breath and said, 'Let me take another crack at it.' When I handed in my revised version, the editor called to say that she and the publisher were exceptionally pleased with the column. It looks like I'll have a new steady gig with her magazine."

9. Offer something surprising (in a good way). "Don't use all the good stuff in the query," freelancer Wayne Curtis suggests. "Leave out some fun surprises for the final piece." That way, your brand-new, well-polished manuscript won't feel like old news to the editor who has been living with your query for a month or two.

If he's really got a jump on his story, Curtis will sometimes surprise his editor by submitting his first 200 to 400 words a week or two before deadline, "just to give the editor some comfort and to allow the art department to start thinking."

10. Show that you care about your work. "We don't change things just for the sake of changing them," Guroff says. "So if a story comes back to you repeatedly with questions and changes, it's because it needs more work before it will fit well in our magazine. A writer who sees such feedback—or *pretends* to see it—as a chance to perfect the piece makes me happy. Someone who turns in a draft and says, 'Do what you want with it,' or tends not to know the answers to follow-up questions off the top of his or her head—indicating a minimum of curiosity about the subject—scares me."

Robert Bittner of Charlotte, Mich., has written for *Pages*, *Preservation*, and other publications. His most recent book is *Your Perfect Job*, a career guide. Visit him on the Web at www.robertbittner.com. This article appeared in *The Writer*, May 2004.

15 WAYS TO FIND TIME TO WRITE

Freelancer and mother of two shares tips on finding the hours you need

by Shirley Jump

If you're like most writers, you're juggling writing with family life, soccer games, dinner preparations, and carpooling. You're probably seeing those writing hours disappear faster than socks in the washing machine, somehow sucked into the vortex of a busy life. Time gets away from you during the day and before you know it, those hours you planned on devoting to researching markets or working on your novel are gone for good.

As a full-time writer and mother of a 4-year-old and a 9-year-old, I know about being busy. Yet I manage to write dozens of articles, two books, and numerous corporate materials each year. Here are some of the ways I've found time to write and tend to family responsibilities.

1. Get up early. I drag myself out of bed at 4:30 every morning. As much as I dislike rising before the sun and the birds, I also know early mornings are the only times when no one will want me to fix them a snack or expect me to answer the phone. For projects that require more concentration, this is the best time for me to work.

2. Make getting up easier. If you are like me, you need serious motivation in the morning. My solution? A coffeepot with a timer and some really good, expensive coffee. I can smell the brew from my room, and I know caffeine is only a few steps away. I also moved my alarm clock away from my bed so I actually have to get up to shut off the buzzer. As a third incentive, I bought a programmable thermostat, so the heat comes on and warms up my office just before I get there.

3. Take work everywhere. When I'm working on a book, I have to cram it in among appointments, kids, and other work. I usually write five pages in the morning, then print them out and take them everywhere I go. Throughout the day, when I catch a few minutes—waiting in the car for my kids to get out of school, for example—I edit those pages and add ideas for the rest of the chapter. Over the course of the day, I can usually sketch out a few more pages.

After the kids go to bed, I input changes and additions. I flesh them out, add a little here and there, pop in some description. In the morning, I start with revising the previous day's work, then write new material. Those little increments of time add up and increase my productivity.

4. Cook as little as possible. Say this to yourself several times: "The Crock-Pot, freezer, and microwave are my friends." Learn to use them and you've shaved hours off the time it takes to feed yourself and your loved ones. Five minutes of prep time, and then the pot does the work for you. You'll have only a pot or two to clean up, and you've eliminated the pre-dinner rush.

5. Hire a cleaning service. When the housework got to be too overwhelming, my husband and I did the math. I calculated how many hours a week I spent on the vacuuming, mopping, bathrooms, and kitchen. Then I figured that against an estimate from a cleaning service. I was surprised to find that the housekeepers *saved* five hours of time but only *cost* one hour of my time (figuring my rate for an hour of writing). The stress-savings of knowing I don't have to worry about the bathrooms is worth every dime.

> As a full-time writer and mother of a 4-year-old and a 9-year-old, I know about being busy. Yet I manage to write dozens of articles, two books, and numerous corporate materials each year.

6. Let the kids fend for themselves. Too often, moms feel we have to do it all—make the sandwich, feed the dog, wash the floor. As my schedule started getting busier, one of the first things I had to learn was that letting the kids do for themselves not only freed me up to work, but taught them responsibility. My 4-year-old doesn't make the neatest sandwich in the world, but he is mighty proud of the one he does make—and he eats the entire thing without being reminded to finish. To me, that's double success.

7. Set goals. Your writing can fall by the wayside if you don't have a deadline to meet. Before I sold my first book, I bought an inexpensive calendar to track my page count for the day. I set a completion date for the book, worked backward, and calculated how many pages per day I needed to complete to get there. This gave me a concrete goal. Granted, the only editor breathing down my neck was myself, but having those little squares to fill in gave me a daily sense of accomplishment.

8. Report in with someone. It's very easy as a writing parent to start to feel isolated and forget there are other writers out there struggling with the same issues. Find another writer in your community and make a weekly date to chat. Online communication is fine, but I find an in-person meeting really forces you to be honest about how much you've been writing.

9. Give the Internet a rest. Use the Internet as an incentive, rather than a procrastination tool. Don't connect until you've hit your page count. If you need some tidbit for research, just leave a hole in your piece and fill it in later.

10. Reward yourself. Chocolate works for me. For you, it might be an hour in the garden or a trip to the movies. Once you achieve a writing goal, pat yourself on the back. All too often, parents forget to do this in the busyness of life.

11. Don't lose sight of the big picture. Every once in a while, step back and do some long-range planning. I do five-year, one-year, and quarterly plans. This helps me see when I'm investing too much time in the wrong direction and getting off track from my writing goals.

12. Get the right tools. Portable word processors, such as QuickPad and AlphaSmart, are great because they're bare bones. No e-mail, no fancy gadgets, just type and upload to the computer later. I take mine everywhere—in the car, to the coffee shop, to the doctor's office. The best part is that I can't edit on it because of the small screen. I can write without thinking and remove that internal editor.

13. Take a notebook everywhere. I mean this one literally. I have notebooks in the car, my purse, the living room, the bedroom, and even the bathroom. When I have an idea, I can jot it down immediately. You never know when a brainstorm is going to happen.

14. Be inventive. When my son was a toddler, he liked to color with me. One day, in the middle of coloring time, I had a phone interview to do. My solution? I dumped a selection of colored pens on the table. I sat near him and did my interview, scribbling on my pad and trading pens with him while I talked. Granted, my notes were tri-colored, but my son was quiet and happy. I've also set up things in my office for my kids to do—crayons, paper, etc. They have chairs and space to get creative, keeping them occupied and the family together.

15. Let go. You don't have to be Super Mom or Super Dad. The house doesn't have to be perfect; the cookies can come from a package. Prioritize what's important and realize that laundry should never be at the top of the list. On the other hand, you don't have to be a workaholic, to take every assignment. Remember to set aside time for fun with your family or to relax.

Shirley Jump of Fort Wayne, Ind., is a prolific freelance writer and author of several forthcoming romantic comedies, including *The Bachelor's Dare* and *The Bride Wore Chocolate.* This article appeared in *The Writer,* July 2003.

SECTION TWO

Get Your Book Published

ELEMENTS OF
A NONFICTION BOOK
PROPOSAL

by Elizabeth Zack

My field of expertise is as an acquiring (and developmental) editor for well over a decade at two very well-known publishing houses. Now I run my own business, offering editorial services to aspiring and previously published authors. For all those years as an acquiring editor, however, I was the one who decided what to buy. Sometimes that choice was easy—and sometimes not.

I spent those years selecting mostly nonfiction works, from health to parenting to self-help to spirituality projects. So I can help you understand why nonfiction editors choose one proposal on a given subject over another. Sure, one proposal might be represented by an agent with whom an editor has a particular affinity, or the writing can be stronger in one proposal than another. But usually, editors buy a particular proposal based on the presentation and the quality of its components. That's often the reason an "auction"—an event in which several publishers try to outbid other publishers for the rights to a particular project—occurs.

So the cardinal rule to remember is that your job as an author is to make the proposal an easy buy for an editor. You want to minimize the chances that the editor who's interested in your work will have to do some side research to convince the team at the publishing company that there's a reason the company should invest in a particular proposal.

Having the following components in your book proposal make an acquiring editor's job easier:

1. Cover letter

Recently some of my clients have read advice that says the cover letter is passé. Don't believe it for a second. If you can write a cover letter that in a sentence describes your project and points out what's unique and saleable about it—do so. If you can't describe your project in a sentence, consider that your project needs more focus. Agents sell books, editors buy books, and sales forces sell books to bookstore buyers often based on a single quality sentence.

Now, if you're lucky enough to have a literary agent representing you, it's possible that your agent will come up with this sentence. But if you provide this single quality sentence first, in the initial query letter to the agent, it could be the reason an agent chooses to represent you and your project.

The cover letter should briefly compare your book to one or two other bestselling works—for example, "It's *Where Angels Walk* meets *Finding Time for Serenity*"—while also pointing out why yours is different or better. The cover letter should also provide a bit of information about you, the author, because when it comes to nonfiction, it pays to be an expert in the field about which you're writing.

2. Title page

Sounds simple, but the title and subtitle of your book can make a huge difference in how the project is perceived, so spend a good amount of time thinking about it. Always be direct and to-the-point in the title—avoid confusion about what the title means.

If you can't figure out what to call your book, err on the side of caution. Be straightforward. Call it *No More Diets* instead of *Choosing to Waist Away*. Make sure that the title offers a promise—*The Seven-Day Pounds-Away Diet* instead of *Thinking About Losing Weight?*

The subtitle should clarify your title even more, pointing out specifics about what's in the book. If the title is *No More Diets*, an appropriate subtitle might be *Making the Pounds Melt Away Through a Unique Two-Week Program*.

And, lastly, make sure that in addition, the title page features your name. If you have professional credentials, be sure to post them after your name, whether you're a Ph.D., M.S.W., or C.D.E.

3. Overview

In this section, talk for a few paragraphs about your book and what it's going to do. In other words, offer a synopsis of your work.

4. The market

Here you must identify who is most likely to buy your book, and cite pertinent statistics that prove the size of the specific target audience. For example, if your project is on diabetes, you could cite close to 16 million Americans living with diabetes today, with possibly millions more yet to be diagnosed. Draw relevant statistics from the Internet, magazines, national associations, and/or surveys, identifying your source when possible. The point of this section is to convince the acquiring editor that there is a large market ready to buy your book right now. And if there have been recent news stories in the media that address your topic, make mention of these as well.

5. The competition

Remember the cardinal rule? Make the proposal an easy buy for the editor. Well, this particular section can really save an editor time and work. He or she will have an easier time of convincing the sales force that a book belongs on the list of a particular publishing house if he or she can prove why it's better than, or different than, other titles on similar topics that are already published. You need to discuss the competition that's already out there, as this competition can do one of two things: (1) convince an editor to buy your work (and an agent to represent you), or (2) provide a reason for an editor to send you a rejection letter (and an agent to say "no thanks").

Start off citing other books available in the marketplace on the same subject. Every time you mention a particular work, write a sentence or two that explains what this book offers and then go on to explain why yours is better, different, and/or more targeted to today's market. For example: does your book offer new research not yet available in the book marketplace? Are you a credentialed author, whereas a person lacking credentials was the author of the competitive title?

Yes, this step requires you to do a little research. But it will be worth it. You may even realize as a result of your search that you need to re-conceptualize your book, to make sure that it offers new information not available in any other published book. Analyze the results of your search—your agent will, and your editor certainly will. Make sure that you can prove there's a need for your book—even if there's a lot of competition out there, or no competition at all.

6. About the author

This section is exactly what it sounds like. It's very important that you have what's called in the publishing industry a "platform." An acquiring editor will be more interested in your project if you have strong credentials in a field or a website of your own that draws weekly or daily traffic. The editor wants to feel that he or she can really trust in what you have to say. Include information here about your background, education, and career. Mention any awards or special notices, and detail why you are an authority on the subject being presented.

If you're not an authority on a subject? Well, if you've written a book about stopping the progression of Parkinson's disease, but don't have any credentials to back it up . . . you may need to pair up with someone—in this case, a noted Parkinson's researcher who agrees with you and can provide the credentials you will need to get your project sold.

7. Promotion

In this section, talk about your ideas for how you can help to promote the book effectively. For example, can you provide a mailing list of addresses for the target audience? Do you have close contacts in the media you can call on to write articles on you and your book when it comes out?

This is an appropriate spot to mention sources that you think would be interested in reviewing your book or doing feature articles on it. For example, if you are writing a soy cookbook, mention that it's a natural review choice for *Vegetarian Times*. If there's a specific television show that your book is appropriate for, point it out. (Everyone mentions *Good Morning America* and *Today*, yet the nationals can only feature a limited number of authors. It's more persuasive to suggest other shows that have a particular relevance to your project's focus.) Lastly, mention any local bookstores that would be willing to host a book signing.

8. Table of contents

Here you'll list the proposed structure for the book. List all the parts (if there are parts or sections) and the chapters. Just as the title of your book should be clear, the same is true of chapter titles.

9. Introduction

This is a key section to provide. The points to cover include an explanation of what the book will offer, why it is timely, who you are, and why you have the experience and passion to write about the subject matter.

10. Sample chapter (or two)

A sample chapter is a necessity; it allows the book editor to get a strong sense of your writing style and tone. Bear in mind that if your book is prescriptive and offers a program, it's wise to select a chapter that is prescriptive in nature. If it's a cookbook, don't include a chapter only with cooking techniques; choose a chapter that has recipes.

11. Media list

If you have appeared on radio or television in the past, cite these appearances. If you've been interviewed in the past, attach news clippings or media tapes. (Many authors misplace or never save such tapes/clippings, but they are valuable resources. They can help a publisher get you placed on a national television show, for example.) If you lecture, be sure to include your lecture schedule (recent past, present, and future).

12. Endorsements

Improve upon the perceived saleability of your project by providing strong endorsement quotes in the actual proposal. Alternatively, it also helps if you simply provide a list of well-respected individuals who would be willing to provide supportive words about your work (but mention only those with whom you have a personal connection; obviously, many celebrities/authorities are too busy or unwilling to offer endorsement quotes to all who inquire).

With these elements in your package, it's much easier to convince an editor to buy (or an agent to represent) your work. Then you will have truly crafted . . . the perfect nonfiction proposal.

Elizabeth Zack, a 16-year veteran of the publishing industry, founded BookCrafters LLC (www.bookcraftersllc.com), a professional editorial services firm that offers advice to writers on how to perfect their manuscripts and craft commercial, saleable book proposals. Prior to starting her own business, Elizabeth was a senior editor for the Ballantine Publishing Group, a division of Random House, and John Wiley & Sons. This article appeared in the book *Making the Perfect Pitch: How to Catch a Literary Agent's Eye*, edited by Katharine Sands (The Writer Books, 2004).

PITCH PERFECT

Write a fiction or nonfiction pitch in three or four easy steps

by Jandy Nelson

Years ago, I received a query letter that began:

> I am a Vietnamese American man, a witness to the Fall of Saigon, a prisoner of war, an escapee, a first-generation immigrant, and an eternal refugee. After my sister committed suicide, I quit my job, sold all my possessions, and embarked on a year-long bicycle journey, back to the land of my birth, to the memories of my sister and the battlefields of my own psyche. *Catfish & Mandala* is my story.

I called for this manuscript immediately—and so did every other agent to whom Andrew X. Pham had sent his letter. His query was "pitch perfect." It simply and elegantly revealed story, style, and most importantly, his authentic narrative voice.

So the love affair with your work begins with the pitch. And despite the fact that at Manus & Associates Literary Agency we get over one thousand submissions a week, we are still looking to fall in love, to be swept off our feet by the promise of a terrific project.

As an agent, I spend a great deal of my time writing pitch letters to editors, so I understand how difficult it can be to encapsulate an epic novel, to reveal the essence of great literary fiction, to determine the audience for prescriptive nonfiction, to do a competitive study of all the other similar books on the shelves. Editors, like agents, are inundated with submissions, and I know my pitch letters need to intrigue, excite, and evoke in the editor the passion that I feel for a project. And so do your letters for us.

An effective pitch goes a long way. If I like your pitch and use it to pitch your book to editors, those editors will then use it with their editorial boards and sales/marketing departments to stir up in-house enthusiasm for the project. And then, if the editor buys the book, that same pitch could be used to inspire the sales force, which in turn uses it with book buyers across the country.

K. M. Soehnlein sent me a query letter years ago for his novel *The World of Normal Boys*. It began:

> When all the kids around him were coming of age, Robin MacKenzie was coming undone.

What a great set-up! I was immediately gripped. When I turned around and pitched the novel to editors, I used the same opening in my letter. When an editor took on the book and began pitching the novel in-house to marketing and publicity people, he used it as well. And now if you look on the book jacket, the flap copy begins with that same wonderful pitch. Your pitches to agents can be the beginning of a very long train of enthusiasm, so it really is worth it to take the same time and care with them as you did in writing your book or proposal.

While there really are no simple rules to follow to write the perfect pitch letter, I am going to give you some brass tacks that might help you get started.

Pitching nonfiction

Fiction and nonfiction pitch very differently (although narrative nonfiction pitches like fiction). Nonfiction pitches need to cover four important elements:

1. What is the concept of the book?
2. Who is the audience and why do they need this book?
3. Why are you an authority? What credentials do you have that make you an expert in this field?
4. What differentiates this book from all other books on the topic?

In addition to these four elements, you will also want to reveal in your nonfiction pitch if you have an author platform. This is an existing audience for your proposed book that comes from your visibility or access to readers. Do you have a lecture circuit? Run workshops? Have a radio show? Do you have additional venues where you can sell your book?

Also, very important in the nonfiction pitch is a great title. I always think of the movie *Shakespeare in Love*, in which they joked that *Romeo and Juliet* was originally called *Ethel, the Pirate's Daughter*. Definitely don't pitch your project to agents with *Ethel, the Pirate's Daughter* as a title; brainstorm with everyone you know until you find your *Romeo and Juliet*.

Here is an example of a strong nonfiction pitch I received:

> *Hot Flashes, Warm Bottles: A Guide for First Time Moms Over Forty* is the first prescriptive guidebook for the multitudes of women who make up the growing ranks of midlife mothers. [Answers: what is the book and who is the audience?] The concerns of these women are unique; they are as different from the concerns of young mothers as they are from older mothers with grown children. [Answers: why does the audience need this book?] *Hot Flashes* combines the candid and often hilarious anecdotes from the women in Nancy's support groups with field-tested and mother-approved advice. [Answers: is the author an authority in the field?] *Hot Flashes* promises to be the bible for this growing demographic of women whose concerns are not yet addressed elsewhere—and who are actively seeking resources. [Answers: are there other competitive titles?]

I asked to see the proposal right away. This simple, straightforward pitch revealed what the book was, who the audience was, and why the book was so important, so topical, and so needed within the targeted community. It revealed the author's expertise and how the book differed from all the other parenting books on the market. All that in four sentences!

Pitching fiction

Pitching fiction (and narrative nonfiction) is trickier. It is less about convincing us there is a market or of your expertise, and more about the quality of your writing and storytelling ability. That said, there are ways more effective than others to pitch fiction.

The biggest mistake I see is writers who confuse a pitch with a synopsis. When pitching your novel, you do not want to give a detailed breakdown of the plot, character motivations, scene descriptions, etc. I know it's daunting to think of breaking down your 400-page masterpiece into a few sentences, but it is imperative. Remember how many queries we pass on in a week!

Many novels can be broken down this way:

Act 1: Set Up (sets the stage: Who are the characters, where are they, what has been happening to them of late?);

Act 2: Hook (a turn of events that is compelling, pivotal in the plot, something which changes the course of the narrative);

Act 3: Resolution (a wrap-up that doesn't give away your ending).

Here is an example of a fiction pitch for *The World of Normal Boys* by K. M. Soehnlein:

> In a time when the teenagers around him are coming of age, Robin Mackenzie is coming undone. [*Set Up.*] A terrible accident has jarringly

awakened the Mackenzie family from the middle-American dream they have been living, and suddenly each member of the family is spinning out of control. [*Hook.*] Through the impeccably authentic narrative voice of thirteen-year-old Robin Mackenzie, Soehnlein tramples over the perfectly mowed lawn of Surburbia in the late 1970s to reveal the emotional complexities that bind and unbind one family. [*Resolution.*]

For *Dream of the Walled City* by Lisa Huang Fleischman:

The daughter of the chief magistrate, Jade Virtue spends the first ten years of her childhood without ever stepping outside the walls of the family's great mansion. [*Set Up.*] But after the mysterious death of her father, she and her family must embark on a new life in a rapidly changing China. [*Hook.*] With exquisite prose, *Dream of the Walled City* recounts the tumultuous life of Jade Virtue as she is swept into the torrent of historical events that mark early twentieth-century China. [*Resolution.*]

Sometimes when pitching fiction or narrative nonfiction, it helps to do a comparative pitch. Lisa Fleischman's *Dream of the Walled City* could be pitched as a Chinese *One Hundred Years of Solitude*, or *The World of Normal Boys* as a gay *The Ice Storm*. But when using a comparative pitch, make sure to be accurate. Don't say you are writing an Irish *Joy Luck Club* when you are writing about a Scottish expedition up Everest. And don't baffle us with an impossible pitch like "my book is *Chicken Soup for the Soul* meets *The Great Gatsby*."

While the author biography is essential for nonfiction pitches, fiction pitch letters are not the place for modesty. Do mention if you've had stories published in magazines, have received an M.F.A., or if you have some experience that gives you an inside look into a particular arena.

For instance, a client of mine, Laurie Lynn Drummond, wrote a collection of short stories, *Anything You Say Can and Will Be Used Against You*, about women cops in Baton Rouge. The fact that she was a cop in Baton Rouge is an essential part of the pitch for her book, even though it is fiction.

These are just some pointers. Ultimately, you need to take the care, the innovation, and the passion with which you wrote your book to write your pitch letter. Your letter can be simple. It can be funny. It can be persuasive. It can be enthusiastic or quirky. It should be whatever works best to introduce your work to the world. Every day, when I go through my mail, I hope there will be a letter that will make my heart beat a little faster.

I am not sure what it is exactly that makes me pick up the phone and call an author in a fit of enthusiasm to see their work, but it happens every day and it happens because of the strength of their letter. I hope tomorrow it will be your letter that does it!

Jandy Nelson is a literary agent with Manus and Associates Literary Agency, Inc., representing authors for over 20 years from offices in New York City and the San Francisco Bay area. Jandy represents both non-fiction (especially narrative nonfiction, memoirs, self-help, and health) and fiction (from literary fiction to multicultural fiction to thrillers). With a background in theater, she also regularly sells her clients' work into the television and feature-film markets. This article appeared in the book *Making the Perfect Pitch: How to Catch a Literary Agent's Eye*, edited by Katharine Sands (The Writer Books, 2004).

5 SECONDS TO CATCH A FICTION EDITOR'S EYE

Learn to develop "bulletproof beginnings" or risk rejection

by Sandy Whelchel

In the hectic world of commercial fiction book publishing, agents and editors can't—and won't—indulge in reading a manuscript that doesn't immediately pique their interest. With slush piles and desks stacked high with solicited and unsolicited works, that first look is the most critical. So it pays to mind what I call the "5-second rule," which is drawn from a conversation I had with a New York editor: *You have five seconds to catch a fiction editor's eye.* That's about one paragraph of your novel.

The editor is the most discerning reader you will ever have. And if you don't approach your story's beginning correctly, that editor may be the *only* reader you ever have. Crafting a great beginning can be a difficult task for a writer. "Hook" is the term most fiction writers use for the initial grabber that keeps the reader involved and turning pages. Some writers write the entire novel before they write that opening hook. For others, hooks seem natural and are the first thing to hit the paper.

But if my experience is any guide, far too many other writers disregard the entire thing and their book fails. Part of my job requires that I participate in reading the hundreds of manuscripts that come into the National Writers Association contests, as well as work tagged for pre-agent reviews. In most years, this averages around 500 manuscripts, in addition to my personal reading, which ranges from 25 to 30 novels a year. From that number, I would offer that perhaps 90 percent of the contest manuscripts lack a compelling hook.

Sometimes, just to satisfy my own curiosity, I'll search for the hook. Usually, it's located in the first 50 pages—but that's too late. Once I located a hook halfway through a 500-page novel! How disappointing for those first-time novelists who will never know that their success was hidden too far back in the manuscript for an editor/reader to find it.

All writing needs a hook, but in commercial fiction the hook is critical. Its purpose is to entice your readers into getting involved in the story so they'll want to keep reading to the end. In short fiction, the hook should appear in the first sentence. Remember the "5-second rule"? That's all the time you have to hook your reader. In book-length commercial fiction, the hook must appear on the first page, and for best effect, in the first few sentences. Hooks should make the reader to want to find an answer. Sometimes they pique the reader's interest and arouse curiosity; sometimes they promise exciting things to come. But they must always get the cogwheels turning enough to keep the reader interested. You must give the reader a reason to begin reading your material and, more importantly, a reason to read to the end.

Writers often protest that, well, the book gets good on page 40. But no editor has the time or inclination to read that far unless they've been drawn into the story from the beginning. In fact, most publishers employ people called "first readers" to winnow the potentially publishable from the uninteresting. In a market where time is money, little time is spent on the dreary.

A writer of my acquaintance once explained her job as a temp for a large publishing house. She was told that when she had finished her typing duties, she should go down to the unsolicited-manuscript room and grab several manuscripts. "Here's a stack of rejection slips," she was told. "If you don't find the work interesting from the first page, stick a rejection slip in and put it back in the return envelope. If the work is good, place it in a stack here for an assistant to read, but there shouldn't be too many in that 'good' stack."

Now, writers may protest the unfairness of this policy, but since you can't change the publishing world, it is far better to change your work.

Even the best speed-readers can't slog through the thousands of manuscripts most publishers receive every year. That's where your attention-grabbing hook comes in. If it is in the first sentence or first paragraph, you've at least managed to get past that initial rejection slip.

Contemporary suspense author Clive Cussler is a master of the hook. In his novel *Cyclops*, he begins the first paragraph with the sentence: "The Cyclops had less than one hour to live." The reader is immediately struck with questions: Why? What is going to happen? How can this be? And the reader is hooked, enticed to read on to find the answers to these questions.

> All writing needs a hook, but in commercial fiction the hook is critical.

Cussler retains his title as master of the hook by also ending the chapter with: "She kept on going, down, down, until her shattered hull and the people it imprisoned fell against the restless sands of the sea floor below, leaving only a flight of bewildered seagulls to mark her fateful passage." Will the reader finish the book? Probably. Only the most jaded reader could put this powerful writing aside and not be haunted by the fateful passing of the Cyclops.

In his bestselling first novel *Open Season*, C.J. Box, who I assisted early in his writing career, begins with, "When a high-powered rifle bullet hits living flesh it makes a distinctive—*pow-WHOP*—sound that is unmistakable even at tremendous distance." What if this powerful opening were hidden after the rather unimpressive citations from the U.S. Government Endangered Species Act Amendments of 1982, which are used on chapter face pages? Would the reader (editor) have lost interest before becoming involved in this enjoyable, fast-paced mystery? Most likely.

Or in Box's second mystery, *Savage Run*, also a bestseller, he begins, "On the third day of their honeymoon, infamous environmental activist Stewie Woods and his new bride, Annabel Bellotti, were spiking trees in the Bighorn National Forest when a cow exploded and blew them up. Until then, their marriage had been happy." That ought to get the reader reading. Note that this is the opening sentence; it isn't hidden on page 2 or 12 or 20. It's right up front to grab your interest.

If you think this requirement is only for mysteries or action-adventure titles, consider the first sentence of Diana Gabaldon's *Outlander*, the first in a best-selling historical romance series: "It wasn't a very likely place for disappearances, at least at first glance."

No matter the genre, great beginnings and the authors who use them are almost always assured an avid readership. Browsing readers have a habit of taking a book off the shelf and reading a paragraph or two before purchasing a book. Authors, and potential authors, need to consider that with the escalating price of books, only the most loyal readers will plunk down their funds unless they are drawn into the book from the very beginning.

Another consideration when writing that great beginning is to keep in mind that the information given in the hook needs to be an integral part of the story, not something dumped on the first page to attract attention. A promise made but not kept will lose your readership for books to come. The editor who becomes interested in the work, only to find that the beginning has nothing to do with the story, won't want to see another book from that author again.

Separating the best manuscripts from the mediocre ones is an easy task if the hook is the criteria. It takes only *five seconds* to determine whether the work is going to interest a reader.

Sandy Whelchel of Parker, Colo., is the author of six nonfiction books and has been executive director of the National Writers Association for the past 12 years. This article appeared in *The Writer*, January 2004.

Bulletproof beginnings

Here are a few things to consider when checking your manuscript before submitting it to a publisher or agent:

• Does your first sentence—or at the very least, first paragraph—draw the reader into the story?

• Does the beginning leave readers with numerous questions that will be answered when they read the work?

• Does your novel start where the action starts?

• Step outside your own work and ask yourself: If I was at a bookstore, would I buy this book if I picked it up and read a few paragraphs?

• If you have a good hook, is the question that you posed in the hook answered in the body of the novel?

—*Sandy Whelchel*

LITERARY CONTESTS: PATHS TO PUBLICATION

Winning a contest can offer prestige and publication

by Katherine Perry Harris

Jill Christman thought her chances of winning a writing contest that offered book publication as a prize were so slim that, when she moved across the country, she didn't even bother sending the contest's sponsor her forwarding address. It wasn't that she was suspicious of such contests; she just didn't expect to win one her first time entering.

The contest's sponsor tracked Christman down at her new job. We have good news, they told her over e-mail; please give us a call.

It was a call Christman was glad she made: Her manuscript, *Darkroom: A Family Exposure*, was selected by Barry Sanders as the winner of the 2001 AWP Award Series (sponsored by the Association of Writers & Writing Programs) in creative nonfiction.

Writers like Christman are not alone in their initial uncertainty about writing contests. As writers, we all hear the traditional skepticism about writing contests: Are they worth it? Are you wasting money sending another entry fee? Should you just as well buy, say, a lottery ticket or a new novel? Are you wasting time mailing manuscript after manuscript to contests when you should be sending elsewhere—to agents, publishers, magazines—or, better yet, when you should be *writing*?

The odds of winning a contest, it seems, may be even slimmer than winning the lottery. Generally speaking, your chances of being published are better if you submit your work to publishers. But what happens to writers like Christman who do win the big money, or in this case, the big book? For those who find success with writing contests, the experience can be extremely satisfying, especially in light of the current climate of large commercial publishing.

"Winning a writing contest that includes publication is like playing a board game where you pick a lucky card that lets you skip to the magic square," says Sara Pritchard, author of *Crackpots*, chosen by Ursula Hegi for the 2002 Bakeless Fiction Prize, sponsored by the Bread Loaf Writers' Conference. "I thank my lucky stars that I won the contest and can sidestep the agent process."

To enter or not to enter?

In recent years, writing contests have become an increasingly popular way for unknown writers to gain recognition and publication. Finding a book-publishing conglomerate to accept a first book—especially a first book of poems or short stories—is becoming more and more difficult given the concern for marketability and the bottom line. "Compared to sending a manuscript to a big publishing house, where it will probably end up in a slush pile, contests are the one scenario in which the odds seem to be much more in the writer's favor," says Brett Ellen Block. His short-story collection, *Destination Known*, was selected by C. Michael Curtis as the winner of the 2001 Drue Heinz Literature Prize, with an award of $10,000.

Contests that award publication allow aspiring writers to find an audience, usually with a small or university press publishing the winning books. "Literary contests judged by a writer provide a rare opportunity to have your work evaluated by someone who is not thinking about [the] market," says Kevin Oderman, whose manuscript *How Things Fit Together* won the 1999 Bakeless Creative Nonfiction Prize, selected by Scott Russell Sanders. According to Ian Pounds, coordinator for the Bakeless Prizes, "Contests are almost the only way *new* or *risky* voices get off the launching pad. The publishing industry then comes a-courting the way Broadway draws from regional not-for-profit theaters in smaller cities."

Learn the basics first

Writers should be aware of the fundamentals of a contest before deciding to enter. First, most writing contests for full-length manuscripts charge an entry fee, which in most cases helps cover administrative costs. The fees range from nothing to $20 for the contests mentioned in this article. Pritchard reminds writers that the fee supports the contest and ensures that it continues, in addition to helping a new writer see her work in print. Guidelines, eligibility, terms of publication, and, of course, prize money also differ from contest to contest. It is always a good idea to contact the contest's sponsor to learn the guidelines.

Also remember that every entrant faces stiff competition. These contests receive many entrants, most of whom are dedicated, talented writers eager to "play the game." The AWP Award Series, for example, attracted more than 1,700 entrants in 2002, including 855 in poetry and 480 in the novel competition. The 2001 Bakeless competition brought in over 1,230 manuscripts, including 700 in poetry and over 450 in fiction.

Clearly, contests are a big investment, both financially and emotionally. With all of these contests and all of these entrants, what are your chances of winning? Is it against all odds, or are those odds realistic?

Like Christman, most recipients of these prizes admit that their chances of winning didn't seem very believable at the time. "I had never entered a contest before, and I certainly never expected my book to win. I wrote it off in my mind because the odds just seemed too unlikely," says Aaron Roy Even. Even's *Bloodroot* won the AWP/Thomas Dunne Books Novel Award in 1999, with an award of $10,000.

Rick Barot echoes Even's doubts. "I was skeptical that I'd win because I'd already heard so many horror stories from my friends about how long it would take to get the book accepted, if ever," says Barot, the author of *The Darker Fall*, which won Sarabande Press' 2001 Kathryn A. Morton Prize in Poetry, selected by Stanley Plumly.

These writers, however, didn't win contests because of sheer luck.

Choosing the right contest

Once you've made the decision to enter a contest, how do you increase your odds of winning? To begin with, consider which contest to enter. Are your chances increased by entering every contest you see advertised, or would it serve you better to be selective?

Contest winners like Pritchard advise against sending to contests left and right, as she did in the beginning. Instead of entering indiscriminately, it's best to narrow the field by doing your homework—just as you would do when researching a story or article, or a magazine to which you submit your best work. You should only enter contests that you would feel truly proud to win, Barot notes. In other words, aim high. Prestige, after all, is one of the reasons why writers enter contests.

"If you're going to enter a literary contest," Even says, "don't submit blind. Make sure the contest matches your work and your expectations. If you've spent 10 years on a novel, you probably don't want to send it to a contest that doesn't offer publication by a decent press."

When researching contests, consider the judge. Many of the contests' judges change from year to year. This could make a difference in how your work is read and treated. If you're unfamiliar with the judges' work, learn about their writing styles. Have they given interviews or written book reviews that reveal their literary tastes? Perhaps a novelist who traditionally writes Southern domestic novels might not be the best reader of your political murder mystery set in a big city. Kate Gadbow considers it a "waste of time to submit work to a contest judged by somebody whose own work might lead you to think they wouldn't understand at all what you're trying to do in yours."

Gadbow followed her own advice and instincts; one factor in her decision to enter a particular contest was a sense of literary connection with the judge, Rosellen Brown. "I'd long admired Brown's work and thought we might share a sensibility," she says. "I knew she would understand [my book] and read it the way I wanted it to be read." Indeed, Brown selected her short novel, *Pushed to Shore*, as the winner of Sarabande's 2001 Mary McCarthy Prize in Short Fiction.

Besides the contest's overall reputation, its sponsor, and the judge, what do you know about previous winners? Have you seen their books in print? Barot asks, "If you enter a contest and you've never seen copies of the books that won earlier, why would you want to give that same fate of invisibility to your book?"

The ticking clock

A contest's deadline often serves as a goal in itself, forcing writers to revise rough writing. For some, the looming deadline of a contest is enough to reevaluate a manuscript long forgotten. These deadlines—unlike the ones you set internally—are not flexible.

"Writing contests are a wonderful inspiration for a person with a rough manuscript to polish things up and send it out by a particular date," Christman says. A recent graduate of a writing program, Christman felt she needed a deadline to revise her thesis and send it out into the world. The deadline for the AWP Award Series proved to be just the trick.

For Gadbow, learning about a contest's page requirement was enough of a push. "I just happened to have a short novel languishing in a drawer," she says. "It was about 30 pages longer than the contest's upper page limit, and I thought cutting it down to the entry size would be a good way for me to get back into it again and tighten it up." The short novel was the same manuscript that later won the Mary McCarthy Prize.

Revision brings you one step closer to a manuscript that is first-rate and contest-ready. Most of the manuscripts other writers submit will be good work, so keep in mind that yours must be better—or, more accurately, the best. "The most important element of contest-entering is writing the best book that you possibly can," Christman says.

After sending out manuscripts left and right, Pritchard realized her work still needed revision—in fact, she says, the stories were sloppy. "They were story collections," she says, "and the stories were not polished. I just wanted to enter." After multiple revisions, her work obviously paid off.

In addition to sending only your best manuscript to contests, also send your best looking. A clean, presentable, and error-free manuscript shows you are serious about the contest and your work.

From entrant to author

When Christman received the e-mail from AWP relaying the good news, she was up all night pondering the number of runners-up. After she received the phone call asking her if she was sitting down, she "cried for about 24 hours. It was an unreal experience."

After the initial shock and excitement of winning sinks in, writers move on to the next phase. Contact with the judge is usually fairly limited, and might include a congratulatory phone call or letter and a review of the book, which is often used later as an introduction or blurb for the jacket. Communication with the sponsor or coordinator is also limited; this may include coordinating advertising and promotion of the book or readings and book signings. The winners then work with the staff of the press to see their manuscript through the publishing process, including editing and possibly some design work.

Involvement during this process varies from individual to individual and press to press. The writers contacted for this article praised each press' level of personal attention, the enthusiastic, dedicated staff, and the variety of options. "University of Massachusetts Press has really given my book a lot of personal attention, and they're not only open to suggestions—they encourage them," says Christie Hodgen, another winner of the AWP Award Series in 2001 for her short-story collection, *A Jeweler's Eye for Flaw*. "For instance, I was able to choose the painting for the cover." Gadbow agrees that "my friends who have published with large commercial publishers have never been given cover options, nor have they been consulted as often."

If you so choose, working with the press allows you to learn more about what it takes to produce a book. "The press has kept me abreast of every step along the way—having me review the cover, showing me the blurbs, etc.," Christman says. She advises new writers to read the contract carefully, ask questions, make sure they're clear on the schedule for their book and what will be expected of them along the way, and take the publicity questionnaire very seriously, which will help with marketing their book.

A book in hand

One of the perks of the process is avoiding the agent track and instead finding an alternative route to publishing. Winning a contest allows writers to skip the business side of writing, an aspect that many find time-consuming, tedious, and dull. Many winners found agents for subsequent work because of the contest, and did not have to spend writing time sorting through reference books, rejection letters, and self-addressed stamped envelopes. "When I read, I want to read Alice Munro, not [a writers handbook]," Pritchard says. "When I write, I want to write stories, not cover letters and synopses."

For some, the prestige of winning a contest helped secure better jobs or raises. Any honor you can add to a resume, query letter, or list of publications is beneficial. The first year Christman was on the academic job market, she had no interviews; after winning the contest, she landed eight and is now teaching creative nonfiction.

But perhaps the most important benefit of winning a contest is the feeling of affirmation and the realization that—finally!—there is an audience that understands your work. Writing is a solitary profession, and it never hurts to receive praise from a jury of your peers.

"You can't win if you don't enter," Christman says. After all, she should know.

Katherine Perry Harris of Columbia, Mo., is a writer and editor for the University of Missouri System and former publications manager for the Association of Writers & Writing Programs, where she served as editor of *The Writer's Chronicle* and coordinator of the AWP Award Series. This article appeared in *The Writer*, October 2003.

Contests

Nearly all of the following sites offer publication and a cash award.

AWP Award Series in Poetry, Short Fiction, Creative Nonfiction, and the Novel (The Association of Writers & Writing Programs)
www.awpwriter.org/contests

The Kathryn A. Morton Prize in Poetry; also, The Mary McCarthy Prize in Short Fiction (Sarabande Books).
www.sarabandebooks.org/contest

Bakeless Literary Prizes (Bread Loaf Writers' Conference)
www.bakelessprize.org

Drue Heinz Literature Prize; also, The Agnes Lynch Starrett Poetry Prize (University of Pittsburgh Press).
www.pitt.edu/~press/awards.html

Iowa Short Fiction Award; also, The John Simmons Short Fiction Award (University of Iowa Press and The Iowa Writers' Workshop)
www.uiowa.edu/~iww/iowashortfiction.htm

The Flannery O'Connor Award for Short Fiction (The University of Georgia Press)
www.uga.edu/ugapress

Books
Grants and Awards Available to American Writers, 2002-2003
(PEN American Center, 22nd edition, ed. by John Morrone)

The Complete Guide to Literary Contests 2001
(Prometheus Books, ed. by Literary Fountain, William F. Fabio, et. al.)

IS A SMALL PRESS A GOOD FIT?

Advice from two authors who successfully published with small imprints

by Tom Bailey and Gary Fincke

Everyone who writes dreams about answering the phone to a "yes" from a major publisher. But sometimes "yes" isn't what it seems to be, and a large publisher isn't as good a way to go as a small one. Here's what we learned from our experiences with smaller presses.

Tom's agent had good news: a major New York publishing house had made a bid on his collection of short stories, *Talking Like an American*. He loaded his family in the car and drove to New York City to meet the editor. She loved the book, she said. Loved it!

But she had a few suggestions. Each of the stories in the collection had a different first-person narrator. She "wondered" if the stories couldn't better be told by the same first-person narrator.

Several of the stories were set in the Mississippi Delta, a few in West Virginia, another in the Adirondacks of upstate New York. She thought it would be "great" if they could all be set in the Delta. She assured Tom that this would make the collection "sell."

Tom cleared his throat and asked her where he was going to find a coal tipple in the Mississippi Delta. As a writer who believed in the pieces he'd worked so hard to make different, he could not do what she asked. At the end of the meeting, they "agreed to disagree." He walked out, having turned down the bid.

Gary's story sounds much the same. "We want to go to auction with this manuscript," his new agent said when she shipped two sample chapters and a book proposal for *Kicking Ass*, his account of his son's rock-'n'-roll life with two signed bands, to 15 New York publishers. He waited for the phone to ring with good news, but when she called, it was to tell him that the publishing houses that were interested thought the manuscript was "too literary" for the market they foresaw. Worse, they wanted Gary to change the focus from "father and son" to a "reportorial account," meaning they didn't think anybody cared about a father's point of view about rock 'n' roll.

The manuscript, unfinished, languished on Gary's desk for months. Then he decided to seek out a publisher on his own, starting with small independent publishers and university imprints that had been receptive to his less marketable short fiction and poetry. The first place Gary sent it was Michigan State University Press. It took five months for them to act, but they decided to publish the book as long as it was both "literary" and kept the "father and son point of view."

Two weeks later, Gary found out he'd won the 2003 Ohio State University Press/The Journal Award for poetry, which meant his collection of poems, *Writing Letters for the Blind*, had not only found a home, but also earned him a $2,000 prize and an assurance of being reviewed. Three weeks after that, the University of Missouri Press told him they wanted to publish his third collection of short stories, *The Stone Child: Stories*. He'd submitted both manuscripts on his own.

And then, as if some sort of literary log jam had been broken, Tom's short-story collection as well as the novel he had recently finished, *The Grace That Keeps This World*, were both accepted by Etruscan Press after he, too, had decided to submit to a small press.

The editors at Etruscan didn't share the concerns of that major publisher he'd turned down. Together, he and they lamented the seemingly long-gone days of the original short-story collections. When Maupassant and Chekhov entitled a collection ". . . *and Other Stories*," they meant it. Much of the joy for the reader was in the many discoveries (of character, of places) that these books of short stories offered. In Etruscan Press, Tom found a match for his vision for "collecting" the various short stories he'd written. And they loved his novel in a way that meant they weren't about to ask him to change the location or the characters.

So between the two of us, five book manuscripts were accepted during the first two months of 2003. It sounds nearly impossible, but looking back, it feels as if the most luck we have had was understanding how our work was better suited to smaller publishers.

Our recent success, however, doesn't mean that getting work accepted by small presses is easy. The competition for spaces on short publication lists is still intense, but our experience has shown us the best ways to go about making the search as productive as possible. Here's what we learned:

1. Find the potential publishers. Know the reference books and magazines that list small and university presses. Particularly helpful is *The International Directory of Little Magazines and Small Presses*.

2. Take the time to learn what each press publishes. They don't all publish poetry, fiction, and creative nonfiction. Some, in fact, publish only scholarly work. The University of Missouri Press, for instance, discontinued its poetry line years ago, but continues to publish collections of short fiction.

3. Send query letters. After you narrow the search, send query letters to determine whether or not the press is currently reading manuscripts. Include your writing credentials. Sending 250 pages of short stories to a press that only publishes two collections a year requires timing as well as quality. Presses answer queries quickly, usually within a few weeks, but a full manuscript may languish for six months without being read.

4. Be ready to submit a manuscript. Once you send a query, be ready to send a completed poetry or fiction manuscript if it is requested. Editors expect to consider a "book manuscript" in these genres. It is sometimes possible, though, to send sample chapters of nonfiction. Initially, Michigan State was receptive to two chapters of *Kicking Ass*, and then they asked to see three more chapters before making a decision.

5. Consider competitions. Some university and small presses hold competitions, especially in poetry, for the small number of places on their lists. Most of the time these have a small fee ($15-$25) to offset expenses and to provide an advance for the winner. While these may seem like "literary lotteries," they are often the likeliest way of being successful with a small press.

6. Expect editorial control. Once you succeed at finding a publisher, a major advantage of working with an independent press is editorial control. None of the New York editors asked us whether we agreed with how they saw our work. All of the small-press editors made suggestions that were left to us to act upon or not.

7. Don't expect to have a bestseller. Small presses may stand behind your book with all their resources, but those resources are often limited. Wide distribution is difficult. Advertising budgets are smaller. Print runs are in the thousands, not hundreds of thousands. There are, however, small presses that, especially in fiction and creative nonfiction, may be willing to try to sell paperback rights to your work to large publishers, giving your work a second chance to be widely distributed.

8. Expect to be involved in the publication process. From advertising the book to securing blurb copy to helping pick out cover art for the book.

9. Finally, support small presses. Buy from presses you think might be interested in your work. Publishing is a business. A purchase from a small press is a vote for the kinds of literary work they publish and helps support other authors like you.

Tom Bailey and **Gary Fincke** both live in Selinsgrove, Pa., and are based at Susquehanna University. Bailey teaches creative writing at the school, and has edited and written two books on fiction writing. In 2004, Etruscan Press published his short-story collection, *Crow Man*, and a novel, *The Grace that Keeps This World*. Fincke directs the university's Writers' Institute and has published 17 books with small presses, including *Writing Letters for the Blind* (poems, Ohio State), *The Stone Child* (stories, Missouri), and *Kicking Ass* (nonfiction, Michigan State). This article appeared in *The Writer*, October 2003.

A GUIDE TO SUCCESSFUL SELF-PUBLISHING

Follow the right path and avoid the pitfalls

by Marilyn Ross

If you've decided to self-publish, you probably reached this decision for several reasons:

1. You want to control your writing/publishing destiny.
2. You desire to get your book out quickly, rather than waiting the 18 months it typically takes trade publishers.
3. You understand the importance of having access to affordable copies of your book to use for promotional purposes.
4. You've heard the stories about how you have to promote your own book anyway, even if it's published by a major house.
5. You realize that if your project is executed properly, you can make a lot more money when you do it yourself.

My goal is to help you streamline the process and make your journey less bumpy. Publishing a book actually is going into business. While the writing may have been fun, perhaps you feel out of your element with the book production, PR, and sales aspects.

You're not alone. Many who follow this path need a hand to avoid the pitfalls along the way.

Let's start at the beginning:

Producing your book

Know your competition. This information can help you "position" your book to be different. Make it easier to use, shorter, longer, funnier, more appealingly designed, filled with extra useful materials. Additions like an appendix, glossary, checklists, sidebars of resources, or true stories to illustrate your points, for example, embellish your manuscript.

But how do you know what's out there? Simple. Go to www.amazon.com and enter your subject. You'll find dozens, maybe hundreds, of similar titles. Notice the sales ranking on Amazon and pay particular attention to the top 10. Download whatever information is available on the book's page for later reference. Now go to a good independent bookstore and visit with the owner or buyer. You want to get his or her recommendation on the three top books in your topic area. Buy them. Study them. Make yours better.

Think marketing from the very beginning. You want to develop what I call a "marketing mind-set." You see, marketing needs to begin the minute you get an idea . . . and it never ends! You can put things in at the writing stage that will help sell books downstream. (I cover this in detail in the book *Jump Start Your Book Sales*, co-authored with my husband, Tom Ross.) Think about your audience: Who will buy this book? How will you reach them? Do they read a certain journal, newsletter, or magazine? Do they belong to a national association? Do they go to specific trade shows? What specialty stores do they frequent?

When I get an idea for a book, I start two folders: one for content and one for marketing. In the early stages, I just drop ideas into my marketing folder. Don't wait until you have a garage full of books—and then start thinking about how to get rid of them.

Write directly to your typical reader. (Women, by the way, buy the most books.) Don't flaunt your vocabulary or use insider jargon. Remember that most people read at the eighth-grade level. Vary the length of your sentences, avoid convoluted sentences, and make frequent paragraph breaks.

Get your manuscript professionally edited and proofread. I've written 13 books, hundreds of articles, newsletters, e-zines, advertising materials, etc. I would never send a book to press without having it professionally edited. (The range of prices for this service is very broad; chances are the cheapest person will be less competent.) As authors, we read the same mistake over and over again in our own manuscript, never realizing it is a boo-boo. We often take things for granted because we know the subject so well, thus confusing our readers. Automated spell-checkers (on our computer) sabotage us by allowing things like "than" when we meant "that." If you miss errors at this point, it is much more expensive to fix them later.

Take the appropriate business steps. You will need to come up with a publishing company name and get an ISBN. This stands for International Standard Book Number, which is to your book what your Social Security number is to you. It's how people find your publishing company and title. And the ISBN people will ask you to fill out an Advance Information Form. This baby is what triggers your listing in the all-important directories: *Forthcoming Books in Print* and *Books in Print*. A Library of Congress Card Number is important if you hope to sell to the library market. You'll also eventually need a Bookland EAN Scanning Symbol for the back of your book cover so bookstores can easily scan in the information. Particulars for all of these important steps are contained in our book *The Complete Guide to Self-Publishing*. To get started on the ISBN, go to www.isbn.org or call 877-310-7333 (toll-free in the United States; others can call 908-286-1090).

Work with an experienced cover designer. Yes, I know your cousin is an illustrator, or your next-door neighbor does graphic design. But do they do books? Someone who is a whiz at logos or brochures can fail dismally at cover design. Your book cover is your salesperson in the bookstore. It has only a few seconds to attract attention. The cover must be easy to read and compelling, the spine copy big and grabbing.

Create a reader-friendly interior. The easiest way to decide how your book should look inside is to go to a bookstore and browse other books. Find one where the interior layout is appealing and use it as a model. Ideally, your book should be typeset in PageMaker, QuarkXPress, InDesign, or one of the other page-layout programs.

Print with a book manufacturer. Here's the area where you can drop a lot more bucks than you need to. I've put projects out to bid and found the high quote to be double the low one. Don't use the corner printer; go to companies that specialize in books. They have the equipment and knowledge to help you avoid problems. Use one of their standard papers rather than requesting something special. Work in even "page signatures": 16, 32, or 64 pages (depending on the trim size of your page).

And here's a tip to save you money and give you a dynamite marketing piece: Have them print an overrun of your cover. Since it's already on the press, all you pay for is the paper.

If you're serious about publishing, I recommend you start with at least 3,000 copies. I know, the thought of having all those books sitting in your garage can be terrifying. But here's the skinny: The more books you print, the lower the unit cost of each book. To be competitive with other books on the subject and to offer the expected industry discounts and not lose money, you almost have to be at this level. Besides, if you're smart, you're going to give away several hundred books to promote your title.

We've been talking so far about traditional printing. Print on Demand (POD) is another popular option today. And for some projects, it's great. If you want a couple hundred copies of a family genealogy, your life story, a church cookbook, or a technical book aimed at a professional audience, for instance, POD is the way to go. Or if you absolutely can't afford self-publishing, you might get your book into shape to present to a trade publisher this way.

But if you want to sell your book in bookstores, POD has some limitations. First, the books are expensive; there are no economies of scale. You'll likely pay around $6 to $12 per book after the setup costs. So you can't afford to give bookstores the 40 percent discount they need, nor the wholesalers the 55 percent they require. And the books are too pricey to send out many for PR purposes. Then there is the returns issue. Most bookstores expect to be able to return books they can't sell, but this usually doesn't work with POD. A final issue to consider is that most POD companies put their own ISBN on your book. Thus, all inquiries about book club sales or bulk premium purchases, for example, will go to them. Since the discount isn't realistic for pursuing these avenues, you'll likely never even hear about the lost opportunity.

Marketing your book

There are as many ways to promote and sell a book as flavors of Baskin-Robbins ice cream. Let's look at the traditional approaches first, then we'll do some "out-of-the-box" thinking and explore other roads to riches.

Before you can launch a PR/sales campaign, though, you need ammunition to capture attention. That comes in the form of promotional materials: a news release, mock review, cover letters, postcards, bookmarks, customer order forms. (The overrun of book covers we discussed earlier is ideal for the latter. Just put your sales blurb and order information on the reverse side.) You will require different PR pieces in your arsenal to approach bookstores, the media, and consumers.

Approaching bookstores. When I speak around the country, people always ask, "How can I get my book in bookstores?" That's the wrong question. The right one is: "How can I get my book *out* of bookstores?" You must drive customer demand with your publicity! Otherwise, the books will just sit on the shelf and eventually be returned.

Frankly, an estimated 52 percent of all books are not sold in bookstores. Sadly, the average American never enters a bookstore. Books are sold via direct mail, through book clubs, in catalogs, on the Internet, in specialty stores, in bulk to companies, at speeches . . . the list goes on and on. My sense is that our time is better spent pursuing these options. When your book catches on, the bookstores will come to you.

Using wholesalers/distributors. It is wise to pursue a few wholesalers and nonexclusive distributors. You can find them in *Literary Market Place*, which is available at most libraries. (Exclusive distribution is another subject entirely, which I don't have space for.) Then when you create demand, they can supply the bookstores. This is easier for everyone and what the stores prefer.

Tapping into libraries. For the right books (ones with no blanks to fill in and on subjects consumers seek), libraries can be a bonanza. There are two major wholesalers that represent small press and self-published books to libraries: Quality Books and Unique Books.

Selling to the K-12 and college market. Your book needn't be a "textbook" to make it in educational circles. I recently had an order from a college bookstore for 15 copies of *Shameless Marketing for Brazen Hussies*. The instructor loved the book and ordered it for her class on entrepreneurship.

My first self-published book was *Discover Your Roots*, a 1978 book about genealogy that piggybacked on the trend created by Alex Haley's *Roots*. We sold thousands of copies to high school history classes.

Reaching nontraditional retail outlets. Remember those specialty stores I mentioned earlier? They can be instrumental in helping you win huge battles in the sales game. Have a book on fishing? Approach places that sell fishing licenses, bait and tackle shops, marinas . . . you get the idea. Is your title about dogs? Outlets like PetsMart, Petco, and individual pet stores might be interested. How about kennel and breed clubs? Veterinarian offices? Humane societies? Go where your potential customers go.

Selling to catalogs. There are over 15,000 catalogs in the United States covering everything from tools to sporting goods, feminine products to inspirational items. Many carry books; some do not—yet. It isn't easy to get into catalogs, but once you do, it's a fabulous way to merchandise your title. After they've tested your product and decided it will work, they place orders month after month, never return books, pay promptly, and give you plenty of free exposure.

Pursuing bulk premium sales. Sometimes companies buy large quantities of books as a consumer goodwill gesture. They resell them to their customers at a big discount or give them away to draw attention to themselves. Pharmaceutical firms, for instance, purchase certain children's books. My friend sold her book about asthma to a pharmaceutical company that manufactured a drug for that ailment. Remember our dog book? Think about pet food manufacturers. The book about fishing? Try high-end fishing-rod manufacturers.

Talk about your subject. Many self-publishers make a lot of money by speaking about their subject. Afterward, they sell books for full retail price at the back of the room. While public speaking certainly isn't for everyone, if you're comfortable in front of people, woo those who might give you a platform. You can also talk on radio and sell books for full price . . . and you don't even have to leave your home or office. Most stations do "phoners" where they call subject experts and interview them.

Now you have a brief overview of how to produce and market your book. Your success will depend on your research, creativity, and tenacity. Good luck!

Marilyn Ross of Buena Vista, Colo., has written and self-published 13 books with her husband, Tom (www.SelfPublishingResources.com), including their bestselling *Complete Guide to Self-Publishing*. This article appeared in *The Writer*, February 2004.

6 ways to get your self-published book reviewed

Reviews sell books. There is no cheaper or more respectable way to promote your book. A good review will provide greater benefits, both in terms of sales and name recognition, than any advertisement you could buy, for no more than the manufacturing cost of a single book plus postage.

In addition, a richly detailed review will provide you with credible promotional material you can use repeatedly. A good review from a newspaper or literary magazine can be the difference between a book that sells and a book that remains completely unknown.

Increasing competition for shrinking review space can make obtaining a review of a new book seem impossible. Many reviewers won't review self-published books, and most can only review about 10 percent of submissions.

Does a new, unknown author have a hope? Yes! Improve your odds as follows:

1. Prepare a tight, carefully constructed synopsis.
This one- or two-paragraph overview of your book should be informative, interesting, well-written, and professional, and it should avoid hype. If possible, include a few brief quotes from pre-publication reviews or a solicited quote from a respected colleague. Never use the words "self-published." You simply run a small publishing company and your book is one of the titles (even if it is the only title).

2. Get a blurb.
A line of praise from a published author can be included with your query. If you don't know other authors, you aren't networking enough! Join a writers group. You can even write to an author whose work you respect and ask for a brief quote. They might refuse, but they might not.

3. Don't skimp on quality.
This is the heart of the prejudice against self-published books. Make sure your book is professionally edited (not by you) and printed on high-quality paper with strong stitched binding. Typos, ink that rubs off, and pages that fall out will kill your chances.

4. Don't skimp on quantity.
Make up a lengthy list of appropriate reviewers. Send a review request with synopsis to the review editors on your list following the protocol in their submission guidelines. If possible, create a run of pre-publication galleys three to six months in advance of publication so you can coordinate reviews with final publication and gather quotes for the back cover. Once

you hear back from the publications you've queried (probably about 10 percent will reply), send books to anyone who shows interest. The cost of a book is negligible when compared to the possible benefits.

5. Be polite and professional.

Reviewers usually have a big stack of books awaiting review, and it is not uncommon to have to wait months. On the other hand, a polite follow-up is fine if coupled with an offer for an interview, a piece of news, or the offer of a giveaway.

6. Don't be fussy.

A local review may be the best way to attract the bigger press, and even small sources may have big followings. Try trade journals specific to your subject, and local papers where you can offer an interview and milk the local angle. Don't neglect the Internet—many respected websites review self-published books. Do a search on "book reviews."

—*Magdalena Ball*

Magdalena Ball of Martinsville, New South Wales, Australia, runs The Compulsive Reader at www.compulsivereader.com, and is the author of *The Art of Assessment: How to Review Anything.* Her award-winning fiction, poetry, reviews, interviews, and essays have appeared in a wide range of online and print publications.

BASICS OF SELF-PROMOTION FOR AUTHORS

by Jessica Hatchigan

Selling your book to a publisher is only Step 1 on the road to a successful career as an author. Step 2 is proving to editors, publishers, and agents (and anyone else who might be paying attention) that you're a marketable commodity. For authors in the early stages of their careers, that means doing all you can to generate respectable sales for your book. For more seasoned authors, it means taking a shot at the bestseller lists.

Yes, that's right: you've got to vacate that rustic retreat, clamber down from the attic, or come on out from the broom closet or wherever else we notoriously shy author types like to hang out when avoiding the limelight. The rules of the game have changed. The romantic scenario of the sensitive author living in solitude flatlined long ago. You're not allowed to stay in sweet seclusion anymore—well, at least not year-round. When your book's out there to be bought, you have to go on the road (whether literally or figuratively) and promote it.

Remember that great catchphrase from the movie *Field of Dreams*, "If you build it, they will come"? Well, get your book published and sit and wait for your customers to come and they may *not* come. But toot your publicity horn and bang your publicity drum and they *will* come, a lot of them to buy. And that is what it's all about.

Like it or not, an author who wants her book to succeed has to find a way to connect with her audience. Unfortunately, authors who receive modest advances for their books—and that's most authors—can expect scandalously little in marketing support from most publishers. (One insider recently told me that many publishing houses today, because their profit margins are so thin, don't even bother to send out review copies of their newbie authors' books.)

So what can the poor author on a shoestring marketing budget do? The answer is, a lot. And the neat thing is that an author doesn't have to—and, in fact, shouldn't—wait for her book to hit the bookstores before she starts promoting her work.

Putting the Internet to work

Author W. Bruce Cameron didn't wait until his book was published to get out there and connect with his target audience. In fact, Cameron began building an audience before he had even written the book that would make him famous.

Cameron's first published book, *8 Simple Rules for Dating My Teenage Daughter*, a humorous guide to parenting two teen daughters, not only became a bestseller but served as the basis for an ABC-TV situation comedy starring John Ritter, which launched in 2002. And Disney recently commissioned Cameron to write a screenplay for a movie based on the book.

For a humorous writer, this is serious success. But only a few years before, Cameron's prospects looked bleak. Back in 1995, he was, in fact, the frustrated author of *nine* unpublished novels, most in the mystery-suspense genre. What happened in 1995 to kick-start Cameron's massive success? "That was the year," he says, "that I realized the Internet makes something possible which hadn't been possible before—which is that a person can actually self-publish, and reach a pretty wide audience."

Unable to sell any of his novels to a publishing house, or to stir up an agent's interest, Cameron decided to publish his own work electronically. He began to produce a free weekly e-mail newsletter, *The Cameron Column*.

That decision coincided with another one: to write the kind of column he himself would enjoy reading. In Cameron's case, that meant sharing his wildly humorous takes on parenthood, the cosmos, and life in general.

Cameron's decision to self-publish was partly a reaction to his frustration over his inability to sell any of his work. But it also was a strategic move. "I knew," he says, "that if I had enough of a fan base, I would be able to attract an agent, or get a publisher to pay attention."

When he launched his newsletter, he had six subscribers. By the end of the first year, his subscriber list had grown to 100. Then momentum kicked in. By 1998, the list had grown to 20,000, and was continuing to grow at a rate of 2,000 subscribers per month. At that point, Cameron approached the *Rocky Mountain News* in Denver with his column. The newspaper, impressed with the column and Cameron's ability to draw a following, signed him up as a regular columnist. His column also began to go out via the Scripps Howard News Service to hundreds of papers.

At the 20,000-subscriber mark, Cameron also approached an agent, who was impressed with the interest he had generated. She eventually took him on as a client and encouraged him in developing "8 Simple Rules" (originally published as a column) into a book proposal, which she successfully sold. The rest is history.

In Cameron's astute hands, the Internet became a powerful tool for building his writing career. "The Internet," he says, "allows you to put your product out there for free so people can sample it. It allows you to get your message and marketing materials—your brand—to the people who will most welcome them. It's your writing style, your voice, and who you are that's going to make you a recognizable author."

How Terry found her groove

Terry McMillan, now a publishing legend for such novels as *Waiting to Exhale* and *How Stella Got Her Groove Back*, is passionate about authors promoting their own work. If McMillan hadn't done everything she could to promote her debut novel, *Mama*, it's quite likely she would have had a much different career.

The astute McMillan had noted the fate of far too many other worthy first-time novelists who had seen their books hitting the remainder racks and going out of print. She knew results like that would dampen any publisher's interest in her future work. (Like the state of Missouri, the literary industry operates very much on a "show-me" dynamic.)

Mama had been purchased for a modest advance ($5,000) and was not envisioned as what the publishing industry calls a "breakout" book; i.e., one that was expected to sell thick and fast. For those reasons, McMillan learned there would be little budget for promoting and publicizing *Mama*. She was told, in effect, that luck and the prevailing winds would determine the fate of her work—and its author. Can we hear a "No way"?

"Get used to hearing, 'We can't, we wish we could, but we can't,'" McMillan said in a 1988 account in *Poets & Writers Magazine*. "You'll do well to do what I did. Take matters into your own hands."

Like any good publicist, McMillan zeroed in on what was unique about her work. She was a black woman who had written a novel about black women's issues. It occurred to her that the black community across America would be interested. She did some research at the library and came up with a list of almost all the black organizations and interest groups across the country, including all black media (TV, radio, newspapers, and magazines), all black colleges, and all black- and women's-studies programs.

McMillan, then an assistant in a legal firm (by day), was not only a speedy typist but had mastered the "mail-merge" feature of her word-processing software. (Mail merge lets you personalize a form letter. In effect, you can send effective, heartfelt, up-close-and-personal notes to hundreds or thousands of people! You also can print out the mailing labels to match.)

The summer before *Mama* was due to hit bookstores, McMillan sent out 4,000 "up-close-and-personal" letters pitching her book—roughly 2,500 to the black organizations she had targeted, another 1,000 to leading independent bookstores, and another 500 or so to authors with whose names she was familiar. She used reference volumes in her local library to get the contact information she needed to compile her mailing lists. (Today, databases are available for purchase and can speed up this chore considerably. See resources listed below under "Mail merge and databases.")

By the end of the summer, McMillan's letters had resulted in scores of invitations from across the country to do readings. She scheduled her own publicity tour and did 39 readings in seven cities. Her editor was so impressed that he convinced her publisher to foot the bill for the tour.

When *Mama* hit the bookstores, it sold out of its first printing (5,000 copies), a truly solid accomplishment for a first-time author.

Hard work, the magic of mail merge, a little legwork at the library, and a good grasp of the law of averages all added up to a crucial end result: McMillan had connected with her audience. She was on her way.

Using your connections

Almost every bestselling author I have interviewed emphasizes, like Cameron, the importance of building a brand. There may be a small number of authors who have enough success and fan base to avoid having to market their books, but until you reach that level, I would advise that you actively find ways to promote your work. "Pull the trigger on every connection that you have," Cameron advises.

He adds: "It's not attractive. I don't pretend it's not obnoxious. I do, though, feel that if this is your dream, then you owe it to yourself to exploit your relationships to fulfill your dream. There are so many people you know who know other people. And you can ask them. You can say, 'Do you know anybody at National Public Radio?' 'Do you know anybody in television?' 'Anybody who knows anybody?' If you know people in other cities, ask, 'What's the bookstore that seems to do the most book signings?' "

And what about the inevitable rejections that come with the pursuit of publicity? "In my opinion, you're not a professional writer if you're wounded or disappointed when you receive a 'no,'" Cameron says. "My nine unpublished books have accumulated so many negative responses from so many publishers and agents that I can fill a closet with them, and I'm to the point now where a 'no' is not even a bump in the road. It's just a 'no.'"

Resources for your own publicity blitz

Are you pumped and ready to publicize? Great! You have an exciting road ahead of you. To speed the process and smooth some bumps you might find along the way, here are a few thoughts and resources:

Pick up some free online publicity pointers.

Online resources abound. The iUniverse website provides valuable marketing tips and resources for newbie self-publicists. Go to www.iuniverse. com/publish and click on "Sales & Marketing Tips." Independent Publisher (www.independentpublisher. com) also offers helpful suggestions. And the online PR firm Talion.com (www.talion.com/resources.htm) offers a fun and enlightening online publicity tutorial called, "Top 10 Publicity Blunders."

Tap into the potential of "mail merge" and databases.

Mail merge works by merging a database of names and addresses with a form letter. This can vastly extend an author's publicity reach. A number of computer user groups offer classes in how to use mail merge. If you're moderately tech-savvy, one half-day course offered by a local organization might bring you up to speed. Call your local community college, or do an online search to find a mail-merge course offering near you. To get online help, Word 2002 users can visit Microsoft's Product Support Services (www.support.microsoft.com) and type "mail merge white paper" into the search box to bring up a link to "Using Mail Merge in Word 2002," a downloadable how-to.

You can either create or buy a database. Some of the best media databases are available online from Bacon's (www.bacons.com/directories/computer.asp). But at $2,000-plus each, they might be too pricey for your budget. As a less expensive alternative, you can purchase one of Bacon's printed media directories ($350 each), and hand-key your selected media contacts' information into a database of your own creation. (Bacon's printed media directories also are available at most library reference departments.) To purchase directories or databases from Bacon's, click on the "Products and Services" bar at www.bacons.com. The Book Marketing Update site (www.bookmarket.com/databases.html) offers databases of top libraries and bookstores ($30-$40 each).

Consider subscribing to PR Leads.

This excellent service, at www.prleads.com, has been highly effective for many professionals. It forwards "leads," which are notices reporters send out requesting input, quotes, and anecdotes from experts on specified topics. (If you've written a book about something, you're an expert.) When you sign up, you indicate your areas of expertise and can then respond to the leads forwarded ($495 a year, or $195 a quarter).

Develop your brand.

If you have the budget, find a graphic artist to create a logo for you. As part of her own branding strategy, bestselling author Brandilynn Collins created the catchphrase "Don't forget to breathe" after several readers told her they held their breath when reading suspenseful passages in her books. Collins had a graphic artist develop a logo incorporating the catchphrase. Her promotional materials (postcards and bookmarks) sport her brand logo. So do all her envelopes, stationery, and mailing labels. Even her bill payments, she says, go out in envelopes bearing the logo.

Make sure your news releases and press kits get noticed.

News releases and press kits are traditional ways to get the word out about your work. But these have to be well-done and strategically prepared or they will be ignored. To make publicity magic happen, your materials must stand out from the pack. There's a simple reason reporters ignore most news releases and press kits: they're overwhelmed by them. An average major daily newspaper receives 500 press releases a day. Media people are looking for reasons to throw these materials away. If you want your news releases or press kits to be among the few that get through, here are some tips:

• **Invest in good stationery**. This is a credibility issue. "Somebody who dresses in the best way they can afford is automatically given more credibility," advises Marisa D'Vari, image expert and the author of *Presentation Magic*. "Bad stationery is an automatic three strikes against you." Whether you order from an online or traditional vendor, make sure you ask to see an approval proof before you finalize your order. If you don't trust your own judgment on eye-catching design and layout, have someone whose judgment you do trust review the proof. Make any changes necessary. (One online site that sells premium stationery online is www. finestationery.com.)

• **Use news-release formats**. A news release is a one- or two-page document. It looks simple, but creating an excellent news release is an art. "The format and content of the press release are crucial in getting the attention of the media," advises Michael Odom, president of Phenix & Phenix Literary Publicists. "Most authors who write their own releases often find them ignored by the media because they did not format them correctly." My book *How to Be Your Own Publicist* provides explicit directions for creating winning news releases. You also can search the Web for online examples of correct news-release formats.

Master the art of writing attention-getting headlines and developing intriguing news "angles."

"There is something to be said for spinning the story or facts about the author to draw the interest of the media," Odom says. "You need to create a compelling argument for why the media should review the book." Mastering the art of developing those all-important angles is crucial. I outline how you can go about this in *How to Be Your Own Publicist*. Perhaps the most helpful exercise is the following: each time you notice an author or book in the media, ask yourself why the media reported on that author or book now, and what approach it took. Learn how to tie news about your book into breaking news stories, or into reports on developing trends.

Include a great "visual" element as part of your press kit.

A great photo of Michael Hoeye, author of the bestselling children's book *Time Stops for No Mouse*, accompanied recent articles about the author. In it, Hoeye's hair bristles straight up from his head—a shock of vivid Crayola orange. It's the kind of photo that makes you look twice—and that's the effect you want. Why not have a photographer take a picture of you that's somehow original—shot through a fisheye lens, or radically foreshortened? You may not want to go this far, but if it fits your brand image, why not make the focal point of the photo your bright orange, lavender, or chartreuse hair?

Give them an "eyeful."

Once your book is on bookstore shelves, attention from TV, radio, newspapers, and magazines can give it "legs"—an expression booksellers use for books that sell well and fast. What's the best way to get on TV? First, do your homework. Watch the show a number of times until you get a good feel for it and where you would fit in. Then call the station and ask for the name of the producer. Prepare a pitch letter that outlines what you have to offer that will be of value to the audience. And mention something visual that you plan to do on the show, D'Vari advises.

Write for trade associations.

That's the advice of Rita Emmett, author of the bestselling *The Procrastinator's Handbook*. Emmett is committed to sending excerpts from her book to magazines, including trade magazines for associations. "It seems as if every occupation has an association, and every association has a magazine desperate for articles," she says. While most trade association magazines don't pay her for her articles, Emmett says, "It's no cost to me, not much work—and it's great publicity for my book."

Promote other authors and experts.

When you call to offer yourself as a resource to media people, also let them know about your networks (organizations and associations you belong to), advises networking expert Susan RoAne, author of *How to Work a Room*. Tell them that if you can't answer a particular question, you'll be happy to refer them to someone you know who can. When you add a touch of selflessness to your dealings with media people, they pick up on it and somewhere down the line, they are more likely to be responsive to you.

Jessica Hatchigan of Ann Arbor, Mich., is an award-winning freelance writer and the author of *How To Be Your Own Publicist*, a guide for owners of small businesses, authors, and entrepreneurs. This article appeared in *The Writer*, September 2003.

PROMOTE YOUR BOOK ONLINE

Creative ways to attract more readers

by Moira Allen

As Karen Wiesner, author of *Weave Your Web: The Promotional Companion to Electronic Publishing*, notes, "The age of handing someone a business card at the point-of-sale when you're at a conference or in passing and saying 'call me' is past. The best tool at anyone's disposal is a Web page. Now we hand out business cards and say, 'Check out my website.' This is where you can show the world all they need to know about you, and how to and *why* to buy your product."

There isn't space here to discuss how to design and build an effective site. (See Resources listed at end of this article for more information.) Suffice to say, an author website must be more than just an electronic "ad" for your book. Nobody surfs the Web looking for ads. They look for content—and the more content you can provide, the more likely you'll be to entice visitors to buy your book.

Many authors recommended posting at least one "free" chapter of your book online—with your publisher's permission. If your book is nonfiction, consider including a FAQ (frequently asked questions) about the topic, articles on related topics, or even a reader Q&A page. If your book is fiction, you may still be able to include useful articles or FAQs; for example, if you've written a Regency romance, consider converting some of the research you must have done for the book into articles that could attract readers to your website. Or consider posting writing tips for would-be authors who might wish to learn the secrets of your success.

Here are some other features authors have built into their websites to attract readers:

Freebies. Julie Hood, author of *The Organized Writer*, offers a free downloadable organization calendar for writers on her site. Others offer bookmarks, bookplates, and other items that can be downloaded or mailed inexpensively.

Prize drawings. Many authors offer a drawing for a free copy of their book—and use the entries to build a promotional mailing list.

Contests. You could offer readers a chance to win a copy of your book, or something related to your book. Karen Wiesner cautions, however, that you shouldn't offer a contest that requires someone to actually *buy* your book (or read it) before they can enter (e.g., a contest that asks readers to write an essay about their favorite chapter in your book). Doing so comes across as blatant self-promotion, alienating potential readers and buyers.

If you're a self-published author, it's easy to give away free copies of your books. If you're not, ask your publisher to give you a few extra author copies for promotional purposes; many will be happy to oblige.

Attracting an audience

Building a website is just the beginning. Carmen Leal, author of *You Can Market Your Book: All the Tools You Need to Sell Your Published Book*, points out that "having a website is meaningless if people don't come to the site regularly and refer others." To bring readers to your site, you must know where those readers can be found. Fortunately, there is a thriving online community for just about any topic you can imagine. To find the community most likely to be interested in your book, search on terms relevant to your topic (e.g., "Regency period" or "Regency romances"). You'll quickly locate sites and discussion lists where potential readers "hang out," chat, and stay informed.

Once you've found that community, here are some ways to tap into it to attract traffic to your own site:

Exchange links with related websites. Don't be afraid to ask for a reciprocal link even from a competing author; most recognize that the benefits of a link swap go both ways.

Write articles or offer a column to newsletters and e-zines that cover your topic. As you begin to explore sites relating to your topic, you may find dozens of small e-mail newsletters that are hungry for material. Most can't pay, but they will be glad to publish original articles or book excerpts in exchange for a byline and link to your site—or even a free classified ad.

Launch your own e-mail newsletter or e-zine. Leal sends out weekly marketing tips from her book—and notes that a newsletter can serve as a marketing vehicle all by itself. She also offers a free "Quote of the Day" on her website and via e-mail. "Many people visit my site daily to read the quote, while others go for the e-mail version. My quote e-mails are forwarded to others by my subscribers, so I am getting untold exposure."

Join a Web ring. As you explore sites related to your topic, you may notice that many belong to Web rings. These rings are a way to bring together a network of related sites. To find out how to get your site listed, click on the "Join the Ring" link on the Web ring banner (usually found near the bottom of the page). Use the ring to find still more sites that might be interested in swapping links with you. Also, check whether sites belong to more than one ring; you may find several that are appropriate for your site.

Promote your website offline as well. Include your Web address on your business card and promotional materials for your book. Make sure your family and friends know where your site is so they can refer people to your page. Include it in your bio whenever you sell an article to a print publication.

One of the best things about this type of electronic promotion is that it can be done for little—or even no—cost. You can host your site on a free service such as Yahoo! Geocities, or Homestead, or pay as little as $9.95 per month to host it on an independent service provider (ISP). Registering your own domain name (e.g., "JoanQAuthor.com" or "MyBookTitle.com") costs less than $25 per year. (You'll need to host your site on an ISP to use your own domain.) Programs like BBEdit (for the Mac) or MS FrontPage (for PCs) make it relatively simple to create your own website—but if you're daunted by the thought of working with HTML, you can usually find an inexpensive, template-based site-development package. (Free hosting services such as Homestead offer free templates, as well.)

The question, however, is not whether you can afford to promote your book on the Internet. Today, as more and more publishers are investing less and less in author promotion, you can't afford not to!

Moira Allen, a contributing editor to *The Writer*, is a freelance writer and the editor of Writing-World.com. She regularly writes items for Miscellany in *The Writer*. Her books include *Starting Your Career As a Freelance Writer*, *Writing.com*, and *The Writer's Guide to Queries, Pitches & Proposals*. She may be reached at moira@writing-world.com. This article appeared in *The Writer*, October 2003.

Resources

"Do You Need an Author Web Site?" by Moira Allen
www.writing-world.com/promotion/website.shtml

Homestead
www.homestead.com

"Nuts and Bolts of an Author Web Site," by Chris Gavaler
www.writing-world.com/promotion/gavaler.shtml

The Organized Writer, by Julie Hood
www.organizedwriter.com

Weave Your Web, by Karen Wiesner
http://karenwiesner.hypermart.net/Eptdg.htm#WEAVE YOUR WEB

Webring
http://dir.webring.com/rw
A site where you can search for and sign up with Web rings on a vast range
of subjects.

*Writing.com: Creative Internet Strategies to Advance Your Writing Career
(2nd Ed.),* by Moira Allen
Offers tips on book promotion, website development, and more.

Writing-World.com: Book Promotion Tips
http://www.writing-world.com/promotion/index.shtml

Yahoo! Geocities
http://geocities.yahoo.com

*You Can Market Your Book: All the Tools You Need to Sell Your Published
Book,* by Carmen Leal
www.writerspeaker.com/YCMYB/YouCan.asp

—*Moira Allen*

A BLUEPRINT FOR WRITERS

11 ways to sustain a long, successful, fulfilling career

by David Poyer

Twenty-seven books don't put me in Alexandre Dumas' or Barbara Cartland's league. But I've been in the business for 25 years now. I've gone through eight publishing companies, four agents, about 30 editors. I've made every mistake that's possible for a writer to make, from signing up with agencies with quill pens as logos to calling a publisher by the name of her main competitor. But the good news is that I've developed a *working philosophy*.

Don't let the word "philosophy" put you off. This won't be an arcane discussion. Rather, it's a set of rules that make the day-to-day job of a career writer go more smoothly. They help me avoid screwups, serve as guard rails when I'm tempted to go off the road, and help me recover gracefully if I do. Here are 11 things I've learned that have helped me sustain my writing career.

1. Expect to dig. The first and most important point is that I expect to "dig." It's Jack London's word, one he picked up in the Klondike gold fields. "Dig is the arcana of literature," London wrote. "There is no such thing as inspiration and very little genius. . . . Dig is a wonderful thing, and will move more mountains than faith ever dreamed of."

I'm continually surprised at the triumph of ego over reality in the case of nine out of ten beginning writers. (And I've known and read hundreds.) They don't seem to understand how many hours of digging it takes to produce an ounce of gold. How many tons of rock you have to sift to find even an industrial-grade diamond. In the worst cases, that's coupled with two other unfortunate delusions: being in love with their own words, and not being familiar with literature.

The writer who doesn't read deeply and widely, who doesn't want to change the first thing he puts down, and who isn't willing to spend hours in a chair grinding over a paragraph until it is not just grammatically correct, but fresh and new and different from every paragraph that's ever existed before—well, he's just wasting his time.

So that's my first point: that I'm going to have to dig. Nothing will come easily. And I wouldn't have it any other way—because that fact alone stops 90 percent of my competition at the starting gate.

2. Keep improving. I try my best to steadily improve the quality of what I produce. Like a good automaker or electronics manufacturer, I upgrade and debug, and try to make each piece better than the one before.

Now, my writing is not *naturally* good. It's repetitious, banal, and cliche-ridden. When I read the first pieces I published, I'm appalled. Because they contain my natural style, without the revision that I've learned I need to bring to it.

But sometimes I wonder: Do I *have* to? Because there are those for whom that first book was just dandy. They were happy with a fast plot and lots of action and cardboard villains. I could have written that way my whole career and maybe sold more copies than I do now.

But that's not how I wanted to spend my life. I held lots of jobs before my novel *The Med* was published and my writing income became enough to live on. But none demanded very much of me, and some were positions of considerable responsibility, in the world's eyes.

Writing is different. No matter how good I get, I can see clearly how short I've fallen of the masters who went before and of those who are writing today. At the same time, occasionally I can shove back from my galleys and feel that the passage I've just read isn't that bad.

How do you improve your writing? Read it aloud to yourself, to a cassette recorder, to friends. Join a workshop. Take a degree in creative writing. If you can't afford the time for a degree, at least audit some classes. Unless you intend to teach, credit is a waste of time for a writer.

Above all, you need to write. Most writers shouldn't send out their first book or short story. They're wasting postage. The hardest digging you'll ever do is teaching yourself to write. Others can help you learn, but they can't teach you, any more than someone can teach you to play the piano. They can show you the notes. How to read music. But you have to teach yourself, week after week, until the knowledge seeps into your fingertips.

But then, very few ideas come from within. Most come from outside, are translated or shaded or reinterpreted in the light of our experience, and then come forth in new vestments. The most creative and original writers who ever lived, the Shakespeares and Austens, used words, plots, and characters other writers before them had created.

You're part of a community of thinkers and creators. This community is as wide as the world and extends as far back in time as history, myth, and speech. Go to conferences, workshops, and presentations. Read not only what you like to read, but different works that present new worlds to you. But always, always work to improve.

3. Give them more than they ask for. Now, this does not mean more *words*, but rather, more quality than what they thought they were buying.

If you're writing articles, do more research than you think necessary. Take more pictures. Do more interviews. Polish harder than you feel that market requires.

One result will be that your work will shine even in an unpromising setting. I've gotten book offers based on short stories and articles. Another benefit is that you'll get invited back by the editor you pleased the first time around. And yet again, it prepares you for more prestigious venues—a glossier or more literary magazine, a better-paying job or a higher class of publisher.

Give the reader more than he expects, too. Even if you're writing thrillers or mysteries or romances, make the work deeper than it needs to be. Most readers won't notice what you're doing. But those who do will appreciate it. You'll become known, like John D. MacDonald, as someone who transcends his genre, humble though it may be.

Really, I'd hope anyone who practices a craft would have this attitude. I hope the surgeon who operates on me aspires to have fewer complications than the average surgeon. I hope my auto mechanic does a better tune-up than I expected. When that happens to you, don't you prize that person? Don't you go back to them the next time? That's just good retailing. Keeping my customer satisfied, being better than the competition—I've *got* to do it. Or you folks will eat my lunch!

4. Make it personal . . . The publishing business is built on personal relationships. I visit Manhattan at least twice a year. Often there's no real reason to. I get phone calls and e-mails every day from my editors and agent. But I need to see them. They need to see me. So I go, and call on everyone I know while I'm there. Just to say hi.

But I don't stop with the editors. There are many others at the publisher's office who'd be overjoyed to have you know their names, shake their hands, send them autographed copies of your books. Editorial assistants, art directors, copy editors, layout people. Not only is it a boost to my oft-pummeled ego, these are the folks in the pipeline going up. Soon these underlings will be editors, then senior editors, and then publishers. Over and over I've run into movers and shakers I first met when they were making Xerox copies, bringing coffee, and answering the phone. Any recognition I've shown them when they were peons, they remember!

5. . . . but not too personal. That said, I continually re-evaluate just how close I get. I'm a loyal guy, and over and over, I've stayed with a situation beyond the point of diminishing returns.

A good author-agent relationship, for example, will usually be closer than that with your editor. She'll set up hotel arrangements for you, take you to lunch, talk heart to heart with you about the work. Over time, this relationship may begin to resemble a friendship. But it's not a friendship, though it may be friendly.

Each of my successive agenting relationships has been less personal and more businesslike. I'd recommend that beginning writers soft-pedal the "friendship" side. Even if you think you have the perfect agent, that may change as your career progresses.

6. Learn how to do everything. Centuries ago, there were only two players in the literature biz: the writer and the printer. Then the humble printer with his ink-stained apron became a publisher. Editors popped up, then sales departments, agents, art directors, legal departments—over time, the business has steadily specialized.

The downside is that as more and more people share the pie, their knowledge of the pie decreases. Their interest in the pie decreases. And very definitely, their concern for the pie decreases. Only the cook still understands and cares about the pie as a whole.

What this means to me is that as those who work downstream of me grow more specialized, I must grow less specialized. I need to be more knowledgeable about the entire publishing and promotion process.

> If you're writing articles, do more research than you think necessary. Take more pictures. Do more interviews. Polish harder than you feel that market requires. One result will be that your work will shine even in an unpromising setting. I've gotten book offers based on short stories and articles.

I can lay out a cover. Not well, but I can do it. (When I forward a book, I often forward a cover concept along with it. Get a scanner and take some time with your word processor's tutorials and you can, too.) I can negotiate a contract. I can discourse on basic book design. I know, more or less, how to allocate resources among print, radio, and Internet media. When I go on tour, I know which stores and media will be best for my book, and usually the names of the managers and the reporters. Did I start out knowing all this? No. I asked questions, read, observed, and took classes.

7. Micro-manage the process. But what, you may ask, is the point? Isn't it the agent's, editor's, or the publicity director's job to take care of your book?

Folks, the unpleasant truth: yours is only one of hundreds of books that will be published that month, and no one else will care about it the way you do. Also remember that publishers operate on a small profit margin. That means they employ entry-level people and burn them out and turn them over. This is a generalization, and I can name a dozen people who are excellent and caring and who have stayed in their positions for years, but there are also folks who are not so excellent, who don't care, and who won't be there three months from now.

That means I want to pay attention to details even after I turn in my manuscript. I don't have to do this, and early in my career I didn't. Those books got lost. They came out with lousy covers, bad layouts, or little or no promotion.

Now I don't look away. To the best of my ability, I track the book through the publishing process. I insist on cover consultation and make sure I get advance sketches. I ask for cover artists, layout people, copy editors by name. I make suggestions and help shape the promotional campaign.

8. Be ready to make changes. You begin with small publishers, and they want you to stay in their stable. But you walk, because to stay with them would be to bury your work forever. You start with an agent and you're friends, but he doesn't have movie contacts and that's what you need.

You'll also find you don't want to work with certain people. It's perfectly acceptable for you to ask for another editor if you're not getting what you need from the first. Or another layout person, or copy editor. You don't have to make a big deal out of it. Just tell your editor in private that you'd rather not have so-and-so as your copy editor. There's no need to complain about what he did, or how stupid he is. He just may not be good with your type of writing or had an off week.

An old show business saw goes: "Be nice to the people you meet on the way up, because you'll meet the same people on the way down." When it's time to say goodbye, I've tried to treat people as I'd want to be treated. A face-to-face meeting, a reasonable, face-sparing explanation of why you're leaving, a sincere thank-you, are just things you owe other human beings.

9. Be ready to walk away. Another lesson I've had to learn is that sometimes the game isn't worth the candle. At some point in your career, you'll be faced with something you really can't live with. It might be a cover you just can't see on your book, or a title that's just too much. An editor who wants to change the central message of your article. A demand for permanent e-rights along with print rights. The alternative is that you lose the deal. This is what the sales department wants, what the contract department has to have, what the newspaper's policy is: you don't have a choice.

I'm here to tell you that you *do* have a choice. Not only that, your choice is clear. Of course, try to compromise first. Negotiate. Be as flexible as you can without giving away what's important. But at the end of the day, you can walk.

And probably you should. For the sake of your own self-respect, and for all the other writers they're doing the same thing to, you *must* walk away from these either-or bad deals.

Here's a secret. Most of the time, once you show backbone, you'll win.

I've had this happen several times. In one case, it was a movie option. I didn't want to give away the rights to my character, along with the (very remunerative) sale of the property under discussion. Both my L.A. agent and the production company advised me that this was universal practice in La-La Land. That if I felt *that* attached to my rights, I'd blow everything. I sweated this out for a couple of days and finally decided to stand my ground. Either I retained rights to the character, selling only film rights for this one story, or the deal was off.

Well, it so happened that Studio X was holding an off-site executive meeting that week. My case went to them. They discussed it and decided to change their policy.

E-rights. For years, one publisher has been trying to get me to sell them e-book rights as part of my contract. I have nothing against e-books, though I find them hard to read. But what I couldn't buy was that they offered the same royalty rate as for a print hardcover. In other words, they were going to sell what I created, without having to print, ship, handle, or return a physical book; but all those savings were going to them, and none to me. They said, sign the contract as it is, or no contract.

I said no.

Silence for a few days. Then the contract arrives with the offending paragraph lined through.

Over and over, I've been confronted with ultimatums from supposedly hardball players that backed down in the end. I think they expect us to buckle. After all, we have no union, no government ministry behind us. But for the same reason, they must think: This guy's holding cards we don't know about. Somebody else must have made an offer.

Now, I *have* lost deals doing this. And I don't do it over minor items. My publishers know me as a pretty easygoing fellow, one who tries hard to meet their requests and necessities. I do it only when essentials are at stake. But usually, when that happens, I win. And even when I don't, there'll be another deal.

Muster the guts to walk away, and you'll win four times out of five.

10. Detach yourself from the outcome. *The Bhagavad Gita* has a wonderful line. "You have a right to your labor. You do not have a right to the fruits of your labor."

Sometimes things go wrong despite me. I can develop personal relationships, micromanage everything, do the best work I can, and still, someone else comes out with a book about the same thing the month before mine. Or a reviewer decides to dance on it for some weird personal reason.

This is a tough struggle for me. When you're a perfectionist, failure feels like personal failure. Rage, guilt, self-reproach, or reproach of others is all too easy. I used to obsess about such things for months. Today I realize the dice just fell against me. At other times, they'll fall my way. Either way, I'm still in the game, and I've done my best.

11. Help other writers. And finally, my philosophy tells me to help other writers. In no other field I know of do the practitioners feel obligated to train their competition, without recompense. But I guess that's the answer: we're not like other practitioners. We're not salesmen, though we have to be salesmen. We're not editors, though we should know how to edit. We're not publicity people, though we should know how to publicize our writing.

In the end, we're artists. We're dedicated to bringing something new into the world—something that will enrich the lives of all who look on what we've created.

I owe almost everything I can do to the thoughts and words of those who've written before me. The only way I can repay any of it is to pass on what I can.

I'm glad to get down on paper a few of the lessons learned that have enabled me to sustain 25 years of the writing life. I doubt I can stand 25 more. But long before then, I hope, I'll be reading your work instead of mine!

David Poyer of Franktown, Va., is the author of 27 books and one of the best-known writers of maritime fiction alive today. His most recent book is titled *A Country of Our Own*. For more information, visit his website at www.poyer.com. This article appeared in *The Writer*, September 2003.

SECTION THREE

The Craft of Writing

A WRITER'S NOTEBOOK

Daily meditations
help liberate your creativity

by Erica Jong

For the last few decades, I have kept little notebooks of inspiration, consolation, and meditation—quotes from others that have awakened the sleeping beast in my mind, poked my imagination into flames, comforted me in times of blockage. These quotes come from everywhere and anywhere—Shunryu Suzuki to Samuel Johnson to Eudora Welty to Muriel Rukeyser. Sometimes they come from friends and family. I write them down in my notebook and annotate them with my own thoughts.

During the same decades that I was compiling these notes, I began to rely on books of inspiration for each day of the year. How wonderful it would be, I thought, if there were a special meditation book made specifically for the creative process, so that each day one could move the mind's muscle, inspire oneself to imaginative labor, impregnate oneself until one heard the fetal heartbeat. Often it's hard to begin work in total solitude, and a writer needs a jump-start.

"Keep a notebook, honey," said Mae West, "and someday it will keep you." West may have meant this in a material sense, but it is also true in a spiritual one. To write is to be reborn, to affirm the self, the soul and the creative spirit.

In that spirit, I've compiled *Writing for Your Life*, a book of my daily meditations on writing. They keep me going in times of depression and sadness when nothing seems worthwhile. I encourage you to keep a similar notebook of inspirational meditations along with your comments. In the meantime, here are a few of my favorites to get you going.

> It is for the artist to proclaim his faith in the everlasting Yes.
>
> —Rabindranath Tagore

Art is essentially saying yes to the universe. In order to create it, you must first say yes to yourself. Creation is self-empowerment. When art succeeds, it empowers others as well because the energy reaches out from the page or canvas. It is an energy exchange. The artist begins the process by saying "yes" to herself.

Get those censors off your shoulders! Banish grandma, grandpa, and the local critic! Imagine your ideal reader. Your ideal reader has a kindly face and thinks your maddest flights of fancy are utterly sane. Because they are. Only by going wild on the page can you find sanity and serenity in life. Have *fun*. This is divine play, not heavy drudgery. The more impishly you play, the more the process works. On the seventh day you can rest. (But you won't need to because play is its own reward, and its own refreshment.)

> Poets have to dream and dreaming in America is no cinch.
>
> —Saul Bellow

Time is not money; time is priceless. And right-brain dream time, alpha-wave time, is the one sort of time most difficult to obtain in a culture that equates busyness (and business) with virtue. Art takes idleness. Creativity flowers when the brain is allowed composting time. The Palm Pilot is the enemy of art. The ringing fax, the ringing telephone, the computer that says "you have mail" are all your enemies. You need silence, long mornings in bed, "complacencies of the peignoir" (as Wallace Stevens says), but above all, dream time.

In America, dream time is suspect. It doesn't seem to yield anything for the ledger, the spreadsheet, the quarterly statement. Even established creators are expected to repeat themselves and produce a predictably marketable commodity. This is killing. All in the sacred name of marketing.

Marketing be damned! The world is in a state of spiritual starvation, and we keep feeding it quarterly statements! There will always be time for business. It is dreams that are fleeting.

> This is also the real secret of the arts—always be a beginner.
>
> —Shunryu Suzuki

Always beginning again, this is the secret the masters know. Writing is practice, but one never becomes perfect.

> First thoughts are also unencumbered by ego, by that mechanism in us that tries to be in control, tries to prove the world is permanent and solid, enduring and logical. The world is not permanent, is ever changing and full of human suffering. So if you express something egoless, it is also full of energy because it is expressing the truth of the way things are.
>
> —Natalie Goldberg

The best art comes from losing control within the context of discipline. The discipline may merely be sitting down at the same time each day, in the same chair and covering pages until you have worked a certain number of hours or produced a certain number of words.

When I am writing fiction, 500 or 1,000 words a day seems to be the most I do. Nonfiction is less stressful, at least for me; my output may be 1,000 to 2,000 words. Poetry, because of its playfulness, seems to be unlimited. It refreshes me to write poetry—but poems only come at times of heightened consciousness.

Create a disciplined context within which you can be free to play. Then play. Give yourself a goal. Usually I write five to ten handwritten pages of fiction a day, then stop. My handwriting is very large, so five to ten pages is only about 500 to 1,000 words. On a "good" day, I write that much in four hours. On a "bad" day, in 10 hours. Sometimes I discover that the "bad" days produced better prose than the "good" days. I'm not in charge. That's the whole point.

> Patch grief with proverbs.
>
> —Cervantes

Writing is balm for grief. Its only two real subjects are death and love. Or love and death. Eros and Thanatos. Which are aspects of each other. We only grieve where we have loved, and only love where there is the potential for grief. Yet we also know that life is a process of learning nonattachment because all things pass, flow, elude our grasp.

This is our human dilemma. We are attachers who must learn nonattachment, lovers who must learn to let go, and grievers who must learn the deep joy that underlies all grief. So we patch grief with proverbs, knowing that the patches barely cover our wounds. The wounds themselves are precious. They hurt us into healing.

> To a poet, nothing can be useless.
>
> —Samuel Johnson

A poet can use a three-legged cat or a sliced lemon glinting in the sunlight. Neruda shows me "a little cathedral" in the sliced lemon, and I have never cut into a lemon since without going to his church. *Look.*

Blake shows you "the world in a grain of sand" and "eternity in a wild flower." What will you show us that we can't see yet?

> Fill your bowl to the brim and it will spill. Keep sharpening your knife and it will blunt. Chase after money and security and your heart will never unclench. Care about people's approval and you will be their prisoner. Do your work, then step back. The only path to serenity.
>
> —Tao Te Ching, translated by Stephen Mitchell

Burn completely in the flame of your own attentiveness. Be present at the desk. Let all five senses work, let the heart open and the third eye see. The fourth dimension is not far off.

Expect nothing from your work except that it consumes you while you are doing it. Do it as well as you can. Then let go of all expectations, both hopes and fears.

In the moments that you achieve this, serenity will be yours. With practice, these moments will multiply.

Energy is eternal delight.

—William Blake

A good sentence—whether prose or poetry—is an energy container, an unsplit atom. When it interacts with the reader, it discharges fireworks.

A book is a box brimming with incendiary material. The reader strikes the match.

One does not choose one's subject matter; one submits to it.

—Gustave Flaubert

All art is born of surrender. You become a writer at that moment when your craft fuses at a white heat with the subject you were born to chronicle. You'll know it when you find your authentic voice and your authentic subject. You'll know it because the hairs will stand up on the back of your neck, a chill will go down your backbone, and a sun will glow in your rib cage. Can it be your heart? Until you reach that point, you're just scribbling.

Chance furnishes me what I need. I am like a man who stumbles along. My foot strikes something, I bend over and it is exactly what I want.

—James Joyce

Look down. Look up. Look straight ahead. Look back.

There are odd bits of research to do. Do you want your characters to go to Morocco? Chances are you'll have to go there, too. Not for the research and the history, but to smell the air, to taste the food, to let the scirocco blow, whistle in your ears.

Atmosphere helps. So does research. But the main stuff you already know. The questions of core and heart are the principal questions. The rest is set design, costume changing, catering.

All you need is a blank piece of paper and a pencil.

—Seymour Mann, my father

Why have I resisted the computer so? I see its magic, its infinite malleability, the joy of creating worlds within words on a starry screen of cosmic blue or green.

I love gadgets—laser printers, scanners, and all that delectable desktop publishing gear.

Yet I will not give up my yellow sheets and my pen that zooms like a toboggan down a frozen slope. And I love my little marbled notebooks, bound in Venetian paper. I can take them anywhere—pool, beach, plane. I need no batteries, no wires, printers, no disks, no surge protector. I *invite* power surges! I welcome hurricanes and blackouts! I will write by the light of one candle. It burns at both ends. Can any computer promise that?

Don't get too hung up on gear. It's the message, not the medium.

The medium is you.

> I must write as though I were a person of importance; and indeed, I am—
> to myself.
>
> —W. Somerset Maugham

When I first began to write, I had been brainwashed to think that *balls* were necessary for the making of literature. Hemingway and Mailer were the rage. As a young female student, I found it difficult to assume a stance of authority. But what is an author if not an authority?

I had to write as if I were a person of importance—but I was only a *girl*. It's a measure of how far we've come that girls now feel empowered to write.

I wrote my first books in fear—terror, in fact. Who was I to be anything so august as an *author*, or to wield anything so phallic as a *pen*?

Gradually I came to realize the truth of Maugham's discovery. I was a person of importance to *myself*. That's where all writing—and all humanity—begins.

> The shaman is the person, male or female, who in his late childhood or
> early youth has an overwhelming psychological experience that turns him
> totally inward. It's a kind of schizophrenic crack-up. The whole unconscious
> opens up and the shaman falls into it.
>
> —Joseph Campbell

Artists are the shamans of our culture. Since we've lost our authentic medicine men, spiritual teachers, sorcerers and witches, we rely more and more upon the artist to fulfill their functions. But when a true artist appears in our midst, instead of rejoicing, we try to kill her with exquisitely contrived ordeals. We try to corrupt her with neglect; if that fails, with attention; with poverty; and if that fails, with riches.

We do this because we have lost sight of the fact that art is not a luxury but a necessity. We believe we can buy spirit the way we can buy everything else.

Spirit is the one thing that cannot be bought. In a society where everyone is a buyer or seller, that makes it deeply suspect.

What you are doing at your desk is not less important than the shaman's vision quest.

Honor it—and yourself.

> If one woman were to tell the truth about her life, the world would split open.
>
> —Muriel Rukeyser

It doesn't get easier to tell the truth. . . . The deeper you go, the harder it gets.

The great revolution of women writing honestly about their lives, their sexual and emotional selves, quickly ossified into convention and was co-opted by formula writers. Female pain and female sexuality became commonplace. Danger became safe. Risk became predictable. A new convention was born: the convention of the confessional novel.

Start again. Go into your heart and find your own truth. That will always be untarnished, fresh, red as arterial blood.

> The secret of being a bore is to tell everything.
>
> —Voltaire

Edit. Edit. Edit. Scrape off the dirt so that the diamonds can shine. A lot of writing is knowing what to take away. Compose with utter freedom and edit with utter discipline.

The two processes must be divorced from each other. Horace once said that a writer must keep his piece nine years. In our instant-gratification world, where novels feed on headlines, nine years seems like an eternity. Still, let some time elapse between initial composition and final editing. When you come back, you will see it with fresh eyes.

> New opinions are always suspected and usually opposed, without any other reason but because they are not already common.
>
> —John Locke

We forget how much courage is required for telling the truth. We forget how high the dues are for making it new in a world that feels more comfortable with old, received ideas, strained through hot water like a used tea bag. It takes courage to live a life. It takes courage to chronicle that life honestly. Honesty is still a risk. It always will be.

The beginning of a novel is a time of awful torment, when you're dealing with a lot of dead pieces and you have to wait and wait for some sort of animation.

—Iris Murdoch

The blank page is terror. The blank screen is, too. How do I dare to impose my prejudices upon it? How do I dare to assume that what I have to say matters to anyone—even me? It's that mysterious leap that distinguishes the dreamer from the doer. I myself always trick myself into starting. "No one will ever read this," I say. "This is just for me." Sometimes I make as many as a dozen starts. Later I realize they were all different ways of sneaking up on the same material. I was stalking my book from many different angles—but I don't see that until I am well and truly launched.

"The last thing we decide about a book is what to put first," said Blaise Pascal. This has always been my experience. If only I could relax and remember that this game of hide and seek with my book is the only way I know of refinding the playfulness that making up requires.

Just keep the thing going any way you can.

—Tennessee Williams

Stand on your head. Dig the garden. Take a plane somewhere. Have a love affair. Just keep the vitality up.

Writers are vampires who feed on human blood for the sake of making the pages fly. We love only our pages—mostly our unwritten pages. The ones already written are taken for granted, like our spouses. Meanwhile, we're always running off in search of excitement to feed the fire. . . . Writers are always at the edge of the inferno, and the fire is licking at our toes. Luckily, this turns us on!

Erica Jong of New York City is the author of eight novels, including *Fear of Flying* and her latest, *Sappho's Leap*, and six volumes of poetry. These excerpts are selected from her work-in-progress, *Writing for Your Life*, and are reprinted here with the permission of the author. © Erica Mann Jong 2003. You can also join her Discussion Forum for writers at www.ericajong.com. This article appeared in *The Writer*, December 2003.

21 rules for writers

1. Have faith—not cynicism.
2. Dare to dream.
3. Take your mind off publication.
4. Write for joy.
5. Get the reader to turn the page.
6. Forget politics (let your real politics shine through).
7. Forget intellect.
8. Forget ego.
9. Be a beginner.
10. Accept change.
11. Don't think your mind needs altering.
12. Don't expect approval for telling the truth.
13. Use everything.
14. Remember that writing is dangerous if it's any good.
15. Let sex (the body, the physical world) in!
16. Forget critics.
17. Tell your truth, not the world's.
18. Remember to be earth-bound.
19. Remember to be wild!
20. Write for the child (in yourself and others).
21. There are no rules.

—*Erica Jong*

A KEY TO SUCCESS: WRITE MORE!

8 ways to boost your productivity

by Lee Tobin McClain

What's the key to writing success? Talent? Intelligence? Creative genius?

None of the above. According to Dean Keith Simonton, a psychologist who has conducted research on creativity for nearly 25 years, creative success correlates most closely with output: the *quantity* of work produced. Artistic and scientific achievers from Picasso to Da Vinci didn't succeed more, percentage-wise, than other now-unknown creators of their eras; while they possessed amazing minds and talents, another large part of their accomplishment is that they simply produced more, and thus had more successes.

As the director of a graduate program in writing, I can vouch for the fact that students who complete more writing projects succeed in getting published more frequently than their slower-writing peers, regardless of talent.

If productivity equals success, how can you increase yours? Here are eight ways, based on many years of writing as well as teaching and observing hundreds of writing students:

1. Build an expectant audience. Many of us are motivated by the expectations of others. We'll do more to fulfill responsibilities or avoid humiliation than we will to fulfill our own dream. If that's your blessing—or your curse—use it. Create an audience for yourself, whether it's a critique group, an editor, or even online subscribers.

Poet Michael Arnzen developed a system for distributing a poem a week from his website, www.gorelets.com, which delivers poetry directly to readers' Palm Pilots or other handheld computers. He solicited subscribers through e-mail and press releases, and once hundreds of people were expecting their weekly poems, Arnzen was committed to delivering. "Knowing my subscribers were always waiting for the next poem in the series drove me to write daily. It was my most productive year as a poet, ever, despite my full-time job," Arnzen says. "And the project brought attention to my other writing, too. I sold three chapbooks this past year, including the poetry series itself."

Critique groups can function the same way. If your group sets up a schedule for distributing work, you feel obligated to fulfill your responsibility. The critiques you receive are almost a bonus compared to the regular production such groups enforce.

For magazine writers—aspiring or published—there's nothing better than landing a few assignments to build an expectant audience and, thus, enhance your productivity. If you're an established writer, play the query-a-day game (see tip No. 3, below) until you have several assignments and deadlines to push you into productivity.

If you're inexperienced, you may have to work on spec or for free. But knowing that an editor, even the editor of the tiny neighborhood newspaper, is expecting your work will jar you into increased productivity, no matter what other demands are made on your time.

2. A gradual increase in your output. Don't try to make a rapid jump in your productivity. Take it slowly. More importantly, take it steadily.

Bestselling novelist Peter Straub compares writing to exercise. "If you spend an hour or two a day writing, fairly soon you will be able to do it for three or four hours each day; and the more you write, the more sheer muscle you develop," he says.

Romance and women's fiction writer Susan Mallery suggests that a very gradual increase in daily pages written can lead to a major boost in quality and quantity of work sold. Her strategy is simple: figure out how many pages you write in each writing session now, and then increase by half a page every few weeks.

Why does it work? "A half page is a manageable goal," Mallery says. "It's so small an increase, it's hard to get excited about it. Yet over time, it makes a huge difference. Those half pages add up without adding stress to the writer."

Mallery ought to know. She's sold more than 80 books to publishers.

The hidden benefit behind Mallery's method is consistency. And consistent writing actually increases quality as well as quantity. "When you write a certain number of pages each day, the story stays 'in place' in the brain," she explains. "That means writing time can be spent on deepening the characterization and enhancing the story rather than trying to remember who these people are and what's happening with the plot."

3. A query a day (games with yourself). If you're trying to make it in magazine writing, you need regular, frequent assignments that will keep you writing. But at the beginning of your career, or during a slump, the assignments can be thin or nonexistent. That's the dangerous point, when it's easy to clean the garage or see the latest flick instead of writing. Soon you can feel like someone who used to write, or used to want to write, instead of feeling like a writer.

At times like this, you need some kind of game to boost your creativity and your career. My favorite is "A Query A Day." All you have to do is produce and mail out one query letter each day, and then you're off the hook and out the door. Conversely, on busy days, when the boss demands the latest report, the spouse threatens to leave, and the teenager wrecks the car, you *still* have to produce that one query.

Benefits are multiple. You get really fast at writing query letters. You get fast at finding markets at the odd moments of your day; I've been known to keep a copy of a writer's handbook in my bathroom.

Best of all, you're planting seeds that will bear fruit for months to come. Inevitably, something hits, and then something else does, and before long, you're so busy writing stories that you have to quit the game. Months later, assignments from the game days will still trickle in. And because you produced so many queries, you probably went off in weird directions; now, you have an assignment to write something out of your own norm, and creativity soars.

Variations for other sorts of writers: Try "A Short Synopsis Per Day," "A Contest Entry Per Day," "A Poem a Day."

4. Multiple projects. When you're working on a long book project, reinforcement and rewards are seriously lacking. If you let discouragement set in, your productivity may dip or plunge.

That's when you need the perspective and refreshment of multiple projects. If you're writing a novel, make use of your background research by submitting short magazine pieces on topics related to your novel's theme. If your book project is nonfiction, see if you can work up a short story or poem—either on the same topic, or on something completely different.

And make sure to submit the other writing somewhere—a contest, a tiny literary magazine, or a newspaper. The opportunity for quicker feedback can give you a boost on your main project. Whether or not you publish any of these side pieces, your big project will benefit from the renewal of interest brought about by your moonlighting.

5. Visualize a compelling future. If you're not producing as much as you want, maybe you're living too much in the present.

Success guru Tony Robbins asserts that you should have enormous goals, the type that will make your palms sweat and your heart race, in order to keep yourself working hard each day. Most people, he maintains, think too small when they think about their future.

"When you write a certain number of pages each day, the story stays 'in place' in the brain."

—Susan Mallery, author of 75 novels

Indeed, successful writers often admit they've been visualizing that place on the bestseller list for years. Before my first book was published, I spent a lot of time looking at the paperback rack, letting my eyes blur so that I could imagine that the latest popular romance was my own.

One day, it was.

So go ahead and picture yourself accepting the Bram Stoker Award, or the Edgar, or the Nebula. Imagine what you'll say when interviewed about your Pulitzer. If your dream is big enough, you'll be motivated to make big efforts at the keyboard today, to make tomorrow's vision come true.

6. Pages, not hours. Should you make yourself sit at the keyboard for two hours each day, or strive for two pages?

Views differ, but I'm a fan of the page count. It's all too easy to sit and daydream away a stint of writing time and produce nothing. But if you know you aren't allowed to leave until you come up with that query, or those three pages, you'll get it done faster. Sometimes what you create will seem to be no good, but you'll find that when you come back later, it's hard to tell the difference between the pages produced quickly and those crafted more slowly.

In any case, bad pages can be fixed. A blank page can't.

7. Book in a week. The book-in-a-week technique is trendy now in the romance-writing community, but dates back to authors like Belgian-born detective writer Georges Simenon. Simenon wrote most of his 500-plus novels in eight to ten days—sans outline, sans pause, and sans computer.

Today's book-in-a-week proponents swear by a similar, if electronically updated, method: they clear their calendars of as much non-writing-related activity as possible in order to fully focus on writing for one week. During that week, they write in every spare moment, whether that means a ten-hour stretch on a Saturday, or writing during commuting time, coffee breaks, their lunch hour, a teenager's soccer game, or a toddler's bath time.

Some really do complete the first draft of an entire book. Others set smaller goals: write an article every day, for example. The point is to push yourself beyond your normal comfort zone, knowing you'll only have to stay there for one week.

The Internet serves as a helpful ally to keep writers motivated for this challenge. "I joined an online book-in-a-week challenge to help me stay the course," one participant explains. "Everyone posted their page totals each evening. Knowing my online friends were doing the same crazy thing, that I'd

> "If you spend an hour or two a day writing, fairly soon you will be able to do it for three or four hours each day; and the more you write, the more sheer muscle you develop."
>
> —Peter Straub, bestselling novelist

have to post my totals each night and that it was only for one week, kept me writing. I wrote an average of 20 pages per day. That's more than I'd ever written before."

This mad rush of writing has several benefits beyond the often-admirable number of pages produced. Focusing on writing as much as possible helps to turn off the internal critic. For this week only, you're not judged on quality, only quantity. For perfectionists, that can be liberating.

April Kihlstrom, who has spoken about book-in-a-week challenges at national conferences, describes quality benefits gleaned from this quantity-related method. A draft written in a short time, she has said, is far more likely to be consistent, passionate, and strong-voiced.

Book in a week isn't for everyone, and it can't be done often, but it may provide the jump-start you need for increasing your productivity.

8. Charts, calendars, and goals. If you're already a working writer, you know that you have to plan out your work; after all, you have deadlines to meet, and editors who will squawk if you don't do so. But if you're still unpublished, you may be meandering along without a real plan, without charting out your goals for yourself.

Get in practice for your future success by setting your own deadlines. That way, when assignments or contracts come, you'll know how quickly you can write, and you'll have faith in your own ability to meet your deadline and follow through on your promises. Plan to finish the picture book this month, the chapter book by spring, the young adult novel by the end of the year. Then figure out how you'll do it with daily page counts marked on a calendar.

As the platitude says, every journey begins with a step. So decide now to put these productivity tips to use. Make a plan about how you'll succeed. As your output increases, watch your career soar along with it.

The beautiful thing about output is that it's something you can control—unlike native intelligence or a good ear for words. If you aren't making it on only a page a week, you have no one to blame but yourself. And when your career takes off due to your increased output, you'll have the satisfaction of knowing that your own hard work made the difference.

Lee Tobin McClain, of Pittsburgh, directs Seton Hill University's long-distance master's program in writing popular fiction. Her teen novels, *My Alternate Life* and *My Abnormal Life*, focus on foster care and adoption. You can visit her website at LeeMcClain.com. This article appeared in *The Writer*, October 2003.

A FICTION WRITER'S CHECKLIST

8 ways to improve your writing

by Sharon Mignerey

Self-editing fiction is one of the most difficult and most useful things we can do. The process helps ensure that what makes it to the page is what we intend. For me, self-editing falls into two categories: storycraft and grammar. (For more on grammar, see page 126.)

I've come up with a list of things to look for in each category, but I share it with a few caveats. First, this is editing. Don't do this during the flush of writing and creating. Second, if you discover that any of these suggestions destroy your personal voice, adapt the techniques so they work for you. And finally, I can share with you only what has worked for me—your personal list may be different than mine.

I find editing for storycraft easier if I make it part of my daily routine. Usually, my day begins by editing what I wrote during the last session, which helps get me limbered up and refreshes my memory about where I left off. As I go through that process, I ask myself the following questions, and then I edit until I'm satisfied, which is never—but I try to get close.

1. Is this section in the right point of view? I'll admit to being a bit of a purist about this—if I start a scene in a particular point of view, my preference is to finish it in that same point of view unless I have an *extremely* good reason to change. The POV character should be either the one with the most at stake or the one with the most interesting observation about what is happening.

2. Have I ended a chapter or a scene in a way that keeps the reader interested? Cliffhangers are used for this very reason—to keep the reader going to find out what happens next.

3. Have I choreographed the scene to create a clear picture of how the characters move through it? Sometimes I'll draw stick figures and a basic diagram so I know where the characters are in relation to one another and their surroundings, then compare that to what I've written.

4. Are my characters thinking too much? Acting too little? Telling what a character is thinking and how she reacts to a situation is easier than describing the situation blow by blow. Showing characters interacting with the story's setting and with one another is a more effective way to communicate what is on their minds than writing interior monologues. You can do this through action and dialogue.

5. Are motivations and emotions clear? Be sure to set up your character's actions so the reader understands why he or she is behaving in a particular way.

6. Is the dialogue realistic? And do my characters sound like themselves rather than me? Since dialogue is supposed to reveal character and propel the plot forward, it's sometimes too easy to get into the mode of ask-a-question and answer-a-question. No matter how much information is conveyed through dialogue, what is said needs to be natural and to mimic how we really talk to each other. Dialogue shouldn't sound like one character interrogating another one.

7. Is dialogue over-attributed? "He said" and "she replied" should be used only enough to make it clear who is talking. Further, whether characters are shouting or whispering should be evident from what they say and how they move through the scene rather than from the attribution. Avoid attributions such as "he replied angrily." Show that your character is angry.

8. Am I peeling the onion? Have I revealed what needs to be known about the character at the time it needs to be known, or have I put in too much backstory too quickly? For example, if the outcome of the climax rests on the hero's being an expert swordsman, his ability needs to be established early. But if he prefers roast chicken to roast beef, that probably doesn't need to be revealed until the moment he's faced with the choice—unless something more important is at stake.

You can use this list to begin one of your own. You'll most likely want to add other elements as you go along. And remember that self-editing is not for the creative process. While you're writing that first draft, kick your self-editor out of your workspace and just write.

Sharon Mignerey, a romance writer, is the author of the Jensen Sister Trilogy: *In Too Deep, Too Close for Comfort*, and *Friend, Lover and Protector*. Her novel *A Sacred Trust* won a National Readers Choice Award. She was the Colorado Romance Writers 2003 Writer of the Year. She lives in Brighton, Colo. This article appeared in *The Writer*, April 2004.

Grammar check

• Own and use Strunk and White's classic little book *The Elements of Style*. Apply the rules of grammar and usage explained there; you'll be just fine.

• Develop a personal list of words and phrases that you overuse and can eliminate from your work without losing meaning. A few of mine include: *just, almost, in order to, so that* (instead of *so*).

• Search for words ending in "ly." During the creation process, you're flying to get the words on the page. But when you self-edit, you can find more precise verbs. For example, you might change "walked slowly" to "ambled." Sometimes you'll choose to leave in the adverbs, but most of the time you'll find that using a stronger verb works better.

• Search for your favorite forms of the "to be" verb: *was, were, is, am, are*. These are *not* indicative of passive writing by themselves, but we often use them as "helper" verbs. With a little editing, many of the "to be" helpers can be taken away so you have "She heard him" rather than "She was hearing him." Don't take the elimination of "to be" verbs to an extreme— sometimes there is no better word.

• Look for sentences that begin with pronouns: *his, her, it, they*. When you find yourself confused about the meaning of a sentence, one common cause is a pronoun with an unclear reference. For example: "A hiker made his way through a forest along a path that traversed a rocky precipice. It smelled strongly of pine." The antecedent for "it" is "precipice," but a pine-smelling precipice seems unlikely and is probably not what the author intended.

• Be consistent. Some style manuals advise always setting off an introductory prepositional phrase with a comma while others say don't. Choose a style and stick to it. If an editor wants a different style, he or she will make the necessary changes.

—*Sharon Mignerey*

CHOOSE & RESEARCH THE RIGHT TOPIC

An interview with Erik Larson

by Ronald Kovach

In his last two books, Erik Larson has proved himself a master at conjuring up a compelling, bestselling nonfiction narrative out of a relatively obscure historical event. This literary slight of hand, he revealed in our interview, begins with a whimsical but purposeful search for a good topic and leads to a focused process of researching his subject.

What "a good topic" means to Larson is a multifaceted one that will allow him to deploy "all the fictional tools" in a strong narrative line, including foreshadowing, time-shifting, and an emphasis on scenes. Pick a bad or too-narrow topic, he says, and you'll wind up with a small book; pick a good subject with many potential paths, and you'll have a rich research and writing project.

In *The Devil in the White City*, a superb narrative which earned a National Book Award nomination, Larson tells a twin tale of Chicago's great fair—the World's Columbian Exposition of 1893—and Dr. Henry Holmes, reputedly the first American urban serial killer. The book underscores how a good storyteller like Larson is a good seducer, hooking the reader from the start with the promise of a rewarding adventure ahead.

Many readers probably open this 400-page book with limited interest in the fair and no knowledge at all of Dr. Holmes. Within a few pages, however, Larson has cast a spell as only a skilled writer and researcher can. By the time we finish his cinematic prologue, he has used well-chosen details to make us appreciate what a colossal undertaking the six-month fair was. Indomitable drive and ambition, great architecture and landscape design, and a monstrous feat of construction all came together to transform swampy wasteland into a

"White City" of grandeur and beauty. The fair comprised more than 200 build-
ings. Entire villages were imported as displays from Egypt, Algeria, and elsewhere. In a nation of 65 million people, the fair recorded 27 million visits.

"Visitors wore their best clothes and most somber expressions, as if entering
a great cathedral," Larson writes. "Some wept at its beauty." Visitors tasted new
foods called Cracker Jack and Shredded Wheat. Larson also uses his prologue
to signal the interesting characters we'll meet in his book, including Frederick
Law Olmsted, Buffalo Bill, Theodore Dreiser, Susan B. Anthony, Thomas
Edison, and Jane Addams. (The famous cast of characters is yet another illustration of how many avenues of exploration Larson's topic opened up.)

The other half of Larson's story is a chilling depiction of Holmes, a con man
of fiendish charm who lured his victims to his World's Fair Hotel, which was
designed for murder and even included a basement crematorium. To better
understand Holmes, whom he calls "a textbook psychopath," Larson gained
vital insights from a forensic psychiatrist who read his first draft.

Larson's previous book was *Isaac's Storm: A Man, a Time, and the Deadliest
Hurricane in History* (1999), a vivid depiction of a great storm that blasted
Galveston, Texas, in 1900, killing 6,000 to 10,000 people.

Larson sees his role as being "an animator of lost stories," adding, "I'm not a
historian; I'm a writer who tries to find stories and bring them to life. I love trying to capture atmosphere, landscape, events, in prose. I love sinking into the
past. What I'm trying to do for my readers is allow them to just fall into another
time, and ideally not emerge until the book is done, with a changed sense of the
past."

Larson lives in Seattle. I spoke to him in Milwaukee, where he expanded on
his search for the right topic and a research process that allows him to bring "a
world" to life.

**Your two historical narratives have a way of making readers wonder
how they ever missed learning about these great subjects. How do you
come up with these obscure but compelling story ideas?**

First of all, I came across both by accident, by luck. However, I have worked
out certain techniques to put myself in the way of luck. One of those is that
when I am looking for an idea, I deliberately put myself into a regimen of just
reading everything I possibly can. I'm lucky to have access to the University of
Washington's Suzzallo Library, and I'll go in there, maybe into the section
where the new science publications arrive, and I will just impressionistically go
through a dozen magazines on things I know nothing about. I'll just sit there
and read through them, looking for interesting things. It rarely does anything
for me, but you never know. It's putting yourself in the way of luck.

Then I will walk among the stacks and at random pull out books and take a
look at them. In the process of that, I'm thinking about things, I'm seeing
things, connections are made. It's like prospecting in a park with one of those
metal detectors, because you just don't know what you are going to find.

So I allocate a lot of time to this process of finding an idea, because it can't be rushed. Because one thing you don't want to do is get stuck with a lousy idea. I know from experience that only a small percentage of the ideas one comes across can live up to the requirements of a strong narrative line, of the kind of structure that will allow all the fictional tools to be deployed.

Always, as you go along, there are things that kind of intrigue you, and you should indulge those feelings. For example, World War II has always been an interest of mine. And when I was looking for ideas for the next book—I'm still in the process of looking—for the first time I read [William Shirer's] *The Rise and Fall of the Third Reich*. No reason; just to read it. And there are half a dozen books that one could write based upon what you come across in that book.

And there are fascinating things in the footnotes—that's often where the best ideas lie, by the way. But professional historians are hamstrung—they have to do certain things. A professional historian doing a look at the world's fair would have to do "the deconstructionist feminist Marxist look at the fair" and put the best stuff in the footnotes. So I always troll the footnotes; I always read the author's notes at the end of the book to find out what's going on. And I came close to having a few good ideas for this next book, whatever it will be, from *The Rise and Fall of the Third Reich*. Then suddenly I was thinking about U-boats, so I tapped into uboat.net on the Internet—fascinating site, everything you'd want to know about U-boats. Stumbled across something there—sort of "maybe, yeah, what about that?" So that's on the plate.

After you've got your idea for a book, what comes next?

You get your idea, you see possibilities, you get excited. Often when I get an idea, it's not something I am incredibly passionate about. It's that I can see somehow that somewhere down the line this is going to become very engaging. I don't wait for passion to happen; the passion will come later if it's a good idea.

Let's say I think Idea X has the possibility to work. The next phase is to do the broad reading, go to the library and read, read, read. Read everything you possibly can. You want to find out what else has been done; you've got to add something new to it, otherwise what's the point?

[At this point] I'm taking notes very impressionistically. What I do is I take those little yellow Post-It notes and, if I'm reading a library book, stick them in the margins and write on the Post-It notes, maybe a little arrow to something that's in the text, and then I photocopy all that, take the Post-Its off, and return it to the library. [Larson sometimes returns from research trips with as many as 800 photocopies.]

And in the first phase, you want to make this as fun and easy as possible, so you don't burn yourself out by taking notes. At this point, you're being creative, trying to figure out the parameters of the story.

And then you start reading on a more focused level, find out what the nuances are. You develop an instinct for the potential for a lot of interesting

paths to be followed. If an idea is too proscribed, if there aren't enough chan-
nels to go down, it's not going to work. You're going to get bored, you're going
to exhaust your material, and you're going to wind up with a very small book.
But if, as you go, you find things swelling and going off in a million directions,
that's good. You want to be intimidated by the material, because that means that
there's heft.

When you're reading, you're just constantly thinking about, what's a great
scene? That's what I look for most of all at this point. And you want to collect a
lot of scenes, because those are your chapters in a work of narrative nonfiction.
This guy gets sick here, or this child dies at this stage of the process—you want
to keep track of those scenes. And once you've amassed a lot of scenes, you're
just about ready to do a proposal, because you know just about everything. You
can see in your mind a kind of structure spreading before you because you've
collected these scenes. If you're thinking cinematically as you're writing scenes,
you are right away creating a world, rather than just doing expository graduate-
student writing.

Ronald Kovach is senior editor of *The Writer*. This is excerpted from an
interview that appeared in *The Writer*, September 2003.

Erik Larson's next book will be another twin tale: of wireless inventor
Guglielmo Marconi and a murderer tracked down with the help of wire-
less technology. The tentative title: *Thunderstruck: A Story of Love, Murder, and
Invention in the Edwardian Age.*

RESEARCH FOR NOVELS

4 rules for finding information to give your fiction depth and veracity

by Shelby Hearon

Everyone expects nonfiction to be chock-full of facts. In the bestselling saga *Seabiscuit*, journalist Laura Hillenbrand researched the history of the three men who brought a small and awkward horse, grandson of Man O'War, to glory, starting back in the years when the first automobiles began to replace the horse and buggy and continuing through the Depression. She has eyewitness accounts, original letters, newspaper stories and extensive documentation of the start of the automotive industry, the terrible life of jockeys, and the breeding and training of thoroughbreds.

In a similar way, the fiction writer must collect an abundance of rich and varied facts in order to create a believable and compelling story that comes to life on the page.

Here are four rules of fact-gathering I swear by, and write by.

1. Discover your facts firsthand. Go where your story is set, walk the ground, eat the food, listen to the talk, read the local paper, take rolls of film, and take notes. Getting facts secondhand is similar to getting your information about the moon from a website on phases of the moon. You can read the scientific information on the positions of the moon, Earth, and sun, and yet end up with nothing close to real, nothing like sitting on the edge of a hillside watching a sliver of the moon rise over the pines or, sleepless, staring out your upstairs window at 2 a.m. and watching the full moon slide out from behind the clouds. You have to gather facts through your own eyes and point of view, because what you notice, what resonates with you personally, will be what stirs the emotions and actions of your fictional people.

I'll give two examples from my own research. Some years ago, I set my novel *Five Hundred Scorpions* in Tepoztlan, a Mexican village near Cuernavaca, about which I had already read three scholarly books, written over a 40-year period. I even had a map of the streets and marketplaces for my expatriate Virginia lawyer to explore. But when I arrived at the actual mountainous town, in the heat of summer, what struck me instantly was: there was no wood anywhere. The townspeople made charcoal to sell from their trees. Poor homes had dirt floors and reed doors; rich homes had quarried stone floors and heavy metal doors. No wood. And that fact, in the course of the novel, gave the presence of a heavy wooden cross inside the church more significance.

Another example of firsthand observation came while working on *Hug Dancing*, set in Waco, Texas, which was, in my university days, a very small, very Baptist town.

In the '90s, it had become part of the central-Texas technology boom. A careful reading of Waco's daily paper and strolls around its streets gave me another glimpse into how the influx of scientists had altered the city. Of all the divergent groups who moved there, the Koreans alone had been taken into the fabric of the town. I knew that my story would have to take place within the Presbyterian Church, because of the long alliance of this congregation with the Koreans, and my narrator became a pastor's wife.

2. Repeat facts in such a way that they deepen the meaning and move the plot as the story develops. Three wonderful contemporary novels illustrate how facts, at first of seemingly little importance and almost randomly acquired, can, when repeated in different scenes with more emphasis and deeper import, become what move the story to its satisfying finish.

I have several times amassed prodigious piles of clippings, overheard conversations, photographs and notes made on-site, without knowing which details I might later need to use.

The narrator in Yann Martel's *Life of Pi* was raised in Pondicherry, India, where his father, once a hotelier, ran a zoo. And so he grew up familiar with the many animals enclosed therein—the late-sleeping elephants, seals, big cats, and bears; the early-rising baboons, macaques, mangabeys, gibbons, giraffes, and mongooses. Only later do we see how desperately every scrap of knowledge he'd learned became a matter of life and death, when he was stranded in a lifeboat with an adult tiger in the middle of the Pacific Ocean.

In *Getting Mother's Body* by Suzan-Lori Parks, Billy Beede, pregnant and living with an aunt and uncle in a rundown trailer in a dusty Texas town, took some pride in the fact that her mama, Willa Mae, dead now six years, was buried according to her wishes wearing her genuine diamond ring and real strand of pearls. Her present concern being to locate the daddy of her child, who had promised to marry her, the matter of her mother rested on the back burner. But when the family learned that Willa Mae's burial spot was about to be plowed under for a supermarket, the aunts, uncles, and cousins all headed for the plot. Unearthing the jewels became central to Billy's survival plan. The author's inclusion of realistic details concerning life in dry small-town Texas and a real cemetery about to be covered over by developers lends her story immediacy, and makes Billy's panic believable.

Finally, in Mark Haddon's amazing first novel, *The Curious Incident of the Dog in the Night-Time*, the rigid rules of the autistic narrator, 15-year-old Christopher, a British schoolboy, seem arbitrary and both sad and funny. Through detail the author shows: why Christopher is good at remembering things; why he likes Sherlock Holmes but not Arthur Conan Doyle; why he hates yellow and brown; why five red cars in a row means it is a super, super day; why he is a whiz at math; and why he likes dogs better than people. Yet as the mystery Christopher is writing (and living) develops, all these unconnected facts lead him not only to its solution but also to an unexpected solution in his own life.

Readers of fiction like to learn something, care about someone, and be surprised by the way things turn out—just as they do in their own lives. Using such well-placed facts is one way to create those experiences for them.

3. Sift your facts for crucial details. Sometimes, a single object will become a sort of shorthand symbol, a talisman, for the central wrenching conflict of your novel. In *Life Estates*, my novel set in South Carolina, Sarah, the narrator, treasures her peach trees. I visited orchards, picked a dozen varieties in the rain, tried out recipes that showed off the taste of each, learned that peach trees must be beaten with newspapers to help them grow strong—all without knowing why the luscious fruit had become so central to my story. But then, when Sarah produced three special peach desserts for her best friend, who was dying, and the ailing woman felt not grateful but unloved, because she had not been given her favorite chocolate treat, I could see that the argument over sweets really had to do with the anguish of leave-taking.

In my latest novel, *Ella in Bloom*, linen dresses became an emblem of my narrator's vain efforts to please her mother. Hearing of her sister's death, Ella stole a linen dress from the vast closet of a wealthy client whose flowers she watered—so she would not be an embarrassment to her mother at the memorial service. Later, she scoured the thrift shops in Old Metairie, La., near New Orleans, where she lived a makeshift life, for a Moygashel linen dress to wear home to Texas for her mother's birthday celebration. (And for this I must have tried on a dozen such garments, to get the weight of the fabric, some sense of the previous owner, the awkwardness of checking price tags.) And so linen dresses became the symbol, the totem, of all the love that Ella wanted and could never get.

4. Gather more facts than you think you need. The marvelous nature of fiction writing is that you don't know what you're looking for until you get into your story. I have several times amassed prodigious piles of clippings, overheard conversations, photographs, and notes made on-site, without knowing which details I might later need to use. I met my new husband while doing research on heart transplants, having watched an actual procedure in Houston. I met and grew deeply attached to four dogs while studying the arduous socializing required for guide dogs, going to puppy socials, watching the nerve-wracking evaluations, and slogging through the hundreds of pages of the puppy-raising manual. For *The Second Dune*, written not long after I'd moved to Texas, I studied fossils, collecting gastropods and pelecypods from the dry limestone escarpment near my back door that had once had been the bottom of a great Cretaceous sea.

What did I need all that information for—on heart surgery, on dogs for the blind, on ancient life? I didn't know until my people came to life on the page, and then I saw that the heart that was transplanted in that novel was not a literal one; that there are a lot of experiences you can use to describe loss, and that giving away an animal you have raised is one; and that for a woman trapped in the expectations of marriage, perceiving the world in geologic time can be a great escape.

Shelby Hearon, the author of 15 novels, recently received the Texas Book Festival award for lifetime achievement. Her latest book is *Ella in Bloom*. An early novel, *The Second Dune*, was reissued in 2004. This article appeared in *The Writer*, April 2004.

WRITING HISTORICAL FICTION

For writers, a key to the future may lie in the past

by John Edward Ames

When I was younger, I wasn't all that keen on history, and even in college I absorbed it by accident more than design. By age 30, however, I was hooked, and by age 40 I was starting to add historical novels (beginning with Westerns) to my overall writing output. By now, I've written novels in five genres, and the historical has emerged as my clear favorite, both as reader and writer.

For most of us who don't start our careers as eager young history majors, it takes time to learn a respectable body of history, and more time still to learn how best to incorporate it into the service of good fiction. But the effort to learn is well worth it because, judging from our popular culture, it seems Americans very much like something that's at least akin to history. And for writers in search of markets, one key to the future may lie in the past.

The demand is impressive when it's toted up. Historical and period movies are well represented at the Oscar ceremonies and are staples in *TV Guide* listings, including a wide variety of Westerns. Most of the major fiction publishers release historical novels, and several paperback houses also have a line of Westerns. Check out a typical issue of *Ellery Queen Mystery Magazine* and you'll find at least two historical mysteries. In fact, a wide range of magazines and other venues—ranging from the Lands' End clothing catalog to *Boys' Life*—pay professional rates for good historical fiction.

If any genre can be said to offer freelancers a favorable supply-and-demand balance, I'd say it's the historical. In part, that's because not all that many writers, especially younger writers, are willing—or interested enough in history—

to develop a few specialized techniques required for writing salable historical fiction.

Yet editorial interest in it remains high, and I bet I know one reason why. It's called a welcome change of perspective. I used to interview fiction editors for the Horror Writers Association newsletter. One common complaint, voiced in some form by many of them, was that they see far too many fiction submissions from writers whose only frame of reference seems to be contemporary TV and movies. From an editor's point of view, perhaps a well-written historical can break up the mind-numbing repetitive monotony.

It's true that writing historical fiction places some unique demands on the writer, including the need to keep reading history. But once you've got the knack, you can expand your repertoire, because period research "recycles" nicely. Once you've amassed useful details from reliable sources, all genres are fair game, and details used in a historical mystery will stand duty in, say, a historical romance, too.

The following pointers are arbitrary and incomplete, but stem directly from my experience as a writer, and avid reader, of historical novels and Westerns.

Remember that fiction trumps facts

In the phrase "historical fiction," fiction is the substantive, the essential element, and historical only the modifier. Accuracy is fine, to a point, but "the facts should never get in the way of the truth," as one screenwriter puts it. More than once I've tossed a book aside when the dialogue becomes a mere excuse for a "facts on file" historical report.

Fiction writers are entertainers, not scholars. The kind of truths creative writers convey is an adjunct to the work of professional historians, not a replication of their efforts. It's our job to evoke the feel of an era, to vitalize dry facts and link the living to the dead through insight, through pity-and-fear catharsis. History should not dominate or overshadow the story, but provide a fascinating backdrop for proving Matthew Arnold right: "The same heart beats in every human breast."

> Fiction writers are entertainers, not scholars. History should not dominate or overshadow the story, but provide a fascinating backdrop.

Or put another way: History tells, but good historical fiction shows. Professional historians, for example, have filled thousands of book and journal pages with research on vigilantism in America. But no list of statistics on lynchings can ever equal the dramatic, gut-wrenching power of Walter Van Tilburg Clark's classic novel *The Ox-Bow Incident*.

This lynch-law parable (which also became an Oscar-nominated film starring Henry Fonda) puts a powerfully human face on all those anonymous victims of "rope justice." After learning that the three drifters they've just hanged are innocent, the "good citizens" who did it are forced to listen as a heartrending farewell letter, written by one of the victims to his wife, is read aloud. The tragedy is compounded when the leader of the lynch mob, unable to bear his shame, commits suicide. The author used the emotional power of fiction, not a flood of facts and footnotes, to breathe life into a dark chapter of American history.

A contemporary writer who excels at providing fascinating period details, while also creating strong reader identification with characters from "days of yore," is Loren D. Estleman, prolific author of Westerns, historicals, and mysteries. In his end-of-an-era Western *Mister St. John*, a celebrated hard-boiled lawman experiences a moment of dark self-insight after infiltrating a criminal gang. It isn't so much fear for his own safety as an irrational dread that he won't be able to cross back over to his own side when the time comes. Association with criminals has awakened something in him that he never felt while actually upholding the law, and it frightens him.

I immediately felt a link to St. John because of my own guilty pleasure at enjoying "mob stories" like *The Sopranos* (even, sometimes, rooting for the bad guys), and because Estleman reminded me that our modern fascination with criminals is perhaps nothing new or alarmingly decadent. In fact, good historical fiction universalizes and humanizes persons and events in a way that "pure history" seldom achieves.

Nothing beats learning directly from the best writers and works of historical tales. Some of my personal favorites include *Deadwood* by Pete Dexter; *Angle of Repose* by Wallace Stegner; *Libbie* by Judy Alter; *Gone with the Wind* by Margaret Mitchell; Estleman's *Aces & Eights*; *Cuba Libre* by Elmore Leonard; and *Red, White, and Blue Murder* by Jeanne M. Dams.

Master idiolect, not dialect

Trying to play professional linguist and master past dialects and diction will only tax most readers' patience and distract from your story. Instead, I recommend a focus on *idiolect*, speech patterns specific to individuals, not groups. Make a core list of authentic period words and phrases to draw from as you compose, assigning some to each major and major-minor character as repetitive traits. That way you can showcase some historical language while also personalizing and distinguishing characters in the reader's mind.

I found making idiolect charts especially helpful when I wrote *Taos Death Cry*, a novel about the celebrated Taos Trappers, a group of intrepid mountain men who explored the American Southwest in the early 19th century. In frontier fiction, it's all too easy for one buckskin-clad "colorful character" to blend in with the others. But in truth, very few individuals speak alike.

So during the pre-writing phase, I consulted a reliable lexicon of words and phrases widely spoken in the early 19th century. I especially looked for high-frequency words and expressions that characters would logically repeat often, such as "I snore!" (a euphemism for the more blasphemous "I swear!") or "Not by a jugful!" (which roughly translates to "No way, buddy!"). It's easy to work such common expressions into almost any remark, and if the writer makes sure only one character tends to repeat "I snore!" it won't take the reader long to identify that speaker from the others.

To further distinguish the half-dozen or so rustic types in *Taos Death Cry*, I gave one character, and only one, some distinctive speech traits of Appalachia. Again I consulted a reliable lexicon, and again I did not try to play linguist and replicate this regional dialect perfectly. I created a pattern based on just a few high-frequency words such as "nary" for never, "high" for near, "Law" or "Laws" for Lord.

It holds for any genre: the best way to forgo all those *he saids/she saids* is to make it clear, from idiolect clues, just who's speaking.

Period details are more useful than abstract history

The best historical fiction I've read spends very little time on the Big Ideas and is instead anchored to mundane details of everyday life which, taken collectively, evoke a strong sense of time and place. Little touches, like the truly tiresome nuisance of having to use buttonhooks to remove shoes in the days before they laced, or the bothersome winter ritual of using a bed-warmer (basically, a pot of hot coals on a long handle) before one could crawl between ice-cold sheets.

I once showed a character muttering curses in the dark because the wick in the coal-oil lamp had just burned out and he had to cut a new wick off his last pair of long johns. A female character in one of my historical romances is reduced to tears because of one of the greatest nuisances of early railroad travel: hot cinders flying out of the smokestack and igniting clothing, in this case ruining her only "going to town" dress. Writers can also have some fun exploiting controversial social issues of the era. One of my flippant male characters is soundly slapped after asking a lady a hotly debated question of the 1860s: "Is it true that tight corset lacings kindle impure desires?"

No matter what era interests them, writers need to become collectors of period data, with special attention to vocabulary, clothing, hairstyles, money and prices, culinary matters, medicine, housing, pastimes, and fads of the era. The possible sources, especially with the Internet, are nearly limitless, the research fascinating and informative.

One enjoyable source that's home delivered is cable TV's History Channel—I often watch it with a notepad on my knee. That's where I first learned, for example, that James Butler "Wild Bill" Hickok didn't wear a holster, but instead shoved his guns into a red sash to gain a fractional second in the "quick draw." (Sadly, I had already written several Wild Bill novels where he's wearing holsters, so three cheers for pen names.)

> The best historical fiction spends very little time on the Big Ideas and is instead anchored to mundane details of everyday life.

Minimize anachronisms in language and world view

Anachronisms, of course, are errors that place persons or things in the wrong period. More than other genres, historical fiction demands careful editing to avoid embarrassing yourself. And you can't count on the overworked copy editor to always save your credibility.

Some errors seem as obvious as clown makeup—after you spot them in print. I sermonize from vast and rueful experience here. I once wrote, describing a battle scene in the 1860s: "The acrid stink of cordite stained the air." Flashy sentence, maybe, but cordite wasn't added to gun powder until decades later. But then, what would you expect from an old pro who once referred to "Oklahoma" when it was still called the Indian Territory?

I'm the one who caught both these clinkers when it was too late to correct them, so obviously I was careless when editing the first time. Fortunately, not all slips are serious or noticed by everyone. Few readers will notice, or mind, if words like "teenager" and "ponytail" (not coined until the 1940s) show up a decade or so earlier. I often see the word hello, for example, used in stories set before the 1870s, even though it actually became established as a way of answering the telephone. Perfection is not our goal, but creating verisimilitude—"the seeming reality"—means working hard to keep "out of time" errors to a minimum.

Another pitfall, related to anachronisms, is generally known as historical chauvinism: imposing contemporary values and worldview on an earlier era when they weren't in fashion. To some extent this pitfall can't be avoided, because we're all children of our time. But we should be especially vigilant to at least monitor our language so the ideas don't sound so contemporary.

Consider, for example, blasphemy or "irreverence toward something considered sacred." A blasphemer nowadays can start a popular website; a few hundred years ago, however, he might well have had a hole bored through his tongue. Remember that language carried greater power (and consequences) during more religious and superstitious ages, especially curses with references to God, Jesus, hell, or damnation. Even as late as 1939, in MGM's production of *Gone with the Wind*, Clark Gable's famous, "Frankly, my dear, I don't give a damn!" was considered daring for its use of the word damn. Which leads nicely to my final suggestion.

Try hard to convey the "grand sweep" of an era

What good is a facts-on-file, dull-and-thudding historical accuracy if a writer fails to create the Zeitgeist, or "spirit of the age?"

Each period in history has its "organizing metaphor." One of my favorite periods, for example, the 1870s and '80s, is sometimes called the "Gilded Age," Mark Twain's way of describing that period's wealth and sense of boundless optimism, as well as its glittering superficiality. Your readers should "feel the age in miniature" when they read your book or story, and the feeling should start early and be periodically reinforced.

My historical novel *The Golden Circle* is set in the heady, intrigue-filled days just before the outbreak of the Civil War. Now and then, I tried to encapsulate the chaos and uncertainty of that time as it was felt by various characters in California. In the epilogue, the final "grand sweep" passage, meant to sound a hopeful note at the dawn of war, occurs in the mind of a Chinese servant as he observes the book's main players assembled for the final time:

> When he saw all of them there in the yard, almost like a painting, Hai Li felt it whole in his heart more than he did as separate words in his mind: Back East in this great but tortured country the terrible trouble had already started. As in his own homeland, blood would beget blood, men would test the limits of depravity and goodness, an entire nation would eventually send its anguished cry to the heavens.
>
> But looking at these faces, he was reminded of the hope that would eventually save mankind from itself: Truth, courage, honor, strength, and from those great virtues would come, after the bloodbath and barbarism and darkness, a great Union with truly free men to match it.

Writing historical fiction isn't for everybody, so those who do develop a skill for it will definitely find receptive markets. The snows of yesteryear have melted, but not our desire to feel the past as an immediate, living experience. Writers who satisfy that desire are fiction specialists who have every right to feel proud, for they are keepers of humanity's collective memory.

John Edward Ames, of New Orleans, is the author of 54 published novels, and has sold over 100 short stories, the most recent to *Arabella Romances* magazine. This article appeared in *The Writer*, November 2004.

MORE THAN A PLACE

5 ways setting enhances your story

by Hal Blythe and Charlie Sweet

Many stories fail to capture the reader's interest even though they have a clear point of view, well-rounded characters, and an interesting plot. What's missing? One key element that writers frequently overlook is setting. They treat it merely as backdrop.

Actually, setting can be so much more effective if it is thought of as a literary Leatherman, a multipurpose tool. When used properly, setting serves the following five functions that will help you create engaging fiction.

Establishes verisimilitude

Every time you begin a story, you open a doorway into a new world. If you want readers to step through that entryway, then you must make that world believable. Often, even a single well-thought-out detail can convince readers that a fictional setting is real.

For example, to encourage our readers to enter the fictional Clement County in Kentucky, we began "Slave Wall" (*Ellery Queen Mystery Magazine*, July 2000) by describing the protagonist crossing a rickety one-lane covered bridge typical of rural Kentucky, which led into a world where time hadn't caught up to the 20th century. This detail also helped our readers cross over from their reality to ours.

Another technique for bringing audiences into an actual location, for instance, is to pick just one recognizable landmark. Have you ever noticed how many movies and TV shows open with an establishing shot of the Golden Gate Bridge, the Eiffel Tower, or Niagara Falls? While the establishing shot is primarily visual, an effective setting in fiction—regardless of where it appears—

appeals to other senses and grounds readers in the familiar. Here are some examples of details that evoke a place:

Smell. Burning rubber at the scene of an accident or the pungent odor of disinfectant that permeates a hospital.

Sound. The din of the crowd at a sporting event or the irritating drip of a leaky faucet in a cold-water flat.

Taste. The acrid taste of smoke in a burning building.

Touch. The feel of a soft leather sofa in an posh apartment.

Physiology. The bone-chilling cold of a playoff game in Green Bay, Wis., or the gut-wrenching heft of salt-water-drenched cargo on the docks.

The more senses you appeal to in your setting, the more you draw your reader into your story. Note how William Faulkner opens his short story "Barn Burning":

> The store in which the Justice of the Peace's court was sitting smelled of cheese. The boy, crouched on his nail keg at the back of the crowded room, knew he smelled cheese, and more: from where he sat he could see the ranked shelves close-packed with the solid, squat, dynamic shapes of tin cans whose labels his stomach read . . .

Without the luxury of a recognizable real setting, Faulkner must use a spate of sensory details to make his post-Civil War general store believable. The nail keg and tin cans appeal to sight, the cheese to smell, and the cans' shapes to the kinesthetic sense. The net result is verisimilitude, convincing the audience of the reality of the situation.

Creates mood and atmosphere

When you invite people into your home, you try to create a dominant impression of the way you live. Proper use of setting can do the same for you as a writer. Like a good decorator, you want to control your readers' responses as they enter your house of fiction.

Proper use of atmosphere suggests to readers how they should react to fiction. It hints at whether the work is to be taken seriously or comically, realistically or romantically. Effective writers use it to play upon readers' emotions.

One of the great masters of mood is Edgar Allan Poe. Note how the opening lines of "The Fall of the House of Usher" establish a feeling of foreboding:

> During the whole of a dull, dark, and soundless day in the autumn of the year, when the clouds hung oppressively low in the heavens, I had been passing alone on horseback, through a singularly dreary tract of country; and at length found myself, as the shades of the evening drew on, within view of the melancholy House of Usher.

How does Poe achieve this eerie effect? Basically by *not* appealing to the senses. First, his narrator can see little (it's a cloudy day) and hear nothing ("soundless"). The narrator has no companion and, with the absence of sense impressions, is entirely alone. Instead of describing the sky, the narrator points out that he is below the "heavens" (by suggestion, hell is also below the heavens). Poe stresses it is also at the end of the cycle of day (late afternoon) and the cycle of the seasons (fall). Nothing is described as growing—i.e., death is all around. The audience's response is conditioned to be much like the narrator's— life is "oppressive" and "dreary." This is not a setting where you would expect something funny to happen.

Shows character traits

The minute you enter a home, you form an impression of its occupant. What kind of person occupies a living room littered with fast-food cartons, clothes draped over chairs and sofas, newspapers and magazines strewn across the threadbare rug? Maybe, instead, it's a well-dusted drawing room with every oil painting hanging straight, fresh-cut flowers spilling out of crystal vases, and objets d'art competing for attention. Is the initial impression the same?

Suppose you want to create two teenage sisters who are very different. You could start with a description of their bedrooms. In the dim light of one, you detail walls covered with Marilyn Manson posters and the cacophonous blare of a boom box. In the other room, you have sunlight streaming in, illuminating a poster of Amy Grant, a single cross, and a collection of candles. Notice that even though neither sister has yet appeared, and you have not made any declarative statement about them, your reader still has a pretty clear idea about their contrasting natures.

Setting suggests a great deal about characters' personalities and goals. It becomes particularly important to characterization when you tell your story in first person. The things you choose to have your narrator notice in the setting often let your reader know a lot more about the character than he knows about himself.

A classic example of this self-characterization through select detail is found in Ralph Ellison's story "Battle Royale," which became the first chapter of *Invisible Man*. In it, Ellison's naive high school senior is invited to a "smoker" thrown by Greenwood's white movers and shakers. To emphasize the African-American teenager's lack of awareness—the crucial point of his character— Ellison has him often describe the scene's characters and events not in clear focus but as hazy. The ballroom is "foggy with cigar smoke," and when the stripper begins her act, he limns "the smoke of a hundred cigars clinging to her like the thinnest of veils." Eventually, the narrator is literally blindfolded, then bloodied so he can barely see. Ultimately, when the narrator delivers his speech on the necessity of humility, Ellison's blurred description of the setting ensures that readers can't help but understand what the naive narrator does not—that he is a victim of white prejudice.

A writer's selection of setting works basically the same way in third-person stories. For instance, in our story "The Turning Point" (*Mike Shayne Mystery Magazine*, July 1980), we carefully chose detail to paint the portrait of Professor Geoffrey Lyons. On his office walls are a medieval cross of gray porcelain, an arbalest, a quiver, a pewter tankard, and a tarnished shield from the Battle of Agincourt. This shows that he is a man lost in the past.

Serves as character

Handled correctly, setting can even play a variety of character roles in your story. The late 19th-century naturalists pictured the environment as a potent force—a Darwinian beast stalking human beings and savagely defeating them. In the hands of Jack London and Joseph Conrad, the snowscape and the ocean were insurmountable characters, the strong who survived. While the sea in "The Open Boat" is certainly the backdrop for the entire tale, Stephen Crane chooses to give it a larger role. The four men in the boat find themselves talking and listening to the waves, thinking about them, and fighting the sea's attempt to drown them. The ocean is an antagonist, the major adversary preventing them from reaching their goal, land.

On the other hand, in *Dances With Wolves*, the Western frontier becomes a companion, a friend that has sustained life for generations. As a result, the Native Americans pray and talk to it reverently.

In Southwest fiction, the desert often has a life of its own. In Louisiana, it's the swamp. In the Northwest, it's the rain forest. You might consider writing a story in which the setting becomes a character, perhaps a rocky crag (Maine), a cave (Kentucky), or level plains (Kansas).

Enhances plot

Maybe the most overlooked function of setting involves the storyline. Used effectively, setting can play any of the following plot roles:

Foreshadowing. "Barn Burning" begins with a makeshift trial set in a general store, where Faulkner has the 10-year-old protagonist focus on two visual details of the setting—a can of ham with scarlet devils on it and a can labeled with the silver curve of fish. These sensory details anticipate the young boy's conflict between evil (*deviled* ham) and good (the fish being the ancient symbol of Christianity).

Building tension. In "The Law of Life," London has his Arctic setting get colder and colder as the abandoned Old Koshkoosh draws closer and closer to death. And in "The Child by Tiger," Thomas Wolfe describes a blizzard in the background to parallel the impending acts of insanity and violence about to attack his peaceful North Carolina town.

Signaling the plot's climax. In "The Storm," as Ben is about to murder his wife, author Malmar McKnight manipulates the setting by having the thunderstorm outside reach its height. Poe has a whirlwind appear when Madeline falls upon her brother Roderick and the House of Usher falls into the tarn.

Pointing to resolution. In how many stories, after the dark night of danger is over, does the storm dissipate, the birds sing, and the sun rise to signal the reader that things will be better for the protagonist? Conversely, to stress disillusionment and despair at the end of "The Swimmer," John Cheever stands the protagonist, Neddy Merrill, in front of his home. It's dark outside and the house is empty and decaying, much like the narcissistic, self-indulgent lifestyle Merrill has led.

Setting can serve you well as a tool in fiction writing. When you read over a scene and feel something is missing, don't overlook this important element.

Hal Blythe and **Charlie Sweet**, who often write under the pseudonym Hal Charles, are professors of English at Eastern Kentucky University. Collaborators for 30 years, they have published 650 pieces and several books. This article appeared in *The Writer*, September 2003.

How to create good settings

Like most tools, setting is not very effective until you've learned how to use it. Here are some basic instructions for getting started:

• Think of setting as more than a physical backdrop for your story.
• Each time you are about to use setting, think about the overall effect you want to achieve.
• Select a few choice details rather than a huge general quantity. Remember, less can be more.
• Try for a variety of sensory details. Don't depend solely on the sense of sight.
• Consider multiple functions for setting. While you're achieving verisimilitude, for instance, you might also be foreshadowing your story's climax and/or helping to develop character.

—*Hal Blythe and Charlie Sweet*

THREE WRITERS ON PLOT

Advice from Dennis Lehane, Gayle Lynds, and Stuart Woods

by Jillian Abbott

A cursory glance at the bestseller list will reveal a common thread: novels that sell well, more often than not, contain, in addition to memorable characters and beautiful language, a gripping plot. To help us get a handle on this important element in fiction, I asked three plot masters—Dennis Lehane, Gayle Lynds, and Stuart Woods—to share the secrets of their craft. The following questions and answers were assembled from in-person and e-mail queries.

What is the place of plot in your fiction?

Dennis Lehane: Starting in the 1960s and continuing through the 1980s, plot became a dirty word in literary circles. Fiction lost its way. A great novel comes when there is beauty of language, illumination of character, and a great plot. All three elements are necessary.

Ideally, plot serves character. If you analyze a story, say *The Silence of the Lambs*, you can begin to see plot as a conflict between a character's wants and needs. Clarice Starling *wants* to catch the killer, Buffalo Bill, and to impress her boss. Yet Clarice is unaware of her deeper *needs* to silence the screaming lambs of her childhood, and to come to terms with her relationship with her father.

Gayle Lynds: Plot is about tying a series of story elements to character. After I have the elements, I live with them awhile until characters start to show themselves to me, and I give my hero, heroine, and villain something each desperately wants. That, of course, creates the crisis of conscience.

Stuart Woods: Plot isn't everything—there's characterization, exposition, observation, and dialogue—but without plot, a book is like a human body without a skeleton. It can't stand up and walk.

How do you approach plotting?

Lehane: I put a character on the page and I have him want something—it could be as simple as a cup of coffee—and he goes out to get that thing. And hopefully, he bumps into another character and then another, and conflict will gradually develop. I'm not a good plotter in the early stage of a novel. The trick is to remind yourself that no one's ever going to see those early stages of a book, so let yourself loose and let your characters loose and see what happens. Then go back and rewrite it all to make it look fluid.

Lynds: Plotting is not a conscious activity. It takes second place to story "elements." My way of finding plot is through what I call elements, which means I find two or three things in which I'm truly interested. In *Mesmerized*, it was the heart-transplant thing, the idea that so many ex-KGB [agents] were retired and living in Washington, and the idea that many government agents use media as a cover. And I wanted to write about an international attorney in D.C.

Woods: Plotting is a process akin to a jazz improvisation: you establish a theme, then improvise on it. I do this on a chapter-by-chapter basis, planning the events that take place, then improvising the writing. I begin this improvisation with a situation (i.e., protagonist discovers skeleton) and build from there.

What is the most common mistake you see beginning writers make in plotting?

Lehane: They either don't have one, in which case their main character sits around thinking and awkwardly telling us, the readers, who he is and what he looks like, or the author starts with a bang, going right into "high-concept" action without us knowing a damn thing about the characters.

Lynds: Timing. When we first begin writing novels, we often either tell too much too soon, or we "save" information for later. From my viewpoint, what's most important is to get the plot and story rolling. After that, the backstory should be earned. In other words, once the book is in full swing, there will be moments when the backstory fits in logically. By the writer's waiting, the reader is already invested and wants to know, which makes the timing appropriate. On the other hand, by withholding clues or other information in an attempt to increase suspense, the author short-changes the book, often making it far too long, too loose, and occasionally confusing.

Woods: Too many writers offer too much information and description, obscuring the bones of their plots.

Is it necessary, in order for a plot to be satisfactorily resolved, that your protagonist get what he or she wants?

Lehane: No. Your [main] characters must get what they need, not what they want.

Lynds: Absolutely not. In fact, if the protagonist always does, suspense goes out the window. Within limits, I agree with Aristotle that the journey is all. But if we know the ending, the journey grows tainted, and our interest declines. I find it far more interesting and useful to have a protagonist who is flawed and fails occasionally throughout the book. By the end, the reader is a bit worried, which again increases suspense. As for endings in which the protagonist takes all, sometimes they work, sometimes not. The integrity of the book is what counts.

Woods: Yes, pretty much, though it shouldn't be too easy.

How can a conflict between what a character wants and what a character needs propel a plot forward?

Lehane: It goes back to the cup of coffee. David Mamet said something I've never forgotten: as long as a character wants something—anything—the audience will be interested. So, as long as the character has a want, the need will grow out of that, organically, and the more you'll figure the character out. Tension will develop for the reader the more elusive the pursuit of both goals is.

Lynds: In *Mesmerized*, a high-flying Washington lawyer receives a heart transplant, which seems to come with its donor's personality, tastes, and history. She desperately wants to return to who and what she was, although that is unrealistic. Finally, the tension between wants and needs reaches an explosive point. She has to put to rest all the intrusive thoughts and the strange ideas that began after her surgery. She can't live as if constantly under siege. After that, she goes in search of her donor, speeding the plot forward.

How did you learn to write compelling plots?

Lehane: The best question I ask myself is: what would a playwright do? Playwrights can only show; they can't tell. Now, I'm a novelist because I occasionally like telling, but it helps if you keep your eye on . . . the constant unfolding of drama.

Lynds: Well, I sure didn't learn about action-adventure in the literary short stories I wrote! Probably my male-pulp-novel era is the closest to training I had. I wrote five Nick Carters, which I figured was a deal, since I was being paid to learn. I was told nothing about plot or much of anything else, except how many words were wanted.

Woods: Lots and lots of reading. As a child, I read horse and dog stories, such as *Lassie Come Home* and *The Black Stallion*. After about the age of six, I was reading Mark Twain and Dickens.

What impact, if any, can setting have on plot, or vice versa?

Lehane: If a novel works, they're all tied together—plot, character, setting, language—and to such a degree, it's hard to pull one from the other. So I wouldn't know how to address that question exactly, except to say if setting works, you don't notice it; if it doesn't work, that's when you notice it.

Lynds: Once again, the Nick Carters demonstrate this connection well. Writing them, I learned very quickly that if I wanted a contract, I needed to come up with a book that took place in an exotic locale that the series had not addressed in a very long time, or at all. So I ended up setting parts of books in Antarctica, the Sudan, Macedonia . . . a host of places I perhaps never would have considered.

The experience taught me to pay attention to scene-setting. To move the plot, to give a sense of freshness, to keep the action going—change the scenery. That forces the author to do some work that lingering in the same spot might not. You must think of a compelling reason for the story to be moved to the new location, and then you must provide a payoff to the readers.

Woods: Place gives your characters mountains to climb and cliffs to fall from.

If plot is the problem, how would you approach a solution?

Lehane: If I have a plotting problem, I usually can't move forward. I block. Then I have to take the time to figure out where I screwed up. Once I've identified it, I go back in and try to fix it. If I'm successful, it's pretty apparent because then I can write again. If I'm not, I'm still blocked.

Lynds: Once I know the plot isn't working in one particular spot, I rethink the book, bringing myself up to date. Often, that's enough to remind me of some thread I've forgotten that can now be brought into play. Other times, I discover the characters are a bit off, doing or saying things that really aren't in character. And finally, it may be simply that I need to be more clever, that a solution simply hasn't occurred to me, and I must be patient with myself and take a walk or a nap or wander around, sometimes for days, until at last I have that eureka moment when I understand a new way of seeing the remainder of the book.

What techniques do you use to create and maintain suspense?

Lehane: Mystic River is constructed around shifting points of view, third person limited, tight on each point-of-view character. This technique not only maintains and extends suspense, but it also drives the plot forward.

Lynds: I have two favorite words, which I have tacked onto my lampshade at eye level. They are "jeopardy" and "menace"—jeopardy refers to the hero and/or heroine, while menace, of course, refers to the villain. The villain has an overriding goal, and that is what drives the plot. To create suspense, the author must understand and respect that villain, and allow the villain to put the protagonist—and society—in jeopardy. Plus, the villain must be smart enough, good enough, with goals frightening enough that he or she is truly menacing.

Will the villain succeed? Will the protagonist succeed? We read books to the very end, biting our nails, to find out the answers to those two questions. In my opinion, they're the foundation of suspense.

Woods: I look upon writing as a kind of magic, and I'm afraid that if I examine it too closely, it might go away.

Jillian Abbott, formerly a columnist for *The Australian*, just finished writing a female action/adventure, *The Leopard's Claw*. This article appeared in *The Writer*, May 2004.

Dennis Lehane is best known for his bestselling novel *Mystic River*, which was a finalist for the PEN/Winship Award, won both the Anthony and the Barry awards for best novel, and is now a Clint Eastwood movie. He has also penned a successful mystery series which includes *A Drink Before the War, Darkness Take My Hand, Sacred, Gone Baby Gone*, and *Prayers for the Rain*. Lehane lives in Boston, where he writes and teaches.

Gayle Lynds has written three international spy thrillers, three novels co-written with the late Robert Ludlum, and five Nick Carter pulp-fiction adventures. She is the first woman to write *New York Times*-bestselling international spy thrillers. Her debut solo thriller, *Masquerade*, was rejected initially because "no women could have written this." Doubleday ultimately published the book in 1996. Her latest novel is *The Coil*, a sequel to *Masquerade*. Lynds lives in California.

Stuart Woods has written more than 27 novels. His first mystery, *Chiefs*, won a Mystery Writers of America Edgar Allan Poe Award. A later book, *Palindrome*, was also nominated for the Edgar. A voracious reader as a child, Woods is now a voracious writer, regularly producing two novels per year. He has two mystery series going (Stone Barrington and Holly Barker). His most recent Holly Barker book is *Blood Orchid*. His 2003 novel is *Capital Crimes*. Woods currently divides his time between Florida (winter), Maine (summer), and New York (spring and fall).

PAINT YOUR PROSE

Add colors to give emotional texture to your story

by Kevin Breen

Adding color to your prose is one way to to infuse your sentences and stories with emotion and texture.

On the sentence level, well-placed color in a descriptive passage can stand out like a bright red cardinal in a wintry forest. In her color-drenched story "Rapture" (*Shenandoah*, Winter 2002), Enid Shomer beautifully describes a drowning woman's memories, which, in the end, are like bits of glass in a kaleidoscope, or like luminous patterns in a cathedral window. Here, the skillful use of color establishes the writer's authority and makes the fictive world flash to life.

The inept use of color, on the other hand, can sap the energy of a passage rather than add to it, or it can immediately brand the writer a novice. Common mistakes include too much use of color (describing the color of every character's pants and shirts); hackneyed uses of color (eyes as green as emeralds); and a fascination with unusual words of color (saffron, argentiferous, chartreuse, etc.), a form of purple prose.

In her award-winning novel *Brokeback Mountain*, Annie Proulx takes the use of color a step beyond the sentence level. Yes, the story is rich with descriptive passages: a tea-colored river, ochre-branched willows, an old photograph where the skin tone has faded to magenta, the blue of a gas stove flame in a bleak trailer, a glassy orange dawn. But what makes Proulx's writing so compelling is that the arresting descriptions also mirror (or strengthen) the emotion of the story. Her descriptions of fires, weather, and landscape all have a somewhat lurid, faded, disquieting aspect to them, qualities present in the larger story of forbidden love.

In *The Great Gatsby*, F. Scott Fitzgerald describes Gatsby's world in radiant colors: Gatsby's chauffeur is dressed in a robin's-egg-blue suit. Gatsby wears pink suits and boasts a wardrobe of fancy shirts that are coral, apple-green, lavender, faint orange, and Indian blue. But when Gatsby's dream fades, the use of bright color is diminished, and the last two chapters are dark, pale, and colorless.

In Haruki Murakami's odd love story "Ice Man" (*The New Yorker*, Feb. 2, 2003), the descriptions are of ice and snow and frost, all shades of white. In other contexts, white could stand for purity and virtue, but in this case it adds force to the story's cold emotional core. The couple ends up in a world of ice, without mirth or festivity, in an "eternal winter" void of color.

Color can also be effective in characterization. My story "Mandala Tower" (published in *Eureka Literary Magazine*), features a complex, flamboyant character, Maud Ballylee, who wears scarlet and indigo sundresses, and amber and silver jewelry. Whenever she is present, bright colors appear. She stands in vivid contrast to the story's main character, a bland, timid man.

A few stories go even further, making color a central theme. In Charlotte Perkins-Gilman's "The Yellow Wallpaper," first published in 1899, a young woman on the verge of a nervous breakdown becomes obsessed with the wallpaper in her bedroom. The wallpaper is an unclean yellow, or in certain lights, a dull orange, which reminds her of sulfur or fungus. The colors symbolize the oppression of women, the patronizing attitude of her husband, and, of course, her descent into madness.

A story by Paul Bowles also takes one color as a central element. In "In the Red Room," parents visiting their son in Sri Lanka are ushered into a strange room, a "blood-colored cubicle," which serves as a kind of shrine. Later in the story, we learn that a terrible murder was committed in this room. The red room stains the entire story with betrayal, adultery, murder, and madness.

In prose, color is language and emotion and characterization, and its creative potential is nearly endless. It can be employed for effects as obvious as description and simple characterization, and as complex as the mysteries of human nature.

Kevin Breen of Grand Rapids, Mich., is a short-story writer whose work has recently appeared in *Aethlon, The Heartlands Today, Emrys Journal*, and *Eureka Literary Magazine*. His articles have appeared in *Poets & Writers Magazine* and the *Los Angeles Times*. This article appeared in *The Writer*, September 2003.

MOVE INTO THE WINNER'S CIRCLE

A judge tells how to make the cut in short-story contests

by Adele Glimm

You've written (and rewritten!) a short story, and you're eager to send it off to one of the many short fiction contests. You hate to think about all those other writers addressing envelopes to the same contest, but they're out there, and they won't go away. So, may the best story win. But which one is the best story? Since your deepest desire is that it be yours, it's time to stop daydreaming about announcing your triumph to family and friends. Instead, try looking at your story as if you were a judge of the contest you're entering.

As one of three judges in a national short fiction contest, I can give you some insight into how the process works.

When we're reading contest submissions, we read each story all the way through, on the theory that a writer may have the kind of talent that doesn't shine until well into the piece but then shines brightly enough to overcome a slow start. Each judge then eliminates those entries that seem clearly not to be winners and does a rough ranking of possible prize stories. Only then do we meet and listen to our fellow judges make a case for their favorites. You'd think, from the differences in our tastes and standards, that we'd never come to a decision without doing battle with sharpened pencil points. But in fact, the same stories tend to rise to the top of our "prizeworthy" lists.

Here are some of the qualities we look for as we pick the winners:

Language

Judge A cares deeply about *language*. English used incorrectly makes her shudder (it was more like an earthquake the day she encountered "in sink" instead of "in sync"). English used not only correctly but with a refined sense of its aesthetic and revelatory capabilities makes her want to cheer. She's hoping for interesting analogies, surprising similes, accurate adjectives (but not too many of them).

Consider some examples by writers who got it supremely right. In his short story "The Girl With a Pimply Face," William Carlos Williams tells of a thick-set man who has "the stability of a cube placed on one of its facets."

In "A Journey," Edith Wharton describes trees and houses seen from a train window as "meaningless hieroglyphs of an endlessly unrolled papyrus."

Language this fresh, this particular, locates readers squarely in the land of literature. We know the stories that contain such writing are worthy of our time and our emotions and may even change our lives. When confronted instead with a phrase like "eyes as round as saucers," we don't expect much pleasure from the story that contains it. A first try at revision might give us something like "eyes as watchful as the full moon."

Few of us can write like Williams or Wharton, but we can all strive for freshness, thus prompting Judge A to place our stories in her "may be prizeworthy" pile. If you toss around tired phrases, she may be too tired to see the brilliance of your characters and plot.

Structure

Judge B is most concerned with *structure*. She is impressed by a story that travels from beginning to end with the craft of a jet pilot taking off, flying the best route to his destination, then landing with finesse. (A crucial difference: it's okay for a story ending to shake up readers.) The point of view of such a story is well chosen and doesn't change arbitrarily. Sections feed smoothly into one another. Every part of the story is relevant to the total effect, the ultimate meaning.

Almost every story worth its ink and paper contains a main character who *wants* something. He or she should also be the character who makes the action of the story happen or, at least, who experiences the major emotions portrayed. In nearly every case, we should see events from this character's point of view.

If your hero is Jen, a pre-med student flattened by an F in chemistry, we don't want to be distracted by the viewpoint of the cafeteria cashier noticing that the skinny, red-haired girl looks melancholy today. We only need the point of view of Jen herself, more determined than ever to make it to med school or else suddenly deciding to drop out in favor of an easier life. (Digression: if we did want the cashier's viewpoint, "melancholy" might or might not be the right word for her to use. Is she a graduate student? A 10th-grade drop-out? An immigrant who enjoys trying out words in her new language? Writers can't relax for a second.)

It would, of course, be possible to write a fine story with two main characters, Jen and the cafeteria cashier, told from alternating points of view. But that's another story and a different structure. William Trevor, one of the finest authors of short stories in English, often writes stories with dual main characters and, therefore, two points of view. In these stories, the problems and emotions of each protagonist are relevant to those of the other. In the early stages of your career, however, the time when you tend to enter contests, it is nearly always preferable to focus on only one character.

Almost every story is a story of change: the structure of Jen's story requires that she change either her ambition or her tactics for achieving it, or at least that she begin to understand the need for change.

Judge B, having read to the end of a story such as Jen's, wants to be left with a sense of earned completion (the story does the earning, not the reader). This does not mean that all plot points must be tidied up or that all (or any) characters' problems are solved.

In his useful book *Techniques of Fiction Writing: Measure and Madness*, Leon Surmelian writes that "at the heart of almost every good story I can think of, there is a discovery or recognition." It is this reward that makes busy readers glad they skipped the evening workout and read the story instead. Readers know instinctively that Jen has to seek her own point of recognition. If the author allows Jen's chemistry professor to dash into the cafeteria to give Jen the news that he mixed up student grades and she really earned an A, readers will think twice before next choosing fiction over free weights.

When Judge B finds a contest entry whose structure moves an interesting main character from an intriguing introduction through a complicating middle and on to a believable point of recognition, she looks forward to defending that story in conference with her two judging colleagues.

That brings me to Judge C—me.

Originality

My main interest is *originality*. I feel cranky when I confront a story with a subject or plot that I've read countless times before. It's often said there are only ten plots in the universe, but certainly there are innumerable subplots, hundreds of ways to treat any situation, new and insightful points to be made about any event life deals our characters or us. Picking up a story from a pile of contest submissions, I'm longing to meet people I haven't just met in the last manuscript or in a book I've been reading. More important, if the characters seem to have dropped in straight from last season's television listings or movies, the story is in danger of dropping into the pile of nonwinners.

Consider an example. You're developing a classic story situation: a teenager upset by his parents' arguments. I strongly suggest those parents fight about some topic *other* than money, alcohol, or the new divorcee up the block who needs male help jump-starting her car and her life. What's an original topic for marital sparring? Well, a difference of opinion on whether to sell the house and travel around the world working in circuses would do it. But don't choose that one. Why not? Because good fiction should be only as original as it can be while still being universal in its appeal. Few spouses fight about such extreme decisions.

The basic emotions of this issue, though, *are* universal: one spouse needs security and stability; the other yearns for risk and adventure. Maybe they fight about whether to leave secure jobs to open a risky business in an unfamiliar area of the country.

As for their teenager, let him *feel* the same universal emotions any teenager would feel (fear of his family falling apart, divided loyalties), but have him do something unexpected rather than, say, drown out the fight with loud music in his room or run out and crash the family car. Once again, as with the cafeteria cashier, the writer comes up against a problem in characterization. What kind of teenager is he? With which parent does he identify? If he, too, values security above all, he may throw himself into school clubs and teams to make it harder for his parents to tear him away. Or perhaps he's bored beyond belief and deliberately sabotages his parents' jobs so they'll be more likely to move.

Emotion

So, you need *language, structure, originality*—and one more thing that all three of us agree is absolutely critical: *emotion*. Whatever else a story tells us, it must tell us how people feel about their lives. The emotions depicted should be gripping but believable; they should be the force behind the actions of the characters.

A useful exercise in learning how emotions are embedded in drama is to rent a video of an unfamiliar movie and watch it without the sound. Notice that universal emotions come through even without words to tell the story: greed, anger, fear, jealousy, passion. Are such easily recognizable emotions animating your story?

Judges are always seeking that indefinable quality that takes the reader's breath away, makes him turn from the last page back to the first to read the story through once more, amazed by the ability of words on paper to create a world.

Even if you don't enter contests, learning to think like a judge will put you a giant step closer to thinking like the editors, who are, after all, also judges of your work. Readers, too, are judges who begin to read a story or a novel and must decide whether to keep reading, whether to buy the book, whether to look for your next work, whether to recommend it to friends.

Like lucky readers, we contest judges are the real prizewinners. We are given the pleasure of discovering works of art.

Adele Glimm has been published in *Ellery Queen Mystery Magazine, Redbook, Cosmopolitan,* and *Epoch.* This article appeared in *The Writer,* May 2004.

What makes a prize-winning story?

- Uses fresh language that delights the reader with surprising and apt analogies, similes, and metaphors.
- Is well structured and cleanly told with respect for language.
- Builds a convincing world with details.
- Peoples its world with breathing, feeling human beings.
- Grips the reader's attention and won't let go.
- Earns the reader's emotional response.
- Tells a story in a way it has never been told before.

Eavesdropping on the judges

Here are a few examples of comments from a short-story contest judging session:

- "A fine writer, but the author runs out of energy and ties up the end too quickly."
- "Good pacing and style, though the end is far too sentimental."
- "Too political—the message is told too bluntly by the author, who should tell it through the characters."
- "Doesn't need the last paragraph (or page, scene)."
- "Point-of-view problems—too much switching, awkwardly done."
- "Interesting idea, but grammar and spelling are too original!"

—*Adele Glimm*

THE WRITING PROCESS

Top authors share advice & tips

compiled by Beth Bakkum

Listen in during the Q&A session of any author's book reading, and you're likely to hear the writers in the audience ask many of the same questions: "Where do you get your ideas?" "Do you write in the morning or the afternoon?" "Do you outline?"

For writers, it's all about the *process*. While every writer ultimately has to determine what works best for him, it never hurts to check out the habits of other successful authors. You might find something worth trying or, at the very least, gain some insight into their creative lives. We've put together this collection of authors' thoughts on the writing process from *The Writer's* monthly "How I Write" column. Read on to learn where top writers find their ideas, what their writing process is like, how they overcome obstacles, and why they spend so much time on revision.

Finding ideas

Susan Orlean

I read the little odd pieces in the newspaper, and pay attention for any wisp of an idea—a handout, a leaflet, a conversation, an advertisement—that might grow into a story. I get lots of stories suggested to me, but they often don't interest me—although every now and again . . . That's why I never turn anyone down who says they have a great idea for me. I think you have to always be paying attention to the world around you, and then ideas will present themselves. (*The Writer*, March 2002)

Ann Rule

I look for an anti-hero or -heroine who seems to have everything in the world the rest of us would be happy with—good looks, money, power, love, charisma. And yet they're not who they seem at all. Once I pick the right subject (I go through 500 cases), I then can count on these people to continue to be outrageous. And all I do is describe how they're acting out behind the perfect mask. (*The Writer*, December 2001)

Lois Lowry

Ideas come by being observant, which all writers are, keeping my eyes, ears, and mind open. That's something that comes to me quite naturally. I travel a lot, often alone. I might watch a family in a restaurant, and I'm interested in how they interact. I'm most interested in the hint that you sometimes get that something is awry in the interaction. You can read that in somebody's posture or a tone of voice. Then the people are gone, but the imagination takes over and begins to fill in the blank spaces. By then, it's become a story in my imagination. (*The Writer*, June 2002)

Terry McMillan

I'm nosy. I'm a good listener. Airplanes are good. Newspaper articles, especially "Dear Abby"! The news. Most often, I just think about people in situations that I don't know if I could handle or tolerate. I worry about them and wonder how they manage. This is usually how a story comes about. (*The Writer*, August 2001)

Antonya Nelson

I grew up in a large family, in a large house. What interests me usually comes back to family. Writing is a process of unveiling my own obsessions and interests—images, overheard conversations, family anecdotes. When the external world and the internal self get into alignment, it's like lightning striking. (*The Writer*, July 2001)

Getting started

Christopher Paolini

Before I started, I studied books on stories and characters and plots. One was *The Writer's Handbook*. And *Story*, by Robert McKee, gave me an idea of story structure. Then I spent an entire month to plot out *Eragon* and the two sequels.

Many writers don't work this way. But for me, I figure out what I'm going to write beforehand, so I'm free to concentrate on presenting it in the most beautiful, eloquent manner possible. You'd never expect a professional singer to compose a song while she sang it. She works it out in advance. (*The Writer*, March 2004)

M. J. Rose

I do a two-page outline [of the novel] with one line describing the main action in each chapter. No details. I see a book like a journey. I like knowing where I'm going to end up before I set forth. It changes like crazy in the writing, but the outline keeps me from getting stuck. Then I revise like a madwoman. I love revising. If I didn't have a deadline on my contracts, I'd never finish. (*The Writer*, February 2003)

Tracy Kidder

For me, the first draft of something is really hard to do. It's usually no good anyway, and overly long. What I tend to do is write really fast so as to prevent remorse for having written badly. At least it didn't take a long time, I say to myself.

It's that rough draft where I have the hardest time staying put. I usually write ten drafts or so of a book. But toward the end, or somewhere in there, it's hard for me to do anything else. Nowadays I can't do it the way I used to, but I used to put in sixteen-hour days sometimes. I loved it, and I still love it. (*The Writer*, April 2004)

The writing process

Thisbe Nissen

Mostly, I try to let whatever's coming just flood its way out, and then I deal with the mess later. I like mess. You can find a lot of good nuggets in the junkyard. Once I've got something, I just keep working it over until I've reached that precarious place where I think maybe it's good, and I think that it's going to lose whatever glimmer of hope it has if I muck with it anymore. Then I try to make myself stop futzing. I find that if I'm too sure of where I'm going with something, then I don't have much interest in going there. The discovery is what's exciting. (*The Writer*, January 2002)

Joyce Carol Oates

I write in longhand. I don't have a word processor. I sometimes write on little notepads and have 60 pages of notes that I spread out and organize [by characters or scenes]. If I had a word processor, I couldn't do that sort of thing. It wouldn't be so physical or visual. I take the strongest parts and build slowly, doing a lot of rewriting as I go along.

I lose myself in the physical world. I describe it very assiduously. When I'm writing fiction, I populate the [narrative] with people who are expressions of a specific place. (*The Writer*, October 2001)

Barbara Parker

After I get an idea of what the book is, I get an idea of the ending. I have no idea of the territory that lies between. You have to fight your way through the wilderness.

At some point, I turn to the bulletin board behind my desk and put up squares of paper representing chapters. I use sticky notes to write down scene plot points or characters and put them in the chapters. You can throw them out or move them. When the entire bulletin board is covered, I'm done. If I raise an issue that is important, I put a red flag on the bulletin board and move it forward until the issue is resolved. (*The Writer*, Oct. 2003)

Dennis Lehane

I write longhand and then try to input it into a computer within 24 hours. I need the flow of a pen across a page; something about a computer screen leaves me feeling self-conscious and boxed in. I plot loosely in advance—I usually know six or seven major structural movements—but I rarely outline unless I've jammed myself up in the middle of a manuscript and don't know how to move forward. I'm a revision fanatic. The early drafts are just pasta on the wall, trying to see what sticks. I find the book through a honing process, going back through the pages and making myself look a lot smarter than I am. (*The Writer*, August 2002)

Suzan-Lori Parks

I work on more than one thing at once. It's like you have a round [tray]—a lazy Susan—and you divide it up into pie wedges. You're sitting at a table and the wedge in front of you is the wedge you're working on right now. Then you write a draft of that. The first wedge for me would be, say, *Getting Mother's Body*. I write a draft of that, and I get to page—whatever—I put it back on the lazy Susan and turn it to the next wedge, a play called *In the Blood*. Then, I turn to another wedge and a draft of *Topdog/Underdog*. Then, I work on *Getting Mother's Body* again.

A lot of times I don't know what I'm doing. I'm wandering through the wilderness of my imagination, so I have no road map. I have very few clues. I'm just wandering, seeing what I can find, what I can hear, what's there. A dead mother's there, a grave. "Oh." A hole which is a portal. "Oh." All that is coming around as I'm wandering through the wilderness, draft after draft. (*The Writer*, January 2004)

Obstacles

Christina Schwarz

It took me a long, long time to write *Drowning Ruth*. I wanted to give up so, so often. Every other week I thought, "What are you doing? This is ridiculous.

You're wasting your time. You're making a fool of yourself." Underneath all that doubt, I knew there was some story there, and if I could just get at it, it would be good.

The same was true for *All is Vanity*. I had a lot of doubts, different ones than I had with the first [book]. But there was something about each of these stories that I knew would be a good novel, if I could just crack it. (*The Writer*, March 2003)

Caroline Hwang

I found myself with the time to write, but I was without a clue as to how to start. After six months, I had maybe a hundred pages, but none of them felt right. At NYU, I was taking a class taught by E.L. Doctorow. I told him how it all just felt futile. He asked me how many pages I had. I told him I had six that I liked. He suggested I skip to a part of the story that excited me, but after all of my years as a journalist, I could write only in a logical, linear way. He asked if I was writing something I would read. It cut me to the quick, because I wasn't. I was writing something I would have read as a grad student, but my tastes had changed dramatically. As a reader, I skim over long descriptions of dust motes swirling in the sunlight, so what was I doing writing them? I realized right then and there that I needed to change my tone and voice to one that was more lighthearted and amusing. (*The Writer*, July 2003)

Revision

Sue Grafton

I confess I'm a prissy little thing. Like Goldilocks, I want every sentence, every scene, and every move in a book to be "just right" before I move on. I revise constantly and only leave a chapter behind when I'm able to read it ten times in a row without changing a word. Even then, I go back, of course, if I realize that I've left something out or need to modify the early sections for consistency. I'm a slow writer but persistent, and that counts for everything. (*The Writer*, May 2002)

Paule Marshall

Writing for me is rewriting because my first drafts are just getting down all kinds of ideas, directions, and thoughts about the book that I think I want to write. Once I get it under way, I discover what I really want to do with it. All kinds of new understandings and ideas emerge as I'm involved in the project. Usually I write several drafts, each one maybe taking over a year.

I try to keep writing and when new information or deeper understanding comes to mind, when there are what I feel are necessary shifts and changes in the plot, I put all of that to the side on separate sheets of paper. I'm a great note-taker.

I try to keep going with the rewriting, then splice in and make changes once I've finished with a chapter or two. For my psychological well-being, I need a sense of moving forward with the book. (*The Writer*, September 2002)

Alan Lightman

When working on the first draft of a novel, I'll make lots of small-scale—local—revisions. Chapter by chapter, line by line. After I've finished the draft, I'll let a few weeks go by and then read the whole book and do a global revision. The local revision is getting the wording of a sentence or a scene right. The global revision is related to getting a character right or a theme expressed the way I want, working on the overall architecture of the book. (*The Writer*, May 2001)

Allison Pearson

I was trained as a copy editor at a newspaper, so I'm a very serious editor of my own material. When I handed in the book, they didn't change anything. Because it's my training, I would revise a lot as I went along. I feel confident if I'm building on a bedrock of stuff that's good rather than coming back to fix it later. I'm sure some people will do that and just get it down and then clean it up. I like to get it really clean and then move on—that gives me a feeling of "at least you've got some good stuff here." (Online Extra, www.writermag.com, February 2004)

Ruth Reichl

At the end, I rewrite and rewrite and rewrite, trying to get rid of all the seductively pretty words, trying to erase the traces of "writing" so the words sound natural. I love it when people say, "It feels as if you just sat down and wrote it in one sitting." There are probably people who can do that, but for me, it takes a great deal of work to make the writing seem effortless. (*The Writer*, November 2002)

Beth Bakkum is editorial associate at *The Writer*. These authors' comments were excerpted from "How I Write" columns that appear as a regular end-page piece in *The Writer*.

CREATING
A WORTHY VILLAIN

Your hero won't be so heroic
if you don't put him to the test

by William G. Tapply

When I finished writing my first novel, I did what most unpublished writers did back then, 20 years ago, before literary agents became the publishers' gate-keepers. I bundled up a chapter with a query letter and sent it directly to several editors.

Rejections, predictably, followed, so I was thrilled when an editor from Scribner's asked to see the whole manuscript. I mailed it out the next day.

I waited for two months, trying not to think about it.

The response, when it arrived, was not exactly what I'd hoped for. "We think you can write," she began, and you didn't need to be Sherlock Holmes to know a "but" was coming, *but*, she went on, *many of the characters are flat, the plot is predictable, the story doesn't generate much tension or suspense, and we knew whodunit from the beginning.*

For a mystery novel, this was not exactly high praise.

The editor—her name was Betsy Rapoport, and she ended up being my beloved editor for seven novels—concluded her note this way: "I can't offer you a contract, and I can make no promises, but if you'd be willing to rewrite your novel I'd be happy to look at it again."

I realized that my novel-writing career had arrived at a turning point: I could revise the book, make it wonderful, get it published, and launch a career; or I could accept the fact that I didn't have what it takes, hide my amateurish mystery novel in a drawer, and live a sensible life.

The choice filled me with dread, because I had no idea what I was doing. But I knew that if I didn't give it my best shot, I'd never find out if I had what it takes to write a saleable novel.

I reread my story and concluded that Betsy was right. It was flat, predictable, and utterly lacking in conflict, tension and suspense.

But how could I fix it?

I kept thinking about her final words. *We knew whodunit from the beginning.*

And then it hit me: all of Betsy's criticisms amounted to the same thing. If the villain was obvious from the beginning, there could be no mystery, and a mystery novel without a mystery could have little tension and suspense—those qualities that compel readers to turn the pages.

In my eagerness to provide lots of clues, to "play fair" with the reader, I had created a villain who looked villainous and acted guilty from the beginning. Any half-witted sleuth should've pegged her immediately.

I had created a story about an oblivious sleuth trying to catch an obvious villain, and the only suspense revolved around the question of just how long it would take my hero to figure out what readers knew from the beginning.

Moreover, when the climax, such as it was, arrived (mercifully), and Brady Coyne, my sleuth, finally confronted Rina, the villain—who by then had committed several murders and told many lies—suddenly and inexplicably gave up, confessed her guilt, and spewed out her entire story.

Simply put, the villain had failed to challenge the hero from beginning to end. She didn't put him to the test. She was unworthy of his best efforts.

The solution was obvious: create a worthy villain, make it hard for my hero, and everything else would take care of itself. It takes a great villain to make a great hero.

So I reinvented Rina. She had committed a murder she believed was necessary and justifiable. She felt no guilt. She was smart, resourceful, and determined to get away with it. She made no mistakes. She was willing to murder again, if that's what it took to preserve her secret.

But when she appeared on the page, she seemed normal. She was a face in a crowd of interesting secondary characters and possible suspects. She gave nothing away. You would never guess what she had done.

Now it took courage and brains and perseverance and a lot of hard sleuthing before Brady found the key piece to the puzzle, and when he finally confronted Rina, she still didn't make it easy for him.

When I finished rewriting my novel, this time with a smart and determined villain, it bore scant resemblance to the story I'd originally submitted to Betsy.

She liked it. She published it. It won an award.

And now, all these years later, the 21st novel in my Brady Coyne series is about to hit the bookstores as I write this. My villains have been cops and lawyers, Vietnam vets and government officials, housewives and teenagers, nurses and businessmen. They are murderers and kidnappers and blackmailers and terrorists. They appear ordinary because they lie and dissemble masterfully. They will do anything to escape detection.

They are worthy villains.

I was lucky that first novel of mine hit the desk of an editor who was willing to give it a second look. It probably deserved to be rejected outright. One way you can avoid that fate—no matter what kind of book you're writing—is to attend to your villains. Make them worthy and good things will naturally follow. For a brief guide to villainy, read on.

The underrated antagonist

In his groundbreaking study *The Hero With a Thousand Faces*, Joseph Campbell argues that all plots are essentially the same: the hero embarks on a quest, encounters obstacles and challenges, and emerges either triumphant or defeated.

Books and articles of writing instruction rightfully emphasize the importance of creating a sympathetic protagonist, a driven hero with strongly felt wants and needs who will strive mightily to fulfill his quest. If the hero is passive and wishy-washy, there won't be much of a story.

In my reading, however, rarely do I find comparable emphasis on the villain—the antagonist who opposes the hero, the character who creates the obstacles, challenges and dangers that make the hero's quest uncertain and difficult. The villain, after all, is the main source of conflict, tension, and suspense—those necessary qualities in all of literature.

Whether your hero wants to win back the love of a mate, escape from prison, rescue a child, nail a serial killer, or save the world, his quest must be difficult and its outcome uncertain if we are to keep turning the pages. That is the job of your antagonist. As Christopher Vogler writes in his essential book *The Writer's Journey*, "The function of the Shadow [villain] in drama is to challenge the hero and give her a worthy opponent in the struggle."

Characteristics of the worthy villain

Shakespeare's Richard III. Dickens' Uriah Heep. Ian Fleming's Goldfinger. Thomas Harris' Hannibal Lecter. All deliciously, exuberantly vile literary villains.

Except in unusual cases, however, the contemporary novelist is better advised to heed the master of suspense. Alfred Hitchcock said, "In the old days, villains had moustaches and kicked the dog. Audiences are smarter today. They don't want their villain to be thrown at them with green limelight on his face. They want an ordinary human being with failings."

"The banality of evil," Hannah Arendt called it in her famous analysis of the Nazi atrocities. Ordinary people performing extraordinarily evil deeds are far more interesting than sneering obvious villains who twirl their moustaches.

Compelling villains are not one-dimensional. Barbara Peters, editor-in-chief of Poisoned Pen Press, told me she looks for novels "where you mourn the victim and empathize to some degree with the villain; that is, the villain is someone fully human and not some cardboard or demonized figure there just for the purposes of the plot. . . . The villain . . . should be someone worthy of the sleuth's intelligence and efforts to apprehend him/her as well as the reader's time and emotional investment."

A villain worthy of the hero's best efforts is able to lose himself in the crowd. He may be a murderer or a rapist, but he manages to appear normal. He deflects suspicion by lying and dissembling expertly.

The worthy villain is not wracked with guilt. In fact, he typically believes he is doing the right—even the heroic—thing. "From his point of view," Vogler says, "a villain is the hero of his own myth, and the audience's hero is his villain."

The villain as hero

Sometimes the hero is not a good guy, nor is the antagonist bent on evil. In fact, a villainous character can serve the function of protagonist, the "good guy," the hero of the story. Compelling novels have been written from the point of view of characters determined to commit crimes. Elmore Leonard and Donald Westlake, for example, often choose as their protagonists small-time hoods and bumbling hit men.

In Lawrence Block's *Small Town*, an ordinary man, grieving over the incomprehensible loss of his wife on Sept. 11, 2001, is plotting his revenge against this horrific injustice. In spite of ourselves, we find ourselves liking and rooting for this tragic figure with an evil plan.

Objectively, the Corleones—Vito, Sonny, and Michael—are villainous characters. But in Mario Puzo's *The Godfather*, the Corleone men are the protagonists. They are the heroes in their own myths.

In these cases, it's the cops and private investigators and FBI agents who are the antagonists—the villains—because their function is to oppose the "heroes."

The worthy villain in mysteries

Conflict between two or more strong forces fuels all stories. Conflict produces uncertainty, tension, and suspense. In mystery novels, the life-and-death contest between a determined sleuth and an equally determined villain, usually a murderer, is the central source of conflict.

The sleuth's quest is to identify the villain, escape the dangers and avoid the pitfalls that threaten him every step of the way, and bring the villain to justice. The hero confronts all obstacles. He risks all dangers. He never quits.

The villain must be equally committed. He will do whatever it takes to get away with murder. "Villains and enemies," Vogler says, "are usually dedicated to the death, destruction, or defeat of the hero."

When both sleuth and villain are highly motivated, it appears to be an equal contest at best. If anything, the villain has the edge. The outcome is uncertain.

If it's to be mysterious, of course, the villain must successfully withhold his identity from both the sleuth and the reader until the climactic revelation. To be worthy of the sleuth's best efforts, the villain must be supremely skilled at lying and must appear ordinary to both sleuth and reader."

By all civilized standards, murderers are evil, but by their own standards, their evil deeds are justified. They believe they are good, even heroic. Their quest is virtuous, and they will not abandon it.

Beginning mystery writers often invent their sleuth first and then try to think up a mystery for him to solve. A better way is to begin with the villain. Imagine him fully. Inhabit his mind. Give him passionate beliefs and powerful wants. Understand him. Make him believable. Then create a scenario in which, if you were him, with the same wants and beliefs, you could imagine yourself committing a murder.

Villains are motivated by the human passions we all feel: love, greed, ambition, fear, envy, betrayal, pride. Remember and relive moments when you've experienced these feelings, and use them to build characters. "I try to get inside the villain's head and think like one," mystery writer Al Blanchard says. "It's always scary to me when a reader tells me I created a good villain. No two villains are alike. Motivation is the key to believability. It's motivation that makes the bad guy come to life."

The worthy villain in thrillers

In mystery novels, readers know only what the hero knows, and they are invited to participate in his sleuthing and detecting. But in thrillers, the identity of the villain, while perhaps unknown to the hero, is either known to the reader from the beginning or revealed early in the story. The story's suspense builds from the uncertainty of whether the villain will succeed in his evil plan before the hero can stop him. Typically, the point of view shifts back and forth between hero and villain.

Thrillers play out as cat-and-mouse games. They are zero-sum games, with only one winner. The villain's triumph means the hero's defeat.

The stakes are often higher in thrillers than in mysteries, and thriller villains are correspondingly bigger, badder, and scarier. They kill without conscience. They are serial killers, assassins, political or religious fanatics, terrorist bombers.

Frederick Forsyth's Jackal, for example, is determined to assassinate President de Gaulle. Ken Follett's Nazi spy "The Needle" wants to deliver information that will change the outcome of World War II. Thomas Harris' Buffalo Bill kills women to harvest their skin. Ian Fleming's Goldfinger plans to rob Fort Knox.

When a flawed, ordinary hero—or even a superhero like James Bond—is matched up against a bigger-than-life villain, the outcome is doubtful and the suspense intense. "The hero has to be powerful and clever," observes mystery writer Hallie Ephron, "so what's the fun if the villain is a wimp? Any game that's too one-sided we turn off before half-time. A worthy villain is absolutely crucial in a suspense/thriller."

But regardless of how psychopathically evil and monomaniacally committed to their purposes they might be, thriller villains would not be worthy unless they were adept at blending into the crowd.

Nor would they be interesting unless they were complicated, multi-layered, and even likable. "My take on villains is that they're not much different than ordinary folk," says novelist Philip R. Craig. "I get this from Dostoyevsky, who thought that murderers were very similar to regular people. When I create a villain, I usually try to make him appear as a normal or even a sympathetic character. Very few of my villains are satanic."

The worthy villain in mainstream novels

Mainstream, or literary, novels depend on conflict, tension, and suspense just as mysteries and thrillers do. But in mainstream fiction, the hero's opposition may come from sources other than a conventional bad guy. The hero confronts his internal psychological conflicts, or he struggles against social, institutional, natural, or cultural forces, or he goes after things that other "good" characters also want.

Alex (not his real name), a promising young writer, recently asked me to critique his novel. It's about an ordinary small-town shopkeeper named Jack whose wife suddenly dies. Soon thereafter, Jack's young daughter, Amanda, accidentally burns down their house, which has been in Jack's family for generations. Jack's goal, the quest that drives the story, is to rebuild the house exactly as it was, to insulate Amanda from all unpleasantness, and thus to restore the familiar normality of his life.

In Alex's first draft, all of the conflict and tension emanated from Jack's fears and obsessions. Nothing external opposed his rebuilding efforts, nor was Amanda in any apparent danger. The result was a smart, entertaining story, but it lacked tension, because readers were given no objective reason to doubt its outcome.

My advice to Alex: personify Jack's struggle by introducing a worthy villain or two. Perhaps a bureaucrat from the Welfare Department appears on the scene, determined to take Amanda away from her distracted and depressed father. Maybe a by-the-numbers building inspector nixes Jack's plans for the house.

Alex tells me that he's working on it.

Melville created Moby Dick to personify Captain Ahab's self-destructive obsession. Ken Kesey's Nurse Ratched, surely one of literature's most delicious villains, personifies the destructive institutional forces of an insane asylum, and metaphorically, of society. Hawthorne's banal Rev. Arthur Dimmsdale stands for the prejudices of Hester Prynne's narrow-minded community. Mark Twain's Injun Joe is the real-life bogeyman that haunts the nightmares of boys like Tom Sawyer.

Mainstream antagonists needn't be evil. Their simple—but vital—function is to oppose the hero. In a story about a divorced woman fighting for custody of her daughter, for example, her ex-husband plays the antagonist's role. If he's a nice guy, a good provider, and a loving father, his claim on the daughter will be strong, putting the outcome in doubt and making him the worthy villain in the wife's story. Told from the husband's point of view, of course, the hero-villain roles would be reversed.

So the job of the villain is to make things hard for your hero. Without an opponent to create problems and obstacles for your hero, there is nothing for readers to worry or care about. Without a villain who is worthy of your hero's best efforts, there is no story. "The villain has to be shaped to suit each story," Barbara Peters says. "There's no single rule how to do it. But he must be worthy of the reader's time and emotional investment. A novel is a journey, and something needs to be drawn from it. The greater the balance between the forces at work in creating the basic conflict that sparks the plot, the higher the reader's level of enjoyment."

William G. Tapply of Hancock, N.H., has published 22 mystery/suspense novels. *Bitch Creek*, due out this fall, will make it 23. He is also the author of *The Elements of Mystery Fiction: Writing a Modern Whodunit* (forthcoming in a new expanded edition from Poisoned Pen Press). This article appeared in *The Writer*, July 2004.

A writer's checklist

How worthy is your villain? Can you answer "yes" to the following questions?

1. Do your villain's goals stand in direct opposition to those of your hero?
2. Is your villain as committed to achieving his goals as your hero is?
3. Is your villain a believable, interesting character in his own right?
4. Are your villain's motivations understandable and coherent?
5. Is your villain skilled at lying and dissembling in order to disguise his acts and purposes?
6. Does your villain avoid making stupid mistakes?
7. Is your villain the equal of your hero, or nearly so, in intelligence, courage, talent, and resourcefulness?
8. Does your villain challenge your hero to test the limits of his own courage and ability?
9. If your villain wins, will your hero necessarily lose?
10. When the pressure's on, does your villain get tougher, smarter, and even more determined?

—*William G. Tapply*

MAKING UP GOOD CHARACTERS

Top writers offer advice on the essential art of characterization

compiled by Ronald Kovach

Plot, setting, dialogue, and style are all important elements of fiction, but many writers and readers would say characterization is its heart and soul. The instinctual tendency of a reader to identify with a fellow (if fictional) human being who is facing an obstacle, making a journey of one type or another, or hoping to survive some dire threat is prime territory for the writer of stories. It is good characters that so often—perhaps most often—sustain our interest through a piece of fiction, and their creation is essential to the developing writer.

Over the last few years, many fine writers have had much to say about the art of characterization in interviews and articles in *The Writer*. To aid you in developing your own characters, we have compiled a sampling of their most pertinent comments. As you'll see from some of the tales below, the characters you create in your imagination might become more real than you'd ever guess.

Building a backstory

Hal Blythe and Charlie Sweet

We suggest that before you begin your story, you establish a fictional biography for your main character. At one extreme, you might think of this bio as a job application for an intelligence agency—providing a full spectrum of detailed information, from physical appearance to educational background, favorite hobbies to preferred authors. Or you may choose to profile only those major traits that define your character's essence—things that might appear in a eulogy. Regardless of which approach you take, you must make one essential decision: you must determine what lies at your character's emotional core.

Ask yourself, what is the one thing that defines my character? What is that character's primary goal in life? Knowing this goal will determine the subsequent choices you make as you create the story in which this character takes center stage.

Once you have a solid understanding of your character and his or her goal (to make the soccer team, to bring Mommy and Daddy back together, to realize her potential as an adult woman), you can begin to devise a plot that reveals your character's attempts to achieve this goal—the struggles, the successes, the failures, the lessons learned. (from their article in *The Writer*, March 2003)

Anne Tyler

I've never thought of my characters in ["ordinary" or "eccentric" terms] or consciously chosen them for such qualities.

What leads me to write about someone is simple curiosity. How would it feel to be so-and-so? What's the relationship of that couple I saw stepping off the bus? Really, it's a decision based not on artistic considerations but on a zest for plain old gossip. I write pages and pages of notes about the characters, much more than will ever be shown in the novel—what kind of childhoods they had, their attitudes toward food and money and clothes, their private anxieties, the things that make them angry. (from an interview by Bethanne Kelly Patrick in *The Writer*, April 2004)

Alan Furst

I always work out all the backstories. I tend to take copious notes about them. Who is this person? Not every character. There are too many characters in the book to do that. Most of the characters—I want to know their history. I want you to know their history.

It can be anything from a three-word history to a ten-paragraph history. It just depends on how important, interesting, and appealing that history is. The reader has to say, "Oh, isn't this great! I'm reading a terrific history of this person." You can't say, "The reader has to learn the history of this person even though it's a boring, stupid history, so I'm just going to impinge upon, demand the reader's good graces for two pages here, while I do this important thing." You can't do that. (from an interview in *The Writer*, May 2003)

M. J. Rose

I don't even try to start a new novel until I've spent six to twelve weeks researching, outlining, and making a scrapbook for my main characters—in other words, procrastinating. . . .

I believe that you need to live with a story and its main characters for a long time and discover as much as you can about them and their world before you actually put fingers to the keyboard. Once I've done a good amount of gathering scrapbook items and making notes, I start to write. (from an interview in *The Writer*, February 2003)

The creative process

Donna Tartt

Character, to me, is the very lifeblood of fiction, and creating character is one of the aspects of writing that I love the most. I love the tradition of Dickens, where even the most minor walk-on characters are somehow alive. To create character, I think, takes a sharp objective eye but also an intuitive intelligence, receptiveness, a willingness to make oneself blank in order to perceive clearly. People are endlessly different. One must see them as they are without projecting one's own values on them. (from an interview by Sarah Anne Johnson in *The Writer*, August 2003)

John Irving

The characters in my novels, from the very first one, are always on some quixotic effort of attempting to control something that is uncontrollable. Some element of the world that is essentially random and out of control. And they're not gonna do it. It's not gonna happen.

I had a doctor's appointment today with my youngest child, and the doctor made an analogy that was just chilling to me—as I think it would be to any parent. Not because the diagnosis was at all serious, but because it speaks to that issue of control. I was looking for a course of medication that we hadn't found. And the doctor said, "The problem with you is that you think you're driving a car. And what you don't understand is that you're driving a boat." The hairs stood up on the back of my neck. I don't like driving a boat. I don't like turning the wheel and then waiting to see what happens.

That's very much like the situation I try to imagine in every novel. I want the principle character—and then the reader—to feel it's okay, I'm in a car. Then, whoops, they're not in a car. (from an interview by Dorman Shindler in *The Writer*, January 2002)

Jonathan Harris

So the question becomes: how does the author of a thriller or fantasy keep the reader's trust? What can be done to convince that reader to keep faith with the story when it dives, as it must, beyond the edge of reason and into the realm of marvelous adventure?

The writer must establish credibility from the start. To do this, I use a technique that I call tethering. This process anchors your story to the concrete world through the use of real elements that resonate with the reader and convince him or her that you know exactly what you are writing about. . . .

A story based around a cannibal psychiatrist with charm and a towering IQ who helps a young female FBI agent catch another serial killer is a leap from the ordinary into the fabulous. But it is a leap that the reader takes willingly on faith. Why? Because Dr. Hannibal Lecter, as written by Thomas Harris in the trilogy of *Red Dragon*, *The Silence of the Lambs*, and *Hannibal*, possesses, without any question, the mind, skills, and knowledge of a brilliant and well-trained psychiatrist. From the first moment that FBI agent Starling, with all the power of her position, goes to interview Lecter in jail, and he succeeds in turning her and the interview inside out—simply by probing her weaknesses with devastating questions—we know that Lecter is for real. We know that Lecter is a force. And once we accept him as credible, we are ready to go along for the ride. (from his article in *The Writer*, December 2003)

Anne Lamott

I didn't know the details of Mattie's life when I started [*Blue Shoe*]. I knew that her world was up in flames, and it's autumn outside, and the trees look like flames. I wanted everything that could be taken away from her to pretty much have been taken away, so that she has given up her husband, she's broke, her mother has just moved out of this house where she grew up. So she moves into the house and what you find is that everything about the house has been designed to cover up the rot and the mildew and the holes and the problems and the family's very poor solutions to its very human and universal problems. I just sort of knew who some of the people were, I knew enough about them to go on. I just took it one day at a time, and screwed up, you know. I believe in a lot of mistakes and false starts and messes. (from an interview in *The Writer*, April 2003)

Jonathan Franzen

Once I have some clear idea of what the book is about, I get a very rough structure. Then, the work for weeks or months is to come up with a topic sentence—something that captures the plight of the characters. For Chip [in *The Corrections*], it was: "He's no good at making money, and he thought it was okay to live the life of the mind." For Gary, it was: "He's struggling to persuade himself that he's not mentally ill."

I think the most important thing—it may sound strange—is to get inside the character to the point that there is a lot of anxiety and shame. The real struggle is to find a dramatic setup and a corresponding tone that make it possible to dwell in that anxiety and shame without feeling icky as a reader. That's a big challenge. My approach to that—pretty much with all the characters—was that when it started seeming funny to me, I knew I was there. If it seemed anguished or earnest, I knew I wasn't there. (from an interview in *The Writer*, February 2002)

Giving your characters freedom

Dean Koontz

To create convincing antagonists, you've got to believe in the reality of evil. If you think evil isn't a real force in the world, if you think everyone could be reformed with enough psychiatric analysis and compassion, you don't understand the darker side of human nature, and your villains won't ring true.

To create convincing protagonists and supporting characters who are complex, realistic, and lovable, you've got to like people, all kinds of people. And when writing, you have to avoid pushing your character along from one calculated plot point to another; give your character free will, as God gave free will to us, for only then will the character act as a real individual, surprising you and your reader.

. . . I read dozens of publications each month—various sciences, history, current events—and odd facts stick with me. They cook in the subconscious, and from time to time they blend together into an edible stew that is a story idea. At that point, I have a premise and often a theme—*The Face* is about many things, for instance, but the themes of redemption and faith are the core of it—but I still do not have a plot. The characters create the plot as they explore their own free will.

The imagination is like a muscle: the more you use it, the better it performs and the quicker you get ideas of a higher caliber. If you aren't getting ideas, the problem isn't usually that you need to "get out of your own way," but that you aren't feeding your subconscious a rich enough diet from which to build stories. (from an interview by Jessica Hatchigan in *The Writer*, December 2003)

J. A. Jance

I've learned to create realistic dialogue that sounds like people talking. Dialogue keeps the plot moving forward. . . . The kind and supportive things characters say to one another or the undermining mean things can reveal more about a character and motivation than whole paragraphs of expository writing. And if one character's line of dialogue stretches to four or five, that isn't dialogue. Real people don't talk in long paragraphs unless they're delivering a speech. . . .

I've learned to trust my characters to tell me when I've gone off track and have them doing something that's wrong or illogical. When that happens, I have to stop, sit back, consider, and then change the most difficult thing there is to change when writing a book—my mind.

It was a shock to me when, 50 pages from the end of my second book, I learned that the person I thought was the killer didn't do it. People have asked me since whether I had to go back and change the clues. "No," I tell them. "It turns out he was innocent the whole time." (from her article in *The Writer*, January 2004)

Anita Shreve

When I begin a novel, I have what I would call a "broad-strokes" outline. I often know my endings. That is, I have an image or even a sentence that I see as the end. But even though I sometimes know my ending, I often have no idea of how I am going to get there. It's the slow unfolding of the characters and the story and the different journeys on which the characters take you that are unpredictable and exciting.

. . . I suppose I could go to a shrink to find out why I am so drawn to the theme of love, with all of its attendant emotions. I don't examine this too closely, for fear of defusing the very thing that makes me want to write. I can tell you, however, that the arena of love is a wonderful place in which to place characters. It's something extraordinary that happens to ordinary people. It's often, as well, a terrific testing ground for moral character. (from an interview by Robert Papinchak in *The Writer*, November 2001)

Carl Hiaasen

Technically, the way I start is usually with, one by one, a cast of characters I'm sort of fiddling with in the back of my head and then on paper—characters I'd like to get on stage and see what happens.

. . . I consider an outline a handcuff. I want to be surprised by my characters; I want to be able to change direction; I want to be able to eliminate characters if they're boring me. Having said this, I understand the value of an outline for a writer whose mind works that way. For some types of novels, it's probably essential.

I can be two-thirds of the way into the book and not know how it's going to end up. I can tell you when I start what the tone is going to be at the end, but in terms of the choreography of the ending or who exactly is left standing and who is in shreds at the end, that I'm not sure of. (from an interview in *The Writer*, June 2003)

Philip Danze

I pay no mind to the axiom, "Write what you know." Adventure stories require that characters be stressed to the point where they reveal their true selves, which would never come to the surface in everyday life.

When writing *Conjuring Maud*, I knew the general direction in which the story was headed and let the characters have enough freedom to work out their lives along logical paths. I felt I had made solid contact with this story. It was very much like making contact with a fastball and watching it sail toward a distant fence. (from an interview in *The Writer*, November 2001)

Ronald Kovach is senior editor of *The Writer*. Excerpts came from interviews conducted by *The Writer* staff, unless otherwise noted.

SECTION FOUR

Writing for Specialized Markets

CREATING CHARACTERS IN POETRY

by Kay Day

The phrase "show, don't tell" resounds in seminars, articles, and classrooms. It's a deceptively simple phrase. When creating character, a poet may find that those three words lead to no small amount of frustration.

Within a poem, the line is the structure that supports the foundation. In poems that involve creating a character, whether the poem is in first person or third person, a number of tools and techniques exist for making the character seem real. A poem succeeds only if the character is round enough to interest the reader.

Consider the monster Grendel in *Beowulf*, the epic poem written between the seventh and tenth centuries. Seamus Heaney's translation was an international bestseller, no small feat for a book of poetry. Grendel still finds favor with readers and critics because of his fierce, malicious deeds that propel the narrative. The epic poem is named for the conquering hero, but the poem itself is remembered for a creature that shredded and devoured brave warriors. Grendel's demonic glory is rendered by a wide range of emotions and actions— his "greedily loping" gait, his "spurned and joyless" demeanor. A long passage early on relates how Grendel delights in picturing the blood and gore he will inflict. When Beowulf reduces the monster to desperation—Grendel "quailed and recoiled" before the victor—character runs full circle from an all-powerful to an impotent creature. Description of Grendel's underwater lair is worthy of a nightmare, illustrating how setting can contribute to character. The fully rendered Grendel anchors the epic poem's endurance.

Poet and critic R. J. McCaffery wryly calls "show, don't tell" an "old writing chestnut." The author of *Chaos Theory and the Knuckleballer* and several other books, McCaffery advises, "Provide evocative detail which suggests information to the reader, and thus engages the reader's imagination in the poem."

In his poem "Eddy's Laundry," McCaffery, who edits a top-notch literary e-zine, *Eye-Dialect* (www.contemporarypoetry.com/dialect), creates a character who works at a Laundromat, yet the character is never labeled. Eddy is rendered whole by his actions, such as, "He tosses lint screen keys on a washer's lid/as he stoops to examine a bare scratch ticket." The reader senses the character's interest in the trivial, a man busy with his duties, but simple-minded enough to examine a throwaway ticket, a man whose career is laundry, as suggested by these lines spoken by the narrator about Eddy:

> Ten years, he told me, two weeks ago,
> ten more to go then—Palm Beach.
> Though, of course, business wouldn't be so good
> as them women wear nothing. But there's fishing—
> he knows a guy who paid off his boat
> with a Grade A Tuna. . . .

Kim Addonizio, whose book *Tell Me* was a 2000 National Book Award finalist, emphasizes that elements of character depend on "description, action, words—these are all ways in which we come to know people." She notes devices for crafting characters include "how they look and the way they present themselves to the world. We know them by what they do and by what they say."

Addonizio, who is also author of the collection *What Is This Thing Called Love*, adds, "Drawing conclusions for readers should be avoided." If you write, "He did bad things, but felt guilty," she says, it "takes the whole experience away from the reader. The writer's job is to show this character doing or remembering those things, and then, to convey the character's experience of guilt through what he says or does." She offers an example she uses with her students, such as asking them about action. "What does it look like?" She says, "That's a question that forces them to think about gesture rather than abstraction. If this guy feels guilty, what can we see him doing that will let us understand how he feels?" She notes, "In poems, the difficulty is greater because you can't go on for pages and pages to establish character. You need to render that character vividly, and quickly."

In her poem "Beer. Milk. The Dog. My Old Man." from her novel in verse, *Jimmy and Rita*, Addonizio, in the final lines, closes out not just one but two characters that the reader can visualize:

> The dog. My old man. He loved
> a cold beer. Sometimes I'd sit up
> at night in the garage and watch
> how he drank it, tipping his head
> way back, and I'd try to drink mine

exactly the same,
but quietly, so he wouldn't notice
and send me away.

For the writer of metrical verse, drawing character can be a double challenge. Alicia (A.E.) Stallings, author of *Archaic Smile* and an editor at *Atlanta
Review*, has won numerous awards for her poetry, among them, the Richard
Wilbur Award. "Basically, the same rules apply for poetry as for fiction," she
explains, "but sometimes a judicious amount of telling is not amiss, frankly. As
for showing, that will tend to come in the nouns and verbs, where adjectives
and adverbs are often closer to telling, in my view. And some of the showing
can be in choices of diction, rather than just action or dialogue or description.
Good prose does this too, of course, but poetry tends to use this more—almost
a personification on the level of the word." As an example, she cites Gwendolyn
Brooks' famous "We Real Cool," where the word "jazz" is used as a verb.

In her poem "Aftershocks," from her collection of the same name, Stallings
creates not one but two characters in such depth that the reader experiences an
intimate kinship. A master poet, she manages this within the form of a sonnet:

Or have we always stood on shaky ground?
The moment keeps on happening: a sound.
The floor beneath us swings, a pendulum
That clocks the heart, the heart so tightly wound,
We fall mute, as when two lovers come
To the brink of the apology, and halt,
Each standing on the wrong side of the fault.

In a sonnet, Stallings says, "you only have some 140-odd syllables to work
with. If it is a drama playing out between two characters, for instance, it is wise
to begin in media res, right in the middle of things, where it gets interesting,
and assume the reader can work out where you are. A dramatic moment helps
you sharpen what each of your characters wants out of a situation. If it is a
monologue, it helps if there is some sort of dramatic irony—a disjunction
between what the speaker wants us to think and what we perceive about him
or her. This again creates tension." And, "If anyone speaks directly in a poem,
their word choices are, of course, vital."

Creating fictional characters within poetry is challenge enough. Consider the
task of rounding characters based on real people. Ruth Daigon, author of
Handfuls of Time and a half-dozen other books, confronted history when she
wrote *Payday at the Triangle*. This book narrates the tragic story of the Triangle
Shirtwaist Factory fire in New York City in 1911. Factory doors were locked
and the windows were shut tight, resulting in the loss of 146 lives. Daigon,
whose awards include the Ann Stanford Poetry Award, couldn't speak for the
characters without knowing the truth.

"I did years of research before the book was completed," she says. "My information was provided by the Kheel Center at Cornell University. There were so many choices to make and I wanted to be certain I had made the right choices." The result of her research and hard work is a stunning collection of history woven as poetry, and the reader cannot help but feel a sense of loss when reading the stories Daigon composed, such as these lines from, "Hyman Meschel, clerk":

> In the hospital, wounds treated, blanketed and warm,
> I breathe in the fresh smell of sheets
> Eyes slowly see the light
> Memory opens wide
> and no one hears my hoarse whispers
> My sister where's my sister . . .

"It was a delicate matter to balance narrative and character," the poet notes, "but by the time I had thoroughly absorbed the account of each character, the description of life before the fire, and what happened during and after, I became each character in my book. I knew how they expressed themselves. I investigated each past life and relationships with the people who had died."

Drawing characters in third person is not the only method of creating a memorable persona. There is also the poem that renders a character either by use of first person or by allowing the character to speak for himself. One powerful poem that creates a character by means of a role is Rhina Espaillat's "For Evan, Who Says I Am Too Tidy," from the book *Where Horizons Go*:

> True, tidy seldom goes where genius goes,
> but then how many do? And heaven knows
> there's work for us who watch the time, the purse,
> the washing of small hands. I've been called worse.

"What's being conveyed," Espaillat says, "is not so much character as role in life. I'm 'Grandma' in this poem, fairly generic and age-determined, concerned, as older people tend to be, not with adventure and excitement, but with the nurturing and the well-being of those in their care. . . . Behind the subject is the sub-subject, the links between one generation and the next, composed of irritation, love, patience, and memory." Espaillat, whose latest book is *Rehearsing Absence*, has garnered many awards, such as the T. S. Eliot Prize and the Richard Wilbur Award. She says characters in poetry are created the same way as in fiction, by "telling details, action, and gesture, and of course, the language itself, its tone, what it suggests above and below the content."

Creating successful characters in poetry depends on more than simply "show, don't tell." Techniques actually involve using both methods successfully, but doing so in balance. Bringing a persona or voice to a level that engages the reader can rest on something as simple as the character examining trash from a floor, or tidying up a room to the point that it irritates a child. Physical confrontation, expressions of mourning by way of monologue, the rendering of a relationship by positioning the reader at an intimate vantage point—each of these mechanisms brings the character to life and allows him to breathe within the single most important element in a poem, the line. And it doesn't hurt to take advice from an expert on character.

In *Poetics*, Aristotle summed up the drawing of character with a simple decree. Above all, he said, "It must be good."

Kay Day has had articles and poetry published in *Miller's Pond* (print edition), *Conspire*, and *Pif*. Her poems appear in a number of anthologies, such as *The Best of Foliate Oak*, and have been read on programs on National Public Radio. She has published three collections of poetry, including *A Poetry Break*. This article appeared in *The Writer*, June 2004.

FIRST-SCENE ESSENTIALS FOR YOUR SCREENPLAY

A script must waste no time in engaging the reader

by Rick Reichman

The first scene of your script determines a thumbs-up or thumbs-down for your work. If your first scene fails to engage a studio or agency editor and make her anxious to get to the next pages, then no other scene, no matter how well done, will be given as much as a dutiful glance.

What, then, are the essential elements that a writer should include to nail a great first scene? One is *prelude*, and the other is *first-scene reversal*.

Prelude

The prelude is the first few pages of your script, and it is important to remember that those pages, no matter when and where the story begins, introduce us to a totally new universe. It may be somewhere in outer space or in Santa Fe, but it is still your—the writer's—outer space or Santa Fe. No one else is familiar with your place, your characters, or their situation. You're asking that we accept a new world and connect with it, or at least get used to it, before the story actually begins. And the best way to introduce your audience to your time, place, people, and situation is to use a bit more detail and description than will be the case in the rest of the script.

At the same time you bring your reader into your creation, you should be introducing other factors that will play a major role in your story. Indeed, your prelude needs to convey visually and/or verbally the story's setting and time, genre, tone, main character, and, most importantly, themes.

Time and location seem easy. After all, the first major slug line gives a time and place—and should include historical time, as well. But remember, a script is written for two audiences: the reader and the movie-goer. So if the slug is written "EXT. NASHVILLE—DAY (WINTER 1951)," that lets the reader know when and where the action is occurring. You must also make sure in the directions that follow, however, to show the viewer that it is winter 1951 in Nashville. It's not that difficult, but many writers simply don't do it.

Next is genre. Is your script a mystery, Western, action adventure, parody, romantic comedy, etc.? Inquiring audiences need to know. Why? Because knowing the genre allows the audience to feel that when they take their seat and buy their $5 popcorn and $3 cola, they have a general idea of the kind of characters, setting, and surprises to expect along the way. After all, you set an entirely different mood and set of expectations if you begin with a vicious ax-to-ax street battle in the Five Points of New York City in 1846, as opposed to opening 100 years later with a Princeton math professor lecturing new students on the importance of mathematicians in World War II and in the present power-struggle with the Russians.

While it's obvious that certain genres such as pirate epics, science fiction, and Westerns are easy to identify the moment the images appear on screen, on paper it is still up to you to give your audience some written evidence as to what type of movie they will be experiencing. How?

I remember one of my students having that very problem. In class, she was reading the opening of her script, which went on for two pages-plus portraying a perfect Christmas setting in a snow-covered suburban neighborhood replete with decorated trees, colorful lights, bright green wreaths, perfectly formed snowmen, and tasteful yard displays. I finally asked, "What kind of film is this?"

"It's a murder mystery," she said.

"Oh. Then perhaps there should be a decapitated snowman," I suggested, "or you could bring us in the back window of someone's house and have the person in the house watching *Rear Window* instead of *It's a Wonderful Life*."

If, on the other hand, you are penning a romantic comedy, you might begin with one of those "dates gone wrong" from the numerous TV dating shows. A drama could open with a car passing or getting caught behind a funeral procession. And a biographical film about a singer might show a concert hall, or, for an astronaut, perhaps a movie theater playing a film about space travel.

The way genre is presented also has an immediate effect on your audience. Whether it takes a serious, comic, absurd, whimsical, or other approach, your tone should fit your plot and, especially, your characters. It should add motivation for an audience to want to stay from prelude to final credits.

It's probably a rule—or should be—that one of your major characters (protagonist or antagonist) is introduced in the first scene. Character introduction, however, can be accomplished many different ways. Physical presence is the most obvious, but other options will also suffice, including discussion of a

The first few pages of every script, no matter when and where its story begins, introduce us to a totally new universe.

character; representation of a character (with, say, her artwork or novel appearing on screen); the character being in a picture, tape, or movie within the film; or even an oblique reference to the character. *Seabiscuit* opens with a short pictorial and verbal history of the hope and opportunities Americans had early in the last century. But it was those hopes and opportunities, and how the stock market crash smashed them, that shaped the fans of Seabiscuit and the people who helped make the horse a star.

While introducing the new world to your audience, the writer also needs to present the themes of his movie. Films from the '80s and early '90s generally accomplished this visually. In *Dead Poets Society*, the themes of tradition, conformity, rigidity, and arrogance—and a hint that they will all be disrupted—are clearly evident in the first minute or so. In *Back to the Future*, the first items we see are clocks, and then "Rube Goldberg" inventions working but producing unintended results. Next, we discover that Einstein is missing, and we hear TV news reporting about some stolen uranium. In *Silence of the Lambs*, Clarise pounds the murky obstacle course running from or to something, exhausted but persistent in her goal, halting only when officially commanded, and adhering strictly to the nearby sign nailed to a tree that posits, "Hurt, Agony, Pain, Love it!"

In all of these openings, the relative themes show up long before the characters actually have something to say. Saying, though, seems to be the trend in more recent films. *Beautiful Mind*, *Minority Report*, *The Hours*, *Spider Man*, *You Can Count on Me*, *Erin Brockovich*, as well as *Seabiscuit*, all open with dialogue or some type of verbal commentary. Staying with this trend or crafting a more visual presentation is your call. But however you decide, you still need to present all the elements that constitute the prelude.

First-scene reversal

The first-scene reversal is the event, incident, or occurrence that truly launches your story. In the opening, your protagonist has a goal she wants to reach. Usually, within seven pages—and certainly no more than ten—an incident, occurrence, or event pulls the protagonist off the original goal (whether she knows it or not) and begins her journey toward a new goal. The remaining pages of your script show how your protagonist achieves her new goal or is ennobled in the effort.

The first-scene reversal can involve, for example, a detective pulled into an unusual case or falsely accused of a crime; a letter that takes a character on an unexpected journey; the nerd being changed into a superhero by some scientific accident; the small-business owner forced into an unsavory pact; the subway rider just missing her train home; or any of the innumerable changes of direction, fortune, and/or plans a character might experience.

Some have labeled this point in the script the inciting incident, but no matter the term, it is the critical point that begins the protagonist's new journey, and that journey will be the crux of your main story.

Writing an engaging opening can't be emphasized enough. I have heard from numerous coverage editors (readers) that if the first scene is good, they'll usually allow for a slightly weaker second or even third scene—as long as the script picks up after that. But if the first scene doesn't work, they say, they won't bother with the rest of the script.

So creating a clear description of time and place, signaling a definitive genre and tone, introducing a major character, and, all the while, visually and/or verbally defining the themes within the first few pages can get the reader involved. Then, just as everyone's gotten comfortable, you twist your main character—and audience—onto a different path and a new goal. This reversal should make your reader eager to turn to the next page and next scene. If your first scene does all this, then it's served you and your story well, and you should be well on your way to producing a winning screenplay.

Rick Reichman of Santa Fe, N.M., is the author of *Formatting Your Screenplay* and teaches screenwriting at the Community College of Santa Fe and at various conferences and workshops across the United States. This article appeared in *The Writer*, January 2004.

KEEP YOUR SCREENPLAY ON TRACK

Avoid these top 22 mistakes

by Staton Rabin

As a veteran story analyst in the film industry who has evaluated thousands of books and screenplays for film studios and agencies, I'm often asked for some kind of "magic formula" that will enable a writer to sell his script.

Is it mainly a good story or great characters that will catch my eye, aspiring screenwriters want to know. Do I have some sort of "check list" of qualities against which I compare screenplays? Will the writer's age, race, or sex work against him? Am I looking for something "commercial," or do smaller, more personal films have a chance? Do my bosses give me "marching orders" and tell me they're looking for one particular genre (horror, romantic comedy, thriller, etc.) over another?

But the most frequent question by far is quite simple: "What makes you give a script a 'Recommend'?"

All of these questions can be answered the same way—and the answer may surprise you. Story analysts who work for film studios or major agencies are not looking for anything in particular—except, of course, a great screenplay. And how do I decide what a great screenplay is? The same way you do. Story analysts are just like anyone else who reads books or goes to the movies. We're looking to get "carried away" by a great story. When your screenplay is great, we almost forget we are "critics" for a while, and get swept up in your thrilling story and fascinating characters.

The only difference between me and the average moviegoer is that I may be able to explain better exactly what it was about a film (structure, characters, dialogue) that made me feel about it the way I do. And if anything about it isn't working, I'll be able to tell you why—and how to fix it. While a screenplay is only a blueprint for a movie rather than the movie itself, reading a great one should be an emotional roller coaster.

That said, any story analyst will tell you that finding a great screenplay is a rare occurrence. In the meantime, we read hundreds of books and scripts a year that leave us cold and functioning in full "critic" mode—which is to say, focusing our full attention on the flaws in your script. And while it's impossible to quantify what makes a great script, or give you some sort of formula for brewing one up, it's very easy to list the kinds of errors that most commonly appear in aspiring screenwriters' work, and that increase the likelihood your material will get a "pass." This list of common mistakes would vary little no matter which experienced industry reader compiled it.

Here are the top 22 mistakes I find in the screenplays that cross my desk every day:

1. Ordinariness. Many writers don't understand just how terrific their work has to be to stand out from the crowd. Every scene—especially the first page—has to be electrifying, or at least surprising or moving, in one way or another, and some scenes have to move people to tears or laughter. The first page should knock a reader out of his or her seat, and so should the rest. Read top produced screenplays—don't just go to see movies—and if your work isn't that good, or almost that good, it won't ever sell. You cannot get away with laziness or lack of talent. If your script is just Okay, or even "good," that's not good enough.

When I teach screenwriting courses, students enter my classroom for the first time and hear the voice of Frank Sinatra. And when they sit down and look at me with puzzled expressions on their faces, wondering if perhaps they've wandered into the school's music-appreciation class by mistake, I point to the CD player with Sinatra's *Fly Me to the Moon* emanating from it, and say: "That's how good you have to be at what *you* do."

2. Lack of story structure. The reason professional screenwriters are paid so much money is that very few amateurs know how to structure a story properly. No matter what else you're good at—dialogue, characters, etc.—you will never sell a script if you can't tell a story using the traditional three-act story structure. And how do you learn how to do this? To some writers it is just, to quote songwriter Irving Berlin, "Doin' what comes natur'lly." Others have to take a screenwriting course or read books on the subject by Syd Field, Lew Hunter, or Michael Hauge. But whether you're born knowing how to structure a story, or you have to learn it from others, it's an essential skill for any screenwriter.

3. Superfluous scenes. I read a lot of scripts that contain scenes showing moving cars (used only to get characters from here to there, rather than for important action or dialogue) and people entering and leaving rooms, or which reveal slow pacing or other poor choices for a story's building blocks. It's important to know which scenes to include in your screenplay and which to leave out, to pick up the action as late as possible in each scene, and to leave the scene as early as possible after conveying what needs to be conveyed. I'm reminded of the old saw about Michelangelo: to carve his famous statue of David, it is said, he took a block of marble and chiseled away anything that didn't look like David. That describes the art of screenwriting. You cut away anything that doesn't serve your story.

4. Chit-chat. Some screenplays have characters who just chat and exchange information or greetings without conveying essential information that propels the plot forward. There's no room for "small talk" in screenplays.

5. Errors of format, grammar, and spelling. It's just as your third-grade teacher always told you: spelling counts. Even if you write a great script, if it's filled with typos and grammatical errors or written in improper screenplay format, you'll have two strikes against you from the moment a Hollywood reader begins reading it. To a story analyst, a writer who hasn't bothered to proofread his script or learn the proper format for screenplays probably hasn't bothered to learn how to write, either. Many books are available on the subject of proper screenplay format—and even software programs that do format for you. And if the spell-check on your computer is inadequate—and it always is—or your grammar leaves much to be desired, hire a copy editor to fix your work before you submit it.

6. Characters who talk alike. Dialogue should be written so that if you cover up the characters' names, you'll still know who's talking. While it's true that the ability to write good dialogue is the least important skill a screenwriter can have (story structure being far more important), it can certainly enhance a good script if you write exceptional dialogue. One way to improve your dialogue is to study how the masters do this. Watch Paddy Chayefsky's *Marty*, for example, and listen for the rhythms and subtext and the way the dialogue provides exposition and reveals character. Another way is to study the way real people talk. Personally, I learn a lot about writing film dialogue by listening to the teenagers talk on the MetroNorth train in New York City.

7. Nothing much happens. The story doesn't move, and it's neither cinematic nor effective in using a visual medium.

8. Unfunny comedy. Don't write a broad comedy unless you are so funny the reader is going to fall off his chair laughing. The ability to make your friends laugh is, by itself, probably not an indication of comic writing talent. (Some people are both funny in person and on the page, but this is rare). Successful comedy writers usually are not funny people in real life.

9. Muddled or derivative thrillers. Don't try to write a mystery or thriller unless you feel you understand the genre and can do something new. These are very difficult scripts to write, and unless you must write in this genre, it's better not to attempt this for a first or second script.

10. Overlong descriptions. Many screenplays I read contain "action lines"—passages that describe what we're seeing and hearing on the screen and include everything but the dialogue—with coy jokes directed at the reader, too many adjectives and characters' thoughts, and too much background or other information that doesn't belong in a script. Though there are exceptions, a good general guideline is: if it won't be seen or heard on the screen, don't describe it in your action lines.

11. Too personal. Despite the edict "Write what you know," you are better off writing a story that isn't about your life. A story about your life is likely to cloud your judgment about what is interesting to an audience and derail your story. Don't work out your personal problems in a screenplay. We readers see too many stories about struggling writers who make deals with the devil, or who make it big and end up sitting around a swimming pool with a bevy of babes in bikinis. Don't use your work to fulfill your own fantasies.

12. Main character isn't in enough personal danger. In any film—whether it's about a lonely, single 34-year-old butcher who can't get a date and fears he'll never get married (*Marty*), or a team of commandos about to storm a fortified enemy camp—the stakes must be high, and the hero must be in jeopardy. Even if that jeopardy is purely emotional, as it is for Marty, rather than physical, we must care about the hero and be on the edge of our seats rooting for him and worrying about whether he'll achieve his goal. This is just as true of romantic dramas or comedies as it is for war movies, thrillers, or detective mysteries.

13. Story wasn't planned well in the concept stage. The concept—the one-sentence "idea" for a film—is either weak or nonexistent, and contains no inherent conflict. If there are problems in your concept, the script will never be any good. All concepts have to contain some sort of difficult conflict or challenge the main character or characters will face, as well as potential for being developed into a two-hour movie.

14. Story doesn't set up fast enough. By page 10, we should at least know the story's setting, the protagonist, and his or her basic problem.

15. Poor choice of subject matter. If friends don't say, "Hey! What a great movie idea," don't write it unless your idea is character-driven and you're sure they'll change their mind after they read your script.

16. Depressing subject. Personally, I tend to "tune out" when I read scripts about people who devolve into self-destruction through drugs, etc. I certainly don't want to deter you from writing the next *Leaving Las Vegas* or *The Grapes of Wrath*. But even serious subjects should be uplifting, not depressing. If you write a character who is depressed, make sure he is "actively depressed" and doing things rather than just sitting at home alone on the couch staring at the TV for two hours.

17. Preachy story. As Sam Goldwyn used to tell his writers, "If you have a message, phone Western Union." If your main purpose in writing your story is to sway people to your view on some political or social cause, you'll have to be a very skilled writer indeed to avoid the pitfall of writing a "preachy" or didactic story that sacrifices drama. *To Kill a Mockingbird*, the moving classic directed by Robert Mulligan and based on the Harper Lee novel, is a good example of how to make a powerful social statement (in this case, about racism) without being "preachy." Don't try to write a script from theme rather than plot unless you're a genius (e.g., your concept can't be "man's inhumanity to man" or some other generality).

18. Main character is not likable. The protagonist can, and even must, be flawed, but he or she must be basically likable, or else fascinatingly evil. There are tried-and-true methods for writing such characters. If you study the first ten or twenty minutes of most movies, you'll discover the kinds of things screenwriters put in their scripts that make you immediately identify with the hero. These can include evidence of the hero's compassion (what the industry calls "pat the dog" scenes) or his appealing sense of humor, his great expertise, his plucky attitude toward setbacks, his oppression (which has not left him spiritually defeated), etc.

Writers use many other techniques to make a film audience immediately like the story's hero—and a good place to find them is by studying old silent comedies by Charlie Chaplin, Buster Keaton, and Harold Lloyd. Even if the main character in your script is a villain, you must make sure the audience identifies with him in some way. If he's a rotten or selfish person and not fascinating and human in his rottenness, then the audience won't like your film.

19. Antagonist or villain is not a strong enough adversary for the hero. If the hero's victory over the villain in your screenplay is a foregone conclusion, there will be no conflict or suspense for your audience. Make your villain almost as clever as, and possibly even more interesting than, your hero.

20. Hero doesn't have to resolve an internal conflict in order to resolve the story's external conflict. The hero's personal flaws must intersect with what he needs to defeat his adversary or solve his problem. A good film to study in this regard is *Witness*, in which John Book (Harrison Ford) is a loner with no wife or children who lives by violence. He's a police officer on the trail of a fellow cop who's a vicious killer. Wounded by gunfire, Book must take refuge in an Amish community, where he falls in love with an Amish woman. It is only when he renounces the violence within himself and learns the power of being part of a tight-knit, peaceful community, that he (with the help of the Amish) is able to defeat the film's villains. The fact that he decides in the end to leave this community doesn't diminish the power of his personal transformation.

21. The character's goal or story purpose is unclear, and he doesn't encounter enough obstacles to achieving it. You can avoid this by applying the principles of traditional story structure to your script.

22. Trying to "direct" the movie by telling actors how to read their lines, where to put the camera, and the like. It's a myth that movie scripts contain camera angles ("close-up," "long shot," etc.). The "spec" screenplay you'll be writing in hopes of selling it to Hollywood is not a shooting script. It should not contain instructions for what the director should do with his camera.

"Wrylies" are the parenthetical instructions ("wryly," "bitterly," etc.) screenwriters sometimes put just above a line of dialogue to tell the actor how to read his line. If you write good dialogue, any good actor should be able to tell how to read the line based on the context and the dialogue itself—he won't need your instructions. The rare exception is when you intend for the dialogue to be read in a way (e.g., sarcastically) that differs dramatically from its surface meaning.

So, while there's no magic formula for writing a script that will sell to Hollywood, if you avoid all these pitfalls you'll greatly increase your chances.

And here's my best tip: don't worry that following the formula of traditional story structure will result in a mundane script. You need a well-structured script the same way a composer needs the correct number of beats per measure. Learn to write a one-sentence story concept, because if you can't write a concept that contains the seeds of character, story, and conflict, you can't write a screenplay that works.

Staton Rabin has been a story analyst for major film companies and individual screenwriters since 1981. She is a senior writer for *Script* magazine and has two young-adult novels, *Betsy and the Emperor* and *Dr. Miracle*, forthcoming from Simon & Schuster/McElderry Books. This article appeared in *The Writer*, March 2004.

Where do I send my screenplay?

Your script is finished. What do you do with it?

• If you're smart, you send it to a qualified story analyst to get an objective evaluation of your screenplay before showing it to film agents or producers. There are many freelance story analysts who work steadily for film studios, major agencies, and independent producers who also do private script analysis for individual screenwriters.

• How do you find these people? Type "script analyst" or "screenplay analysis" into any Web search engine, such as Google.com, and see whose names pop up. You can also check out websites or classified ads in magazines aimed at screenwriters, or call one of the major university film programs. There are many companies aimed at aspiring screenwriters that have websites and a stable of (supposedly) qualified story analysts working for them, and which offer these services for a fee.

• Finding and choosing a qualified story analyst is the same as choosing a qualified doctor: you judge them by their training, professional experience, and referrals. Fees for a screenplay analysis range from a couple hundred dollars to more than $1,000, and analysts vary widely in their quality, the type and length of report they'll write for you, whether their analysis includes a follow-up meeting/discussion, etc.

• Once your script has been analyzed and you've rewritten it as necessary to make it as perfect as you can, then you're ready to send it to producers and agents. Frankly, it is so difficult these days to get a good "Hollywood" agent with clout, you might want to wait till you've already sold a screenplay to a major producer before working with one. At that point, the agents will come to you.

• The best way to approach film producers is to send them a great query letter containing a very brief "pitch" for your screenplay. Never send a producer a screenplay without permission. Some top producers won't even open a letter from a stranger, but many will—and writing a great query is the key to attracting their attention.

Resources

Hollywood Creative Directory
$59.95, or access online version ($249.95) at www.hcdonline.com. Learn the types of films producers have made in the past. Plus, if your script has a great role for a famous actor, you might approach the actor directly, using the directory to find his or her production company.

www.scriptsales.com
www.hollywoodlitsales.com
With these websites, you can check listings of spec or script sales to get names of producers who have recently bought film material, and in what genre.

Variety
The Hollywood Reporter
These two key periodicals will tell you names of producers and their production companies, most of which are in Los Angeles.

www.imdb.com.
An Internet Movie Database that lists just about every movie ever made, plus producers, directors, stars, etc.

—Staton Rabin

PARANORMAL ROMANCE

Stir up a potent brew by adding bizarre events to your love story

by Meg Chittenden

Eight of my 31 novels and a few of my short stories are either paranormal or contain paranormal elements. I have to admit they scared me when I was writing them! Why, then, did I write them? Because the topics—reincarnation, magic, psychics, ghosts, voodoo (what I call "woo-woo" elements)—fascinated me, and I wanted to explore them.

My paranormal novels have sold well, and brought me a bunch of mail, indicating that there is a healthy interest in the topics.

Whenever I give talks about my various books at conferences or conventions, there are always people who ask me when I'm going to write another paranormal story. Interest in this genre is heightened by the popularity of films such as *The Sixth Sense*, *The Blair Witch Project*, *Minority Report*, *Signs*, and, of course, the Harry Potter series. A few years ago, Time-Life tapped into this market with a series of books on such paranormal topics as reincarnation, astral projection, out-of-body experience, extraterrestrials, poltergeists, telepathy, channeling, clairvoyance, psychic healing, the Bermuda Triangle, the great pyramid, ancient astronauts, and the Shroud of Turin.

Fiction publishers are also catching on to the trend. In the past few years, a number of imprints have published paranormal novels, including Leisure Books, LionHearted Publishing, Del Rey Books, ImaJinn Books, DAW Books, and Speculation Press. Silhouette Books is currently reprinting some novels from the Harlequin Dreamscapes series, including my novel *This Time Forever*.

When I began using paranormal elements, I realized that the key to writing good paranormal fiction is to incorporate bizarre, unexplainable events into the narrative without losing believability.

To write a paranormal romance, it isn't necessary to *believe* in paranormal subjects, but it is necessary to *know* something about them, just as it is usually necessary to know something about police procedure, pathology, and abnormal psychology before writing a murder mystery; something about love in all its guises before writing a romance; and something about science before writing science fiction.

A whole world of theory, for example, has been developed around reincarnation. So when I write of it, I generally stick to that theory for the sake of believability. Whatever you are writing about, you have to make the reader believe in the story, the characters, and the plot—at least for the length of the book.

The first paranormal novel I wrote was *The Other Child*, which dealt with voodoo. It came about because I had an elderly neighbor who really liked my little son and daughter. She kept feeding them and giving them presents. Then she started giving me presents. This bothered me. As it turned out, she was just a nice, generous, perfectly harmless woman. But what if she hadn't been? In the book that this unease triggered, I changed the neighbor to a beautiful woman whose child had died.

Later, I was in my local grocery store and overheard a man in a long black coat ask the butcher if he had any animal blood. That made me think about voodoo and then research it. The novel became a story about possession—not just physical possession of the child in the story, but an attempt to have the living child become the possessor of the soul of the dead child. And that's about as woo-woo as you can get.

Otherwise ordinary lives

To make this believable—and here's a key to making a paranormal novel believable—I tried to make the elements that weren't paranormal very ordinary indeed. The mother of the child was a divorcee who was having a love affair with a police officer. The husband of the woman who was practicing the voodoo, though terrified, was a likeable, fairly normal guy. If absolutely everything about the story is unusual or weird, it's difficult for the reader to suspend disbelief.

My next attempt involved reincarnation, which I'd always wanted to look into. In fact, my stories often come out of research. I get interested in something and a story presents itself. It's a backward approach, but it works for me.

What presented itself in this case was a fact—I discovered that Nobel Prize winner John Galsworthy, author of *The Forsyte Saga*, died on my

> To write a paranormal romance, it isn't necessary to believe in paranormal subjects, but it is necessary to know something about them.

birthday. Not the same year, but that didn't matter. I had loved his books when I was younger. Gradually, I developed a plot in which Andrea, a young female author, discovers that her newly published book had been previously written by someone else. Later, she finds out that she had written it herself in a former life, and had been murdered because of it. Andrea is determined to find out who had murdered her. The novel, *Forever Love*, is mostly set in England and goes back and forth between contemporary times and World War II.

The next topic that caught my attention was ghosts. In *When the Spirit Is Willing*, the 19th-century ghost is an American matchmaker, a handy spirit to have around in a romance. I had read books and articles and I had seen movies starring ghosts. These entertainments often stretched the believability quotient far too much. So in *Spirit*, I had my ghost give her opinion on what is possible for ghosts and what isn't.

The Enchanted Bride, a novella, came about from an experience my husband and I had while driving around Cornwall, England. We happened upon some standing stones—the Merry Maiden Stones—in a field by the side of a road. The maidens were females who had danced on the Sabbath and had been turned into stone as punishment. My ghost wasn't one of them, but she had died in that field not too long ago and hadn't quite made it to the other side.

I've had other ghost ideas that I haven't used. I'll tell you about one and you can certainly adapt it you want to. People often make replicas of antique items. It seems to me that if there are any spirits roaming around from that period, they'd be delighted to move into the replica of a house, car, movie theater, live theater, art gallery, restored ghost town, or recovered sunken ship. Lots of possibilities there.

Time travel and reincarnation

Time travel fascinates me, though I haven't written a time-travel novel yet. Reincarnation is similar, but in reincarnation the character stays in this time period while *mentally* experiencing scenes and actions of his or her own life in another time period. The person did, however, actually live previously in that time. When the person is experiencing that former time, he or she feels quite at home, but has no knowledge of the later life. With time travel, the character physically goes backward or forward to another time period, and to a whole other way of life that is very strange to him or her. At the same time, the person knows where he or she really belongs. So in each case, there's a very different approach to the storytelling.

Another thing to bear in mind is that you can use just one woo-woo element in an otherwise "normal" novel. I wrote a romantic suspense novel in which a woman who read tea leaves kept telling the heroine what was going to happen to her. I wrote about a psychic child in an English country-house murder mystery, *The Wainwright Secret*. I didn't know she was psychic until she walked on the scene and started seeing "fuzzy things." Virginia Ellis' wonderful *The Wedding Dress*, a Civil War-era historical romance, is not a paranormal book, but it's a great example of including one unexplainable element. The heroine has a very well-grounded family and a perfectly normal, if difficult, life. But ghosts of soldiers killed in the Civil War show up from time to time, trying to find their way home.

I like to use contrast. If I have something really weird going on, I'd rather have it happen in the daytime with the sun shining than during a thunderstorm in the middle of the night. When you call up a storm, there's a danger of melo-drama.

Here's something else to watch out for if you are writing a paranormal romance: don't forget that you are writing a romance. You need to achieve a balance between the paranormal elements and the love story.

Bestselling author Michael Connelly (*Chasing the Dime* and *Blood Work*) has said that writing a mystery is a lot like the old juggling trick of keeping several plates spinning on top of dowels at the same time, and making sure to keep them all up in the air. Writing a paranormal, or woo-woo, romance, presents a similar challenge.

Meg Chittenden, of Ocean Shores, Wash., has published over 100 short stories and articles, three children's books, and 35 novels that include romance, suspence, mystery, and mainstream titles. This article appeared in *The Writer*, April 2003.

THINK LIKE A TEENAGER

'Get real' to capture the hearts and minds of young adult readers

by Barbara Shoup

I never set out to be a writer of young adult (YA) fiction. Years of teaching high school students had convinced me that teenagers like "real" books, not condescending romantic fluff or preachy stories meant to improve their morals—which is what I thought YA novels were.

My serious teenage readers loved books such as *The Catcher in the Rye*, *A Separate Peace*, and *To Kill a Mockingbird*, and when I was working on *Wish You Were Here*, a novel that explores the after-effects of divorce on 17-year-old Jackson Watt, I hoped they'd love it, too.

Author James Cross Giblin describes YA books as a "kind of bridge for teenage readers between children's and adult fiction." The readers range from 14 to 18 years old.

But if pressed to name the audience I was writing for, I'd have said divorced parents who need to understand what divorce feels like from a kid's point of view. So when my agent read the manuscript and observed that it seemed perfect for the YA market, I was put off by her assessment. As it turns out, my ideas about YA novels being fluffy or preachy were quite wrong.

I entered the YA world when Hyperion Press published *Wish You Were Here* in 1994, and I came to know the work of authors like Chris Crutcher, Laurie Halse Anderson, and Gary Paulson. Their books are every bit as serious as those written for adults—honestly, unflinchingly confronting real, complex issues of the human heart. Some years later, having published two more novels for teenagers, *Stranded in Harmony* and *Vermeer's Daughter*, I'm still not sure why some novels with teenage protagonists are marketed as YAs and others as books for adults, but I've come to understand the common elements of the YA category.

Still growing

The main character in a YA novel is always a young person still being shaped by life in the most fundamental ways. Still grieving over his parents' divorce, Jackson Watt finds his struggle to find his own place in the world complicated by the disappearance of his best friend, his mother's marriage, and his relationships with two girls—one he loves and one who desperately loves him.

Lucas Cantrell, in *Stranded in Harmony*, feels caught in the life everyone has planned for him until he strikes up a friendship with a mysterious woman who gives him the courage to take the first step into what his real life will be.

In *Vermeer's Daughter*, Carelina Vermeer, the plain, stubborn, and dreamy daughter in a contentious household, develops a special relationship with her father, the great 17th-century Dutch painter, who sets her on a path into the wider world of art.

Self-discovery

Self-discovery drives YA novels. As in any novel, a general, overarching question fuels the plot. That question is addressed through a series of scenes that generate more specific questions as the story proceeds and compels the reader to keep turning the pages.

For example, the overarching question in *Stranded in Harmony* is: what happens to a teenage boy who feels hemmed in by the expectations of his family and friends when he meets a woman who recognizes his yearning and sees all he might become? Smaller, more specific questions linger below the surface of the bigger question: Who is the woman on the ridge? Will she help Lucas with his uncle? Can he keep his relationship with her a secret from his girlfriend?

Note that the questions driving the plot are addressed through a *series of scenes*. This is true of all good novels, and especially true if you want to write books teenagers will read. Good scenes present evidence objectively through detail and dialogue, giving readers the freedom and pleasure to come to their own conclusions about what to think and how to feel.

In *Wish You Were Here*, I wanted to show the moment that Jackson began to understand that his friend Brady was arrogant, irrational, and nowhere near as wise as Jackson had believed him to be. So I created a scene in which Brady argued with his father and then just lost it, randomly destroying objects in his father's house, eventually zeroing in on his dad's beloved music collection, methodically ripping the tape from each cassette until "the room was covered with what looked like brown ticker tape."

"I felt paralyzed," says Jackson, witnessing it, "exactly like I used to feel when I was little and something I was watching on TV suddenly turned scary. Just get up and turn it off, I'd tell myself. But I never did. I'd stare at the screen, all the while a dark place opening wider and wider inside me, just like it was now."

Life in the moment

There's a raw, wondering tone to good YA novels, the sense of life being lived now. "When did I change?" reflects Lucas in the beginning of *Stranded in Harmony*. "When did I quit believing that there was a whole world out there, just waiting for me to step into it? When it happened, why didn't I notice it?" A chance meeting with a woman painter who treats her kindly causes Carelina to marvel, "For the first time in my life, I felt as if I were the center of the universe."

Real people with real problems

Thoughts like Carelina's are endearing, but a realistic adolescent character must also reflect the self-absorption, lack of experience, and skewed perspective characteristic of that age. In fact, YA plots hinge on these traits, which create tension in young people's lives and often cause them to behave badly and make terrible mistakes. Set adrift, desperately trying to figure out what to trust and whom to be, Jackson has sex with a girl he doesn't love, drinks, and experiments with marijuana.

The trick is in creating a self-absorbed, difficult teenage character who is also lovable. When Lucas thinks his girlfriend is pregnant, he's mean to her, selfishly obsessing about the impact on his own life, his future. Yet readers root for everything to turn out well for him because they are privy to memories that bring insight to the relationship and thoughts that reflect his guilt and confusion. They see him in action with others, where his best self is revealed. Over the course of the book, they come to their conclusions about him in much the same way they would come to conclusions about real people, through a cumulative series of encounters that clarify and refine their sense of who he really is.

Youthful yearnings

All this is about craft—and craft always matters. But it isn't the only thing that matters in writing for teens. "Hold on to 16 as long as you can," sang rock musician John Mellencamp—and that is at the crux of what all good YA writers do. In fact, they not only remember what it was like to be young, they are incapable of forgetting the terrible, wonderful yearning of that age. They can count on that 16-year-old who lives eternally inside them to recognize and censor an adult voice that creeps between the lines, nagging, bossing kids around, trying to improve them.

Like Stephen King, who remains terrified of the closed closet door of his childhood, the best YA authors write from a time in their own lives that's still emotionally alive for them.

Some years ago, I visited a class of high school juniors who had read *Stranded in Harmony*, and we had a spirited discussion about the book. There was a girl in the back of the room who sat quietly, her head bent, and I wondered if she was even listening. Then, near the end of the period, she raised her hand. "That part when he thought Sara was pregnant?" she said, almost in a whisper. "Well,

I have a baby, and when I read that part, it made me see how my boyfriend felt when he found out. I didn't really know what it was like for him before I read this book."

The bell rang and she was gone before I could thank her for the great gift she had given me by telling me how my book had made a difference in her life.

I realized, once again, that what matters most in writing for young adults is to bring adolescent characters fully to life on the page, let them grapple with the important, always ambiguous human questions, and in so doing, help young readers imagine new, better ways to live their own, real lives.

Barbara Shoup of Indianapolis is the author of six books, including five novels, and has been writer-in-residence at the Writers' Center of Indiana. Her young adult novels, *Wish You Were Here* and *Stranded in Harmony*, were selected as American Library Association Best Books for Young Adults. This article appeared in *The Writer*, October 2003.

TAKE YOUR STORY TO THE CROSSROADS

How to make plot and character come together

by Franny Billingsley

I must open with a confession. Few of the ideas here originated with me. This is a patchwork of scavenged ideas, a scrap of Henry James patched to a shred of folktale. But old ideas can breed original stories. Old ideas lead to undiscovered *Crossroads*—the pulse-points of story—where plot intersects with character.

Why is this intersection vital to your storytelling? Because this is where the meaning of story is revealed. When a character struggles with a dilemma that is precisely calibrated to test his inner nature, the decisions he makes—for good or for evil—illuminate the heart of your story. It is these stories that make the reader gasp with sudden understanding and that resonate long after the book has been closed.

I've assembled below a number of scavenged literary concepts and quotations that helped me reach the Crossroads of my fiction. I hope that these items, along with some examples I provide along the way, can help you find your way to the Crossroads of your own stories.

First, a little more about what I mean by the intersection of plot and character.

The Mind Worm
(from *Story*, Robert McKee)

[M]edieval scholarship devised another ingenious conceit: the Mind Worm. Suppose a creature had the power to burrow into the brain and come to know an individual completely—dreams, fears, strength, weakness. Suppose that this Mind Worm also had the power to cause events in the world. It could then create a specific happening geared to the unique nature of that person that would trigger a one-of-a-kind adventure, a quest that would force him to use himself to the limit, to live to his deepest and fullest. Whether a tragedy or fulfillment, this question would reveal his humanity absolutely. . . . [T]he writer is a Mind Worm.

—from *Story*, by Robert McKee

You must become a Mind Worm. You must burrow into your story until you find the intersection—the Crossroads—of your character's unique nature and unique adventure.

Outer and Inner Stories
(inspired by *The Writer's Journey*, Christopher Vogler)

To begin making your way toward the Crossroads, ask yourself these questions:

What is my character's Outer Story? The "Outer Story" consists of the external events your character faces.

What is my character's Inner Story? The "Inner Story" is your character's journey of inner discovery.

Do the Outer and Inner Stories connect? As an example, let's examine the movie version of *The Wizard of Oz* and ask these questions of Dorothy's adventure.

1. What is Dorothy's Outer Story? She dreams about traveling "over the rainbow," but when she's blown to just such a place (Oz), she struggles to get home.

2. What is Dorothy's Inner Story? Dorothy realizes, "There's no place like home!"

3. Do Dorothy's Outer and Inner Stories connect? Yes. Without the external events—being transported to Oz—Dorothy could never have reached her inner discovery about home.

This is the crucial question. Your character's inner journey must be inextricably linked to his physical journey or you have not done your job as Mind Worm. You have not matched the character's unique nature (Dorothy longing to fly "over the rainbow") with her unique adventure (Dorothy blown "over the rainbow"). Without this connection, your character cannot come to that vital Crossroads of plot and character. The Crossroads is often a place of revelation, or crisis, or decision—or all three. For Dorothy, it is a place of revelation. She stands looking at those ruby slippers, realizing she always had the power to go home. Realizing, "There's no place like home!"

The selkie stories
(from Celtic folklore)

Let's turn now to my second novel, *The Folk Keeper*, to illustrate how I brought my heroine to a Crossroads of plot and character.

> Construct a plot uniquely suited to test your character, and develop a character uniquely tested by your plot.

What was scavenged here? The novel was inspired by stories of the selkies, folkloric creatures that shift between seal and human shape through the magical device of a sealskin. If the sealskin is lost or stolen, the selkie is trapped in human form.

I knew from the outset that my heroine, Corinna, would be half-human/half-selkie, but ignorant of her true nature: she thinks she is human. I knew her Inner Story: Corinna would discover and come to terms with her heritage. But I wrestled with her Outer Story. I could not set Corinna into action. The plot lacked narrative energy—conflict, tension.

After much revision, I summoned the courage to send a draft to my editor, whose response turned the story around. "The main problem," she said, "is that we don't know what Corinna really *wants*. What does she want before she discovers she's part selkie and has to decide where and how to live her life?"

Of course: Give Corinna something she wants! If a character wants something badly, she'll try to get it: She'll *act*. Action generates narrative energy, and if obstacles lie between the character and what she wants, action will generate conflict.

Somehow, then, the idea of the Folk came to me, the idea of dangerous creatures lurking in dark caverns deep below the earth—savage, ravenous creatures, all wet mouth and teeth. The Folk—yes, Corinna would have to respond to the Folk! They would plague her, they would menace her . . . they would give her something to *do*.

The arrival of the Folk gave my story a shot of adrenaline. When they showed up, so did the Folk Keepers, people in charge of pacifying the Folk. This was the answer to my editor's question: I would need to make Corinna want to secure this job, and, once secure, desperate to hold on to it.

Motivation

> Give [your character] a compulsion and turn him loose!
>
> —Ray Bradbury, from Oakley Hall's
> *The Art & Craft of Novel Writing*

I happened upon Bradbury's quote at precisely the right moment during my struggle with *The Folk Keeper*. A compulsion—of course! Corinna not only wants this job, she's obsessed by it. Obsessive characters fascinate us. We turn the pages, suspecting their obsession will lead them into danger.

But the job of Folk Keeper is too dangerous to undertake casually. I had to create a solid motivation to support Corinna's obsession. Corinna, I decided, wants power. And Folk Keepers, who protect their communities from the Folk's savage energy, have power in this society. I also gave Corinna a history to explain her need for power. She's been raised in a foundling home, set to work as a drudge, stripped of all power, all dignity. No wonder she's desperate to be a Folk Keeper: it will rescue her from a life she detests.

Corinna is blind to all hints of her selkie heritage until the villain recognizes who she is and confronts her. Because she stands to inherit an estate the villain had himself hoped to inherit, he throws her into the Caverns to be savaged by the Folk.

There, in the Caverns, Corinna comes to understand that her lust for power has blinded her to her own possibilities—that she has actually disempowered herself. She realizes that only if she sets aside her tough-guy persona to embrace her true self—her poetic self—can she escape both Folk and Caverns.

Illustration of character

What is character but the determination of incident? What is incident but the illustration of character?

—Henry James,
from *The Art of Fiction*

A brilliant idea, beautifully put. An idea, of course, that I turned to my own use.

In the Caverns, Corinna is nothing but the "determination of incident." The plot is nothing but "illustration of character." Corinna encounters her first major Crossroads in the Caverns, a crucial intersection of plot and character. The Caverns, the Folk—these are elements of the plot through which Corinna is moving. But when Corinna finds she can repel the Folk (Outer Story) through her poetry (Inner Story), then plot and character each shape the other.

Let's analyze Corinna's Inner and Outer Stories:

What is Corinna's Outer Story? Corinna has to survive the Folk if she is to escape the Caverns and embrace her true heritage.

What is Corinna's Inner Story? When Corinna meets herself in the Caverns, she realizes that in order to have true power, she has to embrace who she truly is.

Do Corinna's Outer and Inner Stories connect? Yes. Corinna's imprisonment in the Caverns allows her to discover her true self and also to escape.

Deepening the connection between story and character

Inspired by *What's Your Story?* by Marion Dane Bauer.

We have now reached a vital understanding: our character's Inner and Outer Stories must connect. Let us now refine that understanding. Let's ask more questions that will deepen and enrich that connection.

I return to my editor's all-important question: "What does Corinna want?" Bauer's excellent book helped me conceive of this question as not one but three related questions.

What does my character want? This question goes to Outer Story, the real-life action your character plans to take. Let's say your character wants to join a gang. (I plucked this example straight from Bauer's book.)

Why does my character want what he wants? A single desire can spring from several motives: Maybe your character wants to join a gang because it's cool. Or maybe your character wants to join a gang for protection.

What in my character's history explains why he wants what he wants? This is the key to understanding the character's motive.

Maybe your character is socially awkward. Now there's this girl he likes. . . . No wonder he wants to be cool.

Maybe your character's the brainy, scrawny type, always tormented by bigger kids. Now the school bully's after him. No wonder he wants protection.

I propose two additional questions.

Does my character get what he wants? Consider not letting your character get what he wants. Often the most interesting characters take foolish actions (like the kid who wants to join a gang) and leave the story making better choices for themselves.

What is my character's Crossroads? You might call this the climax, where plot and character directly intersect. There is often a crisis; the character is often forced into a decision.

Let's revisit Corinna:

What does Corinna want? She wants to be a Folk Keeper.

Why does Corinna want what she wants? She wants power.

What in Corinna's history explains why she wants power? She's always been disenfranchised, marginalized; she's never had any control over her life.

Does Corinna get what she wants? No. She is not, in the end, a Folk Keeper. She leaves the story making more mature choices.

What is Corinna's Crossroads? I have already mentioned Corinna's Crossroads in the Caverns. But a character may encounter several Crossroads. There is often a final Crossroads where plot and character intersect on the deepest level. It often happens at or toward the end. There is often a crisis; the character often has to make a difficult decision. It is often called the climax. The meaning—theme—of the book is revealed here. The best books never say what they are about. They *show*. When a character makes a decision under pressure, the heart of the story is illuminated.

Corinna has, all along, been confronting questions of identity—is she a Folk Keeper? Is she a selkie? Or is she, perhaps, a human being? This third possibility occurs to her only in the last few pages. She's kept her mind closed against it, even when the romantic hero declares his love (although she reciprocates his affection). Corinna's now stubbornly convinced she's a selkie, just as she was convinced earlier she was a Folk Keeper. But when she dives into the sea, she's caught in a crisis, forced to choose irrevocably between her human and selkie forms, between the cold, wild life of the sea and a life of love on land—of love, and of poetry. Her choice illuminates the meaning of the novel.

As you write, keep your character's final Crossroads clearly in mind. You may not, perhaps, know the Crossroads when you begin. I never do. You may have to work as I do, forward, and then back again. I have to write my way into understanding—understanding what my character wants, understanding her underlying motivation and history, understanding the final Crossroads. Then I work backward, ensuring that everything leads convincingly and inexorably to the place where plot meets character on the deepest level.

A cautionary tale. When I wrote my first novel, *Well Wished*, I had not yet learned the fine art of scavenging; I knew nothing about Inner and Outer Stories. Briefly: the story revolves around a malevolent Wishing Well that will, if it can, twist the meaning of a wish—always with disastrous results. Needy, selfish Nuria ("Miss Grabby Bones") is manipulated into making a wish on behalf of her friend, Catty, who cannot walk. Nuria wishes that Catty regain the use of her legs, but the infelicitous phrasing of her wish allows the Well to switch the girls' bodies. Nuria finds herself stuck in Catty's body, in Catty's wheelchair. The girls can revoke the wish, but Catty, now happily inhabiting Nuria's body, refuses. Nuria, in due course, regains her own body. She also grows and matures, becoming more generous and less of a "Miss Grabby Bones."

What is Nuria's Outer Story? When Nuria makes a foolish wish on the Wishing Well, she gets trapped in Catty's body and has to find her way back into her own.

What is Nuria's Inner Story? She finds herself capable of generosity.

Do Nuria's Outer and Inner Stories connect? No. Nuria's journey into Catty's body doesn't connect with her new maturity. If, however, I'd known then what I know now, I could have made that connection. Consider this statement: "*Nuria* gets stuck in Catty's body." This implies that Nuria brings some personal traits with her to Catty's body, traits that comprise her essence. What are they? Can she still sing? Can she still craft beautiful descriptions of the natural world? If I, as Mind Worm, had presented Nuria as a character wrestling with identity, it would have worked beautifully: When she takes a journey to another body, she discovers the essence of who she is, which could have included her capacity for generosity. But I didn't: Nuria was secure in her identity and so her adventure was not uniquely suited to test her nature.

Tam Lin (a Scottish ballad)

My third novel (in progress) is based on the ballad of Tam Lin, the story of a young man held captive by the fairy queen. His sweetheart, Janet, rescues him by holding onto him, holding physically, no matter what terrifying shape he magically assumes—an adder, a bear, a lump of burning lead.

Briar is the heroine of my twist on this old tale. I always knew Briar's Outer Story: her brother is stolen by the fairies; she must rescue him from fairyland. I could not, however, discover her Inner Story. Corinna embraces her true nature; Dorothy understands the meaning of home. Surely Briar

The decisions [your character] makes at the Crossroads will illuminate the meaning of your story.

must have an Inner Story, but it eluded me.

I struggled with this story for years, just as I had done with *The Folk Keeper*. I eventually sent it to my editor, just as I had done with *The Folk Keeper*. And again, my editor asked me a question:

Editor: "What is the Truth of this story?"

Franny: "The Truth? What do you mean, the Truth?"

Editor: "Think about it."

And I did. I thought about Tam Lin; I thought about Janet, holding him fast. *Holding on*. The Truth came to me then. This is a story about holding on, not a story about change. I had been searching for Briar's Inner Story by asking how she changes. I had not been honoring the Truth of her story. Briar doesn't change, she holds on—holds onto her brother, certainly, but also to her integrity. But this doesn't mean Briar has no Inner Story. She'll come to a Crossroads, a crisis so profound she almost gives up. But like Janet, she'll hold on, despite the obstacles I fling her way, and her triumph will celebrate her adherence to her beliefs. That is the heart of her Inner Story. Briar may not change, but she's confirmed in who she is.

The Steadfast Hero

I mentioned my epiphany about Briar to a writer friend, who said casually, "Oh yeah, she's a Steadfast Hero."

A Steadfast Hero? How could it be that in all my years of scavenging I had never heard of a Steadfast Hero? But now that I had, I set myself to understand it.

Think about *Jane Eyre*. Jane is a Steadfast Heroine. The core of her character is her absolute integrity. She remains true to what she knows to be right, even when it means sacrificing true love. That is her Outer Story. But she comes to a Crossroads, tempted to yield to her love for Mr. Rochester, although they cannot marry. Her integrity is tested; she does not yield: that is her Inner Story. Charlotte Brontë is a Mind Worm. Jane's passion for Mr. Rochester is the very journey calculated to test her integrity: she remains true to herself, which leads us to the "happy-ever-after" ending and to a validation of her principles. Jane's Outer and Inner Stories connect seamlessly.

Set yourself to become a Mind Worm. Construct a plot uniquely suited to test your character, and develop a character uniquely tested by your plot. Remember that once you understand how your plot and character connect, you may have to work backward to develop history and motivation. You may have to work backward to build a foundation that will support the events leading to your Crossroads. Your character may be a Steadfast Hero, or he may be utterly transformed, but he will reach one or more Crossroads where character intersects with plot; and the decisions he makes at the Crossroads will illuminate the meaning of your story.

A disclaimer

I began by letting Robert McKee speak. I'll end by letting John Gardner speak.

> [T]here are no rules for real fiction, any more than there are rules for serious visual art or musical composition. There are techniques—hundreds of them—that, like carpenter's tricks, can be studied and taught . . . but there are no rules. Name one, and instantly some literary artist will offer us some new work that breaks the rule yet persuades us.
>
> —from *The Art of Fiction*, John Gardner

Just as there are Crossroads with no stories, there are stories with no Crossroads. Perhaps you can "persuade" us with the magic of your prose, with your character's riveting voice. I, however, cannot. If you, likewise, find that old ideas inspire your best work, I invite you to scavenge whatever is useful here.

Franny Billingsley of Lake Forest, Ill., is the author of two critically acclaimed children's fantasy novels, *Well Wished*, which *Booklist* named one of its 10 best first novels of the year, and *The Folk Keeper*, which won the Boston Globe-Horn Book Award and was named a Notable Book in Children's Literature by the American Library Association. Visit her on the Web at www.frannybillingsley.com. This article appeared in *The Writer*, June 2004.

PIECES OF THE MYSTERY PUZZLE

Tips on writing mystery fiction

compiled by Elfrieda Abbe

Many writers compare mystery writing to puzzle making. You not only have to solve the puzzle, but you have to create all the parts: sleuths, villains, crimes, motivations, plot twists—and keep the reader interested. One of the best ways to learn how to create the kind of suspense readers can't resist is to see how others who have mastered the craft do it. Here are some tips from the pages of *The Writer*.

On protagonists

Nevada Barr

I didn't think anybody would like Anna Pigeon, because I based her on myself. She's crabby and opinionated. But I found out that all intelligent women are crabby sometimes, are opinionated sometimes, sometimes they want to kill somebody.

She had to evolve, or I'd get bored out of my mind. I was surprised that we evolved in different directions. You write the book, and you're true to your character. At first it's you and that's a piece of cake, but then she starts having relationships that you didn't have and experiences that you didn't have.

[Anna] has become a little harder and a little tougher, because she's been through some tricky times. And my life has gotten easier, more joyous and more soulful. We're still, of course, very connected emotionally and spiritually, because she's my person. But physically and socially, we've gone in different directions. It's really kind of fun. (from an interview at www.writermag.com)

Peter Robinson

When you've written 13 mysteries featuring the same character, one thing you do if you don't want to repeat yourself is dig a little deeper each time. So one thing I've tried to do is peel off more and more layers of [Alan] Banks' life, his personality, his character. And I think that gives the texture and sense of depth you often don't get if, for example, someone is simply using a character to solve a crime. These days, I think readers are far more interested in the detectives' lives. (from an interview in *The Writer*, June 2003)

Sara Paretsky

When I read books with women who are being told they can't do this job or that, that's so passé. I know that [the writers] aren't thinking through what's happened. There are certainly obstacles to women—more now than there were five years ago in different arenas—but the idea that a woman is not taken seriously on the job is so *not true* anymore. You have to be aware of the way those realities are changing. V.I. Warshawski was a pioneer in the fictional world as well as in the real world. She's not a pioneer anymore. She doesn't fight those [feminist] wars anymore. Some things come up. There's certainly a way—like in *Hard Time*—that the fact that she's a woman can make her more physically vulnerable.

It's much more likely at this stage that she'll be challenged as a solo practitioner; to be a small independent [private investigator] in a world of conglomerates is a real battle now. There always has to be conflict because it's that kind of book—conflict-driven. But keeping the conflict based on the reality of the larger world—that's the main thing. (from an interview in *The Writer*, October 2003)

Marcia Muller

Sharon McCone, I decided, was to be as close to a real person as possible. Like real people, she would age, grow, change; experience joy and sorrow, love and hatred—in short, the full range of human emotions. In addition, McCone was to live within the same framework most of us do, complete with family, friends, co-workers, and lovers; each of her cases would constitute one more major event in an ongoing biography. This choice also had a practical basis. In writing crime fiction, the author frequently asks the reader to suspend disbelief in situations that are not likely to occur in real life. Private investigators do not, as a rule, solve dozens of murder cases over the course of their careers. And what few criminals they do encounter do not tend to be as clever and intelligent as their fictional counterparts. To make the story convincing to the reader, the character and day-to-day details of her life had to be firmly grounded in reality. (from her article in *The Writer*, May 1997)

Elizabeth Peters

If the protagonists of the novel are properly conceived, they will behave consistently and comprehensively. Of course, this requirement is true of character development in general, but it is particularly important with series characters, whom the reader comes to know well.

Just because a character is consistent, however, doesn't mean his behavior should always be predictable. In fact, seemingly irrational behavior makes a character more realistic; real people don't always behave sensibly either. Yet, if we examine the true motives that govern their behavior, we find it is not inconsistent, that we ought to have anticipated it. It is the author's task to establish this. The reaction you want from a reader is a shock of surprise, followed immediately by a shock of recognition: "Oh, yes, of course, I ought to have realized . . ." that despite her constant criticism of her son, Amelia would kill to protect him; that though Emerson complains about his wife's recklessness, he is secretly amused by and appreciative of her courage; that while Ramses sounds like a pompous snob, he is as insecure as are most young children. (from her article in *The Writer*, April 1994)

Villains we love to hate

Tess Collins

We've all encountered stereotypical villains in stories. . . . Serial killers are becoming dangerously close to becoming clichés because they are so prevalent in fiction and are rarely portrayed as having comprehensible reasons for their acts. . . . They are simply killing machines.

Complexity, conflict, and empathetic qualities make a good villain. And a good villain is essential to your story. An unpredictable, untrustworthy villain will keep the reader engaged. What he or she will do next must be as thought-provoking as the plot twists and the hero's actions. Being unsure of the villain's future actions makes readers keep reading on and keeps them on edge. Ultimately, despite any empathy they may feel for the villain's situation, readers are forced to root against the villain because of his or her sinister acts. (from her article in *The Writer*, February 2001)

William G. Tapply

Beginning writers tend to worry that unless their villain acts guilty, or appears evil, or has a transparent motive, or is obviously stronger or craftier or more unscrupulous than the other characters, they are not playing fair with their readers. Resist the temptation to throw in clues for your readers' benefit while withholding them from your heroine or hero. And never allow your sleuth to miss a clue that is obvious to your reader. That's giving the reader an unfair advantage—and mystery readers don't want an advantage over the sleuth.

. . . A worthy villain challenges your hero or heroine and leaves the story's outcome in doubt. Match a determined sleuth against a resourceful and clever and equally determined villain and you'll have your readers hooked. (from his book *The Elements of Mystery Fiction*)

Getting the details right

Evan Hunter (Ed McBain)

Anything that ever appears about scientific techniques or DNA or what have you, I will immediately clip out of the paper. I have a whole file on stuff like that.

I also have a friend who's a criminal lawyer and used to be a district attorney, so I will call him and I'll say, "I've got this guy found with 20 pounds of heroin and he claims so and so, *blah, blah, blah*. What's the deal I can offer him?" And he'll say, "Well, why don't you offer him *blah, blah, blah*?" And I'll say, "He won't accept that deal; what can I counter with?" And he'll say, "Why don't you counter with *blah, blah, and blah*?" And we get a whole dialogue going for 20 minutes, plea-bargaining a guy. I think those are some of the best scenes in the 87th Precinct novels. (from an interview in *The Writer*, March 2002)

Ian Rankin

You can keep research as minimal as you like, but your book must read as *authentic*. In other words, the reader must be hoodwinked into thinking you know what you're talking about. A little knowledge will go a long way. Conversely, writers who know too much about a subject can end up putting too much of it into their novels, slowing the story and confusing the reader. The task for the author is to know how much to put in and how much to leave out. I believe in the "less is more" principle. *Showing* is always better than *telling*. Give an example rather than a long explanation. If you have 200 pages of notes on autopsy procedure, fine, but use all of it in a novel and you'll bore the pants off everyone. An autopsy scene of a couple of paragraphs can be every bit as convincing as one of 20 pages, and you stand less risk of descending into tedium or jargon. (from his article in *The Writer*, December 1998)

Putting it together

Gwendoline Butler

Because a mystery story raises questions, you have to be careful of your technique. To my mind, it is vital to know the end before you write the beginning, although within that framework, I like the plot to grow toward its ending. I would feel it dishonest to begin with one murderer in mind, but then to change it halfway through; that would mean that any killer would do, provided there was a surprise. Not everyone would agree with me there. Some writers might consider this too strict a rule.

In my crime novels, the detective is the questioner, so I give him (or her) the focus and tell the story mainly through his or her eyes. You may prefer to have the narrator an innocent before whose eyes the story unfolds, but make sure that such a story is told in the first person. There are drawbacks here: since the narrator cannot be everywhere, he or she will have to rely on reported evidence. (from her article in *The Writer*, November 1999)

P. D. James

Quite often, it takes as long to plot and plan the book as it does to write it. [*A Certain Justice*] begins with a setting, with an idea that I have murder coming right into the heart of chambers, into offices of distinguished lawyers and the striking down of a distinguished criminal lawyer. I had the main idea, which was the setting. Then, of course, [the victim] Venetia came next: her childhood, her life, her relationship with her daughter, with her ex-husband, with her lover, who feels that as a politician it's expedient to return to his wife before the general election, and Venetia's relationship with other lawyers with whom she works. She really is at the heart of the book. (from an interview by Lewis Burke Frumkes in *The Writer*, June 1998)

William G. Tapply

Inexperienced mystery writers often flounder after writing a few scenes because they haven't fully imagined the puzzle that their story is supposed to solve. Or they write a full-length novel full of loose ends, inconsistencies, and irrelevancies. That tightly woven plot, absolutely vital to the mystery novel, just isn't there.

I had those problems in writing my mystery novels until I figured out that plotting the mystery required me to invent two stories . . . the story of what *actually* happened and the story of *detection*. . . . You can't write a whodunit mystery until you know who did it—and why and how and under what circumstances. You have got to know everything about the murder.

. . . One thing all mysteries have in common is the puzzle. Without that whodunit question to drive the plot, it is not, by definition, a mystery. (from his article in *The Writer*, February 2000)

Elfrieda Abbe is editor of *The Writer*. Excerpts are drawn from interviews conducted by *The Writer* staff, unless otherwise credited.

10 things the police wish you'd omit

1. Enough with the donuts. Many of today's law enforcement officers eat salads, work out, and drink bottled water.

2. Overdramatization is a pet peeve of Daryl W. Clemens, author of Crimesandclues.com. He is critical, for example, of storylines like that in the film *Bloodwork*, in which detectives fight over who gets a case. In real life, who wants more work? When the line, "It's right on the line between jurisdictions" came up, Clemens found himself saying to his wife, "Well, kick him over to their side!"

3. Writer Barbara D'Amato would like writers to try not to put a silencer on a revolver. "Since the rotating cylinder is not closed," she notes, "you can't baffle the gases" (and hence sound).

4. The alcoholic cop is a sore point for police officer and author Robin Burcell, who wonders, "Does every star of every police procedural have to be fighting alcoholism?"

5. The lone female detective who proceeds to search an isolated area without calling for backup help is extremely irksome for writer Susan McBride. "I make a conscious effort to keep Maggie Ryan from doing anything truly dangerous on her own," she says. "At the very least, she's alerted her partner or dispatch."

6. Telling the armed suspect to "Drop it, pal" frustrates author Thomas B. Sawyer, who thinks it's better to have the suspect put the gun down rather than take a chance it will discharge wildly when it's tossed.

7. "Police friends of mine are upset that fictional officers hold their guns with their arms away from their body and barrels pointing upward," says Steve Mross, police and court reporter for *The Sentinel-Record* in Hot Springs, Ark. "This is a no-no in training, which they refer to as 'aiming at Jesus.' The gun should be pointed out and down, and then directly ahead to shoot whatever might suddenly appear as danger. Also, police in movies jack a round into the gun chamber before entering a house. Cops always keep a round chambered and ready to go, even when in the holster."

8. "Forget cars that blow up when you shoot them and windshields that shatter," Mross adds. "There will be a bullet hole and spidering, even when glass is hit several times."

(continued)

(10 things, continued)

9. Authors who have police detectives calling suspects "perps" make writers McBride and Rochelle Krich cringe. While that might work for New York, California, and some other parts of the country, it is just not the case everywhere.

10. Cops who don't do paperwork. All of the people questioned for this article maintain that paperwork is an integral part of a police officer's life. There's paperwork related to the Miranda warning given before interrogation; there's paperwork that police turn over to medical personnel at a hospital before interviewing a crime victim; and there's still more paperwork for requisitions and reports.

—*Andrea Campbell*

Andrea Campbell is the author of *Making Crime Pay: The Writer's Guide to Criminal Law, Evidence, and Procedure* and seven other nonfiction books. Her website is www.andreacampbell.com.

WRITING FOR BUSINESS MARKETS

Find the financial angle and expand your freelancing

by Lisa M. Keefe

The worst bit of professional advice I ever received was, "Don't even think about being a business journalist unless you read *BusinessWeek* cover to cover, every week, for fun." (Okay, maybe it wasn't *the* worst advice; my mother thought I should go to law school.)

Almost 20 years have passed since a grad-school adviser dropped those dubious pearls of wisdom on me, and ever since, I have made a steady and better-than-decent living writing, reporting, and editing business stories for newspapers, websites, and consumer and trade magazines.

The recession, the dot-com bust, and the stock market swoon notwithstanding, knowing how to write knowledgeably about business is a lucrative way to expand your freelance markets. Take it from me: good writers with business savvy are hard to find. Business reporting often pays better than other types of writing: $1 to $2 a word for national magazines, 75 cents a word in major local and regional markets. And the possible outlets range from general-interest consumer magazines such as *Redbook* to industry trades and the local newspaper. (As a bonus, once you've established your financial-reporting street creds, you can use them to pitch corporate businesses looking for writers for white papers and advertorials.)

If full-time employment is the goal, fluency in the language of business turns any writer into a valuable utility player. Up until a few years ago, when advertising sales in so many categories took a dive, nobody I knew with financial-reporting expertise went without work involuntarily, at least not for long.

For writers with an interest in the human condition, business reporting is inherently dramatic—ask any divorce lawyer about the emotional investment people make in money. That same passion exists among business owners, executives, consultants, do-gooders, and parents. Yes, Virginia, there are boring business stories, but if nearly all humans have a financial interest, then nearly all things financial have a human side.

The best news for those who, like me, fulfilled their college science and math requirements with Rocks for Jocks classes, is that business reporting does not require a love of advanced mathematics. A grasp of basic arithmetic and ratios will do.

With that in mind, I've devised a five-step road map to developing yourself as a freelance business writer, and listed some markets for your articles.

1. Write what you know

As advice goes, this is an oldie but goodie. Your best start is to look around and find the financial angle on existing aspects of your life. That way, you work with a subject you are already expert in while learning a new skill.

Did you stage a yard sale last summer, but also sell old stuff on eBay? Then you can write about which is most profitable: compare the time invested in each activity, plus the actual cost of selling the goods—making "garage sale" signs vs. the seller's fees on eBay, for example—and subtract them from the money collected from the sale of comparable items. (In business, that's a basic calculation for operating profit.) Possible markets: parenting magazines (everybody unloads kids clothes this way), women's magazines, plus related websites.

If you write about business goods (desks, office supplies), the choices include small-business magazines. Turn your backyard landscaping project into a story, getting high- and low-end bids and calculating the cost of doing it yourself, then comparing what each method would buy. Possible markets: newspapers, home improvement/decorating publications, custom publications such as *Your Home*, distributed to preferred Pier 1 customers. And so on.

2. Learn the lingo

I noted that business reporting doesn't have to be complicated, and truly, a few basics get you started: learning the difference between revenues and profits, between operating profit and net profit, and the meaning of overhead and cash flow. If you cover some industries more regularly, such as retail, you'll need to learn some more specific jargon, like sales per square foot and comparable store sales. If you venture into public-company coverage, you ought to understand what an EBITDA is (a calculation that states "earnings before interest, taxes, depreciation, and amortization") as well as a 10Q (a company's quarterly report filed with the U.S. Securities and Exchange Commission).

Whatever your level of involvement, several volumes exist to help decipher the language. *Wall Street Words: An Essential A to Z Guide for Today's Investor* by David L. Scott is an excellent resource, explaining terms in basic language, even if most are geared toward investing. *Barron's* and *The Wall Street Journal* produce similar specialty dictionaries on financial terminology and use, although they're a bit more technical. The Portable MBA series (Robert F. Bruner, editor) is dull reading but could save you if you are, say, reading up on a company and find something in its history—a complicated bit of financing, for example—that you need to understand more clearly. For fun, I recommend *The Oxford Book of Money* (Kevin Jackson, editor), which is described in the preface as a "book about money and the imagination." It features quotes from various literary works and figures on money and business.

3. Biz reporting for dummies

It's inevitable, though: you will be in an interview discussing something way out of your depth. This is not the time to nod sagely and hope your interviewee doesn't see your rising panic.

Every business journalist has a war story about a time they tried to look smarter than they were. Mine was during an internship in Kalamazoo, Mich., covering a lengthy debate about a complicated municipal bond issue at a local government meeting. I had no idea what they said, but I nodded sagely and wrote it all up. The next day, the editor made me call, and call, and call the village manager to nail down the details. I called her 27 times in a three-hour period. (Did I mention I was near tears?)

Learn from my mistake: always backtrack in an interview to make sure you understand. Don't gloss over a poorly grasped comment and figure you'll straighten it out with the PR rep later; you might miss a great angle on the story—or the whole story. The random executive or business owner will get huffy about your ignorance, but most will truly appreciate the extra care.

4. Look it up

Business reporting requires more backgrounding and pre-interview research from more sources than many other beats. Fortunately, the sources available for this research are many, from websites and databases to people:

The corporate website. For company history, key individuals, press releases, and financials.

Hoover's Online (www.hoovers. com). For free, basic company data such as sales and net profits, names of divisions and affiliates, and a basic overview of the industry and the company. (In-depth information is for subscribers only.)

Newspapers, magazines known for business coverage. Many of these publications, such as *BusinessWeek* and *The New York Times*, make years' worth of archives available online at little or no charge.

Internet search engines. (I recommend Google). A couple of hours spent with your favorite search engine could turn up such interesting tidbits as that bulletin-board list of rants from dissatisfied customers, or the random act of kindness the CEO did for a student at his alma mater.

LexisNexis. This online database of thousands of publications worldwide (www.lexisnexis.com), combined with a Web search, is invaluable for business reporting. Freelance writers can use the database with a credit card and no subscription. There is no charge to conduct a search or view headlines; users pay only for the complete text of articles they view.

Associations. Many do surveys and research, and will gladly offer statistics, trends, and rules-of-thumb that are useful for background. They're also happy to provide an expert.

Among the people whose contact information business reporters should have in their Palm Pilots are:

Analysts. There are buy-side analysts and sell-side analysts, industry analysts and equity analysts, market analysts and technology analysts, to name but a few. Basically, all research the market/company/industry, write reports on trends and developments, and make projections. They're supposed to be independent of the market/company/industry they cover; many are not, yet they still are often a good source of commentary.

Consultants. But make sure you know when they're talking about a client; they often use interviews to sneak in a little PR for the folks who pay the bills.

Lobbyists and advocates. As long as you remember that ax they're grinding, and make sure readers remember it, too, they often are helpful and available sources.

College, university professors. No matter how obscure the issue or trend, it seems an academic somewhere has written a thesis about it.

5. Pitch a hit

The basics of pitching a story to a business publication or section are the same rules for pitching any other type of piece: know the publication, its audience and its voice; be specific about the story and its outline; tell the editor where your story idea fits into the publication. (In addition to reading back issues, click through the publication's website for such background as writer's guidelines, mission statements, and editorial calendars.) Here are some specific business-writing tips, based on my experience:

• Don't make the mistake of pitching a "business" story. "Business" isn't a reporting niche; "personal finance," "local business," and "farm management" are niches, and you must target your query accordingly. As editor of a marketing trade magazine, I am regularly queried on stories about any number of subjects that are unrelated to our mission of "helping marketers do their jobs better every day." I've been pitched articles on investing, saving money with coupons, and airline woes, among others.

• Include enough numbers (sales, sales increases, attendance at trade shows) in your query to show the editor you're knowledgeable on the topic.

• Be as careful about corporate names in your query (and your story) as you are about people's names, for they are often a person's name. A misspelled company name will close that editor off to you forever.

• Don't try to write a story on a subject, company, or person with which you have any kind of personal relationship. Your father's custom-auto paint business is not fodder for a story pitch to the local paper, no matter how quickly it's growing. Bow out of any stories involving your spouse's employer. Writing a profile of the teacher at that elite private school that has a program to teach children about stocks will not get Junior admitted (well, it shouldn't, anyway).

Looking at it the way a businessperson would, developing solid financial reporting skills helps spread your risk and lessen the effects of those economic cycles on your income. And a juicy story about money can have all the scenery-chewing possibilities of an Al Pacino movie. Ultimately, you may find no fascination in following the corporate money trail or learning why one store is going gangbusters in an otherwise deserted mall. But consider that few of the successful business journalists I've known started out covering business: they included TV critics, travel writers, radio personalities, and a few philosophers or poets. You never know until you try.

Lisa M. Keefe of Chicago is the editor of *Marketing News*, the biweekly magazine of the American Marketing Association in Chicago. She previously worked for *Crain's Chicago Business, The Orlando Sentinel,* and *Forbes.* This article appeared in *The Writer,* September 2003.

Where to look for business markets

Local newspapers. A business editor I once met described the Monday edition of her section as the "black hole of copy." Many papers use that Monday issue to run business features—including personal finance, longer profiles, and news analysis—since business news is typically harder to come by over the weekend. Advertisers love it, but editors scramble to come up with the copy, so your best bet for landing those first assignments is for the Monday section.

Local/regional business tabloids. Virtually every mid- and large-size city now has a weekly tabloid covering business news in the area. Contact the editorial office of each individual publication. For example:
• Charlotte, N.C.-based *American City Business Journals, Inc.* (www.bizjournals.com) has more than 40 regional journals in cities from Albany, N.Y., to Wichita, Kan.
• Chicago-based *Crain Communications Inc.* (www.crain.com) has four regional business publications (Chicago, New York, Detroit, Cleveland).

(continued)

(Business markets, continued)

- *Los Angeles Business Journal Associates* (www.labusiness journal.com) has four weekly publications in California (Los Angeles, San Diego, Orange County, and the San Fernando Valley).
- *Business Publications Corp.* owns the *Des Moines* (Iowa) *Business Record* (www.businessrecord.com) and has other area business publications.

Custom publishers. Several companies producing what amount to in-house magazines for clients and customers are scattered throughout the Web, but many are technical. One of them, Imagination Publishing (www.imaginepub.com), has a large percentage of custom magazines, such as those for Pier 1 and Staples, that are more consumer-oriented and less technical. A description of these magazines, their target audience and an editorial overview is on the Imagination website, along with e-mail contact information.

The airline magazines also are custom publications, some of them (United, Delta) produced by Greensboro, N.C.-based Pace Communications Inc. (www.pacepublications.com).

General-interest publications. Some general-interest publications take business articles, including *Redbook* and *Good Housekeeping*. These publications, or whatever your favorite life-management title is, sometimes are ready and lucrative outlets for business reporting.

—*Lisa M. Keefe*

WRITING FOR ALUMNI MAGAZINES

A hidden market

by Bob Guldin

Pity the alumni magazine editors of America. Even though hundreds of them are at prestigious universities directing four-color publications with large circulations and substantial budgets, they get little respect or attention from freelancers.

Jeffrey Charboneau, executive editor of *Syracuse University Magazine*, complains, "We are amazed at how few queries/proposals we receive from writers, considering the hundreds of thousands of SU alumni living all over the world, and also considering that SU offers degrees in English, creative writing, and newswriting, and has an excellent journalism school. That means we have our very own alumni writers not thinking of us!"

Charboneau's complaint is echoed by university-magazine editors around the United States—but what's bad news from the editor's chair is good news if you're a freelance writer looking for professional, attractive, and remunerative venues in which to publish your work. It means there's a whole class of publications—more than 500 throughout the United States—that are "underqueried" and want to hear from you.

Why this lack of attention? In part, it's simply that alumni magazines are not very visible. Few are sold in stores or advertise their existence to the broader public. Hardly any are listed in *The Writer's Handbook* and similar guides.

Beyond that, though, is the well-understood fact that alumni magazines are curious hybrid creatures. Most try to straddle multiple missions for their institution. On one hand, they want to be a fun, attractive, intellectually stimulating read. On the other, they must also be house organs—supporting alumni attendance at Homecoming Weekend, feel-good public relations efforts, and the ever-popular fund-raising (or "advancement") function.

Most university editors are fully aware their publications are seen by some as not quite legitimate, and as a result are hypersensitive to any sign of disrespect. Mary Ruth Yoe, longtime editor of the *University of Chicago Magazine*, complains that some writers have the attitude, "Oh, this is good enough for an alumni magazine—like 'good enough for government work.' But people have to treat our magazine with the same seriousness they would bring to *The New Yorker*."

While Yoe's wish is unlikely to be granted, it does point to Rule No. 1 for the freelancer approaching alumni magazines: give the publication the same level of attention and respect you would a top consumer magazine. Any less, and you're likely to be rejected, just for bad manners.

College and university alumni publications are a remarkably diverse lot. Some are skimpy newsletters or tabloids, entirely staff-written. The more interesting ones from the writer's vantage point are generally four-color magazines with six-figure annual budgets. While some prestigious private universities, including Stanford, Brown, Dartmouth, and Cornell, have excellent magazines, you can't predict the quality of a school's magazine by its ranking in the *U.S. News & World Report* list of best universities. For example, the University of Portland, a small Catholic school in Oregon, consistently wins awards for its creatively edited magazine. Elsewhere, some top universities devote only minimal resources to their magazine.

In terms of content, almost all alumni magazines cover similar beats, including events and developments on campus (e.g., the new astronomy building), faculty achievements and research, and interesting, successful, or even quirky alumni. Some of the best magazines regularly include serious intellectual content.

And since many magazines are closely tied to the school's fund-raising function, lots of ink is devoted to major donors. (And don't sneer—it can be quite a satisfying journalistic feat to find an interesting angle on some generous corporate honcho.)

Just as they vary in quality, college and university magazines vary enormously in pay. While few publicize their rates, you can get some idea simply by looking at the magazine. A hefty, four-color publication with lots of ads is likely to pay reasonably well. Large private universities and the "flagship" campuses of state systems are good bets, while smaller state schools and community colleges often have little or no budget for outside writers. Pay scales at the higher-end magazines tend to run between 50 cents and $1 per published word.

Breaking in

The same guidelines you have encountered many times about how to approach any periodical apply to alumni magazines. First, read several issues of the publication and get a sense of its tone and the kinds of articles it runs. Many magazines have editor's columns—read those. They often give useful hints about the editor's interests and priorities. Of course, this entire process is made easier by the fact that most institutions have large chunks of their magazine's content on the Web.

If you have an idea or two for a potential article, pitch it in a well-written letter and send along a clip or two. Queries should contain a good hook, and should explain why you're the right person to write this piece. Most university editors say they are happy to receive queries by e-mail; phone inquiries can be more problematical.

While contacting an editor with a specific proposal generally works best, some editors, especially those based in smaller towns, may be glad to hear from a skilled local freelancer even without a proposal. Charboneau, the Syracuse editor, says he is trying to build a stable of reliable writers: "Let me know that you exist," he says. "Show me your clips. We need professional writers to do longer pieces."

While some university magazine editors say they favor alumni writers (because they know the territory), virtually all are willing to consider proposals from non-alumni, as well.

Query your alma mater

If you'd like to write for alumni magazines, you'll find that you already have a few built-in starting points.

The first is the college or university you attended. You probably already receive its publication, so dig one up and read it with fresh eyes. Think about remarkable aspects of the school, or inspiring professors, strange alumni, or controversies that roiled the institution. Any of these can be a starting point for a successful query.

As editor of *The George Washington University Magazine* a few years ago, I was approached by a freelance writer (class of '68) who had worked at the college radio station, been a fanatical GW sports fan, and then served in Vietnam. Each aspect of his college or post-college career became the basis for a fine story in our magazine. For example, his article on eight GW alumni who had gone to 'Nam and how the war affected their lives was both moving and very on-target for our readers.

Your second natural connection is the institutions in your immediate area. This is a rich field for two reasons. First, college magazines often run stories with a local angle—how the town or neighborhood has changed, town-gown conflicts, interesting things for alumni to do when they return to campus. In addition, because you live nearby, it's easier for you to explore the campus and get a feel for what's going on there. As one editor told us, "Knowing the culture of the school is huge for us."

When you're on campus, pick up student newspapers and other small publications for faculty and staff. They will often give you insights into hot issues or breaking developments that can be converted into story ideas. College press releases, generally available on the Web, do the same.

Your third natural source of article ideas for alumni magazines is people—particularly people in your area who may be local heroes or newsworthy in any way. And if you are already doing a story on that person, so much the better. As Charboneau suggests, "Whatever assignment a writer tackles, a basic question she or he should ask is, 'What college did you graduate from?' There is a very strong possibility that that person's college has a newsletter or magazine for which the writer may formulate a quick story by using existing interview notes." It's an easy query to write, plus it may lead to additional assignments.

With these logical connections in mind, you may find that querying an alumni magazine—your own or any of the hundreds out there—is a relatively easy task. Just remember to give the editors a full measure of respect (it's not "just an alumni magazine"), and you may open some useful new doors for your writing output.

Bob Guldin, of Takoma Park, Md., is a freelance writer and editor. He was the editor of the *George Washington University Magazine* from 1991 to 1997. This article appeared in *The Writer*, January 2004.

Resources

Your college or university is the easiest place to approach with a query or manuscript. In addition, here are some of the other fine publications in the alumni-magazine market:

Brown Alumni Magazine
www.brownalumnimagazine.com

Cornell Alumni Magazine
www.cornell-magazine.cornell.edu

Johns Hopkins Magazine
www.jhu.edu/~jhumag

Notre Dame Magazine
www.nd.edu/~ndmag

SECTION FIVE

Reference Section

SUBMISSION PROCEDURES

How to look professional
in all your submitted materials

by Philip Martin

Submitting material in good, clean condition is not just a courtesy. As the first impression, it sets the stage for a long relationship with an editor or agent. For this reason alone, you want to put your best foot forward.

But good formatting also has practical implications: it allows your work to be reviewed fully and handled properly. A clean submission allows your initial reviewer (editor, agent, or screener) to compare your work with that of others in the submissions pile (in a way that makes you look good!) and then to make readable copies to share with key colleagues (judges, marketing personnel, outside consultants, etc.) involved in the process,

Everyone prefers to work with writers who conduct themselves professionally. Your submission style communicates at a glance that you know what you are doing. By using proper procedure, you avoid looking amateur or desperate to please. Gimmicks or oddities of any kind (colored paper, glitter, creative typefaces) are usually self-defeating.

Instead, stick with the basics—and let your ideas and writing style speak for themselves.

Publisher/agent guidelines

First: find and follow the available guidelines. When submitting material to a publisher, agent, or contest, look for any written guidelines that specify a desired submission format. Such guidelines might be posted online; go to the website and search for the button or tab that says "information for authors," "submission guidelines," or "how to contact us." Sometimes, guidelines must be requested by sending in an SASE and a letter requesting guidelines. In some cases, you can find details in writer newsletters or market directories in print or online.

For contests, these guidelines are crucial; not following them may get your work tossed immediately. Do you put your name on every page? Or is it required that your name not appear on the work itself, just on cover materials, so the work can be circulated and judged anonymously?

For publishers and agents, it's a matter of understanding and honoring their preferences and needs. Since they get hundreds of submissions weekly, don't you want to start off on their good side?

On the other hand, you may wish to create a standard package that you can send efficiently, perhaps over time, to a number of publishers or agents without tweaking much except the cover letter. In that case, a basic professional approach will usually suffice to keep you out of hot water by avoiding the most common mistakes.

In the absence of other guidelines, here are some basics to follow.

The physical package

Paper stock. To make a good impression, it's fine to use plain white 20-lb. paper; just choose one with a good brightness rating. This rating is marked on the label of papers sold in an office-supply store. A ranking of 92 is ideal, much nicer than the cheapest "photocopy" paper, which is often a little gray. By all means, avoid colored paper.

Print quality. Make sure your print-out is sharp, black, and clean; no streaks, spottiness, or light type. If it doesn't look good to you, it will look worse when it gets photocopied and circulated, as will happen if your submission is of interest.

Binding. Do not bind your pages in any manner. It should not look like a presentation at a board meeting, delivered in a slick binder. Instead, your submission will first get stacked in a pile with many others, often kept in its original envelope. Then, editors or judges may want to select all or part of your manuscript to photocopy and circulate to others. Any substantial binding just gets in the way. It is fine just to paper-clip it all together. For a long submission, you also may want to divide it into major sections using paperclips. These can be slipped on and off easily for photocopying.

Colored pocket folders. One tolerable add-on for a short submission (like a proposal or query) is a brightly colored pocket folder. For packages with many pieces, this allows a few extras to be displayed: an author bio, for instance. It likely will be thrown away at some point, but there can be a brief period when it might call a little more attention to what's inside.

Mailing envelope. The outside packaging has little importance; often it gets discarded by the mail room before the editor sees the work. Package it securely in an envelope large enough to hold your submission as unfolded 8.5" x 11" sheets. A simple bubblewrap mailer is fine for a medium-sized submission.

Plain manila envelopes are fine for a brief query/proposal. For long manuscripts, small mailing boxes are available from the U.S. Post Office.

Mailing method. Super-fast delivery seldom has any value unless there is an actual deadline that you're up against. Editors get a lot of stuff, and usually set aside incoming materials in a pile for a few days before they get to read them.

Handwritten notes on package. One helpful tip: if the material was requested, perhaps at a conference meeting or by e-mail correspondence, say so boldly on the package—*Requested Material*—and also put this right up front on top of the cover page of your submission.

Addressee. Whatever else you do, bend heaven and earth to address your package to the right person, by name (and spell the name right!). If not, your package may or may not get forwarded to the right desk. It definitely makes you look out of touch to send it to someone who has been gone for years. Plus, having the right name clarifies that this is not a mass-mailed proposal. The odds that someone will respond are much greater. How do you find the right name? Start by checking recent guidelines or market listings. But the most reliable way is to first call the publisher's or agent's office with the briefest question: "Can you please confirm the correct name and address for me?"

Return postage and/or stamped envelope. First, follow any published guidelines. In general, today it's common not to include return postage, since it's often cheaper for you to photocopy a new package than to wait to get your submitted material returned, likely in worn condition. It works best just to include your contact information, especially your e-mail address, so an editor or agent can contact you immediately if they wish.

Some authors may wish to add a postcard to be returned immediately with a box to be checked indicating a package was received. Personally, I think that is superfluous. I rarely experience things actually being lost in the mail. If concerned, add a delivery confirmation to your outbound shipping.

Business-like cover letters

Requested material. As noted above, if an editor requested your manuscript in person, by phone, or in writing, then write "Requested Material" on the outside of your envelope. This means your stuff goes into a higher priority pile.

First names. Avoid calling someone by their first names, until you really know the person personally or he or she has offered that first name in prior correspondence.

Business style. This is a business letter. Use single-spacing, with your name and business address (or letterhead), then the date, then their name and business address at the top. Be polite. End by thanking them for their interest.

Short description of your work in first paragraph. Describe your work in one phrase briefly in the first paragraph. What are you submitting? A query for an article? The first three chapters and a synopsis for a science-fiction novel? A proposal for a how-to book on gardening? Five poems for a contest? Many in the publishing business will only read the first paragraph quickly; if it doesn't convince them that your work is in their area of interest, they won't read much more.

Length. In any event, most readers will scan the letter quickly, so it must be direct and clear. For any cover letter, one page is always best. Two is possible, if everything is essential and written very tightly.

Proofreading. Proofread your letter. Believe me, a typo in such a short piece will reflect poorly on you. And if you are new at this, seek feedback from others. This might be the most important writing you do. So show it to a friend, perhaps your spouse or another writer, and ask for helpful suggestions.

Style. Avoid run-on sentences, unnecessary asides, use of ellipses (…) to connect sentence fragments, or use of idiomatic slang ("Hey, I thought you'd like to eyeball this"). This will count as a strike against you. Your submission should be a business-like presentation: not stiff or too formal, but polite, offering your work for their consideration. There are a few exceptions when friendly, humorous, or downright zany presentations work, but I wouldn't count on it unless you know the market and recipient very well.

Word count. If you are proposing or submitting work, give the total word-count up front. For a work to be done, offering a suggested range indicates some flexibility.

Genre. This is not the time to say that your work is hard to describe. Find and pick the closest publishing genre or category. It's always better that your work seems to fit somewhere than not. If you can't sum it up, how will others? If it's a romance that's also a fantasy novel, consider the core interests of the publisher you are submitting it to, and lean in that direction.

Find a hook. Relate your work to other successful work. It often helps to say it's "in the style of" a particular title or author. Is it in the style of Elmore Leonard? Or Elizabeth Berg? Find a one-sentence phrase or hook to encapsulate the most delightful, wonderful nature of your work. How would someone describe it to a friend? Yes, your work is so much more than that single phrase. But distilling it down to a short hook or catch-line is an important exercise.

Besides intriguing an editorial reader, it indicates that you know and care about the importance of a good hook to the success of your endeavor. Browsing customers in a store will respond to it, the marketing department will love it, the editors will be glad that the marketing department loves it, and so on.

Attitude. Never brag about your own work, or use superlatives. *Your* saying it's great won't convince anyone—and will turn many reviewers off. (Never say it's "as good as anything by Elmore Leonard;" instead, just say that it's "in the style of.") If you can find someone with a well-known name or convincing credentials to say that your work is very good, as a blurb, that's acceptable. But *you* should come off as confident, but not arrogant or assuming. Just present yourself in a positive light and lay out your work. The recipient, a professional reader, will see it as their job to decide if it's right for their market.

Enticing. If anything, it's best to say less, in an enticing way. As literary agent Joseph Regal says in his article "The Providential Diamond" in *Making the Perfect Pitch* (Katharine Sands, ed.), your goal isn't to tell everything, it's to make the agent or editor feel like they might be "missing something that just might be very special" if they don't immediately request to see more of your material. Never tell the whole story in your cover letter. Tease a little. Throw out a few gems—a short glimpse of a character in a delightful conundrum, or a personal problem that your self-help book can solve—and ask if they'd like to see more in a full proposal.

Contact info. In your letterhead, provide your complete contact info. Then, in the last paragraph, you might confirm the best way to contact you. By e-mail is often preferred these days: it is quickest and cheapest way for an interested party to contact you. You'd be surprised how often, after your work has sat on a desk in a pile for weeks or months, something is needed ASAP and your work fits the bill. Make sure they can reach you.

Business card. A business card is usually unnecessary. If your letterhead has the same info, save the cards to hand out in person.

Is this a query letter or a submission?

Query letter. If this is a query, your cover letter *is* the query letter. There isn't anything else except maybe a bio sheet. In general, for fiction, you don't query, you just submit the actual material (or a significant sample of it). But for nonfiction, you often must start by sending a query.

For a good example of an article query, see Kelly James-Enger's lead piece in this *Handbook*, "Freelance 101." For proposals and pitches for books, see the pieces written by Elizabeth Zack and Jandy Nelson in the "Get Your Book Published" section.

Submission. If this a submission of fiction (or of nonfiction after someone has gotten your query and responded with "yes, send us more"), publishers will usually specify what they want to see. They might request a synopsis and the first three chapters for a novel. For book-length nonfiction work, they likely will want a chapter outline and a sample chapter.

What is the difference between a synopsis and a chapter outline? A chapter outline is like an expanded Table of Contents in a book—you present each numbered chapter and tell in a few sentences what is in that chapter. A synopsis, on the other hand, is written more like a story; it's a present-tense walk through the book from beginning to end. It highlights key characters, their main issues, and then goes through the book focusing on moments of tension, reversals, and so on.

A full proposal for a nonfiction book can be 30-40 pages long, and follows a certain formula. to write one, refer to a guide for book proposals; two good examples are found in *Jeff Herman's Guide to Book Publishers, Editors, and Literary Agents*, or Michael Larsen's book, *Literary Agents: What They Do,*

How They Do It, and How to Find and Work with the Right One for You.

For general help with pitches, queries, and proposals, Katharine Sands' book, *Making the Perfect Pitch*, offers advice from 40 different perspectives, covering all types of genres and pitching situations.

Basic formatting for manuscript text

Keep it simple. The less formatting, the better. "Plain vanilla" is the way to go. Remember, it should look like a manuscript, not a finished typeset book.

Margins. For letters, a one-inch margin all around is a minumum; margins of 1.25" are nice. For submissions of manuscript text, margins of up to 1.5" allow more room for the editors to make editing marks.

Font/typeface. Courier is still common and fine to use. If the publisher or contest states a preference, follow it. But in most cases, any basic serif font will do. Times Roman is fine and most readable for business letters. Avoid sans serif fonts (Ariel, Helvetica, etc.) as harder to read for long passages. Avoid any font too fancy or stylish. Please, no scripty type. It doesn't help anything and just looks unprofessional.

Type size. 12-point type is ideal for almost all manuscript text. Don't make it smaller; many editors read so much that eye-strain is an issue. Although smaller type can be read, it's just harder. For chapter titles, 14-point is good. For text subheadings, put them in bold.

For a complicated layered structure with many headings and subheads in the text, explain and code them so an editor can recognize the difference between a Level-1 main heading and a Level-2 subhead. No more than 3 layers of headings is usually needed.

For extra elements on a page like headers or footers (see below), 10-point type is ideal, to separate it visually from the main text.

Double-spacing. Double-space anything that you are submitting as a manuscript to be published—and which might need to be edited—i.e., the text of your story or article.

Single-spacing. Business documents usually are single-spaced, unless they are fairly long. These include cover and query letters, brief synopses, chapter outlines, and page elements such as stacked, multi-line headers.

Exceptions. A long piece such as a 30-page book proposal or a six-page synopsis might be double-spaced. Some feel it makes it look less daunting and is easier to read. Personally, I tend to prefer tighter pages, as it allows me to scan the elements more quickly, keeping more related items in proximity.

Justification. Left-justification is the rule. This means the right margin is ragged (the so-called ragged right or *rag right*). That's what you want. It avoids most hyphenation. Basically, you don't want your story or article to look like it has already been published; you want to make it look like a fresh manuscript—with lots of great potential. Publishers will typeset it in the way they like, so almost any extra formatting detracts from that editorial imagination.

Headers. All the pages in multi-page submissions after a cover or title page must include a header that includes the following:
• Author's last name
• Book or story title (brief version, using just a few keywords)
• Page number (sometimes also chapter number for a long work)
In a manuscript, the heading can run as a single long line or as several lines stacked on top of each other.

Words per page. Some feel it is important to have 25 lines per page; figuring that if you use 12-point Courier, with a 10-word per line average, you get a nice 250 words per page. For me and most editors today, this isn't as important as an accurate word count.

Chapters & electronic-file management. For nonfiction, provide each chapter as a separate file. Illustrations or diagrams should be provided separately, each as an individual file; don't embed them in the document, just indicate in your document where Figure 2-1 or Photo 14 goes. For fiction, a single file is okay; if the work is very long, consider several files to divide the book roughly into sections. For short stories: submit a file per story. For poems, don't place more than one poem on a single page, unless they are ultra-short.

Scene changes. To indicate a transition to a new scene or a major shift in time or place, just put in an extra line space by hitting the Return key twice. To emphasize it, add a centered trio of asterisks or pound signs, followed by another line space.

Single-sided only. Always submit everything single-sided. Never submit a two-sided document (printed front and back), which is harder to photocopy or peruse quickly.

Extras: author bio

A useful add-on to include with a initial query is an author bio, a well-designed flyer or text document, that promotes you as an author. A core element is your biographical profile, highlighting your credentials as a writer and an expert in your field. This might include a brief list of the most important places you have been published (short and impressive is better than long and all-inclusive). Also, give contact info (how to reach you or your agent); the address of your professional website if you have one (which might feature clips of your best work or links to online postings of previously published work; a brief description of possibilities for speaking engagements (if you offer these); and perhaps an author photograph.

Feature any testimonials or outstanding reviews of past work; third-party praise for your work is always regarded as far more reliable than your own description of yourself.

If you are a new writer without much much of an established portfolio, this author bio can be downplayed; let your writing speak for itself.

A good author bio sheet or flyer does two things. First, it gives valuable background and credentials. Second, it will impress potential publishers; they will realize that you are a writer who knows how to promote yourself.

Submission tracking & follow-up

Tracking and follow-up. Keep a simple log. Note when each query was sent out, to whom, and when you expect to hear a response. Follow-up, if you wish, in few weeks just to confirm it arrived. Then, wait. If you haven't heard anything after the time a publisher normally says it responds, wait another week, then send a follow-up e-mail or call. If you can't get a response, consider sending the work on to another potential market.

Remember: in a few cases, timing your submission is crucial. Many literary magazines only read work at certain times, usually during the school year. Some periodicals do seasonal themes and must get submissions many months in advance to act on them.

Rejection. When your work comes back or is simply rejected with a brief form letter—and most of the time, it will be—the thing to do is to send it right back out to another prospect. Therefore, develop a list in advance of several potential publishers for each proposal or finished work. Plan to keep sending it out. Many successful writers send it out again on the very same day, certainly the same week.

You will get rejected. It is part of the profession. The only thing it means for sure is that that publisher wasn't buying that type of work at that moment. Many award-winning works have been rejected, sometimes by dozens of publishers, before finding the right place that wanted it.

Have many proposals and queries out there at the same time. A classic beginner's mistake is to send one query, then wait, sometimes months, without getting other works circulating. The pros know that it is a matter of playing the odds. The more work and ideas you have out there in the hands of editors and agents, the better the chance that some of them hit the right persons at the right times.

On the other hand, if specific work isn't accepted over time, at some point you should stick it in a drawer and just send out other, newer work. You can return to the old work later, and many authors do. But for now, move on to the next great article idea or the next story. Your writing will likely get better and more timely, so newer work is more likely to sell than older work.

Never give up. Just get better, heed any feedback, and learn that professional presentation pays off in the end.

Philip Martin of Shorewood, Wis., is author of *The Writer's Guide to Fantasy Literature* (The Writer Books, 2002).

Submission dos and don'ts

Do make sure your submission
- Is well-organized.
- Is clean and professional-looking.
- Is single-sided.
- Is addressed to the right person.
- Includes your contact info, including e-mail address.
- Has a cover letter (or is a query letter) of not more than 1-2 pages that describes what is being submitted.

Most common mistakes
- Cover letters that are too long.
- Typos in cover letter or other elements that should be error-free.
- Unattractive materials from poor-quality printers or with margins or type that are too small.
- Cover letters that are full of hype or too many exclamation points, or too friendly without foundation.
- Cover letters that tell too much, instead of creating interest in reading the actual writing.
- Submissions that make it clear the author did not read the available submission guidelines and didn't really consider whether the market was suitable for the submitted material.
- Submissions (for nonfiction) of complete manuscripts without querying first.

—Philip Martin

BASICS OF COPYRIGHTS & CONTRACTS

An overview for writers

by Tad Crawford

Every writer, from beginner to published professional, must be able to handle the business aspects of writing. In large part, these business aspects require an understanding of copyrights and contracts, since copyrights are what a writer creates (whenever an article, poem, or novel is created) and contracts are the way in which writers and publishers reach the agreements that allow a work to be published and find its audience.

Part 1: Copyright Primer

Copyrights

Copyright protects you from having your writing stolen by someone else. As the copyright owner, you may either allow or prevent anyone else from publishing or making derivations from your work (such as a movie made from a novel). Your copyrights last for your lifetime plus another 70 years, so a successful work may benefit not only you but your heirs as well.

To license any exclusive right of copyright (which means only the licensee can do what the license allows), you or your authorized agent must sign a written license. If no written license is signed, then the usage can at most be nonexclusive (which allows you to license the same usage to more than one party).

Make sure you don't sign a work-for-hire contract or assign all rights in your writing, because then the commissioning party would own the copyright and gain its benefits. A "work-for-hire" contract requires a written agreement, signed by both parties, specifying that the work to be done will be work for hire.

Such a contract should be signed in advance in fairness to the writer. Also, the work to be done must fall into certain categories specified in the copyright law, such as a contribution to a magazine or anthology or a small work done to supplement a larger work. After signing the written contract, the author owns no rights to the finished work. It is like working for an employer who asks you to write something on the job, so that the employer owns the work, not you. Assigning "all rights" creates a very similar situation; once you assign all rights, they are gone and out of your hands entirely. It is better to license the rights only for a specific use.

Registration

You don't have to register your writing to obtain your copyright, because federal law gives you the copyright from the moment you create a work. However, registration with the Copyright Office, which currently costs $30, will help you in the event your work is infringed. You can obtain Copyright Application Form TX by writing to the U.S. Copyright Office, Library of Congress, Washington, D.C. 20559, by calling 202-707-9100, or by downloading off their website at www.copyright.gov/forms. The Copyright Office has numerous helpful circulars that can be requested or downloaded from the website.

Notice on works

It is no longer necessary to place copyright notice either on manuscripts or published works. Since March 1, 1989, the absence of copyright notice cannot cause the loss of the copyright. The lack of notice, however, may give infringers a loophole to try and lessen their damages. So it is still wise to place copyright notice on your works (especially when published) as a visible symbol of your rights as copyright owner. A copyright notice has three elements: 1) "Copyright" or "Copr" or "©"; 2) your name; and 3) the year of first publication.

Infringement

Your work is infringed when someone uses it without your authorization. The test for infringement is whether an ordinary observer would believe one work was copied from another.

The damages for infringement are the actual losses of the person whose work is infringed plus any profits of the infringer. In some cases (especially if the work was registered before the infringement), the court can simply award an amount between $750 and $30,000 for each work infringed. If the infringement is willful, this can be increased to as much as $150,000. Contrary to the beliefs of some Internet enthusiasts, copyright laws do apply to the Internet and unauthorized use of writing on a website is an infringement.

One thing you can do is to search the Web periodically to look for your work being copied and posted illegally. The best way to do this is to search for a distinctive phrase that appears in your work, perhaps in the title, subtitle, or first paragraph. You might be surprised to see your work appearing somewhere you did not expect it to. If so, contact the website administrator, saying that you are the owner of the work being posted, giving notice of infringement, and insisting that the work be withdrawn immediately from the site. Before alleging infringement, it is always wise to consult an attorney (you might check with a volunteer lawyer for an arts group for a recommendation).

Fair use

In some cases, unauthorized use may be a "fair use" and not an infringement. A fair use is a use of someone's else work that is allowed under the copyright law. For example, newsworthy or educational uses are likely to be fair uses. The factors for whether a use is a fair use (and not an infringement) are: 1) the purpose and character of the use, including whether or not it is for profit; 2) the character of the copyrighted work; 3) how much of the total work is used in the course of the use; and 4) what effect the use will have on the market for or value of the work being copied.

There is no word-count formula. It depends on the significance of the portion used, so it might not be "fair use" to quote even a few lines from a poem or a song lyric, whereas you might be able to quote a longer passage from a book-length work. One question to ask is if the work is transformative; that is, are you creating a different kind of work, such as quoting a brief piece of a novel to create a critical review?

One problem is that "fair use" is not a clearly defined right; it's more a defense once you've decided to go ahead and do it. If you are in doubt, the safest strategy is to ask for permission to use the excerpt, in advance, in writing.

Public domain

Since copyright is for a limited term, after the copyright term has ended the written work becomes part of the public domain. Works in the public domain may be freely copied by anyone. Works published in the United States in 1922 or earlier are in the public domain in the U.S. Later works might also be, but they must be reviewed on a case-by-case basis.

Permission

To obtain permission to publish works that are not in the public domain and cannot be used as a fair use, you should use a simple permission form such as that offered in my book, *Business and Legal Forms for Authors and Self-Publishers*. This would set forth what kind of project you are doing, what writing you want to use, what rights you need in the material, what credit line and copyright notice will be given, and what payment, if any, will be made. The person giving permission should sign the permission form.

Often, a permission request should be sent to an author's publisher. Many large publishers have permissions departments. Place your request with plenty of time to spare, as it can take time for large publishers to respond.

Part 2: Contracts Primer

Contracts

Writers should license limited rights of usage in their copyrights, such as first North American serial rights (FNASR), which is the right to be the first magazine in North America to publish the writing.

Typical limitations in a publishing contract are by territory (e.g., "North American"), by language ("English"), by time period ("for a period of one year"), by order (the first publication or a reprint), by exclusivity (exclusive or nonexclusive), by specific format of publication (book, periodical, CD-ROM, website, etc.), by type of printing (hard-copy print version or electronic), and so on. Your copyrights can be subdivided infinitely into any number of such specific, limited rights.

All rights not licensed should be retained by you as the creator. The purpose of contracts is to set out what the parties have agreed to, especially with respect to the crucial issue of what rights are licensed (and whether the license is exclusive, meaning only that particular publication can use the rights, or nonexclusive, meaning that the same rights can be licensed to many publications). After the description of what rights are licensed, the contract should state, "Any usage rights not explicitly licensed hereunder are reserved to the writer."

In general, an author wants to avoiding licensing rights that a publisher really doesn't intend to use or exploit, or that the author can use to his or her own advantage or license elsewhere. And in general, if a publisher wants more rights, such as electronic rights in addition to print rights, it logically should pay something extra for that use.

Other issues in contracts

Contracts also deal with many issues other than the rights to be licensed. For example, a magazine contract should also include a description of the assignment, a due date, a fee, whether certain expenses will be reimbursed, a time for payment, what happens if additional usage is desired beyond the initial license of rights, revisions, copyright notice, authorship credit, what happens in the event of cancellation, which party will obtain any needed permissions and releases, whether the contract will be arbitrated, and miscellaneous issues such as which state's laws will govern the contract and whether any amendments or changes must be in a written document signed by both parties.

Oral vs. written

While oral contracts can be binding, written contracts are much better (and often more enforceable). The problem with oral contracts is that even with the best of intentions, memories fade and people may not recollect the terms in the same way. This can lead to needless disagreements and the loss of clients. A well-drafted written contract memorializes the intention of the parties and serves as a guide to what is expected. That is why the writer should always have a written contract, even for a relatively small assignment.

Book contracts

Moving from magazine to book contracts, the complexity of the contract increases and the contracts will certainly be in writing. The book contract should:

- Cover what rights are licensed;
- Contain a reservation of all other rights to the writer;
- Give a length for the manuscript and any other necessary description of the content; also, give a deadline for delivery;
- Provide who will pay for the index and any expenses such as permissions that must be obtained;
- Give a time window within which the book must be published, provide for royalties, specify an advance—i.e., an amount of money given to the writer (often half on signing the contract and half on delivery of the manuscript) that will later be subtracted from the royalties earned;
- Deal with the sharing of subsidiary rights licensed by the publisher (such as translation rights, dramatizations and audio versions);
- Specify the time for accountings and the right of the writer to inspect the publisher's books;
- Deal with copyright and authorship credit;
- Include a warranty and indemnity in which the writer guarantees that the work is original and doesn't violate anyone's rights;
- Indicate how many copies of the book the writer will receive;
- Plan for what will happen if a revision is necessary;
- Give grounds on which the contract may be terminated;
- Detail the writer's right to buy remainder copies (i.e., copies being sold at very high discounts to clear out inventory) and production materials (such as computer files containing the designed book);
- Determine whether the publisher will be allowed to assign the contract and in what circumstances; and
- Cover such issues as how modifications must be made, where notice should be sent, and which state's laws govern the agreement.

Many of these issues, such as the computation of royalties, can be complex, so you should never hesitate when making contracts to seek expert advice, whether from an attorney or a reference book. For those who might find an attorney difficult to afford, there are volunteer lawyers for the arts in many parts of the United States and Canada. A full listing of these groups can be found at http://dwij.org/matrix/vla_list.html.

Also, literary agents typically know how to negotiate better book contracts for authors. Their fee (a percentage of author income from the book) is often well covered by the improved deal, and they will administer and watch the contract for its duration. To find a literary agent, ask friends for references or look in books to see if an author's agent is thanked in acknowledgements. A listing of major literary agencies can be found at the website of the Association of Authors' Representatives (www.aar-online.org).

Remember, most contracts can be improved for the author to some degree. The so-called "boilerplates" offered by publishers are rarely non-negotiable; this is more accurately a strategy employed by publishers. It is usually expected and seldom considered rude that an author will request some changes and try to negotiate. Some points, called "deal points," are most important and vary from deal to deal depending on the author's circumstances and goals. Deal points might include: the size of the advance, when it will be paid, the royalty rate, the subrights splits, the number of complimentary copies, and the quantity discount for further author purchases.

Other modifications are also possible, if there is a common ground that all parties can agree to. Negotiation requires a willingness to win some points but give on others. It helps to know what is standard, what your bottom line is, what you'd like, and what is a reasonable compromise.

Finally, avoid signing something that you just don't understand. Teach yourself about copyrights and contracts, so that you can enjoy the full fruits of your labors.

Tad Crawford is an attorney and publisher. He is also the author of *Business and Legal Forms for Authors and Self-Publishers* and coauthor (with Kay Murray) of *The Writer's Legal Guide* (both books published by Allworth Press). For more information, go to www.allworth.com.

COMMONLY MISUSED WORDS

Say what you really mean

by Linda Jorgensen

Writers have a lot of techniques at their disposal—subtle interview ploys, a variety of narrative story shapes, dozens of rhetorical and literary devices. But the single most important way to build an effective piece of writing is to use the exact right words to convey meaning.

Entirely obvious, you say? Well, but as an editor, time and again I see intelligent, talented writers failing to say what they meant. They've failed to check a usage guide to *ensure* (not *assure!*)[1] the right choice *between* (not *among!*)[2] two or three commonly misused terms, or to pick the right spelling for a word that's often pronounced wrong.

Dictionaries don't always help: They'll tell you that *compose* and *comprise*[3] are practically synonyms, but literate communicators (such as editors and many readers) know that dictionaries reflect how most people use the English language—which isn't always the same as the best possible usage.

Here are some words that are frequently misused in publications ranging from daily newspapers to textbooks to literary fiction. If you find yourself wrestling with some of these distinctions, why not add them to your personal style sheet? The more you consult your list of confusables, the more attuned you'll become to which words best fit a particular context. I can promise you that will happen.

Why take care with these terms? You'll not only reassure the editors who evaluate the quality of your work (thus perhaps keeping their intervention to a minimum), you'll also develop a sense of nuance and connotation that can only strengthen your writing.

ability, capacity, capability
People can acquire an *ability* ("become capable of doing something"). *Capacity*, however, is inherent potential that can't be acquired (a child's *capacity* to learn language) or indicates the volume some vessel can hold. Using *capacity* when you mean "job" is overkill. *Capability* means "having the necessary skills or attributes to perform a job or task," and it's preferable to *capacity* for that meaning.

affect, effect
Some commentators say this is the most common misusage in the English language. To *affect* something means to have an influence on it. (Giving praise where it's due *affects* performance.) To *effect* something is to cause it to happen, though it can sound slightly pretentious. (To *effect* a good outcome, praise good performance.) *Affect* (in psychology, meaning "emotion" or "expression") and *effect* (meaning "result" or "consequence") are also both nouns.

awhile, a while
Awhile is spelled as one word whenever it isn't modified. (We were gone for *awhile*.) When it's modified, the two-word form a while is required. (We were gone for quite *a while*.)

biennial, semiannual, biannual
Dictionary definitions are ambiguous for these terms—and readers often can't guess from context how they're being used. The best bet is to simply avoid the misleading prefixes *bi*- (*biennial* can mean both "occurring every two years" and "lasting for two years") and *semi*- (*semiannual* can mean "occurring every six months or twice a year"). *Biannual* can mean "occurring twice a year" (same as *semiannual*) or be used as a synonym for *biennial*—which can also mean "lasting for two years." This way lies madness. Just say what you mean: The directory is published every two years.

credible, creditable
Something or someone *credible* is "deserving of belief, trustworthy" (e.g., the testimony given in a courtroom). Something or someone *creditable* is "deemed worthy of limited or qualified praise" (e.g., the so-so but not extraordinary performance by the overworked prosecutor).

credulous, ingenuous, disingenuous
Someone who is *credulous* "believes too easily, without proof" (e.g., the jury members who convict a defendant on circumstantial evidence). Someone who is *ingenuous* is "unsavvy, naive" (e.g., the innocent bystander who picks up the murder weapon and leaves fingerprints). Someone one who is *disingenuous* "pretends innocence or ignorance" in order to circumvent unpleasant facts or

evidence (e.g., the slick defense attorney's "amazement" that anyone would consider his client guilty).

discreet, discretion, discrete

A *discreet* person is someone cautious who "exercises self-restraint in speech and behavior"—i.e., uses *discretion*. The noun isn't related to *discrete*, which describes something or several things that have been "separated into distinct parts."

emigrate (away from), immigrate (into), migrate (from ... to)

People who leave one country are said to *emigrate* from it to enter another. In transit, they are *emigrants*. Once they've arrived where they plan to resettle, they *immigrate* into the new country and might be referred to as *immigrants*. To *migrate* means to travel from one place to another within a general geographical region—country, state, etc.—as seasonal farmworkers (*migrants*) do.

famous, infamous, notorious

Famous means "notable for admirable qualities or actions." Someone considered *infamous* or *notorious* is "well-known for negative traits," such as lying. Often, *notorious* is misused to refer to celebrity or fame (e.g., an actress described as "*notorious* for her beautiful eyes" should be "*famous*" for them instead). It's okay to refer to things that predictably lead to unfortunate consequences as *notorious* (e.g., an annual event *notorious* for causing traffic jams).

ironic, sarcastic, sardonic, cynical

Many of us take our humor dry, with a twist. These terms are used to describe tones of voice, attitudes, comments and other behavior that is perceived as critical or negative. *Ironic* should be used when a remark "attempts to be provocatively amusing by saying the opposite of what is meant." It's wry. A *sarcastic* comment is "marked by bitterness and intended to hurt or sting someone." It's cutting. *Sardonic* is a manner that "shows a scornful facial expression or uses a mocking tone of voice." It's a personal affront combined with a darkly humorous comment. And then there's *cynical*—the attitude of one who believes, as a matter of course, that most things end badly and therefore speaks dismissively of hopes and possibilities. A *cynic* would say that 90 percent of writers routinely disregard the distinctions drawn here.

rack, wrack, wreak

A *rack* is "a frame across which something is tightly stretched." To "*rack* your brains" means to be tormented or strained. A *wrack* is "a wreck." To be driven "to *wrack* and ruin" is to become broken or disabled. To *wreak* havoc is to "inflict a damaging blow," and it's pronounced "reek," not "wreck."

regardless, irregardless

The correct term is *regardless*. *Irregardless* is not a word liked by careful editors, though you will see it in dictionaries. It is considered redundant. I happen to work with one writer who likes to keep me awake and manages to make fun of both anal editors and careless writers by using the term *disirregardless* in his e-mail correspondence. What's a little scary is that's exactly how bogus terms gain credence: we use them and allow others to use them unchallenged. Try that one on an editor who is a good friend, and you'll either get an exploding head or helpless giggling, depending on how many writers misused *comprise* that day.

Note: The source used for this mini-glossary is the consensus-based *New York Public Library Writer's Guide to Style and Usage*, written by EEI Communications staff for HarperCollins and available from EEI Press, www.eeicommunications.com/press. Consult it for further examples and guidance to many other tricky confusable terms.

Linda Jorgensen is the manager of EEI Press, the trade reference publishing division of EEI Communications, the oldest full-service publication services, training, and consulting company on the East Coast. She also edits *The Editorial Eye: Focused on Publications Standards, Practices, and Trends*, a subscription newsletter for writers and editors, and teaches workshops ("Style Summit: The Evolution of English in the Internet Age" and "Editing Stronger Magazines").

[1]You *ensure* ("make sure") that a thing will happen but *assure* ("reassure") a person that it will happen.

[2]You learned in school that *between* is for only two things and *among* is for three or more things. But when you're speaking of a group within which cross-comparisons are being made (between A and B, B and C, A and C, and so on), *among* is correct and preferable.

[3]The whole *comprises* its parts. *Comprised of* is incorrect because it is redundant—*comprised* already means "is composed of." The parts *compose* the whole; the whole cannot be said to be *composed of* its parts, though a synthetic product is "composed of" its elements. Some editors have given up on maintaining this distinction because it's so seldom observed, but those who still do re-a-a-a-lly care about it.

BOOKS & WEBSITES

Recommended resources

compiled by the editors of *The Writer*

The business of writing

The ASJA Guide to Freelance Writing: A Professional Guide to the Business, for Nonfiction Writers of All Experience Levels, edited by Timothy Harper (St. Martin's Griffin). A complete guide to freelancing, with articles by top freelancers. Includes planning a writing business, how to write a magazine query, how to decide if you're ready to go full time, and what you need to know about contracts.

The Complete Guide to Book Marketing, by David Cole (Allworth Press). Helps writers understand the publishing business and book marketing.

The Freelance Success Book: Insider Secrets for Selling Every Word You Write, by David Taylor (Peak Writing Press). Full of "tips on getting assignments and writing great articles . . . shows you how to write effective queries and explains why editors turn down most queries." —Chuck Leddy, *The Writer*

Magazine Editors Talk to Writers, by Judy Mandell (John Wiley & Sons). Top editors—from *Esquire, Parade, Ladies Home Journal*, and other prominent periodicals—discuss the business of magazine publishing and offer tips for writers looking to break into the market.

Ready, Aim, Specialize! Create Your Own Writing Specialty and Make More Money, by Kelly James-Enger (The Writer Books). Successful freelancer

James-Enger tells you how to develop a writing specialty. Includes how to find new markets, 10 hottest specialties, case studies, and hundreds of resources.

The Renegade Writer: A Totally Unconventional Guide to Freelance Writing Success, by Linda Formichelli and Diana Burrell (Marion Street Press). A different take on freelance writing, aimed at helping you to prosper by "breaking the rules."

The Sell Your Novel Tool Kit, by Elizabeth Lyon (Perigee). You've written your novel. Now what? Pick up this book for a step-by-step guide to getting it published. Also see Lyon's *A Writer's Guide to Nonfiction* (Perigee), which takes you through the steps of writing essays, memoirs, self-help, and other nonfiction articles or books. She helps answer these questions: What do I want to say? Who are my readers? What form can my writing take? How can I refine my ideas? Includes chapters on finding new markets and common problems.

The Well-Fed Writer: Financial Self-Sufficiency as a Freelance Writer in Six Months or Less, by Peter Bowerman (Fanove Publishing). A blueprint for building a freelance writing business. Bowerman focuses on writing for corporate clients.

The craft of writing

The Associated Press Stylebook and Briefing on Media Law, edited by Norm Goldstein (Perseus Publishing). The style guide of choice for newspaper and many magazine staffs, organized in dictionary form.

Bird by Bird: Some Instructions on Writing and Life, by Anne Lamott (Anchor Books). A classic, very readable book of writing advice.

The Chicago Manual of Style, 15th ed. (The University of Chicago Press). The classic reference guide for writers and editors, in a newly revised edition.

The Elements of Expression: Putting Thoughts into Words, by Arthur Plotnik (iUniverse). "Written with wit and humor, this compact, accessible guide to expressiveness . . . gives readers a fresh look at how they express (or fail to express) their thoughts and feelings both in writing and speaking." —Ingram Book Group. Also see *The Elements of Editing: A Modern Guide for Editors and Journalists*, by Arthur Plotnik (Pearson).

The Elements of Style, 4th ed., by William Strunk Jr. and E. B. White (Pearson Higher Education). "No book in shorter space, with fewer words, will help any writer more than this persistent little volume." —*The Boston Globe*

How to Read a Poem and Start a Poetry Circle, by Molly Peacock (Riverhead Books). Though meant for aficionados of poetry, this volume, which explains how and why some poems work, is a valuable guide for those who write poetry as well as those who read it.

If You Want to Write: A Book About Art, Independence and Spirit, by Brenda Ueland (Graywolf Press). This small volume is a gem full of inspiration, instruction, and refreshing advice such as: why women who do too much housework should neglect it for their writing. Ueland suggests that all writers develop the fine art of "moodling" and their writing will improve. If you wonder what that is, read the book. You won't regret it. "[T]he best book ever written about how to write." —Carl Sandburg

The Magazine Article: How to Think It, Plan It, Write It, by Peter P. Jacobi (Indiana University Press). The art of article writing is demystified with Jacobi's hands-on and practical approach. Jacobi provides numerous examples of successful articles to illustrate his points.

The Modern Library Writer's Workshop: A Guide to the Craft of Fiction, by Stephen Koch (Modern Library). From 1977 to 1998, Koch taught creative writing at Columbia University. "[S]killfully shows you how to get story ideas, how to develop characters, how to find your 'voice,' how to handle revision, and how to improve . . . all with a profound understanding of the writer's creative process." —Chuck Leddy, *The Writer*

On Becoming a Novelist, by John Gardner (W. W. Norton & Co.). A must-have for aspiring novelists, this book is the product of John Gardner's 20-year career as a fiction writer and creative writing teacher. Also see Gardner's *The Art of Fiction: Notes on Craft for Young Writers* (Vintage).

On Writing: A Memoir of the Craft, by Stephen King (Pocket Books). Advice and reflections on the writing life by one of the bestselling authors of all time.

On Writing Well, 25th Anniversary: The Classic Guide to Writing Nonfiction, by William Zinsser (HarperResource). A must-read for beginners, but a worthwhile, wonderfully written refresher course for more experienced writers. Also see Zinsser's *Writing to Learn* (HarperResource), which focuses on how to write clearly about any subject.

The Plot Thickens: 8 Ways to Bring Fiction to Life, by Noah Lukeman (St. Martin's Press). "[O]ffers a commonsensical approach to plotting—one that begins with an intimate knowledge of characters, then moves on to creating conflict and suspense. After having read thousands of manuscripts, Lukeman knows what works and what doesn't." —Chuck Leddy, *The Writer*

Rules for the Dance: A Handbook for Writing and Reading Metrical Verse, by Mary Oliver (A Mariner Original, Houghton Mifflin). The Pulitzer Prize-winning poet's guide to writing metrical verse. Essential in any poet's library.

Self-Editing for Writers: How to Edit Yourself into Print, by Renni Browne and Dave King (HarperResource). Two top independent editors "teach writers the techniques of the editing trade that turn promising manuscripts into published novels and short stories."

A Short Story Writer's Companion, by Tom Bailey (Oxford University Press). Bailey, a professor who teaches creative writing, walks you through the elements of writing a short story, including character, point of view, plot, setting, and time. He also pays attention to voice, literary techniques, and the idea of fictional truth. The book includes examples and exercises. A real boon to short-story writers.

Writing Fiction: The Practical Guide from New York's Acclaimed Creative Writing School, an anthology from the Gotham Writers' Workshop (Bloomsbury). Devoted to the craft of writing fiction, this volume covers all the bases, including creating characters, focus, point of view, description, dialogue, pacing, and voice.

Writing in General and the Short Story in Particular, by Rust Hills (Mariner Books). A classic guide to writing short stories that explains the essential techniques of fiction.

Inspiration

The Artist's Way: A Spiritual Path to Higher Creativity, by Julia Cameron (J. P. Tarcher). Cameron's bestselling book is the bible on creativity for many artists and writers.

The Courage to Write: How Writers Transcend Fear, by Ralph Keyes (An Owl Book, Henry Holt). Even if you have no fear of writing, Keyes' book is filled with wisdom and encouragement for writers. He interviewed dozens of writers about their greatest fears, such as "Will everyone see through me?" and then offers ways to overcome them.

The Hidden Writer: Diaries and the Creative Life, by Alexandra Johnson (Anchor Books). An inspiring book that shows how writers such as Virginia Woolf, Anais Nin, Katherine Mansfield, and May Sarton have used journaling to enhance their writing.

Take Joy: A Book for Writers, by Jane Yolen (The Writer Books). In eleven sparkling essays, Yolen offers advice that is upbeat, practical, irreverent, often humorous, always heartfelt, and deeply rooted in a true delight in storytelling.

Write Mind, by Eric Maisel (J.P. Tarcher). Maisel lists 299 things writers should never say to themselves, such as: "I will definitely get back to my novel next week" and counters with what they should say instead: "Ready or not, I'm headed for the computer." These short affirmations may give you a jump-start when you need it.

Writing Down the Bones, by Natalie Goldberg (Shambhala Publications). Worth reading for the exercise on "timed writing" alone. In what has become a classic, Goldberg takes a refreshing Zen approach to writing, offering both inspiration and instruction.

Websites

Absolute Write
www.absolutewrite.com
Hosted by Jenna Glatzer, author of *Outwitting Writer's Block* (Lyons Press), this site is for all types of writers, from freelancers to screenwriters. Offers articles, interviews, courses, and market information.

The Academy of American Poets
www.poets.org
Features essays on poetry, biographies of more than 450 poets, texts and audio files of hundreds of poems, and poetry news and events.

American Society of Journalists and Authors
www.asja.org
America's "leading organization of independent nonfiction writers." Membership includes market information, a referral service, seminars, and workshops.

Arts & Letters Daily
www.aldaily.com
Links to hundreds of news sources, including daily highlights of the best articles, reviews, and essays. From *The Chronicle of Higher Education*.

Association of Authors' Representatives
www.aar-online.org
Features a searchable database of member literary agents.

Bartleby
www.bartleby.com
Provides free, searchable access to classic fiction, nonfiction, and reference books.

BookWire
www.bookwire.com
Book publishing news, statistics, and resources for authors, agents, book-sellers, and publishers.

Common Errors in English
www.wsu.edu/~brians/errors/
Should you use "who" or "whom?" Find out on this site, where the differences between oft-confused words are explained.

Cyber Times Navigator
www.nytimes.com/ref/technology/cybertimes-navigator.html
A helpful Web reference page with hundreds of links in a dozen categories, maintained by *The New York Times* for use by its reporters and editors.

Fiction Addiction
www.fictionaddiction.net
Provides resources for fiction writers and readers alike, including how-to articles, author interviews, book reviews, and more.

Fiction Factor
www.fictionfactor.com
E-zine dedicated to the craft of fiction writing.

Freelance Writing
www.freelancewriting.com
Industry news, as well as job and networking opportunities for writers, PR pros, and researchers.

Guru
www.guru.com
Freelancers in the media, finance, IT, marketing, and sales fields can post their resumes and create portfolios for employers to browse.

International Trademark Association
www.inta.org
Is it "laundromat" or "Laundromat"? Search the Trademark Checklist to find the correct usage for 3,000 registered trademarks and service marks.

iTools
www.itools.com/lang
Search for definitions, homonyms, antonyms, and rhymes.

Journalism Jobs
www.journalismjobs.com
The most-visited resource for media jobs, offering jobs and the largest database of resumes for journalists.

Library Spot
www.libraryspot.com
An award-winning research tool with links to hundreds of library and reference sites.

LookSmart's FindArticles
www.findarticles.com
Search and read 3.5 million articles from more than 700 publications.

MediaBistro
www.mediabistro.com
Jobs and resume site for mainly New York media jobs, including print and TV, plus industry news and networking opportunities.

National Writer's Union
www.nwu.org
The "only labor union that represents freelance writers in all genres, formats, and media." Membership includes access to education, grievance, networking, and employment resources.

NewsDirectory
www.newsdirectory.com
Provides links to hundreds of magazines, newspapers, government agencies, and more.

Publishers Weekly
www.publishersweekly.com
The leading publication for the book publishing industry, with news, features, and reviews. Only subscribers of *Publishers Weekly* magazine have complete access to the site.

PubList
www.publist.com
Find addresses, editor contacts, and more with this searchable database of 150,000 magazines, journals, and newsletters.

Refdesk
www.refdesk.com
Provides easy access to hundreds of reference sources.

Science Fiction and Fantasy Writers of America
www.sfwa.org
Provides news and advice about reading, writing, and publishing science fiction and fantasy. Writer Beware section posts information on literary scams, non-paying publishers, and more.

The Scriptorium
www.thescriptorium.net
Monthly e-zine with articles, interviews, writing exercises, and book reviews.

Smart Writers
www.smartwriters.com
Focuses on children's books. Site features monthly journal with the latest news in children's books; sections for writers, educators, and kids.

Society of Children's Book Writers and Illustrators
www.scbwi.org
News, events, and resources for children's book writers and illustrators hosted by the largest children's writing organization in the world.

SPAWN (Small Publishers, Artists and Writers Network)
www.spawn.org
Offers links to research sources, publishers, printers, and the media, and up-to-date market information.

U.S. Copyright Office
www.copyright.gov
News and information related to copyright law, including registration forms, regulations, and copyright records from 1978 to the present.

Web del Sol
www.webdelsol.com
A "literary arts new media complex" featuring links to literary publications, chapbook collections, original fiction, and writing programs.

WorldWide Freelancer
www.worldwidefreelance.com
This monthly e-mail newsletter focuses on non-U.S. markets.

Write From Home
www.writefromhome.com
For freelancers working from home and trying to balance work and family. Features original content, markets, jobs, and calls for submissions.

The Writer
www.writermag.com
Articles, links to literary magazines, conferences, and contests. Lively discussion on topics of interest to writers.

Writers Guild of America
www.wga.org and www.wgaeast.org
Screenwriting news and links. WGA represents writers in the motion picture, broadcast, cable, and new technology industries.

WritersNet
www.writers.net
WritersNet is an Internet directory of writers, editors, publishers, and literary agents. Writers can be listed in a directory of talent and services. You can do an online search for editors and agents.

WritersWeekly
www.writersweekly.com
A weekly e-mail newsletter with four or five markets per issue. The website features updated market information, articles, success stories, books, and courses.

Writers Write
www.writerswrite.com
A great resource for the latest information on books, writing, and publishing.

GLOSSARY

Key terms for writers

Advance—The amount a publisher pays a writer before a book is published; it is deducted from the royalties earned from sales of the finished book.

Agented material—Submissions from literary or dramatic agents to a publisher. Some publishing companies accept agented material only.

All rights—Some magazines purchase all rights to the material they publish, which means that they can use it as they wish, as many times as they wish. They cannot purchase all rights unless the writer gives them written permission to do so.

Assignment—A contract, written or oral, between an editor and writer, confirming that the writer will complete a specific project by a certain date, and for a certain fee.

B&W—Abbreviation for black-and-white photographs.

Book outline—Chapter-by-chapter summary of a book, frequently in paragraph form, allowing an editor to evaluate the book's content, tone, and pacing, and determine whether he or she wants to see the entire manuscript for possible publication.

Book packager—Company that puts together all the elements of a book, from initial concept to writing, publishing, and marketing it. Also called **book producer** or **book developer**.

Byline—Author's name as it appears on a published piece.

Clips—Copies of a writer's published work, often used by editors to evaluate the writer's talent.

Column inch—One inch of a typeset column; often serves as a basis for payment.

Contributor's copies—Copies of a publication sent to a writer whose work is included in it.

Copy editing—Line-by-line editing to correct errors in spelling, grammar, and

259

punctuation, and inconsistencies in style. Differs from **content editing**, which evaluates flow, logic, and overall message.

Copy—Manuscript pages before they are set into type.

Copyright—Legal protection of creative works from unauthorized use. Under the law, copyright is secured automatically when the work is set down for the first time in written or recorded form.

Cover letter—A brief letter that accompanies a manuscript or book proposal. A cover letter is not a query letter (see definition).

Deadline—The date on which a written work is due at the editor's office, agreed to by author and editor.

Developmental Editing—the first round of working with an editor to shape a manuscript, which may involve exploring additions or deletions of substantial portions and dealing with issues of purpose, audience, focus, organization, and overall clarity. After this round is completed, the work may be passed on to a copy-editing round, to clean up and make the language consistent, then proofreading to catch any last errors.

Draft—A complete version of an article, story, or book. First drafts are often called rough drafts.

Electronic rights—Refers to the use of an article in electronic form, rather than hard-copy formats. The scope of what this might cover is open to some interpretation, and it is a good idea to pin down what a publisher means by electronic rights, and what aspect of them they actually intend to utilize, and then consider the fee, advance, or royalty amount being offered.

Fair use—A provision of the copyright law allowing brief passages of copyrighted material to be quoted without infringing on the owner's rights.

Feature—An article that is generally longer than a news story and whose main focus is an issue, trend, or person.

Filler—Brief item used to fill out a newspaper or magazine column; could be a news item, joke, anecdote, or puzzle.

First serial rights—The right of a magazine or newspaper to publish a work for the first time in any periodical. After that, all rights revert to the writer.

FNASR (First North American Serial Rights)—This refers to the specific right to publish an author's work in a serial periodical, in North America, for its first appearance. Thereafter, the right to allow any further reprinting or other use of the work by anyone remains with the author.

Ghostwriter—Author of books, articles, and speeches that are credited to someone else.

Glossy—Black-and-white photo with a shiny, rather than a matte, finish.

Hard copy—The printed copy of material written on a computer.

Honorarium—A modest, token fee paid by a publication to an author in gratitude for a submission.

International reply coupon (IRC)—Included with any correspondence or submission to a foreign publication; allows the editor to reply by mail without incurring cost.

Internet rights—See also electronic rights. This refers to the rights to post an author's work on a website, and possibly to distribute or allow the distribution of the article further via the Internet.

Kill fee—Fee paid for an article that was assigned but subsequently not published; usually a percentage of the amount that would have been paid if the work had been published.

Lead time—Time between the planning of a magazine or book and its publication date.

Libel—A false accusation or published statement that causes a person embarrassment, loss of income, or damage to reputation.

Mass market—Books appealing to a very large segment of the reading public and often sold in such outlets as drugstores, supermarkets, etc.

Masthead—A listing of the names and titles of a publication's staff members.

Ms—Abbreviation for manuscript; mss is the plural abbreviation.

Multiple submissions—Also called **simultaneous submissions**. Complete manuscripts sent simultaneously to different publications. Once universally discouraged by editors, the practice is gaining more acceptance, though some still frown on it. Multiple queries are generally accepted, however, since reading them requires less of an investment in time on the editor's part.

North American (NA)—Sometimes appears as 1st NA; refers the right to publish the North American appearance of a piece of work, leaving the author free to market other appearances of the same work elsewhere. (Rights can be sold or licensed and made specific to any given geographical territory, such as North American, United Kingdom, Turkish, and so on.)

On speculation—Editor agrees to consider a work for publication "on speculation," without any guarantee that he or she will ultimately buy the work.

One-time rights—Editor buys manuscript from writer and agrees to publish it one time, after which the rights revert to the author for subsequent sales.

Op-ed—A newspaper piece, usually printed opposite the editorial page, that expresses a personal viewpoint on a timely news item.

Over-the-transom—Describes the submission of unsolicited material by a freelance writer; the term harks back to the time when mail was delivered through the open window above an office door.

Payment on acceptance—Payment to writer when manuscript is submitted.

Payment on publication—Payment to writer when manuscript is published.

Pen name—A name other than his or her legal name that an author uses on written work.

Print on Demand—a method of printing (for some publishers, it is their main business approach), in which electronic ready-to-print files are stored in a databas, then printed in small numbers, sometimes just as needed to fill actual orders. This is different from "traditional" publishing which prints in larger quantities, often in the thousands of copies, and therefore must estimate demand in advance. Print-on-demand (**POD**) books can be printed in a book-at-a-time (**BAT**) approach, to service a single customer's order.

Public domain—Published material that is available for use without permission, either because it was never copyrighted or because its copyright term is expired, Works published at least 75 years ago are considered in the public domain.

Q-and-A format—One type of presentation for an interview article, in which questions are printed, followed by the interviewee's answers.

Query letter—A letter, usually no longer than one page, in which a writer proposes an article idea to an editor.

Rejection slip—A printed note in which a publication indicates that it is not interested in a submission.

Reporting time—The weeks or months it takes for an editor to evaluate a submission.

Reprint rights—The legal right of a magazine or newspaper to print an article, story, or poem after it has already appeared elsewhere.

Royalty—A percentage of the amount received from retail sales of a book, paid to the author by the publisher. For hardcovers, the royalty is generally 10% on the first 5,000 copies sold; 12 1/2% on the next 5,000 sold; 15% thereafter. Paperback royalties range from 4% to 8%, depending on whether it's a trade or mass-market book.

SASE—Self-addressed, stamped envelope, required with all submissions that the author wishes returned—either for return of material or (if you don't need material returned) for editor's reply.

Slush pile—The stack of unsolicited manuscripts in an editor's office.

Tear sheets—The pages of a magazine or newspaper on which an author's work is published.

Unsolicited submission—A manuscript that an editor did not specifically ask to see.

Vanity publisher—Also called **subsidy publisher**. A publishing company that charges an author all costs of printing his or her book.

Web rights—See Internet rights.

Work for hire—When a work is written on a "for hire" basis, all rights in it become the property of the publisher. Though the work-for-hire clause applies mostly to work done by regular employees of a company, some editors offer work-for-hire agreements to freelancers. Think carefully before signing such agreements, since by doing so you will essentially be signing away your rights to the work.

Worldwide—Refers to the right to publish an article anywhere in the world (however, this right may be subject to other limitations in a contract restricting publication by language, print formats, time period, and so on).

Writers guidelines—A formal statement of a publication's editorial needs, payment schedule, deadlines, and other essential information.

NONFICTION MAGAZINES

NONFICTION MAGAZINES

The magazines in the following list are in the market for freelance articles in many categories. Unless listings state otherwise, a writer should submit a query first, including a brief description of the proposed article and any relevant qualifications or credits. A few editors want to see samples of published work, if available.

Submit photos or slides only if the editor has specifically requested them. A self-addressed envelope with postage sufficient to cover the return of the manuscript or the answer to a query should accompany all submissions.

All information in these lists comes from query responses from the editors, publishers, and directors and from their published guidelines, but personnel and addresses change, as do requirements. No published listing can give as clear a picture of editorial needs and tastes as a careful study of several issues of a magazine, and writers should never submit material without first thoroughly researching the prospective market. If a magazine is not available in the local library or on the newsstand, write directly to the editor for the price of a sample copy. Many companies also offer a formal set of writer's guidelines, available for an SASE (self-addressed, stamped envelope) upon request, or posted on its website.

While some of the more established markets may seem difficult to break into, especially for the beginner, there are thousands of lesser-known publications where editors will consider submissions from first-time freelancers.

All manuscripts must be typed double-space and submitted with self-addressed envelopes bearing postage sufficient for the return of the material. If a manuscript need not be returned, note this with the submission, and enclose an SASE or a self-addressed, stamped postcard for editorial reply. Use good white paper. Always keep a copy, since occasionally material is lost in the mail. Magazines may take several weeks, or longer, to read and report on submissions. If an editor has not reported on a manuscript after a reasonable length of time, write a brief, courteous letter of inquiry.

Some publishers will accept, and may in fact prefer, work submitted on computer disk, usually noting the procedure and type of disk in their guidelines.

ABILITIES

ABILITIES MAGAZINE

Canadian Abilities Foundation, 340 College St., Suite 650, Toronto, Ontario M5T3A9 Canada. 416-923-1885. E-mail: lisa@abilities.ca. Website: www.abilities.ca. Quarterly. Lisa Bendall, Managing Editor. **Description:** For people with disabilities, their families, and professionals engaged in disabilities issues. Covers travel, health, sport, recreation, employment, education, housing, social policy, sexuality, movie/book reviews, profiles; 500-2,000 words; $50-$400. **Columns, Departments:** News and updates (FYI); humor (The Lighter Side). **Queries:** Preferred. **Unsolicited mss:** Accepts. **Rights:** FNAR, non-exclusive electronic.

ABLE

P.O. Box 395, Old Bethpage, NY 11804-0395. 516-939-2253.
E-mail: ablenews@aol.com. Website: www.ablenews.com. Monthly. $15/yr. Circ.: 35,000. Angela Miele Melledy, Publisher/Editor. **Description:** "Positively for, by, and about the disabled." Features news, events, and information of interest to people with disabilities, family and friends, and involved professionals; articles to 500 words; $40/article. **Queries:** Required. **E-Queries:** No. **Unsolicited mss:** Does not accept. **Freelance Content:** 40%. **Payment:** On publication.

ACTIVE LIVING MAGAZINE

Disability Today Publishing Group
2276 Rosendene Rd., St. Ann's, Ontario L0R 1Y0 Canada. 905-957-6016.
E-mail: activeliv@aol.com. Website: www.activelivingmagazine.com. Bimonthly. $19.97/yr. Circ.: Bimonthly. Liz Fleming, Managing Editor. **Description:** Health, fitness, and recreation magazine for people with disabilities. Articles, 750-1,000 words, on improving fitness and mobility, accessible travel and leisure, and new therapeutic and sporting activities. **Tips:** Avoid labeling or condescending language. **Queries:** Preferred. **Payment:** On publication.

CAREERS & THE DISABLED

Equal Opportunity Publications, 445 Broadhollow Rd., Suite 425, Melville, NY 11747-4803. 631-421-9421. E-mail: jschneider@eop.com. Website: www.eop.com. 3x/yr. $10/yr. Circ.: 10,500. James Schneider, Editor. **Description:** Career guidance publication for students and professionals with disabilities. Features role-model profiles and career guidance strategies; 1,000-1,500 words; $.10/word. **Queries:** Preferred. **E-Queries:** Yes. **Unsolicited mss:** Accepts. **Response:** 2 weeks. **Freelance Content:** 60%. **Rights:** FNAR. **Payment:** On publication.

CHALLENGE

Disabled Sports/USA, 9406 N 107th St., Milwaukee, WI 53224-1106. 414-354-0200. E-mail: patty@rspr.com. Website: www.dsusa.org. 3x/yr. $25/yr. Circ.: 25,000. Patty Johnson, Editor. **Description:** Promotes adaptive sports and recreation for kids and adults with physical disabilities—from elite paralympic athletes to youngsters just entering competition. Emphasis on family recreation, fitness training, and activities of DS/USA chapters nationwide. Articles should relate to regional, national, and international competitions. Offers by-line and photo credits only; no monetary payment. **Tips:** "Avoid "gushing" when writing. Disabled athletes are extremely talented, train hard, and set world records close to those of able-bodied contestants. These athletes do not want to be considered as "inspirations" or otherwise presented in a patronizing manner. Use correct terminology relating to disabilities." **Queries:** Required. **E-Queries:** Yes. **Freelance Content:** 10%. **Rights:** None.

CLOSING THE GAP

526 Main St., P.O. Box 68, Henderson, MN 56044. 507-248-3294. E-mail: info@closingthegap.com. Website: www.closingthegap.com. Bimonthly. $34/yr. Circ.: 10,000.

Megan Turek, Managing Editor. **Description:** Newspaper providing practical, up-to-date information on assistive technology products, procedures, and best practices. Feature articles cover how technology enhances the education, vocation, recreation, mobility, communication, etc. of individuals with disabilities. Non-product related articles also used. 800-1,000 words. **Tips:** Use "person first" wording (refer to the person first, followed by disability, e.g., "the boy with a disability"). Original, unpublished material only. No pure research or "one of a kind" product descriptions. Interested only in easily replicated procedures or commercially available products (include price and contact information of producer). **E-Queries:** Yes. **Rights:** All.

DIALOGUE

Blindskills, Inc., P.O. Box 5181, Salem, OR 97304-0181. 503-581-4224, 800-860-4224. E-mail: blindskl@teleport.com. Website: www.blindskills.com. Quarterly. Carol McCarl, Editor. **Description:** Publication for youth and adults who are visually impaired. Covers independence, mobility, career opportunities, educational skills, recreation, technology, health, etc. Also spotlights short pieces of fiction in each issue. Pieces run 800-1,200 words; pay varies. **Tips:** See website for guidelines. **Queries:** Preferred. **SASE Required:** Yes. **Rights:** FNAR. **Payment:** On publication.

INMOTION

Amputee Coalition of America, 900 E Hill Ave., Suite 285, Knoxville, TN 37915. 865-524-8772, ext. 8102. E-mail: carrollnan@aol.com. Website: www.amputee-coalition.org. Bimonthly. $30/yr. Circ.: 40,000. Nancy Carroll, Editor. **Description:** Covers topics of interest to amputees such as new technology, inspirational profiles, etc. Articles, to 2,000 words; $.25/word. **Payment:** On publication.

KALEIDOSCOPE

United Disability Services, 701 S Main St., Akron, OH 44311-1019. 330-762-9755. E-mail: mshiplett@udsakron.org. Website: www.udsakron.org. Semi-annual. Circ.: 1,000. Gail Willmott, Editor-in-Chief. **Description:** Explores the experience of disability through literature and fine arts, from the perspective of individuals, families, health-care professionals, and society. Seeks to challenge and overcome stereotypical, patronizing, sentimental attitudes about disability. Pay $25 and 2 copies. **Fiction:** Character-centered stories, not action pieces. No romance. 5,000 words max. **Nonfiction:** Narratives and articles on experiences and issues of disability. 5,000 words max. **Poetry:** Free verse on disability or written by someone with a disability. Also, short nature poems and light humor. 1-5 poems **Art:** 35mm color, B&W 8x10 glossy; up to $100. **Queries:** Not necessary. **E-Queries:** Yes. **Unsolicited mss:** Accepts. **Response:** Queries 2 weeks, submissions 6 months. **SASE Required:** Yes. **Freelance Content:** 60%. **Rights:** FNASR. **Payment:** On publication. **Contact:** Mildred Shiplett, Editorial Coordinator.

AGRICULTURE & RURAL LIFE

ACRES USA

P.O. Box 91299, Austin, TX 78709-1299. 512-892-4400.
E-mail: editor@acresusa.com. Website: www.acresusa.com. Monthly. $27/yr. Circ.: 11,500. Fred C. Walters, Publisher. **Description:** Articles offer ecological and economical advice for farmers who practice sustainable agriculture. Features hands-on techniques and natural methods for growing crops and raising livestock. **Nonfiction:** Emphasis on commercial production of quality food without use of toxic chemicals; pays $.05/word. **Unsolicited mss:** Accepts. **Payment:** On publication.

AG JOURNAL

Arkansas Valley Journal, P.O. Box 500, La Junta, CO 81050-0500. 719-384-8121.
E-mail: ag-edit@centurytel.net. Website: www.agjournalonline.com. Weekly. $32/yr. Circ.: 10,300. Jeanette Larson, Managing Editor. **Description:** Agriculture news in the Western and Southwestern states. Also covers ag market and pricing trends, grain and forage production, equestrian happenings, equipment for-sale listings, prominent people, etc.; 250-2000 words; $.04/word. **Queries:** Required. **E-Queries:** Yes. **Response:** 2 weeks. **Rights:** All, no reprints. **Payment:** On publication.

AMERICAN BEE JOURNAL

Dadant & Sons, 51 S Second St., Hamilton, IL 62341-1398. 217-847-3324. E-mail: abj@dadant.com. Website: www.dadant.com. Monthly. $22.95/yr. Circ.: 11,000. Joe M. Graham, Editor. **Description:** Publication on beekeeping for both professionals and hobbyists. Offers how-to articles as well as scientific information on disease and treatments. Pays $.75/column inch. **Queries:** Preferred. **Payment:** On publication.

BACKHOME MAGAZINE

Wordsworth Communications, Inc., P.O. Box 70, Hendersonville, NC 28793.
828-696-3838. E-mail: backhome@ioa.com. Website: www.backhomemagazine.com. Bimonthly. $4.95/$21.97. Circ.: 29,000. Lorna K. Loveless, Editor. **Description:** Do-it-yourself information on sustainable, self-reliant living. Offers information and resources on rural land, mortgage-free building, solar/renewable energy, chemical-free gardening, wholesome cooking, home business, home schooling, small livestock, vehicle/workshop projects, family activities. Prefers first-person experiences. Articles run 800-3,000 words; $35/printed page. **Tips:** "Focus not on "dropping out," but on becoming better citizens and caretakers of the planet. Avoid essays." **Queries:** Not necessary. **E-Queries:** Accepts. **Unsolicited mss:** Accepts. **Response:** 2-4 weeks. **SASE Required:** Yes. **Freelance Content:** 80%. **Payment:** On publication.

BEE CULTURE

623 W Liberty St., Medina, OH 44256-2225. 330-725-6677. E-mail: kim@beeculture.com. Website: www.beeculture.com. Monthly. $21.50/yr. Circ.: 13,500. Mr. Kim Flottum, Editor. **Description:** How-to articles on beekeeping, pollination, gardening with bees, nature, etc. Also profiles of commercial operations. Pieces run 1,000-2,000

words; $100-$250. **Tips:** "Writers must know bee and commercial beekeeping. Avoid "How I got started in beekeeping" stories." **Queries:** Preferred. **E-Queries:** Yes. **Unsolicited mss:** Accepts. **Response:** 1-3 months. **SASE Required:** Yes. **Freelance Content:** 25%. **Rights:** FNAR. **Payment:** On publication or negotiated.

BEEF

PRIMEDIA Business Magazines & Media, 7900 International Dr., Suite 300, Minneapolis, MN 55425. 952-851-9329. E-mail: beef@primediabusiness.com. Website: www.beef-mag.com. Monthly. $35/yr. Circ.: 100,000. Joe Roybal, Editor. **Description:** For cattlemen and others in the cattle industy. Covers feeding, cowherds, stock operations, production, animal health, nutrition, finance, marketing, etc. **Queries:** Required. **E-Queries:** Yes. **Unsolicited mss:** Does not accept. **Payment:** On acceptance.

BRAHMAN JOURNAL

American Brahman Breeders Association, 17269 FM 1887, Hempstead, TX 77445. E-mail: jebrockett@aol.com. Website: www.brahman.org/journ.html. Monthly. $25/yr. Circ.: 4,000. Vicki Lambert, Editor. **Description:** "The official publication of the Brahman breed." Covers the Brahman breed of beef cattle and the people involved with them. Articles run 1,200-3,000 words; $100-$250. **Queries:** Preferred. **E-Queries:** No. **Unsolicited mss:** Accepts. **Freelance Content:** 10%. **Rights:** All. **Payment:** On acceptance.

CAPPER'S

Ogden Publications, Inc., 1503 SW 42nd St., Topeka, KS 66609-1265. 785-274-4345. E-mail: cappers@cappers.com. Website: www.cappers.com. Bi-weekly. $27.98/yr. Circ.: 210,000. Ann Crahan, Editor. **Description:** On home and family, for readers in the rural Midwest. **Fiction:** Query first, with brief description. Pays $75-$300. **Nonfiction:** Inspirational, nostalgic, family-oriented, travel, human-interest; 700 words max; $2.50/inch. **Poetry:** Easy to read, down-to-earth themes; 4-6 lines; $10-$15. **Fillers:** Jokes (limit submissions to batches of 5-6; no jokes returned); $2 gift certificate. **Art:** 35mm color slides, transparencies, or sharp color prints, include captions. Pays $10-$40. **Tips:** Query for novel-length manuscripts only; submit all others complete. No simultaneous submissions. **Queries:** Not necessary. **E-Queries:** No. **Unsolicited mss:** Accepts. **Response:** 2-6 months. **SASE Required:** Yes. **Freelance Content:** 25%. **Rights:** FNASR. **Payment:** On publication.

THE CATTLEMAN

Texas & Southwestern Cattle Raisers Assn., 1301 W 7th St., Fort Worth, TX 76102-2604. 817-332-7064. E-mail: lchambers@texascattleraisers.org. Website: www.thecattlemanmagazine.com. $25/yr. Circ.: 15,500. Lionel Chambers, Editor. **Description:** For ranchers who raise beef cattle. **Queries:** Preferred.

COUNTRY
Reiman Publications/Reader's Digest Assn. 5400 S 60th St., Greendale, WI 53129. E-mail: editors@country-magazine.com. Website: www.country-magazine.com. Bimonthly. $16.99/yr. Circ.: 1,500,000. Jerry Wiebel, Editor. **Description:** Articles and photographs describing the allure of country life today. Mostly reader-written. First-person articles; 500-700 words; $75-$200. **Tips:** No articles on farm production techniques. **Queries:** Not necessary. **Unsolicited mss:** Accepts. **Response:** 2 months. **Freelance Content:** 90%. **Payment:** On publication.

COUNTRY FOLK MAGAZINE
HC 77 Box 580, Pittsburg, MO 65724-9717. E-mail: salaki@countryfolkmag.com. Website: www.countryfolkmag.com. 6x/yr. $19.50/yr. Circ.: 10,500. Susan Salaki, Editor. **Description:** True Ozark history stories, old rare recipes, historical photos, and interesting fillers. **Nonfiction:** Ozark history; 800-1,000 words; $5-$25. **Poetry:** Standard rhyming; 3 verses max.; pays complimentary copy. **Tips:** "We only accept traditional poetry and the subject must be about the Ozark region. All of our stories are true, complete with real names and places." **Freelance Content:** 99%.

COUNTRY WOMAN
Reiman Publications/Reader's Digest Assn., 5400 S 60th St., Greendale, WI 53129. 414-423-0100. E-mail: editors@countrywomanmagazine.com. Website: www.countrywomanmagazine.com. Bimonthly. $17.98/yr. Circ.: 1,500,000. Ann Kaiser, Editor. **Description:** For women living in the country or interested in country life. Recipes, craft projects, fiction and nostalgia stories, decorating, profiles of country woman, and poetry. **Fiction:** Wholesome fiction with country perspective or rural theme; 1,000 words; $90-$125. **Nonfiction:** Nostalgia pieces, essays on farm/country life, humorous stories, decorating features, inspirational articles; 750-1,000 words; $50-$75. **Poetry:** Good rhythm and rhyme, seasonal in nature; 12-24 lines; $10-$25. **Queries:** Not necessary. **Unsolicited mss:** Accepts. **Response:** 2-3 months. **SASE Required:** Yes. **Freelance Content:** 90%. **Payment:** On acceptance. **Contact:** Kathleen Zimmer-Anderson, Managing Editor.

DAIRY GOAT JOURNAL
Countryside Publications, Ltd., W11564 State Hwy 64, Withee, WI 54498-9323. 715-785-7979. E-mail: csymag@tds.net. Website: www.dairygoatjournal.com. 6x/yr. $2.50/$21. Circ.: 4,000. Dave Thompson, Editor. **Description:** Magazine for successful dairy-goat owners. Features interesting people and practical husbandry ideas. **Nonfiction:** 1,000-1,500 words. Also fillers and artwork. Pay negotiable. **Tips:** Needs practical stories about goats and their owners; about marketing goat cheese and dairy products. Readership in U.S. and over 70 foreign countries. **Queries:** Preferred. **E-Queries:** No. **Unsolicited mss:** Accepts. **Response:** 2 weeks. **SASE Required:** Yes. **Freelance Content:** 50%. **Rights:** All. **Payment:** On publication.

FARM AND RANCH LIVING

Reiman Media Group, Inc./Reader's Digest Assn., 5400 S 60th St., Greendale, WI 53129. 414-423-0100. E-mail: editors@farmandranchliving.com. Website: www.farmandranchliving.com. Bimonthly. $3.99/$19.98. Circ.: 350,000. Nick Pabst, Editor. **Description:** For U.S. and Canadian families that farm or ranch full-time. Photo-illustrated stories about today's farms, ranchers, includes diaries, rural nostalgia, tractor talk, 4-H, etc.; 1,200 words; $75-$150. **Tips:** "Submit upbeat, positive stories." **Queries:** Not necessary. **E-Queries:** Yes. **Unsolicited mss:** Accepts. **Response:** 4 weeks. **SASE Required:** Yes. **Freelance Content:** 30%. **Rights:** FNAR. **Payment:** On publication.

FARM INDUSTRY NEWS

PRIMEDIA Business Magazines & Media, 7900 International Dr., Suite 300, Minneapolis, MN 55425. E-mail: fin@primediabusiness.com. Website: www.farmindustrynews.com. 12x/yr. $25/yr. Circ.: 250,700. Karen McMahon, Editor. **Description:** For farmers covering new products, machinery, equipment, chemicals, and seeds. **Queries:** Required. **Payment:** On acceptance.

FARM JOURNAL

1818 Market St., Philadelphia, PA 19103-3696. 215-557-8900. E-mail: feedback@agweb.com. Website: www.agweb.com. Monthly. $24.75/yr. Circ.: 445,000. Karen Freiberg, Editor. **Description:** On the business of farming. Articles, 500-1,500 words, with photos; pays $.20-$.50/word. **Queries:** Preferred. **Payment:** On acceptance.

FLORIDA GROWER

Meister Media Worldwide, 1555 Howell Branch Rd., Suite C-204, Winter Park, FL 32789. 407-539-6552. E-mail: flg_edit@meisternet.com. Monthly. Circ.: 12,063. Roy Padrick, Managing Editor. **Description:** The voice of Florida agriculture. Covers all aspects of commercial fruit and vegetable industries. Articles run 1,400 words; $300. **Queries:** Not necessary. **E-Queries:** Yes. **Unsolicited mss:** Accepts. **Freelance Content:** 20%. **Rights:** All. **Payment:** On publication.

HOBBY FARMS

P.O. Box 6050, Mission Viejo, CA 92690. 949-855-8822. E-mail: hobbyfarms@fancypubs.com. Website: www.hobbyfarmsmagazine.com. Bimonthly. $4.99/$23.97. Karen Keb Acevedo, Editor; Toni McAllister, Associate Editor. **Description:** For rural enthusiasts who live on small farms, raise livestock (exotic or traditional), and work their land. Offers informative how-to articles, as well as livestock profiles, crop profiles, event coverage, and regular columns on cooking with farm-fresh ingredients, buying rural property, livestock q&a, etc. Articles run about 2,000 words; $300-$425. **Tips:** "Be familiar with our magazine before sending material. Send sample paragraphs of the article you propose, or a sample of similar articles. Be aware that we are concerned about animal welfare—the proper treatment of livestock is paramount, regardless of whether they are pets or destined for the table." **Queries:** Preferred. **E-Queries:** Yes. **Unsolicited mss:** Accepts. **Response:** 6 weeks. **SASE Required:** Yes. **Freelance Content:** 75%. **Rights:** FNAR.

THE LAND

The Free Press Co., P.O. Box 3169, Mankato, MN 56002-3169. 507-345-4523. E-mail: kschulz@the-land.com. Website: www.the-land.com. Biweekly. $20/yr. Circ.: 35,000. Kevin Schulz, Editor. **Description:** Agricultural and rural-life magazine for Minnesota farm families. **Nonfiction:** On Minnesota agriculture and rural issues, production, how-tos. 500 words; $35-$60. **Queries:** Preferred. **E-Queries:** Yes. **Unsolicited mss:** Does not accept. **Response:** 1-4 weeks. **SASE Required:** Yes. **Freelance Content:** 50%. **Rights:** FNAR. **Payment:** On acceptance.

THE MAINE ORGANIC FARMER & GARDENER

Maine Organic Farmers & Gardeners Assoc., 662 Slab City Rd., Lincolnville, ME 04849. 207-763-3043. E-mail: jenglish@midcoast.com. Website: www.mofga.org. Quarterly. $12/yr. Circ.: 5,000. Jean English, Editor. **Description:** Articles on organic farming/gardening, environmental issues relating to food/health, consumer issues; 250-2,000 words; $.08/word. Also, gardening and farming tips and book reviews. **Tips:** "Avoid rehashing old material. No chemical fertilizers or potato-flake recipes. Our readers know organic methods, and they seek new ideas, new crops, and new cultivation techniques." **Queries:** Preferred. **E-Queries:** Yes. **Unsolicited mss:** Accepts. **Response:** 2-4 weeks. **SASE Required:** Yes. **Freelance Content:** 50%. **Rights:** 1st, reprint. **Payment:** On publication.

NEW HOLLAND NEWS

New Holland, N.A., Inc., P.O. Box 1895, New Holland, PA 17557-0903. 717-393-3821. E-mail: writegm@aol.com. Website: www.newholland.com/na. 8x/yr. Gary Martin, Editor. **Description:** Farm and ruralite features, including rural non-farm and part-time farming, people stories about farm/rural life, ways to improve farm income, second income ideas, etc; 800-1,500 words; $600-$800. **Tips:** No farmer profiles. **Queries:** Preferred. **E-Queries:** Yes. **Unsolicited mss:** Accepts. **Response:** 2 months. **SASE Required:** Yes. **Freelance Content:** 60%. **Rights:** FNAR. **Payment:** On acceptance.

ONION WORLD

Columbia Publishing, 417 N 20th Ave., Yakima, WA 98902-7008. 509-248-2452. E-mail: onionworld@freshcut.com. Website: www.freshcut.com. 8x/yr. $15/yr. Circ.: 5,300. Carrie Kennington, Editor. **Description:** Publication for U.S. and Canadian onion industries (growers, packers, shippers). On onion production, packing, and shipping businesses; varieties grown, challenges, solutions, etc.; to 1,500 words; $5/column inch. **Tips:** Include photos with article. "No meaningless drivel. No gardening articles." **Queries:** Preferred. **E-Queries:** Yes. **Unsolicited mss:** Accepts. **Response:** 1-2 weeks. **SASE Required:** Yes. **Freelance Content:** 25%. **Rights:** FNAR. **Payment:** On publication.

PEANUT FARMER

SpecComm International, Inc., 5808 Faringdon Pl., Suite 200, Raleigh, NC 27609-3930. 919-872-5040. E-mail: editor@peanutfarmer.com. Website: www.peanut-farmer.com. Monthly. $25/yr. Circ.: 17,000. Mary Ann Rood, Editor. **Description:** Offers information on production practices for commercial peanut farmers; 500-2,000 words. **Queries:** Preferred. **E-Queries:** Yes. **Unsolicited mss:** Accepts. **Response:** 2 weeks. **SASE Required:** Yes. **Freelance Content:** 10%. **Rights:** FNAR. **Payment:** On publication.

PROGRESSIVE FARMER

Southern Progress Corp., P.O. Box 2581, Birmingham, AL 35202-2581. 205-877-6415. E-mail: letters@progressivefarmer.com. Website: www.progressivefarmer.com. Monthly. $16/yr. Circ.: 613,000. Jack Odle, Editor. **Description:** Covers new developments in agriculture, rural communities, personal business issues for farmstead and home office, relationships, worker safety, finances, taxes, and regulations. **Queries:** Preferred. **Payment:** On publication.

RURAL HERITAGE

281 Dean Ridge Ln., Gainesboro, TN 38562-5039. 931-268-0655. E-mail: editor@ruralheritage.com. Website: www.ruralheritage.com. Bimonthly. $8/$26. Circ.: 6,700. Gail Damerow, Editor. **Description:** Covers modern farming and logging with horses, mules, and oxen. Articles on draft animal use, training, implements, etc.; 1,200 words; $.05/word. **Queries:** Preferred. **E-Queries:** Yes. **Unsolicited mss:** Accepts. **Response:** Queries 1 week, submissions 3 months. **Freelance Content:** 90%. **Rights:** FNASR. **Payment:** On publication.

RURALITE

Ruralite Services, Inc., P.O. Box 558, Forest Grove, OR 97116. 503-357-2105. E-mail: curtisc@ruralite.org. Website: www.ruralite.org. Monthly. $10/yr. Circ.: 296,800. Curtis Condon, Editor. **Description:** For rural/small-town audiences (OR, WA, ID, WY, NV, northern CA, AK), on issues affecting rural electric cooperatives, rural living, people features, regional history, and celebrations, humorous photos; 400-2,000 words; $50-$400. **Tips:** Readership 55% women, ages 50+. **Queries:** Required. **E-Queries:** Yes. **Unsolicited mss:** Do not accept. **Response:** 1-2 months. **SASE Required:** Yes. **Freelance Content:** 80%. **Payment:** On acceptance.

SHEEP!

Countryside Publications, Ltd., W11564 State Hwy 64, Withee, WI 54498-9323. 715-785-7979. Website: www.sheepmagazine.com. Bimonthly. $21/yr. Circ.: 4,000. Nathan Griffin, Editor. **Description:** For sheep and wool farmers across the U.S. and Canada. Articles on successful shepherds, woolcrafts, sheep raising, sheep dogs; 800-1,500 words; $80-$125. **Tips:** "We are especially interested in people who raise sheep successfully as a sideline enterprise." **Queries:** Preferred. **E-Queries:** No. **Unsolicited mss:** Accepts. **Response:** 1 month. **SASE Required:** Yes. **Freelance Content:** 50%. **Payment:** On acceptance.

SMALL FARM TODAY

3903 W Ridge Trail Rd., Clark, MO 65243-9525. 573-687-3525. E-mail: small-farm@socket.net. Website: www.smallfarmtoday.com. Bimonthly. $4.95/$23.95. Circ.: 12,000. Ron Macher, Editor. **Description:** A "how-to" magazine of alternative and traditional crops, livestock, and direct marketing, to help farmers make their operations profitable and sustainable. **Nonfiction:** Stories about a specific crop, livestock, or marketing method, with how-to and budget information; 1,000-1,800 words; $.35/word. **Tips:** Readers prefer alternative sustainable methods over traditional chemical farming. Sample copy $3. **Queries:** Preferred. **E-Queries:** Yes. **Unsolicited mss:** Accepts. **Response:** Queries 2 months, submissions 4 months. **SASE Required:** Yes. **Rights:** FNAR. **Payment:** On publication.

SMALL FARMER'S JOURNAL

P.O. Box 1627, Sisters, OR 97759-1627. 541-549-2064. E-mail: agrarian@smallfarmersjournal.com. Website: www.smallfarmersjournal.com. Quarterly. $8.50/$30 yr. Circ.: 18,000. Mr. Lynn R. Miller, Editor. **Description:** Covers practical farming for families who own small farms. Subject matter includes natural farming, stock raising, alternative farm research, and research on horses and horsedrawn equipment sales. **Nonfiction:** How-tos, humor, practical work-horse information, livestock and produce marketing, gardening, and articles for the independent family farm. Pay varies. **Tips:** Write of your own farm experiences. Avoid use of chemicals. **Queries:** Not necessary. **E-Queries:** Yes. **Unsolicited mss:** Accepts. **Response:** 3 months. **SASE Required:** Yes. **Freelance Content:** 50%. **Rights:** 1st. **Payment:** On publication.

SUCCESSFUL FARMING

Meredith Corp., 1716 Locust St., Des Moines, IA 50309-3023. 515-284-2853. Website: www.agriculture.com. Monthly. $15/yr. Circ.: 475,000. Loren Kruse, Editor-in-Chief. **Description:** Magazine for farmers and ranchers. Articles focus on successful family farms/businesses (all sizes, all types) that illustrate positive aspects. **Art:** Color transparencies preferred; pay varies. **Tips:** "Provide ideas families can take right to the barn, shop, office, home, and heart to add value to their lives. Measure new practices and trends with dollar signs. Use examples and have multiple sources." **Queries:** Preferred. **E-Queries:** No. **Unsolicited mss:** Accepts. **Response:** 2-7 days. **SASE Required:** Yes. **Freelance Content:** 20%. **Rights:** All. **Payment:** On acceptance. **Contact:** Gene Johnston, Managing Editor.

WALLACES FARMER

Farm Progress Companies, 6200 Aurora Ave., Suite 609E, Urbandale, IA 50322. 515-278-6693. Website: www.wallacesfarmer.com. Monthly. $21.95/yr. Circ.: 62,100. Fran O'Leary, Editor. **Description:** Provides Iowa farmers with useful information on methods and equipment that helps them profitably manage their farming operations. Articles and interviews run 600-700 words. **Tips:** Freelance content limited. **Queries:** Required. **E-Queries:** Yes. **Unsolicited mss:** Accepts. **Freelance Content:** 1%. **Payment:** On acceptance.

THE WESTERN PRODUCER

P.O. Box 2500, 2310 Millar Ave., Saskatoon, Saskatchewan S7K 2C4 Canada. 306-665-3544. E-mail: newsroom@producer.com. Website: www.producer.com. Brenda Washburn. **Description:** On agricultural and rural subjects, preferably with Canadian slant. Articles 600 words or less; $.22/word. Color photos $60-$100. **Payment:** On publication.

ANIMALS & PETS

AKC FAMILY DOG

American Kennel Club, Inc., 260 Madison Ave., New York, NY 10016. 212-696-8321. E-mail: gazette@akc.org. Website: www.akc.org. Quarterly. $8.95/yr. Circ.: 250,000. Erika Mansourian, Features Editor. **Description:** Lifestyle magazine for purebred pet owners. Articles run 1,000-2,500 words; $250-$600. **Queries:** Preferred. **Payment:** On acceptance.

AKC GAZETTE

American Kennel Club, Inc., 260 Madison Ave., New York, NY 10016. 212-696-8321. E-mail: gazette@akc.org. Website: www.akc.org. Monthly. $29.93/yr. Circ.: 60,000. Erika Mansourian, Features Editor. **Description:** Official journal for the sport of purebred dogs. Articles, 1,000-2,500 words, for serious breeders, exhibitors, and judges of purebred dogs; $250-$600. **Queries:** Preferred. **Payment:** On acceptance.

AMERICAN FIELD

American Field Publishing Co., 542 S Dearborn St., Suite 1350, Chicago, IL 60605. 312-663-9797. E-mail: amfieldedit@att.net. Website: www.americanfield.com. 50x/yr. $49/yr. Circ.: 8,000. B.J. Matthys, Managing Editor. **Description:** Short items and anecdotes on hunting dogs and field trials for bird dogs. Yarns on hunting trips, bird-shooting; articles, to 1,500 words, on dogs and field trials, emphasizing conservation of game resources. Pay varies. **Payment:** On acceptance.

AMERICAN TURF MONTHLY

All Star Sports, Inc., 299 East Shore Rd., Suite 204, Great Neck, NY 11023. 516-773-4075. E-mail: editor@americanturf.com. Website: www.americanturf.com. Monthly. $4.95/$42. Circ.: 30,000. James Corbett, Editor. **Description:** The nation's oldest magazine on Thoroughbred racing devoted to the handicapper and racing fan. Articles offer information on systems, angles, wagering strategies, money management, etc. Articles run 1,200-1,500 words; $75/published page. **Tips:** Only uses writers who are experienced with Thoroughbred racing. **Queries:** Preferred. **E-Queries:** Yes. **Unsolicited mss:** Accepts. **Freelance Content:** 50%. **Rights:** All. **Payment:** On publication.

ANIMAL FAIR

Animal Fair Media, P.O. Box 966, New York, NY 10018-0013. 212-629-0392. E-mail: editor@animalfair.com. Website: www.animalfair.com. Quarterly. $11.85/yr. Circ.: 200,000. Heather Klopfer, Managing Editor. **Description:** Lifestyle magazine for people who love animals. Topics include celebrities and their pets, grooming, health, nutrition, etc. **Tips:** "Please keep in mind that most of the magazine is published on the web as far as usage and style goes. If you have an article specifically for the website, contact us about that as well."

ANIMAL PEOPLE

P.O. Box 960, Clinton, WA 98236. 360-579-2505. E-mail: anmlpepl@whidbey.com. Website: www.animalpeoplenews.org. 10x/yr. Circ.: 15,000. Merritt Clifton, Editor. **Description:** Independent newspaper providing original investigative coverage of animal protection worldwide. Articles and profiles of individuals of positive accomplishment, in any capacity that benefits animals or illustrates the intrinsic value of other species. **Tips:** No fiction or poetry. No stories about atrocities, essays on why animals have rights, or material that promotes animal abuse (hunting, fishing, trapping, and slaughter). **Queries:** Preferred. **Payment:** On acceptance.

ANIMALS

Massachusetts Society for the Prevention of Cruelty to Animals, 350 S Huntington Ave., Boston, MA 02130. 617-522-7400. Website: www.mspca.org/animals. Quarterly. $15/yr. Circ.: 50,000. Paula Abend, Editor. **Description:** Informative, well-researched articles, to 2,500 words, on wildlife issues, pet-care topics, and animal protection concerns. **Columns, Departments:** Profiles, 800 words, on individuals who work to make life better for animals, wild or domestic, or to save habitat. Reviews, 300-500 words. **Tips:** "We do not accept personal accounts or favorite pet stories." **Queries:** Required. **E-Queries:** No. **Unsolicited mss:** Accepts. **Response:** 6 weeks. **SASE Required:** Yes. **Freelance Content:** 90%. **Payment:** On acceptance.

APPALOOSA JOURNAL

2720 W Pullman Rd., Moscow, ID 83843. 208-882-5578.
E-mail: journal@appaloosa.com. Website: www.appaloosajournal.com. Monthly. $29.95/yr. Circ.: 22,000. Robin Hendrickson, Editor. **Description:** Official publication of the Appaloosa Horse Club. Covers breeders, trainers, specific training methods, influential horses, youth and non-pro competitors, breed history, trail riding, and artists using Appaloosas as subjects; 1,000-2,000 words; pay varies.

AQUARIUM FISH

Bowtie, Inc., P.O. Box 6050, Mission Viejo, CA 92690. 949-855-8822. E-mail: aquariumfish@fancypubs.com. Website: www.aquariumfish.com. Monthly. Russ Case, Editor. **Description:** On all types of freshwater, saltwater, and pond fish. Articles (with or without color transparencies), 1,500-3,000 words; pay varies. **Tips:** No "pet fish" stories. Send SASE for guidelines. **E-Queries:** Yes. **Payment:** On publication.

THE BARK

2810 Eighth St., Berkeley, CA 94710. E-mail: bark@thebark.com. Website: www.the-bark.com. Quarterly. $15/yr. Circ.: 75,000. Claudia Kawczynska, Editor-in-Chief. **Description:** "We pay homage to the age-old relationship between our two species. We seek to bring our readers a literate and entertaining approach to dog-centric articles and stories." Short stories, essays, and articles run 1,200 words; pay varies. **Tips:** Essay tributes to dogs that have died are discouraged with the exception of tribute section on website. **Response:** 8-12 months. **Payment:** On publication.

BIRD TALK

Bowtie, Inc., P.O. Box 6050, Mission Viejo, CA 92690. 949-855-8822. E-mail: birdtalk@fancypubs.com. Website: www.animalnetwork.com/birds. Monthly. $29.79/yr. Circ.: 160,000. Melissa Kauffman, Editor. **Description:** For pet bird owners on care and feeding, training, safety, outstanding personal adventures, exotic birds in their native countries, profiles of celebrities' pet birds, travel to bird parks or shows. Pays to $.10/word. **Tips:** Good transparencies a plus. **Queries:** Required. **Payment:** On publication.

CALIFORNIA THOROUGHBRED MAGAZINE

California Thoroughbred Breeders Association, 201 Colorado Pl., Arcadia, CA 91007-2604. 626-445-7800. E-mail: ctbainfo@ctba.com. Website: www.ctba.com. Monthly. $45/yr. Circ.: 5,000. Doug Burge, Editor. **Description:** Features an animal husbandry and management series written each month by hands-on practitioners from across the state; veterinary topics and CTBA member profiles.

CAT FANCY

Bowtie, Inc., P.O. Box 6050, Mission Viejo, CA 92690. 949-855-8822. E-mail: letters@catfancy.com. Website: www.catfancy.com. Monthly. $25.97/yr. Circ.: 261,500. Bridget C. Johnson, Editor. **Description:** Covers cat care, health, and culture. Articles run 1,200-1,500 words; $200-$400. **Queries:** Required. **SASE Required:** Yes. **Payment:** On publication.

DOG FANCY

Bowtie, Inc., P.O. Box 6050, Mission Viejo, CA 92690-6050. 949-855-8822. E-mail: dogfancy@fancypubs.com. Website: www.dogfancy.com. Monthly. $27.97/yr. Circ.: 293,500. Allen Reznik, Editor-in-Chief. **Description:** Articles on dog care, health, behavior, grooming, breeds, activities, and events; 850-1,200 words; pay varies. **Tips:** No poetry, fiction, or articles in which the dog speaks as if human. Avoid tributes to dogs that have died or to beloved family pets. **Queries:** Required. **Unsolicited mss:** Does not accept. **Freelance Content:** 80%. **Payment:** On publication.

DOG WORLD

Bowtie, Inc., P.O. Box 6050, Mission Viejo, CA 92690-6050. 949-855-8822. E-mail: dogworld@fancypubs.com. Website: www.dogworldmag.com. Monthly. $28/yr. Circ.: 60,100. Maureen Kochan, Editor. **Description:** For breeders, exhibitors, hobbyists, and professionals in kennel operations, veterinary medical research, grooming, legislation, show awards, training and dog sports; 1,500-5,000 words; pay varies. **Tips:** Written for the serious enthusiast. Seeking in-depth science, training, and health stories. Publishes only one human-interest piece per issue. Does not accept poetry or fiction. **Queries:** Preferred. **E-Queries:** Yes. **Unsolicited mss:** Accepts. **Response:** 4-6 months. **SASE Required:** Yes. **Freelance Content:** 25%. **Rights:** FNAR. **Payment:** On publication.

DOGGONE NEWSLETTER

P.O. Box 19489, Boulder, CO 80308-2498. 303-449-2527. E-mail: roblipete@earthlink.net. Website: www.doggonefun.com. Bimonthly. $25/yr. Circ.: 2,000. Robyn Peters, Editor. **Description:** 16-page publication about fun places to go and cool things to do with dogs. Pieces run 300-800 words; $35-$80. **Tips:** "Our magazine is a must-have for people who can't leave home without the dog!" Avoid humorous articles or those written from the dog's point-of-view. Sample copy $5. **Queries:** Required. **Unsolicited mss:** Does not accept. **Response:** Queries 1 week. **SASE Required:** Yes. **Freelance Content:** 25%. **Payment:** On publication.

EQUUS

PRIMEDIA Enthusiast Group, 656 Quince Orchard Rd., Suite 600, Gaithersburg, MD 20878-1409. 301-977-3900. E-mail: equuslts@aol.com. Website: www.equusmagazine.com. Monthly. $24/yr. Circ.: 148,400. Laurie Prinz, Publisher/Editor. **Description:** On all breeds of horses, covering their health and care as well as the latest advances in equine medicine and research. Articles run 1,000-3,000 words; $100-$400. **Tips:** "Speak as one horseperson to another." **Payment:** On publication.

THE FLORIDA HORSE

Florida Thoroughbred Breeders and Owners Assn., 801 SW 60th Ave., Ocala, FL 34474. 352-732-8858. Website: www.thefloridahorse.com. Michael Compton, Editor. **Description:** On Florida thoroughbred breeding and racing. Also veterinary articles, financial articles, topics of general interest to horse owners and breeders. Articles run 1,500 words; $200-$300. **Queries:** Preferred. **Payment:** On publication.

FRESHWATER AND MARINE AQUARIUM

P.O. Box 487, Sierra Madre, CA 91025-0487. 626-355-6415. E-mail: famamag@aol.com. Website: www.mag-web.com. Monthly. $25/yr. Circ.: 53,000. Patricia Crews, Editor-in-Chief. **Description:** For tropical-fish enthusiasts. How-to articles, varying lengths, on basic, semi-technical, and technical aspects of freshwater and marine aquariology. Pays $50-$350.

GREYHOUND REVIEW

See full listing in Business category.

GUN DOG

PRIMEDIA Enthusiast Group, 6420 Wilshire Blvd., Suite 14, Los Angeles, CA 90048-5502. 323-782-2316. E-mail: gundog@primedia.com. Website: www.gundog-mag.com. Bimonthly. $24.97/yr. Circ.: 49,500. Rick Van Etten, Editor. **Description:** On bird hunting (how-tos, where-tos, dog training, canine medicine, breeding strategy). Also, some fiction and humor. Features, 1,000-2,500 words, with photos; $250-$550. **Payment:** On acceptance.

HORSE & RIDER

See full listing in Sports & Recreation/Outdoors category.

HORSE ILLUSTRATED

Bowtie, Inc., P.O. Box 6050, Mission Viejo, CA 92690. 949-855-8822. E-mail: horseillustrated@fancypubs.com. Website: www.horseillustrated.com. Monthly. $3.99/issue. Circ.: 200,000. Moira C. Harris, Editor. **Description:** For horse owners, covers all breeds, all disciplines. Also, medical care, training, grooming, how-to, and human interest. **Nonfiction:** How-to (horse care/owning horses), training (English and Western); to 2,000 words; $300-$400. **Fillers:** Humor, $50-$75. Cartoons and spot art, $40. **Art:** Illustrations, $100 and up. Photos (slides preferred), $60-$90, $200 for cover. **Tips:** "Our readers are mostly women, ages 18-40, who ride and show for pleasure and are concerned about well-being of their horses." **Queries:** Preferred. **E-Queries:** Yes. **Unsolicited mss:** Accepts. **Response:** 3-6 weeks. **SASE Required:** Yes. **Freelance Content:** 15-20%. **Rights:** FNAR. **Payment:** On publication.

THE HORSE: YOUR GUIDE TO EQUINE HEALTH CARE

The Blood-Horse, Inc., P.O. Box 4680, Lexington, KY 40544-4680. 859-278-2361. E-mail: editorial@thehorse.com. Website: www.thehorse.com. Monthly. $24. Circ.: 41,300. Christy West, Managing Editor. **Description:** Covers equine health for the professional, hands-on horse owner. Prefers "how-to" topics, technical topics, and topical interviews. No first person experiences. Articles run 500-5,000 words; $50-700. **Art:** Accepts color prints, 35mm, or any size transparency. Digital images must be formatted for MAC. Payment for images ranges from $35-350. Do not send originals. **Tips:** See website for calendar of upcoming topics. **Unsolicited mss:** Does not accept. **Rights:** FNAR and electronic. **Payment:** On acceptance.

THE HORSEMEN'S YANKEE PEDLAR

83 Leicester St., North Oxford, MA 01537. 508-987-5886. E-mail: editorial@pedlar.com. Website: www.pedlar.com. Monthly. $18/yr. Circ.: 25,000. Molly Johns, Editor. **Description:** About horses and horsemen in the Northeast. **Nonfiction:** News and feature-length articles, with photos; $.06/word. **Payment:** On publication.

HUNTER AND SPORT HORSE

Silver Square Tech, Inc., 12204 Covington Rd., Fort Wayne, IN 46814-9720. 260-625-4030. E-mail: hshhorse@aol.com. Website: www.hunterandsporthorsemag.com. Bimonthly. $21.95/yr. Circ.: 29,000. Laura Allen, Editor. **Description:** Exclusive editorial and news for the Dressage, Combined Training, and Hunter/Jumper sports. Includes interviews with trainers, judges, and riders in each sport and covers a wide range of interests: humor, opinion, news, products, training ideas, equine health, etc.

I LOVE CATS

16 Meadow Hill Ln., Armonk, NY 10504. 908-222-0990. E-mail: yankee@izzy.net. Website: www.iluvcats.com. Bimonthly. Circ.: 50,000. Lisa Allmendinger, Editor. **Description:** Publication all about cats. **Fiction:** 500-1,000 words. **Nonfiction:** Features, to 1,000 words; pays $40-$125. **Art:** $300 for cover, $50 for inside shots. **Tips:** "We're always on the lookout for interesting, cat-related stories." **Queries:** Preferred. **Payment:** On publication.

MUSHING

See full listing in Sports & Recreation/Outdoors category.

PERFORMANCE HORSE

2895 Chad Dr., P.O. Box 7426, Eugene, OR 97401. 541-341-6508. E-mail: betsy-lynch@performancehorse.com. Website: www.performancehorse.com. Monthly. $24.95/yr. Circ.: 18,000. Betsy Lynch, Editor. **Description:** Seeks to help high-level western performance horse breeders, owners, trainers and competitors to excel in the sports of cutting, reining, and working cow-horses. **Nonfiction:** Training, breeding, management, competitive strategies, how-to; for reining, cutting, and working cow-horse competition; 500-3,000 words; to $500. **Art:** Photos to accompany feature stories and articles; 35mm or larger prints or slides, or hi-res digital (RAW, TIFF, JPEG); pays up to $50. **Queries:** Preferred. **E-Queries:** Yes. **Unsolicited mss:** Accepts. **Response:** 4-6 weeks. **SASE Required:** Yes. **Freelance Content:** 80%. **Rights:** FNASR. **Payment:** On publication.

PET AGE

H.H. Backer Associates Inc., 200 S Michigan Ave., Suite 840, Chicago, IL 60604. 312-663-4040. E-mail: petage@hhbacker.com. Website: www.petage.com. Monthly. Circ.: 23,000. Karen Long MacLeod, Editor-in-Chief. **Description:** Publication for professionals involved in the business of pets and pet supplies. How-to articles on marketing animals and supplies in addition to industry trends and news. Articles run 1,500-2,200 words; $0.15/word. **Queries:** Preferred. **Freelance Content:** 90%. **Payment:** On acceptance.

PET BUSINESS

See full listing in Business category.

PETLIFE

Magnolia Media Group, 3451 Boston Ave., Fort Worth, TX 76116-6330. 817-560-6100. E-mail: awilson@mmgweb.com. Website: www.petlifeweb.com. Bimonthly. $19.99/yr. Circ.: 120,000. Alexis Wilson, Editor. **Description:** For pet owners and enthusiasts on pet health-care, nutrition, training, new products, humor, etc.; 100-

1,500 words; pay varies. **Tips:** "The majority of our audience is women, and they are truly pet lovers. We keep our stories positive—we're animal advocates, but we stay away from political issues. We seek ways to better care for animal companions; heartwarming stories about human/animal bond." **Queries:** Required. **E-Queries:** Yes. **Unsolicited mss:** Does not accept. **Response:** 3-4 weeks. **Freelance Content:** 80%. **Rights:** Worldwide. **Payment:** On publication.

PRACTICAL HORSEMAN
See full listing in Sports & Recreation/Outdoors category.

THE RETRIEVER JOURNAL
Village Press, Inc, 2779 Aero Park Dr., P.O. Box 968, Traverse City, MI 49685. 231-946-3712. E-mail: editor@villagepress.com. Website: www.retrieverjournal.com. Bimonthly. $25.95/yr. Circ.: 16,000. Steve Smith, Editor. **Description:** On topics of interest to hunting retriever owners and breeders. Articles, 1,500-2,200 words; $400 and up. **Queries:** Preferred.

TROPICAL FISH HOBBYIST
T.F.H. Publications, Inc., One TFH Plaza, 3rd & Union Avenues, Neptune City, NJ 07753. 732-988-8400. E-mail: editor@tfh.com. Website: www.tfh.com. Monthly. $4.95/issue. Circ.: 65,000. David Boruchowitz, Editor-in-Chief. **Description:** Covers tropical fish and aquariums. **Nonfiction:** For beginning and experienced tropical and marine fish enthusiasts; 2,500 words; $100-$250. **Fillers:** Cartoons (1/4 page vertical); $25. **Queries:** Not necessary. **E-Queries:** Yes. **Unsolicited mss:** Accepts. **Response:** 60 days. **SASE Required:** Yes. **Freelance Content:** 50%. **Rights:** All. **Payment:** On acceptance.

THE WESTERN HORSEMAN
Cowboy Publishing Group, P.O. Box 7980, Colorado Springs, CO 80933-7980. 719-633-5524. E-mail: edit@westernhorseman.com. Website: www.westernhorseman.com. Monthly. $22/yr. Circ.: 218,500. A.J. Mangum, Editor. **Description:** On the care and training of horses; farm, ranch, and stable management; health care and veterinary medicine. Articles run 1,500 words, pays to $800. Include photos with submission. **Payment:** On acceptance.

YOUNG RIDER
See full listing in Juvenile category.

ARTS & ARCHITECTURE
(For music, dance, etc., see Performing Arts)

AIRBRUSH ACTION
See full listing in Hobbies, Crafts, Collecting category.

THE AMERICAN ART JOURNAL
Kennedy Galleries, Inc., 730 Fifth Ave., New York, NY 10019-4105. 212-541-9600. E-mail: aaj@kgny.com. Website: www.kgny.com. Annual. $35.00/issue. Circ.: 2,000. Jayne A. Kuchna, Editor in Chief. **Description:** American art of 17th through mid-20th centuries. **Nonfiction:** Scholarly articles; 2,000-10,000 words; $200-$500. **Payment:** On acceptance.

AMERICAN INDIAN ART
7314 E Osborn Dr., Scottsdale, AZ 85251-6401. 480-994-5445. Quarterly. $20/yr. Circ.: 25,000. Roanne P. Goldfein, Editorial Director. **Description:** Detailed articles on American Indian arts: painting, carving, beadwork, basketry, textiles, ceramics, jewelry, etc. Articles run 6,000-7,000 words; pay varies. **Queries:** Preferred. **Response:** 6 weeks. **Rights:** FNAR. **Payment:** On publication.

ARCHITECTURE
VNU Business Media, 770 Broadway, New York, NY 10003-9522. 646-654-5766. E-mail: info@architecturemag.com. Website: www.architecturemag.com. Monthly. $42/yr. Circ.: 67,000. C.C. Sullivan, Editor-in-Chief. **Description:** On architectural design, technology, and professional and technical issues. Articles to 2,000 words; $.50/word. **Queries:** Preferred.

ART & ANTIQUES
Trans World Publishing, Inc., 2100 Powers Ferry Rd., Atlanta, GA 30339. 770-955-5656. E-mail: editor@artantiquesmag.com. Website: www.artandantiques.net. 11x/yr. $5/$39.95. Circ.: 150,000. Barbara S. Tapp, Editor-in-Chief. **Description:** For lovers of fine art and antiques. **Nonfiction:** Research articles, art and antiques in context (interiors), overviews, personal narratives; 150-1,200 words; $1/word. **Tips:** Query with resumé and clips. **Queries:** Preferred. **E-Queries:** Yes. **Unsolicited mss:** Accepts. **Response:** 1-2 months. **Freelance Content:** 80%. **Payment:** On acceptance. **Contact:** Patti Verbanas, Managing Editor.

ART PAPERS
Atlanta Art Papers, Inc., P.O. Box 5748, Atlanta, GA 31107-5748. E-mail: editor@artpapers.org. Website: www.artpapers.org. 6x/yr. $7/$35. Circ.: 20,000. Charles Reeve, Ph.D., Editor-in-Chief. **Description:** Southeastern review of regional, national, and international contemporary art. **Nonfiction:** In-depth analyses, readable by the general public, of recent art. Accepts discussions or profiles of individual artists, as well as observations of recent trends; 2,500-3,000 words; $200. Also accepts exhibition reviews; 600-800 words; $40. **Columns, Departments:** Artist profiles, career advice, collector profiles, book reviews, music news, etc. 1,100 words; $100. **Tips:** "Review section emphasizes (but is not limited to) important regional artists who have not found national/international audience." **Queries:** Preferred. **E-Queries:** Yes. **Unsolicited mss:** Accepts. **Response:** 1 month. **SASE Required:** Yes. **Freelance Content:** 95%. **Payment:** 30 days after publication.

ART-TALK

Dandick Company, 4243 N Brown Ave., Scottdale, AZ 85251-3913. 480-948-1799.
E-mail: arttalked@hotmail.com. 9x/yr. $18. Circ.: 40,000. Paul Soderberg, Editor.
Description: Publication for collectors of fine art. Open to articles and fillers; pay
varies. **Payment:** On acceptance.

THE ARTIST'S MAGAZINE

F&W Publications, Inc., 4700 E Galbraith Rd., Cincinnati, OH 45236. 513-531-2690.
E-mail: tamedit@fwpubs.com. Website: www.artistsmagazine.com. Monthly. $27/yr.
Circ.: 195,000. Sandra Carpenter, Editor. **Description:** Written by artists for artists.
Offers instruction for professional success, on painting techniques, media and mate-
rials, design and composition, problem solving, special effects, marketing, and other
business topics. **Tips:** "Best opportunities include: Artist's Life and Business columns.
Writers must be able to write from the artist's viewpoint, using the language of art."
Queries: Preferred. **E-Queries:** No. **Unsolicited mss:** Accepts. **Response:** 90
days. **SASE Required:** Yes. **Freelance Content:** 80%. **Rights:** FNASR. **Payment:**
On publication. **Contact:** Tom Zeit, Senior Editor.

BLACKLINES

2011 Newkirk Ave., Suite 7D, Brooklyn, NY 11226-7423. 718-703-8000. Website:
www.blacklines.net. Quarterly. $32/yr. Circ.: 10,000. Atim Annette Oton, Editor.
Description: Showcases black designers in architecture, interior design, construction, development and the arts. Challenges traditional ideas and perceptions, offers
context for design and means to exchange ideas and information. **Tips:** Send cover
letter and resumé, with 2-5 clips that show ability to interview diverse subjects.
Queries: Preferred. **E-Queries:** Yes. **Unsolicited mss:** Accepts.

CAMERA ARTS

P.O. Box 2328, Corrales, NM 87048-2328. 505-899-8054.
E-mail: camartsmag@aol.com. Website: www.cameraarts.com. Bimonthly. Circ.:
18,000. Tim Anderson, Managing Editor. **Description:** The art and craft of photography in the 21st century. Articles run 1,000-2,000 words; $.25/word. **Tips:** "Before
you write about a photographer, send us a query with samples of his/her artwork first.
If you are a new writer, please send us samples or clips of previous pieces you have
written." **Queries:** Required. **E-Queries:** Yes. **Unsolicited mss:** Accepts.
Response: 2-8 weeks. **SASE Required:** Yes. **Freelance Content:** 80%. **Rights:**
FNAR. **Payment:** On publication.

CLAY TIMES

P.O. Box 365, Waterford, VA 20197. 540-882-3576. E-mail: claytimes@aol.com.
Website: www.claytimes.com. Bimonthly. $5.95/$26. Circ.: 20,000. **Description:**
Pottery information for students, teachers, professionals, and hobbyists. Seeks features on wheel-throwing, handbuilding, glazing, firing, marketing, health/safety, artist
profiles, and how-to, practical application articles with step-by-step instructions;
1,000-1,500 words; pays $75. **Art:** Submit high-quality artwork/photos with how-to

articles. Photos should illustrate a series of steps. **Tips:** "All submissions should be targeted at clay artists of all levels. Assume the reader has no knowledge of the topic you are writing about." **Queries:** Preferred. **E-Queries:** Yes. **Unsolicited mss:** Accepts. **Response:** 1 month. **SASE Required:** Yes. **Freelance Content:** 80%. **Rights:** Exclusive. **Payment:** On publication. **Contact:** Assistant Editor.

THE COMICS JOURNAL

Fantagraphics Books, Inc., 7563 Lake City Way NE, Seattle, WA 98115-4218. 206-524-1967. E-mail: tcjnews@tcj.com. Website: www.tcj.com. Monthly. $50/yr. Circ.: 9,000. Gary Groth, Editor-in-Chief. **Description:** Covers the comics medium as an art form. An eclectic mix of industry news, interviews, criticism, and reviews. Articles run 200-2,000 words; $.04/word. **Queries:** Preferred. **E-Queries:** Yes. **Unsolicited mss:** Accepts. **Response:** 1-2 months. **SASE Required:** Yes. **Freelance Content:** 95%. **Payment:** On publication.

CONTEMPORARY STONE & TILE DESIGN

Business News Publishing , 210 Route 4 East, Suite 311, Paramus, NJ 07652. 201-291-9001. E-mail: michael@stoneworld.com. Website: www.stoneworld.com. Quarterly. $29.95/yr. Circ.: 15,000. Michael Reis, Editor Director/Associate Publisher. **Description:** On using stone in architecture and interior design. Articles, 1,500 words; $6/column inch. **Art:** Photos or drawings. **Payment:** On publication.

DECORATIVE ARTIST'S WORKBOOK

See full listing in Hobbies, Crafts, Collecting category.

DOUBLETAKE

55 Davis Square, Somerville, MA 02144. 617-591-9389. E-mail: dtmag@doubletakemagazine.org. Website: www.doubletakemagazine.org. Quarterly. $32/yr. Circ.: 40,000. Robert Coles, Editor. **Description:** Fiction, poetry, and photography devoted to revealing "extraordinary events and qualities found in everyday life." **Fiction:** Realistic fiction in all its variety. **Nonfiction:** Narrative reporting or personal essays distinguished by documentary, literary, aesthetic, or reportorial excellence. **Queries:** Not necessary. **E-Queries:** No. **Unsolicited mss:** Accepts. **Response:** 3 months. **SASE Required:** Yes. **Freelance Content:** 90%. **Rights:** 1st worldwide English-language serial. **Payment:** On publication.

FIBERARTS

See full listing in Hobbies, Crafts, Collecting category.

PHOTO LIFE

Apex Publications, Inc., One Dundas St. W, Suite 2500, Toronto, Ontario M5G 1Z3 Canada. 418-692-2110. E-mail: editor@photolife.com. Website: www.photolife.com. 6x/yr. $26/yr. Circ.: 55,000. Darwin Wiggett, Anita Dammer, Editors. **Description:** The art, culture, and science of photography. Covers photo techniques, trade information, new equipment, technology, etc. **Tips:** "Writers can break into our market by providing high-quality photography with articles. Our general theme is promoting photography as a universal language—a higher form of self-expression." **Queries:** Preferred. **E-Queries:** Yes. **Unsolicited mss:** Does not accept. **Response:** 1-2 months. **SASE Required:** Yes. **Freelance Content:** 100%. **Rights:** FNAR. **Payment:** On publication. **Contact:** Nicole Richard, Assistant Editor.

POPULAR PHOTOGRAPHY & IMAGING

Hachette Filipacchi Media U.S., Inc., 1633 Broadway, Fl. 43, New York, NY 10019. 212-767-6000. E-mail: popeditor@aol.com. Website: www.popphoto.com. Monthly. $19.94/yr. Circ.: 451,700. John Owens, Editor-in-Chief. **Description:** For serious amateur photographers. Illustrated how-to articles, 500-2,000 words. **Art:** With all photos, submit technical data (camera used, lens, film, shutter speed, aperture, lighting, etc.) to show how picture was made. **Tips:** "We're interested in new, unusual phases of photography not covered previously. No general articles." **Queries:** Required. **Payment:** On acceptance.

PROFESSIONAL PHOTOGRAPHER

Professional Photographers of America, Inc., 229 Peachtree St. NE, Suite 2200 International Tower, Atlanta, GA 30303. 404-522-8600. Website: www.ppmag.com. Monthly. $27/yr. Circ.: 26,000. Cameron Bishopp, Executive Editor. **Description:** Magazine for professional photographers engaged in all types of photography.

SCULPTURE MAGAZINE

International Sculpture Center, 1529 18th St. NW, Washington, DC 20036-1358. 202-234-0555. E-mail: isc@sculpture.org. Website: www.sculpture.org. Monthly. $50/yr. Circ.: 25,000. Glenn Harper, Editor. **Description:** On sculpture, sculptors, collections, books, criticism, technical processes, etc. Pay varies. **Queries:** Preferred. **Unsolicited mss:** Accepts.

SOUTHWEST ART

Active Interest Media, Inc., 5444 Westheimer, Suite 1440, Houston, TX 77056. 713-296-7900. E-mail: southwestart@southwestart.com. Website: www.southwestart.com. Monthly. $5.99/$32.00. Circ.: 65,000. Kristin Bucher, Editor. **Description:** For collectors of Western art (about the West or created, exhibited, or sold in the West). Articles, 1,400 words, on artists, collectors, exhibitions, events, dealers, history, trends in Western American art. Most interested in representational or figurative arts. Pay varies. **Queries:** Preferred. **E-Queries:** No. **Unsolicited mss:** Accepts. **Response:** 4 months. **SASE Required:** Yes. **Freelance Content:** 70%. **Rights:** Exclusive worldwide. **Payment:** On acceptance.

SUNSHINE ARTIST MAGAZINE

Palm House Publishing Co., 3210 Dade Ave., Orlando , FL 32804. 407-228-9772. E-mail: editor@sunshineartist.com. Website: www.sunshineartist.com. Monthly. $34.95/yr. Circ.: 20,000. Bill Sievert, Editor. **Description:** Covers national outdoor art shows, fairs, festivals. Business, education, and art-show focus. **E-Queries:** Yes.

WATERCOLOR
VNU Business Media, 770 Broadway, New York, NY 10003-9522. 646-654-5506. E-mail: mail@myamericanartist.com. Website: www.myamericanartist.com. Quarterly. $23.95/yr. Circ.: 80,000. M. Stephen Doherty, Editor-in-chief. **Description:** Features and articles on watercolor and other water media (gouache, casein, acrylic, etc.). Length and pay varies. **Queries:** Preferred. **Payment:** On publication.

WEST ART
P.O. Box 6868, Auburn, CA 95604-6868. 530-885-0969. Monthly. $16/yr. Circ.: 4,000. Martha Garcia, Editor. **Description:** Tabloid magazine featuring fine arts and crafts (no hobbies). Features run 700-800 words; $.50/column inch. **Queries:** Preferred. **Rights:** All. **Payment:** On publication.

ASSOCIATIONS

AOPA PILOT
See full listing in Aviation category.

CATHOLIC FORESTER
355 Shuman Blvd., P.O. Box 3012, Naperville, IL 60566-7012. 630-983-4900.
E-mail: pbarow@catholicforester.com. Website: www.catholicforester.com.
Quarterly. Circ.: 97,000. Mary Anne File, Editor. **Description:** Full-color, with organizational news, general interest, fiction, and some nonfiction articles for members. **Fiction:** Humor, children, inspirational; 500-1,500 words; $.30/word. **Nonfiction:** Health, fitness, parenting, financial; 500-1,500 words; $.30/word. **Poetry:** Inspirational, religious; 25-50 words; $.30/word. **Queries:** Does Not Accept. **Unsolicited mss:** Accepts. **Response:** 12 weeks. **SASE Required:** Yes. **Freelance Content:** 20%. **Rights:** FNAR. **Payment:** On acceptance. **Contact:** Patricia Baron, Associate Editor.

COLUMBIA
Knights of Columbus, 1 Columbus Plaza, New Haven, CT 06510. 203-752-4398. E-mail: tim.hickey@kofc.org. Website: www.kofc.org. Monthly. $6/yr. Circ.: 1,600,000. Tim S. Hickey, Editor. **Description:** On topics of interest to Knights of Columbus members, their families, and the Catholic layman. Current events, religion, education, art, societal trends, parenting/family life, finances, and Catholic practice and teachings; 500-1,500 words; to $600. **Tips:** Sample copies and guidelines available. **Queries:** Required. **E-Queries:** Yes. **Response:** 2 weeks. **SASE Required:** Yes. **Freelance Content:** 80%. **Payment:** On acceptance.

ELKS
BPO Elks of the USA, 425 West Diversey Parkway, Chicago, IL 60614. 773-755-4900. E-mail: elksmag@elks.org. Website: www.elks.org/elksmag/. 10x/yr. Circ.: 1,100,000. Fred D. Oakes, Editor. **Description:** General interest magazine pub-

lished by the Elks fraternal organization. Typical reader is over 40 with an above-average income and living in a town of 500,000 or less. **Nonfiction:** Authoritative articles (please include sources) for lay person, varied topics: technology, science, sports, history, seasonal. Accepts material related to membership or lodge events; 1,500-2,500 words; $.20/word. **Art:** Cover art; slides, transparencies; $25 per photo. **Tips:** No fiction, travel, business, health, political or religious material, humor, fillers, or poetry. Do not send queries or clips. **Queries:** Does Not Accept. **E-Queries:** No. **Unsolicited mss:** Accepts. **Response:** 1-6 weeks. **SASE Required:** Yes. **Freelance Content:** 30%. **Rights:** FNASR. **Payment:** On acceptance.

HARVARD MAGAZINE

7 Ware St., Cambridge, MA 02138-4037. 617-495-5746.
Website: www.harvardmagazine.com. Bimonthly. $4.95/$30. Circ.: 225,000. John Rosenberg, Editor. **Description:** Articles and profiles on Harvard faculty, staff, students, and alumni. Also, features on research and teaching being conducted in this educational community. **Nonfiction:** Profiles and examples of work and research; 800-10,000 words; $300-$2,000. **Queries:** Required. **E-Queries:** Yes. **Unsolicited mss:** Accepts. **Response:** 1-2 weeks. **SASE Required:** Yes. **Freelance Content:** 50%. **Rights:** One-time. **Payment:** On publication.

KIWANIS

KIWANIS International, 3636 Woodview Trace, Indianapolis, IN 46268-3196. 317-875-8755. E-mail: jbrockley@kiwanis.org. Website: www.kiwanis.org. 10x/yr. $2/issue. Circ.: 240,000. Jack Brockley, Managing Editor. **Description:** Service organization that supports children and young adults around the world. Articles focus on a variety of topics including, family life, small business, international issues, community concerns, health/fitness, and the needs of children (especially under age 6); 1,500-2,000 words; $400-$1,000. No travel pieces, interviews, or profiles. **Tips:** Read sample copy before submitting. "We consider submissions based on two criteria: 1) They should have an overall subject or scope, versus relating to a specific individual, place, or event. 2) They should be applicable to the lives of KIWANIS members and readers." **Queries:** Preferred. **E-Queries:** Yes. **Unsolicited mss:** Accepts. **Response:** 2-4 weeks. **SASE Required:** Yes. **Freelance Content:** 40%. **Rights:** FNAR. **Payment:** On acceptance.

THE LION

300 W 22nd St., Oak Brook, IL 60523-8842. 630-571-5466. E-mail: rkleinfe@lionsclubs.org. Website: www.lionsclubs.org. 10x/yr. $6/issue. Circ.: 510,000. Robert Kleinfelder, Senior Editor. **Description:** Published by Lions Clubs International, reflecting service activities for men and women interested in voluntary community service. **Nonfiction:** Primarily photo stories of Lion's service activities; 300-2,000 words; $300-$700. **Fillers:** Family-oriented humor; 500-1,000 words; $300-$500. **Tips:** No political, religious, or autobiographical topics. **Queries:** Preferred. **E-Queries:** Yes. **Unsolicited mss:** Accepts. **Response:** 1-3 weeks. **SASE Required:** Yes. **Freelance Content:** 20%. **Rights:** All. **Payment:** On acceptance.

MANAGERS REPORT

Advantage Publishing Co., Inc., 1000 Nix Rd., Little Rock, AR 72211. E-mail: info@managersreport.com. Website: www.managersreport.com. Monthly. $18/yr. Circ.: 11,000. Lisa Pinder, Executive Editor. **Description:** For managers and board members of condominiums, homeowners associations, coops and community associations. Motto is "Helping Community Associations Help Each Other." **Nonfiction:** Prefers how-to format, featuring readers and how they resolved problems in their communities. Length varies; $25-$150. **Art:** Prefers photos to accompany all stories; $10. **Tips:** Welcomes new writers. **Queries:** Preferred. **E-Queries:** Yes. **Unsolicited mss:** Accepts. **SASE Required:** Yes. **Freelance Content:** 40%. **Rights:** FNAR. **Payment:** On acceptance.

THE MODERN WOODMEN MAGAZINE

Modern Woodmen of America, P.O. Box 2005, Rock Island, IL 61204-2005. 309-786-6481. Website: www.modern-woodmen.org. Quarterly. Circ.: 400,000. Jill Weaver, Editor. **Description:** Publication for members of Modern Woodmen of America, a fraternal benefit society offering financial services. **Fiction:** Stories that promote family, patriotism, and volunteerism; 1,000 words; $100-$500. **Nonfiction:** Articles on postive family and community life, community service, patriotism, and financial well-being; 1,000 words; $100-$500. **Tips:** Readers mostly middle-class, with kids at home. **Queries:** Not necessary. **E-Queries:** No. **Response:** 4-8 weeks. **Freelance Content:** Less than 5%. **Rights:** One-time. **Payment:** On acceptance. **Contact:** Sharon Snawerdt, Assistant Editor.

NARFE

See full listing in Seniors Magazines category.

THE ROTARIAN

Rotary International, 1560 Sherman Ave., Evanston, IL 60201-4818. 847-866-3000. Website: www.rotary.org. $12/yr. Circ.: 510,000. Vince Aversano, Editor-in-Chief. **Description:** Monthly publication for Rotary members covering international understanding, goodwill and peace, vocational relationships, community life, human relationships, etc. **Queries:** Preferred. **Unsolicited mss:** Accepts. **Contact:** Janice Chambers, Managing Editor.

SCOUTING

Boys Scouts of America, 1325 W Walnut Hill Ln., P.O. Box 152079, Irving, TX 75015-2079. 972-580-2367. Website: www.scoutingmagazine.org. 6x/yr. **Description:** Covers successful program activities conducted by or for Cub Scout packs, Boy Scout troops, and Venturing crews. Also includes features on winning leadership techniques/styles, profiles of outstanding individual leaders, and first-person inspirational accounts of Scouting's impact on an individual, either as a youth or while serving as a volunteer adult leader. **Nonfiction:** Short features, 500-700 words, $300-$700; longer features, up to 1,200 words, $650-$1,000. **Tips:** "Most stories are staff-written or assigned to professional writers. We rely heavily on regional writers to cover an event or activity in a particular part of the country." No fiction or poetry. **Queries:** Required. **Unsolicited mss:** Accepts. **Response:** 3-6 weeks. **SASE Required:** Yes. **Rights:** FNAR. **Payment:** On acceptance for major features; on publication for some unsolicited short features.

THE TOASTMASTER
Toastmasters International, P.O. Box 9052, Mission Viejo, CA 92690-9052. 949-858-8255. E-mail: pubs@toastmasters.org. Website: www.toastmasters.org. Monthly. Circ.: 200,000. Suzanne Frey, Editor. **Description:** On public speaking, leadership, and communication skills. **Nonfiction:** Articles on decision making, leadership, language, interpersonal and professional communication, humor, logical thinking, rhetorical devices, public speaking, profiles of great orators, etc. Payment negotiable upon acceptance; 700-2,200 words. **Tips:** Do not send unsolicited manuscripts via e-mail. **Queries:** Preferred. **E-Queries:** Yes. **Unsolicited mss:** Accepts. **Response:** 3-4 months. **Rights:** varies. **Payment:** On acceptance.

VFW
406 W 34th St., Kansas City, MO 64111. 816-756-3390. E-mail: jcarter@vfw.org. Website: www.vfw.org. Monthly. $15/yr. Circ.: 1,800,000. Richard K. Kolb, Editor. **Description:** Publication focusing on military history and issues relating to veterans and the military. **Nonfiction:** Articles on current foreign policy and defense, along with all veterans' issues; 1,000 words. **Tips:** "Write with clarity and simplicity. Use concrete details and short paragraphs. Use active voice, and avoid flowery prose and military jargon." **Queries:** Preferred. **Unsolicited mss:** Accepts. **Rights:** FNASR. **Payment:** On publication.

WOODMEN
Omaha Woodmen Life Ins. Society, 1700 Farnam St., Omaha, NE 68102. 402-342-1890. E-mail: service@woodmen.com. Website: www.woodmen.com. Billie Jo Faust, Assitant Editor. **Description:** Publication with focus on history, insurance, family, health, science, fraternal lodge activities, etc. Payment negotiable. **Queries:** Preferred. **Payment:** On acceptance.

AUTOMOTIVE

AMERICAN MOTORCYCLIST
13515 Yarmouth Dr., Pickerington, OH 43147. 614-856-1900. E-mail: ama@ama-cycle.org. Website: www.amadirectlink.com. Monthly. $10/yr. Circ.: 245,700. Bill Wood, Managing Editor. **Description:** News, personalities, tours, and events for members of the American Motorcyclist Assn. **Queries:** Preferred. **SASE Required:** Yes. **Payment:** On publication.

AUTO REVISTA

14330 Midway Rd., Suite 202, Dallas, TX 75244-3514. 972-386-0120. E-mail: info@autorevista.com. Website: www.autorevista.com. Weekly. Circ.: 40,000. Kevin Kelly, Editor. **Description:** Free weekly bilingual automotive newspaper.

AUTOMOBILE QUARTERLY

137 E Market St., New Albany, IN 47150. E-mail: editor@autoquarterly.com. Website: www.autoquarterly.com. Quarterly. Mr. Tracy Powell, Managing Editor. **Description:** Journal of automotive history targeting serious enthusiasts and collectors. **Tips:** Prefers hard copy of query with clips. "Please study back issues for desired style and required depth before querying. *AQ* does not repeat specific marque treatments, so studying previous coverage is important." Sample copy $10. **Queries:** Required. **E-Queries:** Yes. **Freelance Content:** 85%.

AUTOMUNDO

2960 SW Eighth St., Fl. 2, Miami, FL 33135. 305-541-4198. E-mail: editor@automundo.com. Website: www.automundo.com. Monthly. $19.95/yr. Circ.: 50,000. Carlos Guzman, Editor. **Description:** Spanish-language publication for auto fans. Articles on makes, models, scenic drives, the latest technology and more.

CAR AND DRIVER

Hachette Filipacchi Media US, Inc., 2002 Hogback Rd., Ann Arbor, MI 48105-9795. 734-971-3600. E-mail: editors@caranddriver.com; spence1cd@aol.com. Website: www.caranddriver.com. Monthly. $21.94/yr. Circ.: 1,300,000. Csaba Csere, Editor-in-Chief. **Description:** "We're mostly staff-written, but always looking for feature writers for non-product pieces—profiles, weird events, little-known historical pieces on auto related subjects." Articles run 2,500 words max. **Tips:** Send query with two clips. **E-Queries:** Yes. **Unsolicited mss:** Does not accept. **Freelance Content:** 5%. **Payment:** On acceptance. **Contact:** Steve Spence, Managing Editor.

CAR CRAFT

PRIMEDIA Enthusiast Group, 6420 Wilshire Blvd., Fl. 10, Los Angeles, CA 90048-5502. 323-782-2000. E-mail: carcraft@primedia.com. Website: www.carcraft.com. Monthly. $19.94/yr. Circ.: 325,000. Terry McGean, Executive Editor. **Description:** Covers high-performance street machines, drag cars, and racing events. Also includes technical pieces and action photos. **Payment:** On publication.

CORVETTE FEVER

PRIMEDIA Enthusiast Group, 6420 Wilshire Blvd., Los Angeles, CA 90048. 661-799-9379. E-mail: cam.benty@primedia.com. Monthly. $3.99/issue. Circ.: 60,000. Cameron Benty, Editor. **Description:** Corvette enthusiast magazine with technical features, vehicle features, personality profiles of significant historical people; 1,500 words; $200/page. **Tips:** "Read the magazine. Submit appropriate queries." **Queries:** Required. **E-Queries:** Yes. **Response:** 6 weeks. **SASE Required:** Yes. **Freelance Content:** 40%. **Rights:** All. **Payment:** On publication.

CYCLE WORLD

Media U.S., Inc., 1499 Monrovia Ave., Newport Beach, CA 92663-2752. 949-720-5300. E-mail: dedwards@hfmus.com. Website: www.cycleworld.com. Monthly. $21.94/yr. Circ.: 325,000. David Edwards, Editor-in-Chief. **Description:** News items on the motorcycle industry, legislation, and trends. Technical and feature articles for motorcycle enthusiasts; 1,500-2,500 words; $100-$200/page. **Queries:** Preferred. **Payment:** On publication.

EASYRIDERS

Paisano Publications, LLC, P.O. Box 3000, Agoura Hills, CA 91376-3000. 818-889-8740. Website: www.easyriders.com. Monthly. $39.95. Circ.: 227,700. Dave Nichols, Editor. **Description:** Hard-hitting, rugged fiction, 1,200-2,000 words, that depicts bikers in a favorable light; humorous bent preferred. Pays $.10-$.25/word. **Payment:** On acceptance.

HOT BIKE

PRIMEDIA Enthusiast Group, 2400 E Katella Ave., Fl. 11, Anaheim, CA 92806. 714-939-2400. E-mail: hot.bike@primedia.com. Website: www.hotbikeweb.com. Monthly. $20.95/yr. Circ.: 57,000. Howard Kelly, Editor. **Description:** Magazine on Harley-Davidson motorcycles (contemporary and antique). Features event coverage on high-performance street and track and sport touring motorcycles; 250-2,500 words; $50-$100/printed page.

HOT ROD MAGAZINE

PRIMEDIA Enthusiast Group, 6420 Wilshire Blvd., Fl. 10, Los Angeles, CA 90048-5502. 323-782-2000. E-mail: hotrod@primedia.com. Website: www.hotrod.com. Monthly. $23.94/yr. Circ.: 709,200. David Freiburger, Editor-in-Chief. **Description:** For automotive enthusiasts on street machines, rods, customs, engine buildups, nostalgia, track and drag racing, trends, etc. **Tips:** "Our freelance content is limited. Writers need either a deep sense of automotive history or hands-on technical know-how." **Queries:** Required. **E-Queries:** Yes. **Unsolicited mss:** Accepts. **SASE Required:** Yes. **Freelance Content:** 10%. **Rights:** All.

MOTOR TREND PRIMEDIA

Enthusiast Group, 6420 Wilshire Blvd., Los Angeles, CA 90048-5515. 323-782-2220. E-mail: motortrend@primedia.com. Website: www.motortrend.com. Monthly. $23.94/yr. Circ.: 1,285,000. Kevin Smith, Editor. **Description:** On autos, auto history, racing, events, and profiles. Articles, 250-2,000 words, photos required; pay varies. **Queries:** Preferred. **Payment:** On acceptance.

MOTORCYCLIST

PRIMEDIA Enthusiast Group, 6420 Wilshire Blvd., Fl. 17, Los Angeles, CA 90048. 323-782-2230. E-mail: mcmail@primediacmmg.com. Website: www.motorcycliston-line.com. Monthly. $11.97/yr. Circ.: 242,000. Mitch Boehm, Editor-in-Chief. **Description:** In-depth information for motorcycle enthusiasts. Includes technical how-to stories, riding tips, gear information, motorcycle tests and useful bike-buying advice. Seeks to help readers maximize their riding experience.

OLD CARS WEEKLY

Krause Publications, Inc., 700 E State St., Iola, WI 54990. 715-445-4612. E-mail: vanbogarta@krause.com. Website: www.oldcarsweekly.com. Weekly. $39.98/yr. Circ.: 76,700. Angelo Van Bogart, Associate Editor. **Description:** On the hobby of collectible cars and trucks (restoration, researching, company histories, collector profiles, toys, etc.). **Nonfiction:** Features, to 2,000 words; pays $.03/word. **Art:** Photos to accompany articles; $5/photo. **Queries:** Preferred.

RIDER

Affinity Group, Inc., 2575 Vista Del Mar Dr., Ventura, CA 93001-3920. 805-667-4100. Website: www.riderreport.com. Monthly. $11.98/yr. Circ.: 140,000. Mark Tuttle Jr., Editor. **Description:** Covers travel, touring, commuting, and camping motorcyclists. Articles to 2,000 words; $100-$750. **Tips:** Editorial guidelines available upon request. **Queries:** Required. **SASE Required:** Yes. **Payment:** On publication.

STOCK CAR RACING MAGAZINE

PRIMEDIA Enthusiast Group, 3816 Industry Blvd., Lakeland, FL 33811-1340. 863-644-0449. E-mail: scrbackfire@primedia.com. Website: www.stockcarracing.com. Monthly. $12/yr. Circ.: 257,296. Larry Cothren, Editor. **Description:** For oval-track enthusiasts. Features technical automotive pieces as well as profiles of interesting NASCAR racing personalities. Articles on stock car drivers, races and vehicles; up to 6,000 words; pay varies.

WOMAN RIDER MAGAZINE

Ehlert Publishing Group, 6420 Sycamore Ln., Suite 100, Maple Grove, MN 55369. 763-383-4400. E-mail: womanrider1@aol.com. Website: www.riderreport.com. Quarterly. $11.95/yr. Circ.: 40,000. Genevieve Schmitt, Editor. **Description:** National motorcycle magazine aimed at women. Focus is on the lifestyle side of motorcycling from a female point-of-view. **Tips:** Seeks people who are motorcylist journalists who can write a mostly third person point of view. First person stories are rarely used. Submit query with bio. **Queries:** Required.

AVIATION

AIR LINE PILOT

Air Line Pilots Assn., P.O. Box 1169, Herndon, VA 20172-1169. 703-481-4460. E-mail: magazine@alpa.org. Website: www.alpa.org. 10x/yr. $32/yr. Circ.: 70,000. J. Gary DiNunno, Editor-in-Chief. **Description:** Industry news, air safety, technology, training, health issues, and other topics related to the piloting profession; 2,000-6,000 words; $200-$600. **Tips:** "Our readers are professional airline pilots and the magazine reflects their interests, concerns, and labor union policies. Therefore our editorial content requires accuracy, knowledge, and an extensive background in piloting." **Queries:** Preferred. **E-Queries:** Yes. **Unsolicited mss:** Accepts. **Response:** 1-2 weeks. **Freelance Content:** 20%. **Rights:** All. **Payment:** On acceptance.

AOPA PILOT
Aircraft Owners and Pilots Assn., 421 Aviation Way, Frederick, MD 21701. 301-695-2350. E-mail: pilot@aopa.org. Website: www.aopa.org. Monthly. $5/issue. Circ.: 400,000. Thomas B. Haines, Editor. **Description:** Nation's leading general aviation magazine. Department and features for private aircraft owners and pilots. Length varies, usually 1,000-1,500 words. **Tips:** Include telephone and/or fax numbers, and your AOPA membership number with all submissions. Do not send orignal art or manuscripts. "We're looking for articles relating to personal flight stories in which a lesson was learned, personal profiles of pilots, and pieces that depict an adventurous destination. Emphasis on aeronautical themes is preferred. **Queries:** Preferred. **E-Queries:** No. **Unsolicited mss:** Accepts. **Payment:** On publication.

AVIATION HISTORY
PRIMEDIA Enthusiast Group, 741 Miller Dr. SE, Suite D-2, Leesburg, VA 20175-8994. 703-771-9400. E-mail: aviationhistory@thehistorynet.com. Website: www.the-historynet.com/aviationhistory. Bimonthly. $23.95/yr. Circ.: 62,500. Arthur H. Sanfelici, Editor. **Description:** On aeronautical history. Submit articles, 3,500-4,000 words, with 500-word sidebars and excellent illustrations. **Queries:** Preferred. **Payment:** On publication.

BUSINESS & COMMERCIAL AVIATION
See full listing in Trade & Technical category.

FLIGHT JOURNAL
Air Age Publishing, 100 E Ridge Rd., Ridgefield, CT 06877-4623. 203-431-9000. E-mail: flightjournal@airage.com. Website: www.flightjournal.com. Bimonthly. $19.95/yr. Circ.: 76,300. Budd Davisson, Editor-in-Chief. **Description:** Covers "the history, the hardware, and the human heart of aviation." Articles, 2,500-3,000 words; pays $600. Tips: Submit 1-page outline.

GENERAL AVIATION NEWS
Flyer Media, Inc., P.O. Box 39099, Lakewood, WA 98439-0099. 253-471-9888. E-mail: janice@generalaviationnews.com. Website: www.generalaviationnews.com. Biweekly. Circ.: 35,000. Janice Wood, Editor. **Description:** Of interest to "general aviation" pilots. Articles run 500-2,500 words; payment negotiable. **Art:** Payment negotiable, usually as part of story fee. **Freelance Content:** 30%. **Payment:** Within one month of publication.

PLANE & PILOT
Werner Publishing Corp., 12121 Wilshire Blvd., Suite 1200, Los Angeles, CA 90025. 310-820-1500. E-mail: editors@planeandpilotmag.com. Website: www.planeandpi-

lotmag.com. Monthly. $16.95/yr. Circ.: 110,000. Lyn Freeman, Editor. **Description:** Aviation-related articles, for pilots of single-engine, piston-powered recreational airplanes. Topics include training, maintenance, travel, equipment, pilot reports. Occasional features on antique, classic, and kit- or home-built aircraft; 1,500-2,500 words; pay varies. **Queries:** Preferred. **Payment:** On publication.

PRIVATE PILOT
Y-Visionary Publishing, L.P., 265 S Anita Dr., Suite 120, Orange, CA 92868. 714-939-9991. E-mail: editorial@privatepilotmag.com. Website: www.privatepilotmag.com. Monthly. $23.97/yr. Circ.: 70,000. Bill Fedorko, Editorial Director. **Description:** General aviation, for pilots and owners of single and multi-engine aircraft, who want to read about places to go, aircraft, and ways to save money. **Nonfiction:** Fly-in destinations, hands-on, how-to, informative articles for pilots, aircraft owners, and aviation enthusiasts; 1,500-3,000 words; $400-$700. **Art:** $300 fee for photography assignments. **Queries:** Preferred. **E-Queries:** No. **Unsolicited mss:** Accepts. **Response:** 2-4 weeks. **SASE Required:** Yes. **Freelance Content:** 80%. **Rights:** FNAR.

BUSINESS

ACCESSORIES MAGAZINE
Business Journals, Inc., 185 Madison Avenue, Fl. 5, New York, NY 10016. 212-686-4412. Website: www.accessoriesmagazine.com. Monthly. $35/yr. Circ.: 20,229. Irenka Jakubiak, Editor-in-Chief. **Description:** For women's fashion-accessories buyers and manufacturers. Profiles of retailers, designers, manufacturers; articles on merchandising and marketing. **Queries:** Preferred. **Payment:** On publication.

ACROSS THE BOARD
845 Third Ave., Fl. 3, New York, NY 10022-6679. 212-339-0214. E-mail: atb@conference-board.org. Website: www.acrosstheboardmagazine.com. 6x/yr. $59/yr. Circ.: 35,000. A. J. Vogl, Editor. **Description:** In-depth articles on business-management and social-policy issues for senior managers of global companies. Presents fresh business ideas and sharp opinions from business management experts. Articles run 1,000-3,500 words; pay varies. **Tips:** "Do not send highly technical pieces nor simple "how-to" pieces on business or market stategy. We prefer pieces that present new ideas that are applicable to real business." **Queries:** Preferred. **E-Queries:** Yes. **Unsolicited mss:** Accepts. **Response:** 2-3 weeks. **Freelance Content:** 70%. **Rights:** FNAR. **Payment:** On acceptance. **Contact:** Vadim Liberman, Assistant Editor.

ALASKA BUSINESS MONTHLY
Alaska Business Publishing Co., P.O. Box 241288, Anchorage, AK 99524-1288. 907-276-4373. E-mail: editor@akbizmag.com. Website: www.akbizmag.com. Monthly. $29.95/yr. Circ.: 10,000. Debbie Cutler, Editor. **Description:** Thorough, objective analysis of issues and trends affecting Alaskan businesses; 500-2,500 words; $100-$300. **Tips:** Query first—on Alaska business topics only. Avoid generalities, need to

be specific for this market. **Queries:** Preferred. **E-Queries:** Yes. **Unsolicited mss:** Accepts. **Response:** 1 month. **Freelance Content:** 80%. **Rights:** All.

ALTERNATIVE ENERGY RETAILER

Zackin Publications, Inc., P.O. Box 2180, Waterbury, CT 06722-2180. 203-755-0158. E-mail: info@aer-online.com. Website: www.aer-online.com. Monthly. $36/yr. Circ.: 14,000. Michael Griffin, Editor. **Description:** For retailers of hearth products (appliances that burn wood, coal, pellets, and gas, also accessories and services). Articles address topics related to the hearth manufacturing and retail industry; 1,500 words. **Art:** Accepts charts, tables, and photographs to illustrate articles. **Tips:** "Articles should focus on the hearth industry, but should not mention the author's company." **Queries:** Preferred. **Payment:** On publication.

AMERICAN BANKER

Thompson Media, One State St. Plaza, Fl. 26, New York, NY 10004. 212-803-8200. Website: www.americanbanker.com. Daily. $795/yr. Circ.: 14,600. David Longobardi, Editor-in-Chief. **Description:** On banking and financial services, technology in banking, consumer financial services, investment products. **Tips:** "Please read our paper before submitting to get a clear idea of the type of stories we publish." **Queries:** Preferred. **Payment:** On publication.

THE AMERICAN SALESMAN

National Research Bureau, 320 Valley St., Burlington, IA 52601. 319-752-5415. Monthly. $56/yr. Circ.: 1,400. Teresa Levinson, Editor. **Description:** For company sales reps. Articles on techniques to increase sales (case histories or public-relations articles), sales seminars, customer service, closing sales, competition, phone usage, managing territory, new sales concepts; 900-1,200 words. **Tips:** Freelance content limited. **Queries:** Preferred. **Unsolicited mss:** Do not accept.

ART BUSINESS NEWS

Advanstar Communications, Inc.
One Park Avenue, Fl. 2, New York, NY 10016-5802. 212-951-6646. E-mail: abn@advanstar.com. Website: www.artbusinessnews.com. Monthly. $43/yr. Circ.: 32,000. Amy Leibrock, Editor-in-Chief. **Description:** For art dealers and framers. Business subjects and trends and events of national importance to the art and framing industry. **Payment:** On publication.

BARRON'S-THE DOW JONES
BUSINESS AND FINANCIAL WEEKLY

Dow Jones & Company, Inc., 200 Liberty St., New York, NY 10281-0099. 212-416-2700. E-mail: editors@barrons.com. Website: www.barrons.com. Weekly. $145/yr. Circ.: 290,955. Edwin A. Finn Jr., President/Editor. **Description:** Provides information on such topics as investing, financial portfolios, industrial developments, market analysis, and electronic investing. **Queries:** Preferred. **Contact:** Richard Rescigno, Managing Editor.

BARTENDER MAGAZINE

Foley Publishing Corporation, P.O. Box 158, Liberty Corner, NJ 07938-0158. 908-766-6006. E-mail: barmag@aol.com. Website: www.bartender.com. $25/yr. Circ.: 149,000. Jaclyn W. Foley. **Description:** On liquor and bartending for bartenders, tavern owners, and owners of restaurants with full-service liquor licenses. **Nonfiction:** General interest, how-to pieces, new products or bartending techniques, interviews, descriptions of unique or interesting bars; 100-1,000 words; $50-$200. **Fillers:** Humor, news, anecdotes; 25-100 words; $5-$25. **Columns, Departments:** 200-1,000 words; $50-$200. **Art:** 8x10 color or B&W glossy prints. **Unsolicited mss:** Accepts. **Response:** 2 months. **Freelance Content:** 100%. **Rights:** FNAR. **Payment:** On publication.

BICYCLE RETAILER AND INDUSTRY NEWS

NBDA Services, Inc., 25431 Cabot Rd., Suite 204, Laguna Hills, CA 92653. 949-206-1677. E-mail: msani@bicyleretailer.com. Website: www.bicycleretailer.com. 18x/yr. $45. Circ.: 12,283. Marc Sani, Publisher; Michael Gamstetter, Editor-in-Chief. **Description:** On employee management, employment strategies, and general business subjects for bicycle manufacturers, distributors, and retailers. Articles, to 1,200 words; pays $.20/word (higher rates by assignment). **Queries:** Preferred. **Payment:** On acceptance.

BLACK ENTERPRISE MAGAZINE

See full listing in Ethnic & Multicultural category.

BOXOFFICE

RLD Communications, Inc., 155 South El Molino Ave., Suite 100, Pasedena, CA 91101. 626-396-0250. E-mail: editorial@boxoffice.com. Website: www.boxoffice.com. Monthly. $40/yr. Circ.: 8,000. Kim Williamson, Editor-in-Chief. **Description:** Business magazine for the movie theatre industry. **Nonfiction:** Interviews, profiles, new products, technical information, and other topics in the movie theatre industry; 800-2,500 words; $.10/word. **Art:** Captions required; 8x10 color or B&W prints; $10 max. **Tips:** No gossip or celebrity news. Content must cover the real issues and trends facing this industry. Submit proposal with resumé and clip samples. **Queries:** Preferred. **E-Queries:** Yes. **Unsolicited mss:** Accepts. **Response:** 1 month. **SASE Required:** Yes. **Freelance Content:** 15%. **Rights:** All, including electronic. **Payment:** On publication. **Contact:** Christine James, Managing Editor.

THE BUSINESS JOURNAL OF CHARLOTTE

American City Business Journals
120 W Morehead St., Suite 200, Charlotte, NC 28202-1844. 704-973-1000.
E-mail: charlotte@bizjournals.com. Website: www.bizjournals.com. Weekly. $49/yr. Circ.: 14,000. Robert Morris, Editor. **Description:** For the business community of metro Charlotte and surrounding areas. Covers manufacturing, marketing, finance, real estate, and other business-related issues.

BUSINESSWOMAN MAGAZINE

Business & Professional Women/USA, 1900 M Street, Washington, DC 20036. 202-293-1100. E-mail: businesswoman@bpwusa.org. Website: www.bpwusa.org. 3x/year. $12/yr. Circ.: 30,000. **Description:** Articles, varying lengths, of concern to working women. Areas of interest: economic equity and security, business practices and management, political activity, work life balance, and women in the workplace.

CHRISTIAN RETAILING

Strang Communications, Inc., 600 Rinehart Rd., Lake Mary, FL 32746. 407-333-0600. E-mail: larry.leech@strang.com. Website: www.christianretailing.com. 20x/yr. $75/yr. Circ.: 10,000. Larry J. Leech II, Managing Editor. **Description:** Covers new products, trends pertaining to Christian books, music, video, children and Spanish, and topics related to running a profitable Christian retail store. Features, 1,500-2,300 words; pays $100-$450. **Payment:** On publication.

CLUB MANAGEMENT

Finan Publishing Co., Inc., 107 W Pacific Ave., St. Louis, MO 63119-2323. 314-961-6644. E-mail: avincent@finan.com. Website: www.club-mgmt.com. Bimonthly. $21.95/yr. Circ.: 16,500. Thomas J. Finan IV, Editor. **Description:** Provides managers of private clubs with information and resources for successful operations. Articles on construction/renovation profiles, insurance, technology, staffing issues, golf-course design and maintenance, special events, maintenance, food/beverage trends, guest-room amenities, spa facilities, outsourcing; 1,500-2,000 words. **Tips:** "Editorial content must be targeted and written in such a way that the busy club manager finds informative, timely, relevant and challenging articles. The magazine's style combines the information-focus of news magazine journals and the reader-friendliness of a consumer magazine." **Queries:** Preferred. **E-Queries:** Yes. **Unsolicited mss:** Accepts. **Response:** 2-3 weeks. **SASE Required:** Yes. **Freelance Content:** 40%. **Rights:** FNAR and electronic. **Payment:** On publication.

COLORADOBIZ

Wiesner Publishing, LLC, 7009 S Potomac St., Suite 200, Englewood, CO 80112. 303-397-7600. Website: www.cobizmag.com. Monthly. $3.95/$22.97. Circ.: 16,700. Robert Schwab, Editor-in-Chief. **Description:** On business in Colorado. Market analysis, economic trends, forecasts, profiles, and individuals involved in business activities; 650-1,200 words; $50-$400. **Tips:** Must target business in Colorado. No general business articles, book reviews, commentaries, syndicated work, humor, poetry. **Queries:** Required. **E-Queries:** Yes. **Payment:** On publication.

CORPORATE GIFT REVIEW

Festivities Publications, Inc., 815 Haines St., Jacksonville, FL 32206. 904-634-1902. Quarterly. $19.95/yr. Circ.: 5,000. Debra Paulk, Editor. **Description:** Innovative tips and how-tos on sales, marketing, management, and operations. Focuses on business gifting. Hard data, stats and research requested. Readers are college-educated, successful business owners. **Tips:** "Avoid generalizations, basic content, and outdated theories." **Queries:** Not necessary. **E-queries:** No. **Unsolicited mss:** Accepts. **Response:** 30 days. **SASE Required:** Yes. **Freelance Content:** 50%. **Rights:** One-time. **Payment:** On publication.

THE COSTCO CONNECTION

Costco Wholesale Corporation, P.O. Box 34088, Seattle, WA 98124-1088. 425-313-6442. E-mail: athompson@costco.com. Website: www.costco.com. Monthly. Free. Circ.: 2,558,800. Anita Thompson, Managing Editor. **Description:** Articles, 100-1,200 words, on small business and Costco members. Pays to $400 and up. Unique editions for members in Canada, UK, Korea, and Puerto Rico. **Queries:** Preferred. **Payment:** On acceptance.

COUNTRY BUSINESS

Emmis Publishing LP, 707 Kautz Rd., St. Charles, IL 60174. 630-377-8000. E-mail: cbiz@sampler.emmis.com. Website: www.country-business.com. Bimonthly. Circ.: 32,000. Susan Wagner, Editor. **Description:** Publication for retailers of country gifts and accessories. Articles feature new products and trends in giftware markets and provide business and marketing advice. **Nonfiction:** Seeking business articles on small business management and retail (e.g. finance, legal, technology, marketing, management, etc); 800-1,800 words; pay varies. **Queries:** Preferred. **E-Queries:** Yes. **Unsolicited mss:** Accepts. **SASE Required:** Yes. **Freelance Content:** 60%. **Payment:** On acceptance.

CRAIN'S CHICAGO BUSINESS

Crain Communications, Inc., 360 N Michigan Ave., Chicago, IL 60601. 312-649-5411. E-mail: editor@chicagobusiness.com. Website: www.chicagobusiness.com. Weekly. $89/yr. Circ.: 50,300. Rance Crain, Publisher/Editor-in-Chief. **Description:** Provides business owners, executives, professionals, and other consumers with articles covering the current news and anyalsis of the business community in the Chicago metro area. **Contact:** Judith Crown, Acting Editor.

CRAIN'S DETROIT BUSINESS

Crain Communications, Inc., 1155 Gratiot Ave., Detroit, MI 48207. 313-446-6000. E-mail: jmelton@crain.com. Website: www.crainsdetroit.com. Weekly. $53/yr. Circ.: 35,700. Cindy Goodaker, Executive Editor. **Description:** Local business publication. **Queries:** Required. **E-Queries:** Yes. **Payment:** On publication.

EMPLOYEE SERVICES MANAGEMENT

Employee Services Management Assn., 2211 York Rd., Suite 207, Oak Brook, IL 60523. 630-368-1280. E-mail: reneemula@esmassn.org. Website: www.esmassn.org. 6x/yr. $52/yr. Circ.: 3,000. Renee Mula, Editor. **Description:** For human resource professionals, employee services professionals, and ESM members. Articles cover topics in relation to recruitment and retention, becoming an employer of choice, work/life issues, employee services, wellness, management and more. Articles run 1,200-2,500 words. **Tips:** Prefers to receive submissions via e-mail. **E-Queries:** Yes.

ENTREPRENEUR MAGAZINE

Entrepreneur Media, Inc., 2445 McCabe Way, Suite 400, Irvine, CA 92614. 949-261-2325. E-mail: pbennett@entrepreneur.com. Website: www.entrepreneur.com. Monthly. $14.97/yr. **Description:** Business information and advice, and innovative strategies for entrepreneurs. Covers all aspects of running and growing a successful business. **Tips:** Read sample issues before submitting. Do not send complete manuscript. "If you're not a regular contributor, include a brief personal bio. Also include contact information so that we may contact you. E-mail address is fine." **Queries:** Required. **Response:** 8-12 weeks. **Payment:** On acceptance. **Contact:** Karen Axelton, Executive Editor; Peggy Reeves Bennett, Articles Editor.

FLORIDA TREND

Trend Magazines, Inc., 490 First Ave. S, St. Petersburg, FL 33701. 727-821-5800. E-mail: mhoward@floridatrend.com. Website: www.floridatrend.com. Monthly. $29.95/yr. Circ.: 51,200. Mark R. Howard, Executive Editor. **Description:** Features articles and profiles on business, technology, the economy, etc. in the state of Florida. Targets businessmen and other professionals who work and reside in this region. **Queries:** Required. **SASE Required:** Yes.

FLOWERS & MAGAZINE

Teleflora, 11444 W Olympic Blvd., Los Angeles, CA 90064. 310-966-3590. E-mail: flowersand@teleflora.com. Website: www.flowersandmagazine.com. Monthly. $52/yr. Circ.: 40,000. Bruce Wright, Editor. **Description:** How-to information for retail florists. **Tips:** Send clips. **Queries:** Preferred. **Payment:** On acceptance.

GIFT BASKET REVIEW

Festivities Publications, Inc., 815 Haines St., Jacksonville, FL 32206-6050. 904-634-1902. E-mail: editorial@festivities-pub.com. Website: www.festivities-pub.com. Monthly. $39.95/yr. Circ.: 15,000. Carol Childers, Editor. **Description:** Covers products, cutting-edge ideas, and up-to-date industry news. **Nonfiction:** Inspiring ideas, professional tips, industry news. **Tips:** "Avoid generalizations and basic content. Submit specific tips and how-tos on sales, marketing, management, and operations. Hard data, stats and research appreciated. Readers are college-educated, successful business owners." **Queries:** Not necessary. **E-Queries:** Yes. **Response:** 30 days. **SASE Required:** Yes. **Freelance Content:** 50%. **Rights:** All, electronic. **Payment:** On publication.

GREENHOUSE MANAGEMENT & PRODUCTION

See full listing in Trade & Technical category.

GREYHOUND REVIEW

National Greyhound Assoc., P.O. Box 543, Abilene, KS 67410-0543. 785-263-4660. E-mail: nga@ngagreyhounds.com. Website: www.ngagreyhounds.com. Monthly. $30. Circ.: 4,000. Gary Guccione, Editor. **Description:** Covers the greyhound racing industry: trade news, special events at tracks, medical news, etc. Intended for greyhound owners, breeders, trainers, and racetrack officials. Articles are generaly how-to pieces, historical/nostalgia, or interviews; 1,000-10,000 words; $85-$150. **Tips:** No general-interest pieces on dogs/pet ownership or on racetrack gambling. **Queries:** Preferred. **E-Queries:** Yes. **Unsolicited mss:** Accepts. **Response:** 2 weeks. **SASE Required:** Yes. **Freelance Content:** 80%. **Rights:** FNAR. **Payment:** On acceptance. **Contact:** Tim Horan, Managing Editor.

GROWERTALKS

Ball Publishing, P.O. Box 9, Batavia, IL 60510-0009. 630-208-9080. E-mail: info@ballpublishing.com. Website: www.growertalks.com. Monthly. $29/yr. Circ.: 10,000. Chris Beytes, Editor. **Description:** For commercial greenhouse growers (not florist/retailers or home gardeners). Covers trends, successes in new types of production, marketing, business management, new crops, and issues facing the industry. **Queries:** Preferred. **Payment:** On publication.

HARVARD BUSINESS REVIEW

Harvard Business School Publishing Corp., 60 Harvard Way, Boston, MA 02163. 617-783-7410. E-mail: hbr_editorial@hbsp.harvard.edu. Website: www.hbsp.harvard.edu. Monthly. $118/yr. Circ.: 249,100. Sarah Cliffe, Executive Editor. **Description:** Targets senior-level managers and CEOs by offering innovative, strategic ideas for managing a large organization. Topics include leadership, strategy, manufacturing, teamwork. Articles written by experts whose ideas and theories for business practice and management have been tested in the real world. **Tips:** Query should be a 3-4 page summary of proposes topic. Include your objective, intended audience, and credentials in proposal. **Queries:** Required. **Response:** 6-8 weeks.

HEARTH & HOME

Village West Publishing, P.O. Box 1288, Laconia, NH 03247-1288. 603-528-4285. E-mail: mailbox@villagewest.com. Monthly. $36/yr. Circ.: 17,000. Richard Wright, Editor. **Description:** Profiles and interviews, with specialty retailers selling both casual furniture and hearth products (fireplaces, woodstoves, accessories, etc.). Articles run 1,000-1,800 words; $150-$250. **Payment:** On acceptance.

HISPANIC BUSINESS

425 Pine Ave., Santa Barbara, CA 93117-3709. E-mail: editorial@hbinc.com. Website: www.hispanicbusiness.com. Monthly. $18/yr. Circ.: 222,900. Jesus Chavarria, Publisher/Editor. **Description:** Features personalities, political agendas, and fascinating stories, with focus on technology and finance. Pays $350 (negotiable). **Tips:** "An ongoing need for experienced freelance writers with expertise and contacts in the Hispanic business market."

HOBBY MERCHANDISER

See full listing in Hobbies, Crafts, Collecting category.

HOMEBUSINESS JOURNAL

Steffen Publishing Co., P.O. Box 403, Holland Patent, NY 13354-0403. 315-865-4100. E-mail: hbj@steffenpublishing.com. Website: www.homebusinessjournal.net. Bimonthly. $18.96/yr. Circ.: 50,000. JoAnne Steffen, Managing Editor. **Description:** Offers quality information and advice for readers in a home business, or those seriously interested in such work, to help them thrive and enjoy working at home. Editorials pertaining to home based business issues; financial, family, health, etc.; 1,000 words; $75. **Tips:** Common mistake is to fail to note the difference in needs between small businesses and home businesses. Welcomes new writers. **Queries:** Required. **E-Queries:** Yes. **Unsolicited mss:** Accepts. **Response:** 4-6 weeks.

HUMAN RESOURCE EXECUTIVE

LRP Publications Co., 747 Dresher Rd. Suite 500, P.O. Box 980, Horsham, PA 19044-0980. 215-784-0910. E-mail: dshadovitz@lrp.com. Website: www.hrexecutive.com. 16x/yr. David Shadovitz, Editor-in-Chief. **Description:** Profiles and case stories, for executives in the human-resource profession. Articles run 1,600-1,800 words; pay varies. **Queries:** Required. **Payment:** On acceptance.

INC.

Gruner + Jahr USA Publishing, 375 Lexington Ave., Fl. 8, New York, NY 10017-5514. 212-499-2000. E-mail: editors@inc.com. Website: www.inc.com. Monthly. $19/yr. Circ.: 680,700. John Koten, Editor-in-Chief. **Description:** Business magazine with helpful how-to articles focusing on small, rapidly-growing, privately-held companies. **Tips:** "We look for stories that are not specific to only one industry. Don't write about products; write about managing the company." **Queries:** Preferred. **E-Queries:** No. **Unsolicited mss:** Accepts. **Response:** 30 days. **SASE Required:** Yes. **Freelance Content:** 3%. **Rights:** FNASR. **Payment:** On publication.

INDUSTRY WEEK

Penton Media, Inc., The Penton Media Building, 1300 E 9th St., Cleveland, OH 44114. 216-696-7000. E-mail: tvinas@industryweek.com. Website: www.industryweek.com. Monthly. Circ.: 233,000. Patricia Panchak, Editor-in-Chief. **Description:** Written for a senior-level management audience, *Industry Week* delivers powerful editorial on the challenges facing today's companies. Articles on manufacturing leadership and management; 1,800-3,000 words; pay varies. **Queries:** Required. **Rights:** All. **Payment:** On acceptance. **Contact:** Tonya Vinas, Managing Editor.

INSTANT & SMALL COMMERCIAL PRINTER

Innes Publishing Company, P.O. Box 7280, Libertyville, IL 60048. 847-816-7900. E-mail: iscpmag@innespub.com. Website: www.innespub.com. Monthly. $110/yr. Circ.: 45,100. Denise Lontz, Editor. **Description:** Covers small commercial and instant printing market. Case histories, how-tos, technical pieces, small-business management; 1,000-5,000 words; pay negotiable. **Queries:** Preferred. **E-Queries:** Yes. **Unsolicited mss:** Accepts. **Response:** 1-6 months. **SASE Required:** Yes. **Freelance Content:** 20%. **Payment:** On publication.

IQ MAGAZINE
Cisco Systems, Inc., 170 W Tasman Dr., MS 8/2, San Jose, CA 95134.
E-mail: iq-editorial@cisco.com. Website: www.cisco.com/go/iqmagazine. Bimonthly.
Circ.: 80,000. Heather Alter, Editor-in-Chief. **Description:** *iQ Magazine* covers how
Internet business strategies can help businesses be more successful: news, analysis,
success stories, interviews, trends, resources, and more. **Tips:** "Please review our
website to see the range of our content, writing style, etc." **E-Queries:** Yes.
Unsolicited mss: Does not accept.

LATIN TRADE
Latin America Media Management, 95 Merrick Way, Suite 600, Coral Gables, FL
33134. 305-358-8373. E-mail: mzellner@latintrade-inc.com. Website: www.latin-
trade.com. Monthly. $44/yr. Circ.: 93,000. Mike Zellner, Editor-in-Chief.
Description: For business persons in Latin America. Covers a wide variety of topics
relating to trade, markets, research, technology and investments. Articles run 800-
2,000 words; $200-$1,000. **Queries:** Required. **E-Queries:** Yes. **Unsolicited mss:**
Does not accept. **Response:** Queries 2 weeks **Freelance Content:** 55%. **Rights:**
All. **Payment:** On publication.

LONG ISLAND BUSINESS NEWS
Dolan Media Company, 2150 Smithtown Ave., Ronkonkoma, NY 11779. 631-737-
1700. E-mail: carl.corry@libn.com. Website: www.libn.com. Weekly. Circ.: 12,000.
John Kominicki, Publisher. **Description:** Covers regional economic and business
news. Tageted towards the business and financial community of Nassau and Suffolk
counties in New York. **Nonfiction:** Articles should cover topics such as finance, technology, health, travel, and the environment and should be aimed at business professionals in this region; $.20-$.30/word. **Tips:** Occasionally works with new writers.
Queries: Preferred. **E-Queries:** Yes. **Response:** 2 weeks. **SASE Required:** Yes.
Rights: One-time. **Payment:** On publication. **Contact:** Carl Corry, Editor.

MANAGE
National Management Assn., 2210 Arbor Blvd., Dayton, OH 45439-1506. 937-294-
0421. E-mail: nma@nma1.org. Website: www.nma1.org. Quarterly. $5/issue. Circ.:
60,000. Douglas E. Shaw, Publisher/Editor. **Description:** Covers human resource
development, team building, leadership skills, ethics in the workplace, law, compen-
sation, and technology; 600-1,000 words; $.05/word. **Queries:** Not necessary. **E-
Queries:** Yes. **Unsolicited mss:** Accepts. **Response:** 3 months. **SASE Required:**
Yes. **Freelance Content:** 60%. **Rights:** FNAR. **Payment:** On acceptance.

MARKETING NEWS
American Marketing Assn., 311 S Wacker Dr. Suite 5800, Chicago, IL 60606-6629.
312-542-9000. E-mail: news@ama.org. Website: www.marketingpower.com.
Biweekly. $100/yr. Circ.: 30,000. Lisa M. Keefe, Editor. **Description:** Authoritative
analysis of news, current trends, and application of developments in marketing profession; also, information on American Marketing Association. **Nonfiction:** Timely

articles on advertising, sales promotion, direct marketing, telecommunications, consumer and business-to-business marketing, and market research; 800-1,200 words; $.80/word. **Tips:** Due to potential conflict of interest, no news stories written by marketing professionals. **Queries:** Preferred. **E-Queries:** Yes. **Unsolicited mss:** Do not accept. **Response:** Queries 6-8 weeks, submissions 2-4 months. **Freelance Content:** 30%. **Rights:** 1st, all media. **Payment:** On acceptance.

THE MEETING PROFESSIONAL

Meeting Professionals International (MPI), 4455 LBJ Freeway, Suite 1200, Dallas, TX 75244-5903. 972-702-3018. E-mail: publications@mpiweb.org. Website: www.mpiweb.org. Monthly. $50/yr. Circ.: 32,000. John Delavan, Managing Editor. **Description:** For meeting professionals. **Tips:** Works only with published writers familiar with the meetings industry. Submit query by e-mail; send resumé and clips by mail (with SASE). **Queries:** Preferred. **E-Queries:** Yes. **Unsolicited mss:** Does not accept. **Response:** 2 weeks. **SASE Required:** Yes. **Freelance Content:** 50%. **Rights:** All. **Payment:** On acceptance.

MODERN PHYSICIAN

Crain Communications, Inc., 360 N Michigan Ave., Fl. 5, Chicago, IL 60601. 312-649-5350. E-mail: moddoc@crain.com. Website: www.modernphysician.com. Monthly. $45/yr. Circ.: 31,400. Joseph Conn, Editor. **Description:** For physician executives. Covers business and management news in addition to stories about how medical practices are changing; 1,000-1,500 words; $.80-$1/word. **Tips:** No product or clinical stories. Welcomes new writers. Check online to see what has already been published. **Queries:** Required. **E-Queries:** Yes. **Unsolicited mss:** Accepts. **SASE Required:** Yes. **Freelance Content:** 30%. **Rights:** All. **Payment:** On acceptance.

MONEY

Time, Inc., 1271 Avenue of the Americas, Fl. 32, New York, NY 10020-1300. 212-552-1212. E-mail: money_letters@moneymail.com. Website: http://money.cnn.com. Monthly. $39.89/yr. Circ.: 1,929,400. Norman Pearlstine, Editor-in-Chief. **Description:** Seeks writers experienced in covering mutual funds for the print media. Send resumé and clips. **Queries:** Preferred. **Contact:** Robert Safian, Managing Editor.

NEEDLEWORK RETAILER

Yarn Tree Designs, P.O. Box 2438, Ames, IA 50010-2438. 515-232-3121. E-mail: info@yarntree.com. Website: yarntree.com/nr.htm. Bimonthly. $12/yr. Circ.: 11,000. Megan Chriswisser, Editor. **Description:** For owners and managers of independent needlework retail stores. Covers new products, trends, and designs in the counted cross-stitch and needlework industry. Also includes information on trade shows. Articles run 500-1,000 words; pay varies. **Tips:** No generic business articles. **Payment:** On acceptance.

THE NETWORK JOURNAL

29 John St., Suite 1402, New York, NY 10038. 212-962-3791. E-mail: editors@tnj.com. Website: www.tnj.com. Monthly. Circ.: 22,000. Rosalind McLymont, Editor. **Description:** for African American small-business owners and professionals. On small-business, personal finance, career management, profiles of entrepreneurs, sales/marketing, etc.; 1,200-1,500 words; $150. **E-Queries:** Yes. **Freelance Content:** 25%. **Rights:** All. **Payment:** On publication.

NSGA RETAIL FOCUS

National Sporting Goods Assn., 1601 Feehanville Dr., Suite 300, Mt. Prospect, IL 60056-6035. 847-296-6742. E-mail: info@nsga.org. Website: www.nsga.org. Bimonthly. Circ.: 2,500. Larry Weindruch, Editor. **Description:** Official publication of NSGA. Covers industry news, consumer trends, management and store operations, and new product development for retailers, wholesalers, manufacturers, and members of NSGA. **Queries:** Required. **E-Queries:** Yes. **Unsolicited mss:** Does not accept. **Response:** Queries 1 week. **SASE Required:** Yes. **Freelance Content:** 15%. **Rights:** 1st and electronic. **Payment:** On publication.

PARTY & PAPER RETAILER

107 Mill Plain Rd., Suite 204, Danbury, CT 06811. 203-730-4090. E-mail: editor@partypaper.com. Website: www.partypaper.com. Monthly. $43/yr. Circ.: 14,500. Nicholas Messina, Managing Editor. **Description:** Retail success stories, trends in the industry (seasonal and everyday), and practical retail advice to party and stationery store owners. Articles cover employee management, marketing, advertising, promotion, finance and legal matters; 800-1,800 words; pay varies. **Tips:** Send query with published clips. **Queries:** Preferred. **Response:** 2 months. **Freelance Content:** 90%. **Rights:** FNAR. **Payment:** On publication.

PET BUSINESS

Macfadden Communications Group, 333 7th Ave., Fl. 11, New York, NY 10001-5004. 212-979-4800. E-mail: dlitwak@petbusiness.com. Website: www.petbusiness.com. 14x/yr. $49.97/yr. Circ.: 24,500. David Litwak, Editor-in-Chief. **Description:** Covers animals and products found in pet stores. Offers research findings, legislative/regulatory actions, and business and marketing tips/trends. **Nonfiction:** Brief, well-documented articles; pays $.10/word, $20/photo. **Payment:** On publication.

PET PRODUCT NEWS

Bowtie, Inc., P.O. Box 6050, Mission Viejo, CA 92690. 949-855-8822. E-mail: cboker@bowtieinc.com. Website: www.petproductnews.com. Monthly. $42/yr. Circ.: 23,000. Carol Boker, Editor. **Description:** Audience is pet-store retailers and managers of such operations, large and small. Includes pet and pet-product merchandising, retailer tips, industry news and opinion. Submit articles with photos; 1,200-1,500 words; $250 and up. **Tips:** No fiction or pet stories. **Queries:** Required. **E-Queries:** Yes. **Unsolicited mss:** Does not accept. **Response:** 2 weeks. **Freelance Content:** 70%. **Rights:** FNASR. **Payment:** On publication.

PHOTO MARKETING

Photo Marketing Assn. International, 3000 Picture Place, Jackson, MI 49201-8898. 517-788-8100. E-mail: pmai_publication@pmai.org. Website: www.pmai.org. Monthly. $50/yr. Circ.: 18,000. Bonnie Gretzner, Managing Editor. **Description:** For owners and managers of camera/video stores or photo processing labs. Business articles, 1,000-2,000 words; pays $150-$500, extra for photos. **Queries:** Preferred. **Unsolicited mss:** Do not accept. **Payment:** On acceptance.

POOL & SPA NEWS

Hanley-Wood LLC, 4160 Wilshire Blvd., Los Angeles, CA 90010. 323-801-4900. E-mail: etaylor@hanley-wood.com. Website: www.poolspanews.com. 2x/month. Circ.: 16,012. Erika Taylor, Editor. **Description:** Provides industry news and feature articles to builders, retailers, technicians, and other pool and spa professionals. Articles cover design, construction, renovation, equipment repair, merchandising, etc. Also provides annual directory, product listings, and technical manuals. **Queries:** Preferred. **Freelance Content:** 15%. **Payment:** On publication.

PRO

Cygnus Business Media, P.O. Box 803, Fort Atkinson, WI 53538. 920-563-6388. Website: www.promagazine.com. 9x/yr. Circ.: 50,000. Noel Brown, Editor-in-Chief. **Description:** On business management for owners of lawn-maintenance firms; 1,000-1,500 words; pays $150-$250. **Queries:** Preferred. **Payment:** On publication.

QUICK PRINTING

Cygnus Business Media, 445 Broadhollow Rd., Melville, NY 11747-3669. 631-845-2700. E-mail: editor@quickprinting.com. Website: www.quickprinting.com. Monthly. $66/yr. Circ.: 48,000. Kelly Campbell, Editor. **Description:** For owners and operators of quick print shops, copy shops, and small commercial printers. How-to pieces on making their businesses more profitable. Also, articles on using computers and peripherals in graphic arts applications. **Tips:** No generic business articles. Currently not buying much freelance material. **Payment:** On publication.

RETAIL SYSTEMS RESELLER

Edgell Communications, 4 Middlebury Blvd., Randolph, NJ 07869. 973-252-0100. E-mail: dbreeman@edgellmail.com. Website: www.retailsystemsreseller.com. Monthly. $95/yr. Circ.: 20,000. Daniel Breeman, Managing Editor. **Description:** Covers news, products, technology and services for value-added resellers and system integrators selling into the retail channel. Focuses retail point-of-sale and payment processing, extending into backend systems and retail supply chain. Articles run 600-1,500 words; $400-$800. **Tips:** Seeking writers who can write for this market and know how to dig as a reporter. No syndicated articles or general business ideas. **E-Queries:** Yes. **Unsolicited mss:** Accepts. **Response:** 60-90 days. **SASE Required:** Yes. **Freelance Content:** 80%. **Rights:** FNAR. **Payment:** On publication.

SALES & MARKETING MANAGEMENT

Bill Communications, Inc., 770 Broadway, New York, NY 10003. 646-654-7606. E-mail: cgalea@salesandmarketing.com. Website: www.salesandmarketing.com. Christine Galea, Managing Editor. **Description:** Provides useful information for sales and marketing executives. Articles focus on best practices, techniques for better job performance, networking with colleagues, and company profiles. **Nonfiction:** Features and short articles; pays varies. **Tips:** Seeks practical "news you can use." **Queries:** Preferred. **Payment:** On acceptance.

SAN FRANCISCO BUSINESS TIMES

American City Business Journals, 275 Battery St., Suite 940, San Francisco, CA 94111. 415-989-2522. E-mail: sanfrancisco@bizjournals.com. Website: www.sanfrancisco.bizjournals.com. Weekly. $82/yr. Circ.: 15,520. Steve Symanovich, Editor. **Description:** Features articles that focus on business, commerce, and technology in the San Francisco Bay area. **Tips:** Limited freelance market. **Queries:** Preferred. **Payment:** On publication.

SIGN BUILDER ILLUSTRATED

Simmons-Boardman Publishing Corp., 345 Hudson St., Fl. 12, New York, NY 10014-4502. 212-620-7200. Website: www.signshop.com. Bimonthly. $21/yr. Circ.: 17,000. Jeff Wooten, Editor. **Description:** How-to articles and editorials relevant to the sign industry; 1,500-2,500 words; $300-$500. **Payment:** On acceptance.

SIGN BUSINESS

National Business Media, Inc., P.O. Box 1416, Broomfield, CO 80038-1416. 303-469-0424. E-mail: ewieber@nbm.com. Website: www.signbusinessmag.com. Monthly. $38/yr. Circ.: 21,000. Edward Patrick Wieber, Editor. **Description:** For sign and related advertising graphics businesses. Prefers step-by-step, how-to features, architectural sign and sign systems profiles; pays $250-$300. **Payment:** On publication.

SMALL BUSINESS OPPORTUNITIES

Harris Publications, Inc., 1115 Broadway, Fl. 8, New York, NY 10010-3455. 212-462-9567. E-mail: sr@harris-pub.com. Website: www.sbomag.com. Bimonthly. $3.25/$14.95. Circ.: 250,000. Susan Rakowski, Editor-in-Chief. **Description:** How-to magazine for entrepreneurs. Articles run 900-1,000 words; $250-$400. **Tips:** Prefers e-queries. "Avoid general articles on small businesses. Our readers look for specifics. Currently we're looking for how-to's, trends, and round-ups." **Queries:** Preferred. **Freelance Content:** 40%. **Payment:** On acceptance.

SOUVENIRS, GIFTS, AND NOVELTIES

Kane Publications, 10 E Athens Ave., Ardmore, PA 19003. 610-645-6940. E-mail: souvnovmag@kanec.com. Tony De Masi, Editor. **Description:** On retailing and merchandising gifts, collectibles, and souvenirs for managers at zoos, museums, hotels, airports, and souvenir stores; 1,500 words; $.12/word.

TANNING TRENDS

Russell Creative Group, P.O. Box 1630, Jackson, MI 49204-1630. 800-652-3269.
E-mail: editor@smarttan.com. Website: www.tanning-trends.com. Monthly. $60/yr.
Circ.: 23,000. Joseph Levy, Executive Editor. **Description:** On small businesses and
skin care for tanning salon owners. Seeks to help salon owners move to the "next
level" of small business ownership. Focuses on business principles, emphasis on public relations and marketing. **Payment:** On publication.

TEA & COFFEE TRADE JOURNAL

Lockwood Publications, Inc., 26 Broadway Fl. 9M, New York, NY 10004. 212-391-
2060. E-mail: editor@teaandcoffee.net. Website: www.teaandcoffee.net. Monthly.
$49/yr. Circ.: 13,000. Jane P. McCabe, Publisher/Editor. **Description:** On issues of
importance to the tea and coffee industry. Articles, 3-5 pages; pays $.20/word.
Queries: Preferred. **Payment:** On publication.

TEENPRENEUR

See full listing in Teens category.

TEXAS TECHNOLOGY

Power Media Group, Inc., 13490 TI Boulevard, Suite 100, Dallas, TX 75243.
972-690-6222. E-mail: editor@thetechmag.com. Website: www.thetechmag.com.
Monthly. $29.95/yr. Circ.: 180,000. Alan Friedrichs, Editor-in-Chief. **Description:**
Publishes multiple editions across Texas. Covers the latest innovations in technology,
consumer trends, new products, etc. Targets general consumers as well as technology
and computer professionals. Pieces run 1,200-3,500 words; $200-$400. **Tips:** "We're
not interested in company or product-specific stories. We want stories on trends and
general topics to appeal to both business and mainstream audiences. Writers who
don't read our publication often send the wrong type of articles." **Queries:** Required.
E-Queries: Yes. **Unsolicited mss:** Accepts. **Response:** 1-2 months. **Freelance
Content:** 95% . **Rights:** FNAR, electronic. **Payment:** On publication.

TEXTILE WORLD

Billian Publishing, Inc., 2100 Powers Ferry Rd., Atlanta, GA 30339. 770-955-5656. E-
mail: editor@textileindustries.com. Website: www.textileworld.com. Monthly. $60/yr.
Circ.: 33,000. **Description:** Business and technical articles that serve textile execu-
tives in their dual roles as technologists and managers; 1,500 words; $200/page.
Queries: Required. **E-Queries:** Yes. **Response:** 4 weeks **Freelance Content:** 5%.
Rights: All. **Payment:** On publication.

TREASURY & RISK MANAGEMENT

Wicks Business Information, 52 Vanderbilt Ave., Suite 514, New York, NY 10017.
212-557-7480. Website: www.treasuryandrisk.com. Monthly. $64/yr. Circ.: 46,000.
Patricia Wechsler, Editor. **Description:** On management for corporate treasurers,
CFOs, and vice presidents of finance. **Tips:** Seeking freelance writers. **Queries:**
Preferred. **Payment:** On acceptance.

VENDING TIMES

Vending Times, Inc., 1375 Broadway, Fl. 6, New York, NY 10018-7001. 212-302-4700. E-mail: editor@vendingtimes.net. Website: www.vendingtimes.com. 14x/yr. $35/yr. Circ.: 17,500. Timothy Sanford, Editor. **Description:** On the business issues of companies providing vending, refreshment, hospitalitity, and catering services. Target audience includes independent and chain vending operators, caterers, suppliers, distributors, and other individuals involved in the food service industry. **Queries:** Preferred. **Payment:** On acceptance.

VIRGINIA BUSINESS

Media General Operations, P.O. Box 85333, Richmond, VA 23293-0001. 804-649-6999. E-mail: jbacon@va-business.com. Website: www.virginiabusiness.com. Monthly. $30/yr. Circ.: 32,000. James Bacon, Publisher/Editor-in-Chief. **Description:** Articles, 1,000-2,500 words, on the business scene in Virginia. Pay varies. **Queries:** Required. **Payment:** On publication.

WOMEN IN BUSINESS

ABWA Company, Inc., P.O. Box 8728, Kansas City, MO 64114-0728. 816-361-6621. E-mail: abwa@abwa.org. Website: www.abwa.org. Bimonthly. $24/yr. Circ.: 43,000. Kathleen Isaacson, Editor. **Description:** How-to business features (trends, small-business ownership, leadership, education, self-improvement, retirement issues, etc.) for working women, ages 35-55. Helps business women of diverse occupations grow personally and professionally. Profiles of ABWA members only; 500-1,000 words; $.20/word. **E-Queries:** Yes. **Unsolicited mss:** Accepts. **Freelance Content:** 2%. **Payment:** On publication.

CAREER & PROFESSIONAL DEVELOPMENT

AMERICAN CAREERS

Career Communications, Inc., 6701 W 64th St., Overland Park, KS 66202. 913-362-7788. Website: www.carcom.com. 2x/yr. Circ.: 500,000. Mary Pitchford, Editor. **Description:** Classroom career-development magazines for elementary, middle, and high school students. Introduces varied careers in different industries that offer realistic opportunities. Articles on resumes, interviews, developing marketable work skills, and making career decisions. Also provides information on a variety of occupations, salaries, and the education/training needed to obtain employment; 300-1,000 words; $100-$450. **Tips:** Send query letter with resumé and writing samples. "We seek stories that reflect racial and gender equality. Some careers require a college degree and some require other backgrounds to enter into the career. We welcome stories that reflect this diversity." **Queries:** Required. **E-Queries:** No. **Unsolicited mss:** Does not accept. **Response:** 1 month. **SASE Required:** No. **Freelance Content:** 50%. **Rights:** All, work-for-hire. **Payment:** Within 30 days of acceptance.

THE BLACK COLLEGIAN
See full listing in Ethnic & Multicultural category.

CAMPUS
Canadian Controlled Media Communications, 5397 Eglinton Ave. W, Suite 101, Toronto, Ontario M9C 5K6 Canada. 416-928-2909. E-mail: turnbull@campus.ca. Website: www.campus.ca. Quarterly. $29.04/yr. Circ.: 130,000. Christian Pierce, Editor. **Description:** Articles to inform, entertain, and educate the student community in Canada. **Queries:** Preferred.

CAREER WORLD
200 First Stamford Place, Stamford, CT 06912-0023. 847-205-3000. E-mail: aflounders@weeklyreader.com. Website: www.weeklyreader.com. Bimonthly. $9.95/yr. Circ.: 87,000. Anne Flounders, Editor. **Description:** Helps junior/senior high school students prepare for college and make career choices. Currenlty seeking gender-neutral articles on specific occupations, career awareness and development, evaluating interests, setting goals, college and tech choices, getting hired, hot jobs, etc. **Tips:** Query with resumé and clips. Sample copies available. **Queries:** Required. **E-queries:** Yes. **Unsolicited mss:** Do not accept. **Response:** 1-6 months. **Freelance Content:** 80%. **Rights:** All. **Payment:** On publication.

CAREERS & COLLEGES
Division of 360 Youth, P.O. Box 22, Keyport, NJ 07735. 732-264-0460. Website: www.careersandcolleges.com. 4x/school year. $6.95/issue. Circ.: 750,000. Paul McKeefry, Publisher. **Description:** Guides high-school juniors and seniors through college admissions process, financial aid, life skills, and career opportunities. **Nonfiction:** Interesting, new takes on college admission, scholarships, financial aid, work skills, and careers. 800-2,500 words; pay varies. **Tips:** Send SASE with $1.95 postage for sample issue. **Queries:** Required. **E-Queries:** No. **Unsolicited mss:** Do not accept. **Response:** 1 month. **Freelance Content:** 80%. **Rights:** FNAR.

CAREERS & THE DISABLED
See full listing in Abilities category.

CIRCLE K MAGAZINE
3636 Woodview Trace, Indianapolis, IN 46268-3196. 317-875-8755. E-mail: ckimagazine@kiwanis.org. Website: www.circlek.org/magazine. 5x/yr. $6/yr. Circ.: 15,000. Shanna Mooney, Executive Editor. **Description:** Official publication of Circle K International (world's largest collegiate service organization). Serious and light nonfiction targeted to college students who are committed to community service and leadership development. Pieces that focus on college lifestyle (trends, friendship, health, technology, etc.) also accepted; 1,500-2,000 words; $150-$400. **Tips:** "Focus on interviews and research, not personal insights. Use illustrative examples and expert quotes." **Queries:** Preferred. **E-Queries:** Yes. **Unsolicited mss:** Accepts. **Response:** 2 months. **Freelance Content:** 60%. **Rights:** FNASR.

COLLEGERECRUITER.COM NEWSLETTER

3109 W 50 St., Suite 121, Minneapolis, MN 55410-2102. 952-848-2211. E-mail: steven@collegerecruiter.com. Website: www.collegerecruiter.com. Steven Rothberg, Publisher. **Description:** Online newsletter offering techniques on seeking employment for students/college grads. Topics include work skills, professional roles and expectations, and resumé/interviewing tips. **Tips:** "We don't offer payment, but we will include byline and a link to the website of your choice."

DIRECT AIM

Communications Publishing Group, Inc., 7300 W 110th St., Fl. 7, Overland Park, KS 66210-2330. 913-317-2888. E-mail: directaim@neli.net. Website: www.neli.net. Quarterly. $9/yr. Circ.: 500,000. Neoshia Michelle Paige, Editor. **Description:** Provides college and career information to Black and Hispanic students who attend colleges, universities, or technical/vocational institutions. **Fiction:** Stories that are historical, cultural, humorous, etc; 500-2,000 words; pay varies. **Nonfiction:** Career preparation, college profiles, financial-aid sources, and interviews with college students from across the U.S. Also accepts pieces on general interest, personal experience, travel, humor, or new products/trends for college students; 750-2,000 words; pay varies. **Fillers:** Humor, anecdotes, newsbreaks; 25-250 words; $25-$100. **Queries:** Required. **Response:** 1 month. **Freelance Content:** 80%. **Rights:** Reprint, work-for-hire.

FLORIDA LEADER

Oxendine Publishing, Inc., 412 NW 16th Ave., P.O. Box 14081, Gainesville, FL 32604-2081. 352-373-6907. E-mail: stephanie@studentleader.com. Website: www.floridaleader.com. 3x/yr. Stephanie R. Reck, Editor. **Description:** Articles focus on student leadership, college success, and career growth in Florida and the Southeast. Targets Florida high school and college students who participate in student government, academic societies, honor societies, community-service organizations, and other student activities. Articles run 800-1,000 words; $35-$75. **Payment:** On publication.

HISPANIC TIMES MAGAZINE

Hispanic Times Enterprises, 3337 W Florida Ave., Hemet, CA 92545-3513. 213-250-4798. 3x/yr. $30/yr. Circ.: 49,000. Gloria J. Davis, Editor. **Description:** Magazine for Hispanic professionals and college students. Focus on careers, businesses, and employment opportunities.

MINORITY ENGINEER

Equal Opportunity Publications, Inc., 445 Broad Hollow Rd., Suite 425, Melville, NY 11747-4803. 631-421-9421. E-mail: jschneider@eop.com. Website: www.eop.com. 3x/yr. Circ.: 17,000. James Schneider, Editor. **Description:** Targets engineering, computer-science, and information technology students and professionals who are Black, Hispanic, Native American, and Asian American. **Nonfiction:** Career opportunities, job-hunting techniques, new technologies, role-model profiles and interviews; 1,000-2,000 words; $.10/word. **Queries:** Preferred. **E-Queries:** Yes. **Unsolicited mss:** Accepts. **Response:** 2 weeks. **SASE Required:** Yes. **Freelance Content:** 60%. **Rights:** FNAR. **Payment:** On publication.

STUDENT LEADER
Oxendine Publishing, Inc., P.O. Box 14081, Gainesville, FL 32604-2081. 352-373-6907. E-mail: anna.campitelli@studentleader.com. Website: www.studentleader.com. 3x/yr. $39/yr. Circ.: 50,000. Anna Campitelli, Associate Editor. **Description:** Covers leadership issues and career and college success for outstanding students who are involved in campus leadership activities. Other topics include promotion, raising money, recruiting volunteers, communicating with administration and the media, etc.; 800-1,000 words; $50-$100. **Tips:** Include quotes from faculty, corporate recruiters, current students, and recent alumni. **Queries:** Required. **Unsolicited mss:** Accepts. **Payment:** On publication.

UCLA MAGAZINE
10920 Wilshire Blvd., Suite 1500, Los Angeles, CA 90024-6517. E-mail: magazine@support.ucla.edu. Website: www.magazine.ucla.edu. Quarterly. $8/yr. Circ.: 235,000. David Greenwald, Editor. **Description:** Focus on people and issues relevant to the university and its primarily alumni readership. Articles include research, profiles and issue-oriented columns. **Queries:** Required. **Unsolicited mss:** Do not accept. **SASE Required:** No. **Freelance Content:** 30%. **Rights:** FNAR. **Payment:** On acceptance.

UNIQUE OPPORTUNITIES
214 S 8th St., Suite 502, Louisville, KY 40202. 502-589-8250.
E-mail: tellus@uoworks.com. Website: www.uoworks.com. Bimonthly. $5/$25. Circ.: 80,000. Mollie V. Hudson, Editor; Bett Coffman, Associate Editor. **Description:** Offers guidance to physicians on career development by providing the economic, business, legal, and career-related issues involved in finding and running a practice. Topics include contract negotiation, practice types, financial matters, legal matters, practice management, etc.; 1,500-3,500 words; $.50-$.75/word. **Queries:** Required. **E-Queries:** Yes. **Response:** 2 months. **SASE Required:** Yes. **Freelance Content:** 45%. **Rights:** FNASR. **Payment:** On acceptance.

COMPUTERS

C/C++ (USERS JOURNAL)
CMP Media LLC, 4601 W 6th St., Suite B, Lawrence, KS 66049-4189. 785-838-7500. E-mail: cujed@cmp.com. Website: www.cuj.com. Monthly. $24.95/yr. Circ.: 43,000. Joe Casad, Editor-in-Chief. **Description:** Features articles and source code on C/C++ and Java programming for professional programmers. Articles should be practical, "how-to" guides that provide sample source code. Algorithms, libraries, frameworks, class designs, book reviews, tutorials, and other special techniques that

solve programming problems are also accepted; 800-2,500 words (80-300 lines of code). **Tips:** Send proposal with 1-2 paragraph abstract, 1-page outline, and brief bio. Prefers to receive proposals and mss. via e-mail. **Queries:** Preferred. **E-Queries:** Yes. **Unsolicited mss:** Does not accept. **Response:** 2-4 weeks.

CLOSING THE GAP
See full listing in Abilities category.

COMPUTER BITS MAGAZINE
P.O. Box 2695, Clackamas, OR 97015. E-mail: editor@computerbits.com. Website: www.computerbits.com. Monthly. $20/yr. Circ.: 25,000. Dennis Bridges, Editor. **Description:** Articles that enhance the computer experience of readers. **Tips:** "We rarely print reviews. We prefer to help our readers use their computers in life and business enhancing ways." **Queries:** Preferred. **Unsolicited mss:** Accepts. **Freelance Content:** 40%. **Rights:** FNAR. **Payment:** On publication.

COMPUTER GRAPHICS WORLD
PennWell Corporation, 98 Spit Brook Rd., Nashua, NH 03062-5737. Website: www.cgw.com. Monthly. $50/yr. Circ.: 48,600. Phil LoPiccolo, Editor-in-Chief. **Description:** On computer graphics technology and its use in science, engineering, architecture, film and broadcast, and interactive entertainment. Computer-generated images. **Nonfiction:** Articles, 800-3,000 words; pays $600-$1,200. **Queries:** Preferred. **Payment:** On acceptance.

COMPUTOREDGE MAGAZINE
P.O. Box 83086, San Diego, CA 92138. 858-573-0315.
E-mail: editor@computoredge.com; submissions@computoredge.com.
Website: www.computoredge.com. Weekly. $35/yr. Circ.: 300,000. Patricia Smith, Editor. **Description:** *ComputorEdge* features non-technical, entertaining articles on computer hardware and software for both average users and experts. **Nonfiction:** Feature articles and columns cover online systems, the Internet, Macintosh systems, common computer problems, etc.; 1,000-1,200 words. **Columns, Departments:** Mac Madness, I Don't Do Windows; 800-900 words. **Tips:** Query via e-mail with brief description of idea and writing credentials. **Queries:** Required. **E-Queries:** Yes. **Unsolicited mss:** Does not accept. **Response:** 1-3 months. **Freelance Content:** 80%. **Rights:** FNASR.

IEEE COMPUTER GRAPHICS AND APPLICATIONS
10662 Los Vaqueros Circle, Los Alamitos, CA 90720. E-mail: cga@computer.org. Website: www.computer.org/cga. Bimonthly. $104/yr. Circ.: 8,000. John C. Dill, Editor-in-Chief. **Description:** Peer-reviewed publication covering the field of computer graphics and applications. Accepts application department proposals that show how computer graphics solve real-world problems; 3,200-5500 words; $400/page. **Tips:** New writers should submit resumé and writing samples. **Rights:** All.

MACWORLD

501 Second St., Fl. 5, San Francisco, CA 94107. 415-243-0505.
E-mail: macworld@macworld.com. Website: www.macworld.com. Monthly.
$34.97/yr. Circ.: 400,000. Jason Snell, Editor-in-Chief. **Description:** Reviews, news, consumer, how-to articles, varying lengths, related to Macintosh computers. Query with clips only. Pays $150-$3,500. **Tips:** "We provide comprehensive coverage of the most innovative and exciting new products developed for the Mac platform. Each month, Macworld's respected experts produce in-depth product reviews, objective lab-based comparisons, compelling features, and practical how-to articles to keep both the professional and expert Mac user up-to-date and productive with the latest technologies." **Queries:** Preferred. **Unsolicited mss:** Does not accept. **Payment:** On acceptance.

NETWORK WORLD

118 Turnpike Rd., Southborough, MA 01772-2104. 508-460-3333.
E-mail: nwnews@nww.com. Website: www.nwfusion.com. Weekly. $95/yr. Circ.: 151,400. John Dix, Editor-in-Chief. **Description:** On applications of communications technology for management level users of data, voice, and video communications systems; to 2,500 words; pay varies. **Payment:** On acceptance.

PEI (PHOTO ELECTRONIC IMAGING)

Professional Photographers of America, Inc., 229 Peachtree St. NE, Suite 2200, Atlanta, GA 30303. 404-522-8600. Website: www.peimag.com. Bimonthly. $20/yr. Circ.: 36,000. Cameron Bishopp, Executive Editor. **Description:** On electronic imaging, computer graphics, desktop publishing, pre-press and commercial printing, latest advances in technology, multimedia, etc.; 1,000-3,000 words; pay varies. **Tips:** Articles by assignment only. **Queries:** Required. **Payment:** On publication.

PEN COMPUTING MAGAZINE

Aeon Publishing Group, 4045 Sunset Lane, Suite A, Shingle Springs, CA 95682-6800. 530-676-7878. Website: www.pencomputing.com. Bimonthly. $18/yr. Circ.: 76,000. Conrad Blickenstorfer, Editor-in-Chief. **Description:** Articles on pen computing technology, PDAs and mobile and wireless computing. Submissions can be in the form of columns, reviews, opinions, or feature articles and should be written for a technically-knowledgeable audience. Payment runs $150-$450 for one page columns and $100-$1,000 for full-length features. **Tips:** "Our readers share a passion for new technology that will help them get their tasks completed faster and more efficiently."

SOFTWARE MAGAZINE

King Content Co., P.O. Box 135, East Walpole, MA 02032. 508-668-9928.
E-mail: lisaz@softwaremag.com. Website: www.softwaremag.com. Quarterly.
John P. Desmond, Publisher/Editorial Director. **Description:** For corporate systems managers and MIS personnel. Features articles on the latest software. **Tips:** E-mail abstract and brief bio to Lisa Zschuschen, Editorial Assistant.

TECHNOLOGY & LEARNING
See full listing in Education category.

TECHNOLOGY REVIEW
Massachusetts Institute of Technology, One Main St., Fl. 7, Cambridge, MA 02142. 617-475-8000. Website: www.technologyreview.com. Robert Buderi, Editor-in-Chief. **Description:** Features general-interest articles on technology and innovation. Pay varies. **Queries:** Preferred. **Payment:** On acceptance.

CONSUMER & PERSONAL FINANCE

THE AMERICAN SPECTATOR
Alfred Regnery, 1611 N Kent St., Suite 901, Arlington, VA 20009. E-mail: editor@spectator.org. Website: www.spectator.org. Monthly. Circ.: 50,000. R. Emmett Tyrrell, Jr., Editor. **Description:** Technical, political, and cultural guide for the investor in the new economy. **Tips:** Query with article clips. Sample copy $5.95. **Queries:** Required. **E-Queries:** No. **Unsolicited mss:** Does not accept. **Response:** 30 days. **Freelance Content:** 50%. **Rights:** All.

CONSUMER REPORTS
Consumers Union of U.S., Inc., 101 Truman Ave., Yonkers, NY 10703-1044. 914-378-2000. Website: www.consumerreports.org. Monthly. $26/yr. Circ.: 4,100,000. Kimberly Kleman, Managing Editor. **Description:** Award-winning journalistic research on health, personal finance, and matters of public policy. Also, independent product-testing reports. **Tips:** "We're mostly staff-written, except for occasional back-of-book columns on health or personal finance. We only work with published writers." **Queries:** Required. **E-Queries:** Yes. **Unsolicited mss:** Accepts. **Response:** 1-3 weeks. **SASE Required:** Yes. **Freelance Content:** 1%. **Rights:** All.

THE DOLLAR STRETCHER
3651 Cortez Row, Bradenton, FL 34210. 941-752-6693. E-mail: gary@stretcher.com. Website: www.stretcher.com. Monthly. $18/yr. Circ.: 45,000. Gary Foreman, Editor. **Description:** Offers practical advice on saving time and money. Articles run 750 words; $.10/word. **Queries:** Not necessary. **Unsolicited mss:** Accepts. **Response:** 2 months. **Freelance Content:** 100%. **Rights:** All. **Payment:** On acceptance.

KIPLINGER'S PERSONAL FINANCE
Kiplinger Washington Editors, Inc., 1729 H Street NW, Washington, DC 20006. 202-887-6400. E-mail: magazine@kiplinger.com. Website: www.kiplinger.com. Monthly. $19.95/yr. Circ.: 1,018,000. Knight Kiplinger, Editor-in-Chief. **Description:** Offers practical advice to individual investors on personal finance issues (investments, mutual funds, insurance, taxes, retirement planning, college loans, etc.). **Tips:** Primarily staff-written, but accepts some material from freelancers. Be familiar with the publication before pitching ideas. **Queries:** Required. **Response:** 1 month.

THE MONEYPAPER

555 Theodore Fremd Ave., Suite B-103, Rye, NY 10580-1451. 914-925-0022. E-mail: moneypaper@moneypaper.com. Website: www.moneypaper.com. Monthly. $90/yr. Vita Nelson, Publisher/Editor. **Description:** Financial news and money-saving ideas. Brief, well-researched articles on personal finance, money management, saving, earning, investing, taxes, insurance, and other related subjects. **Tips:** Include resumé and writing sample. Seeking information about companies with dividend reinvestment plans. **Queries:** Preferred. **Payment:** On publication. **Contact:** David Fish, Executive Editor.

CONTEMPORARY CULTURE

AMERICAN DEMOGRAPHICS

PRIMEDIA Business Magazines & Media, 249 W 17th St., New York, NY 10011. Website: www.demographics.com. Monthly. $59/yr. Circ.: 22,400. John McManus, Editor. **Description:** Articles, 500-2,000 words, on four key elements of a consumer market (size, needs and wants, ability to pay, and how it can be reached). Includes specific examples of how companies market to consumers. Readers include marketers, advertisers, and planners. **Queries:** Preferred.

AMERICAN SCHOLAR

1606 New Hampshire Ave., NW, Washington, DC 20009. 202-265-3808. E-mail: scholar@pbk.org. Website: www.pbk.org. Quarterly. $6.95/issue. Circ.: 25,000. Anne Fadiman, Editor. **Description:** For intelligent people who love the English language. **Nonfiction:** By experts, for general audience; 3,000-5,000 words; $500. **Poetry:** Highly original; to 33 lines; $50. **Queries:** Preferred. **E-Queries:** Yes. **Unsolicited mss:** Accepts. **Response:** 2-4 months. **SASE Required:** Yes. **Freelance Content:** 100%. **Rights:** FNAR. **Payment:** On acceptance.

AMERICAS

19th & Constitution Ave., NW #300, Washington, DC 20036. 202-458-6846. E-mail: americasmagazine@oas.org. Website: www.oas.org. Bimonthly. $18/yr. Circ.: 65,000. James Patrick Kiernan, Editorial Director. **Description:** On a variety of topics (anthropology, the arts, travel, science, etc.) in relation to Latin America and the Caribbean. Articles run 8-10 pages (2,500 words max). **Tips:** Prefers stories that can be well-illustrated. No political material. **Queries:** Required. **Rights:** One-time. **Payment:** On publication. **Contact:** Rebecca Medrano, Managing Editor.

BPM CULTURE MAGAZINE

8517 Santa Monica Blvd., West Hollywood, CA 90069-4107. 310-360-7170. E-mail: info@djmixed.com. Website: www.djmixed.com. 10x/yr. $3.95/$15. Circ.: 45,000. David Ireland, Editor-in-Chief. **Description:** For young adults interested in electronic music, entertainment, video games, DVD's, Internet topics, and other high-tech gadgets. **Tips:** "Understand the culture that we cover—we are a youth culture magazine and are talking to the tastemakers (hip, cool, edgy). Writers should avoid topics geared towards mainstream or older people." **Queries:** Preferred. **Unsolicited mss:** Accepts. **Response:** 5-10 weeks. **SASE Required:** Yes. **Freelance Content:** 70%. **Rights:** One-time. **Payment:** On publication. **Contact:** Rob Simas, Managing Editor.

BRICK

Box 537, Stn Q, Toronto, Ontario M4T 2M5 Canada. E-mail: info@brickmag.com. Website: www.brickmag.com. **Description:** Literary journal for nonfiction. **Tips:** Do not query; prefers complete manuscript. Does not accept fiction of poetry submissions. See guidelines on website. Sample copy $12 (U.S.) plus $3 (U.S.) for shipping. **Queries:** Not necessary. **Response:** 6+ months.

CHRONICLES

The Rockford Institute, 928 N Main St., Rockford, IL 61103-7061. 815-964-5054. E-mail: tri@rockfordinstitute.org. Website: www.chroniclesmagazine.org. Monthly. $39/yr. Circ.: 14,000. Scott Richert, Editor. **Description:** "A Magazine of American Culture." Seeks articles and poetry that display craftsmanship and a sense of form.

THE CIRCLE MAGAZINE

See full listing in Literary Fiction & Poetry category.

COMMONWEAL

475 Riverside Dr., Room 405, New York, NY 10115. 212-662-4200. E-mail: editors@commonwealmagazine.org. Website: www.commonwealmagazine.org. 22x/yr. $3/$47. Circ.: 20,000. Paul Baumann, Editor. **Description:** Review of public affairs, religion, literature and the arts, published by Catholic lay people. **Nonfiction:** On political, religious, social, and literary subjects; 1,000-3,000 words; pays $100. **Poetry:** Submit 5 poems max. (October-May), serious, witty; pays $.75/line. **Columns, Departments:** Brief newsy facts, behind the headlines, reflective pieces; 750-1,000 words; $75. **Tips:** Does not accept simultaneous submissions. "Focus on religion, politics, and culture and how they intertwine." **Queries:** Not necessary. **E-Queries:** Yes. **Unsolicited mss:** Accepts. **Response:** 4-6 weeks. **SASE Required:** Yes. **Freelance Content:** 20%. **Rights:** All. **Payment:** On publication.

FLAUNT

1422 N Highland Ave., Los Angeles, CA 90028-7611. 323-836-1000. E-mail: mail@flauntmagazine.com. Monthly. $50/yr. Circ.: 100,000. Luis Barajas, Editor-in-Chief. **Description:** Photography and writing, also coverage of arts, fashion, architecture, design, and music. Accepts fiction, nonfiction, and puzzles. **Tips:** Send published clips for editor's review. **Queries:** Preferred. **E-Queries:** Yes. **Freelance Content:** 90%. **Rights:** One-time. **Payment:** On publication.

GEIST
Geist Foundation, 1014 Homer St., #103, Vancouver, British Columbia V6B 2W9 Canada. 604-681-9161. E-mail: geist@geist.com. Website: www.geist.com. Quarterly. $16/yr. Circ.: 7,000. Stephen Osborne, Editor-in-Chief. **Description:** "Canadian Magazine of Ideas and Culture." Creative nonfiction (200-1,000 words); excerpts from works in progress (300-1,500 words); and long essays and short stories (2,000-5,000 words). Pay varies. **Tips:** Strongly prefers Canadian content. No e-mail submissions. Sample copy $5. **Queries:** Preferred. **Payment:** On publication.

HISPANIC MAGAZINE
See full listing in Ethnic & Multicultural category.

JUXTAPOZ
High Speed Productions, Inc., 1303 Underwood Ave., San Francisco, CA 94124. 415-822-3083. E-mail: editor@juxtapoz.com. Website: www.juxtapoz.com. Bimonthly. $13.95/yr. Circ.: 70,000. Jamie O'Shea, Editor. **Description:** Publication with focus on modern arts and culture.

LOLLIPOP MAGAZINE
See full listing in Performing Arts category.

NATIVE PEOPLES
See full listing in Ethnic & Multicultural category.

PARABOLA
See full listing in New Age/Spiritual category.

ROLLING STONE
See full listing in Performing Arts category.

RUMINATOR REVIEW
1648 Grand Ave., St. Paul, MN 55105-1804. 651-699-2610.
E-mail: review@ruminator.com. Website: www.ruminator.com. $14/yr. Circ.: 30,000. Margaret Todd Maitland, Editor. **Description:** Quarterly, thematic magazine of book reviews, essays, and interviews. **Art:** B&W, digital, or CRC. **Tips:** "Since each issue is based on a different theme, very few unsolicited reviews are used. But if you've got solid, published clips, send them in with a list of styles and genres you're interested in. If it is a good match, it can lead to an assignment." **Queries:** Preferred. **E-Queries:** Yes. **Response:** 1-2 months. **SASE Required:** Yes. **Freelance Content:** 50%. **Rights:** 1st and 2nd serial.

THE SOUTHWEST REVIEW
Southern Methodist University, P.O. Box 750374, Dallas, TX 75275-0374. 214-768-1037. E-mail: swr@mail.smu.edu. Website: www.southwestreview.org. Quarterly. $6/issue. Elizabeth Mills, Senior Editor. **Description:** Wide-ranging, for adults, on

contemporary affairs, history, folklore, fiction, poetry, literary criticism, art, music, and theater. Prose pieces, 3,500-7,000 words; $100-$300. Poetry, $50-$150. **Tips:** See website for guidelines. **Queries:** Not necessary. **E-Queries:** No. **Unsolicited mss:** Accepts. **Response:** 3 months. **SASE Required:** Yes. **Rights:** FNAR. **Payment:** On publication.

TROIKA
Lone Tout Publications, P.O. Box 1006, Weston, CT 06883. 203-319-0873.
E-mail: submit@troikamagazine.com. Website: www.troikamagazine.com. Quarterly. Circ.: 120,000. Celia Meadow, Editor. **Description:** Cutting-edge, contemporary culture forum with features on the arts, health, science, human interest, international interests, business, leisure, ethics. For educated, affluent baby-boomers, seeking to balance personal achievements, family commitments, and community involvement. Varied length; $200 and up. **Tips:** "We seek to inform, entertain, and enlighten—to be a global voice in a rapidly globalizing world." **Queries:** Not necessary. **E-Queries:** Preferred. **Unsolicited mss:** Accepts. **Response:** Queries 10 days, submissions 3 months. **SASE Required:** Yes. **Freelance Content:** 95%. **Rights:** All. **Payment:** 90 days from publication.

UTNE MAGAZINE
1624 Harmon Pl., Suite 330, Minneapolis, MN 55403-1906. 612-338-5040. E-mail: editor@utne.com. Website: www.utne.com. Bimonthly. $4.99/$19.97. Circ.: 225,000. Karen Olson, Editor. **Description:** Offers alternative ideas and culture, reprinting articles selected from over 2,000 alternative media sources. Also, previously unpublished short pieces, 300-1,000 words. Provocative perspectives, analysis of art and media, down-to-earth news and resources, compelling people and issues. **Tips:** Prefers queries sent via e-mail. **Unsolicited mss:** Does not accept. **Response:** 4-6 weeks. **SASE Required:** Yes. **Freelance Content:** 10%. **Rights:** Nonexclusive worldwide. **Payment:** On publication.

THE WORLD AND I
See full listing in General Interest category.

CURRENT EVENTS & POLITICS

AMERICAN EDUCATOR
See full listing in Education category.

THE AMERICAN LEGION MAGAZINE
P.O. Box 1055, Indianapolis, IN 46206-1055. 317-630-1200.
E-mail: magazine@legion.org. Website: www.legion.org. Monthly. $3.50/$15. Circ.: 2,600,000. John B. Raughter, Editor. **Description:** Covers current world affairs, public policy, and subjects of contemporary interest. Pieces run 750-2,000 words; pay negotiable. **Queries:** Preferred. **E-Queries:** Yes. **Payment:** On acceptance.

BRIARPATCH

Briarpatch Society, 2138 McIntyre St., Regina, Saskatchewan S4P 2R7 Canada. 306-525-2949. E-mail: briarrequest@netscape.net. Website: www.briarpatch-magazine.com. 10x/yr. $3/$24.61. Circ.: 5,000. Debra Brin, Managing Editor. **Description:** Progressive Canadian newsmagazine with a left-wing political slant. Articles on politics, women's issues, environment, labor, international affairs for Canadian activists involved in social-change issues. Also, short reviews of recent books and CDs. **Tips:** "Use journalistic style, with quotes from involved people. We're looking for hard-hitting, thought-provoking stories." **Queries:** Preferred. **E-Queries:** Yes. **Unsolicited mss:** Accepts. **Freelance Content:** 100%. **Rights:** None. **Payment:** In copies.

CALIFORNIA JOURNAL

2101 K St., Sacramento, CA 95816. 916-444-2840. E-mail: edit@californiajournal.com. Website: www.californiajournal.com. Monthly. $39.95. Circ.: 8,000. A.G. Block, Editor. **Description:** Features nonpartisan reports on California government and politics. Articles run 1,000-2,500 words; $300-$1,200. **Queries:** Required. **E-Queries:** Yes. **Unsolicited mss:** Do not accept. **Response:** 1-2 weeks. **SASE Required:** Yes. **Freelance Content:** 30%. **Rights:** All. **Payment:** On publication.

CAMPAIGNS & ELECTIONS

Votenet Solutions, Inc., 2045 15th St. N, Suite 304, Arlington, VA 22201-2614. 703-248-9497. Website: www.campaignline.com. Monthly. $39.95/yr. Circ.: 30,400. Ron Faucheux, Publisher/Editor. **Description:** On strategies, techniques, trends, and personalities of political campaigning. **Nonfiction:** Features, 700-4,000 words; campaign case-studies, 1,500-3,000 words; how-tos, 700-2,000 words, on aspects of campaigning; in-depth studies, 700-3,000 words, on public opinion, election results, and political trends. **Payment:** In copies.

CHRISTIAN SOCIAL ACTION

See full listing in Religion category.

COLUMBIA JOURNALISM REVIEW

Columbia University, 2950 Broadway #207 Journalism Bldg., New York, NY 10027-7004. 212-854-1881. E-mail: cjr@columbia.edu. Website: www.cjr.org. Bimonthly. $27.95/yr. Circ.: 21,700. Gloria Cooper, Deputy Executive Editor. **Description:** Amusing mistakes in news stories, headlines, photos, etc., for "Lower Case" department. Original clippings required. Pays $25. **Payment:** On publication.

COMMENTARY

See full listing in Religion category.

THE CRISIS

See full listing in Ethnic & Multicultural category.

FOREIGN SERVICE JOURNAL

American Foreign Service Assn., 2101 E Street NW, Washington, DC 20037. 202-338-4045. E-mail: journal@afsa.org. Website: www.afsa.org/fsj/index.html. Monthly. $40/yr. Circ.: 13,000. Steve Honley, Editor. **Description:** Covers foreign affairs and the U.S. Foreign Service. **Fiction:** Stories with overseas settings, for fiction issue (summer), submit in April 1; 3,000 words max; $250. **Nonfiction:** On foreign policy and international issues, for Foreign Service and diplomatic community; 2,000-3,000 words; payment negotiable. **Columns, Departments:** Open to short travel pieces about foreign scene, person, place, incident; 600-700 words; $100. **Tips:** "Knowledge of foreign service concerns is essential." **Queries:** Not necessary. **Unsolicited mss:** Accepts. **Response:** 1 month. **Freelance Content:** 25%.

THE FREEMAN: IDEAS ON LIBERTY

The Foundation for Economic Education, 30 S Broadway, Irvington, NY 10533. 914-591-7230. E-mail: fee@fee.org; srichman@fee.org. Website: www.fee.org. Sheldon Richman, Editor. **Description:** On economic, political, and moral benefits of private property, voluntary exchange, individual choice, and limited government. Articles to 2,000 words; $.10/ published word. **Payment:** On publication.

HARPER'S MAGAZINE

Harper's Magazine Foundation, 666 Broadway, Fl. 11, New York, NY 10012-2317. 212-420-5720. E-mail: editorial@harpers.org. Website: www.harpers.org. Monthly. $15/yr. Circ.: 250,000. Lewis H. Lapham, Editor. **Description:** On politics, literary, cultural, scientific issues. **Fiction:** Will consider unsolicited manuscripts, SASE required. **Nonfiction:** Very limited market; 2,000-5,000 words. **Queries:** Required.

HOMELAND DEFENSE JOURNAL

4301 Wilson Blvd., Suite 1003, Arlington, VA 22203. 703-807-2758. E-mail: editor@homelanddefensejournal.com. Website: www.homelanddefensejournal.com. Monthly. Circ.: 20,000. David Silverberg, Editor. **Description:** In-depth analysis of homeland-related topics, the people leading this community, and those that support them. Articles must be unbiased and product-neutral, focused on an event, trend, initiative or project. No simultaneous submissions. Articles run to 1,000 words. **Art:** Provide photos, charts, slides, artwork or any supporting material that would enhance the presentation of the article. **E-Queries:** Yes. **Unsolicited mss:** Accepts. **Rights:** All.

THE HOMELESS REPORTER NEWS-SHEET

P.O. Box 1053, Dallas, TX 75221-1053. Bill Mason, Editor. **Description:** An insider's view and dialogue on solving homelessness. Articles and essays (300-1,500 words) on ways to solve the socio-economic problems of homelessness and poverty. Also human-interest love stories set in that context. **Queries:** Preferred. **E-Queries:** No. **Unsolicited mss:** Accepts. **Payment:** In copies.

IN THESE TIMES

Institute for Public Affairs, 2040 N Milwaukee Ave., Fl. 2, Chicago, IL 60647. 773-772-0100. E-mail: itt@inthesetimes.com. Website: www.inthesetimes.com. Biweekly. $36.95/yr. Circ.: 20,000. Joel Bleifuss, Editor. **Description:** Seeks to inform and analyze popular movements for social, environmental and economic justice in the U.S. and abroad. News reporting, op-eds, and book reviews on left politics, the environment, human rights, labor, etc.; 500-3,000 words; $.12/word. **Tips:** "Avoid excessive editorializing. We look for strong news reporting and writing skills." **Queries:** Preferred. **E-Queries:** Yes. **Unsolicited mss:** Accepts. **Response:** 6-8 weeks. **Freelance Content:** 90%. **Rights:** Reprint. **Payment:** On publication.

LATINO LEADERS

See full listing in Ethnic & Multicultural category.

MIDWEST QUARTERLY

Pittsburg State University, Pittsburg, KS 66762. 620-235-4369.
E-mail: midwestq@pittstate.edu. Website: www.pittstate.edu/engl/midwest.htm.
Quarterly. $15. Circ.: 550. James B. M. Schick, Editor. **Description:** Scholarly articles on contemporary academic and public issues, 18-20 pages. Also accepts poetry, to 70 lines. **Tips:** No payment offered. **Queries:** Preferred. **E-Queries:** Yes. **Unsolicited mss:** Accepts. **Response:** Queries 1 week, submissions 4-6 months. **SASE Required:** Yes.

MONTHLY REVIEW

122 W 27th St., Fl. 10, New York, NY 10001. 212-691-2555.
E-mail: mrmag@monthlyreview.org. Website: www.monthlyreview.org. 11x/yr. $4/$29. Circ.: 7,000. John Bellamy Foster, Editor. **Description:** Analytical pieces on politics, economics, international affairs, and current events, from an independent socialist perspective. Articles run 3,000-4,000 words, book reviews 1,500-2,000 words. Pays $25. **Tips:** "Avoid pieces that date quickly, as it take six months to publish. Looking for solid Marxist analysis." **Queries:** Not necessary. **E-Queries:** Yes. **Unsolicited mss:** Accepts. **Response:** 2 months. **Freelance Content:** 95%. **Payment:** On publication. **Contact:** Claude Misukiewicz, Assistant Editor.

MOTHER JONES

Foundation for National Progress, 731 Market St., Suite 600, San Francisco, CA 94103. 415-665-6637. E-mail: query@motherjones.com. Website: www.motherjones.com. Bimonthly. $5.95/$24. Circ.: 225,000. Roger Cohn, Editor-in-Chief. **Description:** Independent journalism publication focusing on issues of social justice. Features, 1,500-4,000 words, $1,500-$4,000. Short pieces, 100-800 words, $100-$500. Also book, film, and music reviews. **Tips:** "We're looking for investigative reports exposing government cover-ups, corporate malfeasance, scientific myopia, institutional fraud or hypocrisy." **Queries:** Required. **E-Queries:** Yes. **Unsolicited mss:** Do not accept. **Response:** 2-3 months. **SASE Required:** Yes. **Freelance Content:** 95%. **Payment:** On acceptance.

MS. MAGAZINE
See full listing in Women's Publications category.

THE NATION
33 Irving Place, Fl. 8, New York, NY 10003-2332. 212-209-5400. E-mail: info@thenation.com. Website: www.thenation.com. Weekly. $52/yr. Circ.: 139,600. Katrina vanden Heuvel, Editor. **Description:** Politics and culture from a liberal, left perspective, on national and international affairs. Editorials and full-length pieces run 1,500-2,500 words; $75/printed page ($300 max.). **Tips:** "Looking for reporting, with fresh analysis and national significance, on U.S. civil liberties, civil rights, labor, economics, environmental, feminist issues, and the role and future of the Democratic Party." **Queries:** Required. **Unsolicited mss:** Accepts. **SASE Required:** Yes. **Payment:** On publication.

NEW JERSEY REPORTER
Public Policy Center of New Jersey, 36 W Lafayette St., Trenton, NJ 08608. 609-392-2003. E-mail: editor@publicpolicynj.org. Website: www.njreporter.org. Bimonthly. Circ.: 3,200. Mark J. Magyar, Editor. **Description:** In-depth articles, 1,000-4,000 words, on New Jersey politics and public affairs. Pays $175-$800. **Queries:** Required. **Payment:** On publication.

THE NEW YORKER
Condé Nast Publications, Inc., 4 Times Square, Fl. 20, New York, NY 10036. 212-286-2860. Website: www.newyorker.com. Weekly. $49.95/yr. Circ.: 938,600. David Remnick, Editor. **Description:** "We cover the vital stories of our time with intelligence, wit, stylish prose, and a keen eye." **Fiction:** Short stories, humor, and satire. **Nonfiction:** Amusing mistakes in newspapers, books, magazines, etc. Also, political/social essays. Up to 1,000 words. **Poetry:** Send up to 6 poems. **Columns, Departments:** Factual and biographical articles for Profiles, Reporter at Large, etc. Up to 1,000 words. **Tips:** Send all submissions to the appropriate department in the body of an e-mail (not as an attachment). Fiction: fiction@newyorker.com. Talk of the Town: talkofthetown@newyorker.com. Shouts & Murmurs: shouts@newyorker.com. Poetry: poetry@newyorker.com. Letters to the Editor: themail@newyorker.com. **Queries:** Not necessary. **E-Queries:** Yes. **Unsolicited mss:** Does not accept. **Response:** 8 weeks. **Rights:** FNAR. **Payment:** On publication.

THE OLDER AMERICAN
See full listing in Seniors Magazines category.

ONEARTH
See full listing in Environment & Conservation category.

POLICY REVIEW

Hoover Institution, 21 Dupont Circle NW, Suite 310, Washington, DC 20036. 202-466-6730. E-mail: polrev@hoover.stanford.edu. Website: www.policyreview.org. Bimonthly. $6/issue. Circ.: 8,000. Tod Lindberg, Editor. **Description:** Book reviews and full-length articles on public policy; 1,000-5,000 words. **Tips:** Freelance content limited. **Queries:** Preferred. **E-Queries:** Yes. **Unsolicited mss:** Accepts. **Response:** 2-4 weeks. **SASE Required:** Yes. **Freelance Content:** 5%. **Payment:** On publication. **Contact:** Steven Menashi.

THE PROGRESSIVE

409 E Main St., Madison, WI 53703. 608-257-4626.
E-mail: editorial@progressive.org. Website: www.progressive.org. Monthly. $3.50/$32. Circ.: 75,000. Matthew Rothschild, Editor. **Description:** A leading voice for peace and social justice, with fresh and lively commentary on major issues. **Nonfiction:** Investigative reporting; coverage of elections, social movements, foreign policy; interviews, activism, book reviews; $500-$1,300. **Poetry:** On political concerns; $150/poem. **Queries:** Preferred. **Unsolicited mss:** Accepts. **Freelance Content:** 30%. **Payment:** On publication.

REASON

The Reason Foundation, 3415 S Sepulveda Blvd., Suite 400, Los Angeles, CA 90034. 310-391-2245. E-mail: letters@reason.com. Website: www.reason.com. Weekly. Circ.: 60,000. Nick Gillespie, Editor-in-Chief. **Description:** "Free Minds and Free Markets." Looks at politics, economics, and culture from libertarian perspective. Articles 850-5,000 words; pay varies. **Queries:** Preferred. **Payment:** On acceptance.

ROLL CALL

50 F Street NW, Suite 700, Washington, DC 20001. 202-824-6800.
E-mail: letters@rollcall.com. Website: www.rollcall.com. Biweekly. $380/yr. Circ.: 19,400. Morton Kondracke, Executive Editor. **Description:** Covers Capitol Hill. Factual, breezy articles, political or Congressional angle (history, human-interest, political lore, opinion, commentary). **Queries:** Preferred. **Payment:** On publication. **Contact:** Tim Curran, Edtior.

SOCIAL JUSTICE REVIEW

3835 Westminster Pl., St. Louis, MO 63108-3409. 314-371-1653. E-mail: centbur@juno.com. Website: www.socialjusticereview.org. Bimonthly. $20. Circ.: 5,000. Rev. John H. Miller, C.S.C., Editor. **Description:** Focuses on social justice and related issues. Articles should be under 3,000 words; $.02/word. **Tips:** Submissions must be faithful to doctrine of the Catholic Church. **Queries:** Preferred. **E-Queries:** No. **Unsolicited mss:** Accepts. **Response:** 2 weeks. **SASE Required:** Yes. **Freelance Content:** 80%. **Rights:** FNAR. **Payment:** On publication.

TIKKUN

Institute for Labor and Mental Health, 2342 Shattuck Ave., Suite 1200, Berkeley, CA 94704. 510-644-1200. E-mail: magazine@tikkun.org. Website: www.tikkun.org. Bimonthly. $29/yr. Circ.: 20,000. Michael Lerner, Editor. **Description:** Progressive Jewish commentary on politics, culture, and society. Based on the Jewish principle of Tikkun Olam (healing the world), encourages writers to join spirituality to politics, for politics infused with compassion and meaning. **Tips:** Avoid "My trip to Israel (or Eastern Europe/Auschwitz)," "My adult bar mitzvah," "How I became religious." **Queries:** Not necessary. **Unsolicited mss:** Accepts. **Response:** 3-4 months. **SASE Required:** Yes. **Freelance Content:** 20%. **Payment:** In copies.

U.S. NEWS AND WORLD REPORT

1050 Thomas Jefferson St., NW, Washington, DC 20007. 202-955-2000. E-mail: letters@usnews.com. Website: www.usnews.com. Weekly. $34.97/yr. Circ.: 2,201,300. Mortimer B. Zuckerman, Editor-in-Chief. **Description:** Reports on national and international news, politics, business, health, science, technology and social trends. **Queries:** Required. **Unsolicited mss:** Does not accept.

UTNE MAGAZINE

See full listing in Contemporary Culture category.

THE VILLAGE VOICE

Village Voice Media, Inc., 36 Cooper Square, New York, NY 10003.
Website: www.villagevoice.com. Donald H. Forst, Editor-in-Chief. **Description:** Alternative newspaper covering current and controversial topics in New York City. Features reports and criticism on local and national politics. Also reviews on art, music, dance, film, theatre, and other arts. Articles run 500-2,000 words; pays $100-$1,500. **Queries:** Preferred. **SASE Required:** Yes. **Payment:** On publication. **Contact:** Doug Simmons, Managing Editor.

THE WASHINGTON MONTHLY

733 15th St. NW, Suite 520, Washington, DC 20005. 202-393-5155.
E-mail: editors@washingtonmonthly.com. Website: www.washingtonmonthly.com. $5/issue. Paul Glastris, Editor-in-Chief. **Description:** Topical, informative articles, 1,000-4,000 words, on what's going on in Washington (politics/government) or on popular culture. Pays $.10/word, on publication.

THE WORLD AND I

See full listing in General Interest category.

YES! A JOURNAL OF POSITIVE FUTURES

Positive Futures Network, P.O. Box 10818, Bainbridge Island, WA 98110. 206-842-0216. E-mail: editors@yesmagazine.org. Website: www.yesmagazine.org. Quarterly. $24/yr. Circ.: 40,000. Sarah Ruth van Gelder, Executive Editor. **Description:** "We publish stories about people and groups who are addressing the systemic problems that face the world. In doing so, we hope to strengthen the movement to build a more just, sustainable, and compassionate world." Articles run 1,500-2,500 words; $20-$50. **Tips:** Read past articles and guidelines on web before sending queries. Seeks stories that highlight practical solutions rather than expose problems. **Queries:** Required.

YOUTH TODAY

1200 17th St. NW, Fl. 4, Washington, DC 20036. 202-785-0764. E-mail: info@youth-today.org. Website: www.youthtoday.org. 10x/yr. $24.50/yr. Circ.: 30,000. Patrick Boyle, Editor. **Description:** For people who work with kids (8 years old+), on the business of providing youth services. Seeks articles on funding and those that show evidence of "best practices" in serving youth; 1,500-2,000 words; $800-$2,000. **Tips:** "Read stories on our website first. Our readers are managers and frontline youth workers. The stories serve them, not parents and children. Avoid feel-good features." **Queries:** Required. **E-Queries:** Yes. **Unsolicited mss:** Does not accept. **Response:** 2 weeks. **SASE Required:** Yes. **Freelance Content:** 50%. **Rights:** FNAR. **Payment:** On publication.

EDUCATION

AMERICAN EDUCATOR

American Federation of Teachers, 555 New Jersey Ave. NW, Washington, DC 20001-2029. 202-879-4400. Website: www.aft.org. Quarterly. Circ.: 670,000. Ruth Wattenberg, Editor. **Description:** Well-researched news features on current trends and problems in education, education law, professional ethics, etc. Also, essays that explore current social issues relevant to American society. Pieces run 500-2,500 words; $300. **Queries:** Preferred. **Payment:** On publication.

AMERICAN JOURNAL OF HEALTH EDUCATION

AAHPERD, 1900 Association Dr., Reston, VA 20191. 703-476-3400. E-mail: johe@aahperd.org. Website: www.aahperd.org/aahe. Bimonthly. $120/yr. Circ.: 8,000. Becky J. Smith, Executive Editor. **Description:** For health education and promotion specialists in schools, agencies, business, hosipitals, and professional preperation. **Tips:** "All articles undergo peer review. Please submit your manuscript to us online at www.journalsubmit.com or send us a query at ajhe@aahperd.org." Does not offer payment. **Queries:** Preferred.

AMERICAN SCHOOL BOARD JOURNAL

National School Boards Assn., 1680 Duke St., Alexandria, VA 22314-3474. 703-838-6722. E-mail: submissions@asbj.com; editor@asbj.com. Website: www.asbj.com. Monthly. $54/yr. Circ.: 36,000. Sally Zakariya, Editor-in-Chief. **Description:** Informative articles in a practical format regarding educational trends for school board members and administrators.

AMERICAN SCHOOL & UNIVERSITY

PRIMEDIA Business Magazines & Media, 9800 Metcalf, P.O. Box 12901, Overland Park, KS 66212. 913-967-1960. E-mail: asu@primediabusiness.com. Website: www.asumag.com. Monthly. $50/yr. Circ.: 63,540. Joe Agron, Editor-in-Chief. **Description:** Articles and case studies, 1,200-1,500 words, on the design, construction, operation, and management of school and university facilities. **Tips:** Does not offer payment. **Queries:** Preferred.

BLACK ISSUES IN HIGHER EDUCATION

10520 Warwick Ave., Suite B-8, Fairfax, VA 22030-3136. 703-385-2981.
E-mail: hilary@cmabiccw.com. Website: www.blackissues.com. Biweekly. $3.50/$26. Circ.: 12,000. Hilary L. Hurd, Editor. **Description:** News and features on blacks in post-secondary education and public policy. **Nonfiction:** On issues affecting minorities in higher education. **Fillers:** On education and public policy. **Columns, Departments:** Opinion pieces. **Queries:** Preferred. **E-Queries:** Yes. **Unsolicited mss:** Accepts. **Freelance Content:** 40%. **Payment:** On publication.

BOOK LINKS

American Library Assn., 50 E Huron St., Chicago , IL 60611. 312-280-5718.
E-mail: ltillotson@ala.org. Website: www.ala.org/booklinks. Bimonthly. $28.95/yr. Circ.: 31,000. Laura Tillotson, Editor. **Description:** "Connecting Books, Libraries, and Classrooms." Professional journal for K-12 teachers, librarians, parents, educators. Articles should demonstrate ways in which children's and YA thematic literature can be integrated into curriculum for preschool–high school students; 2,000 words; $100. **Tips:** Query first or send draft as an attachment if it is written using Book Links style. **Queries:** Required. **E-Queries:** Yes. **Response:** 6-8 weeks. **Freelance Content:** 90%. **Rights:** All. **Payment:** On publication.

CABLE IN THE CLASSROOM

CCI/Crosby Publishing, 214 Lincoln St., Suite 112, Boston, MA 02134-1348.
617-254-9481. E-mail: cic@ccicrosby.com. Website: www.ciconline.org. Monthly. $25.95/yr. Circ.: 113,100. Al Race, Editor. **Description:** Lists educational cable programming and online resources. Offers tips for finding and using resources effectively and profiles K-12 teachers, librarians, and media specialists who use educational cable technology/programming to benefit students; 500-1,000 words; $250-$500. **Tips:** Articles by assignment only. Don't pitch a story without identifying educators and the classroom cable connection. **Queries:** Required. **Unsolicited mss:** Does not accept. **Response:** 1-3 months. **SASE Required:** Yes. **Freelance Content:** 50%.

CHURCH EDUCATOR

Educational Ministries, Inc., 165 Plaza Dr., Prescott, AZ 86303.
E-mail: edmin2@aol.com. Website: www.educationalministries.com. Monthly. $28/yr. Circ.: 3,000. Robert G. Davidson, Editor. **Description:** Resource for mainline Protestant Christian educators. Focuses on programs used in mainline churches; 200-1,500 words; $.03/word. **Queries:** Not necessary. **E-Queries:** Yes. **Unsolicited mss:**

Accepts. **Response:** Queries 1 week, submissions 3 months. **SASE Required:** Yes. **Freelance Content:** 80%. **Rights:** One Time Rights. **Payment:** On publication.

CLASS ACT

3 River Dale Court, Henderson, KY 42419. E-mail: classact@lightpower.net. Website: www.classactpress.com. 9x/yr. $25/yr. Circ.: 300. Susan Thurman, Editor. **Description:** Newsletter for English and language arts teachers. Provides fun, ready-to-use lessons and units that help teachers make learning language, writing and literature interesting to students. **Nonfiction:** Articles with ideas that teachers can use immediately. "What a Character" (developing characterization); "Writing Similes, Metaphors and Extended Metaphors" 300-1,000 words; $10-$40. **Fillers:** English education related only; 1-2 pages; $10-$20. **Tips:** "Know how to write for teenagers. Humor helps. Avoid telling part of your life as a writer." Accepts e-mail submissions in body of text (no attachments). **Queries:** Not necessary. **E-Queries:** Yes. **Unsolicited mss:** Accepts. **Response:** 1 month. **SASE Required:** Yes. **Freelance Content:** 70%. **Rights:** All. **Payment:** On acceptance.

CLASSROOM NOTES PLUS

National Council of Teachers of English (NCTE)
1111 W Kenyon Rd., Urbana, IL 61801-1096. 217-278-3870.
E-mail: notesplus@ncte.org. Website: www.ncte.org/pubs/journals/cnp. 4x/yr. $60/yr (includes membership). Circ.: 20,500. Editor: Felice A. Kaufmann, NCTE. **Description:** Newsletter offering practical teaching ideas for the secondary classroom. Includes in-depth articles on literature, poetry, and writing. Also provides classroom management tips, recommended websites and resources, and advice for new teachers. **Nonfiction:** Articles must be original, previously unpublished, and identify any necessary sources. **Tips:** See website for specific submission guidelines.

THE CLEARING HOUSE

Heldref Publications, 1319 18th St. NW, Washington, DC 20036. 202-296-6267. E-mail: tch@heldref.org. Website: www.heldref.org. Bimonthly. $14.50/$45. Circ.: 2,000. Sarah Yaussi, Editor. **Description:** Scholarly journal, covers topics for middle-level and high-school teachers and administrators. **Nonfiction:** Scholarly articles on educational trends and philosophy, learning styles, curriculum, effective schools, testing and measurement, instructional leadership; to 2,500 words. **Columns, Departments:** Short articles, new trends; 100-900 words. **Tips:** Writers are generally university professors in education or in-service teachers. **Queries:** Not necessary. **E-Queries:** No. **Unsolicited mss:** Accepts. **Response:** 3-4 months. **SASE Required:** Yes. **Freelance Content:** 100%. **Payment:** In copies.

COLLEGE COMPOSITION AND COMMUNICATION

National Council of Teachers of English (NCTE), 1111 W Kenyon Rd., Urbana, IL 61801-1096. 217-278-3870. Website: www.ncte.org/ccc. 4x/yr. $58/yr. Circ.: 9,500. Editor: Marilyn M. Cooper, Michigan Technological University, Houghton. **Description:** Research and scholarship in composition studies to help college teachers reflect on and improve their practices in teaching writing. The field draws on research and theories from many humanistic disciplines (e.g. English, linguistics, cultural/racial studies, communication, sociology, etc.); so articles may present discussions within any of these fields, if clearly relevant to the work of college writing teachers. **Tips:** See website for specific submission guidelines.

COLLEGE ENGLISH

National Council of Teachers of English (NCTE), 1111 W Kenyon Rd., Urbana, IL 61801-1096. 217-278-3870. E-mail: coleng@scu.edu. Website: www.ncte.org/ce. 6x/yr. $65/yr (includes membership). Circ.: 16,000. Editor: Jean Gunner, Santa Clara University, CA. **Description:** Provides a forum in which scholars working within any of the various subspecialties of the discipline can address a broad cross-section of the profession. Articles on literature, composition, and other disciplinary concerns; open to all theoretical approaches and schools of thought. No practical articles on classroom practice. Readership is broad-based so articles should appeal to nonspecialists as well as specialists in particular areas. **Tips:** See website for specific guidelines.

COMMUNITY COLLEGE WEEK

10520 Warwick Ave., Suite B8, Fairfax, VA 22030-3100. 703-385-2981. E-mail: scottc@cmabiccw.com. Website: www.ccweek.com. Bi-weekly. $40/yr. Circ.: 18,000. Frank Matthews, Publisher/Editor. **Description:** National newspaper covering community, technical, and junior-college issues; 500-700 words; $.35/word. **Tips:** "Always query first by e-mail. Include your resumé and a couple of clips when querying. Please visit our website to see what kind of copy we print before you query." **Queries:** Required. **E-Queries:** Yes. **Unsolicited mss:** Accepts. **Response:** 1-14 days. **SASE Required:** Yes. **Freelance Content:** 95%. **Rights:** FNAR and electronic. **Payment:** On publication. **Contact:** Scott Cech, Editor.

CURRENT HEALTH

The Weekly Reader Corp., 200 First Stamford Place, P.O. Box 120023, Stamford, CT 06912-0023. 203-705-3500. E-mail: smclaughlin@weeklyreader.com. Website: www.weeklyreader.com. 8x/yr. $9.95/yr. Sabrina McLaughlin, Editor. **Description:** For classrooms covering physical and psychological health. Articles on drug education, nutrition, diseases, fitness and exercise, first aid and safety, psychology, and relationships. Printed in two editions (for grades 4-7, and grades 7-12). Articles by assignment only. Pays competitive rates. **Tips:** Must write well for appropriate age level. Send query with resumé and clips. Background in medical writing is ideal. No phone calls. **Unsolicited mss:** Does not accept. **Response:** 1-6 months. **Rights:** All. **Payment:** Within 30 days of acceptance.

DRAMATICS MAGAZINE

See full listing in Performing Arts category.

EARLY CHILDHOOD NEWS

Excelligence Learning Corp., 2 Lower Ragsdale, Suite 125, Monterey, CA 93940. 831-333-2000. E-mail: mshaw@excelligencencemail.com. Website: www.earlychild-hoodnews.com. Bimonthly. Circ.: 50,000. Megan Shaw, Editor. **Description:** For teachers and parents of young children, infants to age 8, on developmentally appropriate activities, behavior, health, safety, and more. **Nonfiction:** Research-based articles on child development, behavior, curriculum, health and safety; 500-2,000 words. **Poetry:** Related to young children (birth-age 6), teaching, educating, or family; 100 words. **Columns, Departments:** Ask the Expert, Problem-Solving Parent, newsletters for child care staff; 500-600 words. **Queries:** Preferred. **E-Queries:** Yes. **Unsolicited mss:** Accepts. **Response:** Queries 6 weeks, submissions 2-3 months. **Freelance Content:** 75%. **Rights:** All. **Payment:** On publication.

EARLY CHILDHOOD TODAY

Scholastic, Inc., 557 Broadway, Fl. 5, New York, NY 10012-3919. 212-343-6100. E-mail: ect@scholastic.com. Website: www.earlychildhoodtoday.com. 8x/yr. $19.95/yr. Circ.: 55,000. Diane Ohanesian, Editor-in-Chief. **Description:** Practical information, strategies, and tips on child development and education for teachers. Also personal stories and program spotlights. Articles run 500-900 words; pay varies.

ENGLISH EDUCATION

National Council of Teachers of English (NCTE), 1111 W Kenyon Rd., Urbana, IL 61801-1096. 217-278-3870. E-mail: engedu@gsu.edu. Website: www.ncte.org/ee. 4x/yr. $55/yr (includes memberships). Circ.: 2,800. Editors: Dana L. Fox, Georgia State University, Atlanta, and Cathy Fleischer, Eastern Michigan University, Ypsilanti. **Description:** Features articles that focus on issues related to the nature of the discipline and the education and development of teachers of English at all levels. **Tips:** See website for specific submission guidelines. **Response:** 3 months.

ENGLISH JOURNAL

National Council of Teachers of English (NCTE), 1111 W Kenyon Rd., Urbana, IL 61801-1096. 217-328-3870. Website: www.ncte.org/ej. 6x/yr. $50/yr (included membership). Circ.: 35,000. Editor: Louann Reid, Colorado State University. **Description:** Professional journal for middle, junior high, and high school teachers, supervisors, and teacher educators. Manuscripts can focus on an upcoming theme or can be used in one of several ongoing features that appear in each issue. **Tips:** See website for specific submission guidelines. **Queries:** Preferred.

ENGLISH LEADERSHIP QUARTERLY

National Council for Teachers of English (NCTE), 1111 W Kenyon Rd., Urbana , IL 61801-1096. 217-278-3870. Website: www.ncte.org/elq. 4x/yr. $18/yr (includes memberships). Circ.: 2,000. Editor: Bonita L. Wilcox, Duquesne University. **Description:** Short articles on a variety of important issues. Seeks to help department chairs, K-12 supervisors, and other leaders in their role of improving the quality of English instruction. **Tips:** See website for specific guidelines.

GIFTED EDUCATION PRESS QUARTERLY

10201 Yuma Ct., Manassas, VA 20109. 703-369-5017.
E-mail: mfisher345@comcast.net. Website: www.giftededpress.com. Quarterly. Circ.: 1,000. Maurice Fisher, Editor. **Description:** Covers the problems and issues of identifying and educating gifted students. Also includes information on teaching science and humanities, home education, and more; 3,500-4,000 words. **Tips:** "We're looking for highly imaginative, knowledgeable authors to write about this field." **Queries:** Required. **E-Queries:** Yes. **Unsolicited mss:** Does not accept. **Response:** 1 month. **SASE Required:** Yes. **Freelance Content:** 50%. **Payment:** In copies.

GREEN TEACHER

95 Robert St., Toronto, Ontario M5S 2K5 Canada. 416-960-1244.
E-mail: info@greenteacher.com. Website: www.greenteacher.com. Quarterly. $26/yr. Circ.: 6,800. Tim Grant, Gail Littlejohn, Editors. **Description:** Teachers, parents, and educators look to this magazine for practical, ready-to-use strategies and activities that educate and promote environmental/global awareness in the classroom. Schoolyard naturalization, green economics, energy education, climate change, rainforest studies, and sustainable food systems; 1,500-3,000 words. **Tips:** Most articles are written by K-12 teachers working in the field of environmental/global education. Does not publish articles about environmental issues, but rather on how to teach about the environment. Submit 1-page outline or summary of article with drawings or photographs. **Queries:** Preferred. **E-Queries:** Yes. **Unsolicited mss:** Accepts. **Response:** Queries 2 weeks, submissions 2-3 months. **Payment:** In copies.

THE HISPANIC OUTLOOK IN HIGHER EDUCATION

210 E State Rt. 4, Suite 310, Paramus, NJ 07652. 201-587-8800.
E-mail: sloutlook@aol.com. Website: www.hispanicoutlook.com. Biweekly. Circ.: 28,000. Adalyn Hixson, Editor. **Description:** On issues, concerns, and potential models to further academic results of Hispanics in higher education. Articles, 1,700-2,000 words; pay varies. **Tips:** Queries should be sent 3 months in advance of tentative submission. **Queries:** Required. **Payment:** On publication.

HOME EDUCATION MAGAZINE

P.O. Box 1083, Tonasket, WA 98855-1083. 509-486-1351.
E-mail: hem@home-ed-magazine.com. Website: www.home-ed-magazine.com. Bimonthly. $32/yr. Circ.: 50,000. Helen Hegener, Publisher. **Description:** Magazine for families who homeschool their children. Seeks submissions from writers who are familiar with homeschooling and who can share the humorous side without being negative about the alternatives. Articles run 1,000-2,000 words; $50-$150. **Tips:** Encourages submissions from homeschooling parents who love to write. Focus on practical experience, not textbook theories. **Queries:** Not necessary. **E-Queries:** Yes. **Unsolicited mss:** Accepts. **Response:** 1-2 months. **SASE Required:** Yes. **Freelance Content:** 60%. **Rights:** FNASR. **Payment:** On acceptance.

INSTRUCTOR

Scholastic, Inc., 524 Broadway, New York, NY 10012. 212-343-6100.
Website: www.scholastic.com/instructor. 8x/yr. $14/yr. Circ.: 218,000. Jennifer
Prescott, Managing Editor. **Description:** Prominent national magazine for K-8
teachers. **Nonfiction:** Topics for teachers (timely issues, classroom ideas, activities,
ways to improve, etc); 800-2,000 words; $500-$1,200. **Fillers:** Cyber Hunt activities
(Internet-based activities); also, short, ready-to-use activities by teachers, for teachers;
100-200 words; $50. **Columns, Departments:** End of the Day (revelatory or
humorous pieces about your experience as a teacher); 400-500 words; $250. **Tips:**
"Keep this in mind: Can a teacher take these ideas into the classroom immediately?"
Queries: Not necessary. **E-Queries:** Yes. **Unsolicited mss:** Accepts. **Response:** 3-
6 months. **SASE Required:** Yes. **Freelance Content:** 80%. **Rights:** All. **Payment:**
On publication.

LANGUAGE ARTS

National Council of Teachers of English (NCTE)
1111 W Kenyon Rd., Urbana, IL 61801-1096. 217-278-3870. E-mail: langarts@u.ari-
zona.edu. Website: www.ncte.org/la. 6x/yr. $65/yr (includes membership). Circ.:
13,500. Coeditors: Kathy G. Short, University of AZ, Tucson; Jean Schroeder, Gloria
Kauffman, Sander Kaser, Tucson Unified School District. **Description:** Professional
journal for elementary and middle school teachers and teacher educators. Provides a
forum for discussion on all aspects of language arts learning and teaching, primarily
as they relate to kids in PreK-8. Covers both theory and classroom practice, highlights
current research, and reviews children's and YA literature, as well as classroom and
professional materials. **Tips:** See website for specific guidelines.

MOMENTUM

National Catholic Educational Assn., 1077 30th St. NW, Suite 100, Washington, DC
20007-3852. 202-337-6232. E-mail: momentum@ncea.org. Website: www.ncea.org.
Quarterly. $20/yr. Circ.: 26,000. Brian Gray, Editor. **Description:** Publication cover-
ing outstanding programs, issues, and research in education. Articles should have relevance to Catholic schools or religious education programs. 500-1,500 words; $50-
$75. **Tips:** No simultaneous submissions. Prefers to receive query via e-mail.
Queries: Preferred. **E-Queries:** Yes. **Payment:** On publication.

RESEARCH IN THE TEACHING OF ENGLISH

National Council of Teachers of English (NCTE)
1111 W Kenyon Rd., Urbana, IL 61801-1096. 217-278-3870.
E-mail: melanie.sperling@ucr.edu. Website: www.ncte.org/rte. 4x/yr. $60/yr. Circ.:
4,500. Editors: Melanie Sperling, University of CA and Anne DiPardo, University of
IA. **Description:** Multidisciplinary journal publishing original research and scholarly
essays on the relationships between language teaching and learning at all levels, preschool through adult. **Tips:** See website for specific submission guidelines.

SCHOLASTIC DYNAMATH

Scholastic, Inc., 557 Broadway, New York, NY 10012-3999. 212-343-6100. E-mail: dynamath@scholastic.com. Website: www.scholastic.com. 8x/yr. Circ.: 200,000. Rebecca Bondor, Editor-in-Chief; Matt Friedman, Editor. **Description:** Offers an engaging mix of humor, news, popular-culture references, and original activities to help readers enjoy learning, while reinforcing and applying key 3rd-6th grade math curriculum concepts. Content must be acceptable for classroom use. **Nonfiction:** Fun math content, tied to current events, popular culture, cool real-life kids, or national holidays (i.e., Martin Luther King Day, President's Day, Thanksgiving); to 600 words; $350-$450/article. **Fillers:** $25-$50 puzzles, to 75 words. **Art:** $50-$400. **Tips:** Dual goals of being entertaining and educational. Need to get style and mathematical grade level just right. Request sample copy to familiarize yourself with unique approach. **Queries:** Preferred. **E-Queries:** Yes. **Unsolicited mss:** Accepts. **Response:** 2 months. **SASE Required:** Yes. **Freelance Content:** 25%. **Rights:** All. **Payment:** On acceptance.

THE SCHOOL ADMINISTRATOR

American Assn. of School Administrators, 801 N Quincy St., Suite 700, Arlington, VA 22203. E-mail: magazine@aasa.org. Website: www.aasa.org. 11x/yr. Members only. Circ.: 23,000. Jay P. Goldman, Editor. **Description:** For school administrators (K-12), on school system practices, policies, and programs with wide appeal. **Nonfiction:** 1,500-3,000 words. **Fillers:** To 400 words. **Columns, Departments:** To 750 words. **Queries:** Preferred. **E-Queries:** Yes. **Unsolicited mss:** Accepts. **Response:** Queries 2 weeks, submissions 8-10 weeks **Freelance Content:** 10%. **Rights:** All. **Payment:** On publication.

SCHOOLARTS

Davis Publications, Inc., 50 Portland St., Worcester, MA 01608-2013. 508-754-7201. E-mail: contactus@davis-art.com. Website: www.davis-art.com. Monthly. $25.50/yr. Circ.: 23,000. Dr. Eldon Katter, Editor. **Description:** On art education in the classroom: successful, meaningful approaches to teaching, innovative projects, uncommon applications of techniques or equipment, etc.; 600-1,400 words; $30-$150. **Queries:** Preferred. **E-Queries:** Yes. **Unsolicited mss:** Accepts. **Response:** 3 months. **SASE Required:** Yes. **Freelance Content:** 85%. **Rights:** All. **Payment:** On publication.

SCIENCE & CHILDREN

National Science Teachers Assn., 1840 Wilson Blvd., Arlington, VA 22201-3000. 703-243-7100. E-mail: s&c@nsta.org. Website: www.nsta.org. 8x/yr. $60/yr. Circ.: 23,500. Christina Ohana, Editor. **Description:** Articles and activities, based on current approaches to instruction and issues in science education. For Pre-K to 8th-grade science teachers. **Queries:** Preferred.

TALKING POINTS

National Council of Teachers of English (NCTE), 1111 W Kenyon Rd., Urbana, IL 61801-1096. 217-278-3870. E-mail: pma8@mindspring.com;koshewa@lclark.edu. Website: www.ncte.org/tp. 2x/yr. $55/yr (includes membership). Circ.: 1,700. Editors: Peggy Albers, Georgia State University, Atlanta, and Allen Koshewa, Lewis and Clark College, Portland, Oregon. **Description:** Helps promote literacy research and the use of whole language instruction in classrooms. Provides a forum for parents, classroom teachers, and researchers to reflect about literacy and learning. **Tips:** See website for specific submission guidelines.

TEACHING ELEMENTARY PHYSICAL EDUCATION

Human Kinetics Publishers, P.O. Box 5076, Champaign, IL 61825-5076. 217-351-5076. E-mail: margeryk@hkusa.com. Website: www.humankinetics.com. Bimonthly. Circ.: 3,500. Margery Kane. **Description:** Resources and ideas on instructional and fun physical-education programs for K-8 phy-ed teachers. **Queries:** Preferred.

TEACHING ENGLISH IN THE TWO-YEAR COLLEGE

National Council of Teachers of English (NCTE)
1111 W Kenyon Rd., Urbana, IL 61801-1096. 217-278-3870.
E-mail: htinberg@bristol.mass.edu. Quarterly. $60/yr. Circ.: 4,500. Editor: Howard Tinberg, Bristol Community College, Fall River, MA. **Description:** For 2-year college teachers and those teaching the first two years of English in 4-year institutions. Seeks articles in all areas of composition (basic, first-year, and advanced); business, technical, and creative writing; and the teaching of literature in the first two college years. Also publishes articles on staffing, assessment, technology, writing program administration, speech, journalism, reading, ESL, etc. **Columns, Departments:** Instructional Notes (short articles describing successful classroom practices); Readers Write (50-200 word comments on published articles or professional issues); What Works for Me (brief descriptions on successful classroom activities, 50-200 words). **Tips:** See website for specific submission guidelines.

TEACHING K-8

Highlights for Children, Inc., 40 Richards Ave., Norwalk, CT 06854-2332. 203-855-2650. Website: www.teachingk-8.com. 8x/yr. $14.97/yr. Circ.: 100,000. Patricia Broderick, Editor. **Description:** Classroom service magazine providing classroom-tested teaching ideas, techniques, etc. for teachers of grades K-8. **Queries:** Not necessary. **E-Queries:** No. **Unsolicited mss:** Accepts. **Response:** 1 month. **SASE Required:** Yes. **Rights:** All. **Payment:** On publication.

TEACHING THEATRE

Educational Theatre Assn., 2343 Auburn Ave., Cincinnati, OH 45219. 513-421-3900. E-mail: jpalmarini@edta.org. Website: www.edta.org. Quarterly. James Palmarini, Editor. **Description:** Journal for middle and high school drama educators. Offers play suggestions, curriculum ideas, classroom exercises, and technical production. **Queries:** Preferred. **E-Queries:** Yes.

TEACHING TOLERANCE

Southern Poverty Law Center, 400 Washington Ave., Montgomery, AL 36104. Website: www.teachingtolerance.org. Semi-annual. Free to educators. Circ.: 600,000. Kelvin Datcher, Director. **Description:** Helps teachers promote interracial and intercultural understanding in the classroom and beyond. Topics include the role of white teachers in multicultural education, creating safe space for refugee students, inclusion for students with disabilities, gay students coming out at school, etc. Articles run 500-3,500 words; $1.25/word. **Tips:** Submit clear focused query. No rhetoric, scholarly analysis, or articles that reinvent the wheel on multicultural education. **Queries:** Preferred. **E-Queries:** Yes. **Unsolicited mss:** Accepts. **Response:** 3 months. **SASE Required:** Yes. **Freelance Content:** 75%. **Rights:** All. **Payment:** On acceptance.

TECH DIRECTIONS

Prakken Publications, 3970 Varsity Dr., Box 8623, Ann Arbor, MI 48107-8623. 734-975-2800. E-mail: susanne@techdirections.com. Website: www.techdirections.com. Susanne Peckham, Editor. **Description:** For teachers in science, technology, and vocational educational fields. Seeking classroom projects for students from upper elementary through community college levels. **Nonfiction:** Articles, 9-12 double-spaced typed pages; $50-$150. **Fillers:** Cartoons (pays $20); puzzles, brainteasers, humorous anecdotes, short classroom activities; (pays $25); humorous anecdotes (pays $5). **Payment:** On publication.

TECHNOLOGY & LEARNING

CMP Media, LLC, 600 Harrison St., Fl. 3, San Francisco, CA 94107-1370. 415-947-6000. E-mail: techlearning_editors@cmp.com. Website: www.techlearning.com. $29.95/yr. Circ.: 85,000. Susan McLester, Editor-in-Chief. **Description:** For K-12 teachers on uses of computers and related technology in the classroom. Human-interest and philosophical articles, how-to pieces, software reviews, and hands-on ideas. Articles should be of general interest to K-12 educators and should encourage them to try new approaches to teaching by using the latest technology in computers, peripherals, integrated learning systems, etc.; 250-2,000 words; pay varies. **Queries:** Required. **E-Queries:** Yes. **Unsolicited mss:** Does not accept. **Response:** 12 weeks. **SASE Required:** Yes. **Payment:** On publication.

TODAY'S CATHOLIC TEACHER

Peter Li Education Group, 2621 Dryden Rd., Dayton, OH 45439. 937-293-1415. E-mail: mnoschang@peterli.com. Website: www.catholicteacher.com. Bimonthly. $14.95/yr. Circ.: 50,000. Mary Noschang, Editor. **Description:** For K-12 educators concerned with private education and particularly Catholic education. **Nonfiction:** Curriculum, classroom management, other articles (religious and non-religious) for classroom teachers in Catholic K-12 schools; articles run 700-3,000 words; $150-$300. **Queries:** Not necessary. **E-Queries:** Yes. **Unsolicited mss:** Accepts. **Response:** 2 months. **SASE Required:** Yes. **Freelance Content:** 80%. **Rights:** FNAR. **Payment:** On publication.

UNIVERSITY BUSINESS

Professional Media Group, 488 Main Ave., Norwalk, CT 06851. 203-847-7200. E-mail: editorial@universitybusiness.com. Website: www.universitybusiness.com. Monthly. Circ.: 34,100. Joseph Hanson, Editor-in-Chief. **Description:** For senior-level administrators in the field of higher education. Focus is on the business side of higher education. Online and print versions.

VOICES FROM THE MIDDLE

National Council of Teachers of English (NCTE)
1111 W Kenyon Rd., Urbana, IL 61801-1096. 217-278-3870. E-mail: cschanche@ncte.org. Website: www.ncte.org/pubs/journals/vm. 4x/yr. $60/yr. Circ.: 10,500. Editor: Kylene Beers, University of Houston, TX. **Description:** Journal for teachers at the middle school level. Based on the premise that middle school teachers face a unique set of circumstances and challenges, this journal presents a variety of voices. Each issue covers one topic/concept related to literacy and learning at the middle school level. Also includes teachers' descriptions of authentic classroom practices, middle school students' reviews of YA literature, a technology column, and reviews of professional resources. Also explores the connections between the theory and practice of each issue's topic. **Tips:** See website for specific submission guidelines.

YOUTH AND CHRISTIAN EDUCATION LEADERSHIP

1080 Montgomery Ave. NE, P.O. Box 2250, Cleveland, TN 37320-2250. 423-478-7597. E-mail: wanda-griffith@pathwaypress.org. Website: www.pathwaypress.org. Quarterly. $8. Circ.: 12,000. Wanda Griffith, Editor. **Description:** For Christian education workers who teach God's word to kids, teens, and adults. Seeks articles that encourage, inform, and inspire those who teach the Bible in local churches; 500-1,000 words; $25-$45. **Queries:** Not necessary. **E-Queries:** Yes. **Unsolicited mss:** Accepts. **Response:** 6-9 weeks. **SASE Required:** Yes. **Payment:** On publication.

ENVIRONMENT, CONSERVATION, NATURE

(See also Sports, Recreation, Outdoors)

ADIRONDACK LIFE

P.O. Box 410, Jay, NY 12941. 518-946-2191. E-mail: gcrane@adirondacklife.com; mthill@adirondacklife.com. Website: www.adirondacklife.com. 8x/yr. $24.95/yr. Circ.: 50,000. **Description:** Outdoor and environmental activities, issues, arts, wilderness/wildlife, and people of the Adirondack Park region of New York State. **Fiction:** Excerpts of upcoming Adirondack and related books; to 4,000 words; $.25/word. **Nonfiction:** Contemporary and historical articles on employment, poverty, prison system, water quality, timber industry, etc.; to 4,000 words; $.25/word. **Columns, Departments:** Profiles of people and places, first-person travel/outdoor historical vignettes; to 2,200 words; $.25/word. **Art:** Color transparencies or B&W prints; $150/full page photo, $400/cover. **Queries:** Preferred. **E-Queries:** Yes. **Unsolicited**

mss: Accepts. **Response:** 2 months. **SASE Required:** Yes. **Freelance Content:** 80%. **Rights:** FNAR. **Contact:** Galen Crane or Mary Thill, Editors.

ALTERNATIVES JOURNAL

Faculty of Environmental Studies, Univ. of Waterloo, Waterloo, Ontario N2L 3G1 Canada. 519-888-4442. E-mail: editor@alternativesjournal.ca. Website: www.alternativesjournal.ca. Quarterly. $25/yr. Cheryl Lousley, Executive Editor. **Description:** Environmental thought, policy, and action. Canadian focus. Feature articles, 4,000 words; notes, 200-500 words; and reports, 750-1,000 words. Pays small honoraria only.

AMERICAN FORESTS

734 15th St. NW, Fl. 8, Washington, DC 20005. 202-737-1944, ext. 203. E-mail: mrobbins@amfor.org. Website: www.americanforests.org. Quarterly. $3/$25. Circ.: 25,000. Michelle Robbins, Editor. **Description:** For people, rural and urban, who share a love for trees and forests. **Nonfiction:** Articles on trees, forests, issues (worldwide); inspirational, educational; 150-2,000 words; $100-$2,000. **Columns, Departments:** Communities (working together on problems); Woodswise (for small-forest owners); Perspectives (current events); Earthkeepers (1-page profiles); Clippings (news briefs). **Tips:** Articles should address one of American forests' focus areas: ecosystem restoration, ecosystem services, wildfire policy, or urban forestry— preferably with an angle that includes the organization's conservation work. No straight travel pieces or fiction. **Queries:** Required. **E-Queries:** Yes. **Unsolicited mss:** Accepts. **Response:** 2-3 months. **SASE Required:** Yes. **Freelance Content:** 75%. **Rights:** One-time, electronic. **Payment:** On acceptance.

ANIMALS

See full listing in Animals & Pets category.

ATLANTIC SALMON JOURNAL

Atlantic Salmon Federation, P.O. Box 5200, St. Andrews, New Brunswick E5B 3S8 Canada. 506-529-4581. E-mail: silverstone@nb.aibn.com. Website: www.asf.ca. Quarterly. Circ.: 11,500. Martin Silverstone, Editor. **Description:** Fishing, conservation, ecology, travel, politics, biology, how-tos, and anecdotes. **Nonfiction:** Articles related to Atlantic salmon; 1,500-3,000 words; $200-$600. **Fillers:** Salmon politics, conservation, and nature; 200-500 words; $100. **Tips:** Sample copy free on request. **Queries:** Preferred. **E-Queries:** Yes. **Payment:** On publication.

AUDUBON

National Audubon Society, 700 Broadway, Fl. 4, New York, NY 10003. E-mail: editor@audubon.org. Website: www.audubon.org. Quarterly. $20/yr. Circ.: 474,000. David Seideman, Editor-in-Chief. **Description:** Conservation and environmental issues, natural history, ecology, and related subjects. Pieces run 150-4,000 words; pay varies. **Tips:** Submit query, clips, and SASE to Editorial Assistant. **Queries:** Required. **Payment:** On acceptance. **Contact:** Audrey Colyar, Editorial Assistant.

BIRD WATCHER'S DIGEST

Parsdon Corp., P.O. Box 110, Marietta, OH 45750-0110. 740-373-5285. E-mail: editor@birdwatchersdigest.com. Website: www.birdwatchersdigest.com. Bimonthly. $19.99/yr. Circ.: 75,000. William H. Thompson III, Editor. **Description:** Bird-watching experiences and expeditions; interesting backyard topics and how-tos. **Nonfiction:** Articles for bird watchers: first-person accounts; profiles of bird species; 600-2,500 words; from $100. **Tips:** Write for guidelines. Submit complete manuscript. **Queries:** Preferred. **Response:** 8 weeks. **SASE Required:** Yes. **Payment:** On publication. **Contact:** Bill Thompson III, Editor.

BIRDER'S WORLD

Kalmbach Publishing Co., 21027 Crossroads Circle, Waukesha, WI 53187. 262-796-8776. E-mail: mail@birdersworld.com. Website: www.birdersworld.com. Bimonthly. $4.95/$22.50. Circ.: 64,000. Charles J. Hagner, Editor. **Description:** On all aspects of birds and birding. Offers tips on birding, attracting and feeding birds, gardening, and travel. Feature articles, 1,600-2,000 words; $400-$500. Also, personal essays, 500-1,500 words. **Queries:** Preferred. **E-Queries:** Yes. **Unsolicited mss:** Accepts. **Response:** 3 months, include SASE (if visuals are sent). **Freelance Content:** 75%. **Rights:** FNAR. **Payment:** On publication.

BLUELINE

See full listing in Literary Fiction & Poetry category.

BUGLE

P.O. Box 8249, Missoula, MT 59807-8249. 406-523-4570. E-mail: bugle@rmef.org. Website: www.rmef.org. Bimonthly. $30/yr. Circ.: 130,000. Dan Crockett, Editor. **Description:** Journal of the Rocky Mountain Elk Foundation. Original, critical thinking about wildlife conservation, elk ecology, and hunting. **Fiction:** Thoughtful elk-hunting stories; human-interest stories; 1,500-4,500 words; $.20/word. **Nonfiction:** About conservation, elk ecology and natural history, elk hunting; 1,500-3,000 words; $.20/word. **Poetry:** 1 page; $100/poem. **Fillers:** Humor. **Columns, Departments:** Essays on hunting or conservation issues; 1,000-3,000 woods; $.20/word. **Tips:** Do not submit how-to pieces. All articles must have a connection to elk. **Queries:** Preferred. **E-Queries:** Yes. **Unsolicited mss:** Accepts. **Response:** 3 months. **SASE Required:** Yes. **Freelance Content:** 80%. **Rights:** FNAR. **Payment:** On acceptance.

CALIFORNIA WILD

California Academy of Sciences, Golden Gate Park, San Francisco, CA 94118-4599. 415-750-7116. E-mail: calwild@calacademy.org. Website: www.calacademy.org. Quarterly. $4/$12.95. Circ.: 30,000. Kathleen Wong, Senior Editor. **Description:** Based at the research facility, natural-history museum, and aquarium in San Francisco's Golden Gate Park. Seeks well-researched articles on natural history and preservation of the environment; 1,000-2,500 words; $.30/word. **Columns, Departments:** Skywatcher; A Closer Look; Wild Lives; In Pursuit of Science. **Tips:**

Prefers queries with clips. New address during rebuilding of Golden Gate site: 875 Howard St., San Franciso, CA 94118. **Unsolicited mss:** Accepts. **Rights:** FNAR. **Payment:** On publication.

CANADIAN GEOGRAPHIC

39 McArthur Ave., Ottawa, Ontario K1L 8L7 Canada. 613-745-4629. E-mail: editorial@canadiangeographic.ca. Website: www.canadiangeographic.ca. Bimonthly. $6.95/$34.95. Circ.: 240,000. Rick Boychuk, Editor. **Description:** Covers Canadian landscape, nature, wildlife, and people. Length and pay varies. **Queries:** Required. **E-Queries:** Yes. **Unsolicited mss:** Do not accept. **Response:** 3 months. **SASE Required:** Yes. **Rights:** FNAR. **Payment:** On publication.

CANADIAN WILDLIFE/BIOSPHERE

Canadian Wildlife Federation, 350 Michael Cowpland Dr., Kanata, Ontario K2M 2W1 Canada. 613-599-9594. E-mail: wild@cwf-fcf.org. $25 (Canada), $37 (outside Canada). Circ.: 20,000. Kendra Toby, Editor. **Description:** On national and international wildlife issues: wild areas, nature-related research, endangered species, wildlife management, land-use issues, character profiles, and science and politics of conservation. **Queries:** Preferred. **Payment:** On publication.

THE CONSERVATIONIST

NY State Dept. of Environmental Conservation
625 Broadway, Albany, NY 12233-4502. 518-402-8047.
E-mail: dhnleson@gw.dec.state.ny.us. Website: www.dec.state.ny.us. Bimonthly. $12/yr. Circ.: 120,000. David H. Nelson, Editor. **Description:** Articles on environmental/conservation programs and policies of New York. Pieces 1,500+ words, $100; 1,500 words or less, $50. **Queries:** Preferred. **Payment:** On publication.

THE COUNTRY CONNECTION

Pinecone Publishing, 691 Pinecrest Rd., Boulter, Ontario K0L 1G0 Canada. 613-332-3651. E-mail: magazine@pinecone.on.ca. Website: www.pinecone.on.ca. 4x/yr. $4.95. Circ.: 5,000. Gus Zylstra, Editor. **Description:** Eco-friendly publication for Ontario. Focuses on nature, heritage, history, nostalgia, environment, country living, the arts, and "green" travel. **Tips:** Canadian material only. Please request writer's guidelines by mail or online for specifications on length/payment/format of articles. Sample copy $5.69. **Queries:** Not necessary. **E-Queries:** Yes. **Unsolicited mss:** Accepts. **Response:** Queries 1 week, submissions to 6 months, SASE (Canadian postage). **Freelance Content:** 75%. **Rights:** FNAR. **Payment:** On publication.

THE DOLPHIN LOG

See full listing in Juvenile category.

E/THE ENVIRONMENTAL MAGAZINE

Earth Action Network, 28 Knight St., Norwalk, CT 06851. 203-854-5559. E-mail: info@emagazine.com. Website: www.emagazine.com. Bimonthly. $3.95/$20. Circ.:

50,000. Jim Motavalli, Editor. **Description:** Focuses on environmental concerns. **Nonfiction:** Features and short pieces, on environmental issues (community gardens, mass transit, global warming, activism, trends, etc.). 400-4,200 words. **Columns, Departments:** Your Health, Money Matters, Eating Right, Going Green, House and Home, Consumer News. 750-1,200 words. **Tips:** "Reporting must be objective. Include quoted sources and end-of-article contact information." Sample copy $5. **Queries:** Preferred. **E-Queries:** Yes. **Unsolicited mss:** Accepts. **Freelance Content:** 60%. **Rights:** FNAR. **Payment:** On publication.

ENVIRONMENT

Heldref Publications, 1319 18th St. NW, Washington, DC 20036-1826. 202-296-6267. E-mail: env@heldref.org. Website: www.heldref.org. Monthly. $5/issue (U.S.); $6.50/issue (Canada). Circ.: 5,000. **Description:** Solid analysis of environmental science and policy issues. **Nonfiction:** On major scientific and policy issues of a significant topic; concise, objective, accurate, jargon-free; use graphics and sidebars for key points; 2,500-4,000 words. **Fillers:** Cartoons; $50. **Columns, Departments:** Education, energy, economics, public opinion; 1,000-1,700 words; $100. **Tips:** Avoid news and feature formats. **Queries:** Required. **E-Queries:** Yes. **Unsolicited mss:** Accepts. **Response:** 6-8 weeks. **Freelance Content:** 98%. **Rights:** FNAR. **Payment:** Varies. **Contact:** Barbara T. Richman, Managing Editor.

GREEN TEACHER

See full listing in Education category.

HIGH COUNTRY NEWS

P.O. Box 1090, Paonia, CO 81428. 970-527-4898. E-mail: editor@hcn.org. Website: www.hcn.org. Biweekly. $32/yr. Circ.: 23,000. Greg Hanscom, Editor. **Description:** Environmental and cultural newspaper covering the American West from the West Coast to the Great Plains. Covers Western environmental and public lands issues, management, rural community, and natural resource issues, profiles of innovators, and Western politics. **Nonfiction:** Well-researched stories on any natural resource (including people, culture and aesthetic values) or environmental topics; 4,000 words; $.25/word and up. **Columns, Departments:** Bulletin boards (book reviews, activist profiles, event announcements); 200 words. Hotlines (news briefs); 250 words. Roundups (topical stories); 800 words. Essays; up to 1,000 words. Pays $.25/word and up. **Art:** Color or B&W prints (8x10 preferred); 35 mm negatives and slides; JPEG files, 300 dpi or higher; $35-$100. **Queries:** Preferred. **E-Queries:** Yes. **Unsolicited mss:** Accepts. **Freelance Content:** 90%. **Payment:** On publication.

THE ILLINOIS STEWARD

See full listing in History category.

MOTHER EARTH NEWS

See full listing in Lifestyle Magazines category.

NATIONAL GEOGRAPHIC KIDS
See full listing in Juvenile category.

NATIONAL GEOGRAPHIC MAGAZINE
National Geographic Society, 1145 17th St. NW, Washington, DC 20036-4688. 202-857-7000. E-mail: editor@nationalgeographic.com. Website: www.nationalgeographic.com. Monthly. $3.95/$29. Circ.: 6,051,160. William Allen, Editor-in-Chief. **Description:** First-person, general-interest, heavily illustrated articles on science, natural history, exploration, environmental conservation, world cultures, and geographical regions. **Tips:** "We're 40% staff-written; the balance of our material is by published authors." **Queries:** Required. **E-Queries:** No. **Unsolicited mss:** Do not accept. **Response:** 4 weeks. **SASE Required:** Yes. **Freelance Content:** 70%. **Rights:** One-time worldwide serial, plus secondary NGS rights. **Payment:** On publication. **Contact:** Oliver Payne, Sr. Editor, Manuscripts.

NATIONAL PARKS
National Parks Conservation Assn., 1300 19th St., NW, Suite 300, Washington, DC 20036-1628. 202-223-6722. E-mail: npmag@npca.org. Website: www.npca.org/magazine. Bimonthly. $25/yr. Circ.: 325,000. Linda M. Rancourt, Editor-in-Chief. **Description:** Covers areas within the national park system. Articles, 1,200-1,500 words, on national park areas, proposed new areas, threats to parks or wildlife, new trends in use, legislative issues, endangered species, etc. **Tips:** "Write for a non-scientific, but well-educated audience. Be specific and include descriptive details and quotes. No "My Trip to..." stories." **Queries:** Required. **E-Queries:** Yes. **Unsolicited mss:** Do not accept. **Response:** 2 months. **SASE Required:** Yes. **Freelance Content:** 60%. **Rights:** FNASR. **Payment:** On acceptance.

NATIONAL WILDLIFE
National Wildlife Federation, 11100 Wildlife Center Dr., Reston, VA 20190-5362. 703-438-6000. E-mail: pubs@nwf.org. Website: www.nwf.org/nationalwildlife. Bimonthly. $20/yr. Circ.: 596,700. Mark Wexler, Editor. **Description:** Covers wildlife and habitat, including conservation; 750-2500 words; $1-$1.25/word. **Tips:** Study the magazine to get a sense of our subject matter and approach before submitting queries. **Queries:** Required. **E-Queries:** Yes. **Unsolicited mss:** Does not accept. **Response:** 6 weeks. **SASE Required:** Yes. **Freelance Content:** 50%. **Rights:** All. **Payment:** On acceptance.

NATURE FRIEND
See full listing in Juvenile category.

ONEARTH
Natural Resources Defense Council, 40 W 20th St., New York, NY 10011. 212-727-4412. E-mail: onearth@nrdc.org. Website: www.nrdc.org/onearth. Quarterly. $12/issue. Circ.: 150,000. Douglas Barasch, Editor-in-Chief. **Description:** Journal of thought and opinion for the general public on environmental affairs, especially on

policies of national and international significance. Strives to be a flagship of environmental thinking and covers critical emerging events and new ideas. **Nonfiction:** Investigative articles, profiles, book reviews, and essays; pay varies. **Poetry:** Conveying emotional and spiritual sources of environmental commitment; $50. **Tips:** "We're a national magazine—no stories with limited, localized perspective. We are less a nature magazine than we are a magazine about environmental issues (politics, policy, etc.)." **Queries:** Required. **Unsolicited mss:** Accepts. **Response:** 6-8 weeks.

ORION

Orion Society, 187 Main St., Great Barrington, MA 01230. 413-528-4422. E-mail: orion@orionsociety.org. Website: www.oriononline.org. Bimonthly. $7/issue. Circ.: 25,000. Jennifer Sahn, Editor. **Description:** Explores the relationship between people and nature. Seeks compelling, reflective writing that explores an alternative worldview with an ecological lens; 600-4,000 words; $.10/word. **Columns, Departments:** Blueprints for Change, Environmental Health, Point-of-View, book reviews; 750 words; $.10/word. **Tips:** "*Orion* is meant as a lively, informative, and provocative dialogue. Review our guidelines before submitting." **E-Queries:** Yes. **Unsolicited mss:** Accepts. **Response:** 10-12 weeks. **SASE Required:** Yes. **Freelance Content:** 20%. **Rights:** FNASR. **Payment:** On publication.

OUTDOOR AMERICA

Izaak Walton League of America, 707 Conservation Ln., Gaithersburg, MD 20878-2983. 301-548-0150. E-mail: oa@iwla.org. Website: www.iwla.org. Quarterly. Circ.: 40,000. Jason McGarvey, Editor. **Description:** Publication of the Izaak Walton League of America. Covers national conservation issues that are top priorities of the league. **Nonfiction:** Public lands management, air quality, water quality, fisheries and game management, outdoor ethics, wildlife habitat conservation, agricultural conservation, open space protection. 1,500-3,000 words; $.25-$.30/word. **Tips:** Send clips. Familiarize yourself with the magazine before sending queries. **Queries:** Preferred. **E-Queries:** Yes. **SASE Required:** Yes.

RANGE MAGAZINE

Purple Coyote Corp., 106 E Adams, Suite 201, Carson City, NV 89706. 775-884-2200. E-mail: bw@rangemagazine.com. Website: www.rangemagazine.com. Quarterly. $3.95/$19.95. Circ.: 21,000. C.J. Hadley, Editor. **Description:** Features controversial issues and provides a forum for opposing viewpoints, seeking solutions to halt the depletion of a national resource: the American cowboy. Devoted to issues that threaten the West, its people, lifestyles, rangelands, and wildlife. Feature articles run 1,500-1,800. **Columns, Departments:** Red Meat Survivors (500 words, interviews with oldtimers, including historic/current photos); $100-$150. **Art:** Original illustrations, slides, high-quality prints; $40-$150. **Tips:** "Submit concise, colorful pieces that address issues affecting those who live on and work the land. Avoid academic, overly technical material." **Queries:** Preferred. **E-Queries:** Yes. **Unsolicited mss:** Accepts. **Response:** 6-10 weeks. **SASE Required:** Yes. **Freelance Content:** 90%. **Rights:** FNAR. **Payment:** On publication.

SIERRA

Sierra Club, 85 2nd St., Fl. 2, San Francisco, CA 94105-3459. 415-977-5656. E-mail: sierra.letters@sierraclub.org. Website: www.sierraclub.org. Bimonthly. $2.95/issue. Circ.: 720,000. Joan Hamilton, Editor. **Description:** Features outstanding nature photography and outdoor recreation/travel information with strong environmental emphasis. **Nonfiction:** Nature and environmental issues; 100-4,000 words; $1/word. **Columns, Departments:** What you can do in your home to make the environment safer; visiting a wild place; environmental problems, policy, etc.; 750-1,500 words; $1/word. **Tips:** "Please send us a query via e-mail." **Unsolicited mss:** Accepts. **Response:** 6-8 weeks. **Freelance Content:** 70%. **Rights:** FNASR and electronic. **Payment:** On acceptance.

SOUTH CAROLINA WILDLIFE

South Carolina Dept. of Natural Resources, P. O. Box 167, Columbia, SC 29202. 803-734-3972. Website: www.scwildlife.com. Bimonthly. $10/yr. Circ.: 60,000. Linda Renshaw, Editor. **Description:** Publication for readers in South Carolina who are interested in the outdoors. Articles run approximately 1,500 words; $.15-$.20/word. **Art:** 35mm or large transparencies; pay varies. **Tips:** Avoid first-person accounts. **Queries:** Preferred. **E-Queries:** Yes. **Unsolicited mss:** Accepts. **Response:** 3-6 weeks. **SASE Required:** Yes. **Freelance Content:** 75%. **Rights:** FNASR. **Payment:** On acceptance. **Contact:** Caroline Foster, Managing Editor.

TEXAS PARKS & WILDLIFE

Fountain Park Plaza, 3000 S Interstate Hwy. 35, Suite 120, Austin, TX 78704. 512-912-7000. E-mail: magazine@tpwd.state.tx.us. Website: www.tpwmagazine.com. Monthly. $19.95/yr. Circ.: 127,300. Susan Ebert, Publisher/Editor. **Description:** Promotes conservation and enjoyment of Texas wildlife, parks, waters, and all outdoors. Features on hunting, fishing, birding, camping, and the environment; 400-1,500 words; $.30-$.50/word. Photos a plus. **Payment:** On acceptance.

VIRGINIA WILDLIFE

4010 W Broad St., Richmond, VA 23230. 804-367-1000. E-mail: lwalker@dgif.state.va.us. Website: www.dgif.state.va.us. **Description:** On fishing, hunting, wildlife management, outdoor safety and ethics, with Virginia tie-in. Articles run 500-1,200 words, $.18/word. Pays extra for color photos. **Queries:** Preferred. **Payment:** On publication.

WHOLE EARTH MAGAZINE

P.O. Box 29198, San Francisco, CA 94129-0198. E-mail: editor@wholeearthmag.com. Website: www.wholeearthmag.com. Quarterly. $24/yr. Circ.: 21,000. Michael Stone, Managing Editor. **Description:** Issues related to the environment/conservation, culture, social change, education, media, technology, medical self-care, and all aspects of creating a more interesting life in a sustainable society. Pay varies for articles. Book reviews and other pieces, $50. **Tips:** Good article material can be found in passionate personal statements or descriptions of the writer's activities in this area. **Queries:** Preferred. **Payment:** On publication. **Contact:** D. Remy, President.

WILDLIFE CONSERVATION MAGAZINE

Wildlife Conservation Society, 2300 Southern Blvd., Bronx, NY 10460-1090. 718-220-5121. E-mail: magazine@wcs.org. Website: www.wcs.org. Bimonthly. $19.95. Circ.: 154,000. Deborah Behler, Editor-in-Chief. **Description:** Popular natural history. First-person articles, based on authors' research and experience. **Nonfiction:** Include personal observations; weave in atmosphere, sights, sounds, smells, colors, weather; if pertinent, include your own feelings; 1,500-2,000 words; $1,500-$2,000. **Columns, Departments:** Wild places; 1,000 words; $750-$1,000. **Tips:** Contribute short news items for Conservation Hotline. **Queries:** Required. **E-Queries:** Yes. **Unsolicited mss:** Accepts. **Response:** 1 month. **SASE Required:** Yes. **Freelance Content:** 75%. **Rights:** FNAR. **Payment:** On acceptance.

WISCONSIN NATURAL RESOURCES

Wisconsin Dept. of Natural Resources, 101 S Webster St., P.O. Box 7921, Madison, WI 53707. 608-266-1510. E-mail: david.sperling@dnr.state.wi.us. Website: www.wnr-mag.com. Bimonthly. $3.50/$8.97. Circ.: 130,000. David L. Sperling, Editor. **Description:** Fosters discussion, understanding, and citizen involvement in resolving outdoor and environmental issues. Also promotes keen outdoor observations, nature appreciation, and agency actitivies which improve outdoor experiences. **Nonfiction:** Discussions of emerging environmental issues such as PDBE contamination, Arsenic in water, powers of observation, hunting ethics, etc.; 1,500-2,200 words. **Fillers:** Nature notes and monographs about individual species; 400-600 words. **Tips:** Does not offer payment. **Queries:** Preferred. **E-Queries:** Yes. **Unsolicited mss:** Accepts. **Response:** Queries 2 weeks, submissions 2-3 months. **SASE Required:** Yes. **Freelance Content:** 20%. **Rights:** One-time.

ETHNIC & MULTICULTURAL

AFRICAN VOICES

See full listing in Literary Fiction & Poetry category.

AIM

P.O. Box 1174, Maywood, IL 60153. 708-344-4414. E-mail: apiladoone@aol.com. Website: www.aimmagazine.org. Quarterly. $5/issue. Circ.: 7,000. Myron Apilado, Editor. **Description:** AIM (America's Intercultural Magazine) is committed to fighting racism. **Fiction:** Short stories reflecting that people from different backgrounds are more alike than different; 3,500 words; $25-$100. **Nonfiction:** 1,000-1,500 words; $15-$25. **Poetry:** 20 lines; $3/poem. **Fillers:** 30 words; $5/piece. **Columns, Departments:** 1,500 words; $15/piece. **Art:** Seeks images promoting racial equality; $10/image. **Queries:** Not necessary. **E-Queries:** No. **Unsolicited mss:** Accepts. **Response:** 1 month. **SASE Required:** Yes. **Freelance Content:** 75%.

ALBERTA SWEETGRASS

Aboriginal Multi-Media Society of Alberta
13245-146th St., Edmonton, Alberta T5L 4S8 Canada. 780-455-2700.
E-mail: edsweet@ammsa.com. Website: www.ammsa.com. Monthly. Circ.: 7,500.
Debora Steel, Editor. **Description:** Newspaper covering Aboriginal issues for communities in Alberta. Interested in news, sports, arts/entertainment, reviews, features, etc. Articles run 500-800 words. No fiction or poetry.

AMERICAN INDIAN ART

See full listing in Arts & Architecture category.

AMERICAN LEGACY

28 W 23rd St., New York, NY 10010-5361. 212-620-2200.
E-mail: amlegacy@americanheritage.com.
Website: www.americanlegacymagazine.com. Quarterly. $2.95/$9.95. Circ.: 508,200.
Audrey Peterson, Editor. **Description:** Covers all aspects of Black history and culture. Articles on people and events that have shaped history for African-Americans; up to 4,000 words; pay negotiable. **Tips:** No lifestyle articles or features on contemporary figures in the Black community unless they have a strong connection with history. Proposals should be one page only plus one page cover letter. **Queries:** Required. **E-Queries:** Yes. **Unsolicited mss:** Accepts. **Response:** 2-4 months. **SASE Required:** Yes. **Freelance Content:** 95%. **Payment:** On acceptance.

AMERICAS

See full listing in Contemporary Culture category.

ASIAN PACIFIC AMERICAN JOURNAL

See full listing in Literary Fiction & Poetry category.

AUTO REVISTA

See full listing in Automotive category.

AUTOMUNDO

See full listing in Automotive category.

AVANCE HISPANO

See full listing in Regional & City Publications category.

THE BLACK COLLEGIAN

IM Diversity, Inc., 909 Poydras St., Fl. 36, New Orleans, LA 70112. 504-523-0154. Website: www.blackcollegian.com. Semiannual. $8/yr. Circ.: 118,000. Preston Edwards Sr., Publisher/Editor. **Description:** On the opportunities and experiences of African-American college students and recent grads in relation to careers and self-development. Provides entry-level career opportunities and methods for preparing to enter the work force. Information on sports, personalities, history, interviews/profiles, opinions, and current events; 900-1,900 words; $100-$500. Also read by faculty, career counselors, and placement directors. **Tips:** "Most of our articles are assigned, but we will consider ideas with a brief, detailed query." **Queries:** Required. **E-Queries:** Yes. **Unsolicited mss:** Does not accept. **Response:** 60 days. **Freelance Content:** 90%. **Rights:** FNAR. **Payment:** On publication.

BLACK ENTERPRISE MAGAZINE

Earl G. Graves Publishing Co., Inc., 130 Fifth Ave., Fl. 10, New York, NY 10011-4306. 212-242-8000. E-mail: edmonda@blackenterprise.com. Website: www.blackenterprise.com. Monthly. $19.95/yr. Circ.: 420,000. Alfred Edmond, Editor-in-Chief. **Description:** On money management, careers, political issues, entrepreneurship, high technology, and lifestyles for black professionals. Also profiles and interviews with successful black professionals. **Queries:** Preferred. **Payment:** On acceptance.

BLACK ISSUES IN HIGHER EDUCATION

See full listing in Education category.

BLACKLINES

See full listing in Arts & Architecture category.

BRAZZIL

2039 N Ave. 52, Los Angeles, CA 90042. 323-255-8062. E-mail: brazzil@brazzil.com. Website: www.brazzil.com. Monthly. $2/issue. Circ.: 12,000. Rodney Mello, Editor. **Description:** Publication printed in English that centers on the politics, way of life, economy, ecology, tourism, music, literature, and arts of Brazil. Some short stories printed in Portuguese. Pieces run 1,000-5,000 words. **Tips:** Liberal viewpoint; controversial material preferred. **Queries:** Not necessary. **E-Queries:** Yes. **Unsolicited mss:** Accepts. **Response:** 2 days. **SASE Required:** Yes. **Freelance Content:** 60%.

CALLALOO

Dept. of English, Texas A&M University, 4227 TAMU, College Station, TX 77843-4227. 979-458-3108. E-mail: callaloo@tamu.edu. Website: http://callaloo.tamu.edu. Quarterly. $12/$40. Circ.: 2,000. Charles H. Rowell, Editor. **Description:** African Diaspora literary journal, with original work by and critical studies of Black writers worldwide. **Fiction:** Fiction, drama; up to 10,000 words. **Nonfiction:** Academic and cultural criticism; up to 10,000 words. **Poetry:** Send up to 10 poems. **Queries:** Not necessary. **E-Queries:** No. **Unsolicited mss:** Accepts. **Response:** 6-8 months. **SASE Required:** Yes. **Freelance Content:** 100%. **Payment:** In copies.

CNEWA WORLD

Catholic Near East Welfare Assoc., 1011 First Ave., New York, NY 10022-4195. 212-826-1480. E-mail: cnewa@cnewa.org. Website: www.cnewa.org. Bimonthly. $2.50/$12. Circ.: 90,000. Michael La Civita, Executive Editor. **Description:** Offers educational profiles of cultures, histories, religions, and social issues of the peoples of Eastern Europe, India, the Middle East and Northeast Africa; to 1,500 words; $.20/word. **Tips:** "Writers and photographers in each Pontifical Mission city and in other CNEWA countries offer the most objective, accurate, sensitive portraits of their subjects." **Queries:** Preferred. **Unsolicited mss:** Accepts. **SASE Required:** Yes. **Freelance Content:** 50%. **Payment:** On publication. **Contact:** Eileen Reinhard.

THE CRISIS

7600 Georgia Ave. NW, Suite 405, Washington, DC 20012. 202-829-5700. E-mail: thecrisiseditorial@naacpnet.org. Website: www.thecrisismagazine.com. Bimonthly. $12/yr. Circ.: 250,000. Victoria Valentine, Editor-in-Chief. **Description:** A journal of civil rights, politics, African American history and culture. Articles range from short briefs to 3,000 word features. **Payment:** On acceptance.

DIRECT AIM

See full listing in Career & Professional Development category.

ESSENCE

See full listing in Women's Publications category.

FACES

See full listing in Juvenile category.

FILIPINAS

1486 Huntington Ave., Suite 300, South San Francisco, CA 94080. 650-872-8660. E-mail: myuchengco@filipinasmag.com. Website: www.filipinasmag.com. Monthly. $2.95/$18. Circ.: 30,000. Mona Lisa Yuchengco, Editor. **Description:** For and about Filipinos and their communities in North America. **Nonfiction:** Profiles on successful Filipino Americans, human-interest stories, issues affecting the Filipino American community; 750-3,000 words; $50-$100. **Art:** Color photos, $25; B&W, $15. **Queries:** Required. **E-Queries:** Yes. **Unsolicited mss:** Accepts. **SASE Required:** Yes. **Freelance Content:** 70%. **Rights:** All. **Payment:** On publication.

FOOTSTEPS

See full listing in Juvenile category.

GERMAN LIFE

Zeitgeist Publishing, 1068 National Hwy, La Vale, MD 21502-7501. 800-875-2997. E-mail: editor@germanlife.com. Website: www.germanlife.com. Bimonthly. $22.95/yr. Circ.: 40,000. Mark Slider, Editor. **Description:** German culture, its past and present, and how America has been influenced by its German immigrants.

Articles on history, travel, people, the arts, and social and political issues; up to 2,000 words; $300-$500. Book reviews and short articles; 250-800 words; $100-$130. **Art:** Photos that capture and/or detail the diversity of German American life and culture; everyday life, landscapes, people, architecture, art, festivals. **Queries:** Preferred. **Response:** 4-6 weeks. **Rights:** First English/German language serial rights.

GOSPEL TODAY
See full listing in Religion category.

HEALTH QUEST
See full listing in Health category.

HEART & SOUL
Vanguarde Media, 315 Park Ave. S, Fl. 11, New York, NY 10010-3654. 646-654-4200. E-mail: heartandsoul@vanguarde.com. Website: www.heartandsoul.com. Monthly. $16.97/yr. Circ.: 308,900. Corynne Corbett, Editor-in-Chief. **Description:** The African-American woman's ultimate guide to total well-being. Health, spirituality, beauty, fitness, relationships, finance, and life issues; 800-1,500 words; pay varies. **Queries:** Preferred. **Payment:** On acceptance.

THE HIGHLANDER
See full listing in History category.

HISPANIC MAGAZINE
Hispanic Publishing Group, 999 Ponce de Leon Blvd., Suite 600, Coral Gables, FL 33134-3037. 305-442-2462. E-mail: editor@hispaniconline.com. Website: www.hispaniconline.com. Monthly. $18/yr. Circ.: 250,000. Carlos Verdecia, Editor. **Description:** General-interest magazine on careers, business, politics, and culture. Confronts issues affecting the Hispanic community, emphasis on solutions rather than problems. Printed in English. **Queries:** Preferred.

HISPANIC BUSINESS
See full listing in Business category.

THE HISPANIC OUTLOOK IN HIGHER EDUCATION
See full listing in Education category.

HISPANIC TIMES MAGAZINE
See full listing in Career & Professional Development category.

INDIA CURRENTS

P.O. Box 21285, San Jose, CA 95151. 408-274-6966.
E-mail: editor@indiacurrents.com. Website: www.indiacurrents.com. 11x/yr.
$19.95/yr. Circ.: 30,200. Ashok Jethanandani, Editor. **Description:** Explores the Indian-American experience. **Fiction:** To 3,000 words; $50-$150. **Nonfiction:** Articles on India culture, arts, and entertainment in the U.S. and Canada. Also, music/book reviews, commentary on events affecting the lives of Indians. Travel articles (first-person stories of trips to India or the subcontinent); to 3,000 words; $50-$150. **Queries:** Preferred. **E-Queries:** Yes. **Unsolicited mss:** Accepts. **Response:** 4 weeks. **SASE Required:** Yes. **Freelance Content:** 60%. **Rights:** FNAR. **Payment:** On publication.

INDIAN LIFE

Box 3765, Redwood Post Office, Winnipeg, MB R2W 3R6 Canada. 204-661-9333.
E-mail: viola.editor@indianlife.org. Website: www.indianlife.org. Bimonthly. $10.
Circ.: 29,000. Viola Fehr, Editor. **Description:** News from across Native North America. **Fiction:** Stories which accurately portray Native Americans; 500-2,000 words; $20-$150. **Nonfiction:** News, first-person views, special features, interviews; 500-1,200 words; $20-$75. **Poetry:** To 100 words; $20-$40. **Tips:** "Writers need to know Native Americans (historical and contemporary). No Native spirituality, politics, land claims." **Queries:** Preferred. **E-Queries:** Yes. **Unsolicited mss:** Accepts. **Response:** 4-8 weeks. U.S. contributors include $2 check with SASE. **Freelance Content:** 20%. **Rights:** FNAR, electronic. **Payment:** On publication.

IRISH AMERICA

875 Sixth Ave., Suite 2100, New York, NY 10001. 212-725-2993.
E-mail: irishamag@aol.com. Website: www.irishamerica.com. Bimonthly. $21.95/yr.
Circ.: 85,000. Patricia Harty, Editor-in-Chief. **Description:** For Irish-American audience on history, sports, the arts, and politics. Articles run 1,500-2,000 words; $.12/word. **Queries:** Preferred. **Payment:** On publication.

IRISH AMERICAN POST

1815 W Brown Deer Rd., Milwaukee, WI 53217. 414-540-6636.
E-mail: editor@irishamericanpost.com. Website: www.irishamericanpost.com.
Martin Hinz, Publisher. **Description:** Online publication for Irish and Irish Americans. Profiles, business stories, sports, travel, politics; 800-1,200 words; $25-$100. Also considers short fiction pieces and poetry. **Tips:** No quaint photos or stories; no "going back home" stories. **Queries:** Preferred.

THE IRISH EDITION

903 E Willow Grove Ave., Wyndmoor, PA 19038-7909. 215-836-4900. Anthony R. Byrne, Editor. **Description:** Short fiction, nonfiction, fillers, humor, and puzzles, for Irish-American and Irish-born readers. Pay negotiable. **Queries:** Preferred. **Payment:** On acceptance.

ITALIAN AMERICA

Order Sons of Italy in America, 219 E Street, NE, Washington, DC 20002. 202-547-2900. E-mail: italianamerica@osia.org. Website: www.osia.org. Quarterly. $12/yr. Circ.: 65,000. Dona De Sanctis, Ph.D., Deputy Executive Editor. **Description:** Covers Italian-American news, history, personalities, culture, etc. Articles on people, institutions, and events of interest to the Italian-American community. Also book reviews. 500-1,200 words; $50-$250. **Tips:** Avoid "My grandmother used to spend hours making her spaghetti sauce . . . " Focus on unique, interesting cultural facets. **Queries:** Preferred. **E-Queries:** Yes. **Unsolicited mss:** Do not accept. **Response:** 2-3 months. **Freelance Content:** 20%. **Rights:** Worldwide non-exclusive. **Payment:** On publication.

JOURNAL OF ASIAN MARTIAL ARTS

See full listing in Sports & Recreation/Outdoors category.

LA FACTORIA DE SONIDO

See full listing in Performing Arts category.

LATIN STYLE MAGAZINE

P.O. Box 2969, Venice, CA 90294-2969. 323-462-4409.
E-mail: info@latinstylemag.com. Website: www.latinstylemag.com. Monthly. Circ.: 120,000. **Description:** Latin arts and entertainment magazine targeting English-speaking Hispanic markets. Covers entertainment, music, fashion, art, and leisure.

LATIN TRADE

See full listing in Business category.

LATINA MAGAZINE

See full listing in Women's Publications category.

LATINA STYLE

See full listing in Women's Publications category.

LATINO LEADERS

520 E Central Pkwy, Suite 117, Plano, TX 75074-5526. 972-633-9991.
E-mail: editor@latinoleaders.com. Website: www.latinoleaders.com. Bimonthly. $9.90/yr. Circ.: 100,000. Nicholas Wilson, Editor. **Description:** Profiles the lives of successful Hispanic-American leaders through inspirational stories that reveal who they really are and how they got to be where they are today. **Columns, Departments:** Mundo Latino (news and events); Up and Coming (Hispanic event guide); Leader of the Past; Leader of the Future; Gallery (photos); Shelf Life (book, movie, music reviews). **E-Queries:** Yes. **Unsolicited mss:** Does not accept. **Response:** Varies.

LILITH

Lilith Publications, Inc., 250 W 57th St., Suite 2432, New York, NY 10107-2420.
212-757-0818. E-mail: lilithmag@aol.com. Website: www.lilithmag.com. Quarterly.
$21/yr. Circ.: 25,000. Susan Weidman Schneider, Editor-in-Chief. **Description:**
Showcases Jewish women writers, educators, and artists; illuminates Jewish women's
lives in their religious, ethnic, sexual, and social-class diversity. **Fiction:** On the lives
of Jewish women; 1,000-2,000 words. **Nonfiction:** Autobiographies, interviews,
social analysis, sociological research, oral history, new rituals, reviews, investigative
reporting, opinion pieces. Also news briefs (500 words) and lists of resources, projects, events. 1,000-2,000 words. **Tips:** Welcomes new writers. **Queries:** Not necessary. **E-queries:** Yes. **Unsolicited mss:** Accepts. **Response:** 12-16 weeks. **SASE
Required:** Yes. **Rights:** FNAR and electronic. **Payment:** On publication.

LIVING BLUES

See full listing in Performing Arts category.

LSR

See full listing in Literary Fiction & Poetry category.

MOMENT

Jewish Educational Ventures, 4710 41st St NW, Washington, DC 20016-1706.
202-364-3300. E-mail: editor@momentmag.com. Website: www.momentmag.com.
Bimonthly. $27/yr. Circ.: 65,000. Hershel Shanks, Editor. **Description:** Sophisticated
articles on Jewish culture, politics, religion, and personalities; 100-3,500 words; pay
negotiable. **Tips:** Looking for fresh angles on Jewish themes. **Queries:** Preferred. **E-
Queries:** Yes. **Unsolicited mss:** Accepts. **Response:** 3-4 months. **SASE Required:**
Yes. **Freelance Content:** 90%. **Rights:** FNASR. **Payment:** On publication.

NA'AMAT WOMAN

350 Fifth Ave., Suite 4700, New York, NY 10118. 212-563-5222.
E-mail: judith@naamat.org. Website: www.naamat.org. Quarterly. $25 members, $10
non-members. Circ.: 20,000. Judith A. Sokoloff, Editor. **Description:** For Jewish
communities, covering varied topics: aspects of life in Israel, Jewish women's issues,
social issues, Jewish art and literature. **Fiction:** 2,000-3,000 words; $.10/word.
Nonfiction: 2,000-3,000 words; $.10-$.12/word. **Columns, Departments:** Book
reviews (800 words) and personal essays (1,200-1,500 words); $.10/word. **Art:** B&W
(hard copy or electronic); $25-$100. **Tips:** "Avoid trite Jewish humor, maudlin fiction,
and war stories." **Queries:** Preferred. **Unsolicited mss:** Accepts. **Response:** 1-3
months. **SASE Required:** Yes. **Freelance Content:** 75%. **Rights:** FNAR.

NATIONAL GEOGRAPHIC MAGAZINE

See full listing in Environment & Conservation category.

NATIVE PEOPLES

Media Concepts Group, Inc.
5333 N 7th St., Suite C-224, Phoenix, AZ 85014-2804. 602-265-4855.
E-mail: editorial@nativepeoples.com. Website: www.nativepeoples.com. Bimonthly.
$4.95/issue. Circ.: 50,000. Daniel Gibson, Editor. **Description:** Dedicated to the
sensitive portrayal of arts and lifeways of the Native peoples of the Americas.
Nonfiction: Artist profiles; issue-oriented pieces with Native American angle; pro-
gram/people profiles in education, health, politics; economic development; 1,000-
3,000 words; $.25/word. **Columns, Departments:** Pathways (travels with Native
site/culture/history focus; Viewpoint (open subject matter); 400-1,200 words;
$.25/word. **Tips:** "Readership is both Native American and those interested in Native
culture. Our stories need to appeal to both, serving as a bridge between cultures."
Queries: Preferred. **E-Queries:** Yes. **Unsolicited mss:** Accepts. **Response:** 4
weeks. **SASE Required:** Yes. **Freelance Content:** 80%. **Rights:** FNAR.

THE NETWORK JOURNAL

The Network Journal Communications, 29 John St., Suite 1402, New York, NY
10038. 212-962-3791. E-mail: editors@tnj.com. Website: www.tnj.com. Monthly.
Circ.: 22,000. Rosalind McLymont, Editor. **Description:** For African American
small-business owners and professionals. On small-business, personal finance, career
management, profiles of entrepreneurs, sales/marketing, etc.; 1,200-1,500 words;
$150. **E-queries:** Yes. **Freelance Content:** 25%. **Rights:** All.

NEW YORK TREND

TTW Associates, Inc., 14 Bond St., Suite 176, Great Neck, NY 11021-2045. 516-466-
0028. E-mail: nytrend@aol.com. Website: www.nytrend.com. Biweekly. $1/$15. Circ.:
61,000. Felicia Persand, Editor. **Description:** On the issues affecting Black and
other minority communities in New York City and other regions across the United
States. Topics include politics, human rights, business, entertainment, and other special features; 800 words; $30. **Tips:** "Avoid fluff writing. We have a strong interest in
hard news and business features." **E-Queries:** Yes. **Unsolicited mss:** Accepts.
Response: 1 week. **Freelance Content:** 50%. **Rights:** 1st print.

RUSSIAN LIFE

P.O. Box 567, Montpelier, VT 05601-0567. 802-223-4955. E-mail: info@rspubs.com.
Website: www.russianlife.net. Bimonthly. $33/yr. Circ.: 15,000. Lina Rozorskaya,
Managing Editor. **Description:** Russian culture, travel, history, politics, art, business,
society. Most stories include professional-quality photos. Articles run 1,000-3,000
words; $.07-$.10/word. **Tips:** No stories about personal trips to Russia, editorials on
developments in Russia, or articles promoting a specific company, organization, or
government agency. We seek to provide coverage of Russia that is free of illusions (but
not blemishes) and full of hope (but not ideology or agendas). Our job is to present a
realistic, truthful, and independent view that balances these realities, providing enjoyable, insightful reading." **Queries:** Required. **E-Queries:** Yes. **Unsolicited mss:**
Accepts. **Response:** 1 month. **SASE Required:** Yes. **Freelance Content:** 75%.

SABOR MAGAZINE
P.O. Box 708, Hollywood, CA 90078-0708. 818-841-2231. E-mail: info@sabor-magazine.com. Website: www.sabormagazine.com. Bimonthly. $26/yr. Circ.: 50,000. Carlos Flores, Editor-in-Chief. **Description:** News and articles on Latin entertainment, including music, dance, night life, resturants, and upcoming events. Also human-interest stories related to Latin culture. Articles to 400 words; $100. **Queries:** Not necessary. **E-Queries:** Yes. **Unsolicited mss:** Accepts. **Response:** 3 days.

SCANDINAVIAN REVIEW
American-Scandinavian Foundation, 58 Park Ave., New York, NY 10016. 212-879-9779. E-mail: info@amscan.org. Website: www.amscan.org. 3x/yr. Circ.: 6,000. Richard J. Litell, Editor. **Description:** Presents the arts, sciences, business, politics, and culture of contemporary Denmark, Finland, Iceland, Norway, and Sweden to a lay audience with interest in Nordic countries. Accepts illustrated articles, essays, and poetry; 1,500-2,000 words; pays $300 honorarium. **Tips:** No original English-language poetry, only Nordic poetry in translation. **Queries:** Preferred. **E-Queries:** Yes. **Response:** 1 month. **SASE Required:** Yes. **Freelance Content:** 50%. **Rights:** One-time. **Payment:** On publication.

SELECCIONES DEL READER'S DIGEST
Readers Digest Assn., One Reader's Digest Rd., Pleasantville, NY 10570-7000. 914-238-1000. Website: www.selecciones.com. Monthly. $19.97/yr. Circ.: 325,000. Genevieve Marlin Fernadez, Managing Editor. **Description:** Spanish-language version of *Reader's Digest*.

SELECTA MAGAZINE
232 Andalusia Ave., Suite 200, Coral Gables, FL 33134-5902. E-mail: selectamag@aol.com. Website: www.revistaselecta.com. Monthly. $36/yr. Circ.: 30,000. **Description:** For upscale Hispanics in the U.S. and Latin America.

TEACHING TOLERANCE
See full listing in Education category.

VISTA
999 Ponce de Leon Blvd., Suite 600, Coral Gables, FL 33134. 305-442-2462. E-mail: editor@vistamagazine.com. Website: www.vistamagazine.com. Monthly. Circ.: 1,000,000. **Description:** News, events, and issues of interest to the Hispanic community throughout the United States. Articles on job advancement, bilingualism, immigration, the media, fashion, education, medicine, sports, food; to 1,500 words. **Queries:** Required. **Unsolicited mss:** Does not accept. **Payment:** On publication.

FAMILY & PARENTING

ADOPTIVE FAMILIES

New Hope Communications, LLC, 42 W 38th St., Suite 901, New York, NY 10018. 646-366-0830. E-mail: letters@adoptivefam.com. Website: www.adoptivefam.com. Bimonthly. $24.95/yr. Circ.: 25,000. Beth Kracklauer, Editor. **Description:** For parents of adoptive children. Topics include middle-school and teen years, relatives and community, adoptive parent support groups, school, foster adoption, transracial adoption, domestic adoption, adoptive parents of color, and other adoptive issues; 1,000-1,500 words; pay negotiable. **Tips:** Prefers queries by fax (646-366-0842) or e-mail. **Queries:** Preferred. **E-Queries:** Yes. **Response:** 6-8 weeks.

AMERICAN BABY

Meredith Corp., 125 Park Ave., Fl. 16, New York, NY 10017. 212-557-6600. Website: www.americanbaby.com. Monthly. $23.94/yr. Circ.: 2,000,000. Judith Nolte, Editor-in-Chief. **Description:** For new or expectant parents on prenatal and infant care. **Nonfiction:** Features, 1,000-2,000 words; personal experience pieces (do not submit in diary format), 900-1,200 words; $800-$2,000. **Columns, Departments:** Crib Notes (news and feature topics); 50-350 words; $500. **Payment:** On acceptance.

ATLANTA PARENT

2346 Perimeter Park Dr., Suite 101, Atlanta, GA 30341-1319. 770-454-7599. E-mail: atlantaparent@atlantaparent.com. Website: www.atlantaparent.com. Monthly. $18/yr. Circ.: 90,000. Liz White, Publisher. **Description:** For parents with children, birth-18 years. On family, child, and parent topics; 300-1,500 words; $15-$35. **Queries:** Preferred. **E-Queries:** Yes. **Unsolicited mss:** Accepts. **Response:** 3-6 months. **SASE Required:** Yes. **Freelance Content:** 50%. **Rights:** One-time. **Payment:** On publication. **Contact:** Amy Dusek, Editor.

BABY TALK

Time, Inc., 530 5th Ave., Fl. 4, New York, NY 10036-5101. 212-522-8989. E-mail: letters@babytalk.com. Website: www.parenting.com. 10x/yr. $19.50/yr. Circ.: 2,000,000. Susan Kane, Editor-in-Chief. **Description:** Pregnancy, babies, baby care, women's health, child development, work and family. Articles by professional writers with expertise and experience; 1,000-3,000 words; pay varies. **Queries:** Required. **E-Queries:** No. **SASE Required:** Yes. **Payment:** On acceptance. **Contact:** Emily Hebert, Editorial Assistant.

BEST WISHES

Family Communications, Inc., 65 The East Mall, Toronto, Ontario M8Z 5W3 Canada. 416-537-2604. E-mail: tracy@parentscanada.com. Website: www.parentscanada.com. Semi-annual. Circ.: 155,000. Tracy Cooper, Editor. **Description:** Publication for new parents written by Canadian health-care professionals.

BIG APPLE PARENT

Family Communications, LLC, 9 E 38th St., Fl. 4, New York, NY 10016. 212-889-6400. E-mail: edit@parentsknow.com. Website: www.parentsknow.com. Monthly. Circ.: 70,000. Helen Rosengren Freedman, Executive Editor. **Description:** Newspaper for New York City parents, with separate editions for Queens and Westchester County. Interviews, news, op-ed pieces; 750 words; $50/piece. **Tips:** "We are looking for news and controversy concerning New York City parenting; we do not need travel, essays, humor, or general child-raising pieces." **Queries:** Not necessary. **E-Queries:** Yes. **Unsolicited mss:** Accepts. **Response:** 1 week. **SASE Required:** Yes. **Freelance Content:** 90%. **Rights:** First (NYC area).

BRAIN, CHILD

P.O. Box 5566, Charlottesville, VA 22905-5566. 434-977-4151. E-mail: editor@brainchildmag.com. Website: www.brainchildmag.com. Quarterly. $5.95/issue. Circ.: 22,000. Jennifer Niesslein, Stephanie Wilkinson, Co-Editors. **Description:** "The Magazine for Thinking Mothers." Explores the personal transformation that motherhood brings. Spotlights women's own view of motherhood. **Fiction:** Literary short stories on an aspect of motherhood; e.g., "The Life Of the Body," by Jane Smiley; 1,500-4,500 words; pay varies. **Nonfiction:** Personal essays, features, book reviews, parodies, debate essays. **Tips:** "We're seeking smart, down-to-earth work that's sometimes funny, sometimes poignant." Send query for features and reviews. Send full manuscript for all other categories. **Queries:** Preferred. **E-Queries:** Yes. **Unsolicited mss:** Accepts. **Response:** 1-3 months. **SASE Required:** Yes. **Freelance Content:** 90%. **Rights:** FNAR and electronic. **Payment:** On publication. **Contact:** Jennifer Niesslein.

CAPPER'S

See full listing in Agriculture & Rural Life category.

CATHOLIC PARENT

Our Sunday Visitor, Inc., 200 Noll Plaza, Huntington, IN 46750-4310. 219-356-8400. E-mail: cparent@osv.com. Website: www.osv.com. Bimonthly. $24/yr. Circ.: 30,000. Woodeene Koenig-Bricker, Editor. **Description:** For Catholic parents. Anecdotal and practical, with an emphasis on values and family life. Features, how-tos, and general-interest articles; 800-1,000 words; pay varies. **Tips:** "Don't preach." **Payment:** On acceptance.

CENTRAL CALIFORNIA PARENT

7638 N Ingram Ave., Suite 101, Fresno, CA 93711-6201. 559-435-1409. E-mail: ccparent@qnis.net. Website: www.ccparent.com. Monthly. $15/yr. Circ.: 40,000. Sally Cook, Publisher/Editor. **Description:** Parenting magazine for families in the Central California region; 500-1,500 words; pay varies. **Queries:** Preferred. **Payment:** On publication.

CENTRAL PENN PARENT

Journal Publications, 101 N Second St., Fl. 2, Harrisburg, PA 17101-1402. 717-236-4300. E-mail: journal@journalpub.com. Website: www.journalpub.com. Monthly. Circ.: 35,000. Karren Johnson, Editor. **Description:** On family and parenting issues in Central Pennsylvania. **Tips:** Welcomes new writers. **Queries:** Required. **E-Queries:** Yes. **Unsolicited mss:** Accepts. **Response:** 3 weeks. **SASE Required:** Yes. **Freelance Content:** 50%. **Rights:** FNAR. **Payment:** On publication.

CHICAGO PARENT

Wednesday Journal, Inc., 141 S Oak Park Ave., Oak Park, IL 60302-2972. 708-386-5555. Website: www.chicagoparent.com. Monthly. $12.95/yr. Circ.: 128,000. Susy Schultz, Editor. **Description:** Magazine for parents in the Chicago metro area.

CHILD

Gruner + Jahr USA Publishing, 375 Lexington Ave., New York, NY 10017. 212-499-2000. E-mail: mailcenter@child.com. Website: www.child.com. 10x/yr. $13.97/yr. Circ.: 1,020,000. Miriam Arond, Editor-in-Chief. **Description:** A sophisticated lifestyle magazine for today's young parents. Welcomes article ideas related to health, nutrition, safety, education, and family life. **Columns, Departments:** Kids' Fashion, Mom's Beauty, Fashion and Home, Pregnancy column, Baby Bytes column, and "What I Wish Every Parent Knew" back-page essay. Also features lifestyle section which includes travel and home design. Fees vary depending upon length and positioning. **Tips:** Accepts requests for guidelines via e-mail, but prefers that queries and manuscripts be sent by regular mail. "Offer news that parents need to know (e.g. options for products/services or ways to preserve precious parenthood time) in a lively, stylish fashion." **Queries:** Preferred. **E-Queries:** Yes. **Unsolicited mss:** Accepts. **Response:** 2 months. **SASE Required:** Yes. **Freelance Content:** 95%. **Rights:** FNAR. **Payment:** On acceptance.

CHILDBIRTH

Meredith Corp., 125 Park Ave., Fl. 16, New York, NY 10017. 212-886-3600. Website: www.americanbaby.com. Semi-annual. Circ.: 2,014,815. Judith Nolte, Editor-in-Chief. **Description:** Magazine for expectant parents. Covers pregnancy, labor, birth, caring for an infant, etc.

CHRISTIAN PARENTING TODAY

Christianity Today International, 465 Gundersen Dr., Carol Stream, IL 60188-2489. 630-260-6200. E-mail: cpt@christianparenting.net. Website: www.christianparenting.net. Bimonthly. $18.95/yr. Circ.: 80,000. Carla Barnhill, Editor. **Description:** Serves the needs of today's families in a positive and practical format. Articles on real-life experiences and the truths of the Bible. **Queries:** Required.

CHRISTIAN SINGLE

See full listing in Religion category.

CITY PARENT

467 Speers Rd., Oakville, Ontario L6K 3S4 Canada. 905-815-0017.
Website: www.cityparent.com. Monthly. $27/yr. Circ.: 205,000. Jane Muller, Editor-in-Chief. **Description:** Offers stories, new-product information, computer news, parenting advice, places to go, and fun things to do with kids. **Queries:** Required. **E-Queries:** Yes. **Unsolicited mss:** Accepts. **Freelance Content:** 50%. **Rights:** All.

CLEVELAND/AKRON FAMILY

TNT Publications, 35475 Vine St., Suite 224, Eastlake, OH 44095. 440-510-2000.
E-mail: editor@tntpublications.com. Monthly. Circ.: 65,000. Frances Richards, Editor. **Description:** For parents in the Cleveland/Akron region. Seeks to encourage positive family interaction. Articles on general topics, area events, trends, and services for area families. Pays $30/article or column. **Queries:** Required. **E-Queries:** Yes. **Unsolicited mss:** Accepts. **Payment:** On publication.

THE COMPLEAT MOTHER

5703 Hillcrest, Richmond, IL 60071. 815-678-7531. E-mail: greg@rsg.org.
Website: www.compleatmother.com. Quarterly. Circ.: 12,000. **Description:** Covers pregnancy, childbirth, and breastfeeding.

COUNTY FAMILIES MAGAZINE

Sherwood Communications, P.O. Box 29, Merritt, MI 49667-0029. 800-892-3208.
E-mail: cf@countyfamilies.com. Website: www.countyfamilies.com. 10x/yr. $15/yr. Circ.: 15,000. Linda Sherwood, Editor. **Description:** Resource for parents in Crawford, Kalkaska, Missaukee, Ogemaw, Roscommon and Wexford counties. On positive parenting and supporting parents in their ongoing endeavor to become better parents; 1,200-1,800 words; $50. **Queries:** Required. **E-queries:** Yes. **Unsolicited mss:** Does not accept. **Response:** 6-8 weeks. **SASE Required:** Yes. **Payment:** 30 days after publication.

DALLAS CHILD

Lauren Publications, Inc., 4275 Kellway Cir., Suite 146, Addison, TX 75001. 972-447-9188. Website: www.dallaschild.com. Monthly. $24/yr. Circ.: 80,000. Shelley Pate, Editor. **Description:** Well-informed, local perspectives on issues affecting families in the Dallas area. Seeks to inform, educate, entertain, and provide a provocative discussion forum amoung parents, the community, and professionals who work with kids. **Queries:** Not necessary. **E-queries:** Yes. **Unsolicited mss:** Accepts.

DALLAS FAMILY

United Parent Publications
1321 Valwood Parkway, Suite 530, Carrollton, TX 75006-8412. 972-488-3555.
E-mail: phwcomments@unitedad.com. Website: www.parenthood.com. Monthly.
$19.95. Circ.: 80,000. Bill Lindsay, Editor-in-Chief. **Description:** For parents in the Dallas metro area.

DOVETAIL

45 Lilac Ave., Hamden, CT 06517. 502-549-5499. E-mail: debitarls@aol.com. Website: www.dovetailinstitute.org. Bimonthly. $29.95/yr. Circ.: 1,000. Debi Tenner, Editor. **Description:** "A Journal by and for Jewish/Christian Families." Resources for dual-faith couples, and their families, friends, and professionals who serve them, from a non-denominational perspective. Readers cover the intermarriage spectrum, including single-faith and dual-faith households. **Nonfiction:** Advice, anecdotes, and research on aspects of interfaith marriage; e.g., "Challah Baking: Thoughts of a Christian Cook," or "Intermarriage in Australia." 800-1,000 words; $25. **Fillers:** Related cartoons, humor, and photos also used. **Tips:** "Have experience or knowledge in the field of intermarriage. Avoid broad generalizations, or strongly partisan religious creeds." **Queries:** Not necessary. **E-Queries:** Yes. **Unsolicited mss:** Accepts. **Response:** Queries 2-4 weeks, submissions 4-6 weeks. **SASE Required:** Yes. **Freelance Content:** 80%. **Rights:** All. **Payment:** On publication.

EXPECTING

Family Communications, Inc., 69 The East Mall, Toronto, Ontario M8Z 5W3 Canada. 416-537-2604. E-mail: info@parentscanada.co. Website: www.parentscanada.com. Semi-annual. Circ.: 292,000. Tracy Cooper, Editor. **Description:** For pregnant Canadian women.

FAITH & FAMILY

Circle Media, Inc., 432 Washington Ave., North Haven, CT 06473. 203-230-3800. E-mail: editor@faithandfamilymag.com. Website: www.faithandfamilymag.com. Bimonthly. $14.95/yr. Circ.: 30,000. Tom and April Hopes, Editors. **Description:** "The Magazine of Catholic Living." How-to articles and interviews of interest to Catholic families, with photos. **Nonfiction:** 1,000-2,000 words; pays $75-$300. **Columns, Departments:** Opinion or inspirational columns, 600-800 words, with strict attention to Catholic doctrine. **Tips:** "We ask for ideas first, not manuscripts." **Queries:** Preferred. **Unsolicited mss:** Does not accept. **Freelance Content:** 70%. **Rights:** FNAR. **Payment:** On publication.

FAMILY

Military Force Features, 65 Washington Ave., Mineola, NY 11001. 516-616-1930. E-mail: hq1@familymedia.com. Website: www.familymedia.com. Monthly. Circ.: 500,000. Don Hirst, Editor. **Description:** Publication for military families. Covers topics of interest to women with children (military lifestyle, home decorating, travel, moving, food, personal finances, career, relationships, family, parenting, health, fitness). **Nonfiction:** Articles, 1,000-2,000 words; pays to $200. **Tips:** Send story idea via e-mail to the editor—do not send written queries or unsolicited manuscripts. **Payment:** On publication.

FAMILY

Kids Monthly Publications, 1122 US Highway 22 W, Mountainside, NJ 07092. 908-232-2913. E-mail: editor@njcountyfamily.com. Website: www.njcountyfamily.com.

Monthly. $18/yr. Circ.: 120,000. Farn Dupre, Editor. **Description:** Parenting magazine for families in North Central New Jersey. Offers information on education, child development, health, safety, and other parenting issues.

FLORIDA FAMILY MAGAZINE
1840 Glengary St., Sarasota, FL 34231-3604. 941-922-5437.
Website: www.floridafamilymagazine.com. Bimonthly. Circ.: 60,000. Emily Leinfuss, Executive Editor. **Description:** For families in and around Sarasota, central Florida, and Tampa. Covers parenting, health, education, family fun, etc.

FOCUS ON THE FAMILY
8605 Explorer Dr., Colorado Springs, CO 80920-1051. 719-531-3400.
E-mail: mathisg@mm.fotf.org. Website: www.family.org. Monthly. Circ.: 2,600,000.
Susan G. Mathis, Editor. **Description:** Provides information for Christian families.

HOMELIFE
LifeWay Christian Resources, One LifeWay Plaza, Nashville, TN 37234-0175.
615-251-2860. E-mail: homelife@lifeway.com. Monthly. Circ.: 400,000.
Description: For Christian families on marriage, parenting, practical concerns, and spiritual emphasis from a biblical perspective. Articles must be consistent with the vision and doctrinal statements of LifeWay Christian Resources. **Tips:** "All articles are by assignment only. We accept queries, but we do not accept freelance submissions or simultaneous submissions. We purchase all rights; no reprints or first rights. Photographers and illustrators must also sign an all-rights contract." Free sample copy upon request. **E-Queries:** Yes. **Unsolicited mss:** Does not accept. **Response:** 8 weeks. **SASE Required:** Yes.

IN THE FAMILY
See full listing in Gay & Lesbian category.

HOUSTON FAMILY
Trader Publishing Co., 11111 Richmond Ave., Suite 130, Houston, TX 77082-6665.
713-266-1885. E-mail: houstonparenting@unitedad.com. Website: www.houstonfamilymagazine.com. Monthly. Circ.: 75,000. Bill Lindway, Editor-in-Chief.
Description: For parents in the Houston area.

L.A. PARENT
Trader Publishing Co., 443 E Irving Dr., Suite D, Burbank, CA 91504-2447
818-846-0400. Website: www.parenthoodweb.com. Monthly. $14/yr. Circ.: 110,000.
Bill Lindsay, Editor-in-Chief. **Description:** On child development, health, nutrition, education, and local travel/activities for parents of children up to age 12. Also publishes *San Diego Parent*, *Parenting* (Orange Co.), and *Arizona Parenting*. **Queries:** Preferred. **Payment:** On acceptance.

LIVING WITH TEENAGERS

LifeWay Christian Resources, One LifeWay Plaza, Nashville, TN 37234-0174. 615-251-2226. E-mail: lwt@lifeway.com. Website: www.lifeway.com. Monthly. $20.25/yr. Circ.: 48,000. Sherrie Thomas, Editor. **Description:** Informs and educates parents of teenagers on how to best deal with typical issues and problems faced by teens. Provides strong Christian emphasis and Biblical solutions.

METROKIDS

Kidstuff Publications, 1080 N Delaware Ave., Suite 702, Philadelphia, PA 19125. 215-291-5560 x102. E-mail: editor@metrokids.com. Website: www.metrokids.com. Monthly. Circ.: 125,000. Tom Livingston, Executive Editor. **Description:** For Delaware Valley area parents with kids, ages 0-16. **Nonfiction:** Parenting subjects in the Philadelphia metro region; 800-1,500 words; $35-$50. **Columns, Departments:** Product reviews, books, music, video, software, health, safety, women's subjects, family finance, travel; 800 words; $35-$50. **Tips:** Prefers to receive query via e-mail; will respond only if interested. **Queries:** Preferred. **E-Queries:** Yes. **Unsolicited mss:** Accepts. **Freelance Content:** 40%. **Rights:** One-time and electronic.

NEW BEGINNINGS

P.O. Box 4079, Schaumburg, IL 60168-4079. 847-519-7730. E-mail: editornb@llli.org. Website: www.lalecheleague.org. Bimonthly. Circ.: 25,000. Kathleen Whitfield, Managing Editor. **Description:** Member publication of La Leche League International, a nonprofit organization. Provides articles and information for women who breastfeed. **Tips:** Does not offer payment for any material.

NEW PARENT

Impact Media Communications, Inc., 10 New King St., White Plains, NY 10604-1205. 914-949-4726. E-mail: knenneker@newparent.com. Website: www.newparent.com. Semi-annual. Circ.: 2,100,000. Kathy Nenneker, Editor. **Description:** For new parents and parents-to-be.

NEW YORK FAMILY

Trader Publishing Co., 141 Halstead Ave., Mamaroneck, NY 10543-2607. 914-381-7474. Website: www.parenthood.com. Monthly. $22/yr. Circ.: 58,000. Heather Hart, Editor-in-Chief. **Description:** Articles related to family life in New York City and general parenting topics. **Payment:** On publication.

NICK, JR.

See full listing in Juvenile category.

NORTHWEST BABY & CHILD

15417 204th Ave. SE, Renton, WA 98059-9021. 425-235-6826. E-mail: editor@nwbaby.com. Website: www.nwbaby.com. Monthly. Circ.: 45,000. Betty Freeman, Editor. **Description:** For parents in Western Washington. **Tips:** Writer's guidelines and editorial calendar available on website. **E-Queries:** Yes.

NORTHWEST FAMILY NEWS

Best Solution Co., 7907 212th St., Suite 201, Edmonds, WA 98026-7525. 425-775-6546. E-mail: nwfamilypub@earthlink.net. Website: www.nwfamily.com. Monthly. $15/yr. Circ.: 50,000. Chris Hopf, Editor. **Description:** Regional parenting and family publication for Western Washington. Nonfiction pieces, $25-$40. Humor, $25-$40. Photos, $5-$20. **Tips:** Send articles in e-mail (no attachments). Include word count. **Queries:** Required. **E-Queries:** Yes. **Unsolicited mss:** Accepts. **Freelance Content:** 65%. **Rights:** One-time (print & electronic).

PARENT CONNECTION

Times Beacon Record Newspapers, P.O. Box 707, Setauket, NY 11733-0769. 631-751-0356. E-mail: parent@tbrnewspapers.com. Website: www.tbrnewspapers.com. Monthly. Circ.: 125,000. Leah Dunaief, Editor. **Description:** For parents in the New York City and surrounding area.

THE PARENT PAPER

North Jersey Media Group, Inc., P.O. Box 471, West Paterson, NJ 07424-0471. 973-569-7000. E-mail: parentpaper@northjersey.com. Website: www.parentpaper.com. Monthly. $25/yr. Circ.: 55,000. Mary Vallo, Editor. **Description:** Parenting magazine for families in New Jersey.

PARENTGUIDE

ParentGuide Network Corp., 419 Park Ave. S., Fl. 13, New York, NY 10016. 212-213-8840. E-mail: editorial@parentguidenews.com. Website: www.parentguidenews.com. Monthly. $19.95/yr. Circ.: 210,000. AnneMarie Evola, Editor. **Description:** For families with kids ages 0-12. Articles on parenting, health, education, child-rearing, etc.; to 1,000 words. **Queries:** Preferred. **E-Queries:** Yes. **Unsolicited mss:** Accepts. **Response:** 1-2 weeks. **SASE Required:** Yes. **Freelance Content:** 80%.

PARENTING

Time, Inc., 530 Fifth Ave., Fl. 4, New York, NY 10036. 212-522-8989. E-mail: youtellus@parenting.com. Website: www.parenting.com. 11x/yr. Circ.: 2,200,000. Janet Chan, Editor-in-Chief. **Description:** Readers are moms (of kids ages newborn-12) as well as expectant moms. Covers the psychological and practical aspects of raising a child, and the emotional issues that face mothers from nurturing their own friendships to juggling the various parts of their lives. **Nonfiction:** On education, health, fitness, nutrition, child development, psychology, and social issues for parents of young children; 1,000-2,500 words for features, 200-500 words for departments. Pay varies. **Queries:** Preferred. **E-Queries:** No. **Unsolicited mss:** Accepts. **Response:** 2 months. **SASE Required:** Yes. **Payment:** On acceptance.

PARENTLIFE

LifeWay Christian Resources, One LifeWay Plaza, MSN 172, Nashville, TN 37234-0172. 615-251-2000. E-mail: parentlife@lifeway.com. Website: www.lifeway.com. Monthly. $19.95/yr. Circ.: 105,000. William Summey, Editor-in-Chief. **Description:**

Christian publication for parents of children ages 0-12. Provides information and education to help parents in each stage of child development. **E-Queries:** Yes. **Contact:** Christi McGuire, Editor.

PARENTS

Gruner + Jahr USA Publishing, 375 Lexington Ave., New York, NY 10017-5514. 212-499-2000. E-mail: mailbag@parentsmagazine.com. Website: www.parents.com. Monthly. $15.98/yr (U.S); $27/yr (Canada). Circ.: 2,237,000. Sally Lee, Editor-in-Chief. **Description:** Features articles on parenting and raising healthy, well-adjusted children. Topics include children's health/safety, behavior, new technology, family life, and travel. **Tips:** See website for writer's guidelines.

PARENTS EXPRESS

Montgomery Newspapers, 290 Commerce Dr., Fort Washington, PA 19034-2400. 215-648-3630. E-mail: wdeluca@montgomerynews.com. Website: www.parents-express.net. Monthly. $24.95/yr. Circ.: 80,000. Wendy DeLuca, Editor. **Description:** For parents in southeastern Pennsylvania and southern New Jersey. Pays $25-$100. **Payment:** On publication.

PARENTS' PRESS

1454 6th St., Berkeley, CA 94710-1431. 510-524-1602. E-mail: parentsprs@aol.com. Website: www.parentspress.com. Monthly. $15. Circ.: 75,000. Dixie Jordan., Editor. **Description:** Parenting newspaper for the San Francisco Bay area. Pays $50 and up. **Tips:** Accepts queries via e-mail, but no attachments. **SASE Required:** Yes. **Freelance Content:** 30%.

PITTSBURGH PARENT

P.O. Box 374, Bakerstown, PA 15007-0374. 724-443-1891. E-mail: pgeditor@nauticom.net. Website: www.pittsburghparent.com. Monthly. Circ.: 50,000. Patricia Poshard, Editor. **Description:** Publication for parents in the Pittsburgh metro area.

QUEENS PARENT

Family Communications, LLC, 9 E 38th St., Fl. 4, New York, NY 10016-0003. 212-889-6400. E-mail: edit@parentsknow.com. Website: www.parentsknow.com. Monthly. $28/yr. Circ.: 70,000. Helen Rosengren Freedman, Executive Editor. **Description:** For parents in the borough of Queens, NYC.

SACRAMENTO SIERRA PARENT MAGAZINE

457 Grass Valley Hwy, Suite 5, Auburn, CA 95603-3725. 530-888-0573. E-mail: ssparent@pacbell.net. Monthly. Circ.: 55,000. **Description:** Provides articles and information to families with children and grandchildren of all ages in the greater Sacramento area. **Nonfiction:** Interested in articles that promote a developmentally appropriate, healthy, and peaceful environment for children. 300-500 words for short pieces; 700-1,000 words for feature articles.

SAN DIEGO FAMILY MAGAZINE

1475 Sixth Ave., Fl. 5, San Diego, CA 92101. 619-685-6970.
Website: www.sandiegofamily.com. Monthly. Circ.: 120,000. Sharon Bay, Publisher
and Editor-in-Chief. **Description:** Family magazine for residents in the San Diego
area. Provides informative, educational articles on parenting with a distinct San Diego
focus. **Tips:** Does not accept phone or e-queries. Submit query by mail with outline,
clips, and SASE for response. See website for submission guidelines. **Queries:**
Required. **E-Queries:** No. **Freelance Content:** 50%. **Rights:** FNAR. **Contact:**
Claire Yezbak Fadden, Editor.

SEATTLE'S CHILD

Trader Publishing Co., 123 NW 36th St., Suite 215, Seattle, WA 98107-4959. 206-
441-0191. E-mail: nweditor@parenthood.com. Website: www.seattleschild.com.
Circ.: 70,000. Wenda Reed, Editor. **Description:** For parents, educators, and childcare providers in the Puget Sound region with kids 14 and under. Investigative reports
and consumer tips on issues affecting families. Also, articles on local events, travel,
theater reviews, health, education, etc. (using local sources). Pieces run 400-2,500
words; $75-$450. **Queries:** Required. **Payment:** On publication.

SINGLE-PARENT FAMILY

Focus on the Family, 8605 Explorer Dr., Colorado Springs, CO 80920-1049. 719-531-
3400. E-mail: singleparent@family.org. Website: www.singleparentfamily.org.
Bimonthly. Circ.: 32,000. Elsa Kok, Editor. **Description:** Information for the
Christian single parent. Addresses issues of divorce, grief, finances, and more. Pay
varies. **Queries:** Preferred. **E-Queries:** Yes. **Unsolicited mss:** Accepts. **SASE
Required:** Yes. **Rights:** FNAR. **Payment:** On acceptance.

SOUTH FLORIDA PARENTING

5555 Nob Hill Rd., Sunrise, FL 33351-4707. 954-747-3050. E-mail: vmccash@sfpar-
enting.com. Website: www.sfparenting.com. Monthly. Circ.: 100,000. **Description:**
For parents in south Florida.

TODAY'S FAMILY

Reminder Publications, Inc., 280 N Main St., East Longmeadow, MA 01028-1814.
413-525-6661. E-mail: news@thereminder.com. Website: www.thereminder.com.
Bimonthly. $9.98/yr. Circ.: 10,000. Elizabeth Wood, Editor. **Description:** Parenting
magazine for Western Massachusetts. Focuses on local news, events, and activities for
families. Columns on family issues, health, day trips, etc. by local writers. **Tips:**
Writers must have expertise on the subject and be from the region (Western Mass.,
Pioneer Valley). Local content, advice written by local experts. **Queries:** Required.
E-Queries: Yes. **Unsolicited mss:** Do not accept. **Response:** 2 weeks. **SASE
Required:** Yes. **Freelance Content:** 10%.

TOLEDO AREA PARENT NEWS

Adams Street Publishing, 1120 Adams St., Toledo, OH 43624. 419-244-9859. E-mail: editor@toledoparent.com. Website: www.toledoparent.com. Monthly. $20/yr. Circ.: 81,000. Eric Lawrence, Editor. **Description:** For parents in Northwest Ohio and Southern Michigan. On parenting, child and family health, and other family topics. Writers must be from the region; 750-1,200 words; $75-$200. **Queries:** Preferred. **Unsolicited mss:** Accepts.

TWINS MAGAZINE

The Business Word, Inc., 11211 E Arapahoe Rd., Suite 101, Centennial, CO 80112-3851. 303-290-8500. E-mail: twins.editor@businessword.com. Website: www.twins-magazine.com. Bimonthly. $25.95/yr. Circ.: 59,000. Sharon Withers, Editor. **Description:** Expert advice from professionals and parents, about the needs of multiple-birth parents. **Nonfiction:** Parenting issues specific to multiples; 1,200 words; $200-$250. **Fillers:** Practical tips (for specific ages: birth-2, 3-4, 5-6); 125-150 words; $20. **Columns, Departments:** Special Miracles (personal experiences); 500-600 words; $40. **Queries:** Preferred. **E-Queries:** Accepts. **Unsolicited mss:** Accepts. **Response:** 3 months. **Freelance Content:** 60%. **Payment:** On publication.

WASHINGTON PARENT

Knollwood Publications, Inc., 4701 Sangamore Rd., #N270, Bethesda, MD 20816-2508. 301-320-2321. E-mail: washpar@washingtonparent.com. Website: www.washingtonparent.com. Monthly. $24/yr. Circ.: 75,000. Margaret Hut, Editor. **Description:** For parents in and around the Washington Metro area, Maryland, and Northern Virginia.

WESTCHESTER PARENT

Family Communications, Inc., 9 E 38th St., Fl. 4, New York, NY 10016-0003. 212-889-6400. E-mail: edit@parentsknow.com. Website: www.parentsknow.com. Monthly. $28/yr. Circ.: 70,000. Helen Rosengren Freedman, Executive Editor. **Description:** For parents in Westchester County, NY.

FILM, TV, ENTERTAINMENT

AMERICAN CINEMATOGRAPHER

ASC Holding Corp., P.O. Box 2230, Los Angeles, CA 90028-4307. 323-969-4333. Website: www.cinematographer.com. Monthly. $40/yr. Circ.: 42,700. Stephen Pizzello, Executive Editor. **Description:** Trade magazine for the cinematography industry. Call for writer's guidelines.

BACK STAGE WEST

VNU Business Media, 5055 Wilshire Blvd., Fl. 5, Los Angeles, CA 90036-6100. 323-525-2356. E-mail: bsweditorial@backstage.com. Website: www.backstage.com. Weekly. $79/yr. Circ.: 12,000. Robert Kendt, Editor-in-Chief. **Description:** Actor's trade paper on the West Coast. Features articles and reviews; pays $.10-$.15/word. **Queries:** Required. **Payment:** On publication.

BOMB

594 Broadway, Suite 905, New York, NY 10012. 212-431-3943. E-mail: info@bomb-site.com. Website: www.bombsite.com. Quarterly. $4.96/$18. Circ.: 25,000. Betsy Sussler, Editor. **Description:** Interviews, varying lengths, on artists, musicians, writers, actors, and directors. Special section in each issue featuring new fiction and poetry. **Fiction:** 20 pages max.; $100. **Poetry:** 10 pages; $100. **Queries:** Preferred. **E-Queries:** Yes. **Unsolicited mss:** Accepts. **Response:** 4 months. **SASE Required:** Yes. **Freelance Content:** 5%. **Rights:** FNASR. **Payment:** On publication. **Contact:** Lucy Raven, Associate Editor.

CINEASTE

304 Hudson St., Fl. 6, New York, NY 10013-1015. 212-366-5720.
E-mail: cineaste@cineaste.com. Website: www.cineaste.com. Quarterly. $6/$20. Circ.: 11,000. Gary Crowdus, Editor-in-Chief. **Description:** Covers the art and politics of the cinema. Views, analyzes, and interprets films. **Nonfiction:** Articles should discuss a film, film genre, a career, a theory, a movement, or related topic, in depth. Interviews with people in filmmaking. 2,000-3,000 words; $75-$100. **Columns, Departments:** 1,000-1,500 words. **Tips:** "Our readers are intelligent general public, sophisticated about art and politics. No matter how complex the ideas or arguments, style must be readable." **Queries:** Preferred. **E-Queries:** Yes. **Unsolicited mss:** Accepts. **Response:** 2-3 months. **SASE Required:** Yes. **Freelance Content:** 50%. **Rights:** FNAR. **Payment:** On publication.

COUNTRY WEEKLY

See full listing in Performing Arts category.

EMMY

Academy of Television Arts and Sciences, 5220 Lankershim Blvd., North Hollywood, CA 91601. 818-754-2800. E-mail: emmymag@emmys.org. Website: www.emmys.tv. Bimonthy. $28/yr. Circ.: 16,000. Gail Polevoi, Editor. **Description:** Television industry magazine for TV professionals and enthusiasts. **Nonfiction:** Profiles and trend stories; 1,500-2,000 words; $900-$1,200. **Columns, Departments:** New writers can break in with Labors of Love or In the Mix filler items; 250-500 words; $200-$400. **Tips:** Writers should have a TV business background. Does not accept academic, fan-magazine, or highly technical articles. **Queries:** Required. **E-Queries:** Yes. **Response:** 4-6 weeks. **SASE Required:** Yes. **Freelance Content:** 80%. **Rights:** FNAR. **Payment:** On publication.

ENTERTAINMENT DESIGN

PRIMEDIA Business Magazines & Media, 249 W 17th St., Fl. 4, New York, NY 10011. 212-204-1819. E-mail: jtien@primediabusiness.com. Website: www.entertainmentdesignmag.com. Jacqueline Tien, Publisher. **Description:** Trade publication on the art and technology of entertainment. Articles cover design, technical, and management aspects of theater, opera, dance, television, and film for those in performing arts and the entertainment trade. Pieces run 500-2,500 words. **Queries:** Preferred. **Payment:** On acceptance.

FANGORIA

Starlog Group, Inc., 475 Park Ave. S., Fl. 7, New York, NY 10016. 212-689-2830. E-mail: tony@starloggroup.com. Website: www.fangoria.com. 10x/yr. $7.99/$39.97. Circ.: 260,000. Anthony Timpone, Editor. **Description:** Nonfiction articles and interviews on horror films, TV series, books, and the artists who create this genre. Emphasizes personalities and behind-the-scenes angles of horror filmmaking. **Nonfiction:** Movie, TV, and book previews; reviews; and interviews connected to upcoming horror films; 2,000-3,000 words; $150-$275. **Tips:** A strong love of the genre is essential. Readers are experts on horror who want to read about the latest films and filmmakers. Website options also open. See website for style and content. **Queries:** Required. **E-Queries:** No. **Unsolicited mss:** Do not accept. **Response:** 6-8 weeks. **SASE Required:** Yes. **Freelance Content:** 92%. **Rights:** All. **Payment:** On publication.

FILM COMMENT

Film Society of Lincoln Center, 70 Lincoln Center Plaza, New York, NY 10023-6595. 212-875-5610. E-mail: filmcomment@filmlinc.com. Website: www.filmlinc.com. Bimonthly. $24.95/yr. Circ.: 45,000. Gavin Smith, Editor. **Description:** On films (new and old, foreign and domestic), also performers, writers, cinematographers, studios, national cinemas, genres. Opinion and historical pieces also used.

FILM QUARTERLY

University of California Press, 2000 Center St., Suite 303, Berkeley, CA 94704-1233. 510-643-7154. Website: www.ucpress.edu/journals/fq. Quarterly. $28/yr. Circ.: 7,600. Ann Martin, Editor. **Description:** Historical, analytical, and critical articles, to 6,000 words. Also, film and book reviews. **Queries:** Preferred.

HEROES FROM HACKLAND

1225 Evans, Arkadelphia, AR 71923. 870-246-6223. 3x/yr. $6.50/$18. Circ.: 150. Mike Grogan, Editor. **Description:** Takes a nostalgic, popular-culture approach to the review of B-movies, cartoons, series books, radio, TV, comic books, and newspaper comic strips. **Nonfiction:** Any fresh article casting light on the popular culture of yesterday and its relation to today; 220-1500 words; $5 and copies. **Poetry:** Nostalgic with a bite, coherent imagery, no impenetrable college quarterly stuff; to 40 lines; $5 and copies. **Fillers:** Vignettes about customs, little-known facts about pop culture icons. **Art:** B&W only; $5/photo. **Tips:** Sample copy $5. **Queries:** Not necessary. **Unsolicited mss:** Accepts. **Response:** 10 days. **SASE Required:** Yes. **Freelance Content:** 75%. **Rights:** 1st. **Payment:** On publication.

ILLINOIS ENTERTAINER
124 W Polk, Suite 103, Chicago, IL 60605-1770. 312-922-9333.
E-mail: editors@illinoisentertainer.com. Website: www.illinoisentertainer.com.
Monthly. $35/yr. Circ.: 70,000. Althea Legaspi, Editor-in-Chief. **Description:** On local and national entertainment (especially alternative music) in the greater Chicago area. Personality profiles, interviews, reviews, etc. Open to non-music/band features, especially of odd, quixotic kind. Pieces run 500-1,500 words; $75. **Tips:** "Send clips (via snail mail) and be patient." **Queries:** Not necessary. **E-Queries:** Yes. **Unsolicited mss:** Accepts. **Response:** 30-90 days. **SASE Required:** No. **Freelance Content:** 70%. **Rights:** FNASR. **Payment:** On publication.

THE INDEPENDENT FILM AND VIDEO MONTHLY
304 Hudson St., Fl. 6, New York, NY 10013. 212-807-1400.
E-mail: editor@aivf.org. Website: www.aivf.org. 10x/yr. $4.95/issue. Circ.: 30,000.
Rebecca Carroll, Editor-in-Chief. **Description:** Publication for active mediamakers on all aspects of independently-produced film and video. Topics include scripting, funding, production techniques, technology, editing, film festivals, distribution, interviews with directors, book reviews, legal issues, media advocacy, etc.; 700-1,300 words. **Queries:** Required. **E-Queries:** Yes. **Unsolicited mss:** Accepts. **Response:** 4 months. **SASE Required:** Yes. **Freelance Content:** 80%. **Rights:** FNAR and electronic. **Payment:** On publication.

KIDS TRIBUTE
See full listing in Juvenile category.

NEW ENGLAND ENTERTAINMENT DIGEST
P.O. Box 88, Burlington, MA 01803. 781-272-2066. E-mail: jacneed@aol.com.
Website: www.jacneed.com. Monthly. $2/$20. Circ.: 5,000. JulieAnn Charest, Editor.
Description: Theater and entertainment news for residents in New England and New York. Professional, regional, college, community and children's theatre, all types of dance, music, film and video; length and pay varies. **Art:** Photographs or illustrations; electronic format; $5/print. **Queries:** Preferred. **E-Queries:** Yes. **Unsolicited mss:** Accepts. **Freelance Content:** 35%. **Payment:** On publication.

PERFORMING ARTS AND ENTERTAINMENT IN CANADA
Canadian Stage & Arts, Ltd., 104 Glenrose Ave., Toronto, Ontario M4T 1K8 Canada.
416-484-4534. Quarterly. $8/yr. Circ.: 40,000. Sarah Hood, Editor. **Description:** Canadian performing arts and entertainment, including theater, music (especially classical, new, jazz, world, and folk), dance, film, TV and related fields. Also profiles, opinion, issues, etc. Especially interested in stories that reflect some aspect of Canadian diversity. Publishes very few reviews. Pieces run 600-1,500 words; $95-$170. **Tips:** Prefers stories with original ideas and opinions, or addressing issues of some complexity or sophistication—not just simple profiles of people or companies. **Queries:** Required. **E-Queries:** Yes. **Unsolicited mss:** Accepts. **SASE Required:** Yes. **Rights:** FNAR, electronic. **Payment:** On publication.

PLAYBILL

Playbill, Inc., 525 Seventh Ave., Suite 1801, New York, NY 10018. 212-557-5757. Website: www.playbill.com. Monthly. $24/yr. Circ.: 1,275,300. Judy Samelson, Editor. **Description:** Increases the understanding and enjoyment of each Broadway production, certain Lincoln Center and Off-Broadway productions, and regional attractions. Also, features about theatre personalities, fashion, entertainment, dining, etc. **Unsolicited mss:** Does not accept.

STAR MAGAZINE

American Media, Inc., 1000 American Media Way, Boca Raton, FL 33464-1000. 561-997-7733. E-mail: letters@starmagazine.com. Website: www.starmagazine.com. Weekly. $47.76/yr. Circ.: 1,385,300. **Description:** On show business and celebrities, health, fitness, parenting, and diet and food.

TV GUIDE

Gemstar-TV Guide International, Inc., 1211 Avenue of the Americas, New York, NY 10036-8701. 212-852-7500. Website: www.tvguide.com. Weekly. $39.88/yr. Circ.: 9,061,600. Michael Lafavore, Editor-in-Chief. **Description:** Short, brightly-written pieces about humorous or offbeat angles of television and industry trends. Most personality pieces are staff-written. **Queries:** Required. **Payment:** On acceptance.

UNIVERCITY

Hadley Media, 21 Mockingbird Hill Rd., Windham, NH 03087-1236. 800-270-2084. E-mail: hadley@univercity.com. Website: www.univercity.com. 8x/yr. Circ.: 40,000. D. Patrick Hadley, Publisher. **Description:** An entertainment magazine for college students. Prints multiple editions (Boston, Chicago, New York). **Tips:** See website for details. Also interested in screenplays for their production company. "Everyone knows how difficult it is to 'break in;' with that in mind, we are committed to discovering new talent that we know exists out there but may not have an 'in.'" **Queries:** Preferred. **E-Queries:** Yes. **Unsolicited mss:** Accepts. **Contact:** Katherine Spafford, Editor-in-Chief.

VIDEOMAKER

P.O. Box 4591, Chico, CA 95927. 530-891-8410. E-mail: editor@videomaker.com. Website: www.videomaker.com. Monthly. Circ.: 91,079. Stephen Muratore, Editor-in-Chief. **Description:** Covers consumer video production: camcorders, computers, tools and techniques. Authoritative how-to articles, instructionals, editing, desktop video, audio/video production, innovative applications, tools and tips, industry developments, new products; to 1,500 words; $.10/word. **Tips:** Unsolicited manuscripts are used only to evaluate queries and are not accepted for print consideration. **Queries:** Preferred. **E-Queries:** Yes. **Unsolicited mss:** Accepts. **Response:** 6-8 weeks. **SASE Required:** Yes. **Freelance Content:** 60%. **Rights:** All and electronic. **Payment:** On publication.

WRITTEN BY

7000 W 3rd St., Los Angeles, CA 90048-4329. 323-782-4522.
E-mail: writtenby@wga.org. Website: www.wga.org. 9x/yr. $40/yr. Circ.: 13,500.
Richard Slayton, Editor. **Description:** Official publication of the Writers Guild of America. Written by and for America's screen and television writers. Feature articles (2,500 words), special reports (1,500-2,000 words), interviews, technical articles, and product reviews. **Tips:** Review previous issues before submitting queries or manuscripts. **Queries:** Required. **Unsolicited mss:** Accepts. **Response:** 8 weeks. **Freelance Content:** 80%. **Rights:** 1st world-wide and electronic. **Payment:** On acceptance.

FITNESS

(see also Health)

ALL FOR YOU

161 Hawkins Circle, Wheaton, IL 60187. 630-668-0439. E-mail: all4youinc@aol.com. Website: www.allforyouweb.com. Monthly. $14.95/yr. Circ.: 10,000. Nancy Thomas, Editor. **Description:** On health, fitness, nutrition, alternative therapies, body/mind/spirit. Highlights local practitioners in the Chicago area. Pays $25/piece. **Tips:** See writer's guidelines on website. **Queries:** Preferred. **E-Queries:** Yes. **Unsolicited mss:** Accepts. **Response:** 1 month. **Freelance Content:** 50%. **Payment:** On publication.

AMERICAN FITNESS

Aerobics and Fitness Assn. of America, 15250 Ventura Blvd., Suite 200, Sherman Oaks, CA 91403-3297. 818-905-0040. E-mail: americanfitness@afaa.com. Website: www.afaa.com. Bimonthly. $48/yr. Circ.: 42,000. Meg Jordan, Editor. **Description:** Trade journal for fitness instructors. **Nonfiction:** Articles on exercise, health, trends in aerobic sports, research, nutrition, class instruction, alternative paths. No first-person stories. 1,200 words; $200/article. **Tips:** Needs research-oriented articles. **Queries:** Required. **E-Queries:** Yes. **Unsolicited mss:** Accepts. **Response:** Between 2 months and a year. **SASE Required:** Yes. **Freelance Content:** 90%. **Rights:** All. **Payment:** On publication.

AMERICAN HEALTH & FITNESS FOR MEN

5775 McLaughlin Rd., Mississauga, Ontario L5R 3P7 Canada. 905-507-3545.
E-mail: editorial@ahfmag.com. Website: www.ahfmag.com. Kerrie-Lee Brown, Editor. **Description:** Men's lifestyle fitness magazine featuring sports commentary, training tips, gear, health, nutrition, fitness breakthroughs, celebrity profiles. Features up to 1,200 words; columns/departments 500-800 words. Pay varies. **Queries:** Not necessary. **E-Queries:** Yes. **Unsolicited mss:** Accepts. **Freelance Content:** 75%. **Rights:** All international. **Payment:** On acceptance.

ENERGY FOR WOMEN

EAS/Muscle Media Publishing, Inc., 555 Corporate Circle, Golden, CO 80401-5621. 303-384-0080. E-mail: editorial@energyforwomen.com. Website: www.energyfor-women.com. Bimonthly. $17.97/yr. Circ.: 400,000. Gretchen Ferraro, Editor-in-Chief. **Description:** For women ages 25-45 who are interested in leading a healthy lifestyle. Editorial provides ways for women to increase their energy and improve their lives by following a consistent nutrition and exercise program. **Nonfiction:** Well-researched, in-depth articles about health, fitness, nutrition, weight-training, cardio, supplementation, motivation, and mind/body issues; 800-2,000 words; $1/word. **Columns, Departments:** Short, catchy, well-researched pieces on training, nutrition, mind/body issues, and health; 300-1,000 words; $1/word. **Tips:** "Read the magazine before submitting. Find out why we're different than other fitness magazines. We're not about quick fixes, fad diets, or the latest celebrity trends. *Energy* is a magazine for real women who want to embrace fitness and health as a lifestyle." **Queries:** Required. **E-Queries:** Yes. **Unsolicited mss:** Does not accept. **Response:** 1 month. **Rights:** FNAR.

FIT PREGNANCY

Weider Publications, Inc., 21100 Erwin St., Woodland Hills, CA 91367-3712. 818-884-6800. E-mail: peg.moline@weiderpub.com. Website: www.fitpregnancy.com. Bimonthly. $9.97/yr. Circ.: 500,000. Peg Moline, Editor-in-Chief. **Description:** Expert advice for the pregnant or postpartum woman and her newborn. Articles, 500-2,000 words, on safe workouts, nutrition, meal plans, medical news, baby care, baby gear, psychology/sex/relationship information, and more. **Queries:** Required. **Unsolicited mss:** Does not accept. **Payment:** On publication.

FITNESS

Gruner + Jahr USA Publishing, 15 E 26th St., New York, NY 10010. 646-758-0430. Website: www.fitnessmagazine.com. Monthly. $3.50/issue. Circ.: 1,500,000. Emily Listfield, Editor-in-Chief. **Description:** For women in their 20's and 30's. Articles on exercise, nutrition, beauty, stress, etc. Also includes features on new products, how-to pieces on exercise, and first-person profiles of individuals with healthy lifestyles; 1,500-2,500 words; $1,500-$2,500. **Tips:** Please contact the appropriate beat editor with story ideas. **Queries:** Required. **Unsolicited mss:** Does not accept. **Response:** 2 months. **SASE Required:** Yes. **Rights:** FNAR. **Payment:** On acceptance. **Contact:** Amy Fishbein (health), Leah McLaughlin (diet/nutrition), Alyssa Shaffer (fitness), Stacy Baker (psychology).

FITNESS PLUS

3402 E Kleindale Rd., Tucson, AZ 85716-1334. 520-881-6696. E-mail: editor@fit-plusmag.com. Monthly. $15/yr. Circ.: 90,000. Kari Redfield, Editor. **Description:** On serious health and fitness training. Articles, 600 words; pay varies. **Queries:** Required. **Payment:** On publication.

FITNESS RX FOR WOMEN

Advanced Research Press, 690 Rt. 25A, Setauket, NY 11733-1200. 631-751-9696. E-mail: editor@musculardevelopment.com. Website: www.fitnessrx.com. Monthly. $4.99/$20.95. Circ.: 307,000. **Description:** For women, featuring well-researched articles on diet, fitness, health, cosmetic enhancement, and sexual fulfillment. Articles run 1,000-2,500 words; $500-$1,500. **Queries:** Preferred. **Payment:** On publication.

IDEA FITNESS JOURNAL

IDEA, Inc., 10455 Pacific Center Ct., San Diego, CA 92121-4339. 858-535-8979. E-mail: member@ideafit.com. Website: www.ideafit.com. Monthly. $50/yr. Circ.: 20,000. Sandy Todd Webster, Editor-in-Chief. **Description:** For the fitness professional. Topics include exercise science, program design, profiles of successful trainers, business/legal/marketing topics, tips for networking, client counseling, new products and research, and training tips. Pay varies. **Queries:** Preferred. **E-Queries:** Yes. **Unsolicited mss:** Accepts. **Response:** 1 month. **SASE Required:** Yes. **Payment:** On publication.

IDEA HEALTH & FITNESS SOURCE

IDEA, Inc., 6190 Cornerstone Ct. E, Suite 204, San Diego, CA 92121-3773. 858-535-8979. E-mail: member@ideafit.com. Website: www.ideafit.com. Monthly. Circ.: 23,000. Sandy Todd Webster, Editor-in-Chief. **Description:** Leading publication for all levels of fitness professionals. Practical articles on new exercise programs, business management, nutrition, health, motivation, sports medicine, group exercise, one-on-one training techniques. Length and pay varies. **Tips:** "Articles must be geared towards exercise studio owners/managers, personal trainers, and fitness instructors. No consumer or general health pieces." **Queries:** Preferred. **E-Queries:** Yes. **Unsolicited mss:** Accepts. **Response:** 2-3 months. **Freelance Content:** 75%. **Rights:** All NA (print and electronic). **Payment:** On acceptance. **Contact:** Cynthia Roth, Editorial Assistant.

MEN'S FITNESS

Weider Publications, Inc./American Media, Inc., 21100 Erwin St., Woodland Hills, CA 91367-3712. 818-884-6800. E-mail: mensfitnesscomments@weiderpub.com. Website: www.mensfitness.com. Monthly. $21.97/yr. Circ.: 677,000. Peter Sikowitz, Editor-in-Chief. **Description:** Authoritative articles on sports, fitness, health, nutrition, and men's issues; 1,500-1,800 words; $500-$1,000. **Tips:** Send clips. **Queries:** Preferred. **Payment:** On acceptance. **Contact:** Dean Brierly, Managing Editor.

MS. FITNESS

P.O. Box 2490, White City, OR 97503-0490. 541-830-0400. E-mail: msfitness@aol.com. Website: www.msfitness.com. 4x/yr. $3.99/$12. Circ.: 150,000. Greta Blackburn, Editor. **Description:** For the dedicated, fit woman of today. Covers all areas of interest including exercise, home equipment, nutrition, fashion and competitions. **Queries:** Not necessary. **E-Queries:** Yes. **Response:** 60-90 days. **SASE Required:** Yes. **Freelance Content:** 50%. **Rights:** None.

MUSCLE & FITNESS

Weider Publications, Inc./American Media, Inc., 21100 Erwin St., Woodland Hills, CA 91367-3712. 818-884-6800. E-mail: jkrumm@weiderpub.com. Website: www.muscle-fitness.com. Monthly. $34.97/yr. Circ.: 410,400. Bill Geiger, Executive Editor. **Description:** Bodybuilding and fitness publication for healthy, active men and women. Covers all areas of bodybuilding, health, fitness, injury prevention and treatment, and nutrition. Feature articles run 1,500-1,800 words; $400-$800. Short pieces and departments run 500-800 words; $360. **Tips:** All features and departments are written on assignment. Send 1-page query with potential sources, qualifications, and recent clips. **Queries:** Required. **Unsolicited mss:** Does not accept. **Rights:** FNAR. **Payment:** On acceptance. **Contact:** Jo Ellen Krumm, Managing Editor.

MUSCLE & FITNESS HERS

Weider Publications, Inc./American Media, Inc., 21100 Erwin St., Woodland Hills, CA 91367-3712. 818-884-6800. E-mail: carey.rossi-walker@weiderpub.com. Website: www.muscle-fitnesshers.com. 10x/yr. Circ.: 253,700. Carey Rossi Walker, Executive Editor. **Description:** Publication for healthy, active women interested in fitness. Weight training, bodybuilding techniques, instructional fitness, health, injury prevention and treatment, and nutrition. Features run 1,500-2,000 words; $400-$800. Shorter pieces and departments run 750-1,000 words; $400. **Tips:** All features and departments are written on assignment. Send 1-page query with potential sources, qualifications, and recent clips. **Queries:** Required. **E-Queries:** No. **Unsolicited mss:** Does not accept. **Rights:** FNAR. **Payment:** On acceptance.

MUSCLE MEDIA

EAS/Muscle Media Publishing, Inc.
555 Corporate Circle, Golden, CO 80401-5621. 303-384-0080.
E-mail: editorial@musclemedia.com. Website: www.musclemedia.com. Bimonthly. $23.97/yr. Circ.: 250,000. Gretchen Ferraro, Executive Editor. **Description:** Health and fitness publication for men.

MUSCULAR DEVELOPMENT

Advanced Research Press, 690 Rt. 25A, Setauket, NY 11733-1200.
631-751-9696. E-mail: editor@musculardevelopment.com.
Website: www.musculardevelopment.com. Monthly. $6.99/$34.97. Circ.: 137,500. Steve Blechman, Editor-in-Chief. **Description:** For serious weight-training athletes, on any aspect of competitive bodybuilding, fat loss, nutrition, and supplementation. Articles run 1,000-2,500 words, with photos; pays $500-$1,500. **Queries:** Preferred.

OXYGEN

5775 McLaughlin Rd., Mississauga, Ontario L5R 3P7 Canada. 905-507-3545. E-mail: editorial@oxygenmag.com. Website: www.oxygenmag.com. Monthly. $19.99/yr. Circ.: 340,000. Nancy LePatourel, Editor-in-Chief. **Description:** Women's health/fitness magazine. Features articles on fitness, health, and nutrition; shorter motivation profiles. Pieces run 1,000-2,000 words; $.50/word. **Tips:** Submit query outlining your topic, the angle you wish to take, and a list of sources. Also include a small paragraph stating why you're qualified to write the article. **Queries:** Required. **E-Queries:** Yes. **Unsolicited mss:** Accepts. **Response:** Queries 2-4 weeks, submissions 1-2 weeks. **Freelance Content:** 60%. **Rights:** FNAR. **Payment:** On acceptance.

PHYSICAL
Basic Mediagroup, Inc., 11050 Santa Monica Blvd., Fl. 3, Los Angeles, CA 90025. 310-445-7500. E-mail: info@physicalmag.com. Website: www.physicalmag.com. Monthly. $15.98/yr. Circ.: 650,000. Bill Bush, Editor-in-Chief. **Description:** Custom publication for General Nutrition Center gold card club members. Covers physical fitness, sports nutrition and body building. **Queries:** Preferred. **E-Queries:** Yes. **Unsolicited mss:** Accepts. **Response:** 1-4 months. **Freelance Content:** 90%. **Rights:** FNASR, electronic. **Payment:** On acceptance.

THE PHYSICIAN AND SPORTSMEDICINE MAGAZINE
McGraw-Hill, Inc., 4530 W 77th St., Suite 350, Minneapolis, MN 55435. 952-835-3222. Website: www.physsportmed.com. Monthly. $48/yr. Circ.: 96,600. Gordon Matheson, Editor-in-Chief. **Description:** News articles, with sports-medicine angle. **Queries:** Preferred. **Payment:** On acceptance. **Contact:** Jim Wappes, Exec. Editor.

SHAPE
Weider Publications, Inc./American Media, Inc., 21100 Erwin St., Woodland Hills, CA 91367-3712. 818-884-6800. Website: www.shape.com. Monthly. $19.97/yr. Circ.: 1,643,800. Anne Russell, Editor-in-Chief. **Description:** Provides women ages 18-34 with tools to create better lives and a deeper understanding of fitness. Uses only solid, well-respected experts in the fields of exercise, health, nutrition, sport, beauty, and psychology. **Nonfiction:** New and interesting ideas on physical and mental aspects of getting and staying in shape; 1,200-1,500 words; pay varies. **Tips:** "*Shape* readers have come to trust us for the final word on the issue most important to them and expect us to present it in a clear, challenging and visually beautiful fashion." **Queries:** Required. **Unsolicited mss:** Does not accept. **Freelance Content:** 70%. **Payment:** On acceptance.

SWEAT MAGAZINE
736 E Loyola Dr., Tempe, AZ 85282. 480-947-3900. E-mail: editor@sweat-magazine.com. Website: www.sweatmagazine.com.. Monthly. $18/yr. Circ.: 60,000. Joan Kay Westlake, Editor. **Description:** Covers amateur sports, outdoor activities, wellness, and fitness, with an Arizona angle. **Nonfiction:** Articles, 500-1,200 words. No self-indulgent or personal tales. Prefers investigative pieces, must relate to Arizona or Arizonans. Pays $35-$100. **Art:** Photos, $20-$100. **Queries:** Required. **Unsolicited mss:** Do not accept. **Payment:** Within 1 month of publication.

TEACHING ELEMENTARY PHYSICAL EDUCATION
See full listing in Education category.

VIM & VIGOR

McMurry Publishing, Inc., 1010 E Missouri Ave., Phoenix, AZ 85014-2602. 602-395-5850. E-mail: careyj@mcmurry.com. Quarterly. $2.95/issue. Circ.: 650,000. Carey E. Jones, Managing Editor. **Description:** A national health and fitness publication with 20 regional editions. **Nonfiction:** Positive articles, with medical facts, healthcare news, medical breakthroughs, exercise/fitness, health trends, wellness, general physical and emotional health, disease updates; written for a general reader. 900-1,500 words; $.80-$1.25/word. **Tips:** No healthcare product promotion, book reviews, personal accounts (unless to illustrate a topic) or unfounded medical claims for disease prevention and treatment. Style is serious, poignant, informative; with a slant that speaks to the reader as "you." Write for an educated reader, but remember to explain scientific terms and complex procedures. **E-Queries:** Yes. **Unsolicited mss:** Do not accept. **Rights:** FNAR, international, and electronic.

WEIGHT WATCHERS MAGAZINE

See full listing in Health category.

FOOD & WINE

BON APPETIT

Condé Nast Publications, Inc., 6300 Wilshire Blvd., Fl. 10, Los Angeles, CA 90048-5204. 323-965-3600. Website: www.bonappetit.com. Monthly. $3.95/$20. Circ.: 1,283,375. Barbara Fairchild, Editor-in-Chief. **Description:** Covers food, entertainment, and travel. **Queries:** Required. **E-Queries:** No. **Unsolicited mss:** Does not accept. **Response:** 4-6 weeks. **SASE Required:** Yes. **Rights:** All. **Payment:** On acceptance. **Contact:** Victoria von Biel, Executive Editor.

BREW YOUR OWN

Battenkill Communications, 5053 Main St., Suite A, Manchester Center, VT 05255. 802-362-3981. E-mail: edit@byo.com. Website: www.byo.com. 8x/yr. Circ.: 40,000. Chris Colby, Editor. **Description:** Practical information for homebrewers. Articles run 1,000-2,500 words; $50-$150. **Queries:** Required. **Payment:** On publication.

CHEF

Talcott Communications Corp., 20 W Kinzie, Fl. 12, Chicago, IL 60610. 312-849-2220. E-mail: rbenes@talcott.com; mwolkoff@talcott.com. Website: www.talcott.com. Monthly. $24/yr. Circ.: 43,600. **Description:** "The Professional Magazine for Chefs." Offers professionals in the foodservice business ideas for food marketing, preparation, and presentation. Chef profiles, foodservice industry and food trends and news. **Nonfiction:** Articles, 800-1,200 words, must include art or art leads; pays $250 to first-time writers, others $350. **Payment:** Up to 30 days after publication.

CHOCOLATIER

Haymarket Group Ltd., 45 W 34th St., Suite 600, New York, NY 10001-3073. 212-239-0855. E-mail: chocmag@aol.com. Website: www.godiva.com. Bimonthly. $21.95/yr. Circ.: 150,000. Michael Schneider, Publisher/Editor-in-Chief. **Description:** Covers chocolate and desserts, cooking/baking techniques, lifestyle, and travel. **Queries:** Required. **Payment:** On acceptance.

COOK'S ILLUSTRATED

Boston Common Press, 17 Station St., Brookline, MA 02445-7995. 617-232-1000. E-mail: cooks@bcpress.com. Website: www.cooksillustrated.com. Bimonthly. $24.95/yr. Circ.: 500,000. Christopher Kimball, Publisher/Editor. **Description:** Articles on techniques of home cooking. Features master recipes based on careful testing, trial and error. **Queries:** Required. **Payment:** On acceptance.

COOKING FOR PROFIT

P.O. Box 267, Fond du Lac, WI 54936-0267. 920-923-3700. E-mail: comments@cookingforprofit.com. Website: www.cookingforprofit.com. Monthly. $24/yr. Circ.: 40,100. Colleen Phalen, Publisher/Editor. **Description:** B2B publication for foodservice professionals. Profiles of successful restaurants, chains, and franchises, schools, hospitals, nursing homes, etc. Also, case studies on energy management in foodservice environment. **Payment:** On publication.

DELICIOUS LIVING

1401 Pearl St., Boulder, CO 80302-5346. 303-939-8440. E-mail: deliciousliving@penton.com. Website: www.deliciouslivingmag.com. Monthly. $24/yr. Circ.: 420,000. Jean Weiss, Editor-in-Chief. **Description:** Lifestyle publication that inspires and motivates readers to lead healthy, conscious, and informed lives. **Tips:** "Our readers are shoppers at natural products stores. Please write to request writer's guidelines." **Queries:** Required. **E-Queries:** Yes. **Rights:** All. **Payment:** On acceptance.

FANCY FOOD & CULINARY PRODUCTS

Talcott Communications Corp., 20 W Kinzie, Fl. 12, Chicago, IL 60610. 312-849-2220, ex.34. E-mail: fancyfood@talcott.com. Website: www.talcott.com. Monthly. $3.95/issue. Circ.: 28,000. John Saxtan, Editor. **Description:** Covers the business of specialty foods, coffee and tea, natural foods, confections, and upscale housewares. Articles run 1,200-1,500 words; $300. **Tips:** Readers are retailers, not consumers. **Queries:** Required. **E-Queries:** Yes. **Unsolicited mss:** Accepts. **Response:** 1 month. **Freelance Content:** 35%. **Rights:** FNASR. **Payment:** On publication.

GOURMET

Condé Nast Publications, Inc., 4 Times Square, Fl. 5, New York, NY 10036-6563. 212-286-2860. Website: www.gourmet.com. Monthly. $12/yr. Circ.: 958,900. Ruth Reichl, Editor-in-Chief. **Description:** "The magazine of good living." Offers cooking tips, recipes, fine food/wine, tips for healthy eating, etc. **Queries:** Preferred. **Unsolicited mss:** Does not accept.

KASHRUS

Yeshiva Birkas Reuven, P.O. Box 204, Brooklyn, NY 11204-0204. 718-336-8544. E-mail: editorial@kashrusmagazine.com. Website: www.kashrusmagazine.com. 5x/yr. $3.75/$18. Circ.: 10,000. Yosef Wikler, Editor. **Description:** Provides up-to-date information to the kosher consumer on food, travel, catering, health issues, mislabeled food products, etc. **Nonfiction:** Articles on food technology, new kosher products, catering, new kitchens, and medicine; 250-1,500 words; $25-$200. **Fillers:** Accepts food-related humor and cartoons. **Art:** Color photos of food, dining, travel, and Israel. Submit on disk or hard copy. **Tips:** "We seek writers who can be sensitive to the feelings of Orthodox Jews." **Queries:** Preferred. **E-Queries:** No. **Unsolicited mss:** Accepts. **Response:** 2 days. **SASE Required:** Yes. **Rights:** FNAR and reprint. **Payment:** On publication.

NORTHWEST PALATE

Pacifica Publishing, Inc., P.O. Box 10860, Portland, OR 97296-0860. 503-224-6039. E-mail: editorial@nwpalate.com. Website: www.nwpalate.com. $4.95/$21. Circ.: 45,000. Cameron Nagel, Publisher/Editor. **Description:** Covers food, wine, and travel in the Pacific Northwest (Oregon, Washington, Idaho, and British Columbia). Articles should be 100-2,000 words; $.25/word. **Tips:** "Writers should familiarize themselves with our content and style. Get a copy of our magazine and also visit our website's back issues to see what we've covered. Please do not submit articles that have no bearing on food, wine, or travel in the Pacific Northwest." **Queries:** Preferred. **E-Queries:** Yes. **Unsolicited mss:** Accepts. **Response:** 1-8 weeks. **SASE Required:** Yes. **Freelance Content:** 80%. **Rights:** FNAR. **Payment:** On publication. **Contact:** Angie Jabine, Managing Editor.

TEA: A MAGAZINE

Olde English Tea Co., P.O. Box 348, Scotland, CT 06264-0348. 860-456-1145. E-mail: teamag@teamag.com. Website: www.teamag.com. Quarterly. $5/$17. Circ.: 12,000. Pearl Dexter, Editor. **Description:** "Focus on tea, not only as a beverage, but as an influence on art, music, literature, history, design, and global societies." Features current trends in health research and tea's impact in relationships, families, and psychological well-being. **Tips:** Does not assign articles to writers and does not accept query letters. Send complete manuscipt; fees are negotiable and may be discussed with the editor. **Unsolicited mss:** Accepts. **Response:** 30 days. **SASE Required:** Yes. **Freelance Content:** 75%. **Payment:** On publication.

TIDINGS

Kylix Media, Inc., 5165 Sherbrooke St. W, Suite 414, Montreal, Quebec H4A 1T6 Canada. 514-481-5892. E-mail: editor@winetidingsmag.com. 8x/yr. $36/yr. Circ.: 19,850. Aldo Parise, Editor-in-Chief. **Description:** Canada's leading national magazine dedicated to food and wine. Articles (1,000-1,500 words, $100-$300), and shorts (400-1,000 words, $30-$150). **Queries:** Preferred. **Payment:** On publication.

VEGETARIAN TIMES

Sabot Publishing, Inc., 301 Concourse Blvd., Suite 350, Glen Allen, VA 23059. 804-346-0990. Website: www.vegetariantimes.com. Monthly. $24.95/yr. Circ.: 321,000. Carla Davis, Managing Editor. **Description:** Articles on vegetarian cooking, nutrition, health and fitness, travel and entertaining. Pay negotiable. **Queries:** Required. **Payment:** On acceptance.

VEGGIE LIFE

EWG Publishing Co., 1041 Shary Circle, Concord, CA 94518. 925-671-9852. E-mail: veggieed@egw.com. Website: www.veggielife.com. Quarterly. $17.97/yr. Circ.: 189,000. Shanna Masters, Editor. **Description:** For people interested in low-fat, meatless cuisine and nutrition. Include 7-8 recipes with submissions; 1,500-2,000 words. **Queries:** Preferred. **Payment:** On publication.

THE WINE NEWS

T.E. Smith, Inc., P.O. Box 142096, Coral Gables, FL 33143-2096. 305-740-7170. E-mail: wineline@aol.com. Website: www.thewinenews.com. Bimonthly. $24/yr. Circ.: 66,000. Kathy Sinnes, Managing Editor. **Description:** Upscale publication that offers commentary, interviews, historical perspectives, and wine recommendations. Targets wine-savvy consumers who look to the magazine for guidance and entertainment in all areas regarding wine. **Tips:** "We publish articles that demonstrate a depth of expertise as well as a distinctive and engaging writing style." **Queries:** Required. **E-Queries:** Yes. **Unsolicited mss:** Accepts. **Response:** 90 days. **Freelance Content:** 10%. **Rights:** One-time. **Payment:** 15 after publication.

WINE SPECTATOR

M. Shanken Communications, Inc., 387 Park Ave. S., New York, NY 10016. 212-684-4224. Website: www.winespectator.com. $40/yr. Circ.: 323,600. Thomas Matthews, Executive Editor. **Description:** On news and people in the wine world, travel, food, and other lifestyle topics. Features, 600-2,000 words, preferably with photos; pays from $400, extra for photos. **Queries:** Required. **Payment:** On publication.

WINEMAKER

Battenkill Communications
5053 Main St., Suite A, Manchester Center, VT 05255. 802-362-3981. E-mail: edit@winemakermag.com.Website: www.winemakermag.com. Bimonthly. Circ.: 35,000. Chris Colby, Editor. **Description:** Practical information for home winemakers. Articles run 1,000-2,500 words; $50-$150. **Queries:** Required. **Payment:** On publication.

WINES & VINES

1800 Lincoln Ave., San Rafael, CA 94901. 415-453-9700. E-mail: edit@winesand-vines.com. Website: www.winesandvines.com. Monthly. Tina Caputo, Managing Editor. **Description:** Trade journal for the grape and wine industry, emphasizing marketing, management, vineyard techniques, and production. Emphasizes technology with valuable, scientific winemaking articles. Articles, 1,000-2,000 words; pays $.15/word. **Tips:** No travel or consumer-oriented articles. "We recommend visiting our website for examples of style and coverage before querying. We prefer queries by e-mail." **Queries:** Required. **E-Queries:** Yes. **Unsolicited mss:** Does not accept. **Payment:** On acceptance.

ZYMURGY

American Homebrewers Assn., Inc., P.O. Box 1679, Boulder, CO 80306-1679. 303-447-0816. E-mail: info@aob.org. Website: www.beertown.org. 6x/yr. $33/yr. Circ.: 24,000. Ray Daniels, Editor-in-Chief. **Description:** Articles appealing to beer lovers and homebrewers. **Queries:** Preferred. **Payment:** On publication.

GAMES & PASTIMES

(See also Hobbies, Crafts, Collecting)

BINGO BUGLE

Frontier Publications, Inc., P.O. Box 527, Vashon, WA 98070-0527. 206-463-5656. Website: www.bingobugle.com. Monthly. Circ.: 1,006,000. Tara Snowden, Editor. **Description:** For bingo players.

THE BRIDGE BULLETIN

American Contract Bridge League, 2990 Airways Blvd., Memphis, TN 38116-3847. 901-332-5586. E-mail: editor@acbl.org. Website: www.acbl.org. Monthly. $20/yr. Circ.: 145,000. Brent Manley, Editor-in-Chief. **Description:** Covers tournament and duplicate bridge. Submit articles that teach or report on trends and issues related to the game. Seeks humor and human-interest pieces as they relate to bridge; $50/page. **Queries:** Required. **E-Queries:** Yes. **Unsolicited mss:** Accepts. **Freelance Content:** 10%. **Rights:** One-time. **Payment:** On publication.

CARD PLAYER

Shulman Media, LLC, 3140 S Polaris Ave., Suite 8, Las Vegas, NV 89102-0008. 702-871-1720. E-mail: info@cardplayer.com. Website: www.cardplayer.com. Biweekly. $109/yr. Circ.: 50,000. Jeff Shulman, CEO. **Description:** For competitive players, on poker events, personalities, legal issues, new casinos, tournaments, strategies and psychology to improve poker play. Articles any length; pay negotiable. **Fillers:** Humor. **Queries:** Preferred. **E-Queries:** No. **Unsolicited mss:** Accepts. **Response:** 1 month. **Freelance Content:** 1%. **Payment:** On publication. **Contact:** Steve Radulovich, Editor-in-Chief.

CASINO PLAYER

Ace Marketing Inc., 5240 S Eastern Ave., Las Vegas, NV 89119-2306. 702-736-8886. E-mail: letters@casinocenter.com. Website: www.casinocenter.com. Monthly. $24/yr. Circ.: 200,000. Adam Fine, Editor-in-Chief. **Description:** For beginning to intermediate gamblers, on slots, video poker, table games, and gaming lifestyle/travel.

Articles, 1,000-2,000 words, with photos; pays from $250. **Tips:** No first-person or real-life gambling stories. **Payment:** On publication.

CHESS LIFE

United States Chess Federation, 3054 US Route 9W, New Windsor, NY 12553-7698. 845-562-8350. E-mail: editor@uschess.org. Website: www.uschess.org. Monthly. $3.75/$45. Circ.: 70,000. Kalev Pehme, Editor. **Description:** Published by United States Chess Federation. Covers news of major chess events (U.S. and abroad), with emphasis on the triumphs and exploits of American players. **Nonfiction:** Articles on news, profiles, technical aspects. Features on history, humor, puzzles, etc.; 500-3,000 words; $100/page. **Art:** B&W glossies, color slides; $25. **Tips:** Does accept fiction. **Queries:** Preferred. **Unsolicited mss:** Accepts. **Payment:** On publication.

COMPUTER GAMES MAGAZINE

The Globe.com, 63 Millet St., Suite 203, Richmond, VT 05477-9492. 802-434-3060. E-mail: editor@cgonline.com. Website: www.cgonline.com. Monthly. $19.97/yr. Circ.: 220,100. Steve Bauman, Editor-in-Chief. **Description:** Publication featuring articles with computer gaming information.

COMPUTER GAMING WORLD

Ziff-Davis Media, Inc., 101 Second St., Fl. 9, San Francisco, CA 94105-3672. 415-357-4900. E-mail: cgwletters@ziffdavis.com. Website: www.computergaming.com. Monthly. $24.94/yr. Circ.: 300,700. Jeff Green, Editor-in-Chief. **Description:** All aspects of computer gaming.

ELECTRONIC GAMING MONTHLY

Ziff-Davis Media, Inc., 101 Second St., Fl. 9, San Francisco, CA 94105-3672. 415-547-8000. E-mail: egm@ziffdavis.com. Website: www.egmmag.com. Monthly. $24.97/yr. Circ.: 528,200. Dan Hsu, Editor-in-Chief. **Description:** Reports on home video console games.

GAMES

Kappa Publishing, P.O. Box 184, Fort Washington, PA 19034-0184. 215-643-6385. E-mail: games@kappapublishing.com. Monthly. $26.95/yr. Circ.: 142,300. R. Wayne Schmittberger, Editor-in-Chief. **Description:** Features and short articles on games and playful, offbeat subjects. Visual and verbal puzzles, pop culture quizzes, brain-teasers, contests, game reviews. **Tips:** Send SASE for guidelines (specify writer's, crosswords, variety puzzles, or brainteasers). **Freelance Content:** 50%. **Payment:** On publication.

JACKPOT!

Morris Specialty Publications, LLC, 6064 Apple Tree Dr., Suite 9, Memphis, TN 38115-0307. 901-360-0777. E-mail: jackpot@bellsouth.net. Website: www.jackpot-magazine.com. Semimonthly. Circ.: 40,000. **Description:** Covers all aspects of casino entertainment, gaming, and food.

POKER PLAYER

3883 W Century Blvd., Inglewood, CA 90303. 310-674-3365. E-mail: srs@gambling-times.com. Website: www.gamblingtimes.com/poker_player. Biweekly. $3.95/issue. Circ.: 37,000. **Description:** Written for the gaming public, this tabloid newspaper provides tournament coverage and poker news/columns from around the world. Articles run 600-700 words; $150/story. **Tips:** "We are a pro-gambling publication that continually improves the expertise and knowledge of our readers. Our writers must be experts in their fields." **Queries:** Preferred. **E-Queries:** Yes. **Unsolicited mss:** Does not accept. **Response:** 30 days. **SASE Required:** Yes. **Freelance Content:** 50%. **Payment:** On publication. **Contact:** Stanley Sludikoff, Editor/Publisher; Joel Gausten, Managing Editor.

POOL & BILLIARD

810 Travelers Blvd. Bldg. D, Summerville, SC 29485. 843-875-5115. E-mail: poolmag@poolmag.com. Website: www.poolmag.com. Monthly. $31.95/yr. Circ.: 18,400. Shari J. Stauch, Executive Editor. **Description:** Consumer and trade magazine for players and others interested in the pool industry. Articles must be relevant to the game of pool. Particular interest in instruction and tourney coverage; 600-2,500 words; $130/page. **Tips:** No fiction or poetry. **Response:** 5 days. **Freelance Content:** 10%.

STRICTLY SLOTS

Casino Publishing Group, 5240 S Eastern Ave., Las Vegas, NV 89119. 702-736-8886. E-mail: letters@casinocenter.com. Website: www.casinocenter.com. Monthly. $24/yr. Circ.: 110,000. Adam Fine, Editor-in-Chief. **Description:** Everything there is to know about all the new slots, slot clubs, promotions, and property profiles. Nonfiction pieces to 1,000 words with photos; pays $.25/word. **Payment:** On publication.

GAY & LESBIAN

THE ADVOCATE

Liberation Publications, Inc., 6922 Hollywood Boulevard, Suite 1000, Los Angeles, CA 90028. 323-871-1225. E-mail: bsteele@advocate.com; info@advocate.com. Website: www.advocate.com. Biweekly. $3.99/$39.97. Circ.: 103,000. Judy Wieder, Editorial Director. **Description:** National news magazine for gay men and lesbians covering news, politics, entertainment, interviews, etc. **Nonfiction:** All nonfiction pieces should employ a specific angle to set the tone and grab the reader's attention; 1,000 words. **Columns, Departments:** My Perspective; one column each issue is written by freelancers; 700 words. **Tips:** Does not accept fiction or simultaneous submissions. **Queries:** Required. **E-Queries:** Yes. **Unsolicited mss:** Does not accept. **Freelance Content:** 50%. **Rights:** FNAR. **Payment:** On publication. **Contact:** Bruce Steele, Editor-in-Chief.

ARISE MAGAZINE
411 Rockmont Circle, Sacramento, CA 95835-1507. 916-454-2781.
E-mail: arise@arisemag.com. Website: www.arisemag.com. Monthly. $35/yr. Circ.: 50,000. MacArthur H. Flournoy, Editor-in-Chief. **Description:** Lifestyle magazine for lesbian, gay, bisexual, and transgender African-Americans. Articles cover health, finance, spirituality, music, travel, politics, and lifestyle issues. Also features poetry and book reviews. Articles run 1,500 words; poetry 500 words. Pay negotiable. **Queries:** Not necessary. **E-Queries:** Yes. **Unsolicited mss:** Does not accept. **Response:** 3 months. **SASE Required:** Yes. **Payment:** On publication.

ECHO MAGAZINE
Ace Publishing, Inc., P.O. Box 16630, Phoenix, AZ 85011-6630. 602-266-0550.
E-mail: editor@echomag.com. Website: www.echomag.com. Biweekly. $55/yr. Circ.: 16,000. **Description:** For gay and lesbian readers in Phoenix metro area and across Arizona. Covers gay-relevant developments in the news, health, entertainment, business, human interest, art features, and op-ed guest column; 800-1,500 words; $30/article. **Tips:** "We are a pro-gay advocacy publication dedicated to informing our readers and helping them find valuable resources. You don't have to be gay to write for us, but you do have to support equality for GLBT persons and be very familiar with the gay community." **Queries:** Preferred. **E-Queries:** Yes. **Response:** 2-4 weeks. **Freelance Content:** 40-50%. **Rights:** All. **Payment:** On publication. **Contact:** Liz Massey or Buddy Early, Managing Editors.

THE GAY & LESBIAN REVEW
P.O. Box 180300, Boston, MA 02118. 617-421-0082. E-mail: hglr@aol.com. Website: www.glreview.com. Bimonthly. $29.70. Circ.: 12,000. Richard Schneider, Editor. **Description:** For the gay and lesbian community, on culture, politics, the arts, and history. Includes reviews of books, film, and art. Articles, 2,000-5,000 words; $100 for feature articles. **Tips:** "Avoid memoirs and overly personal pieces. Articles should deal with issues of lasting significance to GLBT readers." **Queries:** Preferred. **E-Queries:** Yes. **Unsolicited mss:** Accepts. **Freelance Content:** 100%.

GENRE
Window Media, 350 5th Ave., Suite 6917, Empire State Bldg., New York, NY 10118-6917. 212-594-8181. E-mail: genre@genremagazine.com. Website: www.genremagazine.com. Monthly. $19.95/yr. Circ.: 50,000. Tom Eubanks, Editor-in-Chief. **Description:** Fashion, entertainment, travel, fiction, and reviews for gay men. **Fiction:** Short stories with gay themes up to 2,000 words; pay varies. **Nonfiction:** Travel, celebrity interviews, etc.; 300-1,500 words. **Queries:** Preferred. **E-Queries:** Yes. **Unsolicited mss:** Accepts. **SASE Required:** Yes. **Freelance Content:** 60%. **Rights:** Print, electronic. **Payment:** On publication.

IN THE FAMILY
7850 N Silverbell Rd., Suite 114-188, Tucson, AZ 85753. 520-579-8043. Website: www.inthefamily.com. Quarterly. $26/yr. Circ.: 3,000. Laura Markowitz, Editor.

Description: Explores the complex interweave of gay, lesbian, bisexual, transgender, and straight family bonds. Topics include family relationships, couples/intimacy, money, extended family, parenting, therapy, etc. **Fiction:** Short stories with LGBT themes; no erotica. 3,000 words max; $35 plus copies. **Nonfiction:** Articles on LGBT families and/or therapy. 4,000 words max; $35 plus copies. **Columns, Departments:** First-person essays related to LGBT themes. 1,500 words max; $25 plus copies. **Tips:** "We're interested in going beyond coming out stories and exploring the rarely discussed aspect of LGBT people—their relationships, challenges, strengths, etc. We're not interested in celebrity gossip, but offer readers an intelligent, thoughtful view of how sexual and gender orientation affect all members of an extended, nuclear, and affectional family." **Queries:** Not necessary. **E-Queries:** No. **Unsolicited mss:** Accepts. **Response:** 3-5 weeks. **SASE Required:** Yes. **Freelance Content:** 25%. **Rights:** FNAR. **Payment:** On publication.

INSTINCT MAGAZINE
15335 Morrison St., Suite 325, Sherman Oaks, CA 91403-1513. 818-205-9033. E-mail: editor@instinctmag.com. Website: www.instinctmag.com. Monthly. $19.95/yr. Circ.: 62,000. Parker Ray, Editor-in-Chief. **Description:** Seeks gay men's lifestyle pieces, relevant news or investigative pieces, and articles on entertainment, fashion, celebrities, fitness/health, controversial topics; 1,500-2,400 words. **Tips:** "Become familiar with our trademark style. Do not pitch general themes such as dating or first-person columns. We are excited when we hear fresh takes on gay men's lifestyle issues, controversial or against-the-grain viewpoints, and the scoop on upcoming themes. Keep your writing conversational and grounded." **Queries:** Preferred. **E-Queries:** Yes. **Unsolicited mss:** Accepts. **Response:** 90 days. **SASE Required:** Yes. **Freelance Content:** 60%. **Rights:** All. **Payment:** On publication.

THE JAMES WHITE REVIEW
Lambda Literary Foundation, P.O. Box 73910, Washington, DC 20056-3910. 202-682-0952. E-mail: jwr@lambdalit.org. Website: www.lambdalit.org. Quarterly. $4.95/$17.50. Circ.: 3,000. Patrick Merla, Editor. **Description:** Gay men's literary magazine, with fiction, poetry, photography, art, essays, and reviews. Welcomes both unpublished and established writers. **Fiction:** Seeking well-crafted literary fiction with strongly-developed characters; gay themes; to 10,000 words. **Poetry:** Submit up to three poems at a time. **Tips:** "Be patient—we're a small staff with a lot of submissions." **Queries:** Preferred. **E-Queries:** No. **Unsolicited mss:** Accepts. **Response:** Queries 3 weeks, submissions 3-6 months. **SASE Required:** Yes. **Rights:** FNAR. **Contact:** Jonathan Harper, Editorial Assistant.

LAMBDA BOOK REPORT
See full listing in Writing & Publishing category.

METROSOURCE MAGAZINE
180 Varick St., Fl. 5, New York, NY 10014-4606. 212-691-5127. E-mail: rwalsh@metrosource.com. Website: www.metrosource.com. 5x/yr. $4.95/issue. Circ.: 85,000.

Richard Walsh, Editor. **Description:** Lifestyle magazine for gay and lesbian readers. **Nonfiction:** Articles on travel, entertainment, health/fitness, gay adoption, fashion, etc. Also runs profiles of significant people who are gay or lesbian. 1,500-2,000 words. **Queries:** Preferred. **E-Queries:** Yes. **Unsolicited mss:** Does not accept. **Response:** 1 month. **SASE Required:** Yes. **Freelance Content:** 30%.

OUT MAGAZINE
Liberation Publications, Inc., 245 W 17th St., Suite 1200, New York, NY 10011. 212-242-8100. E-mail: blemon@out.com. Website: www.out.com. Monthly. $17.95/yr. Circ.: 136,000. Brendan Lemon, Editor-in-Chief. **Description:** Articles on arts, politics, fashion, finance and other subjects for gay and lesbian readers. No fiction or poetry. Pay varies. **Queries:** Preferred. **Payment:** On publication.

GENERAL INTEREST

AMERICAN HERITAGE
See full listing in History category.

THE ATLANTIC MONTHLY
National Journal Group, Inc., 77 N Washington St., Boston, MA 02114. 617-854-7700. E-mail: letters@theatlantic.com. Website: www.theatlantic.com. Monthly. $24.95/yr. Circ.: 530,000. Cullen Murphy, Editor. **Description:** At the leading edge of contemporary issues. Also, the best in fiction, poetry, travel, food, and humor. **Queries:** Preferred. **E-Queries:** No. **Unsolicited mss:** Accepts. **Response:** 2-4 weeks. **SASE Required:** Yes. **Freelance Content:** 50%. **Rights:** FNAR. **Payment:** On acceptance.

BLACK BOOK
116 Prince St., Fl. 2, New York, NY 10012-3178. 212-334-1800. E-mail: aaron@blackbookmag.com. Website: www.blackbookmag.com. Bimonthly. $18.95/yr. Circ.: 150,000. Aaron Hicklin, Editor-in-Chief. **Description:** General interest lifestyle magazine covering trends, entertainment, arts, beauty and fashion, news, and cutting-edge journalism. Also features some fiction. **Queries:** Preferred.

BUTTON
P.O. Box 26, Lunenburg, MA 01462. E-mail: sally@moonsigns.net. Website: www.moonsigns.net. Annual. Circ.: 1,500. Sally Cragin, Editor. **Description:** "New England's Tiniest Magazine of Poetry, Fiction, and Gracious Living." Short stories, essays, recipes, sheet music, celebrity gossip, book/album reviews, and poetry (no sentimental poems, song lyrics, or centered copy). **Queries:** Not necessary. **E-Queries:** No. **Unsolicited mss:** Accepts. **Response:** 2-3 months. **SASE Required:** Yes. **Freelance Content:** 60%. **Payment:** On publication.

THE CHRISTIAN SCIENCE MONITOR

The Christian Science Publishing Society, One Norway St., Boston, MA 02115. 617-450-2000. Website: www.csmonitor.com. Daily. Paul Van Slambrouck, Editor. **Description:** International daily newspaper covering a wide range of issues and events. Pieces on domestic and foreign affairs, economics, education, environment, law, media, politics, lifestyle trends, women's rights, family issues, community, cultural commentary; 500-1,400 words; $200-$225. **Tips:** See website for specific guidelines for each column/dept.

CHRONOGRAM

Luminary Publishing, P.O. Box 459, New Paltz, NY 12561. 845-255-4711. E-mail: info@chronogram.com. Website: www.chronogram.com. Circ.: 15,000. Brian K. Mahoney, Editor. **Description:** Monthly, based in New York's Hudson Valley, on politics, arts and culture, health, the environment, and regional issues. Publishes short fiction, poetry, first-person pieces, memoirs, and political and cultural reportage. Pays $.10/word. **Tips:** "Our mission is to be an alternative media source to the hulking conglomerates that spew lulling pablum into the general consciousness. We feature people, events, ideas, organizations, opinions, etc. which are sometimes unorthodox. We seek to provide readers with information not offered through mainstream sources. Send pithy queries. No humor or 'occasional' pieces. Send strong writing that speaks for itself. No first-time writers. Query me with an article idea I haven't heard six times before." **Queries:** Required. **Unsolicited mss:** Does not accept. **Response:** 4 weeks. **Freelance Content:** 30%. **Rights:** FNAR.

THE CLEVELAND PLAIN DEALER

1801 Superior Ave., Cleveland, OH 44114. 216-999-4147 or 216-999-4145. E-mail: forum@plaind.com. Website: www.cleveland.com. Daily. **Description:** On variety of subjects: domestic affairs, economics, education, environment, foreign affairs, humor, politics, and regional interest. **Nonfiction:** Op-ed pieces, to 700 words; pays $75. **Tips:** No room for historical pieces not tied to a recent event. **E-Queries:** Yes. **Response:** 7-14 days. **Freelance Content:** 10-15%. **Rights:** Non-exclusive worldwide. **Payment:** On publication.

COLUMBIA

See full listing in Associations category.

CONVERSELY

PMB #121, 3053 Fillmore St., San Francisco, CA 94123. E-mail: query@conversely.com. Website: www.conversely.com. Quarterly. **Description:** Online publication exploring all aspects of relationships between men and women. **Fiction:** Literary stories on male-female relationships; to 3,000 words; $50-$200. **Nonfiction:** Essays and personal stories (memoirs); 500-2,000 words; $50-$200. **Tips:** Submissions are only accepted online at website. Review guidelines before submitting. "We get much more fiction than we can handle, but we don't see enough personal and opinion essays." **Queries:** Not necessary. **E-Queries:** Yes.

Unsolicited mss: Accepts. **Freelance Content:** 70%. **Rights:** 90-day exclusive electronic, non-exclusive thereafter; one-time, non-exclusive print anthology rights.

DETROIT FREE PRESS

600 W Fort St., Detroit, MI 48226. 313-222-6583. E-mail: oped@freepress.com; mccraith@freepress.com. Website: www.freep.com. Daily. **Description:** Newspaper with op-ed page published 6 days/week. Accepts unsolicited manuscripts. **Tips:** "We accept op-ed columns only, 750 words or less. We give preference to local writers. Send submissions via e-mail. If your column is accepted, we will contact you directly. Make sure we have complete name, address, daytime phone, and e-mail address." **Queries:** Preferred. **Payment:** On publication. **Contact:** Linda McCraith.

ELKS

See full listing in Associations category.

FLAUNT

See full listing in Contemporary Culture category.

FRIENDLY EXCHANGE

C-E Publishing, P.O. Box 2120, Warren, MI 48090-2120. 586-753-8326. E-mail: friendlyexchange@aol.com. Website: www.friendlyexchange.com. Quarterly. $20/yr. Circ.: 6,010,900. Dan Grantham, Editor. **Description:** For policyholders of Farmers Insurance Group of Companies. Articles with "news you can use," on home, health, personal finance, travel; 700-1,500 words; $400-$1,000. **Queries:** Required.

GLOBE

American Media, Inc., 1000 American Media Way, Boca Raton, FL 33464-1000. 561-997-7733. E-mail: newstips@globefl.com. Website: www.globemagazine.com. Weekly. $29.97/yr. Circ.: 631,700. Candace Trunzo, Editor. **Description:** Exposés, celebrity interviews, and consumer/human-interest pieces. Articles run 500-1,000 words, with photos; pays $50-$1,500.

GRIT

Ogden Publications, Inc., 1503 SW 42nd St., Topeka, KS 66609-1265. 785-274-4300. E-mail: gritmagazine@grit.com. Website: www.grit.com. Monthly. $27.98/yr. Circ.: 100,000. Ann Crahan, Editor-in-Chief. **Description:** On American life and traditions with stories about ordinary people doing extraordinary things. **Fiction:** Heartwarming stories with a message, upbeat storyline and ending; 1,000-10,000 words; $.10-.$15/word. Payment of $100-$400 made upon acceptance. **Nonfiction:** Features on places or events, unsung heroes, nostalgic remembrances of rural communities and small towns; 500-1,800 words, $.15/word. **Poetry:** Romance; relationships; nature; family interaction; up to 16 lines; $2/line. Payment of $10-$15 made upon acceptance. **Art:** Photos must accompany manuscripts. Include complete caption material. Payment of $50 for front page, $15-$25 inside, made upon publication. **Tips:** Prefers full manuscript with photos. **Queries:** Not necessary. **E-Queries:** No.

Unsolicited mss: Accepts. **Freelance Content:** 90%. **Rights:** FNAR. **Payment:** On acceptance.

HOPE

P.O. Box 160, Brooklin, ME 04616. 207-359-4651. E-mail: info@hopemag.com. Website: www.hopemag.com. Bimonthly. $14.95/yr. Circ.: 18,000. Jon Wilson, Publisher/Editor. **Description:** About people making a difference. Articles run 150-3,000 words; $75-$1,500. **Tips:** Query with clips. No nostalgia, sentimental, political, opinion, or religious pieces. **Queries:** Required. **Payment:** On publication. **Contact:** Kimberly Ridley, Editor.

JOURNAL AMERICA

P.O. Box 459, Hewitt, NJ 07421-3027. 973-728-8355. E-mail: journal@warick.net. Website: www.thejournalamerica.com. Monthly. $19.50/yr. Circ.: 75,000. Glen Malmgren, Editor. **Description:** Covers a variety subjects of interest to the American family. Articles on all aspects of today's demanding lifestyle, with a touch of humor; 200-1,000 words; pay varies. **Queries:** Preferred.

KIWANIS

See full listing in Associations category.

LATIN STYLE MAGAZINE

See full listing in Ethnic & Multicultural category.

NATIONAL ENQUIRER

American Media, Inc., 1000 American Media Way, Boca Raton, FL 33464-1000. 561-997-7733. E-mail: letters@nationalenquirer.com. Website: www.nationalen-quirer.com. Weekly. $63.80/yr. Circ.: 1,775,300. Steve Plamann, Executive Editor. **Description:** Offers topical news, scientific discoveries, human drama, adventure, medical news, personalities, etc. to a mass audience. Also accepts short, humorous or philosophical fillers, witticisms, anecdotes, jokes, tart comments. Original items only. **Queries:** Preferred. **SASE Required:** Yes. **Payment:** On publication.

NEWSWEEK

Newsweek, Inc., 251 W 57th St., Fl. 17, New York, NY 10019-1802. 212-778-4000. E-mail: letters@newsweek.com. Website: www.newsweek.com. Weekly. $42.66/yr. Circ.: 3,125,100. Richard M. Smith, Editor-in-Chief. **Description:** Reports the week's world and national news. Covers politics, the economy, world affairs, business, lifestyle, health, science, the arts, technology, etc. **Columns, Departments:** My Turn (original first-person opinion essays, must contain verifiable facts); 850-900 words; $1,000. Send mss. with SASE. **Response:** 2 months. **Rights:** Non-exclusive worldwide. **Payment:** On publication. **Contact:** Jon Meacham, Managing Editor.

PARADE

Parade Publications, Inc., 711 Third Ave., New York, NY 10017. 212-450-7000. Website: www.parade.com. Weekly. Circ.: 81,000,000. Lee Kravitz, Editor. **Description:** National Sunday newspaper magazine covering subjects of national interest. Factual and authoritative articles on social issues, common health concerns, sports, community problem-solving, and extraordinary achievements of ordinary people; 1,200-1,500 words; pays from $1,000. **Tips:** Query with two writing samples and SASE. "We seek unique angles on all topics." No fiction, poetry, cartoons, games, nostalgia, quotes, or puzzles. **Queries:** Required. **Unsolicited mss:** Does not accept. **Contact:** Steven J. Florio, Assistant Editor.

PEOPLE

Time, Inc., 1271 Avenue of the Americas, New York, NY 10020-1300. 212-522-1212. E-mail: editor@people.com. Website: www.people.com. Weekly. $93/yr. Circ.: 3,550,000. **Description:** Mostly staff-written. Will consider article proposals, 3-4 paragraphs, on timely, entertaining, and topical personalities.

READER'S DIGEST

Readers Digest Assn., Readers Digest Rd., Pleasantville, NY 10570. 914-238-1000. E-mail: letters@rd.com. Website: www.rd.com. Monthly. $2.99/month. Circ.: 12,500,000. Jacqueline Leo, Editor-in-chief. **Description:** Offers stories of broad interest. "Original articles are usually assigned to regular contributors to the magazine. We do not accept or return unpublished manuscripts. We do, however, accept brief electronic queries that clearly detail the article idea—with special emphasis on the arc of the story, your interview access to the main characters, your access to special documents, etc. We look for dramatic narratives, articles about everyday heroes, crime dramas, adventure stories. Include a separate page of your writing credits. We are not interested in poetry, fiction or opinion pieces." **Fillers:** True, never-before-published stories for: Life in These United States; All in a Day's Work; Humor in Uniform; Virtual Hilarity. Previously published or original items for: Laughter, the Best Medicine; Quotable Quotes; short items used at the end of articles. Up to 100 words; $100-$300. **Contact:** Editorial Department.

READER'S DIGEST CANADA

Reader's Digest Assn. Ltd., 1125 Stanley St., Montreal, Quebec H3B 5H5 Canada. 514-940-0751. E-mail: editor@readersdigest.ca. Website: www.readersdigest.ca. Monthly. Circ.: 1,037,305. Murray Lewis, Editor-in-Chief. **Description:** Articles, essays, and human-interest pieces for a general audience. **Nonfiction:** Health/medicine, current events, real-life drama, humor, and ancedotes; 1,000-3,000 words; $1,500. **Fillers:** True, unpublished stories; to 3,000 words; $200. **Tips:** "We offer articles that are strong, sharp, fresh, and forceful. Our feature stories focus on the individual and his or her potential for greatness. Study our magazine and submit a detailed outline of your idea." **Queries:** Required. **E-Queries:** Yes. **Unsolicited mss:** Does not accept. **Response:** 3 weeks. **SASE Required:** Yes. **Freelance Content:** 40%. **Payment:** On acceptance.

THE SATURDAY EVENING POST
Saturday Evening Post Society, 1100 Waterway Blvd., Indianapolis, IN 46202-2174. 317-634-1100. E-mail: letters@satevepost.org. Website: www.satevepost.org. Bimonthly. $14.97/yr. Circ.: 356,000. Cory J. SerVaas, Editor-in-Chief. **Description:** Family-oriented publication covering news in health, medicine, nutrition, and fitness. **Tips:** See website for writer's guidelines. **Queries:** Preferred. **Unsolicited mss:** Accepts. **Response:** 3-6 weeks. **SASE Required:** Yes. **Rights:** All. **Payment:** On publication. **Contact:** Ted Kreiter, Executive Editor.

SELECCIONES DEL READER'S DIGEST
Readers Digest Assn., One Reader's Digest Rd., Pleasantville, NY 10570-7000. 914-238-1000. Website: www.selecciones.com. Monthly. $19.97/yr. Circ.: 325,000. Genevieve Marlin Fernadez, Managing Editor. **Description:** Spanish-language version of *Reader's Digest*.

SELECTA MAGAZINE
See full listing in Ethnic & Multicultural category.

SMITHSONIAN
Smithsonian Institution, MRC 951, P.O. Box 37012, Washington, DC 20013-7012. 202-275-2000. E-mail: articles@simag.si.edu. Website: www.smithsonianmag.com. Monthly. $28. Circ.: 2,000,000. Carey Winfrey, Editor-in-Chief. **Description:** Offers wide-ranging coverage of history, art, natural history, physical science, profiles, etc. **Nonfiction:** History, art, natural history, physical science, profiles; 2,000-5,000 words; pay varies. **Columns, Departments:** "The Last Page;" humorous essays; 550-700 words. **Art:** Photos or illustrations to accompany article, if available; 35mm color transparencies or B&W prints. **Tips:** See website for guidelines. **Queries:** Preferred. **E-Queries:** Yes. **Response:** 6-8 weeks. **SASE Required:** Yes. **Rights:** FNASR. **Contact:** Marlane A. Liddell, Articles Editor.

STAR MAGAZINE
See full listing in Film, TV, Entertainment category.

THE SUN
Sun Publishing Co., 107 N Roberson St., Chapel Hill, NC 27516. 919-942-5282. E-mail: info@thesunmagazine.org. Website: www.thesunmagazine.org. Monthly. $3.95/$34. Circ.: 60,000. Sy Safransky, Editor. **Description:** Essays, stories, interviews, and poetry in which people write of their struggles to understand their lives, often with surprising intimacy. Looking for writers willing to take risks and describe life honestly. **Fiction:** Fiction that feels like a lived experience; to 7,000 words; $300-$750. **Nonfiction:** Personal essays and interviews; to 7,000 words; $300-$1,250. **Poetry:** 1-2 pages; $50-$250. **Art:** B&W photographs only; $50-$200. **Tips:** No journalistic, academic, or opinion pieces. **Queries:** Not necessary. **E-Queries:** No. **Unsolicited mss:** Accepts. **Response:** 3-6 months. **SASE Required:** Yes. **Freelance Content:** 80%. **Rights:** One-time. **Payment:** On publication.

THE WORLD AND I

The Washington Times Corp., 3600 New York Ave. NE, Washington, DC 20002-1947. 202-635-4000. E-mail: editor@worldandi.com. Website: www.worldandi.com. Monthly. $45/yr. Circ.: 16,400. Eric P. Olsen, Associate Executive Editor. **Description:** Scholarly articles on current issues, politics, the arts, science, international cultures, literature, pop culture, etc. Articles should cover current trends in the subject area. Articles run 2,500 words; pay varies. **Tips:** See website for guidelines. **Queries:** Preferred. **Unsolicited mss:** Accepts.

HEALTH

ALTERNATIVE MEDICINE

1650 Tiburon Blvd., Tiburon, CA 94920. 415-789-1405.
E-mail: editor@alternativemedicine.com. Website: www.alternativemedicine.com.
10x/yr. $20/yr. Circ.: 140,000. Clare Ellis, Editor. **Description:** Offers valuable information on effective, nontoxic health care options. Articles promote alternative methods for restoring and maintaining health.

AMERICAN HEALTH & FITNESS FOR MEN

See full listing in Fitness category.

AMERICAN JOURNAL OF HEALTH EDUCATION

See full listing in Education category.

AMERICAN JOURNAL OF NURSING

Lippincott, Williams & Wilkins, 345 Hudson St., Fl. 16, New York, NY 10014. 212-886-1200. E-mail: ajn@lww.com. Website: www.ajnonline.com. Monthly. $29/yr. Circ.: 343,000. Diana Mason, Editor-in-Chief. **Description:** Wide variety of clinical, policy, trends, and professional issues. Feature articles, 2,000-4,000 words; columns, 800-2,000 words. Photos/illustrations encouraged. **Tips:** See website for guidelines. **Queries:** Preferred. **Response:** 2-10 weeks.

AMERICAN MEDICAL NEWS

American Medical Assn., 515 N State St., Chicago, IL 60610. 312-464-4429. Website: www.amednews.com. Weekly. Circ.: 250,000. Kathryn Trombatore, Editor. **Description:** On socioeconomic developments in health care. Seeks well-researched, innovative pieces about health and science from physician's perspective; 900-1,500 words; pays $500-$1,500. **Queries:** Required. **Payment:** On acceptance.

ARTHRITIS TODAY

Arthritis Foundation Inc., 1330 W Peachtree St., NW, Atlanta, GA 30309. 404-872-7100. Website: www.arthritis.org. Bimonthly. $4.95/$20. Circ.: 650,000. Marcy O'Koon Moss, Editor-in-Chief. **Description:** Features on research, care, treatment of arthritis, self-help, how-to, general interest, general health, lifestyle topics (very few inspirational articles). **Tips:** "Our readers are well-informed and desire fresh, in-depth information. We're looking for talented writers/reporters to execute staff-generated ideas. Send published clips." **Queries:** Preferred. **E-Queries:** Yes. **Unsolicited mss:** Accepts. **Response:** 4 weeks. **Freelance Content:** 50%. **Rights:** FNASR. **Payment:** On acceptance.

ASTHMA MAGAZINE

Mosby, Inc., 21 Middle St., Hingham, MA 02043-2829.
Website: www.mosby.com/asthma. Bimonthly. $21/yr. Circ.: 65,000. Rachel Butler, Editor. **Description:** Focuses on ways to manage asthma. Features health and medical news, as well as human-interest stories about children, adults, and the elderly. **Queries:** Required. **Payment:** On acceptance.

BABY TALK

See full listing in Family & Parenting category.

BALANCE MAGAZINE

See full listing in Lifestyle category.

BETTER HEALTH MAGAZINE

Saint Raphael Healthcare System, 1450 Chapel St., New Haven, CT 06511-4405.
203-789-3972. Website: www.srhs.org/betterhealth.asp. Bimonthly. Circ.: 146,000. Cynthia Wolfe Boynton, Editor. **Description:** Wellness and prevention magazine, published by Hospital of Saint Raphael. **Nonfiction:** Upbeat articles to encourage healthier lifestyle, with quotes and narrative from healthcare professionals at Saint Raphael's and other local services. No first-person or personal-experience articles; 1,200-2,500 words; $300-$700. **Tips:** Send $2.50 for sample copy and guidelines. **Queries:** Required. **E-Queries:** No. **Payment:** On acceptance.

BODY & SOUL

See full listing in New Age/Spiritual category.

CONSCIOUS CHOICE

920 N Franklin, Suite 202, Chicago, IL 60610.
E-mail: rebecca@consciouschoice.com. Website: www.consciouschoice.com. Monthly. Circ.: 55,000. Rebecca Ephraim, Editor. **Description:** Issues and information on natural health, natural foods, spirituality, personal growth, social justice, and the environment. Articles run 1,200-2,200 words; $125-$700. **Tips:** Readers are mostly well-educated women with substantial income level. "Generate new and interesting article ideas. Be familiar with the content and style of the magazine. Please note that 70% of our editorial is from local writers." **Queries:** Preferred. **E-Queries:** No. **Unsolicited mss:** Accepts. **Response:** 1-8 weeks. **Freelance Content:** 90%. **Rights:** FNAR and electronic. **Payment:** On publication.

COPING WITH ALLERGIES & ASTHMA

Media America, Inc., P.O. Box 682268, Franklin, TN 37068-2268. 615-790-2400. E-mail: editor@copingmag.com. Website: www.copingmag.com. 5x/yr. $13.95/yr. Circ.: 30,000. Julie McKenna, Editor. **Description:** Publication offering "knowledge, hope, and inspiration to help readers learn to live with their conditions in the best ways possible." Seeks original manuscripts and photography. No payment offered. **Queries:** Not necessary.

COPING WITH CANCER

Media America, Inc., P.O. Box 682268, Franklin, TN 37068-2268. 615-790-2400. E-mail: editor@copingmag.com. Website: www.copingmag.com. Bimonthly. $19/yr. Circ.: 80,000. Julie McKenna, Editor. **Description:** Uplifting and practical articles for people living with cancer. Features medical news, lifestyle issues, and inspiring personal essays. No payment offered.

CURRENT HEALTH

See full listing in Education category.

DIABETES SELF-MANAGEMENT

150 W 22nd St., Suite 800, New York, NY 10011. 212-989-0200. E-mail: editor@diabetes-self-mgmt.com. Website: www.diabetesselfmanagement.com. Bimonthly. $18/yr. Circ.: 465,000. James Hazlett, Editor. **Description:** For individuals who want to know more about controlling and managing their diabetes. **Nonfiction:** How-to articles on nutrition, pharmacology, exercise, medical advances, and self-help; 2,000-2,500 words; pay varies. **Tips:** "Use plain English; avoid medical jargon, but explain technical terms in simple language. Writing style: upbeat, and leavened with tasteful humor where possible. Information should be accurate, up-to-date, and from reliable sources; references from lay publications not acceptable. No celebrity profiles or personal experiences." **Queries:** Required. **E-Queries:** Yes. **Unsolicited mss:** Accepts. **Response:** 3-4 weeks. **SASE Required:** Yes. **Rights:** All. **Payment:** On publication. **Contact:** Ingrid Strauch, Managing Editor.

HEALTH PRODUCTS BUSINESS

Cygnus Business Media, 445 Broad Hollow Rd., Suite 21, Melville, NY 11747. 631-845-2700 x288. E-mail: michael.schiavetta@cygnuspub.com. Website: www.healthproductsbusiness.com. Monthly. Circ.: 18,500. Michael Schiavetta, Editor. **Description:** Helps retailers and manufacturers navigate the challenges of the health and nutrition industry. **Nonfiction:** Stories on health products (supplements, skin/body care, organic food and medicine, sports nutrition, etc.); 1,000-3,000; pay varies. **Tips:** Seeking writers in the industry with credentials and expert knowledge on health/nutrition products. **Queries:** Required. **E-Queries:** Yes. **Unsolicited mss:** Do not accept. **SASE Required:** Yes. **Freelance Content:** 25%. **Rights:** All. **Payment:** On publication.

HEALTH PROGRESS

Catholic Health Assn., 4455 Woodson Rd., St. Louis, MO 63134-3701. 314-427-2500. E-mail: hpeditor@chausa.org. Website: www.chausa.org. Bimonthly. $50/yr. Circ.: 12,000. **Description:** On hospital/nursing-home management and administration, medical-moral questions, health care, public policy, technological developments and their effects, nursing, financial and human resource management for administrators, and innovative programs in hospitals and long-term care facilities. Features run 2,000-4,000 words; pay negotiable. **Queries:** Preferred.

HEALTH QUEST

LEVAS, Inc., 200 Highpoint Dr., Suite 215, Chalfont, PA 18914. 215-822-7935. E-mail: editor@healthquestmag.com. Website: www.healthquestmag.com. Bimonthly. Circ.: 500,000. Gerda Gallop-Goodman, Editor. **Description:** Health and wellness magazine on body, mind, and spirit for African Americans. Covers traditional and alternative medicine. **Queries:** Preferred. **E-Queries:** No. **Unsolicited mss:** Accepts. **Freelance Content:** 20%. **Payment:** On publication.

HEART & SOUL

See full listing in Ethnic & Multicultural category.

HERBALGRAM

American Botanical Council, P.O. Box 144345, Austin, TX 78714-4345. 512-926-4900. E-mail: abc@herbalgram.org. Website: www.herbalgram.org. Quarterly. $29/yr. Circ.: 50,000. Mark Blumenthal, Editor. **Description:** On herb and medicinal plant research, regulatory issues, market conditions, native plant conservation, and other aspects of herbal use. **Payment:** In copies.

HERBS FOR HEALTH

Ogden Publications, Inc., 1503 SW 42nd St., Topeka, KS 66609-1214. 785-274-4300. E-mail: editor@herbsforhealth.com. Website: www.herbsforhealth.com. Bimonthly. $4.99/issue. Circ.: 160,000. KC Compton, Editor-in-Chief. **Description:** Offers information for the general public on the wide range of benefits of herbs, including their role in various healing arts; articles run 500-2,000 words; $.33/word. **Tips:** "List your sources, keep it short, and focus on reader benefit." **Queries:** Preferred. **E-Queries:** Yes. **Unsolicited mss:** Accepts. **Response:** 3 months. **SASE Required:** Yes. **Freelance Content:** 90%. **Rights:** FNASR. **Payment:** On publication.

HOMECARE MAGAZINE

PRIMEDIA Business Magazines & Media, 6151 Powers Ferry Rd. NW, Suite 200, Atlanta, GA 30339. 770-618-0460. E-mail: ppatch@primediabusiness.com. Website: www.homecaremag.com. Monthly. $69/yr. Circ.: 17,400. Paula Patch, Managing Editor. **Description:** Leading resource for the home medical equipment industry. Covers the business of renting and selling home care products/services by featuring industry news, trends, product segment features, and stories with management and operational ideas. Pays up to $.50/word. **Tips:** Seeks writers with experience in this industry. **Queries:** Required. **E-Queries:** Yes. **Unsolicited mss:** Accepts. **Response:** 2-8 weeks. **SASE Required:** Yes. **Freelance Content:** 20%.

LET'S LIVE

11050 Santa Monica Blvd., Fl. 3, Los Angeles, CA 90025. 310-445-7500. E-mail: info@letslivemag.com. Website: www.letsliveonline.com. Monthly. Circ.: 1,700,000. Beth Salmon, Editor-in-Chief. **Description:** Preventive medicine and nutrition, alternative medicine, weight loss, vitamins, herbs, exercise, and anti-aging. Articles run 1,000-1,500 words; pays up to $1,000. **Queries:** Required. **Contact:** Nicole Brechka, Senior Editor; Ayn Nix, Managing Editor.

LISTEN

See full listing in Teens category.

MAMM MAGAZINE

54 W 22nd St., Fl. 4, New York, NY 10010-5811. 646-365-1350. E-mail: editorial@mamm.com. Website: www.mamm.com. Monthly. $17.97/yr. Circ.: 100,000. Gwen Darien, Editor-in-Chief. **Description:** *Mamm Magazine: Women, Cancer, Community* features articles on conventional and alternative treatment, medical news, survivor profiles, investigative pieces, and essays. Pay varies. **Queries:** Preferred. **Payment:** On acceptance. **Contact:** Akiko Takano, Associate Editor.

MANAGED CARE

780 Township Line Rd., Yardley, PA 19067-4200. 267-685-2788. E-mail: editors@managedcaremag.com. Website: www.managedcaremag.com. Monthly. $93/yr., $120 (internationally). Circ.: 60,800. John Marcille, Editor. **Description:** On managed health care, health care financing, and cost-effectiveness. Also, peer-reviewed scientific manuscripts about models of health care delivery and costs associated with them. Articles run 1,000-3,000 words; $.60-$.80/word. **Tips:** "We currently seek writers who cover the business side of health care with an ear to the ground for trends or who can relate interesting case studies involving cost-effective care. Also, looking for academic-style writers willing to contribute scientific or medical review articles for peer review. Please look over our website to get a feel for the kinds of stories we run." **Queries:** Preferred. **E-Queries:** Yes. **Unsolicited mss:** Accepts. **Response:** 1 month. **SASE Required:** Yes. **Freelance Content:** 60%. **Rights:** All. **Payment:** On publication.

MEN'S HEALTH

Rodale Press, Inc., 33 E Minor St., Emmaus, PA 18098. 610-967-5171. E-mail: mhletters@rodale.com. Website: www.menshealth.com. Monthly. $21.94/yr. Circ.: 1,695,500. David Zinczenko, Editor-in-Chief. **Description:** Useful articles, for men ages 25-55, on fitness, health, sex, nutrition, relationships, lifestyle, sports, and travel; 1,000-2,000 words; $.50/word. **Queries:** Required. **E-Queries:** Yes. **Payment:** On acceptance.

MIDWIFERY TODAY
P.O. Box 2672-350, Eugene, OR 97402. 541-344-7438.
E-mail: editorial@midwiferytoday.com. Website: www.midwiferytoday.com.
Description: For birth practitioners on pregnancy, natural childbirth, and breast-feeding. Promotes education and networking between families and midwife praci-tioners. Also features birth-related art, photos, and poetry. Does not offer payment.

THE NEW PHYSICIAN
American Medical Student Assn., 1902 Association Dr., Reston, VA 20191-1502. 703-620-6600. E-mail: tnp@www.amsa.org. Website: www.amsa.org. Monthly. $25/yr. Circ.: 38,000. Rebecca Sernett, Editor. **Description:** On social, ethical, and political issues of interest to medical students. Topics include space medicine, dating in med school, caring for the poor, etc.; to 3,500 words; pay varies. **Tips:** Readers are highly educated, generally in their 20s. **Queries:** Preferred. **Unsolicited mss:** Accepts. **Freelance Content:** 35%. **Rights:** FNAR. **Payment:** On publication.

NUTRITION HEALTH REVIEW
Vegetus Publications, P.O. Box 406, Haverford, PA 19041. 610-896-1853. Quarterly. $3/$24. Andrew Rifkin, Editor. **Description:** Vegetarian-oriented publication. **Nonfiction:** Articles on medical progress, nutritional therapy, genetics, psychiatry, behavior therapy, surgery, pharmacology, animal health; vignettes on health and nutri-tion. **Fillers:** Humor, cartoons, illustrations. **Tips:** "We do not accept material involv-ing subjects that favor animal testing, animal foods, cruelty to animals, or recipes with animal products." Sample copy on request. **Queries:** Required. **Unsolicited mss:** Accepts. **SASE Required:** Yes. **Payment:** On publication.

PATIENT CARE
Advanstar Medical Economics, 5 Paragon Dr., Montvale, NJ 07645-1725. 973-847-5326. E-mail: patientcare@medec.com. Website: www.patientcareonline.com. 12x/yr. $99/yr. Circ.: 135,000. Peter D'Epiro, Managing Editor. **Description:** On medical care, for primary-care physicians. **Tips:** All articles by assignment only. **Queries:** Required. **Unsolicited mss:** Does not accept. **Payment:** On acceptance.

THE PHOENIX
2610 Irving Ave. S, Minneapolis, MN 55408. Monthly. $18/yr. Circ.: 41,000. Julia Edelman, Editor. **Description:** Publication for people working on their physical, mental, emotional and spiritual well-being, seeking peace and serenity. Covers a broad spectrum of recovery, renewal, and growth information. Articles run 800-1,500 words. **Tips:** Contact for upcoming themes. **Queries:** Not necessary. **E-Queries:** Yes. **Unsolicited mss:** Accepts. **Response:** 1 month. **SASE Required:** Yes. **Freelance Content:** 60%. **Rights:** FNAR. **Payment:** On publication.

PREVENTION
Rodale Press, Inc., 33 E Minor St., Emmaus, PA 18098. 610-967-5171.
E-mail: prevention@rodale.com. Website: www.prevention.com. Monthly. $21.97/yr.

Circ.: 3,150,000. Susan Flagg Godbey, Editorial Director. **Description:** Leading magazine for preventative health research and practices. **Tips:** Freelance content limited. **Queries:** Required.

PSYCHOLOGY TODAY

Sussex Publications, Inc., 115 E 23rd St., Fl. 9, New York, NY 10010-6213. 212-260-7210. E-mail: info@psychologytoday.com. Website: www.psychologytoday.com. Bimonthly. $16/yr. Circ.: 323,000. Kaja Perina, Editor-in-Chief. **Description:** On general-interest psychological research. Timely subjects and news. Articles run 800-2,500 word; pay varies.

REMEDY

MediZine, Inc., 298 5th Ave., Fl. 2, New York, NY 10001-4522. 212-695-2223. E-mail: info@medizine.com. Website: www.medizine.com. Quarterly. $12/yr. Circ.: 2,202,900. Kalia Doner, Editor-in-Chief. **Description:** Health and medication issues for readers ages 45 and older. **Queries:** Preferred. **Payment:** On acceptance.

SPIRITUALITY & HEALTH

See full listing in New Age/Spiritual category.

T'AI CHI

See full listing in Sports & Recreation/Outdoors category.

TOTAL HEALTH FOR LONGEVITY

Total Health Communications, Inc., 165 N 100 E, Suite 2, St. George, UT 84770-2505. 435-673-1789. E-mail: thm@infowest.com. Website: www.totalhealth-magazine.com. Bimonthly. $17/yr. Circ.: 64,000. Lyle D. Hurd, Publisher/Editor. **Description:** On preventative health care, fitness, diet, and mental health. Articles run 1,200-1,400 words; $50-$75. **Queries:** Preferred. **Payment:** On publication.

TURTLE MAGAZINE FOR PRESCHOOL KIDS

Children's Better Health Institute, P.O. Box 567, Indianapolis, IN 46206-0567. 317-636-8881. E-mail: t.harshman@cbhi.org. Website: www.turtlemag.org. 8x/yr. $16.95/yr. Circ.: 190,000. Ms. Terry Harshman, Editor. **Description:** Emphasis on health and nutrition for 2- to 5-year-olds. Only new material being accepted at this time is short rebus stories (100-200 words), and short simple poems (4-8 lines). Pays $.22/word for prose, $25 for poetry. **Tips:** Send SASE for guidelines. **Rights:** All. **Payment:** On publication.

VEGETARIAN TIMES

See full listing in Food & Wine category.

VEGETARIAN VOICE

North American Vegetarian Society, P.O. Box 72, Dolgeville, NY 13329-0072. 518-568-7970. E-mail: navs@telenet.net. Website: www.navs-online.org. Quarterly.

$20/yr. Circ.: 8,000. Maribeth Abrams-McHenry, Managing Editor. **Description:** On consumer concerns, health, nutrition, animal rights, the environment, world hunger, etc. Embodies total vegetarian philosophy (all recipes are vegan) and does not support the use of leather, wool, silk, etc. **Payment:** In copies.

VIBRANT LIFE

Review & Herald Publishing Assn., 55 W Oak Ridge Dr., Hagerstown, MD 21740-7301. 301-393-4019. E-mail: vibrantlife@rhpa.org. Website: www.vibrantlife.com. Bimonthly. $19.95/yr. Circ.: 25,000. Charles Mills, Editor. **Description:** Health/fitness magazine combining the physical, mental, and spiritual aspects of a healthy lifestyle in a practical Christian approach. Promotes a vegetarian lifestyle. Articles run 600-2,000 words; $80-$300. **Queries:** Preferred. **Unsolicited mss:** Accepts. **Freelance Content:** 80%. **Rights:** World Serial Rights, reprint.

VITALITY

356 Dupont St., Toronto, Ontario M5R 1V9 Canada. 416-964-0528. E-mail: editorial@vitalitymagazine.com. 10x/yr. $32.10/yr. Circ.: 50,000. Julia Woodford, Editor. **Description:** Canadian natural health magazine and wellness journal. **Nonfiction:** Seeks success stories of people who have overcome a debilitating disease with natural medicine. Also articles on nutritional medicine, consumer information, and emotional wellness; 800-1,800 words; $.10/word (CDN). **Columns, Departments:** News of worthwhile environmental initiatives and solutions; send to attention of "Earthwatch." 800-1,800 words; $.25/word (CDN). **Art:** Submit hard copy or electronic; fees negotiated. **Tips:** Submissions should be double-spaced, one-inch margins, 14 pt. type. **Queries:** Preferred. **E-Queries:** No. **Unsolicited mss:** Accepts. **Response:** 6-8 weeks. **SASE Required:** Yes. **Freelance Content:** 75%. **Payment:** On publication.

WEIGHT WATCHERS MAGAZINE

W/W TwentyFirst Corp., 747 3rd Ave., Fl. 24, New York, NY 10017. 212-370-0644. E-mail: wwmeditor@wwpublishinggroup.com. Website: www.weightwatchers.com. Bimonthly. $16/yr. Circ.: 1,049,000. Nancy Gagliardi, Editor-in-Chief. **Description:** Health, nutrition, fitness, beauty, and weight-loss motivation and success. Pays $1/word. **Tips:** Query with clips required. Guidelines available. **Queries:** Required. **Payment:** On acceptance.

YOGA JOURNAL

2054 University Ave., Suite 600, Berkeley, CA 94704-1059. 510-841-9200. E-mail: editorial@yogajournal.com. Website: www.yogajournal.com. Monthly. $19.95/yr. Circ.: 215,000. Hillari Dowdle, Editor-in-Chief. **Description:** Serves the hatha yoga community. Holistic health, meditation, conscious living, spirituality, and yoga. Articles, 300-6,000 words; pays $75-$3,000. **Queries:** Preferred. **E-Queries:** Yes. **Unsolicited mss:** Accepts. **Response:** 8 weeks. **SASE Required:** Yes. **Freelance Content:** 10%. **Rights:** Non-exclusive worldwide, print and non-print. **Payment:** On acceptance. **Contact:** Nora Isaacs, Managing Editor.

HISTORY

ALABAMA HERITAGE
University of Alabama, P.O. Box 870342, Tuscaloosa, AL 35487-0342. 205-348-7467. Website: www.alabamaheritage.com. Quarterly. $6/$18.95. Donna L. Cox, Editor. **Description:** Lively, well-researched, well-told, true stories of Alabama and Alabamians. **Nonfiction:** Interested in all aspects of Alabama's heritage/culture and of the contributions Alabamians have made to the larger world; 2,500-4,500 words: $200-$400. **Columns, Departments:** Southern Folkways (customs and traditions), Southern Architecture and Preservation, Recollections (history, as viewed by participants), Arts in the South, Alabama Album ("slice of life" photo), Alabama Treasures (artifacts, collections). 250-1,000 words; up to $50. **Tips:** "Excellent visual images (photos, maps, art) must be available to illustrate articles." **Queries:** Required. **E-Queries:** Yes. **Unsolicited mss:** Accepts. **Response:** 4-8 weeks. **Freelance Content:** 90%. **Payment:** On publication.

AMERICA'S CIVIL WAR
PRIMEDIA History Group, 741 Miller Dr. SE, Suite D2, Leesburg, VA 20175. 703-771-9400. E-mail: americascivilwar@thehistorynet.com. Website: www.historynet.com. Bimonthly. $4.99/issue. Circ.: 75,000. Dana B. Shoaf, Managing Editor. **Description:** Popular history for general readers and Civil War buffs, on strategy, tactics, history, narrative. **Nonfiction:** Strategy, tactics, personalities, arms and equipment; 3,500-4,000 words, plus 500-word sidebar; $200-$400. **Columns, Departments:** Up to 2,000 words; $100-$200. **Art:** Cite known color or B&W illustrations, and sources (museums, historical societies, private collections, etc.). **Tips:** Readable style and historical accuracy imperative. Use action and quotes where possible. Attribute quotes, cite major sources. **Queries:** Required. **E-Queries:** Yes. **Unsolicited mss:** Accepts. **Response:** 6 months. **SASE Required:** Yes. **Freelance Content:** 98%.

AMERICAN HERITAGE
Forbes, Inc., 28 W 23rd St., New York, NY 10010-5204. 212-367-3100. E-mail: mail@americanheritage.com. Website: www.americanheritage.com. 6x/yr. $4.95/issue. Circ.: 310,000. Richard F. Snow, Editor. **Description:** Covers the American experience, from serious concerns to colorful sidelights, from powerful institutions to ordinary men and women, using the past to illuminate the present. **Nonfiction:** On the American experience. Annotate all quotations and factual statements; include brief biographical note about yourself. 1,500-6,000 words; pay varies. **Art:** B&W prints, color slides. **Tips:** No fiction or poetry. "We welcome freelancers, but we need detailed queries in advance. Also, consult indexes first." **Queries:** Preferred. **E-Queries:** No. **Unsolicited mss:** Accepts. **Response:** 8-10 weeks. **SASE Required:** Yes. **Freelance Content:** 70%. **Payment:** On acceptance.

AMERICAN HERITAGE OF INVENTION & TECHNOLOGY

Forbes, Inc., 28 W 23rd St., New York, NY 10010. 212-367-3100.
E-mail: mail@americanheritage.com. Website: www.americanheritage.com.
Quarterly. $15/yr. Circ.: 165,000. Frederick Allen, Editor. **Description:** Lively, authoritative prose and illustrations (archival photos, rare paintings), on the history of technology in America, for the sophisticated general reader. Articles run 2,000-5,000 words. **Queries:** Not necessary. **E-Queries:** Yes. **Payment:** On acceptance.

AMERICAN HISTORY

741 Miller Dr. SE, Suite D-2, Leesburg, VA 20175. 703-771-9400.
E-mail: americanhistory@thehistorynet.com. Website: www.thehistorynet.com.
Bimonthly. $4.99/$23.95. Circ.: 95,000. Douglas G. Brinkley, Editor. **Description:** The cultural, military, social and political history of the U.S. for a general audience. Seeks well-researched articles with good focus and strong anecdotal material; 2,000-4,000 words; $400-$600. **Tips:** "We seek tightly focused stories that show an incident or short period of time in history." No travelogues, fiction, or puzzles. **Queries:** Preferred. **E-Queries:** Yes. **Unsolicited mss:** Accepts. **Response:** 10 weeks. **SASE Required:** Yes. **Freelance Content:** 60%. **Rights:** All worldwide. **Payment:** On publication. **Contact:** Philip Brandt George, Associate Editor.

AMERICAN LEGACY

See full listing in Ethnic & Multicultural category.

AMERICAN OUTBACK JOURNAL

See full listing in Regional & City Publications category.

ANCESTRY

360 E 4800 North, Provo, UT 84604. 801-705-7000. E-mail: editoram@ancestry.com. Website: www.ancestry.com. Bimonthly. $24.95/yr. Circ.: 60,000. Jennifer Utley, Managing Editor. **Description:** Family history/genealogy magazine for professional family historians and hobbyists interested in getting the most out of their research. **Nonfiction:** Family articles, especially stories where novel approaches are used to find information on the lives of ancestors; 2,000-2,500 words; $500. **Fillers:** Humorous pieces about pursuit of the author's family history; 600 words; $200. **Art:** Interesting old photographs of ancestors. **Tips:** No typical family histories, only interesting angles on family history, research methods and specific case studies. **Queries:** Preferred. **E-Queries:** Yes. **Unsolicited mss:** Accepts. **Response:** 3 months. **SASE Required:** Yes. **Freelance Content:** 20%. **Rights:** All. **Payment:** On publication.

ANCIENT AMERICAN

P.O. Box 370, Colfax, WI 54730. 715-962-3299.
E-mail: wayne@ancientamerican.com. Website: www.ancientamerican.com.
Bimonthly. $5.50/$29.95. Circ.: 15,000. Frank Joseph, Editor. **Description:** On the prehistory of the American Continent, regardless of presently fashionable beliefs. A public forum for experts and nonprofessionals alike to freely express their views.

Nonfiction: Articles on prehistory in clear, non-technical language, with original color photographs and artwork; 2,000-3,000 words; $50-$150. **Tips:** "Translate complex research into accessible, attractive language with visually appealing format for ordinary readers." **Queries:** Not necessary. **E-Queries:** Yes. **Unsolicited mss:** Accepts. **SASE Required:** Yes. **Freelance Content:** 50%. **Payment:** On publication. **Contact:** Wayne May.

ARMOR MAGAZINE
See full listing in Military category.

THE BEAVER: CANADA'S HISTORY MAGAZINE
Canada's National History Society, 478-167 Lombard Ave., Winnipeg, Manitoba R3B 0T6 Canada. 204-988-9300. E-mail: beaver@historysociety.ca. Website: www.the-beaver.ca. Bimonthly. $4.95/$27.50. Circ.: 49,000. Annalee Greenberg, Editor. **Description:** Canadian history for a general audience. Articles 3,500 words max.; $.30/word. **Tips:** "Combine impeccable research with good nonfiction story-writing skills. See website for our full editorial guidelines." **Queries:** Required. **E-Queries:** No. **Unsolicited mss:** Accepts. **Response:** 6 weeks. **SASE Required:** Yes. **Freelance Content:** 50%. **Rights:** FNASR, electronic. **Payment:** On acceptance.

CALLIOPE
See full listing in Juvenile category.

CAROLOGUE
See full listing in Regional & City Publications category.

CHRONICLE OF THE OLD WEST
P.O. Box 2859, Show Low, AZ 85902. 928-532-2875. E-mail: info@chronicleoftheoldwest.com. Website: www.chronicleoftheoldwest.com. Monthly. $22.50/yr. Circ.: 8,000. Dakota Livesay, Editor. **Description:** 1800s newspaper designed to transport readers back to the Old West. Articles are either currently written as if the event has just occured or reprints of 1800s publications. Each month's edition contains events that took place during the month. Pieces run 800-1,500 words; $.05-$.08/word. No fiction. **Tips:** "We are looking for factual articles about people and events in the Old West from 1845-1899. Articles must be written in newspaper style—as if the writer is reporting on an event that just happened. See our website for complete writer's guidelines and sample issues." **Queries:** Preferred. **E-Queries:** Yes. **Unsolicited mss:** Accepts. **Response:** 4-6 weeks. **SASE Required:** Yes. **Freelance Content:** 30%. **Rights:** FNAR. **Payment:** On publication.

CIVIL WAR TIMES
6405 Flank Dr., Harrisburg, PA 17112. 717-657-9555. E-mail: civilwartimes.magazine@primedia.com. Website: www.thehistorynet.com. 6x/yr. Circ.: 108,000. James Kushlan, Editor. **Description:** Relates the human experience of the American Civil War through lively, nonfiction stories. Relies heavily on primary sources and words of

eyewitnesses. Articles run 2,500-3,000 words; $400-$650. **Tips:** Prefers gripping, quote-rich, well-documented accounts of battles, unusual events, eyewitness accounts (memoirs, diaries, letters), and common soldier photos.

COBBLESTONE
See full listing in Juvenile category.

COLUMBIA: THE MAGAZINE OF NORTHWEST HISTORY
Washington State Historical Society (WSHS) Research Center, 315 N Stadium Way, Tacoma, WA 98403. 253-798-5918. E-mail: cdubois@wshs.wa.gov. Website: www.washingtonhistory.org. Quarterly. $7.50/issue. Circ.: 4,000. Christina Dubois, Managing Editor. **Description:** History publication for the Pacific Northwest. Articles and commentary edited for the general reader. Submissions average 4,000 words. **Queries:** Preferred. **E-Queries:** Yes. **Unsolicited mss:** Accepts. **Response:** 2-4 weeks. **SASE Required:** Yes. **Freelance Content:** 80%. **Rights:** FNAR.

COUNTRY FOLK MAGAZINE
See full listing in Agriculture & Rural Life category.

GOLDENSEAL MAGAZINE
WV Division of Culture & History, The Cultural Center, 1900 Kanawha Blvd. E, Charleston, WV 25305-0300. 304-558-0220. E-mail: goldenseal@wvculture.org. Website: www.wvculture.org/goldenseal. Quarterly. $17/yr. Circ.: 20,000. John Lilly, Editor. **Description:** On traditional West Virginia culture and history. Oral histories, old and new B&W photos, research articles. Features, 3,000 words; shorter articles, 1,000 words. Pays $.10/word. **Payment:** On publication.

GOOD OLD DAYS
306 E Parr Rd., Berne, IN 46711. 260-589-4000.
E-mail: editor@goodolddaysonline.com. Website: www.goodolddaysonline.com.
Monthly. $2.50/issue. Circ.: 200,000. Ken Tate, Editor. **Description:** First-person nostalgia from the "Good Old Days" era (defined as 1929-1955), with particular attention to the period from the Great Depression to the end of World War II. **Nonfiction:** First-person nostalgia within this timeframe; 500-1,500 words; $.04-$.06/word. **Poetry:** Metered and rhymed; 8-24 lines; pay varies. **Columns, Departments:** Good Old Days in the Kitchen, Good Old Days on Wheels; 500-1,500 words; $.04-$.06/word. **Tips:** "Good photos are a key to acceptance of your story. Our readers are generally older, rather conservative. Keep a positive, pleasant tone. Pick out a particular memory and stick to it." **Queries:** Not necessary. **E-Queries:** Yes. **Unsolicited mss:** Accepts. **Response:** 2 months. **SASE Required:** Yes. **Freelance Content:** 85%. **Rights:** All. **Payment:** On acceptance.

HERITAGE QUEST MAGAZINE
See full listing in Hobbies, Crafts, Collecting category.

HERITAGE WRITER

P.O. Box 1339, Albany, OR 97321. 541-730-6450. Monthly. $12/yr. Margaret L. Ingram, Publisher. **Description:** Monthly newsletter for genealogists and historians. Articles include writing personal/family stories, genealogy, scrapbooking, journaling, reunions; spiritual autobiographies; and community/school/church history. No fiction or simultaneous submissions. **Tips:** "Articles from our readers are encouraged. Send #10 SASE for guidelines." **Queries:** Preferred.

THE HIGHLANDER

87 Highland Ave., Hull, MA 02045-1132. 781-925-2100. Website: www.highlandermagazine.com. Bimonthly. $17.50/yr. Circ.: 32,000. Sharon Ray, Editor. **Description:** Covers Scottish heritage (history, clans, families), related to Scotland in the period 1300-1900 A.D. Pieces run 1,500-2,000 words; $185-$250. **Art:** Photos must accompany all manuscripts. Send B&W, color transparencies, maps, or line drawings. **Tips:** "Our focus is not on modern Scotland." **Queries:** Preferred. **E-Queries:** No. **Unsolicited mss:** Accepts. **Response:** Queries 6-8 weeks, submissions 1-2 months. **SASE Required:** Yes. **Payment:** On acceptance.

HISTORY MAGAZINE

Moorshead Magazines, Ltd., 505 Consumers Rd., Suite 500, Toronto, Ontario M2J 4V8 Canada. 416-491-3699. E-mail: magazine@history-magazine.com. Website: www.history-magazine.com. Bimonthly. $5/issue. Circ.: 22,000. Jeff Chapman, Editor. **Description:** Focuses on Western history in the period between early medieval times and the early 1900s. Articles run 500-4,000 words; contact for payment details. **Tips:** Does not accept biographies or descriptions of battles. **Queries:** Preferred. **E-Queries:** Yes. **Unsolicited mss:** Accepts. **Response:** 3 weeks. **Freelance Content:** 90%. **Rights:** First World. **Payment:** On publication.

THE ILLINOIS STEWARD

University of Illinois, 1102 S Goodwin Ave., W503 Turner Hall, Urbana, IL 61801. 217-244-3896. E-mail: karynk@uiuc.edu. Website: http://ilsteward.nres.uiuc.edu. Karyn McDermaid, Managing Editor; Robert Reber; Managing Editor. **Description:** On Illinois history and heritage, with natural-resource stewardship theme. Articles run 1,700-1,800 words; no payment offered. **Tips:** Complimentary copy provided at no charge. **Queries:** Preferred. **E-Queries:** Yes.

MHQ: QUARTERLY JOURNAL OF MILITARY HISTORY

PRIMEDIA History Group, 741 Miller Dr. SE, Suite D-2, Leesburg, VA 20175-8994. 703-771-9400. Website: www.historynet.com/mhq. Quarterly. $69.95/yr. Circ.: 30,000. Rod Paschall, Editor. **Description:** Offers an undistorted view of history, encourages understanding of events, personalities, and artifacts of the past. Open to well-written articles on military history; 5,000-6,000 words; $400-$800. **Queries:** Preferred. **E-Queries:** Yes. **Unsolicited mss:** Accepts. **Response:** 4-8 weeks. **SASE Required:** Yes. **Freelance Content:** 50%. **Payment:** On publication.

MILITARY MAGAZINE

See full listing in Military category.

MONTANA

Montana Historical Society, 225 N Roberts St., P.O. Box 201201, Helena, MT 59601. 406-444-4741. E-mail: cwhitehorn@state.mt.us. Website: www.montanahistoricalsociety.org. Quarterly. $29/yr. Circ.: 10,000. W. Clark Whitehorn, Editor. **Description:** For members of the state historical society and The Western History Assn., covering the history of Montana and the American and Canadian West. Seeks authentic articles on history of the region; new interpretive approaches to major developments in western history. Must use footnotes or bibliography; 3,500-5,500 words. **Queries:** Preferred. **E-Queries:** Yes. **Unsolicited mss:** Accepts. **Response:** 1-3 months. **SASE Required:** Yes. **Freelance Content:** 95%. **Rights:** All.

NAVAL HISTORY

U.S. Naval Institute, 291 Wood Rd., Annapolis, MD 21402-1254. 410-268-6110. Website: www.navalinstitute.org. Bimonthly. $20/yr. Circ.: 40,000. Fred L. Schultz, Editor-in-Chief. **Description:** On international naval and maritime history. Essays, book excerpts, interviews, profiles, personal experience, technical, photo feature; 1,000-3,000 words; pays $300-$500 (assigned articles); $75-$400 (unsolicited). Also, inspirational humor; 50-100 words; $10-$50. **Tips:** "Write a good, concise story; support it with primary sources and good illustrations." **Queries:** Preferred. **E-Queries:** Yes. **Unsolicited mss:** Accepts. **Response:** 1-2 months. **SASE Required:** Yes. **Freelance Content:** 90%. **Rights:** FNASR. **Payment:** On acceptance.

NEBRASKA HISTORY

P.O. Box 82554, Lincoln, NE 68501. 402-471-4748. E-mail: publish@nebraskahistory.org. Website: www.nebraskahistory.org. Quarterly. $30/yr. Circ.: 3,800. Donald B. Cunningham, Editor. **Description:** Seeks well-researched articles, edited documents, and other annotated primary materials on the history of Nebraska and the Great Plains. Articles run 3,000-7,000 words. **Tips:** Rarely publishes family histories or reminiscence. Send submissions by regular mail only; no unsolicited e-mail attachments. **Queries:** Preferred. **Unsolicited mss:** Accepts. **Response:** 1-8 weeks. **SASE Required:** Yes. **Payment:** In copies.

NOW & THEN

See full listing in Regional & City Publications category.

OLD CALIFORNIA GAZETTE

2454 Heritage Park Row, San Diego, CA 92110. 619-491-0099. E-mail: gazettes@sbcglobal.net. Annual. Circ.: 1,000,000. Karen Spring, Publisher. **Description:** Articles on Southern California history, 1800-1920s. Pieces run 500-750 words; $.10/word. **Tips:** $25 bonus for front cover piece. $25 bonus if humorous. **Queries:** Preferred. **E-Queries:** Yes. **Unsolicited mss:** Accepts. **Response:** 1 month. **Freelance Content:** 50%. **Rights:** FNAR. **Payment:** On publication.

OVERLAND JOURNAL

P.O. Box 14707, Spokane, WA 99214. 509-928-9540. E-mail: bob@ahclark.com. Website: www.octa-trails.org. Quarterly. $40 annual membership. Circ.: 2,500. Robert A. Clark, Editor. **Description:** Research and narrative history dealing with Western emigration in the nineteenth century. No payment offered. **Queries:** Preferred. **E-Queries:** Yes. **Unsolicited mss:** Accepts. **Response:** Queries 1 week, submissions 2 months. **SASE Required:** Yes. **Freelance Content:** 5%.

PENNSYLVANIA HERITAGE

Commonwealth Keystone Bldg., Plaza Level, 400 North St., Harrisburg, PA 17120-0053. 717-787-2407. E-mail: miomalley@state.pa.us. Website: www.paheritage.org. Quarterly. Michael J. O'Malley III, Editor. **Description:** Published by Pennsylvania Historical and Museum Commission and the Pennsylvania Heritage Society, to introduce readers to the state's rich culture and historic legacy. Articles on architecture, fine/decorative arts, oral history, folklore, science, travel, technology, natural history, state/local history, etc. Pays $100-$500. **Tips:** "We seek an unusual, fresh angles to make history come to life, including pictorial or photo essays, interviews, travel and destination pieces. Send complete manuscript." **Payment:** On acceptance.

PERSIMMON HILL

1700 NE 63rd St., Oklahoma City, OK 73111. 405-478-6404. E-mail: editor@nationalcowboymuseum.org. Website: www.nationalcowboymuseum.org. Quarterly. $30/yr. Circ.: 15,000. M.J. Van Deventer, Editor. **Description:** Historical and contemporary themes related to the American West, from Hollywood to cowboys. Honors those who have made positive contributions to the West, past or present. **Nonfiction:** On Western history and art, cowboys, ranching, rodeo, and nature; 1,000-1,500 words; $150-$350. **Columns, Departments:** Great hotels and lodgings; entrepreneurs; events, interesting places to visit, personalities; 750-1,000 words; $75-$150. **Art:** Slides, transparencies; up to $50/image. **Tips:** "No stories on western outlaws or 'bad guys' (Billy the Kid) stories." **Queries:** Required. **E-Queries:** Yes. **Unsolicited mss:** Accepts. **Response:** 6-8 weeks. **SASE Required:** Yes. **Freelance Content:** 95%. **Rights:** One-time. **Payment:** On publication.

PRESERVATION

National Trust for Historic Preservation, 1785 Massachusetts Ave. NW, Washington, DC 20036-2117. 202-588-6388. E-mail: preservation@nthp.org. Website: www.preservationonline.org. Bimonthly. $24/yr. Circ.: 185,000. James Conaway, Editor-in-Chief. **Description:** "Encourages a sense of place and passion for historic preservation." Articles on the built environment, place, architecture, preservation issues, and people involved. Mostly freelance. 150-6,000 words; $.50-$1/word. **Queries:** Preferred. **E-Queries:** Yes. **Unsolicited mss:** Accepts. **Response:** Queries 2-3 weeks, submissions 6-8 weeks. **SASE Required:** Yes. **Freelance Content:** 80%. **Rights:** FNAR. **Payment:** On acceptance.

REMINISCE

Reiman Publications/Reader's Digest Assn., 5400 S 60th St., Greendale, WI 53129. E-mail: editors@reminisce.com. Website: www.reminisce.com. Bimonthly. $17.98/yr. Circ.: 1,000,000. Blanche Comiskey, Editor. **Description:** "A stroll down memory lane." Vintage photographs and real-life, first-person stories recall the "good old days" (1960s and back). Articles should have an "I remember" element; 750 words. **Tips:** E-mail or send SASE for submission guidelines. **Queries:** Not necessary. **Unsolicited mss:** Accepts. **Response:** 2 months. **Freelance Content:** 90%.

RENAISSANCE

1450 Barnum Ave., Suite 207, Bridgeport, CT 06610. 800-232-2224. E-mail: editor@renaissancemagazine.com. Website: www.renaissancemagazine.com. Bimonthly. Circ.: 30,000. Kim Guarnaccia, Publisher. **Description:** Renaissance and Medieval history, costuming, heraldry, reenactments, role-playing, and Renaissance faires. **Nonfiction:** Martial arts, travel, interviews, reenactment groups, and reviews of books, music, movies, and games; 3,000 words; $.08/word. **Art:** Prefers electronic format for submissions; pays $8/image. **Tips:** Send query with brief bio and sample article. **Queries:** Preferred. **E-Queries:** Yes. **Unsolicited mss:** Accepts. **Response:** 3-6 weeks. **SASE Required:** Yes. **Freelance Content:** 90%. **Rights:** FNAR.

SOUTH CAROLINA HISTORICAL MAGAZINE

South Carolina Historical Society, 100 Meeting St., Charleston, SC 29401-2299. 843-723-3225. E-mail: info@schistory.org. Website: www.schistory.org. Eric Emerson, Editor. **Description:** Scholarly articles, to 25 pages (with footnotes), on South Carolina history. Review previous issues to be aware of scholarship. Pays in copies.

SOUTHERN OREGON HERITAGE TODAY

See full listing in Regional & City Publications category.

TIMELINE

1982 Velma Ave., Columbus, OH 43211-2497. 614-297-2360. E-mail: timeline@ohiohistory.org. Bimonthly. $6/$30. Circ.: 15,000. Christopher S. Duckworth, Editor. **Description:** Covers the fields of history, prehistory, and natural sciences, directed towards readers in the Midwest. **Nonfiction:** History, politics, economics, social, and natural history for lay readers in Ohio and the Midwest; 1,000-5,000 words. **Tips:** "Your writing style should be simple and direct; avoid jargon." **Queries:** Preferred. **E-Queries:** Yes. **Unsolicited mss:** Accepts. **Response:** 2-3 weeks. **SASE Required:** Yes. **Freelance Content:** 90%. **Rights:** FNAR.

TRUE WEST

P.O. Box 8008, Cave Creek, AZ 85327. 888-687-1881. E-mail: editor@truewestmagazine.com. Website: www.truewestmagazine.com. 10x/yr. Circ.: 157,000. R.G. Robertson, Editor. **Description:** Since 1953, *True West Magazine* has been celebrating the True West lifestyle. **Tips:** "Familiarize yourself with our publication before submitting queries." **Payment:** On publication.

VIETNAM

PRIMEDIA History Group, 741 Miller Dr. SE, Suite D2, Leesburg, VA 20175. 703-771-9400. E-mail: vietnam@thehistorynet.com. Website: www.thehistorynet.com/vn. Bimonthly. $23.95/yr. Circ.: 50,000. David T. Zabecki, Editor. **Description:** First-person and third-person accounts of all historical aspects of the Vietnam War: strategy, tactics, personalities, arms, equipment, etc.; 3,500-4,000 words; $300. **Tips:** Most readers are Vietnam veterans, current military personnel, military historians and enthusiasts. Does not publish fiction, poetry, or "war stories." **Queries:** Preferred. **E-Queries:** Accepts. **Rights:** All worldwide, reprint. **Payment:** On publication.

THE WESTERN HISTORICAL QUARTERLY

Utah State University, Logan, UT 84322-0740. 435-797-1301. E-mail: whq@hass.usu.edu. Website: www.usu.edu/history/whq. Quarterly. Circ.: 2,200. David Rich Lewis, Editor. **Description:** Covers the American West (United States, Canada, and Mexico). Focuses on occupation, settlement, and political, economic, social, cultural and intellectual history. **Nonfiction:** Original articles about the American West, the Westward movement, 20th-century regional studies, Spanish borderlands, Canada, northern Mexico, Alaska, and Hawaii; to 10,000 words; no payment. **Tips:** Prefers descriptive, interpretive, and analytical essays on broad themes; use of primary sources and monographic literature. No multiple submissions. **Queries:** Not necessary. **E-Queries:** Yes. **Unsolicited mss:** Accepts. **Response:** 1 week. **SASE Required:** Yes.

WILD WEST

PRIMEDIA History Group , 741 Miller Dr. SE, Suite D-2, Leesburg, VA 20175-8920. 703-779-8302. E-mail: wildwest@thehistorynet.com. Website: www.thehistorynet.com./wildwest. Bimonthly. $23.95/yr. Circ.: 77,900. Gregory Lalire, Editor. **Description:** History of people, places, battles, and events that led to the taming of the great American frontier. **Nonfiction:** Articles, artwork, and picture essays on life and times of settlers, cowboys, Indians, gunmen, lawmen, all the fascinating characters and aspects of Western lore and culture; 3,500-4,000 words; $200-$400. **Queries:** Preferred. **E-Queries:** Yes. **Unsolicited mss:** Accepts. **Response:** 6 months. **SASE Required:** Yes. **Payment:** On publication.

WORLD WAR II

PRIMEDIA History Group, 741 Miller Dr. SE, Suite D-2, Leesburg, VA 20175. 703-779-8302. E-mail: mhaskew@cowles.com. Website: www.thehistorynet.com. Bimonthly. $27.95. Circ.: 152,300. Chris Anderson, Editor. **Description:** Strategy, tactics, personalities, arms and equipment. **Nonfiction:** Features, 3,500-4,000 words, plus 500-word sidebar; up to $200 **Art:** Cite any color or B&W illustrations, and sources. **Tips:** Readable style and historical accuracy imperative. **Queries:** Preferred. **Unsolicited mss:** Accepts. **Response:** 6 months. **SASE Required:** Yes. **Rights:** Exclusive worldwide. **Payment:** On publication.

HOBBIES, CRAFTS, COLLECTING
(See also Games & Pastimes)

AIRBRUSH ACTION
P.O. Box 438, 3209 Atlantic Ave., Allenwood, NJ 08720. 732-223-7878.
E-mail: editor@airbrushaction.com. Website: www.airbrushaction.com. Bimonthly.
$5.99/$26.95. Circ.: 35,000. Cliff Stieglitz, Editor. **Description:** Showcases innovative airbrush art. Profiles on notable artists, step-by-step how-to articles, columns on T-shirt painting, automotive airbrushing, illustration, and the "kustom kulture" arts. Also, regular Buyer's Guides. **Nonfiction:** Profiles of artists by request only; 1,000-2,000 words; $.15/word. **Queries:** Required. **E-Queries:** Yes. **Unsolicited mss:** Accepts. **Response:** 2 weeks. **SASE Required:** Yes. **Freelance Content:** 50%. **Rights:** All. **Payment:** On publication.

ANCESTRY
See full listing in History category.

ANTIQUE SHOPPE
P.O. Box 2175, Keystone Heights, FL 32656. 352-475-1679.
E-mail: antshoppe@aol.com. Website: www.antiqueshoppefl.com. Monthly. $17.
Circ.: 20,000. Bruce G. Causey, Editor. **Description:** Magazine serving the antique and collection industry. Articles on antiques, collectibles, communities with antique districts, historical locations, local auctions and shows, etc.; 1,000 words; $50. **Queries:** Preferred. **E-Queries:** Yes. **Unsolicited mss:** Accepts. **Freelance Content:** 60%. **Payment:** On publication.

ANTIQUE TRADER
Krause Publications, Inc., 700 E State St., Iola, WI 54990. 715-445-2214.
E-mail: korbecks@krause.com. Website: www.collect.com. Weekly. $37/yr. Circ.: 60,000. Sharon Korbeck, Editor. **Description:** Covers all types of antiques and collectibles. **Nonfiction:** Articles 500-1,200 words; $50-$250. **Rights:** Exclusive. **Payment:** On publication.

ANTIQUE WEEK
DMG World Media, 27 N Jefferson St., P.O. Box 90, Knightstown, IN 46148-1242. 765-345-5133. E-mail: connie@antiqueweek.com. Website: www.antiqueweek.com. Weekly. $37.75/yr. Circ.: 64,000. **Description:** Weekly antique, auction, and collectors' newspaper. **Nonfiction:** Articles, 500-2,000 words, on antiques, collectibles, auction and antique show reports; pays $40-$200 for in-depth articles. **Tips:** Guidelines available. **Queries:** Preferred. **Payment:** On publication. **Contact:** Connie Swaim, Managing Editor.

ANTIQUES & AUCTION NEWS
Engle Printing & Publishing Co., P.O. Box 500, Mount Joy, PA 17552-0500.
717-653-1833. E-mail: antiquesnews@engleonline.com. Website: www.antiquesan-

dauctionnews.net. Weekly. $15/yr. Circ.: 35,000. Denise Sater, Editor. **Description:** Factual articles, 600-1,500 words, on antiques, collectors, collections, and places of historic interest. Pays $18-$40. **Queries:** Required. **Payment:** On publication.

AUTOGRAPH COLLECTOR

Odyssey Publications, Inc., 510A Corona Mall, Corona, CA 92879-1420. 909-371-7137. E-mail: editorev@telus.net. Website: www.autographcollector.com. Monthly. $38/yr. Circ.: 20,000. Ev Phillips, Editor. **Description:** Covers all areas of autograph collecting (preservation, framing, and storage, specialty collections, documents and letters, collectors and dealers). Articles run 1,000-2,000 words; pay varies. **Tips:** Sample copy and guidelines free. **Queries:** Preferred.

BEAD & BUTTON

Kalmbach Publishing Co., 21027 Crossroads Circle, P.O. Box 1612, Waukesha, WI 53187. 262-796-8776. Website: www.beadandbutton.com. 6x/yr. Circ.: 160,000. Mindy Brooks, Editor. **Description:** Illustrated bead projects for enthusiasts: jewelry, home decor, clothing, and more. Also profiles of bead artists and articles on bead history. **Art:** Art is by authors; photo and illustration guidance is by authors; final photos and illustrations are done in-house. **Tips:** Articles are written by artisans in this hobby and freelancers. **Queries:** Required. **E-Queries:** Yes. **Unsolicited mss:** Does not accept. **Response:** 1-2 months. **Rights:** All. **Payment:** On acceptance.

BEADSTYLE MAGAZINE

Kalmbach Publishing Co., 21027 Crossroads Circle, P.O. Box 1612, Waukesha, WI 53187-1612. 262-796-8776. Website: www.beadstylemag.com. 6x/yr. $4.95/$19.95. Linda Augsburg, Editor-at-Large. **Description:** Each issue features 25+ beading projects that are fast, stylish, and offer simple techniques for beginning and seasoned beaders. **Nonfiction:** How-to articles describing how to make beaded jewelry (beginner-level) and short pieces on vintage jewelry, costume jewelry, etc.; 600-800 words. **Tips:** Considers manuscript ideas from project designers only. Include photo or JPEG, brief introduction, list of materials, and step-by-step instructions. See website for guidelines. **Queries:** Not necessary. **Unsolicited mss:** Accepts. **Response:** 2 weeks. **Freelance Content:** 50%. **Rights:** All. **Payment:** On acceptance.

BECKETT BASKETBALL CARD MONTHLY

Beckett Publications, Inc., 15850 Dallas Pkwy., Dallas, TX 75248-3308. 972-91-6657. Website: www.beckett.com. Monthly. $22.50/yr. Circ.: 80,000. Mike Payne, Editor. **Description:** For hobbyists who collect cards and memorabilia. Sports collectibles stories, with a trading card/basketball angle; 800-2,000 words. **Tips:** Promote the hobby in a positive, fun-loving way. **Queries:** Preferred. **E-Queries:** Yes. **Unsolicited mss:** Accepts. **Response:** 10 days. **SASE Required:** No. **Freelance Content:** 30%. **Rights:** All. **Payment:** On publication.

BLADE MAGAZINE

Krause Publications, Inc., 700 E State St., Iola, WI 54945-5010. 715-445-2214. E-mail: blade@krause.com. Website: www.blademag.com. Monthly. $25.98/yr. Circ.: 72,000. Steve Shackleford, Editor. **Description:** For knife makers, collectors, daily knife users, and enthusiasts. Anything new and unusual about handmade and factory knives, historical pieces, interviews, celebrities, values on collectible knives and accessories, tips on use. **Queries:** Preferred. **E-Queries:** Yes. **Unsolicited mss:** Accepts. **Response:** 1-2 months. **SASE Required:** Yes. **Freelance Content:** 5%. **Rights:** All. **Payment:** On publication.

BREW YOUR OWN

See full listing in Food & Wine category.

CAROUSEL NEWS & TRADER

87 Park Ave. W, Suite 206, Mansfield, OH 44902-1612. 419-529-4999. E-mail: cnsam@aol.com. 10x/yr. $3.95/$35. Circ.: 2,500. Walter L. Loucks, Editor. **Description:** Covers all aspects of carousels (Merry-Go-Rounds), including complete machines, individual animals, restoration, history, carving, buy-sell-trade. **Nonfiction:** On carousel history, profiles of operators and carvers, collectors, preservationists, restorationists; 500-1,000 words + photos; $50/printed page. **Queries:** Preferred. **E-Queries:** Yes. **Unsolicited mss:** Accepts. **Response:** 4 weeks. **SASE Required:** Yes. **Payment:** On publication.

CLASSIC TOY TRAINS

Kalmbach Publishing Co., 21027 Crossroads Circle, Waukesha, WI 53187. 262-796-8776. E-mail: editor@classictoytrains.com. Website: www.classictoytrains.com. 9x/yr. $5.50/$39.95. Circ.: 62,000. Neil Besougloff, Editor. **Description:** For enthusiasts of old and new toy trains produced by Lionel, American Flyer, and their competitors. **Nonfiction:** Articles, with photos, on toy train layouts and how-to projects. Also toy train manufacturing history and repair/maintenance. Pays $75/printed page. **Queries:** Preferred. **E-Queries:** Yes. **Unsolicited mss:** Accepts. **Response:** Queries 15 days, submissions 30 days. **Freelance Content:** 60%. **Rights:** All.

CLASSIC TRAINS

Kalmbach Publishing Co., 21027 Crossroads Circle, Waukesha, WI 53187. 262-796-8776. E-mail: rmcgonigal@classictrainsmag.com. Website: www.classic-trainsmag.com. Quarterly. $6.50/$21.95. Circ.: 61,528. Robert S. McGonigal, Editor. **Description:** Celebration of the "golden years" of North American railroading, roughly 1925-1975. **Nonfiction:** First-person recollections of railroaders and railfans, studies of equipment or operations, and photo essays; 500-5,000 words; $.10-$.15/word. **Columns, Departments:** Essays on "fallen flag" (defunct) railroad companies; 1,300 words; $.15/word. **Art:** Prefers prints or transparencies; $30-$100, depending on use. **Tips:** "Our readership is mostly railroad enthusiasts so knowledge of railroading is essential. We do not cover any aspect of railroading today, only railroads in the past." **Queries:** Preferred. **E-Queries:** Yes. **Unsolicited mss:** Accepts.

COLLECTORS NEWS
Collectors News/Pioneer Communications, Inc., P.O. Box 306, 502 2nd St., Grundy Ctr., IA 50638. 319-824-6981. E-mail: collectors@collectors-news.com. Website: www.collectors-news.com. Monthly. $4/$28. Circ.: 10,000. Linda Kruger, Editor. **Description:** Antiques and collectibles magazine for casual collectors and experienced dealers. Accurate information on wide variety of types, market trends, events, and collector interaction. **Nonfiction:** Background of collectibles; how to identify, care for, value items. 20th-century nostalgia, Americana, glass and china, music, furniture, transportation, timepieces, jewelry, farm-related items, and lamps. Articles run 900-1,200 words; $1.10/column inch. **Art:** Quality color or B&W photos. **Queries:** Preferred. **E-Queries:** Yes. **Response:** 2-6 weeks. **SASE Required:** Yes. **Freelance Content:** 30%. **Rights:** FNASR. **Payment:** On publication.

CRAFTING TRADITIONS
Reiman Publications/Reader's Digest Assn.
5400 S 60th St., Greendale, WI 53129. 414-423-0100.
E-mail: editors@craftingtraditions.com. Website: www.reimanpub.com. Bimonthly. $16.98/yr. Circ.: 50,000. Kathleen Zimmer-Anderson, Editor. **Description:** All types of craft designs (needlepoint, quilting, woodworking, etc.) with complete instructions and full-size patterns. **Rights:** All. **Payment:** On acceptance.

CRAFTS MAGAZINE
PRIMEDIA Enthusiast Group, 14901 Heritagecrest Way, Bluffdale, UT 84065-4818. 801-984-2070. E-mail: editor@craftsmag.com. Website: www.craftsmag.com. Monthly. $21.98/yr. Circ.: 350,000. Valerie Pingree, Editor. **Description:** Seeks writers who are professional craft designers and who can write detailed instructions. Interested in crochet, knitting, sewing, embroidery and needlework, decorative painting, beads, papercrafts, seasonal, kitchen crafts, etc. Seeks unique gifts and creative techniques for re-using second hand items. Photos must illustrate steps in making the project. **Tips:** Do not send projects. Submit written query or e-query with photos.

CRAFTS 'N THINGS
Clapper Communications, 2400 Devon, Suite 375, Des Plaines, IL 60018-4618. 847-635-5800. E-mail: craftideas@clapper.com. Website: www.craftideas.com. 8x/yr. $16.97/yr. Circ.: 274,000. Barbara Sunderlage, Editor. **Description:** How-to articles on a variety of crafts, with instructions and photos of finished project. **Tips:** Limited freelance content. **Queries:** Required. **Payment:** On acceptance.

THE CRAFTS REPORT
Crafts Report Publishing Co., Inc., P.O. Box 1992, Wilmington, DE 19899-1992. 302-656-2209. E-mail: editor@craftsreport.com. Website: www.craftsreport.com. Monthly . $29/yr. Circ.: 23,000. Mary Petzak, Editor. **Description:** On the business side of the crafts industry: marketing, growing your craft business, time management, studio safety, retail relationships, features on other crafts professionals at all levels of the field, industry news, etc.

DECORATIVE ARTIST'S WORKBOOK

F&W Publications, Inc., 4700 E Galbraith Rd., Cincinnati, OH 45236-2726. 513-531-2690. E-mail: dawedit@fwpubs.com. Website: www.decorativeartist.com. Bimonthly. $27/yr. Circ.: 84,000. Anne Hevener, Editor. **Description:** Step-by-step how-to articles on decorative painting subjects, including folk art, stroke work, stenciling, fabric painting, and faux finishing methods; 1,000-2,000 words; $200-$300. **Queries:** Required. **Unsolicited mss:** Does not accept. **Response:** 2 weeks. **SASE Required:** Yes. **Freelance Content:** 75%. **Rights:** FNASR.

DOLLS

Jones Publishing Co., Inc., 217 Passaic Ave., Hasbrouck Heights, NJ 07604. 201-393-0336. E-mail: nrdollsmagazine@earthlink.net. Website: www.jonespublishing.com. 10x/yr. $26.95/yr. Circ.: 100,000. Nayda Rondon, Editor. **Description:** Publication for knowledgeable doll collectors. Sharply-focused articles with strong collecting angle and concrete information (value, identification, restoration, etc.). Be sure to include quality slides, transparencies and/or CD with hi-res images (300 dpi), JPEG or TIFF that are at least 4x6 in size. 500-1,500 words; $75-$300. **Queries:** Required.

FAMILY TREE

F&W Publications, Inc., 4700 E Galbraith Rd., Cincinnati, OH 45236. 513-531-2690. E-mail: editor@familytreemagazine.com. Website: www.familytreemagazine.com. Bimonthly. $27/yr. Circ.: 75,000. Allison Stacy, Editor-in-Chief. **Description:** Features articles on how to discover, preserve, and celebrate family history and traditions. **Queries:** Preferred.

FIBERARTS

Sterling Publishing Co., 67 Broadway St., Asheville, NC 28801-2919. 828-253-0467. E-mail: editor@fiberartsmagazine.com. Website: www.fiberartsmagazine.com. 5x/yr. $6/$24. Circ.: 23,700. Sunita Patterson, Editor. **Description:** Covers all fiber-arts: weaving, quilting, embroidery, wearable art, 3-D work, basketry, and more. Readers include professional artists, craftspeople, hobbyists, collectors, and curators. **Nonfiction:** Articles and interviews (outstanding artists and craftspeople, trends and issues, exhibitions, business concerns, historic and ethnic textiles). Articles run 250-2,500 words; $65-$500. **Art:** 35mm slides, transparencies; B&W glossies; electronic images (300+ dpi). No color prints. **Tips:** "Good visuals are key to acceptance. Submit with synopsis, outline, and writing samples. Use accessible, not scholarly, writing tone." **Queries:** Preferred. **E-Queries:** No. **Unsolicited mss:** Accepts. **Response:** 1-2 months. **SASE Required:** Yes. **Freelance Content:** 90%. **Rights:** FNAR.

FINE WOODWORKING
Taunton Press, 63 S Main St., P.O. Box 5506, Newtown, CT 06470-5506.
203-426-8171. E-mail: fw@taunton.com. Website: www.taunton.com. Bimonthly.
Circ.: 295,000. Timothy Schreiner, Publisher. **Description:** Covers high-quality
workmanship, thoughtful designs, and safe and proper procedures for outstanding
results. **Nonfiction:** Articles on basics of tool use, stock preparation and joinery; specialized techniques and finishing; shop-built tools, jigs and fixtures; or any stage of
design, construction, finishing, and installation of cabinetry and furniture. $150/page.
Columns, Departments: Methods of Work, Q&A, Master Class, Finish Line, Tools
& Materials, and Notes & Comment; $10. **Queries:** Required. **Payment:** On publi-
cation. **Contact:** Anatole Burkin, Editor.

FINELINES
P.O. Box 536, Murrysville, PA 15668. 724-387-1269. E-mail: hngoffice@aol.com.
Website: www.historicneedlework.com. Quarterly. $7/issue. Circ.: 4,600. Deborah
Novak Crain, Editor. **Description:** All about historic needlework (1650-1850).
Nonfiction: Travel to historic places with significant needlework; museums; stitching
(samplers, needlework tools, etc.); 500-1,500 words; pay varies. **Queries:** Not neces-
sary. **E-Queries:** Yes. **Unsolicited mss:** Accepts. **SASE Required:** Yes. **Freelance
Content:** 35%. **Rights:** FNAR. **Payment:** On publication.

FINESCALE MODELER
Kalmbach Publishing Co., 21027 Crossroads Circle, Waukesha, WI 53187.
262-796-8776. E-mail: editor@finescale.com. Website: www.finescale.com. 10x/yr.
$4.95/$39.95. Circ.: 60,000. Mark Thompson, Editor. **Description:** Magazine for
scale modelers, including builders of model aircraft, armor, ships, autos, and figures.
Nonfiction: How-to articles for people who make non-operating models of aircraft,
armored vehicles, automobiles, ships, and figures. Photos and drawings should
accompany articles. Also, 1-page model-building hints and tips. Length and pay
varies. **Art:** Prefers color slides, medium-format transparencies, or photo prints. Also
accepts hi-res digital photos. **Tips:** Stories on scale-modeling hobby only. **Queries:**
Preferred. **E-Queries:** Yes. **Unsolicited mss:** Accepts. **Response:** 6 weeks. **SASE
Required:** Yes. **Freelance Content:** 80%. **Rights:** All. **Payment:** On acceptance.

GARDEN RAILWAYS
Kalmbach Publishing Co., P.O. Box 460222, Denver, CO 80246. 303-377-7785.
E-mail: mhorovitz@gardenrailways.com. Website: www.gardenrailways.com.
Bimonthly. Circ.: 37,000. Marc Horovitz, Editor. **Description:** Covers all aspects of
the garden-railroading hobby, including building, operating and landscaping garden
railways. **Nonfiction:** Articles run 500-2,500 words; $45/page (including photos).
Tips: Guidelines available on website or on request. Corporate office: 21027
Crossroads Circle, Waukesha, WI 53187. **Queries:** Required. **E-Queries:** Yes.
Unsolicited mss: Accepts. **Response:** 30 days. **Freelance Content:** 75%. **Rights:**
All, one-time. **Payment:** On acceptance.

GOOD OLD BOAT

7340 Niagara Lane N, Maple Grove, MN 55311-2655. 763-420-8923.
E-mail: karen@goodoldboat.com. Website: www.goodoldboat.com. Bimonthly.
$39.95 in U.S./Canada, $49.95 other. Karen Larson, Editor. **Description:** Articles
and information on upgrading, maintaining and restoring sailboats 10+ years old. Also
profiles influential people who and companies which have helped shape this hobby.
Nonfiction: Technical material relevant to most older sailboats: in-depth, how-to
articles on blister repair, deck delamination repair, tank repair, etc; 3,000-5,000 words.
Also short refit articles, 1,000-2,000 words, and "quick and easy" tips, 300-600 words.
Columns, Departments: Articles or stories on boatowners and their boats, reflections, book reviews, and other features. **Art:** Prefers slides, but also accepts color
prints, B&W photos, and drawings/sketches. Accepts digital 300+ dpi. Pays $100 for
covers, $200 for special photo spreads. **Tips:** Review products and services honestly
for the benefit of fellow readers. "Encourages pride of ownership and reminds sailors
of why they do this work: the joy of sailing and the ability to own a sailboat without
making a half-million-dollar investment." **E-Queries:** Yes. **Response:** 2-6 weeks.
SASE Required: Yes. **Rights:** FNAR. **Payment:** 60 days in advance of publication.

HERITAGE QUEST MAGAZINE

425 N 400 W, Suite 1A, North Salt Lake, UT 84054. 801-677-0048.
E-mail: leland@heritagequest.com. Website: www.heritagequestmagazine.com.
Bimonthly. $6.95/$28. Circ.: 18,000. Leland Meitzler, Publisher/Managing Editor.
Description: Genealogical how-to articles; 1,500-3,000 words; $75/printed page.
Readers range from beginners to professionals. **Queries:** Preferred. **E-Queries:** Yes.
Unsolicited mss: Accepts. **Response:** 90 days. **Freelance Content:** 90%. **Rights:**
All. **Payment:** On publication.

HOBBY MERCHANDISER

Hobby Publications, Inc., Box 102, Morganville, NJ 07751-0102. 800-969-7176.
E-mail: info@hobbymerchandiser.com. Website: www.hobbymerchandiser.com.
Monthly. $20/yr. Circ.: 8,600. Jeff Troy, Editor-in-Chief. **Description:** For the pro-
fessional craft business; also general small-business advice. Articles, 800-1,500 words;
pays $75-$200. **Payment:** On publication.

INTERWEAVE KNITS

Interweave Press, Inc., 201 E 4th St., Loveland, CO 80537-5655. 970-669-7672.
E-mail: knits@interweave.com. Website: www.interweave.com. Quarterly. $24/yr.
Circ.: 60,000. Pam Allen, Editor. **Description:** For those who love to knit. Presents
beautifully finished projects, with clear step-by-step instructions as well as profiles of
people of who love to knit. Pays $100/published page. **Queries:** Preferred. **Payment:**
On publication.

KITPLANES MAGAZINE

531 Encinitas Blvd., Suite 105, Encinitas, CA 92024. 760-436-4747.
E-mail: editorial@kitplanes.com. Website: www.kitplanes.com. Monthly.
$4.99/$29.95. Circ.: 70,000. Brian Clark, Editor. **Description:** For designers,
builders, and pilots of home-built experimental aircraft. Covers all aspects of design,
construction, and performance; 1,500-2,500 words; $70/page. **Tips:** Sample copy $6.
Queries: Preferred. **E-Queries:** Yes. **Unsolicited mss:** Accepts. **Response:**
Queries 2 days, submissions 2 weeks. **SASE Required:** No. **Freelance Content:**
80%. **Payment:** On publication.

KNIVES ILLUSTRATED

Y-Visionary Publishing, L.P., 265 S Anita Dr., Suite 120, Orange, CA 92868. 714-939-
9991. E-mail: knivesillustrated@yahoo.com. Website: www.knivesillustrated.com.
Bimonthly. $19.95/yr. Circ.: 41,100. Bruce Voyles, Editor. **Description:** Source for
new knife information, from both factories and custom builders. Showcases quality
color photos, well-known knife makers, new trends, news from shows, and articles
from industry experts; 900-500 words; $200-$400. **Tips:** "Our readership is extremely
knowledgeable and vocal. Don't proclaim yourself an expert; our readers will know if
you're not. It is highly recommended that you pick up a few copies of the magazine
before querying. However, we always want to find new talent, so it's fairly easy to get
published if you know your stuff." **Queries:** Required. **E-Queries:** Yes. **Unsolicited
mss:** Accepts. **Response:** 2-6 weeks. **Freelance Content:** 85%. **Rights:** All.
Payment: On publication.

LAPIDARY JOURNAL

PRIMEDIA Enthusiast Group, 60 Chestnut Ave., Suite 201, Devon, PA 19333. 610-
964-6300. E-mail: lj.editorial@primedia.com. Website: www.lapidaryjournal.com.
Monthly. $30/yr. Circ.: 58,000. Merle White, Editor-in-Chief. **Description:** All about
amateur and professional jewelry-making.

LOST TREASURE

Lee Harris, P.O. Box 451589, Grove, OK 74345. 918-786-2182. E-mail: managinged-
itor@losttreasure.com. Website: www.losttreasure.com. Monthly. $4.95/$29.95. Circ.:
50,000. Janet Warford-Perry, Managing Editor. **Description:** The treasure hunter's
"magazine of choice." **Nonfiction:** How-tos, legends, folklore, stories of lost treasures; 500-1500 words; $.04/word. **Art:** Cover photos are paid $100. Photos must be
groupings of treasure, 35mm print, negative or slide only, vertical shot, marked with
the author's name and address. **Queries:** Not necessary. **E-Queries:** Yes.
Unsolicited mss: Accepts. **Response:** 1-2 weeks. **Freelance Content:** 35%.
Rights: All. **Payment:** On publication.

MEMORY MAKERS

F&W Publications, Inc., 12365 Huron St., Suite 500, Denver, CO 80234-3438. 303-452-1968. E-mail: editorial@memorymakersmagazine.com. Website: www.memory-makersmagazine.com. 6-7x/yr. $5.95/$30. Circ.: 260,000. Deborah Mock, Editor. **Description:** Magazine on scrapbooking, covering all aspects of the craft (including preservation issues and page ideas). Feature articles run 800-1,000 words. **Columns, Departments:** Departments cover safety issues of products, technology, beginner issues, writing help, and craft ideas; 400-700 words; $200-$350. **Tips:** "Break into our market by offering new and innovative ideas. Avoid very basic scrapbook articles that do not show knowledge of the craft. View a recent issue to get an idea of the topics we cover." **Queries:** Not necessary. **E-Queries:** Yes. **Unsolicited mss:** Accepts. **Response:** 1 month. **Freelance Content:** 40%. **Rights:** 1st world rights.

MINIATURE COLLECTOR

Scott Publications, Inc., 801 W Norton Ave., Suite 200, Muskegon, MI 49441. 231-733-9382. E-mail: contactus@scottpublications.com. Website: www.scottpublications.com. Monthly. $37.95/yr. Circ.: 44,000. Barbara Aardema, Editor. **Description:** Outstanding 1/12-scale and other scale (dollhouse) miniatures and the people who make and collect them. Original, illustrated how-to projects for making miniatures; 800-1,000 words; pay varies. **Queries:** Preferred. **Payment:** On publication.

MODEL AIRPLANE NEWS

Air Age Publishing, Inc., 100 E Ridge Rd., Ridgefield, CT 06877-4623. 203-431-9000. E-mail: man@airage.com. Website: www.modelairplanenews.com. Monthly. $34.95/yr. Circ.: 100,000. Debra Cleghorn, Executive Editor. **Description:** For enthusiasts of radio-controlled model airplanes. Articles include advice from experts in the radio-controlled aviation field; also pieces on design and construction of model airplanes, reviews of new products. Pay varies. **Queries:** Preferred.

MODEL RAILROADER

Kalmbach Publishing Co., 21027 Crossroads Circle, Waukesha, WI 53187. 262-796-8776. E-mail: mrmag@mrmag.com. Website: www.modelrailroader.com. Monthly. $4.95/$39.95. Circ.: 190,000. Terry Thompson, Editor. **Description:** Everything related to the hobby of model railroading. Covers hobby topics with expanded reporting. **Nonfiction:** How-to stories on model railroading; $90/printed page. **Tips:** Authors must be model railroad hobbyists. **Queries:** Preferred. **E-Queries:** Yes. **Unsolicited mss:** Accepts. **Rights:** All. **Payment:** On acceptance.

MODEL RETAILER

Kalmbach Publishing Co., 21027 Crossroads Circle, Waukesha, WI 53187. 262-796-8776. Website: www.modelretailer.com. Monthly. Harold L. Miller, Editor. **Description:** Trade publication for hobby store owners covering the business of hobbies, from financial and shop management issues to industry trends and the latest in product releases. Provides hobby store entrepreneurs with the tools and information they need to be successful retailers. **Nonfiction:** Articles should provide tips or hints on how to be successful in this industry; 1,500 words. **Fillers:** Cartoons and hobby-related jokes; 500 words. **Queries:** Not necessary. **E-Queries:** Yes. **Unsolicited mss:** Accepts. **Response:** 4 weeks. **Freelance Content:** 5%. **Rights:** FNAR and electronic. **Payment:** On acceptance.

MODELER'S RESOURCE
4120 Douglas Blvd., #306-372, Granite Bay, CA 95746-5936. 916-784-9517. E-mail: modres@surewest.net. Website: www.modelersresource.com. Quarterly. Fred DeRuvo, Executive Publisher. **Description:** For builders of models, especially sci-fi, fantasy, vehicular, and figures. Each issue includes previews, photos, reviews, interviews, show coverage, and features on the latest genre kits; 2,000-2,500 words. **Tips:** Occasionally works with new writers. Seeks articles that go beyond the norm. Be clear and concise, yet allow your personal style to flow. "Often, new writers tend to not be instructive enough, or conversely, tend to go off on tangents." **E-Queries:** Yes. **Response:** 2-4 weeks. **SASE Required:** Yes. **Freelance Content:** 10-15%. **Rights:** All. **Contact:** Managing Editor.

NEEDLEWORK RETAILER
See full listing in Business category.

NEW ENGLAND ANTIQUES JOURNAL
Turley Publications, 24 Water St., Palmer, MA 01069. 800-432-3505. E-mail: visit@antiquesjournal.com. Website: www.antiquesjournal.com. Monthly. $3/$22.95. Circ.: 25,000. **Description:** For antiques professionals and casual collectors. Includes event calendars, auction coverage, and more. Also, "Living with Antiques" section with features on preserving and restoring antiques and historic properties. Articles run 2,000 words; $200-$295. **Tips:** Submit well-researched articles with at least 12 high-quality images. **Queries:** Preferred. **E-Queries:** Yes. **Unsolicited mss:** Accepts. **Response:** 1-2 months. **Freelance Content:** 50%. **Payment:** On acceptance.

PETERSEN'S PHOTOGRAPHIC MAGAZINE
PRIMEDIA Enthusiast Group, 6420 Wilshire Blvd., Los Angeles, CA 90048-5502. 323-782-2200. E-mail: photographic@primediacmmg.com. Website: www.photographic.com. Monthly. $11.97/yr. Circ.: 204,500. Ron Leach, Editor-in-Chief. **Description:** On all phases of still photography, for the amateur and advanced photographer. **Payment:** On publication.

PIECEWORK
Interweave Press, 201 E 4th St., Loveland, CO 80537. 970-669-7672. E-mail: piecework@interweave.com. Website: www.interweave.com. Bimonthly. $5.99/$29.95. Circ.: 47,000. Jeane Hutchins, Editor. **Description:** On needlework and textile history. Stories and projects based on makers and techniques from needlework's rich past. **Nonfiction:** Well-researched articles on history of needlework techniques, motifs, and artists; 1,500-2,000 words; $100-$300. **Tips:** Prefers stories with needle-

work projects to demonstrate techniques covered in the article. Contact for upcoming editorial themes. **Queries:** Preferred. **E-Queries:** Yes. **Unsolicited mss:** Accepts. **Response:** Queries 1-2 weeks submissions 1-4 months. **SASE Required:** Yes. **Freelance Content:** 80%. **Rights:** FNAR. **Payment:** On publication.

POPULAR MECHANICS

The Hearst Corp., 810 Seventh Ave., Fl. 6, New York, NY 10019-5818. 212-649-2000. E-mail: popularmechanics@hearst.com; joldham@hearst.com. Website: www.popularmechanics.com. Monthly. $19.97/yr. Circ.: 1,200,000. Joseph Oldham, Editor-in-Chief. **Description:** Latest developments in mechanics, industry, science, telecommunications. **Nonfiction:** Features on hobbies with a mechanical slant; how-tos on home and shop projects; features on outdoor adventures, boating, and electronics. Photos and sketches a plus. 300-1,500 words; to $1,500 (to $500 for short pieces). **Rights:** All. **Payment:** On acceptance. **Contact:** Sarah Deem, Managing Editor.

POPULAR WOODWORKING

F&W Publications, Inc., 4700 E Galbraith Rd., Cincinnati, OH 45236. 513-531-2690. E-mail: popwood@fwpubs.com; kara.gebhart@fwpubs.com. Website: www.popularwoodworking.com. Bimonthly. $23.97/yr. Circ.: 187,200. Steve Shanesy, Editor. **Description:** Projects for the home woodworker. Emphasis on practical techniques that have stood the test of time. How-to (on woodworking projects, with plans), humor (woodworking ancedotes), technical (woodworking techniques); $150/page and up. **Tips:** Tool reviews written in-house. No profiles of woodworkers. Submissions should include materials list, complete diagrams (blueprints not necessary), and discussion of the step-by-step process. "We have become more selective by accepting only practical, attractive projects with quality construction." **Queries:** Preferred. **E-Queries:** Yes. **Unsolicited mss:** Accepts. **Response:** 3-4 months. **SASE Required:** Yes. **Freelance Content:** 30%. **Rights:** 1st worldwide, 2nd. **Payment:** On acceptance. **Contact:** Kara Gebhart, Associate Editor.

QUILTWORKS TODAY

Chitra Publications, 2 Public Ave., Montrose, PA 18801-1220. 570-278-1984. E-mail: chitra@epix.net. Website: www.quilttownusa.com. Bimonthly. $26.95/yr. Circ.: 79,000. **Description:** Colorful pictures, quilting-world news, and projects for traditional and original designs from teachers and talented quilters. Articles on quilt history, techniques, tools, patterns, book/product reviews, etc.; 750-1,500 words; $75. **Tips:** "We offer complete directions and diagrams for completing quilt projects as well as interesting and instructional articles concerning all aspects of quilting. Articles should be informative to quilters, presenting new ideas or techniques." **Queries:** Not necessary. **Unsolicited mss:** Accepts. **Response:** 4 weeks. **SASE Required:** Yes. **Payment:** On publication.

R/C MODELER

R/C Modeler Corp., P.O. Box 487, Sierra Madre, CA 91025. 626-355-1476. E-mail: info@rcmmagazine.com. Website: www.rcmmagazine.com. Monthly. $28/yr. Circ.: 205,000. Patricia E. Crews, Publisher/Editor. **Description:** For the radio-control model aircraft enthusiast. How-to pieces related to radio-control model aircraft, helicopters, boats, cars, etc. Pays $50-$350 for features; $50-$250 for other articles. **Queries:** Not necessary. **E-Queries:** Yes. **Response:** 1-3 weeks. **SASE Required:** Yes. **Freelance Content:** 60%. **Rights:** 1st worldwide. **Payment:** On publication.

RADIO CONTROL CAR ACTION

Air Age, Inc., 100 E Ridge Rd., Ridgefield, CT 06877-4606. 203-431-9000. Website: www.rccaraction.com. Monthly. $34.95/yr. Circ.: 80,000. Peter Vieira, Executive Editor. **Description:** On all aspects of R/C cars including product reviews, how-to articles, race coverage, home-builts and more. Feature articles and columns present technical and general information on building electric and gas RC cars, modifications, modeling equipment, major competitive events, modeling personalities and products. Every issue includes "how-to" articles and in-depth, full-color product evaluations are featured along with many articles for beginners. **Tips:** "Writers must have some sort of RC (radio control) experience. A writing sample should be sent first (using most current issue as a guide) and RC history should be included with sample." **Queries:** Not necessary. **E-Queries:** Yes. **Unsolicited mss:** Accepts. **Rights:** 1st serial publication rights. **Payment:** On publication.

RAILROAD MODEL CRAFTSMAN

Carstens Publications, Inc., P.O. Box 700, Newton, NJ 07860-0700. 973-383-3355. E-mail: bills@rrmodelcraftsman.com. Website: www.rrmodelcraftsman.com. Monthly. $34.95/yr. Circ.: 75,000. William C. Schaumburg, Editor. **Description:** How-to articles on scale model railroading; cars, operation, scenery, etc.

RUBBERSTAMPMADNESS

408 SW Monroe #210, Corvallis, OR 97330. 541-752-0075. E-mail: rsm@rsmadness.com. Website: www.rsmadness.com. Bimonthly. $5.95/$24.95. Circ.: 44,000. Roberta Sperling, Publisher/Editor. **Description:** For rubber stamp artists and collectors. Articles and features explore the creative use of artistic rubber stamps. Issues include stories of artists, new product information, book reviews, convention calendars, a stamp news column, and basic, intermediate, and advanced stamping techniques. **Queries:** Required. **E-Queries:** Yes. **Unsolicited mss:** Does not accept.

RUG HOOKING

Stackpole Magazines, 1300 Market St., Suite 202, Lemoyne, PA 17043. 717-234-5091. E-mail: rughook@paonline.com. Website: www.rughookingonline.com. 5x/yr. $6.95/$27.95. Virginia P. Stimmel, Editor. **Description:** Instructional how-to pieces on rug hooking for beginners and advanced artists. Also, profiles of fiber artists. Articles run 500-3,000 words; pay varies. **Queries:** Preferred. **E-Queries:** Yes. **Unsolicited mss:** Accepts. **Response:** 3 months. **SASE Required:** Yes.

SCALE AUTO

Kalmbach Publishing Co., 21027 Crossroads Circle, Waukesha, WI 53187. 262-796-8776. E-mail: editor@scaleautomag.com. Website: www.scaleautomag.com. 8x/yr. $29.95/yr. Circ.: 30,000. James Haught, Editor. **Description:** For the adult model builder. Features how-to articles, modeling history, contest coverage and kit and product news. **Nonfiction:** To 3,000 words, with photos; pays $60/page. **Tips:** "For how-to articles, the key is including many clean, crisp, step-by-step photos." **Queries:** Required. **E-Queries:** Yes. **Unsolicited mss:** Accepts. **Response:** 90 days. **Freelance Content:** 50%. **Rights:** All. **Payment:** On acceptance.

SEW NEWS

PRIMEDIA Consumer Media & Magazine Group, 741 Corporate Circle, Suite A, Golden, CO 80401. 303-278-1010. E-mail: sewnews@sewnews.com. Website: www.sewnews.com. Monthly. $23.98/yr. Circ.: 173,700. Linda Turner Griepentrog, Editor. **Description:** Seeks articles that teach a specific technique, inspire a reader to try new sewing projects, or inform about an interesting person, company, or project related to sewing, textiles, or fashion. Emphasis on fashion and home decor sewing and sewing-related crafts. Articles, to 3,000 words; pays $25-$400. **Tips:** See website for guidelines. **Queries:** Preferred. **E-Queries:** Yes. **Unsolicited mss:** Do not accept. **Payment:** On acceptance.

SPORTS COLLECTORS DIGEST

Krause Publications, Inc., 700 E State St., Iola, WI 54990. 715-445-2214. E-mail: sports@krause.com. Website: www.krause.com. Weekly. $49.95/yr. Circ.: 30,000. T.S. O'Connell, Editor. **Description:** Articles on old baseball card sets, sports memorabilia, and other collectibles. Pieces run 750-2,000 words; $50-$100. **Art:** B&W photos of unusual collectibles; $25-$150. **Tips:** Sample copy free. **Response:** 5-8 weeks. **Rights:** FNASR. **Payment:** On publication.

TEDDY BEAR AND FRIENDS

Ashton International Media, Inc., P.O. Box 10545, Lancaster, PA 17605-0545. 717-393-8371. Website: www.teddybearandfriends.com. Bimonthly. $17.95/yr. Circ.: 30,000. Michilinda Kinsey, Editor-in-Chief. **Description:** For adult collectors of teddy bears; profiles of artists and manufacturers. **Nonfiction:** Articles, 1,000-1,500 words; pays $.30-$.35/word. **Tips:** Now accepting some fiction or personal-experience stories. **Queries:** Preferred. **Payment:** On publication.

TEDDY BEAR REVIEW

Jones Publishing Co., Inc., N7450 Aanstad Rd., P.O. Box 5000, Iola, WI 54945-5000. 715-445-5000. E-mail: editor@teddybearreview.com. Website: www.teddybearreview.com. Bimonthly. $5.99/$24.95. Circ.: 28,000. Trina Laube, Editor. **Description:** For collectors, bearmakers, and teddy bear and soft sculpture enthusiasts. **Nonfiction:** On antique and contemporary teddy bears for makers, collectors, enthusiasts; 1,200-1,500 words; $200. **Tips:** Looking for articles on artists, manufacturers, and antique bears; prefers specialized topics. Submit photos of bears with queries. Readers treat teddy bears as art. No stories from the bear's point-of-view. **Queries:** Preferred. **E-Queries:** Yes. **Unsolicited mss:** Accepts. **Response:** 8-12 weeks. **SASE Required:** Yes. **Freelance Content:** 70%. **Rights:** All. **Payment:** On acceptance.

THREADS

Taunton Press, 63 S Main St., P.O. Box 5506, Newtown, CT 06470. 203-426-8171. E-mail: th@taunton.com. Website: www.taunton.com. Bimonthly. Circ.: 160,000. Carol Spier, Editor. **Description:** Articles on garment construction and embellishment. **Nonfiction:** Technical pieces on garment construction and embellishment by writers who are expert sewers, quilters, embellishers, and other needle workers. Also covers sewing soft furnishings for home decor; $150/published page.

TRAINS

Kalmbach Publishing Co., 21027 Crossroads Circle, Waukesha, WI 53187. 262-796-8776. E-mail: editor@trainsmag.com. Website: www.trainsmag.com. Monthly. $4.95. Circ.: 120,000. Mark W. Hemphill, Editor. **Description:** Railroad news, features, and stories. **Nonfiction:** History, business analysis, economics, technology, and operations studies of railroads in North America and elsewhere. Occasional first-person recollections. 600-8,000 words; $.10-$.15/word. **Art:** 35mm or medium-format slides; quality 8x10 or larger color and B&W prints; $30-$300. **Tips:** Avoid first-person travelogues or trip reports, unless historical. Writers require a good knowledge of industry and its technology. "We're a technically demanding publication for the railroad industry and knowledgeable railroad enthusiasts." **Queries:** Preferred. **E-Queries:** Yes. **Unsolicited mss:** Accepts. **Response:** Queries 60 days, submissions 90 days. **SASE Required:** Yes. **Freelance Content:** 90%. **Rights:** All (manuscripts), one-time (art). **Payment:** On acceptance.

WATERCOLOR

See full listing in Arts & Architecture category.

WESTERN & EASTERN TREASURES

P.O. Box 219, San Anselmo, CA 94979. 415-454-3936. E-mail: treasurenet@prodigy.net. Website: www.treasurenet.com. Monthly. $4.95/$29.95. Circ.: 100,000. Rosemary Anderson, Editor. **Description:** For metal detectorists, covers all aspects of the hobby. Field-proven advice and instruction; entertaining presentation. **Nonfiction:** Articles new, true and treasure-oriented, from all fields of responsible recreational metal detecting. 1,500 words; $.02-$.04/word. **Art:** Color photo prints/35mm or 300 dpi TIF or JPEG. $5-$7.50, $50-$100 (cover). **Queries:** Not necessary. **E-Queries:** No. **Unsolicited mss:** Accepts. **Response:** 1 month. **SASE Required:** Yes. **Freelance Content:** 100%. **Rights:** All rights reserved. **Payment:** On publication.

WILDFOWL CARVING MAGAZINE

Stackpole, Inc., 1300 Market St. Suite 202, Lemoyne, PA 17043-1420. 717-234-5091. E-mail: wcc@paonline.com. Website: www.wildfowl-carving.com. Quarterly. $29.95/yr. Circ.: 13,000. Candice Tennant, Editor-in-Chief. **Description:** How-to and reference articles on bird carving and collecting antique and contemporary carvings; length and pay varies. **Queries:** Preferred. **Payment:** On acceptance.

WOODWORK

Ross Periodicals, 42 Digital Dr., Suite 5, Novato, CA 94949. 415-382-0580. E-mail: woodwork@rossperiodicals.com. Bimonthly. $4.99/$17.95. Circ.: 70,000. John Lavine, Editor. **Description:** Covers all aspects of woodworking. Assumes medium to advanced understanding in technical articles. Also, artist profiles, reviews. **Nonfiction:** Profiles, technical articles, projects, how-to; also shows, exhibition reviews, etc.; 1,000-4,000 words; $150-$200/printed page. **Queries:** Preferred. **E-Queries:** Yes. **Unsolicited mss:** Accepts. **Freelance Content:** 90%. **Rights:** FNAR. **Payment:** On publication.

YELLOWBACK LIBRARY

P.O. Box 36172, Des Moines, IA 50315. 515-287-0404. Monthly. $36/yr. Circ.: 500. Gil O'Gara, Editor. **Description:** For collectors, dealers, enthusiasts and researchers of children's series books such as Hardy Boys, Nancy Drew, Tom Swift. Dime novels and related juvenile literature also included. **Nonfiction:** Especially interested in interviews with, or articles by, past and present writers of juvenile series fiction; 300-3,000 words. **Tips:** No articles that ridicule the literature or try to fit it into a political, sexual, psychological, or religious context. Nostalgic reflections okay if interesting. **Queries:** Preferred. **E-Queries:** No. **Unsolicited mss:** Accepts. **Response:** 2-7 days. **Freelance Content:** 100%. **Payment:** In copies.

HOME & GARDEN

(See also Lifestyles)

AFRICAN VIOLET MAGAZINE

African Violet Society of America, Inc., 2375 North St., Beaumont, TX 77702. 409-839-4725. E-mail: avsa@earthlink.net. Website: www.avsa.org. Bimonthly. $25/yr. Circ.: 10,000. Ruth Rumsey, Editor. **Description:** On African violets: techniques, methods, history, personal experience, etc.; 700-1,400 words; no payment offered.

THE AMERICAN GARDENER

American Horticultural Society, 7931 E Boulevard Dr., Alexandria, VA 22308-1300. 703-768-5700. E-mail: editor@ahs.org. Website: www.ahs.org. Bimonthly. $4.95. Circ.: 32,000. David J. Ellis, Editor. **Description:** Feature-length articles sought include in-depth profiles of individual plant groups, descriptions of innovative landscape design projects (especially relating to use of regionally native plants or naturalistic gardening), profiles of prominent American horticulturists and gardeners, descriptions of historical developments in American gardening, profiles of unusual public or private gardens, and descriptions of important plant breeding and research programs tailored to a lay audience. **Nonfiction:** Features; 1,500-2,500 words; $300-500. **Columns, Departments:** Natural Connections, Conservationist's Notebook, 600-1,000 words; $150-$200. **Tips:** Request writer's guidelines before querying; in queries authors should describe topic, outline major points to be covered, and explain relevance to a national audience of gardeners. First-time authors should send relevant writing samples and qualifications. **Queries:** Preferred. **E-Queries:** No. **Unsolicited mss:** Accepts. **Response:** 90 days. **SASE Required:** Yes. **Freelance Content:** 75%. **Rights:** FNAR and electronic. **Payment:** On publication.

AMERICAN ROSE

P.O. Box 30000, Shreveport, LA 71130-0030. 318-938-5402. E-mail: ars@ars-hq.org. Website: www.ars.org. Monthly. $37/yr. Circ.: 24,500. Michael C. Kromer, Editor. **Description:** On home rose gardens (varieties, products, helpful advice, rose care, etc.). **Queries:** Preferred.

ATLANTA HOMES AND LIFESTYLES

Weisner Publishing, LLC, 1100 Johnson Ferry Rd., Suite 595, Atlanta, GA 30342-1743. 404-252-6670. Website: www.atlantahomesmag.com. Monthly. $25/yr. Circ.: 32,700. Clint Smith, Editor-in-Chief. **Description:** Original stories with local angle on homes, gardening, food, wine, entertaining, and remodeling; 300-1,200 words; $75-$500. Most pieces are by assignment only. **Queries:** Required. **Unsolicited mss:** Do not accept. **Response:** 3 months. **SASE Required:** Yes. **Freelance Content:** 50%. **Payment:** On acceptance.

BETTER HOMES AND GARDENS

Meredith Corp., 1716 Locust St., Des Moines, IA 50309-3038. 515-284-3000. Website: www.bhg.com. Monthly. $2.99/$19. Circ.: 7,600,000. Karol DeWulf Nickell, Editor-in-Chief. **Description:** Home and family magazine. Covers building/remodeling, decorating, food/entertaining, gardening/outdoor living, money management, health/fitness, and travel. **Tips:** "A freelancer's best chances are in travel, health, parenting, and education. No political subjects, poetry, beauty, or fiction." **Queries:** Preferred. **E-Queries:** No. **Unsolicited mss:** Do not accept. **Response:** 2-3 weeks. **SASE Required:** Yes. **Freelance Content:** 15%. **Rights:** All. **Payment:** On acceptance. **Contact:** Lamont Olson, Managing Editor.

BIRDS AND BLOOMS

Reiman Publications/Reader's Digest Assn., 5400 S 60th St., Greendale, WI 53129. 414-423-0100. E-mail: editors@birdsandblooms.com. Website: www.birdsandblooms.com. Bimonthly. $17.98/yr. Circ.: 1,600,000. Jeff Nowak, Editor. **Description:** For people who love the beauty of their own backyard. Focuses on backyard birding and gardening. **Nonfiction:** First-person experiences from your own backyard; 200-900 words; $100-$200. **Fillers:** 50-300 words; $50-$75. **Art:** Slides or prints; $75-$300. **Tips:** Write conversationally, include tips to benefit readers, keep stories short and to the point. Submit photos. No bird rescue stories. Sample copy $2. **Queries:** Not necessary. **E-Queries:** Yes. **Unsolicited mss:** Accepts. **Response:** Queries 1-2 months, submissions 2-3 months. **SASE Required:** Yes. **Freelance Content:** 25%. **Rights:** FNAR. **Payment:** On publication.

CANADIAN GARDENING

Avid Media, Inc., 340 Ferrier St., Suite 210, Markham, Ontario L3R 2Z5 Canada. 905-475-8440. Website: www.canadiangardening.com. 8x/yr. $24.95/yr. Circ.: 152,000. Aldona Satterthwaite, Editor. **Description:** On gardening in Canada. Presents practical home gardening solutions and seeks to inspire readers with new ideas. Canadian angle imperative. **Nonfiction:** How-to pieces (to 1,000 words) on garden projects, include introduction and step-by-step instructions. Profiles of gardens (to 1,500 words). Pays $125 and up. **Columns, Departments:** 200-400 words. **Queries:** Preferred. **Payment:** On acceptance.

CAROLINA GARDENER

P.O. Box 4504, Greensboro, NC 27404-4504. 336-574-0087. E-mail: editor@carolinagardener.com. Website: www.carolinagardener.com. Bimonthly. $21.95/yr. Circ.: 27,000. L.A. Jackson, Editor. **Description:** Specific to Southeast gardening (profiles of gardens in the region, new cultivars, "good ol' southern heirlooms"). Articles run 750-1,000 words; $175. Slides and illustrations essential. **Queries:** Required. **Payment:** On publication.

COASTAL LIVING

Southern Progress Corp., 2100 Lakeshore Dr., Birmingham, AL 35209-6721. E-mail: jennifer_chappell@timeinc.com. Website: www.coastalliving.com. 8x/yr. $3.95/$18. Circ.: 600,000. Kay A. Fuston, Editor. **Description:** "Coastal Living, the magazine for people who love the coast, celebrates life along our shores. From the inviting homes that fill our pages to the relaxed destinations we discover for our readers and the interesting characters we meet along the way, the magazine reflects not only a lifestyle, but a state of mind." Articles run 800-1,000 words; $1/word. **Tips:** Writer's guidelines available. **Queries:** Required. **E-Queries:** No. **Unsolicited mss:** Does not accept. **Response:** 2-4 weeks **Freelance Content:** 50%. **Rights:** 1st periodical and electronic.

COLORADO HOMES AND LIFESTYLES

Wiesner Publishing, LLC, 7009 S Potomac St., Suite 200, Centennial, CO 80112-4034. 303-397-7600. Website: www.coloradohomesmag.com. 9x/yr. $3.95/$19.97. Circ.: 35,000. Matthew Dakotah, Editorial Director. **Description:** Articles, 1,300-1,500 words, on Colorado homes, design trends, lifestyles, and culture. Features Colorado's finest design and architecture. **Queries:** Required. **E-Queries:** No. **Payment:** On acceptance.

COUNTRY GARDENS

Meredith Corp., 1716 Locust St., Des Moines, IA 50309-3023. 515-284-3515. E-mail: cgardens@mdp.com. Website: www.countryhomemagazine.com. Quarterly. $19.97/yr. Circ.: 350,000. Doug Jimerson, Editor-in-Chief. **Description:** Features gardens that are informal, lush, and old-fashioned. Stories emphasize both inspiration and information. How-tos, profiles of gardeners, garden-related travel, food, projects, decorating, etc.; 750-1,500 words; $500-$1,500. **Queries:** Required.

COUNTRY KITCHENS

Harris Publications, Inc., 1115 Broadway, Fl. 8, New York, NY 10010-2803. 212-807-7100. Semi-annual. Circ.: 325,000. Barbara Jacksier, Editor. **Description:** Offers bright, inviting, and affordable decorating ideas and tips for kitchens. **Queries:** Preferred.

COUNTRY LIVING

The Hearst Corp., 224 W 57th St., New York, NY 10019. 212-649-3500. E-mail: countryliving@hearst.com. Website: www.countryliving.com. Monthly. $3.50/issue. Circ.: 1,700,000. Nancy Mernit Soriano, Editor-in-Chief. **Description:** Covers lifestyle, decorating, antiques, cooking, travel, home building, crafts, and gardens. Articles run 500+ words; pay varies. **Tips:** Avoid grandmother stories. **Queries:** Preferred. **E-Queries:** No. **Unsolicited mss:** Does not accept. **Response:** 8 weeks. **SASE Required:** Yes. **Freelance Content:** 30%. **Rights:** All, 1st serial. **Payment:** On acceptance. **Contact:** Charlotte Barnard, Deputy Editor.

DECOR & STYLE MAGAZINE

2100 Publishing Co., Inc., 337 S Cedros Ave., Suite A1, Solana Beach, CA 92075-1951. 858-755-4534. E-mail: editdept@decorandstyle.com. Website: www.decorandstyle.com. Monthly. $21/yr. Circ.: 50,000. Shana Wilson, Executive Editor. **Description:** On architecture, interior design, and an elegant style of living. Offers both cutting-edge and classic designs. Seeks articles on signature homes, pools and spas, remodeling ideas, home furnishings, art and antiques, home theater, lighting, wine, food, fashion, and entertaining. Features run 2,000-3,000 words; $100-$275. Short articles run 1,000-2,000 words; $100-$200. **Tips:** "We seek material that speaks to affluent, sophisticated, well-traveled homeowners. Avoid how-to articles and do-it-yourself projects." **Queries:** Preferred. **E-Queries:** Yes. **Unsolicited mss:** Accepts. **Response:** 2 months. **Freelance Content:** 40%. **Rights:** All.

ELLE DECOR

Hachette Filipacchi Media U.S., Inc., 1633 Broadway, Fl. 41, New York, NY 10019-6708. 212-767-5800. E-mail: elledecor@hfmus.com. Website: www.elledecor.com. 8x/yr. $29/yr. Circ.: 473,000. Margaret Russell, Editor-in-Chief. **Description:** On designers and craftspeople, and on houses and apartments with notable interior design and/or architecture. Articles run 300-800 words; pays $2/word. **Tips:** Send query via regular mail, include photos of designers and their work. **Queries:** Preferred. **E-Queries:** No. **Payment:** On publication.

FINE GARDENING

Taunton Press, P.O. Box 5506, 63 S Main St, Newtown, CT 06470-5506. 203-426-8171. E-mail: fg@taunton.com. Website: www.finegardening.com. Bimonthly. $29.95/yr. Circ.: 200,000. Todd Meier, Editor. **Description:** For readers with a serious interest in gardening. Focuses on ornamental gardening and landscaping. **Nonfiction:** How-tos, garden design, as well as pieces on specific plants or garden tools. Picture possibilities are essential; 800-2,000 words; $300-$1,200. **Art:** Photos; $50-$500. **Queries:** Required. **Payment:** On acceptance.

GARDEN COMPASS

Streamopolis, 1450 Front St., San Diego, CA 92101. 619-239-2202. E-mail: editor@gardencompass.com. Website: www.gardencompass.com. Bimonthly. $18.50/yr. Circ.: 51,000. Siri Kay Jostad, Editor. **Description:** For California gardening enthusiasts. Features, to 2,000 words. **E-Queries:** Yes. **Freelance Content:** 20%.

GARDEN DESIGN

World Publications, LLC, 460 N Orlando Ave., Suite 200, Winter Park, FL 32789. 407-628-4802. E-mail: editor@gardendesignmag.com. Website: www.gardendesignmag.com. 6x/yr. $23.95/yr. Circ.: 305,600. Bill Marken, Editor-in-Chief. **Description:** On private, public, and community gardens; articles on art and history as they relate to gardens; 500-1,000 words; pays from $1/word. **Payment:** Within 30 days of contract.

GARDEN RAILWAYS

See full listing in Hobbies, Crafts, Collecting category.

GARDEN SHOWCASE

P.O. Box 23669, Portland, OR 97281-3669. 503-684-0153. E-mail: gseditor@gardenshowcase.com. Website: www.gardenshowcase.com. 4x/yr. $9.95/yr. Circ.: 30,000. Lynn Lustberg, Editor. **Description:** Distributed in Oregon and Washington. Features regional plants, gardens, and nurseries, with gardening ideas and examples. **Nonfiction:** Articles on outstanding gardens, etc. 800-1,000 words; $160. **Columns, Departments:** Gardening 101, Speaking Organically, Success with Vegetables; 380-400 words; $100. **Queries:** Preferred. **E-Queries:** Yes. **Unsolicited mss:** Accepts. **Response:** 1-3 months. **SASE Required:** Yes. **Freelance Content:** 100%. **Rights:** FNAR. **Payment:** On publication.

GROWING EDGE MAGAZINE

New Moon Publishing, Inc., P.O. Box 1027, Corvallis, OR 97339-1027. 541-757-2511. E-mail: editor@growingedge.com. Website: www.growingedge.com. Bimonthly. $26.95/yr. Circ.: 20,000. Tom Weller, Editor. **Description:** News and information for indoor and outdoor growers. Covers hydroponic, aquaponic, and soilless greenhouse gardening. Targets both hobby and commercial growers. Articles to 3,000 words; $.20/word. **Art:** Color prints or slides; high-res digital. Pays $25 for inside photo; $175 for cover. **Tips:** "Supply detailed queries first. Know our audience. We do not publish material on traditional, soil-based gardening." **Queries:** Preferred. **E-Queries:** Yes. **Unsolicited mss:** Accepts. **Response:** 1-2 months. **SASE Required:** Yes. **Freelance Content:** 80%. **Rights:** 1st world serial, 1st anthology, and non-exclusive electronic. **Payment:** On publication.

THE HERB COMPANION

Ogden Publications, Inc., 1504 SW 42nd St., Topeka, KS 80537. 785-274-4300. E-mail: editor@herbcompanion.com. Website: www.herbcompanion.com. Bimonthly. $24/yr. Circ.: 100,000. KC Compton, Editor-in-Chief. **Description:** For herb gardeners, cooks, crafters, and general enthusiasts. **Nonfiction:** Practical horticultural information, original recipes using herbs, well-researched historical insights, step-by-step instructions for herbal craft projects, book reviews; 500-2,000 words; $.33/word, negotiable. **Tips:** "Technical accuracy essential. Strive for conciseness, clear organization; include subheads where appropriate, lists of similar information in chart form." **Queries:** Preferred. **E-Queries:** Yes. **Unsolicited mss:** Accepts. **Response:** 1-3 months. **SASE Required:** Yes. **Freelance Content:** 90%. **Payment:** On acceptance.

THE HERB QUARTERLY

EGW Publishing, 1041 Shary Circle, Concord, CA 94518. 925-671-9852. E-mail: jenniferbarrett@earthlink.net. Website: www.herbquarterly.com. Quarterly. Circ.: 36,753. Jennifer Barrett, Editor. **Description:** Covers the practical and professional aspects of herbs. Practical uses, cultivation, gourmet cooking, landscaping, herb tradition, medicinal herbs, crafts ideas, unique garden designs, profiles of experts, and how-tos for the herb lover; 1,500-3,000 words. **E-Queries:** Yes. **Payment:** On publication.

HOME POOL & BAR-B-QUE

Hawks Media Group, Inc., P.O. Box 272, Cranford, NJ 07016-0272. 908-755-6138. E-mail: jeanette@hawksmedia.com. Annual. $10. Circ.: 4,500. Jeanette Hawks, Editor. **Description:** For upscale owners of pools, hot tubs, and spas. **Nonfiction:** Pool experiences, design, landscape, swimwear, recipes, etc.; 1,500 words; $40. **Art:** Photos of pools. spas, and barbecue grills (built-in especially); B&W, color, or digital photos; $10. **Queries:** Preferred. **E-Queries:** Yes. **Unsolicited mss:** Accepts. **Response:** 1 month. **SASE Required:** Yes. **Freelance Content:** 40%. **Rights:** All, may reassign. **Payment:** On publication.

HORTICULTURE, GARDENING AT ITS BEST

F&W Publications, Inc., 98 N Washington St., Boston, MA 02114-1922. 617-742-5600. E-mail: edit@hortmag.com. Website: www.hortmag.com. Bimonthly. $28/yr. Circ.: 209,900. Thomas Fischer, Editor. **Description:** Authoritative, well-written articles on all aspects of gardening; 500-2,500 words; pay varies. **Queries:** Required. **Payment:** On publication.

HOUSE BEAUTIFUL

The Hearst Corp., 1700 Broadway, Fl. 29, New York, NY 10019-5905. 212-903-5084. Website: www.housebeautiful.com. Monthly. $19.97/yr. Circ.: 853,000. Mark Mayfield, Editor-in-Chief. **Description:** Pieces on design, travel, and gardening. **Nonfiction:** A literary, personal memoir, each month, 2,000 words, "Thoughts of Home." Pays $1/word. **Tips:** Send detailed outline and SASE. **Queries:** Preferred. **Payment:** On acceptance.

LANDSCAPE TRADES

See full listing in Trade & Technical category.

LOG HOME DESIGN IDEAS

Active Interest Media, 1620 S Lawe St., Suite 2, Appleton, WI 54915-2411. 920-830-1701. E-mail: editor@aimmedia.com. Website: www.lhdi.com. 9x/yr. $19.95/yr. Circ.: 150,000. Teresa Hilgenberg, Editor. **Description:** For people interested in log homes. **Queries:** Preferred.

LOG HOME LIVING

4125 Lafayette Center Dr., Suite 100, Chantilly, VA 20151-1208. 703-222-9411. E-mail: editor@loghomeliving.com. Website: www.loghomeliving.com. Monthly. $19.95/yr. Circ.: 110,000. Kevin Ireland, Editor-in-Chief. **Description:** For people who own or are planning to build contemporary log homes. Readers are mostly married couples, 30-45 years old, well-educated, do-it-yourselfers. **Nonfiction:** About people who have built modern log homes from manufactured or handcrafted kits. Conversational; describe home, tell how it came to be. Emphasize special elements: intent, design, solutions to problems, features, furnishings, interior design, landscaping; 1,000-2,000 words; $350-$550/article. **Art:** If possible, please include color (professional quality) photos; floor plans, construction costs, schedules a plus. **Tips:** "We seek long-term relationships with contributors who deliver quality work." **Queries:** Preferred. **E-Queries:** Yes. **SASE Required:** Yes. **Freelance Content:** 50%. **Rights:** FNASR. **Payment:** On acceptance.

METROPOLITAN HOME

Hachette Filipacchi Media U.S., 1633 Broadway, Fl. 41, New York, NY 10019-6708. 212-767-6041. Bimonthly. $19.94/yr. Circ.: 604,000. Donna Warner, Editor-in-Chief. **Description:** Interior design and home furnishing articles with emphasis on lifestyle. Service and informational articles on furniture and home products, gardening, food, collecting, trends, etc. **Tips:** Send clips. **Queries:** Preferred. **E-Queries:** No.

MILWAUKEE HOME

Trails Media Group, 6525 W Bluemound Rd. #36, Milwaukee, WI 53213. 414-771-9945. E-mail: kbast@wistrails.com; khansen@wistrails.com. Website: www.milwaukee-home.com. 6x/yr. $4.95/$24.95. Circ.: 15,000. **Description:** Celebrates fine living in southeastern Wisconsin. Readership is primarily upscale women in their 40s who enjoy home and garden designs and are looking for inspiring ideas. Pieces run

500-1,500 words; $.25/word. **Columns, Departments:** Goings On (events); Profiles (people in the home/garden industry, firms, retail outlets, artisans, craftsman, others); Insights (design and décor tips, products, trends, collectibles, artwork, etc.); Indulgence (luxury items); Entertaining (ideas for inspired gatherings, recipes from local culinary talent, etc.); In the Garden (practical and inspired ideas for your garden and landscape); Yard Work (products); Of Historic Note (home/garden area history); Back Door (expert advice). **Tips:** "We work with professional writers who have knowledge or expertise in the areas of homes, gardens, design, architecture, and home entertaining, and who know the Greater Metropolitan Milwaukee area. Please be aware of recent coverage in the magazine." **Queries:** Required. **E-Queries:** Yes. **Unsolicited mss:** Accepts. **Response:** 1-2 months. **SASE Required:** Yes. **Freelance Content:** 80%. **Rights:** FNAR. **Payment:** On publication. **Contact:** Kate Bast, Editor (Features); Kristine Hansen, Assistant Editor (Departments).

NATURAL HOME
Interweave Press, 201 E 4th St., Loveland, CO 80537-5655. 970-669-7672. E-mail: robynl@naturalhomemag.com. Website: www.naturalhomemagazine.com. Bimonthly. $24.95/yr. Circ.: 85,000. Robyn Griggs Lawrence, Editor-in-Chief. **Description:** Promotes earth-inspired living. Features "green," sustainable homes and lifestyles. Articles, 250-1,500 words; $.33-$.50/word. **Tips:** "We need fresh, cutting-edge ideas on green living; also small, newsy items for front-of-the-book Good to Know section. Submit query or complete manuscript. Send e-mail for guidelines." **Queries:** Preferred. **E-Queries:** Yes. **Unsolicited mss:** Accepts. **Rights:** FNAR.

NORTHWEST GARDEN NEWS
Taking Root Publishing, LLC, P.O. Box 18313, Seattle, WA 98118-1104. 206-725-2394. E-mail: norwesgard@earthlink.net. Website: www.northwestgardennews.com. 9x/yr. $20/yr. Circ.: 35,000. Mary Gutierrez, Publisher/Editor. **Description:** Regional magazine with gardening information for gardeners west of the Cascade Mountains in Washington State. Geared toward zone 8 maritime climate. Pieces run 100-500 words; $50-$100. **E-Queries:** Yes. **Unsolicited mss:** Accepts. **Response:** 3 months. **SASE Required:** Yes. **Freelance Content:** 100%. **Payment:** On publication.

OLD HOUSE INTERIORS
Gloucester Publishers, 108 East Main St., Gloucester, MA 01930. 978-283-3200. E-mail: info@oldhouseinteriors.com. Website: www.oldhouseinteriors.com. Bimonthly. $18/yr. Circ.: 124,000. Patricia Poore, Editor-in-Chief. **Description:** On architecture, decorative arts, and history. **Tips:** The most important thing is the art; when proposing an article, know how it should be illustrated. Professional photos not necessary. Query, with clips. **Payment:** On acceptance.

ORGANIC GARDENING MAGAZINE
Rodale Press, Inc., 33 E Minor St., Emmaus, PA 18098. 610-967-8926. E-mail: og@rodale.com. Website: www.organicgardening.com. 6x/yr. $3.99/$24.96. Circ.: 300,000. Scott Meyer, Editor. **Description:** North America's only gardening

magazine dedicated wholly to organic practices. **Nonfiction:** Gardening how-to, solid organic advice; profiles of organic gardens and gardeners; profiles of a vegetable, fruit, or flower. 1,000-1,800 words; $.50-$1/word. **Columns, Departments:** Plants Worth Having; 300 words; $400. **Queries:** Preferred. **E-Queries:** Yes. **Unsolicited mss:** Accepts. **Response:** Queries 8 weeks, submissions 6 weeks. **SASE Required:** Yes. **Freelance Content:** 40%. **Rights:** All. **Payment:** On acceptance.

SEATTLE HOMES & LIFESTYLES

1221 E Pike St., Suite 305, Seattle, WA 98122. 206-322-6699. Website: www.seattlehomesmag.com. 8x/yr. $3.95/$17.97. Circ.: 30,000. Fred Albert, Editor-in-Chief. **Description:** Upscale regional shelter magazine celebrating the best in residential architecture, interior design and gardening, as well as the people, shopping, and pastimes that make the Puget Sound area special. Articles by assignment only; 150-1,500 words; $30-$375. **Tips:** "Send a resumé and three published clips. We will contact the writer with an assignment if we're interested. Seattle-area writers *only*. Queries with story ideas are discouraged." **Queries:** Does not accept. **E-Queries:** No. **Unsolicited mss:** Does not accept. **SASE Required:** Yes. **Freelance Content:** 60%. **Rights:** FNAR, electronic. **Payment:** On acceptance.

SOUTHERN ACCENTS

Southern Progress Corp., 2100 Lakeshore Dr., Birmingham, AL 35209. 205-445-6000. E-mail: letters@southernaccents.com. Website: www.southernaccents.com. Bimonthly. $28. Circ.: 375,000. Julie Goodwin, Managing Editor. **Description:** Celebrates Southern style in interiors, gardens, art, antiques, and entertaining. Focuses on affluent homes and gardens in a 16-state region. Also features the homes of Southerners living abroad and the travel destinations visited by upscale readership. **Nonfiction:** Query first with appropriate story ideas; 800-1,200 words; pay negotiable. **Queries:** Preferred. **SASE Required:** Yes. **Payment:** On acceptance.

STYLE AT HOME

Transcontinental Media, Inc., 25 Sheppard Ave. W, Suite 100, Toronto, Ontario M2N 6S7 Canada. 416-733-7600. E-mail: ghabs@styleathome.com. Website: www.styleathome.com. 10x/yr. $28/yr. Circ.: 230,000. Gail Johnston Habs, Editor. **Description:** Profiles of Canadian homes, renovation, decoration, and gardening. Canadian content and locations only. Articles run 300-800 words; $300-$800 (Canadian). **Tips:** Writer's guidelines available upon request. **Queries:** Preferred. **E-Queries:** Yes. **Payment:** On acceptance.

SU CASA

4100 Wolcott Ave. NE, Suite B, Albuquerque, NM 87109-5838. 505-344-3294. E-mail: cpoling@sucasamagazine.com. Website: www.sucasamagazine.com. 4x/yr. $4.95/$18 (6 issues). Circ.: 39,000. Charles C. Poling, Editor. **Description:** Showcases the style and design of unique homes in the Southwest. **Nonfiction:** Articles on Southwestern architecture and design; profiles of builders, artisans, artists, and craftspeople; interior design; and other home-related topics; 800-2,000 words;

$250-$500. **Art:** Submit 4x5 transparency, 35mm slides, or hi-res scans. Pays $100/photo if stock; $150 for Hasta la Vista. **Tips:** "Our emphasis is New Mexico-based architecture and building. We don't run how-to features or articles on generalized topics like green building or feng shui. Instead, such concepts are embedded in and illustrated by articles on specific homes and communities in the Southwest." **Queries:** Preferred. **E-Queries:** Yes. **Unsolicited mss:** Accepts. **Response:** 2 weeks. **SASE Required:** Yes. **Freelance Content:** 95%.

SUNSET MAGAZINE
See full listing in Lifestyle Magazines category.

VICTORIAN HOMES
Y-Visionary Publishing, LP, 265 S Anita Dr., Suite 120, Orange, CA 92868. 714-939-9991. E-mail: erika.kotite@prodigy.net. Website: www.victorianhomesmag.com. Bimonthly. $3.99/$19.95. Circ.: 80,000. Erika Kotite, Editor. **Description:** Covers the lifestyle of Victorian Revival. Articles explore decoration and architecture of 19th- and early 20th-century homes restored, decorated and lived in by real people, also period museum houses. **Nonfiction:** On interior design, furnishings, gardens, florals, table settings, and decorative accessories. Also, kitchen or bathroom makeovers, whole-house restorations, renovation tips, paint colors/wall coverings, etc.; 1,000-1,500 words; $400-$500. **Columns, Departments:** Victorian furnishings, antiques, collectibles, lighting, flowers, food, etc. **Queries:** Preferred. **E-Queries:** Accepts. **Unsolicited mss:** Accepts. **Response:** 6-8 weeks **Freelance Content:** 80%. **Rights:** All or FNAR. **Payment:** On acceptance.

WATER GARDENING: THE MAGAZINE FOR POND KEEPERS
Pendall Publishing, P.O. Box 607, St. John, IN 46373-0607. 219-374-9419. E-mail: sue@watergardening.com. Website: www.watergardening.com. Bimonthly. $4.99/$24.99. Circ.: 25,000. Susan Speichert, Editor-in-Chief. **Description:** Hobbyist magazine on how to build, design, landscape, and care for ponds and the plants and fish that live in them. Pieces run 500-1,200 words; $150-$250. **Queries:** Preferred. **E-Queries:** Yes. **Unsolicited mss:** Accepts. **Response:** 6 months. **Rights:** FNAR. **Payment:** On publication.

WOMAN'S DAY GARDENING & DECK DESIGN
Hachette Filipacchi Magazines, 1633 Broadway, Fl. 42, New York, NY 10019-6708. 212-767-6000. E-mail: wdsip@hfmus.com. Website: www.womansday.com/specials. 3x/yr. $4.50(U.S.);$4.99(Canada). Circ.: 450,000. Peter Walsh, Editor. **Description:** Special-interest publication offering gardening tips, designs, and solutions to common problems. Also features outdoor furniture, decks, and other outdoor accessories. **Tips:** Include resumé and recent, related, published clips with all queries. No phone calls. **Queries:** Required. **E-Queries:** Yes. **Unsolicited mss:** Does not accept. **Response:** 2 months. **SASE Required:** Yes. **Freelance Content:** 75%. **Rights:** All. **Payment:** On acceptance. **Contact:** Managing Editor.

HUMOR

ANNALS OF IMPROBABLE RESEARCH

P.O. Box 380853, Cambridge, MA 02238. 617-491-4437.
E-mail: air@improbable.com. Website: www.improbable.com. Bimonthly. $29/yr.
Marc Abrahams, Editor. **Description:** Presents the mischievous, funny, and icono-clastic side of science. Features science reports/analysis and humor; 500-2,000 words.
Queries: Preferred. **E-queries:** Yes. **Unsolicited mss:** Accepts.

THE DOOR MAGAZINE

P.O. Box 1444, Waco, TX 76703-1444. E-mail: dooreditor@earthlink.net.
Website: www.thedoormagazine.com. Bimonthly. $5.98/$29.95. Circ.: 10,000. Robert Darden, Senior Editor. **Description:** Religious humor and satire magazine.
Nonfiction: Articles run 250-800 words; $50-$200. Interviews 2,000 words max.; $250. **Art:** Single-panel cartoon gags; $50/piece. **Tips:** "Read the magazine first! Get our guidelines. We're looking for funny stuff about religion with a point! This is not *Guideposts* or *Reader's Digest*. And absolutely, positively, for the last time—no poetry." **E-Queries:** Yes. **Response:** 3 months. **SASE Required:** Yes. **Freelance Content:** 90%. **Rights:** FNAR. **Payment:** On publication.

THE FUNNY TIMES

2176 Lee Rd., Cleveland Heights, OH 44118. 216-371-8600.
E-mail: ft@funnytimes.com. Website: www.funnytimes.com. Monthly. $2.95/$23.
Circ.: 67,000. Ray Lesser, Editor. **Description:** Humor review. **Fiction:** Stories on anything relating to the general human condition: politics, news, relationships, food, technology, pets, work, death, environmental issues, business, religion, seasonal events etc.; 500-700 words; $60. **Nonfiction:** Essays, interviews, book reviews; to 1,000 words. **Art:** Cartoons, 1-2 pages; $30-$50. **Queries:** Not necessary. **E-Queries:** No. **Unsolicited mss:** Accepts. **Response:** 4-6 weeks. **SASE Required:** Yes. **Rights:** FNAR. **Payment:** On publication.

MAD MAGAZINE

E.C. Publications, Inc., 1700 Broadway, Fl. 5, New York, NY 10011.
Website: www.madmag.com. Monthly. **Description:** Humorous pieces (articles, cover ideas, 1-page gags, etc.) on a wide variety of topics/current trends. Include visual elements with submission. Not interested in movie/tv satires, rewritten Mad-like material, poetry, or song parodies. No e-mail, fax, or phone calls. **Art:** Cartoons, 2-8 -panels (not necessary to include sketches with submission). **Tips:** See website for specific guidelines. **Queries:** Preferred. **E-Queries:** No. **Unsolicited mss:** Accepts. **Response:** 8-12 weeks. **SASE Required:** Yes. **Payment:** On acceptance. **Contact:** *MAD* Submissions Editor.

STITCHES

See full listing in Trade & Technical category.

IN-FLIGHT MAGAZINES

ALASKA AIRLINES MAGAZINE
Paradigm Communications Group, 2701 First Ave., Suite 250, Seattle, WA 98121-1125. 206-441-5871. Monthly. $50/yr. Circ.: 45,700. Paul Frichtl, Editor. **Description:** On business, travel, and profiles of regional personalities for West Coast business travelers; 250-2,500 words; pay varies. **Queries:** Preferred. **Payment:** On publication.

AMERICA WEST AIRLINES MAGAZINE
Skyword Marketing, Inc., 4636 E Elwood St., Suite 5, Phoenix, AZ 85040-1963. 602-997-7200. Website: www.skyword.com. Monthly. $29/yr. Circ.: 130,000. Elizabeth Cullum Bonacci, Managing Editor. **Description:** In-flight magazine on travel, lifestyle, business, the arts, technology, personality profiles, etc. **Tips:** "We offer entertaining articles with an emphasis on first-rate reporting and compelling storytelling, including fiction, arts and culture, and thoughtful essays." **Queries:** Required. **E-Queries:** No.

AMERICAN WAY
American Airlines Publishing, 4255 Amon Carter Blvd., MD-4255, Fort Worth, TX 76155. 817-967-1804. E-mail: editor@americanwaymag.com. Website: www.americanwaymag.com. Biweekly. $72/yr. Circ.: 342,600. Sherri Burns, Editor. **Description:** Travel, business, food and wine, health, technology, fitness, personality profiles, and more. **Queries:** Required. **SASE Required:** Yes. **Contact:** Jill Becker, Senior Editor; Richelle Thomson, Senior Editor; Tracy Staton, Senior Editor.

ENROUTE
Spafax Canada, Inc., 4200, Boul. Saint-Laurent, Bureau 707, Montreal, Quebec H2W 2R2 Canada. 514-844-2001. E-mail: info@enroutemag.net. Monthly. $50/yr. Circ.: 200,000. Arjun Basu, Editor-in-Chief. **Description:** Air Canada in-flight magazine on travel and lifestyle.

HCP/ABOARD PUBLISHING
One Herald Plaza, Fl. 3, Miami, FL 33132. 305-376-5258. E-mail: editorial@aboardpublishing.com. Website: www.aboardpublishing.com. **Description:** Publishes custom publications in the travel/tourism industry including 4 inflight publications for Latin America and the Caribbean, and various hotel publications in Central America, the Caribbean, and the U.S. **Nonfiction:** Travel articles on specific Latin American and Caribbean destinations (also some U.S. destinations); general articles on health, business, cuisine; and celebrity interviews (particularly Latin celebrities). **Queries:** Not necessary. **E-Queries:** Yes. **Unsolicited mss:** Does not accept. **SASE Required:** Yes. **Freelance Content:** 70%. **Rights:** All Western Hemisphere. **Payment:** On publication. **Contact:** Abel Delgado (*Explore, Mundo del Sur, Aeropostal*); Rosa Rojas (*Latitudes*); Vanessa Molina (*Discover Charleston, Discover Bermuda, Cabo San Lucas*).

HEMISPHERES

Pace Communications, 1301 Carolina St., Greensboro, NC 27401. 336-378-6065. E-mail: hemiedit@aol.com. Website: www.hemispheresmagazine.com. Monthly. $50/yr. Circ.: 500,000. Randy Johnson, Editor. **Description:** In-flight magazine for United Airlines. **Fiction:** 1,500-3,000 words; pay varies. **Nonfiction:** Articles on universal issues; 2,000-3,000 words; $.75+ per word. **Columns, Departments:** See writer guidelines; 1,500-1,800 words; $.50/word. **Tips:** "We offer a global perspective in a fresh, artful publication." **Queries:** Preferred. **E-Queries:** Yes. **Unsolicited mss:** Accepts. **Response:** 2 months. **SASE Required:** Yes. **Freelance Content:** 95%. **Rights:** 1st worldwide. **Contact:** Selby Bateman, Senior Editor.

HORIZON AIR

2701 First Ave., Suite 250, Seattle, WA 98121-1123. 206-441-5871. Monthly. $45/yr. Circ.: 416,000. Michele Andrus Dill, Editor. **Description:** For travelers in the Northwest, Silicon Valley, California, Arizona, Southern British Columbia, and Southern Alberta. **Nonfiction:** Business, travel, lifestyle, sports, and leisure; 500-750 words; pay varies. **Columns, Departments:** Personal essay on business, travel, life in Northwest; 500-1,500 words. **Art:** Transparencies, slides. **Tips:** Query with samples (photocopies preferred, not originals). **Queries:** Required. **E-Queries:** No. **Unsolicited mss:** Accepts. **Response:** 1-6 months. **SASE Required:** Yes. **Freelance Content:** 80%. **Rights:** FNASR. **Payment:** On publication.

MIDWEST AIRLINES MAGAZINE

Paradigm Communications Group, 2701 First Ave., Suite 250, Seattle, WA 98121. 206-441-5871. Semi-monthly. Eric Lucas, Managing Editor. **Description:** In-flight magazine for Midwest Airlines. Travel stories, business trends, and general features, all with U.S. focus; 300-2,500 words. **Tips:** Keep queries concise. **Queries:** Required. **E-Queries:** No. **Unsolicited mss:** Does not accept. **Response:** 2 months. **SASE Required:** Yes. **Freelance Content:** 80%. **Rights:** FNAR. **Payment:** On publication.

NORTHWEST AIRLINES WORLD TRAVELER

Skies America Publishing Co., P.O. Box 4005, Beaverton, OR 97076-4005. 503-520-1955. E-mail: editors@skies.com. Monthly. $50. Circ.: 350,000. Matt Williams, Editor. **Description:** For passengers of Northwest Airlines.

SKY

Pace Communications, Inc., 1301 Carolina St., Greensboro, NC 27401. 336-378-6065. E-mail: editorial@delta-sky.com. Website: www.delta-sky.com. Monthly. $50. Circ.: 500,000. Duncan Christy, Editorial Director. **Description:** Delta Airlines in-flight magazine. Nonfiction articles on travel, business travel, lifestyle, high tech, sports, arts, food. Pay varies. **Art:** Color slides. **Queries:** Preferred. **Unsolicited mss:** Does not accept. **SASE Required:** Yes. **Payment:** On acceptance.

SOUTHWEST AIRLINES SPIRIT

American Airlines Publishing, 4255 Amon Carter Blvd., Fort Worth, TX 76155.
817-967-1804. E-mail: editors@spiritmag.com. Website: www.spiritmag.com.
Monthly. Circ.: 380,000. **Description:** Travel/lifestlye publication for passengers on
Southwest Airlines.

SPIRIT OF ALOHA

Honolulu Publishing Company Ltd., 707 Richards St., Suite 525, Honolulu, HI
96813. 808-524-7400. E-mail: tchapman@honpub.com. Website: www.spirito-
faloha.com. Tom Chapman, Editor. **Description:** Magazine for Aloha Airlines with
Hawaiian Island focus. **Queries:** Preferred. **E-Queries:** Yes.

US AIRWAYS ATTACHÉ

Pace Communications, Inc., 1301 Carolina St., Greensboro, NC 27401. 336-378-
6065. E-mail: attacheedit@attachemag.com. Website: www.attachemag.com.
Monthly. $50/yr. Circ.: 375,000. Lance Elko, Editor. **Description:** Entertaining arti-
cles for travelers. Ongoing departments, some features. 350-2,000 words; $1/word.
Columns, Departments: Homefront; Sports; Things that Grow; Things that Go;
Golf; Insider's Guide to... (destination piece). **Tips:** Include clips or list of past clients.
Queries: Required. **E-Queries:** Yes. **Unsolicited mss:** Accepts. **Response:** 1-3
months. **SASE Required:** Yes. **Freelance Content:** 60%. **Rights:** Exclusive worldwide for 120 days. **Payment:** On acceptance.

INSPIRATIONAL

BRAVE HEARTS

Ogden Publications, 1503 SW 42nd St., Topeka, KS 66609. 785-274-4300.
E-mail: jteller@grit.com. Website: www.braveheartsmagazine.com. Quarterly. Circ.:
2,000. Ann Crahan, Editor-in-Chief. **Description:** Written by and for ordinary people who have an inspirational message to share. Seeks short manuscripts (up to 900
words), photographs, prayers, and related material on inspirational subjects. Pays $5-
$12/item. **Tips:** "Our magazine is geared to inspire people each time they open it, to
make them smile. We're looking for articles that tug at the heart, that have a message
to impart, that are inspirational. Avoid sappy or maudlin pieces, or illness-of-the week
type of stories." **Queries:** Does not accept. **E-queries:** No. **Unsolicited mss:**
Accepts. **Response:** 3-6 months. **SASE Required:** Yes. **Freelance Content:**
100%. **Rights:** All. **Payment:** On publication. **Contact:** Jean Teller or Traci Smith,
Managing Editors.

DAILY MEDITATION

P.O. Box 2710, San Antonio, TX 78299. 210-735-5247. Semi-annual. $16/yr.
Circ.: 760. Emilia Devno, Editor. **Description:** Offers inspirational, nonsectarian
religious articles that show the way to self-improvement and greater spiritual growth.
Nonfiction: 300-1,600 words; $.02/word. **Poetry:** To 350 words; $.14/line. **Tips:** No

fiction, handwritten material, meditations, photographs, or dated material. **Queries:** Not necessary. **E-queries:** No. **Unsolicited mss:** Accepts. **SASE Required:** Yes. **Rights:** FNASR. **Payment:** On acceptance.

GUIDEPOSTS

16 E 34th St., New York, NY 10016. 212-251-8100. Website: www.guideposts.com. Monthly. $12.97/yr. Circ.: 3,200,000. Edward Grinnan, Editor. **Description:** First-person inspirational magazine about people overcoming challenges through faith. **Nonfiction:** First-person true stories of people who face challenges, fears, illnesses through faith; 500 words and up; $100-$400. **Fillers:** Spiritual quotes; $25. **Columns, Departments:** What Prayer Can Do (power of prayer); Pass It On (people helping people) His Mysterious Ways (more than coincidence). 50-500 words; $25-$100. **Tips:** "Don't tell an entire life story; pick your specific "take-away" message." **E-queries:** No. **Unsolicited mss:** Accepts. **Response:** 3 months. **SASE Required:** Yes. **Freelance Content:** 75%. **Rights:** All. **Payment:** On publication.

IDEALS

535 Metroplex Dr., Suite 250, Nashville, TN 37211. 615-333-0478. Website: www.idealsbooks.com. Bimonthly. $5.95/$19.95. Circ.: 200,000. **Description:** Inspirational, seasonal poetry and prose, with artwork and photography, in turn on Easter, Mother's Day, Country, Friendship, Thanksgiving, and Christmas. **Fiction:** Holiday themes; 800-1,000 words; $.10/word. **Nonfiction:** On issue's theme; 800-1,000 words; $.10/word. **Poetry:** Light, nostalgic pieces; $10/poem. **Queries:** Not necessary. **Unsolicited mss:** Accepts. **Response:** 4-6 weeks. **SASE Required:** Yes. **Rights:** One-time. **Payment:** On publication.

POSITIVE THINKING

66 E Main St., Pawling, NY 12564. 845-855-5000. E-mail: azaengle@guideposts.org. Website: www.guideposts.org. 10x/yr. Circ.: 400,000. Patricia M. Planeta, Editor. **Description:** Magazine with inspirational messages. **Nonfiction:** First-person stories with an emphasis on faith or positive thinking. Also practical how-to pieces; to 2,300 words; pay varies. **Tips:** Send SASE for sample copy or writer's guidelines. **Queries:** Preferred. **E-queries:** Yes. **Unsolicited mss:** Accepts. **Rights:** One-time. **Payment:** On publication. **Contact:** Ann Zaengle.

JUVENILE

AMERICAN GIRL

Pleasant Company Publications, 8400 Fairway Pl., Middleton, WI 53562. 608-836-4848. E-mail: im_agmag_editor@americangirl.com. Website: www.americangirl.com. Bimonthly. $3.95/$22.95. Circ.: 700,000. Kristi Thom, Editor. **Description:** For girls ages 8 and up. **Fiction:** Protagonist should be a girl between 8-12; 2,500 words; pay varies. No science fiction, fantasy, or first romance stories. **Nonfiction:** By assignment only; 150-1,000 words; $1/word. **Fillers:** Visual puzzles, mazes, math puzzles, word games, simple crosswords, cartoons; $50/item. **Columns, Departments:** Girls Express; short profiles of girls doing interesting things; 150 words; $1/word. **Tips:** "The girl must be the story's 'star,' told from her point-of-view. 'Girls Express' offers the best chance to break in." **Queries:** Preferred. **E-Queries:** No. **Unsolicited mss:** Accepts. **Response:** 3 months. **SASE Required:** Yes. **Freelance Content:** 5%. **Payment:** On acceptance.

APPLESEEDS

Carus Publishing Co., 30 Grove St., Peterborough, NH 03458. 603-924-7209. E-mail: swbuc@aol.com. Website: www.cobblestonepub.com. 9x/yr. **Description:** Magazine covering multidisciplinary social studies for kids ages 7-10. **Nonfiction:** Feature articles, profiles, how-to; 150-600 words; $50/page. **Fillers:** Games and activities; 100-300 words; $50/page. **Columns, Departments:** Reading Corner (literature selections, folktales), Your Turn, Experts in Action, The Artist's Eye; 100-600 words; $50/page. **Tips:** All material must be theme-related; see website for upcoming themes. Prefers to receive queries via e-mail. **Queries:** Required. **Rights:** All. **Contact:** Susan Buckley, Editor.

ASK

Carus Publishing Co., 332 S Michigan Ave., Suite 100, Chicago , IL 60604-4416. 312-939-1500. E-mail: ask@caruspub.com. Website: www.cricketmag.com. 9x/yr. $4.95/$32.97. Circ.: 35,000. James L. Plecha, Editor. **Description:** Nonfiction science and discovery magazine for children ages 7-10. **Nonfiction:** Almost all articles commissioned for the theme of the issue; 400-600 words; pay varies. **Tips:** "Writers should study the magazine and guidelines. Articles in *Ask* are clearly written and age appropriate, but do not talk down to children. We look for a lively style that explains the how and why of things. *Ask* raises questions and sparks curiosity on important concepts." **Queries:** Not necessary. **Unsolicited mss:** Accepts. **Response:** 3-4 months. **SASE Required:** Yes. **Freelance Content:** 5%. **Rights:** All.

BABYBUG

Carus Publishing Co., 315 Fifth St., P.O. Box 300, Peru, IL 61354-0300. 815-224-5803, ext. 656. Website: www.cricketmag.com. Monthly. $5/$35.97. Circ.: 48,000. Paula Morrow, Editor. **Description:** Offers simple rhymes and stories that parents will delight in reading to their infants and toddlers. **Fiction:** Very simple and concrete; read-aloud and picture stories for infants and toddlers; 2-8 short sentences; $25. **Nonfiction:** Very basic words and concepts; to 4 short sentences; $25. **Poetry:** Rhythmic, rhyming. Humor or ending with mild surprise a plus; to 8 lines; $25. **Fillers:** Parent/child interactive activities; to 8 lines; $25. **Art:** Art by assignment only; no photos. Submit samples (tear sheets, photocopies) for consideration. Pays $250/page, $500/spread. **Queries:** Does not accept. **E-Queries:** No. **Unsolicited mss:** Accepts. **Response:** 12 weeks. **SASE Required:** Yes. **Rights:** Vary. **Payment:** On publication.

BOYS' LIFE

Boy Scouts of America, P.O. Box 152079, Irving, TX 75015-2079. 972-580-2366. Website: www.boyslife.org. Monthly. $18/yr. Circ.: 1,300,000. Michael Goldman, Senior Editor. **Description:** Magazine for boys ages 7-18. Covers broad range of interests (sports, hobbies, careers, crafts, and special interests of scouting). **Fiction:** 1-2 short stories per issue. Humor, mystery, science fiction, adventure; 1,000-1,500 words; $750 and up. **Nonfiction:** From professional sports to American history to how to pack a canoe, 500-1,500 words; $400-$1,500. Also science, nature, health, sports, aviation, cars, computers, entertainment, pets, history, music, and more; 300-750 words; $150-$400. **Art:** Quality photos only; most work by assignment. **Tips:** "Write for a boy you know who is 12. Use crisp, punchy writing; short, straightforward sentences." See website for writer's guidelines. **Queries:** Required for nonfiction. **Unsolicited mss:** Accepts for fiction only. **Response:** 6-8 weeks. **SASE Required:** Yes. **Freelance Content:** 75%. **Rights:** FNASR. **Payment:** On acceptance. **Contact:** W. E. Butterworth IV, Managing Editor.

BOYS' QUEST

P.O. Box 227, Bluffton, OH 45817-0227. 419-358-4610. E-mail: hsbq@wcoil.com. Website: www.boysquest.com. Bimonthly. $4.95/$22.95. Circ.: 11,000. Marilyn Edwards, Editor. **Description:** Captures interests of all boys with exciting, unique activities and fascinating articles. Each issue focuses on a theme. **Fiction:** Stories on childhood interests, featuring young boys in wholesome childhood activities and pursuits; 350-600 words; $.05/word min. **Nonfiction:** About boys in activities both unusual and worthwhile. Photos with story essential. 500 words; $.05/word min. **Poetry:** $10/poem min. **Fillers:** Puzzles, jokes, riddles, games; $10/puzzle min., varies for other fillers. **Art:** B&W photos, color slides, pen-and-ink illustrations; $5-$35. **Tips:** Readers are boys, ages 8-10. Avoid Halloween, horror, etc. Prefers traditional childhood themes. Buys 3 nonfiction articles for each 1 fiction story. **Queries:** Not necessary. **E-Queries:** No. **Unsolicited mss:** Accepts. **Response:** 4-6 weeks. **SASE Required:** Yes. **Rights:** FNAR. **Payment:** On publication.

CALLIOPE

Cobblestone Publishing, 30 Grove St., Suite C, Peterborough, NH 03458. 603-924-7209. Website: www.cobblestonepub.com. 9x/yr. $29.95/yr. Circ.: 11,000. Charles Baker, Rosalie Baker, Editors. **Description:** "Exploring World History," for ages 8-14. Issues are thematic, exciting, colorful, with maps, timelines, illustrations, and art from major museums. **Fiction:** Authentic historical and biographical fiction, adventure, retold legends, and plays; to 1,000 words; $.20-$.25/word. **Nonfiction:** In-depth nonfiction, biographies; 1,000 words; $.20-$.25/word. **Fillers:** Puzzles and games; activities including crafts, recipes, and woodworking; to 700 words. **Columns, Departments:** Supplemental nonfiction; 300-600 words; $.20-$.25/word. **Art:** Photographs to accompany articles; $25-$100. **Tips:** Contact for upcoming themes. **Queries:** Required. **E-Queries:** No. **Unsolicited mss:** Prefer not to accept. **Response:** 2-4 months. **SASE Required:** Yes. **Freelance Content:** 80%. **Rights:** All. **Payment:** On publication.

CHILDREN'S DIGEST

Children's Better Health Institute, P.O. Box 567, Indianapolis, IN 46206-0567. 317-636-8881. Website: www.childrensdigestmag.org. 6x/yr. $21.95/yr. Circ.: 74,000. Penny Rasdall, Editor. **Description:** Health and fitness magazine for kids ages 10-12. **Fiction:** Stories with a message about health: exercise, sports, safety, nutrition, hygiene, drug education; 500-1,500 words; up to $.12/word. **Nonfiction:** Profiles of famous amateur and professional athletes, "average" athletes (especially kids) who have overcome obstacles to excel in their areas, new or unusual sports, exercise, safety, nutrition, hygiene, drug education; 500-1,000 words; up to $.12/word. **Poetry:** Poetry; $25 and up. **Fillers:** Recipes (healthy ones that kids can make), puzzles, games. **Queries:** Not necessary. **Unsolicited mss:** Accepts. **Response:** 3 months. **SASE Required:** Yes. **Rights:** All.

CHILDREN'S PLAYMATE

Children's Better Health Institute, P.O. Box 567, Indianapolis, IN 46206-0567. 317-636-8881. Website: www.childrensplaymatemag.org. 6x/yr. $16.95/yr. Circ.: 78,000. Terry Harshman, Editor. **Description:** For 6-8 year-olds, emphasizing health, fitness, sports, safety, and nutrition. Offers articles, crafts, recipes, general-interest, and health-related short stories. Also plays, poetry, puzzles, games, and mazes. Pieces should be 500-600 words; $.17/word. **Queries:** Preferred. **Rights:** All. **Payment:** On publication.

CLICK

Carus Publishing Co., 332 S Michigan Ave., Suite 1100, Chicago, IL 60604-4416. 312-939-1500. E-mail: click@caruspub.com. Website: www.cricketmag.com. 9x/yr. $4.95/$32.97. Circ.: 50,000. Marianne Carus, Editor-in-Chief. **Description:** For children ages 3-7. Themes introduce ideas and concepts in natural, physical, or social sciences, the arts, technology, math and history. **Fiction:** Stories that explain nonfiction concepts; 600-1,000 words; pay varies. **Nonfiction:** Articles that explain the how and why of something; 200-400 words; pay varies. **Tips:** See website for theme list and guidelines. **Queries:** Does not accept. **E-Queries:** No. **Unsolicited mss:** Accepts. **Response:** 3-4 months. **SASE Required:** Yes. **Rights:** All.

CLUB CONNECTION

See full listing in Religion category.

CLUBHOUSE JR.

Focus on the Family, 8605 Explorer Dr., Colorado Springs, CO 80920. 719-531-3400. E-mail: mail@fotf.org. Website: www.clubhousemagazine.com/club_jr. Monthly. $1.50/$15. Circ.: 76,000. Annette Bourland, Editor. **Description:** Inspires, entertains, and teaches Christian values to kids ages 4-8. **Fiction:** Fresh, inviting, well-developed characters; fast-paced, interesting story. Stories not explicitly Christian but built on foundations of belief and family values; 250-750 words (for young readers); $125-$300. **Nonfiction:** Articles about real children with interesting experiences. Science and nature told from unique perspective. Use short-caption styled format.

500 max.; $125-$200. **Poetry:** Real-life experience of young children; humorous, descriptive. 250 lines max.; $50-$100. **Fillers:** Puzzles (no crosswords); fun crafts, parent/child together; repetition of images, concise wording, humorous or insightful ending. **Art:** Send samples to Kathleen Gray-Ziegler, Designer. **Queries:** Does not accept. **Unsolicited mss:** Accepts. **Response:** 4-6 weeks. **SASE Required:** Yes. **Freelance Content:** 25%. **Rights:** FNAR. **Payment:** On acceptance.

CLUBHOUSE MAGAZINE

Focus on the Family, 8605 Explorer Dr., Colorado Springs, CO 80920. 719-531-3400. Website: www.clubhousemagazine.org; www.family.org. Monthly. $18/yr. Circ.: 14,000. Jesse Florea, Editor. **Description:** Christian magazine for 8-12 year olds who desire to know more about God and the Bible. We accept stories (fiction and nonfiction), Bible stories, puzzles, crafts, recipes, and cartoons. **Fiction:** 500-1,500 words. **Nonfiction:** Action-oriented Christian stories about children who are wise, brave, funny, or kind; 500-1,500 words; $.15-$.25/word. **Fillers:** 50-100 words; $75. **Tips:** "Avoid poetry, contemporary middle-class family settings, and educational articles that are too technical or informative in nature. Right now our needs include historical fiction, holiday material, mystery stories, and humor with a point." **Response:** 8 weeks. **SASE Required:** Yes. **Freelance Content:** 25%. **Rights:** FNAR. **Payment:** On acceptance. **Contact:** Suzanne Hadley, Associate Editor.

COBBLESTONE

Cobblestone Publishing/Carus Publishing Co., 30 Grove St., Suite C, Peterborough, NH 03458. 603-924-7209. Website: www.cobblestonepub.com. Monthly. $4.95/issue. Circ.: 30,000. Meg Chorlian, Editor. **Description:** American history for kids ages 8-14. **Fiction:** Authentic historical and biographical fiction, adventure, retold legends; up to 800 words; $.20-$.25/word. **Nonfiction:** In-depth nonfiction, plays, first-person accounts, and biographies; 300-800 words; $.20-.$25/word. **Poetry:** Serious or light verse with clear, objective imagery; 30 lines; pay varies. **Fillers:** Crosswords, mazes, picture puzzles; pay varies. **Columns, Departments:** Crafts, recipes, and woodworking projects; pay varies. **Art:** Photographs related to theme; $15-$100. **Queries:** Required. **E-Queries:** Yes. **Unsolicited mss:** Does not accept. **Response:** 2-6 months. **SASE Required:** Yes. **Freelance Content:** 85%. **Rights:** All.

CRICKET

Carus Publishing Co., 315 Fifth St., P.O. Box 300, Peru, IL 61354-0300. 815-224-5803, ext. 656. E-mail: cricket@caruspub.com. Website: www.cricketmag.com. Monthly. $5/$35.97. Circ.: 71,000. Marianne Carus, Editor-in-Chief. **Description:** Folk tales, fantasy, science fiction, history, poems, science, sports, and crafts, for young readers. **Fiction:** Any topic of interest to children; to 2,000 words; $.25/word. **Nonfiction:** Science, biography, history, nature; to 1,500 words; $.25/word. **Poetry:** Brief lyric poems; to 25 lines; $3/line. **Fillers:** Word or math puzzles, recipes, crafts, experiments; 150-200 words; $100. **Tips:** Include bibliography with nonfiction. **Queries:** Does not accept. **E-Queries:** No. **Unsolicited mss:** Accepts. **Response:** 12 weeks. **SASE Required:** Yes. **Freelance Content:** 90%. **Rights:** All.

DIG MAGAZINE

Carus Publishing Co., 30 Grove St. #C, Peterborough, NH 03458-1438. 603-924-7209. Website: www.digonline.com. Bimonthly. $23.95/yr. Circ.: 20,000. Rosalie Baker, Editor. **Description:** For children ages 10-14 on archaeology. Nonfiction pieces run 400-1,000 words; $.20-$.25/word. **Tips:** "Query on a specific upcoming issue; include a bibliography that shows understanding of the topic you are proposing and lists key people in that field." **Queries:** Required. **Unsolicited mss:** Accepts. **Response:** 2-4 months. **SASE Required:** Yes. **Freelance Content:** 80%. **Rights:** All. **Payment:** On publication.

DISCOVERY TRAILS

Radiant Life Resources, 1445 N Boonville Ave., Springfield, MO 65802-1894. 417-862-2781. E-mail: rl-discoverytrails@gph.org. Website: www.radiantlife.org. Quarterly. Circ.: 20,000. Sinda Zinn, Editor. **Description:** Take-home paper for children 10-11 years old, with fiction stories, activities, poems, articles, and puzzles to reinforce daily Christian living. **Fiction:** Stories that promote Christian living through application of Biblical principles by the characters; 700-800 words; $.07-$.10/word. **Nonfiction:** Articles about topics that show God's power, wisdom in creation, or correlation to a relationship with God; 200-400 words; $.07-$.10/word. **Tips:** No Santa, Easter Bunny, or Halloween stories. "We accept e-mail submissions, but don't really want e-mail queries." **Queries:** Not necessary. **E-Queries:** No. **Unsolicited mss:** Accepts. **Response:** 2-4 weeks. **SASE Required:** Yes. **Freelance Content:** 90%. **Payment:** On acceptance.

THE DOLPHIN LOG

Cousteau Society, Inc., 3612 E Tremont Ave., Bronx, NY 10465-2022. 718-409-3370. E-mail: cousteau@cousteausociety.org. Website: www.dolphinlog.org. Bimonthly. $15/yr. Circ.: 80,000. Lisa Rao, Editor. **Description:** On topics related to our global water system (marine biology, ecology, natural history, water-related subjects, etc.) for readers ages 7-13. **Queries:** Preferred. **Payment:** On publication.

FACES

Cobblestone Publishing, 30 Grove St., Suite C, Peterborough, NH 03458-1454. 603-924-7209. E-mail: facesmag@yahoo.com. Website: www.cobblestonepub.com. 9x/yr. $29.95/yr. Circ.: 11,000. Elizabeth Crooker Carpentiere, Editor. **Description:** "People, Places, and Cultures." Introduces young readers (ages 8-14) to different world cultures, religion, geography, government, and art. **Fiction:** Retold folktales, legends, plays; must relate to theme; to 800 words; $.20-$.25/word. **Nonfiction:** In-depth articles on aspect of featured culture; interviews and personal accounts; 600-800 words; $.20-$.25/word. **Fillers:** Activities (crafts, recipes, word puzzles); 100-600 words. **Art:** 35mm; $25-$100. **Tips:** "Avoid judgmental tone. Give our readers a clear image of life in other cultures. Check our website for upcoming themes." **Queries:** Required. **E-Queries:** Yes. **Unsolicited mss:** Accepts. **Response:** Queries 4 weeks, submissions 4 months. **SASE Required:** Yes. **Freelance Content:** 80%. **Rights:** All. **Payment:** On publication.

FOOTSTEPS

Carus Publishing Co., 30 Grove St., Suite C, Petersborough, NH 03458. 603-924-7209. E-mail: cfbaker@meganet.com. Website: www.footstepsmagazine.com. 5x/yr. $23.95/yr. Circ.: 6,000. Charles F. Baker, Editor. **Description:** African American history and heritage for students in grades 4-9. **Fiction:** Authentic retellings of historical and biographical events, adventure, legends; 200-1,000 words; $.20-$.25/word. **Nonfiction:** On issue's theme; 200-1,000 words; $.20-$.25/word. **Fillers:** Activities, short articles, to 600 words. **Art:** Slides, transparencies, digital, prints; pay varies. **Tips:** Cultural sensitivity and historical accuracy required. Contact for upcoming themes. **Queries:** Required. **Unsolicited mss:** Accepts. **Response:** 2-6 months. **SASE Required:** Yes. **Freelance Content:** 90%. **Rights:** All.

THE FRIEND

Church of Jesus Christ of Latter-Day Saints, 50 E North Temple, Fl. 24, Salt Lake City, UT 84150-3226. 801-240-2210. Monthly. $8/yr. Circ.: 245,000. Vivian Paulsen, Managing Editor. **Description:** Nonfiction literary journal for kids up to 12 years of age. No fiction. **Nonfiction:** Articles and stories should be true, focus on character-building qualities and wholesome values without moralizing or preaching. Stories with universal settings, conflicts, and characters. No biographies of living people; 200-300 words, $100; 400+ words, $250. **Poetry:** Poems, uplifting and of substance. Picturable poems suitable for preschoolers of high interest. No nature poems or those with clever play on words; $50. **Fillers:** How-to pieces on various handicraft or homemaking projects. Also, cartoons, games, puzzles, and recipes. **Queries:** Not necessary. **E-Queries:** No. **Unsolicited mss:** Does not accept. **Response:** 8-12 weeks. **Rights:** All. **Payment:** On acceptance.

GIRLS' LIFE

Division of Monarch Publishing Services, Inc., 4517 Harford Rd., Baltimore, MD 21214. 410-426-9600. Website: www.girlslife.com. Bimonthly. $3.50/$14.95. Circ.: 2,000,000. Karen Bokram, Publisher/Editor-in-Chief. **Description:** For girls, ages 10-15, with real information and advice on friends, parents, siblings, guys, school, puberty, and more. Includes profiles of real girls facing real challenges (e.g. young girl traveling through Nepal, young girl battling anorexia). Length and pay varies. **Tips:** No phone calls or e-mail queries. Include resumé, clips, and pitch letter or article. "Freelancers must be familiar with our editorial content, target audience, voice, and language. Read recent issues before pitching. Make sure pitch fits with specific feature, column, or department (celebrity interviews, pop culture, crafts, short profiles, newsworthy tidbits, service-oriented features, friendship features, quizzes, teen-targeted fiction)." **Queries:** Required. **E-Queries:** No. **Response:** 90 days. **SASE Required:** Yes. **Freelance Content:** 30%. **Rights:** All. **Payment:** On publication. **Contact:** Kelly White, Executive Editor.

GUIDE

Review & Herald Publishing Assn., 55 W Oak Ridge Dr., Hagerstown, MD 21740. 301-393-4037. E-mail: guide@rhpa.org. Website: www.guidemagazine.org. Weekly (52x/yr). $43.95/yr. Circ.: 33,000. Randy Fishell, Editor. **Description:** Christian publication for young people, ages 10-14. Adventure, personal growth, Christian humor, inspiration, biography, nature; with spiritual emphasis; 800-1,200 words. True or based-on-true stories only. **Tips:** "Set forth a clearly evident Christian principle without being preachy." Encourages e-mail submissions (attached file or pasted into message). **Queries:** Not necessary. **Unsolicited mss:** Accepts. **Response:** 4-6 weeks. **SASE Required:** Yes. **Freelance Content:** 95%. **Rights:** FNAR, one-time reprint. **Payment:** On acceptance.

GUIDEPOSTS FOR KIDS ON THE WEB

1050 Broadway, Suite 6, Chesterton, IN 46304. 219-929-4429. E-mail: gp4k@guideposts.org. Website: www.gp4k.com. Rosanne Tolin, Managing Editor. **Description:** E-zine for children, ages 7-12. Offers inspiring stories that focus on traditional values as well as other general interest pieces on animals, school, sports, and more. Also has fun puzzles, arts and crafts, quizzes, trivia, animal stories, and interactive features such as a club, discussion boards, and monitored chats. **Fiction:** Stories by noted authors; 500-1,000 words; $100-$250. **Nonfiction:** Profiles of athletes and celebrities (150-500 words) and features that encourage kids to think (250-1,000 words). Pays $100-$250. **Poetry:** 50-150 words; $25-$100. **Fillers:** $25-$150. **Tips:** "We do not consider ourselves a religious e-zine. No Bible-toting kids or preachy stories, please." Include bullets, links, sidebars, etc. **Queries:** Preferred. **E-Queries:** Yes. **Unsolicited mss:** Accepts. **Response:** 6 weeks. **SASE Required:** Yes. **Freelance Content:** 80%. **Rights:** All. **Payment:** On acceptance.

HIGHLIGHTS FOR CHILDREN

803 Church St., Honesdale, PA 18431-1824. 570-253-1080. Website: www.highlights.com. Monthly. $29.64/yr. Circ.: 2,500,000. Christine French Clark, Editor. **Description:** "Fun with a purpose." The stories, Hidden Pictures, jokes, and activities bring engaging entertainment to children, ages 2-12, while developing learning skills. **Fiction:** Humor, mystery, sports, adventure, folktales, world cultures, urban stories. Engaging plot, strong characterization, lively language; to 800 words; $150 and up. **Nonfiction:** Biography, autobiography, arts, science, history, sports, world cultures, up to 800 words. If for younger readers (ages 3-7 years), 500 words or less; $150 and up. **Poetry:** 16 lines, $25 and up. **Fillers:** Crafts (3-7 numbered steps), $30 and up; include a sample; use common household items or inexpensive, easy-to-obtain materials. Holiday/religious/world cultures crafts welcome. **Tips:** "We prefer stories in which protagonist solves a dilemma through his/her own resources. Avoid stories that preach." Prefers complete manuscripts to queries. **Queries:** Not necessary. **E-Queries:** No. **Unsolicited mss:** Accepts. **Response:** 6-8 weeks. **SASE Required:** Yes. **Rights:** All. **Payment:** On acceptance.

HOPSCOTCH

P.O. Box 164, Bluffton, OH 45817-0164. 419-358-4610.
Website: www.hopscotchmagazine.com. Bimonthly. $4.95/$22.95. Circ.: 15,000.
Marilyn Edwards, Editor. **Description:** Written for girls, without the emphasis on fads/fashion, boyfriends, and shopping. Focus is on educational activities and stories. **Fiction:** Features girls in wholesome childhood activities and pursuits; 500 words; $.05/word. **Nonfiction:** Features girls directly involved in an unusual and worthwhile activity; 500 words; $.05/word. **Poetry:** $10/poem **Fillers:** Puzzles, games, crafts, cartoons, recipes. **Art:** Photos are essential. B&W photos, color slides, and illustrations; $5-$35. **Tips:** "Nonfiction pieces make up 75% of our content. Please contact us for upcoming themes." **Queries:** Not necessary. **E-Queries:** No. **Unsolicited mss:** Accepts. **Response:** 4-6 weeks. **SASE Required:** Yes. **Rights:** FNAR.

THE HORN BOOK MAGAZINE

See full listing in Writing & Publishing category.

HUMPTY DUMPTY'S MAGAZINE

Children's Better Health Institute, P.O. Box 567, Indianapolis, IN 46206-0567. 317-636-8881. Website: www.humptydumptymag.org. 6x/yr. $25.95/yr. Circ.: 150,000. Phyllis Lybarger, Editor. **Description:** Encourages kids, ages 4-6, to strive for excellence, with focus on academics, health, personal fitness, medicine, and science. Fiction and nonfiction pieces run 350 words or less; $.22/word. Short verse and narratives, $25/piece. **Fillers:** Games, puzzles, crafts, simple science experiments, healthy and "no-cook" recipes (with minimum adult guidance). Include brief, clear instructions. **Tips:** "Stories should have good 'I can read' quality." **Unsolicited mss:** Accepts. **Response:** 3 months. **SASE Required:** Yes. **Freelance Content:** 25-30%. **Rights:** All. **Payment:** On publication.

JACK AND JILL

Children's Better Health Institute, 1100 Waterway Blvd., P.O. Box 567, Indianapolis, IN 46206-0567. 317-634-1100. Website: www.jackandjillmag.org. 6x/yr. $21.95/yr. Circ.: 200,000. Daniel Lee, Editor. **Description:** For kids, ages 7-10, on health, fitness, science, and general-interest topics. Encourages active, challenging lifestyles, and accomplishment and learning with a hearty helping of fun! **Fiction:** 700 words; $.17/word. **Nonfiction:** On history, biography, life in other countries, etc.; 500 words; $.17/word. **Poetry:** $15-$50. **Fillers:** Games, puzzles, projects, recipes. **Tips:** "Avoid usual topics (e.g. divorce, moving, new kid in school, etc.)." **Queries:** Not necessary. **Unsolicited mss:** Accepts. **Response:** 12 weeks. **SASE Required:** Yes. **Freelance Content:** 50%. **Rights:** All. **Payment:** On publication.

JUNIOR SCHOLASTIC

Scholastic, Inc., 557 Broadway, New York, NY 10012. 212-343-6295.
E-mail: junior@scholastic.com. Website: www.juniorscholastic.com. 17x/yr. $7.75/yr. Circ.: 535,000. Lee Baier, Executive Editor. **Description:** On-the-spot reports from countries in the news. **Queries:** Required. **Payment:** On acceptance.

KIDS TRIBUTE

71 Barber Greene Rd., Don Mills, Ontario M3C 2A2 Canada. 416-445-0544.
Website: www.tribute.ca. Quarterly. $12/yr. Circ.: 300,000. Robin Stevenson, Editor.
Description: Articles on movies and entertainment for young readers, ages 8-13; 350
words; $150-$200 (Canadian). **Queries:** Required. **Payment:** On acceptance.

LADYBUG

Carus Publishing Co., 315 Fifth St., P.O. Box 300, Peru, IL 61354-0300. 815-224-
5803, ext. 656. Website: www.cricketmag.com. Monthly. $5/$35.97. Circ.: 131,000.
Paula Morrow, Editor. **Description:** Stories, poems, songs, games, and adventures
for young children, ages 2-6. Each page illustrated to delight parents and children
alike. **Fiction:** Picture, read-aloud, and early reader stories with lively characters.
Genres: adventure, humor, mild suspense, fairy tales, folktales, contemporary fiction;
to 800 words; $.25/word, $25 min. **Nonfiction:** How-to, informational, and humorous pieces, on age-appropriate topics; to 300 words; $.25/word, $25 min. **Poetry:**
Rhythmic, rhyming, serious, humorous, active; to 20 lines; $3/line, $25 min. **Fillers:**
Rebus, learning activities, games, crafts, songs, finger games. **Tips:** "We're always
looking for more activities." **Queries:** Does not accept. **E-Queries:** No. **Unsolicited
mss:** Accepts. **Response:** 12 weeks. **SASE Required:** Yes. **Freelance Content:**
70%. **Rights:** Vary. **Payment:** On publication.

MAD MAGAZINE

See full listing in Humor category.

MUSE

Carus Publishing Co., 332 S Michigan Ave., Suite 1100, Chicago, IL 60604. 312-939-
1500. E-mail: muse@caruspub.com. Website: www.cricketmag.com. 9x/yr. Diana
Lutz, Editor. **Description:** Focuses on problems connected with a discipline or area
of practical knowledge, for children, ages 10-14. 1,000-2,500 words; $.50/word. **Tips:**
No longer accepts unsolicited manuscripts or queries.

MY FRIEND: THE CATHOLIC MAGAZINE FOR KIDS

Pauline Books & Media, Daughters of St. Paul, 50 Saint Paul's Ave., Boston, MA
02130. 617-522-8911. E-mail: myfriend@pauline.org. Website: www.myfriend-
magazine.org. Monthly. $3.95/issue. Circ.: 10,000. Sr. Maria Grace Dateno, Editor.
Description: "The Catholic Magazine for Kids." Seeks to present "religious truth
and positive values in an enjoyable and attractive way." **Fiction:** Stories with good dialogue, realistic character development and current lingo; 800-1,100 words; $75-$150.
Nonfiction: Fresh perspectives into a child's world: imaginative,unique, challenging,
informative, fun; 800-1,100 words; $75-$150. **Tips:** "We also accept craft ideas. First
send us your idea and if accepted, provide us with a well-made sample." Review sample copy ($2 plus 9x12 SASE) prior to submitting. Guidelines and theme list on web-
site. **Queries:** Not necessary. **E-Queries:** No. **Unsolicited mss:** Accepts.
Response: 3 months. **SASE Required:** Yes. **Freelance Content:** 30%, mostly fiction. **Rights:** First worldwide. **Payment:** On acceptance.

NATIONAL GEOGRAPHIC KIDS

National Geographic Society, 1145 17th St. NW, Washington, DC 20036-4688. 202-857-7000. Website: www.national geographic.com/ngkids. Monthly. $19.95/yr. Circ.: 1,200,000. Melina Bellows, Editor-in-Chief. **Description:** For kids, ages 8-14, who dare to explore. Seeks to increase geographic awareness by inspiring young readers' curiosity, with big, bold photos and fun, fact-filled stories. **Nonfiction:** Adventure, outdoors, sports, geography, history, archaeology, paleontology, human interest, natural history, science, technology. 400-1,200 words; $.80-$1/word. **Tips:** "We work primarily through assignments. We pick up few proposals or manuscripts. We do have submission guidelines and will send a sample copy. Send resumé and relevant clips (hard copy, no e-mail) that show ability to write for kids 8-14." **Queries:** Required. **E-Queries:** No. **Unsolicited mss:** Do not accept. **Response:** 2 months. **SASE Required:** Yes. **Freelance Content:** 90%. **Rights:** All. **Payment:** On publication. **Contact:** Julie Agnone, Executive Editor.

NATURE FRIEND

Carlisle Press, 2673 Township Rd. 421, Sugarcreek, OH 44681. 330-852-1900. Monthly. Circ.: 13,000. Marvin Wengerd, Editor. **Description:** Stories, puzzles, activities, and experiments about nature for children. **Nonfiction:** Articles for children that teach them to be kind to animals, plants, and nature, increase their awareness of God, and illustrate spiritual lessons; 250-1,000 words; $.05/word. **Fillers:** Games, puzzles, and activities concering nature; 150-250 words; $15. **Art:** Photos to accompany mss; transparencies, prints; $35-$50. **Tips:** Send complete manuscript (no queries) via regular mail. Sample copies ($4) and guidelines available. **Queries:** Does not accept. **E-Queries:** No. **Unsolicited mss:** Accepts. **Response:** 4 months. **Freelance Content:** 80%. **Rights:** First or one-time. **Payment:** On publication.

NEW MOON

34 E Superior St. #200, Duluth, MN 55802. 218-728-5507. E-mail: girl@newmoon.org. Website: www.newmoon.org. Bimonthly. $5.50/$29. Circ.: 30,000. Dawn Gorman, Managing Editor. **Description:** Celebrates girls—their accomplishments and efforts to hold onto their voices, strengths, and dreams as they move from being girls to becoming women. **Fiction:** Stories by female authors, with girls as main characters. Fiction should fit theme (see website for upcoming list), for girls ages 8-14; 900 words; $.06-$.10/word. **Nonfiction:** Women's work (profiles a woman and her job, relates to theme); Herstory (profiles a woman from history); Body Language (about puberty, body image, depression, menstruation, etc.); Girls on the Go (by girl or woman adventurers); 600 words; $.06-$.10/word. **Tips:** Sample copy $6.75. **Queries:** Not necessary. **E-Queries:** Accepts. **Unsolicited mss:** Accepts. **Response:** 2 months. **SASE Required:** Yes. **Freelance Content:** 10%. **Rights:** All. **Payment:** On publication.

NICK, JR.

1633 Broadway, Fl. 7, New York, NY 10019-6708. 212-654-6388.
E-mail: nickjr.editors@nick.com. Website: www.nickjr.com. 9x/yr. $17.97/yr. Circ.: 1,000,050. Freddi Greenberg, Editor-in-Chief. **Description:** For parents and their children ages 2-11. Features do-together activities, games, stories, and expert parenting advice and information.

ON THE LINE

616 Walnut Ave., Scottdale, PA 15683. 724-887-8500. E-mail: otl@mph.org. Website: www.mph.org/otl. Monthly. $2.40/$28.50. Circ.: 4,000. Mary Clemens Meyer, Editor. **Description:** For youth, ages 9-14, to reinforce Christian values. Seeks to help upper elementary and junior high school kids understand God, the created world, themselves, and others. **Fiction:** Solving everyday problems, humor, holidays, Christian values; 1,000-1,800 words; $.04-$.05/word. **Nonfiction:** Nature, history, health, howto; 300-500 words; $.04-$.05/word. **Poetry:** Light verse, humor, nature, holidays; 3-24 lines; $10-$25. **Fillers:** Cartoons, crosswords, word finds, scrambled letters, mazes, codes, jokes, riddles, and recipes; $10-$20. **Tips:** "Let the story give the moral subtly; keep it fun." **Queries:** Not necessary. **E-Queries:** Yes. **Unsolicited mss:** Accepts. **Response:** 1 month. **SASE Required:** Yes. **Freelance Content:** 85%. **Rights:** One-time. **Payment:** On acceptance.

PASSPORT

Word Action Publishing Co., 6401 The Paseo, Kansas City, MO 64131. 816-333-7000. E-mail: jjsmith@nazarene.org. Circ.: 18,000. Mike L. Wonch, Editor. **Description:** Newspaper for preteens with resources for spiritual transformation and holy living. Corresponds with WordAction Sunday School materials (for 11-12 year olds). Not accepting submissions at this time. **Contact:** Julie J. Smith, Editorial Assistant.

POCKETS

The Upper Room, 1908 Grand Ave., P.O. Box 340004, Nashville, TN 37203-0004. 615-340-7333. E-mail: pockets@upperroom.org. Website: www.pockets.org. 11x/yr. $19.95/yr. Circ.: 90,000. Lynn Gilliam, Editor. **Description:** Inter-denominational publication promoting the Gospel of Jesus Christ to kids ages 6-11. Readers are kids of many cultures and ethnic backgrounds. These differences should be reflected in the stories (lifestyles, names, living environments, etc.). **Fiction:** Stories to help children deal with everyday life. Prefers real-life settings; no talking animals or inanimate objects; 600-1,400 words; $.14/word. **Nonfiction:** Theme for each issue. Profiles of persons whose lives reflect Christian commitment/values; articles about kids involved in environmental, community, and peace/justice issues. 400-1,000 words; $.14/word. **Fillers:** Puzzles and games (on theme); $25 and up. **Columns, Departments:** Pocketsful of Love and Pocketsful of Prayer; $.14/word. **Tips:** Looking for puzzles and activities on themes (see website). **E-Queries:** No. **Unsolicited mss:** Accepts. **SASE Required:** Yes. **Freelance Content:** 90%. **Payment:** On acceptance.

SCHOLASTIC CHOICES

557 Broadway, New York, NY 10012-3902. 212-343-6434.
E-mail: choicesmag@scholastic.com. Website: www.scholastic.com. 8x/yr.
Circ.: 200,000. Bob Hugel, Editor. **Description:** Classroom magazine aimed at teen audience. Covers life skills, nutrition, health, substance abuse, family issues, peer relationships, careers, and consumer economics. Articles run 800-1,500 words; $600-$1,000. **Queries:** Preferred. **E-Queries:** No. **Unsolicited mss:** Does not accept. **Response:** 2 months. **SASE Required:** Yes. **Freelance Content:** 90%. **Rights:** All. **Payment:** On publication.

SHINE BRIGHTLY

P.O. Box 7259, Grand Rapids, MI 49510. E-mail: sara@gemsgc.org. Website: www.gospelcom.net/gems. Sara Lynne Hilton, Editor. **Description:** Upbeat fiction and features, 500-1,000 words, for Christian girls ages 8-14. Topics include personal life, nature, crafts, etc. Pays $.03/word, extra for photos. Also accepts puzzles; $10-$15. **Tips:** Send SASE for upcoming themes and writer's guidelines. **Queries:** Not necessary. **E-Queries:** No. **Unsolicited mss:** Accepts. **Payment:** On publication.

SKIPPING STONES

P.O. Box 3939, Eugene, OR 97403. 541-342-4956.
E-mail: editor@skippingstones.org. Website: www.skippingstones.org. 5x/yr. $25/yr. Circ.: 2,500. Arun N. Toké, Executive Editor. **Description:** Original writing, art, and photography. **Fiction:** Social awareness, interpersonal relationships; to 750 words. **Nonfiction:** Nature awareness, multicultural education, social responsibility, travelogues, journal entries; to 750 words. **Poetry:** By authors under age 19 only; on nature, social issues, reflections; to 30 lines. **Fillers:** Multicultural, nature; 150 words. **Tips:** "Each year, we also recognize creativity and community service by honoring ten youth groups and children (ages 7-17) with our Youth Honor Awards. We invite writing and art that promote multicultural awareness and/or ecological understanding, sustainable living, creative problem solving, peace, and justice." **Queries:** Not necessary. **Unsolicited mss:** Accepts. **Response:** 1-3 months. **SASE Required:** Yes. **Freelance Content:** 80%. **Rights:** FNASR, reprint. **Payment:** In copies.

SPIDER

Carus Publishing Co., 315 Fifth St., P.O. Box 300, Peru, IL 61354-0300.
815-224-5803, ext. 656. Website: www.cricketmag.com. Monthly. $5/$35.97. Circ.: 79,000. Heather Delabre, Associate Editor. **Description:** Stories, articles, poems, and activities for children. Original artwork fills each issue. **Fiction:** Easy-to-read, realistic stories (fantasy, myths, fairy tales, fables, and science fiction). **Nonfiction:** Interviews, profiles, and how-to articles on science, animals, nature, technology, etc. **Art:** Art (especially children, animals, action, scenes from a story); photography (photo essays or article illustrations), color preferred, B&W considered. **Tips:** Looking for more fiction submissions, also activity ideas, puzzles, and jokes. **Queries:** Does not accept. **E-Queries:** No. **Unsolicited mss:** Accepts. **Response:** 12 weeks. **SASE Required:** Yes. **Freelance Content:** 85%. **Payment:** On publication.

SPORTS ILLUSTRATED FOR KIDS

Time, Inc., 135 W 50th St., Frnt 4, New York, NY 10020-1201. 212-522-1212. E-mail: kidletters@sikids.com. Website: www.sikids.com. Monthly. $2.99/$29.95. Circ.: 1,002,200. Neil Cohen, Managing Editor. **Description:** On the excitement, joy, and challenge of sports, for kids, ages 8-14. Action photos, interactive stories, profiles, puzzles, playing tips. Also, drawings and writing by kids. Articles run 500-700 words; $500-$1,250. **Queries:** Required. **E-Queries:** Yes. **Unsolicited mss:** Accepts. **Response:** 4-6 weeks. **SASE Required:** Yes. **Rights:** Exclusive. **Payment:** 40% on acceptance, 60% on publication. **Contact:** Shawn Nicholls, Editorial Coordinator.

STONE SOUP

P.O. Box 83, Santa Cruz, CA 95063-0083. 831-426-5557.
E-mail: editor@stonesoup.com. Website: www.stonesoup.com. Bimonthly. $5.50/$33. Circ.: 20,000. Gerry Mandel, Editor. **Description:** Stories, poems, book reviews, and art by young writers and artists, ages 8-13. **Fiction:** Personal narratives, arrival stories, family histories, sport stories, science fiction; 2,500 words; $40. **Nonfiction:** Book reviews by children under 14. Prefers writing based on real-life experiences. **Poetry:** Freeverse only; $40. **Art:** Work by kids ages 8-13 only; send 2-3 samples (photocopies ok). **Queries:** Not necessary. **E-Queries:** No. **Unsolicited mss:** Accepts. **Response:** 2-4 weeks. **SASE Required:** No. **Freelance Content:** 100%. **Rights:** All. **Payment:** On publication.

TURTLE MAGAZINE FOR PRESCHOOL KIDS

See full listing in Health category.

U MAGAZINE

9800 Fredericksburg Rd., San Antonio, TX 78288. 800-531-8013.
E-mail: umag@usaa.com. Circ.: 400,000. Julie Finlay, Editor. **Description:** A quarterly 16-page publication on topics of general interest to 9-12 year old dependents of USAA members. Past themes have included citizenship, relationships, saving/managing money, and family business. Articles should run 100-300 words; pay varies. **Tips:** "Know the children's market, including trends among the audience. Be aware, however, that our magazine is not about fashion and doesn't bank on fads or pop culture." **Queries:** Preferred. **E-Queries:** Yes. **Unsolicited mss:** Accepts. **Response:** 6 weeks. **SASE Required:** Yes.

U.S. KIDS: A WEEKLY READER MAGAZINE

Children's Better Health Institute, 1100 Waterway Blvd., P.O. Box 567, Indianapolis, IN 46206-0567. 317-634-1100. E-mail: d.lee@cbhi.org. Website: www.uskids.com. 6x/yr. $21.95/yr. Circ.: 250,000. Daniel Lee, Editor. **Description:** For kids, ages 6-10. True-life stories, science/nature features, health/fitness, kids in the news, color photos, and lots of fun games, activities, and contests. **Fiction:** Science fiction, nature, etc.; 700 words; $.17/word. **Nonfiction:** Looking for profiles on interesting, regular kids (no celebrities), ages 5-10, involved in unusual pursuits (sports, adventures, science); 500-600 words; pay varies. **Tips:** Avoid counterculture, irony/sarcasm, and depressing topics. Stay upbeat and wholesome. **Queries:** Preferred. **E-Queries:** Yes. **Unsolicited mss:** Accepts. **Response:** 12 weeks. **SASE Required:** Yes. **Freelance Content:** 20%. **Rights:** All. **Payment:** On publication.

YES MAG: CANADA'S SCIENCE MAGAZINE FOR KIDS

Peter Piper Publishing, Inc., 3968 Long Gun Place, Victoria, British Columbia V8N 3A9 Canada. 250-477-5543. E-mail: editor@yesmag.ca. Website: www.yesmag.ca. Bimonthly. $3.95/$22 (Canadian). Circ.: 18,000. Shannon Hunt, Editor. **Description:** Canadian children's science magazine. Makes science accessible, interesting, and exciting, for children ages 8-14. Covers science and technology news, do-at-home projects, science-related book and software reviews, profiles of Canadian students and scientists. **Nonfiction:** Science, technology, engineering, and math articles for kids, ages 8-14; 250-1,250 words; $.20/word. **Tips:** Seeking imaginative, fun, well-researched pieces. Be specific in query; ideally send an outline of the article, indicating how you will approach the topic. **Queries:** Preferred. **E-Queries:** Yes. **Unsolicited mss:** Accepts. **Response:** 6 weeks. **SASE Required:** Yes. **Freelance Content:** 60%. **Rights:** One-time. **Payment:** On publication.

YOUNG RIDER

Bowtie, Inc., P.O. Box 8237, Lexington, KY 40533. 859-260-9800. E-mail: yreditor@fancypubs.com. Website: www.youngrider.com. Bimonthly. $15/yr. Circ.: 41,000. Lesley Ward, Editor. **Description:** About horses and children. **Nonfiction:** Horse health, grooming tips, interesting breeds and famous horses, show-ring secrets, how to improve their riding skills, celebrity rider interviews; 1,200 words; $140. **Tips:** Query or send manuscript. **Queries:** Not necessary. **Unsolicited mss:** Accepts. **Payment:** On publication.

LIFESTYLES

7X7 MAGAZINE: SF PEOPLE, STORIES, + STYLE

59 Grant Ave., Fl. 3, San Francisco, CA 94108. 415-362-7797. E-mail: edit@7x7mag.com. Website: www.7x7mag.com. 10x/yr. $3.50/$10. Irene Ricasio Edwards, Executive Editor. **Description:** San Francisco lifestyle magazine with focus on food/wine, travel, fashion design, and local celebrities. **Queries:** Preferred. **E-Queries:** Yes. **Unsolicited mss:** Accepts. **Freelance Content:** 5%. **Rights:** FNAR. **Payment:** On publication. **Contact:** Editorial Dept.

BALANCE MAGAZINE

Beach House Publishing, Inc., P.O. Box 8608, Ft. Lauderdale, FL 33310-8608. 954-382-4325. E-mail: publisher@balancemagazine.com. Website: www.balancemagazine.com. Quarterly. $20/yr. Circ.: 100,000. Susie Levan, Publisher/Editor-in-Chief. **Description:** *Balance Magazine...Personal Growth for Women* is a "health, wealth and happiness" magazine. Strives to provide straightforward, expert and motivational solutions to pressing issues facing baby boomers.

Nonfiction: Short articles on self-development and personal growth; 750-1,500 words. **Tips:** Send submissions in an e-mail attachment. Include 15-word bio. **Queries:** Preferred. **E-Queries:** Yes. **Unsolicited mss:** Accepts.

BLUE MAGAZINE

Blue Media Ventures, Inc., 611 Broadway, Rm. 731, New York, NY 10012. 212-777-0024. E-mail: editorial@bluemagazine.com. Website: www.bluemagazine.com. Bimonthly. $19.95/yr. Circ.: 175,000. Amy Schrier, Editor-in-Chief. **Description:** Explores the world through travel and adventure sports. Described by one reviewer as "National Geographic with a rock-and-roll soundtrack." Features in 3 categories: Blue Planet, Blue Nation, and Blue Asphalt. Exploration is key, whether a profile of coal miners of Bolivia, or inline skating through Central Park. **Tips:** "A well-written query is a good start. Convey your idea in a 500-word pitch; include any appropriate writing samples. We rely on freelance contributions and we're seeking new writers stationed in exotic locales with great stories to tell—who feel that life is, well, an adventure." **Queries:** Preferred. **E-Queries:** Yes. **Unsolicited mss:** Accepts. **Freelance Content:** 100%.

BUDGET LIVING

Budget Living Media, 317 Madison Ave., New York, NY 10017-5204. 212-687-6060. E-mail: editorial@budgetlivingmedia.com. Website: www.budgetlivingmedia.com. Bimonthly. $14.95/yr. Circ.: 450,000. Sarah Gray Miller, Editor-in-Chief. **Description:** Lifestyle magazine people ages 25-40. Features travel, fashion, entertaining, finance, home decorating, etc. **Nonfiction:** Quirky, funny, off-the-beaten trail, personality-driven creative ways of living cheaply (or people who do), with an emphasis on reader service. Also personal essays. Pitch stories with visuals in mind. **Contact:** Alex Bhattacharji, Executive Editor.

DIVERSION

The Hearst Corp., 1790 Broadway, Fl. 6, New York, NY 10019. 212-969-7500. E-mail: sshipman@hearst.com. Website: www.diversion.com. Monthly. $60/yr. Circ.: 200,000. Ed Wetschler, Editor-in-Chief. **Description:** Lifestyle magazine for physicians. Does not accept articles on health-related subjects, but does accept features and profiles of doctors who excel at nonmedical pursuits and who do volunteer medical work. Topics include cars, technology, sports, entertainment, the arts, and broad travel roundups; 1,800 words; $1,000. **Tips:** Query first with brief proposal explaining story focus and include credentials/clips of published work. **Queries:** Required. **E-Queries:** No. **Unsolicited mss:** Accepts. **SASE Required:** Yes. **Payment:** On acceptance.

INSIDE

Jewish Publishing Group, 2100 Arch St., Philadelphia, PA 19103-1308. 215-832-0797. Website: www.jewishexponent.com. Quarterly. $35.95/yr. Circ.: 65,000. Robert Leiter, Editor. **Description:** For Jewish readership in the Philadelphia area. Lifestyle pieces as well as ethnic interest, fashion, home, health, finance, travel, the arts, etc.;

2,000-3,000 words; $350-$500. **Tips:** "Write gracefully for upscale readers. Teach something useful." **Queries:** Preferred. **E-Queries:** Yes. **Unsolicited mss:** Accepts. **Freelance Content:** 80%. **Rights:** FNAR. **Payment:** On publication.

LIVING ABOARD

P.O. Box 91299, Austin , TX 78709-1299. 512-892-4446.
E-mail: editor@livingaboard.com. Website: www.livingaboard.com. Bimonthly.
$18/yr. Circ.: 10,000. Linda Ridihalgh, Editor. **Description:** Lifestyle magazine for those who live or dream of living on their boats. **Nonfiction:** Articles, 1,000-2,000, on personal experience or practical information about living aboard; $.05/word. **Art:** $5/photo, $50/cover photo. **Tips:** Send complete manuscript with bio and credits; e-mail or disk submissions preferred. Photos a big plus. **Payment:** On publication.

MAGICAL BLEND

MB Media, 133-1/2 Broadway St., Chico, CA 95928-5317. 888-296-2442.
E-mail: editor@magicalblend.com. Website: www.magicalblend.com. Quarterly.
$9.95/yr. Circ.: 105,000. Michael Peter Langevin, Editor. **Description:** Offers an entertaining and unique look at modern spiritual lifestyles. Positive, uplifting articles on spiritual exploration, alternative health, social change, self improvement, stimulating creativity, lifestyles, and interviews; 2,000 words max. **Tips:** "No preaching." **Queries:** Does not accept. **Unsolicited mss:** Accepts. **Response:** 1-6 months. **Freelance Content:** 90%. **Payment:** On publication.

MOTHER EARTH NEWS

Ogden Publications, Inc., 1503 SW 42nd St., Topeka, KS 66609-1265. 785-274-4300.
E-mail: letters@motherearthnews.com. Website: www.motherearthnews.com. Bimonthly. $18/yr. Circ.: 375,000. Cheryl Long, Editor-in-Chief. **Description:** Emphasizes resourceful living and country skills for rural residents and urbanites who aspire to a more independent lifestyle. **Nonfiction:** Articles on do-it-yourself living, gardening, home building and repair, natural health, cooking, hobbies, and outdoor living; 300-3,000 words; $.30/word. **Tips:** Review the magazine before submitting. Submit seasonal material five months in advance. **Queries:** Required. **E-Queries:** Yes. **Response:** 6 months. **Payment:** On acceptance.

MOTORHOME

See full listing in Travel Articles category.

NATURAL HOME

See full listing in Home & Garden category.

MOUNTAIN LIVING

Wiesner Publishing, 7009 S Potomac St., Englewood, CO 80112-4037. 303-662-5211.
E-mail: irawlings@mountainliving.com. Website: www.mountainliving.com. 6x/yr.
$3.95/issue. Circ.: 38,000. Irene Rawlings, Editor. **Description:** Features lifestyle pieces for people who live in the mountains or who dream of living there. Articles on

home, garden, travel, architecture, art, and cuisine. **Tips:** Make sure queries reflect the content of the magazine. "Our magazine is very specialized–writers cannot break in without having a sense of the kinds of things we publish. Review a copy of the magazine first and avoid clichés." **Queries:** Required. **E-Queries:** Yes. **Response:** 4 weeks. **Freelance Content:** 50%. **Rights:** FNASR. **Payment:** On acceptance.

REUNIONS MAGAZINE

P.O. Box 11727, Milwaukee, WI 53211-0727. 414-263-4567. E-mail: reunions@execpc.com. Website: www.reunionsmag.com. Bimonthly. $3/$9.99. Circ.: 12,000. Edith Wagner, Editor. **Description:** For persons who are organizing and making decisions for their family, class, military, or other reunions. Seeks tips and techniques (e.g. how to make a memory book sparkle, how to cook for 150 people, where to go/what to do when you get there); clippings (about reunions for us to summarize); funny reunion material; reunion puzzles; and other hot ideas. Prefers short pieces 500 words or less; $5-$10. **Tips:** "We use more short material than long. Subject must be reunions. We're not interested in fiction unless it's reunion stories for kids." **Queries:** Not necessary. **E-Queries:** Yes. **SASE Required:** Yes. **Freelance Content:** 70%. **Rights:** FNAR. **Payment:** On publication.

ROBB REPORT

CurtCo Robb Media, 1 Acton Pl., Acton, MA 01720-3910. 978-264-7500. Website: www.robbreport.com. Monthly. $65/yr. Circ.: 106,500. Larry Bean, Editor. **Description:** Consumer magazine for high-end luxury market. Lifestyles, home interiors, fashion, boats, travel, investment opportunities, exotic automobiles, business, technology, etc.; 150-1,500 words. **Queries:** Required. **E-Queries:** No. **Unsolicited mss:** Accepts. **Response:** 1-3 months. **SASE Required:** Yes. **Freelance Content:** 75%. **Rights:** All. **Payment:** On acceptance.

SOUTHERN ACCENTS

See full listing in Home & Garden category.

SUNSET MAGAZINE

Sunset Publishing Corp., 80 Willow Rd., Menlo Park, CA 94025. 650-321-3600. E-mail: openhouse@sunset.com. Website: www.sunset.com. Monthly. $24/yr. Circ.: 1,477,000. Katie Tamony, Editor-in-Chief. **Description:** Regional magazine for Western America, covering travel and recreation; garden and outdoor living; food and entertaining; building, design, and crafts; 300-1,000 words; $1/word. **Tips:** "We're looking for well-written stories and Travel Guide items offering satisfying travel experiences accomplished in a day or weekend, or as part of a vacation, in the American West or in parts of Canada and Mexico." **Queries:** Preferred. **E-Queries:** No. **Unsolicited mss:** Do not accept. **Response:** 1-3 months. **SASE Required:** Yes. **Freelance Content:** 5%. **Payment:** On acceptance.

TOWN & COUNTRY

The Hearst Corp., 1700 Broadway, New York, NY 10019-5905. 212-903-5000.
E-mail: tnc@hearst.com. Website: www.townandcountrymag.com. Monthly. Circ.:
450,000. Pamela Fiori, Editor. **Description:** General interest articles covering travel,
beauty, fashion, individuals, and the arts. **Tips:** Considers 1-page proposals; include
clips and resumé. Check out a recent issue of the magazine before submitting.
Queries: Required. **Unsolicited mss:** Does not accept. **Freelance Content:** 30%.
Payment: On acceptance.

TRAILER LIFE

TL Enterprises, Inc., 2575 Vista Del Mar, Ventura, CA 93001. 805-667-4100.
E-mail: bleonard@affinitygroup.com. Website: www.trailerlife.com. Monthly.
$3.99/issue. Circ.: 280,000. Barbara Leonard, Editor. **Description:** For RV travelers.
Features on trailers, motorhomes, truck campers, interesting destinations, on-the-
road hobbies, new products, vehicle tests, etc.; 200-2,000 words; $100-$600. **Art:** "We
sometimes buy supplemental art for $75-$250, $500-$700 (cover)." **Tips:** Supply
good 35 mm slides and submit a complete package. **Queries:** Required. **E-Queries:**
No. **Response:** 2-3 weeks. **SASE Required:** Yes. **Freelance Content:** 45%.
Rights: FNAR and electronic. **Payment:** On acceptance.

WHOLE LIFE TIMES

21225 Pacific Coast Hwy, Suite B, P.O. Box 1187, Malibu, CA 90265. 310-317-4200.
E-mail: editor@wholelifetimes.com. Website: www.wholelifetimes.com. Monthly.
Free. Circ.: 58,000. Abigail Lewis, Editor-in-Chief. **Description:** Issues of concern
to "Cultural Creatives"—alternative health/healing, environment, food/nutrition, personal growth, spirituality, and progressive social change. Prefers pieces dealing with
the Southern CA area. **Nonfiction:** To 2,000 words; pays $75-$750 depending on
length and scope of story. **Tips:** Understand the holistic mindset. Readers are fairly
sophisticated; avoid "Yoga 101." **Queries:** Not necessary. **E-Queries:** Yes.
Unsolicited mss: Accepts. **Response:** 1-12 months. **SASE Required:** Yes.
Freelance Content: 75%. **Rights:** FNAR. **Payment:** 30 days after publication.

WIRED

Condé Nast Publications, Inc., 520 Third St., Fl. 3, San Francisco, CA 94107-1815.
415-276-5000. E-mail: editor@wiredmag.com. Website: www.wired.com/wired.
Monthly. $39.95/yr. Circ.: 531,500. Chris Anderson, Editor-in-Chief. **Description:**
Lifestyle magazine for the "digital generation." Discusses the meaning and context of
digital technology in today's world. **Payment:** On acceptance.

MEN'S

BLACK MEN

Great Eastern Color Litho, 210 E State Rt. 4, Suite 211, Paramus, NJ 07652-5103.
201-843-4004. Bimonthly. $4.50/$18. Circ.: 450,000. Kate Ferguson, Editor-in-Chief.

Description: Lifestyle magazine aimed at African American men, age 18-49. Editorial focus is on sex/dating, health/fitness, sports, current events, business, personal finance, community affairs, arts, entertainment, and fashion. **Columns, Departments:** Accepts freelance work for "Sista Speak" department which features issue-oriented essays from women on love, sex, relationships, and other matters of importance to African American men; 750 words. **Tips:** "Avoid submitting/querying articles which don't fit in our format. Writers should submit queries in July and August because September is the month we produce our editorial calendar for the upcoming year. An interesting idea could be picked up and result in an assignment for a writer at this time." **Queries:** Preferred. **E-Queries:** No. **Unsolicited mss:** Accepts. **Rights:** FNAR. **Payment:** On publication.

ESQUIRE

The Hearst Corp., 1790 Broadway, New York, NY 10019-1412. 212-649-4020. E-mail: esquire@hearst.com. Website: www.esquire.com. Monthly. $15.94/yr. Circ.: 724,600. David Granger, Editor-in-Chief. **Description:** For intelligent adult male readers. **Fiction:** Short stories; submit only 1 at a time. No pornography, science fiction, poetry, or "true romance"; pay varies. **Nonfiction:** 2,500-6,500 words; pay varies. **Tips:** Query with clips; unpublished writers, send complete manuscripts. **Queries:** Required. **Payment:** On publication.

GQ: GENTLEMEN'S QUARTERLY

Condé Nast Publications, Inc., 4 Times Square, New York, NY 10036. 212-286-2860. E-mail: gqmag@aol.com. Website: www.gq.com. Monthly. $19.97/yr. Circ.: 775,000. Jim Nelson, Editor-in-Chief. **Description:** General-interest magazine on the life of the man. Covers politics, personalities, lifestyles, trends, grooming, sports, travel, business, and fashion. **Columns, Departments:** Private Lives (essays by men on life); Games (sports); Guy Food (food with recipes); Health; Humor; also on fitness, nutrition, investments, and music. **Tips:** Send clips. **Queries:** Required. **Unsolicited mss:** Does not accept.

HEARTLAND U.S.A.

UST Publishing, 100 W Putnam Ave., Greenwich, CT 06830-5342. 203-622-3456. E-mail: husaedit@att.net. Bimonthly. $12/yr. Circ.: 1,200,000. Brad Pearson, Editor. **Description:** General-interest lifestyle magazine for the active adult male interested in the outdoors. Addresses readers' traditional American lifestyles, interests, and values by providing compelling stories and covering topics such as sports, fishing, hunting, automotive, Western/rodeo, and human interest. Articles run 1,200 words; pays $.25-$1/word. **Tips:** "We are currently overstocked, so we aren't very aggressive in looking for new contributors. We offer a free sample to freelancers and encourage all prospective contributors to review it thoroughly for voice and style." **E-Queries:** Yes. **Response:** 1 month. **SASE Required:** Yes. **Freelance Content:** 95%. **Rights:** FNAR. **Payment:** On acceptance.

MEN'S FITNESS
See full listing in Fitness Magazines category.

MEN'S HEALTH
See full listing in Health category.

MEN'S JOURNAL
Wenner Media, 1290 Avenue of the Americas, Fl. 2, New York, NY 10104-0295. 212-484-1616. E-mail: letters@mensjournal.com. Website: www.mensjournal.com. Monthly. $14.97/yr. Circ.: 653,200. Bob Wallace, Editor-in-Chief. **Description:** Lifestyle magazine for active men, ages 25-49. Articles and profiles on travel, fitness, health, adventure, and participatory sports; 2,000-7,000 words. **Queries:** Required. **Payment:** On acceptance.

PENTHOUSE
General Media Communications, 11 Penn Plaza, Fl. 12, New York, NY 10001-2006. 212-702-6000. Website: www.penthousemag.com. Monthly. $46/yr. Circ.: 641,100. Bob Guccione, Editor-in-Chief. **Description:** Essays, sociological studies, travel, humor, food and fashion, for the sophisticated male. **Fiction:** No unsolicited fiction. **Nonfiction:** General-interest profiles, interviews (with introduction), and investigative or controversial pieces; to 5,000 words; to $1/word. **Queries:** Preferred. **Contact:** Peter Bloch, Editor.

PLAYBOY
730 Fifth Ave., New York, NY 10019-4105. 212-261-5000. E-mail: editor@playboy.com. Website: www.playboy.com. Monthly. Circ.: 3,213,200. **Description:** Magazine for urban men. Publishes nonfiction pieces 3,500-6,000 words, up to $5,000. Also sophisticated fiction, 1,000-10,000 words (5,000 preferred), pays $2,000 for short-shorts. **Queries:** Required. **E-Queries:** No. **Unsolicited mss:** Do not accept. **Response:** 1 month. **SASE Required:** Yes. **Rights:** FNASR. **Payment:** On acceptance. **Contact:** Stephen Randall, Executive Editor; Barbara Wellis, Fiction Editor.

MILITARY

AMERICA'S CIVIL WAR
See full listing in History category.

ARMOR MAGAZINE
U.S. Army Armor Center, Bldg. 1109 A Sixth Ave., Rm. 371, Fort Knox, KY 40121. 502-624-2249. E-mail: armormagazine@knox.army.mil. Website: www.knox.army.mil/armormag. Bimonthly. $20/yr. Circ.: 12,500. Davie Manning, Editor-in-Chief. **Description:** Professional magazine of the Armor Branch for military units and agencies responsible for direct-fire ground combat.

Nonfiction: Military history; research and development of armaments; tactical benefits and strategies, logistics, and related topics. **Art:** Write captions on paper and tape to the back of the photos (don't write on photo backs). Indicate if you want the photos returned. **Tips:** Does not offer payment. **Response:** 2 weeks.

ARMY MAGAZINE

2425 Wilson Blvd., Arlington, VA 22201-3385. 703-841-4300.
E-mail: armymag@ausa.org. Website: www.ausa.org. Monthly. Circ.: 85,000. Mary Blake French, Editor-in-Chief. **Description:** Military subjects, essays, humor, history (especially Korea and World War II), news reports, first-person anecdotes. **Nonfiction:** 1,500 words; $.12-$.18/word. **Fillers:** Cartoons, strong military slant; $35-$50. **Columns, Departments:** Military news, books, commentary (no unsolicited book reviews). **Art:** 35mm slides, 8x10 B&W; 8x10 color glossy prints. Pay varies. **Queries:** Not necessary. **E-Queries:** No. **Unsolicited mss:** Accepts. **Freelance Content:** 70%. **Rights:** All. **Payment:** On publication.

LEATHERNECK MAGAZINE

P.O. Box 1775, Quantico, VA 22134-0776. 703-640-6161.
E-mail: leatherneck@mca-marines.org. Website: www.mca-marines.org. Monthly. $19/yr. Circ.: 96,800. Walter G. Ford, Editor. **Description:** On U.S. Marines. **Nonfiction:** Articles, to 2,500 words, with photos; pays $75/printed page. **Queries:** Preferred. **Payment:** On publication.

MARINE CORPS GAZETTE

P.O. Box 1775, Quantico, VA 22134. 703-640-6161. E-mail: gazette@mca-marines.org. Website: http://mca-marines.org/Gazette/gaz.html. Monthly. $3.50/$32. Circ.: 29,000. Jack Glasgow, Editor. **Description:** Professional journal of U.S. Marines, oriented toward officers and senior enlisted personnel; provides a forum for open discussion and a free exchange of ideas relating to the U.S. Marine Corps and military capabilities. Articles run 750-1,500 words. **Tips:** Does not offer payment. **Queries:** Preferred. **E-Queries:** Yes. **Unsolicited mss:** Accepts. **Response:** 2-4 weeks. **Freelance Content:** 80%. **Rights:** All.

MHQ: QUARTERLY JOURNAL OF MILITARY HISTORY

See full listing in History category.

MILITARY MAGAZINE

2122 28th St., Sacramento, CA 95818. 916-457-8990.
E-mail: generalinfo@milmag.com. Website: www.milmag.com. Monthly. $16/yr. Circ.: 20,000. Armond Noble, Publisher/Editor. **Description:** Military history (WWII, Korea, Vietnam, and today). A conservative publication, prided in printing the truth, dedicated to all who served in the armed forces. **Nonfiction:** Personal war experiences; 4,000 words or less. **Fillers:** Humor in uniform, military humor; 1,000 words or less. **Art:** 200 dpi or better. **Tips:** No payment offered. Sample copy available for no charge. **Queries:** Preferred. **E-Queries:** Yes. **Unsolicited mss:** Accepts.

MILITARY OFFICER
See full listing in Seniors Magazines category.

NATIONAL GUARD
National Guard Assn. of the U.S., One Massachusetts Ave. NW, Washington, DC 20001-1402. 202-789-0031. E-mail: magazine@ngaus.org. Website: www.ngaus.org. Monthly. $20/yr. Circ.: 45,000. Richard Alexander, Publisher. **Description:** Articles on national defense. **Queries:** Preferred. **Payment:** On publication.

SIGNAL
4400 Fair Lakes Ct., Fairfax, VA 22033-3899. 703-631-6100.
E-mail: signal@afcea.org. Website: www.afcea.org/signal. Monthly. $56. Circ.: 30,000. Maryann Lawlor, Senior Editor. **Description:** Communications/electronics issues within the military, industry, and government; 1,400-2,500 words; $650 for 1,800 words. Must include art with submission. **Tips:** Only works with published writers. **Queries:** Required. **E-Queries:** Yes. **Unsolicited mss:** Accepts. **Response:** 1-4 months. **SASE Required:** Yes. **Freelance Content:** 10%. **Rights:** FNAR. **Payment:** On publication.

TIMES NEWS SERVICE
Army Times Publishing Co., Springfield, VA 22159. 703-750-7479.
E-mail: pthompson@atpco.com. Website: www.militarycity.com. Weekly. $2.50/$52. Circ.: 300,000. Phillip Thompson, Lifelines Editor. **Description:** Publishes *Air Force Times*, *Army Times*, *Navy Times*, and *Marine Corps Times* (Gannett weeklies serving the military community, covering breaking developments that affect the careers of readers). **Nonfiction:** Features on contemporary life in the military. Recreation, finances, outdoor life, food/drink, nightlife, relationships, health/fitness, parenting, etc.; to 1,500 words; to $500. **Columns, Departments:** Fitness for young and athletic people; personal finance for moderate incomes; 500 words; $200. **Art:** Color slides, electronic (high-res JPEG); $75/image. **Tips:** Pitch an original story, interesting and entertaining, with a military connection, preferably with military people in the story. **Queries:** Required. **E-Queries:** Yes. **Unsolicited mss:** Does not accept. **Response:** Queries 2-8 weeks, submissions 1-3 weeks. **SASE Required:** Yes. **Freelance Content:** 75%. **Payment:** On acceptance.

VFW
See full listing in Associations category.

VIETNAM
See full listing in History category.

WORLD WAR II
See full listing in History category.

NEW AGE & SPIRITUAL

ALIVE NOW

P.O. Box 34004, Nashville, TN 37203-0004. 615-340-7218. E-mail: alivenow@upper-room.org. Website: www.alivenow.org. Bimonthly. $3.50/$14.95. Circ.: 70,000. Melissa Tidwell, Editor. **Description:** Seeks to nourish people who are hungry for a sacred way of living. Each issue focuses on contemporary topic, explored through prayers, personal experiences, poetry, photographs, and art. **Nonfiction:** Personal experiences of how contemporary issues affect spiritual life, meditations on scripture, prayers, and litanies. 350-600 words; $40-$150. **Poetry:** On the issue's theme; 40 lines or less; $25-$100. **Tips:** "See our website for coming themes. Material unrelated to themes is not considered. Use inclusive language and personal approach. Readership is clergy and lay, across denominations and theological spectrum." **Queries:** Not necessary. **E-Queries:** Yes. **Unsolicited mss:** Accepts. **Freelance Content:** 30%. **Rights:** FNASR. **Payment:** On acceptance.

AQUARIUS: A SIGN OF THE TIMES

1035 Green St., Roswell, GA 30075. 770-641-9055. E-mail: aquarius-editor@mindspring.com. Website: www.aquarius-atlanta.com. Monthly. Free at newsstands; $30/yr. Circ.: 60,000. Kathryn Sargent, Editor. **Description:** Seeks to expand awareness and support readers' spiritual growth. **Nonfiction:** On astrology, divination, alternative spirituality, energy healing, interviews, genetically engineered foods, intentional communities, meditation, yoga, herbs, aromatherapy, etc.; 850 words. **Poetry:** Up to 850 words. **Fillers:** Cartoons, puzzles. **Tips:** Avoid spaceships, aliens, channeled communications, lots of Biblical quotations. "We prefer articles sent via e-mail, pasted into the body of message. Photos with article a plus." **Queries:** Preferred. **E-Queries:** Yes. **Unsolicited mss:** Accepts. **Response:** Queries 1 month, submissions vary. **SASE Required:** Yes. **Freelance Content:** 90%.

BODY & SOUL

New Age Publishing, 42 Pleasant St., Watertown, MA 02472. 617-926-0200. E-mail: editor@bodyandsoulmag.com. Website: www.bodyandsoulmag.com. 8x/yr. $4.99/$14.95. Circ.: 230,000. Seth Bauer, Editor-in-Chief. **Description:** Guide for readers who want to live healthier, more balanced lives. **Nonfiction:** Alternative medicine, natural foods, spirituality, mind/body connection, fitness, greener living; 1,500-3,500 words; up to $1,500. **Fillers:** Short news items; 50-250; $50. **Columns, Departments:** Care (health/fitness/beauty), Choose (home/natural selections), Nourish (food/nutrition), Evolve (mind/spirit/life lessons); 600-1,300 words. Book and music reviews, 200-750 words. **Tips:** Include recent clips and resumé. **Queries:** Preferred. **E-Queries:** No. **Unsolicited mss:** Accepts. **Response:** 8 weeks. **SASE Required:** Yes. **Freelance Content:** 60%. **Rights:** FNASR and electronic. **Payment:** On acceptance. **Contact:** Donna Ress, Assistant Editor.

DREAM NETWORK

1337 Powerhouse Ln., Suite 22, P.O. Box 1026, Moab, UT 84532.
E-mail: publisher@dreamnetwork.net. Website: www.dreamnetwork.net. Quarterly.
$25/yr. H. Roberta Ossana, Editor. **Description:** Features articles, interviews, news
items, photographs, and artwork that inspire, inform, or educate readers on dreams;
1,800 words max; include photos/illustrations. **Tips:** "We serve as a vehicle of creative
and scholarly expression for the growing dream movement. It is our desire to inspire
and educate individuals interested in exploring the meaning and symbolic,
metaphoric language of dreams and their relevance toward individual and cultural
healing and revolution." **Queries:** Not necessary. **Unsolicited mss:** Accepts.
Response: 30-60 days. **SASE Required:** Yes. **Freelance Content:** 50%. **Rights:**
None. **Payment:** In copies.

FATE

P.O. Box 460, Lakeville, MN 55044. 800-728-2730. E-mail: fate@fatemag.com.
Website: www.fatemag.com. Monthly. $4.95/$29.95. Circ.: 20,000. Phyllis Galde,
Editor. **Description:** Covers the strange and unknown, for people willing to believe
that unexplainable things happen. **Nonfiction:** True reports of the strange and
unknown; 1,500-5,000 words; $.10/word. **Fillers:** Briefs on unusual events, odd folk-
lore; up to 1,500 words; $.10/word. **Columns, Departments:** My Proof of Survival
(personal accounts of survival after death); True Mystic Experiences (personal
accounts of unexplained happenings); up to 1,000 words; $25. **Tips:** "Much of our
content is contributed by readers." **Queries:** Preferred. **E-Queries:** Yes. **Response:**
Queries 6 weeks, submissions up to 3 months. **SASE Required:** Yes. **Freelance
Content:** 80%. **Rights:** All. **Payment:** On publication.

THE MOUNTAIN ASTROLOGER

P.O. Box 970, Cedar Ridge, CA 95924.
E-mail: editorial@mountainastrologer.com. Website: www.mountainastrologer.com.
Bimonthly. $7/$36. Circ.: 55,000.**Description:** Astrology magazine featuring arti-
cles, book reviews, humor, and astrological forecasts. **Columns, Departments:**
Article Particles (only area which does not require a query): short anecdotal material,
chart interpretation tips, poetry, humorous pieces, and cartoons. **Art:** Charts and
illustrations to accompany articles. **Queries:** Required. **E-Queries:** Yes.
Unsolicited mss: Does not accept. **Response:** 60 days. **Rights:** One-time.
Contact: Tem Tarriktar, Nan Geary, Janette de Prosse, Editors.

MYSTERIES MAGAZINE

Phantom Press Publications, P.O. Box 490, Walpole, NH 03608. 603-352-1645.
E-mail: editor@mysteriesmagazine.com. Website: www.mysteriesmagazine.com.
Quarterly. Circ.: 15,000. Kim Guarnaccia, Editor/Publisher. **Description:** Articles on
historical mysteries, the paranormal, conspiracies, archaeology, the occult, and scientific discoveries. **Nonfiction:** Feature articles (3,000-5,000 words) and book reviews
(500 words). Pays $.05/word. **Art:** Prefers electronic format for submissions. Pays
$5/image. **Tips:** "Inquire first, preferably by e-mail, with article ideas." **Queries:**

Preferred. **E-Queries:** Yes. **Response:** 3-5 weeks. **SASE Required:** Yes. **Freelance Content:** 60%. **Rights:** FNAR. **Payment:** On publication.

PANGAIA

Blessed Bee, Inc., P.O. Box 641, Point Arena, CA 95468-0641. 707-882-2052. E-mail: editor@pangaia.com. Website: www.pangaia.com. Quarterly. Circ.: 7,000. Anne Newkirk Niven, Publisher. **Description:** Explores Pagan and Gaian Earth-based spirituality. Features essays, poetry, rituals, plays, interviews, articles, and artwork. **Nonfiction:** Activism, ecology, legends, magic, mythology, prayer, rituals, shamanism. 500-5,000 words; $.01/word. **Columns, Departments:** Toe to Toe, Scientific Mysticism, Pathfinders, and Sacred Space. **Tips:** Query for guidelines. **Queries:** Preferred. **Contact:** Elizabeth Barrette, Managing Editor.

PARABOLA

Society for Study of Myth & Tradition, 656 Broadway, New York, NY 10012-2317. 212-505-9037. E-mail: editors@parabola.org. Website: www.parabola.org. Quarterly. $24/yr. Circ.: 40,000. Natalie Baan, Managing Editor. **Description:** "The magazine of myth and tradition." Thematic issues present essays and retellings of traditional myths and fairy tales. Articles on myth, symbol, and spiritual teachings; to 3,000 words. Retellings of traditional stories; to 1,500 words. Pay varies. **Tips:** Contact for upcoming themes and guidelines. Seeks a balance between scholarly and accessible writing, on the ideas of myth and tradition. **Queries:** Preferred.

SAGEWOMAN

Blessed Bee, Inc., P.O. Box 469, Point Arena, CA 95468. 707-882-2052. E-mail: editor@sagewoman.com. Website: www.sagewoman.com. Quarterly. $6.95/$21. Circ.: 25,000. Anne Newkirk Niven, Editor. **Description:** Articles that help women explore spiritual, emotional, and mundane lives and respect all people, creatures, and Earth. "Celebrates the Goddess in every woman." **Nonfiction:** On women's spiritual experience; focuses on issues of concern to pagan and other spiritually-minded women; 1,000-5,000 words. **Tips:** "We prefer inquiries and submissions by e-mail. Please read a copy before submitting; features must be written to an upcoming theme." **Queries:** Not necessary. **E-Queries:** Yes. **Unsolicited mss:** Accepts. **Response:** 1-3 months. **SASE Required:** Yes. **Freelance Content:** 80%. **Rights:** First worldwide serial. **Payment:** On publication.

SCIENCE OF MIND

Science of Mind Publishing, 2600 W Magnolia Blvd., Burbank, CA 91505. 818-526-7757. E-mail: edit@scienceofmind.com. Website: www.scienceofmind.com. Monthly. Circ.: 68,000. Amanda Pisani, Editor-in-Chief. **Description:** Thoughtful perspective on how to experience greater self-acceptance, empowerment, and a meaningful life. **Nonfiction:** Inspiring first-person pieces, 1,000-2,000 words. Interviews with notable spiritual leaders, 3,500 words.

SPIRITUALITY & HEALTH

74 Trinity Pl., New York, NY 10006. E-mail: editor@spiritualityhealth.com. Website: www.spiritualityhealth.com. Betsy Robinson, Managing Editor. **Description:** Covers the people, practices and ideas of the spiritual renaissance in contemporary society and their impact on personal and community well-being. Short department pieces, 100-600 words; features, 1,000-2,500 words. Fees negotiated, based on length, complexity, author experience, etc. **Tips:** "We look for articles that are useful, educational, rich in information, full of news. Read writer's guidelines and be familiar with our magazine. We are not New Age, and your best bet is a short news item with a spiritual angle for Updates & Observations." Rarely accepts features from first-time writers. **Queries:** Preferred. **E-Queries:** Yes.

VENTURE INWARD

215 67th Ave., Virginia Beach, VA 23451. 757-437-7210. E-mail: letters@edgarcayce.org. Website: www.edgarcayce.org. Bimonthly. Circ.: 35,000. Kevin J. Todeschi, Editor-in-Chief. **Description:** Membership magazine for Edgar Cayce organizations (A.R.E., Edgar Cayce Fdn., Atlantic Univ.), on holistic health, spiritual development, mystical experiences, and Cayce philosophy (reincarnation, etc.). **Nonfiction:** Personal mystical or holistic health experiences; to 3,000 words; $300-$400. **Columns, Departments:** Guest Column (opinion, to 800 words); Turning Point (a personal turning-point experience, to 800 words); The Mystical Way (a personal paranormal experience, to 1,500 words); Holistic Health (brief accounts of success using Edgar Cayce remedies); book reviews, to 500 words. Pays $50-$400. **Queries:** Required. **E-Queries:** Yes. **Unsolicited mss:** Do not accept. **Response:** 2-4 weeks. **SASE Required:** Yes. **Freelance Content:** 75%. **Payment:** On publication.

WHOLE LIFE TIMES

See full listing in Lifestyle Magazines category.

PERFORMING ARTS

ACOUSTIC GUITAR

String Letter Publishing, P.O. Box 767, San Anselmo, CA 94979. 415-485-6946. E-mail: editors.ag@stringletter.com. Website: www.acousticguitar.com. Monthly. $29.95/yr. Circ.: 54,600. Scott Nygaard, Editor. **Description:** For players and makers of acoustic guitars. **Tips:** Prefers to receive material from musicians. **Queries:** Preferred.

AMERICAN SQUARE DANCE MAGAZINE

Gramac Printing, 34 E Main, Apopka, FL 32703-5256. 401-647-9688. E-mail: nsd@squaredance.ws. Website: www.squaredance.ws. Monthly. $27.50/yr. Circ.: 12,000. Randy Boyd, Editor. **Description:** For dancers, teachers, callers, and leaders of square dancing. Includes reviews of square and round dance music and listings of square dance festivals.

BACK STAGE

770 Broadway, New York, NY 10003. 646-654-5500. E-mail: seaker@backstage.com. Website: www.backstage.com. Sherry Eaker, Editor in Chief. **Description:** "The Performing Arts Weekly." Service features on learning one's craft, dealing with succeeding in the business, interviews with actors, directors, and playwrights, and industry news/trends. Pay varies. **Queries:** Preferred. **Payment:** On publication.

BLUEGRASS UNLIMITED

P.O. Box 771, Warrenton, VA 20188-0771. 540-349-8181. E-mail: editor@bluegrassmusic.com. Website: www.bluegrassmusic.com. Monthly. $24/yr. Circ.: 27,200. Peter V. Kuykendall, Editor. **Description:** Covers bluegrass and traditional country music. Articles to 3,000 words; $.08-$.10/word. **Queries:** Preferred.

CHART

Chart Communications, Inc.
41 Britain St., Suite 200, Toronto, Ontario M5A 1R7 Canada. 416-363-3101. E-mail: chart@chartattack.com. Website: www.chartattack.com. Monthly. $3.95/$19.95. Circ.: 40,000. Nada Laskovski, Editor. **Description:** Covers Canada's music and pop culture, with slant to the cutting edge. **Queries:** Preferred.

CLAVIER

The Instrumentalist, 200 Northfield Rd., Northfield, IL 60093.
847-446-5000. Website: www.clavier.com. 10x/yr. $19/yr. Circ.: 16,000. Judy Nelson, Editor. **Description:** Professional journal for piano teachers at all levels. **Nonfiction:** Interview/profiles on artists, teachers, composers; teaching articles, music discussion, master classes, and humor pieces for performers and teachers; 8-10 pages; $80-$100/printed page. **Art:** Color prints, $100/full page. **Tips:** Writers should have music degrees. **Queries:** Preferred. **E-Queries:** No. **Unsolicited mss:** Accepts. **Response:** 4-6 weeks. **SASE Required:** Yes. **Freelance Content:** 75%. **Rights:** All. **Payment:** On publication.

COUNTRY WEEKLY

American Media, Inc., 118 16th Ave. S, Suite 230, Nashville, TN 37203.
615-259-1111. Website: www.countryweekly.com. 26x/yr. $46.50/yr. Circ.: 400,000. Rick Taylor, Managing Editor. **Description:** Features on the country music and entertainment industry, with industry news and profiles of musicians and other personalities in the field. **Queries:** Required. **E-Queries:** Yes. **Rights:** All.

DANCE MAGAZINE

MacFadden Communications Group, LLC, 111 Myrtle St., Suite 203, Oakland, CA 94607-2535. 510-839-6060. E-mail: dancemag@dancemagazine.com. Website: www.dancemagazine.com. Monthly. $34.95/yr. Circ.: 55,000. K.C. Patrick, Editor-in-Chief. **Description:** On all aspects of the world of dance: dancers, companies, history, professional concerns, health, news events, etc. **Tips:** Freelance content limited. Sample copy available at no charge. **Queries:** Preferred. **E-Queries:** Yes.

DANCE SPIRIT

Lifestyle Ventures, LLC, 250 W 57th St., Suite 420, New York, NY 10107. 212-265-8890. E-mail: editor@dancespirit.com; sjarrett@lifestyleventures.com. Website: www.dancespirit.com. Monthly. Circ.: 100,000. Caitlin Sims, Editorial Director. **Description:** For dancers of all disciplines. Articles on training, instruction and technique, choreography, dance styles, and profiles of dancers; pay varies. **Payment:** On publication. **Contact:** Sara Jarrett.

DANCE TEACHER

Lifestyle Ventures, LLC, 250 W 57th St., Suite 420, New York, NY 10107-0499. 212-265-8890. E-mail: csims@lifestyleventures.com. Website: www.dance-teacher.com. Monthly. $29.95/yr. Circ.: 20,000. Caitlin Sims, Editor. **Description:** For dance professionals. **Nonfiction:** For educators, students, and professionals; practical information on economic/business issues. Profiles of schools, methods, and people. 500-1,500 words; $100-$300. Photos helpful. **Tips:** All articles must be thoroughly researched. **Queries:** Preferred. **E-Queries:** Yes. **Unsolicited mss:** Accepts. **Freelance Content:** 70%.

DRAMATICS MAGAZINE

Educational Theatre Assn., 2343 Auburn Ave., Cincinnati, OH 45219-2815. 513-421-3900. E-mail: dcorathers@edta.org. Website: www.edta.org. Monthly (September-May). $24/yr. Circ.: 37,000. Don Corathers, Editor. **Description:** Magazine for high school theatre students. **Fiction:** One-act and full-length plays for high school production; $100-$400. **Nonfiction:** Articles on acting, directing, playwriting, and technical subjects. Also interviews and book reviews. Pays $25-$400. **Tips:** Does not publish didactic scripts or musicals. Be aware of the script's production demands. Readers are active theatre students and teachers. **Queries:** Not necessary. **Unsolicited mss:** Accepts. **Freelance Content:** 70%. **Rights:** FNASR. **Payment:** On acceptance.

ELECTRONIC MUSICIAN

PRIMEDIA Business Magazines & Media, P.O. Box 8845, Emeryville, CA 94662-0845. E-mail: emeditorial@primediabusiness.com. Website: www.emusician.com. Monthly. $36/yr. Circ.: 70,000. Steve Oppenheimer, Editor-in-Chief. **Description:** On audio recording, live sound engineering, technical applications, and product reviews. Articles run 1,500-3,500 words; $350-$750. **Payment:** On acceptance.

FLUTE TALK

Instrumentalist Publishing Co., 200 Northfield Rd., Northfield, IL 60093. 847-446-5000. Monthly. $2.50/issue. Circ.: 13,000. Victoria Jicha, Editor. **Description:** Publication for flute teachers or performers. Interviews with players, teachers, composers; other articles on flute playing; 3-5 pages; $90-$100/printed page. **Queries:** Preferred. **E-Queries:** No. **Unsolicited mss:** Accepts. **Response:** Queries 1 week, submissions 1 month. **SASE Required:** Yes. **Payment:** On publication.

GUITAR PLAYER MAGAZINE

United Entertainment Media, Inc., 2800 Campus Dr., San Mateo, CA 94403.
650-513-4300. E-mail: guitplyr@musicplayer.com. Website: www.guitarplayer.com.
Monthly. $24/yr. Circ.: 143,000. Michael Molenda, Editor. **Description:** On guitars
and related subjects. Articles run from 200 words, $100-$600. **Rights:** All. **Payment:**
On acceptance. **Contact:** Emily Fasten, Managing Editor.

GUITARONE

Cherry Lane Magazines, LLC, 6 E 32nd St., Fl. 11, New York, NY 10016-5415.
E-mail: guitarone@cherrylane.com. Website: www.guitaronemag.com. Monthly.
$19.95/yr. Circ.: 141,000. Troy Nelson, Editor-in-Chief. **Description:** Magazine for
serious guitarists. **Queries:** Preferred.

INTERNATIONAL MUSICIAN

American Federation of Musicians, 120 Walton St., Syracuse, NY 13202-1179.
315-422-0900. Website: www.afm.org. Monthly. $25/yr. Circ.: 122,400. Antoinette
Follett, Managing Editor. **Description:** Official publication of AFM. Targets professional musicians. **Queries:** Required. **Payment:** On acceptance.

JAZZIZ

2650 N Military Trail, Suite 140, Boca Raton, FL 33431-6339. 561-893-6868.
E-mail: mail@jazziz.com. Website: www.jazziz.com. Monthly. $69.95/yr. Circ.:
159,000. Michael Fagien, Publisher/Editor. **Description:** Jazz-lifestyle music publication. Features, interviews, profiles, and concept pieces on contemporary smooth
jazz, adult alternative, world-Brazilian, Afro-Cuban, Latin, traditional, and straight
ahead genres of jazz. Pay varies. **Tips:** Send resumé with manuscript. **E-Queries:**
Yes. **Freelance Content:** 80%. **Payment:** On acceptance.

KEYBOARD MAGAZINE

United Entertainment Media, Inc.
2800 Campus Dr., San Mateo, CA 94403-2506. 650-513-4300.
E-mail: keyboard@musicplayer.com. Website: www.keyboardmag.com. Monthly.
$25.95/yr. Circ.: 66,000. Greg Rule, Executive Editor. **Description:** On keyboard
instruments, players, and new technology. **Queries:** Preferred. **Payment:** On
acceptance.

LA FACTORIA DE SONIDO

Barrera Publishing, 43 W 38th St., Fl. 5, New York, NY 10018-1945. 212-840-0227.
Website: www.lafactoriadesonido.com. Bimonthly. $15/yr. Circ.: 120,000. Jennifer
Barrera, Executive Editor. **Description:** Hispanic music and art publication. Music
events, reviews, interviews, fashion and clubs focusing on Hispanic music of all kinds.

LIVING BLUES

University of Mississippi, Hill Hall, Room 301, University, MS 38677. 662-915-5742.
E-mail: lblues@olemiss.edu. Website: www.livingblues.com. Bimonthly. $23.95/yr.

Circ.: 20,000. Brett Bonner, Editor. **Description:** The journal of the African American blues tradition. **Nonfiction:** Interviews, some retrospective, historical articles or investigative pieces; 1,500-10,000 words; pays $75-$200. **Queries:** Preferred.

LOLLIPOP MAGAZINE
P.O. Box 441493, Somerville, MA 02144-0034. 617-623-5319. Website: www.lollipop.com. Quarterly. $15/yr. Circ.: 20,000. Scott Hefflon, Publisher/Editor. **Description:** On music and youth culture. Fiction, essays, and "edgy" commentary. Reviews and interviews related to underground culture. **Queries:** Preferred.

MIX
PRIMEDIA Business Magazines & Media, 6400 Hollis St., Suite 12, Emeryville, CA 94608-1086. 510-653-3307. E-mail: mixeditorial@primediabusiness.com. Website: www.mixonline.com. Monthly. $46/yr. Circ.: 51,700. George Peterson, Editorial Director. **Description:** For professionals, on audio, audio post-production, sound production, live sound, and music entertainment technology. Length and pay varies. **Queries:** Preferred. **Payment:** On publication.

MODERN DRUMMER
12 Old Bridge Rd., Cedar Grove, NJ 07009. 209-239-4140.
E-mail: mdinfo@moderndrummer.com. Website: www.moderndrummer.com. Monthly. $34.97/yr. Circ.: 102,000. Isabel Spagnardi, Publisher/President. **Description:** Features drumming how-tos, interviews, and more. Articles run 500-2,000 words; $50-$500. **Payment:** On publication.

OPERA NEWS
The Metropolitan Opera Guild, Inc., 70 Lincoln Ctr. Plaza, New York, NY 10023-6548. 212-769-7080. E-mail: info@operanews.com. Website: www.operanews.com. Monthly. $30/yr. Circ.: 100,000. Rudolph S. Rauch, Publisher/Editor. **Description:** On all aspects of opera. Articles run 600-2,500 words; pay varies. **Queries:** Preferred.

PERFORMING ARTS AND ENTERTAINMENT IN CANADA
See full listing in Film, TV, Entertainment category.

PLAYS
Sterling Partners, Inc., P.O. Box 600160, Newton, MA 02460. 617-630-9100.
E-mail: lpreston@playsmag.com. Website: www.playsmag.com. Elizabeth Preston, Editor. **Description:** Publishes one-act plays, for production by people ages 7-17. Comedies, dramas, farces, skits, holiday plays. Also adaptations of classics, biographies, puppet plays, creative dramatics. No religious or "adult" themes. Cast should be at least 8 characters. Sets should be within the capabilities of amateur set designers (school teachers, students, volunteers). **Tips:** "Read a copy of our magazine to get a feel for the kinds of plays we publish. Plays should be entertaining, even if there is a moral or message to convey." **Queries:** Required. **E-Queries:** Yes. **Response:** 1-2 weeks. **SASE Required:** Yes. **Freelance Content:** 100%.

ROLLING STONE

Wenner Media, 1290 Avenue of the Americas, Fl. 2, New York, NY 10104. 212-484-1616. E-mail: letters@rollingstone.com. Website: www.rollingstone.com. Biweekly. $19.94/yr. Circ.: 1,250,000. Jann S. Wenner, Editor-in-Chief. **Description:** American music, culture, and politics. **Tips:** No unsolicited manuscripts. Rarely accepts freelance material. Read editorial calendar before pitching ideas. **Queries:** Required.

SHEET MUSIC MAGAZINE

Shacor, Inc., 333 Adams St., Bedford Hills, NY 10507-2001. 914-244-8500. E-mail: editor@sheetmusicmagazine.com. Website: www.sheetmusicmagazine.com. Bimonthly. $19.94/yr. Circ.: 75,000. Edward J. Shanaphy, Editor-in-Chief. **Description:** For amateur and professional musicians. Most content is the actual reproduction of popular songs (words and music). Pieces for pianists, organists, and singers; on musicians, composers, music education, pedagogy; also reviews (to 500 words); no hard rock or heavy metal. 2,000 words; pay varies. **Tips:** Avoid modern rock era subjects. **Queries:** Preferred. **E-Queries:** Yes. **Unsolicited mss:** Accepts. **Response:** 2 months. **SASE Required:** Yes. **Freelance Content:** 50%.

STAGE DIRECTIONS

SMW Communications, Inc., 250 W 57th St., Suite 420, New York, NY 10107. 212-265-8890. E-mail: idorbian@lifestyleventures.com. Website: www.stage-directions.com. 12x/yr. $26/yr. Circ.: 7,000. Iris Dorbian, Editor-in-Chief. **Description:** On directing, costuming, makeup, lighting, set design and decoration, props, special effects, fundraising, and audience development, for readers active in all aspects of community, regional, academic, or youth theater. Submit articles, to 2,000 words; $.10/word. **Tips:** "Short pieces, 700-800 words, are a good way to approach us first."

STORYTELLING MAGAZINE

National Storytelling Network, 101 Courthouse Square, Jonesborough, TN 37659. 423-913-8201. E-mail: nsn@storynet.org. Website: www.storynet.org. Bimonthly. $50/yr. Circ.: 5,000. Nancy Kavanaugh, Editor. **Description:** For the professional storyteller. Articles on the oral tradition; 1,000-2,000 words. Unusual events or applications; 200-400 words. **Queries:** Required. **E-Queries:** Yes. **Unsolicited mss:** Accepts. **Response:** 2 weeks. **Payment:** In copies.

TEACHING THEATRE

See full listing in Education category.

URB MAGAZINE

Native Son Media, Inc., 2410 Hyperion Ave., Los Angeles, CA 90027. 323-993-0291. E-mail: word2urb@urb.com. Website: www.urb.com. 10x/yr. $15.95/yr. Circ.: 70,000. Scott Sterling, Editor. **Description:** On future music culture: electronic dance music, independent hip-hop, and DJ culture. Also, profiles of emerging musicians, singers, and groups. Pays $.10/word. **Tips:** Send published clips. **Queries:** Required. **E-Queries:** Yes. **Response:** 1 month. **Freelance Content:** 80%.

REGIONAL & CITY

(See also: Business, Environment & Conservation, Family & Parenting,
History, Home & Garden, Seniors,
Sports & Recreation, and Travel
for many regional publications)

ALABAMA HERITAGE

See full listing in History category.

ALABAMA LIVING

Alabama Rural Electric Association, P.O. Box 244014, Montgomery, AL 36124. 334-215-2737. E-mail: dgates@areapower.com. Website: www.alabamaliving.com. Monthly. $6/issue. Circ.: 365,000. Darryl Gates, Editor. **Description:** Consumer publication covering topics of interest (history, events, people) to rural and suburban Alabamians. Articles run 500-800 words; $100-$150. **Art:** Outdoor and seasonal scenes with an Alabama angle. Vertical transparencies; $100. **Tips:** "Stick to Alabama topics. Have a source for article, if necessary." **Queries:** Not necessary. **E-Queries:** Yes. **Unsolicited mss:** Accepts. **Response:** Queries 2 weeks, submissions 2 months. **SASE Required:** Yes. **Freelance Content:** 80%. **Payment:** On acceptance.

ALASKA BUSINESS MONTHLY

See full listing in Business category.

ALASKA MAGAZINE

Morris Communications Corp., 301 Arctic Slope Blvd., Suite 300, Anchorage, AK 99518. 907-275-2100. E-mail: donnarae.thompson@alaskamagazine.com. Website: www.alaskamagazine.com. Monthly. $30/yr. Circ.: 185,000. Andy Hall, Editor. **Description:** Covers all aspects of life in Alaska. **Nonfiction:** Articles on well-researched, interesting topics. Travel, historical, interview/profile, personal experience, destination pieces, etc.; 1,000-2,500 words; $380-$950. **Tips:** Send SASE for guidelines. **Queries:** Preferred. **Freelance Content:** 70%. **Payment:** On publication. **Contact:** Donna Rae Thompson, Editorial Assistant.

ALBEMARLE

375 Greenbrier Dr., Suite 100, Charlottesville, VA 22901. 434-817-2000.
E-mail: rhart@cjp.com. Website: www.cjp.com. Bimonthly. Circ.: 10,000. Ruth Hart, Editor. **Description:** Lifestyle magazine highlighting the news and events of Virginia. Topics include health/medicine, the arts, home architecture, interior design, and gardening; pay varies. **Tips:** Write for complete guidelines.

ALBERTA SWEETGRASS

See full listing in Ethnic & Multicultural category.

AMERICAN OUTBACK JOURNAL

New Media Group, 111 W Telegraph St., Suite 202, Carson City, NV 89703. 775-888-9330. E-mail: curt@americanoutback.com. Website: www.americanoutback.com. Curtis Pendergraft, Editor. **Description:** Online publication on the American West. Articles on lore, history, culture, ecology, politics, humor and travel to offbeat Western destinations. **Queries:** Preferred.

ARIZONA HIGHWAYS

Arizona Dept. of Transportation, 2039 W Lewis Ave., Phoenix, AZ 85009. 602-712-2024. E-mail: queryeditor@arizonahighways.com. Website: www.arizonahighways.com. Monthly. $3.99/$21 (US), $31 (Canada). Circ.: 325,000. Robert J. Early, Editor. **Description:** Travel in Arizona (adventure, humor, lifestyles, nostalgia, history, archaeology, Indian culture/crafts, nature, etc.). **Fiction:** Frontier-oriented, must be upbeat and wholesome; 1,800-2,500 words; $.55-$1/word. **Nonfiction:** Travel-adventure, travel-history, travel-destination; personal-experience pieces. Insightful and third-person. 800-1,800 words; $.55-$1/word. **Fillers:** Jokes (humor page); 200 words or less; $50. **Columns, Departments:** Focus on Nature, Along the Way, Back Road Adventures, Hiking, Destination, Humor. Insightful or nostalgic viewpoint. 750 words; $450. **Tips:** "To break in, submit short items to our Off-ramp department. Use active verbs. We do not accept stories on religion, government, or politics." **E-Queries:** Yes. **Unsolicited mss:** Does not accept. **Response:** 30 days or less. **SASE Required:** Yes. **Freelance Content:** 100%. **Payment:** On acceptance.

ARIZONA TRENDS OF THE SOUTHWEST

Dandick Co., P.O. Box 8508, Scottsdale, AZ 85252-8508. 480-948-1799. 10x/yr. $18/yr. Circ.: 34,000. Marnie McGann, Editor. **Description:** Regional magazine on fashion, health, beauty, special events, dining, the performing arts, and much more. **Queries:** Preferred.

ARKANSAS TIMES

Arkansas Writers Project, Inc., P.O. Box 34010, Little Rock, AR 72203. 501-375-2985. E-mail: arktimes@arktimes.com. Website: www.arktimes.com. Weekly. $24/yr. Circ.: 32,700. Max Brantley, Editor. **Description:** On Arkansas history, people, travel, politics. **Payment:** On acceptance.

ASPEN MAGAZINE

720 E Durant Ave., #E-8, Aspen, CO 81611-2071. 970-920-4040. E-mail: edit@aspenmagazine.com. Website: www.aspenmagazine.com. Bimonthly. $4.95/issue. Circ.: 18,500. Janet O'Grady, Editor-in-Chief. **Description:** City and regional news about Aspen, Colorado. **Nonfiction:** Lifestyle articles on Aspen, Snowmass, and the Roaring Fork Valley; outdoor sports, arts, profiles, food and wine, environment news, and photo essays related to Aspen and surrounding area. **Tips:** Sample copy $4.95. **Queries:** Required. **E-Queries:** Yes. **Unsolicited mss:** Does not accept. **Response:** 4 weeks. **SASE Required:** Yes. **Freelance Content:** 30%. **Payment:** 60 days from publication. **Contact:** Dana R. Butler, Managing Editor.

ATLANTA MAGAZINE

Emmis Publishing Corp., 260 Peachtree St., Suite 300, Atlanta, GA 30303.
404-527-5500. Website: www.atlantamagazine.com. Monthly. $19.95/yr. Circ.: 66,000.
Rebecca Burns, Editor-in-Chief. **Description:** Magaizne featuring Atlanta subjects
and personalities. Articles run 1,500-5,000 words; $300-$2,000. **Queries:** Required.
Payment: On acceptance.

ATLANTA HOMES AND LIFESTYLES

See full listing in Home & Garden category.

AVANCE HISPANO

Avance, Inc., 4230 Mission St., San Francisco, CA 94112-1520. 415-585-1080.
Website: www.avancehispano.com. Monthly. $25/yr. Circ.: 30,000. Vanessa Carias,
Publisher/Editor. **Description:** Spanish-language publication for people in the San
Francisco Bay area. Covers education, culture, the arts, science, technology, finance,
management, and law.

BACK HOME IN KENTUCKY

P.O. Box 710, Clay City, KY 40312-0710. 606-663-1011.
E-mail: info@backhomeinky.com. Website: www.backhomeinky.com 6x/yr. $20/yr.
Circ.: 10,000. Jerlene Rose, Publisher/Editor. **Description:** Focuses on Kentucky
destinations, profiles, personal memories, county spotlights, natural history, and nos-
talgia. **Nonfiction:** 400-1,000 words; $25 and up. **Columns, Departments:**
Chronicles (Kentucky history, 400-1,000 words); $25-$100. **Art:** Slides, photos; pays
$25 and up. **Queries:** Not necessary. **E-Queries:** Yes. **Unsolicited mss:** Accepts.
Response: 60 days. **Freelance Content:** 75%. **Payment:** On publication.

BALTIMORE MAGAZINE

1000 Lancaster St., Suite 400, Baltimore, MD 21202-4632. 410-752-4200.
E-mail: iken@baltimoremag.com. Website: www.baltimoremagazine.net. Monthly.
$3.95/$15. Circ.: 65,000. Ken Iglehart, Managing Editor. **Description:** Covers
Baltimore metro area: local people, events, trends, and ideas. **Nonfiction:** Consumer
advice, investigative, lifestyle, profiles, shelter; 250-4,000 words; typically $.30/word.
Columns, Departments: News You Can Use; 800-2,000 words; typically $.30/word.
Tips: Know the product (visit website). Consider short articles for departments; send
query letter and clips. **Queries:** Required. **E-Queries:** Yes. **Unsolicited mss:**
Accepts. **Response:** If editors think pitch might work. **SASE Required:** No.
Freelance Content: 60%. **Rights:** FNASR, reprint. **Payment:** On publication.

BIG SKY JOURNAL

E-Publishing.com, P.O. Box 1069, Bozeman, MT 59771-1069. 406-586-2712.
E-mail: bsj@bigskyjournal.com. Website: www.bigskyjournal.com. Bimonthly. $30/yr.
Circ.: 20,000. Laura M. Hengstler, Editor. **Description:** On Montana art and architecture, hunting and fishing, ranching and recreation. Both fiction (to 4,000 words)
and nonfiction (to 2,500 words). Pay varies. **Queries:** Preferred.

BIRMINGHAM

Birmingham Regional Chamber of Commerce, 505 20th Ave., Suite 151, Birmingham, AL 35203-4606. 205-250-7653. Website: www.bhammag.com. Monthly. $12/yr. Circ.: 12,600. Joe O'Donnell, Editor. **Description:** Regional magazine featuring profiles, business articles, and nostalgia pieces, with local focus. Also, dining, fashion, and general-interest; to 2,500 words; $50-$175. **SASE Required:** Yes. **Payment:** On publication.

BLUE RIDGE COUNTRY MAGAZINE

Leisure Publishing, P.O. Box 21535, Roanoke, VA 24018. 540-989-6138. E-mail: editorial@blueridgecountry.com. Website: www.blueridgecountry.com. 6x/yr. $3.95/$17.95. Circ.: 80,000. **Description:** Covers the history, folklore, travel, cuisine, festivals, outdoor recreation, environmental issues and personalities of the mountain regions of VA, WV, TN, KY, GA, MD, NC, SC, and AL. **Nonfiction:** Features and shorts (with newsy angles) on Applachian-related topics; 150-1,500 words; $50 and up. **Columns, Departments:** News, book reviews, festival features, hikes, environmental and travel news, mountain inn reviews; 150-500 words; $50-$200. **Art:** Transparencies; color prints; B&W prints considered; $25-$100 for photo features. **Tips:** "We often start first-time writers off with short articles, and encourage them to query ideas that will fit our Country Roads, Almanac, Mountain Delicacies, Mountain Inns, and The Hike departments. Photo support is strongly recommended." **Queries:** Preferred. **E-Queries:** Yes. **Unsolicited mss:** Accepts. **Response:** 1-2 months. **Freelance Content:** 90%. **Rights:** FNAR. **Payment:** On publication. **Contact:** Kurt Rheinheimer, Editor-in-Chief; Cara Ellen Modisett, Associate Editor.

BOCA RATON

JES Publishing Corp., 6413 Congress Ave., Suite 100, Boca Raton, FL 33487-2863. 561-997-8683. E-mail: magazine@bocamag.com. Website: www.bocamag.com. Bimonthly. $20/yr. Circ.: 21,400. Marie Speed, Editor-in-Chief. **Description:** Focuses on southern Florida. Regional issues, lifestyle trends, relationships, cuisine, travel, fashion, and profiles of local residents and celebrities; 800-3,000 words; $350-$1,000. **Tips:** Send query with clips. Guidelines available. **Queries:** Required. **SASE Required:** Yes. **Payment:** On acceptance.

THE BOSTON GLOBE MAGAZINE

P.O. Box 2378, Boston, MA 02107-2378. 617-929-2000. Website: www.globe.com/globe/magazine. Weekly. Circ.: 706,000. Doug Most, Editor-in-Chief. **Description:** Covers arts, entertainment, shopping, and news in the Boston area. **Tips:** Send query first. **Queries:** Preferred. **Unsolicited mss:** Accepts. **Response:** 3 weeks. **SASE Required:** Yes. **Freelance Content:** 50%. **Rights:** FNAR. **Payment:** On publication.

BOSTON MAGAZINE

Metrocorp, 300 Massachusetts Ave., Boston, MA 02115. 617-262-9700.
E-mail: editor@bostonmagazine.com. Website: www.bostonmagazine.com. Monthly.
$9/yr. Circ.: 125,000. Jon Marcus, Editor. **Description:** Offers expository features,
narratives, and articles on Boston-area personalities, institutions, and phenomena. No
fiction. 500-700 words, pays $1/word. **Queries:** Required. **Payment:** On publication.

BOSTONIA

Boston University, 10 Lenox St., Brookline, MA 02446-4042. 617-353-3081.
E-mail: bostonia@bu.edu. Website: www.bu.edu/alumni/bostonia/index.html.
Quarterly. Circ.: 230,000. Natalie Jacobsone McCracken, Editor-in-Chief.
Description: "The magazine of culture and ideas." General-interest magazine for
alumni and friends covering politics, literature, music, art, science, and education,
especially from a Boston of BU angle or by alumni. Articles run to 3,000 words; $150-
$2,500. **Queries:** Required.

BUFFALO SPREE

David Laurence Publications, Inc., 6215 Sheridan Dr., Buffalo, NY 14221-4837.
716-634-0820. E-mail: info@buffalospree.com. Website: www.buffalospree.com.
Bimonthly. $12/yr. Circ.: 25,000. Elizabeth Licata, Editor-in-Chief. **Description:**
City/regional magazine for western New York. Articles run 1,800 words; $125-$150.
Queries: Preferred. **Unsolicited mss:** Does not accept. **Freelance Content:** 90%.
Payment: On publication.

CAPE COD LIFE

4 Barlow Landing Rd., Suite 14, P.O. Box 1385, Pocasset, MA 02559-1385.
508-564-4466. E-mail: jrohlf@capecodlife.com. Website: www.capecodlife.com.
8x/yr. $19.75/yr. Circ.: 40,000. **Description:** About life on Cape Cod, Martha's
Vineyard, and Nantucket (past, present and future). Articles on events, business, art,
history, gardening, and lifestyle; 800-2,500 words; $.20-$.25/word. **Queries:**
Preferred. **E-Queries:** Yes. **Unsolicited mss:** Accepts. **Response:** 1-2 months.
SASE Required: Yes. **Freelance Content:** 90%. **Rights:** All. **Payment:** On
acceptance. **Contact:** Janice Randall Rohlf, Senior Editor.

CAROLINA GARDENER

See full listing in Home & Garden category.

CAROLOGUE

South Carolina Historical Society, 100 Meeting St., Charleston, SC 29401-2215. 843-
723-3225. E-mail: info@schistory.org. Website: www.schistory.org. Quarterly. $50/yr.
Circ.: 5,000. Eric Emerson, Editor. **Description:** General-interest articles, to 10
pages, on South Carolina history. **Queries:** Preferred. **Payment:** In copies.

CASCADES EAST

See full listing in Sports & Recreation/Outdoors category.

CENTRAL PA

WITF, Inc., P.O. Box 2954, Harrisburg, PA 17105-2954. 717-221-2800.
E-mail: centralpa@centralpa.org. Website: www.centralpa.org. Monthly. $45. Circ.:
40,000. Gail Huganir, Managing Editor. **Description:** Topics of interest to central
Pennsylvania, including profiles of notable central Pennsylvanians, and broadly based
articles of social interest that "enlighten and inform." Articles, 1,500-3,500 words;
pays $.10/word. **Tips:** "Strong central Pennsylvania connection and excellent writing
essential." **Payment:** On publication.

CHARLESTON MAGAZINE

P.O. Box 1794, Mt. Pleasant, SC 29465-1794. 843-971-9811.
Website: www.charlestonmag.com. Bimonthly. Circ.: 20,000. Darcy Shankland,
Editor. **Description:** General-interest magazine on local topics (people, events, history, etc.). **Tips:** Send SASE for guidelines. **Queries:** Preferred. **Payment:** 30 days
from publication.

CHARLOTTE

Abarta Media, 127 W Worthington Ave., Suite 208, Charlotte, NC 28203-4474.
704-335-7181. E-mail: editor@charlottemag.com. Website: www.charlottemag.com.
Monthly. $17.95/yr. Circ.: 30,000. Richard Thurmond, Editorial Director.
Description: Covers social, economic, and cultural life of Charlotte and surrounding area. Articles on politics, business, art and entertainment, education, sports,
travel, society. Pay varies.

CHESAPEAKE BAY MAGAZINE

See full listing in Sports & Recreation/Outdoors category.

CHICAGO MAGAZINE

Tribune Company, 500 N Dearborn, Suite 1200, Chicago, IL 60610-4901.
312-222-8999. E-mail: letters@chicagomag.com. Website: www.chicagomag.com.
Monthly. $19.90/yr. Circ.: 182,100. Richard Babcock, Editor. **Description:** Covers
topics related to Chicago. Articles run 500-7,000 words; pay varies. **Tips:** Sample copy
$6.45. **Queries:** Required. **E-Queries:** Yes. **Payment:** On acceptance. **Contact:**
Shane Tritsch, Managing Editor.

CHICAGO READER

11 E Illinois St., Chicago, IL 60611. 312-828-0350. E-mail: mail@chicagoreader.com.
Website: www.chireader.com. Weekly. Circ.: 136,000. Kiki Yablon, Managing Editor.
Description: Alternative newspaper for residents in the Chicago area. **Nonfiction:**
News, commentary, opinion, arts and entertainment criticism; 4,000 words and up.
Places to go, things to do, profiles of local people; 400-800 words; $100-$1,000.
Fillers: Lists, charts, short humor; $75. **Columns, Departments:** First Person,
Cityscape, Reading, Neighborhood News; 1,500-2,500. **Art:** Photos, cartoons, illus-
trations; $10-$300. **Queries:** Not necessary. **E-Queries:** Yes. **Unsolicited mss:**
Accepts. **Response:** 3-4 weeks. **Rights:** FNASR. **Payment:** On publication.

CHRONOGRAM
See full listing in General Interest category.

CINCINNATI MAGAZINE
Emmis Publishing Corp.
One Centennial Plaza, 705 Central Ave., Suite 175, Cincinnati, OH 45202-1900. 513-421-4300. E-mail: editors@cintimag.emmis.com. Monthly. $19.95/yr. Circ.: 32,000. Kitty Morgan, Editor. **Description:** Cincinnati people and issues. Pieces run 500-3,500 words; $50-$500. **Tips:** Query with writing sample.

CITY & SHORE
Sun-Sentinel Co., 200 E Las Olas Blvd., Fort Lauderdale, FL 33301-2299. 954-356-4685. Website: www.cityandshore.com. Bimonthly. $25.88/yr. Circ.: 42,000. Mark Gauert, Editor. **Description:** Lifestyle magazine of the Sun-Sentinel. Articles on topics of interest to south Floridians; 1,000-3,000 words; pay varies. **Queries:** Preferred. **Payment:** On acceptance.

COMMON GROUND
P.O. Box 99, 6 W John St., McVeytown, PA 17051-0099. 717-899-6133. E-mail: commonground@acsworld.net. Quarterly. $3.50/$12.95. Circ.: 9,000. Ruth Dunmire, Pam Brumbaugh, Editors. **Description:** Focuses on Pennsylvania's Juniata River Valley. Nonfiction pieces on hiking destinations, local history, personality profiles; $40/printed page. Also accepts short poetry; $5-$25. **Art:** Prints; $15-$25. **Tips:** Send complete manuscript with illustrations on spec. Read magazine for upcoming themes. **Queries:** Does not accept. **E-Queries:** No. **Unsolicited mss:** Accepts. **Response:** 1 month. **SASE Required:** Yes. **Freelance Content:** 90%. **Rights:** FNAR. **Payment:** On publication.

COMMONWEALTH
Massachusetts Institute for a New Commonwealth, 18 Tremont St., Suite 1120, Boston, MA 02108-2301. 617-742-6800. E-mail: editor@massinc.org. Website: www.massinc.org. Quarterly. $50/yr. Circ.: 10,000. Robert Keough, Editor. **Description:** Politics, ideas, and civic life in Massachusetts; 3,000 words and up; $.35-$.50/word. Also, reflective essays on civic life; 800-1,500 words. **Queries:** Preferred. **E-Queries:** Yes. **Unsolicited mss:** Accepts. **Rights:** FNASR. **Payment:** On acceptance.

CONNECTICUT MAGAZINE
Journal Register Company, 35 Nutmeg Dr., Trumbull, CT 06611. 203-380-6600. Website: www.connecticutmag.com. Monthly. $18/yr. Circ.: 86,675. Charles Monagan, Editor. **Description:** Connecticut topics, issues, people, and lifestyles. Pieces run 1,500-3,500 words; $500-$1,200. **Payment:** On acceptance.

THE COUNTRY CONNECTION
See full listing in Environment & Conservation category.

CRAIN'S CHICAGO BUSINESS
See full listing in Business category.

CRAIN'S DETROIT BUSINESS
See full listing in Business category.

DELAWARE TODAY
Today Media, Inc., P.O. Box 2800, Wilmington, DE 19805-0800. 302-656-1809. E-mail: editors@delawaretoday.com. Website: www.delawaretoday.com. Monthly. $18/yr. Circ.: 25,000. Marsha Mah, Editor. **Description:** Service articles, profiles, and other pieces on topics of local interest. **Tips:** Send query with clips. **Queries:** Required. **Unsolicited mss:** Does not accept. **Payment:** On publication.

DURANGO MAGAZINE
Schultz & Associates, Inc., P.O. Box 3408, Durango, CO 81302. 970-385-4030. E-mail: drgomag@animas.net. Website: www.durangomagazine.com. 2x/yr. **Description:** For people who love Durango. Features area attractions, history, people, places, events, and culture.

THE EAST BAY MONTHLY
Klaber Publishing Co., 1301 59th St., Emeryville, CA 94608-2115. 510-658-9811. E-mail: editorial@themonthly.com. Website: www.themonthly.com. Monthly. $12/yr. Circ.: 80,000. Kira Halpern, Editor. **Description:** Regional culture and features magazine. "We use two lengthly feature per month with an emphasis on profiles and first-person essay. Local angle is important. Trend pieces are also desireable as are investigative reportage pieces." Features run 3,000-5,000 words; $350-$700. **Queries:** Required. **E-Queries:** Yes. **Response:** Immediate. **SASE Required:** Yes. **Freelance Content:** 100%. **Rights:** FNAR. **Payment:** On publication.

EMERALD COAST MAGAZINE
Rowland Publishing, Inc., 1932 Miccosukee Rd., P.O. Box 1837, Tallahassee, FL 32302-1837. 850-878-0554. E-mail: editorial@rowlandinc.com. Website: www.rowlandinc.com. Quarterly. $2.95/$16.95. Circ.: 18,500. T. Bart Pfankuch, Editor. **Description:** Lifestyle magazine celebrating life on Florida's Emerald Coast that stretches from Panama City to Pensacola on the Gulf of Mexico coastline. Covers travel, people, business, food/dining, sports, etc. **Queries:** Not necessary. **E-Queries:** Yes. **Unsolicited mss:** Accepts. **Response:** 1 week. **SASE Required:** Yes. **Freelance Content:** 15%. **Payment:** On acceptance.

FLORIDA MONTHLY
Florida Media, Inc., 102 Drennen Road, Suite C-5, Orlando, FL 32806-8502. 407-816-9596. E-mail: editorial@floridamagazine.com. Website: www.floridamagazine.com. Monthly. $21.95/yr. Circ.: 207,400. Amber Billman, Assistant Editor. **Description:** Statewide lifestyle magazine. Articles and columns; 700-2,000 words; pays $.25/word. **Queries:** Preferred. **E-Queries:** Yes. **Unsolicited mss:** Accepts.

Response: 4 weeks. **SASE Required:** Yes. **Freelance Content:** 50%. **Rights:** FNAR. **Payment:** On publication.

FREDERICK
6 N East St., Suite 301, Frederick, MD 21701.
E-mail: dpatrell@fredmag.com. Website: www.fredmag.com. Monthly. $3.50/$24.95. Circ.: 18,000. Dan Patrell, Editor. **Description:** Covers lifestyles and issues in and around Frederick County, Maryland. Articles run 800-3,000 words; $100-$300. **Art:** Electronic, transparencies, slides; $25-$300. **Tips:** "Writers have to know Frederick or Frederick County, know the subject about which they are writing and how it directly affects Frederick/Frederick County." **Queries:** Required. **E-Queries:** Yes. **Unsolicited mss:** Does not accept. **Response:** 1-3 months. **Freelance Content:** 90%. **Rights:** FNASR. **Payment:** On publication.

GARDEN SHOWCASE
See full listing in Home & Garden category.

GEORGIA BACKROADS
P.O. Box 127, Roswell, GA 30077-0127. 770-642-5569.
E-mail: georgiabackroads@georgiahistory.us. Website: www.georgiahistory.us. Quarterly. $4.98/$24. Circ.: 20,000. Olin Jackson, Editor. **Description:** For travelers in Georgia, offering travel destinations, leisure lifestyles, and history; 1,200-3,000 words; $.08-$.15/word. **Queries:** Required. **E-Queries:** Yes. **Unsolicited mss:** Accepts. **Response:** 2-4 weeks. **SASE Required:** Yes. **Freelance Content:** 65%. **Rights:** All. **Payment:** On publication.

GO MAGAZINE
6600 AAA Dr., Charlotte, NC 28212-8250. 704-569-7733.
E-mail: trcrosby@aaaqa.com. Website: www.aaa.com. 6x/yr. Circ.: 785,000. Tom Crosby, Editor. **Description:** For AAA members in North and South Carolina. Features on automotive, finance, insurance, travel, and safety; 750-1,000 words; $150/story. **Queries:** Preferred. **E-Queries:** No. **Unsolicited mss:** Accepts. **Response:** 1-3 weeks. **SASE Required:** Yes. **Freelance Content:** 15%. **Payment:** On publication. **Contact:** Sarah Davis, Associate Editor.

GOLDENSEAL MAGAZINE
See full listing in History category.

GRAND RAPIDS
Gemini Publications, 549 Ottawa NW, Grand Rapids, MI 49503-1444. 616-459-4545.
E-mail: cvalade@geminipub.com. Website: www.geminipub.com. Monthly. $15/yr. Circ.: 20,000. Carole R. Valade, Editor. **Description:** Covers local area. **Nonfiction:** Service articles (dining guide, travel, personal finance, humor) and issue-oriented pieces. Pays $35-$200. **Queries:** Preferred. **E-Queries:** Yes. **Unsolicited mss:** Accepts. **Payment:** On publication.

GULFSHORE LIFE

Gulfshore Media, Inc., 9051 Tamiami Trail N, Suite 202, Naples, FL 34108. 239-594-9980. E-mail: info@gulfshorelifemag.com. Website: www.gulfshorelifemag.com. Monthly. $19.95/yr. Circ.: 30,000. Pam Daniel, Editorial Director. **Description:** On Southwest Florida personalities, travel, sports, business, interior design, arts, history, and nature. Articles run 800-3,000 words; $200. **Queries:** Preferred.

HAWAII

Fancy Publications, Inc., P.O. Box 6050, Mission Viejo, CA 92690-6050. 949-855-8822. E-mail: hawaii@fancypubs.com. Website: www.hawaiimagazine.com. Bimonthly. $20/yr. Circ.: 75,000. June Kikuchi, Editor. **Description:** Written for both residents and visitors. Covers the culture and lifestyle of Hawaii by featuring information on Polynesian heritage and history, current events, restaurants, accommodations, music, festivals, and other activities. **Tips:** Accepts very little freelance material. **Queries:** Preferred. **E-Queries:** No. **Payment:** On publication.

HONOLULU MAGAZINE

PacificBasin Communications, Inc., 1000 Bishop St., Suite 405, Honolulu, HI 96813. 808-537-9500. Website: www.honolulumagazine.com. Monthly. $15/yr. Circ.: 30,000. John Heckathorn, Editor. **Description:** Regional magazine highlighting contemporary life in the Hawaiian Islands with particular emphasis on the area in and around Honolulu. Feature stories on politics, sports, history, people, arts, and events; $500-$900. **Tips:** Include 2-3 published clips with query letter explaining your topic and listing your qualifications. "We are not a travel magazine and our readers know the Islands well. We are not a good market for writers whose knowledge of Hawai'i is superficial." **Queries:** Required. **Rights:** All. **Payment:** On publication. **Contact:** A. Kam Napier, Managing Editor.

HUDSON VALLEY

11 IBM Rd., Suite 108, Poughkeepsie, NY 12601. 845-463-0542. E-mail: rsparling@hvmag.com. Website: www.hudsonvalleymagazine.com. **Description:** Covers Albany, Columbia, Dutchess, Greene, Orange, Putnam, Rensselaer, Rockland, Ulster and Westchester counties in New York state. Features explore the social, cultural and business issues that most affect Valley residents; 1,500 words; $400. **Tips:** Send query with clips. "We guide the reader to great getaways, fascinating people, and the best in arts and entertainment." **Queries:** Required. **Rights:** All. **Payment:** On publication.

ILLINOIS ENTERTAINER

See full listing in Film, TV, Entertainment category.

INDIANAPOLIS MONTHLY

1 Emmis Plaza, 40 Monument Circle, Suite 100 NE, Indianapolis, IN 46204-3019. 317-237-9288. E-mail: contact@indymonthly.emmis.com. Website: www.indianapolismonthly.com. Monthly. $19.95/yr. Circ.: 45,000. Deborah Way, Editor-in-

Chief. **Description:** Profiles, sports, business, travel, crime, controversy, service, first-person essays, book excerpts, etc.; 2,500-4,000 words; $400-$500. **Tips:** All material must have Indianapolis/Indiana focus. **Payment:** On publication.

THE IOWAN

218 6th Ave., Suite 608, Des Moines, IA 50309-4009. 515-282-8220. E-mail: iowan@thepioneergroup.com. Website: www.iowan.com. Bimonthly. $19.95/yr. Circ.: 25,000. Kelly Roberson, Editor. **Description:** Covers history, culture, people, places, and events of Iowa; to 5,000 words; $.30/word. **Queries:** Not necessary. **E-Queries:** Yes. **Unsolicited mss:** Accepts. **Response:** 24 weeks. **SASE Required:** Yes. **Freelance Content:** 80%. **Rights:** One-time NA. **Payment:** On acceptance.

JACKSONVILLE

White Publishing Co., 534 Lancaster St., Jacksonville, FL 32204-4113. 904-396-8666. E-mail: mail@jacksonvillemag.com. Website: www.jacksonvillemag.com. Monthly. $19.90/yr. Circ.: 20,000. Joseph White, Editor. **Description:** Issues and personalities of interest to readers in the greater Jacksonville area. Topics include home/garden, business, health, travel, personal finance, real estate, arts/entertainment, sports, food, etc.; 1,200-2,500 words; $200-$500. **Queries:** Required. **Payment:** On publication.

KANSAS CITY

118 Southwest Blvd., Kansas City, MO 64108. 816-421-4111. E-mail: lelmore@abartapub.com. Website: www.kcmag.com. 12x/yr. $3.50/$12.98. Circ.: 27,000. Leigh Elmore, Editor. **Description:** Celebrates life in Kansas City. **Nonfiction:** Serious piece on local issues, personality profiles, and fun features (Weekend Getaways, etc.); 1,000-3,000 words; $700-$1,000/features. **Columns, Departments:** Excursions (regional travel); Arts (local scene); 1,200 words; $200-$400. **Art:** Prints, transparencies, B&W, jpeg. **Tips:** Avoid generic "fit any market" features. **Queries:** Preferred. **E-Queries:** Yes. **Unsolicited mss:** Accepts. **Response:** 2-4 weeks. **Freelance Content:** 90%. **Rights:** FNAR. **Payment:** On acceptance.

KANSAS! MAGAZINE

Kansas Dept. of Commerce and Housing, 1000 SW Jackson St., Suite 100, Topeka, KS 66612-1324. 785-296-3479. E-mail: ksmagazine@kdoch.state.ks.us. Website: www.travelks.com. Quarterly. $4/$15. Circ.: 45,000. Nancy Nowick Ramberg, Editor. **Description:** Magazine devoted to the state of Kansas. "Our aim is to encourage people to travel through Kansas to experience its rich history, scenic landscape, exciting attractions, and Midwestern hospitality." Length and payment vary. **Tips:** Please avoid politics, religion, sex, and other topics unrelated to travel. **Queries:** Preferred. **E-Queries:** Yes. **Unsolicited mss:** Does not accept. **Freelance Content:** 100%. **Payment:** On acceptance. **Contact:** Shonda Titsworth.

KENTUCKY LIVING

P.O. Box 32170, Louisville, KY 40232. 502-451-2430. E-mail: e-mail@kentuckyliving.com. Website: www.kentuckyliving.com. Monthly. $15/yr. Circ.: 487,000. Paul

Wesslund, Editor. **Description:** On the character and culture of Kentucky. Personalities, history, biography, recreation, travel, leisure; 1,000 words; $450. **Queries:** Preferred. **E-Queries:** Yes. **Unsolicited mss:** Accepts. **Response:** 4-6 weeks. **SASE Required:** Yes. **Freelance Content:** 75%. **Payment:** On acceptance.

KENTUCKY MONTHLY

213 Saint Clair St., Frankfort, KY 40601. 502-227-0053. E-mail: membry@kentucky-monthly.com. Website: www.kentuckymonthly.com. Monthly. $2.95/issue. Circ.: 40,000. Michael Embry, Editor; Stephen M. Vest, Publisher. **Description:** General-interest magazine with focus on the Bluegrass State. **Fiction:** Stories by Kentucky authors or with Kentucky storyline. Has previously published fiction by Sue Grafton, Gwyn Hyman Rubio, and Wendell Berry; 1,000-3,000 words; $50. **Nonfiction:** Profiles of famous Kentuckians, travel, the arts, history, sports, lifestyle, medicine, cooking, gardening, and education. Also features music and book reviews; 300-3,000 words; $25-$300. **Poetry:** Accepts poetry of moderate length; pays in copies. **Art:** Accepts digital photos, prints, and slides; $25/image. **Tips:** "Become familiar with the magazine. Make sure the story will appeal to all areas of the state. Kentucky Monthly is all about Kentucky, so keep that in mind when submitting a query." **Queries:** Preferred. **E-Queries:** Yes. **Unsolicited mss:** Does not accept. **Response:** 6 weeks. **SASE Required:** Yes. **Freelance Content:** 75%. **Rights:** FNAR. **Payment:** On the 15th of the month following publication.

LAKE MICHIGAN TRAVEL GUIDE

Trails Media Group, Inc., 1131 Mills St., Black Earth, WI 53515. 608-767-8000. E-mail: nwood@wistrails.com. Website: www.lakemichigantravelguide.com. Annual. $5.95/issue. Circ.: 60,000. Nick Wood, Editor. **Description:** Focused on unique travel opportunities and interesting destinations in the Lake Michigan region of WI, MI, IL, IN. Publishes regional features as well as brief sketches on culture, events, nature, adventure, dining, lodging, and family fun. 50-3,000 words; $.30/word. **Queries:** Required. **E-Queries:** Yes. **Unsolicited mss:** Does not accept. **Response:** 3-5 months. **SASE Required:** Yes. **Freelance Content:** 100%. **Rights:** FNAR. **Payment:** On publication.

LAKE SUPERIOR

Lake Superior Port Cities, Inc., P.O. Box 16417, Duluth, MN 55816-0417. 218-727-2765. E-mail: edit@lakesuprior.com. Website: www.lakesuperior.com. Bimonthly. $21.95/yr. Circ.: 20,000. Konnie LeMay, Editor. **Description:** Focuses on Lake Superior region (U.S. and Canada) and its peoples. **Nonfiction:** People, events, and places; 1,000-2,000 words; $100-$600. **Fillers:** Short pieces on Lake life; to 600 words; $50-$125. **Columns, Departments:** Science, history, humor, reminiscences; 600-1,500 words; $50-$225. **Art:** Varied formats; $50 all inside shots, color or B&W; $150 cover. **Queries:** Preferred. **E-Queries:** No. **Unsolicited mss:** Accepts. **Response:** 3-6 months. **SASE Required:** Yes. **Freelance Content:** 80%. **Rights:** FNASR. **Payment:** On publication.

LONG ISLAND WOMAN

Box 176, Malverne, NY 11565. E-mail: editor@liwomanonline.com.
Website: www.liwomanonline.com. Monthly. Circ.: 40,000. A. Nadboy, Managing
Editor. **Description:** For educated, active women of the Long Island, NY region.
Service-oriented articles about health, home, beauty, fashion, food, or travel. No fic-
tion or poetry. 500-1,500 words; $35-$150. **Tips:** Does not accept submissions over
2,000 words. No phone calls. See website for specific guidelines. **Queries:** Not nec-
essary. **E-Queries:** Yes. **Unsolicited mss:** Accepts. **Freelance Content:** 40%.
Rights: FNAR. **Payment:** On publication.

THE LOOK

Hawks Media Group, Inc., P.O. Box 272, Cranford, NJ 07016-0272. 908-755-6138.
E-mail: jrhawks@thelookmag.com. Website: www.thelookmag.com. Monthly. Free.
Circ.: 10,000. John R. Hawks, Editor. **Description:** New Jersey entertainment magazine. **Nonfiction:** Articles and profiles on fashion, student life, employment, and
relationships for readers ages 16-26. Also, beach stories about the New Jersey shore.
1,000-2,000 words; $30-$150. **Fillers:** Puzzles, trivia, and quizzes about area people,
places, and events. **Queries:** Preferred. **E-Queries:** Yes. **Unsolicited mss:** Accepts.
Response: 30-60 days. **Freelance Content:** 50%. **Payment:** On publication.

LOS ANGELES MAGAZINE

Emmis Publishing Corp., 5900 Wilshire Blvd., Fl. 10, Los Angeles, CA 90036-5013.
323-801-0100. E-mail: letters@lamag.com. Website: www.losangelesmagazine.com.
Monthly. $9.95/yr. Circ.: 154,000. Kit Rachlis, Editor-in-Chief. **Description:** "The
diary of a great city for those enthralled by what the city has to offer and those overwhelmed by it. An essential guide." Covers politics, business, film, sports, style,
events, places; 400-5,000 words; pay varies. **Tips:** Read the magazine before submitting. **Queries:** Required. **E-Queries:** Yes. **Unsolicited mss:** Accepts. **Response:** 3-
4 weeks. **SASE Required:** Yes. **Freelance Content:** 50%. **Rights:** FNAR.

LOUISVILLE MAGAZINE

137 W Muhammad Ali Blvd., Suite 101, Louisville, KY 40202-1438. 502-625-0100.
E-mail: loumag@loumag.com. Website: www.louisville.com/loumag.html. Monthly.
$3.75/issue. Circ.: 28,000. Bruce Allar, Editor. **Description:** City magazine covering
community issues, personalities, and entertainment in the Louisville area. Articles
run 500-4,000 words; $150-$600. **Queries:** Required. **E-Queries:** Yes. **Unsolicited
mss:** Accepts. **Response:** 60 days. **SASE Required:** Yes. **Freelance Content:**
60%. **Rights:** FNASR. **Payment:** On acceptance.

MEMPHIS

Contemporary Media, Inc., P.O. Box 1738, Memphis, TN 38101-1738. 901-521-9000.
E-mail: memmag@memphismagazine.com. Website: www.memphismagazine.com.
Monthly. $15/yr. Circ.: 21,000. James Roper, Editor. **Description:** Topics related to
Memphis and the Mid-South region: politics, education, sports, business, history, etc.
Tips: Send SASE for guidelines. **Queries:** Required. **Payment:** On publication.

MICHIGAN LIVING

Automobile Club of Michigan, 1 Auto Club Dr., Dearborn, MI 48126-4213. 248-816-9265. E-mail: michliving@aol.com. Bimonthly. $9/yr. Circ.: 1,038,400. Ron Garbinski, Editor. **Description:** Destination travel magazine covering Michigan. Also area and Canadian tourist attractions and recreational opportunities. No foreign destinations. Articles run 300-2,000 words; $55-$500. **Tips:** Send query via e-mail with article idea.

MIDWEST LIVING

Meredith Corp., 1716 Locust St., Des Moines, IA 50309-3038. 515-284-3000. E-mail: mwl@mdp.com. Website: www.midwestliving.com. Bimonthly. $19.97/yr. Circ.: 831,110. Dan Kaercher, Editor-in-Chief. **Description:** Personality profiles and lifestyle articles relating to any or all of the 12 midwest states. Occasionally uses humorous essays. Pay varies. **Rights:** All. **Payment:** On acceptance. **Contact:** Greg Philby, Executive Editor.

MILESTONES

See full listing in Seniors Magazines category.

MILWAUKEE HOME

See full listing in Home & Garden category.

MILWAUKEE MAGAZINE

QuadGraphics, 417 E Chicago St., Milwaukee, WI 53202. 414-273-1101. E-mail: milmag@qg.com. Website: www.milwaukeemagazine.com. Monthly. $3/$19. Circ.: 40,000. John Fennell, Editor. **Description:** In-depth reporting and analysis of issues affecting the Milwaukee metro area. **Nonfiction:** Features, stories, and essays specific to the Milwaukee area; 2,000-5,000 words; $500-$1,000. **Columns, Departments:** Issue-oriented commentary; 900-1200 words; $300-$600. **Queries:** Required. **E-Queries:** Yes. **Unsolicited mss:** Accepts. **SASE Required:** Yes. **Freelance Content:** 50%. **Rights:** FNAR. **Payment:** On publication.

MISSOURI LIFE

P.O. Box 421, Fayette, MO 65248. 660-248-3489. E-mail: info@missourilife.com. Website: www.missourilife.com. Bimonthly. $4.50/$21.99. Circ.: 20,000. Danita Allen, Editor. **Description:** Explores Missouri and its diverse people and places, past and present. History, weekend getaways and day-trips, interesting people and events. Features run 1,000-2,000 words; $.20/word. **Art:** Color slides or digital (300 dpi); $50-$150. **Queries:** Required. **E-Queries:** Yes. **Unsolicited mss:** Accepts. **Response:** 4-6 weeks. **SASE Required:** Yes. **Freelance Content:** 80%.

MONTANA MAGAZINE

P.O. Box 5630, Helena, MT 59604-5630. 406-443-2842. E-mail: editor@montanamagazine.com. Website: www.montanamagazine.com. Bimonthly. $24/yr. Circ.: 42,000. Beverly R. Magley, Editor. **Description:** Full-color photography and articles reflecting the grandeur and personality of Montana. Articles on Montana's culture, history, outdoor recreation, communities, people, contemporary issues, places, events, ecology and conservation; 1,500-2,000 words; $.20/word. **Queries:** Required. **E-Queries:** Yes. **Unsolicited mss:** Accepts. **Response:** 4 months. **SASE Required:** Yes. **Freelance Content:** 90%. **Rights:** One-time.

MPLS.ST. PAUL
220 S 6th St., Suite 500, Minneapolis, MN 55402-4507. 612-339-7571. E-mail: edit@mspmag.com. Website: www.mspmag.com. Monthly. $3.99/issue. Circ.: 72,000. Brian E. Anderson, Editor. **Description:** Covers what is new, exciting, newsworthy in the Twin Cities. **Nonfiction:** Timely local issues, dining/arts/entertainment, home decorating, profiles, etc. **Columns, Departments:** City Limits (news/gossip); About Town (arts and entertainment sidebars). **Queries:** Preferred. **E-Queries:** Yes. **Unsolicited mss:** Accepts. **Response:** 6-8 weeks. **SASE Required:** Yes.

NEBRASKA HISTORY
See full listing in History category.

NEVADA MAGAZINE
401 N Carson St., Suite 100, Carson City, NV 89701-4291. 775-687-5416. E-mail: editor@nevadamagazine.com. Website: www.nevadamagazine.com. Bimonthly. $18.95/yr. Circ.: 84,000. David Moore, Editor. **Description:** On topics related to Nevada such as travel, history, recreation, profiles, humor, and attractions. Articles run 500-1,800 words; pay varies. **Payment:** On publication.

NEW HAMPSHIRE MAGAZINE
150 Dow St., Manchester, NH 03101. 603-624-1442. E-mail: editor@nh.com. Website: www.nhmagazine.com. Monthly. $3.95/$20. Circ.: 26,000. Rick Broussard, Editor. **Description:** Covers people, places, issues and lifestyles of New Hampshire as revealed by the state's best writers, photographers, and artists. **Nonfiction:** Lifestyle, business, and history articles with New Hampshire angle, sources from all regions of the state; 400-2,000 words; $50-$200. **Art:** Prints, slides, negatives, or digital. $25-$300. **Queries:** Preferred. **E-Queries:** Yes. **Unsolicited mss:** Accepts. **Response:** 1 month. **SASE Required:** Yes. **Freelance Content:** 30%. **Rights:** 1st serial and online reprint. **Payment:** On publication.

NEW JERSEY MONTHLY
55 Park Place, P.O. Box 920, Morristown, NJ 07963-0920. 973-539-8230. E-mail: editor@njmonthly.com. Website: www.njmonthly.com. Monthly. $19/yr. Circ.: 94,000. Kate S. Tomlinson, Editor-in-Chief. **Description:** Publication covering trends, people, and news in New Jersey. **Nonfiction:** Well-organized, well-written, thoughtful articles, profiles, and service pieces on just about any topic that is well-grounded in New Jersey; 150-3,000 words; $150-$2,500. **Columns, Departments:** Health, business, education, travel (within NJ), sports, local politics, arts, humor; $400-$1,000. **Tips:** Send query with clips to Christopher Hann, Senior Editor. **Queries:** Preferred. **Contact:** David Chmiel, Editor.

NEW JERSEY REPORTER
See full listing in Current Events, Politics category.

NEW MEXICO
Lew Wallace Bldg., 495 Old Santa Fe Trail, Santa Fe, NM 87501. 505-827-7447. E-mail: submissions@nmmagazine.com. Website: www.nmmagazine.com. Monthly. $4.95/$25.95. Circ.: 118,000. Emily Drabanski, Editor-in-Chief. **Description:** About everything New Mexican (products, places, style, history, books, food, recreation, archaeology, Native American culture and ranch life). **Nonfiction:** Regional interest only; 1,500 words max; $.30/word. **Fillers:** Out-of-the way cafes, unique New Mexicans, and ranch life. **Art:** Slides, transparencies; pay varies. Send c/o Steve Larese, photo editor. **Tips:** "We work about a year in advance. We rarely repeat topics, except for a new, exciting angle. Send in a story idea off the beaten path. We receive too many queries on Santa Fe. Send three writing samples with a well-developed proposal." No poetry. **Queries:** Required. **E-Queries:** No. **Unsolicited mss:** Accepts. **Response:** Queries 1-3 months, submissions 3-6 months. **SASE Required:** Yes. **Freelance Content:** 20%. **Rights:** FNAR. **Payment:** On acceptance.

NEW MEXICO JOURNEY
3333 Fairview Rd., A-327, Costa Mesa, CA 92626. 714-885-2380. Website: www.aaa-newmexico.com. Bimonthly. Circ.: 80,000. Annette Winter, Editor. **Description:** For AAA members. Covers travel, lifestyle and people of New Mexico and surrounding states; 800-1,500 words; pays $1/word. **Columns, Departments:** AutoNews, GoingPlaces; 50-125 words; $1/word. **Tips:** Always looking for stories about offbeat and behind-the-scenes angles on established destinations. **Queries:** Required. **E-Queries:** No. **Unsolicited mss:** Does not accept. **Response:** 8 weeks. **Freelance Content:** 80%. **Rights:** FNAR. **Payment:** On acceptance.

NEW ORLEANS MAGAZINE
MC Media, 111 Veterans Blvd., Metairie, LA 70005. 504-832-3555. E-mail: info@mcmediallc.com. Website: www.neworleansmagazine.com. Monthly. $19.95/yr. Circ.: 40,000. Errol Laborde, Editor. **Description:** On New Orleans area people and issues. Articles, 3-15 triple-spaced pages; pays $15-$500, extra for photos. **Queries:** Preferred. **Payment:** On publication.

NEWPORT LIFE MAGAZINE
101 Malbone Rd., Newport, RI 02840. 401-841-0200. E-mail: magazine@newport-tri.com. Website: www.newportlifemagazine.com. Bimonthly. Circ.: 12,000. Lynne Tungett, Editor. **Description:** On people, places, and attractions of Newport County. **Nonfiction:** General-interest, historical, local profiles, environment, international celebrities, social and political issues; 500-2,500 words. **Columns, Departments:** Sailing, food/wine, home/garden, arts, real estate in Newport County; 200-750 words. **Queries:** Preferred. **SASE Required:** Yes.

NORTH DAKOTA HORIZONS

P.O. Box 1091, Bismarck, ND 58502. 701-355-4458. E-mail: ndhorizons@btinet.net. Website: www.ndhorizons.com. Quarterly. $5/$15. Circ.: 12,000. Andrea Winker Collin, Editor. **Description:** Showcases North Dakota people, places, and events. Articles run 1,000-3,000 words; $100-$300. **Art:** Digital format only; $10-$150/image. **Queries:** Preferred. **E-Queries:** Yes. **Unsolicited mss:** Accepts. **Response:** Up to 1 month. **SASE Required:** Yes. **Freelance Content:** 50%. **Rights:** One-time.

NORTHEAST MAGAZINE

The Hartford Courant, 285 Broad St., Hartford, CT 06115. 860-241-3700. E-mail: northeast@courant.com. Website: www.ctnow.com. Weekly. Circ.: 316,000. Larry Bloom, Editor. **Description:** Sunday magazine for *The Hartford Courant*. Articles spun off news and compelling personal stories; 750-3,000 words; $250-$1,000. **Queries:** Preferred. **E-Queries:** No. **Unsolicited mss:** Accepts. **Response:** 2-3 months. **SASE Required:** Yes. **Freelance Content:** 2%. **Rights:** One-time. **Payment:** On acceptance. **Contact:** Jane Bronfonan, Editorial Assistant.

NOW & THEN

Center for Applachian Studies and Services
P.O. Box 70556, Johnson City, TN 37614-1707. 423-439-5348.
E-mail: woodsidj@mail.etsu.edu. Website: www.cass.etsu.edu/n&t. 3x/yr. $25. Circ.: 1,500. Jane Harris Woodside, Editor. **Description:** Each issue focuses on one aspect of life in Appalachian region (from Northern Mississippi to Southern New York). Previous themes: paying tribute, first person Appalachia, Appalachia and the world, and natural resources. **Fiction:** Must relate to theme of issue and the Appalachian region; 1,500-3,000 words. **Nonfiction:** Articles, interviews, essays, memoirs; 1,000-2,500 words. Also book reviews; 750 words. **Poetry:** Up to 5 poems. **Tips:** Topics can be contemporary or historical. Accepts e-mail submissions for all material except poetry. Sample copy $5. **Queries:** Preferred. **E-Queries:** Yes. **Unsolicited mss:** Accepts. **SASE Required:** Yes.

OHIO

1422 Euclid Ave., Suite 730, Cleveland, OH 44115.
E-mail: editorial@ohiomagazine.com. Website: www.ohiomagazine.com. Monthly. Circ.: 90,000. Richard Osborne, Editorial Director. **Description:** On everything in Ohio—from people and places to food and entertainment. **Nonfiction:** On travel around Ohio with profiles of people, cities, towns, historic sites, tourist attractions, and little-known spots; 1,000-1,200 words. **Tips:** "We seek fresh stories with a decisively different Ohio angle." **Queries:** Preferred. **E-Queries:** Yes. **Unsolicited mss:** Accepts. **Response:** 6 weeks. **SASE Required:** Yes. **Freelance Content:** 25%.

OKLAHOMA TODAY

P.O. Box 1468, Oklahoma City, OK 73101. 405-521-2496.
E-mail: editorial@oklahomatoday.com. Website: www.oklahomatoday.com. 7x/yr. $4.95/$19.95. Circ.: 40,000. Louisa McCune, Editor. **Description:** Explores the peo-

ple, places, history, and culture of Oklahoma. Articles run 250-3,000 words; $50-$750. **Art:** Must evoke a sense of place. Digital, color transparencies, slides, B&W prints; $50-$100/B&W, $50-$750/color. **Tips:** Query with biography and published clips. **Queries:** Preferred. **E-Queries:** Yes. **Unsolicited mss:** Accepts. **Response:** 4-6 months. **SASE Required:** Yes. **Freelance Content:** 80%. **Rights:** First serial worldwide. **Payment:** On publication.

ORANGE COAST MAGAZINE

3701 Birch St., #100, Newport Beach, CA 92660-2618. 949-862-1133. E-mail: dge-orge@orangecoastmagazine.com. Website: www.orangecoastmagazine.com. Monthly. $3.95/issue. Circ.: 52,000. Tina Borgatta, Editor. **Description:** Covers Orange County, CA for educated, sophisticated readers. Local trends, people, news stories, workplace and family issues, etc.; 1,500-3,000 words; $450-$900. **Tips:** Query with cover letter, published clips, and SASE. **Queries:** Required. **E-Queries:** No. **Unsolicited mss:** Accepts. **Response:** 1-2 months. **Freelance Content:** 85%. **Rights:** FNASR; non-exclusive web. **Payment:** On publication. **Contact:** DeAnna George, Managing Editor.

OREGON COAST MAGAZINE

4969 Highway 101, Suite 2, Florence, OR 97439. 541-997-8401. E-mail: theresa@ohwy.com. Website: www.ohwy.com. Bimonthly. $16.95/yr. Circ.: 44,785. Theresa Baer, Editor. **Description:** Covers communities, businesses, people, events, activities, and the natural wonders that make up the Oregon coast. On travel, history, town/city profiles, outdoor activities, events, and nature; 800-1,200 words; $65-$250/feature. Also first-person experiences, 500-1,500 words, with details in sidebars, with slides preferred. **Art:** Some stand-alone photos (verticals); also 2 calendars/yr.; slides and transparencies; $25-75, $325 (cover). **Tips:** Accepts e-queries, but prefers hard copy. **Queries:** Preferred. **Unsolicited mss:** Accepts. **Response:** 2-3 months. **SASE Required:** Yes. **Freelance Content:** 60%. **Rights:** FNAR.

ORLANDO MAGAZINE

Abarta Media, 225 S Westmonte Dr., Suite 1100, Altamonte Springs, FL 32714-4218. 407-767-8338. E-mail: jclark@abartapub.com. Website: www.orlandomag.com. Monthly. $21.95/yr. Circ.: 30,000. James C. Clark, Editor. **Description:** Locally-based articles for residents of Central Florida. Covers news, personalities, health, fashion, and technology. **Tips:** Send clips with query. **Queries:** Preferred.

OUR STATE

P.O. Box 4552, Greensboro, NC 27404-4552. 336-286-0600. E-mail: editorial@ourstate.com. Website: www.ourstate.com. Monthly. $24.95/yr. Circ.: 110,000. Vicky Jarrett, Editor-in-Chief. **Description:** *Our State: Down Home in North Carolina* covers culture, events, travel, food, and folklore in the state; 1,500 words; $125-$500. **Tips:** Most readers are over 50. **Queries:** Preferred. **E-Queries:** Yes. **Unsolicited mss:** Accepts. **Response:** 4-12 weeks. **SASE Required:** Yes. **Freelance Content:** 80%. **Rights:** FNAR. **Payment:** On publication.

OVER THE BACK FENCE

Panther Publishing, 14 S Paint St., Suite 69, P.O. Box 756, Chillicothe, OH 45601. 740-772-2165. E-mail: backfenc@bright.net. Website: www.pantherpublishing.com. Quarterly. **Description:** Serves counties in Southern Ohio. **Nonfiction:** Equated to a friendly and informative conversation with a neighbor about interesting people, places and events; 1,000 words; $.10/word and up, $25 min. **Art:** Photos or illustrations to accompany articles. **Queries:** Required. **Unsolicited mss:** Accepts. **SASE Required:** Yes. **Rights:** One-time. **Payment:** On publication.

PALM SPRINGS LIFE MAGAZINE

Desert Publications, Inc., P.O. Box 2724, Palm Springs, CA 92262. 760-325-2333. E-mail: edit@desert-resorts.com. Website: www.palmspringslife.com. Monthly. $3.95/$38. Circ.: 17,500. Steven Biller, Editor-in-Chief. **Description:** Looks at upscale lifestyle of desert residents. Features celebrity profiles and articles on architecture, fashion, desert ecology, art, interior design, politics, humor, history, etc.; 1,500-2,500 words; $250-$500. **Queries:** Required. **E-Queries:** Yes. **Unsolicited mss:** Accepts. **Response:** 1-2 months. **SASE Required:** Yes. **Freelance Content:** 80%. **Rights:** All. **Payment:** On publication.

PENNSYLVANIA MAGAZINE

P.O. Box 755, Camp Hill, PA 17001-0755. 717-697-4660. E-mail: pamag@aol.com. Website: www.pa-mag.com. Bimonthly. $3.50/$19.97. Circ.: 32,000. Matthew K. Holliday, Editor. **Description:** General-interest magazine for Pennsylvania readership. Topics include people, events, history, scenic photography, etc.; 1,000-2,500 words; $.10-$.12/word. **Tips:** No sports, poetry, hunting, or politics. **Queries:** Preferred. **E-Queries:** Yes. **Unsolicited mss:** Accepts. **Response:** 4-6 weeks. **SASE Required:** Yes. **Freelance Content:** 95%. **Rights:** One-time.

PHILADELPHIA MAGAZINE

Metrocorp, 1818 Market St., Fl. 36, Philadelphia, PA 19103-3638. 215-564-7700. E-mail: editor@phillymag.com. Website: www.phillymag.com. Monthly. $15/yr. Circ.: 119,900. Larry Platt, Editor-in-Chief. **Description:** Covers events and topics in Philadelphia for a sophisticated audience; 1,000-5,000 words. **Queries:** Preferred. **Payment:** On acceptance.

PHOENIX MAGAZINE

Cities West Publishing, 8501 E Princess Dr., Suite 190, Scottsdale, AZ 85255-5480. 480-664-3960. E-mail: phxmag@citieswestpub.com. Monthly. $12.97/yr. Circ.: 60,800. Robert Stieve, Editor. **Description:** Covers the Phoenix metro area. Issues relating to Phoenix and surrounding metro area. Service pieces (where to go, what to do) in the city; 50-2,000 words; pay varies. **Tips:** "Think small; short, timely pieces and profiles are always needed. No personal essays please. Our travel stories are staff-written." **Queries:** Required. **E-Queries:** Yes. **Unsolicited mss:** Do not accept. **Response:** 2-6 weeks. **SASE Required:** Yes. **Freelance Content:** 80%. **Rights:** FNAR. **Payment:** On publication. **Contact:** Kathy Montgomery, Managing Editor.

PITTSBURGH MAGAZINE

WQED Pittsburgh, 4802 Fifth Ave., Pittsburgh, PA 15213-2957.
E-mail: editor@wqed.org. Website: www.wqed.org. Monthly. $3.50/$17.95. Circ.: 46,000. Betsy Benson, Publisher/Editor. **Description:** Covers Pittsburgh and surrounding region. Examines issues and strives to encourage a better understanding of the community by featuring news, service pieces, local celebrity profiles, regional lifestyles, etc.; 500-4,000 words; pay negotiable. **Queries:** Required. **E-Queries:** No. **Unsolicited mss:** Does not accept. **Response:** 2 months. **SASE Required:** Yes. **Freelance Content:** 60%. **Rights:** FNASR. **Payment:** On publication.

PORTLAND MAGAZINE

Sargent Publishing, Inc., 722 Congress St., Portland, ME 04012. 207-775-4339.
E-mail: staff@portlandmagazine.com. Website: www.portlandmagazine.com. 10x/yr. $29/yr. Circ.: 100,000. Colin Sargent, Editor. **Description:** Celebrates the Portland, ME region by providing profiles of businesses and people, columns about life on the waterfront, and features on arts, getaways, maritime history, geography, and cuisine. **Fiction:** Fiction, to 750 words. **Nonfiction:** Articles on local people, legends, culture, trends, etc. **Queries:** Required. **E-Queries:** Yes. **Unsolicited mss:** Accepts.

PROVINCETOWN ARTS

650 Commercial St., Provincetown, MA 02657. 508-487-3167.
E-mail: cbusa@attbi.com. Website: www.provincetownarts.org. Annual. Circ.: 8,000. Christopher Busa, Editor. **Description:** Focuses on Cape Cod's artists, performers, and writers; covers the cultural life of the nation's oldest continuous art colony. **Fiction:** 500-5,000 words; $50-$150. **Nonfiction:** Essays, interviews, journals, performance pieces, profiles, reviews, and visual features. 500-5,000 words; $50-$150. **Poetry:** Up to 3 poems; $25-$100. **Queries:** Not necessary. **E-Queries:** No. **Unsolicited mss:** Accepts. **Response:** Queries 3 weeks, submissions 4 months. **SASE Required:** Yes. **Freelance Content:** 90%. **Payment:** On publication.

RANCH & COVE

P.O. Box 676130, Rancho Santa Fe, CA 92067-6130. 760-942-2330.
E-mail: edit@ranchcove.com. Website: www.ranchcove.com. Monthly. $40/yr. Circ.: 20,000. Collette Stefanko, Editor. **Description:** Regional lifestyle magazines for affluent residents of Rancho Santa Fe, La Jolla, and San Diego's coastal North country. Topics include upscale fashion, travel, golf, shopping, food/wine, autos, antiques, entertainment, spas, gala events, etc.; 500-1,500; $.10/word. **Tips:** "Our audience is affluent—write topics that relate to their lifestyle." **SASE Required:** Yes. **Freelance Content:** 75%. **Rights:** One-time. **Payment:** On publication.

RECREATION NEWS

The Indiana Printing and Publishing Company, Inc., 7339 Hanover Parkway, Greenbelt, MD 20770-3645. 301-474-4600. E-mail: editor@recreationnews.com. Website: www.recreationnews.com. Monthly. $12/yr. Circ.: 110,000. Francis X. Orphe, Editor. **Description:** On recreation and travel around the mid-Atlantic region for government and private sector workers in the Washington, DC area. Covers regional recreational activities, historical sites, fishing, parks, video reviews, weekend getaways, day-off trips, food, etc. Pieces run 900-2,200 words; pays $50 for reprints, $300 for cover features. **Queries:** Preferred. **Unsolicited mss:** Accepts. **Freelance Content:** 85%. **Payment:** On publication.

RHODE ISLAND MONTHLY

Rhode Island Monthly Communications, 280 Kinsley Ave., Providence, RI 02903-1017. 401-277-8200. E-mail: sfrancis@rimonthly.com. Website: www.rimonthly.com. Monthly. $18/yr. Circ.: 42,000. Paula M. Bodah, Editor. **Description:** Features on Rhode Island and southeastern Massachusetts—places, customs, people, and events. **Nonfiction:** Features, from investigative reporting and in-depth profiles to service pieces and visual stories, seasonal material; 2,000-3,000 words; $550-$1,000. **Fillers:** On Rhode Island places, customs, people, events, products and services; 150-500 words; $50-$150. **Tips:** Send clips with query. Sample copy for $3.95 plus postage. **Queries:** Required. **E-Queries:** Yes. **Payment:** On acceptance. **Contact:** Sarah Francis, Managing Editor.

THE ROANOKER MAGAZINE

Leisure Publishing, P.O. Box 21535, Roanoke, VA 24018. 540-989-6138. E-mail: editorial@theroanoker.com. Website: www.theroanoker.com. 6x/yr. $3.95/$14.95. Circ.: 10,722. **Description:** Metropolitan lifestyle magazine covering business, arts and entertainment, personalities, events, and issues in the Roanoke and New River valleys of Virginia. **Nonfiction:** Profiles of area people, travel (regional), human interest, festivals/events, and news; 250-1,500 words; $75 and up. **Columns, Departments:** Shorts on events, festivals, area news, nonprofits; 150-300 words; $50-$100. **Art:** Prints, slides, transparencies, or hi-res digital; $40-$150. **Tips:** "We often start first-time writers off with short articles. Writers should have a familiarity with our coverage area and overall style—metropolitan, city flavor, upbeat and journalistic. Photo support is strongly recommended." **Queries:** Preferred. **E-Queries:** Yes. **Unsolicited mss:** Accepts. **Response:** 1-2 months. **Freelance Content:** 75%. **Rights:** FNAR. **Payment:** On publication. **Contact:** Kurt Rheinheimer, Editor-in-Chief; Norma Lugar, Senior Editor; Cara Ellen Modisett, Associate Editor.

SACRAMENTO

706 56th St., Suite 210, Sacramento, CA 95819. 916-452-6200. E-mail: krista@sacmag.com. Website: www.sacmag.com. Monthly. $12/yr. Circ.: 25,000. Krista Minard, Editor. **Description:** Interesting and unusual people, places, and behind-the-scenes news items. **Nonfiction:** Articles, 1,000-1,500 words, on destinations within a 6-hour drive of Sacramento. Features, 2,500 words, on broad range of topics related to the region. Pay varies. **Columns, Departments:** City Lights, 400 words, $50-$300. **Queries:** Required. **Payment:** On publication.

SAN FRANCISCO MAGAZINE

San Francisco Focus L.L.P., 243 Vallejo St., San Francisco, CA 94111-1511. 415-398-2800. E-mail: letters@sanfran.com. Website: www.sanfran.com. Monthly. $19/yr. Circ.: 133,100. Bruce Kelley, Editor-in-Chief. **Description:** Explores and celebrates San Francisco and the Bay Area. Insightful analysis, investigative reporting, and eye-catching coverage of local food, culture, design, travel, people, and politics. Length and pay vary. **Payment:** On acceptance.

SANDLAPPER, THE MAGAZINE OF SOUTH CAROLINA

P.O. Box 1108, Lexington, SC 29071. 803-359-9954. E-mail: aida@sandlapper.org. Website: www.sandlapper.org. Quarterly. $6/$25. Robert Pearce Wilkins, Editor. **Description:** "*Sandlapper* covers the people, places, history, and culture of South Carolina. No hard news, scandal or controversy, unless historical in nature. Our best writers live here because they understand the lifestyle and culture." Articles run 2,500 max.; $100/page. **Art:** Slides or digital (300 dpi); $100/full page, $50/half page. **Tips:** "Please don't call. Send a well-written query letter that tells us why your idea will excite our readers. Include 2 clips that show writing style. Even though we don't pay well, we have a stable of very fine writers who enjoy working for us, so we can afford to be selective. Also, at our most risqué, we are PG-13. *Sandlapper* is sent to public school classrooms in 3rd and 8th grades—where SC history is target. So we can't make those teachers squirm with 'too-adult' copy." **Queries:** Required. **E-Queries:** Yes. **Response:** 1 month. **SASE Required:** Yes. **Freelance Content:** 70%. **Rights:** FNAR and electronic. **Payment:** Within 1 month of publication.. **Contact:** Aida Rogers, Managing Editor.

SAVANNAH MAGAZINE

P.O. Box 1088, Savannah, GA 31402. 912-652-0293.
E-mail: linda.wittish@savannahnow.com. Website: www.savannahmagazine.com. 8x/yr. $3.95/$18.95. Circ.: 11,000. Linda Wittish, Editor. **Description:** On lifestyles of residents from coastal Georgia and South Carolina low country. **Nonfiction:** On local people, travel destinations (in a day's drive), local history, restaurants, business; 500-2,500 words; $100-$350. **Columns, Departments:** Travel Business; 1,000-1,500; $200-$300. **Queries:** Preferred. **E-Queries:** Yes. **Unsolicited mss:** Accepts. **Response:** 2-4 weeks. **SASE Required:** Yes. **Freelance Content:** 100%. **Rights:** FNAR. **Payment:** On publication.

SEATTLE MAGAZINE

Tiger Oak Publications, Inc., 423 Third Ave. W, Seattle, WA 98119. 206-284-1750. E-mail: editor@seattlemag.com. Website: www.seattlemag.com. Monthly. $18.95/yr. Circ.: 32,000. Rachel Hart, Editor. **Description:** To help people live better in Seattle. City, local issues, home, lifestyle articles on greater Seattle area; 50-2,500 words; $50-$1,200. **Queries:** Required. **E-Queries:** Yes. **Unsolicited mss:** Accepts. **Response:** 3 months. **SASE Required:** Yes. **Freelance Content:** 70%. **Rights:** Exclusive 60 days. **Payment:** 30 days after publication.

SEATTLE WEEKLY

Village Voice Media, Inc., 1008 Western, Suite 300, Seattle, WA 98104. 206-623-0500. E-mail: editorial@seattleweekly.com. Website: www.seattleweekly.com. Weekly. Circ.: 105,000. Audrey Van Buskirk, Editor. **Description:** Newsmagazine offering investigative journalism, political commentary, arts/culture, and other articles and features on the community life and news of the Seattle metro region. **Queries:** Preferred. **Response:** 2-6 weeks. **SASE Required:** Yes. **Payment:** On publication.

SOUTHERN EXPOSURE

Institute for Southern Studies, P.O. Box 531, Durham, NC 27702-0531. 919-419-8311. Website: www.southernstudies.org. Quarterly. $24. Circ.: 5,000. Chris Kromm, Publisher/Editor. **Description:** Forum on "Southern politics and culture." Essays, investigative journalism, oral histories, and personal narratives; 500-3,600 words; $25-$250. **Queries:** Preferred. **Payment:** On publication.

SOUTHERN HUMANITIES REVIEW

See full listing in Literary Fiction & Poetry category.

SOUTHERN OREGON HERITAGE TODAY

Southern Oregon Historical Society, 106 N Central Ave., Medford, OR 97501-5926. 541-773-6536. E-mail: communications@sohs.org. Website: www.sohs.org. Quarterly. $20/yr. Circ.: 2,500. Cynthia Wicklund, Editor. **Description:** On the history of the southern Oregon region (people, places, buildings, and events). Articles run 700-3,500 words; $50-$250. **Tips:** "Make sure there is a storyline, not just a reiteration of facts." **Payment:** On publication.

SPRINGFIELD

P.O. Box 4749, Springfield, MO 65808. 417-831-1600. E-mail: editor@sgfmag.com. Monthly. $16.99/yr. Lin Schneider-House, Associate Editor/Publisher. **Description:** About local people, places, events, and issues. **Nonfiction:** Articles must have a clear link to Springfield, Missouri. Historical/nostalgic pieces and book reviews. **Tips:** Seeking features on Springfield couples at present. **Queries:** Preferred. **E-Queries:** Yes. **Unsolicited mss:** Accepts. **Response:** 2-3 weeks **Freelance Content:** 85%. **Rights:** 1st serial. **Payment:** On publication.

SUSQUEHANNA LIFE

637 Market St., P.O. Box 421, Lewisburg, PA 17837. 570-522-0149. E-mail: info@susquehannalife.com. Website: www.susquehannalife.com. Quarterly. **Description:** Regional magazine highlighting the positive aspects of life in twenty counties in central Pennsylvania. Provides a blend of today's attractions and events with yesterday's history. Also, lifestyle pieces on topics such as gardening, finance, home décor, health, and food.

TALLAHASSEE

Rowland Publishing, Inc., 1932 Miccosokee Rd., P.O. Box 1837, Tallahassee, FL 32302-1837. 850-878-0554. E-mail: bpfankuch@rowlandinc.com. Website: www.rowlandinc.com. Bimonthly. $2.95/$16.95. Circ.: 18,500. T. Bart Pfankuch, Editor. **Description:** Lifestyle magazine celebrating life in Florida's Capital Region. Feature stories on local personalities and current events. Creative nonfiction style of writing preferred; 750-2,000 words; pay varies. **Queries:** Not necessary. **E-Queries:** Yes. **Unsolicited mss:** Accepts. **Response:** 4-6 weeks. **SASE Required:** Yes. **Freelance Content:** 15%. **Payment:** On acceptance.

TEXAS HIGHWAYS

P.O. Box 141009, Austin, TX 78714-1009. 512-486-5858.
E-mail: letters@texashighways.com. Website: www.texashighways.com. Monthly. $17.50/yr. Circ.: 300,000. Jack Lowry, Editor. **Description:** Articles and features on Texas history, travel, and scenery. Travel, historical, cultural, scenic features on Texas; 200-1,800 words; $.40-$.50/word. **Queries:** Required.

TEXAS JOURNEY

AAA Club Services, Inc., P.O. Box 25222, Santa Ana, CA 92799-5222. 714-885-2376. E-mail: journey@aaa-texas.com. Website: www.aaa-texas.com. Bimonthly. Circ.: 583,000. Annette Winter, Editor. **Description:** Publication for AAA Texas members. Articles on cultural travel, consumer travel, the outdoors, personality profiles, auto news in Texas and surrounding states; 1,000-2,000 words; $1/word. **Tips:** Prefers published writers. Seeks stories about offbeat and established destinations. **Queries:** Required. **E-Queries:** No. **Unsolicited mss:** Does not accept. **Response:** 8 weeks. **SASE Required:** Yes. **Freelance Content:** 80%. **Rights:** FNASR.

TEXAS MAGAZINE

801 Texas Ave., Houston, TX 77002. 713-362-7501.
E-mail: ken.hammond@chron.com. Website: www.houstonchronicle.com. Kenneth Hammond, Editor. **Description:** Sunday magazine of the *Houston Chronicle*. "Stories and essays must have Texas angle. We suggest writers e-mail us for specific submission guidelines."

TEXAS MONTHLY

P.O. Box 1569, Austin, TX 78767-1569. 512-320-6900.
E-mail: info@texasmonthly.emmis.com. Website: www.texasmonthly.com. Monthly. $15/yr. Circ.: 301,000. Evan Smith, Editor. **Description:** Covers issues of public concern in Texas. Features on art, architecture, food, education, business, politics, etc. Articles must appeal to an educated Texas audience and have well-researched reporting on issues (offbeat and previously unreported topics, or with novel approach to familiar topics); 2,500-5,000 words; pay varies. **Tips:** No fiction, poetry, or cartoons. **Queries:** Required. **E-Queries:** No. **Unsolicited mss:** Accepts. **Response:** 6-8 weeks. **SASE Required:** Yes. **Payment:** On acceptance.

TORONTO LIFE

St. Joseph Media Ltd., 59 Front St. E, Fl. 3, Toronto, Ontario M5E 1B3 Canada. 416-364-3333. E-mail: editorial@torontolife.com. Website: www.torontolife.com. Monthly. $34/yr. Circ.: 94,100. John Macfarlane, Editor. **Description:** Covers the urban scene in Toronto. Articles run 1,500-4,500 words. **Queries:** Required.

TUCSON LIFESTYLE

Conley Publishing Group, Ltd., 7000 E Tanque Verde, Tucson, AZ 85715. 520-721-2929. E-mail: tucsonlife@aol.com. Monthly. $2.95. Circ.: 34,000. Sue Giles, Editor-In-Chief. **Description:** All about Southern Arizona (businesses, health/wellness, the arts, homes, and gardens, etc.); pieces run 1,000-4,000 words; $125-$500. **Tips:** Base your article on interviews and research. Does not accept travel pieces or anecdotes as articles. **Queries:** Required. **E-Queries:** Yes. **Unsolicited mss:** Accepts. **Response:** 2 weeks. **SASE Required:** Yes. **Freelance Content:** 80%. **Rights:** FNAR. **Payment:** On acceptance. **Contact:** Scott Barker, Executive Editor.

VANCOUVER

Transcontinental Media, Inc., 500-2608 Granville St., Vancouver, British Columbia V6H 3V3 Canada. 604-877-7732. E-mail: mail@vancouvermagazine.com. Website: vancouvermagazine.com. Monthly. $41.95/yr. Circ.: 64,200. Matthew Mallon, Editor. **Description:** City magazine with a focus on urban life (sports, civics, social affairs, business, politics, media, restaurants, fashion, shopping and nightlife). Features and front-of-book pieces, varying lengths; $.50/word. Shorter pieces, 1,500-2,000 words; $.50/word. **Tips:** "Because we're a general-interest magazine, just about anything goes. But keep in mind that you're writing for an affluent, well-educated readership with strong opinions about the city." **Queries:** Preferred. **E-Queries:** Yes. **Unsolicited mss:** Accepts. **Response:** 2+ weeks. **Freelance Content:** 70%. **Rights:** FNASR. **Payment:** On acceptance.

VERMONT LIFE

6 Baldwin St., Montpelier, VT 05602. 802-828-3241. Website: www.vtlife.com. Quarterly. $4.95/$15.95. Circ.: 85,000. Tom Slayton, Editor. **Description:** Explores and celebrates Vermont today by providing quality photographs and articles. **Nonfiction:** Articles about people, places, history, and issues; 200-2,000 words; $100-$700. **Art:** Send slides or transparencies, no prints; $75-$500. **Tips:** No "my recent trip to Vermont" or old jokes, rural homilies. Submit articles that shed light on and accurately reflect Vermont experience today. **Queries:** Preferred. **E-Queries:** Yes. **Unsolicited mss:** Accepts. **Response:** 2-4 weeks. **SASE Required:** Yes. **Freelance Content:** 90%. **Rights:** FNAR. **Payment:** On acceptance.

VERMONT MAGAZINE

P.O. Box 800, Middlebury, VT 05753-0800. 802-388-8480. E-mail: vtmag@sover.net. Website: www.vermontmagazine.com. Bimonthly. $16.95/yr. Circ.: 40,000. Joe Healy, Editor. **Description:** On all aspects of contemporary Vermont (its people, culture, politics, and special places). **Queries:** Preferred. **Payment:** On publication.

THE VILLAGE VOICE
See full listing in Current Events, Politics category.

WASHINGTON FLYER
Metropolitan Washington Airports Authority, 1707 L Street NW, Suite 800, Washington, DC 20036. 202-331-9393. E-mail: jessica@themagazinegroup.com. Website: www.fly2dc.com. Bimonthly. **Description:** For upscale Washington residents and visitors. Dining, entertainment, events in the D.C. area. Briefs and features; 350-1,500 words; $150-$800. **Tips:** Prefers queries via e-mail. **Payment:** On publication. **Contact:** Jessica Bizik, Editor.

THE WASHINGTONIAN
1828 L St. NW, Suite 200, Washington, DC 20036. 202-296-3600. E-mail: editorial@washingtonian.com. Website: www.washingtonian.com. Monthly. $3.95/$29.95. Circ.: 150,000. John Limpert, Editor. **Description:** Covers Washington, D.C. topics. **Queries:** Preferred. **E-Queries:** Yes. **Unsolicited mss:** Accepts. **Response:** 2-8 weeks. **SASE Required:** Yes. **Freelance Content:** 50%. **Rights:** FNASR. **Payment:** On publication.

WISCONSIN MEETINGS MAGAZINE
Trails Media Group, Inc., P.O. Box 317, 1131 Mills St., Black Earth, WI 53515. 608-767-8000. E-mail: nwood@wistrails.com. Website: www.wisconsinmeetings.com. Biannual. Circ.: 10,000. Nick Wood, Editor. **Description:** Provides corporate and association meeting planners with informative features and columns about the meeting industry in WI. **Nonfiction:** Profiles of Wisconsin's big four convention centers. Destination pieces on Lake Geneva, Wisconsin Dells, etc. 500-2,000 words; $.25/word. **Columns, Departments:** Industry trends, outings, team building programs; 750 words; $.25/word. **Queries:** Preferred. **E-Queries:** Yes. **Unsolicited mss:** Does not accept. **Response:** 2-3 months. **SASE Required:** Yes. **Freelance Content:** 75%. **Rights:** FNAR. **Payment:** On publication.

WISCONSIN TRAILS
Trails Media Group, Inc., P.O. Box 317, 1131 Mills St., Black Earth, WI 53515. 608-767-8000. E-mail: hbrown@wistrails.com. Website: www.wistrails.com. Bimonthly. $4.95/$24.95. Circ.: 50,000. Harriet Brown, Editor. **Description:** On Wisconsin people, history, nature, travel/adventure, lifestyle, arts, theater, sports, recreation, home/garden, and business. **Nonfiction:** On the joys and experiences of living in the Badger state (history, wildlife, natural history, environment, travel, profiles, culture). 200-3,000 words; $.25/word. **Fillers:** Quirky Wisconsin news items, crossword puzzles; 50-300 words; $.25/word. **Columns, Departments:** My WI (essays); Discover (events), State Talk (short, quirky news), Profile (noteworthy people), Gone for the Weekend (travel destination), Home & Garden. 50-1,000 words, $.25/word. **Art:** Color transparencies, slides, illustrations (8"x11" largest); pay varies. **Tips:** Most readers are in their 40s and 50s, well-educated, active, and love history/travel. New authors must submit resumé, letter of introduction, and 3 relevant

clips, nonreturnable. See website for guidelines. **Queries:** Required. **E-Queries:** Yes. **Unsolicited mss:** Accepts. **Response:** 3-5 months. **SASE Required:** Yes. **Freelance Content:** 40%. **Rights:** FNAR. **Payment:** On publication.

YANKEE

Yankee Publishing, Inc., P.O. Box 520, Dublin, NH 03444. 603-563-8111. E-mail: queries@yankeepub.com. Website: www.yankeemagazine.com. 10x/yr. $3.99/issue. Circ.: 500,000. Judson D. Hale, Sr., Publisher/Editor-in-Chief. **Description:** On travel and life in New England. Narrative journalism, home and garden, travel, food, etc.; 150-3,000 words. **Queries:** Preferred. **E-Queries:** Yes. **Unsolicited mss:** Accepts. **Response:** 8 weeks. **SASE Required:** Yes. **Freelance Content:** 80%. **Rights:** All. **Payment:** On acceptance.

RELIGION

ADVENTURES

6401 The Paseo, Kansas City, MO 64131. 816-333-7000, ext. 2247. Weekly. Circ.: 14,000. Donna Fillmore, Editor. **Description:** This weekly take-home paper connects Sunday-school learning to life for first and second graders (ages 6-8). Includes fiction/nonfiction short stories, activities, poetry, cartoons, recipes/crafts, and interesting facts/trivia. Bible stories by special assignment only. Issues are thematic. **Tips:** Write for specific guidelines. **Queries:** Preferred. **E-Queries:** Yes. **Response:** 4-6 weeks. **SASE Required:** Yes. **Freelance Content:** 50%. **Rights:** All. **Payment:** On acceptance.

AMERICA

106 W 56th St., New York, NY 10019-3803. 212-581-4640. E-mail: articles@america-magazine.org. Website: www.americamagazine.org. Weekly. $2.75/issue. Circ.: 46,000. Thomas J. Reese, Editor. **Description:** For thinking Catholics and those interested in what Catholics are thinking. Emphasis on social justice and religious/ethical perspectives on current issues facing the church and the world. **Nonfiction:** Features on contemporary issues from a religious and ethical perspective; 1,500-2,000 words. **Poetry:** Serious poetry in contemporary prose idiom, free or formal verse. Submit 2-3 poems, 20-35 lines; $2-$3/line. **Tips:** "No sermons or speeches. Address educated audience who are not experts in your topic." **Queries:** Not necessary. **Unsolicited mss:** Accepts. **Response:** 1-3 weeks. **SASE Required:** Yes. **Freelance Content:** 50%. **Rights:** All. **Payment:** On acceptance.

AMIT

Americans for Israel and Torah, 817 Broadway, New York, NY 10003-4761. 212-477-4720. E-mail: amitmag@amitchildren.org. Website: www.amitchildren.org. Quarterly. Charlotte Schneierson, Editor-in-Chief. **Description:** Mission is to provide information and education to Israel and Jewish people. Topics include Israel, the Middle East, Zionism, parenting, education, history, holidays, travel, culture, etc.

Also, interviews with AMIT students in Israel, book reviews, and features on innovations in education, art, and music. Length and pay varies. **Tips:** "Avoid politics and religion. Focus on innovations in education, and on AMIT students in Israel." **Queries:** Preferred. **E-Queries:** Yes. **Unsolicited mss:** Accepts. **Response:** 2 weeks. **SASE Required:** Yes. **Freelance Content:** 50%.

ANGLICAN JOURNAL

80 Hayden St., Toronto, Ontario M4Y 3G2 Canada. 416-924-9192. E-mail: editor@national.anglican.ca. Website: www.anglicanjournal.com. 10x/yr. $10/yr. Circ.: 243,000. Leanne Larmondin, Editor. **Description:** Newspaper of the Anglican Church of Canada. Provides news and features of the Anglican Church, articles on social and ethical issues, and human-interest pieces. Articles to 1,000 words; $.23/word. **Queries:** Required. **E-Queries:** Yes. **Unsolicited mss:** Does not accept. **Freelance Content:** 15%. **Rights:** FNAR. **Payment:** On publication.

THE ANNALS OF ST. ANNE DE BEAUPRÉ

Redemptorist Fathers, P.O. Box 1000, St. Anne de Beaupré, Quebec G0A 3C0 Canada. 418-827-4538. Monthly. Circ.: 45,000. Father Bernard Mercier, C.Ss.R., Editor. **Description:** Articles, 500-1,500 words, that promote devotion to St. Anne and Christian family values. Pays $.03-$.04/word. **Tips:** No poetry. "We look for work that is inspirational, educational, objective, and uplifting." **Response:** 6 weeks. **Freelance Content:** 80%. **Rights:** FNAR only. **Payment:** On acceptance. **Contact:** Father Roch Achard, Managing Editor.

THE B'NAI B'RITH IJM

B'nai B'rith International, 2020 K St. NW, Washington, DC 20006. E-mail: ijm@bnaibrith.org. Website: www.bnaibrith.org. Quarterly. Circ.: 110,000. Elana Harris, Managing Editor. **Description:** Features general-interest stories of interest to Jewish communities in U.S. and abroad. Topics include politics, religion, the arts, the Middle East, etc; 1,500-2,000 words; $450-$700. **Queries:** Preferred.

THE BANNER

CRC Publications, 2850 Kalamazoo Ave. SE, Grand Rapids, MI 49560-0001. 616-224-0732. E-mail: editorial@thebanner.org. Website: www.thebanner.org. Monthly. $36.95/yr. Circ.: 32,000. John D. Suk, Editor. **Description:** For members of Christian Reformed Church in North America. **Fiction:** to 2,500 words. **Nonfiction:** to 1,800 words; pays $125-$200. **Poetry:** to 50 lines; $40. **Queries:** Preferred. **Payment:** On acceptance.

BIBLE ADVOCATE

P.O. Box 33677, Denver, CO 80233. 303-452-7973. E-mail: bibleadvocate@cog7.org. Website: www.cog7.org/ba. 10x/yr. Circ.: 13,500. Calvin Burrell, Editor. **Description:** Helps Christians understand and obey the Bible. **Nonfiction:** On Bible doctrine, current social and religious issues, everyday-living Bible topics, textual or Biblical book studies, prophecy and personal experience; 1500 words; $25-$55.

Poetry: Free verse, blank verse, and traditional; 5-20 lines; $20. **Fillers:** Facts, inspirational pieces, anecdotes; 100-400 words; $20. **Columns, Departments:** Viewpoint, opinion pieces; 650 words. **Art:** Mac-compatible TIFF or JPEG files, 300 dpi; $10-$35/inside use, $25-$50/cover. **Tips:** No articles on Christmas or Easter. Theme list available. **Queries:** Not necessary. **E-Queries:** Yes. **Unsolicited mss:** Accepts. **Response:** 4-8 weeks. **SASE Required:** Yes. **Freelance Content:** 10-20%. **Rights:** First, reprint, electronic. **Payment:** On publication.

BOOKS & CULTURE: A CHRISTIAN REVIEW
See full listing in Writing & Publishing category.

BREAD FOR GOD'S CHILDREN
P.O. Box 1017, Arcadia, FL 34265-1017. E-mail: bread@sunline.net. 6x/yr.
Circ.: 10,000. Judith M. Gibbs, Editor. **Description:** Christian family magazine with Bible study, stories, teen pages, parent news, ideas, and more. **Nonfiction:** Articles or craft ideas based on Christian principles or activities; how to implement Christian ways into daily living; 600-800 words; $20-$30. **Tips:** Stories must be from a child's point of view, with story itself getting message across; no preaching or moralizing, no tag endings. No stories with speaking animals, occult, fantasy, or romance. "Our purpose is to help Christian families learn to apply God's word in everyday living. We are looking for writers with a solid knowledge of Biblical principles and who are concerned with the youth of today living according to these principles." **Queries:** Not necessary. **E-Queries:** No. **Unsolicited mss:** Accepts. **Response:** 1-6 months. **SASE Required:** Yes. **Freelance Content:** 20%. **Rights:** FNAR.

CADET QUEST
P.O. Box 7259, Grand Rapids, MI 49510. 616-241-5616.
E-mail: submissions@calvinistcadets.org. Website: www.calvinistcadets.org. 7x/yr.
Circ.: 10,000. G. Richard Broene, Editor. **Description:** Christian-oriented magazine for boys, ages 9-14, especially to members of Calvinist Cadet Corps. Purpose: "to show how God is at work in the lives of boys and in the world around them." **Fiction:** Fast-moving stories that appeal to a boy's sense of adventure and humor; 900-1,500 words; pay varies. **Tips:** Send 9x12 SASE for free sample copy and/or upcoming themes. Themes also available on website. E-mail submissions must have text in body of e-mail—no attachments. **Queries:** Not necessary. **Unsolicited mss:** Accepts. **Payment:** On acceptance.

CAMPUS LIFE
See full listing in Teens category.

CATHOLIC DIGEST
Bayard Press, P.O. Box 6001, Mystic, CT 06355. 860-536-2611. E-mail: cdsubmissions@bayard-inc.com. Website: www.catholicdigest.org. Monthly. $2.25/$19.95.
Circ.: 350,000. Joop Koopman, Editor-in-Chief. **Description:** For adult Catholic readers, with general-interest topics on family life, spirituality, science, health, good

works, and relationships. **Nonfiction:** Humor, profiles, how-to, personal experiences; 750-1,500 words; $100-$400. **Fillers:** Up to 500 words; $2/line. **Columns, Departments:** True incidents about good works, parish life, conversion to Catholicism; 100-500 words; $2/line. **Tips:** "We're interested in articles about the family and career concerns of baby boomers looking to improve their lives. Illustrate topic with a series of true-life, interconnected vignettes." **E-Queries:** No. **Response:** 6-8 weeks. **SASE Required:** Yes. **Freelance Content:** 30%. **Rights:** One-time. **Payment:** On acceptance.

CATHOLIC PARENT
See full listing in Family & Parenting category.

CHRISTIAN CAMP & CONFERENCE JOURNAL
P.O. Box 62189, Colorado Springs, CO 80962-2189. 719-260-9400.
E-mail: editor@cciusa.org. Website: www.christiancamping.org. 6x/yr. $26.95/yr. Circ.: 8,700. **Description:** Seeks to inform, inspire, and motivate all who serve in Christian faith-based camps and conference centers, including youth and adult programs. **Fiction:** Only rarely publishes fiction. Pieces must be realistic, and either inspire or encourage Christian camping leaders; 800-1,500 words; $.16/word. **Nonfiction:** How-to (related to organized camping, such as motivating staff or enhancing food service), interview/profile, inspirational (application of Biblical truth to everyday situations in camping), general features (trends in Christian camping). **Tips:** Request publication guidelines and read a sample copy before sending a query. Profiles and interviews are the best bet for freelancers. See website for our editorial calendar and writers' guidelines. **Queries:** Preferred. **E-Queries:** Yes. **Response:** 1 month. **SASE Required:** Yes. **Freelance Content:** 75%. **Rights:** First. **Payment:** On publication. **Contact:** Alison Hayhoe, Editor; Justin Boles, Managing Editor.

THE CHRISTIAN CENTURY
104 S Michigan Ave., Suite 700, Chicago, IL 60603. 312-263-7510.
E-mail: main@christiancentury.org. Website: www.christiancentury.org. Biweekly. $49/yr. Circ.: 30,000. John M. Buchanan, Editor/Publisher. **Description:** Shows how Christian faith calls people to a profound engagement with the world and how people of faith address issues of poverty, international relations, and popular culture. **Nonfiction:** Religious angle on political/social issues, international affairs, culture, the arts, and challenges in everyday lives; 1,500-3,000 words; $75-$200. **Poetry:** Free verse, traditional, haiku. No sentimental or didactic poems; 20 lines; $50. **Art:** Photos, $25-$100. **Tips:** "Many of our readers are ministers or teachers of religion." **Queries:** Preferred. **E-Queries:** Yes. **SASE Required:** Yes. **Freelance Content:** 90%. **Rights:** One-time. **Payment:** On publication.

CHRISTIAN HOME & SCHOOL
Christian Schools International, 3350 E Paris Ave. SE, Grand Rapids, MI 49512. 616-957-1070. Bimonthly. Circ.: 70,000. Gordon L. Bordewyk, Executive Editor. **Description:** For parents in the U.S. and Canada who send their children to

Christian schools and are concerned about challenges facing families today. Pays $175-$250. **Queries:** Preferred. **Payment:** On publication. **Contact:** Roger W. Schmurr, Senior Editor.

CHRISTIAN PARENTING TODAY
See full listing in Family & Parenting category.

CHRISTIAN SINGLE
Lifeway Christian Resources, One LifeWay Plaza, Nashville, TN 37234-0175. Website: www.lifeway.com/christiansingle. Monthly. $20.25/yr. **Description:** For single adults on leisure activities, issues related to single parenting, and life from a Christian perspective. Also offers inspiring personal experiences and humor. Articles run 600-1,200 words; pay varies. **Queries:** Preferred. **Payment:** On acceptance.

CHRISTIAN SOCIAL ACTION
100 Maryland Ave. NE, Washington, DC 20002. 202-488-5631. Bimonthly. Circ.: 50,000. Gretchen Hakola, Editor. **Description:** For United Methodist clergy and lay people interested in the role and involvement of the church in social issues. Seeks stories that educate, analyze, and motivate people to Christian social action on justice and advocacy issues; 1,500-2,000 words; $125-$175. **Queries:** Preferred. **E-Queries:** Yes. **Unsolicited mss:** Does not accept. **Response:** 4-6 weeks. **SASE Required:** Yes. **Freelance Content:** 30%. **Rights:** FNAR. **Payment:** On publication.

CHRISTIANITY TODAY
465 Gundersen Dr., Carol Stream, IL 60188. 630-260-6200. E-mail: letters@christianitytoday.com. Website: www.christianitytoday.com/ctmag. 14x/yr. $24.95/yr. Circ.: 155,000. David Neff, Editor. **Description:** Evangelical Christian publication covering Christian doctrines, current events, news, trends, interpretive essays, etc. from evangelical Protestant perspective; 1,500-3,000 words; $200-$500. **Tips:** "We're seeking Internet-related stories with human interest." **Queries:** Preferred. **E-Queries:** Yes. **Unsolicited mss:** Accepts. **Response:** 3 months. **SASE Required:** Yes. **Freelance Content:** 80%. **Rights:** One-time. **Payment:** On acceptance. **Contact:** Mark Galli, Managing Editor.

CHURCH EDUCATOR
See full listing in Education category.

CLUB CONNECTION
The General Council of the Assemblies of God, 1445 N Boonville Ave., Springfield, MO 65802. 417-862-2781. E-mail: clubconnection@ag.org. Website: www.missionettes.ag.org. Quarterly. Circ.: 12,000. Debby Seler, Editor. **Description:** Magazine for Missionettes (girls ages 6-12). Focuses on the message of salvation. **Fiction:** Short stories; to 700 words; $25-$40. **Nonfiction:** Articles on friends, school, God, family, music, nature, and fun activities; to 700 words; $25-$40. **Poetry:** Leadership/devotional; to 700 words; $25-$40. **Fillers:** Crafts, games, puzzles, snack

recipes, etc.; pays $10. **Queries:** Preferred. **E-Queries:** Yes. **Unsolicited mss:** Accepts. **Freelance Content:** 25%. **Rights:** FNAR. **Payment:** On acceptance. **Contact:** Ranee Carter, Assistant Editor.

CLUBHOUSE JR.
See full listing in Juvenile category.

CLUBHOUSE MAGAZINE
See full listing in Juvenile category.

CNEWA WORLD
See full listing in Ethnic & Multicultural category.

COMMENTARY
165 E 56th St., New York, NY 10022. 212-891-1400. E-mail: editorial@commentarymagazine.com. Website: www.commentarymagazine.com. Monthly. $45/yr. Circ.: 25,000. Neal Kozodoy, Editor. **Description:** Published by the American Jewish Committee. Nonfiction pieces on contemporary issues, Jewish affairs, social sciences, religious thought, and culture. Also open to book reviews and serious fiction, of literary quality, on contemporary social or Jewish issues. **Payment:** On publication.

COMMONWEAL
See full listing in Contemporary Culture category.

THE COVENANT COMPANION
Covenant Publications of the Evangelical Covenant Church, 5101 N Francisco Ave., Chicago, IL 60625. 773-784-3000. E-mail: communication@covchurch.org. Website: www.covchurch.org. Monthly. Circ.: 16,000. **Description:** Discusses issues of faith, spirituality, social justice, local ministry, and the life of the church. Biographical profiles, local church ministries, current issues, and interviews with authors; 1,200-1,800 words; $35-$100. **Tips:** No "rants" about the culture or political agendas. Prefers human-interest pieces or articles on practical spirituality. **Queries:** Not necessary. **E-Queries:** Yes. **Unsolicited mss:** Accepts. **Response:** 4-6 weeks. **SASE Required:** Yes. **Freelance Content:** 40%. **Rights:** FNAR. **Payment:** On publication. **Contact:** Donald J. Meyer, Editor; Jane Swanson-Nystrom, Managing Editor.

CROSS & QUILL
See full listing in Writing & Publishing category.

DAILY MEDITATION
See full listing in Inspiration/Self-Help category.

DECISION
Billy Graham Evangelistic Assn., Two Parkway Plaza, Suite 200, 4828 Parkway Plaza Blvd., Charlotte, NC 28217. E-mail: submissions@bgea.org. Website: www.decision-

mag.org. 11x/yr. $12/yr. Circ.: 1,100,000. Bob Paulson, Managing Editor. **Description:** Offers religious inspirational, personal experience, and how-to articles. **Nonfiction:** Testimonies of people who have become Christians through Billy Graham or Franklin Graham ministries; personal experience articles, with a connection to the Billy Graham Evangelistic Association or Samaritan's Purse, on how God has intervened in a person's daily life or how Scripture was applied to solve a problem; 400-1,500 words; $30-$260. **Poetry:** Free verse and rhymed; 4-16 lines; $.60/word. **Columns, Departments:** Finding Jesus (Stories of people who have become Christians through Billy Graham ministries). 500-600 words; $85. **Tips:** "All articles must have a connection to BGEA or Samarian's Purse, but we want readers to see what God did, not what any organization did." **Queries:** Not necessary. **E-Queries:** Yes. **Unsolicited mss:** Accepts. **Response:** Queries 3 months, submissions 10 months. **SASE Required:** Yes. **Freelance Content:** 10%. **Rights:** FNAR.

DEVO'ZINE

Upper Room Ministries
1908 Grand Ave., P.O. Box 340004, Nashville, TN 37203-0004. 615-340-7247.
E-mail: devozine@upperroom.org. Website: www.upperroom.org. Bimonthly. Sandy Miller, Editor. **Description:** Devotional magazine designed for youth. Weekend feature articles related to theme of the week, with a "twist," 350-500 words; pays $100. Daily meditations, 150-250 words; pays $25. Also, prayers and poems, 10-20 lines. **Queries:** Not necessary. **Unsolicited mss:** Accepts. **SASE Required:** Yes.

DISCIPLESHIP JOURNAL

P.O. Box 35004, Colorado Springs, CO 80935. 719-531-3514. E-mail: djwriters@navpress.com. Website: www.disciplejournal.com. Bimonthly. $4.95/$23.97. Circ.: 130,000. Sue Kline, Editor. **Description:** Articles on Christian growth and practical application of Scripture. **Nonfiction:** Teaching based on Scripture (e.g., what Bible says on forgiveness); how-tos (to deepen devotional life; to reach out in community); 1,000-3,000 words; $.25/word. **Columns, Departments:** On the Home Front (Q&A on family issues); One-to-One (principles for discipling a new believer); DJ+ (up to 500 words, on practical ministry, leading small groups, evangelism, etc.); 750-950 words; $.25/word. **Tips:** First-time writers encouraged to write non-theme articles, on any aspect of living as a disciple of Christ. Seeking articles encouraging involvement in world missions, personal evangelism, and Christian leadership. No testimonies, devotionals, book reviews, or news. **Queries:** Required. **E-Queries:** Yes. **Unsolicited mss:** Does not accept. **Response:** 6 weeks. **SASE Required:** Yes. **Freelance Content:** 80%. **Rights:** FNAR. **Payment:** On acceptance.

DISCOVERY TRAILS

See full listing in Juvenile category.

THE DOOR MAGAZINE

See full listing in Humor category.

DOVETAIL

See full listing in Family & Parenting category.

ENRICHMENT JOURNAL

1445 N Boonville Ave., Springfield, MO 65802-1894. 417-862-2781. E-mail: enrichment@ag.org. Website: www.enrichmentjournal.ag.org. Quarterly. $24/yr. Circ.: 33,000. Gary Allen, Editor. **Description:** Resources to assist Pentecostal ministers in effective ministry. Articles and features on wide range of ministry-related topics; 1,200-2,100 words; $.10/word. **Tips:** Intended readership is Pentecostal/charismatic ministers and church leaders. **Queries:** Not necessary. **E-Queries:** Yes. **Unsolicited mss:** Accepts. **Response:** 1 week. **SASE Required:** Yes. **Freelance Content:** less than 10%. **Rights:** FNAR. **Payment:** On publication. **Contact:** Rick Knoth.

EVANGEL

Light and Life Communications, P.O. Box 535002, Indianapolis, IN 46253-5002. 317-244-3660. Quarterly. $2.25/issue. Circ.: 12,000. Julie Innes, Editor. **Description:** "Devotional in nature, our publication seeks to increase readers' understanding of the nature and character of God and the nature of life lived under the lordship of Christ." **Fiction:** Solving problems through faith; max. 1,200 words; $.04/word. **Nonfiction:** Free Methodist. Personal experience articles; short devotional items, 300-500 words (1,200 max.); $.04/word. **Poetry:** Devotional or nature; 8-16 lines. **Fillers:** Crypto puzzles, cartoons; $10-$20. **Tips:** Send SASE for sample copy and guidelines. **Queries:** Not necessary. **E-Queries:** No. **Unsolicited mss:** Accepts. **Response:** Queries 2 weeks, submissions 6-8 weeks. **SASE Required:** Yes. **Freelance Content:** 100%. **Rights:** One-time. **Payment:** On publication.

EVANGELICAL BEACON

Evangelical Free Church of America, 418 4th St. NE, Charlottesville, VA 22902-4722. E-mail: beacon@efca.org. Website: www.efc.org/beacon.html. Bimonthly. $12/yr. Circ.: 32,000. Diane McDougall, Editor. **Description:** Features news and information from the church. Seeks articles that fit editorial themes. Pieces run 500-2,000 words; $.20/word. **Payment:** On publication.

FAITH & FAMILY

See full listing in Family & Parenting category.

FAITH TODAY

Evangelical Fellowship of Canada, P.O. Box 3745 Markham Industrial Park, Markham, Ontario L3R OY4 Canada. 905-479-5885. E-mail: fteditor@efc-canada.com. Website: www.faithtoday.ca. Bimonthly. Circ.: 20,000. Gail Reid, Managing Editor. **Description:** Seeks to inform, equip, and inspire Christians across Canada. News stories and features on social trends and church trends in Canada. Also, short, quirky items, with photo, on Christianity in Canada; 400-3,000 words; $.20-$.30/word (CDN). **Tips:** No devotionals or generic Christian-living material. Sample copy free on request. **Queries:** Required. **E-Queries:** Yes. **Unsolicited**

mss: Does not accept. **Response:** 3 weeks, SASE required (IRC's). **Freelance Content:** 75%. **Rights:** FNASR. **Payment:** On publication.

THE FAMILY DIGEST

P.O. Box 40137, Fort Wayne, IN 46804. Bimonthly. Circ.: 150,000. Corine B. Erlandson, Manuscript Editor. **Description:** Dedicated to the joy and fulfillment of Catholic family and parish life. Especially looking for upbeat articles which affirm the simple ways in which the Catholic faith is expressed in daily life. **Nonfiction:** Seeking articles on family life, parish life, spiritual life, saints' lives, prayer, how-to, and seasonal (seasonal articles should be submitted 7 months prior to issue date); 650-1,250 words; $40-$60. **Fillers:** Funny and unusual stories drawn from personal, real-life experience; 10-100 words; $25. **Tips:** Writing must have a Catholic theme. Prefers original articles, but will consider reprints of pieces that have appeared in non-competing markets. **Queries:** Not necessary. **E-Queries:** No. **Unsolicited mss:** Accepts. **Response:** 4-8 weeks. **SASE Required:** Yes. **Freelance Content:** 90%. **Rights:** FNAR. **Payment:** 4-8 weeks following acceptance.

FELLOWSHIP

P.O. Box 271, Nyack, NY 10960-0271. 845-358-4601. E-mail: editor@forusa.org. Website: www.forusa.org. Bimonthly. $4.50/$25. Circ.: 9,000. Richard Deats, Editor. **Description:** Magazine of peace, justice, and nonviolence. Published by the Fellowship of Reconciliation, an interfaith, pacifist organization. **Nonfiction:** Articles for a just and peaceful world community; 750-2,500 words. **Art:** B&W photo-essays on active nonviolence, peace and justice, opposition to war. **E-Queries:** Yes. **Unsolicited mss:** Accepts. **Freelance Content:** 25%. **Payment:** In copies and 2 year subscription. Small payment for photos.

FIRST THINGS

Institute on Religion & Public Life, 156 Fifth Ave., Suite 400, New York, NY 10010. 212-627-1985. E-mail: ft@firstthings.com. Website: www.firstthings.com. 10x/yr. Circ.: 32,000. Richard John Neuhaus, Editor-in-Chief. **Description:** General social commentary for academics, clergy, and general-educated readership on the role of religion in public life. Essays and features; 1,500-6,000 words; $400-$1,000. Also features poetry, 4-40 lines. **Tips:** Sample copy free upon request. **Queries:** Required. **E-Queries:** Yes. **Payment:** On publication. **Contact:** Damon Linker, Editor.

FOURSQUARE WORLD ADVANCE

1910 W Sunset Blvd., Suite 400, P.O. Box 26902, Los Angeles, CA 90026. E-mail: comm@foursquare.org. Website: www.foursquare.org. Bill Shepson, Editor. **Description:** Published by the International Church of the Foursquare Gospel. **Tips:** "We do not accept unsolicited manuscripts. However, e-mail queries or letters that briefly describe or outline a proposed article are welcome."

THE FRIEND

See full listing in Juvenile category.

FRIENDS JOURNAL

Friends Publishing Corp., 1216 Arch St., 2A, Philadelphia, PA 19107-2835. 215-563-8629. E-mail: info@friendsjournal.org. Website: www.friendsjournal.org. Monthly. $35/yr. Circ.: 8,000. Susan Corson-Finnerty, Publisher/Executive Editor. **Description:** Reflects Quaker life today by offering commentary on social issues, spiritual reflection, experiential articles, Quaker history, and world affairs. **Nonfiction:** With awareness of Friends' concerns and ways; fresh, nonacademic style; use language that clearly includes both sexes; to 2,500 words. **Poetry:** To 25 lines. **Fillers:** Quaker-related humor, games, and puzzles. **Tips:** Articles with positive approach to problems and spiritual seeking preferred. **Queries:** Not necessary. **E-Queries:** Yes. **Unsolicited mss:** Accepts. **Response:** 3-16 weeks. **SASE Required:** Yes. **Freelance Content:** 70%. **Payment:** None.

GOSPEL TODAY

Horizon Concepts, Inc., 286 Highway 314, Suite C, Fayetteville, GA 30214. 770-719-4825. E-mail: gospeltodaymag@aol.com. Website: www.gospeltoday.com. 8x/yr. $3/$20. Circ.: 50,000. Teresa Hairston, Publisher/Editor. **Description:** "America's leading gospel lifestyle magazine," aimed at African American Christians. Human-interest stories on Christian personalities, events. Book reviews welcome. 1,500-2,000 words; $150-$250. **Tips:** No opinions or poetry. **Queries:** Required. **E-Queries:** Yes. **Unsolicited mss:** Do not accept. **Response:** 6 weeks. **SASE Required:** Yes. **Freelance Content:** 60%. **Rights:** All. **Payment:** On publication.

GROUP MAGAZINE

P.O.Box 481, Loveland, CO 80539-0481. 970-669-3836. E-mail: greditor@grouppublishing.com. Website: www.groupmag.com; www.youthministry.com. Bimonthly. $25.95/yr. Circ.: 50,000. Rick Lawrence, Executive Editor. **Description:** Interdenominational Youth Ministry magazine for leaders of Christian youth. Provides ideas, practical help, inspiration, and training; 500-2,000 words; $125-$350. **Columns, Departments:** Try This One (short ideas for groups: games, fundraisers, Bible study); Hands on Help (tips for leaders). **Tips:** "Use real-life examples, personal experience. Include practical tips, self-quizzes, checklists. Use Scripture." **Queries:** Not necessary. **Unsolicited mss:** Accepts. **Response:** 6-8 weeks. **SASE Required:** Yes. **Freelance Content:** 70%. **Rights:** All. **Payment:** On publication.

GUIDE

See full listing in Juvenile category.

GUIDEPOSTS

See full listing in Inspiration/Self-Help category.

GUIDEPOSTS FOR TEENS

See full listing in Teens category.

HADASSAH

Women's Zionist Organization of America, 50 W 58th St., New York, NY 10019-2505.
212-355-7900. E-mail: zshluker@aol.com. Website: www.hadassah.org. Monthly.
$25/yr. Circ.: 309,000. Alan Tigay, Executive Editor; Zelda Shluker, Managing Editor.
Description: General-interest Jewish feature and literary magazine on issues important to Jewish life. Mission is to challenge, inspire, and inform while reinforcing the
commitment of its readers to Judaism, Zionism, and Israel. **Queries:** Preferred.

INSIGHT

See full listing in Teens category.

JEWISH CURRENTS

Association for Promotion of Jewish Secularism, Inc., 22 E 17th St., #601, New York,
NY 10003. 212-924-5740. E-mail: babush@ulster.net. 6x/yr. $30. Circ.: 2,100.
Lawrence Bush, Editor. **Description:** Articles, reviews, fiction and poetry on Jewish
subjects. Seeks to present a progressive Jewish point-of-view on an issue. **Fiction:**
Jewish angle, humor, contemporary flavor; to 2,500 words. **Nonfiction:** Jewish his-
tory, politics, culture, Yiddish language and literature (in English); to 3,500 words.
Tips: "Our readers are secular, politically liberal." **Queries:** Not necessary.
Unsolicited mss: Accepts. **SASE Required:** Yes. **Payment:** In copies.

THE JEWISH JOURNAL

3580 Wilshire Blvd., Suite 1510, Los Angeles, CA 90010. 213-368-1661. E-mail: edi-
torial@jewishjournal.com. Website: www.jewishjournal.com. **Description:** A nonprofit independent weekly serving the Jewish community of greater Los Angeles.
Welcomes original, insightful, and provocative unsolicited manuscripts. Query first by
e-mail. Payment negotiable.

JOURNAL OF CHRISTIAN NURSING

Nurses Christian Fellowship, P.O. Box 7895, Madison, WI 53707-7895.
608-846-8560. E-mail: jcn.me@ivcf.org. Website: www.ncf-jcn.org. Quarterly. $22.95.
Circ.: 7,000. Judith Shelly, Editor. **Description:** Practical, Biblically-based articles to
help nurses grow spiritually, meet patients' spiritual needs, and face ethical dilemmas.
Nonfiction: Articles should help readers view nursing practice through the eyes of
faith: spiritual care, ethics, values, healing and wholeness, psychology and religion,
personal and professional growth, etc. Priority to nurse authors; work by others considered. 8-12 pages; $25 or less. **Poetry:** 1 page or less; $25. **Tips:** Avoid academic
style. Prefers e-mail submissions sent as an attachment in MS Word. **Queries:** Not
necessary. **E-Queries:** Yes. **Unsolicited mss:** Accepts. **Response:** 2-4 weeks. **SASE
Required:** Yes. **Rights:** 1st time, some reprint. **Payment:** On acceptance.

LEADERSHIP

Christianity Today International
465 Gundersen Dr., Carol Stream, IL 60188. 630-260-6200. E-mail: ljeditor@leader-
shipjournal.net. Website: www.leadershipjournal.net. Quarterly. $24.95/yr. Circ.:

65,000. Marshall Shelley, Editor. **Description:** Provides first-person accounts of real-life experiences in the ministry for church leaders. **Nonfiction:** First-person stories of life in ministry; situation faced, solutions found. Articles must offer practical help (how-to format) for problems church leaders face; 2,000 words; $.15/word. **Tips:** "Avoid essays expounding, editorials arguing, or homilies explaining." **Queries:** Preferred. **E-Queries:** Yes. **Unsolicited mss:** Accepts. **Response:** 3-6 weeks. **SASE Required:** Yes. **Freelance Content:** 30%. **Payment:** On acceptance.

LIBERTY

12501 Old Columbia Pike, Silver Spring, MD 20904-1608. 301-680-6690. E-mail: steeli@nad.adventist.org. Website: www.libertymagazine.org. Bimonthly. Circ.: 200,000. Lincoln Steed, Editor. **Description:** Focuses on religious freedom and church-state relations. Readers are legislators at every level, judges, lawyers, and other leaders. Articles on religious freedom and 1st amendment rights; 1,000-2,500 words; $250+. **Tips:** Submit resumé and clips. **Queries:** Preferred. **E-Queries:** Yes. **Unsolicited mss:** Does not accept. **Response:** 1-3 months. **SASE Required:** Yes. **Freelance Content:** 95%. **Rights:** FNAR. **Payment:** On acceptance.

LIGHT AND LIFE MAGAZINE

Free Methodist Church of North America, P.O. Box 535002, Indianapolis, IN 46253-5002. 317-244-3660. E-mail: llmauthors@fmcna.org. Bimonthly. Circ.: 19,000. Doug Newton, Editor. **Description:** Social and cultural analysis from evangelical perspective. Open to thoughtful articles about practical Christian living; 800-2,000 words. **Queries:** Not necessary. **E-Queries:** Yes. **Unsolicited mss:** Accepts. **Response:** 8-10 weeks. **SASE Required:** Yes. **Rights:** FNAR. **Payment:** On publication.

LIGUORIAN

One Liguori Dr., Liguori, MO 63057. 636-464-2500. E-mail: liguorianeditor@liguori.org. Website: www.liguorian.org. 10x/yr. Circ.: 200,000. William Parker, Editor. **Description:** Faithful to the charism of St. Alphonsus, seeks to help readers develop a personal call to holiness. **Fiction:** Short stories with Catholic content; 1,700-1,900 words; $.12/word. **Nonfiction:** On Catholic Christian values in modern life; 1,700-1,900 words; $.12/word. **Queries:** Preferred. **E-Queries:** Yes. **Unsolicited mss:** Accepts. **Response:** 1-8 weeks. **SASE Required:** Yes. **Freelance Content:** 20-30%. **Payment:** On acceptance.

LIVING LIGHT NEWS

Living Light Ministries, #200, 5306-89 St., Edmonton, Alberta T6E 5P9 Canada. 780-468-6397. E-mail: shine@livinglightnews.org; jeff@livinglightnews.org. Website: www.livinglightnews.org. 7x/yr. $2.50/$19.95. Circ.: 30,000. Jeff Caporale, Editor. **Description:** Family-oriented, contemporary Christian newspaper written primarily for non-Christians as a way of sharing the gospel. **Fiction:** Uses fiction for Christmas issue only. Send Christmas-related material that focuses on the true meaning of Christmas (the birth of Christ) and the values it brings with it. Seeks stories with humor; 300-1,000 words; $.08/word. **Nonfiction:** Powerful testimonials of well-known Christians in music, sports, and entertainment; 300-1,000 words; $.08/word. **Columns, Departments:** Helpful and informative family-related articles; 600-650 words. **Tips:** "See website to view our writer's guidelines and to grasp our editorial vision. We like writers who write with pizzazz!" **Queries:** Preferred. **E-Queries:** Yes. **Unsolicited mss:** Accepts. **Response:** 2-4 weeks, SASE required with Canadian postage or IRC's. **Freelance Content:** 80%. **Rights:** All. **Payment:** On publication.

LIVING WITH TEENAGERS

See full listing in Family & Parenting category.

THE LOOKOUT

Standard Publishing, 8121 Hamilton Ave., Cincinnati, OH 45231. 513-931-4050. E-mail: lookout@standardpub.com. Website: www.lookoutmag.com. Weekly. $29.99/yr. Circ.: 100,000. Shawn McMullen, Editor. **Description:** Focuses on spiritual growth, family issues, people overcoming problems, and applying Christian faith to current issues. Articles run 500-1,800 words; $.05-$.12/word. **Queries:** Preferred. **E-Queries:** Yes. **Unsolicited mss:** Accepts. **Response:** 6-10 weeks. **SASE Required:** Yes. **Rights:** First or reprint. **Payment:** On acceptance.

THE LUTHERAN

Evangelical Lutheran Church in America, 8765 W Higgins Rd., Chicago, IL 60631-4101. 773-380-2540. E-mail: lutheran@elca.org. Website: www.thelutheran.org. Monthly. $15.95/yr. Circ.: 620,000. David L. Miller, Editor. **Description:** Christian ideology, personal religious experiences, social and ethical issues, family life, church, and community of Evangelical Lutheran Church in America. **Nonfiction:** Articles on spirituality and Christian living; describing the unique life, service, challenges and problems of ELCA congregations; describing the life and work of the ELCA and of its institutions, colleges and seminaries. **Columns, Departments:** My View; opinions on a current societal event or issue in the life of this church. **Queries:** Required. **E-Queries:** Yes. **Response:** 1 month. **Rights:** One-time. **Payment:** On acceptance.

MARRIAGE PARTNERSHIP

Christianity Today International, 465 Gundersen Dr., Carol Stream, IL 60188. 630-260-6200. E-mail: mp@marriagepartnership.com. Website: www.marriagepartnership.com. Quarterly. $19.95/yr. Circ.: 57,000. Ginger Kolbaba, Managing Editor. **Description:** Offers realistic, practical, and expert advice for Christian married couples. **Nonfiction:** Related to marriage for men and women who wish to fortify their relationships; 1,000-2,000 words; $.15/word. **Fillers:** Humor welcomed; 1200 words. **Tips:** No simultaneous submissions. **Queries:** Required. **E-Queries:** Yes. **Unsolicited mss:** Does not accept. **Response:** 8 weeks. **SASE Required:** Yes. **Freelance Content:** 25%. **Rights:** FNAR. **Payment:** On acceptance.

MARYKNOLL MAGAZINE

Catholic Foreign Mission Society of America, P.O. Box 311, Maryknoll, NY 10545-0308. 914-941-7590, ext. 2490. E-mail: mklmag@maryknoll.org. Website: www.maryknoll.org. 9x/yr. $10/yr. Circ.: 500,000. Frank Maurovich, Editor. **Description:** Published by the Maryknoll Fathers and Brothers. Christian-oriented publication focusing on the work of missioners overseas; 1,500-2,000 words; $150. **Art:** Prints or slides; $50. **Queries:** Required. **E-Queries:** Yes. **Unsolicited mss:** Does not accept. **SASE Required:** Yes. **Freelance Content:** 5%. **Payment:** On publication.

THE MENNONITE

1700 S Main St., Goshen, IN 46526. 574-535-6052.
E-mail: editor@themennonite.org. Website: www.themennonite.org. $1.50/issue. Circ.: 15,000. Everett Thomas, Editor. **Description:** For members of the Mennonite Church USA. Open to personal stories of Mennonites exercising their faith; 1,400 words; $.07/word. Also accepts poetry, no more than 2 pages; $50-$75. **Tips:** See website for detailed guidelines. **Queries:** Not necessary. **E-Queries:** Yes. **Unsolicited mss:** Accepts. **Response:** 2 weeks. **SASE Required:** Yes. **Freelance Content:** 20%. **Rights:** One-time, electronic. **Payment:** On publication.

MESSENGER OF THE SACRED HEART

661 Greenwood Ave., Toronto, Ontario M4J 4B3 Canada. 416-466-1195. Monthly. Circ.: 11,000. F. J. Power, S. J., Editor. **Description:** For American and Canadian Catholics. Fiction and nonfiction pieces should run about 1,500 words; $.06/word and up. **Payment:** On acceptance.

MINISTRY & LITURGY

Resource Publications, Inc., 160 E Virginia St., Suite 290, San Jose, CA 95112-5848. 408-286-8505. E-mail: mleditor@rpinet.com. Website: www.rpinet.com/ml. Monthly. $50/yr. Circ.: 10,000. Williams Burns, Publisher. **Description:** Practical, imaginative how-to help for Roman Catholic liturgy planners. **Tips:** Sample copy free on request. **Queries:** Required. **E-Queries:** Yes. **Contact:** Donna Cole, Managing Editor.

MOMENT

See full listing in Ethnic & Multicultural category.

MY FRIEND: THE CATHOLIC MAGAZINE FOR KIDS

See full listing in Juvenile category.

NEW WORLD OUTLOOK

The United Methodist Church, 475 Riverside Dr., Rm. 1476, New York, NY 10115. 212-870-3765. E-mail: nwo@gbgm-umc.org. Website: http://gbgm-umc.org/nwo. Bimonthly. $19.95/yr. Circ.: 17,000. Christie R. House, Editor. **Description:** On United Methodist missions and Methodist-related programs and ministries. Focus on national, global, and women's and children's issues, and on men and youth in missions. Articles, 500-2,000 words, illustrated with color photos. **Queries:** Preferred. **Payment:** On publication.

OBLATES

9480 N De Mazenod Dr., Belleville, IL 62223-1094. 618-398-4848.
E-mail: mami@oblatesusa.org. Website: www.oblatesusa.org. **Description:**
Published by the Missionary Association of Mary Immaculate. Seeks articles that
inspire, uplift, and motivate through positive Christian values in everyday life; to 500
words; $150. **Tips:** "Try first-person approach. No preachy, psychological, theological,
or spiritual journey pieces. Christian slant or Gospel message should be apparent, but
subtle." **Queries:** Not necessary. **E-Queries:** No. **Unsolicited mss:** Accepts.
Response: 4-6 weeks. **SASE Required:** Yes. **Freelance Content:** 15%. **Rights:**
FNASR. **Payment:** On acceptance.

ON THE LINE

See full listing in Juvenile category.

OUR SUNDAY VISITOR

200 Noll Plaza, Huntington, IN 46750. E-mail: oursunvis@osv.com. Website:
www.osv.com. Weekly. $2/$37.95. Circ.: 66,000. Gerald Korson, Editor. **Description:**
Reports on national and international news for Catholics, from a sound Catholic per-
spective. **Tips:** Query by mail or e-mail. Place "query" or "manuscript" in subject line.
No phone calls. **Queries:** Preferred. **E-Queries:** Yes. **Unsolicited mss:** Accepts.
Response: 6 weeks. **SASE Required:** Yes. **Freelance Content:** 10%. **Rights:**
FNAR. **Payment:** On acceptance.

PASSPORT

See full listing in Juvenile category.

PASTORAL LIFE

Society of St. Paul, P.O. Box 595, Canfield, OH 44406-0595. 330-533-5503.
E-mail: plmagazine@hotmail.com. Website: www.albahouse.org. Monthly. $20/yr.
Circ.: 1,200. Rev. Matthew Roehrig, SSP, Editor. **Description:** Addresses the issues
of Catholic pastoral ministry. Articles run 1,000-2,500 words; $.04/word. **Tips:** Prefers
query by e-mail. Writer's guidelines available. **Queries:** Preferred. **E-Queries:** Yes.
Unsolicited mss: Accepts. **Payment:** On publication.

THE PENTECOSTAL MESSENGER

Messenger Publishing House, P.O. Box 850, Joplin, MO 64802-0850. 417-624-7050.
E-mail: pm@pcg.org. Website: www.pcg.org. Monthly. Circ.: 5,000. John Mallinak,
Editor. **Description:** Covers issues of Christian commitment. Topics include social
and religious issues and the Bible. Provides articles, human interest features, inspirational stories, and seasonal material. Edited for those in leadership. Articles run 400-
1,200 words; pays $.02/word. **Freelance Content:** 10%. **Payment:** On publication.

POCKETS
See full listing in Juvenile category.

PREACHING
P.O. Box 681868, Franklin, TN 37068-1868. 615-599-9889. E-mail: editor@preaching.com. Website: www.preaching.com. Bimonthly. Michael Duduit, Editor. **Description:** For professional ministers. Each issue contains model sermons which reflect the best of preaching today. Interdenominational, rooted in evangelical convictions. **Nonfiction:** Features (guidance on preaching and worship leadership), 1,750-2,000 words, $50. Sermons, 1,250-1,500 words, $35. **Fillers:** Abridged sermons, 600 words, $20. Children's sermons, 250-300, $10. **Tips:** Virtually all material written by active/retired pastors or seminary faculty; articles by non-ministers rarely accepted. **Queries:** Preferred. **E-Queries:** Yes. **Payment:** On publication.

PRESBYTERIAN RECORD
50 Wynford Dr., Toronto, Ontario M3C 1J7 Canada. 416-441-1111.
E-mail: pcrecord@presbyterian.ca. Website: www.presbyterian.ca/record. 11x/yr. $25/yr (U.S. & Foreign). Circ.: 45,000. David Harris, Editor. **Description:** Published by the Presbyterian Church in Canada. Nonfiction pieces on children and youth ministries, lay ministries, etc. Average length 750 words; $100. **Columns, Departments:** Opinion, Meditation, Spirituality; $100. **Tips:** No fiction. **Queries:** Required. **E-Queries:** Yes. **Unsolicited mss:** Does not accept. **Response:** 1-2 weeks. **SASE Required:** Yes. **Freelance Content:** 10%. **Rights:** One-time. **Payment:** On publication.

PRESBYTERIANS TODAY
Presbyterian Church U.S.A., 100 Witherspoon, Louisville, KY 40202-1396. 502-569-5637. E-mail: today@pcusa.org. Website: www.pcusa.org/today. 10x/yr. $19.95/yr. Circ.: 60,000. Eva Stimson, Editor. **Description:** General-interest magazine for members of the Presbyterian church (U.S.). **Nonfiction:** About Presbyterian people and churches; guidance for daily living; current issues; 1,200-1,500 words; $300. **Fillers:** Humorous anecdotes; 100 words or less; no payment. **Queries:** Preferred. **E-Queries:** Yes. **Unsolicited mss:** Accepts. **Response:** 2-6 weeks. **SASE Required:** Yes. **Freelance Content:** 30%. **Rights:** FNAR.

THE PRIEST
Our Sunday Visitor, Inc., 200 Noll Plaza, Huntington, IN 46750-4304. 260-356-8400. E-mail: tpriest@osv.com. Website: www.osv.com. Monthly. $5/$39.95. Circ.: 7,700. Owen F. Campion, Editor. **Description:** Assists priests, deacons, and seminarians in day-to-day ministry. Historical/nostalgic, humor, inspirational, interview/profile, opinion, personal experience, counseling, administration, theology, etc.; 1,500-2,500 words; $175-$250. **Queries:** Preferred. **E-Queries:** Yes. **Unsolicited mss:** Accepts. **Response:** 5-12 weeks. **SASE Required:** Yes. **Freelance Content:** 25%. **Rights:** FNASR. **Payment:** On acceptance. **Contact:** Murray Hubley, Associate Editor.

PURPOSE
616 Walnut Ave., Scottdale, PA 15683-1999. 724-887-8500. E-mail: horsch@mph.org. Website: www.mph.org. $20.95/yr. Circ.: 10,000. James E. Horsch, Editor. **Description:** Weekly magazine for adults, young and old, general audience with varied interests. Focuses on Christian discipleship—how to be a faithful Christian in the midst of everyday life situations. Uses first-person story form to explore daily issues involved in maintaining a faithful Christian lifestyle. Publication for committed Christians who want to apply their faith in daily life. Suggests ways to resolve life's issues consistent with Biblical principles. **Fiction:** Christian themes to nurture the desire for harmony with neighbors at home to all nations and cultures. **Nonfiction:** Articles to help others grow toward commitment to Christ and the church; 750 words; up to $.05/word. **Poetry:** Positive expression of love and caring; up to 16 lines; $20. **Queries:** Not necessary. **E-Queries:** Yes. **Unsolicited mss:** Accepts. **Response:** Up to 3 months. **SASE Required:** Yes. **Freelance Content:** 90%. **Rights:** One-time. **Payment:** On acceptance.

QUAKER LIFE
Friends United Meeting, 101 Quaker Hill Dr., Richmond, IN 47374-1980. 765-962-7573. E-mail: quakerlife@fum.org. Website: www.fum.org/ql. 10x/yr. $24/yr. Circ.: 7,000. Trish Edwards-Konic, Editor. **Description:** For members of Friends United Meeting, other Friends (Quakers), evangelical Christians, religious pacifists, and those who aspire to live a simple lifestyle. **Nonfiction:** Inspirational, first-person, articles on the Bible applied to daily living, news and analysis, devotional and study articles, and personal testimonies; 750-1,500 words. **Poetry:** Evangelical in nature. **Tips:** Sample copy $2. **Queries:** Not necessary. **E-Queries:** Yes. **Unsolicited mss:** Accepts. **Response:** 2-8 weeks. **SASE Required:** No. **Freelance Content:** 80%. **Rights:** First. **Payment:** 3 copies.

QUEEN OF ALL HEARTS
26 S Saxon Ave., Bay Shore, NY 11706-8993. 631-665-0726. Website: www.montfort-missionaries.com. Bimonthly. Reverend Roger Charest, S.S.M., Managing Editor. **Description:** Publication that covers Marian doctrine and devotion. Particular focus is on St. Louis de Montfort's Trinitarian and Christoecentric approach to Mary in spiritual lives. **Fiction:** 1,500-2,000 words; $40-$60. **Nonfiction:** Essays, inspirational, personal experience; 750-2,000 words; $40-$60. **Poetry:** Free verse; 2 poems max. **Queries:** Preferred. **Unsolicited mss:** Accepts. **Rights:** One-time. **Payment:** On publication.

RECONSTRUCTIONISM TODAY
30 Old Whitfield Rd., Accord, NY 12404. 845-626-2427. E-mail: babush@ulster.net. Website: www.jrf.org. Quarterly. $20/yr. Circ.: 14,000. Lawrence Bush, Editor. **Description:** For the Reconstructionist synagogue movement, with emphasis on creative Jewish living. **Nonfiction:** Personal Jewish journey, with a Reconstructionist connection; 1,000-2,500 words. **Art:** Photographs, illustrations; TIFF, EPS, prints. **Queries:** Preferred. **E-Queries:** Yes. **Unsolicited mss:** Accepts.

REFORM JUDAISM

Union for Reform Judaism, 633 3rd Ave., Fl. 7, New York, NY 10017-6790. 212-650-4240. Website: http://urj.org/rjmag. Quarterly. $3.50/issue. Circ.: 310,000. Aron Hirt-Manheimer, Editor. **Description:** Conveys the creativity, diversity, and dynamism of Reform Judaism. **Fiction:** Thought-provoking, contemporary Jewish fiction; 1,200-2,000 words; $.30/word. **Nonfiction:** 1,200-3,500 words; $.30/word. **Tips:** "Read and understand our publication thoroughly before sending manuscripts. Many freelance submissions are clearly inappropriate. Also, we prefer self-addressed postcards with Yes, No, and Maybe options. This will secure faster response time." **Queries:** Not necessary. **E-Queries:** No. **Unsolicited mss:** Accepts. **Response:** 6-8 weeks. **SASE Required:** Yes. **Freelance Content:** 25%. **Rights:** FNASR. **Payment:** On publication. **Contact:** Joy Weinberg, Managing Editor.

REVIEW FOR RELIGIOUS

3601 Lindell Blvd., St. Louis, MO 63108. 314-977-7363. E-mail: review@slu.edu. Quarterly. David L. Fleming, S.J., Editor. **Description:** Catholic spirituality tradition stemming from Catholic religious communities. **Nonfiction:** Informative, practical, or inspirational articles; 1,500-5,000 words; $6/page. **Queries:** Preferred. **Payment:** On publication.

SACRED JOURNEY

Fellowship in Prayer, 291 Witherspoon St., Princeton, NJ 08542. 609-924-6863. E-mail: editorial@sacredjourney.org. Website: www.sacredjourney.org. 6x/yr. **Description:** Multi-faith journal focusing on spiritual practice, prayer, meditation, and service issues. Articles about spiritual life practiced by men and women of all faith traditions; to 1,500 words. **Tips:** Use inclusive language where possible. See website for guidelines. **Queries:** Not necessary. **E-Queries:** Yes. **Unsolicited mss:** Accepts. **Response:** 2 months. **SASE Required:** Yes. **Freelance Content:** 75%. **Rights:** One-time. **Payment:** In copies.

SEEK

Standard Publishing, 8121 Hamilton Ave., Cincinnati, OH 45231. 513-931-4050. E-mail: dmedill@standardpub.com. Website: www.standardpub.com. Weekly. Circ.: 29,000. Dawn A. Medill, Editor. **Description:** Relates faith in action or Christian living, through inspirational or controversial topics, timely religious issues, and testimonials. Articles run 400-1,200 words; $.07/word for first rights and $.05/word for reprint rights. **Tips:** No poetry or simultaneous submissions. Manuscripts not submitted to the theme list will be returned. Send SASE for a sample copy or a hard copy of guidelines and theme list. E-mail submissions accepted. **Queries:** Does not accept. **E-Queries:** No. **Unsolicited mss:** Accepts. **Response:** 3 months from theme list deadline. **SASE Required:** Yes. **Freelance Content:** 95%. **Rights:** 1st and reprint. **Payment:** On acceptance.

SHARING THE VICTORY

See full listing in Sports & Recreation/Outdoors category.

SIGNS OF THE TIMES

Pacific Press, P.O. Box 5398, Nampa, ID 83653-5398. 208-465-2577.
E-mail: signs@pacificpress.com. Website: www.pacificpress.com. Monthly. $12.49/yr.
Circ.: 200,000. Marvin Moore, Editor. **Description:** For the public, showing the way
to Jesus, based on the beliefs of the Seventh-day Adventist church. Profiles, first-person experiences, health, home, marriage, human-interest, inspirational, etc.; 600-
1,500 words; $.10-$.20/word. **Queries:** Not necessary. **E-Queries:** Yes. **Unsolicited
mss:** Accepts. **Response:** 2-6 weeks. **SASE Required:** Yes. **Freelance Content:**
20%. **Rights:** First. **Payment:** On acceptance.

SPIRITUAL LIFE

2131 Lincoln Rd. NE, Washington, DC 20002-1151. 202-832-8489.
E-mail: editor@spiritual-life.org. Website: www.spiritual-life.org. Quarterly.
$4.75/$18. Circ.: 11,000. Edward O'Donnell, O.C.D., Editor. **Description:** A professional religious journal, with essays on Christian spirituality with a pastoral application to everyday life. Articles run 5,000-8,000 words; $50/page. **Art:** B&W cover;
$100-$200. **Queries:** Not necessary. **E-Queries:** Yes. **Unsolicited mss:** Accepts.
Response: 8-10 weeks. **SASE Required:** Yes. **Freelance Content:** 90%. **Rights:**
FNASR. **Payment:** On acceptance.

ST. ANTHONY MESSENGER

28 W Liberty St., Cincinnati, OH 45202-6498. 513-241-5615.
E-mail: stanthony@americancatholic.org. Website: www.americancatholic.org. Pat
McCloskey, O.F.M. Editor. **Description:** A Catholic family magazine which aims to
help readers lead more fully human and Christian lives by: reporting and putting into
context the major events and movements in a changing Church and world; commenting on matters of significance from the perspective of Christian faith and values;
expanding awareness, tolerance and understanding by presenting the views and
achievements of others through interviews, personality profiles and opinion articles;
enriching, entertaining and informing with fiction, columns, and features. **Tips:**
Readers are people living in families or the family-like situations of Church and community. **Contact:** Amy Luken or Monna Younger, Editorial Assistants.

STANDARD

6401 The Paseo, Kansas City, MO 64131. 816-333-7000.
E-mail: cyourdon@nazarene.org. Website: www.nazarene.org. Weekly. $9.95. Circ.:
150,000. Dr. Everett Leadingham, Senior Editor. **Description:** Denominational
Sunday School take-home paper with leisure reading for adults (generally older adults
with conservative Holiness church background). **Fiction:** Inspirational stories,
Christianity in action; to 1,800 words; $.035/word (1st); $.02/word (reprint). **Poetry:**
Christian themes; 25 lines max; $.25/line (min. $5). **Fillers:** Inspirational; 300-500
words. **Tips:** New writers welcome. Prefers short fiction; avoid fictionalized Bible sto-

ries. **Queries:** Not necessary. **Response:** 3 months. **Freelance Content:** 100%. **Rights:** One-time. **Contact:** Charlie L. Yourdon, Managing Editor.

TEACHERS INTERACTION

Concordia Publishing House, 3558 S Jefferson Ave., St. Louis, MO 63118. 314-268-1083. E-mail: tom.nummela@cph.org. Quarterly. $3.95/$12.95. Circ.: 14,000. Tom Nummela, Editor. **Description:** Builds up volunteer teachers of the faith, and church professionals who support them, in the ministry of sharing ideas, inspirational stories, and education. **Nonfiction:** Practical assistance for volunteer Christian teachers, especially Sunday school. Each issue on a central theme; inquire about upcoming themes; 1,000-1,200 words; $110. **Fillers:** Teachers Interchange (short activities, ideas for Sunday school classes, creative and practical); 150-200 words; $20-$40. **Columns, Departments:** 9 regular columns; 400-500 words; $55. **Art:** Color photos of children, all ages, in Christian educational settings other than day school; seeks to include children with disabilities and children of various ethnic backgrounds; $50-$100. **Queries:** Preferred. **E-Queries:** Yes. **Unsolicited mss:** Accepts. **Response:** 10-30 days. **SASE Required:** Yes. **Freelance Content:** 30%. **Rights:** All. **Payment:** On acceptance.

TIKKUN

See full listing in Current Events, Politics category.

TODAY'S CATHOLIC TEACHER

See full listing in Education category.

TODAY'S CHRISTIAN

Christianity Today International, 465 Gundersen Dr., Carol Stream, IL 60188. 630-260-6200. E-mail: tceditor@todays-christian.com. Website: www.todays-christian.com. Bimonthly. $2.95/$17.95. Circ.: 185,000. Edward Gilbreath, Managing Editor. **Description:** Formerly Christian Reader. Publishes stories that encourage Christians by showcasing stories from the best of Christian media that demonstrate what God is doing in the world today. **Columns, Departments:** Quick Takes, Story Behind the Song; length and payment varies. **Queries:** Not necessary. **E-Queries:** Yes. **Unsolicited mss:** Accepts. **Response:** 6-8 weeks. **SASE Required:** Yes. **Freelance Content:** 60%. **Rights:** 1st NA and electronic.

TODAY'S CHRISTIAN WOMAN

See full listing in Women's Publications category.

TODAY'S PENTECOSTAL EVANGEL

1445 N Boonville Ave., Springfield, MO 65802. 417-862-2781. E-mail: pe@ag.org. Website: www.pe.ag.org. Weekly. $28.99/yr. Circ.: 260,000. Hal Donaldson, Editor. **Description:** For Assembly of God members and potential members. Provides biblical and practical articles to inspire believers. **Nonfiction:** Religious, personal experience, devotional; 800-1,000 words; $.08/word. **Tips:** No queries; send complete manuscript only. **Queries:** Does Not Accept. **E-Queries:** No. **Unsolicited mss:** Accepts. **Response:** Queries 2 weeks, submissions 6 weeks. **SASE Required:** Yes. **Freelance Content:** 5%. **Rights:** 1st and electronic. **Payment:** On acceptance.

TRICYCLE: THE BUDDHIST REVIEW

92 Vandam St., New York, NY 10013. 212-645-1143. E-mail: editorial@tricycle.com. Website: www.tricycle.com. Quarterly. **Description:** Non-profit. Explores the nature of Buddhism in America. Looks at changes when exposed to American traditions, expressions in literature and the arts, and how it can illuminate possibilities facing people today. **Nonfiction:** All submissions must relate to Buddhism. Prefers shorter pieces (3,000 words or less). **Tips:** Prefers to review query before reading manuscript. Send query letter outlining idea, bio information (stating familiarity with subject matter), clips or writing samples, and SASE. **Queries:** Preferred. **E-Queries:** Yes. **Unsolicited mss:** Accepts.

TURNING WHEEL

P.O. Box 3470, Berkeley, CA 94703. 510-655-6169, ext. 303. E-mail: turningwheel@bpf.org. Website: www.bpf.org/bpf. Quarterly. $20/$45. Circ.: 8,000. Susan Moon, Editor. **Description:** Journal of socially engaged Buddhism. Covers issues of social justice and environment from a Buddhist perspective. **Nonfiction:** On social-justice work from a Buddhist perspective. Themes for each issue (e.g., reconciliation, death penalty; medical ethics); 1,800-3,500 words. **Poetry:** Poems related to issue's theme. **Columns, Departments:** Reviews of books and films on social/spiritual issues; 450-850 words. **Tips:** "Submit compelling personal experience, with analytical commentary. Avoid academic prose and new-age mushiness." Also offers $500 Young Writers' Award for one essay in each issue on the theme of that issue. E-mail for guidelines. **Queries:** Preferred. **E-Queries:** Yes. **Unsolicited mss:** Accepts. **Response:** 1-2 months. **SASE Required:** Yes. **Freelance Content:** 40%. **Rights:** One-time. **Payment:** In copies.

U.S. CATHOLIC

Claretian Publications, 205 W Monroe St., Chicago, IL 60606. 312-236-7782. E-mail: editors@uscatholic.org. Website: www.uscatholic.org. Monthly. $22/yr. Circ.: 40,000. Rev. John Molyneux, C.M.F., Editor. **Description:** Celebrates vibrancy and diversity of contemporary Catholicism. Promotes a positive vision of the Catholic faith today. Combines tradition with sense of humor and firm beliefs. **Fiction:** With strong characters that cause readers to stop and consider their relationships with others, the world, and/or God. Overtly religious themes not required; 2,000-4,000 words; $500. **Poetry:** All forms and themes; no light verse; submit 3-5 original poems; up to 50 lines; $75/poem. **Tips:** "We combine tradition with sense of humor and a firm belief that the Catholic faith, well lived, responds to our deepest longings and aspirations." **Queries:** Not necessary. **E-Queries:** Yes. **Unsolicited mss:** Accepts. **Response:** 8-10 weeks. **SASE Required:** Yes. **Freelance Content:** 10%. **Rights:** FNAR. **Payment:** On acceptance.

THE UNITED CHURCH OBSERVER

478 Huron St., Toronto, Ontario M5R 2R3 Canada. 416-960-8500. Website: www.ucobserver.org. 11x/yr. **Description:** On religious trends, human problems, and social issues. Feature articles run 1,000-1,500 words. **Tips:** No poetry. **Queries:** Preferred. **Payment:** On publication.

UNITED SYNAGOGUE REVIEW

155 Fifth Ave., New York, NY 10010. 212-533-7800. E-mail: info@uscj.org. Website: www.uscj.org. 2x/yr. Circ.: 250,000. Ms. Lois Goldrich, Editor. **Description:** Publication of the Conservative Movement, with features related to synagogues, Jewish law, and that organization. **Nonfiction:** Stories about congregational programs or developments in Conservative Judaism; 1,500 words. **Art:** Photographic prints; $200 (cover photo). **Tips:** No payment, but wide exposure to 1 million readers. "Writing should be crisp but not edgy or overly familiar. Our mission is to educate Conservative Jews as to development in their movement. We need a willingness to write stories as directed." **Queries:** Not necessary. **E-Queries:** Yes. **Unsolicited mss:** Accepts. **Response:** Queries immediate, submissions 1-3 months. **Freelance Content:** 25%.

THE WAR CRY

The Salvation Army, P.O. Box 269, Alexandria, VA 22313. 703-684-5500. Website: www.salvationarmyusa.org. Biweekly. $26.50/yr. Circ.: 400,000. Lt. Col. Marlene Chase, Editor-in-Chief. **Description:** Evangelist periodical used to spread the Word of God. Articles must relate to modern life, and offer inspiration, information, or evangelization; essays with insightful perspective on living the Christian life; 800-1,500 words; $.10-$.20/word. **Queries:** Not necessary. **Response:** 4-5 weeks. **SASE Required:** Yes. **Freelance Content:** 10%. **Payment:** On acceptance.

WITH

See full listing in Teens category.

WOMAN'S TOUCH

See full listing in Women's Publications category.

YOUNG SALVATIONIST

See full listing in Teens category.

YOUR CHURCH MAGAZINE

Christianity Today International, 465 Gundersen Dr., Carol Stream, IL 60188.

630-260-6200. E-mail: yceditor@yourchurch.net. Website: www.yourchurch.net. Bimonthly. Circ.: 150,000. Michael J. Schreiter, Managing Editor. **Description:** Trade publication to help church leaders with the business side of ministry. Articles on music and audio, lighting/video, management/administration, church furnishings/buildings/transportation, and finance/law. **Tips:** "Almost all our articles are assigned. Send writing samples and manuscript suggestions via e-mail. Many articles involve interviewing businesspeople, so interview skills are a plus." Sample copy free. **Queries:** Preferred. **Unsolicited mss:** Accepts. **Response:** Queries 1-2 months. **Freelance Content:** 10%. **Rights:** FNAR. **Payment:** On acceptance.

YOUTH AND CHRISTIAN EDUCATION LEADERSHIP
See full listing in Education category.

SCIENCE

21ST CENTURY: SCIENCE AND TECHNOLOGY
P.O. Box 16285, Washington, DC 20041. 703-777-7473. E-mail: tcs@mediasoft.net. Website: www.21stcenturysciencetech.com. Quarterly. $3.50/$25. Circ.: 25,000. Laurence Hecht, Editor-in-Chief. **Description:** Dedicated to the promotion of unending scientific progress, all directed to serve the proper common aims of mankind. **Tips:** "We challenge the assumptions of modern scientific dogma, including quantum mechanics, relativity theory, biological reductionism, and the formalization and separation of mathematics from physics. We demand a science based on constructible (intelligible) representation of concepts, but shun the simple empiricist or sense-certainty methods associated with the Newton-Galileo paradigm." **Queries:** Required. **E-Queries:** Yes. **Unsolicited mss:** Does not accept. **SASE Required:** Yes. **Rights:** One-time. **Payment:** On publication. **Contact:** Marjorie Mazel Hecht, Managing Editor.

AD ASTRA
National Space Society, 600 Pennsylvania Ave. SE, Suite 201, Washington, DC 20003. 202-543-1900. Website: www.nss.org. Quarterly. $38/yr. Circ.: 25,000. Frank Sietzen, Jr., Editor-in-Chief. **Description:** Lively, semi-technical features, on all aspects of international space exploration. Not interested in material on astronomy. Articles run 1,500-3,000 words; $350-$450. **Queries:** Preferred. **E-Queries:** Yes. **Freelance Content:** 80%. **Payment:** On publication.

AIR & SPACE SMITHSONIAN
Smithsonian Institution, P.O. Box 37012, MRC 951, Washington, DC 20013-7012. 202-275-1230. E-mail: editors@airspacemag.com. Website: www.airspacemag.com. Bimonthly. $3.99. Circ.: 225,000. George C. Larson, Editor. **Description:** Original articles on aerospace topics for a lay audience. **Nonfiction:** Feature stories with original reporting, research, and quotes. General-interest articles on aerospace experience, past, present, and future; 2,000-5,000 words; $2,000-$3,500. **Columns,**

Departments: Book reviews, soft news pieces, first-person recollections, and essays; 500-1,500 words; $350-$1,500. **Tips:** "Avoid sentimentalities (the majesty of flight, etc.). Don't rehash—original research only. Send 1-2 page proposal detailing sources and interview list with published clips." **Queries:** Required. **E-Queries:** Yes. **Unsolicited mss:** Accepts. **Response:** 4-8 weeks. **SASE Required:** Yes. **Freelance Content:** 90%. **Rights:** FNASR. **Payment:** On acceptance.

AMERICAN ARCHAEOLOGY

5301 Central Ave. NE #902, Albuquerque, NM 87108-1517. 505-266-9668. E-mail: tacmag@nm.net. Website: www.americanarchaeology.org. Quarterly. $3.95/issue. Circ.: 32,000. Michael Bawaya, Editor. **Description:** On all aspects of archaeology in North America. Nonfiction pieces on excavations and technological advances; 1,500-3,000 words; $600-$1,500. **Art:** Slides or digital photos. Pays $200-$900. **Tips:** "Read an issue of the magazine. Though we're a popular magazine, we have to be sophisticated about archaeology. No personal essays about visits to archaeological sites." **Queries:** Required. **E-Queries:** Yes. **Unsolicited mss:** Does not accept. **Response:** 3 weeks. **SASE Required:** Yes. **Freelance Content:** 60%. **Rights:** FNAR. **Payment:** On acceptance.

AMERICAN HERITAGE OF INVENTION & TECHNOLOGY

See full listing in History category.

ANNALS OF IMPROBABLE RESEARCH

See full listing in Humor category.

ARCHAEOLOGY

Archaeological Institute of America, 3636 33rd St., Long Island City, NY 11106. 718-472-3050. E-mail: editorial@archaeology.org. Website: www.archaeology.org. Bimonthly. $4.95/$20. Circ.: 225,000. Peter A. Young, Editor-in-Chief. **Description:** News magazine about archaeology worldwide. Written for lay people by professionals or writers with a solid knowledge of this field. **Nonfiction:** Profiles, excavation reports, discoveries, photo essays; 500-2,500 words; $500-$1,500. **Columns, Departments:** Multimedia, museum news, book reviews; 500 words; $250-$500. **Queries:** Required. **E-Queries:** Yes. **Unsolicited mss:** Accepts. **Response:** 1 month. **SASE Required:** Yes. **Freelance Content:** 70%. **Payment:** On acceptance.

ASTRONOMY

Kalmbach Publishing Co., 21027 Crossroads Circle, Waukesha, WI 53187. 262-796-8776. E-mail: editor@astronomy.com. Website: www.astronomy.com. Monthly. $5.50/$39.95. Circ.: 150,000. David J. Eicher, Editor. **Description:** Astronomical science and hobby activities, covering our solar system, Milky Way galaxy, black holes, deep-space observing, personality profiles, astronomical travel, etc. **Nonfiction:** Science stories on astronomy, astrophysics, space programs, recent discoveries. Hobby stories on equipment and celestial events; short news items. Features run

2,000-3,000 words; $200-$1,000. **Art:** Photos of astronomical phenomena and other affiliated subjects relating to stories; digital, slides, prints; $25/use. **Queries:** Preferred. **E-Queries:** Yes. **Unsolicited mss:** Accepts. **Rights:** 1st serial, all. **Payment:** On acceptance.

ENVIRONMENT
See full listing in Environment & Conservation category.

NATURAL HISTORY MAGAZINE
Natural History, Inc., Central Park W at 79th St., New York, NY 10024. 212-769-5500. E-mail: nhmag@amnh.org. Website: www.amnh.org/naturalhistory/. Monthly. $30/yr. Circ.: 225,000. Peter Brown, Editor-in-Chief. **Description:** Informative articles (written mostly by scientists) on biological sciences, cultural and physical anthropology, archaeology, earth sciences, astronomy, vertebrates and invertebrates. Pieces run 800-2,500 words; $500-$2,500. **Art:** $350 (full page), $500 (Natural Moment section photo). **Tips:** "Read our magazine first, and research recent articles before sending your query." **Queries:** Preferred. **E-Queries:** No. **Unsolicited mss:** Accepts. **Response:** 4-6 months. **Freelance Content:** 30%. **Rights:** FNAR. **Payment:** On publication.

ODYSSEY
See full listing in Teens category.

POPULAR SCIENCE
Time4 Media, 2 Park Ave., New York, NY 10016-5604. 212-779-5000. E-mail: features@popsci.com. Website: www.popsci.com. Monthly. $13.94/yr. Circ.: 1,485,900. Scott Mowbray, Editor-in-Chief. **Description:** On developments in science and technology. Short illustrated articles on new inventions and products; photo-essays, book excerpt; with photos and/or illustrations; pay varies. **Payment:** On acceptance.

QUEST
P.O. Box 5752, Bethesda, MD 20824-5752. 703-524-2766. E-mail: quest@spacebusiness.com; sjohnson@aero.und.edu. Website: www.spacebusiness.com/quest. $30/yr. Circ.: 1,100. Stephen Johnson, Editor. **Description:** "The History of Spaceflight Quarterly." Strives to capture the stories behind the space industry's triumphs and failures, includes articles and interviews with key people in the field. **Nonfiction:** Features are typically long, peer-reviewed articles written at the level of professional space historians. Interviews from transcribed excerpts from oral interviews are also welcome. 5,000-10,000 words. **Columns, Departments:** Shorter pieces written by students and scholars. Also accepts short "encyclopedia style" reference pieces. Departments include: Human Flight & Robotic Exploration; Military; International; Technology; Business; and Museums & Archives. 750-3,000 words. **Tips:** No payment is offered for any material published. Prior to submitting, authors should e-mail the editor with their proposed story idea. **Queries:** Not necessary. **E-Queries:** Yes. **Unsolicited mss:** Accepts. **Freelance Content:** 100%.

SCIENCE & CHILDREN
See full listing in Education category.

SCIENCE WORLD
Scholastic, Inc., 557 Broadway, Fl. 3, New York, NY 10012-3919. 212-343-6100. E-mail: scienceworld@scholastic.com. Website: www.scholastic.com. Biweekly. $9.25/yr. Circ.: 404,600. Rebecca Bondor, Editor. **Description:** On life science, earth science, physical science, environmental science, or health science, for 7th-10th graders, ages 12-15; 200-750 words; $200-$650. **Tips:** Submit well-researched proposal, with anticipated sources, 2-3 clips of your work, and SASE. Writing should be lively, with an understanding of teens' perspectives and interests.

SCIENTIFIC AMERICAN
415 Madison Ave., New York, NY 10017. 212-754-0550. E-mail: editors@sciam.com. Website: www.sciam.com. Monthly. $34.97/yr. Circ.: 696,000. John Rennie, Editor-in-Chief. **Description:** Addresses all aspects of American scientific endeavor. **Queries:** Preferred.

SKY & TELESCOPE
Sky Publishing Corp., 49 Bay State Rd., Cambridge, MA 02138-1200. 617-864-7360. E-mail: editors@skyandtelescope.com. Website: www.skyandtelescope.com. Monthly. $42.95/yr. Circ.: 111,000. Bud Sadler, Managing Editor. **Description:** Publication for amateur and professional astronomers worldwide. Pays $.25/word. **Columns, Departments:** The Astronomy Scene, Amateur Telescope Making, Astrophotography, Observer's Log, Gallery. Also, 800-word opinion pieces, for Focal Point. **Tips:** When submitting, mention the availability of diagrams and other illustrations. **Queries:** Required. **Payment:** On publication.

TECHNOLOGY REVIEW
See full listing in Computers category.

TIMELINE
See full listing in History category.

UPDATE
2 East 63rd St., New York, NY 10021. 212-838-0230. E-mail: update@nyas.org. Website: www.nyas.org. Dan Van Atta, Editor. **Description:** Magazine for members of the New York Academy of Sciences. Covers all scientific disciplines. **Nonfiction:** Essays and features, 1,000-2,000 words. **Columns, Departments:** Book reviews. **Queries:** Preferred. **Payment:** Honorarium, on publication.

WEATHERWISE
Heldref Publications, 1319 18th St. NW, Washington, DC 20036. 202-296-6267. E-mail: ww@heldref.org. Website: www.weatherwise.org. 6x/yr. Circ.: 20,000. Lynn Elsey, Managing Editor. **Description:** Magazine covering a variety of issues on

weather. Explores current issues and topics in weather and climate, weather history, reviews new books, software, websites, and other media, and answers readers' questions. Articles run 800-2,000 words; pay negotiable. **Queries:** Required. **E-Queries:** Yes. **Unsolicited mss:** Accepts. **Response:** 2 months. **Freelance Content:** 50%. **Rights:** All.

YES MAG: CANADA'S SCIENCE MAGAZINE FOR KIDS
See full listing in Juvenile category.

SENIORS

50 PLUS LIFESTYLES
Oak Creek Publishing, P.O. Box 44327, Madison, WI 53744. 608-274-5200. Monthly. $10/yr. Circ.: 43,000. Anita J. Martin, Editor. **Description:** Newspaper for the active, 50-plus population who reside in and around Dane County, WI. **Tips:** Fax 1-page inquiries to 608-274-5492. Do not send materials through the mail or electronically. **E-Queries:** No.

AARP BULLETIN
AARP Publications, 601 E Street NW, Washington, DC 20049-0001. 202-434-3340. E-mail: bulletin@aarp.org. Website: www.aarp.org/bulletin. Monthly. $12.50/yr. Circ.: 21,068,000. Robert Wilson, Editor. **Description:** Publication of American Association of Retired Persons. **Queries:** Required. **Payment:** On acceptance.

AARP THE MAGAZINE
AARP Publications, 601 E Street NW, Washington, DC 20049-0001. 202-434-6880. Website: www.aarpmagazine.org. Bimonthly. $8/yr. Circ.: 17,183,768. Hugh Delehanty, Editor-in-Chief. **Description:** General-interest membership magazine for members of AARP.

FIFTY PLUS
Richmond Publishing, 1510 Willow Lawn Dr., Suite 203, Richmond, VA 23230-3429. 804-673-5203. E-mail: rpmag@aol.com. Website: www.fiftyplusrichmond.com. Monthly. $15/yr. Circ.: 30,000. George Cruger, Editor. **Description:** Reflects and enhances 50-plus lifestyles in Virginia region, with reader dialogue and input. **Queries:** Required. **E-Queries:** Yes. **Response:** 2-4 weeks. **SASE Required:** Yes. **Rights:** 1st (regional). **Payment:** On publication.

FOREVER YOUNG
467 Speers Rd., Oakville, Ontario L6K 3S4 Canada. 905-815-0017. Website: www.haltonsearch.com. Monthly. $20/yr. Circ.: 580,000. Don Wall, Editor. **Description:** Multi-province Canadian publication for senior citizens. **Queries:** Preferred.

GOOD TIMES
25 Sheppard Ave., Suite 100, Toronto, Ontario M2N 6S7 Canada. 416-733-7600.
E-mail: goodtimes.pub@mail.transcontinental.ca. 11x/yr. $21.95/yr. Judy Brandow,
Editor. **Description:** Canadian lifestyle magazine for retired individuals.
Nonfiction: Celebrity profiles, also practical articles on health, beauty, cuisine, hob-
bies, fashion, leisure activities, travel, taxes, legal rights, consumer protection. 1,300-
1,500 words; $.40/word. **Poetry:** Features some poetry; no payment. **Columns,**
Departments: Health, relationship, travel stories; 1,500-2,000 words; $.40/word.
Tips: Canadian content only. **Queries:** Required. **E-Queries:** No. **Freelance**
Content: 100%. **Rights:** 1st Canadian. **Payment:** On acceptance.

LIFE LINES
Lincoln Area Agency on Aging, 1001 O St., Suite 101, Lincoln, NE 68508-3610. 402-
441-7022. E-mail: lifelines@ci.lincoln.ne.us. Bimonthly. $10/yr. Circ.: 42,000. Dena
Rust Zimmer, Editor. **Description:** Magazine for seniors. Features short stories (to
450 words), poetry (to 40 lines), humor, and regular columns (Sports/Hobbies,
Remember When..., Travels With..., Perspectives on Aging). **Tips:** No payment.

MATURE LIFESTYLES
News Connection USA., Inc., 220 W Brandon Blvd., Suite 203, Brandon, FL 33511.
E-mail: srconnect@aol.com. Website: www.srconnect.com. Monthly. $8/yr. Circ.:
120,000. Kathy Beck, Publisher/Editor. **Description:** Articles, 500-700 words, for
seniors living in Florida. **Tips:** No fiction or poetry. Florida angle required. **Payment:**
On publication.

MATURE LIVING
Lifeway Christian Resources, One LifeWay Plaza, Nashville, TN 37234-0175.
615-251-2485. E-mail: matureliving@lifeway.com. Website: www.lifeway.com.
Monthly. $19.95/yr. Circ.: 325,000. David T. Seay, Editor-in-Chief. **Description:** A
leisure reading magazine focusing on the personal and spiritual needs of senior adults
to encourage growth, hope, and fulfillment in Christian living. **Queries:** Does not
accept. **Unsolicited mss:** Accepts.

MATURE YEARS
United Methodist Publishing House, 201 Eighth Ave. S, Nashville, TN 37203-3919.
615-749-6292. E-mail: matureyears@umpublishing.org. Quarterly. $18/yr. Circ.:
50,000. Mary Catherine Dean, Editor-in-Chief. **Description:** Seeks to help individuals in and near retirement years to understand the appropriate resources of the
Christian faith that can assist them with the specific problems and opportunities of
aging. **Fiction:** Stories with older adult characters in older adult situations; to 2,000
words. **Nonfiction:** Religious and inspirational articles; also, older adults in active
lifestyles; 2,000 words; $.05/word. **Fillers:** Bible puzzles. **Columns, Departments:**
Health/fitness, personal finance, travel, poetry, fiction. **Tips:** Welcomes new writers.
Queries: Preferred. **E-Queries:** Yes. **Unsolicited mss:** Accepts. **Response:** 4-8
weeks. **SASE Required:** Yes. **Rights:** FNAR. **Payment:** On acceptance.

MILESTONES

Philadelphia Corporation for Aging, 642 N Broad St., Philadelphia, PA 19103-3424. 215-765-9000. Website: www.pcaphl.org. Monthly. Circ.: 70,000. Don Harrison, Editor. **Description:** For seniors in the greater Philadelphia area.

MILITARY OFFICER

Military Officers Assn. of America, 201 N Washington St., Alexandria, VA 22314-2539. 703-838-8115. E-mail: editor@moaa.org. Website: www.moaa.org/magazine. Monthly. $24/yr. Circ.: 381,230. Warren S. Lacy, Editor. **Description:** For active duty, reserve/national guard, retired and soon-to-be-retired members of the army, marine corps, navy, air force, coast guard, public health service, or NOAA and their surviving spouses. **Nonfiction:** Current military/political affairs, recent history (especially Vietnam and Korea), retirement topics, and general interest. Original only, no reprints. 1,400-2,500 words; $1,000-$1,800. **Tips:** Active voice, non-technical, with direct quotes. Optimistic, upbeat themes. **Queries:** Required. **E-Queries:** Yes. **Unsolicited mss:** Do not accept. **Response:** 90 days. **Rights:** FNAR, electronic, reprint. **Payment:** On acceptance. **Contact:** Molly Wyman, Managing Editor.

NARFE

National Assn. of Retired Federal Employees, 606 N Washington St., Alexandria, VA 22314. 703-838-7760. Website: www.narfe.org. Monthly. Circ.: 372,000. Margaret M. Carter, Director of Communications/Editor. **Description:** Focuses on issues of interest to retired federal employees.

THE OLDER AMERICAN

Massachusetts Assn. of Older Americans, 108 Arlington St., Boston, MA 02116-5302. 617-426-0804. Quarterly. $50/yr. Circ.: 10,000. Frank Ollivierre, Editor. **Description:** Local, state, and national advocacy and current affairs magazine for older adults.

PITTSBURGH SENIOR NEWS

3345 Evergreen Rd., Pittsburgh, PA 15237-2650. 412-367-2522. Monthly. $15/yr. Circ.: 10,000. Jennifer Kissel, Editor. **Description:** Topics of interest to older adults in the Pittsburgh area.

PLUS MAGAZINE

793 Higuera St., Suite 10, San Luis Obispo, CA 93401. 805-544-8711. E-mail: slojournal@fix.net. Website: www.seniormagazine.com. Monthly. Circ.: 30,000. Steve Owens, Publisher/Editor. **Description:** Entertaining and informative articles for readers ages 50 and older. Book reviews, profiles, travel, business, sports, movies, television, health; 600-1,200 words. **Queries:** Preferred. **E-Queries:** No. **Unsolicited mss:** Accepts. **Response:** 1-2 weeks. **SASE Required:** Yes. **Freelance Content:** 60%. **Rights:** FNAR. **Payment:** On publication.

PRIME TIMES
Times-Beacon-Record Newspapers, P.O. Box 707, East Setauket, NY 11733-0769. 631-751-7744. Monthly. Circ.: 50,000. Lynn Allopenna, Editor. **Description:** For older adults on Long Island, NY.

REMEDY
See full listing in Health category.

SENIOR CONNECTION
News Connection USA, Inc., 220 W Brandon Blvd., Suite 203, Brandon, FL 33511-5100. 813-653-1988. E-mail: srconnect@aol.com. Website: www.srconnect.com. Monthly. $15/yr. Circ.: 120,000. Kathy Beck, Editor. **Description:** General-interest articles, for senior citizens in the west central and Tampa areas of Florida.

SENIOR CONNECTION
Churchhill Publications, P.O. Box 38, Dundee, IL 60118. 847-428-0205. E-mail: churchpb@flash.net. Website: www.seniorconnectionnewspaper.com. Monthly. $18.95/yr. Circ.: 190,000. Peter Rubino, Editor-in-Chief. **Description:** For Catholics, ages 50-plus, with connections to metro Chicago.

THE SENIOR TIMES
Protege, Inc., 435 King St., Littleton, MA 01460. 978-742-9171. E-mail: theseniortimes@aol.com. Monthly. $18/yr. Circ.: 25,000. Jane Jackson, Publisher/Editor. **Description:** For persons ages 50+ who lead active lifestyles. Articles on travel, entertainment, health, finance, senior advocacy issues, opinions, and local personalities. **Art:** Photos; 8x10 B&W; subjects from the greater Boston area (people, places, art); pay negotiable. **Queries:** Not necessary. **E-Queries:** Yes. **Unsolicited mss:** Does not accept. **SASE Required:** Yes. **Payment:** On publication.

SENIOR TIMES
Senior Publishing Co., P.O. Box 30965, Columbus, OH 43230-0965. 614-337-2055. E-mail: seniortimes@insight.rr.com. Monthly. $15.95/yr. Circ.: 60,000. Judith P. Franklin, Editor. **Description:** Ohio's newsmagazine for people over 55.

SENIOR TIMES
Journal News Publishing, P.O. Box 142020, Spokane, WA 99214-2020. 509-924-2440. E-mail: vnh@onemain.com. Monthly. $24/yr. Circ.: 60,000. Mike Huffman, Editor. **Description:** For senior citizens in Washington State.

WHERE TO RETIRE
Vacation Publications, Inc., 1502 Augusta Dr., Suite 415, Houston, TX 77057-2484. 713-974-6903. Website: www.wheretoretire.com. 5x/yr. $19.75/yr. Circ.: 200,000. R. Alan Fox, Publisher/Editor. **Description:** Publication for anyone seeking retirement locale advice.

SPORTS, RECREATION, OUTDOORS

ADVENTURE CYCLIST

Adventure Cycling Association, P.O. Box 8308, Missoula, MT 59807. 406-721-1776. E-mail: mdeme@adventurecycling.org. Website: www.adventurecycling.org. 9x/yr. $30/yr. Circ.: 41,000. Mike Deme, Editor. **Description:** Covers the bicycle adventure travel. Articles run 1,200-2,500 words; $450-$1,500. **Columns, Departments:** Waypoints, Geared Up, Riding Sweep, Cycle Sense, Cyclist's Kitchen, Mechanical Advantage. **Queries:** Not necessary. **E-Queries:** Yes. **Unsolicited mss:** Accepts. **Response:** No guarantee of response. **SASE Required:** Yes. **Freelance Content:** 50%. **Rights:** FNAR. **Payment:** On publication.

AMERICAN FIELD

See full listing in Animals & Pets category.

AMERICAN HANDGUNNER

Publisher's Development Corp., Inc., 12345 World Trade Dr., San Diego, CA 92128. 858-605-0244. E-mail: ed@americanhandgunner.com. Website: www.americanhandgunner.com. Bimonthly. $16.95/yr. Circ.: 171,000. Roy Huntington, Editor. **Description:** Semi-technical articles on shooting sports, custom handguns, gun repair and alteration, handgun matches and tournaments, for lay readers. **Queries:** Required. **Payment:** On publication.

AMERICAN HUNTER

National Rifle Assn. of America, 11250 Waples Mill Rd., Fairfax, VA 22030-9400. 703-267-1300. E-mail: publications@nrahq.org. Website: www.nra.org. Monthly. Circ.: 1,200,000. John Zent, Editor-in-Chief. **Description:** On all aspects of hunting. Includes techniques, equipment, top places to hunt, legislation and current issues, role of hunting in wildlife management. Pieces run 1,800-2,000 words; $800. **Tips:** "We judge submissions based on three criteria: story angle, quality of writing, and quality/quantity of photos." **Queries:** Preferred. **E-Queries:** Yes. **Unsolicited mss:** Accepts. **SASE Required:** Yes. **Freelance Content:** 50%. **Rights:** FNASR.

AMERICAN RIFLEMAN

National Rifle Assn. of America, 11250 Waples Mill Rd., Suite 4, Fairfax, VA 22030-7400. 703-267-1336. E-mail: publications@nrahq.org. Website: www.nra.org. Monthly. $35/yr. Circ.: 1,366,000. Mark Keefe, Executive Editor. **Description:** Articles on use and enjoyment of sporting firearms. **Payment:** On acceptance.

AMERICAN SNOWMOBILER

Kalmbach Publishing Co., 21027 Crossroads Circle, Waukesha, WI 53187. 262-796-8776. Website: www.kalmbach.com. Bimonthly. Circ.: 68,000. Mark Savage, Editor. **Description:** For snowmobile enthusiasts. Covers technical/mechanical information, snowmobile comparisons, how-to information, people involved in sport, travel destinations, etc.

AQUA-FIELD

P.O. Box 575, Navesink, NJ 07752. 17x/yr. Steve Ferber, President. **Description:** Recreation/outdoors publication with how-to features on hunting, fishing, fly-fishing, and outdoor adventure. Interested in new approaches to activities or improvements on tried-and-true methods. Articles run 1,500-3,000 words. **Art:** Color slides or B&W prints. **Queries:** Preferred.

BACKPACKER

Rodale Press, Inc., 33 E Minor St., Emmaus, PA 18098. 610-967-8296. E-mail: editor@backpacker.com. Website: www.backpacker.com. 9x/yr. $19.97/yr. Circ.: 306,500. Jonathan Dorn, Executive Editor. **Description:** On self-propelled backcountry travel (backpacking, kayaking/canoeing, mountaineering; technique, Nordic skiing, health, natural science). Articles run 250-3,000 words; pay varies.

BACKWOODSMAN

P.O. Box 627, Westcliffe, CO 81252. 719-783-9028. E-mail: bwmmag@ris.net. Website: www.backwoodsmanmag@.com. Bimonthly. $4/issue. Circ.: 50,000. Charlie Richie, Editor. **Description:** Historical and how-to articles for the 20th-century frontiersman: muzzleloaders, 19th-century woods lore, early cartridge guns, primitive survival, craft items, American history, gardening, leather crafting, homesteading, log cabin construction, mountain men, Indians, building primitive weapons. Pays in copies and with advertising. **Queries:** Preferred. **E-Queries:** Yes. **Unsolicited mss:** Accepts. **Response:** 7 days. **SASE Required:** Yes. **Freelance Content:** 50%.

BALLOON LIFE

2336 47th Ave. SW, Seattle, WA 98116-2331. 206-935-3649. E-mail: tom@balloon-life.com. Website: www.balloonlife.com. Monthly. $30/yr. Circ.: 3,500. Tom Hamilton, Editor-in-Chief. **Description:** Magazine for those involved in the sport of hot air ballooning. Balloon events/rallies; safety seminars; balloon clubs/organizations; and general-interest stories with interviews or biographies of people who have made a contribution to the sport. Most pieces run 1,000-1,500 words, although shorter articles in the 300 to 500 word range are also considered. Pays $20-$50. **Queries:** Preferred. **E-Queries:** Yes. **Unsolicited mss:** Accepts. **Response:** 2 weeks. **SASE Required:** Yes. **Freelance Content:** 80%. **Rights:** One-time, non-exclusive.

BASSIN'

NatCom, Inc., 15115 S 76th E Ave., Bixby, OK 74008-4114. 918-366-6191. Website: www.ebassin.com. 7x/yr. $15.95/yr. Circ.: 165,000. Jason Sowards, Editor. **Description:** How and where to bass fish, for the amateur fisherman. **Queries:** Preferred. **Payment:** On acceptance.

BAY & DELTA YACHTSMAN

Recreation Publications, Inc., 4090 S McCarran Blvd., Suite E, Reno, NV 89502-7529. 775-353-5100. Website: www.yachtsforsale.com. Monthly. $17.60/yr. Circ.: 30,000. Don Abbott, Publisher/Editor. **Description:** Cruising stories and features, how-to pieces, boat maintenance, with northern California focus. **Queries:** Preferred. **E-Queries:** Yes. **Unsolicited mss:** Accepts. **SASE Required:** Yes.

BICYCLING

Rodale Press, Inc., 135 N Sixth St., Emmaus, PA 18098-0001. 610-967-5171. E-mail: bicycling@rodale.com. Website: www.bicycling.com. Monthly. $19.97/yr. Circ.: 286,800. Steve Madden, Editor. **Description:** For cyclists, on recreational riding, fitness training, nutrition, bike maintenance, equipment and racing. Covers all aspects of sport (road, mountain biking, leisure, etc.). Articles run 500-2,500 words; $50-$2,000. **Tips:** "We prefer queries instead of manuscripts. We're currently looking for interesting cycling personalities and adventure stories." **Queries:** Preferred. **Payment:** On acceptance. **Contact:** Doug Donaldson, Associate Editor.

BIRD WATCHER'S DIGEST

See full listing in Environment & Conservation category.

BIRDER'S WORLD

See full listing in Environment & Conservation category.

BLACK BELT

AIM Publishing, 24900 Anza Dr., Unit E, Valencia, CA 91355. 661-257-4066. E-mail: byoung@sabot.net. Website: www.blackbeltmag.com. Monthly. $32/yr. Circ.: 85,000. Robert Young, Executive Editor. **Description:** Articles related to self-defense (how-tos on fitness and technique; historical, travel, philosophy). Pays $100-$300.

THE BOUNDARY WATERS JOURNAL

9396 Rocky Ledge Rd., Ely, MN 55731. 218-365-6184. E-mail: bwjournal@boundarywatersjournal.com. Website: www.boundarywatersjournal.com. Quarterly. $21/yr. Circ.: 32,000. Stuart Osthoff, Publisher. **Description:** In-depth outdoor guide covering Boundary Waters Canoe Area Wilderness, Quetico Provincial Park, and surrounding Superior National Forest. Topics include camping, fishing, hiking, wildlife, ecology, area history, regional personalities; 1-5 pages; $100-$400. **Tips:** Often needs winter stories. **Queries:** Not necessary. **E-Queries:** Yes. **Unsolicited mss:** Accepts. **Response:** Queries 1-2 weeks, submissions 1-3 months. **SASE Required:** Yes. **Freelance Content:** 50%. **Rights:** FNAR. **Payment:** On publication. **Contact:** Laurie Antonson, Editor.

BOW & ARROW HUNTING

Y-Visionary Publishing, LP, 265 S Anita Dr., Suite 120, Orange, CA 92868. 714-939-9991. E-mail: editorial@bowandarrowhunting.com. Website: www.bowandarrowhunting.com. 9x/yr. $20/yr. Circ.: 90,673. Joe Bell, Editor. **Description:** On bowhunting (profiles and technical pieces), primarily on deer hunting. **Nonfiction:** Articles 1,200-2,500 words, with color slides, B&W, or color photos; pays $250-$500. **Payment:** On publication.

BOWHUNTER

PRIMEDIA Consumer Magazines & Media, 6405 Flank Dr., Harrisburg, PA 17112. 717-657-9555. E-mail: bowhunter_magazine@primediamags.com. Website: www.bowhunter.com. 9x/yr. $3.99/$23.94. Circ.: 160,800. Dwight Schuh, Editor. **Description:** Information for bowhunters, on all aspects of the sport, to entertain and inform readers, making them better bowhunters. **Nonfiction:** General interest, how-to, interview/profile, opinion, personal experience, photo features; 250-2,000 words; $100-$400. **Art:** 35mm slides, 5x7 or 8x10 prints; $75-$250. **Tips:** "Anticipate all questions, then answer them in article or sidebar. Writers must know bowhunting." **Queries:** Preferred. **E-Queries:** Yes. **Unsolicited mss:** Accepts. **Response:** 4-5 weeks. **SASE Required:** Yes. **Freelance Content:** 100%. **Rights:** FNASR, one-time. **Payment:** On acceptance. **Contact:** Jeff S. Waring, Publisher.

BOWHUNTING WORLD

Ehlert Publishing Group, 6420 Sycamore Lane N, Suite 100, Maple Grove, MN 55369-6014. 612-476-2200. Website: www.bowhuntingworld.com. Bimonthly. $20/yr. Circ.: 94,500. Mike Strandlund, Editor. **Description:** How-to articles on bowhunting techniques, feature articles on hunting and the mechanics of archery gear (traditional to high-tech); 1,800-3,000 words. **Tips:** Outline no more than 6 article ideas/query. **Queries:** Preferred. **E-Queries:** Yes. **Unsolicited mss:** Accepts. **Response:** 3-6 weeks. **SASE Required:** Yes. **Freelance Content:** 50%. **Rights:** FNAR. **Payment:** On acceptance.

BOWLERS JOURNAL INTERNATIONAL

122 S Michigan Ave., Suite 1506, Chicago, IL 60603-6194. 312-341-1110. E-mail: email@bowlersjournal.com. Website: www.bowlersjournal.com. Monthly. $24/yr. Circ.: 22,300. Jim Dressel, Editor. **Description:** Covers the bowling industry with features on trends, new products, and management. Articles run 1,200-2,200 words; $75-$250. **Queries:** Required. **E-Queries:** Yes. **Unsolicited mss:** Does not accept. **Payment:** On acceptance.

BOYS' LIFE

See full listing in Juvenile category.

BUCKMASTERS WHITETAIL MAGAZINE

Buckmasters, Ltd., P.O. Box 244022, Montgomery, AL 36124-4022. 334-215-3337. E-mail: dthornberry@buckmasters.com. Website: www.buckmasters.com. 6x/yr. $26/yr. Circ.: 380,000. Darren Thornberry, Managing Editor. **Description:** For serious sportsmen. Hunting how-tos, new biological information about whitetail deer, entertaining stories, "Big Buck Adventures" (details and adventures of the hunt). Articles to 2,000 words; $250-$400. Photos helpful. **Queries:** Required.

CANOE & KAYAK MAGAZINE

PRIMEDIA Enthusiast Group, P.O. Box 3146, Kirkland, WA 98083-3146. 425-827-6363. E-mail: mike@canoekayak.com. Website: www.canoekayak.com. Bimonthly.

$17.95/yr. Circ.: 67,300. Ross Prather, Editor-in-Chief. **Description:** Articles and features on canoeing and kayaking adventures, destinations, boat and equipment reviews, techniques and how-tos, short essays, camping, environment, safety, humor, health, and history. **Nonfiction:** Features (1,500-2,000 words); department pieces (500-1,200 words); $.15/word. **Queries:** Preferred. **Payment:** On publication.

CASCADES EAST

Sun Publishing, 716 NE 4th St., PO Box 5784, Bend, OR 97708-5784. 541-382-0127. E-mail: sunpub@sun-pub.com. Website: www.sun-pub.com. Quarterly. $16/yr. Circ.: 10,000. Geoff Hill, Publisher/Editor. **Description:** Outdoor activities (fishing, hunting, golfing, backpacking, rafting, skiing, snowmobiling, etc.), history, special events, and scenic tours in central Oregon Cascades. **Nonfiction:** 1,000-2,000 words; $.05-$.15/word. **Fillers:** Travel, history, and recreation in central Oregon; $.05-.$15/word. **Queries:** Preferred. **Payment:** On publication.

CHESAPEAKE BAY MAGAZINE

1819 Bay Ridge Ave., Annapolis, MD 21403. 410-263-2662. E-mail: editor@cbmmag.net. Website: www.cbmmag.net. Monthly. $4.99/issue. Circ.: 46,000. T.F. Sayles, Editor. **Description:** For recreational boaters on the Chesapeake Bay. Boating, fishing, destinations, people, history, and traditions of the Chesapeake Bay; to 3,000 words; $75-$800. **Tips:** "Writers need to be familiar with the Chesapeake Bay region and boating. Our readers are well-educated and well-traveled." **Queries:** Preferred. **E-Queries:** Yes. **Unsolicited mss:** Accepts. **Response:** 1-4 weeks. **SASE Required:** Yes. **Freelance Content:** 30%. **Rights:** FNASR. **Payment:** On acceptance. **Contact:** Jane Meneely, Managing Editor.

CROSS COUNTRY SKIER

Cross Country Skier, LLC, P.O. Box 550, Cable, WI 54821-0550. 715-798-5500. E-mail: lou@crosscountryskier.com. Website: www.crosscountryskier.com. Quarterly. $12.97/yr. Circ.: 30,000. Lou Dzierzak, Executive Editor. **Description:** Articles on all aspects of cross-country skiing; to 2,000 words; $200-$400. **Columns, Departments:** Pieces on ski lifestyle, techniques, health/fitness, etc. 1,000-1,500 words; $100-$250. **Tips:** Published November-February. **Queries:** Preferred. **Payment:** On publication.

DAKOTA OUTDOORS

Hipple Publishing Co., P.O. Box 669, 333 W Dakota Ave., Pierre, SD 57501. 605-224-7301. Monthly. $2.25/$10. Circ.: 8,000. Kevin Hipple, Editor. **Description:** Articles on hunting and fishing for outdoorsmen in the Dakotas. Fiction and nonfiction pieces run 1,000-1,500 words; pays $5-$50. **Queries:** Not necessary. **E-Queries:** No. **Unsolicited mss:** Accepts. **Response:** 2 weeks. **SASE Required:** Yes. **Freelance Content:** 75%. **Rights:** One-time. **Payment:** On publication.

DIVER MAGAZINE

Seagraphics Publications Ltd., P.O. Box 1312, Delta, British Columbia V4M 3Y8 Canada. 604-948-9937. E-mail: divermag@axion.net. Website: www.divermag.com. 9x/yr. $18/yr. Circ.: 7,000. **Description:** Illustrated articles on Canadian and North American dive destinations, interviews, personal experiences, ocean science and technology, etc; 500-1,000 words; $2.50/column inch. **Tips:** Does not offer payment for travel articles. **Queries:** Not necessary. **E-Queries:** Yes. **Unsolicited mss:** Accepts. **SASE Required:** Yes. **Freelance Content:** 30%. **Rights:** FNAR. **Payment:** On publication. **Contact:** Peter Vassilopoulos, Editor.

ELYSIAN FIELDS QUARTERLY

Knothole Publishing, P.O. Box 14385, St. Paul, MN 55114-0385. 651-644-8558. E-mail: editor@efqreview.com. Website: www.efqreview.com. Quarterly. $22.50/yr. Circ.: 2,500. Tom Goldstein, Publisher/Editor. **Description:** "The Baseball Review." Literary review for baseball, with essays, poetry, commentary, drama, book reviews, and humor ("anything about baseball is fair game"). Pieces run 400-4,500 words. **Tips:** Must have a passion and appreciation for baseball, and be able to write well. "This is not a journal about hero-worship and nostalgia. Sentimental, ill-conceived, formulaic writing from would-be writers or those looking to publish a 'baseball' story get tossed quickly." **Queries:** Not necessary. **E-Queries:** Yes. **Unsolicited mss:** Accepts. **Response:** 6-9 months (fiction/poetry), 3-4 months (other). **SASE Required:** Yes. **Freelance Content:** 75%. **Rights:** One-time, anthology. **Payment:** In copies.

EXPLORE: CANADA'S OUTDOOR ADVENTURE MAGAZINE

54 Saint Patrick St., Toronto, Ontario M5T 1V1 Canada. 416-599-2000. E-mail: explore@explore-mag.com. Website: www.explore-mag.com. 6x/yr. Circ.: 30,700. James Little, Editor. **Description:** For Canada's active outdoor enthusiasts. Covers adventure travel, hiking, mountain biking, climbing, paddling, winter sports, and more. **Nonfiction:** Features (profiles, adventure stories, destinations). **Columns, Departments:** Explorata (people & outdoor events in the news); The Lowdown (outdoor gear); Techniques; Places to Go; Backcountry (humor). **Queries:** Required. **E-Queries:** Yes.

FIELD & STREAM

Time4 Media, 2 Park Ave., New York, NY 10016-5604. 212-779-5286. E-mail: fsmagazine@aol.com. Website: www.fieldandstream.com. Monthly. $11.97/yr. Circ.: 1,544,000. Sid Evans, Editor. **Description:** The nation's largest hunting and fishing magazine. Tactics/techniques, nostalgia, conservation essays, profiles, humor, cartoons. Also, some fiction with hunting/fishing slant. Length and pay varies. **Queries:** Preferred. **E-Queries:** Yes. **Unsolicited mss:** Accepts. **Response:** 2-4 weeks. **SASE Required:** Yes. **Freelance Content:** 85%. **Rights:** FNAR. **Payment:** On acceptance.

FISHING FACTS

111 Shore Dr., Burr Ridge, IL 60527. 630-887-7722. E-mail: info@midwestout-doors.com. Website: www.fishingfacts.com. Bimonthly. $23.95/yr. Gene Laulunen, Publisher/Editor. **Description:** For the angler who wants to improve skills and maximize success. In-depth articles on fish behavior, techniques for taking fish from all kinds of structure, the latest in fishing products and technology, and simple tips from experts; 750-1,500 words; $30. **Tips:** No elementary fishing techniques or everyday fishing stories. Submit quality, full-color prints with each article. **Queries:** Required. **E-Queries:** Yes. **Unsolicited mss:** Accepts. **Response:** 10 days. **SASE Required:** Yes. **Rights:** FNAR. **Payment:** On publication.

FLY ROD & REEL

Down East Enterprise, Inc., P.O. Box 370, Camden, ME 04843. 207-594-9544. E-mail: pguernsey@flyrodreel.com. Website: www.flyrodreel.com. 6x/yr. $16.67/yr. Circ.: 62,000. Paul Guernsey, Editor-in-Chief. **Description:** Articles and features on fly-fishing and the culture/history of areas being fished; occasional fiction. 2,000-2,500 words; pay varies. **Queries:** Preferred. **Payment:** On acceptance.

FOOTBALL DIGEST

Century Publishing Co., 990 Grove St., Evanston, IL 60201-6510. 847-491-6440. E-mail: cs@centurysports.net. Website: www.centurysports.net. Monthly. $29.95/yr. Circ.: 180,000. William Wagner, Editor-in-Chief. **Description:** For the hard-core football fan. Profiles of pro and college stars, nostalgia, and trends in the sport. **Queries:** Preferred. **Payment:** On publication.

FUR-FISH-GAME

2878 E Main St., Columbus, OH 43209. 614-231-9585. Monthly. $3.99/issue. Circ.: 107,000. Mitch Cox, Editor. **Description:** For serious outdoorsmen of all ages. Covers hunting, trapping, freshwater fishing, predator calling, camping, boating, woodcrafting, conservation, and related topics. **Nonfiction:** Seeking short how-to, humor, and human-interest articles; 2,000-3,000 words; $100-$250. **Art:** Varied photos (close-ups, overall scenes); color slides, B&W, color prints; $25. **Queries:** Required. **E-Queries:** Yes. **Unsolicited mss:** Accepts. **Freelance Content:** 75%. **Rights:** FNAR. **Payment:** On acceptance.

GAME AND FISH

P.O. Box 741, Marietta, GA 30061. 770-953-9222. Website: www.gameandfish.about.com. Monthly. Circ.: 575,000. Ken Dunwoody, Editorial Director. **Description:** Publishes 30 monthly outdoor magazines for 48 states. Articles, 1,500-2,500 words, on hunting and fishing (how-tos, where-tos, and adventure). Profiles of successful hunters and fishermen. No hiking, canoeing, camping, or backpacking pieces. Pays $125-$175 for state-specific articles, $200-$250 for multi-state articles. **Payment:** On acceptance.

GOLF DIGEST

20 Westport Rd., Wilton, CT 06897. 203-761-5100. E-mail: editor@golfdigest.com. Website: www.golfdigest.com. Monthly. $3.99. Circ.: 1,550,000. Jerry Tarde, Editor. **Description:** Covers golf instruction, equipment, and travel. **Tips:** Freelance content limited. **Queries:** Required.

GOLF FOR WOMEN

The Golf Digest Companies, 4 Times Square, Fl. 7, New York, NY 10036. 212-286-3906. E-mail: editors@golfforwomen.com. Website: www.golfforwomen.com. Bimonthly. $16.97/yr. Circ.: 403,500. Susan K. Reed, Editor-in-Chief. **Description:** Golf lifestyle magazine for avid women golfers. Includes travel, instruction, fashion, equipment, news. Query with clips.

GOLF MAGAZINE

Time4Media, 2 Park Ave., New York, NY 10016-5675. 212-779-5000. E-mail: golfletters@golfonline.com. Website: www.golfonline.com. Monthly. $19.94/yr. Circ.: 1,410,000. Kevin Cook, Editor. **Description:** Golf history, travel (places to play around the world), and profiles of professional tour players; short pieces to 500 words; $.75/word. **Queries:** Preferred. **Payment:** On acceptance.

GOLF TIPS

Werner Publishing Corp., 12121 Wilshire Blvd., Fl. 12, Los Angeles, CA 90025-1123. 310-820-1500. E-mail: editors@golftipsmag.com. Website: www.golftipsmag.com. 7x/yr. $17.94/yr. Circ.: 750,000. Dave DeNunzio, Editor. **Description:** Magazine for serious golfers. Includes short "shotmaking" instruction tips, unique golf instruction, golf products, interviews with pro players; 500-1,500 words; $200-$600. **Queries:** Preferred. **Payment:** On publication.

GOLF TODAY

204 Industrial Rd., San Carlos, CA 94070. 650-802-8165. E-mail: bob@golftodaymagazine.com. Website: www.golftodaymagazine.com. Monthly. $22/yr. Circ.: 151,000. Bob Koczor, Editor. **Description:** Golf magazine for players in CA, NV, AZ, and UT. Travel stories, golf tips, product reviews, and guest columns; $5-$15/page. **Tips:** Works with new writers. **Queries:** Not necessary. **E-Queries:** Yes. **Unsolicited mss:** Accepts. **Response:** 1 day. **Freelance Content:** 25%. **Rights:** FNAR. **Payment:** On acceptance.

GUN DIGEST

Krause Publications, Inc., 700 E State St., Iola, WI 54990. 888-457-2873. E-mail: ramagek@krause.com. Website: www.krause.com. Ken Ramage, Editor-in-Chief. **Description:** On guns and shooting, equipment, etc. Seeks well-researched articles, to 5,000 words; pays to $.10/word. **Queries:** Preferred. **E-Queries:** Yes. **Payment:** On acceptance.

GUN DOG
See full listing in Animals & Pets category.

GUNS & AMMO
PRIMEDIA Enthusiast Group, 6420 Wilshire Blvd., Fl. 14, Los Angeles, CA 90048-5502. 323-782-2000. E-mail: gunsandammo@primedia.com. Website: www.gunsandammomag.com. Monthly. $14.97/yr. Circ.: 607,900. Lee Hoots, Editor. **Description:** Technical and general articles on guns, ammunition, and target shooting. **Payment:** On acceptance.

HANG GLIDING & PARAGLIDING MAGAZINE
U.S. Hang Gliding Assn., P.O. Box 1537, Puyallup, WA 98371.
E-mail: editor@ushga.org. Website: www.ushga.org. Monthly. $35/yr. Circ.: 11,000. Dan A. Nelson, Editor. **Description:** Explores all areas of hang gliding, paragliding, and the free flight lifestyle. Articles run 2-3 pages; pays $50. **Queries:** Preferred. **Payment:** On publication.

HORSE & RIDER
PRIMEDIA Enthusiast Group, 4100 International Parkway, Carrollton, TX 75007. 972-309-5700. E-mail: horse&rider@primediamags.com. Website: www.equisearch.com. Monthly. $3.99/$19.95. Circ.: 165,000. Darrell Dodds, Editor/Associate Publisher. **Description:** Educates, informs and entertains competitive and recreational Western riders with training articles, practical stable management techniques, hands-on health care, safe trail riding practices, and coverage of major Western events. **Nonfiction:** Personality profiles, consumer buying advice, and how-tos (training, horse care/horsekeeping); 150-2,000 words; $150-$1,000. **Fillers:** Humorous experiences; 150-1,000 words; $150-$1,000. **Columns, Departments:** Real-life horse stories, trail-riding tips, training tips; 150-1,000 words; pay varies. **Art:** Send query before submitting. Include SASE and photo spec sheet outlining the details of your work. **Tips:** "Please be familiar with our subject matter and style before sending manuscript or query." **Queries:** Preferred. **E-Queries:** No. **Unsolicited mss:** Accepts. **Response:** 3 months. **SASE Required:** Yes. **Freelance Content:** 5%. **Rights:** FNAR. **Payment:** On acceptance.

HOT BOAT
LFP, Inc., 8484 Wilshire Blvd., Suite 900, Beverly Hills, CA 90211-3221. 323-651-5400. E-mail: hbmail@aol.com. Website: www.hotboat.net. Monthly. $23.95/yr. Circ.: 40,000. Chris Davidson, Editor-in-Chief. **Description:** On motorized water sport events and personalities: general-interest, how-to, and technical features. Family-oriented articles, 600-1,000 words; pays $85-$300. **Queries:** Preferred. **Payment:** On publication.

IN-FISHERMAN

PRIMEDIA Enthusiast Group, Two In-Fisherman Dr., Brainerd, MN 56425-8098. 218-829-1648. Website: www.in-fisherman.com. 8x/yr. $16/yr. Circ.: 300,000. Doug Stange, Editor-in-Chief. **Description:** How-to articles on all aspects of freshwater fishing. Also humorous or nostalgic pieces on fishing. Pieces run 1,500-4,500 words; $250-$1,000. **Payment:** On acceptance.

INSIDE TEXAS RUNNING

Runner Triathelete News, P.O. Box 19909, Houston, TX 77224. 281-759-0555. E-mail: rtnews@ix.netcom.com. Website: www.insidetexasrunning.com. 10x/yr. $12. Circ.: 8,000. Lance Phegley, Editor. **Description:** Tabloid newspaper for runners in Texas. **Nonfiction:** Travel pieces for runners attending out-of-town races, unusual runners (not just fast runners), race write-ups, etc.; 300-1,500 words; $300-$1,500. **Columns, Departments:** Short news items for Texas Roundup (2-5 paragraphs max.) **Art:** $10-$25. **Tips:** Avoid "How I ran the marathon" articles or subject matter on other sports. Use quotes. Welcomes new writers with appropriate expertise. **Queries:** Required. **E-Queries:** Yes. **Unsolicited mss:** Accepts. **Response:** 4 weeks. **SASE Required:** Yes. **Freelance Content:** 30%. **Rights:** One-time. **Payment:** On publication.

JOURNAL OF ASIAN MARTIAL ARTS

Via Media Publishing Co., 821 W 24th St., Erie, PA 16502-2523. 814-455-9517. E-mail: info@goviamedia.com. Website: www.goviamedia.com. Quarterly. Michael A. DeMarco, Editor. **Description:** On martial arts and Asian culture: interviews (with scholars, master practitioners, etc.) and scholarly articles based on primary research in key disciplines (cultural anthropology, comparative religion, etc.). **Nonfiction:** Articles, 2,000-10,000 words; pays $150-$500. **Columns, Departments:** Reviews, 1,000 words, of books and audiovisual material; pays in copies. **Response:** 2-8 weeks. **Freelance Content:** 90%. **Payment:** On publication.

JUNIOR BASEBALL

P.O. Box 9099, Canoga Park, CA 91309-0099. 818-710-1234. E-mail: dave@junior-baseball.com. Website: www.juniorbaseball.com. Bimonthly. $3.95/$17.70. Circ.: 50,000. Dave Destler, Editor. **Description:** "America's youth baseball magazine." Targets youth and high school baseball players, coaches, and parents. Articles run 500-2,500 words; pay varies. **Tips:** "Read a few issues to familiarize yourself with our topics, focus, and editorial environment. Writers must know baseball very well! No 'my kid is the next Barry Bonds' articles. No fiction, poems, or tributes." **Queries:** Preferred. **E-Queries:** Yes. **Unsolicited mss:** Accepts. **Response:** 2 weeks. **SASE Required:** Yes. **Freelance Content:** 50%. **Rights:** All. **Payment:** On publication.

KITPLANES MAGAZINE

See full listing in Hobbies, Crafts, Collecting category.

KUNG FU TAI CHI

TC Media, Inc., 40748 Encyclopedia Circle, Fremont, CA 94538. 510-656-5100. E-mail: editor@kungfumagazine.com. Website: www.kungfumagazine.com. Bimonthly. $3.99/$15. Circ.: 45,000. Gene Ching, Associate Publisher. **Description:** Devoted exclusively to Chinese martial arts. Articles run 1,500-2,500 words; $85-$125. **Tips:** "Our readership is very familiar with Chinese martial arts so it's important to consider preceding research. Avoid shameless self-promotion of individual masters and/or styles." **Queries:** Preferred. **E-Queries:** Yes. **Unsolicited mss:** Accepts. **Response:** 1-2 months. **SASE Required:** Yes. **Freelance Content:** 70%. **Rights:** FNAR and electronic. **Payment:** On publication.

LAKELAND BOATING

O'Meara/Brown Publications, Inc., 727 S Dearborn St., Suite 812, Chicago, IL 60605-3827. 312-276-0610. E-mail: lb@omeara-brown.com. Website: www.lakeland-boating.com. Monthly. $21.95/yr. Circ.: 38,200. Matthew Wright, Editor. **Description:** On boating in the Great Lakes and surrounding areas. **Tips:** "We're looking for freelance writers who are also skilled photographers." **Queries:** Required. **E-Queries:** Yes. **Unsolicited mss:** Accepts. **SASE Required:** Yes. **Rights:** FNASR and electronic. **Payment:** On publication.

MICHIGAN OUT-OF-DOORS

Michigan United Conservation Clubs, Inc., P.O. Box 30235, Lansing, MI 48909. 517-371-1041. E-mail: magazine@mucc.org. Website: www.mucc.org. Monthly. $3.50/$25. Circ.: 90,000. Dennis Knickerbocker, Editor. **Description:** On Michigan's natural environment and outdoor recreation, with emphasis on hunting, fishing, and nature study. **Nonfiction:** Informative, entertaining features for sportsmen/women, and all who enjoy the out-of-doors; how-to, investigative, personal adventure, nature lore; 1,000-1,500 words; $90-$200. **Fillers:** Cartoons and line drawings; $30. **Columns, Departments:** By assignment; 700-800 words; $75-$100. **Art:** B&W and color photos; $20-$175. **Queries:** Preferred. **E-Queries:** No. **Unsolicited mss:** Accepts. **Response:** 1-4 months. **SASE Required:** Yes. **Freelance Content:** 75%. **Payment:** On acceptance.

MIDWEST OUTDOORS

Midwest Outdoors, Ltd., 111 Shore Dr., Burr Ridge, IL 60527. 638-887-7722. E-mail: info@midwestoutdoors.com. Website: www.midwestoutdoors.com. Monthly. $2.99/$14.95. Circ.: 36,000. Gene Laululnen, Publisher/Editor. **Description:** Hunting, fishing, and outdoor recreation in the Midwest. Seeks where, when, why, how-to articles; approx. 1,500 words; $30. **Tips:** Avoid first-time experience stories. **E-Queries:** Yes. **Unsolicited mss:** Accepts. **Freelance Content:** 95%. **Rights:** One-time, electronic. **Payment:** On publication.

MOUNTAIN BIKE

Rodale Press, Inc., 135 N 6th St., Emmaus, PA 18049-2441. 610-967-5171. E-mail: mbcrank@mountainbike.com. Website: www.mountainbike.com. 11x/yr. $19.97/yr. Circ.: 150,300. Stephen Madden, Editor-in-Chief. **Description:** On mountain-bike touring; major off-road cycling events; political, sport, or land-access issues; riding techniques; fitness and training tips; 500-2,000 words; $100-$650. **Queries:** Preferred. **Payment:** On publication.

MUSHING

Stellar Communications, Inc., P.O. Box 149, Ester, AK 99725-0149. 907-479-0454. E-mail: editor@mushing.com. Website: www.mushing.com. Bimonthly. $24/yr. Circ.: 6,000. Todd Hoener, Editor-in-Chief. **Description:** Dog-driving how-tos, innovations, history, profiles, interviews, and features related to sled dogs. International audience. **Nonfiction:** 1,000-2,500 words. **Columns, Departments:** Competitive and recreational dog drivers; weight pullers, dog packers, and skijorers; 500-1,000 words. **Art:** 50-80% B&W; $20-$250. **Tips:** "Send your qualifications and clips of previous published work. Also include a short biography. We will work with new and unpublished authors." **Queries:** Preferred. **E-Queries:** Yes. **Unsolicited mss:** Accepts. **Rights:** FNAR. **Payment:** On publication. **Contact:** Deirdre Helfferich, Managing Editor.

MUZZLE BLASTS

National Muzzle Loading Rifle Association, P.O. Box 67, Friendship, IN 47021-0067. 812-667-5131. E-mail: mblastdop@seidata.com. Website: www.nmlra.org. Monthly. $40/yr (members). Circ.: 22,000. Eric A. Bye, Editor. **Description:** Articles on antique muzzleloading guns, gunmakers, events in America's past; how-tos on crafts related to muzzleloaders (gunbuilding, making powder horns, engraving, etc.), safe handling, loading, etc. 1,500-2,000 words; $150-$250. **Art:** Photos, illustrations; must reflect highest standard of safety. **Tips:** Must know muzzleloaders (preferably traditional) and safety. Generally, avoid modern topics. **Queries:** Preferred. **E-Queries:** Yes. **Unsolicited mss:** Accepts. **Response:** 2-6 weeks. **Freelance Content:** 70%. **Rights:** FNAR. **Payment:** On publication.

NEW HAMPSHIRE WILDLIFE

NH Wildlife Federation, 54 Portsmouth St., Concord, NH 03301-5486. 603-224-5953. E-mail: nhwf@aol.com. Website: www.nhwf.org. Bimonthly. $20/yr. Circ.: 7,000. Ken Kreis, Editor-in-Chief. **Description:** First-person experiences on hunting, fishing, trapping and other active outdoor pursuits in New Hampshire. Pieces run 400-1,500 words. No payment offered. **Queries:** Not necessary. **Unsolicited mss:** Accepts.

NORTHEAST OUTDOORS

Woodall Publishing Corp., 2575 Vista Del Mar, Ventura, CA 93001. 805-667-4100. E-mail: editor@woodallpub.com. Website: www.woodalls.com. Monthly. $20/yr. **Description:** On camping and recreational vehicle (RV) touring in northeast U.S.

Prefers how-to, where-to (camp cookery, recreational vehicle hints). Articles run 1,000-2,000 words, preferably with B&W photos; pay varies.

OFFSHORE

500 Victory Rd. Marina Bay, Quincy, MA 02171. 617-221-1400. E-mail: editors@offshoremag.net. Website: www.offshoremag.net. Monthly. $4.50/$19.95. Circ.: 34,000. Betsy Haggerty, Editor. **Description:** For Northeast powerboaters and sailboaters (East Coast from Maine to New Jersey). Topics include destinations (seaports in New England, New York, New Jersey), things to do, places to see, navigation guidelines, first-hand accounts of boating adventures/mishaps, fishing, etc; 1,500-3,000 words; $350-$1,000. **Queries:** Required. **E-Queries:** Yes. **Unsolicited mss:** Accepts. **Response:** 6 weeks. **SASE Required:** Yes. **Freelance Content:** 80%. **Rights:** FNAR. **Payment:** On acceptance.

OUTDOOR CANADA

Avid Media, Inc., 340 Ferrier St., Suite 210, Markham, Ontario L3R 2Z5 Canada. 905-475-8440. E-mail: editorial@outdoorcanada.ca. Website: www.outdoorcanada.ca. 8x/yr. $24/yr. Circ.: 80,800. Patrick Walsh, Editor-in-Chief. **Description:** Articles, 100-4,000 words, on fishing, hunting, and conservation. Payment depends on length and complexity of article; generally around $.50/word. **Tips:** "If you have a story, or story idea, please submit a query letter rather than a completed manuscript."

OUTDOOR WORLD

Krause Publications, Inc., 700 E State St., Iola, WI 54990. 715-445-2214. Website: www.outdoorworldmag.com. Monthly. $4.95/$19.95. Circ.: 200,000. Brian Lovett, Editor. **Description:** Covers the national gamut of hunting, fishing, and outdoor activities. Includes regular columns on bow hunting, big game, bird hunting, bass fishing, big-water angling, turkey hunting, and conservation issues. Stories and articles run 1,500 words. **Queries:** Preferred. **E-Queries:** Yes. **Unsolicited mss:** Accepts. **Response:** 3-4 months. **SASE Required:** Yes. **Freelance Content:** 90%. **Rights:** One-time.

OUTSIDE

Mariah Media, Inc., 400 Market St., Santa Fe, NM 87501-7300. 505-989-7100. E-mail: letters@outsidemag.com. Website: www.outsidemag.com. Monthly. $4.95/$18. Circ.: 650,000. Hal Epsen, Editor. **Description:** Magazine for people with active lifestyles. Covers outdoor sports, adventure travel, personal experience, the environment, outdoor equipment, etc.; 1,500-4,000 words. **Tips:** "Departments are best areas for new writers to break in." **Queries:** Preferred. **Unsolicited mss:** Do not accept. **Response:** 2 months. **SASE Required:** Yes. **Freelance Content:** 90%. **Rights:** FNASR.

PADDLER

Paddlesport Publishing, Inc., P.O. Box 775450, Steamboat Springs, CO 80477. 970-879-1450. Website: www.paddlermagazine.com. Bimonthly. $18/yr. Circ.: 67,800.

Eugene Buchanan, Editor. **Description:** On canoeing, kayaking, rafting, and sea kayaking. Pays $.15-$.25/word. **Tips:** "The best way to break in is to target a specific department such as Hotlines or Paddle People." **Queries:** Preferred. **Payment:** On publication. **Contact:** Frederick Reimers.

PEDAL MAGAZINE
703-317 Adelaide St. W, Toronto, Ontario M5V 1P9 Canada. 416-977-2100. E-mail: pedal@passport.ca. Website: www.pedalmag.com. 6x/yr. $19.95/yr. Circ.: 18,000. Benjamin Sadavoy, Editor. **Description:** Covers all aspects of cycling from mountain bike and road bike adventure touring to recreational cycling and destinations across Canada and abroad. Also features coverage of events, profiles of Canada's top cyclists, product reviews, complete bike tests, maintenance tips, and a calendar of Canadian events. **Tips:** "Our editor is extremely busy. Your chances are better if your query is attention-grabbing and to the point." **Queries:** Preferred. **E-Queries:** Yes. **Unsolicited mss:** Accepts. **Freelance Content:** 100%.

PENNSYLVANIA ANGLER & BOATER
Pennsylvania Fish and Boat Commission, P.O. Box 67000, Harrisburg, PA 17106-7000. 717-705-7835. E-mail: amichaels@state.pa.us. Website: www.fish.state.pa.us. Bimonthly. $9/yr. Circ.: 32,000. Art Michaels, Editor. **Description:** On freshwater fishing and boating in Pennsylvania. Articles, 500-3,000 words, with photos; pays $50-$300. **Queries:** Preferred. **SASE Required:** Yes. **Payment:** On acceptance.

PENNSYLVANIA GAME NEWS
Game Commission, 2001 Elmerton Ave., Harrisburg, PA 17110-9797. 717-787-3745. Monthly. $1.50/issue. Circ.: 120,000. Bob Mitchell, Editor. **Description:** Published by the state Game Commission, to promote wildlife programs, hunting and trapping in the state. **Nonfiction:** On hunting or wildlife,with Pennsylvania interest; 2,000 words; $.08/word. **Tips:** No controversial issues, or technical subjects by freelancers. Avoid "first deer" stories. **Queries:** Not necessary. **E-Queries:** No. **Unsolicited mss:** Accepts. **Response:** 4-6 weeks. **SASE Required:** Yes. **Freelance Content:** 40%. **Rights:** FNAR. **Payment:** On acceptance.

PETERSEN'S BOWHUNTING
PRIMEDIA Enthusiast Group, 6420 Wilshire Blvd., Los Angeles, CA 90048-5515. 323-782-2721. E-mail: bowhunting@primedia.com. Website: www.bowhunting-mag.com. 9x/yr. $3.99/11.97. Circ.: 192,000. Jay Michael Strangis, Editor. **Description:** How-to help for bowhunter enthusiasts. Also, interesting stories about bowhunting. Bowhunting adventure stories. How-to and technical (equipment, products) articles; 2,000 words; $150-$400. **Art:** Photos must accompany all manuscripts; B&W or color prints; $100-$600. **Queries:** Preferred. **E-Queries:** Yes. **Unsolicited mss:** Accepts. **Response:** Queries 3-4 days, submissions 6-7 days. **SASE Required:** Yes. **Freelance Content:** 40%. **Rights:** All, 1st (photos). **Payment:** On acceptance.

PGA MAGAZINE

Great Golf Resorts of the World, Inc., 122 Sycamore Dr., Jupiter, FL 33485-2860. 561-776-0069. Website: www.pga.com. Monthly. $29.95/yr. Circ.: 30,500. Matt Marsom, Editor. **Description:** On golf-related subjects. Articles run 1,500-2,500 words; $300-$500. **Queries:** Preferred. **Payment:** On acceptance.

POWER AND MOTORYACHT

PRIMEDIA Enthusiast Group, 260 Madison Ave., Fl. 8, New York, NY 10016. 917-256-2276. E-mail: diane_byrne@primediamags.com. Website: www.powerandmotoryacht.com. Monthly. Circ.: 157,000. Richard Thiel, Editor. **Description:** For affluent, experienced owners of powerboats, mostly 35 feet and larger. Reaches almost every U.S. owner of a large powerboat, with advice on how to choose, operate, and maintain their boats. Also provides information on where to cruise and how to get the most enjoyment of the lifestyle. **Nonfiction:** Clear, concise, authoritative articles. Include personal experience and information from marine industry experts where appropriate; 800-1,400 words; $500-$1,200. **Tips:** No stories on trailer boats or sailboats. If pitching a cruising story, high-quality, original slides or transparencies must be available as part of the package. Send all queries to Diane M. Byrne, Executive Editor. **Queries:** Required. **E-Queries:** Yes. **Unsolicited mss:** Do not accept. **Response:** Queries 1 month. **SASE Required:** Yes. **Freelance Content:** 20-25%. **Rights:** All. **Payment:** On acceptance. **Contact:** Diane Byrne, Executive Editor.

PRACTICAL HORSEMAN

PRIMEDIA Enthusiast Group, P.O. Box 589, Unionville, PA 19375. 610-380-8977. E-mail: prachorse@aol.com. Website: www.equisearch.com. Monthly. $33/yr. Circ.: 80,000. Mandy Lorraine, Editor. **Description:** How-to articles conveying leading experts' advice on English riding, training, and horse care. **Tips:** Send clips. **Queries:** Preferred. **Payment:** On acceptance.

REAL SPORTS

P.O. Box 8204, San Jose, CA 95155-8204. 408-924-7434. E-mail: freelance@real-sports.com. Website: www.real-sports.com. Quarterly. $9.95/$29.99. Circ.: 150,000. Amy Love, Publisher. **Description:** Authoritative coverage of women's sports. Girls' and women's sports, team sports, professional, collegiate and amateur. Uses action-oriented photographs to show drama of competition. Pieces run 500-2,000 words; $.50/word. **Tips:** Submit original, insightful, realistic portraits of women's sports. **Queries:** Required. **E-Queries:** Yes. **Unsolicited mss:** Do not accept. **Response:** 2 weeks. **SASE Required:** Yes. **Freelance Content:** 70%. **Rights:** FNAR. **Payment:** On publication.

REFEREE

P.O. Box 161, Franksville, WI 53126-0161. 262-632-8855. E-mail: jarehart@referee.com. Website: www.referee.com. Monthly. $5.95/$42.95. Circ.: 35,000. Bill Topp, Editor. **Description:** Magazine for officials at the youth, recreational, high school, collegiate, and professional levels in all sports. Article length varies, pays $.05-$.10/word. **Tips:** "Writers should have knowledge of officiating philosophies, rules, and mechanics. We features sport-specific columns for baseball, basketball, soccer, softball, football. Guidelines available on our website." **Queries:** Preferred. **E-Queries:** Yes. **Unsolicited mss:** Accepts. **Response:** Queries 1-2 weeks, submissions 3-6 weeks. **SASE Required:** No. **Freelance Content:** 30%. **Payment:** On acceptance. **Contact:** Jim Arehart, Associate Editor.

ROCK & ICE

Big Stone Publishing Ltd., 1101 Village Rd., Suite UL-4D, Carbondale, CO 81623. 970-704-1442. E-mail: editorial@rockandice.com. Website: www.rockandice.com. Bimonthly. $29.95/yr. Circ.: 32,000. Duane Raleigh, Publisher/Editor-in-Chief. **Description:** For technical rock and ice climbers (sport climbers, mountaineers, alpinists, and other adventurers). Articles run 500-4,000 words; pays $300/published page. **Queries:** Preferred.

ROCKY MOUNTAIN SPORTS MAGAZINE

2525 15th St., #1A, Denver, CO 80211. 303-477-9770. E-mail: info@rockymountainsports.com. Website: www.rockymountainsports.com. Monthly. Circ.: 90,000. Rebecca Heaton, Editor. **Description:** Sports and lifestyle magazine covering non-team sports and activities in the Rocky Mountain region. **Nonfiction:** Personal experiences, training articles, gear reviews. **Tips:** "Avoid sending completed manuscripts. Ideas need to be Colorado-focused." **Queries:** Preferred. **E-Queries:** Yes. **Unsolicited mss:** Does not accept. **Response:** 2 months. **SASE Required:** Yes. **Freelance Content:** 80%. **Rights:** FNAR. **Payment:** On publication.

RODALE'S SCUBA DIVING

Rodale, Inc., 6600 Abercorn St., Suite 208, Savannah, GA 31405-5834. 912-351-6234. E-mail: edit@scubadiving.com. Website: www.scubadiving.com. Monthly. $21.98/yr. Circ.: 146,826. Buck Butler, Editor. **Description:** For scuba divers of all skill levels. **Queries:** Preferred. **E-Queries:** Yes. **Rights:** All.

RUNNER TRIATHLETE NEWS

14201 Memorial Dr., Suite 204, Houston, TX 77079-6731. 281-759-0555. E-mail: rtnews@ix.netcom.com. Website: www.runnertriathletenews.com. Monthly. $15/yr. Circ.: 13,500. Lance Phegley, Editor. **Description:** Covers running, cycling, triathlons, and duathlons in a 5-state area: TX, LA, AR, OK, NM. Articles on running for road racing, and multi-sport enthusiasts. Pay varies. **Queries:** Preferred. **E-Queries:** Yes. **Unsolicited mss:** Accepts. **Response:** 1-7 days. **Freelance Content:** 40%. **Payment:** On publication.

RUNNER'S WORLD

Rodale Press, Inc., 135 N 6th Street, Emmaus, PA 18098. 610-967-5171. E-mail: rwedit@rodale.com. Website: www.runnersworld.com. Monthly. $18/yr. Circ.: 550,000. David Willey, Editor-in-Chief. **Description:** For recreational runners who train for and race in long-distance events. Length and pay varies. Many stories staff-written or contributed by experts (podiatrists, nutritionists, etc.). **Tips:** See website for guidelines. **Queries:** Required. **E-Queries:** Yes. **Unsolicited mss:** Accepts. **Response:** 2 weeks. **SASE Required:** Yes. **Freelance Content:** 25%. **Rights:** Worldwide. **Payment:** On acceptance. **Contact:** Amby Burfoot, Editor.

RUNNING TIMES

213 Danbury Rd., Wilson, CT 06897-4006. 203-761-1113.
E-mail: editor@runningtimes.com. Website: www.runningtimes.com. 10x/yr.
$3.99/$24.97. Circ.: 70,000. Jonathan Beverly, Editor. **Description:** For the experienced running participant and fan. **Fiction:** Running related, any genre; 1,500-3,000 words; $100-$500. **Nonfiction:** Book excerpts, essays, historical/nostalgic, how-to, humor, inspirational, interview/profile, new product, opinion, personal experience, photo feature, travel, news, reports; 1,500-3,000 words; $100-$500. **Columns, Departments:** Training (short topics on enhancing performance, 1,000 words); Sports-Med (applying medical knowledge, 1,000 words); Nutrition (1,000 words). **Tips:** Get to know runners and running culture, at participant and professional, elite level. No beginner's how-to, generic fitness/nutrition or generic first-person stories. **Queries:** Preferred. **E-Queries:** Yes. **Unsolicited mss:** Accepts. **Response:** 2-6 weeks. **SASE Required:** Yes. **Freelance Content:** 50%. **Rights:** FNAR and electronic. **Payment:** On publication.

SAFARI

Safari Club International, 4800 W Gates Pass Rd., Tucson, AZ 85745. 520-620-1220.
E-mail: sskinner@safariclub.org. Website: www.safariclub.org. Stan Skinner, Managing Editor. **Description:** On worldwide big game hunting and/or conservation projects of Safari Club International's local chapters. Articles run 2,000 words; $300. **Payment:** On publication.

SAIL MAGAZINE

PRIMEDIA Enthusiast Group, 98 N Washington St., Fl. 2, Boston, MA 02114.
617-720-8600. E-mail: sailmail@sailmagazine.com. Website: www.sailmagazine.com. Monthly. $23.94/yr. Circ.: 180,000. Peter Nielsen, Editor-in-Chief. **Description:** On sailboats, equipment, racing, and cruising. How-to articles on navigation, sail trim, etc. Articles run 1,000-2,500 words, with photos; pays $75-$1,000. **Payment:** On acceptance. **Contact:** Amy Ullrich, Managing Editor.

SAILING MAGAZINE

125 E Main St., P.O. Box 249, Port Washington, WI 53074-1915. 262-284-3494.
E-mail: editorial@sailingmagazine.net. Website: sailingonline.com. Monthly. $3.99/issue. Circ.: 43,000. Greta Schanen, Managing Editor. **Description:** Illustrated, for the experienced sailor. Covers cruises, races, boat tests, gear and book reviews, personality profiles; also regular columns. **Nonfiction:** No cruising stories that are just logbooks. No "my first sail" stories. Writers must be familiar with sailing, provide good photos, and write for readers who are also genuine sailors; 200-4,000

words; $125-$600. **Art:** 35 mm transparencies or high-quality digital; $50-$600. **Tips:** "Suggest a story not done in the past four years, include good photographs, and you're in!" **Queries:** Preferred. **E-Queries:** Yes. **Unsolicited mss:** Accepts. **Response:** 2-4 weeks. **Freelance Content:** 60%.

SALT WATER SPORTSMAN

263 Summer St., Boston, MA 02210. 617-303-3660.
E-mail: barry.gibson@time4.com. Website: www.saltwatersportsman.com. Monthly. $4.99/$24.97. Circ.: 170,000. Barry Gibson, Editor. **Description:** Covers marine sport fishing along the coasts of the United States, Canada, the Caribbean, Central America, Bermuda, and occasionally South America and other overseas locations. **Fiction:** Fishing stories, humor, mood, and nostalgia; 1,500-2,000 words; $1,000. **Nonfiction:** How-to and where-to articles; 1,200-1,500 words; $500-$750. **Columns, Departments:** Sportsman's Tips: short how-to-make-it; tackle, rigs, boat equipment; 100-300 words; $150. **Art:** Color slides and prints; $100-$500/inside use, $1,500/cover. **Tips:** No blood and thunder, no overly romantic "remember when." **Queries:** Preferred. **E-Queries:** Yes. **Unsolicited mss:** Accepts. **Response:** 2 weeks. **SASE Required:** Yes. **Freelance Content:** 50%. **Rights:** FNASR. **Payment:** On acceptance.

SCORE GOLF

Canadian Controlled Media Communications, 5397 Eglinton Ave. W, Suite 101, Toronto, Ontario M9C 5K6 Canada. 416-928-2909. Website: www.scoregolf.com. 6x/yr. $14.85/yr. Circ.: 120,000. Robert Weeks, Editor. **Description:** On travel, golf equipment, golf history, personalities, and prominent professionals. Canadian content only. **Nonfiction:** By assignment only; 800-2,000 words; $125-$600. **Fillers:** On Canadian golf scene. Rarely uses humor or poems; 50-100 words; $10-$25. **Tips:** Send query with SASE (include IRCs) and published clips. **Queries:** Required. **Payment:** On publication.

SEA KAYAKER

P.O. Box 17029, Seattle, WA 98127. 206-789-1326.
E-mail: editorial@seakayakermag.com. Website: www.seakayakermag.com. Bimonthly. $23.95/yr. Circ.: 30,000. Christopher Cunningham, Editor. **Description:** For beginning to expert paddlers. Guides sea kayakers through coastal and inland waters and gives readers both entertainment and information. Articles (by assignment only) on sea kayaking (technical, personal experience, profile, review); 1,000-5,000 words; $.15-$.17/word. **Tips:** Combine personal narrative with a sense of place. Send photos with submissions. **Queries:** Preferred. **E-Queries:** Yes. **Unsolicited mss:** Accepts. **Response:** 2 months. **SASE Required:** Yes. **Freelance Content:** 95%. **Rights:** FNASR or second serial. **Payment:** On publication.

SEA MAGAZINE

Duncan McIntosh Co., 17782 Cowan, Suite A, Irvine, CA 92614. 949-660-6150. E-mail: editorial@goboatingamerica.com. Website: www.goboatingamerica.com. Monthly. $3.99/$19.97. Circ.: 50,000. Duncan McIntosh Jr., Publisher/Editor. **Description:** For active West Coast boat owners. Readers are power boaters and sportfishing enthusiasts, Alaska to Mexico, across the Pacific to Hawaii. **Nonfiction:** West Coast boating destination stories, new trends in power boat design, late-season maintenance secrets, how to finance a new boat; 1,200-1,600 words; $250-$400. **Columns, Departments:** Hands-On Boater (do-it-yourself boat maintenance tips); 500-1,200 words; $100-$200. **Art:** 35mm color transparencies or hi-res digital (300 dpi+); $50, $250 (cover). **Tips:** No articles on sailboats, cruise ships, commercial sportfishing party boats, accidents, historic vessels, or chartering. **Queries:** Not necessary. **E-Queries:** Yes. **Unsolicited mss:** Accepts. **Response:** 6 weeks. **Freelance Content:** 60%. **Rights:** FNAR, reprint (print and electronic). **Payment:** On publication. **Contact:** Eston Ellis, Managing Editor.

SHARING THE VICTORY

Fellowship of Christian Athletes, 8701 Leeds Rd., Kansas City, MO 64129. 816-921-0909. E-mail: stv@fca.org; fca@fca.org. Website: www.fca.org. 9x/yr. $2.50/issue. Circ.: 80,000. Jill Ewert, Editor. **Description:** Offers spiritual support and advice to coaches and athletes, and those whom they influence. Also profiles of Christian athletes. Articles run 500-1,000 words; $150-$400. **Tips:** All material must present Christian inspiration. It is preferable that articles and featured individuals show involvement with the ministry of FCA. Send SASE for guidelines. **Unsolicited mss:** Do not accept. **Freelance Content:** 50%. **Payment:** On publication.

SHOTGUN SPORTS

Shotgun Sports, Inc., P.O. Box 6810, Auburn, CA 95604-6810. 530-889-2220. E-mail: shotgun@shotgunsportsmagazine.com. Website: www.shotgunsportsmagazine.com. Monthly. $28/yr. Circ.: 155,000. Frank Kodl, Publisher/Editor. **Description:** On trap and skeet shooting, sporting clays, hunting with shotguns, reloading, gun tests, and instructional shooting. Pay $25-$200 for nonfiction pieces with photos. **Freelance Content:** 100%. **Rights:** FNAR. **Payment:** On publication.

SILENT SPORTS

717 10th St., P.O. Box 152, Waupaca, WI 54981-9990. 715-258-5546. E-mail: info@silentsports.net. Website: www.silentsports.net. **Description:** On bicycling, cross country skiing, running, canoeing, hiking, backpacking, and other "silent" sports. Must have regional (upper Midwest) focus; 1,000-2,000 words; $50-$100 for features, $20-$50 for fillers. **Queries:** Preferred. **Payment:** On publication.

SKATING

U.S. Figure Skating Association, 20 First St., Colorado Springs, CO 80906. 719-635-5200. E-mail: skatingmagazine@usfsa.org. Website: www.usfigureskating.org. 10x/yr. $25/yr (U.S.), $35 (Canada). Circ.: 45,000. Amy Partain, Editor. **Description:**

Communicates information about the sport to USFSA members and figure-skating fans. Promotes USFSA programs, personalities, and trends that affect the sport. **Nonfiction:** Profiles of interesting USFSA members, athletes, judges, etc. Looking for what makes these people unique besides their skating; 1,500 words and up; $75-$150. **E-Queries:** Yes. **Unsolicited mss:** Accepts. **Response:** 1-3 months. **SASE Required:** Yes. **Freelance Content:** 75%. **Rights:** FNASR.

SKI MAGAZINE

Time4 Media, 929 Pearl St., Suite 200, Boulder, Co 80302-5355. 303-448-7600. E-mail: editor@skimag.com. Website: www.skimag.com. 8x/yr. $14.97/yr. Circ.: 455,800. Kendall Hamilton, Editor-in-Chief. **Description:** For experienced skiers: profiles, and destination articles. Articles run 1,300-2,500 words; $.50-$1/word. **Tips:** Send clips. **Queries:** Preferred. **Payment:** On acceptance.

SKI RACING INTERNATIONAL

Inside Communications, Inc., 1830 55th St., Boulder, CO 80301-2700. 303-440-0601. E-mail: sracing@skiracing.com. Website: www.skiracing.com. Weekly. $29.95/yr. Circ.: 30,000. Tim Etchells, Editor. **Description:** On race techniques and conditioning secrets. Coverage of World Cup, pro, collegiate, and junior ski and snowboard competition. Articles by experts, with photos; pay varies.

SKIING MAGAZINE

Time4Media, 929 Pearl St., Boulder, CO 80302-5108. 303-448-7600. E-mail: editor@skiingmag.com. Website: www.skiingmag.com. 7x/yr. $13.94/yr. Circ.: 408,300. Perkins Miller, Editor-in-Chief. **Description:** For the active skier, with destination ideas and instructional tips. Departments include health, fitness, latest trends in skiing industry. Also, profiles of regional runs and their users. **Nonfiction:** Personal adventures on skis, from 2,500 words (no "first time on skis" stories); profiles and interviews, 50-300 words. Pays $150-$300/printed page. **Fillers:** Humorous vignettes, skiing oddities; $.15/word and up. **Tips:** "We're looking for ski adventures that are new, undiscovered, and close to home for most people. Write in first-person." **Queries:** Preferred. **E-Queries:** Yes. **Unsolicited mss:** Accepts. **Freelance Content:** 10%. **Contact:** Helen Olsson, Executive Editor.

SKITRAX

703-317 Adelaide St. W, Toronto, Ontario M5V 1P9 Canada. 416-977-2100. E-mail: skitrax@passport.ca. Website: www.skitrax.com. Quarterly. $13/yr. Circ.: 30,000. Benjamin Sadavoy, Publisher/Editor. **Description:** Official publication of Cross Country Canada and the United States Ski Association. Offers destination and adventure articles. Also features competition coverage of North American and international events, product reviews, a calendar of events, and columns on training, technique, telemarking, masters, waxing, and ski jumping. **Tips:** "Our editor is extremely busy. Your chances are better if your query is attention grabbing and to the point." **Queries:** Preferred. **E-Queries:** Yes. **Unsolicited mss:** Accepts. **Freelance Content:** 100%.

SKYDIVING MAGAZINE

1725 N Lexington Ave., DeLand, FL 32724-2148. 386-736-4793.
E-mail: editor@skydivingmagazine.com. Website: www.skydivingmagazine.com.
Monthly. $4/$20. Circ.: 14,000. Sue Clifton, Editor. **Description:** Techniques, equipment, places, people and events of sport parachuting, written by jumpers for jumpers. Timely news articles on sport and military parachuting; $1/per column inch. **Tips:** Send short bio that shows skydiving experience. **Queries:** Preferred. **E-Queries:** Yes. **Unsolicited mss:** Accepts. **Response:** 2 weeks. **Freelance Content:** 40%. **Rights:** All. **Payment:** On publication.

SNOWBOARDER

PRIMEDIA Enthusiast Group, P.O. Box 1028, Dana Point, CA 92629-5028. 949-496-5922. E-mail: snwbrdrmag@primedia.com. Website: www.snowboarder-mag.com. Bimonthly. $14.97/yr. Circ.: 137,800. Pat Bridges, Editor. **Description:** On snowboarding personalities, techniques, and adventure. Articles, with color transparencies or B&W prints; 1,000-1,500 words; $150-$800. **Payment:** On publication.

SNOWEST

360 B Street, Idaho Falls, ID 83402. 208-524-7000. E-mail: lindstrm@snowest.com. Website: www.snowest.com. 10x/yr. $3.95. Circ.: 150,000. Lane Lindstrom, Editor. **Description:** Family-oriented snowmobile publication for winter recreationists across the U.S. and parts of Canada. **Nonfiction:** Manufacturer reviews, test reports, travel destinations, new product reviews, land use issues, events, technical information, anything related to winter motorized recreation; 2,000 word max.; $100-$300 (with photos). Also, fillers (500-1,500 words). **Art:** Color transparencies (Kodachrome or FujiChrome). **Tips:** Submit 10-15 photos to illustrate a feature, with people involved in every photo; show action; use dawn/dusk for dramatic lighting. **Queries:** Required. **Unsolicited mss:** Accepts. **Rights:** FNASR. **Payment:** On publication.

SOCCER AMERICA

Berling Communications, Inc., P.O. Box 23704, Oakland, CA 94623-0704. 510-528-5000. E-mail: editor@socceramerica.com. Website: www.socceramerica.com. Biweekly. $62/yr. Circ.: 35,000. Mike Woitalla, Executive Editor. **Description:** Soccer news and profiles.

SPORTS ILLUSTRATED

Time, Inc., 135 W 50th St., New York, NY 10020-1201. 212-522-1212. E-mail: letters@si.timeinc.com. Website: www.cnnsi.com. Weekly. $80.46/yr. Circ.: 3,245,900. Norman Pearlstine, Editor-in-Chief. **Description:** Sports news magazine. Articles run 800-1,200 words; pay varies. **Tips:** Limited market; query by mail with clips before submitting. **Queries:** Required. **E-Queries:** No. **Unsolicited mss:** Accepts. **Response:** 4 weeks. **SASE Required:** Yes. **Freelance Content:** Less than 5%. **Rights:** All. **Payment:** On acceptance. **Contact:** Terry McDonell, Managing Editor.

SPORTS ILLUSTRATED FOR KIDS

See full listing in Juvenile category.

SPORTSFAN MAGAZINE

Alan Squire Enterprises, 4948 St. Elmo Ave., Suite 208, Bethesda, MD 20814.
301-986-7901. E-mail: rose@sportsfanmagazine.com. Website: www.sportsfan-magazine.com. Bimonthly. $19.95/yr;$24.95/yr (Canada). Circ.: 80,000. James J.
Patterson, Editor-in-Chief. **Description:** "*SportsFan Magazine* is a DC-based sports publication written by a small, dedicated group of sports lovers whose mission is to chronicle the life and times of America's sports fans." **Poetry:** Regular poetry and prose department with sports-related material. **Fillers:** Accepts sports-related puzzles, humor, illustrations, etc. **Columns, Departments:** Visitor's Locker department features an outside writer in every issue; 1,200-1,300 words. **Tips:** All articles should be fan-focused. **Queries:** Preferred. **E-Queries:** Yes. **Unsolicited mss:** Accepts.
Freelance Content: 50%. **Rights:** FNAR. **Payment:** On publication. **Contact:**
Rose Solari, Senior Editor.

SURFER MAGAZINE

PRIMEDIA Enthusiast Group, P.O. Box 1028, Dana Point, CA 92629.
949-496-5922. E-mail: surferedit@primedia.com. Website: www.surfermag.com.
Monthly. $19.95/yr. Circ.: 118,600. Sam George, Editor. **Description:** Articles on surfers and surfing, 500-5,000 words; pays $.20-$.30/word, $10-$600 for photos.
Payment: On publication.

SURFING

PRIMEDIA Enthusiast Group, P.O. Box 73258, San Clemente, CA 92673. 949-492-7873. E-mail: surfing@primedia.com. Website: www.surfingthemag.com. Monthly.
$21.95/yr. Circ.: 103,000. Evan Slater, Editor-in-Chief. **Description:** For surfing enthusiasts. Offers travel destinations for surfing, surfboard designs and new products, and profiles of well-known surfers. Length and pay vary. **Tips:** No first-person travel articles. **Payment:** On publication.

T'AI CHI

Wayfarer Publications, P.O. Box 39938, Los Angeles, CA 90039. 323-665-7773.
E-mail: taichi@tai-chi.com. Website: www.tai-chi.com. Bimonthly. $20/yr. Circ.:
50,000. Marvin Smalheiser, Editor. **Description:** For persons interested in T'ai Chi Ch'uan (Taijiquan), Qigong, and other internal martial arts, and in similar Chinese disciplines which contribute to fitness, health, and a balanced sense of well being.
Nonfiction: Articles about different internal styles, self-defense techniques, martial arts principles and philosophy, training methods, weapons, case histories of benefits, new or unusual uses for T'ai Chi Ch'uan, interviews; 100-4,500 words; $75-500. **Art:**
4x6 or 5x7 glossy B&W prints. **Tips:** Readers' abilities range from beginners to serious students and teachers. **Queries:** Required. **E-Queries:** Yes. **Unsolicited mss:**
Do not accept. **Response:** 2-3 weeks. **SASE Required:** Yes. **Freelance Content:**
85%. **Rights:** FNAR. **Payment:** On publication.

TENNIS WEEK

Tennis News, Inc., 15 Elm Place, Rye, NY 10580. 914-967-4890.
E-mail: tennisweek@tennisweek.com. Website: www.tennisweek.com. 12x/yr. $4/$40.
Circ.: 107,250. Andre Christopher, Managing Editor. **Description:** Covers the ATP
and WTA (men's and women's professional tours), the tennis industry, major tourna-
ments, new products, retail stores, schedules, scores, rankings, and earnings.
Nonfiction: In-depth, researched articles on current issues and personalities; 1,500-
2,000 words; pay varies. **Queries:** Required. **E-Queries:** Yes. **Unsolicited mss:**
Does not accept. **SASE Required:** Yes. **Rights:** FNAR. **Payment:** On publication.

TEXAS GOLFER

5 Briar Dale Ct., Houston, TX 77027-2904. 713-680-1680.
E-mail: snsmedia@swbell.net. Website: www.texasgolfermagazine.com. Monthly.
$30/yr. Circ.: 55,000. Mike Haines, Editor. **Description:** For Texas golfers, with golf-
course and tournament information, golf tips, and news. Articles run 800-1,500
words. Pay varies. **Tips:** "Most of our freelance work is by assignment." **Queries:**
Required. **E-Queries:** Yes. **Unsolicited mss:** Accepts. **Response:** 2-4 weeks. **SASE
Required:** Yes. **Freelance Content:** 20%. **Rights:** All. **Payment:** On publication.

TRAIL RUNNER

1101 Village Rd., Suite UL-4D, Carbondale, CO 81623. 970-704-1442.
E-mail: mbenge@bigstonepub.com. Website: www.trailrunnermag.com. Bimonthly.
$16.95/yr. Circ.: 27,000. Michael Benge, Editor. **Description:** Feature articles and
news on off-road running. **Queries:** Preferred. **Freelance Content:** 65%.

TRAILER BOATS

Ehlert Publishing, Inc., 20700 Belshaw Ave., Carson, CA 90746-3510. 310-537-6322.
E-mail: editors@trailerboats.com. Website: www.trailerboats.com. Monthly.
$4.99/$16.97. Circ.: 104,000. Ron Eldridge, Editor. **Description:** Technical and
how-to articles on trailer boating (boat, trailer, and tow-vehicle maintenance and
operation, skiing, fishing, cruising, and lifestlye). Also fillers and humor. Pieces run
500-2,000 words; $100-$700. **Queries:** Required. **Unsolicited mss:** Accepts.
Response: 6 weeks. **SASE Required:** Yes. **Freelance Content:** 51%. **Payment:**
On acceptance.

TRIATHLETE

Triathlon Group of North America, 328 Encinitas Blvd., Suite 100, Encinitas, CA
92024-8704. 760-634-4100. Website: www.triathletemag.com. Monthly. $29.95/yr.
Circ.: 44,000. Meredith Hoyer, Editor. **Description:** Covers the sport of triathlon.
Articles, varying lengths, with color slides; pays $.20/word. **Tips:** No "my first
triathlon" stories. **Payment:** On publication.

USA CYCLING

One Olympic Plaza, Colorado Springs, CO 80909-5775. 719-578-4581.
E-mail: media@usacycling.org. Website: www.usacycling.org. Bimonthly. $25/yr.

(nonmembers). Circ.: 49,500. Patrice Quintero, Communications Director. **Description:** On bicycle racing and racers. Contains U.S. cycling news, race coverage and results, features, race information, information on training and coaching. Articles on bicycle racing and racers. **Queries:** Preferred.

USA GYMNASTICS

Pan American Plaza, 201 S Capitol Ave., Suite 300, Indianapolis, IN 46225. 317-237-5050. Website: www.usa-gymnastics.org. Bimonthly. $15/yr. Circ.: 80,000. Luan Peszek, Editor. **Description:** Covers gymnastics, including men's artistic and women's artistic, rhythmic, trampoline, tumbling and sports acrobatics. Coverage of national and international competitions leading up to Olympic Games. In-depth features on athletes and coaches, provides coaching tips. Payment negotiable. **Tips:** Query or call first to discuss article and interest level. Welcomes new writers. **Queries:** Preferred. **E-Queries:** Yes. **Unsolicited mss:** Accepts. **Response:** 4-6 weeks. **SASE Required:** Yes. **Freelance Content:** 10%. **Rights:** FNAR.

VELONEWS

1830 N 55th St., Boulder, CO 80301. 303-440-0601. E-mail: vnedit@7dogs.com. Website: www.velonews.com. 20x/yr. Circ.: 40,000. Kip Mikler, Editor. **Description:** Journal of record for North American bicycle racing, and the world's largest competitive cycling publication. **Nonfiction:** On competitive cycling, training, nutrition; profiles, interviews. No how-to or touring articles; 500-1,500 words; pay varies. **Tips:** Focus on elite, competitive aspect of the sport. **Queries:** Required. **E-Queries:** Yes. **Response:** 1 month. **SASE Required:** Yes. **Freelance Content:** 20%.

THE WATER SKIER

1251 Holy Cow Rd., Polk City, FL 33868-8200. 863-324-4341. E-mail: satkinson@usawaterski.org. Website: www.usawaterski.org. 9x/yr. $3.50/issue. Circ.: 35,000. Scott Atkinson, Editor. **Description:** Published by USA Water Ski, national governing body for competitive water skiing in the U.S. **Nonfiction:** On water skiing (interviews, profiles must be assigned), new products, equipment for boating and water skiing; 1,500-3,000 words; pays $100-$150 (for assigned features). **Art:** Color slides. **Tips:** Submit articles about people involved in the competitive sport. **Queries:** Preferred. **E-Queries:** No. **Unsolicited mss:** Do not accept. **Response:** Queries 1 day, submissions 1 week. **SASE Required:** Yes. **Freelance Content:** 10%. **Rights:** All. **Payment:** On publication.

WATERSKI MAGAZINE

World Publications, LLC, 460 N Orlando Ave., Suite 200, Winter Park, FL 32789. 407-628-4802. E-mail: editor@waterskimag.com. Website: www.waterskimag.com. 8x/yr. $19.97/yr. Circ.: 102,600. Todd Ristorcelli, Editor. **Description:** Waterskiing, wakeboarding, and towed water sports. Instructional features, 1,350 words, including sidebars; $125-$500. Quick tips, 350 words; $35-$125. **Tips:** Travel pieces and profiles by assignment only. **Queries:** Preferred. **Freelance Content:** 25%. **Payment:** On acceptance.

WESTERN OUTDOORS

185 Avenida La Pata, San Clemente, CA 92673. 714-546-4370.
E-mail: lew@wonews.com. 9x/yr. $3.50/$14.95. Circ.: 100,000. Lew Carpenter, Editor. **Description:** On western saltwater and freshwater fishing techniques, tackle, and destinations. Includes the states of California, Oregon, and Washington. Also Alaska, Baja California, and British Columbia. **Nonfiction:** On saltwater or freshwater fishing in the West; facts and comments must be attributed to recognized authorities in their fields; 1,500 words; $450-$600. **Art:** Quality photos and artwork to illustrate articles; $50-$300. **Tips:** Present seasonal materials 6 months in advance. Best time to query is June. **Queries:** Required. **E-Queries:** Yes. **Unsolicited mss:** Does not accept. **Response:** 4-6 weeks. **SASE Required:** Yes. **Freelance Content:** 75%. **Rights:** FNASR. **Payment:** On acceptance.

WESTERN SPORTSMAN

OP Publishing Ltd., 1080 Howe St., Suite 900, Vancouver, British Columbia V6Z 2T1 Canada. 604-678-2586. E-mail: editor@westernsportsman.com. Website: www.westernsportsman.com. Bimonthly. $25/yr. Circ.: 24,683. Tracey Ellis, Coordinating Editor. **Description:** Informative, how-to articles on hunting and fishing in British Columbia, Alberta, Saskatchewan, and Manitoba. Articles run approx. 2,000 words. **Payment:** On publication.

WILDFOWL

PRIMEDIA Enthusiast Group, 6420 Wilshire Blvd., Fl. 14, Los Angeles, CA 90048-5502. 323-782-2173. Bimonthly. $24.97/yr. Circ.: 42,000. Jay M. Strangis, Editor. **Description:** Occasional fiction, humor, related to duck hunters and wildfowl. Pays $400. **Payment:** On acceptance.

WINDSURFING

World Publications, 460 N Orlando Ave., Suite 200, Winter Park, FL 32789-2988. 407-628-4802. E-mail: editor@windsurfingmag.com. Website: www.windsurfingmag.com. 7x/yr. $19.97/yr. Circ.: 68,000. Eddy Patricelli, Editor. **Description:** For experienced boardsailors. Features and instructional pieces ($250-$300) and tips ($50-$75). Pays extra for fast-action photos. **SASE Required:** Yes.

WINDY CITY SPORTS

1450 W Randolph, Chicago, IL 60607. 312-421-1551.
E-mail: jason@windycitysports.com. Website: www.windycitysports.com. Monthly. Circ.: 100,000. Seth Jayson, Managing Editor. **Description:** Covers amateur sports in Chicago and surrounding area. **Tips:** Writers must be knowledgeable in the sport they wish to cover. **Queries:** Preferred. **E-Queries:** Yes. **Unsolicited mss:** Accepts. **Response:** 2 weeks. **SASE Required:** Yes. **Freelance Content:** 25%. **Rights:** FNAR. **Payment:** On publication.

WOODENBOAT

WoodenBoat Publications, Inc., P.O. Box 78, Brooklin, ME 04616. 207-359-4651. E-mail: woodenboat@woodenboat.com. Website: www.woodenboat.com. Bimonthly. $5.99/$29.95. Circ.: 100,000. Matthew Murphy, Editor. **Description:** For wooden boat owners, builders, and designers. Covers design, construction, and maintenance. **Nonfiction:** How-to and technical articles on construction, repair, and maintenance; design, history, and use; profiles of outstanding builders, designers; wooden boat lore. 1,000-5,000 words; $.30/word. **Queries:** Required. **Unsolicited mss:** Accepts. **Response:** 3 months. **SASE Required:** Yes. **Freelance Content:** 70%. **Rights:** 1st worldwide serial. **Payment:** On publication.

YACHTING

Time4Media, 18 Marshall St., Suite 114, Norwalk, CT 06854. 203-299-5900. Website: www.yachtingnet.com. Annual. $5/issue. Circ.: 137,000. Kenny Wooton, Editor-in-Chief. **Description:** Covers news and trends in boating (power, sail, and charter) for the seasoned, upscale boating enthusiast. **Nonfiction:** Articles on upscale, recreational boating—both power and sail; 1,500 words. **Art:** Photos; $350-$1,000. **Tips:** No "how-to" articles. **Queries:** Preferred. **E-Queries:** No. **Unsolicited mss:** Accepts. **Response:** 1-3 months. **Freelance Content:** 15-25%. **Rights:** All. **Payment:** On publication. **Contact:** George Sass, Executive Editor.

TEENS

BREAKAWAY

Focus on the Family, 8605 Explorer Dr., Colorado Springs, CO 80920. 719-531-3400. E-mail: breakaway@family.org. Website: www.family.org. Monthly. $15/yr. Circ.: 100,000. Michael Ross, Editor. **Description:** Readers are Christian boys, ages 12-18. **Fiction:** Stories for young Christian males; to 1,800 words. **Nonfiction:** Real-life adventure articles; to 1,500 words; $.12-$.15/word. **Fillers:** Humor and interesting facts; 500-800 words. **Tips:** No e-mail submissions. Fiction stories not needed at this time. Writer's guidelines w/#10 SASE. Sample copy w/ 8.5x11 SASE and $1.50 check. **Payment:** On acceptance.

BRIO

Focus on the Family, 8605 Explorer Dr., Colorado Springs, CO 80920. 719-531-3400. Website: www.briomag.com. Monthly. $18/yr. Circ.: 200,000. Susie Shellenberger, Editor. **Description:** For Christian teen girls (profiles, how-to pieces, adventures that show the fun Christian teens can have together). **Fiction:** Fiction with realistic character development, good dialogue, and a plot that teen girls will be drawn to. May contain a spiritual slant but should not be preachy; to 2,000 words. **Nonfiction:** Articles; pays $.08-$.12/word. **Fillers:** Short humorous pieces. **Tips:** "*Brio* is aimed at girls ages 12-15 and our second segmented magazine, *Brio & Beyond*, is aimed at girls ages 16-19." **Payment:** On acceptance.

CAMPUS LIFE

Christianity Today International, 465 Gundersen Dr., Carol Stream, IL 60188-2415. 630-260-6200. E-mail: clmag@campuslife.net. Website: www.campuslife.net. 9x/yr. $19.95/yr. Circ.: 100,000. Chris Lutes, Editor. **Description:** Advice on love, sex, self-image, popularity, and other issues of relevance to high school students, with dramatic stories about teens radically changed by their relationship with Jesus Christ. Also, in-depth profiles of Christian musicians. **Fiction:** A 'life lesson' with a Christian world-view, by experienced writers. 2,000 words max.; $.20-$.25/word. **Nonfiction:** First-person stories presenting the lives of teenagers, ordinary or dramatic. 2,000 words max.; $.20-$.25/word. **Tips:** "Avoid religious clichés, misuse of religious language, lack of respect or empathy for teenagers." **Queries:** Required. **E-Queries:** Yes. **Unsolicited mss:** Does not accept. **Response:** 4-6 weeks. **SASE Required:** Yes. **Freelance Content:** 10%. **Rights:** FNAR. **Payment:** On acceptance.

CICADA

Carus Publishing Co., 315 Fifth St., P.O. Box 300, Peru, IL 61354-0300. 812-224-5803, ext. 656. Website: www.cricketmag.com. Bimonthly. $7.95/$35.97. Circ.: 16,000. Marianne Carus, Editor-in-Chief. **Description:** For teens, fiction and poetry that is thought-provoking, yet entertaining, often humorous. Also publishes stories by teens reflecting their own unique perspective. **Fiction:** Literary and genre fiction (realistic, humorous, historical fiction, adventure, science fiction, and fantasy); to 15, 000 words; $.25/word. **Nonfiction:** First-person experiences that are relevant or interesting to teenagers; to 5,000 words; $.25/word. **Poetry:** To 25 lines; $3/line. **Queries:** Does not accept. **E-Queries:** No. **Unsolicited mss:** Accepts. **Response:** 12 weeks. **SASE Required:** Yes. **Freelance Content:** 90%. **Rights:** Vary. **Payment:** On publication. **Contact:** Deborah Vetter.

CLAREMONT REVIEW

4980 Wesley Rd., Victoria, British Columbia V84 1Y9 Canada. 250-658-5221. E-mail: editor@theclaremontreview.ca. Website: www.theclaremontreview.ca. Semi-annual. $10/$18. Circ.: 500. Susan Field, Business Editor. **Description:** Fiction (500-3,000 words) and poetry (to 1 page) by young writers in the English-speaking world, ages 13-19. **Tips:** "We seek fiction with a strong voice and poetry that stirs the heart." No science fiction/fantasy. **Queries:** Not necessary. **Unsolicited mss:** Accepts. **Response:** 6 weeks. **SASE Required:** Yes. **Freelance Content:** 100%.

COLLEGEBOUND TEEN MAGAZINE

Ramholtz Publishing, Inc., 1200 South Ave., Suite 202, Staten Island, NY 10314. 718-761-4800. E-mail: editorial@collegebound.net. Website: www.collegebound-teen.com. $15/yr. Circ.: 725,000. Gina LaGuardia, Editor-in-Chief. **Description:** Provides high school students with an insider's look at all aspects of college life. **Nonfiction:** Real-life student experiences and expert voices dealing with dorm life, choosing the right college, joining a fraternity/sorority, entertainment, fashion/beauty, scholarship strategies, etc.; 600-1,000 words; $75-$100. **Columns, Departments:** Straight Up Strategies, Cash Crunch, Style Scoop; 300-600 words; $50-$75. **Tips:**

Send 2-3 clips or samples of your work (from college newspaper, journalism class, etc.). **Queries:** Preferred. **E-Queries:** Yes. **Unsolicited mss:** Accepts. **Response:** 6-10 weeks. **SASE Required:** Yes. **Freelance Content:** 75%. **Rights:** FNAR. **Payment:** 30 days upon publication.

COSMOGIRL!

The Hearst Corp., 224 W 57th St., Fl. 3, New York, NY 10019-3212. 212-649-3000. E-mail: inbox@cosmogirl.com. Website: www.cosmogirl.com. Monthly. $14.97/yr. Circ.: 1,069,900. Susan Schulz, Editor-in-Chief. **Description:** Teen version of Cosmopolitan, for girls 12-17. Snappy, teen-friendly style. **Nonfiction:** Articles, 900 words, about outstanding young women; first-person narratives of interesting or unusual happenings in the lives of young women; pay varies. **Fillers:** Fillers, 150 words, on ways readers can get involved in social issues. **Queries:** Preferred. **Payment:** On publication.

DEVO'ZINE

See full listing in Religion category.

GUIDEPOSTS FOR TEENS

1050 Broadway, Suite 6, Chesterton, IN 46304. 219-929-4429.
E-mail: gp4t@guideposts.org. Website: www.gp4teens.com. Bimonthly. Circ.: 250,000. Betsy Kohn, Managing Editor. **Description:** Inspirational, general-interest magazine for teen girls (ages 12-18). True stories of adventure, relationships, overcoming. Also, quizzes, do-it-yourself fashion and beauty advice, music reviews, celebrity Q&As, and profiles of role models (celebrities and "real" teens). **Nonfiction:** True first-person dangerous, miraculous, or inspirational stories; ghostwritten by (or for) teens. Protagonist must change in course of the story; must deliver clear inspirational takeaway. **Fillers:** Quizzes (Are you a winner or a whiner? Are you dating a dud?); Celebrity Q&A's, interviews. "Soul Food," short 250 word miraculous stories or "A-Ha" moments, written in first person by (or for) teens. **Tips:** "No preachy religious stories. We need light stories that center around everyday activities (driving, dating, friends, etc.) and milestone events (prom, graduation, etc.)." **Queries:** Preferred. **E-Queries:** Yes. **Unsolicited mss:** Accepts. **Response:** 4-6 weeks. **SASE Required:** Yes. **Freelance Content:** 80%. **Rights:** All. **Payment:** On acceptance. **Contact:** Allison Payne, Associate Editor.

GUMBO

Strive Media Institute Publishing, Inc., 1818 N Dr. Martin Luther King Dr., Milwaukee, WI 53212. 414-374-3511. E-mail: amy@mygumbo.com. Website: www.mygumbo.com. Bimonthly. $15/yr. Circ.: 25,000. Amy Muehlbauer, Managing Editor. **Description:** Multicultural magazine written, edited, and designed for teens by teens. Mission is to teach journalism and design skills to young adults by having them work with adult mentors who are professionals in journalism, graphic design, and photography. Editorial content reflects diversity in a range of subjects such as careers, sports, health, fashion, news, and entertainment. **Tips:** "We do not offer payment as we are published by a non-profit organization. All work is written and edited by teens and is a learning process. Contact the managing editor directly if you are interested in working for Gumbo. Do not send unsolicited material; only assigned articles are published." **Queries:** Required. **E-Queries:** Yes. **Unsolicited mss:** Does not accept. **Response:** 2 weeks. **Rights:** None.

HECKLER
1915 21st St., Sacramento, CA 95814-6813. 916-456-2300. E-mail: info@heckler.com. Website: www.heckler.com. Monthly. $6.99/yr. Circ.: 65,000. Brad Oates, Managing Editor. **Description:** Magazine on the culture of skateboarding, snowboarding, and music. Features, essays, and reviews; to 3,000 words; $15-$75. **Tips:** "We are looking for great interviews with pro skateboarders, snowboarders, or about-to-break bands. Be patient, but be persistent." **Queries:** Preferred. **E-Queries:** Yes. **Unsolicited mss:** Accepts. **Response:** 7 days. **Freelance Content:** 40%. **Rights:** None. **Payment:** On publication.

INSIGHT
Review and Herald Publishing Assoc., 55 W Oak Ridge Dr., Hagerstown, MD 21740-7301. 301-393-4038. E-mail: insight@rhpa.org. Website: www.insightmagazine.org. Weekly. $46.95/yr. Circ.: 20,000. Dwain Neilson Esmond, Editor. **Description:** Magazine for high school and college students on growing in their relationship with God. Articles address typical issues these students face in today's changing society. **Tips:** Accepts poems, stories, and articles written by students in high school/college.

KEYNOTER
Key Club International, 3636 Woodview Trace, Indianapolis, IN 46268. 317-875-8755. E-mail: keynoter@kiwanis.org. Website: www.keyclub.org. 7x/yr. Circ.: 219,000. Amy L. Wiser, Executive Editor. **Description:** For students, ages 13-18, offering informative, entertaining articles on self-help, school, and community issues; 1,200 words; $200-$400. **Tips:** No first-person accounts, fiction, or articles for younger readers. **Queries:** Preferred. **E-Queries:** Yes. **Unsolicited mss:** Accepts. **Response:** Queries 1-4 months, submissions 1 week. **SASE Required:** Yes. **Freelance Content:** 65%. **Rights:** FNASR. **Payment:** On acceptance.

LISTEN
The Health Connection, 55 W Oak Ridge Dr., Hagerstown, MD 21740. 301-393-4010. E-mail: listen@healthconnection.org. Website: www.listenmagazine.org. Monthly. $26.95/yr. Circ.: 50,000. Anita Jacobs, Editor. **Description:** Provides teens with vigorous, positive, educational approach to problems arising from use of tobacco, alcohol, and other drugs. **Fiction:** True-to-life stories; 1,000-1,200 words; $.05-$.10/word. **Nonfiction:** On problems of tobacco, alcohol/drug abuse; personality profiles; self-improvement; drug-free activities; 1,000-1,200 words; $.05-$.10/word. **Poetry:** Open to poems by high-school students only. **Tips:** "Use upbeat approach." **Queries:** Preferred. **E-Queries:** Yes. **Unsolicited mss:** Accepts. **Response:** 2-12 weeks. **SASE Required:** Yes. **Rights:** FNASR. **Payment:** On acceptance.

THE NEW YORK TIMES UPFRONT
Scholastic, Inc., 557 Broadway, New York, NY 10012-3999. 212-343-6100.
E-mail: upfront@scholastic.com. Website: www.upfrontmagazine.com. Biweekly.
$19.95/yr. Circ.: 200,000. David Goddy, Editor-in-Chief. **Description:** News maga-
zine for teenagers. Pieces run 500-1,5000 words; pays $150 and up. **Queries:**
Preferred. **Payment:** On acceptance.

ODYSSEY
Cobblestone Publishing, 30 Grove St., Suite C, Peterborough, NH 03458.
603-924-7209. E-mail: blindstrom@cobblestone.mu.com. Website: www.cobble-
stonepub.com. 9x/yr. Circ.: 21,000. Elizabeth Lindstrom, Editor. **Description:**
Magazine for kids, ages 10-16, on science and technology. **Fiction:** Science-related
stories, poems, science fiction, retold legends, etc., relating to theme; up to 1,000
words; $.20-$.25/word. **Nonfiction:** Subjects directly and indirectly related to theme;
with little-known information (but don't overlook the obvious). 720-950 words; $.20-
$.25/word. **Fillers:** Critical-thinking activities, experiments, models, science fair proj-
ects, etc., for children alone, with adult supervision, or in classroom setting.
Columns, Departments: Far Out; Places, Media, People to Discover; Fantastic
Journeys; 400-650 words. **Tips:** Material must relate to specific theme; contact for
upcoming list. Scientific accuracy, lively approach, and inclusion of research are crucial to being accepted. For fiction, submit manuscript. **Payment:** On publication.

SCHOLASTIC SCOPE
Scholastic, Inc., 557 Broadway, New York, NY 10012-3999. 212-343-6100. E-mail:
scopemag@scholastic.com. Website: www.scholastic.com. 18x/yr. Circ.: 750,000.
Diane Webber, Executive Editor. **Description:** Fiction and nonfiction for 15-18-
year-olds, with 4th-6th grade reading ability. Short stories, 400-1,200 words, on
teenage interests and relationships; family, job, and school situations. Plays to 5,000
words. Pays good rates. **Payment:** On acceptance.

SCIENCE WORLD
See full listing in Science category.

SEVENTEEN
The Hearst Corp., 1440 Broadway, Fl. 13, New York, NY 10018-2301. 212-204-4300.
E-mail: mail@seventeen.com. Website: www.seventeen.com. Monthly. $19.95/yr.
Circ.: 2,432,000. Atoosa Rubenstein, Editor-in-Chief. **Description:** Popular
beauty/fashion magazine for young women, ages 13-21. **Fiction:** "Stories with issues
important and familiar to our readers, that also challenge them and make them
think." **Nonfiction:** Feature stories unique and relevant to teenage girls; 1,000-2,000
words; $1/word. **Columns, Departments:** Features, Guys, Voice, Real Life, To Your
Health, College, Quizzes; 350-500 words. **Tips:** "Story ideas should spring from a
teenage viewpoint and sensibility, not that of parent, teacher, or other adult."
Queries: Required. **Response:** 4-8 weeks. **SASE Required:** Yes. **Freelance
Content:** 30%. **Rights:** FNAR. **Payment:** On publication.

STUDY BREAKS

Shweiki Media, Inc., 4012 Burnet Rd., Austin, TX 78756-3627. 512-450-1114.
E-mail: info@studybreaks.com. Website: www.studybreaks.com. 7x/yr. Circ.: 37,500.
Steve Viner, Publisher/Editor. **Description:** Published in six editions for Texas college students. Covers college life, dating, travel, sports, music, parties, etc. Seeks pieces with humor. **Queries:** Not necessary. **E-Queries:** Yes. **Unsolicited mss:** Accepts. **Payment:** On publication.

SÚPERONDA

Hispanic Business, Inc., 425 Pine Ave., Santa Barbara, CA 93117-3709.
805-964-4554. E-mail: editorial@hbinc.com. Website: www.superonda.com. 5x/yr.
$12/yr. Circ.: 100,000. Jesus Chavarria, Publisher/Editor. **Description:** English-language magazine geared toward U.S. Hispanics (in college or college-bound) ages 18-24. Features, 600-1,800 words; columns, 600 words; pays to $.75/word. **Queries:** Required. **E-Queries:** Yes. **Unsolicited mss:** Does not accept. **Response:** 30-60 days. **Freelance Content:** 80%. **Rights:** All. **Payment:** On publication.

TEEN

Hearst Communications, Inc., 3000 Ocean Park Blvd., Suite 3048, Santa Monica, CA 90405. 310-664-2950. Website: www.teenmag.com. Quarterly. Circ.: 600,000. Jane Fort, Editor-in-Chief. **Description:** Established in 1955, Teen is now the little-sister publication to *Seventeen* and *CosmoGirl* magazines, appealing to young teens interested in fashion, beauty, body image, and empowerment. Nonfiction and some short fiction; pay varies. **Queries:** Preferred. **Payment:** On publication.

TEEN INK

Young Author's Foundation, P.O. Box 610030, Newton, MA 02461-0030.
617-964-6800. E-mail: editor@teenink.com. Website: www.teenink.com. 10x/yr.
$25/yr. Circ.: 175,000. Kate Dunlop Seamans, Editor. **Description:** Magazine written by teens for teens. Features fiction, nonfiction, poetry, and art. Receives 40,000 submission/yr. **Tips:** "Our magazine is written entirely by teenagers, ages 13-19." Does not offer payment. **Queries:** Not necessary. **E-Queries:** Yes. **Unsolicited mss:** Accepts. **Freelance Content:** 100%.

TEEN VOICES

Women Express, Inc., 80 Summer St., Boston, MA 02110. 617-426-5505.
E-mail: teenvoices@teenvoices.com. Website: www.teenvoices.com. Quarterly.
$2.95/$19.95. Circ.: 25,000. Ellyn Ruthstrom, Managing Editor. **Description:** Written by, for, and about teenaged and young-adult women. Offers a place to share thoughts with others the same age. **Fiction:** Short stories, any subject and length. **Nonfiction:** About any important issue or experience. **Poetry:** "Your feelings, thoughts, etc." **Columns, Departments:** Opinions/editorial pieces. **Tips:** Be honest and candid. Appreciates material that promotes feminism, equality, and self-esteem. **Queries:** Not necessary. **E-Queries:** Yes. **Unsolicited mss:** Accepts. **Response:** 3-5 days. **SASE Required:** No. **Rights:** FNAR. **Payment:** In copies.

TEENPRENEUR

Earl G. Graves Publishing Co., Ltd., 130 5th Ave., Fl. 10, New York, NY 10011-4355. 212-242-8000. Website: www.blackenterprise.com. 6x/yr. Circ.: 450,000. Alfred Edmond, Editor-in-Chief. **Description:** For African-American teens interested in business.

TWIST

Bauer Publishing Co., 270 Sylvan Ave., Englewood Cliffs, NJ 07632-2523. 201-569-6699. E-mail: twistmail@twistmagazine.com. Website: www.twistmagazine.com. Monthly. $9.97/yr. Circ.: 300,000. Janet Giovanelli, Editor-in-Chief. **Description:** On relationships, entertainment, fitness, fashion, and other topics, for today's young women. **Tips:** Mostly staff-written; queries with clips required.

WHAT MAGAZINE

108-93 Lombard Ave., Winnipeg, Manitoba R3B 3B1 Canada. 204-985-8160. E-mail: what@whatmagnet.com. Website: www.whatmagnet.com. Bimonthly. $14/yr. Circ.: 250,000. Barbara Chabai, Editor. **Description:** Canadian teen pop-culture magazine (including music, movie and TV interviews, typical issues and themes affecting readers, ages 13-19). **Nonfiction:** Charged, edgy, unconventional, from pop culture to social issues; 450 words and up; pay negotiable. **Tips:** Query with working story title, 1-sentence explanation of angle, justification and proposed treatment, potential contacts, proposed length. Welcomes new writers. **Queries:** Required. **E-Queries:** Yes. **Unsolicited mss:** Do not accept. **Response:** 1-2 months. **SASE Required:** Yes. **Freelance Content:** 60%. **Rights:** 1st Canadian. **Payment:** On publication.

WITH

722 Main St., P.O. Box 347, Newton, KS 67114. 316-283-5100. Website: www.with-online.org. Bimonthly. $26.95/yr. Circ.: 5,000. Carol Duerksen, Editor. **Description:** "The Magazine for Radical Christian Youth." Seeks to "empower teens to be radically committed to Jesus Christ, peace, justice, and sharing God's good news through words and action." **Fiction:** First-person stories; 1,500 words; $100. **Nonfiction:** Creative, "inside the life of a teen," first-person preferred. Avoid preaching. Themes: Roots and Wings, Jesus, Christmas, and service/mission; 1,500 words; pay varies. **Fillers:** Wholesome humor and poetry. **Art:** 8x10 B&W. **Queries:** Not necessary. **E-Queries:** Yes. **Unsolicited mss:** Accepts. **Response:** 1 month. **SASE Required:** Yes. **Freelance Content:** 20%. **Rights:** FNAR and electronic. **Payment:** On acceptance.

YM

Gruner + Jahr USA Publishing, 15 E 26th St., Fl. 14, New York, NY 10010-1505. 646-758-0555. Website: www.ym.com. Monthly. $20/yr. Circ.: 2,206,000. Christina Kelly, Editor-in-Chief. **Description:** Fashion, beauty, boys, advice, and features for girls, ages 12-24. **Queries:** Required. **Unsolicited mss:** Accepts. **Response:** 1-2 months. **Freelance Content:** 40%. **Payment:** On publication.

YOUNG AND ALIVE
P.O. Box 6097, Lincoln, NE 68506. E-mail: editor@christianrecord.org. Quarterly. Circ.: 25,000. Gaylena Gibson, Editor. **Description:** Publication for young adults who are blind or visually impaired. Presents material from a non-denominational, Christian viewpoint and features articles on adventure, biography, camping, careers, health, history, hobbies, holidays, marriage, nature, practical Christianity, sports, and travel. Features run 800-1,400 words; pay varies. **Art:** Slides or prints; $10/photo. **Queries:** Not necessary. **E-Queries:** No. **Unsolicited mss:** Accepts. **Response:** 12 months. **SASE Required:** Yes. **Freelance Content:** 90%. **Rights:** One-time. **Payment:** On acceptance.

YOUNG SALVATIONIST
The Salvation Army, P.O. Box 269, Alexandria, VA 22313-0269. 703-684-5500. Website: www.salvationarmyusa.org. 10x/yr. Circ.: 48,000. Laura Ezzell, Managing Editor. **Description:** For teenagers, seeks to teach Christian view of everyday living. **Fiction:** Uses some fiction; 500-1,200 words; $.15/word. **Nonfiction:** Articles (to 1,000-1,500 words); short-shorts, first-person testimonies (600-800 words). Pays $.15/word ($.10/word for reprints). **Tips:** Write for theme list or sample issue. **SASE Required:** Yes. **Freelance Content:** 80%. **Payment:** On acceptance.

TRADE & TECHNICAL

9-1-1 MAGAZINE
Official Publications, Inc., 18201 Weston Place, Tustin, CA 92780-2251. 714-544-7776. E-mail: publisher@9-1-1magazine.com. Website: www.9-1-1magazine.com. Randall D. Larson, Editor. **Description:** Trade magazine for emergency communications management, covering the skills, training, and equipment which 9-1-1 and public safety dispatch professionals have in common. "We run stories on provocative issues and cover major incidents from both a responder and a communications standpoint." Features run 1,000-2,500 words; $.10-$.20/word. **Tips:** "We are looking for writers knowledgable in this field. As a trade magazine, stories should be geared for professionals in the emergency services and dispatch field, not the general reader." No poetry or fiction. **Rights:** FNAR. **Payment:** On publication.

ABA JOURNAL
American Bar Association, 750 N Lake Shore Dr., Fl. 6, Chicago, IL 60611. 312-988-6018. E-mail: abajournal@abanet.org. Website: http://www.abajournal.com. Monthly. $75/yr. Circ.: 376,000. Danial Kim, Editor; Debra Cassens, Managing Editor. **Description:** Includes news of current developments in the law, U.S. Supreme Court news and stories providing ideas and tools to help lawyers become better lawyers. Does not accept "Top Tips" stories aimed at readers in any office setting, stories that mark the anniversary of major Supreme Court cases, or opinion pieces. **Nonfiction:** News or short pieces about trends in legal practice; 650-3,000 words; $250-$2,000. **Tips:** "Our readership is lawyers, and we are interested only in stories

for lawyers. We want experienced journalists who have at least written for legal news publications. Read our magazine and e-report. Pitch ideas that make sense for us. Don't pitch ideas we've already covered." **Queries:** Preferred. **E-Queries:** Yes. **Response:** 1 week. **SASE Required:** No. **Freelance Content:** 5%. **Rights:** All. **Payment:** On acceptance. **Contact:** Sarah Randag, releases@abanet.org.

AMERICAN CITY & COUNTY

PRIMEDIA Business Magazines & Media, 6151 Powers Ferry Rd. NW, Suite 200, Atlanta, GA 30339-2927. 770-955-2500. E-mail: bwolpin@primediabusiness.com. Website: www.americancityandcounty.com. Monthly. $67/yr. Circ.: 73,800. Bill Wolpin, Editorial Director. **Description:** On local government issues (wastewater, water, solid waste, financial management, information technology, etc.). Articles run 600-2,500 words. **Tips:** Readers are elected and appointed local government officials.

AMERICAN COIN-OP

Crain Communications, Inc., 500 N Dearborn St., Suite 1000, Chicago, IL 60610-4964. 312-337-7700. Website: www.crain.com. Monthly. $39/yr. Circ.: 16,800. Paul Partika, Editor. **Description:** On successful coin-operated laundries (management, promotion, decor, maintenance). Send SASE for guidelines. **Queries:** Preferred.

AMERICAN DEMOGRAPHICS

See full listing in Contemporary Culture category.

AMERICAN LAUNDRY NEWS

500 N Dearborn St., Suite 1000, Chicago, IL 60610. 312-337-7700. E-mail: laundrynews@crain.com;bbeggs@crain.com. Monthly. $39/yr. Circ.: 16,000. Bruce Beggs, Editor. **Description:** Laundry and linen management, including institutional, commercial and industrial laundries, and uniform rental and linen supply companies. **Nonfiction:** New technology, industry news and trends, profiles; 1,000-2,000 words; to $.22/word. **Art:** Color prints; $25-$50. **Tips:** "We do not cover the drycleaning or coin-operated laundry segments of our industry." Sample copy for $6 and 10x13 SASE. **Queries:** Preferred. **E-Queries:** Yes. **Unsolicited mss:** Accepts. **Response:** 1 month for queries, 2 months for submissions. **SASE Required:** Yes. **Freelance Content:** 10%. **Rights:** All. **Payment:** On publication.

AMUSEMENT TODAY

Amusement Today, Inc., P.O. Box 5427, Arlington, TX 76005-5427. 817-460-7220. E-mail: info@amusementtoday.com. Website: www.amusementtoday.com. Monthly. $40/yr. Circ.: 2,500. Gary Slade, Editor-in-Chief. **Description:** Trade publication for those who work in the amusement industry.

AREA DEVELOPMENT

400 Post Ave., Westbury, NY 11590-2289. 516-338-0900. E-mail: gerri@areadevelopment.com. Website: www.areadevelopment.com. Monthly. Circ.: 45,500. Geraldine Gambale, Editor. **Description:** Covers site-selection and facility-planning issues for

executives at industrial companies. Stories on location issues for industrial companies (site selection, real estate, taxes, labor, energy, environment, government regulations, etc.); 2,000 words; $.30-$.40/word. **Tips:** No "puff" promotional material about particular areas or communities. **Queries:** Preferred. **E-Queries:** Yes. **Unsolicited mss:** Accepts. **Freelance Content:** 90%. **Payment:** On publication.

AUTOMATED BUILDER

CMN Publishing Division, 1445 Donlon St., Suite 16, Ventura, CA 93003-5640. 805-642-9735. E-mail: info@automatedbuilder.com. Website: www.automatedbuilder.com. Monthly. Circ.: 25,000. Don Carlson, Editor. **Description:** On home manufacturers and dealers. Technical articles on methods, materials, and technologies for in-plant building industry; 750-1,000 words; $300. **Queries:** Required. **Unsolicited mss:** Accepts. **Response:** 10 days. **SASE Required:** Yes. **Freelance Content:** 10%. **Payment:** On acceptance.

BUILDER

Hanley-Wood, LLC, One Thomas Cir. NW, Suite 600, Washington, DC 20005-5802. 202-452-0800. Website: www.builderonline.com. 16x/yr. $29.95/yr. Circ.: 142,900. Boyce Thompson, Editor-in-Chief. **Description:** On trends and news in home building (design, marketing, new products, etc.). Articles to 1,500 words; pay negotiable. **Queries:** Preferred. **Payment:** On acceptance.

BUSINESS & COMMERCIAL AVIATION

McGraw-Hill, Inc., 4 International Dr., Suite 260, Rye Brook, NY 10573-1065. 914-933-7600. E-mail: feedback@aviationnow.com. Website: www.aviationnow.com/bca. Monthly. $60/yr. Circ.: 50,000. William Garvey, Editor-in-Chief. **Description:** For pilots, on use of private aircraft for business transportation. Articles to 2,500 words, with photos; pays $100-$500. **Queries:** Preferred. **Payment:** On acceptance.

CALIFORNIA LAWYER

Daily Journal Corp., 1145 Market St., Fl. 8, San Francisco, CA 94103. 415-252-0500. E-mail: tema_goodwin@dailyjournal.com. Website: www.dailyjournal.com. Monthly. $5/$75. Circ.: 140,000. Peter Allen, Editor. **Description:** General-interest magazine covering legal issues. Combines hard-hitting legal news, case commentary and technology coverage. **Nonfiction:** Features, 1,000-3,000 words; $500-$2,500. **Columns, Departments:** News, commentary, features, essays, legal advice, technology, book reviews; 500-1,500 words; $50-$500. **Tips:** "The best way to break in is to start with something small in news section." **Queries:** Preferred. **E-Queries:** Yes. **Unsolicited mss:** Accepts. **Response:** 1-6 weeks **Freelance Content:** 80%. **Payment:** On acceptance. **Contact:** Tema Goodwin, Managing Editor.

CLEANING & MAINTENANCE MANAGEMENT

National Trade Publications, 13 Century Hill Dr., Latham, NY 12110-2197. 518-783-1281. Website: www.cmmonline.com. Monthly. $45/yr. Circ.: 41,300. Paul Amos, Editor-in-Chief. **Description:** On managing efficient cleaning and custodial/maintenance operations. Also provides technical/mechanical how-to articles. Articles run 500-1,200 words; pays to $300 for commissioned features. **Queries:** Preferred. **Payment:** On publication.

COAL PEOPLE MAGAZINE

P.O. Box 6247, Charleston, WV 25362. 304-342-4129. E-mail: cmp@newwave.net. Website: www.coalpeople.com. 10x/yr. $2.50/issue. Circ.: 10,500. **Description:** A combination of human interest features on coal personalities, operations, and businesses servicing the coal mining industry. Updated news features and calendars are featured monthly. Pieces run 500 words; $80. **Tips:** Avoid political subjects and negative environmental issues. **E-Queries:** Yes. **Response:** 3 months. **SASE Required:** Yes. **Freelance Content:** 50%. **Rights:** FNAR. **Payment:** On publication. **Contact:** Christina Karawan, Managing Editor.

COLLEGE STORE EXECUTIVE

P.O. Box 1500, Westbury, NY 11590. 516-334-3030. Website: www.ebmpubs.com. 8x/yr. $40/yr. Circ.: 9,000. Ken Baglino, Editor. **Description:** Features news, profiles, articles, etc. for the college store industry. **Tips:** No general business or how-to articles. **Queries:** Preferred. **Payment:** On publication.

CONTRACT MANAGEMENT

National Contract Management Assoc. (NCMA), 8260 Greensboro Dr., Suite 200, McLean, VA 22102. 800-344-8096. E-mail: cm@ncmahq.org. Website: www.ncmahq.org. Monthly. $158/yr. Circ.: 22,000. Amy Miedema, Editor-in-Chief. **Description:** Provides comprehensive reporting on current issues and trends relevant to both public and private sectors of the profession. **Nonfiction:** Business best practices, management/organizational articles, contracts interest, professional development; 2,000 words; pay varies. **Columns, Departments:** Opinion pieces, information for small businesses, legal scholars' research, varied feature material; 1,000 words; pay varies. **Tips:** "We seek clearly written business articles that appeal to contract management professionals of all levels." **Queries:** Preferred. **E-Queries:** Yes. **Unsolicited mss:** Accepts. **Response:** 1-3 weeks. **SASE Required:** No. **Freelance Content:** 3%. **Rights:** All. **Payment:** On publication.

CONVENIENCE STORE NEWS

VNU Business Media, 770 Broadway, New York, NY 10003-9522. 646-654-4500. E-mail: info@csnews.com. Website: www.csnews.com. 15x/yr. $89/yr. Circ.: 80,400. Claire Pumplin, Editor-in-Chief. **Description:** Publication covering the convenience store and petroleum marketing industry. Provides news, research, trends, and best-practice information to convenience store and petroleum chain executives, store owners and managers, suppliers, and distributors. **Queries:** Preferred. **Contact:** John Lofstock, Senior Editor.

COOKING FOR PROFIT

See full listing in Food & Wine category.

DAIRY FOODS

1050 Illinois Route 83, Suite 200, Bensenville, IL 60106-1096. 630-616-0200. E-mail: phillipsd@bnp.com. Website: www.dairyfoods.com. Monthly. $100/yr. Circ.: 20,840. David Phillips, Editor. **Description:** On innovative dairies, processing operations, marketing, new products for milk handlers and makers of dairy products. Articles run 2,500 words. No payment offered.

DEALERSCOPE

North American Publishing Co., 401 N Broad St., Fl. 5, Philadelphia, PA 19108. 215-238-5300. Website: www.dealerscope.com. Monthly. Circ.: 22,000. Grant Clauser, Editor-in-Chief. **Description:** On new consumer electronics, computer and electronics products, and new technologies. **Tips:** Query with resumé and clips. **Payment:** On publication.

DENTAL ECONOMICS

Penwell, P.O. Box 3408, Tulsa, OK 74101-3408. 918-835-3161. Website: www.dentaleconomics.com. Monthly. $88/yr. Circ.: 101,700. Joseph A. Blaes, DDS, Editor-in-Chief. **Description:** On business side of dental practice, patient and staff communication, personal investments. **Payment:** On acceptance.

DISPLAY & DESIGN IDEAS

VNU Business Publications, 1115 Northmeadow Pkwy, Roswell, GA 30076-3857. 770-569-1540. E-mail: jclark@ddimagazine.com. Website: www.ddimagazine.com. Monthly. Circ.: 21,500. RoxAnna Sway, Editor. **Description:** A national retail interior design magazine for visual merchandisers and store planners/designers. Reports on new retail store design, design trends, merchandising strategies, and product information. **Nonfiction:** Stories on new, cutting-edge store design, with special attention to visual merchandising, fixtures, flooring, lighting and ceiling and wall treatments. 1,000 words; fees negotiable. **Art:** Sumbit at least 2-3 high-quality, color photos with each article. **Tips:** Articles should quote at least three different sources. **Queries:** Required. **E-Queries:** Yes. **Unsolicited mss:** Does not accept. **Response:** 1-2 weeks. **Freelance Content:** 30%. **Rights:** Unlimited. **Payment:** On publication. **Contact:** Julie Clark, Senior Editor.

DRUG TOPICS

Advanstar Communications, Inc., 5 Paragon Dr., Montvale, NJ 07645. 201-358-7258. E-mail: drug.topics@medec.com. Website: www.drugtopics.com. Biweekly. $61/yr. Circ.: 116,800. Harold E. Cohen, Editor. **Description:** Covers pharmacy news, issues, trends, products, marketing for pharmacists, buyers, wholesalers, academia, and others; 750-2,000 words. **Tips:** Payment is offered for commissioned articles only. **Queries:** Required. **Rights:** First. **Payment:** On acceptance.

ELECTRONIC INFORMATION REPORT

PRIMEDIA Business Magazines & Media, P.O. Box 4234, Stamford, CT 06907-0234. 203-358-4100. E-mail: eir@simbanet.com. Website: www.simbanet.com.

Weekly. Linda Kopp, Executive Editor. **Description:** Covers all aspects of the marketing of electronic information.

ELECTRONIC MUSICIAN
See full listing in Performing Arts category.

ENGINEERED SYSTEMS
Business News Publishing Co., LLC, P.O. Box 2600, Troy, MI 48007-2600. 248-244-6400. E-mail: beverlyr@bnp.com. Website: www.esmagazine.com. Monthly. $58/yr. Circ.: 57,500. Robert C. Beverly, Editor. **Description:** Articles, case histories, news, and product information related to engineered HVAC systems in commercial, industrial, or institutional buildings. **Tips:** "We encourage e-mail inquiries. Our website can provide a feel for our content and style." **Queries:** Preferred. **E-Queries:** Yes. **Payment:** On publication.

THE ENGRAVERS JOURNAL
P.O. Box 318, Brighton, MI 48116. 810-229-5725. E-mail: editor@engraversjournal.com. Website: www.engraversjournal.com. Monthly. Mike Davis, Publisher; Sonja Davis, General Manager. **Description:** Trade magazine for engravers featuring articles on small business operations. Pays $75-$300. **Queries:** Preferred. **E-Queries:** No. **Unsolicited mss:** Accepts. **Freelance Content:** 60%. **Rights:** Varies. **Payment:** On acceptance. **Contact:** Claudia Sinta, Managing Editor.

ENTERTAINMENT DESIGN
See full listing in Film, TV, Entertainment category.

FIRE CHIEF PRIMEDIA
Business Magazines & Media, 330 N Wabash, Suite 2300, Chicago, IL 60611. E-mail: jwilmoth@primediabusiness.com. Website: www.firechief.com. Monthly. $54/yr. Circ.: 52,600. Janet Wilmoth, Editor. **Description:** For fire officers. **Nonfiction:** Training, safety and health, communications, fire investigation, finance and budgeting, professional development, incident command, hazmat response, vehicle maintenance; 1,000-5,000 words; to $.30/word. **Columns, Departments:** Training Perspectives, EMS Viewpoint, Sound Off; 1,000-1,800 words. **Queries:** Preferred. **SASE Required:** Yes. **Payment:** On publication.

FIREHOUSE
Cygnus Business Media, 445 Broad Hollow Rd., Suite 21, Melville, NY 11747. 631-845-2700. E-mail: harvey.eisner@cygnuspub.com. Website: www.firehouse.com. Monthly. $30/yr. Circ.: 100,000. Harvey Eisner, Editor-in-Chief. **Description:** For firefighters and fire buffs; seeks to educate, inform and entertain. **Nonfiction:** Coverage of major fires and disasters, apparatus and equipment, communications, training, law, safety, EMS, etc; 500-2,000 words. **Art:** Prefers color photos, illustrations, charts, and diagrams. **Queries:** Required. **E-Queries:** Yes. **Rights:** FNAR. **Payment:** On publication.

FOOD MANAGEMENT

Penton Media, 1300 E 9th St., Cleveland, OH 44114-1503. 216-696-7000.
E-mail: fmeditor@aol.com. Website: www.foodservicesearch.com. Monthly. $70/yr.
Circ.: 47,800. John Lawn, Editor-in-Chief. **Description:** On food service in hospitals, nursing homes, schools, colleges, prisons, businesses, and industrial sites. Covers trends, legislative issues, how-tos, management, and retail-oriented food service pieces. **Queries:** Required.

FOUNDATION NEWS & COMMENTARY

Council on Foundations, 1828 L Street NW, Washington, DC 20036. 202-466-6512.
E-mail: fnceditor@cof.org. Website: www.foundationnews.org. Bimonthly. $60/yr.
Circ.: 10,000. Allan Clyde, Editor. **Description:** Covers the world of grant making, for professional grant makers, volunteer trustees, and grant seekers. Articles run 1,200-3,000 words; payment varies. **Tips:** Avoid fundraising topics. **Queries:** Required. **E-Queries:** Yes. **Unsolicited mss:** Accepts. **Freelance Content:** 25%. **Rights:** All. **Payment:** On acceptance.

GLASS DIGEST

Ashlee Publishing Company, Inc., 18 E 41st St., Fl. 20, New York, NY 10017-6222.
212-376-7722. E-mail: publisher@ashlee.com. Website: www.ashlee.com. Monthly. $40/yr. Circ.: 12,300. Jordan Wright, Publisher. **Description:** On building projects and glass/metal dealers, distributors, storefront and glazing contractors; 1,200-1,500 words. **Payment:** On publication. **Contact:** Gregg Wallis, Managing Editor.

GOVERNMENT EXECUTIVE

National Journal Group, Inc., 1501 M St. NW, Suite 300, Washington, DC 20005-1700. 202-739-8500. E-mail: govexec@govexec.com. Website: www.govexec.com. Monthly. $48/yr. Circ.: 70,000. Timothy Clark, President/Editor. **Description:** Publication for civilian and military government workers at the management level. Aricles run approx. 1,500-3,000 words.

GREENHOUSE MANAGEMENT & PRODUCTION

P.O. Box 1868, Fort Worth, TX 76101-1868. David Kuack, Editor. **Description:** For professional greenhouse growers. **Nonfiction:** How-tos, innovative production or marketing techniques; 500-1,800 words. **Art:** Color slides or electronic images; $50-$300. **Queries:** Preferred. **Unsolicited mss:** Accepts. **Payment:** On acceptance.

HAUNTED ATTRACTION MAGAZINE

Prion, Inc., P.O. Box 220286, Charlotte, NC 28222-0286. 704-366-0875.
E-mail: info@hauntedattraction.com. Website: www.hauntedattraction.com.
Quarterly. $6.99/$25. Circ.: 5,000. Leonard Pickel, Editor-in-Chief. **Description:** Trade publication for the haunted house industry. **Nonfiction:** Spotlights on haunted attractions; how-tos on props and effects for haunted attractions; to 3,000 words; no payment offered. **Queries:** Preferred. **E-Queries:** Yes. **Unsolicited mss:** Accepts. **Freelance Content:** 90%. **Contact:** Leonard Pickel.

HEALTH PRODUCTS BUSINESS
See full listing in Health category.

HEATING/PIPING/AIR CONDITIONING ENGINEERING
Penton Media, 1300 E 9th St., Cleveland, OH 44114-1501. 216-696-7000. E-mail: hpac@penton.com. Website: www.hpac.com. Monthly. $65/yr. Circ.: 56,000. Michael G. Ivanovich, Editor. **Description:** On heating, piping, and air conditioning systems and related issues (indoor air quality, energy efficiency), for industrial plants and large buildings only. Articles, to 3,500 words; pays $70/printed page. **Queries:** Preferred.

THE HOME SHOP MACHINIST
Village Press, Inc., 2779 Aero Park Dr., Traverse City, MI 49686. 231-946-3712. E-mail: nknopf@villagepress.com. Website: www.homeshopmachinist.com. Bimonthly. $5.95. Circ.: 36,000. Neil A. Knopf, Editor. **Description:** Publishes how-to articles for serious machinists and hobbyists. **Nonfiction:** Machine how-to projects. Photos, drawings and text required. No people profiles; $40/page. **Art:** $9/photo. **Tips:** Write in first person only; accuracy and detail essential. **Queries:** Preferred. **E-Queries:** Yes. **Unsolicited mss:** Accepts. **Response:** 1-4 weeks. **SASE Required:** Yes. **Freelance Content:** 95%. **Rights:** FNASR. **Payment:** On publication.

HOSPITALS & HEALTH NETWORKS
One N Franklin St., Fl. 29, Chicago, IL 60606. 312-893-6800. E-mail: bsantamour@healthforum.com. Website: www.hhnmag.com. Monthly. $80/yr. Circ.: 71,600. Bill Santamour, Managing Editor. **Description:** For health-care executives and hospital administrators on financing, staffing, coordinating, and providing facilities for health-care services; 250-1,800 words; pay varies. **Unsolicited mss:** Does not accept. **Payment:** On publication.

HYDROPONIC RETAILING IN THE USA
New Moon Publishing, Inc., P.O. Box 1027, Corvallis, OR 97339-1027. 541-757-2511. Website: www.growingedge.com. Quarterly. Circ.: 1,200. **Description:** News and information for the hydroponic retail store. Articles, 1,500-2,000 words, on running a business, employee relations, retailing problems and issues, and retail point of sale technology. Pays $150. **Art:** Color prints or slides; high-res digital. Pays $25 for inside photos; $150 for cover. **Queries:** Preferred. **E-queries:** Yes. **Response:** 2-3 months. **SASE Required:** Yes. **Freelance Content:** 50%. **Rights**: 1st world serial.

IDEA HEALTH & FITNESS SOURCE
See full listing in Fitness Magazines category.

INDUSTRIA ALIMENTICIA
Stagnito Communications, Inc., 155 Pfingsten Rd., Suite 205, Deerfield, IL 60015. 847-205-5660. Website: www.stagnito.com. Monthly. Circ.: 45,000. **Description:** Spanish-language publication. Covers the food-processing industry in Latin America. **Contact:** Elsa Rico-Torres.

INK MAKER

Cygnus Business Media, 445 Broad Hollow Rd., Suite 21, Melville, NY 11747-3601. E-mail: info@inkmakeronline.com. Website: www.inkmakeronline.com. Monthly. $66/yr. Circ.: 5,000. Linda M. Casatelli, Editor. **Description:** Reports on trends, technology, and news in the printing ink industry. Features both technical and non-technical pieces for ink manufacturers and printers. Also includes interviews with printers from across the country. **Queries:** Required. **Unsolicited mss:** Accepts. **Response:** 2-3 weeks. **Freelance Content:** 30%. **Rights:** FNAR.

INTERCOM

See full listing in Writing & Publishing category.

INTERNAL MEDICINE WORLD REPORT

Medical World Communications, 241 Forsgate Dr., Jamesburg, NJ 08831-1385. 732-656-1140. Website: www.imwronline.com. Monthly. $180/yr. Circ.: 100,300. Dalia Buffery, Editor. **Description:** Provides practicing internists with relevant clinical news. Articles based on scientific presentations at medical conferences or reports in major medical journals; up to 600 words; $.50/word. **Tips:** No articles on animal or test-tube studies. No articles of a promotional nature, such as those reporting on talks given at events sponsored by drug companies. Welcomes new writers. **Queries:** Preferred. **E-Queries:** Yes. **Unsolicited mss:** Accepts. **Response:** 1 week. **SASE Required:** Yes. **Freelance Content:** 90%. **Rights:** All (print and electronic). **Payment:** On publication.

JOURNAL OF EMERGENCY MEDICAL SERVICES (JEMS)

525 B Street, Suite 1900, Carlsbad, CA 92101. 800-266-5367. Website: www.jems.com. Monthly. $29.97/yr. Circ.: 40,000. A.J. Heightman, Editor-in-Chief. **Description:** A leading voice in emergency medicine and prehospital care. Readers include EMTs, paramedics, nurses, physicians, EMS managers, administrators, and educators. **Nonfiction:** On provider health and professional development; innovative applications of EMS; interviews/profiles, new equipment and technology; industry news and commentary; $200-$400. **Columns, Departments:** $150-$200/department; $25/news item. **Art:** Only real-life EMS action shots; completed model release form must accompany photos when appropriate. $150-$400 (cover). **Queries:** Preferred. **E-Queries:** Yes. **Unsolicited mss:** Accepts. **Response:** 3 months. **Freelance Content:** 70%. **Payment:** On publication.

JUNGLE LAW

632 Broadway, Fl. 7, New York, NY 10012-2614. 212-352-0840. E-mail: editors@junglemediagroup.com. Website: www.junglelawonline.com. Monthly. $12. Circ.: 132,000. Ryan D'Agostino, Editor-in-Chief. **Description:** Publication for law students. Seeks to provide professionals with the tools they need to be succesful. Online and print versions. **Queries:** Preferred. **Unsolicited mss:** Accepts. **SASE Required:** Yes.

LANDSCAPE TRADES

Landscape Ontario Horticulture Trades Assn., 7856 Fifth Line S., RR4, Milton, Ontario L9T 2X8 Canada. 905-875-1805. E-mail: linerskine@landscapeontario.com. Website: www.landscapetrades.com. 9x/yr. $45/yr. Circ.: 8,000. Sarah Willis, Editorial Director. **Description:** Articles on landscape design, construction, and maintenance. Also, pieces on retail and wholesale nursery industries. **Queries:** Required. **Unsolicited mss:** Does not accept. **Response:** 2-3 weeks. **Freelance Content:** 50%. **Rights:** FNAR. **Payment:** On publication. **Contact:** Linda Erskine.

LP-GAS

Advanstar Communications, Inc., 7500 Old Oak Blvd., Cleveland, OH 44130. 440-891-2616. E-mail: phyland@advanstar.com. Website: www.lpgasmagazine.com. $30/yr. Circ.: 14,500. Patrick Hyland, Editor. **Description:** On LP-gas dealer operations: marketing, management, etc. **Nonfiction:** Articles, 1,500-2,500 words, with photos; pays flat fee schedule. **Queries:** Preferred. **Payment:** On acceptance.

MACHINE DESIGN

Penton Media, Inc., Penton Media Bldg., 1300 E 9th St., Cleveland, OH 44114-1503. 216-696-7000. E-mail: mdeditor@penton.com. Website: www.machinedesign.com. Semi-monthly. $105/yr. Circ.: 185,000. Ronald Khol, Editor. **Description:** On mechanical and electromechanical design topics for engineers. Covers electric/electronics, fluid power, automotive, fastening and joining, aerospace, manufacturing, management, mechanical, CAD/CAM. Articles, to 10 typed pages; pay varies. **Queries:** Preferred. **Payment:** On publication.

MAINTENANCE TECHNOLOGY

1300 S Grove Ave., Suite 105, Barrington, IL 60010-5246. 847-382-8100. E-mail: editors@mt-online.com. Website: www.mt-online.com. Monthly. Circ.: 54,000. Robert C. Baldwin, Editor. **Description:** Technical articles with how-to information to increase reliability and maintainability of electrical and mechanical systems and equipment. Readers are managers, supervisors, and engineers in all industries and facilities. **Queries:** Preferred. **Payment:** On acceptance.

MIDWIFERY TODAY

See full listing in Health category.

NAILPRO

Creative Age Publications, Inc, 7628 Densmore Ave., Van Nuys, CA 91406-2042. 818-782-7328. E-mail: nailpro@creativeage.com. Website: www.nailpro.com. Monthly. $24/yr. Circ.: 58,140. Jodi Mills, Executive Editor. **Description:** Magazine for nail professionals covering new products, techniques, business-building ideas, and other beauty industry news. **Tips:** "Writers must have a knowledge of the beauty industry and specifically the nailcare industry." **Queries:** Preferred. **E-Queries:** Yes. **Unsolicited mss:** Accepts. **Response:** 2 weeks. **Freelance Content:** 80%. **Rights:** All. **Payment:** On acceptance.

NATIONAL FISHERMAN
Diversified Business Communications, Inc., P.O. Box 7438, Portland, ME 04101-3919. 207-842-5606. E-mail: editor@nationalfisherman.com. Website: www.nationalfisherman.com. Monthly. $22.95/yr. Circ.: 38,000. Jerry Fraser, Editor-in-Chief. **Description:** For commercial fishermen and boat builders. Articles run 200-2,000 words; $4-$6/inch. **Queries:** Preferred. **Payment:** On publication.

THE NORTHERN LOGGER AND TIMBER PROCESSOR
NL Publishing, Inc., P.O. Box 69, Old Forge, NY 13420-0069. 315-369-3078. E-mail: nela@telnet.net. Monthly. $12/yr. Circ.: 12,865. Eric A. Johnson, Editor. **Description:** Covers the forest-product industry. Features run 1,000-2,000 words; pays $.15/word. **Queries:** Preferred. **Payment:** On publication.

P.I. MAGAZINE
4400 Route 9 S, Suite 1000, Freehold, NJ 07728-7198. 732-308-3800. E-mail: info@pimagazine.com. Website: www.pimagazine.com. Bimontly. $39/yr. Circ.: 10,000. Jimmie Mesis, Publisher/Editor. **Description:** Journal for professional investigators. Profiles of PI's, with true accounts of their most difficult cases. Pays $100-$200. **Tips:** No fiction. **Payment:** On publication.

PIZZA TODAY
Macfadden Protech, LLC, 908 S 8th St., Suite 200, Louisville, KY 40203-3357. 812-949-0909. Website: www.pizzatoday.com. Monthly. $29.95/yr. Circ.: 41,000. Jeremy White, Executive Editor. **Description:** On pizza business management for pizza entrepreneurs. Articles on food preparation, marketing strategies, business management, hiring and training, etc.; 500-1,500 words; $.50/word. **Tips:** Send query by e-mail, fax, or mail. **Queries:** Preferred. **Payment:** On acceptance.

POLICE AND SECURITY NEWS
1208 Juniper St., Quakertown, PA 18951. 215-538-1240. E-mail: jdevery@policeandsecuritynews.com. Website: www.policeandsecuritynews.com. Bimonthly. $18/yr. Circ.: 22,000. James Devery, Editor. **Description:** Trade publication for the law enforcement industry. Targets middle and upper management professionals within both the public and private law enforcement and security industries. **Nonfiction:** Law enforcement and security related articles directed toward middle and upper management covering all areas. Written for experts in a manner which non-experts can comprehend. 500-3,000 words; $.10/word. **Tips:** Submit query, cover letter, complete manuscript, bio, and SASE. **Queries:** Preferred. **E-Queries:** Yes. **Unsolicited mss:** Accepts. **Response:** 1-2 weeks. **Freelance Content:** 50%. **Rights:** FNAR. **Payment:** On publication.

POOL & BILLIARD
See full listing in Games & Pastimes category.

PRACTICE STRATEGIES

American Optometric Assn., 243 N Lindbergh Blvd., St. Louis, MO 63141. 314-991-4100 ext.267. E-mail: rfpieper@theaoa.org. Website: www.aoanet.org. Monthly. Members. Circ.: 33,000. Bob Pieper, Editor. **Description:** Published by a section of the Journal of American Optometric Assn., on practice management and business issues (insurance, motivating staff, government health programs, etc.). **Queries:** Preferred. **E-Queries:** Yes. **Unsolicited mss:** Accepts. **Response:** 1 month. **Freelance Content:** 25%. **Rights:** All. **Payment:** On publication.

PRECISION MANUFACTURING

Synergy Resource Group, Inc., 3131 Fernbrook Lane, Suite 111, Plymouth, MN 55447. E-mail: liz@mpma.com. Website: www.mpma.com. 8x/yr. Circ.: 7,700. Liz Kuntz, Editor-in-Chief. **Description:** For manufacturing job shops in the states of Minnesota, Wisconsin, Iowa, North Dakota, and South Dakota. Focus is on trends, personalities, and successes in the manufacturing industry. **Nonfiction:** Seeking skilled writers for profile pieces and industry-related articles; length varies. **Tips:** Welcomes new writers. **Queries:** Required. **E-Queries:** Yes. **Unsolicited mss:** Accepts. **Response:** 2-4 weeks. **SASE Required:** Yes. **Freelance Content:** 50%. **Rights:** One-time and reprint. **Payment:** On publication.

REMODELING

Hanley Wood Magazines, One Thomas Cir. NW, Suite 600, Washington, DC 20005. 202-452-0390. E-mail: salfano@hanleywood.com; chartman@hanleywood.com. Website: www.remodelingmagazine.com. Monthly. Circ.: 80,000. Sal Alfano, Editor-in-Chief; Christine Hartman, Managing Editor. **Description:** Publication for full-service remodeling contractors. Articles (by assignment only) on industry news for residential and light commercial remodelers; 250-1,700 words. **Queries:** Required. **E-Queries:** Yes. **Unsolicited mss:** Does not accept. **Response:** 1 month. **Freelance Content:** 10%. **Payment:** On acceptance.

REPLACEMENT CONTRACTOR

Hanley Wood Magazines, One Thomas Cir. NW, Suite 600, Washington , DC 20005. 202-452-0390. Monthly. Circ.: 22,500. Sal Alfano, Editor-in-Chief; Jim Cory, Editor. **Description:** For roofing, siding, decking, and window replacement contractors. **Nonfiction:** Articles (by assignment only) on industry news and issues for residential and light commercial exterior replacement remodelers; 250-2,500 words. **Queries:** Required. **E-Queries:** Yes. **Unsolicited mss:** Does not accept. **Response:** 1 month. **Freelance Content:** 40%. **Payment:** On acceptance.

REVISTA AEREA

Strato Publishing Co., Inc., 405 E 56th St., Apt. 4E, New York, NY 10022-2430. 212-223-2707. E-mail: revistaaerea@revistaaerea.com. Website: www.revistaaerea.com. Bimonthly. $50/yr. Circ.: 11,200. Elaine Asch-Root, Editor. **Description:** Covers both military and commercial aviation industries in Latin America, and other countries where Spanish is the primary language.

RV BUSINESS

TL Enterprises, Inc., 2575 Vista Del Mar Dr., Ventura, CA 93001. 800-765-1912.
E-mail: rvb@tl.com. Website: www.rvbusiness.com. Monthly. $48/yr. Circ.: 21,000.
John Sullaway, Editor. **Description:** For the RV industry offering news and product-
related features. Also covers legislative matters affecting the industry. Articles, to
1,500 words; pay varies. **Tips:** No generic business features.

SOUTHERN LUMBERMAN

P.O. Box 681629, Franklin, TN 37068-1629. 615-791-1961. E-mail: ngregg@south-
ernlumberman.com. Website: www.southernlumberman.com. Monthly. $23/yr. Circ.:
15,500. Nanci P. Gregg, Editor. **Description:** For owners and operators of small- to
medium-sized sawmills. Looking for features on sawmills with description of equipment and tips from owner/manager on how to work efficiently, and how to save and
make money; 500-2,500 words; $100-$300. **Queries:** Preferred. **E-Queries:** No.
Unsolicited mss: Accepts. **Response:** 4-6 weeks. **SASE Required:** Yes.
Freelance Content: 45%. **Rights:** FNASR. **Payment:** On publication.

STITCHES

240 Edward St., Aurora, Ontario L4G 3S9 Canada. 905-713-4336.
E-mail: simon@stitchesmagazine.com. Website: www.stitchesmagazine.com.
Monthly. $40/yr (Canada), $45 (U.S.). Circ.: 39,000. Peter Cocker, Publisher.
Description: "The Journal of Medical Humor." Specializes in humor and lifestyle
pieces for physicians. **Fiction:** To 2,000 words; $.35/word (Canada), $.25/word (U.S.).
Nonfiction: To 2,000 words. **Poetry:** Shorter; $.50/word (Canada), $.40/word (U.S.).
Art: Cartoons only. $50 (Canada), $40 (U.S.). **Queries:** Not necessary. **E-Queries:**
Yes. **Unsolicited mss:** Accepts. **Freelance Content:** 95%. **Rights:** FNASR.
Payment: On publication. **Contact:** Simon Hally, Editor.

STONE WORLD

Business News Publishing, 210 E State Rt 4, Suite 311, Paramus, NJ 07652-5103.
201-291-9001. E-mail: info@stoneworld.com. Website: www.stoneworld.com.
Monthly. Circ.: 21,000. Michael Reis, Associate Publisher/Editor. **Description:** On
new trends in installing and designing with stone. For architects, interior designers,
design professionals, and stone fabricators and dealers. 750-1,500 words; pays $6/col-
umn inch. **Queries:** Preferred. **Payment:** On publication.

TECHNICAL COMMUNICATION

See full listing in Writing & Publishing category.

TODAY'S FACILITY MANAGER

Group C Communications, Inc., P.O. Box 2060, Red Bank, NJ 07701. 732-842-7433.
Website: www.todaysfacilitymanager.com. Circ.: 50,000. Matt Stansberry, New
Products Editor. **Description:** News and new-product information for in-house, on-
site facility professionals. Articles run 1,000-1,500 words; pays flat fee. **Tips:**
Welcomes new writers. Requires solid research and reporting skills. **Queries:**

Required. **E-Queries:** Yes. **Unsolicited mss:** Does not accept. **SASE Required:** Yes. **Freelance Content:** 10%. **Payment:** 30 day after publication.

TOURIST ATTRACTIONS AND PARKS

Kane Publications, 10 E Athen Ave., Suite 208, Ardmore, PA 19003. 610-645-6940. E-mail: tapmag@kanec.com. Website: www.touristattractionparks.com. Scott C. Borowsky, Executive Editor. **Description:** On successful management of parks, entertainment centers, zoos, museums, arcades, fairs, arenas, and leisure attractions. Articles run 1,500 words; $.12/word. **Queries:** Preferred. **Payment:** On publication.

WASTE AGE

PRIMEDIA Business Magazines & Media, 6151 Powers Ferry Rd. NW, Suite 200, Atlanta, GA 30339-2941. 770-618-0112. E-mail: bwolpin@primediabusiness.com. Website: www.wasteage.com. Monthly. $55/yr. Circ.: 40,000. Bill Wolpin, Editorial Director. **Description:** Covers collection, transfer, processing,and disposal of waste. Case studies; analysis of news, trends, products, people, and events; how-to articles with solutions to problems in the field. Most pieces run 1,500-2,500 words. **Queries:** Required. **E-Queries:** Yes. **Unsolicited mss:** Accepts. **Response:** 2 months. **SASE Required:** Yes. **Rights:** Worldwide. **Payment:** On publication.

WOODSHOP NEWS

Soundings Publications, LLC, 10 Bokum Rd., Essex, CT 06426-1536. 860-767-8227. E-mail: editorial@woodshopnews.com. Website: www.woodshopnews.com. Monthly. $3.95/$21.95. Circ.: 77,700. A.J. Hamler, Editor. **Description:** Business advice for professional woodworkers; profiles of shops with unique businesses, furniture lines, or stories; economics and marketing techniques applicable to small and medium size woodworking shops; trends in woodworking equipment, new technology, and construction techniques. Articles to 1,400 words; $150-$500. **Tips:** Seeks profiles of woodworkers outside the Northeast region. **Queries:** Preferred. **Unsolicited mss:** Accepts. **Payment:** On publication.

WORKBOAT

Diversified Business Communications, Inc., P.O. Box 1348, Mandeville, LA 70470-5844. 985-626-0298. E-mail: workboatmagazine@aol.com. Website: www.workboat.com. Monthly. $49/yr. Circ.: 22,000. David Krapf, Editor. **Description:** Current, lively information for workboat owners, operators, crew, suppliers, and regulators. Covers construction and conversion, diesel engines and electronics, politics and industry, unusual vessels, new products, etc.; features (to 2,000 words) and shorts (500-1,000 words); pay varies. **Queries:** Preferred. **Payment:** On publication.

TRAVEL

AAA GOING PLACES

1515 N Westshore Blvd., Tampa, FL 33607. 813-289-1391.
E-mail: sklim@aaasouth.com. Website: aaagoingplaces.com. Bimonthly. Circ.: 4,000,000. Sandy Klim, Editor. **Description:** On domestic travel and lifestyle, for AAA Members. **Nonfiction:** Well-researched domestic and international travel, automotive, lifestyle. 3rd-person preferred; 800-1,200 words; $200-$400. **Tips:** Prefers general, rather than niche, travel stories to a destination, with an angle; e.g., Washington D.C., "The Monuments," rather than the annual art exhibit at Lincoln Memorial. Weekend or weeklong vacation ideas for seniors and families. Fun vacation stops, a little unusual but with lots to offer ("Hershey, PA: something for everyone"). **Queries:** Not necessary. **E-Queries:** Yes. **Unsolicited mss:** Accepts. **Response:** Queries 6 months, submissions 3 months. **SASE Required:** Yes. **Freelance Content:** 50%. **Rights:** 1st, web and reprint rights, some reprints from local markets. **Payment:** On acceptance.

AAA MIDWEST TRAVELER

Automobile Club of Missouri, 12901 N Forty Dr., St. Louis, MO 63141. 314-523-7350. E-mail: mright@aaamissouri.com. Website: www.aaatravelermags.com. Bimonthly. Circ.: 461,000. Michael J. Right, Editor. **Description:** For AAA members in Missouri and parts of Illinois, Indiana and Kansas. Seeks lively writing to encourage readers to take the trip they've just read about. Include useful information (travel tips). AAA properties preferred. 1,200-1,500 words; $150-$350. **Queries:** Preferred. **E-Queries:** No. **Unsolicited mss:** Accepts. **Response:** 4-6 weeks. **SASE Required:** Yes. **Freelance Content:** 80%. **Rights:** FNAR, reprint, electronic. **Payment:** On acceptance.

AAA SOUTHERN TRAVELER

12901 N Forty Dr., St. Louis, MO 63141. 314-523-7350. Website: www.aaatravelermags.com. Bimonthly. $3/issue. Circ.: 180,000. Michael Right, Editor. **Description:** For members of AAA in Arkansas, Louisiana, and Mississippi. Articles run 1,200 words; pays $300. **Tips:** Call or write for current editorial calendar. **Queries:** Preferred. **E-Queries:** Yes. **Unsolicited mss:** Does not accept. **Response:** Queries 2-4 weeks. **Freelance Content:** 90%. **Rights:** FNAR and electronic. **Payment:** On acceptance. **Contact:** Deborah Reinhardt, Managing Editor.

ARIZONA HIGHWAYS

See full listing in Regional & City Publications category.

ASU TRAVEL GUIDE

A S U Travel Guide, Inc., 1525 Francisco Blvd. E, San Rafael, CA 94901-5539. 415-459-0300. E-mail: staff@asutravelguide.com. Website: www.asutravelguide.com. Quarterly. $34.95/yr. Circ.: 42,000. Christopher Gil, Managing Editor. **Description:** Publication for airline employees. Features travel information including bargains and discounts. Articles 1,800 words; $200. **Tips:** "Do not write about specific hotels, etc. Airline employees get deals, so a discount sidebar is written by the editor. Send copies of previously written travel articles." **Queries:** Required. **E-Queries:** Yes. **Unsolicited mss:** Does not accept. **Response:** 2 weeks. **SASE Required:** Yes. **Freelance Content:** 85%. **Rights:** FNAR. **Payment:** On acceptance.

BRITISH HERITAGE

PRIMEDIA Enthusiast Group, 6405 Flank Dr., Harrisburg, PA 17112-2750. 717-657-9555. E-mail: britishheritage.magazine@primediamags.com. Website: www.britishheritage.com. Bimonthly. $25.90/yr. Circ.: 77,485. Bruce Heydt, Managing Editor. **Description:** Travel articles on places to visit in the British Isles. Writers should include detailed historical information in a "For the Visitor" sidebar; 800-1,500 words; $100-$200. **Payment:** On acceptance.

CARIBBEAN TRAVEL AND LIFE

World Publications, 460 N Orlando Ave., Winter Park, FL 32789. 407-628-4802. E-mail: editor@caribbeantravelmag.com. Website: www.caribbeantravelmag.com. 9x/yr. $23.95/yr. Circ.: 150,000. Bob Friel, Editor. **Description:** For the upscale traveler, on travel, recreation, leisure, and culture in the Caribbean, the Bahamas, and Bermuda. Topics include sports, adventure, travel, shopping, dining, arts and entertainment, and sightseeing suggestions; 150-3,000 words; pays $75-$2,000. **Tips:** No general queries, i.e. "traveling to the Bahamas." Read the magazine first and send published clips. **E-Queries:** Yes. **Payment:** On publication.

CLUBMEX NEWSLETTER

International Gateway Insurance Brokers, Inc., 3450 Bonita Rd., Suite 103, Chula Vista, CA 91910. 619-422-3022. E-mail: ckelleher@igib.com. Website: www.igib.com. Bimonthly. $12.95/yr. Chuck Stein, Editor. **Description:** Stories on specific travel destinations in Mexico. Articles must tell readers where to go, what to see, where to stay and shop, and describe other interesting things to do (example: a trip to Mexico's magnificent Copper Canyon). **Nonfiction:** Articles on retirement areas, fishing, camping, swimming, lodging, wind surfing, snorkeling, boating, restaurants, shopping, whale watching, events/fiestas, and interesting people. Prefers pieces that involve travel by auto, RV, or other road-use vehicle. 300-1,000 words; $65 for cover story, $50 for interior. **Tips:** "Our parent company specializes in Mexico Tourist Automobile Insurance, so our editorial content contains information on Mexico travel. The essential purpose of our newsletter is to encourage our readers to drive into Mexico." **Queries:** Preferred. **E-Queries:** Yes. **Unsolicited mss:** Accepts. **SASE Required:** Yes. **Freelance Content:** 100%. **Payment:** On publication. **Contact:** Cecilia Kelleher.

COAST TO COAST

2575 Vista del Mar Dr., Ventura, CA 93001. 805-667-4100. E-mail: vlaw@affinity-group.com. Website: www.rv.net. 8x/yr. $4/$28. Circ.: 150,000. Valerie Law, Editorial Director. **Description:** Membership magazine for a network of upscale RV resorts across North America. Focuses on travel and outdoor recreation. **Nonfiction:** Essays on travel, recreation, and good times. Destination features on a North American city or region. Activity/recreation features introduce a sport, hobby, or other diversion. Also, features on RV lifestyle; 1,200-3,000 words; $300-$600. **Art:** Slides, digital images, prints; $75-$600. **Queries:** Not necessary. **E-Queries:** Yes. **Unsolicited mss:** Accepts. **SASE Required:** Yes. **Freelance Content:** 75%. **Rights:** FNAR. **Payment:** On acceptance.

CORPORATE & INCENTIVE TRAVEL MAGAZINE

Coastal Communications Corp., 2650 N Military Trail, Suite 250, Boca Raton, FL 33431-6390. 561-989-0600. E-mail: ccceditor1@att.net. Website: www.corporate-inc-travel.com. Monthly. Circ.: 40,000. **Description:** ABC audited for meeting and incentive travel planners and key executives responsible for meeting decisions. Articles range monthly from in-depth how-tos to issue-oriented features, examinations of professional concerns, thoroughly researched destination reports, and columns by industry experts. **E-Queries:** Yes.

CRUISE N' TRAVEL EN ESPANOL

Independent Publishing Co., Inc., 10371 SW 44th St., Miami, FL 33165-5607. 305-221-3186. Quarterly. $10/yr. Circ.: 35,000. Hilda Inclan, Editor-in-Chief. **Description:** Getaway magazine for affluent Hispanic travelers. **Nonfiction:** Stories describing destinations, cruises, airlines, casinos, hotels, restaurants, festivals, shopping, and other travel-related topics. **Columns, Departments:** Health tips and health-related stories for travelers. **Tips:** "Writers should be sensitive to the needs of the demanding traveler accustomed to quality and class. Articles written in Spanish are preferred, but stories in English will also be accepted provided the writer is agreeable to translation." Phone calls welcome. **Queries:** Preferred. **E-Queries:** No. **Freelance Content:** 80%. **Rights:** None.

CRUISE TRAVEL

World Publishing Company, 990 Grove St., Evanston, IL 60201. 847-491-6440. E-mail: cruise-editor@centurysports.net. Website: www.cruisetravelmag.com. Bimonthly. $29.95/yr. Circ.: 172,000. Charles Doherty, Editor-in-Chief. **Description:** Ship-, port-, and cruise-of-the-month features, 800-2,000 words; cruise guides; cruise roundups; cruise company profiles; travel suggestions for one-day port stops. Photo-features strongly recommended; pay varies. **Tips:** Query by mail only, with sample color photos. **Queries:** Preferred. **Payment:** On publication.

ELITE TRAVELER

801 Second Ave., New York, NY 10017. 212-986-5100. E-mail: editor@elite-traveler.com. Website: www.elite-traveler.com. 6x/yr. $150/yr. Circ.: 129,316. **Description:** *Elite Traveler* serves affluent consumers. Categories covered include luxury leisure travel destinations, hotels, board meetings, family travel, spas, golf, jets, yachting and luxury cruising, wine, technology, autos, security, finance, dining, fashion. Length and pay vary (often $1/word). **Tips:** "Be familiar with

our style and audience before querying." **Queries:** Preferred. **E-Queries:** Yes. **Unsolicited mss:** Does not accept. **Response:** 2 weeks. **SASE Required:** No. **Freelance Content:** 60%. **Rights:** None. **Payment:** On publication. **Contact:** Laura Hughes, Editorial Director; Mike Espindle, Managing Editor.

ENDLESS VACATION

Resort Condominums International, Inc., 9998 N Michigan Rd., Carmel, IN 46032-9640. E-mail: julie.woodard@rci.com. Website: www.rci.com. Bimonthly. $84/yr. Circ.: 1,500,000. **Description:** Magazine for frequent travelers (timeshare owners) with features on where to go and what to do on vacation. **Nonfiction:** Focus is primarily on domestic vacation travel, with some mainstream international vacation articles. Features should cover new and interesting vacation options, with a solid angle. 1,000-2,000 words; $800-$1,500. **Columns, Departments:** Weekend travel destinations, health and safety on the road, family vacationing articles, cruise stories, celebrity-focused destinations, short travel news-oriented and service pieces, hot news tips and travel trends; 500-1,200 words; $100-$1,200. **Art:** Travel-oriented photos (landscapes, scenics, people, activities, etc.). **Tips:** "Write for doers, not dreamers. We seek activities in which readers can participate." **Queries:** Preferred. **E-Queries:** No. **Response:** 4-8 weeks. **Freelance Content:** 90%. **Rights:** FNAR. **Payment:** On acceptance. **Contact:** Julie Woodard, Senior Editor.

EPICUREAN TRAVELER

Fezziwig Publishing Co., 740 Stetson St., Moss Beach, CA 94038. 650-728-5389. E-mail: editor@epicurean-traveler.com. Website: www.epicurean-traveler.com. $28/yr. Circ.: 25,000. Scott Clemens, Publisher/Editor. **Description:** Quarterly print magazine and e-zine featuring articles on luxury travel with a special emphasis on food and wine. **Tips:** Editorial calendar is currently full, but will consider queries. All articles must have a connection to the local food/wine of a particular region or area. **Queries:** Required. **E-Queries:** Yes. **Response:** 6 weeks. **Freelance Content:** 75%. **Rights:** 1st electronic. **Payment:** On publication.

FAMILY MOTOR COACHING

8291 Clough Pike, Cincinnati, OH 45244-2796. 513-474-3622. E-mail: magazine@fmca.com. Website: www.fmca.com. Monthly. $3.99/$27. Circ.: 140,000. Robbin Gould, Editor. **Description:** Offers articles on motorhome travel for members of the Family Motor Coach Association and other RV enthusiasts. **Nonfiction:** Travel articles keyed to noteworthy sites, attractions, and events that are accessible by motorhome, as well as personality profiles of travelers who have interesting uses for their motorhomes. Also technical articles relating to motorhome maintenance, do-it-yourself projects, motorhome components and accessories; 1,200-2,000 words; pays $50-$500. **Art:** Articles with photos preferred. Prefers transparencies, but accepts color prints and 4x6 digital images with 300+ dpi. **Queries:** Preferred. **E-Queries:** Yes. **Unsolicited mss:** Accepts. **Response:** 4-12 weeks. **SASE Required:** Yes. **Rights:** FNASR and electronic. **Payment:** On acceptance.

HIGHWAYS

P.O. Box 8545, Ventura, CA 93002-8545. 805-667-4100. Website: www.goodsamclub.com/highways. 11x/yr. $20/yr. Circ.: 1,000,000. Dee Reed, Managing Editor. **Description:** Published for Good Sam Club, world's largest recreation vehicle owner's organization. Articles on outdoor recreation and RV industry news, travel destination and technical features; $300 and up. **Tips:** Does not accept unsolicited manuscripts via e-mail. "Study recent issues before sending queries. Conduct research to understand what the RV market is all about. We're different from most travel magazines, and we're certainly not an automotive publication. We fill a large niche in the travel industry." **Queries:** Required. **E-Queries:** Yes. **Unsolicited mss:** Do not accept. **Response:** 4-8 weeks. **SASE Required:** Yes. **Freelance Content:** 40%. **Rights:** FNAR and electronic. **Payment:** On acceptance.

HILL COUNTRY SUN

P.O. Box 1482, Wimberley, TX 78676. 512-847-5162.
E-mail: allan@hillcountrysun.com. Website: www.hillcountrysun.com. Monthly. Allan C. Kimball, Editor. **Description:** Tourist-oriented magazine covering the Central Texas Hill Country. **Nonfiction:** On interesting things to do, places to visit or interesting people who live in the Hill Country. Include logistical information (where, what, when, how to get there, etc.) and photos with all submissions. 500-700 words; $40-$50. **Tips:** Query first with 3-4 ideas. No first-person accounts, fiction, or poetry. **Queries:** Required. **Unsolicited mss:** Does not accept.

THE INTERNATIONAL RAILWAY TRAVELER

P.O. Box 3747, San Diego, CA 92163. 619-260-1332. E-mail: irteditor@aol.com. Website: www.irtsociety.com. Monthly. $69/U.S., $79/Canada. Circ.: 5,000. Gena Holle, Editor. **Description:** Train-travel stories from around the world. **Nonfiction:** Anything involving trains, from luxury to seat-of-the-pants trips. Hotels with a rail history, sightseeing by tram or metro. Articles must be factually sound, with ample logistical detail so readers can easily replicate the author's trip; 300-1,200 words; $.03/word. **Art:** B&W glossies, transparencies, color prints, or digital (300 dpi) stored in a compressed file format. Pays $10 inside stories, $20 for cover. **Tips:** "Your travel stories need not be written chronologically. Try building your story around a few key points or impressions from your trip. Read our publication. Our most valued writers know our readers well. They write with verve and wit, and yet are scrupulously accurate. Their love of and genuine interest in rail travel in all its forms shines through all of their stories." **Queries:** Preferred. **E-Queries:** Yes. **Unsolicited mss:** Accepts. **Response:** 2 months. **SASE Required:** Yes. **Freelance Content:** 80%. **Rights:** FNASR, electronic. **Payment:** Within 1 month of cover date.

INTERVAL WORLD

Interval International, Inc., 6262 Sunset Dr., Miami, FL 33143-4843.
E-mail: intervaleditors@interval-intl.com. Website: www.intervalworld.com. Quarterly. Circ.: 1,000,035. Amy Drew Thompson, Managing Editor. **Description:** For time-share vacationers. **Tips:** No phone calls or faxes.

ISLANDS

Islands MediaCorp, 6309 Carpinteria Ave., Carpinteria , CA 93013. 805-745-7100. E-mail: islands@islands.com. Website: www.islandsmag.com. 8x/yr. $24/yr. Circ.: 230,000. James Badham, Editor-in-Chief. **Description:** *"Islands* covers islands around the world in stories that get at the essence of the place covered. Photos and narratives take readers to warm popular islands like Bora-Bora and Hawaii, cold places like Aleutians and Iceland, and off-the-beaten-track islands everywhere." **Nonfiction:** Illuminate what makes a place tick through strong narrative-based writing. Profiles of unforgettable people; 850-3,500 words; $.50/word and up. **Columns, Departments:** Horizons (short, quirky island-related items); 50-250 words. **Tips:** Break in by writing for Horizons, Crossroads (essays), IslandWise (500-word quick-hit profiles of places). Does not assign major features to unfamiliar writers. Do not query by phone. **Queries:** Preferred. **E-Queries:** Yes. **Unsolicited mss:** Accepts. **Response:** 3 months. **SASE Required:** Yes. **Freelance Content:** 90%. **Rights:** All. **Payment:** On acceptance.

LONG WEEKENDS

Great Lakes Publishing Co., 1422 Euclid Ave., Cleveland, OH 44115. 216-771-2833. E-mail: editorial@ohiomagazine.com. Website: www.long-weekends.com. Semi-annual. Circ.: 200,000. Miriam Carey, Editor. **Description:** Travel magazine covering unusual destinations in 8 states: NY, PA, WV, OH, IN, KY, IL, MI. Looking for off-the-beaten-path destinations, privately-owned inns, and unusual B&Bs. **Tips:** "We look for good, solid queries backed up by three clips from regional publications. Avoid pitching anything 'mainstream.' Visit our website for guidelines and to search past articles." **Queries:** Required. **Unsolicited mss:** Does not accept. **Response:** 3 months. **Freelance Content:** 80%. **Rights:** FNAR. **Payment:** On publication.

MICHIGAN LIVING

See full listing in Regional & City Publications category.

MOTION SICKNESS

See full listing in Literary Fiction & Poetry category.

MOTORHOME

TL Enterprises, Inc., 2575 Vista Del Mar, Ventura, CA 93001. 805-667-4100. E-mail: bhampson@affinitygroup.com. Website: www.motorhomemagazine.com. Monthly. $26/yr. Circ.: 150,000. Bruce Hampson, Managing Editor. **Description:** Covers destinations for RV travelers. Also, activities, hobbies, how-tos, motorhome tests, RV product evaluations, technical theory features, legislative updates, special events, and profiles of celebrities who own motorhomes. Articles run 150-2,000 words; $100-$600. **Columns, Departments:** Crossroads—varied topics: unique motorhomes to great cafes, museums to festivals; with 1-2 good color transparencies; 150 words; $100. Quick Tips—do-it-yourself ideas for motorhomes, no photo, just a sketch if necessary; 150 words; $25-$100. **Art:** 35mm slides preferred. **Tips:** "Departments are easiest way to break in. Readers are active travelers; most retirees, but more baby boomers entering the RV lifestyle, so some articles directed to novices and families. No diaries or product tests." **Queries:** Preferred. **E-Queries:** Yes. **Unsolicited mss:** Accepts. **Response:** 3-4 weeks. **SASE Required:** Yes. **Freelance Content:** 65%. **Payment:** On acceptance.

NATIONAL GEOGRAPHIC ADVENTURE

National Geographic Society, 104 W 40th St., Fl. 19, New York, NY 10018. 212-790-9020. E-mail: adventure@ngs.org. Website: www.nationalgeographic.com/adventure. 10x/yr. $9.97/yr. Circ.: 450,000. Jim Meigs, Executive Editor. **Description:** Covers adventure destinations and trends (adventure travel, though doable, is designed to push the envelope a little more on the experience). Destinations are 65% domestic, the remainder international. Also covers gear and technology trends, popular adventurers, breaking news topics on adventure and outdoor issues, and lesser-known historical tales. **Nonfiction:** Features, 1,500-6,000 words. Some examples: diving near Australia's Ningaloo Reef; paddling on New England's Merrimack River, climbing Mt. Kilimanjaro, rafting the Gauley River, America's Top National Parks, fast weekend escapes. **Columns, Departments:** Adventure travel service, profiles, opinion, news, commentaries. **Tips:** "Writing that inspires travelers to go places and do things, while entertaining readers who don't travel." **Queries:** Required. **Unsolicited mss:** Does not accept. **Freelance Content:** 75%.

NATIONAL GEOGRAPHIC TRAVELER

National Geographic Society, 1145 17th St. NW, Washington, DC 20036. 202-857-7000. E-mail: traveler@nationalgeographic.com. Website: nationalgeographic.com/traveler. 8x/yr. $17.95/yr. Circ.: 738,900. Keith Bellows, Editor. **Description:** Most articles by assignment only; query first with 1-2-page proposal, resumé, and published clips required. **Nonfiction:** Articles 1,500-4,000 words; pays $1/word. **Payment:** On acceptance.

NATIONAL MOTORIST

National Automobile Club, 1151 Hillsdale Blvd., Foster City, CA 94404. 650-294-7000. E-mail: editor@nationalmotorist.com. Website: www.nationalmotorist.com. Quarterly. $2/yr (part of membership dues). Circ.: 38,000. Tom Inglesby, Editor. **Description:** Articles on motoring and travel in the U.S. and Internationally with emphasis on the West. Covers car care, news, California laws on motoring, history of the West and related information for California motorists. Illustrated articles, 600-1,200 words; pays $.20-$.40/word, extra for photos (digital images preferred). **Tips:** Prefers queries by e-mail. **Payment:** On acceptance.

NORTHWEST TRAVEL

4969 Highway 101, #2, Florence, OR 97439. 800-348-8401. E-mail: theresa@ohwy.com. Website: www.northwestmagazines.com. Bimonthly. Circ.: 50,000. Stefani Blair, Stefanie Griesi, Judy Fleagle, Editors. **Description:** Where to go and what to see in Oregon, Washington, Idaho, British Columbia, Western Montana, sometimes Alaska. Every article has a travel connection; each issue has detailed drive guide to one area. **Nonfiction:** First-person experience. Put details in sidebars; 500-1,500 words; $65-$350/feature. **Fillers:** Worth a Stop; $50. **Art:** Seeking terrific slides of wildlife, artsy or dramatic scenery shots. Also does 2 annual calendars. Send slides or transparencies; $25-$75 ($325 cover). **Tips:** "Submit written queries for action-oriented stories, not armchair travel brochures." **Queries:** Preferred. **Unsolicited mss:** Accepts. **Response:** 2-3 months. **SASE Required:** Yes. **Freelance Content:** 60%. **Rights:** FNAR. **Payment:** On publication.

RIDER
See full listing in Automotive category.

ROMANTIC DESTINATIONS
6254 Poplar Ave., Suite 200, Memphis, TN 38119-4723. 901-761-1505.
E-mail: info@southernbride.com. Website: www.southernbride.com. 2x/yr.
$4.95/issue. Circ.: 60,000. Sherra Meyers, Editor. **Description:** Romantic travel magazine focusing on places for romantic getaways, honeymoons, and wedding destinations. **Nonfiction:** Stories from brides and/or grooms sharing their experiences of wedding planning and honeymoon planning. 500-1,000 words; $.75/word or flat fee. **Columns, Departments:** 200-400 words, flat fee. **Queries:** Preferred. **Unsolicited mss:** Accepts. **Freelance Content:** 50%. **Payment:** On publication.

ROUTE 66 MAGAZINE
P.O. Box 66, Laughlin, NV 89028-9790. 702-299-0856.
E-mail: info@route66magazine.com. Website: www.route66magazine.com.
Quarterly. $16/yr. Circ.: 35,000. Paul Taylor, Publisher. **Description:** Features articles on travel and life along Route 66 between Chicago and Los Angeles. Articles run 1,500-2,000 words; pays $20/column. **Queries:** Preferred. **Payment:** On publication.

RV JOURNAL
P.O. Box 7675, Laguna Niguel, CA 92607. 949-489-7729.
E-mail: editor@rvjournal.com. Website: www.rvjournal.com. Quarterly. $12.50/yr.
Circ.: 140,000. Dina Todd, Editor. **Description:** Features travel and destination articles for RV travelers in NM, AZ, NV, UT, CA, OR, and WA. Pieces run 800-1,000 words. **Tips:** Submit query with bio and samples of previously published work. Priority is given to articles that accompany high-quality, color photographs. **Queries:** Required. **Unsolicited mss:** Accepts. **Rights:** FNAR.

SOUTH AMERICAN EXPLORERS
South American Explorers Club, 126 Indian Creek Rd., Ithaca, NY 14850-1310.
607-277-0488. E-mail: don@saexplorers.org. Website: www.saexplorers.org.
Quarterly. $22/yr. Circ.: 8,600. Don Montague, Editor. **Description:** Feature articles on scientific studies, travel, historical personalities, archaeology, exploration, social sciences, peoples and culture, etc. **Nonfiction:** Length varies from 1,200-10,000 words; $50-$250. **Art:** Photos, sketches, maps. **Tips:** Write or e-mail for guidelines and sample issue. **Queries:** Preferred. **E-Queries:** Yes. **Unsolicited mss:** Accepts.

SPECIALTY TRAVEL INDEX

305 San Anselmo Ave., #309, San Anselmo, CA 94960. 800-442-4922.
E-mail: info@specialtytravel.com. Website: www.specialtytravel.com. Biannual.
$6/issue. Circ.: 35,000. **Description:** Travel directory listing 350 worldwide opera-
tors. Also provides travel articles for consumers and travel agents. **Nonfiction:**
Stories on special interest, adventure-type travel, from soft adventures (e.g., cycling
through French wine country) to daring exploits (an exploratory river-rafting run in
Pakistan). Varied styles okay (first-person, descriptive); in general, not written in the
present tense, but with a lively immediacy; 1,250 words; $300. **Tips:** Always seeking
off-the-beaten-path perspectives. Query with published clips. **Queries:** Preferred.
E-Queries: Yes. **Unsolicited mss:** Accepts. **Response:** 3-6 months. **SASE
Required:** Yes. **Freelance Content:** 80%. **Payment:** On acceptance. **Contact:**
Risa Weinreb, Editor.

TRAILER LIFE

See full listing in Lifestyle Magazines category.

TRANSITIONS ABROAD

P.O. Box 745, Bennington, VT 05201.
E-mail: editor@transitionsabroad.com. Website: www.transitionsabroad.com.
Bimonthly. $4.95/$28. Circ.: 25,000. Sherry Schwarz, Editor. **Description:** For overseas travelers of all ages who seek information on enriching, in-depth experiences of
different cultures. Includes features with practical focus on work, study, travel, and
living abroad. **Nonfiction:** Practical how-to travel articles; 800-1,000 words; $2/col-
umn inch. **Columns, Departments:** Info exchange letters (200-300 words, free subscription); Itineraries (up to 500 words, $25-$50). **Tips:** Eager for new writers with
information not usually found in guidebooks. Also seeking special expertise on cultural travel opportunities for specific groups: seniors, students, families, etc. No journal writing; no U.S. travel. Send all material electronically. **Queries:** Not necessary.
E-Queries: Yes. **Unsolicited mss:** Accepts. **SASE Required:** Yes. **Freelance
Content:** 65%. **Rights:** FNAR. **Payment:** On publication.

TRAVEL AMERICA

Century Publishing Co., 990 Grove St., Evanston, IL 60201-4370. 847-491-6440.
E-mail: rmink@centurysports.net. Website: www.travelamerica.com. Bimonthly.
$5.99/$29.95. Circ.: 241,000. Randy Mink, Editor. **Description:** Consumer travel
magazine, exclusively U.S. destinations. **Nonfiction:** General destination stories;
1,000 words; $300. **Columns, Departments:** If You Only Have a Day (in any city);
500-600 words; $150-$175. **Art:** Slides, usually with text package; individual photos
$25-$35. **Tips:** Submit short 1-page stories on narrow topics. Sample copy $5 with
SASE. **Queries:** Not necessary. **E-Queries:** No. **Unsolicited mss:** Accepts.
Response: 2-6 weeks. **SASE Required:** Yes. **Freelance Content:** 80%. **Rights:**
FNAR. **Payment:** On publication.

TRAVEL + LEISURE

American Express Publishing Corp., 1120 Avenue of the Americas, New York, NY 10036-6700. 212-382-5600. E-mail: tlquery@amexpub.com. Website: www.travelandleisure.com. Monthly. $43/yr. Circ.: 1,000,000. Nancy Novogrod, Editor-in-Chief. **Description:** Provides practical advice for leisure travelers and information on international travel destinations, luxury lodgings, nightlife, art, architecture, and travel-related fashion and products. Articles run 1,000-4,000 words; $1,000-$5,000. **Tips:** Limited market. Departments are the best chance for new writers. Writers should have same sophistication and travel experience as our readers. **Queries:** Required. **E-Queries:** Yes. **Unsolicited mss:** Does not accept. **Response:** 2-4 weeks. **SASE Required:** Yes. **Freelance Content:** 95%. **Rights:** 1st. **Payment:** On acceptance.

TRAVEL SMART

P.O. Box 397, Dobbs Ferry, NY 10522. 800-327-3633. E-mail: travel.now@aol.com. Website: www.travelsmartnewsletter.com. Nancy Dunnan, Publisher/Editor. **Description:** Newsletter featuring interesting, unusual, or economical destinations. Offers useful travel-related tips and practical consumer information for vacation or business travel. Prefers short pieces, 250-1,000 words; $50-$150. **Tips:** Give specific details on hotels, restaurants, transportation, e.g.costs, telephone numbers and websites. Query for longer pieces. **Payment:** On publication.

WEEKEND ADVENTURES

Away Media, LLC, P.O. Box 1895, Cumberland, MD 21501-1895. 301-722-3533. E-mail: info@wamonline.com. Website: www.wamonline.com. Quarterly. Steven B. Leyh, Publisher. **Description:** Travel publication focusing on vacation destinations in Western Maryland, the Potomac Highlands of West Virginia, and the Laurel Highlands of Pennsylvania. Pays $50 for features of 1,000+ words. **Tips:** "Articles include outdoor adventures, historical places, dining out, getaways, day trips, equipment, attractions, etc. We try to help our readers understand the outdoors better, to help our readers relax, and live better, and to make our mountain communities a better place to live." **E-Queries:** Yes. **Rights:** FNASR, electronic. **Payment:** On publication.

WESTWAYS

Automobile Club of Southern California, P.O. Box 25222, Santa Ana, CA 92799-5222. 714-885-2376. E-mail: westways@aaa-calif.com. Website: www.aaa-calif.com. Bimonthly. Circ.: 3,328,000. John Lehrer, Editor-in-Chief. **Description:** Travel articles, on southern California, the West, greater U.S., and foreign destinations; 1,000-2,500 words; pays $1/word. **Queries:** Preferred. **Payment:** On acceptance.

WEDDING

BRIDAL GUIDE
RFP, LLC, 3 E 54th St., Fl. 15, New York, NY 10022. 212-838-7733.
Website: www.bridalguide.com. Bimonthly. $18.95/yr. Circ.: 250,000. Diane Forden, Editor-in-Chief. **Description:** Covers wedding topics including wedding fashions, home design, travel, marriage/relationship issues, etc. Accepts queries for articles on marriage/relationships/sexuality, wedding planning, budgeting and travel; 1,000-2,000 words; pays $.50/word.

BRIDE & GROOM
415 Boston Turnpike, Suite 104, Shrewsbury, MA 01545.
E-mail: bgeditor@townisp.com. Website: www.originalweddingexpo.com. 3x/yr.
Circ.: 50,000. Lisa Dayne, Editor. **Description:** Provides comprehensive planning information to Central Massachusetts' engaged couples. **Nonfiction:** Articles that focus on the various aspects of wedding planning; 500-1,000 words; $100-$200. **Queries:** Preferred. **E-queries:** Yes. **Unsolicited mss:** Accepts. **Response:** 2-4 weeks. **SASE Required:** Yes. **Freelance Content:** 50%. **Rights:** First and reprint. **Payment:** On publication.

BRIDE'S
Condé Nast Publications, Inc., 4 Times Sq., New York, NY 10036. 212-286-7528.
E-mail: letters@brides.com. Website: www.brides.com. Bimonthly. $18/yr. Circ.: 450,000. Millie Martini Bratten, Editor-in-Chief. **Description:** For engaged couples or newlyweds on wedding planning, relationships, communication, sex, finances, religion, and in-laws; 800-3,000 words; $1+/word. **Queries:** Preferred. **Unsolicited mss:** Accepts. **Payment:** On acceptance. **Contact:** Nancy Mattia, Senior Editor.

MODERN BRIDE
Condé Nast Publications, Inc., 4 Times Sq., New York, NY 10036. 212-286-2860.
E-mail: readermail@modernbride.com. Website: www.modernbride.com. Bimonthly. $11.97/yr. Circ.: 406,000. Antonia Van der Meer, Editor-in-Chief. **Description:** For bride and groom, on wedding planning, financial planning, juggling career and home, etc. Articles run 1,500-2,000 words; $600-$1,200. Also, short humorous pieces for brides, 500-1,000 words. **Payment:** On acceptance.

SOUTHERN BRIDE
6254 Poplar Ave., Suite 200, Memphis, TN 38119-4723. 901-761-1505.
E-mail: info@southernbride.com. Website: www.southernbride.com. $4.95/issue. Circ.: 140,000. Sherra Meyers, Editor. **Description:** Bridal publication primarily circulated throughout the Southeast that shows the trends and traditions of the South. Stories from brides and/or grooms sharing their experience of wedding nuptials and honeymoon planning; 500-1,000 words; $.75/word or flat fee. **Queries:** Preferred. **Unsolicited mss:** Accepts. **Freelance Content:** 50%. **Rights:** FNAR. **Payment:** On publication.

WEDDINGBELLS

34 King St. E, Suite 1200, Toronto, Ontario M5C 2X8 Canada. 416-363-1574.
E-mail: editorialdept@weddingbells.com. Website: www.weddingbells.com.
Semiannual. Circ.: 350,000. Crys Stewart, Editor. **Description:** U.S. publication
offering pre- and post-wedding lifestyle and service journalism to bridal couples.
Nonfiction pieces by assignment only. **Tips:** Send resumé and copies of published
work. **Queries:** Not necessary. **Unsolicited mss:** Does not accept. **Contact:**
Michael Killingsworth, Managing Editor.

WOMEN'S

BBW: BIG BEAUTIFUL WOMAN

Aeon Publishing Group, P.O. Box 1297, Elk Grove, CA 95759. 916-684-7904.
Website: www.bbwmagazine.com. Bimonthly. $14.95/yr. Circ.: 100,000. Sally E.
Smith, Editor-in-Chief. **Description:** Magazine for women ages 25-45, especially
those that are plus-size. Includes interviews with successful women who are plus-size.
Queries: Preferred. **Payment:** On publication.

BUSINESSWOMAN MAGAZINE

See full listing in Business category.

CHATELAINE

Rogers Media, Inc., One Mount Pleasant Rd., Toronto, Ontario M4Y 2Y5 Canada.
416-764-1888. E-mail: editors@chatelaine.com. Website: www.chatelaine.com.
Monthly. $3.50/issue (Canadian). Circ.: 700,000. Rona Maynard, Editor.
Description: On health, fitness, women transforming their lives, practical, fresh
advice on everyday challenges and opportunites faced by readers; 500-2,500 words;
$500 and up. Health is the only topic currently open to freelancers. **Tips:** "Our mag-
azine empowers Canada's busiest women to create the lives they want. It speaks to
the strength of the inner woman—her passion, purpose, and sense of possibility."
Queries: Required. **E-Queries:** No. **Unsolicited mss:** Accepts. **Response:** 6
weeks. **SASE Required:** Yes. **Freelance Content:** 75%. **Rights:** FNAR.
Payment: On acceptance.

COMPLETE WOMAN

Associated Publications, Inc., 875 N Michigan Ave., Suite 3434, Chicago, IL 60611.
312-266-8680. Bimonthly. $3.99/issue. Circ.: 500,000. Bonnie L. Krueger, Editor.
Description: Practical advice for women on love, sex, careers, health, and personal
relationships. **Nonfiction:** Articles (include how-to sidebars) with practical advice for
women; 1,000-2,000 words. **Tips:** Query with clips. **Queries:** Required. **E-Queries:**
No. **Unsolicited mss:** Accepts. **Response:** 90 days. **Freelance Content:** 90%.
Rights: One-time, all rights. **Payment:** On acceptance. **Contact:** Lora Wintz,
Executive Editor.

COSMOPOLITAN

The Hearst Corp., 224 W 57th St., New York, NY 10018. 212-649-3570. Website: www.cosmopolitan.com. Monthly. $24.97/yr. Circ.: 3,021,720. Kate White, Editor-in-Chief. **Description:** On issues affecting young career women, with emphasis on beauty, health, fitness, career, relationships, and personal life.

COUNTRY WOMAN

See full listing in Agriculture & Rural Life category.

ELLE CANADA

Transcontinental Media, Inc., 25 Sheppard Ave. W, Suite 100, Toronto, Ontario M2N 6S7 Canada. 416-227-8212. E-mail: rsilvan@ellecanada.com. Website: www.elle-canada.com. Monthly. $19.95/yr. Circ.: 100,000. Rita Silvan, Editor-in-Chief. **Description:** Women's magazine featuring fashion, beauty, and trends. Seeks articles on hard-to-get items, unique stories, and interviews with celebrities or designers; 500-1,500 words; pay varies. **Tips:** "A good idea is always considered even from a first-time writer. Make sure there's a point and tell us why our readers would take an interest in your topic. Make sure you convey what they can get out of the story for themselves." **Queries:** Preferred. **E-Queries:** Yes. **Unsolicited mss:** Accepts. **Response:** 1-2 months. **SASE Required:** Yes. **Freelance Content:** 80%. **Rights:** Exclusive. **Payment:** On acceptance.

ESSENCE MAGAZINE

Essence Communications, Inc., 1500 Broadway, Fl. 6, New York, NY 10036. 212-642-0600. E-mail: info@essence.com. Website: www.essence.com. Monthly. $20/yr. Circ.: 1,061,700. Diane Weathers, Editor-in-Chief. **Description:** National magazine for African-American women. Features provocative articles on personal development, relationships, wealth building, work-related issues, parenting, health, political and social issues, travel, art, etc. Also, cover stories on African-American celebrities. Features run 1,200+ words, departments run 400+ words and up. Pay varies ($1/word minimum). **Queries:** Required.

EXECUTIVE WOMAN

Powerhouse Communications Group, 6025 Flewellyn Rd., Suite 125, Ottawa, Ontario K2S 1B6 Canada. 613-831-0980. E-mail: editorial@sympatico.ca. Website: www.executivewoman.com. Monthly. $89/yr. Circ.: 300,000. Patricia den Boer, Editor-in-Chief. **Description:** Written for the professional career woman. Covers business, career, health/nutrition, finance, and wellness topics. Focuses on ways to manage role overload, family issues, management challenges, and personal life. Also profiles leading female executives, managers, and business owners in Canada/U.S.

FAMILY CIRCLE

Gruner + Jahr USA Publishing, 375 Lexington Ave., New York, NY 10017-5514. 212-499-2000. E-mail: fcfeedback@gjusa.com. Website: www.familycircle.com. 15x/yr. $2.50/issue. Circ.: 4,500,000. Susan Ungaro, Editor-in-Chief. **Description:**

Covers women who have made a difference. Also marriage, family, childcare/elder-care issues, consumer affairs, psychology, and humor. **Nonfiction:** Useful articles for all phases of a woman's life; true life, dramatic narratives; 1,000-2,000 words; $1/word. **Fillers:** Humor about family life; 750 words. **Columns, Departments:** Full Circle (current issues affecting families); 750 words. **Tips:** Often uses new writers in "Women Who Make A Difference" column. **Queries:** Required. **E-Queries:** No. **Unsolicited mss:** Accepts. **Response:** 4 weeks. **SASE Required:** No. **Freelance Content:** 80%. **Rights:** One-time, electronic. **Payment:** On acceptance.

FIRST FOR WOMEN

Bauer Publishing Co., 270 Sylvan Ave., Englewood Cliffs, NJ 07632-2521. 201-569-6699. E-mail: editor@firstforwomen.com. 17x/yr. $34/yr. Circ.: 1,542,000. Carol Brooks, Editor-in-Chief. **Description:** Reflects concerns of contemporary women; 1,500-2,500 words; pay varies. **Queries:** Preferred. **E-Queries:** Yes. **Response:** 2 months. **Payment:** On acceptance.

GLAMOUR

Condé Nast Publications, Inc., 4 Times Square, New York, NY 10036. 212-286-2860. E-mail: letters@glamour.com. Website: www.glamour.com. Monthly. $18/yr. Circ.: 2,300,000. Cynthia Leive, Editor-in-Chief. **Description:** On careers, health, psychology, politics, current events, interpersonal relationships, for women ages 18-35; from 1,000 words; pays from $500. **Tips:** Fashion, entertainment, travel, food, and beauty pieces are staff-written. **Queries:** Required. **Payment:** On acceptance.

GOLF FOR WOMEN

See full listing in Sports & Recreation/Outdoors category.

GOOD HOUSEKEEPING

The Hearst Corp., 250 W 55th St., New York, NY 10019-5288. 212-649-2200. E-mail: ghkletters@hearst.com. Website: www.goodhousekeeping.com. Monthly. $21.97/yr. Circ.: 4,690,500. Ellen Levine, Editor-in-Chief. **Description:** Expert advice on marriage/family, finances, health, etc. **Columns, Departments:** Better Way (consumer pieces), 300-500 words. Profiles (on people involved in inspiring, heroic, fascinating pursuits), 400-600 words. My Story (first-person or as-told-to, in which a woman (using her real name) tells how she overcame a difficult problem. **Queries:** Required. **E-Queries:** No. **Response:** 2-3 months. **SASE Required:** Yes.

HARPER'S BAZAAR

The Hearst Corp., 1700 Broadway, Fl. 37, New York, NY 10019-5905. 212-903-5000. E-mail: editors@harpersbazaar.com. Website: www.harpersbazaar.com. Monthly. $19.97/yr. Circ.: 742,000. Glenda Bailey, Editor-in-Chief. **Description:** For active, sophisticated women. Articles on the arts, world affairs, travel, families, education, careers, health, sexuality; 1,500-2,500 words; pay varies. **Tips:** Send query with proposal of 1-2 paragraphs; include clips. **Queries:** Required. **Unsolicited mss:** Does not accept. **SASE Required:** Yes. **Payment:** On acceptance.

LADIES' HOME JOURNAL

Meredith Corp., 125 Park Ave., Fl. 20, New York, NY 10017-5516. 212-557-6600.
E-mail: lhj@mdp.com. Website: www.lhj.com. Monthly. $15.97/yr. Circ.: 4,101,400.
Diane Salvator, Editor-in-Chief. **Description:** Information on topics of interest to
today's woman. Most readers are in their 30s, married, and working at least part-time.
Fiction: Accepts short fiction pieces through agents only. **Nonfiction:** Articles on
health, psychology, human-interest stories, etc.; 1,000-3,000 words; pay varies.
Columns, Departments: Parenting, health, and first-person drama; 150-1,500
words. **Tips:** "We seek human-interest pieces, shorter items, and new twists on established themes." **Queries:** Preferred. **E-Queries:** No. **Unsolicited mss:** Accepts.
Response: 4-8 weeks. **SASE Required:** Yes. **Freelance Content:** 70%. **Rights:**
All. **Payment:** On acceptance.

LATINA MAGAZINE

Latina Media Ventures, 1500 Broadway, New York, NY 10036-4015. 212-642-0200.
E-mail: editor@latina.com. Website: www.latina.com. 11x/yr. $20/yr. Circ.: 250,000.
Sylvia Martinez, Editor-in-Chief. **Description:** Bilingual lifestyle magazine for
Hispanic women in the U.S. Features articles on Latina fashion, beauty, culture, and
food. Also runs celebrity profiles and interviews.

LATINA STYLE

1730 Rhode Island Ave. NW, Suite 1207, Washington, DC 20036-3109. 202-955-
7930. E-mail: editor@latinastyle.com. Website: www.latinastyle.com. 6x/yr. Circ.:
150,000. Robert Bard, Publisher. **Description:** For the contemporary Latina
woman, showcases Latina achievements in business, science, civic affairs, education,
entertainment, sports, arts and culture. Also, covers career opportunities, finance,
technology, travel, beauty/fashion, food, health/fitness, and book and film reviews.
Pieces run 300-2,000 words; pay varies. **Queries:** Preferred. **E-Queries:** Yes.
Unsolicited mss: Accepts. **Response:** 2 months, SASE optional. **Freelance
Content:** 20%. **Rights:** FNAR. **Payment:** 30 days post-publication.

LILITH

Lilith Publications, Inc., 250 W 57th St., Suite 2432, New York, NY 10107-2420.
212-757-0818. E-mail: lilithmag@aol.com. Website: www.lilithmag.com. Quarterly.
$21/yr. Circ.: 25,000. Susan Weidman Schneider, Editor-in-Chief. **Description:**
Showcases Jewish women writers, educators, and artists; illuminates Jewish women's
lives in their religious, ethnic, sexual, and social-class diversity. **Fiction:** On the lives
of Jewish women; 1,000-2,000 words. **Nonfiction:** Autobiographies, interviews,
social analysis, sociological research, oral history, new rituals, reviews, investigative
reporting, opinion pieces. Also news briefs (500 words) and lists of resources, projects, events. 1,000-2,000 words. **Tips:** Welcomes new writers. **Queries:** Not necessary. **E-Queries:** Yes. **Unsolicited mss:** Accepts. **Response:** 12-16 weeks. **SASE
Required:** Yes. **Rights:** FNAR and electronic. **Payment:** On publication.

MAMM MAGAZINE
See full listing in Health category.

MORE
Meredith Corp., 125 Park Ave., New York, NY 10017. 212-455-1190.
E-mail: more@mdp.com. Website: www.moremag.com. 10x/yr. Circ.: 850,000. Susan
Crandell, Editor. **Description:** Sophisticated and upscale editorial for women of the
baby-boomer generation. Features essay, interviews, etc.; little service/how-to pieces.
Queries: Preferred. **E-Queries:** Yes. **Unsolicited mss:** Accepts. **Response:** 3
months. **SASE Required:** Yes. **Rights:** All. **Payment:** On acceptance.

MOTHERING
P.O. Box 1690, Santa Fe, NM 87504-1690. 505-984-8116.
E-mail: info@mothering.com. Website: www.mothering.com. Bimonthly. $18.95/yr.
Circ.: 70,000. Melissa Chianta, Managing Editor. **Description:** On natural family liv-
ing, covering topics such as pregnancy, birthing, parenting, etc. Articles to 2,000
words; pays $200-$500. **Queries:** Preferred. **Payment:** On publication.

MS. MAGAZINE
Feminist Majority Foundation, 433 S Beverly Dr., Beverly Hills, CA 90212-4401.
310-556-2515. E-mail: info@msmagazine.com. Website: www.msmagazine.com.
Quarterly. $25/yr. Circ.: 110,000. Elaine Lafferty, Editor-in-Chief. **Description:** On
feminism, women's roles, and social change. Nonfiction articles and essays on national
and international news reporting, profiles, theory, and analysis. Also accepts short fiction and poetry. **Tips:** Query with resumé, published clips, and SASE. **Queries:**
Required. **Response:** 12 weeks. **Contact:** Manuscripts Editor.

NA'AMAT WOMAN
350 Fifth Ave., Suite 4700, New York, NY 10118. 212-563-5222.
E-mail: judith@naamat.org. Website: www.naamat.org. Quarterly. $25 members, $10
non-members. Circ.: 20,000. Judith A. Sokoloff, Editor. **Description:** For Jewish
communities, covering varied topics: aspects of life in Israel, Jewish women's issues,
social issues, Jewish art and literature. **Fiction:** 2,000-3,000 words; $.10/word.
Nonfiction: 2,000-3,000 words; $.10-$.12/word. **Columns, Departments:** Book
reviews (ca. 800 words); Personal essays (ca. 1,200-1,500 words); $.10/word. **Art:**
B&W (hard copy or electronic); $25-$100. **Tips:** "Avoid trite Jewish humor, maudlin
fiction, and war stories." **Queries:** Preferred. **Unsolicited mss:** Accepts. **Response:**
1-3 months. **SASE Required:** Yes. **Freelance Content:** 75%. **Rights:** FNAR.
Payment: On publication.

PLAYGIRL
801 Second Ave., Fl. 9, New York, NY 10017. 212-661-7878. Monthly. $4.99. Circ.:
350,000. Michele Zipp, Editor-in-Chief. **Description:** Women's magazine focusing
on sex, relationships, and women's health. **Fiction:** Erotic first-person fiction. Female
perspective for Fantasy Forum section; 800-1,200 words. **Nonfiction:** Articles, 750-

3,000 words, on women's issues, sexuality, relationships, and celebrities, for women ages 18 and up. **Fillers:** Quizzes. **Tips:** "Easiest way to break in is to write for Fantasy Forum." **Queries:** Preferred. **E-Queries:** No. **Unsolicited mss:** Accepts. **Response:** 2-3 months. **Freelance Content:** 20%. **Payment:** On publication.

PRIMAVERA

Box 37-7547, Chicago, IL 60637. Annual. $10. Circ.: 1,000. **Description:** Original fiction (to 25 pages) and poetry that reflects the experience of women of different ages, races, sexual orientations, social classes. **Tips:** Encourages new writers. Does not accept material that is confessional, formulaic, or scholarly. **Queries:** Not necessary. **E-Queries:** No. **Unsolicited mss:** Accepts. **Response:** Queries 2 weeks, submissions 1-6 months. **SASE Required:** Yes. **Freelance Content:** 100%. **Rights:** FNAR. **Payment:** In copies.

REDBOOK

The Hearst Corp., 224 W 57th St., Fl. 6, New York, NY 10019-3212. 212-649-3450. E-mail: redbook@hearst.com. Website: www.redbookmag.com. Monthly. $15.97/yr. Circ.: 2,269,000. Ellen Kunes, Editor-in-Chief. **Description:** On subjects related to relationships, marriage, sex, current social issues, crime, human interest, health, psychology, and parenting. **Fiction:** Fresh, distinctive short stories, of interest to women. No unsolicited poetry, novellas, or novels; query first. Pays from $1,500 for short stories (to 25 pages). **Nonfiction:** Articles, 1,000-2,500 words; dramatic inspirational narratives, 1,000-2,000 words; pay varies. **Tips:** Send published clips, writing samples. **Queries:** Preferred. **Response:** 12 weeks. **SASE Required:** Yes. **Payment:** On acceptance.

ROOM OF ONE'S OWN

See full listing in Literary Fiction & Poetry category.

SAGEWOMAN

See full listing in New Age/Spiritual category.

SELF

Condé Nast Publications, Inc., 4 Times Square, New York, NY 10036-6522. 212-286-2860. E-mail: comments@self.com. Website: www.self.com. Monthly. $16/yr. Circ.: 1,332,800. Lucy Danziger, Editor-in-Chief. **Description:** Covers all aspects of healthy lifestyle, with latest information on health, fitness, nutrition, mental wellness, beauty and style. **Tips:** Pitch stories with a news hook. Send queries via regular mail. **Queries:** Preferred. **E-Queries:** No. **Unsolicited mss:** Accepts. **Response:** 1 month. **SASE Required:** Yes. **Freelance Content:** 75%. **Rights:** FNAR. **Payment:** On acceptance. **Contact:** Dana Points, Executive Editor.

SNAP

Perigraph Ltd., Box 130-2137 33rd Ave. SW, Calgary, Alberta T2T 1Z7 Canada. 403-243-1769. E-mail: editorial@snapmagazine.com. Website: www.snapmagazine.com.

Quarterly. Circ.: 30,000. Carolyn Fleming, Editor-in-Chief. **Description:** For professional women, covers new business developments, technology, and developments in design and culture. Also, profiles of people making an impact in these areas, and articles on music, books, and art. **Tips:** "We write about what is really new, so the stories we want are those that cover what no one else has covered yet. If you are a writer who can spot what is hot now, you might have a story for us. Please send brief, concise story ideas describing your intended focus, and whom you intend to interview. Back up your ideas with facts and figures and give us some information on your writing experience." **Queries:** Required. **E-Queries:** Yes. **Unsolicited mss:** Does not accept. **Response:** 4 weeks. **Rights:** FNAR.

SO TO SPEAK
See full listing in Literary Fiction & Poetry category.

TODAY'S CHRISTIAN WOMAN
Christianity Today International, 465 Gundersen Dr., Carol Stream, IL 60188. 630-260-6200. E-mail: tcwedit@christianitytoday.com. Website: www.todayschristianwoman.com. Bimonthly. $5/issue. Circ.: 250,000. Jane Johnson Struck, Editor. **Description:** For women, ages 20-40, on contemporary issues and hot topics that impact their lives. Provides depth, balance, and Biblical perspective to women's daily relationships. **Nonfiction:** Articles to help women grow in their relationship to God, and to provide practical help on family/parenting, friendship, marriage, health, single life, finances, and work; 1,000-1,800 words. **Tips:** Does not accept poetry, fiction, or Bible studies. Looking for humor, issues/hot topics, and "My Story" articles. **Queries:** Required. **E-Queries:** Yes. **Unsolicited mss:** Does not accept. **Response:** 8 weeks. **SASE Required:** Yes. **Rights:** FNAR. **Payment:** On acceptance. **Contact:** Holly Robaina, Assistant Editor.

VOGUE
Condé Nast Publications, Inc., 4 Times Square, New York, NY 10036-6518. 212-286-2860. E-mail: voguemail@aol.com. Website: www.vogue.com. Monthly. $28/yr. Circ.: 1,257,700. Anna Wintour, Editor-in-Chief. **Description:** General features for the contemporary woman. Articles, to 1,500 words, on fashion, beauty, arts/entertainment, travel, medicine, and health. **Queries:** Preferred. **Contact:** Laurie Jones, Managing Editor.

WISCONSIN WOMAN
Plus Publications, P.O. Box 230, Hartland, WI 53029-0230. 262-367-5303. E-mail: 50plus@pitnet.net. Monthly. $14.95/yr. Circ.: 30,000. Michele Hein, Editor-in-Chief. **Description:** Publication featuring news about women in the four county Metro Milwaukee area.

WOMAN'S OWN
Harris Publications, Inc., 1115 Broadway, Fl. 8, New York, NY 10010-2803. 212-807-7100. E-mail: info@womansown.com. Website: www.womansown.com. Bimonthly.

$11.97/yr. Circ.: 253,000. Lynn Varacalli, Editor-in-Chief. **Description:** Inspirational, practical advice on relationships, career, and lifestyle choices for women ages 25-35. Topics: staying together, second marriages, working women, asserting yourself, meeting new men, sex, etc. **Queries:** Preferred. **Payment:** On acceptance.

WOMAN'S TOUCH

1445 Boonville, Springfield, MO 65802-1894. E-mail: womanstouch@ag.org. Website: www.womanstouch.ag.org. 6x/yr. $9.95/issue. Circ.: 12,000. Darla Knoth, Managing Editor. **Description:** Inspirational ministry magazine for Christian women. **Nonfiction:** About triumph in times of trouble, celebrity interviews with women leaders, cooking, reaching the unchurched, testimonies, unique activities for women's groups or mature singles; 800 words; $20-$40. **Tips:** Seeking articles with fresh themes. Publishes some book excerpts. **Queries:** Required. **E-Queries:** Yes. **Unsolicited mss:** Does not accept. **Response:** 12 weeks. **Freelance Content:** 20%. **Rights:** One-time. **Payment:** On publication.

WOMAN'S WORLD

Bauer Publishing Co., 270 Sylvan Ave., Englewood Cliffs, NJ 07632-2521. 201-569-6699. Weekly. $59.80/yr. Circ.: 1,612,000. Stephanie Saible, Editor-in-Chief. **Description:** For middle-income women, ages 18-60. **Fiction:** Fast-moving short stories (1,400 words) with light romantic theme. Prefers dialogue-driven to propel the story. Also, mini-mysteries (1,000 words) with "whodunit" or "howdunit" theme. No science fiction, fantasy, horror, ghost stories, or gratuitous violence. Pays $1,000 for romantic short stories; $500 for mini-mysteries. **Nonfiction:** Love, romance, careers, medicine, health, psychology, family life, travel, etc. Also, dramatic stories of adventure or crisis and investigative reports. 1,000-1,300 words; $250-$900. **Tips:** Queries required for nonfiction pieces. **Payment:** On acceptance.

WOMEN IN BUSINESS

See full listing in Business category.

WOMEN TODAY

Box 300, Stn. A, Vancouver, British Columbia V6C 2X3 Canada. 604-514-2000, ext. 252. E-mail: editor@womentodaymagazine.com. Website: www.womentoday-magazine.com. Monthly. Claire Colvin, Editor. **Description:** E-zine for women on health, relationships, career, self-esteem, family, fashion, cooking. Features journalistic, nonfiction articles for a global audience. **Tips:** Submit e-query with brief synopsis, length, and contact information. **Queries:** Required. **E-Queries:** Yes. **Response:** 6-8 weeks. **Rights:** One-time.

WORKING MOTHER

Working Mother Media, 260 Madison Ave., Fl. 3, New York, NY 10016-2401. 212-351-6400. E-mail: editors@workingmother.com. Website: www.working-mother.com. Monthly. $9.97/yr. Circ.: 944,700. Jill Kirshenbaum, Editor-in-Chief. **Description:** Helps working women balance their professional life, family life, and inner life. Offers solutions to the stress that comes with juggling both family and career. Articles run 700-1,500 words. **Tips:** Send queries first. Enclose clips of previously published work. "It's best to be familiar with the tone and content of our publication before querying." **Queries:** Required. **E-Queries:** No. **Response:** 3 months. **Rights:** All. **Contact:** Christine L. Ford, Managing Editor.

WRITING & PUBLISHING

AMERICAN JOURNALISM REVIEW

University of Maryland, 1117 Journalism Bldg., Suite 2116, College Park, MD 20742-7111. 301-405-8803. E-mail: editor@ajr.umd.edu. Website: www.ajr.org. Bimonthly. $24. Circ.: 25,000. Rem Rieder, Editor. **Description:** Covers print, broadcast, and online journalism. Articles, 500-5,000 words, on trends, ethics, and coverage that falls short. Pay varies. **Queries:** Required. **E-Queries:** Yes. **Unsolicited mss:** Accepts. **Freelance Content:** 70%. **Rights:** Print and electronic. **Payment:** On publication.

AUTHORSHIP

National Writers Assn., 3140 S Peoria St., #295, Aurora, CO 80014-3178. 303-841-0246. E-mail: authorship@nationalwriters.com. Website: www.nationalwriters.com. Quarterly. $2.95/$20. Circ.: 6,200. **Description:** For writers at all levels and all areas of interest. **Nonfiction:** How-to articles for writers; 800-1,200 words; $10. **Poetry:** Accept poems that focus on writing and the writing process; to 40 lines; $10. **Fillers:** On writing and writers; 2-4 lines; $10 for bundles of 5. **Tips:** "Do not submit 'How I Became a Success' stories. We seek short (1,000 words) author interviews, humor, and well-written how-to pieces. Sidebars with story are appreciated." **Queries:** Preferred. **E-Queries:** Yes. **Unsolicited mss:** Accepts. **Response:** Queries 2-4 weeks, submissions 2-4 months. **SASE Required:** Yes. **Freelance Content:** 75%. **Rights:** FNAR. **Payment:** On publication. **Contact:** Sandy Whelchel.

BLOOMSBURY REVIEW

Owaissa Communications Co., Inc., 1553 Platte St., Suite 206, Denver, CO 80202. 303-455-3123. E-mail: bloomsb@aol.com. Bimonthly. $3/issue. Circ.: 50,000. Marilyn Auer, Editor. **Description:** Book reviews, literary features, interviews, and essays; 600 words or more; $10-$40. Also, poetry, $5/poem. **Queries:** Preferred. **E-Queries:** Yes. **Unsolicited mss:** Accepts. **Response:** 2 months. **SASE Required:** Yes. **Freelance Content:** 25%. **Rights:** FNAR. **Payment:** On publication.

BOOK LINKS

See full listing in Education category.

BOOK/MARK QUARTERLY REVIEW

P.O. Box 516, Miller Place, NY 11764. 631-331-4118. E-mail: cyberpoet@msn.com. Quarterly. $3.50/$12. Circ.: 850. Mindy Kronenberg, Editor-in-Chief. **Description:** Publishes reviews of books and magazines by small presses and non-corporate publishing entities. Welcomes inquiries regarding reviews, books (especially those by local writers), and internship possibilites for students. Reviews run 600-950 words. **Tips:** "We welcome reviews from all serious contributors. Writers who catch our attention are those that articulate important points on the books they're reviewing. We recommend reviewing an issue of *Book/Mark* to get an idea of our format and style." **Queries:** Preferred. **E-Queries:** Yes. **Unsolicited mss:** Accepts. **Response:** Queries 2-4 weeks, submissions immediately. **SASE Required:** Yes. **Freelance Content:** 80%. **Payment:** In copies.

BOOKPAGE

ProMotion, Inc., 2143 Belcourt Ave., Nashville, TN 37212. 615-292-8926. E-mail: lynn@bookpage.com. Website: www.bookpage.com. Monthly. $25/yr. Circ.: 500,000. Lynn Green, Editor. **Description:** Consumer-oriented newspaper used by booksellers and libraries to promote new titles and authors. Provides book reviews, 400 words, $20/review. **Tips:** Query with writing samples and areas of interest; editor will make assignments for reviews. **Queries:** Required. **Freelance Content:** 90%.

BOOKS & CULTURE: A CHRISTIAN REVIEW

Christianity Today International, 465 Gundersen Dr., Carol Stream, IL 60188. 630-260-6200. E-mail: bceditor@booksandculture.com. Website: www.christianity.net. Bimonthly. $24.95/yr. Circ.: 12,000. David Neff, Executive Editor. **Description:** Magazine with emphasis on Christian books, culture, and religion.

BYLINE

ByLine Press, P.O. Box 5240, Edmond, OK 73083-5240. 405-348-5591. E-mail: mpreston@bylinemag.com. Website: www.bylinemag.com. Monthly. $24/yr. Circ.: 3,500. Marcia Preston, Editor. **Description:** Publication for writers. **Fiction:** Genre, mainstream, literary, humor; 2,000-4,000 words; $100. **Nonfiction:** Articles on the craft and business of writing; 1,500-1,800 words; $75. **Poetry:** About writing or the creative process; 30 lines max; $10. **Columns, Departments:** End Piece, humorous or motivational (700 words, $35); First $ale (250-300 words, $20); Great American Bookstores! (500-600 words, $35-$40); Only When I Laugh, writing-related humor (50-400 words, $15-$25). **Tips:** "Queries preferred for feature articles only. Include practical information that can help writers succeed." Accepts queries via e-mail, but not submissions. **Queries:** Preferred. **E-Queries:** Yes. **Unsolicited mss:** Accepts. **Response:** 4-6 weeks. **SASE Required:** Yes. **Freelance Content:** 80%. **Rights:** FNAR. **Payment:** On acceptance.

C/OASIS

491 Moraga Way, Orinda, CA 94563. E-mail: eide491@earthlink.net. Website: www.sunoasis.com/oasis.html. Monthly. David Eide, Editor; Vicki Goldsberry, Poetry Editor. **Description:** Original stories, poetry, essays, as well as insightful articles about electronic publishing, legal issues, and job markets; 700-3,000 words; $10-$20. **Tips:** Send poetry submissions to redmuse@austin.rr.com c/o Vicki Goldsberry. **E-Queries:** Yes. **Unsolicited mss:** Accepts.

CANADIAN WRITER'S JOURNAL

White Mountain Publications, Box 1178, , New Liskeard, Ontario POJ 1PO Canada. 705-647-5424. E-mail: cwj@cwj.ca. Website: www.cwj.ca. Bimonthly. Circ.: 350. Deborah Ranchuk, Managing Editor. **Description:** Digest-sized magazine emphasizing short "how-to" articles targeted for the Canadian writer. **Nonfiction:** Any subject related to writing, from generating ideas to marketing and publishing; 400-2,000 words; $7.50/page. Book reviews, 250-500 words, on books about writing or books published in Canada. **Tips:** Prefers electronic submissions. "Be specific and consise. Use your personal experience and achievements. Avoid overworked subjects (overcoming writer's block, handling rejection, finding time to write, etc.)." See guidelines on website. **Queries:** Not necessary. **E-Queries:** Yes. **Unsolicited mss:** Accepts. **Response:** 2 months, SASE required (include IRCs). **SASE Required:** Yes. **Freelance Content:** 75%. **Payment:** On publication.

CATHOLIC LIBRARY WORLD

Catholic Library Assn., 100 North St., Suite 224, Pittsfield, MA 01201-5109. 413-443-2CLA. E-mail: cla@cathla.org. Website: www.cathla.org. Quarterly. $60/yr. Mary E. Gallagher, SSJ, General Editor. **Description:** Articles, reviews, and association news for school, academic, and institutional librarians/archivists. **Tips:** No payment offered. **Queries:** Not necessary. **E-Queries:** Yes. **Unsolicited mss:** Accepts. **Contact:** Jean R. Bostley, SSJ.

CHILDREN'S BOOK INSIDER

901 Columbia Rd., Ft. Collins, CO 80525-1838. 800-807-1916. E-mail: mail@write4kids.com; laura@write4kids.com. Website: www.write4kids.com. Monthly. Jon Bard, Managing Editor. **Description:** Provides the "inside scoop" on publishing books for children. Accepts queries for how-to articles on writing children's books. **Tips:** Send SASE with $.60 postage for sample copy. **E-Queries:** Yes. **Contact:** Laura Backes.

CHILDREN'S WRITER

Institute of Children's Literature, 93 Long Ridge Rd., West Redding, CT 06896-0811. 800-443-6078. E-mail: informationservices@childrenswriter.com. Website: www.childrenswriter.com. Monthly. $24/yr. Susan M. Tierney, Editor. **Description:** 12-page newsletter reporting on the marketplace for children's writing. Pieces run 850-2,000 words; pays $200-$300. **Queries:** Preferred. **Response:** 1 month. **SASE Required:** Yes. **Rights:** FNAR.

CROSS & QUILL

Christian Writers Fellowship International, 1624 Jefferson Davis Rd., Clinton, SC 29325. 864-697-6035. E-mail: cqarticles@aol.com. Website: www.cwfi-online.org. Bimonthly. $20/yr. Circ.: 1,000. **Description:** *Cross & Quill: The Christian Writers Newsletter* informs, instructs, and encourages Christians in publishing to produce writing of the highest Biblical and professional standards **Nonfiction:** 200-1,000 words; $5-$25 depending upon need for editing. **Poetry:** 12 lines; $5. **Fillers:** 100

words; $5. **Tips:** "We lean toward informative, how-to articles rather than personal experience or reflection pieces. Please keep in mind our audience. We only publish articles, poetry, and fillers that relate to writing and the writing life." **E-Queries:** Yes. **Response:** 2 months. **SASE Required:** Yes. **Freelance Content:** 75%. **Rights:** FNAR, reprint. **Payment:** On publication. **Contact:** Sandy Brooks, Editor.

EDITOR & PUBLISHER

VNU Business Media, 770 Broadway, Fl. 7, New York, NY 10003. 646-654-5270. E-mail: edpub@editorandpublisher.com. Website: www.editorandpublisher.com. Weekly. $99/yr. Circ.: 18,100. Sid Holt, Editor-in-Chief. **Description:** On the newspaper industry: newspaper websites, features, how-tos, opinion pieces, etc. **Tips:** Send complete manuscripts. **Payment:** On publication.

THE EDITORIAL EYE

EEI Communications, 66 Canal Center Plz, Suite 200, Alexandria, VA 22314-5507. 703-683-0683. E-mail: press@eeicommunications.com. Website: www.eeicommunications.com/eye. Monthly. $99/yr. Circ.: 2,400. Linda Jorgensen, Editor. **Description:** Resource for editors, writers, managers, journalists and educators on publications standards, practices, and trends. Focuses on clear writing, intelligent editing, project management, changing grammar/usage rules and conventions, and quality control priorities.

FOLIO: THE NEW DYNAMICS OF MAGAZINE PUBLISHING

PRIMEDIA Business Magazines & Media, 261 Madison Ave., Fl. 9, New York, NY 10016-2303. 212-716-8585. E-mail: foliomail@primediabusiness.com. Website: www.foliomag.com. Monthly. $96/yr. Circ.: 9,300. Geoffrey Lewis, Editorial Director. **Description:** For the magazine publishing executive.

FOREWORD

ForeWord Magazine, Inc., 129 1/2 Front St., Traverse City, MI 49684-2508. 231-933-3699. E-mail: alex@forewordmagazine.com. Website: www.forewordmagazine.com. 6x/yr. $10/$40. Circ.: 20,000. Alex Moore, Managing Editor. **Description:** Trade journal for librarians and booksellers. Reviews new titles from independent publishers and university presses. **Tips:** Sample copy $10, plus $2 S&H. **Queries:** Required. **E-Queries:** Yes. **Unsolicited mss:** Accepts.

THE HORN BOOK MAGAZINE

56 Roland St., Suite 200, Boston, MA 02129. 617-628-0225. E-mail: info@hbook.com. Website: www.hbook.com. Bimonthly. $9.75/$48. Circ.: 16,000. Roger Sutton, Editor. **Description:** Critical review of new children's/YA books. Also, editorials, columns, and articles about children's literature. **Nonfiction:** Critical essays on children's literature and related subjects for librarians, teachers, parents; up to 2,800 words. **Queries:** Not necessary. **E-Queries:** Yes. **Unsolicited mss:** Accepts. **Response:** 4-6 months. **SASE Required:** Yes.

INTERCOM

Society for Technical Communication, 901 N Stuart St., Suite 904, Arlington, VA 22203-1822. 703-522-4114. E-mail: intercom@stc.org. Website: www.stc.org. 10x/yr. Circ.: 20,000. Maurice Martin, Editor. **Description:** Industry information for technical writers, publishers, and editors.

LAMBDA BOOK REPORT

Lambda Literary Foundation, P.O. Box 73910, Washington, DC 20056-3910. 202-462-7924. E-mail: lbreditor@lambdalit.org. Website: www.lambdalit.org. Monthly. $34.95/yr. Circ.: 8,000. Jim Marks, Editor. **Description:** Reviews and features on gay and lesbian books. Articles run 250-1,500 words. **Queries:** Preferred.

LITERARY TRAVELER

P.O. Box 400272, North Cambridge, MA 02140-0003. 617-628-3504. E-mail: francis@literarytraveler.com. Website: www.literarytraveler.com. Linda McGovern, Editor. **Description:** Online publication featuring articles about writers or places that have literary significance. Pays $5-$25. **Tips:** See website for specific guidelines. **Queries:** Preferred. **E-Queries:** Yes. **Unsolicited mss:** Accepts.

LOCUS

Locus Publications, P.O. Box 13305, Oakland, CA 94661. 510-339-9196. E-mail: locus@locusmag.com. Website: www.locusmag.com. Monthly. Circ.: 8,000. Jennifer A. Hall, Executive Editor. **Description:** Covers industry news for profesional writers and publishers of science fiction and fantasy. **Tips:** Sample copy $5.95 plus $2 shippling/handling. **E-Queries:** No.

NEWSLETTER ON NEWSLETTERS

P.O. Box 348, Rhinebeck, NY 12572. 845-876-5222. Website: www.newsletterbiz.com. Semi-monthly. Paul Swift, Publisher/Editor. **Description:** For professionals involved in publishing newsletters and specialized information, both in print and online.

OHIO WRITER

Poets' & Writers' League of Gr. Cleveland, 12200 Fairhill Rd., Townhouse 3-A, Cleveland, OH 44120. 216-421-0403. E-mail: pwlgc@yahoo.com. Website: www.pwlgc.com. 6x/yr. Circ.: 1,000. Darlene Montonaro, Editor. **Description:** Features, interviews, how-tos, and articles relevant to writing in Ohio. **Tips:** See website for complete guidelines. Sample copy $3. **Queries:** Required. **Response:** 3 months. **Freelance Content:** 5%. **Rights:** Revert to author after publication. **Payment:** On publication.

ONCE UPON A TIME

553 Winston Ct., St. Paul, MN 55118. 651-457-6223. E-mail: audreyoutat@comcast.net. Website: http://onceuponatimemag.com. Quarterly. $26/yr. Circ.: 1,000. Audrey B. Baird, Editor. **Description:** Support magazine that provides wisdom and

advice for those who write and illustrate for children. **Nonfiction:** Writing and/or illustrating how-tos (plotting, character development, revising, dialogue, how you work, handle rejections, the story behind your book, etc.; 100-900 words. **Poetry:** On related topics; 30 lines. **Tips:** Use friendly style, with tips and information that really work. **E-Queries:** No. **Unsolicited mss:** Accepts. **Response:** 1 month. **SASE Required:** Yes. **Freelance Content:** 50%. **Rights:** One-time. **Payment:** In copies.

POETS & WRITERS

Poets & Writers, Inc., 72 Spring St., New York, NY 10012-4019. 212-226-3586. E-mail: editor@pw.org. Website: www.pw.org/mag. $4.95/$17.95. Circ.: 70,000. Therese Eiben, Editor. **Description:** Bimonthly trade magazine for writers of poetry, fiction, and creative nonfiction. Profiles of contemporary authors, essays on the creative process of writing, and articles with practical applications for both emerging and established writers; 500-3,500 words. **Tips:** Does not cover any type of genre fiction, children's literature, or screenwriting/playwriting. **Queries:** Preferred. **E-Queries:** Yes. **Unsolicited mss:** Accepts. **Response:** 4-6 weeks. **SASE Required:** Yes. **Freelance Content:** 95%. **Rights:** FNASR. **Payment:** On publication.

PUBLISHERS WEEKLY

Reed Business Information, 360 Park Ave. S, New York, NY 10010-1710. 646-746-6400. Website: www.publishersweekly.com. Weekly. $199/yr. Circ.: 34,400. Nora Rawlinson, Editor-in-Chief. **Description:** Seeks essays, 900 words, on current issue or problem facing publishing and bookselling for "My Say" column. Articles for "Booksellers' Forum" may be somewhat longer. Pay varies. **Contact:** Daisy Maryles, Executive Editor.

Q B R THE BLACK BOOK REVIEW

ALEP Inc., 9 W 126th St., Fl. 2, New York, NY 10027-3810. 212-348-1681. E-mail: mrodz@qbr.com. Website: www.qbr.com. Bimonthly. $4.95/$16. Circ.: 56,000. Max Rodriguez, Editor-in-Chief. **Description:** Highlights books written by black writers or for a black audience. Features reviews, interviews, writing contests, and literary events. Covers all genres—fiction, nonfiction, poetry, YA, biography/memoir, classics. Reviews should be close to 700 words; $25/review. **Queries:** Preferred. **E-Queries:** Yes. **Unsolicited mss:** Accepts. **Response:** 1-2 months. **SASE Required:** Yes. **Freelance Content:** 100%. **Rights:** None. **Payment:** On publication.

QUILL & QUIRE

St. Joseph's Corp., 70 The Esplanade #210, Toronto, Ontario M5E 1R2 Canada. 416-360-0044. E-mail: info@quillandquire.com. Website: www.quillandquire.com. Quarterly. $59.95/yr (Canadian), $95/yr (non-Canadian). Circ.: 6,000. Scott Anderson, Editor. **Description:** Trade publication for the Canadian publishing industry. Offers books news, author interviews, and reviews of Canadian books. Written for writers, publishers, editors, librarians, and booksellers. **Queries:** Required. **E-Queries:** Yes. **Unsolicited mss:** Does not accept.

ROMANTIC TIMES BOOKCLUB
55 Bergen St., Brooklyn, NY 11201. 718-237-1097.
E-mail: rtinfo@romantictimes.com. Website: www.romantictimes.com. Monthly.
$43/yr. Circ.: 100,000. Kathryn Falk, Founder/CEO. **Description:** Topics on the
romance-fiction and women's fiction publishing industry.

SCBWI BULLETIN
Society of Children's Book Writers and Illustrators
8271 Beverly Blvd., Los Angeles, CA 90048. 323-782-1010. E-mail: stephen-
mooser@scbwi.org. Website: www.scbwi.org. Bimonthly. **Description:** "We welcome submissions of interest to our illustrator and writer members." Pays $50 plus
SCBWI membership. **Art:** Pays $10/drawing for line art; $25 for B&W cover photo.
Queries: Preferred. **E-Queries:** Yes. **Rights:** FNAR. **Contact:** Stephen Mooser.

SCR(I)PT
5638 Sweet Air Rd., Baldwin, MD 21013. 888-245-2229 ext. 202.
E-mail: editor@scriptmag.com. Website: www.scriptmag.com. Bimonthly.
Description: Seeking writers presently working in the film industry to contribute
articles on the craft and business of screenwriting. Interested in feature articles and
interviews. Print articles run 2,000-3,000 words; $.05-$.08/word. Also web articles,
$25-$50/piece. **Queries:** Preferred. **E-Queries:** Yes. **Unsolicited mss:** Accepts.
Response: 4-6 weeks. **SASE Required:** Yes.

SMALL PRESS REVIEW
Dustbooks, P.O. Box 100, Paradise, CA 95967. 530-877-6110.
E-mail: directories@dustbooks.com. Website: www.dustbooks.com. Bimonthly.
$25/yr. Circ.: 2,500. Len Fulton, Editor. **Description:** Features reviews and news
about small presses and magazines. **Nonfiction:** Reviews and essays on small-press
literary books, publishers, and small-circulation magazines; 200 words. **Tips:** Sample
copy free on request. **Queries:** Preferred. **E-Queries:** Yes.

SOCIETY OF CHILDREN'S BOOK WRITERS & ILLUSTRATORS
8271 Beverly Blvd., Los Angeles, CA 90048. 323-782-1010. E-mail: scbwi@scbwi.org.
Website: www.scbwi.org. Monthly. **Description:** Articles pertinent to writers and/or
illustrators of children's books. Pays $50/article. **Art:** Pays $10 for line drawings; $25
for B&W cover photo. **Queries:** Required. **Rights:** FNAR.

TECHNICAL COMMUNICATION
Society for Technical Communication, 106 Buckingham Mews, Macon, GA 31220.
478-301-2299. E-mail: george@ghayhoe.com. Website: www.stc.org. Quarterly. Circ.:
25,000. George Hayhoe, Editor. **Description:** Industry information for technical
writers, publishers, and editors. Features research results, technical communication
theory, case studies, tutorials related to new laws, standards, requirements, techniques, or technologies, bibliographies, and bibliographic essays on technical communication. **Queries:** Not necessary. **E-Queries:** Yes. **Unsolicited mss:** Accepts.

VERBATIM

4907 N Washtenaw Ave., Chicago, IL 60625. 773-275-1516.
E-mail: editor@verbatimmag.com. Website: www.verbatimmag.com. Quarterly.
$7/$25. Circ.: 1,500. Erin McKean, Editor. **Description:** "The Langauge Quarterly."
On language and linguistics, written for a general audience. **Nonfiction:** Seeks interesting, well-written articles on language. Topics include spelling reform, palindromes,
names, and citation finding. To 2,500 words; $75-$400. **Poetry:** Light verse only,
specifically about language; to 30 lines; $75. **Fillers:** Cryptic crosswords only; $25-
$100. **Tips:** "Avoid lamentations about declining language standards. Also, no puns,
homonyms, or Shakespeare. Humor always a plus!" **Queries:** Required. **E-Queries:**
Yes. **Unsolicited mss:** Accepts. **Response:** 1-3 months. **Freelance Content:** 80%.
Rights: All. **Payment:** On publication.

THE WIN-INFORMER

Writers Information Network, A Professional Association for Christian Writers, P.O.
Box 11337, Bainbridge Island, WA 98110. 206-842-9103. E-mail: writersinfonet-
work@juno.com. Website: www.christianwritersinfo.net. Bimonthly. $40/yr. Circ.:
1,000. Elaine Wright Colvin, Editor. **Description:** Christian writers networking magazine with professional development in writing and marketing tips. **Nonfiction:** Up-
to-date market information, CBA industry news/trends, how-to advice, ethics, contracts, author/editor relations, book reviews, and information on clubs, groups, and
conferences; 50-800 words; $20-$50 and/or subscription. **Tips:** Submit articles in the
body of an e-mail; do not send attachments or printed version. Include bio with publishing credits. **Queries:** Not necessary. **Freelance Content:** 30%. **Rights:** FNAR.

THE WRITER

Kalmbach Publishing Co., 21027 Crossroads Circle, Waukesha, WI 53187.
262-796-8776. E-mail: queries@writermag.com. Website: www.writermag.com.
Monthly. Circ.: 40,000. Elfrieda Abbe, Editor. **Description:** Founded in 1887, the
magazine uses articles and interviews that focus on the process of writing.
Nonfiction: Articles, to 2,500 words. How-to, marketing ideas, publishing trends,
profiles and book reviews. Payment depends on length and complexity of article. $50-
$75 for reviews; $100-$500 for features and columns. **Tips:** "E-mail submissions are
fine. Send to queries@writermag.com. Be sure to list your e-mail address in the body
of message. Do not send clips. If we like your idea, we'll request samples of your
work." Sample copy $4.95, plus tax, S/H.

WRITER'S BLOCK MAGAZINE

300-30 Murray St., Ottawa, Ontario K1N 5M4 Canada.
E-mail: dgoldberger@niva.com. Website: www.writersblock.ca. Circ.: 42,000. Dalya
Goldberger, Managing Editor. **Description:** *Writer's Block* is the only Canadian
web magazine that explores ideas that matter most to Canadians in the writing trade.
Each quarterly issue offers information, insight, and opinions that help define the
environment in which we work, learn, and create." Aimed at established and aspiring
Canadian writers. Fiction and poetry also accepted. 2,500 words max; offers byline.

THE WRITER'S CHRONICLE

Association of Writers & Writing Programs, MSN 1E3, George Mason University, Fairfax, VA 22030. E-mail: awpchron@gmu.edu. Website: www.awpwriter.org/magazine. 6x/yr. Circ.: 24,000. **Description:** Essays, articles, and news on writing. Designed to inform and entertain writers, students, editors, and teachers. **Nonfiction:** Information on grants, awards, fellowships, articles, news, and reviews. Pays $8 per 100 words, or as negotiated. **Queries:** Preferred. **E-Queries:** Yes.

WRITER'S DIGEST

F&W Publications, Inc., 4700 E Galbraith Rd., Cincinnati, OH 45236. 513-531-2690. E-mail: writersdig@fwpubs.com. Website: www.writersdigest.com. Monthly. $27/yr. Circ.: 175,000. Kristin Godsey, Editor. **Description:** Covers all aspects of the American writing market. Feature articles on the craft of writing fiction, nonfiction, essays, scripts/screenplays, etc. Also covers the business side of professional writing and provides up-to-date paying markets seeking material. **E-Queries:** Yes. **Freelance Content:** 70%. **Rights:** FNASR. **Payment:** On acceptance.

WRITERS' JOURNAL

Val-Tech Media, P.O. Box 394, Perham, MN 56573-0394. 218-346-7921. E-mail: writersjournal@lakesplus.com. Website: www.writersjournal.com. Bimonthly. $4.99/$19.97. Circ.: 26,000. Leon Ogroske, Editor. **Description:** Publication for writers (including professional communicators, independent/self-publishers, editors, teachers, poets) covering the business side of writing, all types of publishing (traditional, self, electronic, POD), writing skills/composition, etc; 1,000-2,000 words. **Tips:** "Our audience wants to learn how to become better writers and seeks advice on how to get published. We are especially interested in pieces explaining unusual and unique methods of earning income writers can use while practicing and honing their skills." **E-Queries:** Yes. **Unsolicited mss:** Accepts. **Response:** Queries 6 weeks, submissions 5 months. **SASE Required:** Yes. **Rights:** One-time. **Payment:** On publication.

WRITERSWEEKLY.COM

Booklocker.com, Inc., P.O. Box 2399, Bangor, ME 04402. E-mail: angela@writersweekly.com. Website: www.writersweekly.com. **Description:** Features new freelance jobs and paying markets in weekly Wednesday issue. Free of charge. **Tips:** "The highest-circulation freelance writing e-zine in the world."

WRITING THAT WORKS

Communications Concepts, Inc., 7481 Huntsman Blvd. #720, Springfield, VA 22153. 703-643-2200. E-mail: concepts@writingthatworks.com. Website: www.writingthatworks.com. **Description:** Newsletter on practical business and organizational writing and related editing and publishing. Covers writing techniques, style issues, managing publications, online publishing, PR/marketing, etc. Pieces run 200-500 words.

FICTION & POETRY
MAGAZINES

FICTION & POETRY MAGAZINES

The following section presents a list of magazines whose primary focus in most cases is publishing fiction and poetry. The fiction usually appears in the form of short stories; however, some magazines also publish excerpts from novels and longer works.

The list is divided into markets for specific genres of fiction. These include: Fiction for Young Writers, Literary Magazines, Mystery & Detective, Romance & Confession, and Science Fiction & Fantasy.

The largest number of magazines are found in the Literary Magazine portion. These independent and college journals often publish not only fiction and poetry but also a potent range of creative nonfiction essays on varied cultural topics, as well as book reviews and interviews with authors and artists.

Although payment from these relatively small magazines, which range in circulation from 300 to 10,000, is modest (often in copies only), publication can begin to establish a writer's serious literary credentials and often will help bring the work of a beginning writer to the attention of editors at larger magazines. Notably, some of America's leading authors still contribute work to the smaller literary magazines. Together with emerging new voices, they form a community of writers whose only criteria are excellence and the elevation of stimulating thought in literary discourse.

These literary journals, little magazines, and college quarterlies welcome work from novices and pros alike; editors are always interested in seeing traditional and experimental fiction, poetry, essays, reviews, short articles, criticism, and satire. As long as the material is well-written, the fact that a writer has not yet been widely published doesn't adversely affect his or her chances for acceptance.

Most of these literary publications have small budgets and staffs, so they may be slow in their reporting time; several months is not unusual. In addition, some (particularly the college-based magazines) do not read manuscripts during the summer.

Publication may also lead to having one's work chosen for reprinting in one of the prestigious annual collections of work from the little magazines.

For a complete list of the thousands of literary publications and little magazines in existence, writers may wish to consult such comprehensive reference works as *The International Directory of Little Magazines and Small Presses*, published annually by Dustbooks (P.O. Box 100, Paradise, CA 95967) and available at many public libraries.

FICTION FOR YOUNG WRITERS

CICADA

Carus Publishing Co., 315 Fifth St., P.O. Box 300, Peru, IL 61354-0300. 812-224-5803, ext. 656. Website: www.cricketmag.com. Bimonthly. $7.95/$35.97. Circ.: 16,000. Marianne Carus, Editor-in-Chief. **Description:** For teens, fiction and poetry that is thought-provoking, yet entertaining, often humorous. Also publishes stories by teens reflecting their own unique perspective. **Fiction:** Literary and genre fiction (realistic, humorous, historical fiction, adventure, science fiction, and fantasy); to 15,000 words; $.25/word. **Nonfiction:** First-person experiences that are relevant or interesting to teenagers; to 5,000 words; $.25/word. **Poetry:** To 25 lines; $3/line.

Queries: Does not accept. **E-Queries:** No. **Unsolicited mss:** Accepts. **Response:** 12 weeks. **SASE Required:** Yes. **Freelance Content:** 90%. **Rights:** Vary. **Payment:** On publication. **Contact:** Deborah Vetter.

CLAREMONT REVIEW

4980 Wesley Rd., Victoria, British Columbia V84 1Y9 Canada. 250-658-5221. E-mail: editor@theclaremontreview.ca. Website: www.theclaremontreview.ca. Semiannual. $10/$18. Circ.: 500. Susan Field, Business Editor. **Description:** Fiction (500-3,000 words) and poetry (to 1 page) by young writers in the English-speaking world, ages 13-19. **Tips:** "We seek fiction with a strong voice and poetry that stirs the heart." No science fiction/fantasy. **Queries:** Not necessary. **Unsolicited mss:** Accepts. **Response:** 6 weeks. **SASE Required:** Yes. **Freelance Content:** 100%.

GUMBO

Strive Media Institute Publishing, Inc., 1818 N Dr. Martin Luther King Dr., Milwaukee, WI 53212. 414-374-3511. E-mail: amy@mygumbo.com. Website: www.mygumbo.com. Bimonthly. $15/yr. Circ.: 25,000. Amy Muehlbauer, Managing Editor. **Description:** Multicultural magazine written, edited, and designed for teens by teens. Mission is to teach journalism and design skills to young adults by having them work with adult mentors who are professionals in journalism, graphic design, and photography. Editorial content reflects diversity in a range of subjects such as careers, sports, health, fashion, news, and entertainment. **Tips:** "We do not offer payment as we are published by a non-profit organization. All work is written and edited by teens and is a learning process. Contact the managing editor directly if you are interested in working for Gumbo. Do not send unsolicited material; only assigned articles are published." **Queries:** Required. **E-Queries:** Yes. **Unsolicited mss:** Does not accept. **Response:** 2 weeks. **Rights:** None.

NEW MOON

34 E Superior St. #200, Duluth, MN 55802. 218-728-5507. E-mail: girl@newmoon.org. Website: www.newmoon.org. Bimonthly. $5.50/$29. Circ.: 30,000. Dawn Gorman, Managing Editor. **Description:** Celebrates girls—their accomplishments and efforts to hold onto their voices, strengths, and dreams as they move from being girls to becoming women. **Fiction:** Stories by female authors, with girls as main characters. Fiction should fit theme (see website for upcoming list), for girls ages 8-14; 900 words; $.06-$.10/word. **Nonfiction:** Women's work (profiles a woman and her job, relates to theme); Herstory (profiles a woman from history); Body Language (about puberty, body image, depression, menstruation, etc.); Girls on the Go (by girl or woman adventurers); 600 words; $.06-$.10/word. **Tips:** Sample copy $6.75. **Queries:** Not necessary. **E-Queries:** Accepts. **Unsolicited mss:** Accepts. **Response:** 2 months. **SASE Required:** Yes. **Freelance Content:** 10%. **Rights:** All. **Payment:** On publication.

SKIPPING STONES

P.O. Box 3939, Eugene, OR 97403. 541-342-4956.
E-mail: editor@skippingstones.org. Website: www.skippingstones.org. 5x/yr. $25/yr. Circ.: 2,500. Arun N. Toké, Executive Editor. **Description:** Original writing, art, and photography. **Fiction:** Social awareness, interpersonal relationships; to 750 words. **Nonfiction:** Nature awareness, multicultural education, social responsibility, travelogues, journal entries; to 750 words. **Poetry:** By authors under age 19 only; on nature, social issues, reflections; to 30 lines. **Fillers:** Multicultural, nature; 150 words. **Art:** Original B&W or color prints with captions or photo essays. **Tips:** "Each year, we also recognize creativity and community service by honoring 10 youth groups and children (ages 7-17) with our Youth Honor Awards. We invite writing and art that promote multicultural awareness and/or ecological understanding, sustainable living, creative problem solving, peace, and justice." **Queries:** Not necessary. **E-Queries:** Accepts. **Unsolicited mss:** Accepts. **Response:** 1-3 months. **SASE Required:** Yes. **Freelance Content:** 80%. **Rights:** FNASR, reprint. **Payment:** In copies.

SPANK! YOUTH CULTURE ONLINE

Ububik, #505, 300 Meredith Rd., Calgary, Alberta T2E 7A8 Canada. 403-217-0468. E-mail: happyrandom@spankmag.com. Website: www.spankmag.com. Stephen R. Cassady, Editor. **Description:** E-zine written by youth for youth, for ages 14 to 24. Only accepts submissions from youth.

STONE SOUP

P.O. Box 83, Santa Cruz, CA 95063-0083. 831-426-5557. E-mail: editor@stonesoup.com. Website: www.stonesoup.com. Bimonthly. $5.50/$33. Circ.: 20,000. Gerry Mandel, Editor. **Description:** Stories, poems, book reviews, and art by young writers and artists, ages 8-13. **Fiction:** Personal narratives, arrival stories, family histories, sport stories, science fiction; 2,500 words; $40. **Nonfiction:** Book reviews by children under 14. Prefers writing based on real-life experiences. **Poetry:** Free verse only; $40. **Art:** Work by kids ages 8-13 only; send 2-3 samples (photocopies ok). **Tips:** Sample copy $4. **Queries:** Not necessary. **E-Queries:** No. **Unsolicited mss:** Accepts. **Response:** Queries 2-3 weeks, submissions 4 weeks. **SASE Required:** No. **Freelance Content:** 100%. **Rights:** All. **Payment:** On publication.

STORYWORKS

Scholastic, Inc., 557 Broadway, New York, NY 10012. 212-343-6100. E-mail: storyworks@scholastic.com. Website: www.scholastic.com/storyworks. Bimonthly. Circ.: 270,000. Lauren Tarshis, Editor. **Description:** Language arts magazine for kids ages 8-12. **Queries:** Required. **Unsolicited mss:** Does not accept.

TEEN INK

Young Author's Foundation, P.O. Box 610030, Newton, MA 02461-0030. 617-964-6800. E-mail: editor@teenink.com. Website: www.teenink.com. 10x/yr. $25/yr. Circ.: 175,000. Kate Dunlop Seamans, Editor. **Description:** Magazine written by teens for teens. Features fiction, nonfiction, poetry, and art. Receives 40,000 submissions/yr.

Tips: "Our magazine is written entirely by teenagers, ages 13-19." Does not offer payment. **Queries:** Not necessary. **E-Queries:** Yes. **Unsolicited mss:** Accepts. **Freelance Content:** 100%.

TEEN VOICES

Women Express, Inc., 80 Summer St., Boston, MA 02110. 617-426-5505. E-mail: teenvoices@teenvoices.com. Website: www.teenvoices.com. Quarterly. $2.95/$19.95. Circ.: 25,000. Ellyn Ruthstrom, Managing Editor. **Description:** Written by, for, and about teenaged and young-adult women. Offers a place to share thoughts with others the same age. **Fiction:** Short stories, any subject and length. **Nonfiction:** About any important issue or experience. **Poetry:** "Your feelings, thoughts, etc." **Columns, Departments:** Opinions/editorial pieces. **Art:** Digital file (TIFF or EPS), or hard copy. **Tips:** Be honest and candid. Appreciates material that promotes feminism, equality, and self-esteem, "You're more than just a pretty face." **Queries:** Not necessary. **E-Queries:** Yes. **Unsolicited mss:** Accepts. **Response:** 3-5 days. **SASE Required:** No. **Rights:** FNAR. **Payment:** In copies.

LITERARY MAGAZINES

13TH MOON

University of Albany, SUNY, Dept. of English, HU 378, Albany, NY 12222. 518-442-5593. E-mail: moon13@albany.edu. Website: www.albany.edu/13thMoon. Annual. $10/issue. Circ.: 500. Judith Emlyn Johnson, Editor. **Description:** Feminist literary journal, with literature and graphic arts by contemporary women. Seeks to draw attention to neglected categories of women artists. **Fiction:** 5 pages. **Nonfiction:** Feminist nonfiction on women's issues. **Poetry:** Women's reflections on global issues; 3-5 poems. **Tips:** Themed issues; accepts submissions September-May. "*13th Moon* has a historical and ongoing commitment to publishing the work of minority women, lesbians, and women of color." **Queries:** Preferred. **E-Queries:** No. **Unsolicited mss:** Accepts. **SASE Required:** Yes. **Freelance Content:** 100%. **Rights:** One-time. **Payment:** In copies.

96 INC.

P.O. Box 15559, Boston, MA 02215. 617-267-0543. Website: www.96inc.com. Annual. $15/yr. Circ.: 3,000. **Description:** Dedicated to publishing new voices and integrating established and novice writers. **Fiction:** All types, no restrictions on style or subject; to 3,000 words. **Nonfiction:** Stories with useful information for other writers (new publishers, etc.); to 2,500 words. **Queries:** Preferred. **E-Queries:** No. **Unsolicited mss:** Accepts. **Response:** 6-12 months. **SASE Required:** Yes. **Rights:** One-time. **Payment:** In copies. **Contact:** Vera Gold or Nancy Mehegan.

AFRICAN AMERICAN REVIEW

Saint Louis Univ., Shannon Hall 119, 220 N Grand Blvd., St. Louis, MO 63103-2007. 314-977-3688. E-mail: weixlmj@slu.edu. Website: http://aar.slu.edu. Quarterly. Circ.:

1,882. Joe Weixlmann, Ph.D., Editor. **Description:** "As the official publication of the Division of Black American Literature and Culture of the Modern Language Association, African American Review promotes a lively exchange among writers and scholars in the arts, humanities, and social sciences who hold diverse perspectives on African American literature and culture." **Fiction:** 2,500-5,000 words; $25-$50. **Nonfiction:** 2,500-5,000 words; $30-$80. **Poetry:** Any length; $25. **Queries:** Not necessary. **E-Queries:** Yes. **Unsolicited mss:** Accepts. **Response:** Queries 2 days, submissions 6 months. **SASE Required:** Yes. **Freelance Content:** 100%. **Rights:** FNAR. **Payment:** On publication. **Contact:** Aileen Keenan, Managing Editor.

AFRICAN VOICES

270 W 96th St., New York, NY 10025. 212-865-2982. E-mail: africanvoices@aol.com. Website: www.africanvoices.com. Quarterly. $3/$12. Circ.: 20,000. Carolyn A. Butts, Editor. **Description:** Literary magazine with fiction, nonfiction, poetry, and visual arts by people of color. **Fiction:** Humorous, erotic, and dramatic fiction by ethnic writers. All themes, subjects, and styles, emphasis on style and technique. 500-2,000 words. **Nonfiction:** Investigative articles, artist profiles, essays, book reviews, and first-person narratives. 500-2,500 words. **Poetry:** All styles; avant-garde, free verse, haiku, light verse, traditional. Submit up to 5 poems, 3 pages max. **Art:** B&W photos. **Queries:** Preferred. **E-Queries:** Accepts. **Unsolicited mss:** Accepts. **Response:** Queries 6 weeks, submissions 6-12 weeks. **SASE Required:** Yes. **Freelance Content:** 80%. **Rights:** FNAR. **Payment:** In copies. **Contact:** Kim Horne, fiction; Layding Kalbia, poetry; Debbie Officer, book reviews.

AFRO-HISPANIC REVIEW

Dept. of Romance Languages, U. Missouri, 143 Arts & Science Building, Columbia, MO 65211. 573-882-5040. E-mail: lewism@missouri.edu. 2x/yr. $15/yr. Circ.: 310. Marvin A. Lewis, Editor. **Description:** Literary fiction, poetry, and essays that focus on the literature and culture of Afro-Latin America. Main emphasis is on literary analysis and criticism of works by African diasporan authors living in the Spanish Caribbean, Central America, and South America. **Fiction:** Stories that deal with the Black experience in Spanish America; 1-20 pages. **Nonfiction:** Book reviews and scholarly articles treating literary works by black writers of Spanish expression in the Americas; 20 pages. **Poetry:** Poems that deal with the black experience in Spanish America. **Tips:** Does not offer payment for work published. Academic audience. "We do not accept fiction or poetry that fall outside our area of focus. Our journal's reputation is of sufficient stature in the scholarly arena that it's well-known both here and abroad." **Queries:** Preferred. **E-Queries:** No. **Unsolicited mss:** Accepts.

AGNI

Boston Univ., Creative Writing Program, 236 Bay State Rd., Boston, MA 02215. 617-353-7135. E-mail: agni@bu.edu. Website: www.bu.edu/agni. Semi-annual. $9.95/$17. Circ.: 4,000. Sven Birkerts, Editor. **Description:** Print and online magazine featuring contemporary literature by established and new writers, on literary and political subjects, to engage readers in a broad cultural conversation. Accepts fiction, poetry, and nonfiction pieces on a group of books (not reviews of single books) or broader cultural or literary issues. Length varies. Pays $20-$150 ($10/page). **Tips:** Reviews submissions between September 1-May 31. **Queries:** Not necessary. **E-Queries:** No. **Unsolicited mss:** Accepts. **Response:** 2-4 months. **SASE Required:** Yes. **Freelance Content:** 15%. **Rights:** FNASR, anthology. **Payment:** On publication.

AGNIESZKA'S DOWRY

A Small Garlic Press, 5445 N Sheridan, #3003, Chicago, IL 60640-7477. E-mail: marek@enteract.com; ketzle@ketzle.net. Website: www.asgp.org. $6/issue. Marek Lugowski, katrina grace craig (no caps), Editors. **Description:** Poetry community publishing online literary journal (permanently) and as chapbooks (being kept in print indefinitely). **Tips:** Submit material via e-mail only to both editors. Does not accept hard copy. Follow specific guidelines posted on website. **Payment:** In copies.

ALASKA QUARTERLY REVIEW (AQR)

University of Alaska-Anchorage, 3211 Providence Dr., Anchorage, AK 99508. 907-786-6916. E-mail: ayaqr@uaa.alaska.edu. Website: www.uaa.alaska.edu/aqr. Semi-annual. $6.95/$10. Circ.: 3,500. Ronald Spatz, Editor. **Description:** "One of the nation's best literary magazines" (*Washington Post Book World*). **Fiction:** Experimental and traditional literary forms. No romance, children's, or inspirational/religious; up to 20,000 words. **Nonfiction:** Literary nonfiction, essays, and memoirs; up to 20,000 words. **Poetry:** Avant-garde, free verse, traditional. No light verse. 10 poems max. **Tips:** Send manuscript via regular mail. **Queries:** Not necessary. **Unsolicited mss:** Accepts. **SASE Required:** Yes. **Freelance Content:** 95%. **Rights:** FNAR. **Payment:** In copies.

ALLIGATOR JUNIPER

Prescott College, 220 Grove Ave., Prescott, AZ 86301. 928-350-2012. E-mail: aj@prescott.edu. Website: www.prescott.edu/highlights/aj.html. Annual. $7.50/$12. Circ.: 600. Miles Waggener, Managing Editor. **Description:** Literary journal that seeks to create a bridge between the arts and the environment. Features B&W photography, fiction, creative nonfiction, and poetry. **Fiction:** 30 pages max; pays $10/story. **Nonfiction:** 30 pages max; pays $10/story. **Poetry:** 5 poems or 5 pages; pays $10 per 5 poems or pages. **Tips:** "We select work based on merit. Occasional theme issues. Please see our guidelines before submitting." **Queries:** Not necessary. **E-Queries:** No. **Unsolicited mss:** Accepts. **Response:** 3-6 months. **Freelance Content:** 100%. **Rights:** FNAR. **Payment:** On acceptance.

AMERICAN BOOK REVIEW

Illinois State Univ., Unit for Contemporary Literature, Campus Box 4241, Normal, IL 61790-4241. E-mail: rakaise@ilstu.edu. Website: www.litline.org/abr. Bimonthly. $4/issue. Circ.: 5,000. Ron Sukenick, Publisher. **Description:** Literary book reviews and essays on literature; 750-1,250 words; $50. **Queries:** Preferred. **E-Queries:** Yes. **Response:** 1-4 weeks. **SASE Required:** Yes. **Freelance Content:** 20%. **Payment:** On publication. **Contact:** Rebecca Kaiser, Managing Editor.

AMERICAN LITERARY REVIEW

Univ. of North Texas, P.O. Box 311307, English Dept., Denton, TX 76203. 940-565-2755. E-mail: americanliteraryreview@yahoo.com. Website: www.engl.univ.edu/alr. Bi-annual. $5/$10. Circ.: 500. Corey Marks, Editor. **Description:** Literary journal with fiction, creative nonfiction, and poetry. Both in print and online. **Queries:** Not necessary. **Unsolicited mss:** Accepts. **Response:** 3 months. **SASE Required:** Yes. **Freelance Content:** 90%. **Rights:** FNASR. **Payment:** In copies.

THE AMERICAN POETRY REVIEW

117 S 17th St., Suite 910, Philadelphia, PA 19103. 215-496-0439. E-mail: dbonanno@aprweb.org. Website: www.aprweb.org. Bimonthly. $3.95/issue. Circ.: 17,000. **Description:** Premier forum for contemporary poetry, since 1972. Send up to 4 poems, any length; pays $1.60/line. Also runs literary criticism, interviews, essays, social commentary. **Tips:** Do not send manuscript by fax or e-mail. **Queries:** Not necessary. **E-Queries:** No. **Unsolicited mss:** Accepts. **Response:** 8-10 weeks. **SASE Required:** Yes. **Rights:** FNASR. **Payment:** On publication. **Contact:** Stephen Berg, David Bonanno, Arthur Vogelsang.

ANCIENT PATHS

P.O. Box 7505, Fairfax Station, VA 22039. E-mail: ssburris@msn.com. Website: www.literatureclassics.com/ancientpaths. Annual. $5/year or $9.50/2 years. Circ.: 175. Skylar Hamilton Burris, Editor. **Description:** Poetry, stories, art, and reviews. **Fiction:** Short stories, novel excerpts; prefers third-person; to 2,500 words. **Nonfiction:** Creative nonfiction/personal narratives; to 2,500 words. Chapbook reviews; to 500 words. **Poetry:** Free verse or formal (ballads, sonnets, quatrains, etc.); to 60 lines. **Art:** B&W. **Tips:** Largely Judeo-Christian themes and readers. No sex or profanity. No polemics. "We seek quality literature, not just literature that mentions Christ. Combine sound and meaning. Don't be pretentious or shallow. Avoid focusing on specific denomination." **Queries:** Not necessary. **E-Queries:** Yes. **Unsolicited mss:** Accepts. **Response:** 3-4 weeks. **SASE Required:** Yes. **Freelance Content:** 99%. **Rights:** One-time. **Payment:** One copy and $1-$3.

ANOTHER CHICAGO MAGAZINE

3709 N Kenmore, Chicago, IL 60613-2905. E-mail: editors@anotherchicagomag.com. Website: www.anotherchicagomag.com. Semiannual. $14.95. Circ.: 2,000. Barry Silesky, Editor. **Description:** Literary publication featuring poetry, fiction, and commentary. Also, issues feature an occasional interview with a noted writer, translations, reviews of current literature, and an 8-page center photography folio. **Fiction:** Quality literary fiction that is urgent, new, or worldly; to 25 pages. **Columns, Departments:** Reviews of current fiction and poetry; 500 words. **Art:** B&W photography; 8 photos (from a single artist) in each issue. **Tips:** Reviews work from February 1-August 31. "We seek unusual, engaged work of highest quality only." **Queries:** Not necessary. **E-Queries:** No. **Unsolicited mss:** Accepts. **Response:** Submissions 10+ weeks. **SASE Required:** Yes. **Freelance Content:** 10%. **Rights:** FNASR. **Payment:** On publication.

ANTHOLOGY, INC.

P.O. Box 4411, Mesa, AZ 85211-4411. 480-461-8200. E-mail: info@anthology.org. Website: www.anthology.org. 4x/yr. $4.95/$18. Circ.: 1,000. **Description:** Poetry, prose, and art from new and emerging writers and artists from around the world. **Fiction:** Any genre; 5,000 words. **Nonfiction:** Any genre; 5,000 words. **Poetry:** Any style; up to 100 lines. **Tips:** No graphic horror or pornography. Avoid cliché and trick endings. **Queries:** Not necessary. **E-Queries:** No. **Unsolicited mss:** Accepts. **Response:** 60-90 days. **SASE Required:** Yes. **Freelance Content:** 90%. **Rights:** FNAR. **Payment:** In copies. **Contact:** Sharon Skinner, Executive Editor; Elissa Harris, Prose Editor; Trish Justrish, Poetry Editor.

ANTIETAM REVIEW

Washington County Arts Council, 41 S Potomac St., Hagerstown, MD 21740. 301-791-3132. Annual. $8.40/issue. **Description:** Quality short fiction, poetry, and B&W photos that have not been previously published. **Fiction:** Well-crafted, any subject. Prefers short stories, but will consider a novel excerpt if it works as an independent piece; to 5,000 words; $100/story plus 2 copies. **Nonfiction:** Creative nonfiction. **Poetry:** Submit up to 3 poems, to 30 lines; $25/poem plus 2 copies. **Tips:** Accepts material September 1-December 1. **Queries:** Not necessary. **E-Queries:** No. **Unsolicited mss:** Accepts. **Response:** 3-6 months. **SASE Required:** Yes. **Freelance Content:** 90%. **Rights:** FNAR. **Payment:** On publication. **Contact:** Mary Jo Vincent, Business Manager.

THE ANTIGONISH REVIEW

St. Francis Xavier University, P.O. Box 5000, Antigonish, NS B2G 2W5 Canada. 902-867-3962. E-mail: tar@stfx.ca. Website: www.antigonishreview.com. Quarterly. $24/yr (Canada); $30/yr (US). Circ.: 950. B. Allan Quigley, Jeanette Lynes, Co-Editors. **Description:** Poetry, short stories, essays, book reviews. **Fiction:** 2,000-5,000 words; $50. **Nonfiction:** 2,000-5,000 words; $50-$150. **Poetry:** Any subject, any point of view. **Tips:** Considers stories from anywhere, original or translations, but encourages Atlantic Canadians and Canadian writers, and new and young writers. No submissions accepted by e-mail. **Queries:** Preferred. **Unsolicited mss:** Accepts. **Response:** 4-6 months, SASE required (IRC's). **Freelance Content:** 100%. **Payment:** On publication.

ANTIOCH REVIEW

P.O. Box 148, Yellow Springs, OH 45387. 937-769-1365. Website: www.antioch.edu/review. Quarterly. $40/yr. Circ.: 5,100. Robert S. Fogarty, Editor. **Description:** Fiction, essays, and poetry from emerging and established authors. **Fiction:** Intelligent, compelling stories written with distinction; to 8,000 words; $10/page. **Nonfiction:** Social sciences, humanities, literary journalism; to 8,000 words; $10/page. **Poetry:** 3-6 poems; $10/page. **Tips:** "Read an issue of magazine to obtain a good idea of subjects, treatment, and lengths." **Queries:** Not necessary. **E-Queries:** No. **Unsolicited mss:** Accepts. **Response:** 12-14 weeks. **SASE Required:** Yes. **Freelance Content:** 100%. **Payment:** On publication.

APALACHEE REVIEW

P.O. Box 10469, Tallahassee, FL 32302. 2x/yr. **Description:** Literary journal for poetry, fiction, and creative nonfiction. Accepts simultaneous submissions. No e-mail submissions. Sample copy $5. **Unsolicited mss:** Accepts. **SASE Required:** Yes.

ARKANSAS REVIEW: A JOURNAL OF DELTA STUDIES

P.O. Box 1890, Arkansas State University, State University, AR 72467. 870-972-3043. E-mail: tswillia@astate.edu. Website: www.clt.astate.edu/arkreview. 3x/yr. $7.50/$20. Circ.: 500. Tom Williams, General Editor. **Description:** Regional studies journal focusing on 7-state Mississippi River Delta. Publishes academic articles, interviews, reviews, fiction, poetry, and B&W visual art. **Tips:** "We have an interdisciplinary academic audience. All material must have regional focus." **Queries:** Not necessary. **E-Queries:** Yes. **Unsolicited mss:** Accepts. **Freelance Content:** 50%. **Rights:** FNAR. **Payment:** In copies.

ART TIMES

P.O. Box 730, Mt. Marion, NY 12456. 845-246-6944.
E-mail: info@arttimesjournal.com. Website: www.arttimesjournal.com. 11x/yr. Circ.: 27,000. Raymond J. Steiner, Editor. **Description:** Commentary resource on fine and performing arts. **Fiction:** No excessive sex, violence, racist themes; up to 1,500 words; $25 and subscription. **Nonfiction:** Feature essays are staff-written. **Poetry:** All forms, up to 20 lines. Pays in copies. **Queries:** Not necessary. **E-Queries:** No. **Unsolicited mss:** Accepts. **Response:** 6 months. **SASE Required:** Yes. **Freelance Content:** 100%. **Rights:** FNASR. **Payment:** On publication.

ASCENT

Concordia College, English Dept., 901 Eighth St. S, Moorhead, MN 56562. 218-299-4000. Website: www4.cord.edu/english/ascent/. 3x/yr. $12/yr. Circ.: 750. W. Scott Olsen, Editor. **Description:** Literary magazine with fiction, essays, and poetry. No reviews or editorial articles. Submit complete manuscripts with SASE. **Tips:** Review copy of magazine before submitting. **E-Queries:** No. **Payment:** In copies.

ASIAN PACIFIC AMERICAN JOURNAL

Asian American Writers' Workshop, 16 W 32nd St., Suite 10A, New York, NY 10001. 212-494-0061. E-mail: apaj@aaww.org. Website: www.aaww.org. Hanya Yanagihara, Editor. **Description:** Short stories, excerpts from longer fiction works, and poetry by emerging or established Asian American writers. **Tips:** Send 4 copies of each piece submitted, in all genres. Submit up to 10 poems. **Queries:** Preferred. **Payment:** In copies.

AURA LITERARY ARTS REVIEW

University of Alabama-Birmingham, HUC 135, 1530 3rd Ave. S, Birmingham, AL 35294. 205-934-3216. Semi-annual (Spring and Fall issues). $6/issue. Circ.: 500. Christopher Giganti, Editor-in-Chief. **Description:** Student-produced magazine for written and visual art. Fiction and nonfiction up to 10,000 words. Poetry up to 10 pages. **Queries:** Not necessary. **E-queries:** No. **Unsolicited mss:** Accepts. **Response:** 2 months. **SASE Required:** Yes. **Payment:** In copies.

THE BALTIMORE REVIEW

P.O. Box 410, Riderwood, MD 21139. E-mail: susanmd@e-global.com. Website: www.baltimorereview.org. 2x/yr. $7.95/$14.70. Circ.: 1,000. **Description:** Literary journal showcasing a provocative mix of poetry, fiction, and creative nonfiction. Poetry should be 1-2 pages; fiction and nonfiction no more than 6,000 words. **Tips:** "Be an avid reader of the type of publication in which you'd like your work to appear. Support the literary community and improve your own chances for success by purchasing, and reading, literary journals. Keep the creativity in the work, not in how you approach editors. Be professional." **Queries:** Not necessary. **E-Queries:** No. **Unsolicited mss:** Accepts. **Response:** 2-4 months. **SASE Required:** Yes. **Rights:** FNAR. **Payment:** In copies. **Contact:** Susan Muaddi Darraj, Editor.

BARROW STREET

P.O. Box 1831, Murray Hill Station, New York, NY 10156. E-mail: info@barrowstreet.org. Website: www.barrowstreet.org. **Description:** Literary journal publishing poetry. Send 3-5 poems (no more than 7 pages) with cover letter. **Tips:** Does not accept electronic submissions. Simultaneous submissions accepted with notice. **E-Queries:** No. **Response:** 3-5 months. **SASE Required:** Yes. **Payment:** In copies.

THE BEACON STREET REVIEW

Emerson College, WLP Dept., 120 Boylston St., Boston, MA 02118. Website: http://pages.emerson.edu/publications/bs. Semiannual. $6/$10. Circ.: 1,000. **Description:** New fiction, creative nonfiction, and poetry. Send up to 5 poems for poetry, up to 25 pages for prose. **Tips:** No e-mail submissions or queries. Send SASE or e-mail for guidelines. Annual Editor's Choice Awards chosen from published works. **Queries:** Not necessary. **E-Queries:** No. **Unsolicited mss:** Accepts. **Rights:** FNAR. **Payment:** On publication. **Contact:** Megan Weireter.

THE BEAR DELUXE MAGAZINE

P.O. Box 10342, Portland, OR 97296. 503-242-1047. E-mail: bear@orlo.org. Website: www.orlo.org. Biannual. $16/4 issues. Circ.: 19,000. Tom Webb, Editor. **Description:** Explores environmental issues through the creative arts. **Fiction:** Environmental themes; 750-4,000 words; $.05/word. **Nonfiction:** News, reporting, interviews; seeks cultural connections to environmental issues; 200-4,000 words; $.05/word. **Poetry:** 3-5 poems, up to 50 lines; $10. **Fillers:** First-person opinion pieces, short news pieces, cartoons; 100-750 words; $.05/word, $10/cartoon. **Columns, Departments:** Portrait of an Artist, Technology, Reporter's Notebook; 100-1,500 words; $.05/word. **Art:** B&W and color photos, illustrations, cartoons, paintings, etc.; $30. **Queries:** Preferred. **E-Queries:** Yes. **Unsolicited mss:** Accepts. **Response:** 6 months. **SASE Required:** Yes. **Freelance Content:** 50%. **Rights:** FNAR. **Payment:** On publication.

BELLEVUE LITERARY REVIEW

New York School of Medicine, Dept. of Medicine, 550 First Avenue, OBV-A612, New York, NY 10016. 212-263-3973. E-mail: info@blreview.org. Website: www.blreview.org. 2x/yr. $7/issue. Circ.: 4,000. Danielle Ofri, Editor-in-Chief. **Description:** *"The Bellevue Literary Review* is a forum for illuminating humanity and human experience. We invite submissions of previously unpublished works of fiction, nonfiction, and poetry that touch upon relationships to the human body, health, illness, and healing. We encourage creative interpretation of these themes." Prose should be no longer than 5,000 words, poetry no more than 1 page/poem (submit up to 3). **Tips:** Online submissions now accepted. See website for full submission guidelines. **Queries:** Not necessary. **E-Queries:** Yes. **Unsolicited mss:** Accepts. **Response:** 3-5 months. **SASE Required:** Yes. **Rights:** FNAR. **Payment:** In copies.

BELLINGHAM REVIEW

Western Washington University, MS-9053, Bellingham, WA 98225. 360-650-4863. E-mail: bhreview@cc.wwu.edu. Website: www.wwu.edu/~bhreview. Semiannual. Brenda Miller, Editor-in-Chief. **Description:** Journal for fiction, poetry, and creative nonfiction. **Tips:** Also sponsors the Annie Dillard Award for Nonfiction, the Parallel Award for Poetry, and the Tobias Wolff Award for Fiction. Cash award of $1,000 and publication. Send SASE or visit website for guidelines. **Queries:** Does not accept. **E-Queries:** No. **Unsolicited mss:** Accepts. **Response:** 3 months. **SASE Required:** Yes. **Freelance Content:** 100%. **Rights:** FNAR. **Payment:** On publication.

BELLOWING ARK

P.O. Box 55564, Shoreline, WA 98155. 206-440-0791. E-mail: bellowingark@comcast.net (inquiries only). Bimonthly. $4/$18. Circ.: 850. Robert R. Ward, Editor. **Description:** Literary magazine following the Romantic tradition. **Fiction:** Short fiction, portraying life as positive and meaningful; length varies. **Poetry:** Any style or length. **Queries:** Not necessary. **E-Queries:** Yes. **Unsolicited mss:** Accepts. **Response:** 2-4 months. **SASE Required:** Yes. **Freelance Content:** 95%. **Rights:** First, reprint. **Payment:** In copies.

BELOIT FICTION JOURNAL

Beloit College, Box 11, 700 College St, Beloit, WI 53511. 608-363-2577. E-mail: mccownc@beloit.edu. Website: www.beloit.edu/~english/bfjournal.htm. Annual. $15/issue. Clint McCown, Editor. **Description:** Publishes literary fiction, any theme (no genre fiction). Submit stories between 1-40 pages (average 15 pages). Interested in new and established writers. **Tips:** Send work between August 1-December 1. "Submit with a great opening line, original language, strong forward movement. No pornography, political propaganda, or religious dogma." **Queries:** Not necessary. **E-Queries:** No. **Unsolicited mss:** Accepts. **Response:** 2-4 weeks. **SASE Required:** Yes. **Payment:** In copies. **Contact:** Heather Skyler, Managing Editor.

BELOIT POETRY JOURNAL

P.O. Box 151, Farmington, ME 04938. 207-778-0020. E-mail: sharkey@maine.edu. Website: www.bpj.org. Quarterly. $5/$18. Circ.: 1,300. Lee Sharkey, John Rosenwald, Editors. **Description:** Publishes the best poems received, without bias as to length, form, subject, or tradition. Looking to discover new voices. **Tips:** "Avoid lineated journal entries, clichés, self-absorbed 'how I feel' verse. A strong poem needs fresh insight and a distinctive music. All book reviews are written by our reviews editor." Does not accept electronic submissions. **Queries:** Not necessary. **E-Queries:** No. **Unsolicited mss:** Accepts. **Response:** Up to 4 months. **SASE Required:** Yes. **Payment:** In copies.

BIBLIOPHILOS

200 Security Bldg., Fairmont, WV 26554. 304-366-8107. Quarterly. $5/$18. Circ.: 350. Dr. Gerald J. Bobango, Editor. **Description:** Scholastically-oriented literary journal. "We seek to promote the worldview of the pre-1960s, to show importance of books and scholarly endeavor (and to encourage people to relegate their PCs and laptops to the dustbin)." **Fiction:** Stories about growing up in rural West Virginia in the 1930s and WWII; people with traditional values; stories of love and kindness; to 3,000 words; $5-$25. **Nonfiction:** Documented reviews of history, literature, and literary criticism needed (e.g., Mona Lisa's Landscape: a study of the painting's background; Cruising With the Cruisers: on Caribbean cruises, sociology of passenger and crew); 3,000 words; $5-$25. **Fillers:** "Hemingway and Faulkner Reminisce About the Prom," in their respective style; 25-300 words; $5-$10. **Columns, Departments:** Book reviews, poetry, opinion. **Art:** B&W photos; $5-$25. **Tips:** Read the journal before submitting. Send for specifications and sample issue. On the west coast contact Susanne Olson, Director of West Coast operations, Bibliophilos, P.O. Box 39843, Griffith Station, Los Angeles, CA 90039. **Queries:** Required. **E-Queries:** No. **Unsolicited mss:** Does not accept. **Response:** 2-4 weeks. **SASE Required:** Yes. **Freelance Content:** 50%. **Rights:** FNASR. **Payment:** On publication.

BIGNEWS

Mainchance/Grand Central Neighborhood Social Services Corp., 302 E 45th St., New York, NY 10017. 212-883-0680. E-mail: bignewsmag@aol.com. Website: www.mainchance.org/bignews. Monthly. $1/$25. Circ.: 25,000. Ron Grunberg, Editor. **Description:** Literary magazine featuring fiction, nonfiction, and artwork. Typical article runs 1,000-5,000 words; $50/article. **Tips:** "Please read our content online to get an idea of what we are looking for. We focus on the outcast or outsider point of view." **Queries:** Not necessary. **E-Queries:** Yes. **Unsolicited mss:** Accepts. **Response:** Queries 2 days, submissions 2 weeks. **Freelance Content:** 75%. **Rights:** FNAR and electronic. **Payment:** On publication.

BIRMINGHAM POETRY REVIEW

University of Alabama-Birmingham, English Dept., HB 205, 1530 3rd Ave. S, Birmingham, AL 35294-1260. 205-934-4250. Website: www.uab.edu/english/bpr. Semi-annual. $2. Circ.: 750. **Description:** Perfect-bound 60-64 page journal of poetry and reviews. **Queries:** Not necessary. **E-Queries:** Yes. **Unsolicited mss:** Accepts. **Response:** 4-12 weeks. **SASE Required:** Yes. **Freelance Content:** 100%. **Rights:** FNAR. **Payment:** In copies. **Contact:** Robert Collins or Adam Vines, Editors.

BITTER OLEANDER

4983 Tall Oaks Dr., Fayetteville, NY 13066-9776. 315-637-3047. E-mail: info@bitteroleander.com. Website: www.bitteroleander.com. Bi-annual. $8/$15. Circ.: 1,200. Paul B. Roth, Editor. **Description:** Imaginative poetry, fiction, interviews with known and new writers whose work is featured. 128 pages. **Fiction:** Original, imaginative, aware of language as possibility instead of an enslavement; 2,500 words. **Poetry:** Imaginative, concentration on the concrete particular. **Tips:** Seeking more contemporary poetry in translation. No confessional storytelling, overly abstract poetry. **Response:** 1-4 weeks. **SASE Required:** Yes. **Freelance Content:** 80%. **Rights:** All, revert back to author. **Payment:** In copies.

BLACK BEAR REVIEW

1916 Lincoln St., Croydon, PA 19021-8026. E-mail: editor@blackbearreview.com. Website: www.blackbearreview.com. Biannual. $12/yr. Circ.: 750. Ave Jeanne, Editor. **Description:** International literary magazine for the concerned poet and artist. **Tips:** Prefers poems on social and environmental concerns. Avoid traditional forms. Submissions by e-mail only. **Queries:** Not necessary. **E-Queries:** Yes. **Unsolicited mss:** Does not accept. **Response:** 1 week. **SASE Required:** Yes. **Freelance Content:** 100%. **Rights:** FNASR. **Payment:** In copies.

BLACK WARRIOR REVIEW

P.O. Box 862936, Tuscaloosa, AL 35486-0027. 205-348-4518. E-mail: bwr@ua.edu. Website: http://webdelsol.com/bwr. Bi-annual. $14/yr. Circ.: 2,000. Dan Kaplan, Editor. **Description:** Publishes contemporary fiction, poetry, nonfiction, art, interviews, reviews, and photography. Seeks work from emerging and established writers. "Only send your best work." **Tips:** No unsolicited e-mail submissions. See website for guidelines. **Queries:** Not necessary. **E-Queries:** Yes. **Unsolicited mss:** Accepts. **Response:** 2-5 months. **SASE Required:** Yes.

BLUE UNICORN

22 Avon Rd., Kensington, CA 94707. 510-526-8439. 3x/yr. $7/$18. Circ.: 500. Ruth G. Iodice, Editor. **Description:** Has published many of the nation's best poets over the past 25 years. **Poetry:** Well-crafted poems, in form or free verse, also expert translations. Shorter is better. **Tips:** "Study great poets, but develop your own voice; avoid copying whatever is popular. The sound of a poem helps make it memorable." **Queries:** Preferred. **E-Queries:** No. **Unsolicited mss:** Accepts. **SASE Required:** Yes. **Freelance Content:** 100%. **Rights:** FNAR. **Payment:** In copies.

BLUELINE

English Dept., SUNY, Potsdam, NY 13676. 315-267-2043. E-mail: blueline@potsdam.edu. Website: www.potsdam.edu/engl/blueline. Annual. $10/yr. Circ.: 600. Rick Henry, Editor. **Description:** Poems, stories, and essays on the Adirondack and regions similar in geography and spirit, or on the shaping influence of nature. **Fiction:** To 3,500 words. **Nonfiction:** On Adirondack region or similar areas; to 3,500 words. **Poetry:** Submit up to 5 poems; to 75 lines. **Tips:** Accepts submissions from September 1-December 1 only. **Queries:** Not necessary. **E-Queries:** Yes. **Unsolicited mss:** Accepts. **Rights:** FNASR. **Payment:** In copies.

BOSTON REVIEW

Boston Critic, Inc., MIT, 30 Wadsworth St., E53, Room 407, Cambridge, MA 02139. 617-258-0805. E-mail: review@mit.edu. Website: www.bostonreview.net. Bimonthly. Circ.: 20,000. Deborah Chasman, Josh Cohen, Editors. **Description:** Political, literary, and cultural journal. Open to poetry, fiction (1,200-5,000 words), and nonfiction (politics, literature, art, music, film, photography, and culture). **Queries:** Preferred. **Rights:** FNASR. **Contact:** Joshua J. Friedman, Managing Editor.

BOULEVARD

6614 Clayton Rd. #325, Richmond Heights, MO 63117. 314-862-2643. Website: www.richardburgin.com. 3x/yr. $8/$15. Circ.: 4,000. Richard Burgin, Editor. **Description:** A literary review magazine publishing fine, established writers and new writers with exceptional promise. Recent authors: Joyce Carol Oates, Stephen Dixon, Ha Jin, Alice Hoffman, and Alice Adams. **Fiction:** Well-constructed, moving stories, in an original voice; to 30 typed pages; $50-$350. **Nonfiction:** Literary, film, music, criticism, travel pieces, memoirs, philosophical or social issues. **Poetry:** No light verse. Submit up to 5 poems of up to 200 lines; $25-$250/poem. **Tips:** No science fiction, erotica, westerns, horror, romance, or children's stories. **Queries:** Not necessary. **E-Queries:** No. **Unsolicited mss:** Accepts. **Response:** Queries 1 week, submissions 1-2 months. **SASE Required:** Yes. **Freelance Content:** 85%. **Rights:** FNAR. **Payment:** On publication.

BRIAR CLIFF REVIEW

Briar Cliff University, 3303 Rebecca St., Sioux City, IA 51104. E-mail: currans@briarcliff.edu. Website: www.briarcliff.edu/bcreview. **Description:** Eclectic literary and cultural magazine featuring poetry, fiction, essays, and book reviews. Also nonfiction pieces (to 6,000 words) on Siouxland history or humor/satire. **Tips:** Manuscripts read August-October. **Payment:** In copies. **Contact:** Tricia Currans-Sheehan, Editor; Jeanne Emmons, Poetry Editor; Phil Hey, Fiction Editor.

BRIDGE

119 N Peoria, #3D, Chicago, IL 60607. 312-421-2227.
E-mail: submissions@bridgemagazine.org. Website: www.bridgemagazine.org. Triannual. Michael Workman, Publisher/Editor-in-Chief. **Description:** A magazine based on "the simple belief that separate fields of inquiry can and should be thought

of as having shared horizons." **Fiction:** Realistic fiction; 2,000-5,000 words. **Nonfiction:** Critical nonfiction; 2,000-5,000 words. **Tips:** See website for specific submission guidelines. **Queries:** Preferred. **SASE Required:** Yes.

CAIRN

St. Andrews College, 1700 Dogwood Mile, Laurinburg, NC 28352. 910-277-5310. E-mail: cairn@sapc.edu. Website: www.sapc.edu. Annual. $8/issue. Circ.: 1,000. April Link, Matt Phelps, Editors. **Description:** Features fiction, nonfiction, poetry, and book reviews. **Tips:** "*Cairn* is a literary journal that seeks quality work. Recent contributors have been Dana Gioia, Robert Creeley, Richard Blanco, Ted Enslin, and Jean Monahan. We read manuscripts from September to December." **Queries:** Not necessary. **E-Queries:** No. **Unsolicited mss:** Accepts. **Response:** 4 months. **SASE Required:** Yes. **Payment:** In copies. **Contact:** Editorial Dept.

CALIFORNIA QUARTERLY

California State Poetry Society, P.O. Box 7126, Orange, CA 92863. 949-854-8024. E-mail: jipalley@aol.com. Quarterly. $7/$25. Circ.: 250. Julian Palley, Editor. **Description:** "California State Poetry Quarterly." Submit up to 6 poems, to 40 lines on any subject or style. Pays one copy. **Queries:** Not necessary. **Unsolicited mss:** Accepts. **Response:** 5-6 months. **SASE Required:** Yes. **Freelance Content:** 100%.

CALYX JOURNAL

P.O. Box B, Corvallis, OR 97339. 541-753-9384. E-mail: calyx@proaxis.com. Website: www.proaxis.com/~calyx. Biannual. $9.50/issue. Circ.: 5,000. Beverly McFarland, Senior Editor. **Description:** Journal of art and literature by women, with poetry, prose, art, and book reviews. Presents wide spectrum of women's experience, especially work by unheard voices (new writers, women of color, working-class, older women). **Fiction:** 5,000 words. **Nonfiction:** 5,000 words. **Poetry:** 6 poems max. **Art:** Color cover, plus 16 pages of B&W art. **Tips:** Submit prose and poetry October 1-December 31. Art submissions accepted anytime. Send query for book reviews only. **Queries:** Not necessary. **Unsolicited mss:** Accepts. **Response:** 6-8 weeks. **SASE Required:** Yes. **Payment:** In copies.

THE CAPE ROCK

Southeast Missouri State University, Dept. of English, Cape Girardeau, MO 63701. 573-651-2500. E-mail: hhecht@semo.edu. Bi-annual. $5/$7. Circ.: 500. Harvey E. Hecht, Editor. **Description:** Poetry journal, with photography. **Poetry:** To 70 lines; pays $200 for "Best in issue." **Art:** A series of 12-15 B&W photos, featuring a sense of place; $100. **Tips:** Manuscripts read August-April. **Queries:** Not necessary. **E-Queries:** Yes. **Unsolicited mss:** Accepts. **Response:** Queries 1-2 weeks, submissions 2-4 months. **SASE Required:** Yes. **Rights:** All. **Payment:** In copies.

THE CAPILANO REVIEW

2055 Purcell Way, North Vancouver, British Columbia V7J 3H5 Canada. 604-984-1712. E-mail: tcr@capcollege.bc.ca. Website: www.capcollege.bc.ca/dept/TCR. 3x/yr. $9/$25. Circ.: 900. Sharon Thesen, Editor. **Description:** Innovative poetry, fiction, drama, and work in the visual media, in a cross-disciplinary format. **Fiction:** To 6,000 words (drama, to 10,000 words); $50-$200 (Canadian). **Poetry:** 5-6 poems; $50-$200 (Canadian). **Tips:** Does not accept simultaneous submissions. "We look for work pushing beyond the boundaries of traditional art and writing." **Queries:** Not necessary. **E-Queries:** No. **Unsolicited mss:** Accepts. **Response:** 4 months, SASE with Canadian postage or IRCs required. **Rights:** FNASR. **Payment:** On publication. **Contact:** Carol L. Hamshaw, Managing Editor.

THE CARIBBEAN WRITER

University of the Virgin Islands, RR02, Box 10,000, Kingshill St. Croix, Virgin Islands 00850. 340-692-4152. E-mail: submit@thecaribbeanwriter.com, qmars@uvi.edu. Website: www.thecaribbeanwriter.com. Annual. $12/issue; $20/ 2 yr. individual subscription; $40/ 2 yr. institutional subscription. Circ.: 1,200. Marvin E. Williams, Editor. **Description:** Literary anthology with Caribbean focus. **Fiction:** Personal essays, also one-act plays (max. 3,500 words or 10 pages), or up to 2 short stories (15 pages or less); Caribbean experience or heritage central. **Poetry:** Caribbean focus; submit up to 5 poems. **Tips:** Original, unpublished work only (if self-published, give details). Blind submissions policy: print only the title on your manuscript; give your name, address, e-mail and any other contact information on a separate sheet. Revolving deadline November 30. **Queries:** Not necessary. **E-Queries:** Yes. **Unsolicited mss:** Accepts. **SASE Required:** Yes. **Freelance Content:** 80%. **Rights:** One-time. **Payment:** In copies. **Contact:** Ms. Quilin Mars.

CAROLINA QUARTERLY

CB#3520 Greenlaw Hall, UNC-Chapel Hill English Dept., Chapel Hill, NC 27599-3520. E-mail: cquarter@unc.edu. Website: www.unc.edu/depts/cqonline. Amy Weldon, Editor. **Description:** Features poetry, fiction, nonfiction, and artwork by new and established writers. **Fiction:** Short stories and novel excerpts; up to 25 pages. **Nonfiction:** Personal essays, memoirs, book reviews. **Poetry:** Up to 6 poems. **Art:** Painting, photography, drawings **Tips:** Manuscripts not read May, June, and July. Accepts queries, but not submissions, via e-mail. Sample copy $5. **Queries:** Not necessary. **E-Queries:** Yes. **Unsolicited mss:** Accepts. **Response:** 4-6 months. **SASE Required:** Yes.

CHARITON REVIEW

English Department, Brigham Young University, Provo, UT 84602. Semiannual. Circ.: 700. Jim Barnes, Editor. **Description:** Quality poetry and fiction and contemporary translations. To 6,000 words; $5/printed page. **Tips:** "The only guideline is excellence."

THE CHATTAHOOCHEE REVIEW

Georgia Perimeter College, 2101 Womack Rd., Dunwoody, GA 30338-4497. E-mail: gpccr@gpc.edu. Website: www.chattahoochee-review.org. Quarterly. $6/$16. Lawrence Hetrick, Editor. **Description:** Promotes fresh writing by emerging and established voices. **Fiction:** To 5,000 words; $20/page. **Nonfiction:** $15/page, reviews $50. **Poetry:** $30/poem. **Tips:** Also hosts annual Lamar York Prize for Nonfiction. See website for details. **Queries:** Not necessary. **Response:** 1-16 weeks. **SASE Required:** Yes. **Freelance Content:** 80%. **Rights:** FNAR. **Payment:** On publication.

CHELSEA

P.O. Box 773, Cooper Station, New York, NY 10276-0773. Semiannual. $8/$13. Circ.: 2,100. Alfredo de Palchi, Editor. **Description:** New and established voices in literature. Eclectic, lively, sophisticated, with accent on translations, art, and cross-cultural exchange. Pays $15/page, plus 2 copies. **Fiction:** Mainstream, literary; to 25 pages. **Nonfiction:** Essays, memoirs; to 25 pages. **Poetry:** Traditional, avant-garde; 5-8 poems. **Columns, Departments:** Book reviews, by assignment only. **Art:** Submit slides; color (cover), B&W inside. **Tips:** Interested in avant-garde: original ideas and use of language. Send for sample, $6. **Queries:** Not necessary. **E-Queries:** No. **Unsolicited mss:** Accepts. **Response:** 1-5 months. **SASE Required:** Yes. **Rights:** FNAR. **Payment:** On publication.

CHIRON REVIEW

702 N Prairie, St. John, KS 67576-1516. 620-786-4955. E-mail: chironreview@hotmail.com. Website: www.geocities.com/soho/nook/1748/. Quarterly. $5/$15. Circ.: 2,000. Michael Hathaway, Publisher/Editor. **Description:** Publication featuring a wide range of contemporary creative writing (fiction and nonfiction, traditional and offbeat) including artwork and photography of featured writers. Also provides news and literary reviews. **Fiction:** Contemporary fiction; 700-3,000 words. **Nonfiction:** Essays, interviews, and reviews of literary books and magazines; 500-1,000 words. **Poetry:** Send 5 poems. **Tips:** Does not accept e-mail, simultaneous or previously published submissions. **Queries:** Not necessary. **Unsolicited mss:** Accepts. **Response:** 2-8 weeks. **SASE Required:** Yes. **Freelance Content:** 100%. **Rights:** One-time. **Payment:** In copies.

CIA-CITIZEN IN AMERICA, INC

30 Ford St., Glen Cove, NY 11542. 516-759-8718. E-mail: ciamc@webtv.net. 9x/yr. John J. Maddox, Magazine Coordinator. **Description:** Fiction and nonfiction, to 2,000 words. Poetry to 100 words. Prefers self photos to be published with articles. Fillers accepted. Pays $40-$100. **Tips:** Queries required for e-mail only. Include brief bio with age stated.

CIMARRON REVIEW
Oklahoma State University, 205 Morrill Hall, Stillwater, OK 74078-4069. E-mail: cimarronreview@yahoo.com. Website: http://cimarronreview.okstate.edu. Quarterly. Circ.: 600. E.P. Walkiewicz, Editor. **Description:** Poetry, fiction, and essays. Seeks work with individual, innovative style and contemporary themes. Pays two copies and 1-year subscription. **Tips:** "We're open to anything fresh, exciting, savvy." Accepts simultaneous submissions. Read a sample copy ($7) before submitting. **Queries:** Not necessary. **E-Queries:** No. **Unsolicited mss:** Accepts. **Response:** 1-6 months. **SASE Required:** Yes. **Rights:** FNASR. **Payment:** In copies.

THE CIRCLE MAGAZINE
173 Grandview Rd., Wernersville, PA 19565. 610-823-2707. E-mail: circlemag@aol.com. Website: www.circlemagazine.com. Quarterly. $4/$15. Circ.: 4,000. **Description:** Literary magazine featuring short fiction, poetry, columns, and reviews. **Fiction:** Odd, witty, satirical. No religious pieces. 700-4,500 words. **Nonfiction:** Music, political, personal. Query first. **Poetry:** Any length/style, leans toward free verse. Send 3-5 poems. **Tips:** *"The Circle . . .* where culture and subculture meet . . . is an independent literary zine which answers to no one. We enjoy laughing. We enjoy thinking. We're not politically correct. We are, however, choosy and charming." **Unsolicited mss:** Accepts. **Response:** Queries 1-2 weeks, submissions 3-6 months. **SASE Required:** Yes. **Freelance Content:** 50%. **Payment:** In copies. **Contact:** Penny Talbert, Editor; Michael Clipman, Poetry Editor.

COLORADO REVIEW
Colorado State University, English Dept., Fort Collins, CO 80523. 970-491-5449. E-mail: creview@colostate.edu. Website: www.coloradoreview.com. 3x/yr. $9.50/$24. Circ.: 1,300. Stephanie G'Schwind, Editor. **Description:** Fiction, poetry, and personal essays by new and established writers. Seeking work that is vital, imaginative, highly realized, and avoids mere mannerism to embody human concern. Fiction and nonfiction to 20 pages. Poetry length varies. Pays $5/page. **Art:** Slides, $100 (cover). **Tips:** Simultaneous submissions ok, but writers must notify CR immediately if work is accepted elsewhere. Reading period, September-April only; submissions sent outside this period are returned unread. **Queries:** Not necessary. **E-Queries:** No. **Unsolicited mss:** Accepts. **Response:** Queries 2-4 weeks, submissions 4-8 weeks. **SASE Required:** Yes. **Rights:** FNAR. **Payment:** On publication.

COLUMBIA: A JOURNAL OF LITERATURE AND ART
Columbia University, 415 Dodge Hall, 2960 Broadway, New York, NY 10027. 212-854-4216. E-mail: columbiajournal@columbia.edu. Website: www.columbia.edu/cu/arts/journal. Annual. **Description:** Literary journal, with contemporary poetry, fiction, and creative nonfiction from established and emerging voices. Edited by students in Columbia's MFA writing program. **Fiction:** No restrictions (avoid children's stories or genre pieces). Open to experimental writing, mainstream narratives, work that takes risks; 25 pages or less. **Nonfiction:** Same as fiction (no reviews or academic criticism); 20 pages or less. **Poetry:** Wide range of

forms and styles; 4 poems max. **Tips:** No electronic submissions. See website for specific guidelines. **Queries:** Not necessary. **Unsolicited mss:** Accepts. **Response:** 1-3 months. **SASE Required:** Yes. **Rights:** FNAR. **Payment:** In copies. **Contact:** Poetry or Prose Editor.

COMBAT

P.O. Box 3, Circleville, WV 26804. E-mail: majordomo@combat.ws. Website: www.combat.ws/. Quarterly. **Description:** The literary expression of battlefield touchstones; wartime insights and experiences. Fiction and nonfiction to 4,000 words; poetry to 400 words. **Tips:** Read submission guidelines. **Queries:** Not necessary. **E-Queries:** Yes. **SASE Required:** Yes. **Freelance Content:** 90%. **Rights:** FNASR.

CONCHO RIVER REVIEW

Angelo State University, English Dept., San Angelo, TX 76909. 325-942-2273. E-mail: me.hartje@angelo.edu. Bi-annual. $8/$14. Circ.: 300. Terry Dalrymple, Fiction Editor. **Description:** Literary journal with fiction, essays, poetry, and book reviews. **Fiction:** Traditional stories with strong sense of conflict, finely-drawn characters, and crisp dialogue; 1,500-5,000 words. **Nonfiction:** Critical papers, personal essays, and reviews; 1,500-5,000 words. **Poetry:** Send 3-5 poems at a time; 1 page or less. **Queries:** Not necessary. **E-Queries:** Yes. **Unsolicited mss:** Accepts. **Response:** Queries 2-4 weeks, submissions 3-6 months. **SASE Required:** Yes. **Freelance Content:** 100%. **Rights:** FNAR. **Payment:** In copies.

CONDUIT

510 8th Ave. NE, Minneapolis, MN 55413. 612-326-0995. Website: www.conduit.org. 2x/yr. $8/issue. Circ.: 800. William D. Waltz, Editor. **Description:** Seeks previously unpublished poetry, prose, artwork, and B&W photography. Submit 3-5 poems or 1 prose piece (up to 3,500 words). **Tips:** "*Conduit* is a lively literary journal featuring innovative work by emerging and established writers. We dedicate 75% of our pages to poetry." **Queries:** Not necessary. **E-Queries:** Yes. **Unsolicited mss:** Accepts. **Response:** 6 weeks-6 months. **SASE Required:** Yes. **Freelance Content:** 75%. **Rights:** FNAR.

CONFLUENCE

P.O. Box 336, Belpre, OH 45714-0336. E-mail: wilmaacree@charter.net; confluence1989@yahoo.com. Annual. $5/issue. Circ.: 1,000. Wilma Acree, Editor. **Description:** Presents the work of emerging and established authors. **Fiction:** Literary fiction; to 5,000 words. **Nonfiction:** Interviews, essays; to 5,000 words. **Poetry:** Lyric, narrative poetry with fresh images. No rhymed poetry unless of exceptional quality; to 60 lines. **Tips:** No previously published work or simultaneous submissions. Cover letter with short bio and complete contact info required. **Queries:** Not necessary. **E-Queries:** Yes. **Unsolicited mss:** Accepts. **Response:** Queries 1 month, submissions 1-5 months. **SASE Required:** Yes. **Freelance Content:** 80%. **Rights:** FNAR. **Payment:** In copies.

CONFRONTATION

Long Island University, C.W. Post of L.I.U., Dept. of English, Brookville, NY 11548. 516-299-2720. E-mail: martin.tucker@liu.edu. Semiannual. $10. Circ.: 2,000. Martin Tucker, Editor. **Description:** Literary magazine with poetry, fiction, essays, and memoirs. Also, original work by famous and emerging writers. **Fiction:** To 30 pages; $25-$150. **Nonfiction:** Mostly memoirs. Other nonfiction, including reviews, is assigned; $25-$150. **Poetry:** Pays $10-$100. **Tips:** Send query for nonfiction material only. Accepts queries via e-mail, but not submissions. Manuscripts read September-May only. **Unsolicited mss:** Accepts. **Response:** Queries 2-4 weeks, submissions 6-8 weeks. **SASE Required:** Yes. **Freelance Content:** 75%. **Rights:** FNASR. **Payment:** On publication.

THE CONNECTICUT POETRY REVIEW

P.O. Box 818, Stonington, CT 06378. J. Claire White, Harley More, Editors. **Description:** Poetry, 5-20 lines; pays $5/poem. Reviews, 700 words; pays $10. **Tips:** Manuscripts read September-January, and April-June. **Payment:** On acceptance.

CONNECTICUT RIVER REVIEW

Connecticut Poetry Society, P.O. Box 4053, Waterbury, CT 06704-0053. E-mail: editorcrr@yahoo.com (for queries only). Annual. $12/yr. Circ.: 500. Sue Holloway, Editor. **Description:** National journal of poetry in print since 1978. Poetry accepted from both professionals and new writers. Submit up to 3 poems (any form/subject, 40 lines max.) between October 1-April 15. Upon notifiction of acceptance, poems must be submitted electronically or on disk. Include contact information and SASE. Accepts simultaneous submissions with notice. **Tips:** "Poems are reviewed by both an editorial board and an editor, so 'making the cut' requires charming an informed, diverse audience—use fresh language!" **SASE Required:** Yes. **Payment:** In copies.

COTTONWOOD MAGAZINE

University of Kansas, 1301 Jayhawk Blvd., Room 400, Kansas Union, Lawrence, KS 66045. 2x/yr. **Description:** Publishes new and well-known writers. No rhymed poetry. Kansas and Midwestern focus. Photos, graphics, and book reviews from Midwest presses also accepted. **Fiction:** Work from experience; no contrived or slick fiction. Submit only 1 story at a time. 1,500-8,000 words. **Poetry:** Submit up to 5 poems; 10-80 lines. **Art:** Photos, other graphic arts. **Tips:** Published work eligible for annual awards. **E-Queries:** No. **Response:** 3-6 months. **SASE Required:** Yes. **Rights:** FNAR. **Payment:** In copies.

CRAB CREEK REVIEW

P.O. Box 840, Vashon Island, WA 98070. Website: www.crabcreekreview.org. Semiannual. Circ.: 600. **Description:** Original poetry, short fiction, and artwork. No simultaneous submissions. **Fiction:** Up to 6,000 words. **Poetry:** Up to 5 poems. Translations welcome. **Art:** B&W photography, pen or brushwork, preferably drawn to 9x6. **Response:** 2-4 months. **SASE Required:** Yes. **Rights:** FNAR. **Payment:** In copies. **Contact:** Submissions Editor.

THE CREAM CITY REVIEW

Univ. of WI-Milwaukee, English Dept., P.O. Box 413, Milwaukee, WI 53201. 414-229-4708. E-mail: creamcity@uwm.edu. Website: www.uwm.edu/dept/english/ccr. Semi-annual. $8/$15. Circ.: 700. Erica Wiest, Editor. **Description:** Literary journal with fiction, nonfiction, poetry, interviews, and book reviews. **Queries:** Not necessary. **E-Queries:** No. **Unsolicited mss:** Accepts. **Response:** Queries 2 weeks, submissions 3-8 months. **SASE Required:** Yes. **Freelance Content:** 100%. **Rights:** FNAR. **Payment:** In copies.

CREATIVE NONFICTION

5501 Walnut, Suite 202, Pittsburgh, PA 15232. 412-688-0304. E-mail: creative.nonfiction@verizon.net. Website: www.creativenonfiction.org. 3x/yr. $10/$29.95. Circ.: 4,000. Lee Gutkind, Editor-in-Chief. **Description:** Literary journal, devoted exclusively to non-fiction. Personal essays, memoirs, literary journalism, profiles of creative nonfiction authors, book reviews. **Nonfiction:** Prose, rich with detail and distinctive voice on any subject; seeking essays based on research; $10/page. **Tips:** "Material can be personal, but must reach out universally in some way." **Queries:** Not necessary. **E-Queries:** Yes. **Unsolicited mss:** Accepts. **Response:** 3 months. **SASE Required:** Yes. **Freelance Content:** 95%. **Rights:** FNASR, reprint. **Payment:** On publication.

CUTBANK

University of Montana, English Dept., Missoula, MT 59812. 406-243-6156. E-mail: cutbank@selway.umt.edu. Website: www.umt.edu/cutbank. Biannual. $6.95/$12. Circ.: 1,000. Elizabeth Conway, Editor-in-Chief. **Description:** Fiction, poetry, and artwork. **Tips:** "Request a sample copy to see what we publish." **Queries:** Not necessary. **E-Queries:** No. **Unsolicited mss:** Accepts. **Response:** 3-4 months. **SASE Required:** Yes. **Freelance Content:** 90%. **Payment:** In copies.

DESCANT

T.C.U. Box 297270, Fort Worth, TX 76129. 817-257-6537. E-mail: d.kuhne@tcu.edu. Website: www.eng.tcu.edu/journals/descant/index.html. Annual. $12. Circ.: 750. Dave Kuhne, Editor; Lynn Risser, Editor. **Description:** Seeks quality work in traditional or innovative form. **Fiction:** No restrictions; most stories under 5,000 words. **Poetry:** Fewer than 60 lines. **Tips:** Submit September-April only. **Queries:** Not necessary. **E-Queries:** No. **Unsolicited mss:** Accepts. **Response:** 6-8 weeks. **SASE Required:** Yes. **Freelance Content:** 100%. **Rights:** FNAR. **Payment:** In copies.

DESCANT

P.O. Box 314, Station P, Toronto, Ontario M5S 2S8 Canada. 416-593-2557. E-mail: descant@web.net. Website: www.descant.on.ca. Quarterly. Circ.: 2,000. Karen Mulhallen, Editor. **Description:** Literary journal publishing new and established writers and artists. Considers original, unpublished submissions of poetry, short stories, essays, plays, interviews, musical scores, novel excerpts, and visual arts. **Tips:** No simultaneous submissions. Does not accept electronic submissions. **SASE Required:** Yes.

THE DISTILLERY

Motlow State Community College, P.O. Box 8500, Dept. #210, Lynchburg, TN 37352-8500. 931-393-1700. Website: www.mscc.cc.tn.vs/distillery/. Semiannual. $9/$15. Circ.: 500. Dawn Copeland, Editor. **Description:** Literary journal of poetry, fiction, nonfiction, art, and photography. **Fiction:** Literary, emphasis on style, character, voice; 4,000 words. **Nonfiction:** Creative nonfiction, with a sense of style. Critical and personal essays; 4,000 words. **Poetry:** Voice, style, and image; any length. **Tips:** Avoid warmed-over exercises in Kmart realism. No simultaneous submissions. **Queries:** Not necessary. **E-Queries:** No. **Unsolicited mss:** Accepts. **Response:** 2-4 months. **SASE Required:** Yes. **Rights:** FNAR. **Payment:** In copies.

DOUBLE DEALER REDUX

The Pirate's Alley Faulkner Society, Faulkner House, 624 Pirate's Alley, New Orleans, LA 70116. 504-586-1609. E-mail: faulkhouse@aol.com. Website: www.wordsandmusic.org. Annual. Circ.: 7,500. Rosemary James, Supervising Editor. **Description:** Poems, short stories, essays, and critical reviews, also portions of novels and novellas. **Tips:** Has published entire novellas with author's permission. **Queries:** Preferred. **Unsolicited mss:** Does not accept. **Payment:** In copies.

DREAMS & VISIONS

Skysong Press, 35 Peter St. S, Orillia, Ontario L3V 5A8 Canada. E-mail: skysong@bconnex.net. Website: www.bconnex.net/~skysong. Semi-annual. $4.95/issue. Circ.: 200. Steve Stanton, Editor. **Description:** *Dreams & Visions: New Frontiers in Christian Literature* features short literary fiction from a Christian perspective (science fiction, humor, fantasy, magic realism, contemporary, inspirational). No genre excluded. **Fiction:** Based on Biblical norms or traditions, but portraying spiritual truths in new, innovative ways; 2,000-6,000 words; $.01/word. **Tips:** Sample copy $4.95 or writer's package of 4 back issues w/guidelines $10. **Queries:** Not necessary. **E-Queries:** Yes. **Unsolicited mss:** Accepts. **Response:** SASE w/Canadian postage or $1 (US). **Freelance Content:** 100%.

EPOCH

Cornell University, 251 Goldwin Smith Hall, Ithaca, NY 14853-3201. 607-255-3385. Triannual. $6.50/$11. Circ.: 1,000. Michael Koch, Editor. **Description:** Serious fiction, poetry, and personal essays. Pays $5-$10/page. **Queries:** Not necessary. **E-Queries:** No. **Unsolicited mss:** Accepts. **Response:** 4-6 weeks. **SASE Required:** Yes. **Freelance Content:** 100%. **Rights:** FNAR. **Payment:** On publication.

EUREKA LITERARY MAGAZINE

Eureka College, 300 E College Ave., Eureka, IL 61530. 309-467-6336. E-mail: llogsdon@eureka.com. Biannual. $7.50/issue. Circ.: 500. Loren Logsdon, Editor. **Description:** Publishes well-written, thought-provoking stories (2-28 pages) and poetry (any length). **Queries:** Not necessary. **E-Queries:** Yes. **Unsolicited mss:** Accepts. **Response:** Queries 2-3 weeks, submissions 4-5 months. **SASE Required:** Yes. **Freelance Content:** 100%. **Rights:** One-time. **Payment:** In copies.

EVENT
Douglas College, P.O. Box 2503, New Westminster, British Columbia V3L 5B2 Canada. 604-527-5293. E-mail: event@douglas.bc.ca. Website: http://event/douglas.bc.ca. 3x/yr. Circ.: 1,250. Cathy Stonehouse, Editor. **Description:** Mostly fiction, poetry, and creative nonfiction. **Fiction:** Readable, stylish, with well-handled characters and strong point-of-view; submit up to 2 short stories; 5,000 words max; $22/page ($500 max.). **Nonfiction:** Personal essays, memoirs, travel accounts, literary; 5,000 words max; $22/page ($500 max.). **Poetry:** Appreciate strong narrative, sometimes confessional modes. Eclectic, always open to content that invites involvement; submit 3-8 poems. **Art:** For cover only; $150. **Tips:** Hosts annual *Event* Creative Nonfiction Contest with $1,500 in prizes. Also offers optional critique service to writers ($100 fee). **Queries:** Not necessary. **Unsolicited mss:** Accepts. **Response:** 1-6 months. SASE required with IRC's. **Freelance Content:** 85%. **Rights:** FNASR. **Payment:** On publication.

EXQUISITE CORPSE
P.O. Box 25051, Baton Rouge, LA 70802. E-mail: submissions@corpse.org. Website: www.corpse.org. Andrei Codrescu, Editor. **Description:** Fiction, nonfiction, and poetry for "a journal of letters and life." B&W photos and drawings. Read the magazine before submitting. **Tips:** Send all material via e-mail. Does not accept hard copy. Refer to website for updated submission guidelines. **Queries:** Required.

FICTION
English Dept., The City College of New York, Convent Ave. at 138th St., New York, NY 10031. 212-650-6319. E-mail: fictionmagazine@yahoo.com. Website: www.fictioninc.com. 2-3x/yr. $10/issue. Circ.: 600. Mark Jay Mirsky, Editor. **Description:** Short fiction from both new and published authors. Seeks material that is new and experimental. **Tips:** Manuscripts not accepted May 15-September 1. **Queries:** Not necessary. **E-Queries:** No. **Unsolicited mss:** Accepts. **Response:** 4-6 months. **SASE Required:** Yes. **Freelance Content:** 100%. **Rights:** All.

FIELD: CONTEMPORARY POETRY AND POETICS
Oberlin College Press, 10 N Professor St., Oberlin, OH 44074. 440-775-8408. E-mail: oc.press@oberlin.edu. Website: www.oberlin.edu/ocpress. Biannual. $14/yr. Circ.: 1,250. David Young, David Walker, Martha Collins, Pamela Alexander, Editors. **Description:** Contemporary poetry, poetics, and translations. Seeks to be at forefront of what is happening in poetry. Fall issue features symposium on a famous writer, Spring issue features reviews. **Poetry:** Varied formats, length. Submit 3-5 poems; pays $15/page, plus copies and subscription. **Tips:** Accepts queries via e-mail, but not submissions. **E-Queries:** Yes. **Unsolicited mss:** Does not accept. **Response:** 4-6 weeks. **SASE Required:** Yes. **Payment:** On publication. **Contact:** Linda Slocum, Managing Editor.

FINE MADNESS

P.O. Box 31138, Seattle, WA 98103-1138. E-mail: beastly@oz.net. Website: www.fine-madness.org. Annual. $7/$12. Circ.: 1,000. **Description:** International poetry by writers, well-known and new, highly original in language and content. **Poetry:** Form open, strong sense of language, original imagery. **Tips:** No simultaneous submissions. "Avoid concrete poetry, light verse, topical poetry, or over-dependence on form. We prefer lyrical poems that use language in thoughtful and thought-provoking ways." **Queries:** Preferred. **E-Queries:** Yes. **Unsolicited mss:** Accepts. **Response:** Queries 1-2 months, submissions 3-4 months. **SASE Required:** Yes. **Freelance Content:** 100%.

FIRST INTENSITY

P.O. Box 665, Lawrence, KS 66044-0665. 785-479-1501.
E-mail: leechapman@aol.com. Annual. $14/issue. Circ.: 300. Ms. Lee Chapman, Editor. **Description:** Literary journal with poetry, short fiction, prose poetry, book reviews, interviews. Essays on poetics, writing, writers, visual artists. Submit up to 10 pages of material. **Tips:** Seeking serious, experimental work, nothing "mainstream." Readership tends to be college-educated and serious about writing. **Queries:** Not necessary. **E-queries:** Yes. **Unsolicited mss:** Accepts. Response: 8-10 weeks. **SASE Required:** Yes. **Freelance Content:** 50%. **Payment:** In copies.

THE FIRST LINE

Blue Cubicle Press, P.O. Box 250382, Plano, TX 75025-0382.
E-mail: submission@thefirstline.com; info@thefirstline.com. Website: www.thefirst-line.com. Quarterly. $3/$10. Circ.: 250. David LaBounty, Jeff Adams, Editors. **Description:** Celebrates the first line. Provides a forum for discussing favorite lines and different short stories stemming from a common first line. **Fiction:** All stories must stem from the same first line; 300-3,000 words. **Nonfiction:** Essays about a first line from book or story; 300-1,000 words. **Queries:** Not necessary. **E-Queries:** Yes. **Unsolicited mss:** Accepts. **Response:** 2-6 weeks. **SASE Required:** Yes. **Freelance Content:** 100%. **Rights:** Negotiable. **Payment:** $10/story and 1 copy. **Contact:** Robin LaBounty, Manuscript Coordinator.

FIVE POINTS

MSC 8R0318, Georgia State University, 33 Gilmer St. SE, Unit 8, Atlanta, GA 30303-3083. Website: www.webdelsol.com/Five_Points. 3x/yr. $7/$20. Circ.: 2,000. David Bottoms, Editor. **Description:** Quality fiction, poetry, essays, and interviews. Writing must have original voice, substance and significance. **Fiction:** 7,500 words; $15/page, $250 max. **Nonfiction:** Personal essays, literary essays, and creative nonfiction; 7,500 words; $15/page, $250 max. **Poetry:** 100 lines max. per poem; $50/poem. **Art:** Photos (slides or prints) only. Paintings and illustrations sometimes considered. Pay varies. **Tips:** "No limitations on style or contents. Our only criterion is excellence." Reading period between September 1-April 30. **Queries:** Not necessary. **E-Queries:** No. **Unsolicited mss:** Accepts. **Response:** 2-3 months. **SASE Required:** Yes. **Freelance Content:** 10%. **Rights:** FNAR. **Payment:** On publication.

FLINT HILLS REVIEW

Bluestem Press, Emporia State University, Dept. of English, Box 4019, Emporia, KS 66801-5087. 316-341-5216. Website: www.emporia.edu/fhr. Annual. Circ.: 500. **Description:** Writing, from and about Kansas and the Great Plains region, conveying a strong sense of place. **Fiction:** Place-focused writing about or set in the region. **Nonfiction:** Interviews, essays; offers annual prize of $200. **Poetry:** Strong imagery, fidelity to place. **Art:** Place-based B&W photos, ideally which redefine the region. **Tips:** Do not send genre fiction, religious writing, or unsolicited critical essays or interviews (query first for these). "Correspond via e-mail if you have specific questions. Write for our guidelines. Send copies of your work that seem appropriate to our mission of showcasing place-based writing." **Queries:** Not necessary. **E-queries:** Yes. **Unsolicited mss:** Accepts. **Response:** 2-6 months. **SASE Required:** Yes. **Freelance Content:** 5%. **Rights:** FNAR. **Payment:** In copies.

THE FLORIDA REVIEW

University of Central Florida, English Dept., Orlando, FL 32816. 407-823-2038. Biannual. $8/$15. Circ.: 1,500. Jeanne M. Leiby, Editor. **Description:** Literary journal with mainstream and experimental fiction. Also nonfiction and poetry. Prose should be no more than 10,000 words. **Queries:** Not necessary. **Unsolicited mss:** Accepts. **Response:** 1-2 months. **SASE Required:** Yes. **Rights:** FNAR. **Payment:** In copies. **Contact:** Kereth Cowe-Spigai.

FLYWAY: A LITERARY REVIEW

Iowa State University, 206 Ross Hall, Ames, IA 50011. E-mail: flyway@iastate.edu. Website: www.flyway.org. Triannual. $18/yr. Circ.: 500. Stephen Pett, Editor. **Description:** Quality poetry, nonfiction, and fiction by new and established writers. **Fiction:** Literary fiction up to 20 pages. **Nonfiction:** Personal essays up to 20 pages. **Poetry:** Ambitious; "open to all poetry that takes its experience seriously, including humorous poems." **Art:** "We are always looking for cover art. Send slides or photos of work." **Queries:** Not necessary. **E-Queries:** No. **Unsolicited mss:** Accepts. **Response:** 2 weeks. **SASE Required:** Yes. **Freelance Content:** 90%. **Rights:** One-time. **Payment:** In copies.

THE FOLIATE OAK

University of Arkansas, Arts and Humanities, Monticello, AR 71656. 870-460-1247. E-mail: foliateoak@uamont.edu. Website: www.uamont.edu/foliateoak/. Monthly. Diane Payne, Faculty Advisor. **Description:** Literary journal for new and established writers. Accepts submissions electronically September-May. **Fiction:** No genre, racist, homophobic, maudlin writing; to 3,500 words. **Nonfiction:** Creative nonfiction to 3,500 words. **Poetry:** Submit up to 5 poems. **E-Queries:** Yes. **Response:** 1 month. **Payment:** In copies.

FOLIO

American University, Dept. of Literature, Washington, DC 20016. Website: www.foliojournal.org. Bi-annual. $12/yr. Circ.: 500. **Description:** Quality fiction, creative nonfiction, poetry, translations, and B&W photos. Prose to 3,500 words, poetry to 5 poems. **Tips:** Submissions read September 1-March 1. **Queries:** Not necessary. **E-Queries:** No. **Unsolicited mss:** Accepts. **Response:** 2-6 months. **SASE Required:** Yes. **Freelance Content:** 90%. **Payment:** In copies.

FOOTSTEPS

Footsteps Press, P.O. Box 75, Round Top, NY 12473.
E-mail: krause5@francomm.com. Website: www.footstepspublishing.com. Bill Munster, Editor. **Description:** "We are now looking for material only related to horror, sci fi, and fantasy. Submit interviews, bits of novels, short stories." Query with complete manuscript and SASE. Send hard copy only. Pays flat fee. **Tips:** Material submitted may be on any topic. Also looking for anything related to poems about movies or prose poems. No rhymed poems.

THE FORMALIST

320 Hunter Dr., Evansville, IN 47711. $7.50 (sample)/$14/year (2 issues). William Baer, Editor. **Description:** Well-crafted poetry in a contemporary idiom which uses meter and traditional poetic conventions in vigorous and interesting ways. Especially interested in sonnets, couplets, tercets, ballads, the French forms etc. Also interested in metrical translations of major, formalist, non-English poets.Does not accept haiku, sestinas, or syllabic verse. Does not have any interest in erotica, blasphemy, vulgarity, or racism. No simultaneous submissions, previously published work, or disk submissions. Submit 3-5 poems with SASE. **Tips:** Offers Howard Nemerov Sonnet Award, $1,000. **Queries:** Not necessary. **Response:** 8 weeks. **SASE Required:** Yes. **Payment:** In copies.

FOURTEEN HILLS

San Francisco State University, Creative Writing Dept., 1600 Holloway Ave., San Francisco, CA 94132-1722. 415-338-3083. E-mail: hills@sfsu.edu. Website: www.14hills.net. Biannual. $7/issue, $12/yr. Circ.: 600. Jason Snyder, Editor-in-Chief. **Description:** Innovative fiction, poetry, drama, and interviews. Seeking matter or styles overlooked by traditional journals. **Fiction:** Up to 5,000 words **Poetry:** Submit up to 5 poems **Queries:** Not necessary. **E-Queries:** No. **Unsolicited mss:** Accepts. **Response:** Queries 2 weeks, submissions up to 10 months **Rights:** FNAR. **Payment:** In copies.

FROGPOND

Haiku Society of America, P.O. Box 2461, Winchester, VA 22604-1661. 540-722-2156. E-mail: ithacan@earthlink.net; redmoon@shentel.net. Website: www.hsa-haiku.org. 3x/yr. $28/yr (US). Circ.: 1,000. Jim Kacian, Editor. **Description:** Features haiku and related forms; $1/poem. Also articles, essays, and reviews. **Tips:** Know what is current in contemporary haiku. "We are the largest journal published outside of Japan and have been in operation since 1968. The most important English-Language Haiku journal in the world." **E-Queries:** Yes. **Unsolicited mss:** Accepts. **Response:** 2-3 weeks. **SASE Required:** Yes. **Freelance Content:** 95%. **Rights:** FNAR. **Payment:** On acceptance.

FROM THE ASYLUM

P.O. Box 3662, Galveston, TX 77552. 409-741-0868.
E-mail: fta@fromtheasylum.com. Website: www.fromtheasylum.com. Monthly. Katherine Sanger, Editor. **Description:** "Literary e-zine that runs the gauntlet of strange to bizarre and then some. Fiction, poetry, you name it." Open length and style; pays $5 plus 2 copies of yearly anthology in which work appears. **Tips:** "We're not looking for graphic sex or extreme violence unless its extremly important to the story, and even then we probably don't want it. We prefer the Alfred Hitchcock school of thought—it's scarier if you don't see it. Check out our most recent stories to see what types of things we want, and if you're not sure, feel free to send it along anyway. We respond within a month, and don't mind simultaneous submissions." **Queries:** Not necessary. **E-Queries:** Yes. **Unsolicited mss:** Accepts. **Response:** 1 month. **SASE Required:** Yes. **Freelance Content:** 100%. **Rights:** One-time electronic, one-time anthology. **Payment:** On acceptance.

FUGUE

University of Idaho, English Dept., Brink Hall, Room 200, Moscow, ID 83844-1102. E-mail: ronmcf@uidaho.edu. Website: www.uidaho.edu/ls/eng/fugue. Semiannual. $6/issue. Circ.: 300. Ron McFarland, Faculty Advisor. **Description:** Dedicated to new voices and quality writing. **Fiction:** Well written, traditional as well as experimental; up to 6,000 words; $20. **Nonfiction:** Creative nonfiction; up to 6,000 words; $20. **Poetry:** Any length and topic; submit up to 4 poems at a time; $10. **Art:** Seeking cover art; $50. **Tips:** "Don't send more than one genre together. Avoid cliché or worn-out language. We're looking for new, innovative, edgy pieces." **Queries:** Not necessary. **E-queries:** No. **Unsolicited mss:** Accepts. **Response:** 2-4 months. **SASE Required:** Yes. **Freelance Content:** 20%. **Rights:** One-time, reverts with credit. **Payment:** On publication.

FUTURES MYSTERIOUS ANTHOLOGY

3039 38th Ave. S, Minneapolis, MN 55406-2140. 612-724-4023. E-mail: babs@suspenseunlimited.net; babs@fmam.biz. Website: www.fmam.biz. Quarterly. Circ.: 4,500. **Description:** 138 pages of short fiction, primarily mystery, also horror, sci-fi, some literary, poetry, and puzzles. Most stories run 500-12,000 words. **Art:** Illustrations and cartoons. **Tips:** "We seek writers and artists with the fire to fly!—this magazine is where the seasoned meet with those first timers (Starting Line) to make magic." Read sample issue and check guidelines (online and inside front cover) before submitting. **Queries:** Not necessary. **Freelance Content:** 99%. **Contact:** Barbara (Babs) Lakey, Owner/Publisher; RC Hildebrandt, Poetry Editor; Mark Orr, Senior Mystery Fiction Editor; Daniel Blackston, Senior Speculative Fiction Editor.

THE GEORGIA REVIEW

University of Georgia, Athens, GA 30602-9009. 706-542-3481.
E-mail: garev@uga.edu. Website: www.uga.edu/garev. Quarterly. $9/issue. Circ.:
5,500. T.R. Hummer, Editor. **Description:** An eclectic blend of essays, fiction,
poetry, book reviews, and visual art. **Fiction:** Short stories, no novel excerpts;
$40/page. **Nonfiction:** Essays, no book chapters; $40/page. **Poetry:** $3/line **Art:**
Cover plus 8-page interior portfolio, each issue; $450 for the 9 images. **Tips:** Accepts
material August 16-May 14 only. Query for book reviews, send complete manuscript
for all else. **E-Queries:** No. **Response:** Queries 1-2 weeks, submissions 1-3 months.
SASE Required: Yes. **Freelance Content:** 80%. **Payment:** On publication.

GETTYSBURG REVIEW

Gettysburg College, Gettysburg, PA 17325. 717-337-6770.
Website: www.gettysburgreview.com. Quarterly. $6/$24. Circ.: 3,500. Peter Stitt,
Editor. **Description:** Quality poetry, fiction, essays, essay reviews, and graphics by
beginning and established writers and artists. **Fiction:** Literary fiction, fresh and sur-
prising, including novel excerpts; 1,000-20,000 words; $25/printed page. **Nonfiction:**
Varied (memoir, literary criticism, creative nonfiction, other); 3,000-7,000 words;
$30/printed page. **Poetry:** All styles and forms; $2.50/line. **Tips:** Manuscripts read
September-May. **Queries:** Not necessary. **E-Queries:** No. **Unsolicited mss:**
Accepts. **Response:** Queries 2-3 weeks, submissions 3-6 months. **SASE Required:**
Yes. **Freelance Content:** 100%. **Rights:** FNASR. **Payment:** On publication.
Contact: Mark Drew, Assistant Editor.

GLIMMER TRAIN STORIES

Glimmer Train Press, Inc., 1211 NW Glisan St., Suite 207, Portland, OR 97209.
503-221-0836. E-mail: info@glimmertrain.com. Website: www.glimmertrain.com.
Quarterly. $9.95/$32. Circ.: 18,000. Linda Burmeister Davies, Editor. **Description:**
Literary short stories by established and emerging writers—"a feast of fiction." Stories
should be 1,200-8,000 words; $500/story. **Tips:** All stories must be submitted online;
see website for specific submission guidelines. **Queries:** Not necessary. **E-Queries:**
No. **Unsolicited mss:** Accepts. **Response:** 3 months. **SASE Required:** Yes.
Freelance Content: 100%. **Rights:** FNAR. **Payment:** On acceptance.

GRAIN MAGAZINE

P.O. Box 67, Saskatoon, Saskatchewan S7K 3K1 Canada. 306-244-2828. E-mail:
grainmag@sasktel.net. Website: www.grainmagazine.ca. Quarterly. $9.95/$26.95.
Circ.: 1,500. Kent Bruyneel, Editor. **Description:** Canadian literary magazine publishing original work only, no reprints. Publishes new emerging writers, and established writers from Canada and around the world. Original work only, no reprints.
Fiction: Literary fiction in any style, well-crafted stories. No mainstream romance or
historical fiction; to 30 pages. **Nonfiction:** Creative nonfiction; to 30 pages. **Poetry:**
Submit up to 8 poems. Avoid avant garde, but does publish work that pushes boundaries. Favors thoughtful work that takes risks. **Tips:** "Pay attention to a story's subtext.
We prefer imaginative fiction, even quirky. Flaws we see most often are: a lack of

understanding of and attention to a story's subtext; expository writing; a lack of deftness with language; and stories written by writers who have not read enough fiction and are therefore not fluent in form." **Queries:** Not necessary. **Unsolicited mss:** Accepts. **Response:** 3 months, include SASE (IRC's) or e-mail address for reply. **Freelance Content:** 100%. **Rights:** 1st Canadian serial. **Payment:** On publication.

GRAND STREET

214 Sullivan St., 6C, New York, NY 10012. 212-533-2944.
E-mail: info@grandstreet.com. Website: www.grandstreet.com. Biannual. Jean Stein, Editor. **Description:** Art, fiction, nonfiction, and poetry. Accepts unsolicited poetry, any length; $3/line. **Queries:** Not necessary. **E-Queries:** No. **Response:** Queries 7 days, submissions 8-16 weeks. **SASE Required:** Yes. **Payment:** On publication.

GRASSLANDS REVIEW

P.O. Box 626, Berea, OH 44017. E-mail: grasslandsreview@aol.com. Website: http://grasslandsreview.blogspot.com. Semiannual. $12/yr. Laura Kennelly, Editor. **Description:** Encourages new writers. Seeks "imagination without sloppiness, ideas without lectures, and delight in language." Short stories 1,000-3,500 words. Poetry any length. **Tips:** Accepts manuscripts postmarked March or October only. **Queries:** Not necessary. **Response:** 6-12 months. **SASE Required:** Yes. **Payment:** In copies.

GREEN MOUNTAINS REVIEW

Johnson State College, Johnson, VT 05656. 802-635-1350.
E-mail: gmr@badger.jsc.vsc.edu. Biannual. $7/$14. Circ.: 1,700. **Description:** Poems, stories, and creative nonfiction by well-known and promising new authors. Also, interviews, literary criticism, and book reviews. **Fiction:** Wide range of styles and subjects; to 30 pages. **Nonfiction:** Interviews with writers and literary essays; to 30 pages. **Poetry:** Any type. **Art:** B&W photos. **Tips:** Publishes 2% of submissions. Occasionally features special-theme issues. **Queries:** Not necessary. **E-Queries:** No. **Unsolicited mss:** Accepts. **Response:** 3-6 months. **SASE Required:** Yes. **Freelance Content:** 80%. **Rights:** FNASR. **Payment:** In copies. **Contact:** Neil Shepard, Poetry Editor; Tony Whedon, Fiction Editor.

THE GREENSBORO REVIEW

Dept. of English, 134 McIver Bldg., UNCG, P.O. Box 26170, Greensboro, NC 27402-6170. E-mail: jlclark@uncg.edu. Website: www.uncg.edu/eng/mfa. Semiannual. $5/$10. Circ.: 800. Jim Clark, Editor. **Description:** Quality fiction (any theme/subject/style, to 7,500 words) and poetry (style and length varies). **Tips:** Original work only; no multiple submissions. **Queries:** Not necessary. **E-Queries:** No. **Unsolicited mss:** Accepts. **Rights:** FNASR. **Payment:** In copies.

GULF COAST

University of Houston, English Dept., Houston, TX 77204-3013. 713-743-3223. E-mail: editors@gulfcoastmag.org. Website: www.gulfcoastmag.org. Biannual. $8/issue. Circ.: 1,500. Sasha West, Managing Editor. **Description:** Journal of literary fiction, nonfiction, poetry, and fine art. **Tips:** Accepts queries via e-mail, but not manuscripts. **Queries:** Not necessary. **E-Queries:** Yes. **Unsolicited mss:** Accepts. **Response:** 3-6 months. **SASE Required:** Yes.

HAPPY

240 E 35th St., Suite 11A, New York, NY 10016. . E-mail: bayardx@aol.com. Biannual. $20/issue, $60/4 issues. Circ.: 350. Bayard, Editor. **Description:** General-interest publication. **Fiction:** Original work only. No racist, sexist, or pornographic material; 500-6,000 words; $.01-$.05/word. **Tips:** "Avoid being dull, dim-witted, boring." **Queries:** Not necessary. **E-Queries:** No. **Unsolicited mss:** Accepts. **Response:** 1 week. **SASE Required:** Yes. **Freelance Content:** 100%. **Rights:** One-time. **Payment:** On publication.

HARP-STRINGS

P.O. Box 640387, Beverly Hills, FL 34464. E-mail: verdure@digitalusa.net. Quarterly. $3.50/$12. Circ.: 105. Madelyn Eastlund, Editor. Description: Seeks poetry: narrative, lyrics, ballads, sestinas, rondeau redoubles, blank verse, villanelles, sonnets, prose poems, etc. 14-80 lines. Tips: No trite, broken prose masquerading as poetry; no confessions or raw-guts poems. No simultaneous submissions. Reads only in February, May, July, and November. Queries: Not necessary. E-Queries: Yes. Unsolicited mss: Accepts. Freelance Content: 100%. Rights: One-time and electronic. Payment: In copies.

HAWAI'I REVIEW

University of Hawaii, Dept. of English, 1733 Donaggho Rd., Honolulu, HI 96822. 808-956-3030. E-mail: hi-review@hawaii.edu. Website: www.hawaii.edu/bop/hr.html. Biannual. $10/issue. Circ.: 1,000. Michael Pulelua, Editor. **Description:** Literary poetry, fiction, nonfiction, and reviews. **Fiction:** Up to 20 pages. **Nonfiction:** Up to 20 pages. **Tips:** Submissions accepted year-round. **Queries:** Not necessary. **E-Queries:** Yes. **Unsolicited mss:** Accepts. **Response:** Queries 2-3 weeks, submissions 3-6 months. **SASE Required:** Yes. **Rights:** FNAR.

HAYDEN'S FERRY REVIEW

The Virginia G. Piper Center for Creative Writing, Arizona State University, P.O. Box 871502, Tempe, AZ 85287-1502. 480-965-1243. E-mail: hfr@asu.edu. Website: www.haydensferryreview.com. Biannual. $7.50/$14. Circ.: 1,300. **Description:** Literary and art magazine featuring quality art, poetry, fiction, and creative nonfiction by new and established artists and writers. Pays $25/page ($100 max.). Submit no more than 6 poems. **Tips:** Accepts queries via e-mail, but not submissions. **Queries:** Not necessary. **E-Queries:** Yes. **Unsolicited mss:** Accepts. **Response:** Queries 1 week, submissions 8-12 weeks. **SASE Required:** Yes. **Freelance Content:** 80%. **Rights:** FNASR. **Payment:** On publication. **Contact:** Poetry or Fiction Editor.

HEAVEN BONE

P.O. Box 486, Chester, NY 10918. E-mail: heavenbone@aol.com. Annual. $10/issue. Circ.: 2,500. Steve Hirsch, Editor. **Description:** Poetry, fiction, reviews, and artwork with emphasis on surreal, beat, experimental, and Buddhist concerns. **Fiction:** 2,500-10,000 words. **Nonfiction:** Essays on creativity, philosophy, and conciousness studies, relating to writing. 7,500 words. **Poetry:** Surreal, experimental, visual, neo-beat, and Buddhist imagery and themes. **Art:** Any digital or traditional format. **Tips:** "Despite 'Heaven' in title, we are not a religious publication." **Queries:** Preferred. **E-Queries:** Yes. **Unsolicited mss:** Accepts. **Response:** Queries 3 weeks, submissions up to 12 months. **SASE Required:** Yes. **Rights:** FNASR. **Payment:** In copies.

THE HOLLINS CRITIC

Hollins University, P.O. Box 9538, Roanoke, VA 24020. 540-362-6275. E-mail: acockrell@hollins.edu. Website: www.hollins.edu. 5x/yr. $6/issue. Circ.: 500. R. H. W. Dillard, Editor. **Description:** Features an essay on a contemporary fiction writer, poet, or dramatist (cover sketch, brief biography, and book list). Also book reviews and poetry. Reviews poetry submissions from September-December 15 only. Does not accept unsolicited reviews or essays (accepts for poetry only). $25/poem, does not pay for book reviews. **Tips:** Sample copy $1.50. **Queries:** Not necessary. **E-Queries:** No. **Unsolicited mss:** Accepts. **Response:** 2 months. **SASE Required:** Yes. **Freelance Content:** 100%. **Rights:** FNAR. **Payment:** On publication.

HUDSON REVIEW

684 Park Ave., New York, NY 10021. 212-650-0020.
Website: www.hudsonreview.com. Quarterly. $9/$32. Circ.: 5,000. Paula Deitz, Editor. **Description:** Fiction, poetry, essays, book reviews; criticism of literature, art, theatre, dance, film, and music; and articles on contemporary culture. **Tips:** Accepts unsolicited manuscripts on the following schedule: Nonfiction, January 1-March 31; Poetry, April 1-June 30; Fiction, September 1-November 30. **Queries:** Preferred. **E-Queries:** No. **Unsolicited mss:** Accepts. **Response:** 3 months. **SASE Required:** Yes. **Payment:** On publication.

THE ICONOCLAST

1675 Amazon Rd., Mohegan Lake, NY 10547-1804. Bimonthly. $2.50/$15. Circ.: 700. Phil Wagner, Editor. **Description:** For readers and writers of original work bypassed by corporate and institutional publications. **Fiction:** Literary stories, plots, and ideas with active characters engaged with the world; 100-3,500 words; $.01/word. **Nonfiction:** Nothing topical, fashionable, political, or academic; 100-3,500 words; $.01/word. **Poetry:** Well-crafted, with something to say; send 2-5 poems; to 2 pages; $2-$5/poem. **Fillers:** Humor (nothing silly, self-consciously zany); 20-2,000 words; $.01/word. **Tips:** "Write well, be sincere, act professionally. We do not want manuscripts that have been mass-mailed to other publications at the same time." **Queries:** Not necessary. **E-Queries:** No. **Unsolicited mss:** Accepts. **Response:** Queries 1 week, submissions 1 month. **SASE Required:** Yes. **Freelance Content:** 90%. **Rights:** FNASR. **Payment:** On publication.

ILLYA'S HONEY

Dallas Poets Community, P.O. Box 700865, Dallas, TX 75370. E-mail: info@dallaspoets.org. Website: www.dallaspoets.org. Quarterly. $6/$18. Circ.: 150. Ann Howells, Wesley Hartman, Editors. **Description:** Mostly poetry, some micro-fiction. Pays one copy. **Fiction:** Flash fiction, sharp, well-crafted; up to 200 words. **Poetry:** Any form, any subject; prefers free verse. **Queries:** Not necessary. **Unsolicited mss:** Accepts. **Response:** 4-6 months. **SASE Required:** Yes. **Freelance Content:** 98%. **Rights:** FNAR.

INDIANA REVIEW

Indiana University, Ballantine Hall 465, 1020 E Kirkwood Ave., Bloomington, IN 47405. 812-855-3439. Website: www.indiana.edu/~inreview. Semiannual. $9/$16. Circ.: 2,000. Esther Lee, Editor. **Description:** Publication for both emerging and established writers. Features quality writing within a wide aesthetic. **Fiction:** Daring stories which integrate theme, language, character, and form, with consequence beyond the world of its narrator; up to 40 pages. **Nonfiction:** Lively essays on engaging topics. Interviews with established writers and book reviews; to 30 pages; $5/page and copies. **Poetry:** Intelligent form and language, with risk, ambition, and scope. **Queries:** Not necessary. **Unsolicited mss:** Accepts. **Response:** Queries 1 week, submissions 3-4 months. **SASE Required:** Yes. **Freelance Content:** 98%. **Rights:** FNASR. **Payment:** On publication. **Contact:** Poetry or Fiction Editor.

INTERIM

University of Nevada, Dept. of English, Las Vegas, NV 89154-5011. Annual. Claudia Keelan, Editor. **Description:** Features poetry (any form or length) and fiction (to 7,500 words). Also book reviews and essays. Will not be accepting unsolicited manuscripts until September 2005. **Payment:** In copies.

INTERNATIONAL POETRY REVIEW

University of North Carolina, Dept. of Romance Languages, Greensboro, NC 27402-6170. Biannually. Circ.: 200. Kathleen Koestler, Editor. **Description:** Features work that crosses language barriers to present the voices of poets in different countries. **Nonfiction:** Book reviews and short essays; to 1,500 words. **Poetry:** Original English poems and contemporary translations from other languages. **Tips:** Prefers material with cross-cultural or international dimension. **Queries:** Preferred. **Unsolicited mss:** Accepts. **Payment:** In copies.

IOWA REVIEW

University of Iowa, 308 EPB, Iowa City, IA 52242. 319-335-0462. E-mail: iowa-review@uiowa.edu. Website: www.uiowa.edu/~iareview. Triannual. $7.95/$20. Circ.: 3,000. David Hamilton, Editor. **Description:** Publishes essays, poems, stories, and reviews. Material can be any length. Pays $25 for first page and $15 for each additional page. **Queries:** Not necessary. **E-Queries:** Accepts. **Unsolicited mss:** Accepts. **Response:** 1-4 months. **SASE Required:** Yes. **Freelance Content:** 98%. **Rights:** FNASR. **Payment:** On publication.

JOURNAL OF NEW JERSEY POETS

County College of Morris, English Dept. B-300, 214 Center Grove Rd., Randolph, NJ 07869. 973-328-5471. E-mail: szulauf@ccm.edu. Website: www.ccm.edu/humanities/humanities/journal/html. Annual. $10/issue. Circ.: 900. Sander Zulauf, Editor. **Description:** Regional poetry magazine dedicated to the works of poets and artists who live or have lived in New Jersey. Supported by the college's Center for Teaching Excellence. **Nonfiction:** Essays on poetry and book reviews on new work by New Jersey poets; to 1,500 words. **Poetry:** Send up to 3 poems at a time (no epics). **Tips:** New Jersey not required as subject matter. "We seek mature, lively, accomplished work appealing to a large audience." **Queries:** Not necessary. **E-Queries:** No. **Unsolicited mss:** Accepts. **SASE Required:** Yes. **Freelance Content:** 100%. **Rights:** FNASR. **Payment:** In copies.

JUBILAT

University of Massachusetts-Dept. of English, Bartlett 482, Amherst, MA 01003-0515. Website: www.jubilat.org. $6/issue. Circ.: 1,200. Robert N. Casper, Publisher. **Description:** Poetry, art, and short nonfiction on poetry or other subjects. Does not publish short stories. Send one prose piece and/or 3-5 poems; mail genres seperately. **Tips:** Read a sample issue before submitting. No electronic submissions. **Unsolicited mss:** Accepts. **Response:** 3-5 months. **SASE Required:** Yes.

KALLIOPE

Florida Community College at Jacksonville, 11901 Beach Blvd., Jacksonville, FL 32245. 904-646-2081. Website: www.fccj.org/kalliope. Semiannual. $16/yr. Circ.: 1,600. Mary Sue Koeppel, Editor. **Description:** *Kalliope: a journal of women's literature & art* features poetry, short fiction, interviews, reviews, and visual art by women. Open to experimental forms. **Fiction:** Well-constructed literary work; to 2,500 words. **Nonfiction:** Interviews with writers and/or artists; 200-2,500 words. **Poetry:** Submit in groups of 3-5. **Art:** Submit in groups of 4-10 works. B&W professional quality, glossy, or prints from negatives. **Tips:** Include SASE and a short contributor's note with all submissions. **Queries:** Not necessary. **E-Queries:** No. **Unsolicited mss:** Accepts. **Response:** Queries 1-3 weeks, submissions 6 months. **Freelance Content:** 100%. **Rights:** FNAR. **Payment:** In copies.

KARAMU

Eastern Illinois University, English Dept., Charleston, IL 61920. 217-581-6297. Annual. $7.50. Circ.: 500. Olga Abella, Editor. **Description:** Publishes poetry, fiction, and creative nonfiction. **Fiction:** Stories that capture something essential about life, beyond the superficial, and develop genuine voices; 3,500 words. **Nonfiction:** Any subject with the exception of religion and politics; 3,500 words. **Tips:** Avoid rhyming poetry or didactic prose. Recent sample copies available for $7.50; back issues 2 for $6. **Queries:** Preferred. **E-Queries:** No. **Unsolicited mss:** Accepts. **Response:** Queries 2-3 days, submissions 4-6 months. **SASE Required:** Yes. **Freelance Content:** 100%. **Rights:** One-time. **Payment:** In copies.

KARITOS REVIEW

N4714 Skinner Hollow Rd., Monroe, WI 53566. E-mail: editor@karitos.com.
Website: www.karitos.com. Annual. $3. Circ.: 250. Chris Wave, Managing Editor.
Description: Literary magazine with fiction, essays, and poetry. Send 3 submissions
only. **Tips:** "Our readership is multicultural and evangelical. Our festival has a theme
each year (2001 is 'A Joyous Journey Through Customs and Cultures'), but submissions need not reflect this. Taboos—any kind of religious stereotype; anything anti-
Christian." **Queries:** Not necessary. **E-Queries:** Yes. **Unsolicited mss:** Accepts.

KELSEY REVIEW

Mercer County Community College, P.O. Box B, Trenton, NJ 08690. 609-586-4800
x3326. E-mail: kelsey.review@mccc.edu. Website: www.mccc.edu. Annual. Circ.:
2,000. Robin Schore, Editor. **Description:** Literary journal exclusively for writers living or working in Mercer Country, N.J. Features fiction, essays, poetry, and B&W line
art. Submit prose up to 2,000 words, poetry up to 6 poems. **Tips:** Deadline May 1.
Responds by June 30. **Queries:** Not necessary. **Unsolicited mss:** Accepts.
Freelance Content: 100%. **Rights:** None. **Payment:** In copies.

THE KENYON REVIEW

104 College Dr., Gambier, OH 43022-9623. 740-427-5208.
E-mail: kenyonreview@kenyon.edu. Website: www.kenyonreview.org. Quarterly.
$8/issue. Circ.: 6,000. Meg Galipault, Managing Editor. **Description:** Features new
writing from emerging and established writers. Short Fiction and essays: to 7,500
words; $10/page. **Poetry:** to 10 pages; $15/page. Plays: to 35 pages; $10/page.
Excerpts: to 35 pages from larger works; $10/page. Translations of poetry and short
prose; $10/page. **Tips:** "Because of our editor's sabbatical, unsolicited manuscripts
received after March 31, 2003 will not be read until September 1, 2004." Guidelines
can be found on website. **Queries:** Not necessary. **E-Queries:** No. **Response:** 1-4
months. **SASE Required:** Yes. **Freelance Content:** 90%. **Rights:** First. **Payment:**
On publication. **Contact:** David H. Lynn, Editor.

KIMERA

N 1316 Hollis St., Spokane, WA 99201. 509-326-6641.
E-mail: editor@js.spokane.wa.us. Website: http://js.spokane.wa.us/kimera. Annual.
$10/yr. Circ.: 300. Jan Strever, Editor. **Description:** For fine writing, in print and
online. Uses John Locke's premise,"Where is the head with no chimeras?" Features
short fiction (no erotica) and poetry. Avoid poems that have a "message." **Tips:** "We
look for those flights of fancies that all of us have. Our major requirement is that the
writing sent to us should attend to the language, as it is our medium." **Queries:** Not
necessary. **E-Queries:** Accepts. **Unsolicited mss:** Accepts. **Response:** 3 months.
SASE Required: Yes. **Freelance Content:** 100%. **Rights:** 1st, electronic.
Payment: In copies.

THE KIT-CAT REVIEW

244 Halstead Ave., Harrison, NY 10528. 914-835-4833. Quarterly. $7/$25. Circ.: 500. Claudia Fletcher, Editor. **Description:** Literary journal seeking excellence and originality. **Fiction:** E.g., "The Heisenberg Approach," a fictional excerpt from Werner Heisenberg's diary; to 5,000 words, prefers shorter. **Nonfiction:** "Wishing for Miracles: Tijuana Interviews," a piece about life in modern-day Tijuana; to 6,000 words, prefer shorter. **Poetry:** All types and lengths, except greeting card or deliberately obscure. **Tips:** Avoid O. Henry-type endings. No excessive vulgarity or profanity. Sample copy $7. **Queries:** Not necessary. **E-Queries:** No. **Unsolicited mss:** Accepts. **Response:** 2-4 week. **SASE Required:** Yes. **Freelance Content:** 100%. **Rights:** 1st, one-time. **Payment:** On acceptance.

KUUMBA

BLK Publishing, Inc., P.O. Box 83912, Los Angeles, CA 90083-0912. 310-410-0808. E-mail: newsroom@blk.com. Website: www.blk.com. Biannual. $2.95/issue. Circ.: 37,000. Reginald Harris, Editor. **Description:** Poetry journal of the black lesbian and gay community. Seeks submissions that relate to coming out, family, community, substance abuse, relationships, etc. **E-Queries:** Yes. **Response:** 6 weeks. **SASE Required:** Yes. **Freelance Content:** 10%. **Rights:** FNAR. **Contact:** Alan Bell.

THE LARCOM REVIEW

P.O. Box 161, Prides Crossing, MA 01965. 978-927-8707. E-mail: amp@larcompress.com. Website: www.larcompress.com. Semi-annual. $12/$20. Circ.: 300. Susan Oleksiw, Editor. **Description:** Publishes contemporary short fiction, poetry, and essays about New England life written by residents of this region and those who live outside. **Fiction:** Stories range from pieces on family life to suspense mystery fiction, from short shorts to longer tales to be savored over an evening; 3,000 words; $25. **Nonfiction:** Entertaining, accessible essays and articles. Interviews and book reviews assigned; 3,000 words; $25. **Art:** Prints, slides, illustrations, and B&W art; $25. **Tips:** Seeking stories on all aspects of life in 6 states, including stories by New Englanders living elsewhere. Don't submit fiction and nonfiction together. **Queries:** Not necessary. **E-Queries:** No. **Unsolicited mss:** Accepts. **Response:** 3-4 months. **SASE Required:** Yes. **Rights:** FNAR. **Payment:** On publication.

THE LAUREL REVIEW

Greentower Press, Northwest Missouri State University, Dept. of English, Maryville, MO 64468. 816-562-1265. Semiannual. Circ.: 900. Rebecca Aronson, John Gallaher, Nancy Mayer, Co-editors. **Description:** Literary journal featuring poetry, fiction, and creative nonfiction. Open to submission between September-May. **Response:** Within 4 months. **Payment:** In copies.

THE LEDGE

40 Maple Ave., Bellport, NY 11713. Annual. $8.95/issue. Circ.: 1,500. Timothy Monaghan, Editor. **Description:** Seeks exceptional contemporary poetry and fiction. No restrictions on style or form. **Queries:** Not necessary. **E-Queries:**

No. **Unsolicited mss:** Accepts. **Response:** Queries 2-3 weeks, submissions 3 months. **SASE Required:** Yes. **Freelance Content:** 100%. **Rights:** FNASR. **Payment:** In copies.

LIGHT

P.O. Box 7500, Chicago, IL 60680. 847-853-1028. Website: www.lightquarterly.com. Quarterly. $6/$20. Circ.: 1,000. John Mella, Editor. **Description:** Literary journal devoted exclusively to light verse. Also features some reviews and essays. **Tips:** "Think James Thurber, E. B. White, Ogden Nash, etc. If it has wit, point, edge, or barb, it has a home here." See website for guidelines. **Queries:** Preferred. **E-Queries:** No. **Unsolicited mss:** Accepts. **Response:** Queries 1-4 months. **Payment:** In copies.

LITERAL LATTÉ

61 Fourth Ave., Suite 240, New York, NY 10003.
E-mail: litlatte@aol.com. Website: www.literal-latte.com. Jenine Gordon Bockman, Editor. **Description:** Online literary journal featuring short stories, poetry, essays, and art. Also prints an annual anthology. **Fiction:** Varied styles; the word is as important as the tale; 6,000 words. **Nonfiction:** Personal essays, all topics; thematic book reviews done as personal essays; 6,000 words. **Poetry:** All styles; 2,000 words max. **Fillers:** Intelligent literary cartoons. **Art:** Photocopies or slides (of photos, drawings, paintings, B&W or color). Open to styles, abstraction to photorealism. **Tips:** Always looking for new talent. Also hosts annual fiction and poetry contests ($1,500 in prizes for each). **Queries:** Not necessary. **Unsolicited mss:** Accepts. **Response:** 3-6 months. **Rights:** FNASR. **Payment:** On publication.

LITERARY MAGAZINE REVIEW (LMR)

Univ. of Wisconsin, English Dept., 410 S Third St., River Falls, WI 54022. 715-425-3173. E-mail: jennifer.s.brantley@uwrf.edu. Website: www.uwrf.edu/lmr. Quarterly. Circ.: 350. **Description:** Reviews periodicals that publish poetry and creative prose. **Tips:** "*LMR* is now in its twentieth year as a valuable resource for writers and readers seeking the best literary magazines. Reviewing both newcomers and older magazines, *LMR* is the best place to find what to read and where to submit." **Queries:** Required. **E-Queries:** Yes. **Response:** 1 month. **SASE Required:** Yes. **Rights:** FNAR. **Payment:** In copies. **Contact:** Dr. Jenny Brantley, Editor.

THE LITERARY REVIEW

Fairleigh Dickinson University, Mail Code M-GH2-01, 285 Madison Ave., Madison, NJ 07940. 973-443-8564. E-mail: tlr@fdu.edu. Website: www.theliteraryreview.org. Quarterly. $7/issue. Circ.: 2,000. Rene Steinke, Editor. **Description:** International journal of poetry, fiction, essays, and contemporary reviews. Prose any length, poetry up to 5 poems. **Tips:** Submissions are read between September 1 and May 31 only. **Queries:** Not necessary. **E-Queries:** Yes. **Unsolicited mss:** Accepts. **Response:** Queries 1 week, submissions 12-16 weeks. **SASE Required:** Yes. **Rights:** FNAR. **Payment:** In copies.

LONG SHOT

P.O. Box 6238, Hoboken, NJ 07030. Website: www.longshot.org. Semiannual. $8/issue, $24/2 yr. (4 issues). Circ.: 1,500. Editorial Board. **Description:** Features raw, graphic, exuberant poetry devoid of pretense . **Fiction:** To 10 pages **Nonfiction:** To 10 pages. **Poetry:** To 8 pages. **Art:** B&W photos, drawings. **Queries:** Not necessary. **E-Queries:** No. **Unsolicited mss:** Accepts. **Response:** 8-12 weeks. **SASE Required:** Yes. **Freelance Content:** 20%. **Payment:** In copies.

THE LONG STORY

18 Eaton St., Lawrence, MA 01843. 978-686-7638. E-mail: rpburnham@mac.com. Website: www.longstorymagazine.com. $6/issue. Circ.: 1,000. R.P. Burnham, Editor. **Description:** Stories with a moral/thematic core, particularly about poor and working-class people. 8,000-12,000 words (occasionally to 20,000). **Queries:** Not necessary. **E-Queries:** No. **Unsolicited mss:** Accepts. **Response:** 2 months. **SASE Required:** Yes. **Freelance Content:** 95%. **Rights:** FNAR. **Payment:** In copies.

LSR

P.O. Box 440195, Miami, FL 33144. 305-447-3780. 2x/yr. $6. Circ.: 3,000. Nilda Cepero, Editor/Publisher. **Description:** Publishes poetry, book reviews, interviews, and line art. (Formerly known as *Latino Stuff Review.*) **Nonfiction:** Book reviews or interviews, to 750 words. **Poetry:** Submit up to 4 poems, 5-45 lines each. Style, subject matter, and content open, prefers contemporary with meaning and message. No pornographic, religious, or surreal poetry. **Art:** Line artwork; submit up to 5 illustrations on 3.5 inch disk (to be printed 6 inch x 6 inch on cover, 8 inch x 10 inch on full-page inside). **Tips:** Cover letter required, include SASE and bio. "Read as many current poetry magazines as you can." **Queries:** Not necessary. **E-Queries:** No. **Unsolicited mss:** Accepts. **Response:** 9 months. **SASE Required:** Yes. **Freelance Content:** 100%. **Rights:** FNAR. **Payment:** In copies.

LYNX EYE

Scribblefest Literary Group, 542 Mitchell Dr., Los Osos, CA 93402. 805-528-8146. E-mail: pamccully@aol.com. Quarterly. $7.95/$25. Circ.: 500. Pam McCully, Editor. **Description:** Features stories, poetry, essays, and B&W artwork in both familiar and experimental formats. **Fiction:** Short stories, vignettes, novel excerpts, one-act plays, belles lettres, and satires; 500-5,000 words; $10/piece and copies. **Nonfiction:** Essays only; 500-5,000 words. **Poetry:** 30 lines. **Art:** B&W drawings only. **Tips:** Avoid memoirs and autobiographical pieces. **Queries:** Not necessary. **E-Queries:** No. **Unsolicited mss:** Accepts. **Response:** 12 weeks. **SASE Required:** Yes. **Freelance Content:** 100%. **Rights:** FNASR. **Payment:** On acceptance.

MALAHAT REVIEW

University of Victoria, P.O. Box 1700, Stn CSC, University of Victoria, Victoria, British Columbia V8W 2Y2 Canada. 250-721-8524. E-mail: malahat@uvic.ca. Website: www.malahatreview.com. Quarterly. $10/$30 (Canadian). Circ.: 1,000. John Barton, Editor. **Description:** Short fiction, nonfiction, poetry, and reviews of Canadian fiction or books of poetry. Seeks balance of views and styles by established and new writers. Pays $30/page. **Queries:** Not necessary. **E-Queries:** Yes. **Unsolicited mss:** Accepts. **Response:** Up to 3 months. **SASE Required:** Yes. **Freelance Content:** 100%. **Rights:** 1st worldwide. **Payment:** On acceptance.

MANOA: A PACIFIC JOURNAL OF INTERNATIONAL WRITING
University of Hawaii Press, English Dept., 1733 Donaghho Rd, Honolulu, HI 96822. 808-956-3070. E-mail: fstewart@hawaii.edu. Website: www.hawaii.edu/mjournal. Semiannual. Circ.: 2,500. Frank Stewart, Editor. **Description:** Literary journal featuring fiction, poetry, translations, essays, interviews, and artwork. **Fiction:** To 30 pages; $20-$25/page. **Nonfiction:** Essays, to 25 pages; book reviews (4-5 pages, pays $50). **Poetry:** Submit 4-6 poems; $50. **Tips:** "Our journal contains a high proportion of international writers; definitely not for beginners." No e-mail submissions. **Queries:** Preferred. **E-Queries:** No. **Payment:** On publication.

MANY MOUNTAINS MOVING
420 22nd St., Boulder, CO 80302. 303-545-9942. E-mail: mmm@mmminc.org. Website: www.mmminc.org. 6x/yr. $4/$18. Circ.: 3,000. Naomi Horii, Editor. **Description:** Literary journal of diverse contemporary voices, from diverse cultural backgrounds. Fiction and nonfiction to 20,000 words. Poetry any length, 3-10 poems. No payment offered. **Tips:** Only interested in excellent quality work. Accepts unsolicited material May-August only. Contact for upcoming themes. Sample copy $7.50. **Queries:** Not necessary. **E-Queries:** No. **Unsolicited mss:** Accepts. **Response:** Submissions 4 months. **SASE Required:** Yes. **Freelance Content:** 100%.

THE MARLBORO REVIEW
P.O. Box 243, Marlboro, VT 05344. Website: www.marlbororeview.com. Biannual. Ellen Dudley, Editor. **Description:** Literary journal of poetry, fiction, essays, translations, reviews, and interviews. **Fiction:** To 30 pages. **Nonfiction:** Literary/personal essays only; to 30 pages. **Poetry:** Any length. **Art:** For cover; film or camera-ready. **Tips:** Interested in cultural, philosophical, and scientific issues as seen from the writer's perspective. "We look for good, strong writing." Also sponsors an annual poetry competition. **Queries:** Not necessary. **E-Queries:** Yes. **Unsolicited mss:** Accepts. **Response:** Queries 1 month, submissions 3 months. **SASE Required:** Yes. **Freelance Content:** 80%. **Rights:** FNAR. **Payment:** In copies.

THE MASSACHUSETTS REVIEW
University of Massachusetts, South College, Amherst, MA 01003-9934. 413-545-2689. E-mail: massrev@external.umass.edu. Website: www.massreview.org. Quarterly. **Description:** Literary publication for writers of fiction, nonfiction, and poetry. **Fiction:** Short fiction; 15-25 pages; $50. **Nonfiction:** Essays, translations, interviews; $50. **Poetry:** $.35/line ($10 min.). **Tips:** Reviews material October 1-June 1. **Payment:** On publication. **Contact:** Editorial Board.

METAL SCRATCHES

9251 Lake Dr. NE, Forest Lake, MN 55025. E-mail: metalscratches@aol.com. Semi-annual. $4/$9. Circ.: 100. Kimberly Mark, Editor. **Description:** "*Metal Scratches* is an experimental literary magazine exploring the darker side of humanity. We publish short prose only. We're also looking for B&W drawings for cover art." **Fiction:** Stories that show the darker side of humanity, behaviors that would surpise others, strong character development. 3,500 words max. **Tips:** "Avoid horror and shock. Give us something new that is creepy or dark. Don't be afraid to submit. We love to publish stories that others will not." Sample copy $2. **Queries:** Not necessary. **E-Queries:** Yes. **Unsolicited mss:** Accepts. **Response:** 1 month. **SASE Required:** Yes. **Freelance Content:** 100%. **Rights:** One-time. **Payment:** In copies.

MICHIGAN QUARTERLY REVIEW

University of Michigan, 3574 Rackham Bldg., 915 E Washington St., Ann Arbor, MI 48109-1070. E-mail: mqr@umich.edu. Website: www.umich.edu/~mqr. Laurence Goldstein, Editor. **Description:** Contemporary literary journal featuring fiction, scholarly essays, creative nonfiction, and poetry. Pays $8-$10/page. No electronic sub-missions. **Tips:** Also offers prize for best fiction and best poetry published in the jour-nal each year. Sample copy $5. **Queries:** Not necessary. **E-Queries:** No. **Unsolicited mss:** Accepts. **Response:** 6 weeks. **SASE Required:** Yes. **Payment:** On publication.

MID-AMERICA POETRY REVIEW

P.O. Box 575, Warrensburg, MO 64093-0575. 660-747-4602. 3x/yr. $6/$15. Robert C. Jones, Editor. **Description:** Publishes free verse, lyrical, and narrative poetry. "Many of the poems we publish focus on pastoral/rural themes or our relationship to the nat-ural world." **Tips:** Send SASE for response only; unaccepted submissons recycled. **Queries:** Not necessary. **E-Queries:** No. **Unsolicited mss:** Accepts. **Response:** 2-4 weeks. **Freelance Content:** 100%. **Rights:** FNAR. **Payment:** 2 copies plus $5 per accepted poem.

MID-AMERICAN REVIEW

Bowling Green State University, Dept. of English, Bowling Green, OH 43403. 419-372-2725. E-mail: mikeczy@bgnet.bgsu.edu. Website: www.bgsu.edu/midamerican-review. 2x/yr. Circ.: 2,000. Mike Czyzniejewski, Editor. **Description:** High-quality fiction, 10-20 pages, poetry, articles, translations, and reviews of contemporary writ-ing. Fiction, to 5,000 words; pays to $50, dependent on funding. Review/articles, 500-2,500 words. **Tips:** Manuscripts read September-May. Query for longer works. **Response:** 1-4 months **Payment:** In copies.

MINDPRINTS

Allan Hancock College, Learning Assistance Program, 800 South College Dr., Santa Maria, CA 93454-6399. 805-922-6966 ext. 3274. E-mail: pafahey@hancock.cc.ca.us. Annual. $6. Circ.: 600. Paul Fahey, Editor. **Description:** Literary journal. Short fic-tion, memoirs, poetry, and art for writers and artists with disabilities and those with an interest in this field. Showcases a variety of talent from this diverse population. **Fiction:** Short-short fiction, flash fiction; 250-750 words. **Nonfiction:** Short memoir, creative nonfiction (often disability-related); 250-750 words. **Poetry:** Rhymed and prose; to 35 lines. **Art:** B&W photos and artwork. **Tips:** "We look for fiction and memoir of universal appeal, short pieces with a strong voice, a narrowness of focus and rich detail—fully dimensional writing with a beginning, middle and end, works that are brief, profound and surprising." E-mail submissions are accepted only from writers and artists who reside outside the U.S. **Queries:** Not necessary. **Unsolicited mss:** Accepts. **Response:** Queries 1 week, submissions 3 months. **SASE Required:** Yes. **Rights:** One-time rights. **Payment:** One copy.

THE MINNESOTA REVIEW

University of Missouri, Dept. of English, 110 Tate Hall, Columbia, MO 65211. 573-882-3059. E-mail: editors@theminnesotareview.org. Semiannual. $30/2 yr. Circ.: 1,300. Jeffrey Williams, Editor. **Description:** A journal of committed writing, progressive in nature, committed to socialist and feminist writing. (Note: does not have a Minnesota focus; was founded there, but later moved and kept name.) **Fiction:** Political, experimental; to 5,000 words. **Nonfiction:** Essays and reviews. **Poetry:** Political; 1-10 pages. **Tips:** "Many of our issues are organized around a special topic." Sample copy $15. **Queries:** Not necessary. **E-Queries:** No. **Unsolicited mss:** Accepts. **Response:** Queries 2-4 weeks, submissions 4-6 weeks. **SASE Required:** Yes. **Freelance Content:** 100%. **Payment:** In copies.

MISSISSIPPI REVIEW

Center for Writers, University of Southern Mississippi, Southern Sta., Box 5144, Hattiesburg, MS 39406-5144. 601-266-4321. E-mail: rief@netdoor.com. Website: www.mississippireview.com. Frederick Barthelme, Editor. **Description:** Literary journal featuring poetry and fiction. **Tips:** Annual fiction/poetry competition; deadline, October 1. Pays $1,000 for each winning story and poem.

THE MISSOURI REVIEW

University of Missouri-Columbia, 1507 Hillcrest Hall, Columbia, MO 65211. 573-882-4474. Website: www.missourireview.com. Triannual. $7.95/$22. Circ.: 6,500. Speer Morgan, Editor. **Description:** Literary magazine with contemporary fiction, poetry, interviews, book reviews, and personal essays. **Poetry:** 6-14 pages of poetry by 3-5 poets each issue; pays $30/page. **Queries:** Not necessary. **E-Queries:** No. **Response:** 6-8 weeks. **SASE Required:** Yes. **Freelance Content:** 90%. **Rights:** All; revert to author. **Payment:** On publication.

MODERN HAIKU

Box 68, Lincoln, IL 62656. Website: www.modernhaiku.org. 3x/yr. $22/yr. Circ.: 780. Lee Gurga, Editor; Charles Trumball, Associate Editor; Lidi Rozmus, Art Editor. **Description:** International journal of English-language haiku and translations, book reviews, articles, and essays. **Nonfiction:** Articles and essays related to haiku; $5/page. **Poetry:** Haiku and senryu; $1/poem. **Tips:** "No sentimental, pretty-pretty, or pseudo-Japanese work. Write about what you actually experience, not about an exotic, imaginary place. Juxtaposition of disparate perceptions that form a harmony is desirable." **Queries:** Not necessary. **E-Queries:** No. **Unsolicited mss:** Accepts. **Response:** 2 weeks. **SASE Required:** Yes. **Freelance Content:** 90%. **Rights:** FNAR.

MOTION SICKNESS

4117 SE Division St., #417, Portland, OR 97202.
E-mail: editor@motionsickmag.com. Website: www.motionsickmag.com. Steve Wilson, Editor. **Description:** Quarterly, with slant towards travel and tourism. Articles, essays, fiction, poetry, and narratives. Also, book reviews, media criticism, art and cartoons. No destination articles. Features, 500-5,000 words. Pays $10-$50. **Tips:** "We seek material that addresses the effect tourism has on a region, the change in economy, environment, language, morals, etc. Address travel from the standpoint of immigrants, bus drivers, guest-house employees. We want cultural reportage about travel and tourism, stories of bad trips, humorous looks at disaster, narratives that experiment with form and style, and accounts of the travels of people from other cultures. Open to different styles and genres, but lean toward the satirical and literary." **Queries:** Not necessary. **Unsolicited mss:** Accepts. **Rights:** FNAR.

MUDLARK

University of North Florida/Dept. of English, 4567 St. Johns Bluff Rd. S, Jacksonville, FL 32224-2645. E-mail: mudlark@unf.edu. Website: www.unf.edu/mudlark. William Slaughter, Editor. **Description:** Online journal featuring poetry and nonfiction essays on poetry. "*Mudlark: An Electronic Journal of Poetry & Poetics* considers accomplished work that locates itself anywhere on the spectrum of contemporary practice." **Tips:** "To submit or not to submit? Take a good look at *Mudlark*. Spend some time on the website. Then make your decision. The work of hobbyists and lobbyists is not for us. The poem is the thing at *Mudlark*, and the essay about it." **Queries:** Not necessary. **E-Queries:** Yes. **Unsolicited mss:** Accepts. **Response:** 1-30 days. **Freelance Content:** 100%.

NATURAL BRIDGE

University of Missouri-St. Louis/Dept. of English, 8001 Natural Bridge Rd., St. Louis, MO 63121-4499. 314-516-5517. E-mail: natural@jinx.umsl.edu. Website: www.umsl.edu/~natural. Biannual. $8/issue. Ryan Stone, Editor. **Description:** Literary short fiction, personal essays, poetry, and poetry translations. **Tips:** Submission periods are July 1-August 31, and November 1-December 31. Simultaneous submissions accepted. **E-Queries:** No. **Payment:** In copies.

NEBO

Arkansas Tech University, Dept. of English, Russellville, AR 72801-2222. E-mail: michael.ritchie@mail.atu.edu. Biannual. $10/annual. Circ.: 100. Michael Ritchie, Editor. **Description:** Publishes fiction and poetry. Prefers new writers. **Fiction:** Experimental short fiction, realistic fiction; to 2,000 words. **Poetry:** Formal, metered verse; experimental free verse. **Queries:** Not necessary. **E-Queries:** No. **Unsolicited mss:** Accepts. **Response:** Up to 3 months. **SASE Required:** Yes. **Rights:** FNAR. **Payment:** In copies.

NEBRASKA REVIEW

University of Nebraska-Omaha, Writer's Workshop, FAB 212, Omaha, NE 68182-0324. 402-554-3159. E-mail: jreed@unomaha.edu. Bi-annual. $8/$15. Circ.: 1,000. James Reed, Editor. **Description:** Contemporary fiction, poetry, and creative non-fiction. **Fiction:** Literary mainstream; 7,500 words. **Nonfiction:** Creative nonfiction and personal essays; 7,500 words. **Poetry:** Contemporary, literary; 5-6 pages max. **Tips:** "We have eclectic tastes, professional, non-dogmatic; in fiction, we seek strong voices." General inquiries accepted via e-mail, but not submissions. Sample copy $4.50. **Queries:** Not necessary. **E-Queries:** Yes. **Unsolicited mss:** Accepts. **Response:** Submissions 3-6 months. **SASE Required:** Yes. **Freelance Content:** 100%. **Rights:** FNAR. **Payment:** In copies.

NEW DELTA REVIEW

Louisiana State University, 15 Allen Hall, Dept. of English, Baton Rouge, LA 70803. 225-578-4079. Website: http://english.lsu.edu/journals/ndr. Semiannual. $7/$12. Circ.: 500. Brock Hamlin, Ronlyn Domingue, Editors. **Description:** Literary journal, focusing especially on work of new and established writers. **Fiction:** Short stories; 6,000 words. **Nonfiction:** Creative nonfiction, interviews, reviews (no academic essays); 5,000 words. **Poetry:** Submit up to 4 poems, any length; also translations. **Art:** Cover art and 8 color slides of artwork (mostly paintings, but will consider all visual media). **Queries:** Not necessary. **E-Queries:** No. **Unsolicited mss:** Accepts. **Response:** Queries 1 week, submissions 3 months. **SASE Required:** Yes. **Freelance Content:** 95%. **Rights:** FNAR and electronic. **Payment:** In copies.

NEW ENGLAND REVIEW

Middlebury College, Middlebury, VT 05753. 802-443-5075. E-mail: nereview@middlebury.edu. Website: www.middlebury.edu/~nereview. Quarterly. $8/issue. Circ.: 2,000. Stephen Donadio, Editor. **Description:** Short stories, short-shorts, novellas, and excerpts from novels. Also, long and short poems, interpretive and personal essays, book reviews, critical reassessments, and letters from abroad. **Fiction:** 10,000 words; $10/page. **Nonfiction:** Exploration of all forms of contemporary cultural expression; 10,000 words; $10/page. **Poetry:** Submit up to 6 poems, any length; $10/page, $20 min. **Queries:** Not necessary. **E-Queries:** No. **Unsolicited mss:** Accepts. **Response:** Queries 2 weeks, submissions 12 weeks. **SASE Required:** Yes. **Payment:** On publication.

NEW ENGLAND WRITERS NETWORK

P.O. Box 483, Hudson, MA 01749-0483. E-mail: newneditor@aol.com. Website: www.newnmag.net. $20/yr. Glenda Baker, Editor-in-Chief. **Description:** Literary journal with fiction, nonfiction, and poetry. **Fiction:** Short stories, novel excerpts, to 2,000 words. All genres (no pornography or excessive violence); pays $10.

Nonfiction: Personal, humorous essays, to 1,000 words; pays $5 **Poetry:** Upbeat, positive, to 32 lines; pays $5. **Tips:** June-August reading period. **Queries:** Not necessary. **E-Queries:** No. **Unsolicited mss:** Accepts. **Payment:** On publication.

NEW LETTERS

University of Missouri-Kansas City, University House, 5101 Rockhill Rd., Kansas City, MO 64110-2499. 816-235-1168. E-mail: newletters@umkc.edu. Website: www.newletters.org. Quarterly. $5/$17. Circ.: 5,000. Robert Stewart, Editor-in-Chief. **Description:** "Poetry, fiction, art, and essays with fresh, sophisticated writing." **Fiction:** Any style, subject, or genre; to 5,000 words. **Nonfiction:** Essays, profiles; to 5,000 words. **Poetry:** Submit 3-6 poems. **Tips:** Do not query or send manuscript via e-mail. Also offers annual contests for poetry, ficton, and creative nonfiction. **Queries:** Not necessary. **Unsolicited mss:** Accepts. **Response:** 3 months. **SASE Required:** Yes. **Freelance Content:** 50%. **Rights:** FNAR. **Payment:** On publication. **Contact:** Aleatha Ezra, Assistant Managing Editor.

NEW YORK STORIES

LaGuardia Community College, English Dept., E-103, 31-10 Thompson Ave., Long Island City, NY 11101. E-mail: nystories@lagcc.cuny.edu. Website: www.newyorkstories.org. 3x/yr. $5.95/issue. Circ.: 1,500. Daniel Caplice Lynch, Editor-in-Chief. **Description:** Publishes 6-8 short stories per issue as well as nonfiction pieces relating to New York City. Accepts simultaneous submissions. **Fiction:** Experimental or mainstream fiction; no genre fiction. Stories can be set anywhere; to 6,000 words; $100-$500. **Nonfiction:** Creative nonfiction set in NYC or with NYC theme; to 6,000 words; $100-$500. **Art:** B&W artwork with NYC theme; to $200. **Tips:** "Be fresh in your approach. NYC-centered nonfiction gets an especially close look since we get suprisingly few submissions in that category. Stories that touch on NYC's diversity, offbeat situations, and humor are always welcome. But if your talents lead you in other directions, we're still interested." **Queries:** Not necessary. **Unsolicited mss:** Accepts. **Response:** Queries 1 week, submissions 3-6 months. **SASE Required:** Yes. **Freelance Content:** 100%. **Rights:** FNASR. **Payment:** On publication.

NIMROD

University of Tulsa, 600 S College Ave., Tulsa, OK 74104-3189. 918-631-3080. E-mail: nimrod@utulsa.edu. Website: www.utulsa.edu/nimrod. Semiannual. $17.50/yr. Circ.: 3,000. Dr. Francine Ringold, Editor. **Description:** Quality prose and fiction by emerging writers of contemporary literature. **Fiction:** Quality fiction (no genre fiction), vigorous writing with believable characters and dialogue; 7,500 words max. **Nonfiction:** Vivid essays related to annual theme; 7,500 words max. **Poetry:** 1,900 words max. **Queries:** Not necessary. **E-Queries:** Yes. **Unsolicited mss:** Accepts. **Response:** 6-8 weeks. **SASE Required:** Yes. **Freelance Content:** 100%. **Rights:** FNAR. **Payment:** In copies.

NO EXPERIENCE REQUIRED

P.O. Box 131032, The Woodlands, TX 77393-1032. E-mail: nerzine@yahoo.com. 3x/yr. $5/$15. Circ.: 300. **Description:** Small literary magazine for new and undiscovered writers. **Fiction:** All genres; 15 pages maximum. **Poetry:** All forms; 90 lines. **Art:** Publishes in B&W. Art must be no smaller than 5x7, and no larger than 9x12. **Tips:** Make sure submissions are free of major spelling/grammar errors. No pornography. "Our purpose is not only to publish new and undiscovered writers, but to offer advice that they may need to achieve in the future. Due to the growing number of submissions, we can no longer offer comments or suggestions." **Queries:** Not necessary. **E-Queries:** No. **Response:** 6 months. **SASE Required:** Yes. **Freelance Content:** 100%. **Rights:** FNAR. **Payment:** In copies.

THE NORTH AMERICAN REVIEW

University of Northern Iowa, 1222 W 27th St., Cedar Falls, IA 50614-0516. E-mail: nar@uni.edu. Website: webdelsol.com/NorthAmReview/NAR/. Bimonthly. $22/yr. Vince Gotera, Editor. **Description:** Poetry, fiction, nonfiction, and art on contemporary North American concerns and issues, especially environment, gender, race, ethnicity, and class. No simultaneous submissions. **Fiction:** Literary realism, multicultural, or experimental; up to 12,000 words; $5/350 words. Submit January through March only. **Nonfiction:** Creative nonfiction, journals and diaries, letters, memoirs, profiles; nature, travel, and science writing; also literary journalism and essays; up to 12,000 words; $5/350 words. **Poetry:** Traditional or experimental, formal or free verse (closed or open form); submit 3-6 poems; $1/line. **Tips:** "We like stories with strong narrative arc and sense of humor." **Queries:** Not necessary. **Unsolicited mss:** Accepts. **Response:** 3 months. **SASE Required:** Yes. **Freelance Content:** 80%. **Rights:** FNASR. **Payment:** On publication.

NORTH CAROLINA LITERARY REVIEW

East Carolina University, Bate Building, English Dept., Greenville, NC 27858-4353. 252-328-1537. E-mail: bauerm@mail.edu.edu. Website: www.ecu.edu/nclr. Annual. Circ.: 750. **Description:** By and about North Carolina writers. Covers North Carolina history, culture, and literature. Mostly nonfiction, accepts some poetry and fiction. Pays $50/story or illustration. **Tips:** Sample copy available for $15. **Queries:** Not necessary. **Response:** 3 months **Rights:** FNAR. **Payment:** On publication.

NORTH DAKOTA QUARTERLY

University of North Dakota, Grand Forks, ND 58202-7209. 701-777-3322. E-mail: ndq@und.nodak.edu. Website: www.und.nodak.edu/org/ndq. Quarterly. $8/sample, $12/special issue. Circ.: 700. Robert W. Lewis, Editor. **Description:** Fiction, nonfiction, poetry, reviews, and criticism, often from unique perspective of the Northern Plains. **Tips:** "The list of *North Dakota Quarterly* authors is long and illustrious: Louise Erdrich, Larry Woiwode, Kathleen Norris, Garrison Keillor, and Thomas McGrath." **Queries:** Not necessary. **E-Queries:** Yes. **Unsolicited mss:** Accepts. **Response:** Queries 2-4 weeks, submissions 2-4 months. **SASE Required:** Yes. **Freelance Content:** 75%. **Rights:** FNASR. **Payment:** In copies.

NORTHWEST REVIEW

369 PLC, University of Oregon, Eugene, OR 97403. 541-346-3957. E-mail: jwitte@uoregon.edu. Website: http://darkwing.uoregon.edu/~engl/deptinfo/nwr.html. 3x/yr. $8/$22. Circ.: 1,000. John Witte, Editor. **Description:** "One of the nation's most distinguished reviews, our publication offers a forum for talented emerging young writers." Submit fiction and poetry of any length. Also open to eclectic commentary and essays. **Queries:** Not necessary. **E-Queries:** No. **Unsolicited mss:** Accepts. **Response:** Queries immediately, submissions 8-10 weeks. **SASE Required:** Yes. **Freelance Content:** 100%. **Rights:** FNASR. **Payment:** In copies.

NOTRE DAME REVIEW

University of Notre Dame, 840 Flanner Hall, Notre Dame, IN 46556. Website: www.nd.edu/nndr/review.htm. Biannual. $8/$15. Circ.: 2,000. Kathleen Canavan, Senior Editor. **Description:** Literary magazine featuring fiction and poetry of any length. Also runs long and short reviews by assignment. **Tips:** Send query for reviews, complete manuscript for all else. **E-Queries:** No. **Unsolicited mss:** Accepts. **Response:** Queries 1 month, submissions 3-5 months. **SASE Required:** Yes. **Freelance Content:** 60%. **Rights:** FNASR. **Payment:** On publication.

OASIS

P.O. Box 626, Largo, FL 33779-0626. 727-345-8505. E-mail: oasislit@aol.com. Website: www.oasislit.com. Triannual. $25/yr. Circ.: 300. Neal Storrs, Editor. **Description:** Stories and poetry, some nonfiction. **Fiction:** Style paramount, any length. **Poetry:** Free verse with a distinct, subtle music. No old-fashioned rhymes or rhythms. **Queries:** Not necessary. **E-Queries:** Yes. **Unsolicited mss:** Accepts. **Response:** Usually within 1 day. **SASE Required:** Yes. **Freelance Content:** 95%. **Rights:** FNAR.

OFFERINGS

P.O. Box 1667, Lebanon, MO 65536. Quarterly. $5/$16. Circ.: 75. Velvet Fackeldey, Editor. **Description:** Quality poetry, all forms; 30 lines max. **Tips:** Overstocked with nature poetry. Send SASE for writer's guidelines. **Queries:** Not necessary. **E-Queries:** No. **Unsolicited mss:** Accepts. **Response:** 4-6 weeks. **SASE Required:** Yes. **Freelance Content:** 100%. **Rights:** FNAR. **Payment:** No payment.

THE OLD RED KIMONO

Humanities Div., Floyd College, P.O. Box 1864, Rome, GA 30162. E-mail: napplega@mail.fc.peachnet.edu. Annual. $5. Circ.: 1,400. La Nelle Daniel, Nancy Applegate, Faculty Editors. **Description:** Poems and short stories of all types. Fiction should be 1,500 words or less. **Tips:** Local writers constitute 50% of journal. Sponsors annual Paris Lake Poetry Contest. **Queries:** Not necessary. **E-Queries:** Yes. **Unsolicited mss:** Accepts. **Response:** 8 weeks. **SASE Required:** Yes. **Freelance Content:** 100%. **Rights:** FNAR. **Payment:** In copies.

OREGON EAST

Eastern Oregon University, Hoke #304, One University Blvd., La Grande, OR 97850. 541-962-3787. E-mail: oe@eou.edu. Annual. $5. Circ.: 1,000. Eden Kruger, Editor. **Description:** Short fiction, flash fiction, nonfiction, 1-act plays and poetry. Prose should not exceed 3,000 words. Poetry can be any form (no greeting card verse), up to 60 lines. **Art:** Photos of original graphics should be B&W glossies, 4x5 or 5x7, high contrast. Slides also welcomed. Include titles or captions. **Queries:** Not necessary. **E-Queries:** Yes. **Unsolicited mss:** Accepts. **Response:** 2-3 months. **SASE Required:** Yes. **Freelance Content:** 100%. **Rights:** FNAR. **Payment:** In copies.

OSIRIS

P.O. Box 297, Deerfield, MA 01342. 413-774-4027. Semiannual. $7.50/issue. Circ.: 1,000. Andrea Moorhead, Editor. **Description:** A multilingual, international poetry journal. Features contemporary, foreign poetry in original language (English and French are the principle languages of this journal). Other works appear in original language with facing-page translation in English. Length varies. **Tips:** "We seek poetry that is well-crafted, non-narrative, and lyrical. Translators need to secure permission of both poet and publisher. Ask for a sample copy." **Queries:** Not necessary. **E-Queries:** No. **Unsolicited mss:** Accepts. **Response:** 4-8 weeks. **SASE Required:** Yes. **Freelance Content:** 30%. **Payment:** In copies.

OTHER VOICES

University of Illinois-Chicago, Dept. of English (M/C 162), 601 S Morgan St., Chicago, IL 60607. 312-413-2209. E-mail: othervoices@listserv.uic.edu. Website: www.othervoicesmagazine.org. Semiannual. $7/issue. Circ.: 1,500. Gina Frangello, Editor. **Description:** Literary journal. **Fiction:** Literary short stories, novel excerpts, 1-act plays; traditional or experimental; no genre fiction; to 7,500 words. **Nonfiction:** Book reviews, interviews with esteemed fiction writers. **Tips:** Accepts manuscripts between October 1-April 1 only. **Queries:** Not necessary. **E-Queries:** No. **Unsolicited mss:** Accepts. **Response:** 3 months. **SASE Required:** Yes. **Freelance Content:** 100%. **Rights:** First serial. **Payment:** In copies.

THE OXFORD AMERICAN

303 President Clinton Ave., Little Rock, AR 72201. 501-907-6418. Website: www.oxfordamericanmag.com. $29.95. Circ.: 45,000. Marc Smirnoff, Editor. **Description:** "The Southern Magazine of Good Writing." General-interest magazine that explores the American South through good writing. Features fiction, nonfiction, and poetry. **Poetry:** 3-5 poems, any length; $125/poem. **Tips:** "Writers should always learn a little bit about the homes where their writing ends up. Writers should only send their beloved work to magazines to which they feel a special kinship." **Queries:** Not necessary. **E-Queries:** No. **Unsolicited mss:** Accepts. **Response:** Queries vary, submissions up to 3 months. **SASE Required:** Yes. **Freelance Content:** 50%. **Rights:** FNASR. **Payment:** On publication.

OYSTER BOY REVIEW

P.O.Box 77842, San Francisco, CA 94107-0842.
E-mail: editors@oysterboyreview.com; fiction@oysterboyreview.com. Website: www.oysterboyreview.com. Quarterly. Damon Sauve, Publisher. **Description:** "Literary magazine, in print and online, featuring the underrated, ignored, misunderstood, and varietal." See website for guidelines. **Tips:** No simultaneous submissions or previously published work. Mss read January–September. **Queries:** Not necessary. **E-Queries:** Yes. **Unsolicited mss:** Accepts. **Response:** 3-6 months. **SASE Required:** Yes. **Rights:** FNASR. **Payment:** In copies.

PAINTBRUSH

Truman State University, Language & Literature Division, Kirksville, MO 63501. 660-785-4185. Website: www.paintbrush.org. Annual. $15/yr. Circ.: 500. Ben Bennani, Editor. **Description:** International journal of poetry and translation. **Poetry:** Serious, original, highly imaginative work. Submit 3-5 poems with cover letter. **Queries:** Preferred. **E-Queries:** Yes. **Unsolicited mss:** Accepts. **Response:** 10 weeks. **SASE Required:** Yes. **Freelance Content:** 60%. **Rights:** FNAR. **Payment:** In copies.

PAINTED BRIDE QUARTERLY

Rutgers Univ., English Dept., Armitage Hall, Camden, NJ 08102. 856-225-6129.
E-mail: pbq@camden.rutgers.edu. Website: www.pbq.rutgers.edu. Annual. $15/yr. Circ.: 1,500. Marion Wrenn, Editor. **Description:** Literary journal of fiction and poetry, both print and online. **Fiction:** Any genre; up to 5,000 words. **Nonfiction:** Essays and reviews; up to 3,000 words. **Poetry:** Length varies, no more than 5 poems. **Art:** B&W photos, etchings, lithographs, line drawings. **Tips:** Does not accept electronic submissions. **Queries:** Not necessary. **E-Queries:** Yes. **Unsolicited mss:** Accepts. **Response:** 3 months. **SASE Required:** Yes. **Freelance Content:** 100%. **Rights:** FNAR. **Payment:** On publication.

PALO ALTO REVIEW

Palo Alto College, 1400 W Villaret, San Antonio, TX 78224-2499. 210-921-5017. E-mail: professor78224-par@yahoo.com. Semiannual. $5.00. Circ.: 500. Ellen Shull, Editor. **Description:** Articles, essays, memoirs, plus a few poems and short fiction on varied historical, geographical, scientific, mathematical, artistic, political, and social topics. **Fiction:** No experimental or excessively avant-garde fiction. **Nonfiction:** Original, unpublished articles and interviews. **Poetry:** Submit 3-5 poems, to 50 lines. **Columns, Departments:** Food for Thought (200-word think pieces); reviews, to 500 words, of books, films, videos, or software. **Art:** Photo essays welcome. **Tips:** A "journal of ideas." Send SASE for upcoming themes. **Payment:** In copies.

PANGOLIN PAPERS

P.O. Box 241, Nordland, WA 98358. 360-385-3626. E-mail: trtlbluf@olympus.net. Triannual. $7.95/$20. Circ.: 400. Pat Britt, Editor. **Description:** Literary short stories, to 8,000 words. **Tips:** No poetry, genre fiction, or essays. **Queries:** Not necessary. **E-Queries:** No. **Unsolicited mss:** Accepts. **Response:** 3 months. **SASE Required:** Yes. **Rights:** FNAR. **Payment:** In copies.

THE PARIS REVIEW

541 E 72nd St., New York, NY 10021. 212-861-0016. E-mail: queries@theparisreview.com. Website: www.parisreview.com. Quarterly. $12/$40. Circ.: 12,000. Brigid Hughes, Executive Editor. **Description:** International literary magazine featuring high-quality fiction, poetry, interviews, and essays from established and emerging writers/artists. Accepts unsolicited manuscripts for short fiction and poetry only. **Tips:** Annual prizes, in several categories, up to $1,000. **Queries:** Not necessary. **E-Queries:** Yes. **Unsolicited mss:** Accepts. **Response:** Queries 2-3 weeks, submissions 3-4 months. **SASE Required:** Yes. **Freelance Content:** 75%. **Rights:** FNAR. **Payment:** On publication.

PARNASSUS: POETRY IN REVIEW

205 W 89th St., Apt. 8F, New York, NY 10024-1835. 212-362-3492. E-mail: parnew@aol.com. Website: www.parnassuspoetry.com. Semiannual. $12-$15. Circ.: 2,500. Herbert Leibowitz, Editor. **Description:** For in-depth analysis of contemporary books of poetry. **Nonfiction:** Critical essays and reviews on contemporary poetry. No academic or theoretical work, looks for criticism that is colorful, idiosyncratic, well-written; 20-25 pages; $150. **Poetry:** Mostly by request; $25/page. **Queries:** Not necessary. **E-Queries:** Yes. **Unsolicited mss:** Accepts. **Response:** 2 months. **SASE Required:** Yes. **Freelance Content:** 100%. **Rights:** All, reverts to author. **Payment:** On publication.

PARTING GIFTS

3413 Wilshire, Greensboro, NC 27408. Website: www.marchstreetpress.com. Semiannual. $9. Robert Bixby, Editor. **Description:** Literary journal featuring fiction (500-1,000 words) and poetry (up to 50 lines). **Tips:** Manuscripts read January-June. **Queries:** Not necessary. **E-Queries:** Yes. **Unsolicited mss:** Accepts. **Response:** Queries 1 day, submissions 1 week. **SASE Required:** Yes. **Freelance Content:** 100%. **Rights:** FNAR. **Payment:** In copies.

PASSAGES NORTH

Northern Michigan University, Dept. of English, Gries Hall, 1401 Presque Isle Ave., Marquette, MI 49855. 906-227-1203. E-mail: passages@nmu.edu. Website: myweb.nmu.edu/~passages. Annual. $13. Circ.: 1,000. Kate Hanson, Editor. **Description:** Literary fiction, poetry, and nonfiction for established and emerging writers. **Fiction:** Submit one short story (no genre fiction); to 5,000 words. **Nonfiction:** Interviews, essays, literary nonfiction; to 5,000 words. **Poetry:** Up to 6 poems, up to 100 lines. **Tips:** Submissions read September 1-April 15 only. Include brief cover letter with contact information. **Queries:** Not necessary. **E-Queries:** No. **Unsolicited mss:** Accepts. **Response:** 6-8 weeks. **SASE Required:** Yes. **Freelance Content:** 95%. **Rights:** FNAR. **Payment:** In copies.

PATERSON LITERARY REVIEW

Poetry Center at Passaic County Community College, 1 College Blvd., Paterson, NJ 07505-1179. 973-684-6555. E-mail: mgillan@pccc.cc.nj.us. Website: www.pccc.cc.nj.us/poetry. Annual. $10/issue. Circ.: 1,000. Maria Mazziotti Gillan, Editor. **Description:** Literary publication of poetry, fiction, book reviews, articles, and artwork. **Fiction:** 1,500 words. **Nonfiction:** 1,000 words. **Poetry:** 100-line limit. **Queries:** Not necessary. **E-Queries:** No. **Unsolicited mss:** Accepts. **Response:** 6 months. **SASE Required:** Yes. **Freelance Content:** 100%. **Rights:** FNAR.

PEARL

3030 E Second St., Long Beach, CA 90803. 562-434-4523. E-mail: pearlmag@aol.com. Website: www.pearlmag.com. Biannual. $8/$18. Circ.: 700. Marilyn Johnson, Joan Jobe Smith, Editors. **Description:** Contemporary poetry and short fiction. **Fiction:** Accessible humanistic fiction, related to real life. Ironic, serious, and intense, humor and wit welcome; 1,200 words. **Poetry:** Humanistic; to 40 lines. **Art:** B&W. **Queries:** Not necessary. **E-Queries:** Yes. **Unsolicited mss:** Accepts. **Response:** Queries 1 week, submissions 6-8 weeks. **SASE Required:** Yes. **Freelance Content:** 100%. **Rights:** FNAR. **Payment:** In copies.

PEDESTAL MAGAZINE.COM

228 E Park Ave., Charlotte, NC 28203. 704-643-0244. E-mail: pedestalmagazine@aol.com. Website: www.thepedestalmagazine.com. Bimonthly. Circ.: 10,000. John Amen, Editor. **Description:** Online literary magazine featuring new and established visual artists and writers of poetry, fiction, and nonfiction. Each issue includes an in-depth interview with a featured writer and visual artist with examples of their work. **Fiction:** All types of fiction including literary, experimental, science fiction, and fantasy. Preference leans towards pieces that cross genres and do not fall into one specific category; to 6,000 words; $.05/word. **Nonfiction:** Accepts academic/scholarly pieces, as well as those that focus on issues of aesthetics, psychology, philosophy, and religion; to 6,000 words; $.05/word. **Poetry:** Open to a wide variety of poetry, ranging from the highly experimental to the traditionally formal; $30-$60/poem. **Art:** Accepts art submissions for inclusion in gallery. Artists should query before sending work. **Tips:** "We are looking for freshness, clarity, poignance. Writers should try to avoid cliches, sentimentality, or inflated drama. We look for a unique piece." **Queries:** Not necessary. **E-Queries:** Yes. **Unsolicited mss:** Accepts. **Response:** Queries 1 week, submissions 6-8 weeks. **Freelance Content:** 100%. **Payment:** 30 days after publication.

PEREGRINE

Amherst Writers & Artists, P.O. Box 1076, Amherst, MA 01004. 413-253-3307. E-mail: awapress@aol.com. Website: www.amherstwriters.com. Annual. $12/issue. Circ.: 1,000 .Pat Schneider, Editor. **Description:** Features poetry, fiction, and short personal essays. **Fiction:** All styles, forms, and subjects; 3,000 words. **Nonfiction:** Short personal essays; to 1,500 words. **Poetry:** No greeting-card verse; 70 lines (3-5 poems). **Tips:** *"Peregrine* has provided a forum for national and international writers for 23 years, and is committed to finding exceptional work by new as well as established writers. We seek work that is unpretentious and memorable. We welcome work reflecting diversity of voice. We do not accept work by or for children." Submissions must be postmarked October 1-April 1. **Queries:** Not necessary. **E-Queries:** No. **Unsolicited mss:** Accepts. **Response:** 2-3 months after deadline. **SASE Required:** Yes. **Payment:** On publication. **Contact:** Nancy Rose, Managing Editor.

PERMAFROST

University of Alaska–Fairbanks, English Dept., P.O. Box 75720, Fairbanks, AK 99775-0640. 907-474-5398. Website: www.uaf.edu/english/permafrost. Annual. $10/issue. **Description:** International literary journal for the arts. Fiction, nonfiction, poetry, and artwork of emerging and established writers and artists. **Fiction:** To 30 pages; avoid genre fiction (horror, sci-fi, fantasy). **Nonfiction:** To 30 pages. **Poetry:** To 5 poems. **Tips:** Alaskan themes discouraged. Reading period is September 1-March 1. **Queries:** Not necessary. **E-Queries:** No. **Unsolicited mss:** Accepts. **Response:** 3 months. **SASE Required:** Yes. **Rights:** FNAR. **Payment:** In copies.

PHANTASMAGORIA

Century College/English Dept., 3300 Century Ave. N, White Bear Lake, MN 55110. 651-779-3410. E-mail: allenabigail@hotmail.com. Semiannual. $9/$15. Circ.: 1,000. Abigail Allen, Editor. **Description:** Accepts previously unpublished short stories or poems of literary merit. **Fiction:** Short stories to 4,000 words. Submit only one story at a time. **Poetry:** 100 lines or fewer. Submit no more than six poems at a time. **Tips:** Send SASE for reply; faxed or e-mailed submissions will not be read. **Queries:** Not necessary. **E-Queries:** No. **Unsolicited mss:** Accepts. **Freelance Content:** 98%. **Rights:** FNAR. **Payment:** In copies.

THE PIKEVILLE REVIEW

Pikeville College, Humanities Division, 147 Sycamore St., Pikeville, KY 41501. 606-218-5002. E-mail: eward@pc.edu. Website: www.pc.edu. Annual. $4/issue. Circ.: 500. Elgin M. Ward, Editor. **Description:** Contemporary fiction, poetry, creative essays, and book reviews, for Kentucky writers and others. **Tips:** Open to new and unpublished writers. **Queries:** Not necessary. **E-Queries:** Yes. **Unsolicited mss:** Accepts. **Response:** Queries 2 weeks, submissions 30-60 days. **SASE Required:** Yes. **Payment:** On publication.

PINDELDYBOZ

23-55 38th St., Astoria, NY 11105. E-mail: pindeldyboz@pindeldyboz.com. Website: www.pindeldyboz.com. 1x/yr. $12. Whitney Pastorek, Editor. **Description:** Previously unpublished literary fiction from established and up-and-coming authors. **Queries:** Not necessary. **E-Queries:** Yes. **Unsolicited mss:** Accepts. **Freelance Content:** 100%. **Rights:** FNASR. **Payment:** In copies.

THE PLASTIC TOWER

P.O. Box 702, Bowie, MD 20718. E-mail: rscottk@aol.com. Quarterly. $2.50/$8. Circ.: 250. Roger Kyle-Keith, Carol Dyer, Editors. **Description:** Fun, irreverent, but serious about bringing enjoyable poetry to the public. **Nonfiction:** Reviews of literary and poetry magazines; 100 words. **Poetry:** Eclectic, all types of poetry, from sonnets to free verse to limericks; 40 lines max. **Art:** 10-15 small B&W illustrations per issue. **Tips:** "Develop a fresh and unique voice, and you will eventually prevail." **Queries:** Not necessary. **E-Queries:** No. **Unsolicited mss:** Does not accept. **Response:** Queries 1 month, submissions 6 months. **SASE Required:** Yes. **Freelance Content:** 80%. **Rights:** FNAR. **Payment:** In copies.

PLEIADES

Central Missouri State Univ., Dept. of English, Warrensburg, MO 64093. 660-543-8106. E-mail: kdp8106@cmsu2.cmsu.edu. Website: www.cmsu.edu/engl-phil/pleiades.html. 2x/yr. $6/$12. Circ.: 3,000. Kevin Prufer, Editor. **Description:** Traditional and experimental poetry, fiction, criticism, translations, and reviews. Cross-genre especially welcome. Prose up to 10,000 words; poetry any length. **Tips:** Considers simultaneous submissions. "We are interested in a very wide range of styles, genres, themes and writers. In the last year, work first printed in *Pleiades* has been taken for *The Best American Poetry* and *The Pushcart Prize Anthology*, among others." **E-Queries:** No. **Unsolicited mss:** Accepts. **Response:** 1-2 months. **SASE Required:** Yes. **Freelance Content:** 85%. **Rights:** FNASR, electronic. **Payment:** On publication.

PLOUGHSHARES

Emerson College, 120 Boylston St., Boston, MA 02116-4624. 617-824-8753. E-mail: pshares@emerson.edu. Website: www.pshares.org. 3x/yr. $10.95/issue. Circ.: 6,000. Don Lee, Editor. **Description:** Publishes compelling fiction and poetry. Each issue is guest-edited by a prominent writer. **Fiction:** To 30 pages; pays $25/printed page ($50 min., $250 max.). **Poetry:** Send 1-3 poems; $25/printed page. **Tips:** No genre work, unsolicited book reviews, or criticism. Reviews submissions postmarked August 1-March 31 only. Submissions received April-July are returned unread. **Queries:** Not necessary. **E-Queries:** No. **Unsolicited mss:** Accepts. **Response:** 3-5 months. **SASE Required:** Yes. **Rights:** FNASR. **Payment:** On publication.

POEM

Huntsville Literary Association, P.O. Box 2006, Huntsville, AL 35804. Semiannual. $20. Circ.: 400. Rebecca Harbor, Editor. **Description:** Publishes serious poetry. **Poetry:** Traditional forms and free verse. Poems characterized by compression, rich vocabulary, significant content, and evidence of a "tuned ear and practiced pen." Submit 3-5 poems. **Tips:** Send cover letter instead of query. **Queries:** Not necessary. **E-Queries:** No. **Unsolicited mss:** Accepts. **Response:** 4-6 weeks. **SASE Required:** Yes. **Rights:** FNAR. **Payment:** In copies.

POET LORE

The Writer's Center, 4508 Walsh St., Bethesda, MD 20815. 301-654-8664. E-mail: postmaster@writer.org. Website: www.writer.org. Biannual. $9/issue. Circ.: 400. Editors: Rick Cannon, E. Ethelbert Miller, Jody Bolz. **Description:** Contemporary poetry by both new and established writers. Also timely reviews of new poetry and books about poetry/poets. **Tips:** "Inviting all types of poetry, the editors of *Poet Lore* look for a high level of craftsmanship, and imaginative use of language and image." **Queries:** Not necessary. **E-Queries:** Yes. **Unsolicited mss:** Accepts. **Response:** 2-3 months. **SASE Required:** Yes. **Rights:** FNASR, anthology. **Payment:** In copies. **Contact:** Dee Dee Clendenning, Managing Editor.

POETRY LETTER

California State Poetry Society, P.O. Box 7126, Orange, CA 92863. 949-854-8024. Quarterly. $7/$25. Circ.: 250. Russell Salamon, Editor. **Description:** Literary journal. Submit up to 6 poems, to 40 lines on any subject or style. Pays one copy. **Queries:** Not necessary. **Unsolicited mss:** Accepts. **Response:** 5-6 months. **SASE Required:** Yes. **Freelance Content:** 100%.

POETRY MAGAZINE

The Poetry Foundation, 1030 N Clark St., Suite 420, Chicago, IL 60610. 312-787-7070. E-mail: poetry@poetrymagazine.org. Website: www.poetrymagazine.org. Monthly. $3.75/issue. Circ.: 12,000. **Description:** Literary journal for and about poetry. Poems may be any length; $6/line. Also prose, $150/page. **Queries:** Not necessary. **E-Queries:** No. **Unsolicited mss:** Accepts. **Response:** 4 months. **SASE Required:** Yes. **Freelance Content:** 100%. **Payment:** On publication.

THE PORTLAND REVIEW

Portland State University, P.O. Box 347, Portland, OR 97207-0347. 503-725-4533. E-mail: kfriedman@earthlink.net. Website: www.portlandreview.org. 3x/yr. $8/issue. Circ.: 500. Kevin Friedman, Editor; Andrew M. Roberts, Assistant Editor. **Description:** Short fiction, poetry, reviews, interviews, and art for a literary and academic audience. Submit fiction up to 20 pages; nonfiction and poetry any length. **Tips:** "We support new and emerging writers, as well as established authors." **Queries:** Not necessary. **Unsolicited mss:** Accepts. **Response:** 1-5 months. **SASE Required:** Yes. **Rights:** FNAR. **Payment:** On publication. **Contact:** Fiction Editor or Poetry Editor.

POTOMAC REVIEW

Montgomery College, Paul Peck Humanities Institute, 51 Mannakee St., Rockville, MD 20850. 301-251-7417. Website: www.meral.com/potomac. Semiannual. $10/$15. Circ.: 1,500. Eli Flam, Editor. **Description:** Regionally rooted, with a conscience, a lurking sense of humor, and a strong environmental/nature bent. **Fiction:** Vivid, with ethical depth and in Flannery O'Connor's words "the vision to go with it." 3,000 words. **Nonfiction:** 3,000 words. **Poetry:** Poems that educate, challenge, or divert in fresh ways; up to 3 poems, 5 pages. **Art:** B&W photos, drawings, and prints. Query first. **Tips:** Contact for upcoming themes. **Queries:** Not necessary. **E-Queries:** No. **Unsolicited mss:** Accepts. **Response:** 2-3 months. **SASE Required:** Yes. **Freelance Content:** 75%. **Rights:** FNAR. **Payment:** In copies.

THE PRAIRIE JOURNAL OF CANADIAN LITERATURE

P.O. Box 61203, Brentwood Post Office, Calgary, AB T2L 2K6 Canada. E-mail: prairiejournal@yahoo.com. Website: www.geocities.com/prairiejournal. Semiannual. $4/issue. Circ.: 600. A. Burke, Editor. **Description:** Devoted to new, previously unpublished writing. **Fiction:** Literary; any length, pay varies. **Nonfiction:** Essays, reviews, and interviews on Canadian subjects. **Poetry:** Any length. **Art:** B&W photos. **Tips:** No simultaneous submissions. Accepts general inquries via e-mail, but not submissions. Sample copy $6. **Queries:** Not necessary. **E-Queries:** Yes. **Unsolicited mss:** Accepts. **Response:** 2-3 months, include SASE (IRC's). **Freelance Content:** 100%. **Rights:** First. **Payment:** On publication.

PRAIRIE SCHOONER

Univ. of Nebraska, P.O. Box 880334, 201 Andrews Hall, Lincoln, NE 68588. 402-472-0911. E-mail: kgrey2@unl.edu. Website: www.unl.edu/schooner/psmain.htm. Quarterly. $9/$26. Circ.: 3,000. Hilda Raz, Editor. **Description:** Contemporary poetry, fiction, essay, and reviews. **Fiction:** Short stories; 18-25 pages. **Nonfiction:** Essays, book reviews, translations; 15-25 pages. **Poetry:** Submit 5-7 poems at a time. **Tips:** Annual prizes for work in the magazine, $200-$1,000. **Queries:** Not necessary. **E-Queries:** No. **Unsolicited mss:** Accepts. **Response:** Queries 3 weeks, submissions 3-4 months. **SASE Required:** Yes. **Rights:** All, electronic, can revert to author. **Payment:** In copies. **Contact:** Kelly Grey Carlisle, Managing Editor.

PUCKERBRUSH REVIEW

76 Main St., Orono, ME 04473-1430. 207-866-4868. Semiannual. $6/issue. Circ.: 300. Constance Hunting, Editor. **Description:** Literary poetry, fiction, interviews, reviews, translations, and essays (personal or literary). Also publishes literary news from specific regions or countries. Pays 2 copies. **Queries:** Preferred. **E-Queries:** No. **Unsolicited mss:** Accepts. **Response:** 1 month. **SASE Required:** Yes. **Freelance Content:** 90%.

PUDDING MAGAZINE

Innovative Writers Programs, 81 Shadymere Ln., Columbus, OH 43213.
614-986-1881. E-mail: info@puddinghouse.com. Website: www.puddinghouse.com.
$8.95/issue; 4/$29. Circ.: 1,000. Jennifer Bosveld, Editor. **Description:** *Pudding Magazine: The International Journal of Applied Poetry* features mostly poetry, but also short-short stories, essays, writing exercises, and mini-reviews. **Nonfiction:** Articles/essays on poetry and intentional living, social concerns, poetry applied to the times of our lives; 500-2,500 words. **Poetry:** On popular culture, social concerns, and personal struggle. **Columns, Departments:** Reviews of poetry books. **Tips:** Featured poet in each issue receives $10 and 4 copies. **E-Queries:** No. **Unsolicited mss:** Accepts. **Response:** 1 day. **SASE Required:** Yes. **Freelance Content:** 98%. **Payment:** In copies.

PUERTO DEL SOL

New Mexico State Univ.
Dept. of English, MSC 3E, Box 30001, Las Cruces, NM 88003-8001. 505-646-2345. E-mail: puerto@nmsu.edu. Website: www.nmsu.edu/~puerto/welcome.html. Kevin McIlvoy, Editor-in-Chief. **Description:** Features poetry, short stories, personal essays, novel excerpts, book reviews, photo-essays, translations, and other artwork. Short stories and personal essays (to 30 pages); excerpts (to 65 pages). **Tips:** Manuscripts read September 1-February 1. **Response:** 3-5 months. **SASE Required:** Yes. **Payment:** In copies.

QUARRY

P.O. Box 1061, Kingston, Ontario K7L 4Y5 Canada. 613-548-8429.
E-mail: info@quarrypress.com. 3x/yr. Circ.: 1,200. Suzanne Garret, Editor. **Description:** Literary magazine publishing innovative fiction, poetry, and essays by Canadian writers. **Tips:** Seeking talented new writers.

QUARTER AFTER EIGHT

Ohio University, 102 Ellis Hall, Athens, OH 45701. 740-593-2827. E-mail: quarter-aftereight@hotmail.com. Website: www.quarteraftereight.org. Annual. $10. Circ.: 1,000. Hayley Haugen, Co-Editor. **Description:** Literary journal with fiction (experimental or sudden) and nonfiction (essays, criticism, commentary, interviews). Pieces should be 10,000 words max. **Tips:** Also sponsors annual prose contest with $300 prize. Send SASE for details. **Queries:** Not necessary. **E-Queries:** No. **Unsolicited mss:** Accepts. **Response:** 12-16 weeks. **SASE Required:** Yes. **Rights:** FNAR. **Payment:** In copies.

QUARTERLY WEST

255 S Central Campus Dr., Dept. of English-LNCO 3500, Salt Lake City, UT 84112-9109. 801-581-3938. Website: www.utah.edu/quarterlywest. Semi-annual. $7.50/$12. Circ.: 1,600. David Hawkins, Editor. **Description:** Literary journal, for new writers and established authors. **Fiction:** Shorts and longer fiction, that play with form and language, not bound by convention; 500-6,000 words; pay varies. **Nonfiction:**

Memoir, book reviews, essays; 500-6,000 words. **Poetry:** Up to 5 pages, 3 poems. **Tips:** No "Western" themes or religious verse. **Queries:** Not necessary. **E-Queries:** No. **Unsolicited mss:** Accepts. **Response:** 6-8 months. **SASE Required:** Yes. **Freelance Content:** 75%. **Payment:** On publication.

QUEEN'S QUARTERLY

Queens University, 144 Barrie St., Kingston, Ontario K7L 3N6 Canada. 613-533-2667. E-mail: qquarter@post.queensu.ca. Website: http://info.queensu.ca/quarterly. Quarterly. $20/yr. Circ.: 2,700. Boris Castel, Editor. **Description:** Nonfiction (covering a wide range of topics) and fiction. **Fiction:** In English and French; to 5,000 words; to $300. **Nonfiction:** To 5,000 words; to $400. **Poetry:** Send up to 6 poems; to $400. **Art:** B&W art; to $400. **E-Queries:** Yes. **Payment:** On publication.

RAMBUNCTIOUS REVIEW

1221 W Pratt Blvd., Chicago, IL 60626. Annual. $4/issue. Circ.: 500. **Description:** Features new and established writers of poetry and fiction. **Tips:** Also hosts yearly themed contests with cash prizes. Send SASE for information. **Queries:** Not necessary. **E-Queries:** No. **Unsolicited mss:** Accepts. **Freelance Content:** 100%. **Rights:** FNASR. **Payment:** In copies. **Contact:** Editorial Board.

RATTAPALLAX

532 La Guardia, Suite 353, New York, NY 10012. 212-560-7459. E-mail: info@rattapallax.com. Website: www.rattapallax.com. 2x/yr. $7.95/issue. Circ.: 2,000. Martin Mitchell, Alan Cheuse, Editors. **Description:** Literary magazine featuring modern poetry and prose. Each issue comes with a CD containing selected poets reading their work. **Queries:** Not necessary. **E-Queries:** No. **Unsolicited mss:** Accepts. **Response:** 3-6 months. **SASE Required:** Yes. **Freelance Content:** 5%. **Rights:** FNAR. **Payment:** In copies.

RATTLE

13440 Ventura Blvd., Suite 200, Sherman Oaks, CA 91423. 818-986-3274. E-mail: stellasuel@aol.com. Website: www.rattle.com. 2x/yr. $8/issue. **Description:** Features poetry, translations, reviews, essays, and interviews. **Nonfiction:** Essays on any subject that pertains to writing; to 2,000 words. Reviews should be on poetry books; to 400 words. **Poetry:** Open to any type or form of contemporary poetry. Prefers shorter poems, but will read and consider everything. **Tips:** Send cover letter, bio, and SASE with submission. Does not accept previously published work or simultaneous submissions. **Queries:** Not necessary. **E-Queries:** Yes. **Unsolicited mss:** Accepts. **Payment:** In copies. **Contact:** Alan Fox, Editor; Stellasue Lee, Poetry Editor.

REAL

Stephen F. Austin State University, P.O. Box 13007, SFA Sta., Nacogdoches, TX 75962. 936-468-2059. E-mail: real@sfasu.edu. Semiannual. $20. Circ.: 400. David R. Dickerson, Managing Editor. **Description:** Short fiction, poetry, and criticism. **Fiction:** Realistic portrayal of human situations; to 5,000 words. **Nonfiction:** Well-written, scholarly articles; to 5,000 words. **Poetry:** Imagistic verse, not just reformatted prose; to 100 lines. **Art:** B&W photography and line drawings. **Queries:** Not necessary. **E-Queries:** No. **Unsolicited mss:** Accepts. **Response:** Queries 1 week, submissions 4-6 weeks. **SASE Required:** Yes. **Freelance Content:** 100%. **Payment:** In copies.

RED CEDAR REVIEW

Michigan State Univ., Dept. of English, 17-C Morrill Hall, E. Lansing, MI 48824-1036. 517-355-1707. E-mail: rcreview@msu.edu. Website: www.msu.edu/~rcreview. Biannual. $5/$6. Meg Sparling, Editor. **Description:** Publishes poetry, fiction, and creative nonfiction of all genres by both published and unpublished authors. **Fiction:** 5,000 words max. **Nonfiction:** Creative nonfiction; 5,000 words max. **Poetry:** Submit up to 5 poems. **Queries:** Preferred. **E-Queries:** Yes. **Unsolicited mss:** Accepts. **Response:** Queries 3 weeks, submissions 3 months. **SASE Required:** Yes. **Payment:** In copies.

RED ROCK REVIEW

English Dept. 12A, Community College of Southern Nevada
3200 E Cheyenne Ave., North Las Vegas, NV 89030. 702-651-4094.
E-mail: richard_logsdm@ccsn.nevada.edu. Semiannual. $5.50/$10. Circ.: 1,000. Dr. Richard Logsdon, Editor. **Description:** Featuring work by new and well-established writers. **Fiction:** Mainstream fiction; 5,000 words. **Nonfiction:** Reviews and interviews with literary artists; 2,000 words. **Poetry:** Up to 60 lines. **Tips:** Does not accept e-mail submissions. **Queries:** Not necessary. **E-Queries:** Yes. **Unsolicited mss:** Accepts. **Response:** Queries 2 weeks (e-mail responses sooner), submissions 3 months. **SASE Required:** Yes. **Freelance Content:** 60%. **Rights:** FNAR. **Payment:** In copies.

RED WHEELBARROW

De Anza College, 21250 Stevens Creek Blvd., Cupertino, CA 95014. 408-864-8600. E-mail: splitterrandolph@fhda.edu. Annual. $7.50/issue. Circ.: 500. Randolph Splitter, Editor. **Description:** Fiction, poetry, creative nonfiction, photography, comics, and drawings. Submit prose (to 4,000 words) or poetry (up to 5 poems). **Art:** B&W drawings, comics, and other visual art forms. **Tips:** Accepts work in September-January only. Diverse voices welcome. "Please note our publication is not affiliated with Red Wheelbarrow Press or any other similarly named publication." Accepts queries and submissions via e-mail. Include SASE or e-mail address for reply. **Unsolicited mss:** Accepts. **Response:** 2-6 months. **Freelance Content:** 95%.

RHINO

P.O. Box 591, Evanston, IL 60204. Website: www.rhinopoetry.org. Annual. $10/yr. Circ.: 1,000. Editors: Deborah Rosen, Alice George, Kathleen Kirk, and Helen Degen Cohen. **Description:** Poetry, translations, and short-short fiction. Occasionally publishes a short essay on poetry. Send 3-5 poems or 1-2 short prose pieces (250-650 words). **Tips:** "We encourage adventurous writing in love with language." Reads material between April 1-October 1 only. See guidelines on website. **Queries:** Not necessary. **E-Queries:** No. **Unsolicited mss:** Accepts. **Response:** In up to 6 months. **SASE Required:** Yes. **Payment:** In copies.

RIVER CITY

University of Memphis, Dept. of English, Memphis, TN 38152. 901-678-4591. E-mail: rivercity@memphis.edu. Website: www.people.memphis.edu/~rivercity. Semiannual. $7/$12. Circ.: 1,200. Dr. Mary Bryce Leader, Editor. **Description:** Literary journal of the University of Memphis featuring original short stories, nonfiction, and poetry. **Art:** Photos, B&W or color; illustrations, B&W. **Tips:** "Avoid sentimentality, push the limits of the language." Now publishing non-thematic issues. **Queries:** Not necessary. **E-Queries:** Yes. **Unsolicited mss:** Accepts. **Response:** 1-3 months. **SASE Required:** Yes. **Rights:** One-time.

RIVER OAK REVIEW

P.O. Box 3127, Oak Park, IL 60303. E-mail: info@riveroakarts.org. Website: www.riveroakarts.org. Semiannual. Marylee MacDonald, Editor. **Description:** Fiction, poetry, and creative nonfiction. Limit prose to 20 pages; poetry to batches of no more than 4. **Tips:** No criticism, reviews, or translations. **Payment:** In copies.

RIVER STYX

634 N Grand Blvd., Fl. 12, St. Louis, MO 63103. 314-533-4541. Website: www.riverstyx.org. Triannual. $7/$20. Circ.: 1,500. Richard Newman, Editor. **Description:** International, multicultural literary journal. Fiction, poetry, essays, and art by emerging and established writers and artists. Fiction and nonfiction should run 30 pages or less, poetry format is open. **Queries:** Not necessary. **E-Queries:** No. **Unsolicited mss:** Accepts. **Response:** 3-5 months. **SASE Required:** Yes. **Rights:** FNAR. **Payment:** On publication.

ROANOKE REVIEW

221 College Ln., Salem, VA 24153. 540-375-2380. Annual. $13/2 years. Circ.: 300. Paul Hanstedt, Editor. **Description:** Literary magazine featuring fiction (to 7,500 words) and poetry (to 100 lines). **Tips:** Accepts material September 1-February 28. **Queries:** Not necessary. **Unsolicited mss:** Accepts. **Payment:** In copies.

ROCKFORD REVIEW

Rockford Writers' Guild, P.O. Box 858, Rockford, IL 61105. Website: www.writersguild1.tripod.com. 3x/yr. $6/$20. Circ.: 750. David Ross, Editor. **Description:** Literary journal featuring poetry and prose. **Fiction:** 1,000 words. **Nonfiction:** Essays, short plays; 1,000 words. **Poetry:** Experimental or traditional, to 30 lines (shorter preferred); up to 3 poems. **Tips:** Two Editor's Choice Prizes awards $25/issue. **Queries:** Not necessary. **E-Queries:** No. **Unsolicited mss:** Accepts. **Response:** Queries 2 weeks, submissions 2 months. **SASE Required:** Yes. **Rights:** FNAR. **Payment:** In copies.

ROOM OF ONE'S OWN

P.O. Box 46160, Sta. D, Vancouver, British Columbia V6J 5G5 Canada. E-mail: contactus@roommagazine.com. Website: www.roommagazine.com. Quarterly. $22/yr (Can.), $25 (U.S.). **Description:** Short stories, poems, art, and reviews by, for, and about women. **Fiction:** To 5,000 words. **Nonfiction:** Creative nonfiction and essays; to 5,000 words. **Poetry:** Prefers groups of poems, rather than single poems. **Columns, Departments:** Book reviews; to 700 words. **Art:** Seeking original art and photography (by female artists) on the female experience. Send slides, photos, or photocopies. **Tips:** Payment is $35 CDN, 1-year subscription, and two copies; or payment all in copies, plus 1-year subscription. **E-Queries:** No. **Unsolicited mss:** Accepts. **Response:** Include SASE (Canadian postage or IRC's). **Rights:** FNASR. **Contact:** Editorial Collective.

SANSKRIT LITERARY-ARTS

University of North Carolina-Charlotte, 168 Cone University Center, Charlotte, NC 28223. 704-687-2326. E-mail: sanskrit@email.uncc.edu. Website: www.uncc.edu/sanskrit. Annual. $10. Circ.: 3,500. David M. Hill, Editor-in-Chief. **Description:** Short fiction and short-shorts (to 3,500 words), and poetry of all forms (prefers free form, modern, with concert imagery). **Tips:** Annual deadline first Friday in November. Send cover letter and 30-70 word bio with submission. **Queries:** Not necessary. **E-Queries:** Yes. **Unsolicited mss:** Accepts. **Freelance Content:** 100%. **Rights:** FNAR and electronic.

THE SEATTLE REVIEW

University of Washington, Padelford Hall, Box 354330, Seattle, WA 98195-4330. 206-543-2302. E-mail: seaview@english.washington.edu. Website: http://depts.washington.edu/engl/seaview1.html. 2x/yr. **Description:** Poetry, prose, interviews, creative nonfiction, artwork (color or B&W). Submissions should not exceed 20-22 pages. **Tips:** Manuscripts read October-May only. Sample copy $7. **SASE Required:** Yes. **Payment:** In copies.

SENECA REVIEW

Hobart & William Smith Colleges, Geneva, NY 14456. 315-781-3392. E-mail: senecareview@hws.edu. Website: www.hws.edu/senecareview. Biannual. $7/$11. Circ.: 1,000. Deborah Tall, Editor. **Description:** A journal of poetry and lyric essays. Special interest in translations. **Tips:** No simultaneous submissions; one submission per annual reading period. **Queries:** Not necessary. **E-Queries:** No. **Unsolicited mss:** Accepts. **Response:** 2-3 months. **SASE Required:** Yes. **Freelance Content:** 100%. **Rights:** FNAR. **Payment:** In copies and a 2-year subscription.

THE SEWANEE REVIEW

University of the South, 735 University Ave., Sewanee, TN 37383-1000. Website: www.sewanee.edu/sreview/home.html. Quarterly. $8.50/sample issue; $9.50/issue outside USA. Bob Jones, Managing Editor. **Description:** Literary publication. Considers only unpublished original work. Query for essays (7,500 words or less) and reviews; submit complete manuscript for fiction (3,500 to 7,500 words) and poetry (6 poems, 40 lines or less). **Tips:** Do not submit between June 1 and August 31. No simultaneous or electronic submissions. **E-Queries:** No. **Response:** 4-6 weeks. **SASE Required:** Yes.

SHENANDOAH

The Washington and Lee University Review, Matlingly House, 2 Lee Ave., Washington and Lee University, Lexington, VA 24450-0303. 540-458-8765. Website: http://shenandoah.wlu.edu. Triannual. $22/yr. Circ.: 1,800. R. T. Smith, Editor. **Description:** A literary journal that publishes poems, essays, and reviews which display passionate understanding, formal accomplishment, and serious mischief. **Fiction:** $25/page. **Nonfiction:** Criticism, essays, interviews; $25/page. **Poetry:** $2.50/line. **Tips:** Submissions accepted September 1-May 30. Sample copy $8. **Queries:** Not necessary. **E-Queries:** No. **Unsolicited mss:** Accepts. **Response:** 8 weeks. **SASE Required:** Yes. **Freelance Content:** 80%. **Rights:** FNASR. **Payment:** On publication.

SLIPSTREAM

P.O. Box 2071, Niagara Falls, NY 14301. 716-282-2616. E-mail: editors@slipstream-press.org. Website: www.slipstreampress.org. Annual. $20. Circ.: 1,000. Robert Borgatti, Dan Sicoli, Livio Farallo, Editors. **Description:** Poetry, short fiction, and graphics not normally found in mainstream publications. Prose up to 15 pages, poetry 1-6 pages. **Art:** Send photocopies of B&W photos/graphics. **Tips:** No rhyming, religious, or trite verse. **Queries:** Not necessary. **Unsolicited mss:** Accepts. **Response:** 1-6 weeks. **SASE Required:** Yes. **Freelance Content:** 100%. **Rights:** FNAR. **Payment:** In copies. **Contact:** Dan Sicoli.

THE SMALL POND

P.O. Box 664, Stratford, CT 06615. 203-378-4066. 3x/yr. $4/$10. Circ.: 300. Napoleon St. Cyr, Editor. **Description:** Literary journal with interesting, sometimes quirky fiction and poetry. **Fiction:** 2,500 words max. **Nonfiction:** Anything interesting; 2,500 words. **Poetry:** Any style, subject; 100 lines. **Tips:** Avoid bleeding hearts. **Queries:** Not necessary. **E-Queries:** No. **Unsolicited mss:** Accepts. **Response:** Queries 2-5 days, submissions 2-5 weeks. **SASE Required:** Yes. **Freelance Content:** 100%. **Rights:** All. **Payment:** In copies.

SNAKE NATION REVIEW

Snake Nation Press, Inc., 110 West Force St., Valdosta, GA 31601. 229-244-0752. E-mail: jeana@snakenationpress.org. Website: www.snakenationpress.org. 3x/year. $6/$20. Circ.: 2,000. Jean Arambula, Editor. **Description:** General-interest literary magazine featuring unpublished/underpublished writers. Open to new and experimental writing. Send SASE for guidelines. Editor's choice for each category (poetry, fiction, art, or photos) receives $100, all others are paid in copies. **Queries:** Not necessary. **E-Queries:** Yes. **Unsolicited mss:** Accepts. **Response:** 3-6 months. **Freelance Content:** 100%. **Rights:** One-time.

SNOWY EGRET

P.O. Box 29, Terre Haute, IN 47808. Biannual. $15/$25. Circ.: 400. Philip Repp, Editor. **Description:** Oldest independent U.S. journal of nature writing. Emphasis on natural history and human beings in relation to nature from literary, artistic, philosophical, pyschological, and historical perspectives. Pays $2/page for fiction and nonfiction, $4/poem or page for poetry, plus two contributor's copies. **Fiction:** Characters who relate strongly to nature and grow in understanding of themselves and the world; 500-10,000 words. **Nonfiction:** Essays on the natural world and humans' relationship to it with detailed observations from author's own experience; 500-10,000 words. **Poetry:** Nature-oriented poems. **Columns, Departments:** "Woodnotes." First-hand experiences with landscape or wildlife encounters; 250-2,000 words. **Tips:** "Submit freshly observed material, with plenty of description and/or dialogue." **Queries:** Not necessary. **E-Queries:** No. **Response:** 2-8 weeks. **SASE Required:** Yes. **Freelance Content:** 95%. **Rights:** FNAR. **Payment:** On publication.

SO TO SPEAK

George Mason University, 4400 University Dr., MS2D6, Fairfax, VA 22030-4444. 703-993-3625. E-mail: sts@gmu.edu. Website: www.gmu.edu/org/sts. Bi-annual. $6/$11. Circ.: 1,300. Kirsten Hilgeford, Editor. **Description:** Feminist journal of language and arts, concerned with the history of women, of feminists, and looking to see the future through art. Includes fiction, poetry, nonfiction, reviews, visual arts (B&W). **Fiction:** Literary, feminist; to 5,000 words. **Nonfiction:** Literary, lyrical, critical; reviews (feminist books and hypertext); to 4,000 words. **Poetry:** Literary, feminist; experimental, lyrical, narrative. **Art:** B&W art, seeking color cover art. **Tips:** "This is a feminist journal. Ours is a vision of memory and prophesy." **Queries:** Not necessary. **E-Queries:** No. **Unsolicited mss:** Accepts. **Response:** 3-4 months. **SASE Required:** Yes. **Payment:** In copies.

SONORA REVIEW

University of Arizona, Dept. of English, Tucson, AZ 85721. 520-624-9192. E-mail: sonora@u.arizona.edu. Website: www.coh.arizona.edu/sonora. Melissa Koosmann and Matt Sadler, Editors-in-Chief. **Description:** Features stories, poems, memoirs, personal essays, and creative nonfiction. Does not usually consider genre material (mystery, romance, etc.). Send complete manuscript. Fiction and nonfiction, 8,000 words max. Poetry, 12 pages max. Accepts simultaneous submissions. **Tips:** Manuscripts read year-round. **Queries:** Not necessary. **Unsolicited mss:** Accepts. **Response:** 2-3 months. **SASE Required:** Yes. **Rights:** FNAR. **Payment:** 2 copies.

SOU'WESTER

Southern Illinois University—Edwardsville, Edwardsville, IL 62026-1438. 618-650-3190. Biannual. Circ.: 300. Allison Funk, Geoff Schmidt, Editors. **Description:** Small literary magazine publishing fiction, poetry, essays, and book reviews. **Queries:** Not necessary. **E-Queries:** No. **Response:** Submissions 3 months. **Rights:** All. **Payment:** In copies.

SOUTH CAROLINA REVIEW

Clemson University, Dept. of English, Clemson, SC 29634-0523. 864-656-5399. E-mail: cwayne@clemson.edu. Website: www.clemson.edu/caah/cedp/scrintro.htm. Semiannual. Circ.: 450. Wayne Chapman, Editor. **Description:** Fiction, essays, reviews, interviews, and poems. **Tips:** Does not accept unsolicted submissions via e-mail. **Queries:** Preferred. **E-Queries:** No. **Unsolicited mss:** Does not accept. **Response:** Queries 1-2 weeks, submisssions 1-2 months. **SASE Required:** Yes. **Freelance Content:** 90%. **Rights:** World. **Payment:** In copies.

SOUTH DAKOTA REVIEW

University of South Dakota, English Dept., 414 E Clark St., Vermillion, SD 57069-2390. 605-677-5184. E-mail: sdreview@usd.edu. Website: www.usd.edu/sdreview. Quarterly. $10/$30. Brian Bedard (bbedard@usd.edu), Editor. **Description:** Literary journal featuring fiction, creative nonfiction, and poetry. Accepts professional quality work from new, established, and emerging writers from all regions, with some special though not exclusive interest in western regional works. For fiction and nonfiction, send only 1 piece at a time (1,500-6,000 words); for poetry, send 3-5 poems. Include short cover letter, bio, and SASE. **Tips:** "We are a well-known literary magazine aimed at a well-educated audience, many of whom have a special interest in contemporary writing about the Great Plains and the American West. We look for substantial storyline, convincing characterization, authentic sense of place in fiction, and creative use of language in poetry." **Queries:** Not necessary. **E-Queries:** No. **Unsolicited mss:** Accepts. **Response:** 4-10 weeks. **Freelance Content:** 90%. **Rights:** FNASR. **Payment:** In copies and 1-year subscription.

SOUTHERN HUMANITIES REVIEW

9088 Haley Center, Auburn Univ., Auburn, AL 36849. E-mail: shrengl@auburn.edu. Quarterly. $5/$15. Circ.: 700. Dan R. Latimer, Virginia M. Kouidis, Co-editors. **Description:** Scholarly literary magazine featuring fiction (3,500-15,000 words), nonfiction essays and criticism (3,500-15,000 words), and poetry (up to 2 pages). **Queries:** Not necessary. **E-Queries:** Yes. **Unsolicited mss:** Accepts. **Response:** Queries 1-2 weeks, submissions 1-3 months. **SASE Required:** Yes. **Freelance Content:** 70%. **Rights:** 1st, reverts to author. **Payment:** In copies.

SOUTHERN POETRY REVIEW

Armstrong Atlantic State University, Dept. of Languages, Literature, & Philosophy, 11935 Abercorn St., Savannah, GA 31419. Website: www.spr.armstrong.edu. Robert Parham, Editor. **Description:** Welcomes previously unpublished poetry submissions any length, style, or content. Send 3-5 poems max. No fiction, essays, or reviews. Send hard copy only. **Tips:** Manuscripts read year-round. Also sponsors the Guy Owen Prize. **Queries:** Not necessary. **Unsolicited mss:** Accepts. **Freelance Content:** 100%. **Rights:** FNAR. **Payment:** Two copies.

THE SOUTHERN REVIEW

Louisiana State University, 43 Allen Hall, Baton Rouge, LA 70803. 225-578-5108. Website: www.lsu.edu/thesouthernreview. Quarterly. Circ.: 3,100. John Easterly, Associate Editor. **Description:** Literary publication of contemporary literature, with special interest in Southern culture and history. **Fiction:** 4,000-8,000 words; $12/page. **Nonfiction:** Essays; 4,000-10,000 words; $12/page. **Poetry:** To 4 pages; $20/page. **Tips:** "We seek craftsmanship, technique, and seriousness of subject matter." **Queries:** Preferred. **Response:** 2 months. **SASE Required:** Yes. **Rights:** FNASR. **Payment:** On publication.

SOW'S EAR POETRY REVIEW

355 Mt. Lebanon Rd., Donalds, SC 29638-9115. 276-628-2651. E-mail: errol@kitenet.net. Quarterly. $5/$15. Circ.: 600. Errol Hess, Managing Editor. **Description:** Contemporary poetry (any style or length, up to 5 poems), essays, reviews, and B&W prints or drawings. **Tips:** "We're looking for poems that make the strange familiar or the familiar strange, that connect the little story of the text and the big story of the human situation." **Queries:** Not necessary. **E-Queries:** Yes. **Unsolicited mss:** Accepts. **Response:** Queries 1 week, submissions 3-6 months. **SASE Required:** Yes. **Freelance Content:** 100%. **Rights:** FNASR. **Payment:** In copies.

SPINDRIFT

Shoreline Community College, 16101 Greenwood Ave. N, Shoreline, WA 98133. 206-546-5864. E-mail: spindrift@shore.ctc.edu. Annual. $8/issue. Circ.: 400. Gary Parks, Faculty Advisor. **Description:** Literary, mainstream, and experimental fiction and poetry. Prose to 4,500 words. "*Spindrift* is an award winning literature and art magazine. We publish authors and artists from all over the country and world." **Tips:** Study sample issue ($2) before submitting. Submit September-January only. **Queries:** Not necessary. **Unsolicited mss:** Accepts. **Response:** 8 weeks. **SASE Required:** Yes. **Freelance Content:** 100%. **Rights:** FNAR.

SPINNING JENNY

P.O. Box 1373, New York, NY 10276. E-mail: info@blackdresspress.com. Website: www.blackdresspress.com. Annual. $8/issue. Circ.: 1,000. C.E. Harrison, Editor. **Description:** Poetry, some fiction. **Tips:** No simultaneous submissions. **Queries:** Not necessary. **E-Queries:** No. **Unsolicited mss:** Accepts. **Response:** 12 weeks. **SASE Required:** Yes. **Payment:** In copies.

THE SPOON RIVER POETRY REVIEW

4240 Dept. of English, Illinois State University, Normal, IL 61790-4240. 309-438-7906. Website: www.litline.org/spoon. 2x/yr. $10/$15. Circ.: 1,200. Dr. Lucia Getsi, Editor. **Description:** Features poetry (original and translations) from established and emerging poets. **Tips:** "We accept around 1% of all submissions." **Queries:** Does not accept. **Unsolicited mss:** Accepts. **Response:** 2 months. **SASE Required:** Yes. **Payment:** In copies.

STAND

Virginia Commonwealth University, Dept of English, Box 2005, Richmond, VA 23284-2005. 804-828-1331. Website: www.people.vcu.edu/~dlatane/stand.html. Quarterly. $12/$49.50. Circ.: 7,500. **Description:** Literary magazine featuring fiction (to 10,000 words) and poetry (to 250 lines). No genre writing. **Tips:** "We're probably not the right market for new writers." UK address: School of English, University of Leeds, Leeds, LS2 9JT, stand@leeds.ar.uk. **Queries:** Not necessary. **E-Queries:** Yes. **Unsolicited mss:** Accepts. **Response:** 1-3 months. **SASE Required:** Yes. **Freelance Content:** 60%. **Payment:** On publication. **Contact:** Matthew Welton, John Whale, David Latané.

STORYHOUSE.COM

4019 SE Hawthorne Blvd., Portland, OR 97214. 503-233-1144. E-mail: submissions@storyhouse.com. Website: www.storyhouse.com. Todd Cowing, Esther Cowing, Editors. **Description:** An online retailer of fresh roasted coffee in the Pacific Northwest. Seeks original art, stories, poems, letters, and essays for coffee-can labels. Current needs: short-short/flash fiction, especially flash romance, serialized flash, and mysteries. Also well-argued essays or academic pieces. See website for word count and pay rates. **Tips:** All material (queries and submissions) must be submitted via e-mail. See submission guidelines on website. **Queries:** Preferred. **E-Queries:** Yes. **Unsolicited mss:** Accepts. **Rights:** Author retains copyright. **Payment:** On acceptance.

STORYQUARTERLY

431 Sheridan Rd., Kenilworth, IL 60043. 847-256-6998. E-mail: storyquarterly@yahoo.com (business correspondence only). Website: www.storyquarterly.com. $10/issue. Circ.: 6,000. Editor/Publisher: M. M. M. Hayes; Associate Editors: Dan Gutstein, Katherine Hughes. **Description:** *StoryQuarterly*, an annual anthology of short stories, publishes contemporary American and international literature of high quality in a full range of styles and forms. Submit short stories, short-shorts, or novel excerpts. Also looking for translation of contemporary work, and photojournalism. Pieces should be 100-10,000 words. No genre fiction. **Tips:** "We accept online submissions (through our website) only, unless no computer access, or if manuscript exceeds 8,000 words. These may be sent to our office and we will send response if SASE is included. We read submissions October 1-March 31 only." **Queries:** Not necessary. **Unsolicited mss:** Accepts, online only. **Rights:** One-time. **Payment:** 10 copies and life subscription ($350 value).

STORYTELLER

858 Wingate Dr., Ottawa, Ontario K1G 1S5 Canada. **Description:** General fiction magazine seeking humor, adventure, mystery, drama, suspense, horror, science fiction, and fantasy. Do not submit material that falls too far within any one of these genres. Submissions must be fiction (2,000-6,000 words) and have Canadian connection. **Tips:** Read a sample issue before submitting material. Does not accept simultaneous submissions. **Rights:** FNAR.

SUB-TERRAIN

P.O. Box 3008 MPO, Vancouver, British Columbia V6B 3X5 Canada. 604-876-8710. E-mail: subter@portal.ca. Website: www.subterrain.ca. 3x/yr. $3.95 (U.S.) $4.95 (Canada). Circ.: 5,000. Brian Kaufman, Editor. **Description:** "Strong words for a polite nation." Publishes fiction, poetry, photography and graphics from uprising Canadian, U.S., and international writers and artists. Fiction, 3,000 words max. No unsolicited poetry. **Tips:** "We seek work with a point-of-view and some passion, on issues of pressing importance (especially with urban slant). No bland, flowery, universal work that says nothing in style or content. Challenge conventional notions of what fiction is or should be and do so with a social conscience. We provide an eclectic fusion of fiction, poetry and commentary aimed at an educated, curious reader." **Queries:** Preferred. **E-Queries:** Yes. **Unsolicited mss:** Accepts. **Response:** Queries 1-2 weeks, submissions 4-6 months, SASE required (IRC's). **Freelance Content:** 85%. **Rights:** FNAR. **Payment:** On publication.

SYCAMORE REVIEW

Purdue Univ., Dept. of English, 500 Oval Dr., West Lafayette, IN 47907-2038. 765-494-3783. E-mail: sycamore@purdue.edu. Website: www.sla.purdue.edu/sycamore. Biannual. $7/$12. Circ.: 700. Sean M. Conrey, Editor. **Description:** Literary journal featuring fiction, poetry, essays, interviews, and translations. **Queries:** Not necessary. **Unsolicited mss:** Accepts. **Response:** Queries 1-2 weeks, submissions 3-4 months. **SASE Required:** Yes.

TALKING RIVER REVIEW

Lewis-Clark State College, 500 Eighth Ave., Lewiston, ID 83501. 208-799-2301. Biannual. $7/$14. Circ.: 500. **Description:** Publishes the best work from established and first-time writers. **Fiction:** Short stories, up to 25 pages. **Nonfiction:** Literary essays, up to 25 pages. **Poetry:** Any style, 1-5 pages. **Tips:** Send only your best work. Reads manuscripts September 1-April 1. **Queries:** Does not accept. **E-Queries:** No. **Unsolicited mss:** Accepts. **Response:** Submissions 3-4 months. **SASE Required:** Yes. **Freelance Content:** 100%. **Rights:** FNAR. **Payment:** In copies.

TAR RIVER POETRY

East Carolina University, Dept. of English, Greenville, NC 27858-4353. 252-328-6046. Biannual. $12/yr.,$20/2 years. Circ.: 700. Peter Makuck, Editor. **Description:** Formal and open form poetry, reviews, and interviews. **Poetry:** Strong imagery, figurative language; to 6 pages. **Tips:** "No sentimental, flat poetry. Emphasize the visual." **Queries:** Not necessary. **E-Queries:** No. **Unsolicited mss:** Accepts. **Response:** Queries 1 week, submissions 4-6 weeks. **SASE Required:** Yes. **Freelance Content:** 100%. **Payment:** In copies.

TERRA INCOGNITA

P.O. Box 150585, Brooklyn, NY 11215-0585. 718-492-3508. E-mail: terraincognitamagazine@yahoo.com. Website: www.terra-incognita.com. Annual. $9/issue. Circ.: 500. **Description:** International online and print journal publishing poetry, fiction, essays, articles, and interviews in English and Spanish. Also art and photography. **Fiction:** Short stories, novel excerpts, plays; 5,000 words. **Nonfiction:** Articles, essays, interviews; 3,500-5,000 words. **Poetry:** Send up to 7 poems; to 100 lines each. **Columns, Departments:** Reviews; 1,000 words. **Art:** B&W; slides or photos. **Tips:** "Writers should submit work that they believe in deeply, that they've worked on carefully and that has a unique voice. They should avoid sending material that is technically weak." **Queries:** Preferred. **Unsolicited mss:** Accepts. **Response:** 1-3 months. **SASE Required:** Yes. **Freelance Content:** 75%. **Rights:** FNASR. **Payment:** In copies. **Contact:** Alexandra Van de Kamp, Poetry Editor; William Glenn, Prose Editor.

THE TEXAS REVIEW

Sam Houston State University, English Dept., P.O. Box 2146, Huntsville, TX 77341-2146. 936-294-1992. E-mail: eng_pdr@shsu.edu. Website: www.shsu.edu/~www_trp. Semiannual. $20/yr. Circ.: 1,200. Paul Ruffin, Editor. **Description:** Literary journal of poetry, fiction, and nonfiction. **Tips:** "We do not read manuscripts between May 1-September 1. **Queries:** Not necessary. **E-Queries:** Yes. **Unsolicited mss:** Does not accept. **Response:** Queries 1 week, submissions 6-8 weeks. **SASE Required:** Yes. **Rights:** FNAR.

THEMA

P.O. Box 8747, Metairie, LA 70011-8747. 504-887-1263. E-mail: thema@cox.net. 3x/yr. $8/$16. Circ.: 300. Virginia Howard, Editor. **Description:** Each issue is a stand-alone, thematic anthology. Provides a forum for writers, and source material for teachers of creative writing. **Fiction:** Less than 6,000 words (20 pages); $10-$25. **Nonfiction:** Less than 6,000 words. **Poetry:** 3-page max; $10. **Tips:** Request upcoming themes. **Queries:** Not necessary. **E-Queries:** Yes. **Unsolicited mss:** Accepts. **Response:** Queries 2 weeks, submissions 4 months. **SASE Required:** Yes. **Freelance Content:** 99%. **Rights:** One-time. **Payment:** On acceptance.

THIRD COAST

Western Michigan Univ., Dept. of English, Kalamazoo, MI 49008-5331. Website: www.wmich.edu/thirdcoast. Biannual. $6/$11. Circ.: 1,000. Glenn Deutsch, Editor. **Description:** Literary review (fiction, creative nonfiction, poetry) for contemporary writers/readers. **Tips:** Address submissions to appropriate section editor: fiction, creative nonfiction, or poetry. Accepts simultaneous submissions with notice. **Queries:** Not necessary. **E-Queries:** No. **Unsolicited mss:** Accepts. **SASE Required:** Yes. **Freelance Content:** 95%. **Rights:** FNASR. **Payment:** On publication.

THOUGHTS FOR ALL SEASONS

86 Leland Rd., Becket, MA 01223. $6/issue. Circ.: 1,000. Prof. Michel P. Richard, Editor. **Description:** Irregular serial publication that celebrates the epigram, of 2-4 lines, as a literary form. Includes humor and satire. **Poetry:** Rhyming, quatrains, limericks, nonsense verse with good imagery; to 1 page. **Columns, Departments:** Thematic by issue; to 10 pages. **Queries:** Not necessary. **E-Queries:** No. **Response:** 21 days. **SASE Required:** Yes. **Freelance Content:** 60%. **Payment:** In copies.

THE THREEPENNY REVIEW

P.O. Box 9131, Berkeley, CA 94709. 510-849-4545.
Website: www.threepennyreview.com. Quarterly. $25/yr. Circ.: 9,000. Wendy Lesser, Editor. **Description:** "Literary and immensely readable" (*Publishers Weekly*). Offers reviews of the arts. Features new poetry, short stories, memoirs, and essays. **Fiction:** To 5,000 words; pays up to $200. **Nonfiction:** Essays on books, theater, film, dance, music, art, television, and politics; 1,500-3,000 words; pays up to $200. **Poetry:** To 100 lines; pays $100. **Tips:** Manuscripts read September-May. **Queries:** Preferred. **Response:** 2 months. **SASE Required:** Yes. **Payment:** On acceptance.

TIGHTROPE

Swamp Press, 15 Warwick Ave., Northfield, MA 01360. Annual. $6/issue. Circ.: 300. Ed Rayher, Editor. **Description:** Letterpress magazine featuring poetry (any length) with original graphics. **Queries:** Preferred. **E-Queries:** No. **Unsolicited mss:** Do not accept. **Response:** 1-2 months. **SASE Required:** Yes. **Rights:** FNAR. **Payment:** In copies.

TIMBER CREEK REVIEW

8969 UNCG Station, Greensboro, NC 27413. 336-334-2952.
E-mail: timber_creek_review@hoopsmail.com. Quarterly. $4.50/$16. Circ.: 180. J. M. Freiermuth, Editor; Roslyn Willett, Associate Editor. **Description:** Short stories, poetry, and occasional literary nonfiction. **Fiction:** 2,500-7,500 words (average 4,000 words); $10-$35. **Nonfiction:** 2,500-5,000 words; $10-$35. **Poetry:** 3-30 lines; pays single copy. **Tips:** No reprints. Do not send query, but include cover letter with your submission. **Unsolicited mss:** Accepts. **Response:** 3-6 months. **SASE Required:** Yes. **Freelance Content:** 100%. **Rights:** FNAR.

TRIQUARTERLY

Northwestern University, 629 Noyes St., Evanston, IL 60208-4302. 847-491-4170. Website: www.triquarterly.org. 3x/yr. $11.95. Circ.: 4,000. Susan Firestone Hahn, Editor. **Description:** Not-for-profit literary magazine featuring previously unpublished fiction, poetry, literary essays, and artwork. **Fiction:** Literary fiction only (no genre); $5/page. **Poetry:** Serious, aesthetically informed, inventive; $.50/line. **Tips:** Accepts material October-March only. **Queries:** Not necessary. **E-Queries:** No. **Unsolicited mss:** Accepts. **Response:** 12 weeks. **SASE Required:** Yes. **Freelance Content:** 70%. **Rights:** FNASR. **Payment:** On publication.

TWO RIVERS REVIEW

P.O. Box 158, Clinton, NY 13323. E-mail: tworiversreview@juno.com. Website: http://trrpoetry.tripod.com/tworiversreview/index.html. Biannual. $6/$12. Circ.: 400. Philip Memmer, Editor. **Description:** Poetry that displays strong craft and clear language. Submit up to 4 poems at a time (no more than 3 times/calendar year). **Tips:** No e-mail submissions. Manuscripts without SASE are discarded. **Queries:** Not necessary. **E-Queries:** Yes. **Unsolicited mss:** Accepts. **Response:** 3-8 weeks. **SASE Required:** Yes. **Freelance Content:** 80%. **Rights:** FNAR. **Payment:** In copies.

VERMONT INK

P.O. Box 3297, Burlington, VT 05401-3297. E-mail: vermontink@aol.com. Website: www.vermontink.com. Donna Leach, Editor. **Description:** Quarterly publication featuring short stories and poetry. **Fiction:** Uses well-written, entertaining, and basically G-rated stories. Accepts adventure, historical, humor, mainstream, mystery and suspense, regional interest, romance, science fiction, and Westerns; 1,000-3,000 words; ¼ to ½ cent/word. **Poetry:** Upbeat and humorous; 4-20 lines; $5. **Tips:** Send complete manuscript, cover letter, short bio and SASE. Sample copy $4. **Queries:** Not necessary.

VERSE

University of Georgia, English Dept., Athens, GA 30602. 3x/yr. $8/$18. Circ.: 1,000. Brian Henry, Andrew Zawacki, Editors. **Description:** Poetry, criticism, and interviews with poets. Focus is international and eclectic, and favors the innovative over the staid. **Nonfiction:** Essays on poetry, interviews, and reviews. **Poetry:** Up to 5 poems. **Queries:** Not necessary. **Unsolicited mss:** Accepts. **Response:** Queries 2 months, submissions 1-4 months. **SASE Required:** Yes. **Freelance Content:** 75%. **Rights:** FNAR. **Payment:** In copies.

VESTAL REVIEW

2609 Dartmouth Dr., Vestal, NY 13850. E-mail: editor@stny.rr.com. Website: www.vestalreview.net. Quarterly. Circ.: 2,000. Mark Budman, Sue O'Neill, Editors. **Description:** Features flash fiction, any genre; under 500 words; $.03-$.10/word and a contributor's copy. **Tips:** Seeking literary stories; no children's stories or syrupy romance. E-mail submissions only. See website for details on submission deadlines and manuscript formatting. Sample copy $5 postpaid. Subscription $15/year. Please write the check to Mark Budman. **Queries:** Not necessary. **E-Queries:** Yes. **Unsolicited mss:** Accepts. **Response:** 2 months. **Freelance Content:** 100%. **Rights:** 1st electronic.

THE VIRGINIA QUARTERLY REVIEW

One W Range, P.O. Box 400223, Charlottesville, VA 22904-4223. 434-924-3124. Website: www.virginia.edu/vqr. Quarterly. $5/$18. Circ.: 4,000. Ted Genoways, Editor. **Description:** A journal of literature and discussion. **Fiction:** Quality fiction; $100/page. **Nonfiction:** Serious essays, articles on literature, science, politics, economics, etc; 3,000-6,000 words; $100/page. **Poetry:** $5/line. **Queries:** Preferred. **Unsolicited mss:** Accepts. **Payment:** On publication.

WASCANA REVIEW

Univ. of Regina, Dept. of English, Regina, Saskatchewan S4S 0A2 Canada. 306-585-4302. E-mail: michael.trussler@uregina.ca. Website: www.uregina.ca./english/wrhome.htm. Biannual. $5/issue. Circ.: 250. Michael Trussler, Editor. **Description:** Poetry and short fiction that combines craft with risk, pressure with grace. Wide variety of themes. **Fiction:** Fiction that displays an honest, meaningful grasp of human experience and of individuals' struggles to relate to themselves and the world around them; 5,000 words; $3/page. **Nonfiction:** Cutting-edge literary criticism; articles on contemporary short fiction and poetry; 7,500 words; $3/page. **Poetry:** Poetry of high artistic merit; up to 6 poems; $10/page. **Queries:** Not necessary. **E-Queries:** Yes. **Unsolicited mss:** Accepts. **Response:** Queries 1 week, submissions 2 months. **SASE Required:** Yes. **Freelance Content:** 100%. **Rights:** FNASR. **Payment:** On publication.

WEBER STUDIES

Weber State Univ., 1214 University Circle, Ogden, UT 84408-1214. E-mail: weber-studies@weber.edu. Website: www.weberstudies.weber.edu. Quarterly. Circ.: 1,000. Brad L. Roghaar, Editor. **Description:** Features narratives, critical commentary/opinion, fiction and poetry. Subjects deal with the environment and culture of the contemporary American West. **Fiction:** 5,000 words; $100-$150. **Nonfiction:** 5,000 words; $100-$150. **Poetry:** Submit multiple poems, up to 6 poems or 200 lines; $25-$70. **Queries:** Not necessary. **Unsolicited mss:** Accepts. **Response:** Queries 1 week, submissions 3-4 months. **SASE Required:** Yes. **Freelance Content:** 80%. **Rights:** 1st and Web archive. **Payment:** On publication.

WEST BRANCH

Bucknell University, Bucknell Hall, Lewisburg, PA 17837-2029. 570-577-1853. E-mail: westbranch@bucknell.edu. Website: www.bucknell.edu/westbranch. Semiannual. $6/$10. Circ.: 700. Paula Closson Buck, Editor. **Description:** Literary magazine accepting original, unpublished poetry, fiction, literary nonfiction, and book reviews. Pays $10/page ($20 min/$100 max). **Fiction:** Realistic and avant-garde. **Nonfiction:** Format open. **Poetry:** No confessional verse. **Tips:** Please query for book reviews only; send complete mss. for all else. Sample copy $3. **Queries:** Not necessary. **E-Queries:** Yes. **Unsolicited mss:** Accepts. **Response:** 1 month. **SASE Required:** Yes. **Freelance Content:** 90%. **Rights:** FNAR.

WESTERN HUMANITIES REVIEW

University of Utah, 255 S Central Campus Dr., Room 3500, Salt Lake City, UT 84112. 801-581-6070. E-mail: whr@mail.hum.utah.edu. Website: www.hum.utah.edu/whr. Biannual. $16/yr. Barry Weller, Editor. **Description:** Fiction, nonfiction, and poetry for educated readers. Pays $5/page, dependent on funding. **Fiction:** Literary fiction, exciting and original (no genre fiction). **Nonfiction:** On humanities issues. **Tips:** Reviews submissions September-May; all other submissions returned unread. **Queries:** Not necessary. **E-Queries:** No. **Unsolicited mss:** Accepts. **Response:** 2-10 weeks. **SASE Required:** Yes. **Rights:** FNAR. **Payment:** On publication.

WHETSTONE

Barrington Area Arts Council, P.O. Box 1266, Barrington, IL 60011. 847-382-5626. E-mail: baacouncil@aol.com. Annual. $7. Circ.: 850. Dale Griffith, Editor-in-Chief. **Description:** Poetry, short fiction, novel excerpts, and creative fiction, from established and emerging artists across the country. **Fiction:** Character-driven prose that tells truth in detail; 5,000 words; pay varies. **Poetry:** Concrete rather than abstract;

submit up to 5 poems. **E-Queries:** Yes. **Unsolicited mss:** Accepts. **Response:** Queries 2 weeks, submissions 5 months. **SASE Required:** Yes. **Freelance Content:** 100%.

WILLOW SPRINGS

MS-1, Eastern Washington University, 705 W First, Spokane, WA 99201. 509-623-4349. Biannual. $6/$11.50. Circ.: 1,200. Jennifer Davis, Editor. **Description:** Poetry, short fiction, and nonfiction, of literary merit. **Tips:** No simultaneous submissions. Submit prose and poetry in separate envelopes. Manuscripts read September 15-May 1. **Queries:** Not necessary. **E-Queries:** No. **Unsolicited mss:** Accepts. **Response:** 4-8 weeks. **SASE Required:** Yes. **Freelance Content:** 100%. **Rights:** FNAR. **Payment:** In copies.

WIND

P.O. Box 24548, Lexington, KY 40524. E-mail: wind@wind.org.
Website: www.wind.wind.org. 3x/yr. $15/yr. Circ.: 500. Chris Green, Editor; Arwen Donahue, Fiction Editor; Rebecca Howell, Poetry Editor. **Description:** Features short stories, poems, and essays. Reviews of books from small presses and news of interest to the literary community are also included. **Fiction:** Any style, genre, or subject matter; to 3,000 words. **Nonfiction:** Open to essays on any topic, literary or otherwise; to 3,000 words. **Poetry:** Accepts any subject matter, style, poetic form, etc.; 3-5 poems, any length. **Art:** Send copies of B&W artwork, any theme. **Tips:** "Publishing a wide scope of work from diverse communities, we operate on the metaphor of neighborly conversation between writers about the differing worlds in which they live. Perhaps the most important thing to do is to listen to the conversation first!" **Queries:** Required. **E-Queries:** No. **Unsolicited mss:** Accepts. **Freelance Content:** 80%. **Rights:** FNASR. **Payment:** In copies.

WINDSOR REVIEW

University of Windsor, Dept. of English, Windsor, Ontario N9B 3P4 Canada. 519-253-3000. E-mail: uwrevu@uwindsor.ca. Website: www.windsorreview.com. Biannual. $15/issue. Circ.: 500. Marty Gervais, Editor. **Description:** Literary fiction and poetry. **Fiction:** Literary fiction; up to 5,000 words; $25/story plus 1 yr. subscription. **Nonfiction:** Interviews with well-known writers; 3,000-7,000 words; $50. **Poetry:** All types; experimental, concrete or traditional; $10/poem plus 1 yr. subscription. **Art:** B&W preferred; $100-$200. **Tips:** Does not accept e-mail submissions, but will accept e-queries regarding submission status, etc. **Queries:** Not necessary. **E-Queries:** Yes. **Unsolicited mss:** Accepts. **Response:** Submissions 1-3 months. **SASE Required:** Yes. **Freelance Content:** 90%. **Rights:** FNAR. **Payment:** On publication.

WITNESS

Oakland Community College, 27055 Orchard Lake Rd., Farmington Hills, MI 48334. 734-996-5732. E-mail: stinepj@umich.edu. Website: www.webdelsol.com/witness. Semi-annual. Peter Stine, Editor. **Description:** Literary journal featuring fiction, poetry, essays, memoirs, and artwork. **Fiction:** Fiction, 5-20 pages; pays $6/page. **Nonfiction:** Essays, 5-20 pages; pays $6/page. **Poetry:** Submit up to 3 at a time; pays $10/page. **Tips:** Accepts simultaneous submissions. Do not submit material electronically. **Payment:** On publication.

THE WORCESTER REVIEW
6 Chatham St., Worcester, MA 01609.
Website: www.geocities.com/Paris/LeftBank/6433. Annual. $20. Rodger Martin, Editor. **Description:** Literary journal featuring fiction, poetry, and critical essays on poetry with New England connection. Submit fiction and nonfiction pieces of 4,000 words or less, and no more than 5 poems. **Tips:** Sample copy $6. **Queries:** Not necessary. **E-Queries:** No. **Unsolicited mss:** Accepts. **Response:** 9 months. **SASE Required:** Yes. **Rights:** FNAR. **Payment:** In copies.

XAVIER REVIEW
Xavier Review Press, Box 110-C, Xavier University, 1 Drexel Dr., New Orleans, LA 70125-1098. 504-483-7303. E-mail: rskinner@xula.edu. 2x/yr. $5/$10. Richard Collins, Editor. **Description:** Seeks fiction, poetry, short drama, and nonfiction essays and criticism that focus on AfricanAmerican studies, the Deep South, and the Caribbean. Submit fiction and nonfiction up to 4,000 words. For poetry, send 2-3 short poems, or 1 long poem (up to 3 pages). **Tips:** "Read several back issues. Don't send material that is obviously not within our stated interests." **Queries:** Not necessary. **E-Queries:** Yes. **Unsolicited mss:** Accepts. **Response:** Queries 30 days, submissions 60 days. **Freelance Content:** 90%. **Rights:** FNAR. **Payment:** In copies.

THE YALE REVIEW
Yale University, P.O. Box 208243, New Haven, CT 06520-8243. 203-432-0499. Website: www.yale.edu/yalereview. Quarterly. $28/yr. Circ.: 6,000. J. D. McClatchy, Editor. **Description:** Literary magazine with fiction ($400/story), nonfiction ($500/piece), and serious poetry (pay varies). **Tips:** See magazine to get an idea of the kind of material they seek. **Queries:** Not necessary. **E-Queries:** No. **Unsolicited mss:** Accepts. **Response:** 1-3 months. **SASE Required:** Yes. **Freelance Content:** 30%. **Rights:** FNASR. **Payment:** On publication.

YEMASSEE
University of South Carolina, Dept. of English, Columbia, SC 29208. 803-777-2085. Website: www.cla.sc.edu/engl/index.html. Biannual. $15 ($7 student). Circ.: 500. Carl Jenkinson, Editor; Jill Carroll, Editor. **Description:** Literary journal of poetry, short fiction, one-act plays, brief essays, and interviews. **Fiction:** Short, smart, accessible, character-driven; to 5,000 words. **Nonfiction:** Literary reviews, interviews with literary figures; to 3,000 words. **Poetry:** No fixed length; prefers poems under 3 pages. **Tips:** Offers $200 award for fiction and poetry in each issue. "We are committed to publishing the work of emerging writers as well as established writers. Try us!" **Queries:** Not necessary. **E-Queries:** No. **Unsolicited mss:** Accepts. **Response:** 2 months. **SASE Required:** Yes. **Freelance Content:** 100%. **Rights:** FNAR.

ZOETROPE: ALL STORY

916 Kearny St., San Francisco, CA 94133. 415-788-7500. E-mail: info@all-story.com. Website: www.all-story.com. Quarterly. Circ.: 30,000. Francis Ford Coppola, Publisher. **Description:** Literary publication of stories and one-act plays no longer than 7,000 words. **Queries:** Does not accept. **E-Queries:** No. **Unsolicited mss:** Accepts. **Response:** 5 months. **SASE Required:** Yes. **Rights:** FNASR. **Payment:** On acceptance.

ZYZZYVA

P.O. Box 590069, San Francisco, CA 94159-0069. 415-752-4393.
E-mail: editor@zyzzyva.org. Website: www.zyzzyva.org. 3x/yr. $11/$24. Circ.: 4,000. Howard Junker, Editor. **Description:** Journal of West Coast writers and artists featuring fiction (no novel excerpts), nonfiction essays, and poetry. Pays $50/piece. **Tips:** Accepts material only from current West Coast (California, Oregon, Washington, Hawaii, Alaska) residents. **Queries:** Not necessary. **E-Queries:** No. **Unsolicited mss:** Accepts. **Response:** 1 month. **SASE Required:** Yes. **Freelance Content:** 85%. **Rights:** FNASR. **Payment:** On publication.

MYSTERY & DETECTIVE

COZY DETECTIVE MYSTERY

Ink Publications, 686 Jakes Ct., McMinnville, OR 97128-2546.
E-mail: detectivemag@onlinemac.com.
Website: www.angelfire.com/ms/COZYDETECTIVE. 3-5x/yr. $4.95/issue. Tom Youngblood, Editor. **Description:** Mystery stories by new authors breaking into the genre. Stories must be heavy on character and mystery content. **Tips:** No stories over 6,000 words. Also seeks cartoons, poems, and reviews. **Queries:** Preferred. **E-Queries:** Yes. **Unsolicited mss:** Accepts. **Response:** 6 weeks. **SASE Required:** Yes. **Rights:** FNASR. **Payment:** In copies.

ELLERY QUEEN'S MYSTERY MAGAZINE

Dell Magazines, 475 Park Ave. S, Fl. 11, New York, NY 10016. Website: www.the-mysteryplace.com. 10x/yr. $3.99/$43.90. Circ.: 180,780. Janet Hutchings, Editor. **Description:** A short-story mystery magazine. Mystery and crime. **Fiction:** Police procedurals, private-eye stories, tales of suspense, traditional whodunits, cozies; 250-20,000 words (usually 2,500-8,000 words); $.05-$.08/word. **Tips:** Interested in new authors. Seeks private-eye stories (avoid sex, sadism, sensationalism for its own sake). "We are always in the market for the best detective, crime, and mystery stories being written today." Sample copy for $5. **Queries:** Not necessary. **E-Queries:** No. **Unsolicited mss:** Accepts. **Response:** 3 months. **SASE Required:** Yes. **Freelance Content:** 95%. **Rights:** FNASR. **Payment:** On acceptance.

HARDBOILED

Gryphon Books, P.O. Box 209, Brooklyn, NY 11228-0209. Website: www.gryphon-books.com. $10/issue, $35/4 issues. Gary Lovisi, Editor. **Description:** "We seek hard-hitting crime fiction by new masters. Mind-blasting nonfiction and riveting private eye and crime stories." **Fiction:** Cutting-edge crime fiction, with impact; to 3,000 words. **Tips:** "If you want to write for *Hardboiled*, I suggest you try a subscription" **Queries:** Preferred. **E-Queries:** No. **Unsolicited mss:** Accepts. **Response:** Queries 2-4 weeks, submissions 6 weeks. **SASE Required:** Yes. **Freelance Content:** 35%. **Rights:** FNAR.

ALFRED HITCHCOCK'S MYSTERY MAGAZINE

Dell Magazines, 475 Park Ave. S, Fl. 11 , New York, NY 10016. Website: www.the-mysteryplace.com. 12x/yr, with 2 double issues. $3.99/issue, $5.99/double issue. **Description:** Original mystery short stories. Well-plotted, plausible mystery, suspense, detection, and crime stories. Ghost stories, humor, futuristic, or atmospheric tales considered if they include a crime (or the suggestion of one); to 12,000 words, pay varies. **Tips:** Submissions by new writers strongly encouraged. No reprints. **Queries:** Not necessary. **E-Queries:** No. **Unsolicited mss:** Accepts. **Response:** 3 months. **SASE Required:** Yes. **Freelance Content:** 100%. **Rights:** Anthology, foreign serial. **Payment:** On acceptance.

NEW MYSTERY MAGAZINE

101 W 23rd St., New York, NY 10011-2490. E-mail: editorial@newmystery.com. Quarterly. $37.77/yr. Circ.: 100,000. Charles Raisch, Editor. **Description:** Mystery, crime, detection, and suspense short stories. **Fiction:** Prefers sympathetic characters in trouble, visual scenes; 2,000-6,000 words; pays to $500. No true crime stories. **Columns, Departments:** Book reviews, 250-2,000 words, of upcoming or recent novels. **Tips:** Send $8 and 9x12 SASE for contributor's packet (includes sample copy). **Payment:** On publication.

OVER MY DEAD BODY!

P.O. Box 1778, Auburn, WA 98071-1778. E-mail: omdb@worldnet.att.net. Website: www.overmydeadbody.com. Quarterly. $5.95/$20. Circ.: 1,000. Cherie Jung, Editor. **Description:** Mystery, suspense, and crime fiction and nonfiction. **Fiction:** Mystery or crime-related fiction, from cozy to hardboiled, including suspense, and cross-over mysteries; 750-4,000 words; $.01/word. **Nonfiction:** Author profiles/interviews, mystery-related travel articles; 500 words and up; $10-$25. **Queries:** Required. **E-Queries:** Yes. **Unsolicited mss:** Accepts. **Response:** 4-6 weeks. **SASE Required:** Yes. **Freelance Content:** 100%. **Rights:** FNASR. **Payment:** On acceptance. **Contact:** Fiction Editor or Feature Editor.

THE STRAND

P.O. Box 1418, Birmingham, MI 48012-1418. 248-788-5948. E-mail: strandmag@worldnet.att.net. Website: www.strandmag.com. Quarterly. $24.95/yr. Circ.: 16,000. Andrew Gulli, Editor. **Description:** Mystery stories, detective stories, tales of terror and the supernatural. Featured pieces are modeled after the writing styles of Sir Arthur Conan Doyle, Daphne du Maurier, and Robert Louis Stevenson. Stories run 3,000-5,000 words; $25-$150. **Tips:** Send SASE for guidelines. **Queries:** Not necessary. **Unsolicited mss:** Accepts. **Response:** 4-10 weeks. **SASE Required:** Yes. **Rights:** FNASR. **Payment:** On publication.

ROMANCE & CONFESSION

ARABELLA ROMANCES

1735 Market St., Suite A-523, Philadelphia, PA 19103. 215-525-1223. E-mail: submissions@arabellamagazine.com. Website: www.arabellamagazine.com. **Description:** Provides a mix of romantic fiction and nonfiction. **Fiction:** Short romantic fiction of 750-4,500 words in any romantic genre; pays $0.10/word. **Nonfiction:** Tantalizing recipes for a romantic dinner or brunch for two; length 500-750 words. Romantic travel features; query first. **Unsolicited mss:** Accepts. **Response:** 2-4 months. **SASE Required:** Yes. **Rights:** All.

BLACK ROMANCE/BRONZE THRILLS

333 Seventh Ave., Fl. 11, New York, NY 10001-5004. 212-979-4800. Bimonthly. $19/yr. Circ.: 70,000. Lisa Finn, Editor. **Description:** Short, first-person romantic fiction for African American women. Stories should be 19-21 pages. Some nonfiction pieces on relationships, spicing up sex/romance, tips on dating, beauty, etc. **Tips:** Avoid cultural stereotypes. Stories should be juicy (mild sex scenes), romantic, but not offensive. **Queries:** Not necessary. **E-Queries:** Yes. **Unsolicited mss:** Accepts. **Response:** 3-4 weeks. **SASE Required:** Yes. **Freelance Content:** 100%. **Rights:** All. **Payment:** On publication.

BLACK SECRETS

333 Seventh Ave., Fl. 11, New York, NY 10001-5004. 212-780-4800. Monthly. $11/yr. Circ.: 70,000. Takesha Powell, Editor. **Description:** Short fiction with romantic and erotic themes for African-American women. Pays $100/story. **Queries:** Required. **E-Queries:** Yes. **Unsolicited mss:** Accepts. **SASE Required:** Yes. **Freelance Content:** 100%. **Rights:** All. **Payment:** On publication.

INTIMACY

333 Seventh Ave., Fl. 11, New York, NY 10001. 212-780-3500. Bimonthly. $2.99/issue. Circ.: 50,000. Takesha D. Powell, Editor. **Description:** Short, first-person romantic fiction for African American women, ages 18-45. Stories must have contemporary plot with 2 romantic/intimate love scenes; 19-21 pages. **Tips:** "Avoid clichés, profanity, and stereotypes." **Queries:** Not necessary. **E-Queries:** Yes. **Unsolicited mss:** Accepts. **Response:** 3-4 weeks. **SASE Required:** Yes. **Freelance Content:** 100%. **Rights:** All. **Payment:** On publication.

ROMANCE AND BEYOND

3527 Ambassador Caffery Pkwy., PMB 9, Lafayette, LA 70503-5130. 337-991-9095. E-mail: rbeyond@aol.com. Website: www.romanceandbeyond.com. Annual. Softcover Anthology $9.99. Mary Tarver, Editor. **Description:** Speculative romantic short stories and poetry, combining elements of romance with science fiction, fantasy, and the paranormal. **Fiction:** Up to 10,000 words. **Poetry:** Length varies; pays in copies. **Tips:** Reading period February-May. Annual contest: October-January. "Internal conflict created by attraction between hero and heroine. Tone can be dark to humorous, but story must be a romance with happy ending. Sources of external conflict left to your imagination, the more original the better." **Queries:** Not necessary. **E-Queries:** No. **Unsolicited mss:** Accepts. **Response:** 4 months. **SASE Required:** Yes. **Freelance Content:** 100%. **Rights:** One-time. **Payment:** On acceptance.

TRUE CONFESSIONS

333 Seventh Ave., Fl. 11, New York, NY 10001-5004. 212-979-4800. Monthly. Pat Byrdsong, Editor. **Description:** First-person, true-to-life stories that reflect the lives of working-class families. Romance, mystery, modern social problems, etc. Stories run 1,000-7,000 words. Confessions: Emotionally charged stories with a strong emphasis on characterization and well-defined plots are preferred. Stories should be intriguing, suspenseful, humorous, romantic, or tragic. Pays $.03/word. **Tips:** Seeks more 3,000-5,000 word stories and stories about African, Latina, and Asian Americans. Prefers queries via e-mail prior to submitting. If e-mail is not available, send complete manuscript. Sample copy $3. **Unsolicited mss:** Accepts. **Response:** 90 days. **Freelance Content:** 95%. **Rights:** All. **Payment:** One month after publication.

TRUE LOVE

333 Seventh Ave., Fl. 11, New York, NY 10001-5004. 212-979-4800. Monthly. $10.97. Circ.: 225,000. Alison Way, Editor. **Description:** Fresh, young, true-to-life stories, on love and topics of current interest. Pays $.03/word. **Tips:** Must use past tense and first-person style. **Payment:** On publication.

TRUE ROMANCE

333 Seventh Ave., Fl. 11, New York, NY 10001. 212-979-4800. Monthly. $2.99/issue. Circ.: 225,000. Pat Vitucci, Editor. **Description:** Dramatic stories of personal redemption, romance, family relationships, humor, women's issues. **Fiction:** Topical stories based on news events; intriguing subjects; 5,000-10,000 words; $.03/word. **Poetry:** Up to 24 lines; $10-$30. **Columns, Departments:** Cupid's Corner (photo and 1,000 words), $50; Passages (to 2,000 words), $50-$100; The Way I Lived It, first or third person fiction (2,000-4,000 words), $100-$150. **Tips:** "Our readers must sympathize with the narrator. Stories are to be first-person narrative. Please read an issue or two before submitting." **Queries:** Preferred. **E-Queries:** Yes. **Unsolicited mss:** Accepts. **Response:** 8-12 months. **SASE Required:** Yes. **Freelance Content:** 100%. **Payment:** On publication.

TRUE STORY

333 Seventh Ave., Fl. 11, New York, NY 10001-5004. Monthly. Circ.: 580,000.
Description: Features true stories about the issues that face us today: parenthood, relationships, careers, family affairs and social concerns. **Nonfiction:** Subject matter can range from romance to tear-jerkers, and everything in between. All stories must be written in the first person and range from 2,000-10,000 words. Pays $0.05/word. **Queries:** Not necessary. **Unsolicited mss:** Accepts. **Freelance Content:** 80%. **Rights:** All. **Payment:** One month after publication.

SCIENCE FICTION & FANTASY

ABSOLUTE MAGNITUDE

DNA Publications, Inc., P.O. Box 2988, Radford, VA 24143. 540-763-2925. E-mail: absolutemagnitude@dnapublications.com. Website: www.dnapublications.com. Quarterly. Warren Lapine, Publisher/Editor/Art Director. **Description:** Full-size quarterly that features character-driven, technical science fiction. **Fiction:** No fantasy, horror, satire, or funny science fiction. Seeks tightly-plotted stories with well-developed characters. Characters should be the driving force behind the main action in the story. 1,000-25,000 (3,000-8,000 words preferred) words; $.02-$.06/word. **Tips:** Do not submit material via e-mail. See website for specific submission guidelines. **Queries:** Not necessary. **Rights:** FNASR. **Payment:** On publication.

ANALOG SCIENCE FICTION AND FACT

475 Park Ave. S, Fl. 11, New York, NY 10016. 212-686-7188. E-mail: analog@dell-magazines.com. Website: www.analogsf.com. 10x/yr. $3.99/$43.90. Circ.: 50,000. Stanley Schmidt, Editor. **Description:** Science fiction, with strong characters in believable future or alien settings. Home to many of science fiction's foremost writers, with long tradition of discovering and cultivating new talent. **Fiction:** Short stories, 2,000-7,500 words; novelettes, 10,000-20,000 words; serials, to 80,000 words. Pays $.04-$.08/word. **Nonfiction:** Future-related articles; 4,000 words; $.06/word. **Poetry:** $1/line. **Tips:** Queries required for serials and nonfiction only. **Queries:** Preferred. **E-Queries:** No. **Unsolicited mss:** Accepts. **Response:** 1 month. **SASE Required:** Yes. **Freelance Content:** 100%. **Rights:** FNASR, nonexclusive foreign serial. **Payment:** On acceptance.

ARTEMIS: SCIENCE FICTION FOR A SPACE-FARING AGE

1380 E 17 St., Suite 201, Brooklyn, NY 11230-6011.
Website: www.lrcpublications.com. Quarterly. $5.95/$15. Circ.: 8,000. Ian Randal Strock, Editor. **Description:** Artemis is a stand-alone part of the Artemis Project—a commercial venture to establish a lunar colony. **Fiction:** Near-term, near-Earth, hard science fiction; up to 15,000 words; $.03-$.05/word. **Nonfiction:** Articles for readers interested in knowning how to get to, build, or live in a lunar colony. Also pieces on commercial space and manned space travel. Up to 5,000 words; $.03-$.05/word. **Columns, Departments:** "News Notes" news related to commercial/manned space

and the Moon. **Tips:** "You want me to read your manuscript? Do me the courtesy of reading my magazine. Full writers' guidelines are available on the website." **Queries:** Not necessary. **E-Queries:** No. **Unsolicited mss:** Accepts. **Response:** 1-3 months. **SASE Required:** Yes. **Freelance Content:** 90%. **Payment:** On acceptance.

ASIMOV'S SCIENCE FICTION MAGAZINE

475 Park Ave. S, Fl. 11, New York, NY 10016. 212-686-7188. E-mail: asimovs@dell-magazines.com. Website: www.asimovs.com. 10x/yr. Circ.: 40,000. Gardner Dozois, Editor. **Description:** Short, character-oriented science fiction and fantasy. **Fiction:** Stories in which characters, rather than science, provide main focus for reader's interest. Mostly serious, thoughtful fiction, some humorous; to 30,000 words; $.06-$.08/word. **Poetry:** Up to 40 lines; $1/line. **Tips:** "Borderline fantasy is fine, but no sword and/or sorcery. No explicit sex or violence." **Queries:** Does not accept. **E-Queries:** No. **Unsolicited mss:** Accepts. **Response:** 2-3 months. **SASE Required:** Yes. **Freelance Content:** 90%. **Rights:** First English Rights, nonexclusive reprint rights. **Payment:** On acceptance.

DRAGON

Paizo Publishing, LLC, 3245 146th Pl. SE, Suite 110, Bellevue, WA 98007. E-mail: dragon@paizo.com. Website: www.paizo.com. Monthly. $37.95/yr. Circ.: 60,000. Matthew Sernett, Editor. **Description:** On fantasy and science fiction role-playing games. **Fiction:** Short fiction on sword and sorcery, horror, humor; up to 5,000 words; $.05/word. **Nonfiction:** Idea generators, new rules; up to 4,000 words; $.05/word. **Art:** Photos, illustrations, cartoons. **Tips:** Review guidelines on website before querying. Send all queries via e-mail. **Queries:** Required. **E-Queries:** Yes. **Unsolicited mss:** Does not accept. **Rights:** First worldwide or all.

DREAMS OF DECADENCE

DNA Publications, Inc., P.O. Box 2988, Radford, VA 24143-2988. 540-763-2925. E-mail: dreamsofdecadence@dnapublications.com. Website: www.dnapublications.com. Angela Kessler, Editor/Art Director. **Description:** Quarterly digest devoted to vampire poetry and fiction. **Fiction:** Original, well-written short stories. Emphasis is on dark fantasy rather than horror. Seeks unique ideas, original story concepts, and well-developed characters. Do not send stories with overused plots or themes. 1,000-15,000 words; $.01-$.05/word. **Poetry:** Seeks all forms of poetry relating to vampires. Poems should be not be horrific in nature, but should be explicitly vampiric. Up to 2 pages; $3-$20/poem. **Tips:** Do not submit material via e-mail. See website for guidelines. **Queries:** Not necessary. **E-Queries:** No, **Rights:** FNASR. **Payment:** On publication.

FLESH AND BLOOD

121 Joseph St., Bayville, NJ 08721. E-mail: horrorjack@aol.com. Website: www.fleshandbloodpress.com. 4x/yr. Circ.: 1,000. Jack Fisher, Editor-in-Chief; Robert Swartwood, Senior Editor; Teri A. Jacobs, Assistant Editor. **Description:** Dark fantasy, bizarre, and supernatural stories. Despite name, prefers

work that is subtle, magic realism, bizarre eccentric, avant-garde, or any mix thereof. **Fiction:** Currently seeking horror/dark fantasy work. Should have one or more of the following elements: dark fantastic, surreal, supernatural, bizarre, offbeat. 6,000 words max.; $.04-$.05/word. **Tips:** "Do not exceed maximum word count. Stories should be unique, entertaining, and imaginative. The more descriptive and dark, the better. Avoid stories with insane main characters; about obese people who eat others or who are evil; stories not set in the modern day; over-used vampire, werewolf stories; tales about evil gods and their followers; based solely on monsters; excessive gore, blood, sex, etc. Be sure to include SASE and brief letter listing previous publication credits." **Queries:** Not necessary. **E-Queries:** Yes. **Unsolicited mss:** Accepts. **Response:** 2 months. **SASE Required:** Yes. **Rights:** FNASR. **Payment:** On publication.

HADROSAUR TALES

Hadrosaur Productions, P.O. Box 2194, Mesilla Park, NM 88047-2194. E-mail: hadrosaur.productions@verizon.net. Website: www.hadrosaur.com. 3x/yr. $6.95/$15. Circ.: 150. David Summers, Editor. **Description:** Short stories and poetry. **Fiction:** Literary science fiction and fantasy. Contemporary or historical fiction welcome if it includes a mythic or science-fictional element. Psychological or character-oriented horror considered; no graphic violence; to 6,000 words; $6/story. **Poetry:** Poems with science fiction/fantasy imagery and themes; to 50 lines; $2/poem. **Art:** Pen-and-ink line drawings (cover). **Tips:** Avoid cliche-fantasy. **Queries:** Not necessary. **E-Queries:** Yes. **Unsolicited mss:** Accepts. **Response:** 1-6 weeks. **SASE Required:** Yes. **Freelance Content:** 100%. **Rights:** One-time. **Payment:** On acceptance.

LEADING EDGE

3146 JKHB, Provo, UT 84602. E-mail: tle@byu.edu. Semiannual. $12 (3 issues). Circ.: 500. Kristina Kugler, Editor. **Description:** Science fiction and fantasy. Publishes many new writers. **Fiction:** To 17,000 words; $.01/word ($10-$100). **Nonfiction:** On science fiction, fantasy, or author interviews; to 10,000 words; pays in copies. **Poetry:** Length varies; $10/poem. **Columns, Departments:** Book reviews; to 2,000 words; pays in copies. **Tips:** Does not accept submissions by e-mail. Sample copy for $4.95. "Avoid rehashed plots, poor mechanics, poor plot resolution. No sex, graphic violence, or strong language." **Queries:** Not necessary. **E-Queries:** No. **Unsolicited mss:** Accepts. **Response:** 2-3 months. **SASE Required:** Yes. **Freelance Content:** 100%. **Rights:** FNASR. **Payment:** On publication.

MAGAZINE OF FANTASY & SCIENCE FICTION

P.O. Box 3447, Hoboken, NJ 07030. E-mail: fandsf@aol.com. Website: www.fsf-mag.com. Monthly. $3.99/issue (U.S.), $4.99/issue (Canada). Circ.: 40,000. Gordon Van Gelder, Editor. **Description:** Devoted to speculative fiction. **Fiction:** Prefers character-oriented stories. Science fiction element may be slight, but present; to 25,000 words; $.05-$.08/word. **Tips:** "We receive a lot of fantasy submissions, but we're looking for more science fiction and humor." **Queries:** Does not accept. **E-Queries:** No. **Unsolicited mss:** Accepts. **Response:** 8 weeks. **SASE Required:** Yes. **Rights:** Worldwide serial, and option on anthology. **Payment:** On acceptance.

MYTHIC DELIRIUM

DNA Publications, Inc., P.O. Box 13511, Roanoke, VA 24034-3511.
E-mail: mythicd2001@yahoo.com. Website: www.mythicdelirium.com. Biannual.
Mike Allen, Editor/Art Director. **Description:** Seeks science fiction, fantasy, horror, and cross-genre poetry. Particular interest in poetry that employs well use of rhyme or traditional form. Prefers material that is under 40 lines. Pays $5 for poems under 40 lines; $10 for poems over 40 lines. **Tips:** Do not submit material via e-mail. See website for specific guidelines. **Payment:** 30 days after publication.

NIGHT TERRORS

1202 W Market St., Orrville, OH 44667-1710. 330-683-0338.
E-mail: dedavidson@night-terrors-publications.com.
Website: www.night-terrors-publications.com. Annual. $6/issue. Circ.: 1,000. Mr. D.E. Davidson, Editor. **Description:** Short stories of psychological horror, the supernatural, or occult. Emphasis on "continuing terror"; stories should have beginning, middle, and end, but in the end, the terror/threat should not be resolved. Pieces run 2,000-5,000 words. **Tips:** "We prefer stories which make the reader think and grow edgy, not those which make them flinch or grow nauseous." **Queries:** Not necessary. **E-Queries:** Yes. **Unsolicited mss:** Accepts. **Response:** Queries 1 week, submissions 12 weeks. **SASE Required:** Yes. **Freelance Content:** 95%. **Rights:** FNASR. **Payment:** In copies.

OF UNICORNS AND SPACE STATIONS

1472 West 2450 South, Woods Cross, UT 84087. Semiannual. $4/$16 (4 issues). Circ.: 200. Gene Davis, Editor. **Description:** Science fiction and fantasy magazine for adults with a family-oriented writing style. **Fiction:** Science fiction or fantasy, sometimes a little horror; 250-5,000 words; $.05/word. **Poetry:** Prefers fixed form poetry; any reasonable length; $.05/word, $5 max. **Art:** B&W line art. **Queries:** Not necessary. **E-Queries:** Yes. **Unsolicited mss:** Accepts. **Response:** 3 months. **SASE Required:** Yes. **Freelance Content:** 100%. **Payment:** On publication.

ON SPEC

P.O. Box 4727, Edmonton, AB T6E 5G6 Canada. 780-413-0215. E-mail: onspec@onspec.ca, onspec@canada.com. Website: www.onspec.ca. Quarterly. $22/yr. Circ.: 1,500. Diane Walton, Editor. **Description:** Seeks original, unpublished speculative fiction and poetry by Canadian authors. **Fiction:** Science fiction, fantasy, horror, ghost stories, fairy stories, magic realism, speculative fiction; to 6,000 words; C$50-C$180. **Nonfiction:** By assignment only. **Poetry:** Science fiction, fantasy themes; blank, free verse, discursive prose; to 100 lines; C$20. **Fillers:** Science fiction, fantasy, horror, ghost stories, fairy stories, magic realism, speculative fiction; to 1,000 words; C$50. **Art:** Illustrations by assignment; B&W photos; $50/inside use, $200/cover. **Tips:** Does not consider e-mail or fax submissions. Welcomes non-Canadian authors, but content must remain 80% Canadian. Sample copy $7. **Queries:** Not necessary. **E-Queries:** Yes. **Unsolicited mss:** Accepts. **Response:** 2-3 months. **SASE Required:** Yes. **Rights:** FNASR. **Payment:** On acceptance.

OUTER DARKNESS

1312 N Delaware Pl., Tulsa, OK 74110. 918-832-1246. Quarterly. $3.95/issue ($4.95 by mail). Circ.: 500. Dennis Kirk, Editor. **Description:** "Where Nightmares Roam Unleashed," horror and science fiction. Also poetry, cartoons, and interviews. **Fiction:** Traditional horror and science fiction; to 5,000 words. **Nonfiction:** Interviews with authors, artists, editors; to 1,500 words. **Poetry:** Some free verse, prefers traditional rhyming; to 30 lines. **Art:** All stories illustrated, submit sample work. **Queries:** Not necessary. **E-Queries:** No. **Response:** Queries 2 weeks, submissions 8-12 weeks. **SASE Required:** Yes. **Freelance Content:** 25%. **Rights:** FNAR. **Payment:** In copies.

REALMS OF FANTASY

Sovereign Media Co., 441 Carlisle Dr., Herndon, VA 20170-4884. 703-471-1556. E-mail: realmsoffantasy@aol.com. Website: www.rofmagazine.com. Bimonthly. $16.95/yr. Circ.: 112,000. Shawna McCarthy, Editor. **Description:** Devoted to fantasy fiction and artwork. Heroic, contemporary, traditional, feminist, dark, light; up to 10,000 words; $.03-$.05/word. **Tips:** No standard science-fiction stories (alien worlds, technology-driven, etc.). **Queries:** Not necessary. **Unsolicited mss:** Accepts. **SASE Required:** Yes.

THE SILVER WEB

Buzzcity Press, P.O. Box 38190, Tallahassee, FL 32315. 850-385-8948. E-mail: buzzcity@yourvillage.com. Ann Kennedy, Editor. **Description:** Fantastical fiction, including science fiction, dark fantasy, etc. **Tips:** Currently not accepting unsolicited submissions. **Queries:** Preferred.

SPACE AND TIME

138 W 70 St. 4B, New York, NY 10023-4468. Website: www.cith.org/space&time.html. Biannual. $5/issue. Circ.: 2,000. Gordon Linzner, Editor. **Description:** Science fiction, fantasy, horror, and things that fall between the cracks. Also, a healthy selection of poetry (same genre), along with the occasional short feature. **Fiction:** Science fiction, fantasy, horror; to 10,000 words; $.01/word. **Poetry:** All styles and forms (rhymed, unrhymed, etc.). **Art:** B&W artwork assigned, to illustrate specific stories. Send photocopied samples; $10. **Tips:** Avoid clichés. No media fiction. Appreciates material that deserves to be in print, but which other magazines don't quite know what to do with. **Queries:** Not necessary. **E-Queries:** No. **Unsolicited mss:** Accepts. **Response:** 1-4 months. **Freelance Content:** 99%. **Rights:** FNASR. **Payment:** On publication.

STRANGE HORIZONS

E-mail: editor@strangehorizons.com. Website: www.strangehorizons.com. Weekly. Susan Groppi, Editor-in-Chief. **Description:** E-zine of speculative and science fiction. Features art, articles, fiction, poetry, and reviews. **Fiction:** To 9,000 words; pays $.05/word. **Nonfiction:** Articles, 1,000-5,000 words; pays $50/article. **Poetry:** To 100 lines; pays $20/poem. **Columns, Departments:** Art and book reviews, 750-1,000 words; pays $20/review. **Art:** Commissioned illustrations; $75/illustration. **Tips:** No simultaneous submissions. All material must be submitted electronically to the appropriate address: fiction@strangehorizons.com; poetry@strangehorizons.com; gallery@strangehorizons.com; articles@strangehorizons.com; reviews@strangehorizons.com. See website for specific guidelines. **E-Queries:** Yes. **Rights:** 1st, worldwide (exclusive for 2 months, then reverts to author).

TALEBONES

Fairwood Press, 5203 Quincy Ave. SE, Auburn, WA 98092. E-mail: info@talebones.com. Website: www.talebones.com. Quarterly. $6/$20. Circ.: 1,000. Patrick Swenson, Honna Swenson, Editors. **Description:** Science fiction and dark fantasy. **Fiction:** Sci-fi and dark fantasy stories with a punch, often slanted toward darker fiction; 6,000 words; $.01-$.02/word. **Poetry:** All suitable forms and themes; $10. **Fillers:** Cartoons; $10. **Art:** Most formats; $15-$50. **Tips:** "Send us your cover letter, but keep it to the point." **Queries:** Not necessary. **E-Queries:** Yes. **Unsolicited mss:** Accepts. **Response:** 1-8 weeks. **SASE Required:** Yes. **Rights:** FNASR. **Payment:** On acceptance.

WEIRD TALES

DNA Publications, Inc., 123 Crooked Ln., King of Prussia, PA 19406-2570. 610-275-4463. E-mail: weirdtales@comcast.net. Website: www.weird-tales.com. Bimonthly. $5.95/$20. Circ.: 10,000. George Scithers, Darrel Schweitzer, Editors/Art Directors; Diane Weinstein, Art Director. **Description:** Publication seeking short stories and poetry in fantasy-based horror, heroic fantasy, and exotic mood pieces. Rarely buys material that does not present fantasy elements. **Tips:** Send hard copy of manuscript; do not send via e-mail. E-mail or send SASE for submission guidelines. **Queries:** Not necessary. **Unsolicited mss:** Accepts. **Response:** Queries 1 week, submissions 1-3 months. **SASE Required:** Yes. **Freelance Content:** 90%. **Rights:** FNASR. **Payment:** On publication.

BOOK PUBLISHERS

GENERAL ADULT BOOKS

This and the two following sections feature publishers, in turn, of general adult books, juvenile books, and religious books. These lists include a wide range of options, from some of the largest trade publishers to a selected list of many smaller presses and university presses.

Many publishers are willing to consider either unsolicited queries or manuscripts, but an increasing number have a policy of only reading submissions sent to them via literary agents. Since finding an agent willing to take on a new writer's work is not always an easy task, many writers still choose to present their manuscripts directly to publishers.

Before even considering submitting a complete manuscript to an editor, it is always advisable to send a brief query letter describing the proposed book, and an SASE. The letter should also include information about the author's special qualifications for dealing with the particular topic covered, as well as any previous publication credits. An outline of the book (or a synopsis for fiction) and a sample chapter may also be included.

While it is common courtesy to submit a book manuscript to only one publisher at a time, it is often acceptable to submit the same query or proposal in advance to more than one editor simultaneously, as it takes an editor less time to review a query and respond with some indication of further interest. When sending simultaneous queries, however, always state clearly in your letter that you are doing this.

With any submission of manuscript materials to a publisher, be sure to enclose sufficient postage for the manuscript's return.

Royalty rates for hardcover books usually start at 10% of the retail price of the book and increase after a certain number of copies have been sold. Paperbacks generally have a somewhat lower rate, about 5% to 8%. Smaller presses and university presses sometimes base their royalty on net receipts (i.e., what they get after discounts), rather than the retail price (the "list price" printed on the book). It is customary for the publishing company to pay the author a cash advance against royalties when the book contract is signed or when the finished manuscript is received. Some publishers pay on a flat-fee basis.

Writers seeking publication of book-length poetry manuscripts are encouraged to consider contests that offer publication as the prize (see Prizes, in Other Markets & Resources).

ABBEVILLE PUBLISHING GROUP

116 W 23rd St., Suite 500, New York, NY 10011. 646-375-2039.
E-mail: abbeville@abbeville.com. Website: www.abbeville.com. **Description:** Fine art and illustrated books on art/architecture, children's, decorative arts, design, music/media, animals, sports, gardening, travel, etc. **Proposal Process:** Does not accept unsolicited submissions or proposals.

A CAPPELLA BOOKS

Chicago Review Press, 814 N Franklin St., Chicago, IL 60610. 312-337-0747.
Website: www.ipgbook.com. **Description:** Nonfiction titles on music, performing
arts, and film. **Books Statistics:** 8 titles/yr; 30-40% by first-time authors; 50% unagented. **Proposal Process:** Submit query, 2 sample chapters, and SASE. Responds
in 1 month to queries. **Payment:** Royalty.

A.R.E. PRESS

Edgar Cayce's Assn. for Research & Enlightenment, 215 67th St., Virginia Beach, VA
23451-2061. E-mail: arepress@edgarcayce.org. Website: www.edgarcayce.org. Ken
Skidmore, Senior Editor. **Description:** Publishes materials that center on spirituality and self-help. **Books Statistics:** 12 titles/yr. **Sample Titles:** *God at the Speed of
Light* by T. Lee Baumann, M.D.; *12 Positive Habits of Spiritually Centered People*
by Mark Thurston and Sarah Thurston.

ABINGDON PRESS

The United Methodist Publishing House, 201 Eighth Ave. S, P.O. Box 801, Nashville,
TN 37203. 615-749-6301. Website: www.abingdonpress.com. **Description:** General-
interest books: mainline, social issues, marriage/family, self-help, exceptional people,
etc. **Proposal Process:** Query with outline and 1-2 sample chapters. **Payment:**
Royalty. **Sample Titles:** *What About the Soul? Neuroscience and Christian
Anthropology* by Joel Green; *What Do Other Faiths Believe?* by Paul E. Stroble.
Tips: Guidelines available. **Contact:** Robert Ratcliff, Ph.D., Senior Editor (academic
and professional books); Charles Puskas, Senior Editor (reference books); Ron Kidd,
Senior Editor (general interest books); Peg Augustine, Editor (children's books).

HARRY N. ABRAMS, INC.

La Martiniere Groupe, 100 Fifth Ave., New York, NY 10011. 212-206-7715. E-mail:
submissions@abramsbooks.com. Website: www.abramsbooks.com. Mark McGowan,
Publisher. **Description:** Illustrated art books on a variety of subjects including art
history, fine art, folk art, photography, history, performing arts, comics, architecture,
food/wine, nature, jewelry/fashion, interior design, museum collections, pop culture,
science, sports. Also publishes art books for children, calendars, and journals. **Books
Statistics:** 200 titles/yr. **Proposal Process:** Submit outline, sample chapters, and
illustrations. **Payment:** Royalty. **Sample Titles:** *The Comics: Since 1945* by Brian
Walker; *New York from the Air: An Architectural Heritage* by John Tauranac; *What
Is Design Today* by George H. Marcus. **Contact:** Eric Himmel, Editor-in-Chief.

ACADEMIC PRESS

A Harcourt Science and Technology Company/Elsevier Science, 525 B St., Suite
1900, San Diego, CA 92101-4495. 619-231-0926. E-mail: ap@acad.com. Website:
www.academicpress.com. **Description:** Scientific/technical books, journals, textbooks, and other reference materials for research scientists, students, and professionals who work in the fields of life sciences, physical sciences, engineering, mathematics, computer sciences, and social/behavorial sciences. **Proposal Process:** Submit 1-

2 page prospectus summarizing the topic and approach of manuscript; detailed chapter outline; description of audience and competing titles; and curriculum vitae. **Sample Titles:** *Origins of Life on the Earth and in the Cosmos* by Geoffrey Zubay; *Electronics and Communications for Scientists and Engineers* by Martin Plonus; *Earth Magnetism* by Wallace Hall Campbell. **Contact:** Books Editorial Dept.

ACADEMY CHICAGO PUBLISHERS

363 W Erie St., Chicago, IL 60610. 312-751-7300.
E-mail: info@academychicago.com. Website: www.academychicago.com. Anita Miller, Senior Editor. **Description:** General adult fiction (classic mysteries, Victorian classics) and nonfiction (history, biography, travel, film/video, Celtic, and Arthurian). Special interest in books by and about women. No how-to, explicit sex, grotesque violence, sci-fi, or horror. **Books Statistics:** 11 titles/yr. **Proposal Process:** Query with 4 sample chapters and SASE. No electronic submissions. See website for guidelines. **Sample Titles:** (Nonfiction) *Looking Backward: Stories from Chicago's Jewish Past* by Walter Roth; *Over Sand & Sea* by Patrick Pfister. (Fiction) *Letters in the Attic* by Bonnie Shimko. **Contact:** Jordan Miller, Vice President/Publicity.

ADAMS MEDIA CORPORATION

57 Littlefield St., Avon, MA 02322. 508-427-7100. Website: www.adamsmedia.com. Gary M. Krebs, Director of Publishing. **Description:** Nonfiction trade paperbacks in the categories of self-help, how-to, relationships, parenting, inspiration, popular reference, business, small business, careers, and personal finance. **Books Statistics:** 150 titles/yr. **Proposal Process:** Query with outline, sample chapters, and SASE. Accepts simultaneous queries, but not e-queries. Hard copy only. Responds in 1 month. **Payment:** Advance/royalty or work-for-hire.

ADAMS-BLAKE PUBLISHING

8041 Sierra St., Suite 102, Fair Oaks, CA 95628. 916-962-9296.
Website: www.adams-blake.com. Monica Blane, Senior Editor.
Description: Technical subjects for the corporate market. Books on business, careers, and technology. **Books Statistics:** 5 titles/yr (100 submissions); 90% by first-time authors; 100% unagented. **Proposal Process:** Query with outline. Accepts simultaneous queries, but not e-queries. Responds in 4 weeks. **Payment:** Royalty, 10-15% net. **Tips:** Narrow market—technical titles sold to the corporate market for very high prices.

ADAMS-HALL PUBLISHING

P.O. Box 491002, Los Angeles, CA 90049. 800-888-4452. Sue Ann Bacon, Editorial Director. **Description:** Business and personal finance books with wide market appeal. **Proposal Process:** Query with proposed book idea, list of current competitive titles, author qualifications, description of why your book is unique, and SASE. Does not accept complete manuscript. **Payment:** Royalty.

ADDICUS BOOKS, INC.

P.O. Box 45327, Omaha, NE 68145. 402-330-7493. E-mail: info@addicusbooks.com. Website: www.addicusbooks.com. Rod Colvin, Publisher. **Description:** Independent press publishing nonfiction titles on economics, investing, business, self-help, health, how-to, and regional topics. **Books Statistics:** 5-10 titles/yr; 70% by first-time authors; 60% unagented. **Proposal Process:** Submit 1-page overview, chapter outline, 2-3 sample chapters, description of intended audience, estimated word/photo count, and bio/resumé. Also accepts 1-page e-queries (no attachments). **Payment:** Royalty. **Sample Titles:** *A Simple Guide to Thyroid Disorders* by Paul Ruggieri, M.D. **Contact:** Susan Adams, Managing Editor.

ADVENTURES UNLIMITED PRESS

P.O. Box 74, Kempton, IL 60946. 815-253-6390. Website: www.adventuresunlimitedpress.com. **Description:** Nonfiction material on Atlantis, ancient civilizations, science, alternative science and health, conspiracy, UFOs, etc.

AEGIS PUBLISHING GROUP LTD

796 Aquidneck Ave., Newport, RI 02842-7246. 401-849-4200. E-mail: aegis@aegisbooks.com. Website: www.aegisbooks.com. Robert Mastin, Publisher. **Description:** Books on telecommunications and data networking. Materials target both industry professionals and general consumers. **Sample Titles:** *Telecom Made Easy* by June Langhoff; *The Cell Phone Buyer's Guide* by Penelope Stetz.

AERONAUTICAL PUBLISHERS

One Oakglade Circle, Hummelstown, PA 17036-9525. 717-566-0468. E-mail: aeronauticalpubs@aol.com. Website: www.aeronauticalpublishers.com. Mike Markowski, Publisher; Marjie Markowski, Editor-in-Chief. **Description:** How-to, general, and semi-technical. Subjects include aviation history, hobbies, recreation, radio control, free flight, indoor models, micro radio control, homebuilt aircraft, ultralights, and hang gliders. **Proposal Process:** Query with SASE. Prefers hard copy. Responds in 2 months. See website for guidelines. **Sample Titles:** *Flying Models* by Don Ross; *Birdflight as the Basis of Aviation* by Otto Lilienthal. **Tips:** "Our focus is on books of short to medium length that will serve the emerging needs of the full-scale and model aviation community, as well as aviation history. We also want to help youth get started, while enhancing everyone's enjoyment of the hobby. We are looking for authors that are passionate about aviation, and will champion the messages of their books."

AFRICA WORLD PRESS, INC.

541 W Ingham Ave., Suite B, Trenton, NJ 08638. 609-695-3200. E-mail: awprsp@africanworld.com. Website: www.africanworld.com. Kassahun Checole, Publisher. **Description:** Publisher of nonfiction and poetry. Material focuses on African, African American, Caribbean, and Latin American issues. **Proposal Process:** Query. **Payment:** Royalty. **Sample Titles:** *The Challenges of History and Leadership in Africa: The Essays of Bethwell Allan Ogot* edited by Toyin Falola and Atieno Odhiambo.

AFRICAN AMERICAN IMAGES

1909 W 95th St., Chicago, IL 60643. 773-445-0322. E-mail: aai@africanamericanimages.com. Website: www.africanamericanimages.com. **Description:** Adult and children's nonfiction Africentric books. **Books Statistics:** 6 titles/yr (100 submissions); 50% by first-time authors; 80% unagented. **Proposal Process:** Query with complete manuscript. Considers simultaneous queries. Prefers hard copy. Guidelines available. **Payment:** Royalty (10% net). **Tips:** "Write to promote self-esteem, collective values, liberation, and skill development." **Contact:** Editorial Dept.

AHSAHTA PRESS

MFA Program, Boise State University, Dept. of English, 1910 University Dr., Boise, ID 83725-1525. 208-426-2195. E-mail: ahsahta@boisestate.edu. Website: ahsahtapress.boisestate.edu. Janet Holmes, Director. **Description:** Trade paperback books specializing in poetry. **Books Statistics:** 3 books/yr (300 submissions); 50% by first-time authors; 100% unagented. **Proposal Process:** Send complete manuscript. No electronic queries; hard copy only. Responds in 3 months. **Payment:** Annual royalty.

ALASKA NORTHWEST BOOKS

Graphic Arts Center Publishing Co., P.O. Box 10306, Portland, OR 97296-0306. 503-226-2402. E-mail: triciab@gacpc.com. Website: www.gacpc.com. Tricia Brown, Acquisitions Editor. **Description:** Regional nonfiction about Alaska for a general audience. Specializes in history, natural history, biography, travel, Native heritage, cooking, guidebooks, factbooks, and children's books by Alaskans and about Alaska. **Books Statistics:** 6-8 titles/yr (250 submissions); 10% by first-time authors; 90% unagented. **Proposal Process:** Send cover letter, complete outline with ideas for photos/illustrations, TOC, author bio with examples of previous publications, market analysis, photocopies or slides of artwork, and SASE. Responds in 6 months. **Payment:** Pays royalty (10-12% net). **Sample Titles:** *A Place Beyond: Finding Home in Arctic Alaska* by Nick Jans; *Alaska's Natural Wonders: A Guide to the Phenomena of the Far North* by Robert Armstrong and Marge Hermans; *Baked Alaska: Recipes for Sweet Comforts from the North Country* by Sarah Eppenbach. **Tips:** "Avoid poetry, adult fiction, and native 'legend' written by non-Native Americans. Children's book authors should avoid partnering with an illustrator before submission has been accepted."

ALBION PRESS

4532 W Kennedy Blvd., Suite 233, Tampa, FL 33609. 813-805-2665.
E-mail: mcgregpub@aol.com. Dave Rosenbaum, Acquisitions.
Description: Nonfiction titles with emphasis on sports and true crime. No fiction. **Books Statistics:** 12 titles/yr (300 submissions); 50% by first-time authors; 50% unagented. **Proposal Process:** Query with outline, sample chapters, and SASE. Accepts simultaneous and electronic queries. Prefers hard copy. Responds in 2 months. **Payment:** Royalty.

ALGONQUIN BOOKS OF CHAPEL HILL

A Division of Workman Publishing Co., P.O. Box 2225, Chapel Hill, NC 27515-2225. 919-967-0108. E-mail: dialogue@algonquin.com. Website: www.algonquin.com. Shannon Ravenel, Managing Editor. **Description:** Trade books, literary fiction and nonfiction, for adults. **Proposal Process:** Send query for fiction and book proposal for nonfiction. Responds in 6 weeks. **Sample Titles:** *The Last Girls* by Lee Smith; *Hollow Ground* by Stephen Marion.

ALLWORTH PRESS

10 E 23rd St., Suite 510, New York, NY 10010-4402. 212-777-8395. E-mail: pub@allworth.com. Website: www.allworth.com. Nicole Potter, Editor. **Description:** Nonfiction titles on business and self-help that target artists, designers, photographers, writers, and film/tv/performing artists. **Books Statistics:** 42 titles/yr. **Proposal Process:** Query with outline and sample chapters. **Payment:** Royalty. **Sample Titles:** *Creative Careers in Hollywood* by Laurie Scheer; *Design Humor: The Art of Graphic Wit* by Steven Heller.

ALPINE PUBLICATIONS, INC.

P.O. Box 7027, Loveland, CO 80537. 970-667-9317. E-mail: alpinepubl@aol.com. Website: www.alpinepub.com. B.J. McKinney, Publisher. **Description:** Nonfiction books for youth and adults on dogs and horses. Topics include breeding, care, training, health, management, etc. No fiction, poetry, humor, personal experience, or photo essays. **Books Statistics:** 6-8 titles/yr (50 submissions); 50% by first-time authors; 100% unagented. **Proposal Process:** Submit query, outline, and 3 sample chapters and SASE. Accepts simultaneous queries. Prefers hard copy. Responds in 6-8 weeks. **Payment:** Royalty. **Sample Titles:** *Amost a Whisper: A Holistic Approach to Working With Your Horse* by Sam Powell; *The Alaskan Malamute* by Barbara A. Brooks and Sherry E. Wallis. **Tips:** Accepts queries via e-mail, but not submissions.

ALYSON PUBLICATIONS

Division of Liberation Publications, Inc. 6922 Hollywood Blvd., Suite 1000, Los Angeles, CA 90028. 323-860-6074. E-mail: mail@alyson.com. Website: www.alyson.com. Angela Brown, Editor-in-Chief. **Description:** Gay, lesbian, bisexual, and transgender fiction (novels, mysteries, erotica) and nonfiction (biography/memoir, history, humor, self-help, politics/queer theory, relationships). Also publishes children's and YA titles with gay/lesbian themes. **Proposal Process:** Send query with summary, chapter outline, and SASE. Do not send sample chapters or complete manuscript. Simultaneous queries accepted with notice. Responds in 2-4 months. **Payment:** Royalty. **Sample Titles:** (Nonfiction) *The Power of a Partner: Creating and Maintaining Healthy Gay and Lesbian Relationships* by Dr. Richard Pimental-Habib, Ph.D.; (Fiction) *Light, Coming Back* by Ann Wadsworth; (Children's) *Heather Has Two Mommies* by Lesléa Newman. **Tips:** See website for guidelines.

AMACOM BOOKS

American Management Assn., 1601 Broadway, Fl. 9, New York, NY 10019.
212-903-8391. Website: www.amacombooks.org. Adrienne Hickey, Editorial
Director. **Description:** Solution-oriented nonfiction on a variety of business issues
including finance/accounting, computers/technology, human resources, communication, international relations, marketing, advertising, small business, sales, project
management, and customer service. **Proposal Process:** Send formal proposal outlining content, approach, intended audience, and competing titles. Also include
TOC, sample chapters, and resumé/curriculum vitae. **Sample Titles:** *Creating a
Total Rewards Strategy* by Todd M. Manus; *Delivering Knock Your Socks Off
Service* by Ron Zemke. **Tips:** See website for specific guidelines.

AMADEUS PRESS, LLC

512 Newark Pompton Turnpike, Pompton Plains, NJ 07444. 973-835-6375.
E-mail: jcerullo@amadeuspress.com. Website: www.amadeuspress.com.
Carol Flannery, Editorial Director. **Description:** Full-service trade publisher producing books, CDs, and DVDs for a wide audience of discerning music lovers (classical, opera, and tradition music of the world) and professionals as well as fans and
admirers of the performing arts. **Proposal Process:** Send proposal with letter
describing purpose and audience, TOC, 1-2 sample chapters, sample illustrations,
bio/resume, and schedule for completing manuscript. Responds in 8-12 weeks.

AMBER BOOKS

1334 E Chandler Blvd., Suite 5-D67, Phoenix, AZ 85048. 480-460-1660.
E-mail: amberbk@aol.com. Website: www.amberbooks.com. Tony Rose, Publisher.
Description: Publishes African American self-help books, career-guide books, and
biographies on successful entertainment personalities. Aims to publish materials that
help African Americans earn an income, obtain education, and find the empowerment to succeed. **Sample Titles:** *Wake Up and Smell the Dollars! Whose Inner City
is this Anyway?* by Dorothy Pitman Hughes; *Beautiful Black Hair* by Shamboosie;
*The African-American Teenager's Guide to Personal Growth, Health, Safety, Sex, &
Survival* by Debrah Harris-Johnson; *Yes, Yes, Yes: The Unauthorized Biography of
Destiny's Child* by Kelly Kenyatta.

AMERICAN INSTITUTE OF AERONAUTICS
AND ASTRONAUTICS, INC.

1801 Alexander Bell Dr., Suite 500, Reston, VA 20191-4344. 703-264-7505.
Website: www.aiaa.org. Elaine Camhi, Editor-in-Chief. **Description:** Materials on
aerospace technology. Publications include the AIAA Educational Series, Progress in
Astronautics and Aeronautics, several general-interest aerospace publications, and
technical journals.

AMERICAN PARADISE PUBLISHING

P.O. Box 781, St. John, USVI 00831. 304-779-4257.
E-mail: info@americanparadisepublishing.com. Website: www.americanparadis-epublishing.com. Pamela Gaffin, Editor. **Description:** Nonfiction on the U.S. Virgin Islands aimed at Caribbean readers and tourists. Guidebooks, cookbooks, how-to, and books on sailing, yacht cruising, hiking, snorkeling, sportfishing, local history, and West Indian culture. **Proposal Process:** Query with outline and sample chapters. **Payment:** Royalty. **Tips:** "We seek useful, practical books that help our Virgin Island readers lead better and more enjoyable lives."

AMERICAN PSYCHIATRIC PUBLISHING, INC.

American Psychiatric Assn., 1000 Wilson Blvd., Suite 1825, Arlington, VA 22209. 703-907-7322. Website: www.appi.org. Robert E. Hales, M.D., M.B.A., Editor-in-Chief. **Description:** Publisher of books (professional, reference, and academic), journals, and other media related to psychiatry, mental health, behavioral and social sciences, and medicine. **Proposal Process:** Submit completed author questionnaire, detailed chapter outline, curriculum vitae, and brief prospectus stating why APPI should publish the book. **Payment:** Royalty. **Sample Titles:** *Manual of Clinical Psychopharmacology* by Alan F. Schatzberg, M.D. **Contact:** John McDuffie, Editorial Director (703-907-7892).

ANDREWS MCMEEL PUBLISHING

Andrews McMeel Universal, 4520 Main St., Kansas City, MO 64111. 816-932-6700. Website: www.amuniversal.com/amp. **Description:** Publisher of best-sellers, humor collections, general nonfiction trade, gift books, and calendars. **Proposal Process:** Does not accept unsolicited manuscripts. All material must be submitted through a literary agent. **Sample Titles:** *Dear Mom* by Bradley Taylor Greive.

ANDROS BOOK PUBLISHING

P.O. Box 12080, Prescott, AZ 86304. 520-778-4491. E-mail: androsbks@aol.com. Website: www.hometown.aol.com/androsbks. Susanne Bain, Publisher. **Description:** Small publishing house specializing in home schooling, school choice, and parental involvement in education. **Proposal Process:** Send proposal letter, two sample chapters and TOC, and SASE. **Tips:** "We currently seek uplifting material about home school and positive parental involvement in children's education or school choice issues. Looking less for feel-good works than for 'how-to or how we do it.' Looking for personal experience."

ANHINGA PRESS

P.O. Box 10595, Tallahassee, FL 32302-0595. 850-521-9920.
E-mail: info@anhinga.org. Website: www.anhinga.org. Rick Campbell, Editorial Director. **Description:** Publishes books of contemporary poetry. **Books Statistics:** 4 titles/yr (750 submissions); 50% by first-time authors; 99% unagented. **Proposal Process:** Query or send complete manuscripts with SASE. Accepts simultaneous queries, but not e-queries. Responds in 6 weeks. **Payment:** Royalty or flat fee.

THE ANONYMOUS PRESS

332 Bleecker St., #631, New York, NY 10014. Gil Bonner, Acquisitions. **Description:** Nonfiction on topics of conspiracy, cover-ups, true history (not propaganda), counter-culture, anarchy, Zoroastrianism, etc. **Books Statistics:** (500 submissions); 100% by first-time authors. **Proposal Process:** Send query via regular mail. **Payment:** Royalty, 10-20%.

ANVIL PRESS

P.O. Box 3008, MPO, Vancouver, British Columbia V6B 3X5 Canada. 604-876-8710. E-mail: info@anvilpress.com. Website: www.anvilpress.com. Brian Kaufman, Editorial Director. **Description:** Fiction, poetry, creative nonfiction, some nonfiction contemporary, and progressive literature. **Books Statistics:** 8-10 titles/yr (200 submissions); 80% by first-time authors; 100% unagented. **Proposal Process:** Query with outline and sample chapters. Considers simultaneous queries and e-queries (no attachments). Responds in 4-6 months. **Payment:** Royalty, 10-15% net. Flat fee advance, $200-$500. **Sample Titles:** *Intensive Care* by Alan Twigg; *The Beautiful Dead End* by Clint Hutzulak. **Tips:** Canadian authors only. "Avoid sending formulaic writing. We're looking for originality in style and voice, contemporary modern."

APA BOOKS

American Psychological Assn., 750 First St. NE, Washington, DC 20002-4242. 202-336-5500. Website: www.apa.org. **Description:** Nonfiction titles reflecting current research and discovery in the field of psychology. Materials have scholarly, professional focus. Also publishes children's books under the Magination Press imprint and adult self-help titles under the APA LifeTools imprint. **Proposal Process:** Submit prospectus with curriculum vitae. Prospectus should include TOC, purpose, audience, market anaylsis, anticipated length, proposed schedule, and the theories or ideas that will be explored in the book. **Sample Titles:** (APA Books) *Behavioral Genetics in the Postgenomic Era* by Robert Plomin, Ph.D., et al. (Magination Press) *Jenny is Scared! When Sad Things Happen in the World* by Carol Shurman, Ph.D. (APA LifeTools) *Forgiveness Is a Choice: A Step by Step Process for Resolving Anger and Restoring Hope* by Robert D. Enright, Ph.D.

APERTURE

20 East 23rd St., New York, NY 10010. 212-505-5555. E-mail: editorial@aperture.org. Website: www.aperture.org. Ray K. Metzker. **Description:** Photography books. **Proposal Process:** Submit 1 page synopsis; hard copy only. Include delivery memo that describes work, format, and the number of images, SASE. Allow 6-8 weeks for response.

APPALACHIAN MOUNTAIN CLUB BOOKS

5 Joy St., Boston, MA 02108. 617-523-0655. Website: www.outdoors.org. Beth Krusi, Publisher/Editor. **Description:** Regional (New England) and national nonfiction titles, 175-350 pages, for adults, juveniles and young adults. Topics include guidebooks on non-motorized backcountry recreation, nature, outdoor recreation skills

(how-to books), mountain history/biography, search and rescue, conservation, and environmental management. **Books Statistics:** 12 titles/yr (40 submissions); 75% by first-time authors. **Proposal Process:** Query with outline and sample chapters. Accepts simultaneous queries. Responds in 3 months. **Payment:** Royalty. **Sample Titles:** *Quiet Water Canoe Guide: New York* by John Hayes and Alex Wilson; *Women on High: Pioneers of Mountaineering* by Rebecca A. Brown; *River Days: Exploring the Connecticut River from Source to Sea* by Michael Tougias. **Tips:** See website for complete submission guidelines. **Contact:** Editorial Department.

APPLAUSE THEATRE & CINEMA BOOKS

Hal Leonard Corp., 151 W 46th St., Fl. 8, New York, NY 10036. 212-575-9265. Website: www.applausepub.com. Glenn Young, Publisher; Michael Messina, Managing Director. **Description:** Publishes biographies, reference materials, and guide books in the fields of stage, cinema, and entertainment. Topics include acting, music/literature, memoir, humor, biography, television, playwriting and screenwriting, Shakespeare, etc. **Sample Titles:** *At This Theatre: 100 Years of Broadway Shows, Stories and Stars* by Louis Botto with Robert Viagas; *The Unseen Force: The Films of Sam Raimi* by John Kenneth Muir.

APPLEWOOD BOOKS, INC.

128 The Great Rd., P.O. Box 365, Bedford, MA 01730. 781-271-0055. E-mail: applewood@awb.com. Website: www.awb.com. **Description:** Adult nonfiction on culture, nostalgia, history, literature, cooking, travel, sports, self-help, biography, etc. **Books Statistics:** 40 titles/yr.

AQUAQUEST PUBLICATIONS, INC.

P.O. Box 700, Locust Valley, NY 11560. 516-759-0476.
E-mail: editorial@aquaquest.com. Website: www.aquaquest.com.
Description: Nonfiction titles on underwater adventures and scuba diving. Books cover a range of underwater and marine topics such as travel, diving, shipwrecks, marine life, historical, technical, photography, and fiction. **Sample Titles:** *Diving Micronesia* by Eric Hanauer; *Solo Diving, 2nd Ed: The Art of Underwater Self-suffiency* by Robert Von Maier.

ARCADE PUBLISHING, INC.

141 Fifth Ave., New York, NY 10010. 212-475-2633.
E-mail: info@arcadepub.com. Website: www.arcadepub.com. Richard Seaver, President/Editor-in-Chief. **Description:** Adult nonfiction in the areas of business, travel, history, art, biography, African American studies, women's studies, religion, philosophy, science, technology, and true crime. Also publishes fiction, poetry, and literature/essays. **Sample Titles:** *Lovesong: Becoming a Jew* by Julius Lester; *Race Manners* by Bruce A. Jacobs; *The Women Who Wrote the War* by Nancy Caldwell Sorel; *Hitler's Gift: The True Story of the Scientists Expelled by the Nazi Regime* by Jean Medawar and David Pyke. **Tips:** Does not accept unsolicited submissions. **Contact:** Darcy Falkenhagen, Associate Editor.

ARCADIA PUBLISHING

Tempus Publishing, 2 Cumberland St., Charleston, SC 29401. 843-853-2070. Website: www.arcadiapublishing.com. **Description:** Nonfiction regional history titles. Publishes *Images of America* and *Making of America* series. Other topics include Native America, the Civil War, sports, college history, postcard history, aviation, and motoring. **Books Statistics:** 800 titles/yr; 85% by first-time authors; 95% unagented. **Proposal Process:** Query with SASE. See website for list of regional acquisition editors. **Sample Titles:** *Irish Chicago* by John Gerard McLaughlin; *McDonough County Historic Sites* by John E. Hallwas.

ARSENAL PULP PRESS

103-1014 Homer St., Vancouver, British Columbia V6B2W9 Canada. 604-687-4233. E-mail: contact@arsenalpulp.com. Website: www.arsenalpulp.com. **Description:** Literary fiction and nonfiction in the areas of gay/lesbian, cultural studies, pop culture, cooking, visual art, politics, and regional topics (particularly British Columbia). No genre fiction or children's books. **Proposal Process:** Send cover letter with synopsis, writing sample (50-60 pages), and SASE. No submissions by fax or e-mail. Considers proposals from Canadian authors only with the exception of anthologies. Responds in 3 months. **Sample Titles:** *The Garden of Vegan* by Tanya Barnard and Sarah Kramer; *Out/Lines: Underground Gay Graphics from Before Stonewall* by Thomas Waugh; *Vancouver: The Unknown City* by Sarah Reeder and John Mackie. **Tips:** Currently not accepting poetry.

ARTE PUBLICO PRESS

University of Houston, 452 Cullen Peformance Hall, Houston, TX 77204-2004. 713-743-2843. E-mail: submapp@mail.uh.edu. Website: www.artepublicopress.com. Dr. Nicolas Kanellos, Founder/Director. **Description:** Contemporary and recovered literature by U.S. Hispanics, in both Spanish and English, with a focus on children's, women's, and civil rights literature. "Pinata Books." Novels, short stories, poetry, drama, nonfiction, and autobiographies. **Books Statistics:** 30 titles/yr (200 submissions); 80% by first-time authors; 20% unagented. **Proposal Process:** Query with outline, sample chapters, and SASE. No simultaneous or electronic queries. Hard copy only. Responds in 6 months. **Payment:** Royalty. **Sample Titles:** (Adult Fiction) *Close to the Heart* by Diane Gonzales; (Children's) *La Tierra de las Adivinanzas/The Land of the Riddles* by Cesar Villareal Elisondo. **Tips:** Looking for work by and about Hispanics in the U.S.

ARTECH HOUSE PUBLISHERS

Horizon House Publications, Inc., 685 Canton St., Norwood, MA 02062. 781-769-9750. Website: www.artechhouse.com. Mark Walsh, Senior Acquisitions Editor. **Description:** Professional-level books on telecommunications, wireless, microwave, radar, computer security, and software engineering. **Sample Titles:** *Running the Successful Hi-Tech Project Office* by Eduardo Miranda; *Centrex or PBX: The Impact of IP* by John R. Abrahams.

ARTISAN

Division of Workman Publishing Co., 708 Broadway, New York, NY 10003-9555. 212-254-5900. E-mail: artisaninfo@workman.com. Website: www.artisanbooks.com. **Description:** Illustrated nonfiction on art/architecture, biography/memoir, cooking, food/wine, crafts, gardening, film/tv, music, history, pets, sports, and travel. **Proposal Process:** Prefers to see as much of completed project as possible. Send copies of photos or illustrations (no originals). Does not accept submissions via e-mail, fax, or disk. Include SASE. **Sample Titles:** *Melons for the Passionate Grower* by Amy Goldman; *The French Laundry Cookbook* by Thomas Keller. **Contact:** Editorial Dept.

ASM PRESS

American Society for Microbiology, 1752 N St. NW, Washington, DC 20036. 202-737-3600. E-mail: books@asmusa.org. Website: www.asmpress.org. **Description:** Reference manuals, scholarly monographs, and textbooks for the molecular biology and microbiological sciences. **Proposal Process:** Submit proposal with clear explanation of how book will be beneficial to the microbiology community. Also include market analysis, TOC, and current curriculum vitae. **Tips:** See website for detailed submission guidelines. **Contact:** Holly L. Koppel, Production/Marketing Assistant.

AUGSBURG FORTRESS, PUBLISHERS

100 S Fifth St., Suite 700, P.O. Box 1209, Minneapolis, MN 55440-1209. 612-330-3300. E-mail: booksub@augsburgfortress.org. Website: www.augsburgbooks.com. **Description:** Publishes books that focus on faith in daily life, Biblical studies, history of Christianity, theology, ethics, etc. **Tips:** See website for specific guidelines.

AVALON BOOKS

Thomas Bouregy & Co., Inc., 160 Madison Ave., New York, NY 10016. 212-598-0222. E-mail: avalon@avalonbooks.com. Website: www.avalonbooks.com. Erin Cartwright-Niumat, Editorial Director. **Description:** Hardcover secular romances, mysteries and westerns for the library market. **Books Statistics:** 60 titles/yr (1,500 submissions); 65% by first-time authors; 80% unagented. **Proposal Process:** Query with first 3 chapters and outline. Responds in 1 month to queries; 6-8 months to mss. Send SASE for guidelines. **Payment:** Advance plus royalty, 5-15%. **Sample Titles:** *A Wanted Man* by Nancy J. Parra; *Willow* by Carolyn Brown; *A Hanging in Hidetown* by Kent Conwell. **Tips:** "No old-fashioned, predictable, formulaic books. Avoid graphic or premarital sex or sexual tension in your writing."

AVALON TRAVEL PUBLISHING

1400 65th St., Suite 250, Emeryville, CA 94608. 510-595-3664. E-mail: acquisitions@avalonpub.com. Website: www.travelmatters.com/acquisitions. Rebecca Browning, Acquisitions Editor. **Description:** Travel guides, 200-800 pages. Most titles fit into one of the following series: Adapter Kit, The Dog Lover's Companion, Foghorn Outdoors, Moon Handbooks, Moon Metro, Rick Steves, and Road Trip USA. No fiction, children's books, or travelogues/travel diaries. **Proposal Process:** Visit website for detailed proposal instructions. Do not call. **Payment:** Royalty.

AVANT-GUIDE TRAVEL BOOKS

Empire Press Media, 350 Fifth Ave., Empire State Bldg., Suite 7815-78th Fl., New York, NY 10118. 212-563-1003. E-mail: editor@aventguide.com. Website: www.avantguide.com. Dan Levine, Editor; Marilyn Wood, Editor. **Description:** Travel guidebooks. **Books Statistics:** 16 titles/yr (50 submissions); 50% by first-time authors; 100% unagented. **Proposal Process:** Query by e-mail. Considers simultaneous queries. Responds in 1 week to e-queries, 3 months to material sent by regular mail. **Payment:** Flat fee, $10,000-$20,000. **Tips:** "Please send only manuscripts that are travel guidebooks. We'll consider guides of other types if they are style-driven and fit into our publishing program. No phone calls please."

AVERY

Penguin Group (USA) Inc., 375 Hudson St., Fl. 4, New York, NY 10014. 212-366-2806. Website: www.penguin.com. John Duff, Publisher; Eileen Bertelli, Associate Publisher. **Description:** Trade books in alternative health, health, fitness, nutrition, and healthy cooking. **Books Statistics:** 25 titles/yr; 50% by first-time authors; 25% unagented. **Proposal Process:** Query with outline or sample chapters. **Payment:** Royalty. **Sample Titles:** *Prescription for Nutritional Healing* by Phyllis Balch, CMC, and James Balch, M.D.; *The Food Carb Cookbook* by Sandra Woodruff, M.S., R.D. **Contact:** Dara Stewart, Editor; Kristen Jennings, Associate Editor.

BAEN BOOKS

P.O. Box 1403, Riverdale, NY 10471-0671. 718-548-3100. Website: www.baen.com. Jim Baen, Editor-in-Chief. **Description:** Strongly plotted science fiction; innovative fantasy. **Books Statistics:** 120 titles/yr (5,000 submissions); 5% by first-time authors; 50% unagented. **Proposal Process:** Query with synopsis and manuscript. **Payment:** Advance and royalty. **Sample Titles:** *War of Honor* by David Weber. **Tips:** Send SASE or check website for guidelines.

BALLANTINE BOOKS

The Ballantine Publishing Group/Random House, Inc., 1745 Broadway , New York, NY 10019. 212-782-9000. Website: www.randomhouse.com. Leona Nevler, Editor. **Description:** General fiction and nonfiction. **Proposal Process:** Accepts material through literary agents only.

BANTAM DELL PUBLISHING GROUP

Random House, Inc., 1745 Broadway, New York, NY 10019. 212-782-9000. Website: www.bantamdell.com. **Description:** Executive Vice President and Deputy Publisher: Nita Taublib. Acquisitions: Toni Burbank (self-help, health/medicine, nature, spirituality, philosophy); Jackie Cantor (general commercial fiction, literary fiction, women's fiction, memoir); Tracy Devine (narrative nonfiction, history, adventure, military, science, general upscale commercial fiction, women's fiction, suspense); Anne Groell (fantasy, science fiction); Ann Harris (general commercial, literary, science, medicine, politics); Susan Kamil (The Dial Press, literary fiction and nonfiction); Robin Michaelson (health, women's health, child care/parenting, psychology, self-help); Bill Massey (thrillers, suspense, historical, military, nature/outdoors, adventure, popular science); Kate Miciak (mystery, suspense, historical fiction); Wendy McCurdy (romance, women's fiction); Danielle Perez (suspense/thrillers, women's fiction, inspiration/spirituality, self-help, personal development, health, animals); Beth Rashbaum (health, psychology, self-help, women's issues, Judaica, history, memoir). Imprints: Bantam, Dell, Delacorte Press, Delta, The Dial Press. **Sample Titles:** *The Cottage* by Danielle Steel (Delacorte, fiction); *A Painted House* by John Grisham (Dell, fiction); *Body of Lies* by Iris Johansen (Bantam, fiction); *Love, Greg and Lauren* by Greg Manning (Bantam, nonfiction); *Safe Harbor* by Luanne Rice (Bantam, fiction); *The Wisdom of Menopause* by Christiane Northup, M.D. (Bantam, nonfiction); *Inside Delta Force* by Eric Haney (Delacorte, nonfiction); *American Chica* by Marie Arana (The Dial Press, fiction).

BARBOUR PUBLISHING: HEARTSONG PRESENTS

Barbour Publishing, Inc., P.O. Box 719, Uhrichsville, OH 44683. 740-922-6045. E-mail: info@heartsongpresents.com. Website: www.barbourbooks.com or www.heartsongpresents.com. Rebecca Germany, Acquisitions Editor. **Description:** Adult mass-market inspirational romance (contemporary and historical). **Books Statistics:** 52 titles/year (300 submissions), 15% first-time authors, 90% unagented. **Proposal Process:** Query with outline (1-2 pages), 2-3 sample chapters. Accepts simultaneous queries, but not e-queries. Prefers hard copy. Responds in 3-4 months. **Payment:** Royalty (8% net). **Tips:** SASE for guidelines.

BARD PRESS

LongStreet Press, 2974 Hardman Ct. NE, Atlanta, GA 30305-3425. 800-927-1488. E-mail: ray@bardpress.com. Website: www.bardpress.com. **Description:** High-quality business and self-help books. **Books Statistics:** 3-4 titles/yr. **Proposal Process:** Submit short query with title, subject, and market. **Sample Titles:** *Owners Manual for the Personality at Work* by Pierce J. Howard, Ph.D. and Jane Mitchell Howard, M.A.; *Masters of Networking* by Ivan R. Misner, Ph.D. and Don Morgan, M.A.

BARNES & NOBLE PUBLISHING

122 Fifth Ave., New York, NY 10011. 212-633-3300. **Description:** Nathaniel Marunas, Editorial Director (music, gardening, food, art/architecture, nature, sports, illustrated books); Rick Campbell, VP Trade Publishing (reference, history, biography, humor); Sui Mon Wu, Senior Editor (self-help, New Age, humor, health); Stuart Miller, Publisher (reprints of literature, history, philosophy, puzzle books); Jeanette Limondjian, VP Coeditions (illustrated books). **Proposal Process:** No unsolicited manuscripts.

BARRICADE BOOKS, INC.

185 Bridge Plaza N, Suite 308-A, Fort Lee, NJ 07024. 201-944-7600. E-mail: cstuart@barricadebooks.com. Website: www.barricadebooks.com. Carole Stuart, Publisher. **Description:** Nonfiction on arts and entertainment, self-help, biography, humor, natural science, New Age, health, sexuality, religion, psychology,

current events, and politics. Seeks material of a controversial nature; does not publish fiction, poetry or children's books. **Books Statistics:** 20 titles/yr (200 submissions); 25% by first-time authors; 60% unagented. **Proposal Process:** Submit query, outline, 1-2 sample chapters, and SASE. Hard copy format preferred. Responds in 3-4 weeks. **Payment:** Royalty with nominal advance. **Sample Titles:** *My Face for the World to See* by Liz Renay; *Murder at the Conspiracy Convention* by Paul Krassner; *I Escaped From Auschwitz* by Rudolf Vrba; *Surviving Terrorism* by Rainer Stahlberg. **Tips:** "We look for unique, controversial nonfiction. Avoid subjects that are widely covered in the press or in other books. Writing should be short with easy-to-understand sentences."

BARRON'S EDUCATIONAL SERIES, INC.

250 Wireless Blvd., Hauppauge, NY 11788. 631-434-3311. E-mail: info@barronseduc.com. Website: www.barronseduc.com. Wayne Barr, Director of Acquisitions. **Description:** Juvenile nonfiction (science, nature, history, hobbies, and how-to), fiction for middle-grade students and teens, and picture books for ages 3-6. Also publishes adult nonfiction (test preparation, business, pet care, childcare, cookbooks, foreign languages). **Proposal Process:** Query with SASE. See guidelines.

WILLIAM L. BAUHAN, PUBLISHER

P.O.Box 443, Dublin, NH 03444. 877-832-3738.
E-mail: info@bauhanpublishing.com. Website: www.bauhanpublishing.com. William L. Bauhan, Editor. **Description:** Publishes biographies, fine arts, gardening, architecture, and history books, with an emphasis on New England. **Proposal Process:** Submit query with outline and sample chapter. **Sample Titles:** *Once: As it Was* by Griselda Jackson Ohannessian; *An Historical Guide to Rhode Island Stained Glass* by Paul Norton; *Some Sense of Transcendence* by Douglas Worth.

BAY SOMA PUBLISHING

444 De Haro St., Suite 130, San Francisco, CA 94107. 415-252-4350.
E-mail: info@baybooks.com. Website: www.baybooks.com. Floyd Yearout, Editor. **Description:** Publishes hardcover, trade paperback, coffeetable, and full-color illustrated books. Topics include gardening, interior design, and cookbooks. Also publishes companion books to television shows and other media programming. **Books Statistics:** 15 titles/yr (100 queries); 10% by first-time authors. **Payment:** Royalties vary substantially. Offers $0-$25,000 in advance. **Sample Titles:** *Compact Living* by Jane Graining; *Party! Food* by Lorna Wing; *Color in the Garden* by Nori and Sandra Pope. **Tips:** "Authors should submit ideas or outlines with biographical information and a rationale as to why the book will sell."

BAYLOR UNIVERSITY PRESS

P.O. Box 97363, Waco, TX 76798-7363. 254-710-3164.
E-mail: carey_newman@baylor.edu. Website: www.baylorpress.com. Carey C. Newman, Editor. **Description:** Scholarly nonfiction, especially religion, history, and church-state issues. **Proposal Process:** Query with outline. **Payment:** Royalty.

BEACON PRESS
25 Beacon St., Boston, MA 02108-2892. 617-742-2110. Website: www.beacon.org. Helene Atwan, Director. **Description:** General nonfiction and fiction. Subject matter includes world affairs, women's studies, anthropology, history, philosophy, religion, gay and lesbian studies, nature writing, African American studies, Latino studies, Asian American studies, and Native American studies. **Proposal Process:** Send query letter, book proposal, and curriculum vitae. Do not send entire manuscript and do not submit via e-mail or fax. Prefers agented submissions. **Sample Titles:** *Choosing Naia: A Family's Journey* by Mitchell Zuckoff; *Free for All: Defending Liberty in America Today* by Wendy Kaminer.

BEHRMAN HOUSE INC.
11 Edison Place, Springfield, NJ 07081. 973-379-7200. Website: www.behrman-house.com. David Behrman, Acquisitions. **Description:** Hebrew language and Judaica textbooks for children. Adult Jewish nonfiction. **Books Statistics:** 20 titles/yr (200 submissions); 20% by first-time authors; 95% unagented. **Proposal Process:** Query with outline and sample chapters. **Payment:** Flat fee or royalty.

BELLWETHER-CROSS PUBLISHING
18319 Highway 20 W, East Dubuque, IL 61025. 815-747-6255. E-mail: jsheldon@bellwethercross.com. Website: www.bellwethercross.com. Jana Sheldon, Acquisitions Editor. **Description:** College textbooks and lab manuals related to environmental science, biology, botany, astronomy, oceanography, business, etc. Also computer software related to the publishing industry. **Books Statistics:** 55 titles/yr (600 submissions); 100% by first-time authors; 100% unagented. **Proposal Process:** For educational materials, query with proposed book idea, list of current competitive books, and bio. For trade nonfiction, query with outline and sample chapters. Send SASE for return of all materials. Prefers electronic format. Accepts simultaneous queries. Responds within 2 weeks. **Payment:** Royalty. **Sample Titles:** *Daring To Be Different* by James A. Hatherley; *Palaces Under the Sea* by Joe Strykowski and Rena Bonem, Ph.D.

BENJAMIN CUMMINGS
Pearson plc, 1301 Sansome St., San Francisco, CA 94111. 415-402-2500. Website: www.aw.com/bc. Frank Ruggirello, VP/Editorial Director. **Description:** Educational nonfiction. Publishes textbooks and other materials on chemistry, health/kinesiology, life science, physics, and astronomy. **Proposal Process:** Send formal prospectus, TOC, sample chapters, and curriculum vitae to the appropriate editor. See website for detailed guidelines and staff listings.

THE BERKLEY PUBLISHING GROUP
Penguin Group (USA) Inc., 375 Hudson St., New York, NY 10014. 726-282-5074. E-mail: online@penguinputnam.com. Website: www.penguinputnam.com. Denise Silvestro, Senior Editor. **Description:** General-interest fiction and nonfiction; science fiction, suspense, mystery and romance. Publishes both reprints and originals.

Paperback books, except for some hardcover mysteries and science fiction. Imprints include Ace Books, Diamond, Jam, Jove, Perigee, and Riverhead Books. **Books Statistics:** 800 titles/yr. **Proposal Process:** Submit through agent only.

BERKSHIRE HOUSE PUBLISHERS

480 Pleasant St., Suite 5, Lee, MA 02138. 413-243-0303. E-mail: info@berkshire-house.com. Website: www.berkshirehouse.com. Philip Rich, Editorial Director. **Description:** Publishes a series of regional travel guides and books on specific destinations of unusual charm and cultural importance in the Berkshires and New England. Also publishes regional cookbooks and books on country inns and country living. **Books Statistics:** 8-10 titles/yr (300 submissions); 10% by first-time authors; 97% unagented. **Proposal Process:** Send query letter, outline, prospectus, and sample chapter. Considers simultaneous and electronic queries. Responds in 4 weeks. **Payment:** Royalty. **Sample Titles:** *The Berkshire Book: A Complete Guide* by Lauren Stevens; *New England Cooking: Seasons and Celebrations* by Claire Hopley. **Tips:** "Avoid submitting general cookbooks (i.e. those not related to travel, etc.), memoirs, autobiographies, and biographies and history titles that are unrelated to New England. We do not accept children's books, poetry or fiction (with the possible exception of a novel related to this region)."

BERRETT-KOEHLER PUBLISHERS INC.

235 Montgomery St., Suite 650, San Francisco, CA 94104. 415-288-0260. E-mail: bkpub@bkpub.com. Website: www.bkconnection.com. Jeevan Sivasubramaniam, Managing Editor. **Description:** Books on the workplace, business, and organizations. Seeks to publish work that inspires a more humane, ethical, and globally-conscious world. **Proposal Process:** Send proposal, outline, and 2-4 sample chapters. Make sure proposal states the need for your topic, the intended audience, your knowlege base and credentials, suggested marketing ideas, and an estimated timetable for completing the work. **Sample Titles:** *Change is Everybody's Business* by Pat McLagan; *Repacking Your Bags* by Richard J. Leider and David A. Shapiro.

THE BESS PRESS

3565 Harding Ave., Honolulu, HI 96816. 808-734-7159.
E-mail: editor@besspress.com. Website: www.besspress.com. .Reve Shapard, Editor. **Description:** Nonfiction titles on Hawaii and the Pacific for adults and children. Topics include arts/crafts, biography/memoir, cooking, gardening/plant life, humor, travel, language, and Pacific Island studies. **Proposal Process:** Send query with outline. Hard copy. **Payment:** Royalty.

BEYOND WORDS PUBLISHING, INC.

20827 NW Cornell Rd., Suite 500, Hillsboro, OR 97124. 503-531-8700.
E-mail: info@beyondword.com. Website: www.beyondword.com. Jenefer Angell, Adult Acquisitions Editor. **Description:** Photography, children's books, and books on personal growth, women, and spirituality. **Books Statistics:** 15-20 titles/yr (4,000 submissions); 90% by first-time authors; 75% unagented. **Proposal Process:** Submit

outline and 3 sample chapters for adult titles; complete manuscript for juvenile titles. Include SASE with all material. Accepts simultaneous queries, but not e-queries. Send only hard copy. Responds in 3-4 months. **Payment:** Royalty. **Sample Titles:** (Adult nonfiction) *Spiritual Writing: From Inspiration to Publication* by Deborah Levine Herman. (Children's) *It's Your Rite: Girls Coming of Age Stories*. **Tips:** No adult fiction, poetry, or fiction stories by children. Looking for original and creative children's stories. **Contact:** Barbara Leese, Children's Managing Editor.

BICK PUBLISHING HOUSE

307 Neck Rd., Madison, CT 06443. 203-245-0073. E-mail: bickpubhse@aol.com. Website: www.bickpubhouse.com. Dale Carlson, President. **Description:** Books, 64-250 pages, for teens and adults on science, philosophy, psychology, wildlife rehabilitation, and special needs/disabilities. **Proposal Process:** Submit outline and sample chapters. **Payment:** Royalty.

BILINGUAL REVIEW PRESS

Hispanic Research Center, Arizona State University, P.O. Box 872702, Tempe, AZ 85287-2702. 480-965-3867. E-mail: brp@asu.edu. Website: www.asu.edu/brp. **Description:** High-quality fiction, nonfiction, and poetry. Titles are by or about U.S. Hispanics. Publishes both established and emerging writers. **Books Statistics:** 8-10 titles/yr. **Sample Titles:** *Night Watch* by Reinaldo Bragado Bretaña; *Renaming Ecstasy: Latino Writings on the Sacred* edited by Orlando Ricardo Menes.

BINFORD & MORT PUBLISHING

5245 NE Elam Young Pkwy., Suite C, Hillsboro, OR 97124. 503-844-4960. E-mail: polly@binfordandmort.com. Website: www.binfordandmort.com. Pam Henningsen, Publisher. **Description:** Nonfiction on the Pacific Northwest. **Books Statistics:** 10 titles/yr (200 submissions); 5% by first-time authors; 90% unagented. **Proposal Process:** Send query. Accepts simultaneous queries, but not e-queries. Prefers electronic or hard-copy format. Responds in 3 months. **Payment:** Pays royalty, typically 5-10% range. **Tips:** Does not accept children's stories or poetry.

JOHN F. BLAIR, PUBLISHER

1406 Plaza Dr., Winston-Salem, NC 27103-1470. 336-768-1374. Website: www.blairpub.com. Carolyn Sakowski, Editor. **Description:** Biography, history, folklore, travel, and books with Southeastern focus. **Proposal Process:** Send query via regular mail. Does not accept electronic submissions. **Payment:** Royalty. **Sample Titles:** *Romantic Virginia* by Andrea Sutcliffe; *Voices from the Trail of Tears* edited by Vicki Rozema.

BLOOMBERG PRESS

Bloomberg LP, 100 Business Park Dr., P.O. Box 888, Princeton, NJ 08542-0888. 609-750-5070. E-mail: press@bloomberg.com. Website: www.bloomberg.com/books. Kathleen Peterson, Senior Acquisitions Editor. **Description:** Nonfiction, varying lengths, on topics such as investing, finance, and business. **Proposal Process:** Query with outline and sample chapter or send complete manuscript. Include SASE. **Payment:** Royalty.

BLOOMSBURY USA

175 5th Ave., Suite 300, New York, NY 10010. E-mail: info@bloomsburyusa.com. Website: www.bloomsburyusa.com. **Description:** High-quality publisher of fiction and nonfiction. **Sample Titles:** *City of Masks* by Daniel Hecht; *Rough Amusements* by Ben Neihart. **Tips:** See website for detailed guidelines.

BLUE HERON PUBLISHING

1234 SW Stark St., Portland, OR 97205. 503-221-6841. E-mail: submissions@blue-heronpublishing.com. Website: www.greatnorthwestbooks.com. Daniel Urban, Editorial Director. **Description:** Books on creative and technical writing; books on teaching writing and English; political mysteries and suspense novels; Northwestern and Western fiction for adults, universities and high schools (especially multicultural themes); original cookbooks; guides and how-to books that address such issues as health, wellness, finance, travel, career, and lifestyle. **Books Statistics:** 10-12 titles/yr. (400-500 submissions). **Proposal Process:** Query with outline and SASE. Accepts simultaneous and electronic queries. Responds in 2-4 months. **Payment:** Royalty. **Sample Titles:** (Fiction) *Ricochet River* by Robin Cody; *Boomboom* by Joseph Ferone. (Nonfiction) *Pebbling the Walk: Surviving Cancer Caregiving* by Steve Reed; *The Two Guys Gourmet* by Paul R. Zeissler and Kevin M. Doolan. **Tips:** Not accepting queries or manuscripts at this time. See website for updates and guidelines. **Contact:** Dennis Stovall, Publisher.

BLUEFISH RIVER PRESS

P.O. Box 1398, Duxbury, MA 02332. 781-934-5564. E-mail: info@bluefishriver-press.com. Website: www.bluefishriverpress.com. **Description:** Serious fiction and books on sports with particular emphasis on baseball. **Books Statistics:** 5 titles/yr (100 submissions); 50% by first-time authors; 50% unagented. **Proposal Process:** Submit query via e-mail. Accepts simultaneous queries. Responds in 1 week. **Payment:** Royalty 7-15%. **Contact:** David Pallai, President.

BONUS BOOKS

875 N Michigan Ave., Suite 1416, Chicago, IL 60611. E-mail: bb@bonus-books.com. Website: www.bonusbooks.com. Devon Freeny, Managing Editor. **Description:** Nonfiction trade books, both paperback and hardcover. Subjects include entertainment/pop culture, automotive, biography, current events, journalism, cooking, games/gambling, health, personal finance, regional and local topics, and sports. **Books Statistics:** 20-30 titles/yr (600-800 submissions); 20% by first-time authors; 80% unagented. **Proposal Process:** Query with complete manuscript and SASE. Simultaneous and e-queries accepted. Prefers hard copy. **Payment:** Royalty. **Sample Titles:** (Journalism) *Best Newspaper Writing* edited by Keith Woods; (Gaming) *Get the Edge at Roulette* by Christopher Pawlicki; (Regional) *Chicago the Beautiful* by Kenan Heise; (Entertainment) *Hal Lifson's 1966* by Hal Lifson.

BOOK PUBLISHING CO.
415 Farm Rd., P.O. Box 99, Summertown, TN 38483. 931-964-3571.
E-mail: info@bookpubco.com. Website: www.bookpubco.com. **Description:** Books on vegetarian nutrition and cooking, alternative health, and Native American history and culture. **Sample Titles:** *Plants of Power* by Alfred Savinelli; *Apple Cider Vinegar for Weight Loss and Good Health* by Cynthia Holzapfel.

BOWTIE PRESS
Bowtie, Inc., P.O. Box 6050, Mission Viejo, CA 92690. 949-855-8822.
E-mail: bowtiepress@fancypubs.com. Website: www.bowtiepress.com. **Description:** Nonfiction books on pets, motorcycles, hobby farming, and horses. **Books Statistics:** 20 titles/yr. **Proposal Process:** Send summary of manuscript with outline, descriptions of illustrations and appendices, market analysis, bio/resume listing expertise and previous publishing credits, and SASE. Does not accept electronic submissions. **Sample Titles:** *Careers with Horses* by Vicki Hogue; *Proficient Motorcycling* by David L. Hough; *Advice from the Doggy Lama* by Bob Lovka.

BRANDEN PUBLISHING CO.
P.O. Box 812094, Wellesley, MA 02482. 781-235-3634.
E-mail: branden@branden.com. Website: www.branden.com. Adolfo Caso, Editorial Department. **Description:** Trade publisher of fiction, children's books/YA, and nonfiction on sports, crime/law, military, international/political studies, Italian American studies, health/medicine, and reference. **Sample Titles:** *The Kaso English to Italian Dictionary* by Adolf Caso; *The Freedom Stairs* by Marilyn Weymouth Seguin.

BRASSEY'S, INC.
22841 Quicksilver Dr., Dulles, VA 20166. 703-661-1548.
E-mail: djacobs@booksintl.com. Website: www.brasseysinc.com.
Don McKeon, VP/Publisher. **Description:** Nonfiction, 35,000-200,000 words, on history (especially military history), national/international affairs, foreign policy, intelligence, defense, aviation, biography, and sports. **Books Statistics:** 80 titles/yr (900 submissions); 10% by first-time authors; 80% unagented. **Proposal Process:** Send query with synopsis, author bio, outline, 2 sample chapters, and SASE. Accepts e-queries, but prefers hard copy. Responds in 2 months. **Payment:** Advance and royalty. **Sample Titles:** *Fragments of Grace: My Secret Search for Meaning in the Strife of South Asia* by Pamela Constable; *Al Qaeda's Great Escape: The Military and the Media on Terror's Trail* by Philip Smucker. **Contact:** Donald Jacobs, Associate Acquisitions Editor.

GEORGE BRAZILLER, PUBLISHER
171 Madison Ave., New York, NY 10016. 212-889-0909. George Braziller, Publisher. **Description:** Fiction, nonfiction, international literature, art, architecture. **Proposal Process:** Send proposal with sample chapters and CV to editor's attention.

BREAKAWAY BOOKS

P.O. Box 24, Halcottsville, NY 12438. 212-898-0408.
E-mail: garth@breakawaybooks.com. Website: www.breakawaybooks.com.
Garth Battista, Publisher. **Description:** Fiction and essays on sports, specifically on the experience of being an athlete. Also publishes illustrated storybooks for kids ages 3-8, all dealing with sports (particularly running, cycling, swimming, triathlon, canoeing, kayaking, and sailing). **Books Statistics:** 8 titles/yr; 80% by first-time authors; 80% unagented. **Proposal Process:** Query (preferably by e-mail) with outline and sample chapters. Include SASE if submitting by mail. Accepts simultaneous queries. **Payment:** Royalty. **Tips:** Literary writing of the highest quality. No genre stories, how-tos, or celebrity bios. "Our goal is to bring to light literary writing on the athletic experience."

BRICK TOWER PRESS

1230 Park Ave., New York, NY 10128. 212-427-7139. Website: www.bricktowerpress.com. **Description:** Cookery, gardening, autobiography, military and maritime history. **Sample Titles:** (Cooking) *Fresh Bread Companion* by Liz Clark; (Maritime) *Return of the Coffin Ships-The Derbyshire Enigma* by Bernard Edwards; (Biography) *Reflexions* by Richard Olney.

BRISTOL PUBLISHING ENTERPRISES

2714 McCone Ave., Hayward, CA 94545. 800-346-4889. Website: www.bristolpublishing.com. Aidan Wylde, Editor. **Description:** Cookbooks, craftbooks, health, and pet care. **Books Statistics:** 12-20 titles/yr (300 submissions); 18% first-time authors; 100% unagented. **Proposal Process:** Query with outline, sample chapters, and SASE. Accepts simultaneous queries, but not e-queries. Prefers hard copy. **Payment:** Royalty. **Sample Titles:** *Quick & Easy Low-Carb Recipes* by Joanna White; *Quick & Easy Pasta Recipes* by Coleen and Bob Simmons; *Gourmet Dog Biscuits* by Sondra Macdonald. **Tips:** See website for guidelines.

BROADWAY BOOKS

Doubleday Broadway Publising Group/Random House, Inc.
1745 Broadway, New York, NY 10019. 212-782-9000.
Website: www.randomhouse/broadway. **Description:** Adult nonfiction; small and very selective fiction list. **Proposal Process:** No unsolicited submissions. Query first.

BROWNTROUT PUBLISHERS, INC.

P.O. Box 280070, San Francisco, CA 94128-0070. 650-340-9800.
E-mail: production@browntrout.com. Website: www.browntrout.com. **Description:** Publishes fine art and photography in the format of calendars, books, and postcard books. **Proposal Process:** Accepts submissions from professional photographers only. Photographers should send query letter with tear sheets or samples if available. Material cannot be returned.

BUCKNELL UNIVERSITY PRESS

Bucknell University, Lewisburg, PA 17837. 570-577-3674. Website: www.departments.bucknell.edu/univ_press. Greg Clingham, Director. **Description:** Scholarship and criticism in English, American and comparative literature, theory and cultural studies, history, philosophy, modern languages (especially Hispanic and Latin American studies), anthropology, political science, classics, cultural geography, or any combination of the above. **Books Statistics:** 38 titles/yr (500 submissions); 50% by first-time authors; 99% unagented. **Proposal Process:** Query with outline and sample chapters. No simultaneous or electronic queries. Hard copy only. Responds in 1 month to proposals, 3-4 months to manuscripts. **Payment:** Royalty, 10% net. **Sample Titles:** *Being in Common: Nation, Subject, and Community in Latin American Literature and Culture* by Silvia Rosman; *Freedom, Slavery, and Absolutionism: Corneille, Pascal, Racine* by Zia Elmarsafy. **Tips:** "Excellent scholarship in the humanities and related social sciences; no 'popular' material."

BUILDERBOOKS.COM

National Assn. of Home Builders, 1201 15th St. NW, Washington, DC 20005-2800. 800-368-5242. E-mail: publishing@nahb.org. Website: www.builderbooks.com. **Description:** Publishes educational print and electronic products for builders, remodelers, developers, sales/marketing professionals, and consumers in the residential construction industry. **Books Statistics:** 25 titles/yr; 99% unagented. **Proposal Process:** Query with outline and sample chapter. Responds in 1-2 months. **Payment:** Royalty. **Sample Titles:** *Pro Builder: Business Planning* by Steve Maltzman and Mike Benshoof; *Decorating with Architechtural Trimwork* by Jay Silber. **Tips:** Writers must be experts. **Contact:** Dean Innerarity (dinnerarity@nahb.org); Doris M. Tennyson, Senior Acquisitions Editor (dtennyson@nahb.org).

BULFINCH PRESS

Time Warner Book Group, 1271 Avenue of the Americas, New York, NY 10020. 212-522-8700. Website: www.bulfinchpress.com. Michael L. Sand, Executive Editor. **Description:** Illustrated fine art and photography books, coffee table books, and books on photojournalism, painting, and design. **Books Statistics:** 70-80 titles/yr. **Proposal Process:** Query with outline or proposal, sample artwork and text (no originals), author/artist bio, and SASE. Accepts simultaneous queries, but not e-queries. Responds in 1-4 weeks. **Sample Titles:** *Stanley Kubrick: A Life in Pictures* by Christiane Kubrick; *The Breathing Field: Yoga as Art* by Wyatt Townley. **Tips:** "Visual material is crucial." **Contact:** Jared Silverman, Dept. Assistant.

BULL PUBLISHING

P.O.Box 1377, Boulder, CO 80304. 800-676-2855. E-mail: bullpublishing@msn.com. Website: www.bullpub.com. Jim Bull, Publisher. **Description:** Health, child care, nutrition, and self-help. **Sample Titles:** *Habits Not Diets: The Secret to Lifetime Weight Control* by James M. Ferguson, M.D.; *Hormonal Balance: Understanding Hormones, Weight, and Your Metabolism* by Scott Isaacs, M.D.

BURFORD BOOKS

32 Morris Ave., Springfield, NJ 07081. 973-258-0960.
Website: www.burfordbooks.com. Peter Burford, Acquisitions Editor. **Description:** Books on sports, the outdoors, military history, food, and wine. **Books Statistics:** 25 titles/yr (250 submissions); 50% by first-time authors; 50% unagented. **Proposal Process:** Query with outline. Considers simultaneous queries. Prefers hard-copy format. Responds in 3 weeks. **Payment:** Royalty. **Sample Titles:** *The GPS Handbook* by Bob Egbert; *The Really Useful Little Book of Knots* by Peter Owen. **Tips:** Seeks well-written books on practically anything that can be done outside.

BURNHAM PUBLISHERS

111 N Canal St., Suite 955, Chicago, IL 60606. 312-930-9446.
Richard Meade, Senior Editor. **Description:** College textbooks in the fields of political science, archaeology, psychology, sociology, and mass communications. **Books Statistics:** 30 titles/yr (200 queries); 90% unagented. **Proposal Process:** Submit query, 2 sample chapters, curriculum vitae, and SASE. Responds in 1 month to queries. **Sample Titles:** *Living Off Crime* by Ken Tunnell; *History of Nazi Germany* by Joseph Bendersky; *Cities in the Third Wave* by Leonard Ruchelman. **Tips:** Welcomes new submissions; virtually all manuscripts are written by college professors.

BUTTE PUBLICATIONS, INC.

P.O. Box 1328, Hillsboro, OR 97123-1328. 503-648-9791. Website: www.buttepublications.com. **Description:** Publishes material related to deafness and education, especially for teachers of PreK-12 students. Also publishes college textbooks and resources for parents and professionals. Concentration is on the reading and writing aspects of teaching children who are deaf.

C&T PUBLISHING

1651 Challenge Dr., Concord, CA 94520. E-mail: ctinfo@ctpub.com.
Website: www.ctpub.com. Darra Williamson, Editor-in-Chief. **Description:** Quilting books, 48-200 finished pages. Focus is how-to, although will consider picture, inspirational, or history books on quilting. **Proposal Process:** Send query, outline, or sample chapters. Simultaneous queries considered. **Payment:** Royalty. **Sample Titles:** *Q is For Quilt* by Diana McClun and Laura Nownes; *America From the Heart* by Karey Bresenhan; *15 Two-Block Quilts* by Claudia Olson.

CAMBRIDGE UNIVERSITY PRESS

40 W 20th St., New York, NY 10011-4211. 212-924-3900. Website: www.cup.org.
Richard Ziemacki, Director. **Description:** Scholarly books and college textbooks. Subjects include the behavioral, biological, physical, and social sciences. Also computer science and technology, as well as the humanities such as literature, music, and religion. **Sample Titles:** *Life at the Limits: Organisms in Extreme Environments* by David A. Wharton; *The Cambridge Illustrated History of Religions* edited by John Bowker; *Handbook for Academic Authors* by Beth Luey.

CAREER PRESS/NEW PAGE BOOKS

3 Tice Rd., Franklin Lakes, NJ 07417. 201-848-0310. E-mail: mlewis@nisusa.net. Website: www.careerpress.com. Michael Lewis, Acquisitions Editor. **Description:** Adult nonfiction books on business, career, education, personal finance, and reference. Seeks to publish high-quality work that will help improve the lives of their readers. **Proposal Process:** Prefers complete manuscript, but will consider proposals. Include TOC, estimated book length, two complete sample chapters, author bio, market analysis, and previously published clips. Responds within 30 days.

CAROUSEL PRESS

P.O. Box 6038, Berkeley, CA 94706-0038. 510-527-5849. E-mail: carole@carousel-press.com. Website: www.carousel-press.com. Carole T. Meyers, Publisher. **Description:** U.S. and Europe round-up travel guides. **Books Statistics:** 1-2 title/yr (100 submissions); 50% by first-time authors; 75% unagented. **Proposal Process:** Send letter, TOC, sample chapter, and SASE. Simultaneous and electronic queries accepted. Prefers hard copy. **Payment:** Modest advance and royalty. **Tips:** "We publish 1-2 new books each year and will consider out-of-print books that the author wants to update."

CARROLL AND GRAF PUBLISHERS, INC.

Avalon Publishing Group, 161 William St., Fl. 16, New York, NY 10038. 646-375-2570. Website: www.avalonpub.com. Tina Pohlman, Senior Editor. **Description:** General fiction and nonfiction. **Books Statistics:** 120 titles/yr; 10% by first-time authors. **Proposal Process:** No unagented submissions.

CARSON-DELLOSA PUBLISHING CO., INC.

P.O. Box 35665, Greensboro, NC 27425. 336-632-0084. Website: www.carsondellosa.com. Pam Hill, Product Acquisitions. **Description:** Supplemental educational materials, including teacher resource books, activity books, and student workbooks, for PK-8th grade teachers. **Books Statistics:** 100 titles/yr. **Proposal Process:** Contact for submission guidelines. **Tips:** "We also have a Christian products division. We welcome book proposals and manuscripts from teachers and writers. Note that we do not accept fiction, children's storybooks, or poetry."

CASSANDRA PRESS

P.O. Box 150868, San Rafael, CA 94915. 415-382-8507. E-mail: starvibe@indra.com. Fred Rubenfeld, President. **Description:** Publisher of New age, holistic health, metaphysical, and psychological books. **Books Statistics:** 2-3 titles/yr; 50% by first-time authors; 50% unagented. **Proposal Process:** Query with outline and sample chapters, or complete manuscript. Include SASE. Accepts simultaneous queries, but not e-queries. Prefers hard copy format. **Payment:** Royalty, 6-8%. **Contact:** Editorial Dept.

THE CATHOLIC UNIVERSITY OF AMERICA PRESS

240 Leahy Hall, 620 Michigan Ave. NE, Washington, DC 20064. 202-319-5052. E-mail: cua-press@cua.edu. Website: www.cuapress.cua.edu. David J. McGonagle, Director. **Description:** Scholarly works related to the humanities, namely ecclesiastical and secular history, literature, political theory, philosophy, social studies, and theology. **Books Statistics:** 25 titles/yr; 50% by first-time authors; 100% unagented. **Proposal Process:** Submit abstract or TOC, resumé, and list of previous publications. **Sample Titles:** *The Orphans of Byzantium* by Timothy S. Miller; *Fiction, Intuition, and Creativity* by Angela Hague.

CCLS PUBLISHING HOUSE

Cultural Center for Language Studies, 3191 Coral Way, Suite 114, Miami, FL 33145. 305-529-8563. E-mail: info@cclscorp.com. Website: www.cclscorp.com. Luiz Goncalves, President. **Description:** Language school and publishing house whose focus is to teach and create both multimedia and print language-instruction materials for students learning English or Spanish.

CHAMPION PRESS, LTD

4308 Blueberry Rd., Fredonia, WI 53021. Website: www.championpress.com. **Description:** Nonfiction titles in the areas of cooking, fitness, self-help, new and innovating home management topics. Also publishes a limited number of education and homeschooling titles. No longer seeking submissions in fiction, poetry, or parenting. **Proposal Process:** Send proposal including market anaylsis, marketing plan and ideas, bio with credentials, first 3 chapters, and SASE. Do not phone or e-mail. **Sample Titles:** *The Complete Crockery Cookbook* by Wendy Louise; *Squeezing Your Size 14 Self Into a Size 6 World* by Carrie Myers Smith; *The Frantic Family Cookbook* by Leanne Ely. **Tips:** "Please follow our guidelines and be familiar with the types of books we publish prior to sending your project our way."

CHARLES RIVER MEDIA

10 Downer Ave., Hingham, MA 02043. 781-740-0400. Website: www.charlesriver.com. **Description:** Books on web design, programming, networking, game development, and graphics.

CHECKMARK BOOKS

Facts On File, Inc., 132 W 31st St., New York, NY 10001-2006. 212-967-8800. E-mail: jchambers@factsonfile.com. Website: www.factsonfile.com. James Chambers, Editor-in-Chief. **Description:** Focuses on careers, education, health, popular history and culture, fashion, and fitness. Looking for materials that fit a particular market niche that are high-quality, with a strong reference component. **Proposal Process:** Query with sample chapters or outline. **Payment:** Advance against royalty. **Tips:** Does not publish memoirs, autobiographies, or fiction.

CHELSEA GREEN PUBLISHING CO.

P.O. Box 428, White River Junction, VT 05001. 802-295-6300.
E-mail: mbrant@chelseagreen.com. Website: www.chelseagreen.com. Marcy Brant,
Editorial Assistant. **Description:** Independent publisher specializing in nonfiction
books on environmental issues. Also publishes cookbooks, biographies, and reference
titles. **Books Statistics:** 15-20 titles/yr; 30% by first-time authors; 85% unagented.
Proposal Process: Submit brief proposal, TOC, sample chapter, description of previously published works and SASE. **Sample Titles:** *This Organic Life* by Joan Dye
Gussow; *The Slow Food Guide to New York City* by Patrick Martins and Ben Watson;
The Solar House: Passive Heating and Cooling by Dan Chiras. **Tips:** "We are an environmental publisher of titles with a strong, practical orientation. Topics include
organic agriculture and food, shelter, renewable energy, and right livelihood."

CHICAGO REVIEW PRESS

814 N Franklin St., Chicago, IL 60610. 312-337-0747. Website: www.chicagoreview-
press.com. Cynthia Sherry, Editorial Director. **Description:** Nonfiction in the areas
of parenting, how-to, popular science, biography/memoir, general nonfiction, and
other regional topics. Also activity books for kids. **Proposal Process:** Query with outline, resumé, competition survey, and sample chapters. Enclose SASE for response in
8-10 weeks.

CHINA BOOKS & PERIODICALS, INC.

2929 24th St., San Francisco, CA 94110-4126. 415-282-2994. E-mail: info@china-
books.com. Website: www.chinabooks.com. Greg Jones, Senior Editor. **Description:**
Books on all subjects relating to China, Chinese culture, and Chinese-American history. Adult nonfiction of varying lengths, also juvenile picture books, fiction, nonfiction, and YA books. **Books Statistics:** 3 titles/yr; 50% by first-time authors; 95% unagented. **Payment:** Royalty, 6-8% of net. **Sample Titles:** *Rise of Digital China* by E.
Wong and G. Lee; *Healing Energy* by Virginia Newton. **Tips:** No novels or poetry.
No "My trip to China" proposals.

CHRONICLE BOOKS

85 Second St., Fl. 6, San Francisco, CA 94105. 415-537-3730.
E-mail: frontdesk@chroniclebooks.com. Website: www.chroniclebooks.com.
Description: Fiction, children's books, giftbooks, and nonfiction titles on art, photography, architecture, design, travel, nature, and food. **Proposal Process:** Send
proposal (complete manuscript for fiction) with SASE. Proposal should include cover
letter with brief description of project, outline, introduction, sample text/chapters,
sample illustrations/photographs (duplicates, not originals), market analysis, and brief
bio. **Tips:** Does not publish romances, science fiction, fantasy, westerns, or other
genre fiction. **Contact:** Editorial Dept.

CLARKSON POTTER/PUBLISHERS

The Crown Publishing Group/Random House, Inc., 201 E 50th St., New York, NY
10022. 212-751-2600. Website: www.randomhouse.com. Lauren Shakely, Senior Vice

President/Editorial Director. **Description:** Illustrated trade books about such topics as cooking, gardening, and decorating. **Proposal Process:** Submissions accepted through agents only. **Sample Titles:** *Eden on Their Minds: American Gardeners with Bold Visions* by Starr Ockenga; *The Art of Expecting* by Veronique Vienne.

CLEAR LIGHT PUBLISHERS

823 Don Diego, Santa Fe, NM 87501-4224. 800-253-2747.
E-mail: clpublish@aol.com. Website: www.clearlightbooks.com. Harmon Houghton, Publisher. **Description:** Focuses on Southwestern themes, especially Native American cultures. Publishes nonfiction, fiction, picture books, and young adult books. Fiction includes: multicultural, historical, inspirational and regional. Seeking nonfiction mss on history, multicultural, ethnic issues, nature, religion, biographies of Native Americans. **Proposal Process:** Query with SASE.

CLEIS PRESS, INC.

P.O. Box 14684, San Francisco, CA 94114-0684. 415-575-4700. Website: www.cleis-press.com. Frederique Delacoste, Acquisitions Editor. **Description:** Lesbian and gay studies, literature by women, human rights, sexuality, and travel. Fiction and non-fiction, 200 pages. No poetry. **Payment:** Royalty. **Tips:** Enclose return postage with all submissions or material will not be returned.

CLOVER PARK PRESS

P.O. Box 5067-T, Santa Monica, CA 90409-5067. 310-452-7657. E-mail: clover-parkpr@earthlink.net. Website: http://home.earthlink.net/~cloverparkpr. Martha Grant, Acquisitions Editor. **Description:** Nonfiction adult books on California (history, natural history, travel, culture, or the arts), biography of extraordinary women, nature, travel, exploration, and scientific/medical discovery. **Proposal Process:** Query with outline, sample chapter, author bio, and SASE.

COFFEE HOUSE PRESS

27 N Fourth St., Suite 400, Minneapolis, MN 55401. 612-338-0125.
Website: www.coffeehousepress.org. Allan Kornblum, Publisher. **Description:** Publishes literary novels, full-length short story collections, poetry, essays, memoir, and anthologies. **Books Statistics:** 12 titles/yr (5,000 submissions); 20% by first-time authors; 20% unagented. **Proposal Process:** Query with sample chapters (20-30 pages) and SASE. Considers simultaneous queries. Send hard copy only; do not send via e-mail or fax. Responds in 4-6 weeks to queries, 4-5 months to manuscripts. **Payment:** Royalty. **Sample Titles:** *The Impossibly* by Laird Hunt; *That Kind of Sleep* by Susan Atefat-Peckman; *Circle K Cycles* by Karen Tei Yamashita; *The Man Who Swam With Beavers* by Nancy Lord. **Tips:** No genre fiction (mysteries, gothic romances, westerns, science fiction) or books for children.

COLLECTOR BOOKS

A Division of Schroeder Publishing Co., P.O. Box 3009, Paducah, KY 42002. 270-898-6211. E-mail: editor@collectorbooks.com. Website: www.collectorbooks.com. Gail Ashburn, Editor. **Description:** Publishes books for dealers and collectors on items such as dolls, toys, antiques, Depression glass, pottery and porcelain, china and dinnerware, quilts, jewelry, furniture, and other memorabilia. **Books Statistics:** 50 titles/yr (400 submissions); 50% by first-time authors. **Proposal Process:** Submit proposal with resumé or brief bio, outline, fully developed introduction, and at least one fully developed chapter accompanied by sample photos. For value guide proposals, please include a sample price guide for every item pictured with explanation of how you arrived at those prices. Responds in 3 weeks. **Payment:** Royalty 5% of retail price. **Sample Titles:** *Collector's Encyclopedia of Depression Glass* by Gene Florence; *Star Wars Super Collector's Wish Book* by Geoffrey Carlton.

COLLECTORS PRESS, INC.

P.O. Box 230986, Portland, OR 97281. 503-684-3030.
E-mail: info@collectorspress.com. Website: www.collectorspress.com. Richard Perry, Publisher. **Description:** "We are an award-winning publisher of nostalgic art and retro cooking books. We do not publish fiction or children's books." **Books Statistics:** 20 titles/yr; 50% by first-time authors; 80% unagented. **Proposal Process:** Send proposal. Include SASE for return of manuscript. **Payment:** Flat fee or royalty. **Sample Titles:** *Come Fly With Us! A Global History of the Airline Hostess* by Johanna Omelia and Michael Waldock; *Road Trip America* by Andrew Wood; *Retro Pies: A Collection of Celebrated Family Recipes* by Linda Everett; *Retro Romance: Classic Tips for Today's Couples* by Cheryl and Joe Homme. **Tips:** See website for details.

CONARI PRESS

Imprint of Red Wheel/Weiser, LLC, 368 Congress St., Boston, MA 02210.
617-542-1324. Website: www.redwheelweiser.com. Ms. Pat Bryce, Editor.
Description: Publishes books on health, personal growth, spirituality, women's issues, and relationships. **Proposal Process:** Submit outline, sample chapters, and 6-1/2" x 9-1/2" SASE. Hard copy only. Accepts simultaneous queries, but not e-queries. Responds in 3-6 months. **Payment:** Royalty. **Tips:** "Please visit our website for detailed submission guidelines. Before submitting any materials, please study our books in a bookstore, library, or publisher's catalog."

CONFLUENCE PRESS

Lewis-Clark State College, 500 Eighth Ave., Lewiston, ID 83501-2698. 208-792-2336. E-mail: conpress@lcsc.edu. Website: www.confluencepress.com. James R. Hepworth, Editor. **Description:** Trade poetry, fiction, novels, essays, literary criticism, photography, art, science, and folklore. Special interest in the literature of the contemporary and American West. **Books Statistics:** 2 titles/yr (1,000 submissions); 50% by first-time authors; 75% unagented. **Proposal Process:** Send query with formal cover letter and SASE. Accepts simultaneous queries. Prefers hard copy. Responds in 6 weeks. **Payment:** Royalty. **Sample Titles:** (Fiction) *The Wild Awake* by Paulann Petersen; (Song Lyrics) *Earth & Sky: The Laurie Lewis Songbook* by Laurie Lewis; (Poetry) *Even in Quiet Places* by William Stafford. **Tips:** "We are currently seeking writing about the contemporary American Northwest."

CONTEMPORARY BOOKS

Imprint of McGraw-Hill Professional, Prudential Plaza, 130 E Randolph St., Suite 900, Chicago, IL 60601. 312-233-6520. **Description:** Nonfiction trade books with a strong focus on sports and fitness, parenting, self-help, general reference, health, careers, foreign language, and dictionaries. **Books Statistics:** 400 titles/yr (600 submissions); 10% by first-time authors; 20% unagented. **Proposal Process:** Query with outline. Prefers hard copy. Considers simultaneous queries. **Payment:** Royalty 7.5% list paper, 10-15% list cloth or flat fee-typical range is $1,000-$4,000. **Sample Titles:** *Mindgames: Phil Jackson's Long Strange Journey* by Roland Lazenby; *Successful Direct Marketing Methods* by Bob Stone.

CONTINUUM INTERNATIONAL PUBLISHING GROUP

370 Lexington Ave., Suite 1700, New York, NY 10017. 212-953-5858. Website: www.continuumbooks.com. **Description:** General-interest trade titles, scholarly titles, and reference materials in the areas of literature, the arts, history, religion, philosophy, and social issues. **Proposal Process:** Query with SASE. **Sample Titles:** *All about Oscar* by Emanuel Levy; *Truly Our Sister: A Theology of Mary in the Communion of Saints* by Elizabeth A. Johnson. **Contact:** Evander Lomke, Vice President/Senior Editor; Frank Oveis, Vice President/Senior Editor.

COPPER CANYON PRESS

P.O. Box 271, Port Townsend, WA 98368. 360-385-4925.
E-mail: poetry@coppercanyonpress.org. Website: www.coppercanyonpress.org. Sam Hamill, Editor. **Description:** Poetry publisher. **Books Statistics:** 18 titles/yr (1,000 submissions); 10% by first-time authors; 95% unagented. **Proposal Process:** No unsolicited manuscripts. **Payment:** Royalty. **Sample Titles:** *Cool, Calm & Collected* by Carolyn Kizer; *Spring Essence: The Poetry of Ho Xuan Huong* translated by John Balaban. **Tips:** Currently not accepting unsolicited manuscripts; check website for updates. Also offers annual Hayden Carruth Award for first, second and third books. **Contact:** Michael Wiegers.

COUNCIL OAK BOOKS

1615 S Baltimore, Suite 3, Tulsa, OK 74119. 918-587-6454. E-mail: pmillichap@gigplanet.com. Website: www.counciloakbooks.com. Paulette Millichap, Editor. **Description:** Distinguished nonfiction books based in personal, intimate history (letters, diaries, memoir and first-person adventure/travel); Native American history and spiritual teachings; small inspirational gift books; unique vintage photo books and Americana. **Books Statistics:** 10 titles/yr (300 submissions); 25% by first-time authors; 75% unagented. **Proposal Process:** Query with outline and SASE. Do not send complete manuscript. Accepts simultaneous and electronic queries. Prefers hard copy. **Payment:** Royalty. **Sample Titles:** *The Blessing: A Memoir* by Gregory

Orr. **Tips:** No fiction, poetry, or children's books. "We're looking for unique, elegant voices whose history, teachings and experiences illuminate our lives."

COUNTERPOINT PRESS

Member of the Perseus Book Group, 387 Park Ave. S, New York, NY 10016. 212-340-8138. Website: www.counterpointpress.com. **Description:** Serious literary works in the areas of history, philosophy, art, nature, science, poetry, and fiction. **Sample Titles:** *Deus Lo Volt* by Evan S. Connell; *Appetites* by Caroline Knapp. **Contact:** Acquisitions Editor.

THE COUNTRYMAN PRESS, INC.

W.W. Norton & Co., P.O. Box 748, Woodstock, VT 05091. 802-457-4826. Website: www.countrymanpress.com. **Description:** Publishes nonfiction material on New England history and culture. Topics include country living, gardening, nature and the environment, and travel. Also publishes regional guidebooks on hiking, walking, canoeing, kayaking, bicycling, mountain biking, cross-country skiing, and flyfishing for all parts of the U.S. **Proposal Process:** Submit query or outline, 3 sample chapters, and SASE. **Payment:** Royalty.

CRAFTSMAN BOOK COMPANY

6058 Corte del Cedro, P.O. Box 6500, Carlsbad, CA 92018. 760-438-7828. E-mail: jacobs@costbook.com. Website: www.craftsman-book.com. Laurence D. Jacobs, Editor. **Description:** Construction manuals for the professional builder and contractor. **Books Statistics:** 12 titles/yr (30 submissions); 90% by first-time authors; 100% unagented. **Proposal Process:** Query with outline and SASE. Simultaneous and electronic queries accepted. Prefers hard copy format. **Payment:** Royalty. **Sample Titles:** *Contractor's Plain-English Legal Guide* by Queda Story; *Contractor's Guide to Quickbooks Pro* by Karen Mitchell. **Tips:** "We're looking for simple, practical hands-on text written in the second person. Only material for the professional builder. No handyman or do-it-yourself material."

CRANE HILL PUBLISHERS

3608 Clairmont Ave., Birmingham, AL 35222. 205-714-3007. E-mail: cranies@crane-hill.com. Website: www.cranehill.com. **Description:** History, biography/memoir, folklore, cookbooks, art, photography, humor, travel, and mind/body/spirit. "We search for quality books that reflect the history, perceptions, experience, and customs of people in regional locales around the U.S." **Payment:** Royalty. **Sample Titles:** *A Morning Cup of Yoga* by Jane Trechsel; *Whistlestop Cafe Cookbook* by Mary Jo Smith McMichael; *Lighthouse Ghosts* by Norma Elizabeth and Bruce Roberts.

CREATIVE HOMEOWNER

Division of Federal Marketing Corp., 24 Park Way, P.O. Box 38, Upper Saddle River, NJ 07458-0038. 201-934-7100. E-mail: sharon.ranftle@creativehomeowner.com. Website: www.creativehomeowner.com. Timothy O. Bakke, Editorial Director. **Description:** Books on lifestyle for the home and garden. Topics include interior design/decorating, gardening/landscaping, and home improvement/repair. **Books Statistics:** 12-16 titles/yr (20-30 submissions); 70% by first-time authors; 98% unagented. **Proposal Process:** Query. Accepts simultaneous and electronic queries. Prefers hard copy. Responds in 2-4 months. **Payment:** Royalty or flat fee. **Sample Titles:** *Decorating with Architectural Trimwork* by Jay Silber. **Tips:** Avoid passive voice. Prefers straightforward, expository, instructional text in clear language. **Contact:** Sharon Ranftle.

CREATIVE PUBLISHING INTERNATIONAL

18705 Lake Drive E, Chanhassen, MN 55317. 952-936-4700. Website: www.creativepub.com. **Description:** How-to books, as well as books on nature, photography, and wildlife books for children and adults under the NorthWord Press imprint. Also offers multilingual educational, nonfiction books and multimedia products for children, teachers, and parents under the Two-Can imprint.

CROSS CULTURAL PUBLICATIONS, INC.

P.O. Box 506, Notre Dame, IN 46556. 219-273-6526. E-mail: crosscult@aol.com. Website: crossculturalpub.com. Cyriac K. Pullapilly, General Editor. **Description:** All academic disciplines, also general-interest books. Special interest in intercultural and interfaith issues. Prefers books that push the boundaries of knowledge and existing systems of religion, philosophy, politics, economics, ethics, justice and arts (whether through fiction, nonfiction, or poetry). **Books Statistics:** 30 titles/yr (5,000 submissions); 30% by first-time authors; 90% unagented. **Proposal Process:** Send proposal with TOC, resumé, and SASE. Considers simultaneous and electronic queries. Prefers hard copy. **Payment:** Royalty. **Tips:** "Our primary concern is subject matter, then organization, clarity of argument, literary style. No superficially argued books."

THE CROSSING PRESS

Ten Speed Press, P.O. Box 7123, Berkeley, CA 94707. 510-559-1600.
E-mail: elaine@crossingpress.com. Website: www.crossingpress.com.
Elaine Goldman Gill, Publisher. **Description:** Publisher of books, vidoes, and audios on natural and alternative health, spirituality, personal growth, self-help, empowerment, and cookbooks. **Proposal Process:** Submit proposal with outline, market analysis, sample chapters, and author bio. Responds in 8 weeks. **Payment:** Royalty. **Sample Titles:** *Pocket Herbal Reference Guide* by Debra St. Claire; *Natural Healing for Dogs & Cats* by Diane Stein; *A Magical Guide to Love & Sex* by Cassandra Eason; *Wicca: The Complete Craft* by D.J. Conway. **Tips:** No longer accepts fiction, poetry, or calendars. **Contact:** Acquisitions Editor.

CUMBERLAND HOUSE PUBLISHING

431 Harding Industrial Dr., Nashville, TN 37211. 615-832-1171. E-mail: info@cumberlandhouse.com. Website: www.cumberlandhouse.com. Tilly Katz, Acquisitions Editor. **Description:** Nonfiction titles in history, sports, and cooking. Also publishes some mystery titles and Christian titles. **Books Statistics:** 60 titles/yr (1,300 submis-

sions); 50% by first-time authors; 75% unagented. **Proposal Process:** Query with outline. No simultaneous or electronic queries. Hard copy only. Responds in 3-6 months. **Payment:** Royalty. **Sample Titles:** *Stonewall Jackson's Book of Maxims* by James Robertson Jr.; *Goodnight John-Boy* by Earl Hamner and Ralph E. Giffin. **Tips:** No poetry or westerns. Considers fiction, but stronger interest in nonfiction.

CURBSTONE PRESS

321 Jackson St., Willimantic, CT 06226. 860-423-5110. E-mail: info@curbstone.org. Website: www.curbstone.org. Judith Doyle, Alexander Taylor, Co-Directors. **Description:** Fiction, creative nonfiction, poetry books, and picture books that reflect a commitment to social change, with an emphasis on contemporary writing from Latin America and Latino communities in the U.S. **Proposal Process:** Query with 10-20 sample pages. Does not accept complete manuscripts. Hard copy only. **Payment:** Royalty. **Sample Titles:** *My Mother's Island* by Marnie Mueller; *Maroon* by Danielle Legros Georges. **Tips:** Also sponsers the Miguel Mármol Prize for Latina/o First Fiction. **Contact:** Alexander Taylor, Co-Director.

DA CAPO PRESS

Perseus Books Group, 11 Cambridge Center, Cambridge, MA 02142. 617-252-5200. Website: www.dacapopress.com. **Description:** General nonfiction on film, dance, theatre, history, literature, art, sports, African American studies, pregnancy, parenting, health, fitness, and relationships. **Books Statistics:** 60 titles/yr (250 submissions). **Proposal Process:** Query with outline, sample chapters and author bio/curriculum vitae. Accepts simultaneous queries, but not e-queries. Hard copy only. Responds in 2-3 months. **Payment:** Royalty. **Contact:** Dan O'Neil.

DALKEY ARCHIVE PRESS

The Center for Book Culture, ISU Campus Box 8905, Normal, IL 61790-8905. 309-438-7555. E-mail: contact@dalkeyarchive.com. Website: www.dalkeyarchive.com. John O'Brien, Founder/Publisher. **Description:** Mostly publishes reprints of literary works and translations from the past 100 years. Publishes some original, avant-garde, experimental fiction. **Books Statistics:** 2-4 original titles/yr. **Proposal Process:** Query with SASE via regular mail. No unsolicited manuscripts. Responds in 2-4 months. **Contact:** Submissions Editor.

THE DANA PRESS

The Dana Foundation, 900 Fifteenth St., NW, Washington, DC 20005. 202-737-9200. E-mail: lbarnes@dana.org. Website: www.dana.org/books/press. **Description:** Publishes health and popular science books about the brain for the general reader.

JOHN DANIEL AND CO.

Daniel & Daniel Publishers, Inc., P.O. Box 21922, Santa Barbara, CA 93121. 805-962-1780. E-mail: dandd@danielpublishing.com. Website: www.danielpublishing.com. John Daniel, Publisher. **Description:** Publishes in the field of belles lettres: literary fiction, poetry, memoirs, and essays. "Belles lettres, for us, means stylish and elegant writing. We are looking for good writing that works, poetry that sings, memoirs and essays that make us think." **Books Statistics:** 4 titles/yr (5,000 submissions); 25% by first-time authors; 100% unagented. **Proposal Process:** For novels, nonfiction, and short stories, send synopsis or outline and no more than 50 sample pages. For poetry, send 12-15 sample poems. Send hard copy only; does not accept material via e-mail, fax, or phone. Accepts simultaneous queries. Responds in 4 weeks. **Payment:** Royalty. **Sample Titles:** (Fiction) *The House on Q Street* by Ann L. McLaughlin; *Unplugged* by Paul McComas; (Poetry) *Go Where the Landshed Takes You* by Jane Glazer; (Essays) *Keeping Warm: Selected Essays and Stories* by Max Schott. **Tips:** Does not accept children's books, genre fiction, cookbooks, or how-to books. See website for specific submission guidelines.

JONATHAN DAVID PUBLISHERS, INC.

68-22 Eliot Ave., Middle Village, NY 11379. 718-456-8611. E-mail: info@jdbooks.com. Website: www.jdbooks.com. Alfred J. Kolatch, Editor-in-Chief. **Description:** Nonfiction titles on sports, reference, and biography. Area of specialization is popular Judaica. **Books Statistics:** 25 titles/yr; 25% by first-time authors; 90% unagented. **Proposal Process:** Query with brief synopsis, TOC, sample chapter, resumé, and SASE. No simultaneous queries. Accepts e-queries, but prefers hard copy. **Payment:** Royalty or outright purchase. **Sample Titles:** (Sports) *New York Yankees: Seasons of Glory* by William Hageman and Warren Wilbert; (Biography) *Great African-American Women* by Darryl Lyman; (Judaica) *Greatest Jewish Stories* by David Patterson.

DAVIES-BLACK PUBLISHING

Division of Consulting Psychologists Press, Inc., 3803 E Bayshore Rd., Palo Alto, CA 94303. 650-969-8901. E-mail: clk@starband.net. Website: www.cpp-db.com. Connie Kallback, Acquisitions Editor. **Description:** Professional and trade titles in business and careers with a focus on leadership and management, organization development, human resource development, career management, and professional improvement. **Sample Titles:** *What's Your Type of Career?* by Donna Dunning; *Breakthrough Creativity* by Lynne C. Levesque; *Successful Woman's Guide to Working Smart* by Caitlin Williams.

DAVIS PUBLICATIONS, INC.

50 Portland St., Worcester, MA 01608. 508-754-7201. Website: www.davis-art.com. Claire M. Golding, Editor-in-Chief. **Description:** Books, 100-300 manuscript pages, for the art education market. Most titles are for teachers of art, grades K-12. Must have an educational component. **Proposal Process:** Query with outline and sample chapters c/o Claire M. Golding.

DAW BOOKS, INC.

Penguin Group (USA) Inc., 375 Hudson St., Fl. 3, New York, NY 10014-3658. 212-366-2096. E-mail: daw@us.penguingroup.com. Website: www.dawbooks.com. Elizabeth R. Wollheim, Publisher. **Description:** Specializes in science fiction and fantasy. Most books are targeted to an adult audience, however some are appropriate for young adults as well. **Proposal Process:** Send complete manuscript with SASE. Responds in 3 months. **Sample Titles:** *The Saga of the Renunciates* by Marion Zimmer Bradley; *The Lost Dragons of Barakhai* by Mickey Zucker Reichert. **Tips:** Does not accept short stories, novellas, or poetry. **Contact:** Submissions Editor.

DEARBORN TRADE PUBLISHING, INC.

A Kaplan Professional Company, 155 N Wacker Dr., Chicago, IL 60606-1719. 312-836-4400. E-mail: hull@dearborn.com. Website: www.dearborntrade.com. Don Hull, Editorial Director. **Description:** Professional and consumer books on investing, real estate, sales and marketing, general management, and business. **Proposal Process:** Query with outline and sample chapters. **Payment:** Royalty and flat fee.

IVAN R. DEE, PUBLISHER

Member of the Rowman & Littlefield Publishing Group, 1332 N Halsted St., Chicago, IL 60622-2637. 312-787-6262. E-mail: editorial@ivanrdee.com. Website: www.ivanrdee.com. Ivan R. Dee, President/Publisher; Hilary Meyer, Managing Editor. **Description:** Serious nonfiction for general readers. Topics include history, biography, politics, literature, and theatre. Imprints: New Amsterdam Books and J.S. Sanders & Co. **Books Statistics:** 60 titles/yr (1,000 submissions). **Proposal Process:** Query with outline, sample chapters, and SASE. Accepts simultaneous queries. Does not accept electronic submissions. **Payment:** Royalty. **Sample Titles:** *Oppenheimer* by Jeremy Bernstein; *The Fourth Network* by Daniel M. Kimmel.

DEL REY BOOKS

An Imprint of the Random House Publishing Group, 1745 Broadway, Fl. 18, New York, NY 10019. 212-782-8393. E-mail: delrey@randomhouse.com. Website: www.delreydigital.com. Betsy Mitchell, VP & Editor-in-Chief; Shelly Shapiro, Editorial Director. **Description:** Science fiction, fantasy, media tie-ins, manga, alternate history, horror, young adult fantasy, 60,000-120,000 words, average. **Books Statistics:** 75 titles/yr; 10% by first-time authors; 0% unagented. **Proposal Process:** No unsolicited manuscripts; accepts agented submissions only. **Payment:** Royalty. **Sample Titles:** *Perdido Street Station* by China Mieville; *Altered Carbon* by Richard K. Morgan. **Contact:** Steve Saffel, Chris Schluep, Keith Clayton.

DELACORTE PRESS

Bantam Dell Publishing Group/Random House, Inc., 1745 Broadway, New York, NY 10019. 212-782-9140. Website: www.bantamdell.com. Leslie Schnur, Editor-in-Chief. **Description:** Imprint of The Bantam Dell Publishing Group. Commercial fiction (romance, historical, mystery) and nonfiction (politics/current affairs, psychology, parenting, self-help, and true crime). **Proposal Process:** Accepts material from literary agents only. **Sample Titles:** (Fiction) *Sometimes I Dream in Italian* by Rita Ciresi; *The Thief-Taker* by T.F. Banks. (Nonfiction) *For the Bride* by Colin Cowie; *How to Think Like Leonardo Da Vinci* by Michael Gelb.

DELMAR LEARNING

Division of Thompson Learning, 5 Maxwell Dr., Clifton Park, NY 12065. 800-998-7498. E-mail: info@delmar.com. Website: www.delmar.com. **Description:** Technical nonfiction textbooks for post-secondary learning institutions. Topics include agriscience, electronics, graphic design, nursing, allied health, cosmetology, travel/tourism, etc. **Proposal Process:** Author guidelines available in PDF format on website.

DELTA BOOKS

Bantam Dell Publishing Group/Random House, Inc., 1540 Broadway, New York, NY 10036. 212-782-9140. Website: www.bantamdell.com. **Description:** Imprint of The Bantam Dell Publishing Group. Biography/memoir, literary fiction, short story collections, and women's fiction. **Proposal Process:** Accepts material from literary agents only. **Sample Titles:** *Shopaholic Ties the Knot* by Sophie Kinsella; *Paradise Park* by Allegra Goodman.

THE DERRYDALE PRESS

Rowman & Littlefield Publishing Group, 4501 Forbes Blvd., Suite 200, Lanham, MD 20706. 301-459-3366. Website: www.derrydalepress.com. **Description:** Primarily nonfiction on travel, hunting, fishing, food/wine, nature, archery, golf, and games/hobbies. Also publishes some fiction with themes on hunting/fishing. **Proposal Process:** Submit description (outlining your qualifications, competing titles, target audience, and length), TOC, 1-2 sample chapters, and introduction or overview if available. Accepts simultaneous submissions with notice. **Sample Titles:** *True North: Reflections on Fishing and a Life Well Lived* by Jack Kulpa; *Tigers of the Sea* by Colonel Hugh D. Wise. **Contact:** Bethany Perry.

DEVIN-ADAIR PUBLISHERS, INC.

P.O. Box A, Old Greenwich, CT 06870. 203-622-1010. J. Andrassi, Editor. **Description:** Books on conservative affairs, Irish topics, photography, Americana, self-help, health, gardening, cooking, and ecology. **Proposal Process:** Send outline, sample chapters, and SASE. **Payment:** Royalty.

THE DIAL PRESS

Bantam Dell Publishing Group/Random House, Inc., 1745 Broadway, New York, NY 10019. 212-782-9000. Website: www.bantamdell.com. Susan Kamil, VP/Editorial Director. **Description:** Imprint of The Bantam Dell Publishing Group. Quality literary fiction and nonfiction, on subjects that include biography, Americana, contemporary culture, government/politics, history, memoirs, psychology, women's issues/studies. **Books Statistics:** 6-12 titles/yr; 75% by first-time authors. **Proposal Process:** Accepts material from literary agents only. **Sample Titles:** *American Chica* by Marie Arana; *Franklin Flyer* by Nicholas Christopher.

THE DONNING CO.

184 Business Park, Suite 206, Virginia Beach , VA 23462. 757-497-1789.
E-mail: info@donning.com. Website: www.donning.com. Scott Rule, Marketing
Director. **Description:** Publishes coffee-table pictorial histories of local communities, colleges, businesses, and regional heritage. **Proposal Process:** Query with outline and sample chapters. **Payment:** Royalty. **Sample Titles:** *The History of Wilmington Country Club: Its First 100 Years* by Dr. Joseph B. Dietz Jr.; *Our Time: Celebrating 75 Years of Learning and Leading* by Wendy Adair and Oscar Gutierrez.

DORCHESTER PUBLISHING CO., INC.

Dorchester Publishing Co., Inc., 200 Madison Ave., Suite 2000, New York, NY 10016.
212-725-8811. Website: www.dorchesterpub.com. Alicia Condon, VP/Editorial
Director. **Description:** Mass-market paperback in the categories of historical fiction, historical romance, paranormal romance, futuristic romance, contemporary romance, young adult romance, horror, thrillers, and Westerns. Imprints: Leisure, Love Spell, and SMOOCH. **Books Statistics:** 250 titles/yr (2,500 submissions); 10% by first-time authors; 30% unagented. **Proposal Process:** Submit query or synopsis with first 3 chapters and SASE. Manuscripts range from 45,000-100,000 words depending on genre. Responds in 8 months. **Payment:** Royalty. **Sample Titles:** *Dark Destiny* by Christine Feehan; *To Wake the Dead* by Richard Laymon; *The Year My Life Went Down the Loo* by Katie Maxwell. **Tips:** See website for specific submission guidelines for each genre. **Contact:** Micaela Bombard or Jessica McDonnell.

DORLING KINDERSLEY

Pearson plc, 375 Hudson St., New York, NY 10014. 212-213-4800.
Website: www.dk.com. **Description:** Picture books and fiction for middle-grade and older readers. Also, illustrated reference books for both adults and children.
Proposal Process: Send outline and sample chapter. **Payment:** Royalty or flat fee.

DOUBLEDAY

Doubleday Broadway Publishing Group/Random House, Inc., 1745 Broadway, New York, NY 10019. 212-782-9000. Website: www.randomhouse.com. William Thomas, V.P./Editor-in-Chief. **Description:** Publishes high-quality fiction and non-fiction. Publishes hardcover and trade paperback originals and reprints. **Tips:** Does not respond to unsolicited submissions or queries.

DOVER PUBLICATIONS, INC.

31 E 2nd St., Mineola, NY 11501. 516-294-7000. E-mail: dover@inch.com. Website: www.doverpublications.com. Paul Negri, Editor-in-Chief. **Description:** Children's books, coffee table books, cookbooks, biographies, and adult nonfiction on a wide variety of subjects. **Books Statistics:** 600 titles/yr. **Proposal Process:** Query with SASE. **Payment:** Offers advance. **Sample Titles:** *Engineering and Technology, 1650-1750: Illustrations and Texts from Original Sources* by Martin Jensen.

DOWN THERE PRESS

938 Howard St., Suite 101, San Francisco, CA 94103. 415-974-8985, ext. 205.
E-mail: downtherepress@excite.com. Website: www.goodvibes.com/dtp/dtp.
Description: Nonfiction titles for both children and adults addressing self-awareness
and sexual health issues. Also publishes collections of erotic fiction. **Proposal
Process:** Send cover letter, TOC, sample chapters and SASE. **Sample Titles:** *A
Kid's First Book About Sex* by Joani Blank; *Good Vibrations* by Joani Blank.

THOMAS DUNNE BOOKS.

St. Martin's Press, 175 Fifth Ave., New York, NY 10010. 212-674-5151. Thomas L.
Dunne, Publisher. **Description:** Adult fiction (mysteries, trade, etc.) and nonfiction
(history, biographies, science, politics, humor, etc.). **Proposal Process:** No unsolicited manuscripts. Agented queries only. **Payment:** Royalty.

DUQUESNE UNIVERSITY PRESS

600 Forbes Ave., Pittsburgh, PA 15282. 412-396-6610.
Website: www.dupress.duq.edu. Susan Wadsworth-Booth, Director. **Description:**
Scholarly publications in the humanities and social sciences; creative nonfiction
(book-length only) by emerging writers.

DURBAN HOUSE PUBLISHING

7502 Greenville Ave., Suite 500, Dallas, TX 75231. 214-890-4050. E-mail: info@dur-
banhouse.com. Website: www.durbanhouse.com. Robert Middlemiss, Editor-in-
Chief. **Description:** Quality fiction (suspense/thriller, mystery, historical, main-
stream/contemporary, literary) and nonfiction (self-help, how-to, women's issues,
memoirs, contemporary, true crime). **Books Statistics:** 10-20 titles/yr. **Proposal
Process:** Fiction: query with 3 sample chapters, synopsis, and brief bio. Nonfiction:
query with proposal, sample chapters, brief bio, and details of marketing platform.
Sample Titles: (Fiction) *Samsara* by John Hamilton Lewis; *No Ordinary Terror* by
J. Brooks Van Dyke; *Hands of Vengeance* by Richard Sand. (Nonfiction) *Behind the
Mountain* by Nick Williams; *What Makes a Marriage Work* by Malcolm Mahr.

EAGER MINDS PRESS

Hambleton-Hill Publishing, 1501 County Hospital Rd., Nashville, TN 37218.
615-254-2451. **Description:** Seeks submissions from members of the Society of
Children's Book Writers and Illustrators, agented authors, and published writers who
can submit a list of writing credits. **Contact:** Dayne Kellon, Assistant Publisher.

EAKIN PRESS

Sunbelt Media, Inc., P.O. Box 90159, Austin, TX 78709-0159. 512-288-1771. Website:
www.eakinpress.com. **Description:** Regional publisher of both adult and children's
titles on the history and culture of the Southwest. Particular emphasis on Texas and
Oklahoma. **Books Statistics:** 65 titles/yr (1,200 submissions); 40% by first-time
authors; 1% unagented. **Proposal Process:** Query with synopsis, brief bio, and publishing credits. Does not accept material electronically. Responds in 3 months. See

website for detailed guidelines. **Payment:** Royalty. **Sample Titles:** *The Last Cowboy* by Davis L. Ford. **Contact:** Angela Buckley, Associate Editor.

EASTERN WASHINGTON UNIVERSITY PRESS

Eastern Washington University, 705 W First Ave., Spokane, WA 99201. 509-623-4286. E-mail: ewupress@ewu.edu. Website: www.ewupress.ewu.edu. **Description:** Poetry, poetry translations, fiction, and nonfiction. **Books Statistics:** 6 titles/yr (75 submissions). **Proposal Process:** Query with complete manuscript and outline. Prefers hard copy format. Accepts simultaneous queries. Responds in 4-6 months. **Payment:** Royalty. **Sample Titles:** *If Rock & Roll Were a Machine* by Terry Davis; *The Prince and the Salmon People* by Claire Rudolf Murphy.

ECLIPSE PRESS

1736 Alexandria Dr., Lexington, KY 40504. 859-278-2361. E-mail: info@eclipsepress.com. Website: www.eclipsepress.com. Jacqueline Duke, Editor. **Description:** Books on equine and equine-related subjects, including Thoroughbred racing, breeding, handicapping, English sport horses and disciplines, Western sport horses and disciplines, horse health care, and individuals interested in horses. **Proposal Process:** Send brief synopsis, resumé or bio, outline/TOC, sample chapters, list of similar titles currently on the market, and SASE. Do not submit material via e-mail. **Sample Titles:** *Racing to the Table: A Culinary Tour of Sporting America* by Margaret Guthrie; *Feeling Dressage* by Ruth Sabine Schaefer.

ECW PRESS

2120 Queen St. E, Suite 200, Toronto, Ontario M4E 1E2 Canada. 416-694-3348. E-mail: info@ecwpress.com. Website: www.ecwpress.com. Jack David, Publisher. **Description:** Trade books on poetry, fiction, pop culture, sports, travel, and celebrity bio. **Books Statistics:** 40 titles/yr (1,000 submissions). **Proposal Process:** Query first. See website for specific guidelines. **Sample Titles:** *Hawksley Burns for Isadora* by Hawksley Workman; *From Someplace Else: A Memoir* by Ralph Osborne; *Ghost Rider: Travels on the Healing Road* by Neil Peart. **Tips:** Unsolicted manuscripts accepted. **Contact:** Michael Holmes, Poetry/Fiction Editor; Jennifer Hale, Nonfiction/Pop Culture Editor.

ENTREPRENEUR PRESS

2445 McCabe Way, Fl. 4, Irvine, CA 92614. 949-261-2325. E-mail: jcalmes@entrepreneur.com. Website: www.entrepreneur.com. Mike Drew, Marketing Director. **Description:** Nonfiction general and small business trade books. Areas include: business skills, motivational as well as how-to and general business including leadership, marketing, accounting, finance, new economy and business growth and start-ups, customer relations, innovation, stock market and online trading. **Books Statistics:** 15-20 titles/yr (600 submissions); 30% by first-time authors. **Proposal Process:** Query with outline, sample chapters, and SASE. Accepts simultaneous and electronic queries. Responds in 2 weeks. **Payment:** Royalty, range is 5-15%. **Contact:** Jere L. Calmes, Editorial Director.

EPIC PUBLISHING CO.

2101 S Pioneer Way, Las Vegas, NV 89117-2944. 702-248-7263.
E-mail: info@epicpublishing.com. Website: www.epicpublishing.com. **Description:** Fiction, nonfiction, children's books, and biographies.

EPICENTER PRESS, INC.

P.O. Box 82368, Kenmore, WA 98028. 425-485-6822.
E-mail: info@epicenterpress.com. Website: www.epicenterpress.com. Kent Sturgis, Publisher. **Description:** Quality nonfiction trade books emphasizing Alaska. Regional press whose interests include but are not limited to the arts, history, environment, and diverse cultures and lifestyles of the North Pacific and high latitudes.

PAUL S. ERIKSSON, PUBLISHER

P.O. Box 163, Forest Dale, VT 05745. 802-247-4210. **Description:** Publishes general nonfiction and some fiction. **Proposal Process:** Send outline and cover letter and 3 chapters, SASE required. **Payment:** Royalty. **Contact:** Editorial Department.

M. EVANS & CO., INC.

216 E 49th St., New York, NY 10017. 212-688-2810. E-mail: editorial@mevans.com. Website: www.mevans.com. **Description:** Small commercial publisher of general nonfiction with an emphasis on health, cooking, history, relationships, current affairs, how-to, and crime. Also publishes small list of adult commercial fiction. No poetry or belles letters. **Books Statistics:** 30 titles/yr (500 submissions); 10-20% by first-time authors; 10% unagented. **Proposal Process:** Query with outline, sample chapters, and SASE. Accepts simultaneous and electronic queries. Hard copy preferred. **Payment:** Royalty. **Sample Titles:** *Hidden Agenda: How the Duke of Windsor Betrayed the Allies* by Martin Allen; *Dreams From the Other Side* by Alex Lukeman, Ph.D.; *Amazingly Simple Lessons We Learned After Fifty* by William B. Toulouse. **Tips:** "Open to adult books for which we can identify a market." **Contact:** P.J. Dempsey or Matt Harper, Editorial Dept.

EXCALIBUR PUBLICATIONS

P.O. Box 89667, Tucson, AZ 85752-9667. 520-575-9057.
E-mail: excalibureditor@earthlink.net. Alan M. Petrillo, Editor. **Description:** Military history, history of battles, military and historical personalities, firearms, arms and armour. **Books Statistics:** 4-6 titles/yr; 60% by first-time authors; 95% unagented. **Proposal Process:** Query with outline or synopsis, first 2 chapters, and SASE. If artwork is part of package, include samples. Accepts simultaneous queries, including e-queries. Responds in one month. **Payment:** Royalty. **Tips:** Seeking well-researched and documented work. The writer should have a mastery of the subject matter. Unpublished writers are welcome and strongly encouraged.

FACTS ON FILE, INC.

132 W 31st St., Fl. 17, New York, NY 10001. 212-967-8800.
E-mail: llikoff@factsonfile.com. Website: www.factsonfile.com. Laurie Likoff,

Editorial Director. **Description:** Reference books on science, health, literature, language, history, the performing arts, ethnic studies, popular culture, and sports, etc. **Books Statistics:** 100-150 titles/yr (200-250 submissions); 10% by first-time authors; 30% unagented. **Proposal Process:** Query with outline, sample chapter, and SASE. Unsolicited synopses welcome. Accepts simultaneous queries and e-queries. Responds in 4-6 weeks. **Payment:** Royalty. **Sample Titles:** *Encyclopedia of The World's Nations*; *Encyclopedia of American War Heroes*; *Encyclopedia of Ancient Egypt*. **Tips:** Strictly a reference and information publisher. (No fiction, poetry, computer books, technical books, or cookbooks.)

FAIR WINDS PRESS

33 Commercial St., Gloucester, MA 01930-5089. 978-282-9590. Website: www.fairwindspress.com. **Description:** Publishes material on New Age, spirituality, and health. **Sample Titles:** *Earl Mindell's Diet Bible* by Earl Mindell, R.Ph., Ph.D.; *Yoga Burns Fat* by Jan Maddern; *Pilates Back Book* by Tia Stanmore.

FAIRVIEW PRESS

2450 Riverside Ave., Minneapolis, MN 55454. 800-544-8207.
E-mail: press@fairview.org. Website: www.fairviewpress.org. Lane Stiles, Director.
Description: Grief/bereavement, aging/seniors, caregiving, palliative and end of life care, and health/medicine (including complementary medicine). Also topics of interest to families, including childcare/parenting, psychology, self-help/inspirational, and spirituality. **Books Statistics:** 10-20 titles/yr (2,500 submissions); 50% by first-time authors; 70% unagented. **Proposal Process:** Query with sample chapters or complete manuscript, include SASE. Accepts simultaneous queries, but not e-queries. Hard copy only. **Tips:** No fiction; no longer acquiring children's picture books or adult memoirs.

FALCON PUBLISHING

The Globe Pequot Press, 246 Goose Ln., Guilford, CT 06437. 203-458-4500. Website: www.falcon.com. Scott Adams, Senior Acquisitions Editor. **Description:** Nonfiction titles on nature, outdoor recreation, travel, cooking, regional history, and Western Americana. **Books Statistics:** 130 titles/yr. **Proposal Process:** Send brief synopsis, TOC, sample chapter, description of target audience and competing titles, bio/resume, and SASE. Address material to: Submissions Editor [+ category]. Responds in 6-8 weeks.

FARRAR, STRAUS, & GIROUX, INC.

19 Union Square W, New York, NY 10003. 212-741-6900.
E-mail: fsg.editorial@fsgee.com. Website: www.fsgbooks.com. **Description:** Literary fiction, nonfiction, poetry, and children's books. **Books Statistics:** 175 titles/yr. **Proposal Process:** Query with cover letter, outline, sample chapters, resumé or CV, and SASE. Responds in 2-3 months. **Sample Titles:** *The Time of Our Singing* by Richard Powers; *Second Founding: New York City and the Reconstruction of American Democracy* by David Quigley.

FAWCETT/IVY BOOKS

The Ballantine Publishing Group/Random House, Inc., 201 E 50th St., Fl. 9, New York, NY 10022. **Description:** Adult mysteries, regencies, and historical romances, 75,000-120,000 words. **Proposal Process:** Acquisitions through agents. Query with outline and sample chapters. Responds in 3-6 months. **Payment:** Royalty. **Contact:** Editorial Dept.

FREDERICK FELL PUBLISHERS, INC.

2131 Hollywood Blvd., Suite 305, Hollywood, FL 33020. 954-925-5242. E-mail: info@fellpub.com. Website: www.fellpub.com. Barbara Newman, Acquisitions Editor. **Description:** New Age, self-help, how-to, business, hobbies, and inspirational. **Books Statistics:** 40 titles/yr (2,000 submissions); 50% by first-time authors; 90% unagented. **Proposal Process:** Query with sample chapters and SASE. Accepts simultaneous queries, but not e-queries. Prefers hard copy. Responds in 2 months. **Payment:** Royalty. **Sample Titles:** *The Greatest Salesman in the World* by Og Mandino; *The Tiniest Acorn* by Marsha T. Danzig. **Tips:** "Seeking experts in all genres to help to make 'Fell's Official Know-It-All Guides' series grow." **Contact:** Julia Drimus, Assistant Editor.

THE FEMINIST PRESS

The Graduate Center, CUNY, 365 Fifth Ave., Suite 5406, New York, NY 10016. 212-817-7920. Website: www.feministpress.org. Jean Casella, Publisher. **Description:** Educational press publishing books by and about multicultural women. Strives to resurrect the voices of women that have been repressed and silent. Publishes reprints of significant "lost" fiction, original memoirs, autobiographies, biographies, multicultural anthologies, nonfiction, and educational resources. **Tips:** Particular interest in international literature. Accepts no original fiction by U.S. authors; reprints and imports only. Accepts only e-mail queries of 200 words. See website for submission guidelines.

FERGUSON PUBLISHING CO.

200 W Jackson Blvd., Fl. 7, Chicago, IL 60606. 312-692-1000. Website: www.fergpubco.com. Andrew Morkes, Managing Editor. **Description:** Nonfiction for the juvenile, young adult and college markets relating to career preparation and reference.

FINDHORN PRESS LTD.

305A The Park, Findhorn, Forres IV36 3TE Scotland, UK. 0144-1309-690582. E-mail: info@findhornpress.com. Website: www.findhornpress.com. Terry Bogliolo, Publisher. **Description:** Nonfiction on self-help, health/healing, spirituality, music, and dance. **Books Statistics:** 18 titles/yr. **Proposal Process:** Send short synopsis via e-mail. Does not accept unsolicited manuscripts. **Sample Titles:** *In Search of the Magic Findhorn* by Karin Bogliolo; *Flight into Freedom and Beyond* by Eileen Caddy.

FIREBRAND BOOKS

2232 S Main St., Ann Arbor, MI 48103. 248-738-8202.
Website: www.firebrandbooks.com. Karen Oosterhous, Publisher. **Description:**
Fiction and nonfiction—all with emphasis on feminist and/or lesbian themes.
Payment: Royalty. **Sample Titles:** (Nonfiction) *Eight Bullets: One Woman's Story of Surviving Anti-Gay Violence* by Claudia Brenner with Hannah Ashley. (Fiction) *And Then They Were Nuns* by Susan J. Leonardi.

FITZROY DEARBORN PUBLISHERS

919 N Michigan Ave., Suite 760, Chicago, IL 60611-1427. 312-587-0131.
Website: www.fitzroydearborn.com. **Description:** Publishes library reference books on a variety of acadmic subjects including the arts, humanities, business, and science.

FODOR'S TRAVEL PUBLICATIONS

Random House Information Group/Random House, Inc., 1745 Broadway, New York, NY 10019. 212-572-8702. E-mail: kcure@fodors.com. Website: www.fodors.com. Karen Cure, Editorial Director. **Description:** Publishes fact-packed travel guidebook series, covering destinations around the world. Every book is highly detailed. Both foreign and US destinations. **Books Statistics:** 40 titles/yr (100 submissions); 100% unagented. **Proposal Process:** Query first, then send an outline and writing sample. Accepts simultaneous queries, but not e-queries. Prefers hard copy. Responds in 2-10 weeks. **Payment:** Flat fee, depending on the work performed. **Sample Titles:** *Fodor's Paris 2003* by Fodor's; *Escape to Northern New England* by Fodor's. **Tips:** "Avoid pitching general-interest guidebooks to destinations we already cover. Avoid travel literature and other personal narratives."

FORDHAM UNIVERSITY PRESS

University Box L, 2546 Belmont Ave., Bronx, NY 10458-5172. 718-817-4795.
E-mail: manuscripts@fordhampress.com. Website: www.fordhampress.com. Saverio Procario, Director. **Description:** Scholarly nonfiction in the humanities, social sciences, philosophy, theology, history, communications, economics, sociology, business, politcal science, law, literature, and the fine arts. Also publishes regional material on metro New York and books of interest to the general public. **Sample Titles:** *From First to Last: The Life of William B. Franklin* by Mark A. Snell; *The State of the Union: New York and the Civil War* edited by Harold Holzert. **Contact:** Anthony Chiffolo, Acquisitions Editor.

FORGE BOOKS

Tom Doherty Associates, LLC, 175 Fifth Ave., New York, NY 10010. 212-388-0100.
E-mail: inquiries@tor.com. Website: www.tor.com. Melissa Ann Singer, Senior Editor. **Description:** General fiction and limited nonfiction. From 80,000 words. **Proposal Process:** Send cover letter, complete synopsis, first 3 chapters, and SASE. Responds in 6-9 months. **Payment:** Advance and royalties. **Tips:** "For a complete listing of submission guidelines, please see our website."

FORUM

Prima Publishing, 3000 Lava Ridge Ct., Roseville, CA 95661. 916-787-7000. Website: www.primapublishing.com. David Richardsom, Editor. **Description:** Serious nonfiction on current affairs, business, public policy, libertarian/conservative thought, high-level management, individual empowerment, and historical biography. **Proposal Process:** Submit outline, sample chapters, market research, and SASE. Accepts simultaneous queries. Prefers hard copy. **Payment:** Royalty and flat fee, standard range.

WALTER FOSTER PUBLISHING, INC.

23062 La Cadena Dr., Laguna Hills, CA 92653. 949-380-7510. E-mail: info@walterfoster.com. Website: www.walterfoster.com. **Description:** How-to art and craft instruction books for artists of all ages and all skill levels.

FOUR WALLS EIGHT WINDOWS

39 W 14th, #503, New York, NY 10011. 212-206-8965. E-mail: edit@4w8w.com. Website: www.4w8w.com. **Description:** Popular science, history, biography, and politics. **Books Statistics:** 30 titles/yr (5,000 submissions); 15% by first-time authors; 10% unagented. **Proposal Process:** Query with outline and SASE. Accepts simultaneous queries. Accepts queries via e-mail, but not submissions. Prefers hard copy. Responds in 2 months. **Payment:** Royalty. **Tips:** "Visit our website for complete submission guidelines. Please note that we do not accept poetry or any commercial fiction such as romance, mysteries, thrillers, etc."

FOUR WAY BOOKS

P.O. Box 535, Village Station, New York, NY 10014. 212-334-5430. E-mail: four_way_editors@yahoo.com. Website: www.fourwaybooks.com. Martha Rhodes, Director/Founding Editor. **Description:** Nonprofit literary press accepting unsolicited poetry, short fiction, and novellas during the month of June. **Books Statistics:** 6-8 titles/yr. **Proposal Process:** Refer to guidelines on website before submitting. **Sample Titles:** *New Messiahs* by Henry Israeli; *Six Small Fires* by Paul Jenkins; *The Little Bat Trainer* by Gwen Ebert. **Tips:** "You may submit to our contest each year—the Intro Prize run alternately with the Levis Prize—and you may submit outside the contest in June. Please see our guidelines for specifics."

OLIN FREDERICK, INC.

P.O. Box 547, Dunkirk, NY 14048. 716-672-6176. E-mail: magwynne@olinfrederick.com. Website: www.olinfrederick.com. **Description:** Political nonfiction as well as biography, history, economics, health/medicine, business, and other subjects. Also political fiction and poetry, all with focus on "revealing the truth about issues in the government." **Proposal Process:** Query with outline, synopsis, author bio, and SASE. Do not send sample chapters unless requested. **Payment:** Royalty. **Sample Titles:** *A Woman's Odyssey* by Erika Hansen; *Flag Mischief* by Douglas Campbell; *Secret Players* by Carl A. Nelson. **Contact:** Editorial Director.

W.H. FREEMAN & CO. PUBLISHERS

41 Madison Ave., Fl. 37, New York, NY 10010. 212-576-9400.
Website: www.whfreeman.com. John Michael, Executive Editor. **Description:** Textbooks and educational materials with strong emphasis in the sciences and mathematics. Also publishes serious nonfiction for the general reader on topics such as nature/environment, astronomy, current events, anthropology, health, and psychology. Imprints: Computer Science Press and Scientific American Books. **Proposal Process:** Query with formal proposal and credentials. **Sample Titles:** *Universe: Stars and Galaxies* by Roger Freedman and William Kaufmann; *Physical Chemistry* by Peter Atkin and Julio DePaula; *The Basics of Abstract Algebra* by Paul Bland.

FULCRUM PUBLISHING, INC.

16100 Table Mountain Parkway, Suite 300, Golden, CO 80403. 303-277-1623.
E-mail: fulcrum@fulcrum-books.com. Website: www.fulcrum-books.com. Daniel Forrest-Bank, Managing Editor; Katie Raymond, Associate Managing Editor. **Description:** Adult trade nonfiction with focus on western regional topics (gardening, travel, nature, history, education, Native American culture). **Proposal Process:** Send cover letter, sample chapters, TOC, author credentials, and market analysis. **Payment:** Royalty. **Sample Titles:** *Our Stories Remember: American History, Culture, and Values through Storytelling* by Joseph Bruchac; *Wild Women of the Old West* by Richard W. Etulain and Glenda Riley.

GALLOPADE INTERNATIONAL

665 Highway 74 S, Suite 600, Peachtree City, GA 30269. 770-631-4222.
E-mail: info@gallopade.com. Website: www.gallopade.com. **Description:** "We are an award-winning company that publishes educational supplements on a variety of topics for all 50 states and the increasingly popular Carole Marsh Mysteries series." Also publishes full-color pocket guides, activity books, maps, stickers, etc.

GEMSTONE PRESS

A Division of LongHill Partners, Inc., Sunset Farm Offices, P.O. Box 237, Woodstock, VT 05091-0237. 802-457-4000. Website: www.gemstonepress.com. **Description:** Nonfiction titles on jewelry, gems, gemology. **Proposal Process:** Send cover letter, TOC, introduction, 2 sample chapters, and SASE. Hard copy only. Responds in 3 months. **Tips:** "GemStone Press books are designed to help consumers and those who work in the gem trade increase their understanding, appreciation, and enjoyment of jewelry, gems, and gemology. Our books our easy to read, easy to use. They are designed for the person who does not have scientific or technical background." **Contact:** Submissions Editor.

GLENBRIDGE PUBLISHING LTD.

19923 E Long Ave., Centennial, CO 80016. 720-870-8381. E-mail: glenbr@eazy.net.
Website: www.glenbridgepublishing.com. James A. Keene, Editor. **Description:** Nonfiction titles on self-help, business, education, food, history, music, health and medicine. **Books Statistics:** 4-6 titles/yr (15,000 submissions); 85% first-time

authors; 98% unagented. **Proposal Process:** Query with sample chapter and SASE. Accepts simultaneous queries. Responds in 1 month. **Payment:** Royalty. **Sample Titles:** (Self-Help) *Three Minute Therapy: Change Your Thinking, Change Your Life* by Dr. Michael Edelstein with David R. Steele. (Food) *Ice Cream: The Whole Scoop* by Gail Damerow; *Flying the Stock Market* by Franklin Reick with Bruce Siminoff. **Contact:** Mary B. Keene, President.

THE GLOBE PEQUOT PRESS

P.O. Box 480, Guilford, CT 06437. 203-458-4500. E-mail: info@globepequot.com. Website: www.globepequot.com. Shelley Wolf, Submissions Editor. **Description:** Nonfiction with national and regional focus. Topics include regional travel, outdoor recreation, natural history field guides, regional cookbooks, popular regional history, regional humor. **Proposal Process:** Query with 1-page synopsis, definition of target audience, TOC or outline, sample chapter, resumé, and analysis of competing titles. **Payment:** Royalty or flat fee. **Sample Titles:** *Arizona Curiosities* by Sam Lowe; *It Happened in New Jersey* by Fran Capo; *Hiking Arkansas* by Janie and Wyatt Jones.

DAVID R. GODINE PUBLISHER

9 Hamilton Place, Boston, MA 02108. 617-451-9600. E-mail: info@godine.com. Website: www.godine.com. **Description:** Fiction, nonfiction, poetry, photography, children's books, cookbooks, and translations. **Books Statistics:** 20 titles/yr (800-1,000 submissions). **Proposal Process:** No unsolicited manuscripts. Accepts material from literary agents only.

GOLDEN WEST PUBLISHERS

4113 N Longview, Phoenix, AZ 85014. 602-265-4392. E-mail: office@goldenwest-publishing.com. Website: www.goldenwestpublishers.com. Hal Mitchell, Editor. **Description:** Cookbooks, nonfiction Western history titles, and travel books. Currently seeking writers for state and regional cookbooks. **Proposal Process:** Query. **Payment:** Royalty or flat fee.

GOOD BOOKS

P.O. Box 419, Intercourse, PA 17534-0419. 717-768-7171. Website: www.goodbks.com. Merle Good, Publisher. **Description:** General nonfiction on crafts, how-to, family/parenting, cooking, Americana, children's, and inspirational topics. **Sample Titles:** *Awash with Color: Watercolor Wall Quilts* by Judy Turner; *Fix-It and Forget-It: Recipes for Entertaining* by Phyllis Pellman Good and Dawn J. Ranck. **Contact:** Phyllis Pellman Good, Senior Editor.

GOSPEL LIGHT PUBLICATIONS/REGAL BOOKS

1957 Eastman, Ventura, CA 93003-7383. 805-644-9721. Website: www.gospellight.com. **Description:** Sunday school curriculum, teacher training resources, and inspirational Biblical books for pastors and church leaders. **Proposal Process:** Send cover letter with outline, 2-3 sample lessons, and SASE. Currently not accepting manuscripts for Regal. **Sample Titles:** *Blessing Your*

Children: How You Can Love the Kids in Your Life by Jack W. Hayford; *The Worship Warrior: How Your Prayer and Worship Can Protect Your Home and Community* by Chuck D. Pierce. **Tips:** Does not accept unsolicited manuscripts.

GRAYWOLF PRESS

2402 University Ave., Suite 203, St. Paul, MN 55114. 651-641-0077. Website: www.graywolfpress.org. Fiona McCrae, Publisher. **Description:** Literary fiction (short story collections and novels), poetry, and essays. **Books Statistics:** 20 titles/yr (3,000 submissions); 20% by first-time authors; 50% unagented. **Proposal Process:** Send SASE for guidelines. Responds in 3 months to queries. **Payment:** Royalty; offers advance.

GREAT QUOTATIONS PUBLISHING

8102 Lemont Rd., Suite 300, Woodridge, IL 60517. 630-390-3586. E-mail: greatquotations@yahoo.com. Ringo Suek, Editor. **Description:** Gift book with humorous, inspiration and business categories. 100-150 pages with short sentences. **Books Statistics:** 50 titles/yr (250 submissions); 50% by first-time authors; 70% unagented. **Proposal Process:** Query with outline and sample chapters or send complete manuscript, include SASE. **Payment:** Royalty and flat fee. **Sample Titles:** *The Secret Language of Women: A Humorous Guide to Understanding Women* by Sherrie Weaver.

GREENHAVEN PRESS

Imprint of The Gale Group, 15822 Bernardo Center Dr., Suite C, San Diego, CA 92127. E-mail: chandra.howard@thomson.com. Website: www.gale.com/greenhaven. **Description:** Series publisher of anthologies for high school and college-level readers, most notably the Opposing Viewpoints series. Anthologies cover current events and controversies, historical events, and geo-political issues. **Proposal Process:** Seeks freelance writers to research, edit, and write on work-for-hire basis. Grad students, professors, and professional researchers preferred. Send query letter and resumé/curriculum vitae via e-mail. No unsolicited manuscripts. **Payment:** Flat fee. **Contact:** Chandra Howard, Senior Acquisitions Editor.

GREENLINE PUBLICATIONS

P.O. Box 590780, San Francisco, CA 94159-0780. 415-386-8646. E-mail: info@greenlinepub.com. Website: www.greenlinepub.com. **Description:** Books that appeal to travelers in search of distinct experiences. "In the next several months, we will be releasing more travel guides in two categories: The Greenline Historic Travel Guide series and The Fun Also Rises series. **Sample Titles:** *The Fun Seeker's North America* by Alan Davis; *The 25 Best World War II Sites, Pacific Theater: The Ultimate Traveler's Guide to the Battlefields, Monuments and Museums* by Chuck Thompson.

GREENWOOD PUBLISHING GROUP
88 Post Rd W, Westport, CT 06881. 203-226-3571 ext. 3390.
Website: www.greenwood.com. **Description:** Professional and scholary nonfiction reference titles/textbooks on business, economics, natural science, law, the humanities, and the social sciences. **Tips:** See website for specific submission guidelines. Submit book proposal to one editor only.

GREYSTONE BOOKS
Douglas & McIntyre Publishing Group, 2323 Quebec St., Suite 201, Vancouver, British Columbia V5T 4S7 Canada. 604-254-7191. E-mail: dm@douglas-mcintyre.com. Website: www.greystonebooks.com. **Description:** Nonfiction on natural history, natural science and environmental issues, popular culture, health, and sports. **Books Statistics:** 30 titles/yr. **Sample Titles:** *The Sacred Balance* by David Suzuki; *Gordie: A Hockey Legend* by Roy MacSkimming.

GRIFFIN PUBLISHING GROUP
18022 Cowan, Suite 202, Cowan, CA 92614. 949-263-3733.
E-mail: griffinbooks@griffinpublishing.com. Website: www.griffinpublishing.com.
Robin Howland. **Description:** Books on business/finance, education, the Olympics, sports/fitness, health/nutrition, and general trade. **Sample Titles:** *Journey of the Olympic Flame* by US Olympic Committee; *How to Get Kids to Eat Great and Love It!* by Christine Wood.

GROVE/ATLANTIC, INC.
841 Broadway, New York, NY 10003. 212-353-7960. Joan Bingham, Executive Editor.
Description: Distinguished fiction and nonfiction. **Books Statistics:** 60 titles/yr. 10-15% of books by first-time authors. **Proposal Process:** Query. No unsolicited manuscripts. **Payment:** Royalty.

GRYPHON HOUSE, INC.
P.O. Box 207, Beltsville, MD 20704. 301-595-9500. E-mail: kathyc@ghbooks.com.
Website: www.gryphonhouse.com. Kathy Charner, Editor-in-Chief. **Description:** Early childhood learning and activity books for teachers and parents.

HANCOCK HOUSE PUBLISHERS
1431 Harrison Ave., Blaine, WA 98230-5005. 604-538-1114.
E-mail: david@hancockhouse.com. Website: www.hancockhouse.com. **Description:** Adult nonfiction: guidebooks, biographies, natural history, popular science, conservation, animal husbandry, and falconry. **Proposal Process:** Query with outline and sample chapters or send complete manuscript. Simultaneous queries considered. **Payment:** Royalty.

HARBOR PRESS, INC./HARBOR HEALTH

P.O. Box 1656, Gig Harbor, WA 98335. 253-851-5190.
E-mail: submissions@harborhealth.com. Website: www.harborpress.com. Debby Young, Senior Editor. **Description:** Books on health, diet, psychology, parenting, self-improvement, etc. **Proposal Process:** Query with TOC, 2 sample chapters, and bio/resume. Send all submissions c/o Debby Young, Senior Editor at 5 Glen Dr., Plainview, NY 11803. See website for specific guidelines. **Sample Titles:** *Smart Buys Drug-Wise* by Lee Haak and Rick Melcher.

HARCOURT INC.

15 E 26th St., New York, NY 10010. 212-592-1045.
Website: www.harcourtbooks.com. Lori Benton, VP/Publisher. **Description:** General trade adult and children's books. **Books Statistics:** 120 titles/yr; 5% by first-time authors. **Proposal Process:** No unsolicited manuscripts, queries, or illustrations. Accepts work from agents only. **Payment:** Royalty.

HARLEQUIN ENTERPRISES, LTD.

225 Duncan Mill Rd., Don Mills, Ontario M3B 3K9 Canada. 416-445-5860. Website: www.eharlequin.com. Donna Hayes, President/Publisher; Isabel Swift, VP Editorial.. **Description:** Women's fiction (romance, action adventure, mystery). **Proposal Process:** Query appropriate editor, include SASE. **Sample Titles:** (Silhouette Books) *The Courage to Dream* by Margaret Daley; (Red Dress Ink) *Fashionistas* by Lynn Messina; (Mira Books) *Home Before Dark* by Susan Wiggs. **Contact:** Randall Toye, Gold Eagle Books (series action adventure fiction) and Worldwide Mystery (contemporary mystery fiction). Tara Gavin, Harlequin Books (contemporary and historical series romance), Red Dress Ink (20-something fiction), Silhouette Books (contemporary romance series), and Steeple Hill (contemporary inspirational romance series). Dianne Moggy, Mira Books (women's fiction, contemporary/historical drama, family sagas, romantic suspense, and relationship novels).

HARPERCOLLINS PUBLISHERS

10 E 53rd St., New York, NY 10022-5299. 212-207-7000.
Website: www.harpercollins.com. **Description:** High-quality book publisher with many imprints. **Proposal Process:** Adult trade books, send to Managing Editor for Fiction, Nonfiction (biography, history, etc.). For reference books: submissions from agents only. For college texts: address queries to College Dept. (no unsolicited manuscripts; query first).

HARPERPRISM

HarperCollins Publishers, 10 E 53rd St., New York, NY 10022-5299. 212-207-7000. John Douglas, Executive Editor. **Description:** Science fiction/fantasy.

HARVARD BUSINESS SCHOOL PRESS

60 Harvard Way, Boston, MA 02163. 617-783-7500. Website: www.hbsp.harvard.edu. Hollis Heimbouch, Editorial Director. **Description:** Professional nonfiction titles on business and management. **Sample Titles:** *The Company of the Future: How the Communications Revolution is Changing Management* by Frances Cairncross.

HARVARD COMMON PRESS

535 Albany St., Boston, MA 02118-2500. 617-423-5803. E-mail: bshaw@harvard-commonpress.com. Website: www.harvardcommonpress.com. Bruce Shaw, Publisher. **Description:** Adult nonfiction on childcare/parenting, health, gardening, and cooking. **Books Statistics:** 15 titles/yr; 25% by first-time authors; 40% unagented. **Proposal Process:** Send outline, analysis of competing books, and sample chapters or complete manuscript with SASE. **Payment:** Royalty. **Sample Titles:** *The Ultimate Rotisserie Cookbook* by Diane Phillips; *The Wild Vegetarian Cookbook* by Steve Brill; *The Birth Partner* by Penny Simkin, P.T.; *The Hummingbird Garden* by Mathew Tekulsky. **Contact:** Pamela Hoenig, Executive Editor.

HARVARD UNIVERSITY PRESS

79 Garden St., Cambridge, MA 02138-1499. 617-495-2600. Website: www.hup.harvard.edu. Mary Ann Lane, Managing Editor. **Description:** Scholarly books and serious works of general interest in the humanities, the social and behavioral sciences, the natural sciences, and medicine. Does not normally publish poetry, fiction, festschriften, memoirs, symposia, or unrevised doctoral dissertations.

HATALA GEROPRODUCTS

P.O. Box 42, Greentop, MO 63546. E-mail: editor@geroproducts.com. Website: www.geroproducts.com. Mark Hatala, Ph. D., Editor. **Description:** Books of interest to older (60+) adults. Nonfiction in the areas of senior relationships, advice, health/medicine, humor, travel, "how-to," and also some fiction (romance or erotica). **Books Statistics:** 1-2 titles/yr (30 submissions); 30% by first-time authors; 100% unagented. **Proposal Process:** Send outline with sample chapters. Considers simultaneous queries. Responds in 1-2 months. **Payment:** Royalty, 5-7.5% retail. Advance usually $250-500. **Sample Titles:** (Nonfiction) *Seniors in Love* by Robert Wolley; *The ABC's of Aging* by Dr. Ruth Jacobs. (Fiction) *Romance Is In the Air* by Ginger Binkley. **Tips:** All books are large print, so manuscripts should be around 50,000 words. Audience is men and woman (but particularly women) over age 60. Books need to be pertinent to the lives of older Americans.

HATHERLEIGH PRESS

5-22 46 Ave., Suite 200, Long Island, NY 11101. 212-832-1584. E-mail: lori@hatherleigh.com. Website: www.hatherleighpress.com. Lori Baird, Editorial Director. **Description:** Nonfiction titles on health, fitness, diet, exercise, and cooking. Publishes "Living With" series of chronic illness books. **Books Statistics:** 25 titles/yr (100 submissions); 5% by first-time authors; 99% unagented. **Proposal Process:** Query with sample chapters, TOC, market analysis, and SASE.

Considers simultaneous and electronic queries. Prefers hard copy. Responds in 3-6 months. **Payment:** Royalty or flat fee. **Sample Titles:** *The Body Sculpting Bible For Men/Women* by James Villepigue and Hugo Rivera; *Ski Flex* by Paul Frediani and Harald Harb. **Tips:** "No first-person accounts, e.g., 'How I survived this illness.' It helps if you can bring a celebrity draw to the project. Experts in the fields of health and fitness who can write are very desirable."

HAWORTH PRESS, INC.
10 Alice St., Binghamton, NY 13904-1580. 607-722-5857.
Website: www.haworthpress.com. Bill Palmer, Managing Editor. **Description:** Scholarly and trade press interested in adult nonfiction and GLBT fiction. Topics include psychology, spirituality, social work, gay/lesbian studies, women's studies, and family/marital relations. Also covers some subject matter related to recreation and entertainment. **Proposal Process:** Send outline with sample chapters or complete manuscript. **Payment:** Royalty.

HAY HOUSE, INC.
P.O. Box 5100, Carlsbad, CA 92018-5100. 760-431-7695.
E-mail: slittrell@hayhouse.com. Website: www.hayhouse.com. Shannon Littrell, Submissions Editor. **Description:** Publishes books that center on the topics of self-help, New Age, transformational, and alternative health. **Books Statistics:** 45 titles/yr (2,000 submissions); 2% by first-time authors; 10% unagented. **Proposal Process:** Accepts submissions from agents only. **Payment:** Royalty. **Tips:** "Audience is concerned with the planet, the healing properties of love, and self-help principles. Readers are interested in taking more control of their lives. Research the market thoroughly to make sure that there aren't too many books already on the subject that you're interested in writing about. Make sure to have a unique slant on ideas." No poetry, children's books, or books of quotations.

HAZELDEN PUBLISHING
The Hazelden Foundation, 15251 Pleasant Valley Rd., P.O. Box 176, Center City, MN 55012-0176. 800-328-9000. E-mail: info@hazelden.org. Website: www.hazelden.org. **Description:** Self-help books, curricula, videos, audios, and pamphlets relating to addiction, recovery, spirituality, mental health, and family issues. **Proposal Process:** Query with outline and sample chapters. Considers simultaneous queries. **Payment:** Royalty.

HEALTH COMMUNICATIONS, INC.
3201 SW 15th St., Deerfield Beach, FL 33442. 800-851-9100. Website: www.hci-books.com. Bret Witter, Editorial Director; Allison Janse, Executive Editor; Susan Heim, Religion Editor; Elisabeth Rinaldi, Editor. **Description:** Nonfiction in the areas of self-help, child guidance/parenting, health/medicine, and women's issues/studies. **Books Statistics:** 50 titles/yr. **Proposal Process:** See website for guidelines. Responds in 3 months to queries and proposals.

HEALTH INFORMATION PRESS

Practice Management Information Corp., 4727 Wilshire Blvd., #300, Los Angeles, CA 90010. 323-954-0224. Website: www.medicalbookstore.com. Kathryn Swanson, Acquisitions Editor. **Description:** Nonfiction titles on health/medicine for a general audience. **Proposal Process:** Query with outline and sample chapters. Manuscripts average 250 pages. **Payment:** Royalty. **Tips:** "Simplify complicated health and medical issues so that consumers can make informed decisions about their health and medical care."

HEALTH PRESS

P.O. Box 37470, Alburquerque, NM 87176-7470. 505-888-1394.
E-mail: goodbooks@healthpress.com. Website: www.healthpress.com. K. Frazier, Editor. **Description:** Health-related adult and children's books, 100-300 pages. "We're seeking cutting-edge, original manuscripts that will excite, educate, and help readers." Author must have credentials, or preface/intro must be written by M.D., Ph.D., etc. Controversial topics are desired; must be well researched and documented. **Proposal Process:** Submit outline, TOC, first chapter, and SASE. **Payment:** Royalty.

HEARST BOOKS

The Hearst Corp., 959 8th Ave., New York, NY 10019. 212-649-2000.
E-mail: hearstbooks@hearst.com. Website: www.hearstbooks.com. Jacqueline Deval, Vice President/Publisher. **Description:** Publishes general trade nonfiction titles in conjuction with Hearst magazines. Subject matter includes how-to, cooking, decorating/interior design, crafts, gardening, lifestyle, etc. **Books Statistics:** 30 titles/yr.

HEBREW UNION COLLEGE PRESS

3101 Clifton Ave., Cincinnati, OH 45220. 513-221-1875 ext. 293.
E-mail: hucpress@phuc.edu. Barbara Selya, Acquisitions Editor. **Description:** Scholarly Jewish publisher on very specific topics in Judaic studies. Target audience is mainly rabbis and professors. **Books Statistics:** 4 titles/yr (15 submissions); 100% unagented authors. **Proposal Process:** Query with outline and sample chapters. Prefers hard copy. Responds in 1 week. **Tips:** No Holocaust memoirs or fiction.

HEIMBURGER HOUSE PUBLISHING CO.

7236 Madison St., Forest Park, IL 60130-1765. 708-366-1973.
E-mail: heimbrgrhouse@aol.com. Website: www.heimburgerhouse.com.
Description: Model and prototype railroad books. Also publishes magazines, maps, cookbooks, books on California and Colorado history, and historical hobby books. **Sample Titles:** *The American Streamliner, Postwar Years* by Donald J. Heimburger and Carl R. Byron; *The Milwaukee Road 1928-1985* by Jim Scribbins.

HEINEMANN

Reed Elsevier USA, Inc., 361 Hanover St., Portsmouth, NH 03801. 603-431-7894. Website: www.heinemann.com. **Description:** Practical theatre, drama education, professional education, K-12, and literacy education. **Books Statistics:** 80-100 titles/yr; 50% by first-time authors; 75% unagented. **Proposal Process:** Submit cover letter, statement of objectives, TOC, sample chapters, resumé or curriculum vitae, and SASE. **Tips:** Welcomes first-time authors. See website for guidelines.

HEMINGWAY WESTERN STUDIES SERIES

Boise State University, 1910 University Dr., Boise, ID 83725. 208-426-1999. Website: www.boisestate.edu/hemingway/series.htm. Tom Trusky, Editor. **Description:** Publishes artists and writers of eccentric format books (multiple editions) relating to Rocky Mountain environment, race, religion, gender, and other public issues.

HENRY HOLT AND CO.

115 W 18th St., New York, NY 10011-4113. 212-886-9200. E-mail: info@hholt.com. Website: www.henryholt.com. Sara Bershtel, Acquisitions. **Description:** Distinguished works of biography, history, fiction, current events, and natural history. **Proposal Process:** Prefers submissions from literary agents.

HERITAGE HOUSE PUBLISHING CO. LTD

The Heritage Group, #301-3555 Outrigger Rd., Nanoose Bay, British Columbia V9P 9K1 Canada. 250-468-5328. E-mail: editorial@heritagehouse.ca. Website: www.heritagehouse.ca. Vivian Sinclair, Managing Editor. **Description:** Publisher of BC history, biography, recreation guides, nautical subjects, and special-interest titles. Dedicated to publishing nonfiction by Canadian authors. **Books Statistics:** 10-15 titles/yr; 50% by first-time authors; 100% unagented. **Proposal Process:** Submit introduction, TOC, 2-3 sample chapters, and SASE. **Sample Titles:** *Fort Steele: Gold Rush to Boom Town* by Naomi Miller; *Magnificently Unrepentant: The Story of Merve Wilkinson and Wildwood* by Goody Niosi. **Tips:** See website for specific submission guidelines.

HEYDAY BOOKS

P.O. Box 9145, Berkeley, CA 94709. 510-549-3564. E-mail: heyday@heydaybooks.com. Website: www.heydaybooks.com. Malcolm Margolin, Publisher. **Description:** Titles on California history, culture, natural history, literature, art, poetry, California Native American life, and other regional topics. **Books Statistics:** 20 titles/yr **Sample Titles:** *The High Sierra of California* by Gary Snyder and Tom Killion. **Contact:** Jeannine Gendar, Editorial Director.

HIGGINSON BOOK CO.

148 Washington St., Salem, MA 01970. 978-745-7170. E-mail: acquisitions@higginsonbooks.com. Website: www.higginsonbooks.com. Lauren Companeschi, Editor. **Description:** Nonfiction genealogy and local history only, 20-1,000 pages. Specializes in reprints. **Proposal Process:** Query with outline, sample chapters, and SASE. Accepts simultaneous queries. Prefers e-queries. Responds in 1 month. **Payment:** Royalty. **Tips:** Specialty press-genealogies and local history only.

HILL STREET PRESS

191 E Broad St., Suite 209, Athens, GA 30601-2848.
E-mail: editorial@hillstreetpress.com. Website: www.hillstreetpress.com. Judy Long, Editor-in-Chief. **Description:** Nonfiction titles in history, music, pop culture, cooking/food, gardening, sports, business, journalism, gay/lesbian, gender studies, memoir, and biography. Many titles have regional or international focus. Also publishes some literary fiction from previously published authors. **Books Statistics:** 20 titles/yr (500 submissions); 10% by first-time authors; 10% unagented. Most manuscripts range from 50,000-85,000 words. **Proposal Process:** Submit query, 1-page synopsis, 3 sample chapters, complete author bio with resumé, and SASE. Do not send complete manuscript. Do not send material electronically; hard copy only. Responds in 3-6 months. **Payment:** Annual royalty (8-10%). **Sample Titles:** *Before Scarlett: Girlhood Writings of Margaret Mitchell* by Margaret Mitchell. **Tips:** Not accepting fiction submissions at this time. Does not publish poetry, children's books, science fiction, horror, or romance. Review guidelines on website prior to submitting material.

HIPPOCRENE BOOKS

171 Madison Ave., New York, NY 10016. 212-685-4371.
E-mail: hippocrene.books@verizon.net. Website: www.hippocrenebooks.com.
Description: Foreign language dictionaries and learning guides; trade nonfiction, including bilingual anthologies of classic poetry, proverbs and short stories; international cookbooks; history, military history, WWII and Holocaust studies; Polish-interest titles, and Judaic interest titles. **Books Statistics:** 50 titles/yr (200-300 submissions); 80% by first-time authors; 90% unagented. **Proposal Process:** Send query letter describing project and its marketability, with projected TOC. Accepts simultaneous queries. Prefers hard copy. Responds in 1-2 months. **Payment:** Royalty, typically 6-10%. Flat Fee $500-$1,500. **Sample Titles:** (Cooking) *Flavors of Burma: Cuisine and Culture from the Land of Golden Pagodas* by Susan Chan; (Language) *Beginner's Swedish* by Scott Mellor; (History) *Romania: An Illustrated History* by Nicolae Klepper. **Contact:** Rebecca Cole (cooking, travel, biography, history), Nicholas Williams (foreign lang./dictionaries), Anne Kemper (illustrated histories).

HOHM PRESS

P.O. Box 2501, Prescott, AZ 86302. 928-778-9189. Website: www.hohmpress.com.
Regina Sara Ryan, Senior Editor. **Description:** Nonfiction titles on nutrition, natural health, transpersonal psychology, religious studies, enneagrams, parenting, women's studies, and music. No children's books. **Proposal Process:** Submit cover letter with summary, outline, sample chapter, and SASE.

HOLLOWAY HOUSE PUBLISHING CO.

8060 Melrose Ave., Los Angeles, CA 90046-7082. 323-653-8060.
Website: www.hollowayhousebooks.com. **Description:** Publishes African American, American Indian, gambling, fiction, and nonfiction. **Books Statistics:** 16 titles/yr. **Sample Titles:** *The New Book of the Navajo* by R.F. Locke; *Dorothy Dandridge* by Earl Mills.

HOME PLANNERS

One Thomas Circle NW, Suite 600, Washington, DC 20005. 202-452-0800. E-mail: lbellamy@homeplanners.com. Website: www.eplans.com. Linda Bellamy, Executive Editor. **Description:** How-to reference materials on planning and design for homes, landscapes, and outdoor projects. **Books Statistics:** 12-15 titles/yr. **Proposal Process:** Query with SASE.

HOMESTEAD PUBLISHING

P.O. Box 193, Moose, WY 83012. 307-733-6248. Carl Schreier, Publisher. **Description:** Fiction, guidebooks, art, history, travel, natural history, how-to, and biography. **Payment:** Royalty. **Tips:** Second office: Homestead Publishing, 1068 14th St., San Francisco, CA 94114.

HOUGHTON MIFFLIN CO.

222 Berkeley St., Boston, MA 02116-3764. 617-351-5100. Website: www.hmco.com. Janet Silver, VP/Publisher, Adult Trade. **Description:** Trade literary fiction, nonfiction, biography, history, science, gardening, nature books, cookbooks. Adult fiction/nonfiction to 100,000 words. **Books Statistics:** 100 original titles/yr. **Proposal Process:** No unsolicited manuscripts. Considers material from literary agents only. **Tips:** Unsolicited manuscripts are generally rejected.

HOUGHTON MIFFLIN CO./TRADE & REFERENCE DIVISION

222 Berkeley St., Boston, MA 02116-3764. 617-351-5000. Website: www.hmco.com. **Description:** Quality adult and children's fiction, nonfiction and reference materials. Imprints include Houghton Mifflin, Mariner, Clarion, American Heritage, Chambers, Larousse, and Kingfisher.

HOWELL PRESS

1713-2D Allied Ln., Charlottesville, VA 22903. 434-977-4006. E-mail: rhowell@howellpress.com. Website: www.howellpress.com. Ross A. Howell, Jr., Editorial Director. **Description:** Illustrated books and gift books on history, transportation, aviation, quilts, and topics of regional interest. **Books Statistics:** 8-10 titles/yr (300 submissions); 60% first-time authors; 95% unagented. **Proposal Process:** Query with outline and sample chapters. Considers simultaneous and electronic queries. Prefers hard copy. **Payment:** Royalty. **Tips:** For our Gourmet & Gift category we look for humorous or novelty ideas. Aviation History is an important subject area for our program.

HP BOOKS

The Putnam Berkley Group/Penguin Putnam, Inc., 375 Hudson St., New York, NY 10014. E-mail: online@penguinputnam.com. Website: www.penguinputnam.com. **Description:** How-to titles on cooking and automotive topics. **Proposal Process:** Query with SASE. **Contact:** Editorial Dept.

HUMAN KINETICS PUBLISHERS, INC.

P.O. Box 5076, Champaign, IL 61825-5076. 217-351-5076. E-mail: hk@hkusa.com. Website: www.humankinetics.com. Rainer Martens, President. **Description:** Reference, text, trade, and coaching materials on health, medicine, recreation, and sports. **Books Statistics:** 100 titles/yr; 30% by first-time authors; 90% unagented. **Proposal Process:** Submit outline with sample chapters and artwork.

HUNTER HOUSE PUBLISHERS

P.O. Box 2914, 1515 1/2 Park St., Alameda, CA 94501-0914. 510-865-5282. E-mail: acquisitions@hunterhouse.com. Website: www.hunterhouse.com. Jeanne Brondino, Acquisitions Editor. **Description:** Nonfiction materials for families and communities on topics such as health, self-help/personal growth, sexuality/relationships, violence intervention/prevention, activity books for teachers, and counseling resources. **Books Statistics:** 21 titles/yr (300 submissions); 5% by first-time authors; 80% unagented. **Proposal Process:** Query for guidelines, then submit complete proposal. Accepts simultaneous and electronic queries. Prefers hard copy. Responds in 2-3 months. **Payment:** Royalty, 12% of net. **Sample Titles:** *The Worried Child* by Paul Foxman, Ph.D. **Tips:** Absolutely no fiction, autobiographies/memoirs, or personal stories.

HUNTER PUBLISHING, INC.

239 S Beach Route, Hobe Sound, FL 33455. 772-546-7986. E-mail: comments@hunterpublishing.com. Website: www.hunterpublishing.com. Michael Hunter, Acquisitions Department. **Description:** Travel guides to various destinations around the world. **Books Statistics:** 70 titles/yr (300 submissions); 40% by first-time authors; 90% unagented. **Proposal Process:** Query with outline and SASE. Accepts simultaneous and electronic queries. Responds in 2 weeks. **Payment:** Royalty. **Tips:** "Do not send travelogues."

IDEA GROUP PUBLISHING

Idea Group, Inc., 701 E Chocolate Ave., Suite 200, Hershey, PA 17033-1240. 717-533-8845. Website: www.idea-group.com. **Description:** Publisher of journals, cases, and books on information science, education, technology, and management. **Proposal Process:** Submit 2-4 page proposal with suggested titles (3-5), introduction, list of objectives, target audience, current competitors, TOC, and timetable. **Contact:** Senior Academic Editor.

IMPACT PUBLISHERS, INC.

P.O. Box 6016, Atascadero, CA 93423-6016. 805-466-5917. E-mail: editor@impact-publishers.com. Website: www.impactpublishers.com. Melissa Froehner, Publisher. **Description:** Popular and professional psychology books, from 200 pages. Titles on personal growth, relationships, families, communities, and mental health for adults. Nonfiction children's books for "Little Imp" series on issues of grief, self-esteem, and coping with difficult issues such as divorce. **Proposal Process:** Query with outline and sample chapters. **Payment:** Royalty. **Tips:** "Writers must have advanced degrees and professional experience in human-service fields."

INDIANA UNIVERSITY PRESS
601 N Morton St., Bloomington, IN 47404-3797. 812-855-8817.
E-mail: iupress@indiana.edu. Website: www.indiana.edu/~iupress. Jane Lyle, Managing Editor. **Description:** Scholarly nonfiction, especially Jewish studies, literary criticism, music, history, women's studies, African American studies, science, philosophy, African studies, Middle East studies, Russian studies, anthropology, regional, etc. **Proposal Process:** Query with outline and sample chapters. **Payment:** Royalty. **Sample Titles:** *Seizing the New Day: African Americans in Post-Civil War Charleston* by Wilbert L. Jenkins.

INDO US BOOKS
37-46 74th St., Jackson Heights, NY 11372. 718-899-5590.
Website: www.indousbooks.com. **Description:** Books and journals on philosophy, health, herbals, music, beauty care, and religion. Seeks to bring the culture of India closer to those living in the United States.

INNER OCEAN PUBLISHING INC.
P.O. Box 1239, Makawao, HI 96768. 808-573-8000. Website: www.innerocean.com. John Elder, Publisher; Karen Bouris, Associate Publisher. **Description:** Nonfiction titles in women's issues, personal growth, spirituality, sexuality, environmental and political call-to-action genres. **Proposal Process:** Query with outline and sample chapters. Accepts simultaneous queries. **Payment:** Royalty. **Sample Titles:** *Spiritual Gardening* by Peg Streep.

INNER TRADITIONS INTERNATIONAL
One Park St., P.O. Box 388, Rochester, VT 05767. 802-767-3174.
E-mail: info@innertraditions.com. Website: www.innertraditions.com. Jon Graham, Acquisitions Editor. **Description:** Nonfiction titles on indigenous cultures, perennial philosophy, visionary art, ancient mysteries, spiritual traditions of the East and West, holistic health/healing, sexuality, and self-development. Seeks to "help transform our culture philosophically, environmentally, and spiritually." **Books Statistics:** 60 titles/yr (10,000 submissions); 30% by first-time authors; 65% unagented. **Proposal Process:** Query with outline, sample chapters, and SASE. Accepts simultaneous and electronic queries. Prefers hard copy. Responds in 6-12 weeks. **Payment:** Royalty. **Contact:** Jeanie Levitan.

INNISFREE PRESS, INC.
Inner Ocean Publishing, Inc., P.O. Box 1239, Makawao, HI 96768.
Website: www.innisfreepress.com. John Elder, Publisher. **Description:** Nonfiction titles in women's issues, personal growth, spirituality, sexuality, environmental and political call-to-action genres. No novels, poetry, or children's books. **Proposal Process:** Query with outline and sample chapters. Accepts simultaneous queries. **Payment:** Royalty.

INTERLINK PUBLISHING

46 Crosby St., Northampton, MA 01060. 413-582-7054. E-mail: info@interlink-books.com. Website: www.interlinkbooks.com. Pam Thompson, Acquisitions Editor. **Description:** Independent publisher specializing in world travel, world history and politics, and translated fiction. Uses 3 imprints: Crocodile Books, Interlink Books, Olive Branch Press. **Books Statistics:** 50 titles/yr (2,000 submissions); 5% by first-time authors; 50% unagented. **Proposal Process:** Query with outline, 2 sample chapters, and SASE. No e-queries; hard copy only. Responds in 4-6 months. **Payment:** Royalty, 5-10%. **Sample Titles:** *The Arabs in Isreal* by Azmi Bishara; *Paris by Bistro* by Christine Graf and Dennis Graf; *The Great Terror War* by Richard Falk. **Tips:** "Please study our list carefully before sending your submission."

INTERNATIONAL MARINE

The McGraw-Hill Companies, P.O. Box 220, Camden, ME 04843. 207-236-4838. E-mail: alex_barnett@mcgraw-hill.com. Website: www.internationalmarine.com. Jonathan Eaton, Editorial Director. **Description:** Nonfiction titles on boating (sailing and power). **Sample Titles:** *One Minute Guide to the Nautical Rules of the Road* by Charlie Wing. **Contact:** Tristram Coburn, Acquisitions Editor.

ISI BOOKS

Imprint of the Intercollegiate Studies Institute, 3901 Centerville Rd., P.O. Box 4431, Wilmington, DE 19807-0431. 302-652-4600. E-mail: booklist@isi.org. Website: www.isibooks.org. **Description:** Interdisciplinary nonfiction titles in the humanities and social sciences that explore current political, economic, and social issues.

JAI PRESS, INC.

Elsevier Science, Ltd., 655 Avenue of the Americas, New York, NY 10010-5107. 203-323-9606. E-mail: jai@jaipress.com. Website: www.jaipress.com. Roger A. Dunn, Managing Director. **Description:** Research and technical reference books on such subjects as business, economics, management, sociology, political science, computer science, life sciences, and chemistry. **Proposal Process:** Query or send complete manuscript. **Payment:** Royalty.

JALMAR PRESS

The B.L. Winch Group, Inc., P.O. Box 370, Fawnskin, CA 92333. E-mail: jalmarpress@att.net. Website: www.jalmarpress.com. Susanna Palomones, Editor. **Description:** Activity-driven books that help kids develop their social, emotional, ethical, and moral skills that lead to academic achievement and lifelong learning. **Books Statistics:** 10 titles/yr (200 submissions); 1-2% by first-time authors; 100% unagented. **Proposal Process:** Query with complete manuscript, include SASE. Accepts simultaneous and electronic queries. Prefers hard copy. Responds in 4-6 weeks. **Payment:** Royalty. **Tips:** Does not publish children's story books. Market is teachers and school counselors.

JEWISH LIGHTS PUBLISHING

A Division of LongHill Partners, Inc., Sunset Farm Offices, Route 4, P.O. Box 237, Woodstock, VT 05091. 802-457-4000. E-mail: submissions@jewishlights.com. Website: www.jewishlights.com. **Description:** Nonfiction in the areas of spirituality, Jewish life cycle, theology, philosophy, healing/recovery, gardening, cooking, history, and travel. Also publishes reference materials and resources for Jewish pastoral leaders and books for children and youth. **Proposal Process:** For adult nonfiction, send cover letter, TOC, introduction, 2 sample chapters, and SASE. For children's books under 40 pages, send entire text. No electronic submissions; hard copy only. Responds in 3 months. **Sample Titles:** *The Women's Haftarah Commentary: New Insights From Women Rabbis on the 54 Weekly Haftarah Portions, The 5 Megillot & Special Shabbatot* edited by Rabbi Elyse Goldstein; *The Jewish Dream Book: The Key to Opening the Inner Meaning of Your Dreams* by Vanessa L. Ochs with Elizabeth Ochs. **Contact:** Submissions Editor.

JIST PUBLISHING

8902 Otis Ave., Indianapolis, IN 46216-1033. 317-613-4200. E-mail: info@jist.com. Website: www.jist.com. **Description:** Nonfiction books and materials in the areas of career, job search, business, and families in crisis. **Books Statistics:** 35 titles/yr (60+ submissions). **Proposal Process:** Query with outline and sample chapters. No simultaneous or electronic queries. Prefers hard copy. Responds in 14-16 weeks. **Payment:** Royalty or flat fee basis. **Sample Titles:** *300 Best Jobs Without a Four-Year Degree* by Michael Farr and LaVerne L. Ludden, Ed.D. **Tips:** See website for guidelines. **Contact:** Lori Cates Hand (Trade Editor), Susan Pines (Reference Books Editor), Randy Haubner (Workbook Editor).

THE JOHNS HOPKINS UNIVERSITY PRESS

2715 N Charles St., Baltimore, MD 21218. 410-516-6900. Website: www.press.jhu.edu/press. Trevor Lipscombe, Editor-in-Chief. **Description:** Scholarly nonfiction in the following areas: classics, history of science/medicine/technology, history, literary criticism, political science, religious studies, and science. **Proposal Process:** Unsolicited queries and proposals are accepted, but no unsolicited poetry or fiction. No e-mail submissions. Hard copy only. Include resumé, description of the project, sample text and descriptive TOC.

JOHNSON BOOKS

Johnson Publishing Co., 1880 S 57th Ct., Boulder, CO 80301. 303-443-9766. E-mail: books@jpcolorado.com. Steve Topping, Editorial Director. **Description:** Nonfiction titles on environmental subjects, archaeology, geology, natural history, astronomy, travel guides, outdoor guidebooks, fly fishing, and regional topics. **Proposal Process:** Send proposal. **Payment:** Royalty.

JONA BOOKS

P.O. Box 336, Bedford, IN 47421. 812-278-9512. E-mail: jonabook@kiva.net. Website: www.jonabooks.com. Marina Guba, Editor. **Description:** Sci-fi, mystery, historical fiction, horror, true crime, law enforcement, Old West and military history. 50,000 word minimum. **Books Statistics:** 50 titles/yr (800 submissions); 35% by first-time authors; 80% unagented. **Proposal Process:** Query with outline, sample chapters, and SASE. Accepts simultaneous and electronic queries. Prefers hard copy. **Payment:** Royalty. **Tips:** "We're looking for more true crime, stories of individual soldiers and true stories from the Old West. Fiction should be based on historical events. We're also now accepting some nonfiction projects, but our base is still the categories listed above."

THE JOSEPH HENRY PRESS
National Academies Press, 500 Fifth St. NW, Washington, DC 20001. 202-334-3336. E-mail: smautner@nas.edu. Website: www.nap.edu. Stephen Mautner, Executive Editor. **Description:** Publishes general trade nonfiction titles that address topics in science, technology, and health. **Books Statistics:** 12-15 titles/yr. **Proposal Process:** Send initial inquiry via e-mail. **Tips:** Extremely selective in choosing authors. Most acquisitions are either commissioned or come through agents.

JOVE BOOKS
The Putnam Berkley Group/Penguin Putnam, Inc., 375 Hudson St., New York, NY 10014. E-mail: online@penguinputnam.com. Website: www.penguinputnam.com. **Description:** Fiction and nonfiction. **Proposal Process:** Query first. Does not accept unsolicited manuscripts.

KALMBACH PUBLISHING CO.
21027 Crossroads Circle, Waukesha, WI 53187. 262-796-8776. E-mail: books@kalmbach.com. Website: www.kalmbachbooks.com. Candice St. Jacques, Editor-in-Chief. **Description:** Publisher of reference materials and how-to books for serious hobbyists in two main lines: 1. Rail fan, model railroading, plastic modeling, and toy train collecting/operating. 2. Beading and fashionable jewelry-making. **Books Statistics:** 20 titles/yr (100 submissions); 50% by first-time authors; 80% unagented. **Proposal Process:** Send query first. Upon approval, follow with detailed outline and complete sample chapter including photos, drawings, and how-to text. Accepts simultaneous and electronic queries. Prefers hard copy. Responds in 2 months. **Payment:** Royalty, 10% on net price. **Sample Titles:** (Trains) *Build a Better Toy Train Layout* by Dick Christianson and John Grams; *Legendary Lionel Trains* by John Grams and Mark Thompson. (Beading) *Chic & Easy Beading* by Alice Korach; *Basic Beadweaving Stitches* by Alice Korach. **Tips:** "Our books are about half text and half illustrations. Authors must be able to furnish good photographs and rough drawings. We welcome telephone inquiries to save time, misconceptions, and wasted work."

KAR-BEN PUBLISHING
Division of Lerner Publishing Group, 6800 Tildenwood Ln., Rockville, MD 20852. 800-452-7236. E-mail: karben@aol.com. Website: www.karben.com. Judyth Groner, Madeline Wikler, Editorial Directors. **Description:** Picture books, fiction, and nonfiction on Jewish themes for preschool and elementary children (to age 9). **Books**

Statistics: 10-12 titles/yr (50-100 queries and 300-400 mss/yr); 5% by first-time authors; 100% unagented. **Proposal Process:** Send complete manuscript with SASE. **Payment:** Flat fee or royalty. **Sample Titles:** *Keeping The Promise* by Tami-Lehman Wilzig; *It's Seder Time* by Latifa Berry Kropf.

KENSINGTON PUBLISHING CORP.
850 Third Ave., New York, NY 10022. 212-407-1500.
Website: www.kensingtonbooks.com. Michaela Hamilton, Editor-in-Chief.
Description: Fiction: historical romance, erotica, women's contemporary, mysteries/thrillers, horror, westerns, mainstream. Nonfiction: narrative, traditional health, alternative health, pets, New Age/occult, spirituality, self-help, psychology, sex/relationships, pop culture, film/entertainment, gambling, true crime, current events/politics, military, business, sports, women's issues, cooking, biography, Judaica. Also, both fiction and nonfiction in gay/lesbian, Asian, and African American studies. Imprints: BET/Sepia, Arabesque, Dafina, Regency Romance, Brava, Strapless, Zebra, Pinnacle, Kensington, Citadel, and Lyle Stuart. **Books Statistics:** 600 titles/yr. **Proposal Process:** Prefers to receive submissions through literary agents. Considers unsolicited manuscripts for Arabesque and Regency Romance imprints only. **Sample Titles:** *About Face* by Fern Michaels; *Cry Me a River* by Ernest Hill.

KENT STATE UNIVERSITY PRESS
P.O. Box 5190, 307 Lowry Hall, Terrace Dr., Kent, OH 44242-0001. 330-672-7913. E-mail: ksupress@kent.edu. Website: www.kentstateuniversitypress.com. Joanna Hildebrand Craig, Editor-in-Chief. **Description:** Interested in high-quality, scholarly works in history and literary criticism, American studies, regional topics for Ohio and the Midwest, biographies, and general nonfiction. **Proposal Process:** Submit letter of inquiry. No faxes, phone calls, or e-mail submissions. **Sample Titles:** *History in Bones* by Juliana Gray Vice; *Blood & Ink: An International Guide to Fact-Based Crime Literature* by Albert Borowitz; *Not All Politics is Local: Reflections of a Former County Chairman* by William D. Angel Jr.

KEY PORTER BOOKS
70 The Esplanade, Toronto, Ontario M5E 1R2 Canada. 416-862-7777.
E-mail: info@keyporter.com. Website: www.keyporter.com. **Description:** General-interest nonfiction (politics, current events, natural history, self-help, health, environment, food/wine, gardening, business, sports, biography/memoir); literary fiction; and children's books. No unsolicited materials. **Sample Titles:** (Fiction) *Remember Me* by Trezza Azzopardi. (Environment) *Dancing at the Dead Sea: Tracking the World's Environmental Hotspots* by Alanna Mitchell. (Children's) *Play Ball! Rosie in Chicago* by Carol Matas.

KIPLINGER BOOKS

1729 H St. NW, Washington, DC 20006. 202-887-6680.
E-mail: dharrison@kiplinger.com. Website: www.kiplinger.com/books. **Description:** Publishes material on personal finance and business management. **Sample Titles:** *Kiplinger's Practical Guide to Your Money* by Ted Miller; *Switching Careers* by Robert K. Otterbourgh; *Making Money in Real Estate* by Carolyn Janik.

KIVAKI PRESS

P.O. Box 1053, Skyland, NC 28776. 828-274-7941. E-mail: gray3@juno.com.
Website: www.kivakipress.com. Fred Gray, Publisher. **Description:** Nonfiction books for the academic, holistic health, and environmental markets covering such topics as person/place narratives, ecological restoration, deep ecology, and indigenous epistemologies. **Books Statistics:** 1-4 titles/yr (20-30 submissions). **Proposal Process:** Submit outline with sample chapters. Send hard copy or electronic version. **Payment:** Royalty, 10-15% **Sample Titles:** *Look to the Mountain: An Ecology of Indigenous Education* by Gregory Cajete, Ph.D.; *Igniting the Sparkle: An Indigenous Science Education Model* by Gregory Cajete, Ph.D.

KLUWER ACADEMIC PUBLISHERS

233 Spring St., Fl. 7, New York, NY 10013-1570. 212-620-8000.
E-mail: info@plenum.com. Website: www.wkap.nl. **Description:** Trade nonfiction, approximately 300 pages, on popular science, criminology, psychology, social science, anthropology, health, the humanities, engineering and law. Imprints include Kluwer Academic, Plenum Publishing, and Kluwer Law International. **Proposal Process:** Query with outline and SASE. Hard copy only. **Payment:** Royalty.

ALFRED A. KNOPF, INC.

The Knopf Publishing Group/Random House, Inc., 1745 Broadway, New York, NY 10019. 212-782-9000. Website: www.randomhouse.com/knopf. **Description:** Distinguished adult fiction and general nonfiction (biography/memoir, nature, history, travel, food/wine). **Proposal Process:** Query for nonfiction. **Sample Titles:** *Mark Twain: An Illustrated Biography* by Geoffrey C. Ward; *Paperboy: Confessions of a Future Engineer* by Henry Petroski. **Contact:** Editorial Board.

KRAUSE PUBLICATIONS, INC.

700 E State St., Iola, WI 54990-0001. 715-445-2214. Website: www.krause.com.
Description: How-to books, hobby books, Standard Catalogs, price guides. Topics include antiques and collectibles, toys, records, comics, automotive, numismatics, outdoors, guns, knives, sewing, quilting, needlework, beading, ceramics. **Books Statistics:** 190 titles/yr; 95% unagented. **Contact:** Paul Kennedy (antiques and collectibles); Julie Stephanie (sewing, quilting, beading, ceramics, needlework); Donald Gulbrandsen (firearms, outdoors, transportation).

LANGENSCHEIDT PUBLISHING GROUP
46-35 54th Rd., Maspeth, NY 11378. 718-784-0055. E-mail: feedback@langenscheidt.com. Website: www.langenscheidt.com. Sue Pohja, Aquisitions Editor. **Description:** Travel guides, phrasebooks, foreign language dictionaries, travel reference titles, and language audio. Imprints: Berlitz Publishing, Hammond World Atlas, Insight Guides, American Map, Hagstrom Map, ADC Map, Creative Sales, Arrow Map. **Sample Titles:** *Hawaii Insight Guide* by Scott Rutherford; *Cape Cod & The Islands Street Atlas*.

LANTERN BOOKS
1 Union Square W, Suite 201, New York, NY 10003. 212-414-2275. E-mail: editorial@booklightinc.com. Website: www.lanternbooks.com. **Description:** Books on spirituality, health and healing, animal advocacy, religion, social thought, and vegetarianism.

LARK BOOKS
Sterling Publishing, 67 Broadway, Asheville, NC 28801. 828-253-0467. E-mail: nicole@larkbooks.com. Website: www.larkbooks.com. Nicole Tuggle, Acquisitions Editor. **Description:** Distinctive books for creative people in crafts, how-to, leisure activities, and gardening. **Proposal Process:** Query with outline. **Payment:** Royalty.

LAST GASP OF SAN FRANCISCO
777 Florida St., San Francisco, CA 94110. 415-824-6636. E-mail: gasp@lastgasp.com. Website: www.lastgasp.com. **Description:** Publisher and distributor of books, comics, and magazines that reflect an eclectic mix of topics. Subject matter includes pop culture, fashion, horticulture, occultism, literature, erotica, art, and humor. **Sample Titles:** *Mini-Mod Sixties* Book by Samantha Bleikorn.

LAWRENCE HILL BOOKS
814 N Franklin, Chicago, IL 60610. 312-337-0747. E-mail: frontdesk@ipgbook.com. Website: www.ipgbook.com. Linda Matthews, Publisher. **Description:** Publishes titles on Black and African American topics and interests.

LECTORUM PUBLICATIONS, INC.
Scholastic, Inc., 524 Broadway, New York, NY 10012-3999. 212-965-7466. E-mail: crivera@scholastic.com. Website: www.lectorum.com. **Description:** Publisher and distributor of children's books written or translated in Spanish. **Sample Titles:** *La Historia de Johnny Appleseed* translated by Teresa Mlawer; *Calor: A Story of Warmth For All Ages* by Amado Pena.

LIBRA PUBLISHERS, INC.
3089C Clairemont Dr., Suite 383, San Diego, CA 92117. 858-571-1414. William Kroll, Editorial Director. **Description:** Nonfiction titles on behavioral and social sciences, medical topics, and general interest. Also publishes fiction, poetry, and professional journals.

LINTEL

24 Blake Ln., Middletown, NY 10940. 845-342-5224.
Description: Poetry and experimental fiction. **Proposal Process:** No unsolicited manuscripts. **Payment:** Royalty. **Contact:** Joan Dornhoefer, Editorial Assistant.

LIPPINCOTT WILLIAMS & WILKINS PUBLISHING

323 Norristow Rd., Suite 200, Ambler, PA 19002. 215-646-8700.
Website: www.lww.com. **Description:** Information for practicing nurses, nursing students, and other healthcare professionals.

LITTLE, BROWN AND COMPANY

Time Warner Book Group, 1271 Avenue of the Americas, New York, NY 10020. 212-522-8700. Website: www.twbookmark.com. Michael Pietsch, Senior VP/Publisher.
Description: Fiction and nonfiction in the areas of biography/memoir, history, current affairs, health/fitness, reference, science, sports, self-help/inspirational. **Proposal Process:** No unsolicited manuscripts. Accepts agented queries only. **Sample Titles:** *The Lovely Bones* by Alice Sebold; *An Unfinished Life* by Robert Dallek; *All He Ever Wanted* by Anita Shreve.

LITTLE, BROWN & CO. BOOKS FOR YOUNG READERS

Time Warner Book Group, 1271 Avenue of the Americas, New York, NY 10020. 212-522-8700. Website: www.twbookmark.com. Megan Tingley, Editor-in-Chief.
Description: Picture books, chapter books, general Megan Tingley books, and YA fiction/nonfiction. **Proposal Process:** No unsolicited or unagented queries/manuscripts. **Sample Titles:** *Gossip Girl* by Cecily von Ziegesar; *Look-Alikes Christmas* by Joan Steiner. **Contact:** Children's Editorial Dept.

LLEWELLYN PUBLICATIONS.

Llewellyn Worldwide, Ltd., P.O. Box 64383, St. Paul, MN 55164-0383. 800-THE-MOON. E-mail: nancym@llewellyn.com. Website: www.llewellyn.com. Nancy J. Mostad, Acquisitions Manager. **Description:** Fiction and nonfiction in the New Age Sciences: alternative health, astrology, crafts, divination, magick and shamanism, nature religions and lifestyles, paranormal, spiritist and mystery religions, spiritual science, and tantra. Also fiction/nonfiction on occult, fantasy, and other metasphysical topics for middle grade and high school readers. **Books Statistics:** 100 titles/yr (2,500 submissions); 100% by first-time authors; 99% unagented. **Proposal Process:** Send either complete manuscript or proposal with cover letter, outline, and sample chapters. Accepts simultaneous and electronic queries. Responds in 2 weeks. See website for specific submission guidelines. **Payment:** Royalty. **Sample Titles:** (Adult nonfiction) *Spirit of the Witch: Religion & Spirituality in Contemporary Witchcraft* by Raven Grimassi. (YA Fiction) *Blue is for Nightmares* by Laurie Faria Stolarz. **Tips:** "We are interested in any story as long as the theme is authentic occultism, and the work is entertaining and educational."

LONE PINE PUBLISHING

1808 B St. NW, Suite 140, Auburn, WA 98001. 253-394-0400.
E-mail: hibach@lonepinepublishing.com. Website: www.lonepinepublishing.com.
Description: Publishes books on nature, gardens, and outdoor recreation. Also ghost stories and popular history.

LONELY PLANET PUBLICATIONS

150 Linden St., Oakland, CA 94607. 510-893-8555. E-mail: info@lonelyplanet.com.
Website: www.lonelyplanet.com. Todd Sotkiewicz, President, General Manager USA.
Description: Travel guides, phrasebooks, maps, restaurant and activity guides, and other travel series.

LONGSTREET PRESS, INC.

2974 Hardman Ct. NE, Atlanta, GA 30305. 770-980-1488.
E-mail: info@longstreetpress.com. Scott Bard, Publisher/President. **Description:**
General fiction and nonfiction, humor, sports, food/wine, art/photography, and children's books. **Proposal Process:** Query with outline, sample chapters, and SASE.
Accepts very little fiction, and only through an agent. Responds in 5 months.
Payment: Royalty. **Sample Titles:** *The Millionaire Next Door* by Thomas Stanley;
Fuqua A Memoir by J.B. Fuqua.

LOTUS PRESS INNER WORLDS MUSIC

P.O. Box 325, Twin Lakes, WI 53181. 262-889-8561.
E-mail: lotuspress@lotuspress.com. Website: www.lotuspress.com. **Description:**
Nonfiction titles on alternative health, aromatherapy, and herbalism.

LOUISIANA STATE UNIVERSITY PRESS

P.O. Box 25053, Baton Rouge, LA 70894-5053. 225-578-6295.
E-mail: lsupress@lsu.edu. Website: www.lsu.edu/lsupress. Mary Katherine Callaway,
Director. **Description:** Scholarly adult nonfiction, dealing mainly with the U.S.
South, its history and its culture. **Proposal Process:** Query with outline and sample chapters. **Payment:** Royalty.

THE LYONS PRESS

An Imprint of The Globe Pequot Press
246 Goose Lane, Guilford, CT 06437. 203-458-4500. E-mail: info@lyonspress.com.
Website: www.lyonspress.com. **Description:** Jay Cassell, Editorial Director (fishing, hunting, survival, military, history); Tom McCarthy, Senior Editor (sports/fitness, history, outdoor adventure, memoirs); George Donahue, Senior Editor (military history, martial arts, narrative nonfiction, sports, travel, current affairs); Jay McCullough, Editor (narrative nonfiction, travelogues, adventure, military espionage, international current events, history); Ann Treistman, Editor (narrative nonfiction, travelogues, adventure, sports, animals, cooking); Holly Rubino, Production Editor (narrative nonfiction, home); Lisa Purcell, Editor-at-Large (history, adventure, narrative nonfiction, cooking); Steven D. Price, Editor-at-Large (horses and horsemanship); Lilly Golden,

Editor-at-Large (fiction, memoirs, narrative nonfiction); Alicia Solis, Managing Editor. **Books Statistics:** 300 titles/yr (200 submissions); 50% by first-time authors; 30% unagented. **Proposal Process:** Send query with outline, sample chapters, or complete manuscript. Accepts simultaneous queries, but not e-mailed manuscripts. Responds in approximately 8 weeks. **Payment:** 5-10% royalty on wholesale price. Offers $2,000-$7,000 advance.

MACADAM/CAGE PUBLISHING
155 Sansome St., Suite 550, San Francisco, CA 94104. 415-986-7502.
E-mail: info@macadamcage.com. Website: www.macadamcage.com. Patrick Walsh, Editor; Anika Streitfeld, Editor; Kate Nitze, Assistant Editor. **Description:** Literary, historical, mainstream, contemporary fiction, and narrative nonfiction such as memoirs. **Books Statistics:** 30-35 titles/yr; 75% first-time authors. **Proposal Process:** Query with bio, cover letter with estimated word count, three sample chapters, and SASE for reply. Does not accept electronic submissions. Responds in 3-4 months. **Payment:** Royalty. **Sample Titles:** *Ella Minnow Pea* by Mark Dunn; *Beautiful Girls* by Beth Ann Bauman. **Tips:** No sci-fi, romance, religion, poetry, self-help, or New Age material.

MACMILLAN REFERENCE USA
The Gale Group, 300 Park Ave. S, Fl. 9, New York, NY 10010. 917-534-2100.
E-mail: frank.menchaca@gale.com. Frank Menchaca, Vice President. **Description:** Multi- and single-volume titles for junior high, high school, college and public libraries, primarily in science and social studies areas.

MADISON BOOKS
5360 Manhattan Circle #100, Boulder, CO 80303. 303-543-7835. Rick Rinehart, Editorial Director/Acquisitions. **Description:** Adult trade nonfiction on music, art, biography, history, and literature. **Books Statistics:** 4 titles/yr. **Proposal Process:** Query with outline, sample chapters, and SASE. Accepts simultaneous queries, but not e-queries. Responds in 2-4 months. **Payment:** Royalty. **Tips:** Submit work with a journalistic style. **Contact:** Mandy Phillips, Editorial Assistant.

MANDALA PUBLISHING
17 Paul Dr., San Rafael, CA 94903. 415-460-6112.
E-mail: info@mandala.org. Website: www.mandala.org. Lisa Fitzpatrick, Acquisitions Editor. **Description:** Books on East Indian art, culture, and philosophy. **Proposal Process:** Submit synopsis, TOC, and sample chapter. **Sample Titles:** *Prince of Dharma: The Illustrated Life of Buddha* by Ranchor Prime; *Practical Yoga: Yoga Cures for Daily Life* by James Bae.

MARION STREET PRESS, INC.
P.O. Box 2249, Oak Park, IL 60303. 708-445-8330. E-mail: edavis@marionstreet-press.com. Website: www.marionstreetpress.com. Ed Avis, Editor. **Description:** Books on writing and journalism. **Books Statistics:** 5 titles/yr (10 submissions/yr);

50% by first-time authors; 100% unagented. **Proposal Process:** Send query via e-mail. Accepts simultaneous queries. Responds in 30 days. **Payment:** Royalty, 7%. **Sample Titles:** *Championship Writing: 50 Ways to Improve Your Writing* by Paula LaRocque; *Math Tools for Journalists* by Kathleen Woodruff Wickham; *Pen & Sword: A Journalist's Guide to Covering the Military* by Ed Offley. **Tips:** "We publish practical, how-to books for writers and journalists. Book proposals should have a specific, identifiable market."

MARVEL ENTERPRISES INC.

10 E 40th St., New York, NY 10016. 212-576-4001. Website: www.marvel.com. **Description:** Publisher of comic books. **Proposal Process:** Accepts artwork from letterers, pencilers, and inkers. Accepts unsolicited written material, but not character ideas. For information on how to submit writing samples, please review submission guidelines on website. All written submissions must include a signed Marvel Idea Submission Form, available on website.

MCFARLAND & COMPANY, INC.

P.O. Box 611, Jefferson, NC 28640. 336-246-4460. E-mail: info@mcfarlandpub.com. Website: www.mcfarlandpub.com. **Description:** Nonfiction, primarily scholarly and reference. Very strong lists in general reference, performing arts, baseball, and history (U.S., world, medieval, Civil War). Also has strong interest in automotive history. **Books Statistics:** 250 titles/yr. **Tips:** "We seek thorough, authoritative coverage of subjects not already exhausted by existing books. We sell mostly to libraries and individuals interested in specialized topics. See our website for submission guidelines." **Contact:** Steve Wilson, Senior Editor; Virginia Tobiassen, Editorial Development Chief; Gary Mitchem, Assistant Editor.

MCGRAW HILL/OSBORNE MEDIA

2100 Powell St., Fl. 10, Emeryville, CA 94608. 510-420-7700. Website: www.osborne.com. Roger Stewart, Editorial Director. **Description:** General computer books, from beginner to technical levels. Subject areas: networking, programming, databases, certification, applications, Internet, e-business, robotics, consumer technologies. **Books Statistics:** 200 titles/yr (1,000 submissions); 15% by first-time authors; 30% unagented. **Proposal Process:** Query. Prefers electronic format. Simultaneous queries accepted. Responds in 1-2 weeks. **Payment:** Royalty (10-15% of net). **Tips:** "Avoid topics that are already over-published. Knowledge of audience and technical proficiency are crucial. First-time authors should be prepared to submit sample chapters." **Contact:** Roger Stewart (Consumer), Wendy Rinaldi (Programming), Tracy Dunkelberger (Networking), Gareth Hancock (Certification).

MCGREGOR PUBLISHING

4532 W Kennedy Blvd., Suite 233, Tampa, FL 33609. 813-805-2665. E-mail: mcgregpub@aol.com. Dave Rosenbaum, Acquisitions. **Description:** Publishes nonfiction only, with an emphasis on sports and true crime. **Books Statistics:** 12 titles/year (300 submissions), 50% first-time authors, 50% unagented. **Proposal**

Process: Query with outline, sample chapters, and SASE. Accepts simultaneous and electronic queries. Prefers hard copy. Responds in 2 months. **Payment:** Royalty.

MEL BAY PUBLICATIONS INC.
4 Industrial Dr., Pacific, MO 63069. 636-257-3970. E-mail: email@melbay.com. Website: www.melbay.com. **Description:** Publishes music books, videos, CDs, DVDs, and material on instruments.

MENASHA RIDGE PRESS
P.O. Box 43673, Birmingham, AL 35243. 205-322-0439.
E-mail: info@menasharidge.com. Website: www.menasharidge.com. Russell Helms, Acquisitions Editor. **Description:** How-to and where-to guidebooks to all outdoor, high adventure sports and activities. Limited nonfiction about adventure sports and general travel books. **Books Statistics:** 20 titles/yr (60 submissions); 15% by first-time authors; 90% unagented. **Proposal Process:** Query with outline and sample chapter. Considers simultaneous and electronic queries. Responds in 1-3 months. **Payment:** Royalty, 10% range. **Sample Titles:** *Mountain Bike! A Manual of Beginning to Advanced Techniques* by William Nealy; *The Best in Tent Camping: Wisconsin* by Johnny Molloy. **Tips:** "Examine the market to truly evaluate whether your book is unique."

MENTOR BOOKS
Penguin Group (USA) Inc., 375 Hudson St., New York, NY 10014. 212-366-2000. Website: www.penguinputnam.com. **Description:** Nonfiction for the college and high-school market. **Proposal Process:** Query required. **Payment:** Royalty.

MEREDITH CORP. BOOK PUBLISHING
1716 Locust St., Des Moines, IA 50309-3023. 515-284-3000. Website: www.meredith.com. Linda Cunningham, Editor-in-Chief. **Description:** Books on gardening, crafts, decorating, do-it-yourself, cooking, health, etc. **Tips:** Limited market. Most titles are staff-written.

MERIWETHER PUBLISHING LTD
Contemporary Drama Service, 885 Elkton Dr., Colorado Springs, CO 80907. 719-594-4422. E-mail: merpcds@aol.com. Website: www.meriwetherpublishing.com. **Description:** Nonfiction titles on theater and peforming arts, mostly for educational markets. Also publishes plays and musicals for production. **Sample Titles:** *Sketch-O-Frenia: Fifty Short and Witty Satirical Sketches* by John Dessler and Lawrence Phillis; *Group Improvisation: The Manual of Ensemble Improv Games* by Peter Gwinn. **Contact:** Dianne Bundt, Editorial Assistant.

MICHIGAN STATE UNIVERSITY PRESS
1405 S Harrison Rd., Suite 25, East Lansing, MI 48823-5202. 517-355-9543. E-mail: msupress@msu.edu. Website: www.msupress.msu.edu. Martha Bates, Acquisitions Editor. **Description:** Scholarly nonfiction with concentrations in his-

tory, regional history, women's studies, African American history, and contemporary culture. Also publishes series on Native American studies, rhetoric, and poetry. **Books Statistics:** 35 titles/yr (2,400 submissions); 75% first-time authors, 100% unagented. **Proposal Process:** Query with complete manuscript. Simultaneous queries accepted. Responds in 2 months. Hard copy preferred. **Payment:** Royalty. **Sample Titles:** *The Low Road: A Scottish Family Memoir* by Valerie Miner; *Routes of Passage: Rethinking the African Diaspora* by Ruth Simms Hamilton. **Tips:** "We seek lucid writing, original perspective, and original scholarship."

MID-LIST PRESS

4324 12th Ave. S, Minneapolis, MN 55407-3218. Website: www.midlist.org.
Description: Literary fiction (novels and short fiction collections), poetry, and creative nonfiction. Does not publish anthologies, so do not send individual short stories or poems. **Books Statistics:** 5 titles/yr (3,000 submissions); 80% first-time authors; 99% unagented. **Payment:** Royalty. **Sample Titles:** *The Last Cigarette* by Jason Waldrop; *The Sincere Cafe* by Leslee Becker. **Tips:** "We're interested in submissions of the highest literary quality. Read some of the books we've published in the past to get a sense of our standards." Guidelines available online or with SASE.

THE MIT PRESS

5 Cambridge Center, Cambridge, MA 02142. 617-253-5646.
Website: www.mitpress.mit.edu. Larry Cohen, Editor-in-Chief. **Description:** Books on computer science/artificial intelligence; cognitive sciences; economics; finance; architecture; aesthetic and social theory; linguistics; technology studies; environmental studies; and neuroscience.

MODERN LANGUAGE ASSOCIATION

Modern Language Assn. of America, 26 Broadway, Fl. 3, New York, NY 10004-1789. 646-576-5000. Website: www.mla.org. **Description:** Publishes books, periodicals, a newsletter, and style guides for students and teachers focusing on language, literature, grammar, and composition.

MONTANA HISTORICAL SOCIETY

P.O. Box 201201, Helena, MT 59620. E-mail: cwhitehorn@state.mt.us.
Website: www.montanahistoricalsociety.org. W. Clark Whitehorn, Editor.
Description: Publishes books on Montana and western history. **Books Statistics:** 3 titles/yr (20 submissions); 10% by first-time authors; 100% unagented. **Proposal Process:** Query with outline, sample chapters, and SASE. No simultaneous queries. Accepts e-queries, but prefers hard copy. **Payment:** Royalty. **Sample Titles:** *Mavericks: The Lives and Battles of Montana's Political Legends* by John Morrison and Catherine Wright Morrison; *Girl From the Gulches: The Story of Mary Ronan* edited by Ellen Baumler; *Christmastime in Montana* by Dave Walter; *Hope in Hard Times: New Deal Photographs of Montana, 1936-1942* by Mary Murphy. **Tips:** Looking for well-researched, well-written cultural and environmental history. Writers should avoid overexposed topics like western gunfighting.

MONTEREY BAY AQUARIUM PRESS

886 Cannery Row, Monterey, CA 93940. 831-648-4847.
E-mail: mgelizondo@mbayaq.org. Website: www.montereybayaquarium.org.
Description: Publishes titles on natural history and conservation of the oceans for both adults and children.

WILLIAM MORROW AND CO., INC.

HarperCollins Publishers, 10 E 53rd St., New York, NY 10022. 212-207-7000.
Website: www.harpercollins.com. Michael Morrison, Editorial Director.
Description: Adult fiction and nonfiction. **Proposal Process:** Query.

MOTORBOOKS INTERNATIONAL

Motorbooks International/MBI Publishing Co., Galtier Plaza, Suite 200, 380 Jackson St., St. Paul, MN 55101-3885. E-mail: trade@motorbooks.com. Website: www.motorbooks.com. **Description:** Books on automotive, motorcycle, tractor, railroading, truck, boating, aviation, and military.

MOUNTAIN PRESS PUBLISHING

1301 S 3rd W, P.O. Box 2399, Missoula, MT 59806. 406-728-1900.
E-mail: info@mtnpress.com. Website: www.mountain-press.com. Lynn Purl, Science Editor; Gwen McKenna, History Editor; Jennifer Carey, Geology Editor.
Description: Nonfiction trade books for general audiences, primarily adults. Considers proposals for projects in natural history (including field guides for plants, wildlife, etc.), western history, or frontier history. No technical earth science or ecology. **Books Statistics:** 12 titles/yr (150 submissions); 20% by first-time authors; 90% unagented. **Proposal Process:** Query with outline, sample chapters, and SASE. Simultaneous and electronic queries accepted. Responds in 1-12 weeks. **Payment:** Royalty. **Sample Titles:** *Loons: Diving Birds of the North* by Donna Love; *Custer: A Photographic Biography* by Bill and Jan Moeller; *Roadside Geology of Wisconsin* by Robert H. Dott, Jr. and John W. Attig.

THE MOUNTAINEERS BOOKS

1001 SW Klickitat Way, Suite 201, Seattle, WA 98134. 206-223-6303.
E-mail: acquisitions@mountaineersbooks.org.
Website: www.mountaineersbooks.org. **Description:** Nonfiction on the outdoors involving noncompetitive, non-motorized, self-propelled activities such as mountain climbing, hiking, walking, skiing, canoeing, kayaking, and snow shoeing. Also publishes environmental and conservation subjects, narratives of expeditions, and adventure travel. **Books Statistics:** 30 titles/yr (400-500 submissions); 50% by first-time authors; 90% unagented. **Proposal Process:** Query with outline, sample chapters, and SASE. Accepts simultaneous and electronic queries. Prefers hard copy. Responds in 2-4 months. **Payment:** Royalty, typical range is $2,400-$4,500. **Sample Titles:** *Rock Climbing: Mastering Basic Skills* by Craig Luebben; *Backpackers: Light Hiking* by Karen Berger. **Contact:** Cassandra Conyers, Acquisitions Editor; Christine Hosler, Assistant Acquisitions Editor.

MOYER BELL LIMITED

549 Old North Road, Kingston, RI 02881-1220. 401-294-0106. Website: www.moyer-bell.com. Britt Bell, Publisher. **Description:** Adult fiction, nonfiction, and poetry. **Tips:** Call for submission guidelines.

MUSEUM OF NEW MEXICO PRESS

228 East Palace Ave., Santa Fe, NM 87501. 505-827-6455. E-mail: mwachs@oca.state.nm.us. Website: www.mnmpress.org. Mary Wachs, Editorial Director. **Description:** Publisher of art and photography on Native America and the Hispanic Southwest. **Proposal Process:** Submit proposal with resumé or curriculum vitae. Include TOC, a sample chapter, and samples of artwork if material is illustrated.

MUSTANG PUBLISHING CO., INC.

P.O. Box 770426, Memphis, TN 38177. 901-684-1200. E-mail: info@mustangpublishing.com. Website: www.mustangpublishing.com. Rollin A. Riggs, Acquisitions Editor. **Description:** General nonfiction for readers ages 18 to 50. **Books Statistics:** 4 titles/yr (1,000 submissions); 75% by first-time authors; 100% unagented. **Proposal Process:** Query with outline, sample chapters, and SASE. Accepts simultaneous queries, but not e-queries. Responds in 2-3 months. **Payment:** Royalty, 6-8% net. **Tips:** No travel or memoirs. No phone calls.

MY BYLINE MEDIA

P.O. Box 14061, Surfside Beach, SC 29587. Website: www.mybylinemedia.com; www.writingcareer.com. Brian S. Konradt, Publisher. **Description:** Nonfiction titles that cover the writing trade. Topics include all kinds of writing (screen, business, fiction, magazine, technical, corporate, copywriting, etc.), the publishing industry, journalism, public relations, freelancing, etc. No fiction or poetry. **Books Statistics:** 12 titles/yr; 0% by first-time authors; 100% unagented. **Proposal Process:** Query with complete manuscript. Prefers electronic format. Considers simultaneous submissions. Responds in 2-4 weeks. **Payment:** Royalty, 50%. **Sample Titles:** *Writing Industry Reports* by Jennie S. Bev; *Freelance Writing for Vet Hospitals* by Stanley Burkhardt. **Tips:** "Our books cover the entire spectrum of writing. We only accept material by experienced and published authors. Our goal is to help writers master their writing careers, whether they are freelancers, staff writers, or hobbyists with a passion for writing."

THE MYSTERIOUS PRESS

Time Warner Book Group, 1271 Avenue of the Americas, New York, NY 10020. 212-522-7200. Website: www.mysteriouspress.com. Kristen Weber, Editor. **Description:** Publishes mystery, suspense, and crime novels. **Books Statistics:** 20 titles/yr. **Proposal Process:** Agented manuscripts only. **Payment:** Royalty. **Sample Titles:** *Open and Shut* by David Rosenfelt; *Dead Midnight* by Marcia Muller.

NATUREGRAPH PUBLISHERS

P.O. Box 1047, Happy Camp, CA 96039. 530-493-5353. E-mail: nature@sisqtel.net. Website: www.naturegraph.com. Barbara Brown, Editor. **Description:** Publishes adult nonfiction books under two main categories: natural history and nature; and Native American culture, outdoor living, land, and Indian lore. **Books Statistics:** 2-3 titles/yr (400 submissions); 100% by first-time authors; 100% unagented. **Proposal Process:** Query with outline and SASE. Accepts simultaneous queries, but not e-queries. Responds in 1 month. **Payment:** Royalty. **Sample Titles:** *The Winds Erase Your Footprints* by Shiyowin Miller; *Anasazi Legends* by Lou Cuevas; *Greengrass Pipe Dancers* by Lionel Little Eagle; *Scenic Byways of Northern California* by Marie Webster Weisbrod. **Tips:** No children's books.

THE NAVAL INSTITUTE PRESS

US Naval Institute, 291 Wood Rd., Annapolis, MD 21402-5034. 410-268-6110. E-mail: esecunda@usni.org. Website: www.usni.org. Paul Wilderson, Executive Editor. **Description:** Nonfiction (60,000-100,000 words) on naval history, seamanship and navigation, reference, professional guides, ship guides, biographies, textbooks and other topics of current interest. Occasional military fiction (75,000-110,000 words). **Proposal Process:** Send detailed prospectus with sample chapters, chapter outlines, a list of sources, curriculum vitae, and cover letter. Submit hard copy only. Do not send original artwork or photographs; photocopies only. **Payment:** Royalty. **Sample Titles:** *Advance Force-Pearl Harbor* by Burl Burlingame; *Fight for the Sea: Naval Adventure from WWII* by John Frayn Turner; *Under Two Flags: The American Navy in the Civil War* by William M. Fowler.

NEW HARBINGER PUBLICATIONS

5674 Shattuck Ave., Oakland, CA 94609-1662. 510-652-0215. E-mail: tesilya@newharbinger.com. Website: www.newharbinger.com. Catharine Sutker, Acquisitions Manager. **Description:** Self-help psychology books, workbooks on life issues, women's topics and balanced living. Read by lay people and used by mental health professionals. **Books Statistics:** 45 titles/yr (600+ submissions); 75% by first-time authors; 90% unagented. **Proposal Process:** Query with an outline and sample chapters. Responds in 1 month. **Payment:** Royalty 10% of net cash receipts. **Sample Titles:** *The Relaxation and Stress Reduction Workbook* by Martha Davis, Ph.D., et. al.; *The Anxiety and Phobia Workbook* by Edmund H. Bourne, Ph. D. **Contact:** Tesilya Hanauer, Acquisitions Editor.

NEW HORIZON PRESS

P.O. Box 669, Far Hills, NJ 07931. 908-604-6311. E-mail: nhp@newhorizonpressbooks.com. Website: www.newhorizonpressbooks.com. Dr. Joan Dunphy, Editor-in-Chief. **Description:** True stories of crime/justice, medical dramas, psychological thrillers, and courageous individuals in extraordinary circumstances. Also publishes nonfiction on current issues (self-help, minority concerns, politics, health, environment, animal rights) and books for children that teach tolerance, coping, and crisis skills. **Books Statistics:** 12 titles/yr; 90% first-time authors; 50% unagented.

Proposal Process: Query with outline, sample chapters, and SASE. Accepts simultaneous and electronic queries. Prefers hard copy. Responds in 4 weeks. **Payment:** Royalty. **Sample Titles:** *Healing Journeys: How Trauma Survivors Learn to Live Again* by Linda Daniels, Psy.D.; *Changing Course: One Woman's True-Life Adventures as a Merchant Marine* by Jeanne Marie Lutz. **Tips:** "We seek nonfiction stories of courageous individuals with an intense human interest appeal. We also publish investigative journalism that probes important public issues."

THE NEW PRESS

450 W 41st St., Fl. 6, New York, NY 10036. 212-629-8802. Website: www.thenewpress.com. Andre Schiffrin, Director. **Description:** Serious nonfiction in the fields of history, politics, African American studies, economics, labor, multicultural education, media, and Latin American studies, among others. Does not publish U.S. fiction or poetry, but has a program in international fiction. **Books Statistics:** 50 titles/yr (several hundred submissions); 20% by first-time authors; 50% unagented. **Proposal Process:** Send query. Simultaneous queries considered, but not e-queries. Responds in 2 months. **Payment:** Royalty. **Sample Titles:** (Fiction) *Absolute Perfection of Crime* by Tanguy Viel; (Nonfiction) *American Power and the New Mandarins: Historical and Political Essays* by Noam Chomsky; *Crossing Into America: The New Literature of* Immigration edited by Louis Mendoza and S. Shankar. **Tips:** "See website or request a print catalog to get an idea of the type of material we publish."

NEW VICTORIA PUBLISHERS

P.O. Box 27, Norwich, VT 05055. 802-649-5297. E-mail: newvic@aol.com. Website: www.newvictoria.com. Rebecca Béguin, Acquisitions Editor. **Description:** Publishes mysteries and lesbian novels. **Books Statistics:** 6 titles/yr (150-200 submissions); 2-3% by first-time authors; 100% unagented. **Proposal Process:** Query with outline, sample chapters, and SASE. Accepts simultaneous queries, but not e-queries. Prefers hard copy. Responds in 2-3 weeks. **Payment:** Royalty, 10%.

NEW WORLD LIBRARY

14 Pamaron Way, Novato, CA 94949. 415-884-2100. Website: www.newworldlibrary.com. Georgia Hughes, Editorial Director. **Description:** General trade nonfiction in the areas of spirituality, self-help, parenting, women's studies, alternative health, religion, enlightened business, animal spirituality, and multicultural studies. No personal memoirs or fiction. **Books Statistics:** 35 titles/yr (2,000 submissions); 10% by first-time authors; 30% unagented. **Proposal Process:** Query with sample chapters, outline, and SASE. Accepts simultaneous queries, but not e-queries. Prefers hard copy. Responds in 90 days. **Payment:** Royalty.

NEW YORK UNIVERSITY PRESS

838 Broadway, Fl. 3, New York, NY 10003. 212-998-2575.
E-mail: nyupress.info@nyu.edu. Website: www.nyupress.org. **Description:** Scholarly nonfiction in history, law, religion, media studies, cultural studies, sociology, politics, anthropology, and psychology. No fiction or poetry. **Proposal Process:** Submit pro-

posal with sample chapters and curriculum vitae. Enclose SASE for return of materials. Responds in 6 weeks. **Sample Titles:** *Irving Howe: A Life of Passionate Dissent* by Gerald Sorin; *Voicing Chicana Feminisms: Young Women Speak Out on Sexuality and Identity* by Aida Hurtado.

NEWCASTLE PUBLISHING
19450 Greenbriar Dr., Tarzana, CA 91356-5524. 818-787-4378. Daryl Jacoby. **Description:** Nonfiction manuscripts, 200-250 pages, for older adults on personal health, health care issues, psychology, and relationships. No fads or trends. **Proposal Process:** Simultaneous queries considered. **Payment:** Royalty. **Tips:** "We want books with a long shelf life."

NEWMARKET PRESS
18 E 48th St., Fl. 15, New York, NY 10017. 212-832-3575. E-mail: mailbox@newmarketpress.com. Website: www.newmarketpress.com. Shannon Berning, Assistant Editor. **Description:** Nonfiction on health, psychology, self-help, child care, parenting, music, film, and personal finance. **Proposal Process:** Submit cover letter with concise 1-page summary of project and your qualifications, TOC, marketing analysis including similar or competing titles, and sample chapters (or complete manuscript). **Payment:** Royalty. **Sample Titles:** *Kids & Sports* by Eric Small, M.D., FAAP; *The Healing Touch for Dogs* and *The Healing Touch for Cats* by Dr. Michael W. Fox; *Stress Relief* by Georgia Witkin, Ph.D.; *The West Wing Script Book* by Aaron Sorkin.

NICOLAS-HAYS INC.
P.O. Box 2039, York Beach, ME 03910-2039. 207-363-1558. E-mail: nhi@ici.net. Website: www.nicolashays.com. **Description:** Books on Jungian psychology, Eastern philosophy, and women's psycho-spirituality.

NO STARCH PRESS
555 De Haro St., Suite 250, San Francisco, CA 94107. 415-863-9900. E-mail: info@nostarch.com. Website: www.nostarch.com. **Description:** Publisher of computer books. **Books Statistics:** 25 titles/yr.

NOLO
950 Parker St., Berkeley, CA 94710. 510-549-1976. Website: www.nolo.com/manuscripts.cfm. **Description:** Publisher of self-help legal books and software for consumers, small businesses, and nonprofit organizations. **Contact:** Acquisitions Editor.

NORTH COUNTRY PRESS
P.O. Box 546, Unity, ME 04988-0546. 207-948-2208. E-mail: ncp@unisets.net. Patricia Newell / Mary Kenney, Publishers. **Description:** Nonfiction with a Maine and/or New England tie-in with emphasis on the outdoors; also limited fiction (Maine-based mysteries). **Proposal Process:** Query with SASE, outline, and sample chapters. No unsolicited manuscripts. **Payment:** Royalty. **Tips:** "We publish high-quality books for people who love New England."

NORTHEASTERN UNIVERSITY PRESS

360 Huntington Ave., 416 CP, Boston, MA 02115. 617-373-5480.
Website: www.nupress.neu.edu. Robert Gormley and Sarah Rowley, Editors.
Description: Nonfiction trade and scholarly titles, 50,000-200,000 words, in music, criminal justice, women's studies, ethnic studies, law and society, political science, American studies, and American history. **Proposal Process:** Submit query with outline and sample chapter. **Payment:** Royalty.

NORTHERN ILLINOIS UNIVERSITY PRESS

310 N 5th St., DeKalb, IL 60115. 815-753-1826. Website: www.niu.edu/univ_press.
Mary L. Lincoln, Editorial Director. **Description:** Publishes nonfiction titles on history, politics, anthropology, archaeology, and literary and cultural studies. **Books Statistics:** 22 titles/yr (500 submissions); 50% by first-time authors; 90% unagented. **Proposal Process:** Query with outline and sample chapters. Accepts simultaneous and electronic queries. Prefers hard copy.

NORTHWESTERN UNIVERSITY PRESS

629 Noyes St., Evanston, IL 60208. 847-491-5313.
E-mail: nupress@northwestern.edu. Website: www.nupress.northwestern.edu. Sue Betz, Executive Editor. **Description:** Trade and scholarly books. **Sample Titles:** *Bridges of Memory: Chicago's First Wave of Black Migration* by Timuel Black; *The Nature of Truth* by Sergio Troncoso.

NORTHWORD PRESS

Creative Publishing International, 18705 Lake Dr. East, Chanhassen, MN 55317.
Website: www.northwordpress.com. **Description:** Adult and children's nonfiction on nature and wildlife topics. **Books Statistics:** 15-20 titles/yr (500 submissions); 10% by first-time authors; 35% unagented. **Proposal Process:** Send query, outline, and sample chapters for adult nonfiction. Send query only for children's proposals. Accepts simultaneous queries. Responds in 90 days. **Payment:** Royalty on 1/2 of projects, 5% list. Flat fee on 1/2 of projects; $3,000-$10,000. **Sample Titles:** (Adult) *America From 500 Feet!* by Bill and Wesley Fortney; *The Heart of a Champion* by Frank Deford; (Children's) *Trout, Trout, Trout!* by Eve Bunting. **Tips:** No poetry or personal memoirs/essays on nature. Also, no "green" or animal rehabilitation stories. **Contact:** Bryan Tranden (adult titles) or Aimee Jackson (children's titles).

W.W. NORTON AND CO., INC.

500 Fifth Ave., New York, NY 10110. E-mail: manuscripts@wwnorton.com. Website: www.wwnorton.com. Starling Lawrence, Editor-in-Chief. **Description:** High-quality literary fiction and nonfiction. **Proposal Process:** Send outline, 1 sample chapter, and SASE to Editorial Dept. Accepts brief e-mail submissions (no longer than 6 pages). **Tips:** No occult, paranormal, religious, genre fiction (formula romance, science fiction, westerns), arts and crafts, YA, or children's books.

O'REILLY & ASSOCIATES

1005 Gravenstein Hwy N, Sebastopol, CA 95472. 707-827-7000. E-mail: proposals@oreilly.com. Website: www.oreilly.com. **Description:** Nonfiction titles on computer technology. **Proposal Process:** Send formal proposal. State how you are qualified by outlining your technical experience as well as your experience as a writer. **Sample Titles:** *C++ in a Nutshell* by Ray Lischner; *Head First Java* by Kathy Sierra and Bert Bates. **Tips:** "We are the premier information source for leading-edge computer technologies. Our company's books bring to light the knowledge of technology innovators. O'Reilly books, known for the animals on their covers, occupy a treasured place on the shelves of the developers building the next generation of software."

OHIO UNIVERSITY PRESS/SWALLOW PRESS

Scott Quadrangle, Athens, OH 45701. 740-593-1155. Website: www.ohiou.edu/oupress. David Sanders, Director. **Description:** Ohio University Press: Scholarly nonfiction, 300-400 manuscript pages. Especially interested in Victorian studies, contemporary history, regional studies, and African studies. Swallow Press: General-interest nonfiction and frontier Americana. **Proposal Process:** Query with outline and sample chapters. **Payment:** Royalty. **Sample Titles:** *Women, Work, and Representation: Needlewomen in Victorian Art and Literature* by Lynn M. Alexander. **Tips:** Also hosts annual Hollis Summers Poetry Award Competition. See guidelines at website.

ONJINJINKTA PUBLISHING

The Betty J. Eadie Press, 909 SE Everett Mall Way, Suite A120, Everett, WA 98208. 425-290-7809. E-mail: peter@onjinjinkta.com. Website: www.onjinjinkta.com. Peter Orullian, Senior Editor. **Description:** Nonfiction books with inspiration or spiritual content, must contain redeeming themes. Publishes nonfiction aimed at strengthening virtues, also books whose topics extoll family values. **Books Statistics:** 8 titles/yr (2,000 submissions); 80% by first-time authors; 70% unagented. **Proposal Process:** Query with outline and sample chapters. **Payment:** Royalty/advance. **Tips:** No New Age books or category fiction. "We seek books with clearly defined subject matter, authoritative writing, and original approaches to classic themes of spirituality." **Contact:** Tom Eadie, Submissions Editor.

OPEN COURT PUBLISHING CO.

332 S Michigan Ave., Suite 1100, Chicago, IL 60604. 312-939-1500. Website: www.opencourtbooks.com. David Ramsay Steele, Editor. **Description:** Scholarly books on philosophy, Eastern thought, and related areas. Trade books of a thoughtful nature on music, social issues, Jungian thought, psychology, education, social issues, and contemporary culture. **Books Statistics:** 20 titles/yr (1,200 submissions); 20% by first-time authors; 70% unagented. **Proposal Process:** Send sample chapters with outline, resumé, and SASE. No simultaneous or electronic queries. Prefers hard copy. Response time varies. **Payment:** Royalty. **Sample Titles:** *The World of the Rings: Language, Religion, and Adventure in Tolkien* by Jared Lobdell.

ORCHISES PRESS

P.O. Box 20602, Alexandria, VA 22320-1602. 703-683-1243.
E-mail: lathbury@gmu.edu. Website: http://mason.gmu.edu/~rlathbur. Roger Lathbury, Editor. **Description:** Original poetry, essays, some humor, textbooks, reprints. No fiction, children's books, or cookbooks. **Books Statistics:** 5-8 titles/yr (500 submissions); 20-40% by first-time authors; 90% unagented. **Proposal Process:** Query with sample chapters or complete manuscript, include SASE. Accepts simultaneous queries, but not e-queries. Hard copy only. **Payment:** Royalty. **Tips:** "For poetry, we're a hard market—unless some work has appeared in serious magazines of national stature (*The Atlantic Monthly*, *Poetry*, *The New Yorker*) chances are slim. Poetry must be technically adroit, intellectually precise and sophisticated."

OREGON STATE UNIVERSITY PRESS

101 Waldo Hall, Corvallis, OR 97331-6407. 541-737-3873. E-mail: mary.braun@oregonstate.edu. Website: http://oregonstate.edu/dept/press. Mary Elizabeth Braun, Acquisitions Editor. **Description:** Scholarly nonfiction and books of importance to the Pacific Northwest, especially those dealing with the history, natural history, culture, and literature of the region; environmental history; or with natural resource issues. **Books Statistics:** 15 titles/yr. **Proposal Process:** Query with summary of manuscript. Responds in 10-12 weeks. **Payment:** Royalty. **Sample Titles:** *Oregon's Promise: An Interpretive History* by David Peterson Del Mar; *Frigid Embrace: Politics, Economics, and Environment in Alaska* by Stephen Haycox. **Tips:** See guidelines on website.

THE OVERLOOK PRESS

Peter Mayer Publishers, Inc., 141 Wooster St., Fl. 4, New York, NY 10012.
212-673-2210. E-mail: overlook@netstep.net. Website: www.overlookpress.com. Tracy Carns, Editor. **Description:** Literary fiction, fantasy/science fiction, and foreign literature in translation. General nonfiction, including art, architecture, design, film, history, biography, crafts/lifestyle, gay/lesbian, martial arts, Hudson Valley regional interest, and children's books. **Proposal Process:** Query with outline, sample chapters, and SASE. Does not accept query letters and submissions via e-mail. **Payment:** Royalty. **Sample Titles:** *The Corruption of American Politics* by Elizabeth Drew; *Icons of the Twentieth Century* by Barbara Cady.

OXFORD UNIVERSITY PRESS

198 Madison Ave., New York, NY 10016. 212-726-6000. Website: www.oup.com/us.
Description: Serious nonfiction, trade, and academic books in the humanities and social sciences; college textbooks, medical, scientific, technical and reference books. **Books Statistics:** 1,500 titles/yr; 40% by first-time authors; 80% unagented. **Proposal Process:** Query. **Payment:** Royalty. **Sample Titles:** *Gone to Texas: A History of the Lone Star State* by Randolph B. Campbell; *All Shook Up: How Rock n' Roll Changed America* by Glenn C. Altschuler.

PANTHEON BOOKS

The Knopf Publishing Group/Random House, Inc., 1745 Broadway, New York, NY 10019. 212-782-9000. Daniel Frank, Editorial Director. **Description:** Contemporary literary fiction, graphic novels, and nonfiction in the areas of current affairs, literature, the arts, business, travel, nature, science, and history. **Proposal Process:** Query with SASE. **Payment:** Royalty. **Sample Titles:** *Waiting* by Ha Jin; *Hidden Power: Presidential Marriages That Shaped Our Recent History* by Kati Marton.

PARA PUBLISHING

P.O. Box 8206-238, Santa Barbara, CA 93118-8206. 805-968-7277.
E-mail: info@parapublishing.com. Website: www.parapublishing.com. Dan Poynter, Publisher. **Description:** Adult nonfiction books on parachutes and skydiving only. Author must present evidence of having made at least 1,000 jumps. **Proposal Process:** Query. **Payment:** Royalty.

PARAGON HOUSE PUBLISHERS

2285 University Ave. W, Suite 200, St. Paul, MN 55114-1635. 651-644-3087.
Website: www.paragonhouse.com. Rose Yokoi, Editorial Director. **Description:** Reference and scholarly titles in the areas of biography, history, philosophy, psychology, religion, spiritual health, political science and international relations. **Books Statistics:** 12-15 titles/yr (2,500-3,000 submissions); 80% by first-time authors; 90% unagented. **Proposal Process:** Query with abstract of project. Include summary of your premise, main arguments, and conclusion. Does not accept e-mail submissions. Responds in 3 months. Guidelines available on website. **Payment:** Royalty, typically 10% net. **Sample Titles:** *Politics of Parenting* by William B. Irvine; *Oneness Perceived* by Jeffrey Eisen. **Tips:** "No fiction, poetry, or New Age materials. We seek scholarly nonfiction of cultural and intellectual appeal with international and interdisciplinary character."

PARENTING PRESS

P.O. Box 75267, Seattle, WA 98125. 206-364-2900.
E-mail: office@parentingpress.com. Website: www.parentingpress.com. Carolyn J. Threadgill, Publisher. **Description:** Nonfiction titles on child guidance, parent education, emotional competency, and children's safety. Books offer concrete skills modeling and problem-solving processes and acknowledge the importance of feelings and teaching responsibility. **Books Statistics:** 6 titles/yr (500+ submissions); 80% by first-time authors. **Proposal Process:** Query with outline, sample chapters and SASE. Accepts simultaneous and electronic queries. Prefers hard copy. Responds in 6 weeks. See website for detailed guidelines. **Payment:** Royalty. **Sample Titles:** *I'm Mad* by Elizabeth Crary; *Taking No for an Answer and Other Skills Children Need* by Laurie Simons. **Tips:** "Our niche is building social skills, dealing with feelings, and preventing abuse. We seek authors with expertise derived from working with children."

PAUL DRY BOOKS
117 S 17th St., Suite 1102, Philadelphia, PA 19103. 215-732-9939.
E-mail: editor@pauldrybooks.com. Website: www.pauldrybooks.com. Paul Dry, Publisher. **Description:** Literary fiction and nonfiction. **Sample Titles:** *Hotel Kid: A Times Square Childhood* by Stephen Lewis; *For Solo Violin* by Aldo Zargani.

PAVEMENT SAW PRESS
P.O. Box 6291, Columbus, OH 43206. 614-445-0534.
E-mail: editor@pavementsaw.org. Website: www.pavementsaw.org. David Baratier, Editor. **Description:** Nonprofit organization publishing collections of poetry. **Books Statistics:** 7-8 titles/yr (700 submissions); 50% by first-time authors; 100% unagented. **Payment:** Royalty or flat fee ($1,000).

PEACHPIT PRESS
Pearson plc, 1249 Eighth St., Berkeley, CA 94710. 510-524-2178. E-mail: proposals@peachpit.com. Website: www.peachpit.com. **Description:** Books on computer and graphic-design topics. **Proposal Process:** Query with outline and sample chapters for manuscripts, 100-1,100 words, or submit proposal via e-mail. **Sample Titles:** *Before & After Page Design* by John McWade.

PEARSON EDUCATION INC.
One Lake St., Upper Saddle River, NJ 07675. 201-236-7000. Website: www.pearsoned.com. **Description:** Intergrated educational textbooks, assessment tools, and educational services.

PELICAN PUBLISHING CO., INC.
P.O. Box 3110, Gretna, LA 70054. 504-368-1175. Website: www.pelicanpub.com. Nina Kooij, Acquisitions Editor. **Description:** General trade nonfiction. Travel guides (destination-specific, no travelogues); children's books (holiday, ethnic or regional); popular history (not scholarly); and cookbooks (cuisine-specific). **Books Statistics:** 95 titles/yr (5,000 submissions); 10% by first-time authors; 90% unagented. **Proposal Process:** Query with outline, sample chapters, and SASE. No simultaneous or electronic queries. Hard copy only. See complete guidelines on website. **Payment:** Royalty. **Sample Titles:** *Festivals of Lite Kosher Cookbook* by Gail Ashkanazi-Hankin; *The Influence of Air Power upon History* by Walter J. Boyne; *Country Music Night Before Christmas* by Thomas N. Turner. **Tips:** No autobiographical material.

PENGUIN PUTNAM INC.
Pearson plc, 375 Hudson St., New York, NY 10014. 212-366-2000.
Website: www.penguinputnam.com. Phyllis Gran, President. **Description:** General interest fiction and nonfiction paperbacks. Owns several imprints and trademarks including Berkley Books, Dutton, Grosset & Dunlap, New American Library, Penguin, Philomel, G.P. Putnam's Sons, Penguin Putnam Books for Young Readers, Riverhead Books, and Viking. **Payment:** Royalty.

THE PENNSYLVANIA STATE UNIVERSITY PRESS
University Support Bldg. 1, Suite C, 820 N University Dr., University Park, PA 16802. 814-865-1327. Website: www.psupress.org. Peter Potter, Editor-in-Chief. **Description:** Scholarly nonfiction in the areas of art history, East European studies, gender studies, history, Latin American studies, law, philosophy, political science, religion, and sociology. **Proposal Process:** Query with outline and SASE. Considers simultaneous queries. **Payment:** Royalty.

THE PERMANENT PRESS
4170 Noyac Rd., Sag Harbor, NY 11963. 631-725-1101. Website: www.thepermanentpress.com. Judith Shepard, Editor. **Description:** Literary fiction. Original and arresting adult novels. **Books Statistics:** 12 titles/yr (6,000-7,000 submissions); 30-40% by first-time authors; 70% unagented. **Proposal Process:** Send query, sample chapters, and SASE. Accepts simultaneous queries, but not e-queries. Prefers hard copy. **Payment:** Royalty. **Sample Titles:** *Angels in the Morning* by Sash Troyan; *A Week in Winter* by Barth Landor; *My Brother's Passion* by D. James Smith **Tips:** "We seek distinctive writing style and original voice in adult fiction."

PERSPECTIVES PRESS
P.O. Box 90318, Indianapolis, IN 46290-0318. 317-872-3055. E-mail: ppress@iquest.net. Website: www.perspectivespress.com. Pat Johnston, Publisher. **Description:** Nonfiction books on infertility, adoption, and closely related reproductive health and child welfare issues (foster care, etc.). **Proposal Process:** Query. **Payment:** Royalty. **Tips:** "Read our guidelines before submitting."

PETERSON'S
Thompson Learning, 2000 Lenox Dr., Fl. 3, Princeton Pike Corporate Center, Lawrenceville, NJ 08648. 609-896-1800. Website: www.peterson.com. **Description:** Books and online products that offer information on colleges, universities, test preparation, study abroad, summer opportunities, graduate programs, and career exploration. **Books Statistics:** 200 titles/yr (250-300 submissions). **Payment:** Work-for-hire. **Contact:** Del Franz, Editor-in-Chief.

PHILOMEL BOOKS
Penguin Young Readers Group/Penguin Group (USA) Inc., 345 Hudson St., New York, NY 10014. 212-414-3610. Website: www.penguinputnam.com. Patricia Lee Gauch, Editorial Director. **Description:** Juvenile picture books and young adult fiction, particularly fantasy and historical. Fresh, original work with compelling characters and sense of the dramatic. **Proposal Process:** Query. **Contact:** Michael Green, Senior Editor.

PINEAPPLE PRESS
P.O. Box 3889, Sarasota, FL 34230. 941-359-0886. E-mail: info@pineapplepress.com. Website: www.pineapplepress.com. June Cussen, Editor. **Description:** Trade fiction and nonfiction about Florida. **Books Statistics:** 20 titles/yr (1,500 submissions); 75%

by first-time authors; 99% unagented. **Proposal Process:** Query with outline, sample chapters, and SASE. Accepts simultaneous queries, but not e-queries. Prefers hard copy. **Payment:** Royalty. **Tips:** "We're looking for excellent books on Florida."

PLATYPUS MEDIA
627 A Street NE, Washington, DC 20002. 202-546-1674.
E-mail: info@platypusmedia.com. Website: www.platypusmedia.com. Dia Michels, President. **Description:** Adult nonfiction titles on women's health, breastfeeding, and family life. Also publishes children's books (with accompanying activity guides) that explore the theme of families. Currently not accepting unsolicited manuscripts.

PLAYERS PRESS, INC.
P.O. Box 1132, Studio City, CA 91614. 818-789-4980. Robert Gordon, Editor.
Description: Publishes plays and musical books on the performing arts, theatre, film, television, costumes, makeup, technical theatre, technical film, etc. **Books Statistics:** 30 titles/yr (1,000 submissions); 60% by first-time authors; 80% unagented. **Proposal Process:** Query with manuscript-size SASE and 2 #10 SASE's for correspondence. Include bio/resumé. No simultaneous or electronic queries. Responds in 3 weeks to queries, 1-3 months to submissions. **Payment:** Royalty.

POCKET BOOKS
Simon & Schuster, Inc., 1230 Avenue of the Americas, New York, NY 10020.
212-698-7000. Maggie Crawford, V.P./Editorial Director. **Description:** Publisher of adult fiction. **Proposal Process:** Accepts material from literary agents only. **Payment:** Royalty. **Sample Titles:** *The Summerhouse* by Jude Deveraux.

POISONED PEN PRESS
6962 E First Ave., Suite 103, Scottsdale, AZ 85251.
E-mail: editor@poisonedpenpress.com. Website: www.poisonedpenpress.com.
Description: Adult mysteries on crime and detection. **Books Statistics:** 3-5 titles/month. **Proposal Process:** See website or send SASE for guidelines. **Payment:** Royalty. **Sample Titles:** *Silver Lies* by Ann Parker; *Dead Man's Touch* by Kit Ehrman. **Contact:** Editorial Review Committee.

POLESTAR
Imprint of Raincoast Books
9050 Shaughnessy St., Vancouver, British Columbia V6P 6E5 Canada. 604-323-7100.
E-mail: info@raincoast.com. Website: www.raincoast.com. Lynn Henry, Associate Publisher. **Description:** Poetry, adult and juvenile/teen fiction, sports, juvenile/teen nonfiction, and general trade nonfiction. **Proposal Process:** No unsolicited manuscripts, query letters only. List previous writing or publishing experience. For illustrated material, send samples only. Do not send original artwork or slides. Include SASE. Responds in 8-16 weeks. See submission guidelines on website for further information. **Sample Titles:** *The Five Books of Moses Lapinsky* by Karen X. Tulchinsky; *Beatrice Chancy* by George Elliot Clarke.

POMEGRANATE

Pomegranate Communications, Inc., P.O. Box 808022, Petaluma, CA 94975-8022. 707-586-5500. E-mail: info@pomegranate.com. Website: www.pomegranate.com. **Description:** Nonfiction titles on a variety of subjects including history, multicultural studies, women's studies, photography, music, and humor. Special emphasis on art.

PONCHA PRESS

P.O. Box 280, Morrison, CO 80465. 303-697-2384.
E-mail: bosgood@ponchapress.com. Website: www.ponchapress.com. Barbara Osgood-Hartness, Editor-in-Chief. **Description:** Fiction and nonfiction. **Books Statistics:** 3 titles/yr. **Proposal Process:** Currently not accepting manuscripts. **Sample Titles:** (Nonfiction) *An English Experience* by Marge D. Hansen; (Fiction) *The Gold of El Negro* by Michael C. Haley.

POPULAR PRESS

University of Wisconsin Press, 1930 Monroe St., Fl. 3, Madison, WI 53711.
E-mail: tmbrock@wisc.edu; rbrowne@mailstore.bgsu.edu. Tricia Brock, Acquisitions Editor; Ray B. Browne, Pat Browne, General Editors, Bowling Green, OH. **Description:** General and specific, trade and scholarly studies on contemporary and classic popular culture subjects (tv/film, celebrities, religion, literature, women's studies/masculinities, biography), fiction and memoir high in popular culture content considered (200-400 pages). **Books Statistics:** 10-15 titles/yr (400 submissions); 50% by first-time authors. **Proposal Process:** Send 1-3 page query with outline/TOC and bio/curriculum vitae via regular mail or pasted into body of e-mail (no attachments). No simultaneous or electronic manuscript submissions. Responds in 3-6 months. **Payment:** Royalty.

POSSIBILITY PRESS

One Oakglade Circle, Hummelstown, PA 17036-9525. 717-566-0468.
E-mail: possibilitypress@aol.com. Website: www.possibilitypress.com.
Mike Markowski, Publisher; Marjie Markowski, Editor-in-Chief. **Description:** How-to, self-help, inspirational. Subjects include business, popular psychology, current significant events, success/motivation, entrepreneurship, sales/marketing, networking, MLM, home-based business topics, and human-interest success stories. Also some fiction that teaches lessons about life and success. **Books Statistics:** 5-10 titles/yr (1,000 submissions); 90% by first-time authors; 95% unagented. **Proposal Process:** Query with SASE. Prefers hard copy. Responds in 2 months. See website for guidelines. **Sample Titles:** (Nonfiction) *Leading Leaders to Leadership* by John Fuhrman. (Fiction) *The Millionaire Mentor* by Greg S. Reid. **Tips:** "Our focus in on creating short to medium length bestsellers by authors who speak and consult. We're looking for authors who are passionate about making a difference in the world. To be considered, the author needs to be entrepreneurially-minded and self-motivated enough to champion his/her book's message via radio, TV, and print media."

PRAEGER PUBLISHERS

Greenwood Publishing Group, Inc., 88 Post Rd. West, Westport, CT 06881-5007. 203-226-3571. Website: www.praeger.com. **Description:** Scholarly and professional nonfiction in the humanities and social sciences. Particular interest in military/history, psychology, business, current affairs, politics/international relations, performing arts, and literature. **Proposal Process:** Query with outline. **Payment:** Royalty. **Sample Titles:** *The United Nations and Iraq: Defanging the Viper* by Jean E. Krasno and James S. Sutterlin.

PRESTEL PUBLISHING

900 Broadway, Suite 603, New York, NY 10003. 212-955-2720. E-mail: sales@prestel-usa.com. Website: www.prestel.com. **Description:** Books on art, architecture, and photography. **Sample Titles:** *Xtreme Interiors* by Courtenay Smith and Annette Ferrara; *Representing the State: Capital City Planning in the Early Twentieth Century* by Wolfgang Sonne.

PRICE STERN SLOAN, INC.

The Putnam Berkley Group/Penguin Putnam, Inc., 345 Hudson St., New York, NY 10014. 212-414-3610. Website: www.penguinputnam.com. Jon Anderson, Publisher. **Description:** Witty and quirky novelty juvenile titles. Imprints include Troubador Press, Wee Sing, and MadLibs. **Proposal Process:** No unsolicited manuscripts accepted. Query first. **Payment:** Royalty. **Sample Titles:** *The Ghost Hunter's Handbook* by Rachel Dickenson; *Haunted Mad Libs* by Roger Price, et al. **Tips:** No novels or picture books.

PRIMA PUBLISHING

3000 Lava Ridge Ct., Roseville, CA 95661. 916-787-7000. Website: www.primapublishing.com. Alice Feinstein, Editorial Director. **Description:** Nonfiction books in diverse areas including health, parenting and education, business and current affairs. **Proposal Process:** Query with outline, sample chapter, and market research. Responds in 6-8 weeks. Hard copy format preferred. **Payment:** Royalty and flat fee, standard range. **Sample Titles:** *Maximize Your Presentation Skills* by Ellen A. Kaye; *Encyclopedia of Sports and Fitness Nutrition* by Liz Applegate, Ph.D. **Contact:** David Richardson, Denise Sternad, Jamie Miller, Jennifer Base Sander.

PRIMER PUBLISHERS

5738 N Central Ave., Phoenix, AZ 85012. 602-234-1574. E-mail: info@primerpublishers.com. Website: www.primerpublishers.com. Bill Fessler, Acquisitions Editor. **Description:** Travel and regional subjects, especially about the Southwest U.S. Also publishes history (20th century, World War II, and Middle East conflicts), and "Living the Simple Life" philosophical writings. No fiction. General adult audience. **Books Statistics:** 5-10 titles/yr (20 submissions); 50% by first-time authors; 99% unagented. **Proposal Process:** Send query, outline, and sample chapters if available. Prefers hard copy. No simultaneous queries. Responds in 1 month. **Payment:** Royalty (8% net) or flat fee.

PRINCETON ARCHITECTURAL PRESS

37 E Seventh St., New York, NY 10003-8027. 212-995-9620.
Website: www.papress.com. **Description:** Architecture and graphic design books including architectural monographs, cities and landscapes, guidebooks, history, theory and professional practice.

PRINCETON UNIVERSITY PRESS

41 William St., Princeton, NJ 08540. 609-258-4900.
Website: www.pup.princeton.edu. Sam Elworthy, Editor-in-Chief. **Description:** Scholarly and scientific books on all subjects. **Proposal Process:** Submit brief proposal with curriculum vitae. **Sample Titles:** *Women Don't Ask: Negotiation and the Gender Divide* by Linda Babcock and Sara Laschever; *Ancient Wine: The Search for the Origin of Viniculture* by Patrick E. McGovern.

PROJECT MANAGEMENT INSTITUTE PUBLISHING DIVISION

Four Campus Blvd., Newtown Square, PA 19073-3299. 610-356-4600. E-mail: pmihq@pmi.org. Website: www.pmi.org. **Description:** Books and resources on project management and general business/management.

PROMETHEUS BOOKS

59 John Glenn Dr., Amherst, NY 14228. 716-691-0133. Website: www.prometheus-books.com. **Description:** Popular science, social sciences, New Age, religion, psychology, current events, humanism, health, biographies, politics, education and children's titles.

PRUETT PUBLISHING CO.

7464 Arapahoe Rd., Suite A-9, Boulder, CO 80303. 303-449-4919. E-mail: pruettbks@pruettpublishing.com. Website: www.pruettpublishing.com. Jim Pruett, Acquisitions Editor. **Description:** Nonfiction books and guides dealing with the Rocky Mountain West. Subjects include outdoor recreation travel and history, hiking, flyfishing, nature, and the environment. Also publishes textbooks on the history of Colorado for grade school students. **Books Statistics:** 10 titles/yr (300 submissions); 50% by first-time authors; 90% unagented. **Proposal Process:** Send proposal with brief summary, outline/TOC, 1-2 sample chapters, examples of artwork, market anaylsis, and bio/resume. Send electronic or hard copy. **Payment:** Royalty, net 10-12%. **Sample Titles:** *Yellowstone: Portraits of a Fly-Fishing Landscape* by John Juracek; *Montana Disasters: Fire, Floods, and Catastrophes* by Molly Searl; *Lessons of Fairsized Creek: 12 Ways to Catch More Trout on the Fly* by John Huber.

PUCKERBRUSH PRESS

76 Main St., Orono, ME 04473-1430. 207-581-3832. Constance Hunting, Editorial Director. **Description:** Publishes poetry, fiction, and belles lettres. **Books Statistics:** 3 titles/yr (500 submissions); 60% by first-time authors; 100% unagented. **Proposal Process:** Send query with complete manuscript and SASE. Accepts simultaneous queries, but not e-queries. Responds in 3 months. **Payment:** Royalty, range

10% net. **Sample Titles:** (Poetry) *Settling* by Patricia Ranzoni. (Fiction) *The Crow on the Spruce* by Chenoweth Hall. **Tips:** Literary only. Avoid crime, incest, prison, detective, police, mystery, and religious themes.

PURDUE UNIVERSITY PRESS

Purdue University, South Campus Courts, Building E, 509 Harrison St., West Lafayette, IN 47907-2025. 765-494-2038. E-mail: pupress@purdue.edu. Website: www.thepress.purdue.edu. **Description:** "Dedicated to the dissemination of scholarly and professional information, the Press provides quality resources in several key subject areas including aging, agriculture, business, technology, health, veterinary medicine and other challenging disciplines in the humanities and sciences."

QUILL DRIVER BOOKS/WORD DANCER PRESS, INC.

1831 Industrial Way, Suite 101, Sanger, CA 93657. 559-876-2170. E-mail: info@quilldriverbooks.com. Website: www.quilldriverbooks.com. Stephen Blake Mettee, Publisher. **Description:** Biographies, how-to books, self-help for seniors, parenting, the craft of writing, and California regional topics. **Books Statistics:** 12 titles/yr (500 submissions); 60% by first-time authors; 95% unagented. **Proposal Process:** Send query with nonfiction book proposal and SASE for reply. Prefers hard copy. Considers simultaneous submissions. **Payment:** Royalty, 4-10%. **Sample Titles:** *It's Never Too Late to Be Happy: Repreparing Yourself For Happiness* by Muriel James; *Answers to Satisfy the Soul* by Jim Denney. **Tips:** Does not publish poetry, children's books, or fiction.

QUIXOTE PRESS

1854 345th Ave., Wever, IA 52658. 319-372-7480. E-mail: maddmack@interl.com. Bruce Carlson, President. **Description:** Adult fiction and nonfiction including humor, folklore, and regional cookbooks. **Proposal Process:** Query with sample chapters and outline. **Payment:** Royalty.

RAGGED MOUNTAIN PRESS

The McGraw-Hill Companies, P.O. Box 220, Camden, ME 04843. 207-236-4837. E-mail: alex_barnett@mcgraw-hill.com. Website: www.raggedmountainpress.com. Jonathan Eaton, Editorial Director. **Description:** Nonfiction titles on a variety of outdoor activities (fishing, camping, sea kayaking, survival techniques, RV living, etc.) **Sample Titles:** *The Backpacker's Handbook* by Chris Townsend; *The Essential Wilderness Navigator: How to Find Your Way in the Great Outdoors* by David Seidman. **Contact:** Alex Barnett, Acquisitions Editor.

RAINBOW BOOKS, INC.

P.O. Box 430, Highland City, FL 33846-0430. 863-648-4420. E-mail: rbibooks@aol.com. Betsy Lampe, Editorial Director. **Description:** Primarily nonfiction with a small list of mystery fiction. **Books Statistics:** 15-20 titles/yr (600 submissions); 85% first-time authors; 99% unagented. **Proposal Process:** Query with outline, sample chapters, and SASE. Accepts simultaneous queries, but not e-queries. Prefers hard copy. **Payment:** Royalty. **Tips:** Looking for a broad range of nonfiction books. In mystery fiction, primarily seeking "cozies" of no more than 70,000 words. Send SASE for guidelines. **Contact:** Jamie Peters, Assistant Editor.

RAINCOAST BOOKS

9050 Shaughnessy St., Vancouver, British Columbia V6P 6E5 Canada. 604-323-7100. E-mail: infor@raincoast.com. Website: www.raincoast.com. Lynn Henry, Associate Publisher. **Description:** Regional, national, and international titles on the environment, social issues, natural history, sports, and travel. Also, children's books, adult fiction and nonfiction. No genre fiction. **Proposal Process:** No unsolicited manuscripts, query letters only. List previous writing or publishing experience. For illustrated material, send samples only. Do not send original artwork or slides. Include SASE. Responds in 8-16 weeks. See submission guidelines on website for additional information. **Sample Titles:** *Mount Appetite* by Bill Gaston; *A Reckless Moon* by Dianne Warren.

THE READER'S DIGEST ASSOCIATION, INC.

Readers Digest Rd., Pleasantville, NY 10570-7000. 914-238-1000. Website: www.rd.com. **Description:** Publishes books on health, home improvement, gardening, cooking, etc; children's books; Select Editions (condensed books); reading series; Young Families products; music collections; home videos; and other special-interest magazines.

RED HEN PRESS

P.O. Box 3537, Grand Hills, CA 91394. 818-831-0649. E-mail: editors@redhen.org. Website: www.redhen.org. Mark E. Cull, Editor; Kate Gale, Editor. **Description:** Literary fiction (novels, short fiction, gay/lesbian), poetry, memoirs, essays, literary criticism. **Books Statistics:** 12 titles/yr (2,000 submissions); 15% by first-time authors. **Proposal Process:** Send sample chapters via regular mail. **Payment:** Royalty, 10% of sales. **Sample Titles:** (Poetry) *Daphne's Lot* by Chris Albani; (Fiction) *Talking Heads: 77* by John Domini.

RED MOON PRESS

P.O. Box 2461, Winchester, VA 22604-1661. 540-722-2156. E-mail: redmoon@shen-tel.net. **Description:** Publishes books, anthologies, and individual volumes of contemporary haiku.

RED SAGE PUBLISHING

P.O. Box 4844, Seminole, FL 33775. 727-3847. Website: www.redsagepub.com **Description:** Books of ultra-sensual fiction written for the adventurous woman. **Books Statistics:** 2 titles/yr; 50% by first-time authors. **Proposal Process:** Accepts unsoliced manuscripts. No simultaneous submissions. See website for guidelines. **Tips:** "We look for character-driven stories that concentrate on the love and sexual relationship between hero/heroine. Author voice, excellent writing, and strong emotions all are important ingredients." **Contact:** Alexandria Kendall, Publisher.

THE RED SEA PRESS

11 Princess Rd., Trenton, NJ 08648. 609-844-9583.
E-mail: awprsp@africanworld.com. Website: www.africanworld.com. Kassahun Checole, Publisher. **Description:** Adult nonfiction, 360 double-spaced manuscript pages. Focus on nonfiction material with a specialty on the Horn of Africa. **Proposal Process:** Query. **Payment:** Royalty.

RED WHEEL

Imprint of Red Wheel/Weiser, LLC, 368 Congress St., Boston, MA 02210. 617-542-1324. Website: www.redwheelweiser.com. Ms. Pat Bryce, Editor. **Description:** Publishes spirituality, inspirational, and self-help books. **Proposal Process:** Submit outline, sample chapters, and 6-1/2" x 9-1/2" SASE. Hard copy only. Accepts simultaneous queries, but not e-queries. Responds in 3-6 months. **Payment:** Royalty. **Tips:** "Please study our books in a bookstore, library, or publisher's catalog."

REDMOND TECHNOLOGY PRESS

Redmond Technology Press, 8581 154th Avenue Northeast, Redmond, WA 98052. 425-861-9628. E-mail: editor@redtechpress.com. Website: www.redtechpress.com. **Description:** Publishes computer books aimed at the mainstream business user.

REGNERY PUBLISHING, INC.

One Massachusetts Ave., NW, Washington, DC 20001. 202-216-0600.
Website: www.regnery.com. Harry Crocker, Executive Editor. **Description:** Nonfiction titles on current affairs, politics, history, biography and other subjects. The Lifeline Press imprint publishes health titles. **Books Statistics:** 35 titles/yr. **Proposal Process:** Send query with outline and SASE. Hard copy only. Authors must have major media credibility or experience. **Payment:** Royalty.

RIO NUEVO PUBLISHERS

451 N Bonita Ave., Tucson, AZ 85745. 520-623-9558. E-mail: info@rionuevo.com. Website: www.rionuevo.com. **Description:** Nonfiction on the American Southwest. **Sample Titles:** *Celebrating Guadalupe* by Jacqueline Orsini Dunnington; *Clouds for Dessert: Sweet Treats from the Wild West* by Susan Lowell. **Tips:** "Our mission is to publish compelling and visually exciting books about the places, people, and things that make the American Southwest so distinctive." **Contact:** Lisa Cooper, Editorial Dept.; Tracy Vega, Marketing Dept.

RISING TIDE PRESS

P.O. Box 30457, Tucson, AZ 85751. 520-888-1140.
E-mail: books@risingtidepress.com. Website: www.risingtidepress.com.
Brenda Kazen, Editorial Director. **Description:** Lesbian/feminist fiction and nonfiction. Books for, by, and about women. Fiction, romance, mystery, and young adult and adventure, science fiction/fantasy. **Books Statistics:** 6-10 titles/yr (3,000 submissions); 75% by first-time authors; 95% unagented. **Proposal Process:** Query with sample chapters and SASE. Responds in 2-3 months. **Payment:** Royalty.

RIVER CITY PUBLISHING

1719 Mulberry St., Montgomery, AL 36106. 877-408-7078.
E-mail: agordon@rivercitypublishing.com. Website: www.rivercitypublishing.com.
Ashley Gordon, Editor. **Description:** Fiction, nonfiction (emphasizes regionally related travel, history, art, and culture), poetry, children's books with strong crossover appeal to an adult market. **Proposal Process:** Fiction: send at least the first five chapters. Nonfiction: send outline with 3-5 sample chapters. Hard copy only. See website for complete submission guidelines. **Tips:** Most books tend to reflect the South. Generally publishes authors who have been published before but offers a "best first novel" contest in odd-numbered years. Biographies and memoirs should clearly place the subject in the context of an important era or historical event in the South. No textbooks, genre fiction, YA material, self-help, how-to, religious, business, education, medical, or psychology.

RIVERHEAD BOOKS

The Putnam Berkeley Group/Penguin Putnam, Inc., 375 Hudson St., New York, NY 10014. Website: www.penguinputnam.com. Julie Grau, Cindy Spiegel, Co-Editorial Directors. **Description:** Quality fiction and nonfiction. **Proposal Process:** Accepts material from literary agents only. **Payment:** Royalty. **Sample Titles:** *Blue Shoe* by Anne Lamott; *My Dream of You* by Nuala O'Faolain. **Contact:** Alex Morris, Editorial Assistant.

RIVERWOOD BOOKS

P.O. Box 3400, Ashland, OR 97520. 541-488-6415.
E-mail: steve@whitecloudpress.com. Steven Scholl, Publisher. **Description:** General trade nonfiction (health, family, relationships, travel, memoirs, history), fiction, children's, young adult, and poetry.

RIZZOLI INTERNATIONAL PUBLICATIONS, INC.

300 Park Ave. S, New York, NY 10010. 212-387-3620. Charles Miers, Publisher.
Description: Illustrated books on art, architecture, and lifestyle. **Proposal Process:** Query with SASE. Considers simultaneous queries. Accepts e-queries, but prefers hard copy. Response time varies. **Tips:** Does not publish fiction or children's books. Books are highly illustrated in the categories of art, architecture, and lifestyle. **Contact:** David Morton, Sr. Editor, Architecture; Eva Prinz, Editor, Art.

ROBERTS RINEHART PUBLISHERS

5360 Manhattan Circle #101, Boulder, CO 80303. E-mail: rrinehart@rowman.com.
Description: Nonfiction titles on Ireland and Irish life, natural history, and museum catalogs.

ROBINS LANE PRESS

A Division of Gryphon House, Inc., P.O. Box 207, Beltsville, MD 20705. 301-595-9500. E-mail: info@robinslane.com. Website: www.robinslane.com. **Description:** "Timely, unique books on subjects of interest to today's parents." **Books Statistics:** 4

titles/yr (100 submissions); 75% by first-time authors; 90% unagented. **Proposal Process:** Query with outline and sample chapters if available. Considers simultaneous queries and e-queries. Prefers hard copy. Responds in 6-8 weeks. **Sample Titles:** *Snacktivities! 50 Edible Activities for Parents and Children* by MaryAnn F. Kohl and Jean Potter; *The Simpler Family: A Book of Smart Choices and Small Comforts for Families Who Do Too Much* by Christine Klein. **Contact:** Acquisitions Editor.

ROC

Penguin Group (USA) Inc., 375 Hudson St., New York, NY 10014. 212-366-2000. Website: www.penguinputnam.com. Laura Anne Gilman, Executive Editor; Jennifer Heddle, Editor. **Description:** Publisher of science fiction and fantasy. **Proposal Process:** Strongly discourages unsolicited submissions. "Most of our acquisitions come via reputable literary agents." **Payment:** Standard royalties. **Sample Titles:** *Drinking Midnight Wine* by Simon R. Green; *The Dragon Delasangre* by Alan F. Troop; *Conquistador* by S.M. Stirling.

ROCKPORT PUBLISHERS/ROTOVISION

33 Commercial St., Gloucester, MA 01930-5089. 978-282-9590. E-mail: info@rockpub.com. Website: www.rockpub.com. **Description:** Graphic design, interior design, architecture, fine arts, crafts, etc.

RODALE BOOKS

Division of Rodale Press, Inc., 400 S 10th St., Emmaus, PA 18098. 610-967-5171. Website: www.rodale.com. **Description:** General trade nonfiction. No fiction, poetry, or screenplays. **Proposal Process:** Send complete proposal package that includes a book prospectus, outline (with headings and subheadings), 1 or more sample chapters, resumé/bio listing credentials, market analysis with competing titles, and SASE. **Tips:** "Our mission is to inspire and enable people to improve their lives and the world around them, and to show them how they can use the power of their bodies and minds to make their lives better. We're looking for authors who can dig deeply for facts and details, report accurately, and write with flair." **Contact:** Heather Jackson, Executive Editor (women's health/fitness, general trade, senior health, and weight loss); Margot Schupf, Executive Editor (organics, gardening, lifestyle, cooking); Ellen Phillips, Executive Editor, (home arts and pet care); Jeremy Katz, Executive Editor (men's health, men's sports/fitness, science/technology, finance); Lou Cinquino, Senior Editor (parenting); Jennifer Kushnier, Associate Editor (general health, self-help/inspiration, biography/memoir, relationships, current affairs, the environmental sciences, general business, psychology).

RODMELL PRESS

2147 Blake St., Berkeley, CA 94704-2715. 510-841-3123.
E-mail: rodmellprs@aol.com. Website: www.rodmellpress.com. Donald Moyer, Editor. **Description:** Books on yoga, Buddhism, and aikido.

ROUGH GUIDES

345 Hudson St., Fl. 4, New York, NY 10014. 212-414-3635.
E-mail: mail@roughguides.com. Website: www.roughguides.com. **Description:** Guides and phrase books for independent travel. Also publishes reference titles on a wide range of subjects including music, film, the Internet, and computers.

ROUTLEDGE

Taylor & Francis Group, 29 W 35th St., New York, NY 10001. 212-216-7800. E-mail: doconnor@routledge-ny.com. Website: www.routledge-ny.com. **Description:** Trade, academic, professional books in the humanities and social sciences.

ROWMAN & LITTLEFIELD PUBLISHERS INC.

4720 Boston Way, Lanham, MD 20706. 301-459-3366.
E-mail: nrothschild@rowman.com. Website: www.rowmanlittlefield.com.
Description: Innovative and thought-provoking books for an educated audience.
Books Statistics: 1,000 titles/yr. **Payment:** Offers advance.

ROYAL FIREWORKS PUBLISHING

1 First Ave., P.O. Box 399, Unionville, NY 10988. 845-726-4444.
E-mail: rfpress@frontiernet.net. Charles Morgan, Editor. **Description:** Books for gifted children, parents, and teachers. Also publishes teen and adult novels in the genres of science fiction, mystery, thriller, and historic Americana. **Books Statistics:** 100 titles/yr (2,000 submissions); 40% by first-time authors; 95% unagented. **Proposal Process:** Submit complete manuscript with brief plot overview. No simultaneous or electronic queries. Responds in 3 weeks. **Payment:** Royalty. **Tips:** "We're looking for historical fiction, books on growing up, books about kids solving problems, science fiction, and mystery-adventure."

RUMINATOR BOOKS

1648 Grand Ave., St. Paul, MN 55105. 651-699-7038. E-mail: books@ruminator.com.
Website: www.ruminator.com. Pearl Kilbride, Editor. **Description:** Publishes fiction and memoirs on contemporary affairs, cultural criticism, travel essays, nonfiction, and international literature. No genre fiction, self-help, children's books, or poetry. Prefers books that examine the human experience or comment on social and cultural mores. **Proposal Process:** Query with outline and sample chapters.

RUNNING PRESS

125 S 22nd St., Philadelphia, PA 19103-4399. 215-567-5080.
E-mail: comments@runningpress.com. Website: www.runningpress.com. Ellen Beal, Editorial Director. **Description:** Illustrated nonfiction titles for adults and children. Publishes educational, inspirational, pop culture-oriented, historical nonfiction, self-help, Miniature Editions™, and creative how-to kits for children and adults. **Proposal Process:** Query with outline/TOC and 2-3 page writing sample. Accepts simultaneous queries, but not e-queries. Prefers hard copy. Responds in 4 weeks. **Payment:** Royalty or flat fee. **Tips:** No fiction or poetry. **Contact:** Juliana Rosati.

RUTGERS UNIVERSITY PRESS

100 Joyce Kilmer Ave., Piscataway, NJ 08854-8099. 732-445-7762.
Website: rutgerspress.rutgers.edu. Leslie Mitchner, Editor-in-Chief. **Description:**
Scholarly publisher of religion, history of medicine, biological sciences, media studies, art, literature, history, gender studies, and multicultural studies. Also interested in
general studies that have a strong scholarly basis. **Books Statistics:** 90 titles/yr (1,200
submissions); 35% by first-time authors; 85% unagented. **Proposal Process:** Query
with outline and sample chapters. Send Humanities proposals to Molly Baab; Science
and Social Sciences proposals to Adi Hovav. Accepts simultaneous queries, but not e-
queries. Prefers hard copy. Responds in 3-4 weeks. **Payment:** Royalty. **Sample
Titles:** *The Body Electric: An Anatomy of the New Bionic Senses* by James Geary;
Born to Belonging: Writing on Spirit and Justice by Mab Segrest; *Backroads, New
Jersey: Driving at the Speed of Life* by Mark Di Ionno. **Tips:** "Avoid anything too jar-
gon-laden. We are most interested in projects with a strong scholarly foundation."
Contact: Molly Baab, Editorial Assistant.

RUTLEDGE HILL PRESS

Division of Thomas Nelson Publishers, P.O. Box 141000, Nashville, TN 37214-1000.
615-902-2333. E-mail: tmenges@rutledgehillpress.com. Website: www.rutledgehill-
press.com. Lawrence M. Stone, Publisher. **Description:** General nonfiction, self-
help/reference, inspirational/gift books, cookbooks, fitness and health. **Books
Statistics:** 40 titles/yr (1,000 submissions); 35% by first-time authors; 70% unagented. **Proposal Process:** Query with outline, sample chapters and SASE. Accepts
simultaneous and electronic queries. Prefers hard copy. **Payment:** Flat fee. **Tips:**
Interested in adult nonfiction. **Contact:** Tracey Menges.

RYLAND PETERS & SMALL INC.

519 Broadway, Fl. 5, New York, NY 10012. 646-613-8682.
E-mail: info@rylandpeters.com. Website: www.rylandpeters.com. **Description:**
Publisher of stationery and illustrated gift books on cookery, gardening, lifestyle and
interior design.

SAGE PUBLICATIONS, INC.

2455 Teller Rd., Thousand Oaks, CA 91320. 805-499-0721.
E-mail: info@sagepub.com. Website: www.sagepub.com. **Description:** Nonfiction
books and materials for researchers, professionals, scholars, policymakers, and students. Subject matter includes aging/gerontology, anthropology/archaeology, the arts,
ethnic/cultural studies, business, communications, counseling/psychology, education,
social work, politics, engineering, history, science, and mathematics. **Books
Statistics:** 200 titles/yr. **Proposal Process:** Send formal book proposal to the appropriate editor. See website for staff listing and more specific guidelines. **Sample
Titles:** *Human Genetics for the Social Sciences* by Gregory Carey; *Critical Issues in
Crime and Justice* by Albert R. Roberts. **Contact:** Editorial Acquisitions Dept.

SANDLAPPER PUBLISHING CO, INC.

P.O. Box 730, Orangeburg, SC 29116-0730. E-mail: agallmanl@mindspring.com.
Amanda Gallman, Managing Editor. **Description:** Publisher of nonfiction books on
South Carolina history, culture, and cuisine. **Proposal Process:** Query with outline,
sample chapters, and SASE. No phone calls.

SANTA MONICA PRESS

P.O. Box 1076, Santa Monica, CA 90406. 310-230-7759. E-mail: books@santamoni-
capress.com. Website: www.santamonicapress.com. **Description:** Lively and modern how-to books, literary nonfiction, and books on pop culture, film, music, theater,
and television. **Proposal Process:** Send cover letter and outline indicating the nature
and scope of each chapter. Include 2 sample chapters and photocopies of any photographs or illustrations. State in cover letter the intended audience, explanation as to
why book is unique, summary of competing books, anticipated length, brief bio, and
complete contact info. Include SASE with appropriate postage. No phone calls.
Sample Titles: *James Dean Died Here: The Locations of America's Pop Culture
Landmarks* by Chris Epting; *Footsteps in the Fog: Alfred Hitchcock's San Francisco*
by Jeff Kraft and Aaron Leventhal.. **Contact:** Acquisitions Editor.

SARABANDE BOOKS INC.

2234 Dundee Rd., Suite 200, Louisville, KY 40205. 502-458-4028.
E-mail: sarabandeb@aol.com. Website: www.sarabandebooks.org. **Description:**
Nonprofit literary press publishing poetry, short fiction, and creative nonfiction.
Proposal Process: Open submissions during the month of September only. Query
with 10 poems, a single story, or section of novella/short novel. Send complete man-
uscript only if requested. **Sample Titles:** (Fiction) *Bloody Mary* by Sharon Solwitz;
(Poetry) *The Day Before* by Dick Allen. **Tips:** Also offers the Kathryn A. Morton
Prize in Poetry and the Mary McCarthy Prize in Short Fiction.

SASQUATCH BOOKS

119 S Main St., Suite 400, Seattle, WA 98104. 206-467-4300.
E-mail: books@sasquatchbooks.com. Website: www.sasquatchbooks.com. Gary Luke,
Editor. **Description:** Regional titles covering the west coast of the U.S. only. Topics
include food, travel, gardening, pop culture, literary nonfiction, and children's books.
Books Statistics: 40 titles/yr; 30% by first-time authors; 30% unagented. **Proposal
Process:** Query with SASE. No e-queries or phone calls. Hard copy only. Responds
in 3 months. **Payment:** Royalty. **Tips:** Regional only (Pacific NW, Alaska, and
California).

SCARECROW PRESS

4501 Forbes Blvd., Suite 200, Lanham, MD 20706. 301-459-3366.
Website: www.scarecrowpress.com. **Description:** Single volume reference titles; historical dictionaries (of countries, religious, organizations, wars, movements, cities, and
ancient civilizations); scholarly, professional, and textbooks in selected disciplines.
Books Statistics: 175 titles/yr; 20% by first-time authors; 95% unagented. **Proposal**

Process: Query with subject matter, scope and intended purpose of your manuscript. Accepts e-queries. Responds in 2-4 months. **Payment:** Royalty. **Tips:** See guidelines. **Contact:** Bruce Phillips (music); Stephen Ryan (film); Kim Tabor (YA literary criticism reference titles, historical dictionaries); Sue Easun (information studies, military history, children's literary criticism); Melissa Ray (all other inquiries).

SCHIFFER PUBLISHING LTD

4880 Lower Valley Rd., Atglen, PA 19310. 610-593-1777.
E-mail: info@schifferbooks.com. **Description:** Books on collectibles, antiques, military history, arts/crafts, art/design, and New Age topics.

SCHOLASTIC, INC.

524 Broadway, New York, NY 10012-3999. 212-965-7287.
Website: www.scholastic.com. Dorothy Coe, Editorial Coordinator.
Description: Books for K-8 teachers, curriculum coordinators, staff developers, and pre-service educators; Activity/Resource books in all curriculum areas; Teaching Strategies Books: strategies and lessons for new practices; Theory and Practice Books: written by academic professionals, thoroughly discuss current research and translate into practice. **Proposal Process:** Query with outline, sample chapters or activities, contents page, and resumé. **Payment:** Flat fee or royalty.

SCOTT FORESMAN

1900 E Lake Ave., Glenview, IL 60025. Website: www.scottforesman.com.
Susanne Singleton, Publisher. **Description:** Publisher of elementary textbooks on reading, language arts, science, mathematics, social studies, music, and bilingual studies. **Proposal Process:** Considers authors with proper educational credentials only. Submit resumé if qualified. Does not publish children's literature or unsolicited manuscripts. **Payment:** Royalty or flat fee.

SEAL PRESS

300 Queen Anne Ave. N, #375, Seattle, WA 98109. 206-722-1838.
E-mail: leslie.miller@avalonpub.com. Website: www.sealpress.com. Leslie Miller, Senior Editor. **Description:** Publishes titles ranging from literary fiction to health, pop culture, women's studies, parenting and travel/outdoor adventure. Currently focusing acquisitions in two popular series: Adventura (focuses on women's travel/adventure writing) and Live Girls (showcases the voices of modern feminism). **Books Statistics:** 25 titles/yr (1,500 submissions); 20% by first-time authors; 20% ungented. **Proposal Process:** Send query only. No electronic queries. Prefers hard copy. Responds in 2 months. **Payment:** Royalty, 7.5% net.

SEVEN LOCKS PRESS

3100 W Warner Ave., Suite 8, Santa Ana, CA 92704. 714-545-2526.
E-mail: sevenlocks@aol.com. Website: www.sevenlockspublishing.com. James C. Riordan, Publisher. **Description:** Nonfiction on contemporary topics, self-help issues, public affairs, and critical issues of our time. Also some fiction.

SEVEN STORIES PRESS

140 Watts St., New York, NY 10013. 212-226-8760. E-mail: info@sevenstories.com. Website: www.sevenstories.com. Daniel Simon, Acquistions Editor. **Description:** Small press publishing literary fiction and nonfiction in the areas of activism and politics. **Books Statistics:** 25 titles/yr; 20% by first-time authors; 15% unagented. **Proposal Process:** Does not read unsolicted manuscripts. **Payment:** Royalty, 7-15%. **Sample Titles:** *The War on the Bill of Rights* by Nat Hentoff; *Popular Music from Vittula* by Mikael Niemi.

SHAMBHALA PUBLICATIONS, INC.

Horticultural Hall, 300 Massachusetts Ave., Boston, MA 02115. 617-424-0030. E-mail: editors@shambhala.com. Website: www.shambhala.com. Peter Turner, President/Executive Editor. **Description:** Nonfiction titles on Eastern religion, especially Buddhism and Taoism, as well as psychology, self-help, arts, literature, health/healing, and Eastern philosophy. **Proposal Process:** Query with outline, author bio, TOC, and three sample chapters. **Payment:** Flat fee and royalty. **Contact:** Katie Keach.

SIERRA CLUB BOOKS

85 Second St., San Francisco, CA 94105. Phone: 415-977-5500. Fax: 415-977-5792. E-mail: danny.moses@sierraclub.org. Website: www.sierraclub.org/books. Danny Moses, Editor-in-Chief. **Description:** Nonfiction about nature, ecology, and environmental issues for a general audience. Also publishes children's books. **Books Statistics:** 15 titles/yr (1,000 submissions); 10-20% by first-time authors; 40-50% unagented. **Proposal Process:** Send outline and sample chapter. Considers simultaneous and electronic queries. Prefers electronic format. Responds in 1 month. **Payment:** Royalty. **Sample Titles:** *Downhill Slide: Why the Corporate Ski Industry Is Bad for Skiing, Ski Towns, and the Environment* by Hal Clifford; *Breaking Gridlock: Moving Transportation That Works* by Jim Motavalli. **Tips:** Currently not accepting unsolicited manuscripts or proposals for children's books. **Contact:** Editorial Department.

SIGNATURE BOOKS PUBLISHING LLC

564 West 400 North, Salt Lake City, UT 84116-3411. 801-531-1483. E-mail: people@signaturebooks.com. Website: www.signaturebooks.com. George Smith, President. **Description:** Fiction, nonfiction, essays, and humor on Western and Mormon Americana. Seeks to present history and culture in a scholary, professional manner. **Proposal Process:** Submit query letter outlining thesis or plot with resumé or curriculum vitae. Does not accept unsolicited manuscripts. **Payment:** Royalty. **Sample Titles:** *Mormon Mavericks* by John Sillito. **Contact:** Ron Priddis, Editor.

SILMAN-JAMES PRESS

3624 Shannon Rd., Los Angeles, CA 90027. Phone: 323-661-9922; Fax: 323-661-9933. E-mail: silmanjamespress@earthlink.net. Gwen Feldman, Jim Fox, Co-Publishers. **Description:** Books on film, filmmaking, the motion picture industry, music, and the performing arts. Also includes Siles Press imprint which publishes books on chess and other general nonfiction subjects. **Books Statistics:** 8 titles/yr; 40% by first-time authors; 90% unagented. **Proposal Process:** Query with outline and sample chapters. Accepts phone queries. Responds in 2-12 weeks. **Payment:** Royalty. **Sample Titles:** *Improvisation Technique for the Performing Actor in Film, Theatre, and Television* by Stephen Book; *In the Blink of an Eye: A Perspective on Film Editing* by Walter Murch.

SILVER LAKE PUBLISHING

2025 Hyperion Ave., Los Angeles, CA 90027. 323-663-3082. E-mail: theeditors@silverlakepub.com. Website: www.silverlakepub.com. James Walsh, Publisher. **Description:** Nonfiction on personal finance, small business management, consumer reference, and popular economics. **Books Statistics:** 8-10 titles/yr. **Proposal Process:** Send cover letter with outline, 2 sample chapters, and bio/resume. No electronic submissions. Responds in 6-8 weeks. **Sample Titles:** *Under 40 Financial Planning Guide: From Graduation to Your First Home* by Cornelius P. McCarthy. **Tips:** Study recent books published to get a sense of what material they are interested in. **Contact:** Kristin Loberg, Editor or Megan Thorpe, Editor.

SILVERBACK BOOKS INC.

55 New Montgomery St., Suite 503, San Francisco, CA 94105. 415-348-8595. E-mail: info@silverbackbooks.com. Website: www.silverbackbooks.com. **Description:** Publisher of cookbooks. **Sample Titles:** *Cooking With Friends* by Trish Dessire; *Zone Perfect Cookbook* by Kristy Walker.

SIMON & SCHUSTER

1230 Avenue of the Americas, New York, NY 10020. 212-698-7000. Website: www.simonsays.com. Alice Mayhew, Editorial Director. **Description:** High-quality fiction and nonfiction. **Proposal Process:** No unsolicited manuscripts. Accepts material from literary agents only. **Sample Titles:** (Fiction) *The Gold Swan* by James Thayer; *Down by the River: Drugs, Money, Murder, and Family* by Charles Bowden.

SMITH AND KRAUS, INC.

P.O. Box 127, Lyme, NH 03768. 603-643-6431. E-mail: sandk@sover.net. Website: www.smithkraus.com. Marisa Smith, Publisher. **Description:** Publishes monologue and scene anthologies, biographies of playwrights, translations, books on career development (in theater) and the art of theater, and teaching texts for young actors (K-12). **Books Statistics:** 30 titles/yr (500+ submissions); 20% by first-time authors; 50% unagented. **Proposal Process:** Query with SASE. No simultaneous queries. Accepts hard copy and brief e-queries (1-2 pages). Responds in 1-2 months. **Payment:** Royalty and flat fee. **Tips:** "We seek material of interest to the theatre community." Does not accept full-length and one-act plays unless the play in question has been produced within the year and is therefore eligible for the "Best Scene and Monologue" Series for the Year.

GIBBS SMITH, PUBLISHER

P.O. Box 667, Layton, UT 84041. 801-544-9800. E-mail: info@gibbs-smith.com. Website: www.gibbs-smith.com. Suzanne Taylor, Editorial Director. **Description:** Interior design books, cookbooks, gift books, architecture guides, monographs, children's picture and activity books, and other materials related to home and hearth and culture/lifestyle. **Tips:** "We're looking for fresh insights into home decorating and inspirational stories that can be illustrated and sold as adult gift books, suitable for any occasion."

SMITHSONIAN BOOKS

750 Ninth St. NW, Suite 4300, Washington, DC 20560-0950. 202-275-2300. E-mail: inquiries@sipress.si.edu. **Description:** General trade and illustrated books in American studies, natural sciences, photography, aviation and spaceflight history, and anthropology.

SNOW LION PUBLICATIONS

P.O. Box 6483, Ithaca, NY 14851. 607-273-8519. E-mail: tibet@snowlionpub.com. Website: www.snowlionpub.com. **Description:** Publishes titles exclusively on Tibetan Buddhism. **Sample Titles:** *The Wheel of Time Sand Mandala* by Barry Bryant; *The Art of Peace* edited by Jeffrey Hopkin.

SOHO PRESS

853 Broadway, New York, NY 10003. 212-260-1900. E-mail: soho@sohopress.com. Website: www.sohopress.com. Juris Jurjevics, Publisher. **Description:** Adult literary fiction, mysteries, nonfiction memoirs, travel books, and materials on social and cultural history. **Books Statistics:** 50 titles/yr (2,000 submissions); 50% by first-time authors; 10% unagented. **Proposal Process:** Query with first 3 sample chapters, brief plot outline, and list of previously published credits. Considers simultaneous queries, but not e-queries. Hard copy only. Responds in 2 months. **Payment:** Royalty (net 10%,12.5%, 15%). **Sample Titles:** (Fiction) *After* by Phyllis Reynolds Naylor; (Crime Fiction) *Maisie Dobbs* by Jacqui Winspear; (Memoir) *Grace: An American Woman in China, 1934-1974* by Eleanor McCallie Cooper and William Liu. **Tips:** No mass-market, how-to, cooking, or religious titles.

SOURCEBOOKS CASABLANCA

Sourcebooks, Inc., P.O. Box 4410, Naperville, IL 60567-4410. 603-961-3900. E-mail: todd.stocke@sourcebooks.com. Website: www.sourcebooks.com. Todd Stocke, Editorial Director. **Description:** The nonfiction, relationships/love imprint of Sourcebooks, Inc. **Proposal Process:** Query with outline and sample chapters. **Payment:** Royalty. **Sample Titles:** *LUV Questions* by Cyndi Haynes.

SOURCEBOOKS, INC.

P.O. Box 4410, Naperville, IL 60567-4410. 630-961-3900. E-mail: todd.stocke@sourcebooks.com. Website: www.sourcebooks.com. Todd Stocke, Editorial Director. **Description:** General-interest nonfiction titles in a wide range of categories: reference, history, sports, self-help/psychology, personal finance, small business, marketing/management, parenting, health/beauty, relationships, biography, gift books, and women's issues. Launched a fiction imprint, Sourcebooks Landmark, in 2001. **Books Statistics:** 120 titles/yr (3,000+ submissions); 10% by first-time authors; 20% unagented. **Proposal Process:** Query with outline, sample chapters, and SASE. Accepts simultaneous queries, but not e-queries. **Payment:** Royalty. **Sample Titles:** (Fiction) *The Blue Moon Circus* by Michael Raleigh. (Nonfiction) *Bargain Beauty Secrets* by Diane Irons. **Tips:** "We believe in authorship. We work with our authors to develop great books that find and inspire a wide audience. We believe in helping our authors' careers and recognize that a well-published, successful book is often a cornerstone. We seek authors who are as committed as we are and we ask our prospective authors to do their research."

SOUTH END PRESS

7 Brookline St., Cambridge, MA 02139-4146. 617-547-4002.
Website: www.southendpress.org. **Description:** Nonprofit, collectively run book publisher committed to the politics of radical social change. Encourages critical thinking and consecutive action on the key political, cultural, social, economic, and ecological issues shaping life in the United States and in the world. **Books Statistics:** 10 titles/yr (1,000 submissions); 5% by first-time authors; 95% unagented. **Proposal Process:** Query with sample chapters. Accepts simultaneous queries. Responds in 6-8 weeks. **Payment:** Royalty.

SOUTHERN ILLINOIS UNIVERSITY PRESS

P.O. Box 3697, Carbondale, IL 62902-3697. 618-453-2281. E-mail: kageff@siu.edu. Website: www.siu.edu/~siupress. Karl Kageff, Senior Editor. **Description:** Nonfiction on the humanities, 200-300 pages. **Proposal Process:** Query with outline and sample chapters. **Payment:** Royalty. **Sample Titles:** *Chicago Death Trap: The Iroquois Theatre Fire of 1903* by Nat Brandt.

SOUTHERN METHODIST UNIVERSITY PRESS

P.O. Box 750415, Dallas, TX 75275-0415. 214-768-1433.
E-mail: klang@mail.smu.edu. Website: www.smu.edu/press. Kathryn Lang, Acquisitions Editor. **Description:** Publishes literary fiction, books on life in the Southwest (both fiction and nonfiction), and books on film, theatre, and the performing arts. Also nonfiction titles on medical humanities issues, ethics, and death/dying. Establishing a new Sports series and interested in both fiction and nonfiction titles. **Books Statistics:** 10-12 titles/yr (2,500 submissions); 80% by first-time authors; 90% unagented. **Proposal Process:** Query with outline and sample chapters. Accepts simultaneous queries. Hard copy only. Responds in 1 month. **Payment:** Royalty (net 10%).

SPECTACLE LANE PRESS

P.O. Box 1237, Mt. Pleasant, SC 29466. 843-971-9165. E-mail: jaskar44@aol.com. James A. Skardon, Editor. **Description:** Humor, text, and cartoons. Subject matter varies, including satire, self help, business, lifestyle, sports, and television topics. **Books Statistics:** 1-3 titles/yr (300 submissions); 90% by first-time authors; 90% unagented. **Proposal Process:** Query with outline, sample chapters, and SASE. Accepts e-queries, but not simultaneous queries. Responds in 2-4 weeks. **Payment:** Advance against royalty. **Tips:** "Humor should be current and sophisticated, nothing scatological. Writing should be clear, straightforward, well-organized, with base of solid expertise on nonhumor subjects."

SPHINX PUBLISHING

Imprint of Sourcebooks, Inc., P.O. Box 4410, Naperville, IL 60567-4410. 630-961-3900. E-mail: dianne.wheeler@sourcebooks.com. Website: www.sourcebooks.com. Dianne Wheeler, Editor. **Description:** Nonfiction books on legal self-help in subjects including personal affairs, business, parenting, and real estate. **Proposal Process:** Query with outline and sample chapters. **Payment:** Royalty.

SPINSTERS INK

191 University Blvd. #300, Denver, CO 80206. 303-761-5552.
E-mail: fempres@aol.com. Website: www.spinsters-ink.com. Sharon Silvas, Editorial Director. **Description:** Adult fiction and nonfiction books, 250+ pages, that deal with social justice and/or significant issues in women's lives from a feminist perspective and encourage change and growth. **Books Statistics:** 6 titles/yr; 50% by first-time authors; 80% unagented. **Proposal Process:** Query with outline via e-mail (no mail requests). Considers simultaneous queries. Responds in 90 days. **Payment:** Royalty. **Tips:** Not accepting new material until 2005.

SQUARE ONE PUBLISHERS INC.

115 Herricks Rd., Garden City Park, NY 11040. 516-535-2010.
E-mail: sq1info@aol.com. Website: www.squareonepublishers.com. **Description:** Nonfiction on vintage poster art, collectibles, cooking, general interest, history, how-to, parenting, self-help, health, etc.

ST. MARTIN'S PRESS

175 Fifth Ave., New York, NY 10010. 212-674-5151. Website: www.stmartins.com.
Description: Trade nonfiction (history, multicultural studies, pop culture, the arts, science, business, professional), popular and literary fiction, and scholarly titles/reference titles/college textbooks. Also publishes a small list of for young readers. **Proposal Process:** No unsolicited submissions. Accepts work from literary agents only. **Payment:** Royalty. **Sample Titles:** (Fiction) *Sons of Fortune* by Jeffrey Archer; (Nonfiction) *Atkins for Life* by Robert C. Atkins, M.D.

STACKPOLE BOOKS

5067 Ritter Rd., Mechanicsburg, PA 17055. 717-796-0411.
E-mail: jschnell@stackpolebooks.com. Website: www.stackpolebooks.com. Judith Schnell, Editorial Director. **Description:** Nonfiction on the outdoors, nature, birding, fishing, fly fishing, climbing, paddling, sports, sporting literature, history, and mil-

itary reference. **Books Statistics:** 90 titles/yr (150 submissions); 20% by first-time authors; 70% unagented. **Proposal Process:** Submit queries with sample chapters to acquisitions editor for the line: Mark Allison (nature), Judith Schnell (fishing/sports), Chris Evans (History), Kyle Weaver (Pennsylvania). No simultaneous or electronic queries. Hard copy only. **Payment:** Royalty; advance or flat fee. **Tips:** No poetry, cookbooks, fiction, or books on crafts. History books must have some original research involved. **Contact:** Acquisitions Editor.

STANFORD UNIVERSITY PRESS
1450 Page Mill Rd., Palo Alto, CA 94304. 650-723-9434.
Website: www.sup.org. Norris Pope, Editor. **Description:** Furthers the University's research and teaching mission primarily through books of significant scholarship. Also publishes some professional books, advanced textbooks, and intellectually serious popular works. **Books Statistics:** 120 titles/yr (2,000 submissions); 35% by first-time authors; 95% unagented. **Proposal Process:** Query with outline and sample chapters. Accepts simultaneous queries, but not e-queries. Hard copy only. Response time varies. **Payment:** Royalty. **Tips:** No original fiction or poetry.

STARRHILL PRESS
River City Publishing, 1719 Mulberry St., Montgomery, AL 36106. 877-408-7078.
E-mail: jdavis@rivercitypublishing.com. Website: www.rivercitypublishing.com.
Jim Davis, Editor. **Description:** Titles on art, gardening, health, history, literature, music, and travel. **Tips:** Generally publishes authors with extensive track records.

STATE UNIVERSITY OF NEW YORK PRESS
90 State St., Suite 700, Albany, NY 12207. 518-472-5000.
Website: www.sunypress.edu. James H. Peltz, Editor-in-Chief.
Description: Publishes scholarly and trade books in the humanities and social sciences. **Books Statistics:** 180 titles/yr (2,500 submissions); 99% unagented. **Proposal Process:** Query with outline and sample chapters. Accepts simultaneous queries, but not e-queries. Responds in 4-6 weeks. **Payment:** Royalty (typically 5-10%). **Tips:** "We generally publish books for a scholarly audience, with perhaps some potential for crossover to general trade."

STEERFORTH PRESS
25 Lebanon St., Hanover, NH 03755. 603-643-4787. Website: www.steerforth.com.
Chip Fleischer, Publisher. **Description:** Adult nonfiction and some literary fiction. Serious works of history, biography, politics, current affairs. **Proposal Process:** Does not accept unsolicited proposals or manuscripts.

STEINER BOOKS/ANTHROPOSOPHIC PRESS
400 Main St., Rear Annex, MA 10230. 413-528-8233.
E-mail: service@steinerbooks.org. Website: www.steinerbooks.org. **Description:** Publisher of Rudolf Steiner's works on anthroposophy. Also publishes materials on spirituality, religion, philosophy, and psychology. Imprint: Lindisfarne.

STEMMER HOUSE PUBLISHERS, INC.

4 White Brook Rd., Gilsom, NH 03448. 800-345-6665.
Website: www.pathwaybook.com. Craig Thoon, IV, Editorial Director. **Description:** Publishes the International Design Book Series (illustrated books on the design and architecture of various countries including Africa, Asia, Native American, etc) and general nonfiction on nature/environment issues for kids. **Books Statistics:** 4-8 titles/yr (2,000+ submissions); 50% by first-time authors; 95% unagented. **Proposal Process:** Query with sample chapters and SASE. Considers simultaneous and electronic queries. Prefers hard copy. **Payment:** Royalty, 5%-10% net. **Tips:** "We look for books with at least 30 years' staying power, and therefore print on acid-free paper as part of that commitment."

STERLING PUBLISHING

387 Park Ave. S, New York, NY 10016. 212-532-7160.
Website: www.sterlingpub.com. **Description:** Nonfiction on a wide variety of topics: how-to, hobby, woodworking, alternative health/healing, fiber arts, crafts, wine, nature, oddities, puzzles, juvenile humor and activities, juvenile nature/science, Celtic topics, gardening, pets, recreation, sports and games books, reference, and home decorating. **Proposal Process:** Query with outline, sample chapter, and sample illustrations. Include SASE for return of materials. No electronic submissions; hard copy only. **Payment:** Royalty. **Tips:** Unsolicited manuscripts accepted, please accompany with an SASE. **Contact:** Acquisitions Committee.

STONEYDALE PRESS PUBLISHING CO.

523 Main St., Stevensville, MT 59870. 406-777-2729. E-mail: info@stoneydale.com. Website: www.stoneydale.com. Dale A. Burk, Publisher. **Description:** Publishes adult nonfiction, primarily how-to, on outdoor recreation with special emphasis on big game hunting. Also publishes some regional history of the Northern Rockies. Specialized market. **Proposal Process:** Send query with outline and sample chapters. **Payment:** Royalty.

STOREY PUBLISHING

210 Mass Moca Way, North Adams, MA 01247. 413-346-2100.
Website: www.storey.com. Deborah Balmuth, Editorial Director. **Description:** Nonfiction how-to books in the areas of gardening, crafts, natural health, building, pets/animals, and nature. Also gift books and juvenile nature books. **Books Statistics:** 40 titles/yr; 50% by first-time authors; 80% unagented. **Proposal Process:** Send query with outline, sample chapters, and SASE. Accepts simultaneous queries, but not e-queries. Hard copy only. Responds in 2-3 months. **Payment:** Royalty or flat fee. **Tips:** Well-researched competitive analysis and clearly defined "hook" to make proposed book stand out from competition. Clear, hard-working content, with imaginative presentation. **Contact:** Deborah Burns (equine, animals, nature); Gwen Steege (gardening, crafts); Andrea Dodge (cooking, wine, beer).

STORMLINE PRESS

P.O. Box 593, Urbana, IL 61801. E-mail: ray@raybial.com.
Raymond Bial, Publisher/Editor. **Description:** Publishes primarily regional nonfiction on language, literature, history, and photography. **Books Statistics:** 1-2 titles/yr; 10% first-time authors; 10% unagented. **Proposal Process:** Query with outline, sample chapters, and SASE. Accepts simultaneous queries, but not e-queries. Prefers hard copy. **Payment:** Royalty. **Sample Titles:** (Nonfiction) *When the Waters Recede* by Dan Guillory. (Fiction) *Silent Friends* by Margaret Lacey. **Tips:** "We publish distinctive works of literary and artistic value, with emphasis on rural and small town. Please review our books to gain a sense of the type of material we publish. We are a very small publisher and do not have the staff to respond to inquiries or submissions. We do not accept unsolicited manuscripts—publication by invitation only."

STRAWBERRY HILL PRESS

Strictly Book Promotions, Inc., 21 Isis St., Suite 102, San Francisco, CA 94103.
415-626-2665. E-mail: strictly@bookpromo.com. Daniel F. Vojir, Editor.
Description: Nonfiction: biography, autobiography, history, cooking, health, how-to, philosophy, performance arts, and the Third World. **Proposal Process:** Query with sample chapters, outline, and SASE. **Payment:** Royalty.

STRING LETTER PUBLISHING

255 West End Avenue, San Rafael, CA 94901. 415-485-6946.
E-mail: books@stringletter.com. Website: www.stringletter.com.
Description: Publisher of contemporary adult music.

SUCCESS SHOWCASE PUBLISHING

131 W Sunburst Ln., Suite 220, Tempe, AZ 85284. 480-831-8334. E-mail: info@confessionsofshamelessselfpromoters.com. Website: www.confessionsofshamelessselfpromoters.com. **Description:** Publishes books on successful marketing strategies.

SUMMIT BOOKS

Simon & Schuster Trade/Simon & Schuster, Inc., 1230 Avenue of the Americas, New York, NY 10020. 212-698-7000. Website: www.simonsays.com. **Description:** General-interest fiction and nonfiction of high literary quality. No category books. **Proposal Process:** Query through agents only. **Payment:** Royalty.

SUMMIT UNIVERSITY PRESS

P.O. Box 5000, Corwin Springs, MT 59030-5000. 406-848-9295. E-mail: info@summituniversitypress.com. Website: www.summituniversitypress.com. **Description:** Books on spirituality and personal growth. **Sample Titles:** *Emotions: Transforming Anger, Fear, and Pain* by Marilyn C. Barrick, Ph.D.; *Your Seven Energy Centers* by Elizabeth Clare Prophet and Patricia R. Spadaro.

SUNDANCE PUBLISHING/NEWBRIDGE EDUCATIONAL

P.O. Box 740, Northborough, MA 01532-0740. 800-343-8204.
Website: www.sundancepub.com. Sherry F. Litwach, Product Development.
Description: K-8 curriculum materials for reading and language arts, including
guides, to accompany quality children's, young adult, and adult literature. **Payment:**
Flat fee only.

SYBEX INC.

1151 Marina Village Parkway, Alameda, CA 94501. 510-523-8233. E-mail: proposals@sybex.com. Website: www.sybex.com. Jordan Gold, VP/Publisher. **Description:**
Nonfiction titles on computers and software. **Books Statistics:** 180 titles/yr.

SYRACUSE UNIVERSITY PRESS

621 Skytop Rd., Suite 110, Syracuse, NY 13244-5290. 315-443-5534.
E-mail: msevans@syr.edu. Website: http://sumweb.syr.edu/su_press/. Mary Selden
Evans, Executive Editor. **Description:** Scholarly general and regional nonfiction.
Proposal Process: Send formal prospectus with abstract, curriculum vitae, sample
chapter, TOC, and introduction. Responds in 4-8 weeks. **Sample Titles:** *Painting the
Middle East* by Ann Zwicker Kerr; *Voices from Iran: The Changing Lives of Iranian
Women* by Mahnaz Kousha; *My War: A Memoir of a Survivor of the Holocaust* by
Edward Stankiewicz; *All In One Breath: Selected Poems* by Harry C. Staley.

THE TAUNTON PRESS INC.

63 S Main St., Newtown, CT 06470. 203-426-8171.
E-mail: tt@taunton.com. Website: www.taunton.com.
Description: Books on home design, fiber arts, woodworking and gardening.

TAYLOR TRADE PUBLISHING

Rowman & Littlefield Publishing Group, 4501 Forbes Blvd., Suite 200, Lanham, MD
20706. 301-459-3366. Website: www.rlpgbooks.com. **Description:** Adult trade nonfiction on sports, gardening, history, entertainment, health, family matters, nature,
regional interest. **Books Statistics:** 100 titles/yr. **Proposal Process:** Send outline of
manuscript with sample chapters.

TEACHERS COLLEGE PRESS

1234 Amsterdam Ave., New York, NY 10027. 212-678-3929.
E-mail: tcpress@tc.columbia.edu. Website: www.teacherscollegepress.com.
Brian Ellerbeck, Executive Acquisitions Editor. **Description:** Books and materials
that focus on all areas of education including curriculum, leadership, teacher education, early childhood, child development, language, literacy, etc. Also publishes materials on psychology, sociology/culture, history, philosophy, and women's studies.
Books Statistics: 60 titles/yr. **Sample Titles:** *Creating Solutions that Heal: Real-
Life Solutions* by Lesley Koplow; *The Children Are Watching: How the Media Teach
About Diversity* by Carlos E. Cortes; *Language of Learning* by Karen Gallas.

TEHABI BOOKS

Tehabi Books, 4920 Carroll Canyon Road, San Diego, CA 92121-3735. 858-450-9100. E-mail: nancy.cash@tehabi.com. Website: www.tehabi.com. **Description:** Books on history, travel, sports, personalities, nature, and wildlife.

TEMPLE UNIVERSITY PRESS

Temple University, 1601 N Broad St., USB 306, Philadelphia, PA 19122-6099. 215-204-8787. E-mail: tempress@temple.edu. Website: www.temple.edu/tempress. Janet Francendese, Editor-in-Chief. **Description:** Academic nonfiction in the fields of history, political science, sociology, anthropology, law, education, cinema, disabilities, multicultural studies, gay/lesbian, and women's studies. Also publishes a strong list of regional and sports titles for a general audience. **Proposal Process:** Send query or proposal with outline and sample chapters. Hard copy only. **Payment:** Royalty. **Sample Titles:** *Larry Kane's Philadelphia* by Larry Kane and Dan Rather; *The Sons and Daughters of Los: Culture and Community in L.A.* by David E. James.

TEN SPEED PRESS

P.O. Box 7123, Berkeley, CA 94707. 510-559-1600. Website: www.tenspeed.com. Lorena Jones, Editorial Department. **Description:** Career and business books, cookbooks, and general nonfiction. Imprints: Celestial Arts, Crossing Press, and Tricycle Press. **Books Statistics:** 150 titles/yr (5,000 submissions); 30% by first-time authors; 60% unagented. **Proposal Process:** Query with outline, sample chapters, and SASE. Responds in 6 weeks. **Payment:** Royalty. **Sample Titles:** *What Color is Your Parachute?: A Practical Manual for Job-Hunters and Career Changes* by Richard Nelson Bolles; *Odd Jobs: Portraits of Unusual Occupations* by Nancy Rica Schiff. **Tips:** "Familiarize yourself with our house and our list before submitting mss. Provide a rationale for why we are the best publishing house for your work."

TEXAS A&M UNIVERSITY PRESS

John H. Lindsey Building, Lewis St., 4354 TAMU, College Station, TX 77843. 979-845-1436. E-mail: dlv@tampress.tamu.edu. Website: www.tamu.edu/upress. Mary Lenn Dixon, Editor-in-Chief. **Description:** American and military history, Eastern European studies, presidential studies, anthropology, natural history, literary fiction, and Southwestern and Western studies. **Proposal Process:** Submit proposal including synopsis, TOC, intended audience, competing titles currently on the market, resumé or curriculum vitae, and sample chapters. **Sample Titles:** *A Southern Family in White and Black* by Douglas Hales; *American Military Aviation in the 20th Century* by Charles J. Gross. **Contact:** Diana L. Vance, Editorial Assistant.

THAMES & HUDSON INC.

500 Fifth Ave., New York, NY 10110. 212-354-3763. E-mail: bookinfo@thames.wwnorton.com. Website: www.thamesandhudsonusa.com. **Description:** Illustrated books on art, architecture, decorative arts, design, fashion, photography, travel, history, archaeology, spirituality, and natural history. **Proposal Process:** Send letter of inquiry before submitting material.

THIRD WORLD PRESS

P.O. Box 19730, Chicago, IL 60619.
E-mail: twpress3@aol.com. Website: www.thirdworldpressinc.com.
Haki R. Madhubuti, Publisher. **Description:** Progressive Black Publishing. Adult fiction, nonfiction, poetry, and YA material. **Books Statistics:** 20 titles/yr; 20% by first-time authors; 80% unagented. **Proposal Process:** Query with outline. Send SASE or e-mail for guidelines. **Payment:** Royalty. **Contact:** Gwendolyn Mitchell, Editor.

THORSONS

4720 Boston Way, Lanham, MD 20706. 301-731-9526.
E-mail: karen.kreiger@harpercollins.uk. Website: www.thorsons.com. **Description:** Publishes material on health, personal development, alternative health, inspiration, sex, parenting, psychology, religion, self-help, and spirituality.

THUNDER'S MOUTH PRESS

Avalon Publishing Group, 245 W 17th St., Fl. 11, New York, NY 10011.
212-981-9919. Website: www.avalonpub.com. **Description:** Adult trade books in a variety of subject areas. Concentrates heavily on pop culture, current events, contemporary culture, fantasy and role-playing games, and biography. **Books Statistics:** 75 titles/yr; 10% by first-time authors; 0% unagented. **Proposal Process:** Send query with sample chapters. No simultaneous or electronic queries. Response time varies.

TILBURY HOUSE

2 Mechanic St., #3, Gardiner, ME 04345. 207-582-1899.
E-mail: tilbury@tilburyhouse.com. Website: www.tilburyhouse.com.
Jennifer Bunting, Publisher; Audrey Maynard, Children's Book Editor. **Description:** Small, independent publisher. Children's picture books (w/ possibility of teacher's guide) that deal with cultural diversity or nature/environment. Adult nonfiction titles on Maine and the Northeast. **Proposal Process:** Query with outline and sample chapters. Prefers hard copy format. Will not open e-mail attachments. Accepts unsolicited manuscripts. **Payment:** Pays on publication. **Sample Titles:** (Adult) *On Wilderness: Voices from Maine* edited by Phyllis Austin, Dean Bennett, and Robert Kimber; *Down on the Island, Up on the Main: A Recollected History of South Bristol, Maine* by Ellen Vincent. (Children's) *Life Under Ice* by Mary Cerullo; *The Carpet Boy's Gift* by Pegi Deitz Shea.

TIMBER PRESS, INC.

133 SW Second Ave., Suite 450, Portland, OR 97204-3527. 503-227-2878.
E-mail: info@timberpress.com. Website: www.timberpress.com. Neal Maillet, Executive Editor. **Description:** Publishes high-quality books on plants and flowers for gardeners, horticulturists, and botanists. **Proposal Process:** Send proposal including cover letter outlining purpose and audience, TOC, 1-2 sample chapters, sample illustrations, bio/resume, and estimated timetable for completing the project. Responds in 8-12 weeks. **Sample Titles:** *The Gardener's Guide to Growing Dahlias* by Gareth Rowlands; *Portraits of Himalayan Flowers* by Toshio Yoshida.

TOKYOPOP

Mixx Entertainment, Inc., 5900 Wilshire Blvd., Suite 2000, Los Angeles, CA 90036-5020. 323-692-6700. E-mail: info@tokyopop.com. Website: www.tokyopop.com. **Description:** Japanese Manga, graphic novels and comic books.

TOR BOOKS

Tom Doherty Associates, LLC, 175 Fifth Ave., New York, NY 10010. 212-388-0100. E-mail: inquiries@tor.com. Website: www.tor.com. Patrick Nielsen Hayden, Senior Editor. **Description:** Science fiction, fantasy, and horror. From 80,000 words. **Proposal Process:** Send cover letter, complete synopsis, first 3 chapters, and SASE. Responds in 6-9 months. **Payment:** Advance and royalties. **Tips:** "For a complete listing of submission guidelines, please see our website."

TORCHLIGHT PUBLISHING INC.

P.O. Box 52, Badger, CA 93603. 559-337-2200. E-mail: torchlight@spiralcomm.net. Website: www.torchlight.com. **Description:** Features articles on health and vegetarianism, leadership, motivation and self-improvement, spirituality and religion, etc. **Contact:** Susanne Bolte.

TORMONT/BRIMAR PUBLICATIONS

338 Saint Antoine St. East, Montreal, Quebec H2Y 1A3 Canada. 514-954-1441. E-mail: dianem@tormont.ca. Website: www.tormont.com. Diane Mineau, Editorial Director. **Description:** Children's books, cookbooks, dictionaries, encyclopedias, and general interest books.

TOUCHWOOD EDITIONS

The Heritage Group, #6-356 Simcoe St., Victoria, British Columbia V8V 1L1. 250-360-0829. E-mail: touchwoodeditions@shaw.ca. Website: www.touchwoodeditions.com. Vivian Sinclair, Managing Editor. **Description:** Nonfiction titles on nautical subjects, history, and biography with British Columbia focus. Emphasis on creative nonfiction; also interested in historical fiction. **Books Statistics:** 8-10 titles/yr; 50% by first-time authors; 100% unagented. **Proposal Process:** Submit query with outline and 2-3 sample chapters. No e-queries; hard copy only. **Payment:** Royalty.

TOWLEHOUSE PUBLISHING

394 W Main St., B-9, Hendersonville, TN 37075. 615-822-6405. E-mail: vermonte@aol.com. Website: www.towlehouse.com. **Description:** Nonfiction publisher specializing in "Potent Quotables" and the *Good Golf!* series. Also looking for timely and compelling books on American trends and issues from a conservative and/or Christian perspective. Also publishes sports books.

TRAFALGAR SQUARE PUBLISHING

P.O. Box 257, Howe Hill Rd., North Pomfret, VT 05053. 802-457-1911. E-mail: tsquare@sover.net. Website: www.trafalgarsquarebooks.com or www.horse-andriderbooks.com. **Description:** Books on horses, horse riding, and other equestrian topics. **Sample Titles:** *Centered Riding 2: Further Exploration* by Sally Swift; *Right From the Start: Create a Sane, Soft, Well-Balanced Horse* by Michael Schaffer; *It's Not Just About the Ribbons* by Jane Savoie; *The Downunder Difference* by Clinton Anderson.

TRANSACTION PUBLISHERS

Rutgers State University, 35 Berrue Circle, Piscataway, NJ 08854. 732-445-2280. E-mail: trans@transactionpub.com. Website: www.transactionpub.com. **Description:** Nonfiction in the social sciences: economics, political science, history, sociology, anthropology, psychology, etc. **Sample Titles:** *The First New Nation* by Seymour Martin Lipset; *Justice and the Politics of Memory* by Gabriel R. Ricci.

TRIUMPH BOOKS

601 South LaSalle St., Suite 500, Chicago, IL 60605. 312-939-3330. Website: www.triumphbooks.com. Thomas Bast, Editorial Director. **Description:** Books on sports, recreation, and popular culture. **Proposal Process:** Query with SASE or submit proposal with outline, 1-2 sample chapters, and art/illustrations. **Sample Titles:** *Few and Chosen* by Whitey Ford.

TURTLE POINT PRESS

233 Broadway, Rm 946, New York, NY 10514. 212-285-1019. Website: www.turtle-point.com. Jonathan D. Rabinowitz, President. **Description:** Publisher of forgotten, literary fiction—historical and biographical. Also some contemporary fiction and poetry. Imprints: Book & Co. and Helen Marx Books. **Proposal Process:** Query with sample chapters. Considers simultaneous queries. **Payment:** Royalty.

TURTLE PRESS

S.K. Productions, P.O. Box 290206, Wethersfield, CT 06129-0206. 860-721-1198. E-mail: editorial@turtlepress.com. Website: www.turtlepress.com. Cynthia Kim, Editor. **Description:** Publishes books on mind-body, Eastern philosophy, holistic fitness, and martial arts. **Books Statistics:** 4-8 titles/yr (350 submissions); 40% by first-time authors; 90% unagented. **Proposal Process:** Query with outline, sample chapters, and SASE. Simultaneous and electronic queries accepted but prefers hard copy. Responds in 2-4 weeks. **Payment:** Royalty. **Sample Titles:** *Martial Arts Instructor's Desk Reference* by Sang H. Kim; *Fighting Science* by Martina Sprague; *Perfecting Ourselves: Coordinating Body, Mind, and Spirit* by Aaron Hoopes.

TUTTLE PUBLISHING

153 Milk St., Fl. 5, Boston, MA 02109-4809. 617-951-4080. E-mail: info@tuttlepublishing.com. Website: www.tuttlepublishing.com. **Description:** Publishes titles on various aspects of Asian culture, including cooking, martial arts, interior design, origami, language, travel, religion, and philosophy. **Contact:** Editoral Acquisitions.

TWO-CAN PUBLISHING

Zenith Entertainment, Ltd., 234 Nassau St., Princeton, NJ 08542. 609-921-6700. E-mail: tomhaworth@two-canpublishing.com. Website: www.two-canpublishing.com. **Description:** "Books that absorb, entertain, inform and explain for children, teachers and parents around the world." Publishes illustrated educational books and multimedia products for kids ages 3-13 on topics such as animals, botany, geography, history, math, nature, reference, and science. **Sample Titles:** *A First Look at Animals* series; *Me and My Pet* series; *Sports Club* series.

ULYSSES TRAVEL GUIDES

4176 St.-Denis St., Montreal, Quebec H2W 2M5 Canada. 514-843-9882.
E-mail: info@ulysses.ca. Website: www.ulyssesguides.com. **Description:** Travel guidebooks that offer cultural and tourist information for various regions. **Sample Titles:** *Canadian French for Better Travel* by Cindy Garayt; *Bed and Breakfast in Ontario* by Julia Roles; *Hiking in Ontario* by Tracey Arial.

THE UNIVERSITY OF AKRON PRESS

374-B Bierce Library, Akron, OH 44325-1703. 330-972-5342.
E-mail: uapress@uakron.edu. Website: www.uakron.edu/uapress. .Michael J. Carley, Editor. **Description:** Publishes 5 nonfiction series: poetry; Ohio history and culture; technology and the environment; law, politics, and society; international, political, and economic history. **Books Statistics:** 12 titles/yr (100 submissions); 40% by first-time authors; 100% unagented. **Proposal Process:** Query with outline and sample chapters. Simultaneous and electronic queries accepted. Prefers hard copy. Responds in 1-2 months. **Payment:** Royalty. **Tips:** See website for submission guidelines.

UNIVERSITY OF ALABAMA PRESS

20 Research Dr., Tuscaloosa, AL 35487-0380. 205-348-1561.
E-mail: jknight@uapress.ua.edu. Website: www.uapress.ua.edu. Judith Knight, Acquisitions Editor. **Description:** Scholarly and general regional nonfiction. Submit work to appropriate editor: Daniel J.J. Ross (history, military history, Latin American history, and Jewish studies); Curtis Clark (African American, Native American and women's studies, public adminstration, theater, English, rhetoric and communication); Judith Knight (archaeology and anthropology). **Books Statistics:** 55 titles/yr; 50% by first-time authors; 90% unagented. **Proposal Process:** Send cover letter, curriculum vitae, outline, sample chapter(s), and a prospectus outlining the proposed length, illustrations, etc. **Payment:** Royalty, 5-10%.

UNIVERSITY OF ARIZONA PRESS

355 S Euclid Ave., Suite 103, Tucson, AZ 85719. 520-621-1441.
E-mail: szuter@uapress.arizona.edu. Website: www.uapress.arizona.edu. Christine Szuter, Director/Editor-in-Chief. **Description:** Scholarly and popular nonfiction: Arizona, American West, anthropology, archaeology, environmental science, geography, Latin America, Native Americans, natural history, space sciences, western and environmental history. **Proposal Process:** Query with outline, sample chapters, and

current curriculum vitae or resumé. **Payment:** Royalty. **Sample Titles:** *Science in the American Southwest: A Topical History* by George E. Webb; *Enduring Seeds: Native American Agriculture and Wild Plant Conservation* by Gary Paul Nabhan. **Contact:** Patti Hartmann or Yvonne Reineke, Acquiring Editors.

UNIVERSITY OF ARKANSAS PRESS

The University of Arkansas, 201 Ozark Ave., Fayetteville, AR 72701-1201. 479-575-3246. E-mail: uaprinfo@cavern.uark.edu. Website: www.uapress.com. Lawrence J. Malley, Director/Editor-in-Chief. **Description:** Scholarly nonfiction and poetry. **Proposal Process:** Send query with SASE. **Payment:** Royalty.

UNIVERSITY OF CALIFORNIA PRESS

2120 Berkeley Way, Berkeley, CA 94720. 510-642-4247. E-mail: askucp@ucpress.edu. Website: www.ucpress.edu. Lynne Withey, Director. **Description:** Scholarly and general-interest books in the fields of anthropology, art, art history, Asian studies, California natural history guides, classics, co-publications, film, food studies, history, Mark Twain series, Middle Eastern studies, music, poetry, public health, religion, regional studies, and sociology. **Proposal Process:** Send letter of introduction, curriculum vitae, TOC, and sample chapter. Proposals via e-mail or phone not accepted. **Sample Titles:** *Safe Food* by Marion Nestle; *Pathologies of Power* by Paul Farmer; *Winslow Homer* by Elizabeth Johns.

UNIVERSITY OF CHICAGO PRESS

1427 E 60th St., Chicago, IL 60637-2954. 773-702-7700. Website: www.press.uchicago.edu. **Description:** Scholarly, nonfiction, advanced texts, monographs, clothbound and paperback, reference books.

UNIVERSITY OF GEORGIA PRESS

330 Research Dr., Athens, GA 30602-4901. 706-369-6130. E-mail: books@uga-press.uga.edu. Website: www.ugapress.org. Nicole Mitchell, Director. **Description:** Scholarly and creative nonfiction with particular interests in Southern and American history and literature, environment/natural history, multicultural studies, women's studies, civil rights, folklore, biography/memoir, life sciences, pop culture, and regional topics. **Proposal Process:** Query with outline, sample chapters, and curriculum vitae. Responds in 1 month. **Sample Titles:** *The Lonely Hunter: A Biography of Carson McCullers* by Virginia Spencer Carr; *Beyond Atlanta: The Struggle for Racial Equality in Georgia, 1940-1980* by Stephen G.N. Tuck. **Tips:** Also sponsors the Flannery O'Connor Award for Short Fiction and Contemporary Poetry Series Competition. Please visit website for contest submission guidelines.

UNIVERSITY OF HAWAI'I PRESS

2840 Kolowalu St., Honolulu, HI 96822. 808-956-8694. Website: www.uhpress.hawaii.edu. Patricia Crosby, Pam Kelly, Keith Leber, Masako Ikeda, Editors. **Description:** Scholarly books on East Asian, Southeast Asian, Asian American, Hawaiian and Pacific studies from disciplines as diverse as the arts, history, language, literature, natural science, philosophy, religion, and the social sciences. **Proposal Process:** Query with outline and sample chapters. **Payment:** Royalty.

UNIVERSITY OF ILLINOIS PRESS

1325 S Oak St., Champaign, IL 61820-6903. 217-333-0950. E-mail: uipress@uiuc.edu. Website: www.press.uillinois.edu. Willis G. Regier, Director/Editor-in-Chief. **Description:** Scholarly and regional nonfiction. **Proposal Process:** Query with cover letter, TOC, 1-2 sample chapters, and curriculum vitae. Does not accept simultaneous submissions. Responds in 3 weeks. **Payment:** Royalty. **Sample Titles:** *Art and Freedom* by E.E. Sleinis.

UNIVERSITY OF IOWA PRESS

119 W Park Rd., 100 Kuhl House, Iowa City, IA 52242-1000. 319-335-2000. E-mail: holly-carver@uiowa.edu. Website: www.uiowapress.org. Holly Carver, Director. **Description:** Scholarly nonfiction in the areas of poetry/literature, biography/memoir, theatre, archaeology/anthropology, Americana, natural history, and regional topics related to Midwestern life and culture. **Payment:** Accepts book proposals from recognized experts. Send 300-500 word description of book, TOC, curriculum vitae, and market analysis. Responds in 5-6 weeks. **Sample Titles:** *Birth: A Literary Companion* by Kristin Kovacic and Lynne Barrett.

UNIVERSITY OF MASSACHUSETTS PRESS

P.O. Box 429, Amherst, MA 01004-0429. 413-545-2217. E-mail: wilcox@umpress.umass.edu. Website: www.umass.edu/umpress. Bruce Wilcox, Director. **Description:** Scholarly and general-interest books. Also material in African American studies, American studies, architecture and environmental design. **Proposal Process:** Query with SASE.

UNIVERSITY OF MINNESOTA PRESS

111 Third Ave. S, Suite 290, Minneapolis, MN 55401-2520. 612-627-1970. Website: www.upress.umn.edu. Doug Armato, Editorial Director. **Description:** Nonprofit publisher of selected general-interest books and academic books for scholars. Areas of emphasis include American studies, anthropology, art and aesthetics, cultural theory, film and media studies, gay/lesbian studies, geography, literary theory, political and social theory, race and ethnic studies, sociology and urban studies. Does not accept original fiction or poetry. **Books Statistics:** 110 titles/yr; 50% by first-time authors; 99% unagented. **Proposal Process:** Query with outline, detailed prospectus or introduction, TOC, sample chapter, and resumé. Considers simultaneous queries, but not e-queries. Responds in 4-6 weeks. **Payment:** Royalty, 6-10% net. **Sample Titles:** *Inside the Ropes with Jesse Ventura* by Tom Hauser; *Harmful to Minors: Protecting Children from Sex* by Judith Levine; *Screenstyle: Fashion and Femininity in 1930's Hollywood* by Sarah Berry. **Tips:** "The Press maintains a longstanding commitment to publishing books that focus on Minnesota and the Upper Midwest, including regional nonfiction, history, and natural science."

UNIVERSITY OF MISSOURI PRESS

2910 LeMone Blvd., Columbia, MO 65201-8227. 573-882-7641.
E-mail: upress@umsystem.edu. Website: www.system.missouri.edu/upress. Beverly Jarrett, Clair Willcox, Acquisitions. **Description:** Scholarly books on American and European history; American, British, and Latin American literary criticism; political philosophy; intellectual history; regional studies; and short fiction.

UNIVERSITY OF NEBRASKA PRESS

233 N 8th St., Lincoln, NE 68588. 402-472-3581. E-mail: lrandolph1@unl.edu. Website: www.nebraskapress.unl.edu. Gary Dunham, Editor-in-Chief. **Description:** Scholarly and trade fiction and nonfiction in a wide range of areas including agriculture, Native studies, history, literature, music, sports history, political science, and multicultural studies. Also publishes titles on regional topics about the culture and history of the Great Plains and the American West. **Books Statistics:** 90 titles/yr; 20% by first-time authors; 75% unagented authors. **Proposal Process:** Query with outline, sample chapters, and SASE. No unsolicited manuscripts or simultaneous queries. **Payment:** Royalty. **Sample Titles:** *In the Shadow of Memory* by Floyd Skloot; *Local Wonders: Seasons in the Bohemian Alps* by Ted Kooser. **Tips:** No poetry or children's books. **Contact:** Ladette Randolph, Executive Editor.

UNIVERSITY OF NEVADA PRESS

MS 166, Reno, NV 89557. 775-784-6573. Website: www.nvbooks.nevada.edu. Joanne O'Hare, Director and Editor-in-Chief. **Description:** Publishes fiction and nonfiction. Nonfiction topics include environmental studies, geography, anthropology, history, biography, natural history, regional (Nevada and the West), mining, gaming, and Basque studies. **Proposal Process:** Query first, with outline or TOC, synopsis, sample chapter, estimated length, completion date of manuscript, and resumé. **Payment:** Royalty.

UNIVERSITY OF NEW MEXICO PRESS

MSC01 1200, 1 University of New Mexico, Albuquerque, NM 87131-0001. 505-277-2346. E-mail: unmpress@unm.edu. Website: www.unmpress.com. Luther Wilson, Director. **Description:** Scholarly nonfiction on social and cultural anthropology, archaeology, Latin American and American history, art, photography, biography, fiction, and poetry. **Proposal Process:** Query. **Payment:** Royalty.

UNIVERSITY OF NORTH CAROLINA PRESS

P.O. Box 2288, Chapel Hill, NC 27515-2288. 919-966-3561.
E-mail: uncpress@unc.edu. Website: www.uncpress.unc.edu. David Perry, Editor-in-Chief. **Description:** General-interest books (75,000-125,000 words) on the lore, crafts, cooking, gardening, travel, and natural history of the Southeast. No fiction or poetry, or memoirs of living persons. **Proposal Process:** Query. **Payment:** Royalty.

UNIVERSITY OF NORTH TEXAS PRESS

P.O. Box 311336, Denton, TX 76203-1336. 940-565-2142.
Website: www.unt.edu/untpress. Ronald Chrisman, Director. **Description:**
Nonfiction on military history, Texas history, multicultural topics, and women's history. **Books Statistics:** 16 titles/yr (250 submissions); 95% unagented. **Proposal Process:** Query with sample chapters. Do not send complete manuscript. Accepts e-queries, but not simultaneous queries. Responds in 2 weeks. **Payment:** Royalty.
Sample Titles: *The Light Crust Doughboys Are on the Air: Celebrating Seventy Years of Texas Music* by John Dempsey; *Interpreters with Lewis and Clark: The Story of Sacagawea and Toussaint Charbonneau* by Dale Nelson. **Tips:** "We prefer writing that has scholarly rigor, yet still appeals to a general audience. Avoid personal narrative, unless needed to make an analytical point. No memoirs. We prefer subjects of regional (Southwest) interest."

UNIVERSITY OF NOTRE DAME PRESS

University of Notre Dame, 310 Flanner Hall, Notre Dame, IN 46556. 574-631-6346.
Website: www.undpress.nd.edu. Rebecca DeBoer, Executive Editor. **Description:**
Academic books, hardcover and paperback, on the following topics: philosophy, Irish studies, literature, theology, international relations, medieval studies, sociology and general interest.

UNIVERSITY OF OKLAHOMA PRESS

1005 Asp Ave., Norman, OK 73019-6051. 405-325-2000.
E-mail: cerankin@ou.edu. Website: www.oupress.com. Charles E. Rankin, Associate Director/Editor-In-Chief. **Description:** Books, to 350 pages, on the American West, Indians of the Americas, classical studies, literary criticism, natural history, political science, and Native American and Chicano literature. **Proposal Process:** Query.
Payment: Royalty. **Sample Titles:** *Blood of the Prophets* by Will Bagley; *Spain in the Southwest* by John Kessell; *Diminished Democracy* by Theda Skocpol.

UNIVERSITY OF PENNSYLVANIA PRESS

4200 Pine St., Philadelphia, PA 19104-4011. 215-898-6261.
E-mail: custserv@pobox.upenn.edu. Website: www.upenn.edu/pennpress. Eric Halpern, Editor. **Description:** Scholarly nonfiction. **Proposal Process:** Query.

UNIVERSITY OF PITTSBURGH PRESS

3400 Forbes Ave., Pittsburgh, PA 15260. 412-383-2456.
Website: www.pitt.edu/~press. Cynthia Miller, Director. **Description:** Scholarly nonfiction (philosophy of science, Latin American studies, political science, urban environmental history, culture, composition, and literacy).

UNIVERSITY OF TENNESSEE PRESS

Conference Center Bldg., Suite 110, Knoxville, TN 37996-4108. 865-974-3321.
E-mail: danforth@utk.edu. Website: www.utpress.org. Scot Danforth, Acquisitions Editor. **Description:** Scholarly and general-interest titles in the areas of American

studies: African American studies, Appalachian studies, archaeology, architecture, Civil War studies, folklore, history, literary studies, material culture, and religion. Also publishes regional academic and trade books dealing with Appalachia, Tennessee and the South. **Books Statistics:** 35-40 titles/yr; 99% unagented. **Proposal Process:** Query with SASE. Accepts simultaneous and electronic queries. **Payment:** Royalty. **Tips:** Scholarly treatment, unique contributions to scholarship. Readable style. Authors should avoid formatting their manuscripts (making them look like books). Sample material should be double spaced on 8 1/2x11 paper.

UNIVERSITY OF TEXAS PRESS

University of Texas, P.O. Box 7819, Austin, TX 78713-7819. 512-232-7600. E-mail: utpress@uts.cc.utexas.edu. Website: www.utexas.edu/utpress. Theresa May, Editor-in-Chief. **Description:** Scholarly nonfiction in the areas of Latin American/Latino studies, Native American studies, anthropology, Texana, natural science and history, environmental studies, Classics, Middle Eastern studies, Jewish studies, film and media studies, gender studies, Texas architecture, and photography/art. **Books Statistics:** 90-100 titles/yr (800 submissions); 5% by first-time authors; 98% unagented. **Proposal Process:** Query with proposal and SASE. Accepts simultaneous and electronic queries. Responds in 3 months. No phone calls. **Payment:** Royalty. **Tips:** No fiction (except occasional translation of literature, Latin American or Middle Eastern) or poetry. **Contact:** Allison Faust, Associate Editor or Wendy Moore, Assistant Editor.

UNIVERSITY OF TORONTO PRESS

10 St. Mary St., Suite 700, Toronto, Ontario M4Y 2W8 Canada. 416-978-2239. E-mail: utpbooks@utpress.utoronto. Website: www.utpress.utoronto.ca. Bill Harnum, Senior Vice-President. **Description:** Scholary and general trade titles, and academic journals. Subjects include philosophy, social sciences, classical and Medieval studies, language, literature and literary theory, gay and lesbian studies, religion, music, education, history, etc. **Books Statistics:** 140 titles/yr. **Proposal Process:** Submit query with outline and sample chapters. Accepts unsolicited manuscripts. **Sample Titles:** *Indigenous Difference and the Constitution of Canada* by Patrick Macklem; *Colour-Coded: A Legal History of Racism in Canada, 1900-1950* by Constance Backhouse; *On the Edge of Empire: Gender, Race, and the Making of British Columbia, 1849-1871* by Adele Perry.

UNIVERSITY OF UTAH PRESS

1795 E South Campus Dr., Rm. 101, Salt Lake City, UT 84112. 801-581-6771. Website: www.upress.utah.edu. Peter DeLafosse, Acquisitions Editor. **Description:** Scholarly nonfiction in anthropology/archaeology, linguistics, Mesoamerica, Native America, western history, and natural history. Also publishes Utah and regional guidebooks, nature writing, ecocriticism, and creative nonfiction relating to nature and the environment, and regional general-interest titles. **Proposal Process:** Submit curriculum vitae with either complete manuscript or book prospectus. **Payment:** Royalty. **Sample Titles:** *Chauvet Cave: The Art of Earliest Times* by Jean Clottes;

The Broken Land: Adventures in Great Basin Geology by Frank DeCourten; *Butch Cassidy Was Here: Historic Inscriptions of the Colorado Plateau* by James H. Knipmeyer. **Contact:** Editorial Dept.

THE UNIVERSITY OF VIRGINIA PRESS

P.O. Box 400318, Charlottesville, VA 22904-4318. 434-924-1373. E-mail: bz2v@virginia.edu. Website: www.upress.virginia.edu. Boyd Zenner, Acquisitions Editor. **Description:** Generally scholarly nonfiction and regional general interest books with emphasis on history, literature and environmental studies. **Proposal Process:** Send 2-4 page narrative description stating book's purpose, intent, and audience, list of primary and secondary sources, chapter by chapter outline, estimated length, estimated schedule for completion, sample chapters, and updated curriculum vitae. **Sample Titles:** *Apostles of Disunion: Southern Secession Commissioners and the Causes of the Civil War* by Charles Dew; *Lifeboat* by John R. Stilgoe; *An American Cutting Garden: A Primer for Growing Cut Flowers Where Summers Are Hot and Winters Are Cold* by Suzanne McIntire.

UNIVERSITY OF WISCONSIN PRESS

University of Wisconsin, 1930 Monroe St., Fl. 3, Madison, WI 53711-2059. 608-263-1012. E-mail: uniscpress@uwpress.wisc.edu. Website: www.wisc.edu/wisconsinpress/. Raphael Kadushin, Acquisitions Editor. **Description:** Trade nonfiction (biography, natural history, poetry, social issues), scholarly nonfiction (anthropology, cinema, literature, rhetoric, multicultural studies, history, the environment, political science), and regional titles on the Midwest. **Books Statistics:** 80 titles/yr. **Proposal Process:** Submit formal book proposal with current curriculum vitae and list of 5 expert sources who could serve as potential readers. Be sure to address the essence or theme of manuscript along with intended audience and competing titles. **Sample Titles:** *Old World Wisconsin: Around Europe in the Badger State* by Fred L. Holmes; *Iran: From Religious Dispute to Revolution* by Michael M.J. Fischer. **Tips:** See website for specific guidelines.

UNIVERSITY PRESS OF COLORADO

5589 Arapahoe Ave., 206C, Boulder, CO 80303. 720-406-8849. E-mail: sandy@upcolorado.com. Website: www.upcolorado.com. Darrin Pratt, Editorial Director. **Description:** Scholarly nonfiction in archaeology, environmental studies, local interest titles, history of the American West, and mining history. **Books Statistics:** 16 titles/yr. **Proposal Process:** Query with outline and sample chapters. Accepts simultaneous and electronic queries. Prefers hard copy. **Sample Titles:** *Hiking Circuits in Rocky Mountain National Park* by Jack P. and Elizabeth D. Hailman; *Bats of the Rocky Mountain West: Natural History, Ecology, and Conservation* by Rick A. Adams. **Tips:** "We are currently not taking submissions for fiction, biographies and memoirs." **Contact:** Sandy Crooms, Acquisitions Editor.

UNIVERSITY PRESS OF FLORIDA

15 NW 15th St., Gainesville, FL 32611-2079. 352-392-1351.
E-mail: mb@upf.com. Website: www.upf.com. Meredith Morris-Babb, Editor-in-Chief. **Description:** Scholarly and general interest titles in archaeology, anthropology, history, women's studies, literature, and regional topics. Does not accept fiction. **Books Statistics:** 80 titles/yr (800 submissions); 15% first-time authors; 95% unagented. **Proposal Process:** Query with outline, sample chapters, and SASE. Accepts simultaneous and electronic queries. Prefers hard copy. **Payment:** Royalty. **Sample Titles:** (History) *Colonial Plantations and Economy in Florida* edited by Jane G. Landers; (Archaeology) *Spanish Colonial Gold Coins in the Florida Collection* by Alan K. Craig; (General Interest) *Beyond Theme Parks: Exploring Central Florida* by Benjamin D. Brotemarkle.

UNIVERSITY PRESS OF KANSAS

2501 W 15th St., Lawrence, KS 66049-3905. 785-864-4154. E-mail: upress@ku.edu. Website: www.kansaspress.ku.edu. Michael Briggs, Editor-in-Chief. **Description:** General interest trade and academic books specializing in American history/culture, military history, legal studies, Western Americana, politics/presidential studies, and the Great Plains and Midwest regions. **Proposal Process:** Submit 500-2,500 word proposal outlining the thesis of the project, intended audience, overall significance, and methods of research. Include TOC and author bio with qualifications. Accepts proposals via e-mail, but not attached partial or complete manuscripts. **Sample Titles:** *The Modern American Presidency* by Lewis L. Gould; *The Zapruder Film: Reframing JFK's Assassination* by David Wrone; *Brown vs the Board of Education: Caste, Culture,and the Constitution* by Robert J. Cottrol and Raymond T. Diamond.

THE UNIVERSITY PRESS OF KENTUCKY

663 S Limestone St., Lexington, KY 40508-4008. 859-257-5200.
E-mail: ghenr2@uky.edu. Website: www.kentuckypress.com. Stephen Wrinn, Director. **Description:** Scholarly nonfiction in the areas of biography/memoir, enviromental studies, medicine/health, film studies, folklore, military history, and political science. Also publishes regional nonfiction related to Kentucky and the Ohio Valley, the Applachian Mountains, and the South. **Proposal Process:** Query with curriculum vitae, sample chapter, and SASE. **Sample Titles:** *The Sheriff: America's Defense of the New World Order* by Colin S. Gray; *Godfather: The Intimate Francis Ford Coppola* by Gene D. Phillips. **Tips:** Does not accept fiction, poetry, or drama.

UNIVERSITY PRESS OF MISSISSIPPI

3825 Ridgewood Rd., Jackson, MS 39211-6492. 601-432-6205.
E-mail: press@ihl.state.ms.us. Website: www.upress.state.ms.us. Seetha Srinivasan, Director. **Description:** Scholarly and trade titles in American literature, history, and culture, Southern studies, African American, women's and American studies, pop culture, folklife, art/architecture, natural sciences, health, and other liberal arts.

UNIVERSITY PRESS OF NEW ENGLAND

One Court St., Suite 250, Lebanon, NH 03766. 603-448-1533.
E-mail: university.press@dartmouth.edu. Website: www.upne.com. Phyllis Deutsch, Editor. **Description:** Nonfiction titles on nature and the environment, fiction of New England, Jewish studies, women's studies, American studies, and maritime studies. **Books Statistics:** 80 titles/yr (3,000 submissions); 30% by first-time authors; 80% unagented. **Proposal Process:** Send query. No simultaneous or electronic queries. Hard copy only. Responds in 3-6 months. **Payment:** Royalty, 0-10% net. **Sample Titles:** *The Bellstone: The Greek Sponge Divers of the Aegean* by Michael Kalafatas; *New England Weather, New England Climate* by Gregory A. Zielinski and Barry D. Keim; *The Jews of Prime Time* by David Zurawik. **Contact:** Ellen Wicklum, Editor; John Landrigan, Editor.

UPSTART BOOKS

P.O. Box 800, W5527 Hwy. 106, Fort Atkinson, WI 53538-0800. 920-563-9571. Website: www.highsmith.com. Matt Mulder, Publisher. **Description:** Activity and curriculum resource books, 48-240 pages, for librarians and teachers of pre-K-12. Focuses on reading activities, Internet skills, library skills, and storytelling activity books. **Books Statistics:** 15 titles/yr (250 submissions); 30% by first-time authors; 100% unagented. **Proposal Process:** Query with outline and sample chapters. Accepts simultaneous and electronic queries accepted. Prefers hard copy. Responds in 1 month. **Payment:** Royalty. **Tips:** No books for children.

VAN DER PLAS PUBLICATIONS

1282 7th Ave., San Francisco, CA 94122. 415-665-8214. E-mail: rob@vanderplas.net. Website: www.vanderplas.net. Rob van der Plas, Publisher/Editor. **Description:** General and sports-related material on bikes/biking, golf, and baseball. **Sample Titles:** *Cycling for Profit: How to Make a Living With Your Bike* by Jim Gregory; *Lance Armstrong's Comeback from Cancer* by Samuel Abt; *Performance Cycling: The Scientific Way to Improve Your Cycling Performance* by Stuart Baird.

VANDAMERE PRESS

P.O. Box 149, St. Petersburg, FL 33731. 727-556-0950.
Website: www.vandamere.com. Arthur Brown, Publisher/Editor-in-Chief.
Description: History, biography, disability studies, health care issues, military, fiction, and the Nation's Capital for a national audience. **Books Statistics:** 10 titles/yr (2,500 submissions); 10% by first-time authors; 75% unagented. **Proposal Process:** Query with outline, sample chapters, and SASE. Simultaneous queries accepted. Does not accept material sent electronically or by registered/certified mail. Responds in 1-6 months. **Payment:** Royalty. **Sample Titles:** (Washington D.C. regional) *Two Hundred Years: Stories of the Nation's Capital* by Jeanne Fogle; (History) *Americans Behind the Barbed Wire: WWII Inside a German Prison Camp* by J. Frank Diggs; (Disability) *Black Bird Fly Away: Disabled in an Able-Bodied World* by Hugh Gregory Gallagher.

VELOPRESS

1830 N 55th St., Boulder, CO 80301. 303-440-0601. E-mail: velopress@7dogs.com. Website: www.velopress.com. **Description:** Books for cyclists and multi-sport athletes. **Sample Titles:** *Tour de France 2002: The Official Guide* by Jacques Augendre; *Inside Triathlon Training Diary* by Joe Friel; *Eddy Merckx: The Greatest Cyclist of the 20th Century* by Rik Vanwalleghem.

VERSO

180 Varick St., Fl. 10, New York, NY 10014. 212-807-9680.
E-mail: versony@versobooks.com. Website: www.versobooks.com.
Description: Books with a radical or leftist perspective on topics in the social sciences, humanities, and politics. **Proposal Process:** Submit proposal with short overview of book's main themes, TOC, brief bio of author/contributors, target markets, potential competitors, and intended timetable. Limit proposal to 10 pages; do not send complete manuscript. Include SASE for response. **Sample Titles:** *Cultural Resistance Reader* edited by Stephen Duncombe; *Legalize This! The Case for Decriminalizing Drugs* by Douglas Husak; *Banking on Death: Or, Investing in Life: The History and Future of Pensions* by Robin Blackburn.

VIKING

Penguin Group (USA) Inc., 375 Hudson St., New York, NY 10014. 212-366-2000. Website: www.penguin.com. Paul Slovak, Vice President/Publisher. **Description:** Fiction and nonfiction, including psychology, sociology, child-rearing and development, cookbooks, sports, and popular culture. **Proposal Process:** Query with SASE. **Payment:** Royalty. **Sample Titles:** (Nonfiction) *Bamboozled at the Revolution: How Big Media Lost Billions in the Battle for the Internet* by John Motavalli; (Fiction) *Women About Town* by Laura Jacobs.

VINTAGE ANCHOR PUBLISHING

The Knopf Publishing Group/Random House, Inc., 1745 Broadway, New York, NY 10019. 212-782-9000. Website: www.randomhouse.com. Martin Asher, Editor-in-Chief. **Description:** Adult trade paperbacks and reprints. Quality fiction, serious nonfiction, multicultural, sociology, psychology, philosophy, women's interest, etc. Includes Anchor Books and Vintage Books imprints. **Books Statistics:** 200 titles/yr (700 queries/yr); 5% by first-time authors; 0% unagented. **Proposal Process:** Accepts submissions from literary agents only. **Sample Titles:** (Nonfiction) *The Beauty of the Husband: A Fictional Essay in 29 Tangos* by Anne Carson; (Fiction) *On the Yankee Station* by William Boyd.

VITAL HEALTH PUBLISHING

P.O. Box 152, Ridgefield, CT 06877. 203-894-1882. E-mail: info@vitalhealth.net. Website: www.vitalhealth.net. David Richard, Publisher. **Description:** Promotes health and wellness through books, videos, and other products that focus on the integration of mind, body, and spirit. **Sample Titles:** *Facets of a Diamond, Reflections of a Healer* by John Diamond, MD; *Our Children's Health: America's Kids in*

Nutritional Crisis and What You Can Do to Help by Bonnie Minsky, MA, MPH, LCN, and Lisa Holk, ND; *Trace Your Genes to Health* by Chris Reading, MD.

VOYAGEUR PRESS
123 N Second St., Stillwater, MN 55082. 651-430-2210. E-mail: mdregni@voyageur-press.com. Website: www.voyageurpress.com. Michael Dregni, Editorial Director. **Description:** Books, 15,000-100,000 words, on nature and the environment, country living and farm heritage, travel and photography, and regional history. "Photography—contemporary and/or historical—is very important for most of our books." **Proposal Process:** Query with outline and sample chapters. See guidelines. **Payment:** Royalty.

W. WHORTON & COMPANY
1900 E 87th St., Chicago, IL 60617. 773-721-7500. E-mail: will.horton@gte.net. **Description:** Publisher of educational books and materials.

WALDMAN HOUSE PRESS INC.
525 N Third St., Minneapolis, MN 55401-1201. 612-341-4044. E-mail: nedw@wald-manhouse.com. Ned Waldman. **Description:** Gift books and children's books.

WALKER AND CO.
104 Fifth Ave, Fl. 7, New York, NY 10011. 212-727-8300. Website: www.walker-books.com; www.walkeryoungreaders.com. **Description:** Adult nonfiction on history, science, math, technology, biography and health. Also books for young readers (picture books, middle grade fiction, YA novels). **Books Statistics:** 60 titles/yr; 5% by first-time authors. **Proposal Process:** Query with synopsis and SASE. Accepts simultaneous queries, but not e-queries. Prefers hard copy. **Payment:** Royalty. **Sample Titles:** (Adult Nonfiction) *Edison & the Electric Chair* by Mark Essig; *The Book Nobody Read* by Owen Gingerich. (Juvenile) *One Witch* by Laura Leuck and Steven Schindler. **Tips:** No adult fiction, poetry, travel, photo books, or New Age. No juvenile fantasy, science fiction, series, folk tales, fairy tales, myths/legends, textbooks, novelties, or horror. **Contact:** Jacqueline Johnson (Adult Nonfiction); Emily Easton (Juvenile).

WARNER BOOKS
Time & Life Bldg., 1271 Avenue of the Americas, New York, NY 10020. 212-522-7200. Website: www.twbookmark.com. Maureen Egen, President. **Description:** Hardcover, trade paperback and mass market paperback, reprint and original, fiction and nonfiction, audio books and gift books. **Books Statistics:** 250 titles/yr. Publishes book 2 years after acceptance. **Payment:** Royalty. **Sample Titles:** *All the Sundays Yet to Come* by Kathryn Bertine. **Tips:** Does not accept unsolicited manuscripts or proposals.

WARWICK PUBLISHING INC.

Warwick Communications, Inc., 161 Frederick St., Suite 200, Toronto, Ontario M5A 4P3 Canada. 416-596-1555. E-mail: jennifer@warwickgp.com. Website: www.warwickgp.com. **Description:** General-interest nonfiction with a focus on sports, food/wine, history, current events, art/architecture, photography, and personal finance. **Proposal Process:** Send query with brief outline/TOC, and SASE. Responds within 3 months. **Sample Titles:** *The World Cup of Hockey* by Joe Pelletier and Patrick Houda; *Icewine: The Complete Story* by John Schreiner. **Tips:** Does not accept proposals for fiction, poetry, drama, or children's picture books.

WASHINGTON STATE UNIVERSITY PRESS

P.O. Box 645910, Pullman, WA 99164-5910. 800-354-7360. E-mail: wsupress@wsu.edu. Website: www.wsupress.wsu.edu. Glen Lindeman, Editor. **Description:** Books on Northwest history, prehistory, natural history, culture and politics, 200-500 pages. Focus is on the greater Pacific Northwest region: Washington, Idaho, Oregon, western Montana, and Alaska. **Proposal Process:** Query. **Payment:** Royalty.

WASHINGTON WRITERS PUBLISHING HOUSE

P.O. Box 15271, Washington, DC 20003. **Description:** Poetry and fiction by writers in the greater Washington, DC and Baltimore area only. **Proposal Process:** Query with SASE. Submission guidelines available.

WATSON-GUPTILL PUBLICATIONS

770 Broadway, New York, NY 10003. 646-654-5000. E-mail: info@watsonguptill.com. Website: www.watsonguptill.com. **Description:** Illustrated and nonfiction, instructional books on art, photography, graphic design, home decor, crafts, music, film, theatre, performing arts, architecture, and interior design, as well as children's books. **Proposal Process:** Query to Editorial Dept. with proposal, detailed outline, author bio, sample text and artwork (no originals). No telephone or e-mail submissions or queries.Responds in 6-8 weeks. **Payment:** Royalty. **Tips:** "Demonstrate the need in the marketplace for your book." **Contact:** Editorial Department.

WAYNE STATE UNIVERSITY PRESS

4809 Woodward Ave., Detroit, MI 48201-1309. Website: wsupress.wayne.edu. Jane Hoehner, Director/Acquistions. **Description:** Scholarly nonfiction in the areas of Jewish history, arts and culture, African American studies, film/television, fairy-tale studies, literature (German and Renaissance), childhood studies, labor and urban studies, and speech/language pathology. Also publishes regional titles on Michigan, Detroit, and the Great Lakes. **Books Statistics:** 30-40 titles/yr (150 submissions). **Proposal Process:** Query with proposal and SASE. Prefers hard copy. Accepts e-queries. No simultaneous submissions. **Sample Titles:** *Spirit Possession in Judaism* by Matt Goldish; *AIA Detroit: The American Institute of Architects Guide to Detroit Architecture* by Eric J. Hill and John Gallagher. **Tips:** No fiction. **Contact:** Kathryn Wildfong, Acquisitions Editor; Annie Martin, Assistant Acquisitions Editor.

WEISER BOOKS

Imprint of Red Wheel/Weiser, LLC, 368 Congress St., Boston, MA 02210. 617-542-1324. Website: www.redwheelweiser.com. Ms. Pat Bryce, Editor. **Description:** Nonfiction titles on metaphysical topics such as Magic, Wicca, Tarot, Astrology, and Qabalah. **Proposal Process:** Submit outline, sample chapters, and SASE. Hard copy only. Accepts simultaneous queries, but not e-queries. Responds in 3-6 months. **Payment:** Royalty. **Tips:** "Please visit our website for detailed submission guidelines. Before submitting any materials, please study our books in a bookstore, library, or publisher's catalog."

WELDON OWEN PUBLISHING

814 Montgomery St., San Francisco, CA 94133-5111. 415-291-0100. E-mail: info@weldonowen.com. Website: www.weldonowen.com. **Description:** High-quality illustrated reference books.

WESLEYAN UNIVERSITY PRESS

110 Mount Vernon St., Middletown, CT 06459-0433. 860-685-2420. E-mail: tradko@wesleyan.edu. Website: www.wesleyan.edu/wespress. Tom Radko, Director. **Description:** Scholarly press focusing on poetry, music, dance, performance arts, film, psychology, and science fiction. **Books Statistics:** 40 titles/yr (1,500 submissions); 1% by first-time authors; 97% unagented. **Proposal Process:** Query with outline, sample chapters, and SASE. Accepts simultaneous and electronic queries. Prefers hard copy. Responds in 2-4 weeks. **Payment:** Royalty. **Tips:** Write for a complete catalog and submission guidelines. **Contact:** Suzanna Tamminen, Editor-in-Chief.

WESTCLIFFE PUBLISHERS

P.O. Box 1261, Englewood, CO 80150-1261. 303-935-0900. E-mail: editor@westcliffepublishers.com. Website: www.westcliffepublishers.com. Linda Doyle, Associate Publisher. **Description:** High-quality nature and landscape photography books, trail and travel guides, and books with regional focus. **Proposal Process:** Submit proposal with brief description of concept of book, TOC, sample chapter(s), bio/resume, and target market. **Sample Titles:** *Colorado Caves: Hidden Worlds Beneath the Peaks* by Richard J. Rhinehart; *Arizona's Best Wildflower Hikes: The Desert* by Christine Maxa; *Montana and Idaho's Continental Divide Trail* by Lynna and Leland Howard. **Contact:** Managing Editor.

WESTERN EDGE PRESS/SHERMAN ASHER PUBLISHING

P.O. Box 31725, Santa Fe, NM 87501. 505-988-7214. E-mail: westernedge@santafe.net. Website: www.shermanasher.com. Jim Mafchir, Publisher. **Description:** Small press publishing nonfiction (Jewish studies, Southwest studies, cats and humor, art, Latin American studies, literature, craft of writing, Northern New Mexico Hispanic and Pueblo culture, and erotica); poetry (collections and anthologies); and memoirs. Also publishes in bilingual format. **Books Statistics:** 4-8 titles/yr; 0% by first-time authors; 100% unagented. **Proposal Process:** Send query with outline, credentials, and no more than 50 pages of sample text; include SASE. E-mail queries accepted, but should be brief and should not contain attachments. Does not accept any unsolicited manuscripts. Responds in 3 months. **Payment:** Varies per project/author. **Sample Titles:** (Nonfiction) *Invisible Dreamer: Memory, Judaism and Human Rights* by Marjorie Agosin; *Found Tribe: Jewish Coming Out Stories* edited by Lawrence Schimel. (Humor) *Vanity in Washington* by Peggy VanHulsteyn. (Poetry) *Written With a Spoon: A Poet's Cookbook* edited by Nancy Fay and Judith Rafaela. **Tips:** Currently not accepting poetry; send queries for nonfiction only.

WESTVIEW PRESS

Perseus Book Group, 5500 Central Ave., Boulder, CO 80301. 303-444-3541. E-mail: wvproposal@perseusbooks.com. Website: www.westviewpress.com. **Description:** Academic, professional and reference books in the social sciences, humanities, and science. **Books Statistics:** 100 titles/yr. **Proposal Process:** Send query via e-mail. **Sample Titles:** *Blood Diamonds: Tracing the Deadly Path of the World's Most Precious Stones* by Greg Campbell; *A Delicate Balance: What Philosophy Can Tell Us About Terrorism* by Trudy Govier; *Kitchen Table Entrepreneurs: How Eleven Women Escaped Poverty and Became Their Own Bosses* by Martha Shirk and Anna Wadia.

WESTWINDS PRESS

Graphic Arts Center Publishing Co., P.O. Box 10306, Portland, OR 97296-0306. 503-226-2402. E-mail: tricia@gacpc.com. Website: www.gacpc.com. Tricia Brown, Acquisitions Editor. **Description:** Regional nonfiction about the western United States for a general audience. Specializes in history, natural history, biography/memoir, travel, guidebooks, factbooks, cooking, and children's books. **Books Statistics:** 5-7 titles/yr (100 submissions); 10% by first-time authors; 90% unagented. **Proposal Process:** Send cover letter, complete outline with ideas for photos/illustrations, TOC, author bio with examples of previous publications, market analysis, photocopies or slides of artwork, and SASE. Responds in 6 months. **Payment:** Royalty (10-12% net). **Sample Titles:** *Heaven on the Half Shell: The Story of the Northwest's Love Affair with the Oyster* by David G. Gordon; *The Great Northwest Nature Factbook: A Guide to the Region's Remarkable Animals, Plants & Natural Features* by Susan Ewing. **Tips:** "Avoid poetry, adult fiction, and native 'legend' written by non-Native Americans. Children's book authors should avoid partnering with an illustrator before submission has been accepted."

WHITE CLOUD PRESS

P.O. Box 3400, Ashland, OR 97520. 541-488-6415. E-mail: sscholl@jeffnet.org. Website: www.whitecloudpress.com. Steven Scholl, Publisher. **Description:** Nonfiction on religion, current events, travel, memoirs and mythology. **Sample Titles:** *The Unlimited Mercifier* by S. Hirtenstein; *The Garden of Life* by Stephen Mason.

WHITECAP BOOKS

351 Lynn Ave., North Vancouver, British Columbia V7J 2C4 Canada. 604-980-9852. E-mail: whitecap@whitecap.ca. Website: www.whitecap.ca. Robert McCullough, Publisher; Robin Rivers, Editorial Director. **Description:** Juvenile fiction and non-fiction (nature-oriented), 32-84 pages. Also publishes adult books, varying lengths, on gardening, cookery, and regional subjects. **Proposal Process:** Query with TOC, synopsis, and 1 sample chapter. **Payment:** Royalty and flat fee. **Tips:** "Please visit our website to view our current catalog and submission guidelines."

WHITSTON PUBLISHING CO.

1717 Central Ave., Suite 201, Albany, NY 12205. 518-452-1900. E-mail: whitston@capital.net. Website: www.whitston.com. Michael Laddin, Publisher. **Description:** Nonfiction, scholarly, reference, literary criticism, and anthologies. **Books Statistics:** 20 titles/yr (200 submissions); 100% unagented. **Proposal Process:** Query with outline, sample chapters or complete manuscript, and SASE. No simultaneous or electronic queries. Hard copy only. Responds in 3-12 months. **Payment:** Royalty.

WILDCAT CANYON PRESS

2716 Ninth St., Berkeley, CA 94710. 510-848-3600. E-mail: info@wildcatcanyon.com. Website: www.wildcatcanyon.com. **Description:** Books on relationships, fashion, self-care, and parenting.

WILDERNESS PRESS

1200 5th St., Berkeley, CA 94710. 510-558-1666. E-mail: editor@wildernesspress.com. Website: www.wildernesspress.com. **Description:** Guides and how-to books on outdoor activities. No narratives. **Books Statistics:** 12 titles/yr; 25% by first-time authors. **Proposal Process:** Send query. Prefers either electronic or hard copy. See website for guidelines. **Payment:** Royalty, typically 10-12%.

JOHN WILEY & SONS, INC.

111 River St., Hoboken, NJ 07030. 201-748-6000. E-mail: info@wiley.com. Website: www.wiley.com. Gerard Helferich, Publisher, General Interest Books. **Description:** History, biography, memoir, popular science, health, self-improvement, reference, African American, narrative nonfiction, business, computers, cooking, architecture/graphic design, and children's nonfiction. **Books Statistics:** 1,500 titles/yr. **Proposal Process:** Query with outline. Prefers electronic format. Simultaneous queries accepted. Responds in 2-4 weeks. **Payment:** Royalty, range varies. **Sample Titles:** (Adult) *The Inextinguishable Symphony: A True Story of Love and Music in Nazi Germany* by Martin Goldsmith; *The Power of Gold: The History of an Obsession* by Peter L. Bernstein; *Splendid Soups* by James Peterson. (Children's) *New York Public Library Amazing Explorers* by Brendon January; *Revolutionary War Days* by David C. King.

WILEY/HALSTED

John Wiley & Sons, Inc., 111 River St., Hoboken, NJ 07030. 201-748-6000. E-mail: info@wiley.com. **Description:** Publishes textbooks, educational materials, and reference books. **Proposal Process:** Query. **Payment:** Royalty.

WILLOW CREEK PRESS

P.O. Box 147, Minocqua, WI 54548. 715-358-7010. E-mail: books@willowcreekpress.com. Website: www.willowcreekpress.com. Andrea Donner, Editor. **Description:** Trade nonfiction on outdoor sports/travel, wildlife, pets (dogs, cats, horses), gardening, food/wine, and other general-interest topics. **Books Statistics:** 20 titles/yr; 30% by first-time authors; 80% unagented. **Proposal Process:** Prefers to see detailed outline, sample chapter, and SASE instead of general query. Accepts simultaneous queries, but not e-queries. Responds in 4-6 weeks. **Payment:** Royalty. **Sample Titles:** *What Dogs Teach Us* by Glenn Droomgoole; *Garden Birds of America* by George H. Harrison; *Keller's Outdoor Survival Guide* by William Keller. **Tips:** "Avoid long letters explaining your work and what will be written; let the writing speak for itself."

WILSHIRE BOOK CO.

12015 Sherman Rd., North Hollywood, CA 91605-3781. 818-765-8579. E-mail: mpowers@mpowers.com. Website: www.mpowers.com. Melvin Powers, Publisher. **Description:** Nonfiction titles, from 50,000 words, on self-help, motivation/inspiration, recovery, psychology, personal success, entrepreneurship, humor, Internet marketing, mail order, horsemanship. Also publishes some fictional allegories, from 25,000 words, that teach principles of psychological growth or offer guidance in living. **Books Statistics:** 25 titles/yr (2,000 submissions); 80% by first-time authors; 75% unagented. **Proposal Process:** Query with SASE or submit outline, 3 sample chapters, author bio, or market analysis. **Payment:** Royalty and advance. **Sample Titles:** *The Princess Who Believed in Fairy Tales* by Marcia Grad; *The Knight in Rusty Armor* by Robert Fisher; *Think & Grow Rich* by Napoleon Hill. **Tips:** "Writing and publishing must be a team effort. We need you to write what we can sell. We suggest that you read the successful books that are similar to the manuscript you want to write. Analyze them to discover what elements make them winners. Duplicate those elements in your own style, using a creative approach and fresh material, and you will have written a book we can catapult onto the bestseller list."

WINDHAM BAY PRESS

P.O. Box 1198, Occidental, CA 95465-1198. 707-823-7150. E-mail: ellnsearby@aol.com. **Description:** Publishes travel guidebooks. **Tips:** Does not solicit manuscripts.

WINDSWEPT HOUSE PUBLISHERS

P.O. Box 159, Mount Desert, ME 04660. 207-244-5027. E-mail: windswt@acadia.net. Website: www.booknotes.com/windswept. Mavis Weinberger, Acquisitions Editor. **Description:** Adult and children's books (all ages), mostly relating to the Maine/New

England region: novels, poetry, nature, history. **Books Statistics:** 4 titles/yr. **Proposal Process:** No unsolicited manuscripts. Send SASE for guidelines. **Payment:** Royalty, to 10%. No flat fee. **Tips:** Children's books needing pictures should come complete with illustrations.

THE WINE APPRECIATION GUILD LTD
360 Swift Ave., South San Francisco, CA 94080. 415-866-3020.
E-mail: info@wineappreciation.com. Website: www.wineappreciation.com.
Description: Publishes books on wine.

WOODBINE HOUSE
6510 Bells Mill Rd., Bethesda, MD 20817. 301-897-3570.
E-mail: info@woodbinehouse.com. Website: www.woodbinehouse.com. Nancy Gray Paul, Acquisitions Editor. **Description:** Publishes books for or about children with disabilities only. Current needs include parenting, reference, special education, and high-low books. **Proposal Process:** Query or submit complete manuscript with SASE. See guidelines. **Payment:** Royalty.

WORDWARE PUBLISHING
2320 Los Rio Blvd., Suite 200, Plano, TX 75074. 972-423-0090.
E-mail: gbivona@wordware.com. Website: www.republicoftexaspress.com.
Ginnie Bivona, Acquisitions Editor. **Description:** Publishes books related to Texas, history, ghost stories, humor, travel guides, and general-interest topics. No fiction or poetry. **Books Statistics:** 30 titles/yr (100+ submissions); 50% by first-time authors; 90% unagented. **Proposal Process:** Query with outline and SASE. Accepts simultaneous and electronic queries. Prefers hard copy. **Payment:** Royalty. **Sample Titles:** (Nonfiction) *The Laughing Gas: The Best of Maxine* by Marian Henley; *Texas Money: All the Law Allows* by Mona D. Sizer; *Ghosts of North Texas* by Mitchel Whitington; (Children's) *Real Kids, Real Adventures in Texas*. **Tips:** "We are looking for interesting, entertaining books for the mainstream reader. We do not publish family memoirs unless they are famous, or better yet, infamous."

WORKMAN PUBLISHING CO., INC.
708 Broadway, New York, NY 10003-9555. 212-254-5900.
E-mail: info@workman.com. Website: www.workman.com. Susan Bolotin, Editor-in-Chief. **Description:** Nonfiction and calendars for adult and juvenile markets. **Books Statistics:** 40 books/yr, 70 calendars/yr. **Proposal Process:** Query with outline, sample chapters, and SASE. Considers simultaneous queries, but not e-queries. Hard copy only. Response time varies. **Payment:** Royalty or flat fee, range varies. **Sample Titles:** *The Dinner Doctor* by Anne Byrn; *Stich n' Bitch: The Knitter's Handbook* by Debbie Stoller; *The What to Expect Babysitter's Handbook* by Heidi Murkoff; *Granny's Purse* by P. Hanson. **Tips:** See website for details.

WORLD LEISURE CORP.

177 Paris St., Boston, MA 02128. 617-569-1966. E-mail: editor@worldleisure.com. Website: www.worldleisure.com. **Description:** Publishes nonfiction titles in the areas of travel and downhill skiing/snowboarding. Also publishes gift books. **Sample Titles:** *Great Nature Vacations With Your Kids* by Dorothy Jordan; *All-Terrain Skiing: Body Mechanics and Balance from Powder to Ice* by Dan Egan.

WORLDWIDE LIBRARY

Harlequin Enterprises, Ltd.
225 Duncan Mill Rd., Don Mills, Ontario M3B 3K9 Canada. 416-445-5860.
E-mail: feroze_mohammed@harlequin.ca. Feroze Mohammed, Editorial Director.
Description: Action adventure, paramilitary adventure, science fiction, and post nuclear holocaust fiction. Imprints: Gold Eagle Books, Worldwide Mystery. **Books Statistics:** 36 titles/yr; 1% by first-time authors; 99% unagented. **Proposal Process:** Query with outline and sample chapters. Accepts simultaneous queries, but not e-queries. Hard copy only. Responds in 3 months. **Payment:** Flat fee. Typical range: $3,000-$6,000.

YALE UNIVERSITY PRESS

302 Temple St., New Haven, CT 06520-9040. 203-432-0960.
Website: www.yale.edu/yup. Jonathon Brent, Editorial Director. **Description:** Publishes scholarly texts and general-interest nonfiction. **Books Statistics:** 250 titles/yr; 15% by first-time authors; 85% unagented. **Proposal Process:** Send cover letter, prospectus, and curriculum vitae. If available, send TOC, a sample chapter, estimated length and intended audience, and accompanying artwork. Does not accept unsolicited manuscripts. **Payment:** Royalty. **Sample Titles:** *Why Terrorism Works* by Alan M. Dershowitz; *Benjamin Franklin* by Edmund S. Morgan; *New York: Capital of Photography* by Max Kozloff. **Contact:** Gretchen Ring, Assistant.

YMAA

4354 Washington St., Roslindale, MA 02131. 617-323-7215.
E-mail: ymaa@aol.com. Website: www.ymaa.com. David Ripianzi, Acquisitions Director. **Description:** Nonfiction titles on Asian healing, health, spirituality, and martial art disciplines. **Books Statistics:** 25% by first-time authors; 100% unagented. **Payment:** Royatly, 10%. **Sample Titles:** *Taiji Sword, Classical Yang Style* by Dr. Yang, Jwing-Ming; *Inside Tai Chi: Hints, Tips, Training and Process for Students and Teachers* by John Loupos.

ZEPHYR PRESS

50 Kenwood #1, Brookline, MA 02445. 617-713-2813. E-mail: editor@zephyr-press.org. Website: www.zephyrpress.org. Christopher Mattison, Managing Editor. **Description:** Independent publisher of literature in English translation and con-temporary English-language poetry. **Books Statistics:** 9 titles/yr (100 submissions); 40% by first-time authors; 100% unagented. **Proposal Process:** Submit sample chapters. Considers simultaneous queries. **Payment:** Royalty, 7%. **Sample Titles:**

The Boy Who Catches Wasps by Duo Duo; *Salute-To Singing* by Gennady Aygi; *Courting Laura Providencia* by Jack Pulaski.

ZOO PRESS
P.O. Box 3528, Omaha, NE 68103. 402-770-8104. E-mail: editors@zoopress.org. Website: www.zoopress.org. **Description:** "We're a literary book publisher striving to expose the best English-language writers. We promote work that displays quality—by quality we mean originality, formal integrity, rhetorical variety, authenticity, and aesthetic beauty." **Books Statistics:** 10 titles/yr. **Proposal Process:** See website for guidelines. **Tips:** Publishes heavily from submissions to annual contests: The Paris Review Prize in Poetry, The Kenyon Review Prize in Poetry for a First Book, and The Zoo Press Prizes for Short Fiction and Novel.

JUVENILE BOOKS

Children's book publishing is big business, and getting bigger. With the blockbuster sales of the *Harry Potter* series by author J.K. Rowling, writing children's books has once again been shown to be a legitimate avenue to literary fame and, on occasion, fortune. In fact, curiously, some studies suggest that many children's books are sold to adults who intend to keep the books for themselves, making the question of what makes a children's book hit the bestseller lists an interesting one. For instance, the Dr. Seuss book, *Oh, The Places You'll Go!*, is a perennial favorite as a college graduation gift, although the sales show up in the children's book category.

The market for juvenile books is very diverse. Children's books range from colorful board books for toddlers to social-realism novels for young adults on subjects that just a few decades ago were taboo. Many books are issued in series, while others are released as stand-alone titles.

However, as in all areas of publishing, while there is tremendous diversity across the field, there is also increasing specialization by individual publishers. Each seeks to find its own profitable niche within that broad expanse of interest.

Before sending off materials, it is important to study each publisher under consideration very carefully. Start by getting a copy of their guidelines for author queries and submissions; often these can be found on their website. Also, request a catalog.

The publisher's catalog is one of the best vehicles to understand precisely the kind of books a publisher is acquiring. A marketing tool, a publisher's catalog reveals the special appeal that each book holds for the publisher and—it hopes—for bookstore buyers, librarians, and many eventual readers. A publisher's catalog tells how each book is different from (or similar to) others in the field. Reading a catalog carefully can help you understand clearly the kind of books a publisher is seeking.

As always, before you send a query letter or other materials, you may wish to get the name of the current editor at the publishing house who is in charge of the particular line or type of book that you are proposing. If this information is not available on the website, make a very brief phone call. Explain your project in just one or two sentences, ask whom to send the query (or manuscript) to, confirm the address, and then thank the receptionist and hang up. Do not try to harangue an editor or pitch your proposal on the phone; a busy editor seldom has time to listen to your idea, and you will not be as convincing as you can be by presenting a professional, well-written query that can be studied at leisure. Trying to pitch an idea on the phone is usually just the best way to annoy an editor.

Be polite, be professional, and remember to target your writing, making sure the language, style, and content are appropriate to your target readers.

ABDO PUBLISHING

Subsidiary of Abdo Consulting Group, Inc., 4940 Viking Dr., Suite 622, Edina, MN 55435. 612-831-1317. E-mail: info@abdopub.com. Website: www.abdopub.com. Paul Abdo, Editor-in-Chief. **Description:** Nonfiction material for children in grades preK-8. Topics include biography, history, geography, science, social studies, and sports. **Books Statistics:** 200 titles/yr. **Proposal Process:** Send resumé via e-mail. No unsolicited manuscripts. **Sample Titles:** *Cats* Series by Stuart A. Kallen; *Oceans & Seas* by Kate A. Furlong; *Holidays* by Julie Murray.

ACCORD PUBLISHING LTD

1732 Wazee St., Suite 202, Denver, CO 80202-1284. 303-298-1300. Website: www.accordpublishing.com. Ken Fleck. **Description:** Children's books, calendars, and educational materials.

ADVANCE PUBLISHING

6950 Fulton St., Houston, TX 77022. 713-695-0600. E-mail: info@advancepublishing.com. Website: www.advancepublishing.com. **Description:** Children's picture books, junior biographies, and educational texts and materials.

ALL ABOUT KIDS PUBLISHING

117 Bernal Rd. #117, PMB 405, San Jose, CA 95119. 408-846-1833. E-mail: mail@aakp.com. Website: www.aakp.com. Linda Guevara, Editor. **Description:** Picture books, board books, chapter books, and how-to books. **Books Statistics:** 6 titles/yr. **Proposal Process:** Write or see website for guidelines. **Sample Titles:** *The Moon Smiles Down* by Tony Waters; *A My Name is Andrew* by Mary McManus Burke; *Swim, Swam, Swum* by Roy Marsaw.

ATHENEUM BOOKS FOR YOUNG READERS

Simon & Schuster Children's Publishing/Simon & Schuster, Inc., 1230 Avenue of the Americas, New York, NY 10020. 212-698-7200. Website: www.simonsays.com. **Description:** Picture books, juvenile fiction, and nonfiction as well as illustrated collections for preschool to high-school age children. **Proposal Process:** Query with SASE. No unsolicited manuscripts. **Sample Titles:** *Olivia* by Ian Falconer; *The House of the Scorpion* by Nancy Farmer; *Dovey Coe* by Francis O'Rourk Dowell; *Beautiful Blackbird* by Ashley Bryan. **Contact:** Ginee Seo, Associate Publisher; Caitlyn Dlouhy, Executive Editor.

AVISSON PRESS, INC.

3007 Taliaferro Rd., Greensboro, NC 27408. 336-288-6989. Martin L. Hester, Editor. **Description:** YA biography only. Special interest in women and minorities, but is open to any good subject matter. **Books Statistics:** 6-8 titles/yr (750 submissions); 25% by first-time authors; 80% unagented. **Proposal Process:** Query with outline or sample chapter, bio, and SASE. Accepts simultaneous queries, but not e-queries. Responds in 2 weeks. **Payment:** Royalty. **Sample Titles:** *The Experimenters: Twelve Great Chemists* by Margery Evernden; *Eight Who Made A Difference: Pioneer Women in the Arts* by Erica Stux; *Prince of the Fairway: The Tiger Woods Story* by Allison Teague. **Tips:** Some literary topics and books by assignment only.

BANTAM BOOKS FOR YOUNG READERS

Random House Children's Books/Random House, Inc., 1745 Broadway, New York, NY 10019. 212-782-9000. Website: www.randomhouse.com/kids. **Description:** Movie tie-ins, and media-driven projects. Not seeking manuscripts at this time. **Tips:** Illustrators and photographers should contact Isabel Warren-Lynch, Executive Director, Art & Design. Responds only if interested. Samples returned with SASE. Pays by the project or royalties.

BLACK BUTTERFLY CHILDREN'S BOOKS

Writers and Readers Publishing, Inc., 62 E Starrs Plain Rd., Danbury, CT 06810. 203-744-6010. Deborah Dyson, Editor. **Description:** Titles featuring black children and other children of color, ages 9-13, for Young Beginners series. Picture books for children to age 11; board books for toddlers. **Proposal Process:** Send query with SASE. **Payment:** Royalty.

BLACKBIRCH PRESS

Imprint of The Gale Group, 15822 Bernardo Center Dr., Suite C, San Diego, CA 92117. E-mail: chandra.howard@thomson.com. **Description:** Nonfiction series publisher for primary and middle-grade readers, 2,500-13,000 words. Innovative series include *Made in the U.S.A.*, *Triangle Histories*, *Giants of Science*, and *History's Villains*. **Proposal Process:** Seeks experienced freelance writers for work-for-hire projects. Send query letter, resumé, and list of publications via e-mail. No unsolicited manuscripts. **Payment:** Flat fee. **Contact:** Chandra Howard, Senior Acquisitions Editor.

BLOOMSBURY CHILDREN'S BOOKS

Bloomsbury Publishing PLC, 175 Fifth Ave., Suite 712, New York, NY 10010. Website: www.bloomsbury.com/usa/childrens. Victoria Wells Arms, Editorial Director. **Description:** Picture books, literary nonfiction, and YA fiction (fantasy, mysteries, and historical fiction). **Proposal Process:** Send complete manuscript for picture books, query with synopsis and 10 sample pages for longer works (both fiction and nonfiction). Include SASE. Responds in 20 weeks. **Sample Titles:** *Polly's Picnic* by Richard Hamilton; *Goodnight Lulu* by Paulette Bogan.

THE BLUE SKY PRESS

Scholastic Inc., 557 Broadway, New York, NY 10012. 212-343-6100. Website: www.scholastic.com. Bonnie Verburg, Editorial Director. **Description:** Children's picture books and novels for ages 0-12. **Books Statistics:** 12 titles/yr; 10% by first-time authors; 10% unagented. **Proposal Process:** Query with SASE. **Tips:** Limited market.

BOOKS FOR YOUNG READERS

Henry Holt and Company, 115 W 18th St., New York, NY 10011. 212-886-9200. Website: www.henryholt.com/byr. **Description:** Picture books, fiction, and nonfiction on a wide variety of topics, and for kids of all ages. No textbooks, board/novelty books, activity books, or instructional books. **Proposal Process:** Open to both solicited and unsolicited manuscripts. However, no multiple or simultaneous submissions will be accepted. Send complete manuscript with brief cover letter, list of previously published works, and SASE (for return of manuscript) via regular mail. No e-mail, fax, disk, or CD submissions accepted. Responds in 3-4 months. **Tips:** Send Xeroxes, prints, or slides of art (no originals). Do not submit illustrations with picture books unless you are the illustrator.

BOYDS MILLS PRESS

Highlights for Children, 815 Church St., Honesdale, PA 18431. 570-253-1164. E-mail: admin@boydsmillspress.com. Website: www.boydsmillspress.com. **Description:** Children's books of literary merit, from picture books to novels. **Books Statistics:** 60 titles/yr (14,400 submissions); 40% by first-time authors; 60% unagented. **Proposal Process:** Send outline and sample chapters for YA novels and nonfiction. Send complete manuscripts for all other categories. Hard copy only. Does not accept simultaneous queries. Responds in 30 days. **Sample Titles:** *Girls: A to Z* by Eve Bunting; *A Cold Snap* by Audrey B. Baird; *Volcanoes* by David L. Harrison. **Tips:** Varied literary fiction. Avoid well-worn themes; no series or romances.

BROWN BARN BOOKS

Pictures of Record, Inc., 119 Kettle Creek Rd., Weston, CT 06883. 203-227-3387. E-mail: editorial@brownbarnbooks.com. Website: www.brownbarnbooks.com. Nancy Hammerslough, Editor-in-Chief. **Description:** New publisher specializing in quality young adult (and older) books. **Proposal Process:** Query with outline and SASE. Authors may send query/outline via e-mail (in body of text, not as attachment). **Payment:** Royalty. **Tips:** "We are in the market for good manuscripts aimed at kids 12 or older."

CANDLEWICK PRESS

2067 Massachusetts Ave., Cambridge, MA 02140. 617-661-3330. E-mail: bigbear@candlewick.com. Website: www.candlewick.com. Karen Lotz, President/Publisher; Elizabeth Bicknell, Editorial Director/Associate Publisher. **Description:** High-quality children's books and YA fiction. Also publishes picture books for ages birth-8. **Proposal Process:** Currently not accepting unsolicited manuscripts. **Sample Titles:** *Guess How Much I Love You* by Sam McBratney and Anita Jeram; *Because of Winn-Dixie* by Kate DiCamillo; *Feed* by M.T. Anderson. **Tips:** Humorous and/or non-rhyming picture-book texts about universal childhood experiences. High-quality literary fiction for YA readers.

CAPSTONE PRESS

151 Good Counsel Dr., P.O. Box 669, Mankato, MN 56002. E-mail: freelance.writing@capstone-press.com. Website: www.capstone-press.com. Helen Moore, Acquisitions Editor. **Description:** Nonfiction children's books for schools and libraries. Content includes curriculum-oriented topics, sports, and pleasure-reading materials. **Books Statistics:** 400 title/yr. **Proposal Process:** Send

resumé and writing sample only; does not accept submissions or proposals. E-queries okay for potential assignments. Send either electronic or hard copy. Responds in 4-6 weeks. **Payment:** Flat fee. **Sample Titles:** (Grades 3-9) *Stealth Bombers: The B-2 Spirits* by Bill Sweetman. (Grades 2-6)*The Boyhood Diary of Charles Lindbergh* by Megan O'Hara. **Tips:** "We do not accept fiction or poetry. We do hire freelance authors to write titles on assignment."

CAROLRHODA BOOKS, INC.

Division of Lerner Publishing Group, 241 First Ave. N, Minneapolis, MN 55401. 612-332-3344. Website: www.lernerbooks.com. Zelda Wagner, Submissions Editor. **Description:** Publishes hardcover originals for kids ages 4-12 in the areas of biography, science, nature, history, and historical fiction. **Books Statistics:** 50 titles/yr (2,000 submissions); 10% by first-time authors; 90% unagented. **Proposal Process:** Submissions are accepted in the months of March and October only. Work received in any other month will be returned unopened. SASE required for authors who wish to have their material returned. Responds in 2-6 months. **Sample Titles:** *Smile a Lot* by Nancy Carlson; *Emergency* by Margaret Mayo; *Ladybugs* by Mia Posada.

CARTWHEEL BOOKS

Scholastic, Inc., 557 Broadway, New York, NY 10012. 212-343-6100. Website: www.scholastic.com. Ken Geist, Editorial Director. **Description:** Picture, novelty, and easy-to-read books, to about 1,000 words, for children, preschool to third grade. No novels or chapter books. Royalty or flat fee.

CHARLESBRIDGE PUBLISHING

85 Main St., Watertown, MA 02472. 617-926-0329. E-mail: tradeeditorial@charlesbridge.com. Website: www.charlesbridge.com. **Description:** Nonfiction and fiction children's picture books. **Books Statistics:** 25 titles/yr (2,500-3,000 submissions); 10% by first-time authors; 20% unagented. **Proposal Process:** Send complete manuscript. Exclusive submissions only: must indicate on envelope and cover letter. Include SASE. **Payment:** Royalty. **Tips:** Not acquiring board books, folktales, alphabet books, or nursery rhymes at this time. **Contact:** Submissions Editor.

CHELSEA HOUSE PUBLISHERS

2080 Cabot Blvd., Suite 201, Langhorne, PA 19047-1813. E-mail: nnardonne@chelseahouse.com. Website: www.chelseahouse.com. Sally Cheney, VP Product Development/Editorial Director. **Description:** Quality nonfiction books for children and young adults. Features biographies, sports, multicultural studies, science and high-school/college-level literary criticism. Grade range K-12. **Books Statistics:** 350 titles/yr (500+ submissions); 25% by first-time authors; 98% unagented. **Proposal Process:** No unsolicited manuscripts. Query with outline, 2 sample chapters, and SASE. Accepts simultaneous and electronic queries. Prefers electronic format. Do not send complete manuscript unless requested. **Payment:** Pays flat fee. **Tips:** No autobiographical or fictionalized biography. Writing should be clear and direct, but lively. **Contact:** Noelle Nardone, Program Coordinator.

CHILD AND FAMILY PRESS

Child Welfare League of America, 440 First St. NW, Fl. 3, Washington, DC 20001-2085. 202-942-0263. E-mail: ptierney@cwla.org. Website: www.cwla.org. Peggy Porter Tierney, Assistant Director. **Description:** Positive, upbeat picture books for children. **Books Statistics:** 5 titles/yr (2,000 submissions); 25% by first-time authors; 90% unagented. **Proposal Process:** Send complete manuscript. Prefers hard copy. No query letters or phone calls. Considers simultaneous submissions. Responds in 6 months. **Payment:** Royalty. **Tips:** "Avoid anything too cutesy, moralistic, or patronizing."

CHILDREN'S BOOK PRESS

2211 Mission St., San Francisco, CA 94110. E-mail: cbookpress@cbookpress.org. Website: www.cbookpress.org. Ina Cumpiano, Senior Editor. **Description:** Bilingual and multicultural picture books, 750-1,500 words, for children in grades K-6. Publishes contemporary stories reflecting the traditions and culture of people of color and new immigrant communities in the U.S. Seeks to help encourage a more international, multicultural perspective on the part of all young people. **Proposal Process:** Query. **Payment:** Advance on royalty. **Tips:** See website for specific guidelines.

CHILDREN'S PRESS

Scholastic, Inc., 90 Sherman Turnpike, Danbury, CT 06816. 203-797-3500. Website: www.grolier.com. John Sefridge, Publisher. **Description:** Science, social studies, and biography, to 25,000 words, for supplementary use in libraries and classrooms. **Payment:** Royalty or outright purchase. **Tips:** Currently overstocked; not accepting unsolicited manuscripts. No phone inquiries.

CHOUETTE PUBLISHING

4710, Saint-Ambroise St., Bureau 225, Montreal, Quebec H4C 2C7 Canada. 514-925-3325. Website: www.chouettepublishing.com. Christine L'Heureux, President/Publisher. **Description:** Picture and activity books for children ages 0-6.

CLARION BOOKS

A Division of Houghton Mifflin Co., 215 Park Ave. S, New York, NY 10003. 212-420-5889. Website: www.hmco.com. Dinah Stevenson, VP/Associate Publisher and Editorial Director. **Description:** Publishes picture books, nonfiction, and fiction for both children and teens (birth-18). **Books Statistics:** 50-60 titles/yr (1,000+ submissions); 5% by first-time authors; 50-75% unagented. **Proposal Process:** Send query with complete manuscript. No unsolicited material. Accepts simultaneous queries, but not e-queries. **Payment:** Royalty. **Sample Titles:** *Hot Day on Abbott Avenue* by Karen English, illustrated by Javaka Steptoe; *Words West: Voices of Young Pioneers* by Ginger Wadsworth. **Tips:** "Research the types of books we publish before submitting." **Contact:** Jennifer Greene, Jennifer Wingertzahn, Lynne Polvino.

CRABTREE PUBLISHING CO.

PMB 16A, 350 Fifth Ave., Suite 3308, New York, NY 10118. 212-496-5040; 800-387-7650. E-mail: editor@crabtreebooks.com. Website: www.crabtreebooks.com. **Description:** Colorful nonfiction children's books featuring sports, science, social studies, art, and biographies. **Sample Titles:** *Fun With Dolphins* by Bobbie Kalman.

CREATIVE TEACHING PRESS

Creative Teaching Press, Inc., The Learning Works, 15342 Graham St., Huntington Beach, CA 92649-1111. 714-895-5047. E-mail: webmaster@creativeteaching.com. Website: www.creativeteaching.com. **Description:** Publisher of educational books and materials.

CRICKET BOOKS

Carus Publishing Co., 30 Grove St., Suite C, Peterborough, NH 03458. 603-924-7209. Website: www.cricketbooks.net. **Description:** Picture books, chapter books, and middle-grade novels for children ages 7-14. **Books Statistics:** 10 titles/yr (5,000 submissions). **Proposal Process:** Nonfiction: send query with outline, sample chapters, and SASE. Fiction: send query with outline, complete manuscript, and SASE. Considers simultaneous queries, but not e-queries. Prefers hard copy. Responds in 4 months to proposals, 6 months to manuscripts. **Payment:** Royalty, typical range 10%. **Tips:** "As of March 31, 2003, Cricket Books is temporarily not accepting unsolicited manuscripts. Please see our website for details and updates." **Contact:** Submissions Editor.

CROWN BOOKS FOR YOUNG READERS

Random House Children's Media Group/Random House, Inc., 1540 Broadway, Fl. 19, New York, NY 10036. 212-782-9000. Website: www.randomhouse.com. **Description:** Children's nonfiction (science, sports, nature, music, and history) and picture books for ages 3 and up. Send complete manuscript and SASE for picture books. **Contact:** Editorial Dept.

DAWN PUBLICATIONS

12402 Bitney Springs Rd., Nevada City, CA 95959. 800-545-7475. Website: www.dawnpub.com. Glenn J. Hovemann, Editor. **Description:** Nature-awareness/natural science illustrated picture-books for children. No talking animals, fantasies, or legends. **Books Statistics:** 6 titles/yr; 60% by first-time authors. **Proposal Process:** Submit complete manuscript. Hard copy only. Responds in 2-3 months. Writer's guidelines available on website. **Payment:** Royalty. **Sample Titles:** *Around One Cactus* by Anthony Fredericks.

DELACORTE BOOKS FOR YOUNG READERS

Random House Children's Books/Random House, Inc., 1745 Broadway, Fl. 9, New York, NY 10019. 212-782-9000. Website: www.randomhouse.com/kids. **Description:** Distinguished literary fiction and commercial fiction for the middle grade and young adult categories. **Proposal Process:** Currently not accepting unsolicited manuscripts. However, open to submissions for the Delacorte Dell Yearling Contest for a First Middle Grade Novel and the Delacorte Press Contest for a First Young Adult Novel. See website for guidelines. **Tips:** Illustrators and photographers should contact Isabel Warren-Lynch, Executive Director, Art & Design. Responds only if interested. Samples returned with SASE. Pays by the project or royalties.

DELL DRAGONFLY BOOKS FOR YOUNG READERS

Random House Children's Books/Random House, Inc., 1745 Broadway, New York, NY 10019. 212-782-9000. Website: www.randomhouse.com/kids. **Description:** Quality reprint paperback imprint for picturebook paperback books. **Proposal Process:** Does not accept manuscripts. **Tips:** Illustrators and photographers should contact Isabel Warren-Lynch, Executive Director, Art & Design. Responds only if interested. Samples returned with SASE. Pays by the project or royalties.

DELL LAUREL LEAF BOOKS FOR YOUNG READERS

Random House Children's Books/Random House, Inc., 1745 Broadway, New York, NY 10019. 212-782-9000. Website: www.randomhouse.com/teens. **Description:** Quality reprint paperback imprint for young adult books. **Proposal Process:** Does not accept manuscripts. **Tips:** Illustrators and photographers should contact Isabel Warren-Lynch, Executive Director, Art & Design. Responds only if interested. Samples returned with SASE. Pays by the project or royalties.

DELL YEARLING BOOKS

Random House Children's Media Group/Random House, Inc., 1745 Broadway, New York, NY 10019. Website: www.randomhouse.com/kids. **Description:** Quality reprint paperback imprint for middle-grade paperback books. **Proposal Process:** Does not accept manuscripts. **Tips:** Illustrators and photographers should contact Isabel Warren-Lynch, Executive Director, Art & Design. Responds only if interested. Samples returned with SASE. Pays by the project or royalties.

DIAL BOOKS FOR YOUNG READERS

Penguin Young Readers Group/Penguin Group (USA) Inc., 345 Hudson St., New York, NY 10014. Website: www.penguinputnam.com. Lauri Hornik, Editorial Director. **Description:** Lively, unique picture books for children ages 2-8, and middle grade and young adult novels. **Proposal Process:** Picture books: send complete manuscript. Novels: send outline and two sample chapters. Include SASE for response and return of manuscript. Responds within 4 months.

DOUBLEDAY BOOKS FOR YOUNG READERS

Random House Children's Books/Random House, Inc., 1745 Broadway, New York, NY 10019. 212-782-9000. Website: www.randomhouse.com/kids. **Description:** Trade picture books for kids ages 3-8. **Proposal Process:** Not accepting any unsolicited picture book manuscripts at this time. **Tips:** Illustrators and photographers should contact Isabel Warren-Lynch, Executive Director, Art & Design. Responds only if interested. Samples returned with SASE. Pays by the project or royalties.

DUTTON CHILDREN'S BOOKS

Penguin Young Readers Group/Penguin Group (USA) Inc., 345 Hudson St., New York, NY 10014. 212-414-3700. Website: www.penguin.com. Stephanie Owens Lurie, Publisher. **Description:** Trade children's books for ages 0-18. Publisher's list includes board books, picture books, early readers, chapter books, novels, and nonfiction. Titles are sold to bookstores, schools and libraries. **Tips:** "We're seeking clever wordsmiths who can tell a compelling story, with distinctive style and memorable characters that learn or change in the course of the story."

EDUPRESS

208 Avenida Fabricante, Suite 200, San Clemente, CA 92672-7536. 949-366-9499. E-mail: kathy@edupressinc.com. Website: www.edupressinc.com. **Description:** Hands-on, educational activities and materials for Pre-K through middle school teachers. Includes resources for language arts, math, reading, science, social studies, art, and early childhood. **Proposal Process:** Send partial or complete manuscript with cover letter that includes outline, synopsis, and author bio. Responds in 2-4 months. **Payment:** Purchases all rights to material; does not pay royalties. **Contact:** Kathy Rogers.

EERDMANS BOOKS FOR YOUNG READERS

William B. Eerdmans Publishing Co., 255 Jefferson Avenue, SE, Grand Rapids, MI 99503. 616-459-4591. Website: www.eerdmans.com/youngreaders. Judy Zylstra, Editor-in-Chief. **Description:** High-quality picture books, novels, and biographies for kids of all ages. Some titles have spiritual themes, others deal with historical events or social concerns. **Books Statistics:** 12-15/yr. **Proposal Process:** Send complete manuscript for picture books and those under 200 pages. For longer books, send query letter and 3-4 sample chapters. Responds in 2-3 months. **Tips:** Currently seeking stories with depth, "tales worth telling," works that delight in life's joys, but also offer honest hope and comfort in the face of life's challenges.

ENSLOW PUBLISHERS, INC.

40 Industrial Rd., P.O. Box 398, Berkeley Heights, NJ 07922-0398. 908-771-9400. Website: www.enslow.com. **Description:** Juvenile and YA nonfiction for schools and public libraries. Primarily biography, holiday/customs, current issues, science, math, technology, sports, history, and health/drug education. No fiction or picture books. **Books Statistics:** 175 titles/yr; 50% by first-time authors; 99% unagented. **Proposal Process:** Send query with outline and sample chapters. No electronic or simultaneous queries. Prefers hard-copy format. **Payment:** Royalty or flat fee. **Sample Titles:** *American Women of Flight: Pilots and Pioneers* by Henry M. Holden; *Benjamin Franklin: Inventor and Patriot* by Carin T. Ford. **Tips:** "We're always seeking new or established authors who can write nonfiction in an interesting and exciting manner. Propose a new title for an existing series, or possibly a new series idea."

EVAN-MOOR EDUCATIONAL PUBLISHERS

18 Lower Ragsdale Dr., Monterey, CA 93940. 831-649-5901.
E-mail: editorial@evan-moor.com. Website: www.evan-moor.com. **Description:**
Educational books and materials for grades PreK-6. Content covers reading, writing,
math, geography, social studies, science, arts and crafts, dramatic plays, and thematic
units. **Books Statistics:** 40-60 titles/yr.

DAVID FICKLING BOOKS

31 Beaumont St., Oxford, OX1 2NP England. 0-1865-339000. Website: www.david-
ficklingbooks.co.uk. **Description:** High-quality fiction and picture books for kids
ages 0-18. **Proposal Process:** Send synopsis, first few chapters, and SASE. **Contact:**
Editor.

FIREFLY BOOKS LTD

3680 Victoria Park Ave., Toronto, Ontario M2H 3K1 Canada. 416-499-8412. E-mail:
valerie@fireflybooks.com. Website: www.fireflybooks.com. Valerie Hatton, Publicity
Manager. **Description:** Books on a variety of topics including cooking, gardening,
astronomy, health, natural history, reference, and sports. Also publishes children's
books and calendars.

FITZHENRY & WHITESIDE

195 Allstate Parkway, Markham, Ontario L3R 4T8 Canada. 905-477-9700. Website:
www.fitzhenry.ca. **Description:** Adult nonfiction in a variety of subjects including
reference and natural science. Also publishes textbooks (geography and history) and
children's books (biography, fiction, nonfiction). **Sample Titles:** (Adult) *Get Back to
Work: A No-Nonsense Guide for Finding Your Next Job Fast* by Charles Grossner,
Leo Spindel, and Harvey Glasner; (Children's) *A Company of Fools* by Deborah
Ellis.

FREE SPIRIT PUBLISHING

217 Fifth Ave. N, Suite 200, Minneapolis, MN 55401-1724. 612-338-2068. E-mail:
help4kids@freespirit.com. Website: www.freespirit.com. **Description:** Award-winning publisher of books for parents, teens, educators, counselors and everyone else
who cares about kids. **Sample Titles:** *The Complete Guide to Service Learning:
Proven, Practical Ways to Engage Students in Civic Responsibility, Academic
Curriculum, & Social Action* by Cathryn Berger Kaye, M.A. **Tips:** "Our emphasis is
on positive self esteem, self awareness, stress management, school success, peace-
making and violence prevention, social action, creativity, family and friends and special needs (i.e., gifted and talented children with learning differences)."

FRONT STREET BOOKS

862 Haywood Rd., Asheville, NC 28806. 828-236-3097.
E-mail: contactus@frontstreetbooks.com. Website: www.frontstreetbooks.com. Joy
Neaves, Editor. **Description:** Independent publisher of books for children and
young adults. **Books Statistics:** 10-15 titles/yr; 30% by first-time authors; 90% una-

gented. **Payment:** Royalty. **Sample Titles:** *Hammer Soup* by Ingrid and Dieter Schubert; *The Yellow Balloon* by Charlotte Dematons. **Tips:** No longer accepting picture book manuscripts. See website for guidelines.

GARETH STEVENS PUBLISHING

WRC Media, Inc., 330 West Olive St., Suite 100, Milwaukee, WI 53212. 414-332-3520. E-mail: info@gspub.com. Website: www.garethstevens.com. Mark Sachner, Creative Director. **Description:** Quality educational books (arts/crafts, nature, science, social studies, history, Spanish/bilingual, and atlas/reference) and fiction for children ages 4-16. Specifically targets the school and public library educational market. **Books Statistics:** 400 titles/yr. **Sample Titles:** *Animals I See at the Zoo* by JoAnn Early Macken; *Native American Peoples*; *World Almanac Library of the States*; *Creature Features* by Nicola Whittaker.

GREENE BARK PRESS INC.

P.O. Box 1108, Bridgeport, CT 06601-1108. 203-372-4861. Website: www.greenebarkpress.com. Thomas J. Greene, Publisher. **Description:** Children's picture books for ages 3-9. **Books Statistics:** 1-6 titles/yr. **Proposal Process:** Send cover letter with brief synopsis including the authors' background, name, address, etc. Send copies of artwork (do not send originals) if available. SASE required for response. **Payment:** Does not give royalty advances. Authors are given 10% royalty; illustrators are either paid flat fee or royalty between 3%-5%. **Tips:** Prefers artwork to accompany mansuscript, but will not disqualify submissions without art. Do not send queries by telephone, fax, or e-mail. Rarely publishes juvenile novels. **Contact:** Michele Hofbauer, Associate Publisher.

GREENWILLOW BOOKS

HarperCollins Publishers, 1350 Avenue of the Americas, New York, NY 10019. 212-261-6627. Website: www.harperchildrens.com. **Description:** Children's books and picture books for all ages. Fiction and nonfiction. **Books Statistics:** 40 titles/yr; 2% by first-time authors; 70% unagented. **Proposal Process:** Currently not accepting unsolicited material. **Payment:** Royalty.

GROSSET & DUNLAP PUBLISHERS

Penguin Young Readers Group/Penguin Group (USA) Inc., 345 Hudson St., New York, NY 10014. Website: www.penguinputnam.com. Debra Dorfman, President/Publisher. **Description:** Mass-market children's books. **Proposal Process:** Does not accept unsolicited manuscripts. Material from literary agents only. **Payment:** Royalty. **Sample Titles:** *Anyone But Me* (Katie Kazoo Switcheroo) by Nancy Krulik; *Hank Zipzer* by Henry Winkler and Lin Oliver.

HARCOURT TRADE CHILDREN'S BOOKS

Harcourt Inc., 525 B St., Suite 1900, San Diego, CA 92101-4495. 619-261-6616. Website: www.harcourtbooks.com. **Description:** Juvenile fiction and nonfiction for beginning readers through young adults. Imprints include Gulliver Books, Red

Wagon Books, Odyssey Classics, Silver Whistle, Magic Carpet Books, Harcourt Children's Books, Harcourt Young Classics, Green Light Readers, Harcourt Paperbacks, Voyager Books/Libros Viajeros. **Proposal Process:** No unsolicited submissions or queries. Accepts work from agents only. **Sample Titles:** *lizards, frogs, and polliwogs* by Douglas Florian; *Stella's Dancing Days* by Sandy Asher.

HARPERCOLLINS CHILDREN'S BOOKS

HarperCollins Publishers, 1350 Avenue of the Americas, New York, NY 10019. 212-261-6500. Website: www.harperchildrens.com. Kate Morgan Jackson, Editor-in-Chief. **Description:** Publishes 525-550 hardcover and paperback titles/year in the following categories. Fiction: picture books, chapter books, middle-grade, young adult, early readers. Nonfiction: picture books, middle grade, young adult. Novelty: board books, novelty books, TV/movie tie-ins. Imprints include: HarperTrophy, HarperTempest, Avon, HarperFestival, Greenwillow Books, Joanna Cotler Books, Laura Geringer Books, Katherine Tegen Books. **Sample Titles:** *I'm Gonna Like Me: Letting Off a Little Self-Esteem* by Jamie Lee Curtis; *And God Cried, Too: A Kid's Book of Healing and Hope* by Marc Gellman. **Tips:** "HarperCollins Children's Books is not accepting unsolicited and/or unagented manuscripts or queries. Unfortunately, the volume of these submissions is so large that we cannot give them the attention they deserve. Such submissions will not be reviewed or returned."

HOLIDAY HOUSE, INC.

425 Madison Ave., New York, NY 10017. 212-688-0085. **Description:** General juvenile fiction and nonfiction. **Books Statistics:** 60 titles/yr (8,000 submissions); 1-5% by first-time authors; 70% unagented. **Proposal Process:** Query with SASE. **Payment:** Royalty. **Contact:** Acquisitions Editor.

HUMANICS PUBLISHING GROUP

12 S Dixie Hwy, Suite 200-203, Lake Worth, FL 33460. 800-874-8844. E-mail: humanics@mindspring.com. Website: www.humanicslearning.com. W. Arthur Bligh, Editor. **Description:** Nonfiction titles on self-help, philosophy, and spirituality. Also teacher resources (pre-K to 3). **Books Statistics:** 20 titles/yr (600 submissions); 70% by first-time authors; 90% unagented. **Proposal Process:** Query with outline, sample chapters, and SASE. Accepts e-queries, but no simultaneous queries. Prefers hard copy. **Payment:** Royalty. **Tips:** Interested in books that provide help, guidance, and inspiration.

ILLUMINATION ARTS PUBLISHING

P.O. Box 1865, Bellevue, WA 98009. 425-644-7185. E-mail: liteinfo@illumin.com. Website: www.illumin.com. Ruth Thompson, Editorial Director; Terri Cohlene, Creative Director; Trey Bornmann, Marketing Director. **Description:** Publishes uplifting/spiritual children's picture books. **Books Statistics:** 4 titles/yr (2,000 submissions). **Proposal Process:** Prefers manuscripts to 1,000 words. No electronic submissions. Include SASE for response. **Sample Titles:** *All I See is a Part of Me* by Chara M. Curtis; *The Errant Knight* by Ann Tompert.

SARA JORDAN PUBLISHING

M.P.O. Box 490, Niagara Falls, NY 14302-0490. 905-938-5050.
Website: www.songsthatteach.com. **Description:** Educational materials with particular emphasis on music and songs that teach. **Proposal Process:** Does not accept unsolicted manuscripts or illustrations.

JUST US BOOKS

356 Glenwood Ave., Fl. 3, East Orange, NJ 07017. 973-672-7701. E-mail: justusbook@aol.com. Website: www.justusbooks.com. Cheryl Willis Hudson, Editorial Director. **Description:** Specializes in Black-interest books for children: picture books, poetry, and chapter books for middle readers. **Books Statistics:** 4-6 titles/yr **Proposal Process:** Query with a one-page synopsis and an SASE. **Sample Titles:** *Bright Eyes, Brown Skin* by Cheryl Willis Hudson; *Annie's Gift* by Angela Medearis.

KIDHAVEN PRESS

Imprint of The Gale Group, 15822 Bernardo Center Dr., Suite C, San Diego, CA 92117. E-mail: chandra.howard@thomson.com. Website: www.gale.com/kidhaven. **Description:** Nonfiction series publisher for primary grade readers, 2,500-5,000 words. Popular series include *Nature's Predators*, *Wonders of the World*, *Seeds of a Nation*, and *Animals with Jobs*. **Proposal Process:** Seeks freelance writers for work-for-hire projects. Send query letter, resumé, brief writing sample, and/or list of publications. No unsolicited manuscripts. **Payment:** Flat fee. **Contact:** Chandra Howard, Senior Acquisitions Editor.

ALFRED A. KNOPF AND
CROWN BOOKS FOR YOUNG READERS

1745 Broadway, 9-3, New York, NY 10019. 212-782-9000. Website: www.randomhouse.com/kids. **Description:** Distinguished juvenile fiction and nonfiction for kids ages 0-18. Send query letter with SASE. Address envelope to Acquisitions Editor. **Tips:** Illustrators and photographers should contact Isabel Warren-Lynch, Executive Director, Art & Design. Responds only if interested. Samples returned with SASE. Pays by the project or royalties.

WENDY LAMB BOOKS

Random House Children's Books/Random House, Inc., 1745 Broadway, New York, NY 10019. 212-782-9000. Website: www.randomhouse.com/kids. Wendy Lamb, Editorial Director/Acquisitions Editor; Alison Root, Editorial. **Description:** Literary fiction and nonfiction for readers ages 8-12 and 12-15. **Books Statistics:** 12 titles/yr (300-400 submissions). **Proposal Process:** Query via e-mail or regular mail. **Payment:** Royalty. **Tips:** Illustrators and photographers should contact Isabel Warren-Lynch, Executive Director, Art & Design. Responds only if interested. Samples returned with SASE. Pays by the project or royalties.

LEARNING HORIZONS

One American Rd., Cleveland, OH 44144. 216-252-7300. Website: www.learning-horizons.com. **Description:** Supplemental education materials for children in preK-6 covering language, math, science, and social studies.

LEE & LOW BOOKS

95 Madison Ave., New York, NY 10016. 212-779-4400 x24. E-mail: lmay@leeandlow.com. Website: www.leeandlow.com. Louise E. May, Executive Editor. **Description:** Quality children's book publisher specializing in multicultural themes. **Books Statistics:** 12-15 titles/yr (1,500 submissions); 35% by first-time authors; 80% unagented. **Proposal Process:** Send hard copy of manuscript with SASE. See website for details. **Payment:** Advance/royalty. **Tips:** No folk tales or animal stories. Seeking character-driven realistic fiction about children of color, with special interest in stories set in contemporary U.S. and nonfiction picture books with a multicultural focus. "Lee and Low is dedicated to publishing culturally authentic literature. The company makes a special effort to work with writers and artists of color and encourages new voices."

LEGACY PRESS

P.O. Box 261129, San Diego, CA 92196. 858-668-3260. Christy Scannell, Editorial Director. **Description:** Christian nonfiction for kids ages 2-12. **Books Statistics:** 10/yr (300 submissions); 50% by first-time authors; 100% unagented. **Proposal Process:** Submit outline with sample chapters. Considers simultaneous queries. Responds in 3 months. **Sample Titles:** *The Christian Girl's Guide to Being Your Best*. **Tips:** "Please request our guidelines and catalog before submitting. Visit a Christian bookstore and understand the niche market we work with."

LERNER PUBLICATIONS

Division of Lerner Publishing Group, 241 First Ave. N, Minneapolis, MN 55401. 612-332-3344. Website: www.lernerbooks.com. Jennifer Zimian, Submissions Editor. **Description:** Publishes primarily nonfiction for readers of all grade levels. List includes titles encompassing nature, geography, natural and physical science, current events, ancient and modern history, sports, world cultures and numerous biography series. No alphabet, puzzle, song or textbooks, religious subject matter or plays. **Proposal Process:** Submissions are accepted in the months of March and October only. Work received in any other month will be returned unopened. SASE required for authors who wish to have their material returned. No phone calls. Responds in 2-6 months.

ARTHUR A. LEVINE BOOKS

Scholastic, Inc., 557 Broadway, New York, NY 10012. 212-343-4436. Website: www.scholastic.com. Arthur A. Levine, Editorial Director. **Description:** Picture books and literary fiction for children of all ages. **Books Statistics:** 15 titles/yr. **Proposal Process:** Query before sending submission. First-time authors welcome. **Sample Titles:** *The Hickory Chair* by Lisa Rowe Fraustino.

LITTLE SIMON

Simon & Schuster Children's Publishing/Simon & Schuster, Inc., 1230 Avenue of the Americas, New York, NY 10020. Website: www.simonsayskids.com. Cindy Eng Alvarez, Vice President/Editorial Director. **Description:** Novelty books, board books, pop-up books, lift-the-flap, and touch-and-feel books. Audience is children 6 months-8 years. No picture or chapter books. **Proposal Process:** Query with SASE. **Sample Titles:** *A Is for Animals* by David Pelham; *A Charlie Brown Christmas* by Charles M. Schulz; *'Twas the Day After Christmas: A Lift-the-Flap Story* by Mavis Smith.

LOBSTER PRESS

1620 Sherbrooke St. W, Suite C, Montreal, Quebec H3H 1C9 Canada. 514-904-1100. E-mail: operations@lobsterpress.com. Website: www.lobsterpress.com. **Description:** High-quality children's books including picture books, travel guides for kids, *Millennium Generation* series, and *Pet-Sitters' Club* series. Also publishes travel guides, adult nonfiction, self-help, and illustrated titles. **Books Statistics:** 25 titles/yr (200 queries and 1,500 mss/yr); 90% by first-time authors; 75% unagented. **Payment:** Royalty. **Tips:** Not accepting unsolicited manuscripts at the present time.

LUCENT BOOKS

Imprint of The Gale Group, 15822 Bernardo Center Dr., Suite C, San Diego, CA 92127. E-mail: chandra.howard@thomson.com. Website: www.gale.com/lucent. **Description:** Nonfiction series publisher for junior high and middle-grade readers, 18,000-25,000 words. Highly regarded series include the *Overview* series, *The Way People Live*, *Teen Issues*, *Modern Nations*, and the *American War Library*. Topics include current issues, political, social, historical, and environmental topics. **Proposal Process:** Seeks skilled freelance writers for work-for-hire projects. Send query letter, resumé, and list of publications via e-mail. No unsolicited manuscripts. **Payment:** Flat fee. **Contact:** Chandra Howard, Senior Acquisitions Editor.

MAGINATION PRESS

American Psychological Assn., 750 First St. NE, Washington, DC 20002. 202-218-3982. Website: www.maginationpress.com. Darcie Conner Johnston, Managing Editor. **Description:** Publishes illustrated story books and nonfiction of a clearly psychological nature for children. Picture books for children 4-11; fiction for children 8-12; nonfiction for children 4-18. **Books Statistics:** 8-12 titles/yr (700 submissions); 50% by first-time authors; 95% unagented. **Proposal Process:** Submit complete manuscript; include SASE if material needs to be returned. Accepts simultaneous queries, but not e-queries. Hard copy only. Responds in 3-6 months. **Payment:** Royalty. **Sample Titles:** *Jenny is Scared* by Carol Schuman; *The Year my Mother was Bald* by Ann Speltz. **Tips:** "We're looking for strong self-help and psychological content in stories that focus on an issue that affects children, plus engaging writing. Many of our books are written by medical or mental-health professionals." No YA fiction, chapter books, or poetry.

MARGARET K. MCELDERRY BOOKS

Simon & Schuster, 1230 6th Ave., New York, NY 10020. 212-698-2761. Website: www.simonsayskids.com. Emma D. Dryden, Vice President/Editorial Director. **Description:** Books for kids of all ages, infant through YA. Literary hardcover trade, fiction, nonfiction, and some poetry. **Books Statistics:** 30-35 titles/yr (4,000 queries); 35% by first-time authors; 50% unagented. **Proposal Process:** Query with outline and sample chapters. Accepts simultaneous queries. Responds in 1-2 months. Guidelines available. **Payment:** Advance/royalty. **Tips:** "We're looking for unique perspectives on unique topics of interest to children. We don't accept science fiction, but we do publish some fantasy." **Contact:** Sarah Nielsen, Assistant Editor.

MEADOWBROOK PRESS

5451 Smetana Dr., Minnetonka, MN 55343. 952-930-1100. E-mail: awiechmann@meadowbrookpress.com. Website: www.meadowbrookpress.com. Christine Zuchora-Walske, Editorial Director. **Description:** Books on relationships, parenting, pregnancy/childbirth, party planning, humorous poetry for children, and children's activities. **Books Statistics:** 20 titles/yr (600 submissions); 80% by first-time authors; 90% unagented. **Proposal Process:** Send query with SASE via regular mail. Simultaneous queries accepted. Currently not accepting unsolicited manuscripts or queries for adult fiction, adult poetry, humor, and children's fiction. Responds in 4 months. **Payment:** Royalty or flat fee. **Sample Titles:** (Adult nonfiction) *Discipline without Shouting or Spanking* by Jerry Wyckoff, Ph.D. and Barbara C. Unell; *Reflections for Expectant Mothers* by Ellen Sue Stern; (Children's) *Funny Little Poems for Funny Little People* by Bruce Lansky. **Contact:** Angela Wiechmann, Editor.

MILKWEED EDITIONS

1011 Washington Ave. S, Suite 300, Minneapolis, MN 55415. 612-332-3192. E-mail: editor@milkweed.org. Website: www.milkweed.org. H. Emerson Blake, Editor-in-Chief. **Description:** Literary fiction; literary nonfiction about the natural world; poetry; literary novels for middle graders (ages 8-13). **Books Statistics:** 17 titles/yr (3,000 submissions); 40% by first-time authors; 50% unagented. **Proposal Process:** Query with SASE. Accepts simultaneous queries, but not e-queries. Responds in 2-6 months. See website for specific submission guidelines. **Payment:** Royalty. **Sample Titles:** (Fiction) *Distant Music* by Lee Langley; (Nonfiction) *Toward the Livable City* edited by Emilie Buchwald; (Young Adult) *The Trouble with Jeremy Chance* by George Harrar. **Tips:** "We're looking for a fresh, distinctive voice. No genre fiction, picture books, etc. We seek to give new writers a forum; publishing history isn't as important as excellence and originality." **Contact:** Elisabeth Fitz, First Reader.

THE MILLBROOK PRESS

P.O. Box 335, 2 Old New Milford Rd., Brookfield, CT 06804. 203-740-2220. Website: www.millbrookpress.com. Kristin Vibbert, Manuscript Coordinator. **Description:** Children's book publisher, with 3 imprints: Copper Beech, Twenty-First Century, and Roaring Brook. Quality nonfiction for the school and library market for grades PreK-

6. Main market is elementary schools, but titles range from infant picture books to YA historical fiction. **Books Statistics:** 150 titles/year (5,000 submissions), 50% by first-time authors, 75% unagented. **Proposal Process:** Query with outline, sample chapters, and SASE. Accepts simultaneous queries, but not e-queries. Responds in 1 month. **Payment:** Royalty or flat fee. **Sample Titles:** *Cats and Kids* by Allen H. Hudelhoff; *The Tooth Fairy Tells All* by Cynthia L. Copeland; *Apple Cider Making Days* by Ann Purmell. **Tips:** Send SASE for guidelines or catalog, or check website.

MONDO PUBLISHING

980 Avenue of the Americas, Fl. 2, New York, NY 10018. 212-268-3560. Don L. Curry, Executive Editor. **Description:** Children's trade and educational. Picture books, nonfiction, and early chapter books for readers ages 4-12. "We seek beautiful books that children can read on their own or have read to them, and enjoy over and over." **Books Statistics:** 50 titles/yr (1,000 submissions); 30% by first-time authors. **Proposal Process:** Send SASE with request for submission guidelines. Query with complete manuscript. No electronic queries. Hard copy only.

NATIONAL GEOGRAPHIC SOCIETY

1145 17th St. NW, Washington, DC 20036-4688. 202-828-5492.
E-mail: jtunstal@ngs.org. Nancy Feresten, Editorial Director. **Description:** Nonfiction books in the areas of history, adventure, biography, multicultural themes, science, nature, and reference for children ages 4-14. **Books Statistics:** 25 titles/yr (1,000 submissions); 5% by first-time authors; 50% unagented. **Proposal Process:** Query with complete manuscript and SASE. Accepts simultaneous queries. Hard copy only. Responds in several months. **Payment:** Royalty or flat fee. **Tips:** "We like a strong writer's voice telling an interesting story on a subject of interest to young people." **Contact:** Jo Tunstall, Editor.

THE OLIVER PRESS, INC.

Charlotte Square, 5707 W 36th St., Minneapolis, MN 55416-2510. 952-926-8981.
E-mail: queries@oliverpress.com. Website: www.oliverpress.com. **Description:** Collective biographies for middle and high school students. Currently offering 6 different curriculum-based series such as *Business Builders and Innovators* (history of technology). Ages 10-young adult. **Proposal Process:** Submit proposals for books on people who have made an impact in such areas as history, politics, crime, science, and business. Include SASE. Accepts simultaneous and electronic queries. **Payment:** Royalty or flat fee. **Tips:** "Book proposals should fit one of our existing series; provide brief summaries of 8-12 people who could be included. We're looking for authors who thoroughly research their subject and are accurate and good storytellers." No fiction, picture books, or single-person biographies. **Contact:** Jenna Anderson, Editor; Denise Sterling, Editor; Megan Rocker, Associate Editor.

ORCA BOOK PUBLISHERS

P.O. Box 468, Custer, WA 98240-0468. 250-380-1229. E-mail: orca@orcabook.com. Website: www.orcabook.com. **Description:** Publishes children's picture books, young readers and juvenile fiction, and YA fiction. **Proposal Process:** Considers work from Canadian authors only. Query with 1-page cover letter and SASE. Do not fax or e-mail. No simultaneous queries. **Tips:** Manuscripts can also be sent to Canadian office: P.O. Box 5626, Victoria, BC V8R 6S4.

RICHARD C. OWEN PUBLISHERS, INC.

Children's Book Dept., P.O. Box 585, Katonah, NY 10536. 914-232-3903. Website: www.rcowen.com. Janice Boland, Children's Book Editor; Amy Finney, Project Editor/Professional Materials. **Description:** Fiction and nonfiction for kids in grades K-2 as well as professional resources for teachers and educators. **Books Statistics:** 15 titles/yr (1,000 submissions); 95% by first-time writers; 100% unagented. **Proposal Process:** Query with complete manuscript. Accepts simultaneous queries, but not e-queries. Prefers hard-copy format. Send SASE for guidelines. **Payment:** Royalty for writers. Flat fee for illustrators. **Sample Titles:** (Children's) *Star Pictures* by Julieanne Darling; (Professional) *How Children Learn to Read* by John W.A. Smith and Warwick B. Elley. **Tips:** "We seek brief, original, well-structured children's books that youngsters in grades K-2 can read by themselves. Also short, high-interest articles, stories for children, ages 7-8. Writing should be fresh and energetic with a clear style and voice. We especially seek nonfiction about history, geography, and science for very young children ages 5-7."

PACIFIC VIEW PRESS

P.O. Box 2657, Berkley, CA 94702. Website: www.pacificviewpress.com. Pam Zumwalt, Acquisitions Editor. **Description:** Small publishing house specializing in nonfiction for kids ages 8-12. Main focus in on the culture and history of countries of the Pacific Rim, especially China. **Sample Titles:** *Exploring Chinatown: A Children's Guide to Chinese Culture* by Carol Stepanchuk; *Cloud Weavers: Ancient Chinese Legends* by Rena Krasno and Yeng-Fong Chiang.

PEACHTREE PUBLISHERS

1700 Chattahoochee Ave., Atlanta, GA 30318-2112. 404-876-8761. E-mail: hello@peachtree-online.com. Website: www.peachtree-online.com. **Description:** Children's picture books, chapter books, and YA books; adult self-help in education, parenting, psychology, and health; guides to the American South (hiking, fishing, walking). **Proposal Process:** Send full manuscript or 3 sample chapters plus TOC and SASE. Send all submissions via U.S. mail; no e-mail or fax queries/submissions. Responds in 4-6 months. **Sample Titles:** (Children's) *The Sunsets of Miss Olivia Wiggins* by Lester L. Laminack. **Tips:** Strong writing with unique subject matter or approach. No adult fiction, fantasy, sci-fi, romance, anthologies, poetry or short stories. **Contact:** Helen Harriss.

PINATA BOOKS
Arte Publico Press, University of Houston, 452 Cullen Performance Hall, Houston, TX 77204-2004. 713-743-2841. Website: www.artepublicopress.com. Nicolas Kanellos, President. **Description:** Children's and YA literature by U.S. Hispanic authors. **Proposal Process:** Query with outline and sample chapters, or send complete manuscript. **Payment:** Royalty. **Sample Titles:** *Jumping Off to Freedom* by Anilu Bernardo; *Alicia's Treasure* by Diane Gonzales Bertrand; *Mexican Ghost Tales of the Southwest* by Alfred Avila.

PIPPIN PRESS
229 E 85th St., New York, NY 10028. 212-288-4920. Barbara Francis, Editor-in-Chief. **Description:** Publishes early chapter books, middle group fiction, unusual nonfiction for children ages 7-12, and occasional picture books. Also publishes humor for all ages. **Books Statistics:** 6 titles/yr (3,000 submissions); 10% by first-time authors; 90% unagented. **Proposal Process:** Query with SASE. No unsolicited manuscripts. No simultaneous or electronic queries. **Payment:** Royalty. **Tips:** "We're looking for childhood memoirs and small chapter books (64-96 pages) on historical events in which young people are the heroes." **Contact:** Joyce Segal, Senior Editor.

PLEASANT COMPANY PUBLICATIONS
8400 Fairway Pl., Middleton, WI 58562-0998. 608-836-4848. Website: www.americangirl.com/corp. **Description:** Historical fiction, contemporary fiction, and contemporary advice and activity for girls ages 7-13. Also publishes books on parenting and family issues. **Proposal Process:** Fiction: send complete manuscript of 25,000-40,000 words. Nonfiction: send query with outline, sample chapters, and list of previous publications. Include SASE with all submitted material. Responds in 12-16 weeks. **Payment:** Royalty or flat fee. **Sample Titles:** *The American Girls Collection* series by Valerie Tripp; the *Amelia* series by Marissa Moss; *The Girls of Many Lands* series; *What I Wish You Knew* by Dr. Lynda Madison. **Tips:** Small "concept-driven" list. Does not accept picture books or manuscripts for *The American Girls Collection*. See website for specific guidelines. **Contact:** Submissions Editor.

PUFFIN BOOKS
Penguin Young Readers Group/Penguin Group (USA) Inc., 345 Hudson St., New York, NY 10014-3647. 212-414-3600. Website: www.penguinputnam.com/yreaders. Tracy Tang, President/Publisher. **Description:** Children's novels, picture books, chapter books, easy-to-reads, and lift-the-flap books. **Proposal Process:** Query or send complete manuscript, include SASE. No picture book manuscripts. **Contact:** Kristin Gilson, Executive Editor; Sharyn November, Senior Editor.

G.P. PUTNAM'S SONS BOOKS FOR YOUNG READERS
Penguin Young Readers Group/Penguin Group (USA) Inc., 345 Hudson St., Fl. 14, New York, NY 10014. 212-366-2000. Website: www.penguinputnam.com. Nancy Paulsen, President/Publisher. **Description:** Publishes general trade nonfiction and fiction for ages 2-18. Mostly picture books and middle-grade novels. **Books**

Statistics: 45 titles/yr (12,000 submissions); 5% by first-time authors; 50% una-gented. **Proposal Process:** Children's novels: query with synopsis and 3 sample chapters. Picture books: send complete manuscript (if less than 10 pages). Considers simultaneous queries, but not e-queries. Prefers hard copy. Responds in 1-3 months. **Payment:** Royalty. **Sample Titles:** *Saving Sweetness* by Diane Stanley; *Amber Brown Sees Red* by Paula Danziger. **Tips:** "Multicultural books should reflect different cultures accurately, but unobtrusively. Stories about children who are physically or cognitively disabled should portray them accurately, without condescension. Avoid series, romances. We accept very little fantasy."

RAINBOW BRIDGE PUBLISHING

P.O. Box 571470, Salt Lake City, UT 84157-1470. 800-598-1441. E-mail: mail@rbp-books.com. Website: www.rbpbooks.com. George Starks, Associate Publisher. **Description:** Parent and teacher resource materials for students between preschool and eighth grade. Topics include math, reading, writing, science, geography and language arts. Imprints: Skill Mill (provides educational content for mass-market audiences) and Federal Education Publishing (provides educational content for Federal and school programs).

RAINBOW PUBLISHERS

P.O. Box 261129, San Diego, CA 92196. 858-668-3260. Website: www.rainbowpub-lishers.com. Christy Scannell, Editorial Director. **Description:** Reproducible activity books for Christian teachers in church, school, and home settings. Materials target kids ages 2-12. **Books Statistics:** 16/yr (300 submissions); 50% first-time authors; 100% unagented. **Proposal Process:** Submit outline and sample chapters. Considers simultaneous queries. Responds in 3 months. **Payment:** Flat fee of $640 or more. **Sample Titles:** *Undercover Heroes of the Bible* (4-book series); *Instant Bible Lessons* (7-book series). **Tips:** "Please request our guidelines and catalog before submitting. We only accept book proposals; we do not buy individual ideas such as one game or one craft."

RAINTREE

15 E 26th St., New York, NY 10010. 646-935-3702. Website: www.raintreesteck-vaughn.com. Eileen Robinson, Editorial Director. **Description:** Children's nonfiction in series only. No single titles. All published books are curriculum-oriented. **Books Statistics:** 200 titles/yr (500 submissions). Considers some first-time authors; almost all unagented. **Proposal Process:** Query with outline, sample chapters, and SASE. Accepts simultaneous queries with notice. No e-queries. Responds in 2-4 months. **Payment:** Flat fee (varies).

RANDOM HOUSE/
GOLDEN BOOKS YOUNG READERS GROUP

Random House Children's Media Group/Random House, Inc., 1745 Broadway, New York, NY 10019. 212-782-9000. Website: www.randomhouse.com/kids. Kate Klimo, VP/Publisher; Mallory Loehr, VP/Editor-in-Chief, Random House; Amy Jarashow,

Associate Publisher, Golden Books; Cathy Goldsmith, VP/Associate Publisher/Art Director, Vice President/Publisher. **Description:** Color and activity books; board games and novelty books; fiction and nonfiction for beginning readers; hardcover and paperback for kids ages 7-YA. **Proposal Process:** No unsolicited manuscripts. Agented material only.

MORGAN REYNOLDS, INC.

620 S Elm St., Suite 223, Greensboro, NC 27406. 336-275-1311.
E-mail: editors@morganreynolds.com. Website: www.morganreynolds.com. John Riley, Publisher. **Description:** Lively, well written biographies and histories for young adults. Suitable subjects include important historical events and important historical and contemporary figures. **Books Statistics:** 20 titles/yr (300 submissions); 50% by first-time authors; 90% unagented. **Proposal Process:** Query with outline, sample chapters, and SASE. Considers simultaneous and electronic queries. Prefers hard copy. Responds in 1 month. **Payment:** Royalty. **Sample Titles:** *Curious Bones: Mary Anning and the Birth of Paleontology* by Thomas W. Goodhue; *Remarkable Journeys: The Story of Jules Verne* by William Schoell; *Gwendolyn Brooks: Poet from Chicago* by Martha E. Rhynes. **Tips:** YA nonfiction only. Avoid eccentric topics, autobiographies, and "cute" writing styles. Market includes libraries, both public and middle/high school. **Contact:** Laura Shoemaker, Editor.

RISING MOON

Northland Publishing, 2900 N Fort Valley Rd., Flagstaff, AZ 86001. 928-774-5251.
E-mail: editorial@northlandpub.com. Website: www.northlandpub.com. Theresa Howell, Children's Editor. **Description:** Picture books for children ages 5-8. Interested in material with Southwest themes and contemporary bilingual Spanish/English themes. **Books Statistics:** 10-12 titles/yr (3,000 submissions); 25% unagented. **Proposal Process:** Accepts unsolicited manuscripts. Considers simultaneous queries, but not e-queries. Prefers hard copy. Responds in 3 months. **Payment:** Royalty or flat fee. **Sample Titles:** *Kissing Coyotes* by Marcia Vaughan; *Do Princesses Wear Hiking Boots?* by Carmela LaVigna Coyle; *My Best Friend Bear* by Tony Johnston. **Tips:** "Please submit through your agent, and review our guidelines carefully first."

THE ROSEN PUBLISHING GROUP

29 E 21st St., New York, NY 10010. 212-777-3017. Kathy Kuhtz Campbell, Managing Editor. **Description:** Publishes nonfiction children and YA titles for the school and library market. Rosen books encompass a wide variety of topics and issues that affect young people's lives in the areas of careers, guidance, science, health, history, social studies, art, culture, and sports. Imprints: PowerPlus Books, a 12-book series of nonfiction titles correlated to the curriculum for students in grades 4-8. Buenas Letras, books designed for Spanish-speaking students and students learning Spanish in the U.S. **Books Statistics:** 200 titles/yr. **Proposal Process:** Query via regular mail. No e-queries. **Payment:** Royalty and/or flat fee. **Tips:** Nonfiction work-for-hire series format (6 books to a series).

SANDCASTLE PUBLISHING

1723 Hill Dr., P.O. Box 3070, South Pasadena, CA 91031-6070. E-mail: www.sand-castle-online.com. **Description:** Specializes in books that introduce children and teens to the performing arts. Fiction and nonfiction titles range from easy reading to young adult. **Sample Titles:** *Sensational Scenes for Teens* by Chambers Stevens; *Magnificent Monologues for Kids* by Chambers Stevens.

SCHOLASTIC PRESS

An imprint of Scholastic, Inc., 557 Broadway, New York, NY 10012. 212-343-6100. Website: www.scholastic.com. Elizabeth Szabla, Editorial Director; Dianne Hess, Executive Editor; Tracy Mack, Executive Editor; Lauren Thompson, Senior Editor. **Description:** Picture book fiction and nonfiction; literary middle grade and young adult fiction (no genre or series); books dealing with key relationships in children's lives; and books with unique approaches to biography, history, math, or science. **Books Statistics:** 40-50 titles/yr (4,000+ submissions); 5-7% by first-time authors; 0-1% unagented. **Proposal Process:** Will only accept submissions from literary agents or previously published authors. Query with outline and sample chapters. Hard copy only. Considers simultaneous submissions. Responds to queries 1-4 weeks, submissions 6-12 months. **Sample Titles:** *Dear Mrs. LaRue* by Mark Teague; *A Corner of the Universe* by Ann M. Martin; *Max's Logbook* by Marissa Moss. **Tips:** No board books/flap books, resources for teachers or librarians, genre or series fiction, poetry, fairy tales, books similar to existing successful titles, or didactic books that carry heavy moral theme. **Contact:** Jennifer Rees, Associate Editor.

SEASTAR BOOKS

11 E 26th St., Fl. 17, New York, NY 10010. Andrea Spooner, Editor-in-Chief. **Description:** Literary children's hardcover books, picture books and middle-grade fiction/nonfiction. **Proposal Process:** Accepts submissions from SCBWI members only.

SHOE STRING PRESS

2 Linsley St., North Haven, CT 06473-2517. 203-239-2702. E-mail: books@shoe-stringpress.com. Website: www.shoestringpress.com. Diantha C. Thorpe, Editor. **Description:** Books for children and teenagers, including juvenile nonfiction for ages 10 and older. Resources that share high standards of scholarship and practical experience for teachers and librarians. Imprints include Linnet Books, Archon Books, and Linnet Professional Publications. **Proposal Process:** Submit outline and sample chapters. **Payment:** Royalty.

SILVER MOON PRESS

160 Fifth Ave., Suite 622, New York, NY 10010. 212-242-6499. E-mail: mail@silver-moonpress.com. Website: www.silvermoonpress.com. Hope Killcoyne, Editor; David S. Katz, Publisher. **Description:** American historical/biographical fiction with young protagonists, for children ages 8-12. Also educational test prep material/English language arts, and social studies. **Books Statistics:** 6-12 titles/yr (75-100 submissions);

80% by first-time authors; 80% unagented. **Proposal Process:** Query with outline and sample chapters. Accepts simultaneous queries. Prefers hard copy. Responds in 1-3 months. **Payment:** Royalty. **Contact:** Karin Lillebo.

SIMON & SCHUSTER BOOKS FOR YOUNG READERS

Simon & Schuster Children's Publishing/Simon & Schuster, Inc., 1230 Avenue of the Americas, New York, NY 10020. 212-698-2851. Website: www.simonsays.com. Elizabeth Law, Vice President/Associate Publisher. **Description:** Fiction (picture books and YA novels) and nonfiction for kids in grades PreK-12. **Proposal Process:** Query with SASE. Guidelines available. **Sample Titles:** (Fiction) *Jumpman* by James Valentine; (Picture Book) *I Dream of Trains* by Angela Johnson, illustrated by Loren Long. **Contact:** David Gale, Editorial Director; Paula Wiseman, Books Director; Kevin Lewis, Executive Editor.

SOUNDPRINTS

353 Main Ave., Norwalk, CT 06851. 203-846-2274. E-mail: ben.nussbaum@sound-prints.com. Website: www.soundprints.com. Ben Nussbaum, Assistant Editor. **Description:** Books on wildlife and history to educate and entertain. "Manuscript must have an exciting storyline while at the same time be based on fact and supported by careful research." **Books Statistics:** 50 titles/yr (100 submissions); 100% una-gented. **Proposal Process:** Does not accept unsolicted manuscripts due to the specific guidelines for each series. Submit published writing samples for review. **Payment:** Flat fee. **Sample Titles:** *Smithsonian Oceanic Collection, Smithsonian's Backyard, Smithsonian Prehistoric Pals, Smithsonian Let's Go To The Zoo!, Smithsonian's Odyssey Collection, Soundprints' Read-and-Discover.* **Tips:** Catalog available upon request.

SPORTS PUBLISHING LLC

804 N Neil, Champaign, IL 61820. 217-363-2072. E-mail: submissions@sportspub-lishingllc.com. Website: www.sportspublishingllc.com. Scott Rauguth, Director of Acquisitions. **Description:** Leading publisher of regional and national sports covering a wide range of sports. *Kids Superstars* series for readers in grades 3-5.

STORY LINE PRESS

Three Oaks Farm, P.O. Box 1240, Ashland, OR 97520-0055. 541-512-8792. Website: www.storylinepress.com. Robert McDowell, Editorial Director. **Description:** Fiction, nonfiction, and poetry of varying lengths. **Books Statistics:** 12 titles/yr (8,000 submissions); 10% by first-time authors; 80% unagented. **Proposal Process:** Query with outline, sample chapters and SASE. Accepts simultaneous and electronic queries. Prefers hard copy. **Payment:** Royalty.

STUDIO MOUSE

353 Main Ave., Norwalk, CT 06851. 203-846-2274. E-mail: ben.nussbaum@sound-prints.com. Website: www.soundprints.com. Ben Nussbaum, Assistant Editor. **Description:** Books feature characters of the world of Walt Disney. "Manuscripts

focus on the importance of learning the alphabet, numbers, colors, shapes, and first words while entertaining the reader with fun images of Walt Disney characters." **Books Statistics:** 50 titles/yr (100 submissions); 100% unagented. **Proposal Process:** Does not accept unsolicted manuscripts due to the specific guidelines for each series. Submit published writing samples for review. **Payment:** Flat fee. **Sample Titles:** *First Words, Family Matters, Count Up and Down, Early Learning, Reading to Grow, Kindness Counts, Healthy Kids and Friends Collections*. **Tips:** Catalog available upon request.

TEACHER CREATED MATERIALS

6421 Industry Way, Westminster, CA 92683. Website: www.teachercreated.com. **Description:** Quality resource books covering all areas of the educational curriculum. Books are created by teachers for teachers and parents. **Proposal Process:** Send 10-12 sample pages, tenative TOC, summary of audience, content, and objectives, and SASE. Mail materials to P.O. Box 1040, Huntington Beach, CA, 92647. Does not accept electronic submissions.

TIME-LIFE FOR CHILDREN

Time-Life, Inc., 2000 Duke St., Alexandria, VA 22314. 703-838-7000. Website: www.timelife.com. Mary J. Wright, Managing Editor. **Description:** Juvenile books. Publishes series of 12-36 volumes (no single titles). Author must have a series concept. **Proposal Process:** Does not accept unsolicited material.

MEGAN TINGLEY BOOKS

Little, Brown & Co. Children's Publishing, 1271 Avenue of the Americas, New York, NY 10020. Website: www.twbookmark.com/childrens. Megan Tingley, Editor-in-Chief. **Description:** Fiction and nonfiction for preschoolers through young adults. Mainly picture books. No mystery or romance. **Proposal Process:** Agented submissions only.

TRICYCLE PRESS

Ten Speed Press, P.O. Box 7123, Berkeley, CA 94707. 510-559-1600. Website: www.tenspeed.com. Nicole Geiger, Publisher. **Description:** Novels for young readers (ages 8-12); picture books (ages 3+); board books (ages 0-3); and "real life" books (ages 3-13) for kids and parents on important growing-up issues. **Books Statistics:** 20 titles/yr (8,000-10,000 submissions); 15-20% first-time authors; 50% unagented. **Proposal Process:** No queries. Send outline and sample chapters for novels and longer nonfiction; complete manuscript for picture books. No electronic queries or faxed submissions. Hard copy only. Responds in 12-24 weeks. **Payment:** Royalty, 15-20% net. **Sample Titles:** *Pretend Soup and Other Real Recipes: A Cookbook for Preschoolers* by Mollie Katzen and Ann Henderson. *Don't Laugh at Me* by Steve Seskin and Allen Shamblin; *Hey, Little Ant* by Phillip and Hannah Hoose. **Tips:** See website for specific submission guidelines.

TROLL COMMUNICATIONS
100 Corporate Dr., Mahwah, NJ 07430. 201-529-4000. Website: www.troll.com.
M. Francis, Editor. **Description:** Juvenile fiction and nonfiction. **Proposal Process:** Submit query letter. **Payment:** Royalty or flat fee. **Sample Titles:** *Treasures in the Dust* by Tracy Porter; *In the Forest of the Night* by Amelia Atwater-Rhodes.

TUNDRA BOOKS
McClelland & Stewart
481 University Ave., Suite 900, Toronto, Ontario M5G 2E9 Canada. 416-598-4786. E-mail: mail@mcclelland.com. Website: www.tundrabooks.com. Kathy Lowinger, Publisher. **Description:** Fiction, nonfiction, books for young adults, myths and legends, history, and picture books. **Tips:** Currently not accepting unsolicited manuscripts.

TURTLE BOOKS
866 United Nations Plaza, Suite 525, New York, NY 10017. 212-644-2020.
Website: www.turtlebooks.com. John Whitman, Publisher. **Description:** Children's picture books only. **Proposal Process:** Submit complete manuscript with SASE. **Payment:** Royalty. **Sample Titles:** *The Lady in the Box* by Ann McGovern; *The Legend of Mexicatl* by Jo Harper.

TWENTY-FIRST CENTURY BOOKS
The Millbrook Press, P.O. Box 335, 2 Old New Milford Rd., Brookfield, CT 06804. 203-740-2220. Website: www.millbrookpress.com. Kristen Vibbert, Manuscript Coordinator. **Description:** Curriculum-oriented publisher for the school and library market, focusing on current issues, U.S. history, science, biography and social studies, etc. **Books Statistics:** 135 titles/yr (2,000 submissions). **Proposal Process:** Query with outline. Considers simultaneous queries, but not e-queries. Hard copy only. Responds in 2-3 months. **Payment:** Royalty. **Tips:** Accepts full submissions through agents only. Requires proposals with strong tie to curriculum for grades 5 and up. Picture books, activity books, parent's guides, etc. will not be considered. Send SASE for guidelines or catalog.

VIKING CHILDREN'S BOOKS
Penguin Young Readers Group/Penguin Group (USA) Inc., 345 Hudson St., New York, NY 10014. Website: www.penguinputnam.com. **Description:** "Viking Children's Books is currently not accepting unsolicited manuscripts. Thank you."

ALBERT WHITMAN & CO.
6340 Oakton St., Morton Grove, IL 60053. 847-581-0033. Website: www.albertwhitman.com. Kathleen Tucker, Editor-in-Chief. **Description:** Picture books for ages 2-8. Also novels, biographies, mysteries, and nonfiction for middle-grade readers. **Proposal Process:** Send complete manuscript for picture books, 3 chapters and outline for longer fiction; query for nonfiction. Do not e-mail or fax.

WILEY CHILDREN'S BOOKS

John Wiley & Sons, Inc., 111 River St., Hoboken, NJ 07030. 201-748-6088. Website: www.wiley.com. **Description:** Nonfiction books, 96-128 pages, for children 8-15. **Proposal Process:** Query. **Payment:** Royalty.

WILLIAMSON PUBLISHING CO.

P.O. Box 185, Charlotte, VT 05445. 802-425-2102.
Website: www.williamsonbooks.com. Susan Williamson, Editorial Director.
Description: How-to-do-it learning books based on a philosophy that says "learning is exciting, mistakes are fine, and involvement and curiosity are wonderful." **Books Statistics:** 15 titles/yr (800-1,000 submissions); 50% by first-time authors; 90% unagented. **Proposal Process:** Query with outline and sample chapters. No simultaneous or electronic queries. Hard copy only. Responds in 3-4 months. **Payment:** Royalty or flat fee. **Tips:** "We're looking for knowledgeable writers who know their subject and understand how kids learn. Writing should be filled with information supported by how-to activities that make learning a positive and memorable experience. All of our books are written directly to kids, although they are also often used by teachers and parents. We're also looking for illustrators who work in B&W and can combine how-to illustrations along with a sense of 'kid' humor."

WIZARDS OF THE COAST, INC.

P.O. Box 707, 1801 Lind Avenue, SW, Renton, WA 98055. 425-226-6500. Website: www.wizards.com/books. **Description:** Publisher of shared-world fantasy and science fiction series. **Proposal Process:** Series are developed in-house and writers are hired on work-for-hire basis only. Send writing sample (short stories accepted), cover letter with brief description, credentials, and SASE. No phone calls. Responds in 12-18 weeks. **Sample Titles:** *Lord of Stormweather* by Dave Gross; *Emperor's Fist* by Scott McGough.

RELIGIOUS BOOKS

Religious book publishing is growing by leaps and bounds. In the 21st century, it ranges from books on Jewish traditions to Christian devotionals, from picture books for children to religious romances, from scholarly works on theology to the popular prophesy of the fictional *Left Behind* series (published by Tyndale House), found high on *The New York Times* bestseller lists.

Clearly, each publisher of religious books has a distinctive mission, often with a specialized sense of ideal approach and language to be used. Publishers expect their authors to be knowledgeable about readers' needs, to be familiar with the appropriate methods and concerns required for any book in this field to succeed.

Perhaps even more so than for other markets, before sending off materials, research each publisher under consideration carefully. Request a catalog, and get a copy of their guidelines for queries and submissions (often found on publisher websites). Be sure to send an SASE with your query, as well as sufficient return postage for any subsequent materials or illustrations sent.

JASON ARONSON, INC.

230 Livingston St., Northvale, NJ 07647-1726. 201-767-4093. Website: www.aronson.com. Dana Salzman, Associate Publisher. **Description:** Nonfiction on all aspects of Jewish life, including such topics as anti-Semitism, the Bible, Hasidic thought, genealogy, medicine, folklore and storytelling, interfaith relations, the Holocaust, the Talmud, women's studies, and travel. **Proposal Process:** Send complete manuscript or query with outline and sample chapters. **Payment:** Royalty.

BAKER BOOKS

P. O. Box 6287, Grand Rapids, MI 49516-6287. 616-676-9185. Website: www.bakerbooks.com. Don Stephenson, Director of Publications. **Description:** Hardcover and trade paperbacks in both fiction and nonfiction categories: trade books for the general public; professional books for church and parachurch leaders; texts for college and seminary classrooms. Topics include contemporary issues, women's concerns, parenting, singleness, Bible study, Christian doctrine, reference books, books for pastors and church leaders, textbooks for Christian colleges and seminaries, and literary novels focusing on women's concerns. **Books Statistics:** 250 titles/yr; 10% by first-time authors; 65% unagented. **Sample Titles:** *I Am With You Always* by Chip Ingram; *Transformed for Life* by Derek Prince; *Night Whispers* by Jennie Afman Dimkoff. **Tips:** Does not accept unsolicited proposals.

BETHANY HOUSE PUBLISHERS

11400 Hampshire Ave. S, Minneapolis, MN 55438. 952-829-2500. Website: www.bethanyhouse.com. **Description:** Religious fiction and nonfiction. Adults: personal growth, devotionals, women's issues, spirituality, contemporary issues. Adult manuscripts should be 75,000 words or longer. Typical novels range up to 125,000 words. Children and teens: first chapter books, 6,000-7,500 words, of Biblical lessons and Christian faith for ages 7-10; imaginative stories and believable characters, 20,000-40,000 words, for middle-grade readers; and at least 40,000-word stories with strong plots and realistic characters for teens of ages 12-17. **Proposal Process:** Does not accept unsolicited manuscripts or book proposals. Does accept 1-page facsimile proposals directed to Adult Nonfiction, Adult Fiction, or YA/Children editors. See website for current fax number. Continues to accept queries, proposals, and manuscripts through established literary agents, recognized manuscript services, and writer's conferences attended by editorial staff. **Sample Titles:** (Nonfiction) *The Eyes of the Heart* by Tracie Peterson; (Fiction) *The Covenant* by Beverly Lewis; (Youth) *Long Shot* by Sigmund Brouwer.

BLUE DOLPHIN PUBLISHING, INC.

P.O. Box 8, Nevada City, CA 95959-0008. 530-265-6925. E-mail: bdolphin@netshel.net. Website: www.bluedolphinpublishing.com. Paul M. Clemens, President. **Description:** Books, 200-300 pages, on comparative spiritual traditions, lay and transpersonal psychology, self-help, health, healing, and other topics help people grow in their social awareness and conscious evolution. **Proposal Process:** Query with outline, sample chapters, and SASE. Responds in 3-6 months. **Payment:** Royalty.

BROADMAN AND HOLMAN PUBLISHERS

127 Ninth Ave. N, Nashville, TN 37234-0115. Website: www.broadmanholman.com. Leonard G. Goss, Editorial Director. **Description:** Adult trade, children's, academic, religious, and inspirational fiction and nonfiction. **Books Statistics:** 100 titles/yr. **Proposal Process:** Query with SASE. Guidelines available. **Payment:** Royalty. **Sample Titles:** *The Beloved Disciple* by Beth Moore; *The Jericho Sanction* by Oliver North; *The Little Style Guide to Great Christian Writing and Publishing* by Leonard and Carolyn Goss.

CHRISTIAN PUBLICATIONS, INC.

3825 Hartzdale Dr., Camp Hill, PA 17011. 717-761-7044. E-mail: editorial@christianpublications.com. Website: www.christianpublications.com. **Description:** Adult nonfiction from an evangelical Christian viewpoint, centering on personal spiritual growth often with a "deeper life" theme. **Books Statistics:** 15 titles/yr (250 submissions); 65% by first-time authors; 99% unagented. **Proposal Process:** Query with outline, proposal, two sample chapters, and SASE. Accepts simultaneous queries. Prefers hard copy. Responds in 4-6 weeks. **Payment:** Royalty, 10% net. **Sample Titles:** *Seeking the Unseen God* by Marty Berglund; *The Attributes of God* by A.W. Tozer; *Father's Love Letter: An Intimate Message from God to You* by Barry Adams. **Tips** "We're interested in Bible-based books on spiritual growth, Christian living, family, marriage, home schooling, leadership, inspirational, devotional. We're also looking for well-written books on Christian history for youth and/or adults. Please do not send personal experience stories." **Contact:** Lauraine Gustafson, Managing Editor; Gretchen Nesbit, Assistant Editor.

CONCORDIA PUBLISHING HOUSE

3558 S Jefferson Ave., St. Louis, MO 63118-3968. 314-268-1187. E-mail: brandy.overton@cph.org. Website: www.cph.org. **Description:** Nonfiction on Christian living, inspiration, parenting, literature/arts, spirituality, and culture. Also publishes children's/YA titles, devotionals, pastoral/professional resources, day school and Sunday school curriculum and resources, multiethnic materials, music/hymnals, and Bible study/Bible reference materials. **Proposal Process:** Sumbit brief cover letter with resumé, outline, short sample of manuscript, and SASE. Responds in 8-12 weeks. **Payment:** Royalty. **Sample Titles:** (Adult Nonfiction) *Christianity in an Age of Terrorism* by Gene Edward Veith. (YA) *Teens Pray* by Edward C. Grube. (Children's) *The Very First Christmas* by Paul L. Maier. **Tips:** Does not accept poetry, drama, adult fiction, biographies, or short stories. See website for submission guidelines. **Contact:** Editorial Assistant.

THE CROSSROAD PUBLISHING CO.

481 8th Ave., Suite 1550, New York, NY 10001. 212-868-1801.
E-mail: ask@crossroadpublishing.com. Website: www.crossroadpublishing.com.
Description: Publisher of spiritual and religious titles. **Books Statistics:** 55 titles/yr **Proposal Process:** Query with brief description, TOC, approximate word count, estimated timetable, intended audience, resumé or curriculum vitae, and writing sample (no more than 2 chapters). **Sample Titles:** *Awake in The Spirit* by M. Basil Pennington; *Faith That Makes Sense* by Robert J. Cormier.

DEVORSS & CO.

1046 Princeton Dr., Marina del Rey, CA 90292. 310-822-8940.
E-mail: service@devorss.com. Website: www.devorss.com. **Description:** Nonfiction titles on metaphysical, spiritual, inspirational, New Age, and self-help topics. **Proposal Process:** Write for guidelines. Send SASE for reply and return of materials. **Sample Titles:** *The Little Book of Candle Power* by Carli Logan; *How to be Healthy Wealthy Happy* by Raymond Charles Barker; *Expressions of Oneness* by Jean Shorter; *The Invisible String* by Patrice Karst.

WILLIAM B. EERDMANS PUBLISHING CO., INC.

255 Jefferson Ave. SE, Grand Rapids, MI 49503. 616-459-4591. E-mail: info@eerdmans.com. Website: www.eerdmans.com. Jon Pott, Editor-in-Chief. **Description:** Publishes nonfiction books that focus on Christian theology, religious history and biography, ethics, philosophy, literary studies, and spiritual growth. Also publishes children's books, Biblical reference, and ministry resources. **Proposal Process:** Send query letter explaining the content of the book, intended audience, estimated length, and your qualifications for writing the material. Also state how the book is different from other books currently available on the subject. Include TOC, sample chapters, and SASE. **Payment:** Royalty. **Sample Titles:** *The Dwelling of the Light: Praying with Icons of Christ* by Rowan Williams; *Inge: A Girl's Journey Through Nazi Europe* by Inge Joseph Bleier and David E. Gumpert. **Tips:** Does not respond to submissions sent by e-mail or fax.

FORTRESS PRESS

P.O. Box 1209, Minneapolis, MN 55440. 612-330-3300. E-mail: submissions@augsburgfortress.org. Website: fortresspress.com. **Description:** Academic and ecumenical publisher of books in religion, with focus in the following: Biblical studies, Christian theology (including historical, feminist, and contextual theologies), ethics, history of Christianity, Judaism, religion and science, African American religion, and pastoral resources. **Books Statistics:** 60 titles/yr; 10% or less by first-time authors. **Proposal Process:** Send bio with curriculum vitae, working title, 250-word description stating thesis, TOC, intended audience, list of competing titles currently on the market, 1-3 sample chapters, and SASE. **Payment:** Royalty. **Sample Titles:** *Writings of the New Testament* by Luke Timothy Johnson; *The Prophetic Imagination* by Walter Brueggemann; *Models of God* by Sallie McFague.

GENESIS PUBLISHING CO., INC.

36 Steeple View Dr., Atkinson, NH 03811. 603-362-4121. E-mail: genesis@genesisbook.com. Website: www.genesisbook.com. Gerard M. Verschuuren, President. **Description:** Adult fiction and nonfiction, especially on the topics of religion and philosophy. **Proposal Process:** Query with SASE. **Payment:** Royalty.

GOOD NEWS PUBLISHERS/CROSSWAY BOOKS

1300 Crescent St., Wheaton, IL 60187. 630-682-4300. E-mail: editorial@gnpcb.org. Website: www.crosswaybooks.org. **Description:** Publishes books with an Evangelical Christian perspective. Fiction (historical, action/adventure, contemporary/Christian realism, YA), nonfiction (Christian living, Biblical teaching, evangelism, Christian truth), and a select number of academic/professional volumes. **Books Statistics:** 85 titles/yr. **Proposal Process:** Send 1-2 page synopsis (preferably chapter by chapter), 2 sample chapters, and SASE. Does not accept e-mail or fax submissions. Do not send complete manuscript. Responds in 4-6 months. **Sample Titles:** *Jesus Driven Ministry* by Ajita Fernado; *Holiness by Grace: Delighting in the Joy That is Our Strength* by Bryan Chapell. **Tips:** See guidelines on website before submitting. **Contact:** Jill Carter, Editorial Administrator.

HACHAI PUBLISHING

156 Chester Ave., Brooklyn, NY 11218. 718-633-0100. E-mail: info@hachai.com. Website: www.hachai.com. D.L. Rosenfeld, Editor. **Description:** Publishes Judaica children's picture books for readers ages 2-8. Interested in stories that convey traditional Jewish experience in modern times, traditional Jewish observance such as holidays and year-round mitzvahs, and positive character traits. **Books Statistics:** 4 titles/yr (300 submission); 60% by first-time authors; 90% unagented. **Proposal Process:** Query or send complete manuscript, and SASE. Accepts simultaneous queries, but not e-queries. Hard copy only. Responds in 6 weeks. **Payment:** Flat fee. **Tips:** "We do not accept fantasy, animal stories, romance, violence, or preachy sermonizing."

HARPER SAN FRANCISCO

HarperCollins Publishers, 353 Sacramento St., Suite 500, San Francisco, CA 94111-3653. 415-477-4400. Website: www.harpersf.com. **Description:** Books on spirituality and religion. "We strive to be the preeminent publisher of the most important books across the full spectrum of religion and spiritual literature, adding to the wealth of the world's wisdom by respecting all traditions." **Books Statistics:** 70 titles/yr; 5% by first-time authors. **Proposal Process:** No unsolicited manuscripts. Accepts material from literary agents only. **Sample Titles:** *The Brother of Jesus* by Hershel Shanks and Ben Witherington III; *Slow Way Home* by Michael Morris; *When Religion Becomes Evil* by Charles Kimball; *Tantrika* by Asra Nomani; *Christmas in Harmony* by Philip Gulley; *100 Simple Secrets of Great Relationships* by David Niven. **Contact:** Acquisitions Editor.

HARVEST HOUSE PUBLISHERS

990 Owen Loop N, Eugene, OR 97402-9173. 541-343-0123.
Website: www.harvesthousepublishers.com. **Description:** Publisher of Evangelical Christian books. **Books Statistics:** 160 titles/yr. **Proposal Process:** Does not accept unsolicited submissions. Recommends using Evangelical Christian Publishers Association (ECPA). Website www.ecpa.org or the Writer's Edge, P.O. Box 1266, Wheaton, IL. 60189. **Tips:** "We provide high-quality books and products that glorify God, affirm Biblical values, help people grow spiritually strong, and proclaim Jesus Christ as the answer to every human need."

JOURNEYFORTH BOOKS

Bob Jones University Press, 1700 Wade Hampton Blvd., Greenville, SC 29614. 864-370-1800, ext. 4350. E-mail: jb@bjup.com. Website: www.bjup.com/books. **Description:** Christian publisher. Books for young readers, ages 6-teen, that reflect "the highest Christian standards of thought, feeling, and action." **Books Statistics:** 10 titles/yr (500 submissions). **Proposal Process:** Submit synopsis and the first five chapters. Accepts simultaneous queries. **Payment:** Negotiable—royalty or flat fee. **Sample Titles:** *Tommy's Clubhouse* by Sharon Hambrick; *Fanny Crosby: Queen of Gospel Songs* by Rebecca Davis; *The Slide* by Catherine Farnes; *The Children of the Storm* by Natasha Vins. **Tips:** "Secular conflicts are considered, but only within the context of a Christian worldview. Avoid modern humanistic philosophy in stories; instead, emphasize a Biblically conservative lifestyle that best serves the individual and society. The writing must be excellent and the story engaging. We are not currently accepting picture books." **Contact:** Nancy Lohr, Acquisitions Editor.

JUDSON PRESS

American Baptist Churches, P.O. Box 851, Valley Forge, PA 19482-0851. 610-768-2109. E-mail: randy.frame@abc-usa.org. Website: www.judsonpress.com. Randy Frame, Editor. **Description:** Resources to enhance individual Christian living and the life of the church. **Books Statistics:** 15 titles/yr (700 submissions); 20% by first-time authors; 90% unagented. **Proposal Process:** Query with proposal, TOC, estimated length of book, sample chapters, target audience, expected completion date, and bio. Simultaneous queries accepted. Accepts queries via e-mail, but not proposals/submissions. Prefers hard copy. **Payment:** Royalty. **Sample Titles:** *Before We Say I Do: 7 Steps to a Healthy Marriage* by Marvin A. McMickle; *Addicted to Hurry: Spiritual Strategies for Slowing Down* by Kirk Byron Jones. **Tips:** "Avoid life stories or poetry. Looking for unusually good writing and original ideas."

KREGEL PUBLICATIONS

P.O. Box 2607, Grand Rapids, MI 49501-2607. 616-451-4775.
Website: www.kregelpublications.com. Dennis Hillman, Publisher. **Description:** Evangelical Christian publisher interested in pastoral ministry, Christian education, family and marriage, contemporary issues, women's issues, devotional books, and biblical studies. Also publishes adult and juvenile fiction (with solid Christian message), children's literature, and academic titles. No poetry, autobiographies, general fiction, or cartoons. **Proposal Process:** Accepting query letters only. Should include summary, target audience, and brief author bio. Allow 3 months for response. See website for guidelines. **Payment:** Royalty. **Sample Titles:** *Eusebius* translated by Paul Maier; *A Different Kind of Laughter: Finding Joy and Peace in the Deep End of Life* by Andy Cook; *Unveiling Islam* by Ergen Caner and Emir Caner; *Romance Rustlers and Thunderbird Thieves* by Sharon Dunn. **Contact:** Acquisitions Editor.

LOYOLA PRESS

3441 N Ashland Ave., Chicago, IL 60657-1397. 773-281-1818.
E-mail: editorial@loyolapress.com; durepos@loyolapress.com. Website: www.loyola-press.org. Jim Manney, Editorial Director. **Description:** Publishes Christian books and resources for the general trade. Titles cover gift/inspiration, prayer, spirituality, Catholic life, history, theology, Jesuit or Ignatian spirituality, and spiritual direction. **Books Statistics:** 40 titles/yr (500-600 submissions); 25% by first-time authors; 50% unagented. **Proposal Process:** Send proposal with 1-2 sample chapters and SASE. Simultaneous and electronic queries accepted. Prefers hard copy. Responds in 6-8 weeks. **Payment:** Royalty, typically industry standard. **Sample Titles:** *The New Faithful* by Colleen Carroll; *Heroic Leadership* by Chris Lowney; *Go in Peace* by John Paul II. **Tips:** Does not accept academic material, poetry, children's books, or fiction. See website for guidelines. **Contact:** Joseph Durepos, Acquisitions Editor.

MOODY PUBLISHERS

820 N LaSalle Blvd., Chicago, IL 60610-3284. 312-329-8047.
E-mail: acquisitions@moody.edu. Website: www.moodypublishers.org. **Description:** Evangelical Christian books in categories such as Christian living, women, marriage/family, finances, and fiction. **Proposal Process:** Considers agented proposals only. No phone calls. **Tips:** "We seek to educate and edify the Christian and to evangelize the non-Christian by ethically publishing conservative, evangelical Christian literature and other media for all ages around the world." **Contact:** Acquisitions Coordinator.

MOREHOUSE PUBLISHING

4775 Linglestown Rd., Harrisburg, PA 17112. 717-541-8130.
E-mail: dfarring@morehousegroup.com. Website: www.morehousepublishing.com.
Debra Farrington, Publisher and Editorial Director. **Description:** An Episcopal publisher specializing in books on spirituality, Anglican studies, professional books for clergy, and Episcopal adult formation materials. **Books Statistics:** 30-35 titles/yr (500-750 submissions); 60% by first-time authors; 90% unagented. **Proposal Process:** Query with cover letter, brief proposal, resumé, short book description, outline, market analysis, sample chapters (20 pages). Accepts simultaneous queries, but not e-queries. Responds in 4-6 weeks. **Tips:** No fiction or poetry. "We are currently not accepting children's book manuscripts."

MULTNOMAH PUBLISHERS, INC.

P.O. Box 1720, Sisters, OR 97759. 541-549-1144.
Website: www.multnomahbooks.com. **Description:** Evangelical, Christian publishing house. **Proposal Process:** Submit 2-3 sample chapters with outline, cover letter, and SASE. No unsolicited manuscripts. **Payment:** Royalty. **Sample Titles:** *Reflections on the Savior* by Max Lucado; *31 Days of Power: Learning to Live in Spiritual Victory* by Ruth Myers. **Tips:** "Multnomah Books are message-driven, clean, moral, uplifting fiction and nonfiction." Currently not accepting proposals for biographies, poetry, or children's books.

THOMAS NELSON BOOKS

P.O. Box 141000, Nashville, TN 37214-1000. Website: www.thomasnelson.com.
Description: Nonfiction adult inspirational, motivational, devotional, self-help, Christian living, prayer, and evangelism titles. **Books Statistics:** 40-50 titles/yr. **Proposal Process:** Query with SASE. No unsolicited manuscripts. All submissions must come through an agent. **Payment:** Royalty. **Sample Titles:** *Wild at Heart* by John Eldredge; *Seeking His Face* by Charles F. Stanley. **Contact:** Acquisitions Editor.

NEW CANAAN PUBLISHING CO.

P.O. Box 752, New Canaan, CT 06840. E-mail: djm@newcanaanpublishing.com.
Website: www.newcanaanpublishing.com. Kathy Mittelstadt, Editor. **Description:** Children's books for readers ages 5-16. Also YA fiction/nonfiction and Christian titles. **Books Statistics:** 3-4 titles/yr (120 submissions); 50% by first-time authors; 100% unagented. **Proposal Process:** Submit complete manuscript with SASE. Accepts simultaneous queries, but not e-queries. Hard copy only. Responds in 6 months. **Payment:** Royalty. **Sample Titles:** (Nonfiction) *Rock Your World* by Bill Scott; *Dynamic Evangelism* by Luke Tamu. (Children's) *Little Red Baseball Stockings and Other Stories* by Nathan Zimelman; *Olive the Orphan Reindeer* by Michael Christie. **Tips:** Seeking strong educational and moral content.

NEW LEAF PRESS, INC./MASTER BOOKS

P.O. Box 726, Green Forest, AR 72638. 870-438-5288. E-mail: nlp@newleafpress.net. Website: www.newleafpress.net. Roger Howerton, Acquisitions Editor. **Description:** New Leaf Press: nonfiction titles, 100-400 pages, on Christian living as well as gift books and devotionals. Master Books: nonfiction titles related to creationism, including children's books, scholarly works and books for the layman. No poetry, fiction, or personal stories. **Books Statistics:** 30-35 titles/yr (500-600 submissions); 15% by first-time authors. **Proposal Process:** Query with outline and sample chapters. Accepts simultaneous queries. Responds in 3 months. **Payment:** Royalty, 10% of net. **Sample Titles:** (New Leaf Press) *Come Home to Comfort* by Sharon Hoffman; *G.I. Joe & Lillie* by Joseph S. Bonsall; (Master Books) *Exploring the World Around You* by Gary Parker; *Grand Canyon: A Different View* by Tom Vail. **Tips:** "Tell us why this book is marketable and to which market(s) it is directed. How will it fulfill the needs of Christians? We endeavor to publish books which will bring the lost to Christ and balance to the body of Christ."

NORTH STAR PUBLICATIONS INC.

P.O. Box 227, East Sandwich, MA 02537-0227. 508-420-6188. E-mail: norbook@aol.com. Website: www.northstarpublications.com. **Description:** Books on psychology, health, spirituality, inspirational, and some biography.

OUR SUNDAY VISITOR PUBLISHING

200 Noll Plaza, Huntington, IN 46750. 219-356-8400. E-mail: booksed@osv.com. Website: www.osv.com. Jacquelyn Lindsey, Mike Dubruiel, Beth McNamara, Acquisitions Editors. **Description:** Nonfiction Catholic-oriented books of various lengths. **Books Statistics:** 40-50 titles/yr (500+ submissions); 10% by first-time authors; 100% unagented. **Proposal Process:** Query with outline, market analysis, and SASE. Responds in 3 months. **Payment:** Royalty.

PARACLETE PRESS

P.O. Box 1568, Orleans, MA 02653. 508-255-4685. E-mail: mail@paracletepress.com. Website: www.paracletepress.com. Editorial Review Committee. **Description:** An ecumenical publisher specializing in full-length, nonfiction and literary fiction for the adult Christian market. **Books Statistics:** 20 titles/yr (150-250 submissions). **Proposal Process:** Query with summary of proposed book and its target audience, estimated length of book, TOC, and 1-2 sample chapters. Accepts simultaneous queries. Responds in 8 weeks. **Payment:** Royalty.

PAULINE BOOKS & MEDIA

Daughters of St. Paul, 50 Saint Paul's Ave., Jamaica Plain, MA 02130-3491. 617-522-8911. Website: www.pauline.org. **Description:** Roman Catholic publications for both adults and children.

PAULIST PRESS

997 Macarthur Blvd., Mahwah, NJ 07430. 201-825-7300.
Website: www.paulistpress.com. **Description:** Adult nonfiction, 120-250 pages, on ecumenical theology, Roman Catholic studies, liturgy, spirituality, church history, ethics, religious education, and Christian philosophy. Also publishes a limited number of religious story books for children. HiddenSpring imprint publishes general religious trade books. **Proposal Process:** For adult books, query with SASE. For juvenile books, submit complete manuscript, with one sample illustration. No simultaneous submissions. **Payment:** Flat fee or royalty. **Sample Titles:** *The Unity of the Bible: Exploring the Beauty and Structure of the Bible* by Duane L. Christensen; *Carmelite Prayer: A Tradition for the 21st Century* edited by Keith J. Egan. **Contact:** Lawrence Boadt, Editorial Director.

QUEST BOOKS

Theosophical Publishing House, 306 W Geneva Rd., P. O. Box 270, Wheaton, IL 60189-0270. 630-665-0130. Website: www.questbooks.net. Brenda Rosen, Acquisitions Editor. **Description:** Nonfiction books on Eastern and Western religion and philosophy, holistic health, healing, transpersonal psychology, men's and women's spirituality, creativity, meditation, yoga, ancient wisdom. **Proposal Process:** Query with outline and sample chapters. **Payment:** Royalty or flat fee. **Contact:** Karen Schweizer.

SAINT MARY'S PRESS

Christian Brothers of the Midwest Province, 702 Terrace Heights, Winona, MN 55987-1320. 800-533-8095. Website: www.smp.org. Lorraine Kilmartin, Editor-in-Chief. **Description:** Nonprofit Catholic publisher developing materials in 5 lines: Catholic high school religion textbooks and resources; parish religious education and youth ministry resources; the Bible and supplemental resources; family faith-life resources; and teen spirituality resources.

SCHOCKEN BOOKS

The Knopf Publishing Group/Random House, Inc., 299 Park Ave., New York, NY 10171. 212-572-2838. Website: www.schocken.com. Susan Ralston, Editorial Director. **Description:** Fiction and nonfiction books of Jewish interest. **Books Statistics:** 9 titles/yr. **Proposal Process:** Query with outline and sample chapters. Accepts simultaneous queries, but not e-queries. Prefers hard copy. Responds in 1 month. **Payment:** Royalty. **Sample Titles:** *Living a Life That Matters* by Harold Kushner; *The Jewish Holiday Kitchen* by Joan Nathan; *How to Be a Jewish Parent* by Anita Diamant. **Tips:** Looking for well-written fiction, history, biography, current affairs of Jewish interest for general readers. **Contact:** Altie Karper, Editor; Cecelia Cancellaro, Editor.

SHAW BOOKS

WaterBrook Press, 2375 Telstar Dr., Suite 160, Colorado Springs, CO 80920-3669. 719-590-4999. Website: www.shawbooks.com. Elisa Fryling Stanford, Editor. **Description:** Nonfiction books with a Christian perspective. **Books Statistics:** 25 titles/yr; 20% by first-time authors; 50% unagented. **Proposal Process:** Query with SASE. **Payment:** Flat fee or royalty. **Sample Titles:** *Simple Acts of Moving Forward* by Vinita Hampton Wright; *New Way to Be Human* by Charlie Peacock.

ST. ANTHONY MESSENGER PRESS

28 W Libery St., Cincinnati, OH 45202. 513-241-5615. E-mail: stanthony@ameri-cancatholic.org. Website: www.americancatholic.org. Lisa Biedenbach, Editorial Director. **Description:** Inspirational nonfiction for Catholics. Supports a Christian lifestyle in our culture by providing material on scripture, church history, education, practical spirituality, parish ministries, and family-based religious education pro-grams. Also publishes liturgy resources, Franciscan resources, prayer aids, and chil-dren's books. **Proposal Process:** Query with 500-word summary. **Payment:** Royalty.

STANDARD PUBLISHING

8121 Hamilton Ave., Cincinnati, OH 45231. 513-931-4050. Website: www.standard-pub.com. **Description:** Christian children's materials: books, board books, picture books, coloring books, and Christian church curriculum/teacher resources. **Books Statistics:** 70 titles/yr (2,000 submissions); 15% by first-time authors; 80% una-gented. **Proposal Process:** Query with outline. Simultaneous queries accepted. Responds in 3 months. **Payment:** Royalty (typically 5-10%) and flat fee (varies). **Tips:** "Study our products before submitting. Call or write for up-to-date guidelines."

TYNDALE HOUSE PUBLISHERS, INC.

351 Executive Dr., Carol Stream, IL 60188. 630-668-8300.
E-mail: manuscripts@tyndale.com. Website: www.tyndale.com.
Description: General-interest titles for the evangelical Christian market including fiction (romance, suspense, historical), general nonfiction (home/family, devotional, motivational, Christian growth, humor), Bibles and Bible reference, and children's books. **Books Statistics:** 300+ titles/yr; 5% by first-time authors; 3% unagented. **Proposal Process:** No unsolicited manuscripts or proposals. Responds in 3-4 months to queries. Send SASE or see website for guidelines. **Payment:** Royalty. **Sample Titles:** (Fiction) *The Priest* by Francine Rivers; (Nonfiction) *Beyond Belief to Convictions* by Josh D. McDowell and Bob Hostetler; *The Miracle of Motivation* by George Shinn; (Children's) *Before I Dream Bible Storybook* by Karyn Henley. **Tips:** Does not accept curriculum, plays, poetry, sermons, or music.

UAHC PRESS

633 Third Ave., New York, NY 10017. 212-650-4120. E-mail: uahcpress@uahc.org. Website: www.uahcpress.com. Rabbi Hara Person, Editorial Director. **Description:** Publishes trade books and textbooks of Jewish interest for preschool through adult readers. **Books Statistics:** 18 titles/yr (300 submissions); 17% by first-time authors;

100% unagented. **Proposal Process:** Query with outline and sample chapters. Considers simultaneous queries. Prefers hard copy. Responds in 4-8 weeks. **Payment:** Royalty. **Sample Titles:** (Nonfiction) *The Reform Judaism Reader: North American Documents* by Michael A. Meyer and W. Gunther Plaut; *Jewish Living: A Guide to Contemporary Reform Practice* by Mark Washofsky; (Children's) *Solomon and the Trees* by Matt Biers-Ariel. **Tips:** Seeking books dealing with Jewish topics in areas of textbooks for religious school classrooms, children's trade books, and adult nonfiction.

UPPER ROOM BOOKS

Division of Upper Room Ministries, 1908 Grand Ave., Nashville, TN 37212. 615-340-7332. Website: www.upperroom.org. JoAnn Miller, Executive Editor. **Description:** Focuses on Christian spiritual formation (families, churches, small groups, congregational leaders, and individuals). **Books Statistics:** 15 titles/yr (300 submissions); 2% by first-time authors; 100% unagented. **Proposal Process:** Query with outline, 2 sample chapters, and 2 SASEs (notification and return of submission). Prefers electronic submissions. Considers simultaneous queries. See guidelines on website. **Payment:** Royalty. **Sample Titles:** *The Art of Spiritual Direction: Giving and Receiving Spiritual Guidance* by W. Paul Jones; *Called By a New Name: Becoming What God Has Promised* by Gerrit Scott Dawson; *Abundance: Joyful Living in Christ* by Marilyn Brown Oden. **Tips:** Keep these categories in mind: Opening Our Hearts and Minds to God, Walking Together with Christ, Preparing the Spiritual Way for Emerging Generations, Maturing as Spiritual Leaders, and Realizing Our Oneness in Christ. No fiction or poetry.

W PUBLISHING GROUP

Thomas Nelson, Inc., 402 BNA Drive, Suite 600, Nashville, TN 37214. 615-902-2105. Website: www.wpublishinggroup.com. David L. Moberg, Publisher. **Description:** Christian titles on apologetics/theology, Bible/Bible reference, career/personal finance, Christian living, devotionals, fiction, marriage/family, men, ministry, women, and youth. **Proposal Process:** Does not accept unsolicited manuscripts. **Payment:** Royalty. **Sample Titles:** *A Love Worth Giving* by Max Lucado; *Great Lives Volume 6: Paul* by Charles R. Swindoll; *Strong Women, Soft Hearts* by Paula Rinehart.

WESTMINSTER JOHN KNOX PRESS

Presbyterian Publishing Corporation, 100 Witherspoon St., Louisville, KY 40202. 502-569-5613. Website: www.presbypub.com. **Description:** Publisher of academic nonfiction in Biblical studies, theology, church history, homiletics, ethics, and religious studies. **Proposal Process:** Send curriculum vitae, TOC, one-page summary, introduction or sample chapter (only one or two chapters, please), and SASE to Lori Dowell, Editorial Dept., at above address, or via e-mail to ldowell@presbypub.com. Responds in 6-8 weeks. **Payment:** Royalty. **Sample Titles:** *Soul Feast: An Invitation to the Christian Spiritual Life* by Marjorie Thompson; *The Gospel According to the Simpsons* by Mark I. Pinsky; *Christian Doctrine* by Shirley C. Guthrie.

ZONDERKIDZ

Zondervan Publishing, 5300 Patterson Avenue SE, Grand Rapids, MI 49530. 616-698-6900. Website: www.zondervan.com. **Description:** Publishes children's books based on Christian values. **Tips:** See website for specific submission guidelines. Prospective writers must follow guidelines exactly, or submissions will go unread. **Contact:** Julie Marchese, Editorial Assistant.

ZONDERVAN

HarperCollinsPublishers, 5300 Patterson SE, Grand Rapids, MI 49530. 616-698-6900. E-mail: zpub@zondervan.com. Website: www.zondervan.com. Diane Bloem, Manuscript Editor. **Description:** General fiction and nonfiction for children and adults in the Christian publishing market. **Books Statistics:** 150 titles/yr. **Proposal Process:** Query with outline and sample chapters. Considers simultaneous queries. Does not accept manuscripts or queries via e-mail. No poetry, drama, sermons, cookbooks or dissertations. **Sample Titles:** *Purpose Driven Life* by Rick Warren; *Courageous Leadership* by Bill Hybels. **Tips:** Does not accept unsolicited manuscripts and proposals sent by air or surface mail. Authors may submit their work by faxing their proposals to 616-698-3454, c/o Book Proposal Review Editor; or they may submit work electronically to First Edition, The ECPA Manuscript Service at www.ecpa.org.

OTHER MARKETS
& RESOURCES

AGENTS

As the number of book publishers that will consider only agented submissions grows, more writers are turning to agents to sell their manuscripts. The following list includes agents that handle literary work, agents that handle dramatic work, and those that handle both. Submission procedures, commission rates, and organizations to which the agent(s) is a member are also included in each listing. Since agents derive their income from the sales of their clients' work, they must represent writers who are selling fairly regularly to good markets. Nonetheless, many of the agents listed here note they will consider unpublished writers. Always query an agent first, and enclose a self-addressed, stamped envelope—most agents will not respond without it. Do not send any sample material until the agent has requested it.

Be wary of agents who charge fees for reading manuscripts. The agents listed below have indicated they do not charge reading fees; however, it is typical for many agents to charge their clients for copyright fees, manuscript retyping, photocopies, copies of books for use in the sale of other rights, and long-distance calls.

To learn more about agents and their role in publishing, the Association of Authors' Representatives, Inc., (AAR) publishes a canon of ethics as well as an up-to-date list of members. Write to: Association of Authors' Representatives, P.O. Box 237201, Ansonia Station, New York, NY 10023, or visit their Web site: www.aar-online.org.

Another good source which lists agents and their policies is *Literary Market Place*, a directory found in most libraries.

ABRAMS ARTISTS AGENCY

275 Seventh Ave., Fl. 26, New York, NY 10001. 646-486-4600.
Description: Plays and screenplays. Receives 1,000 queries/submissions per year. Unpublished writers considered. **Submissions:** Query with synopsis, up to 10 sample pages, bio/resumé, and SASE. Accepts simultaneous queries, but not e-queries. **Commission:** 10% feature screenplays, 15% books. **Contact:** Charmaine Ferenczi, Maura Teitelbaum.

MIRIAM ALTSHULER LITERARY AGENCY

53 Old Post Rd N, Red Hook, NY 12571. 845-758-9408.
Description: Serious literary fiction, serious commercial fiction and nonfiction, memoirs, general nonfiction, and narrative nonfiction. Receives 3,000 queries/yr; 275 submissions/yr. Accepts unsolicited queries, but not manuscripts. Unpublished writers considered. **Submissions:** Query with SASE. Accepts simultaneous queries, but no fax or e-queries. Responds in 3 weeks. **Commission:** 15% domestic, 20% foreign. **Member:** AAR. **Tips:** No romance, science fiction, self-help, spiritual, mystery, fantasy, poetry, screenplays, how-to, or techno-thrillers. **Contact:** Miriam Altshuler.

MICHAEL AMATO AGENCY

1650 Broadway, Suite 307, New York, NY 10019-6833. 212-247-4456.
Website: www.amatoagency.tvheaven.com.
Description: Screenplays. **Submissions:** Query with SASE.

MARCIA AMSTERDAM AGENCY

41 W 82 St., #9A, New York, NY 10024-5613. 212-873-4945.
Description: Adult and YA fiction, mainstream nonfiction, and screenplays and teleplays in the categories of comedy and romance. Receives 14,000 submissions/yr. Accepts 2-5% of unsolicited material. Accepts unsolicited queries, but not manuscripts. Considers unpublished writers. **Submissions:** Query with bio/resumé and SASE. Accepts simultaneous queries, but not e-queries. Responds within 2 weeks. **Commission:** 10% screen/television, 15% books, 20% foreign. **Member:** Signatory of WGA. **Contact:** Marcia Amsterdam.

ARTISTS & ARTISANS INC.

45 W 21st St., Fl. 3, New York, NY 10010.
Website: www.artistsandartisans.com. **Description:** Quality adult trade fiction and nonfiction. **Submissions:** Send standard query letter with description of project, author bio, and SASE. Authors can also submit online by visiting website. Usually responds in 1 week. **Contact:** Adam Chromy.

THE AXELROD AGENCY

55 Main St., P.O. Box 357, Chatham, NY 12037. 518-392-2100.
E-mail: steve@axelrodagency.com. **Description:** Fiction and nonfiction. Does not accept unsolicited manuscripts. **Submissions:** Send query with SASE. Responds in 3 weeks to queries, 6 weeks to manuscripts. **Commission:** 15% domestic, 20% foreign. **Member:** AAR. **Contact:** Steven Axelrod.

MALAGA BALDI LITERARY AGENCY

233 W 99th St., 19C, New York, NY 10025. 212-222-3213.
E-mail: mbaldi@nyc.rr.com. **Description:** Quality literary adult fiction and nonfiction. Receives thousands of queries/submissions per year. Accepts 2% of unsolicited material. Considers unsolicited queries/manuscripts. Unpublished writers considered. **Submissions:** "Send query first; if we are interested, we will ask for proposal, outline, and sample pages for nonfiction, complete manuscript for fiction." Accepts simultaneous queries, but not e-queries. Responds in 10 weeks. **Commission:** 15%. **Tips:** Always send SASE with query letter. Always send SASE jiffybag with full submission for safe return of manuscript. **Contact:** Malaga Baldi.

BALKIN AGENCY, INC.

P.O. Box 222, Amherst, MA 01004. 413-548-9835.
E-mail: balkin@crocker.com. **Description:** Specializes in adult nonfiction, professional books, and college textbooks. Does not accept unsolicited manuscripts. **Submissions:** Query with outline, 1 sample chapter, and SASE. **Commission:** 15% domestic, 20% foreign. **Member:** AAR. **Contact:** Rick Balkin.

LORETTA BARRETT BOOKS, INC.

101 Fifth Ave., Fl. 11, New York, NY 10003. 212-242-3420.
Description: Specializes in adult fiction and nonfiction. Does not accept unsolicited

manuscripts. **Submissions:** Send query with SASE. For fiction, include synopsis; for nonfiction, include outline and sample chapters. No e-mail or fax queries. **Commission:** 15% domestic, 20% foreign. **Member:** AAR. **Contact:** Loretta Barrett, Nick Mullendore.

BIG SCORE PRODUCTIONS

P.O. Box 4575, Lancaster, PA 17604. 717-293-0247.
E-mail: bigscore@bigscoreproductions.com.
Website: www.bigscoreproductions.com. **Description:** All types of fiction and nonfiction. No poetry, erotica, or alternative lifestyle. Represents 30-50 clients. 25% of clients are new or previously unpublished writers. Welcomes new writers. **Submissions:** Send query or proposal with outline and TOC. Prefers to receive submissions via e-mail; do not send attachments unless requested. **Commission:** 15% domestic. **Contact:** David Robie, Sharon Hanby-Robie.

BLEECKER STREET ASSOCIATES, INC.

532 LaGuardia Place, Suite 617, New York, NY 10012. 212-677-4492.
Description: Represents 25% fiction (mystery/suspense, women's novels, literary) and 75% nonfiction (biography, business, parenting, cooking/food, current affairs, Judaica, military, finance, health/medicine, nature/environment, history, how-to, New Age, pop culture, psychology, science/technology, self-help, sociology, sports, women's studies, politics). Receives 5,000+ queries/yr; 200 submissions/yr. Accepts 2% of unsolicited material. Accepts unsolicited queries, but not manuscripts. Unpublished writers considered. **Submissions:** Query with bio/resume and SASE. Accepts simultaneous queries, but no phone, fax, or e-queries. Responds in 2-4 weeks. **Commission:** 15% domestic, 25% foreign. **Member:** AAR, MWA, RWA. **Tips:** "Do not call us with book ideas. Contact us via a query letter. Ditto on fax and e-mail—we will not respond." **Contact:** Agnes Birnbaum.

REID BOATES LITERARY AGENCY

69 Cooks Crossroad, Pittstown, NJ 08867-0328. 908-730-8523.
Description: Adult mainstream nonfiction only. No unsolicited manuscripts or proposals. Unpublished writers considered. **Submissions:** Send query with SASE via regular mail. Does not accept simultaneous queries or e-queries. **Commission:** 15% domestic, 20% foreign. **Contact:** Reid Boates.

BOOKSTOP LITERARY AGENCY

67 Meadow View Rd., Orinda, CA 94563. 925-254-2664.
E-mail: info@bookstopliterary.com. Website: www.bookstopliterary.com.
Description: Juvenile and young adult fiction and nonfiction, also illustration for children's books. Unpublished writers considered. **Submissions:** Send complete manuscript for fiction; sample chapters and outline for nonfiction. No queries necessary. No e-mail submissions accepted. **Commission:** 15%. **Contact:** Kendra Marcus.

GEORGES BORCHARDT, INC.
136 E 57th St., New York, NY 10022. 212-753-5785.
Description: Fiction and nonfiction. Does not accept unsolicited manuscripts.
Commission: 15% domestic. **Member:** AAR.

BRANDT & HOCHMAN LITERARY AGENTS
1501 Broadway, New York, NY 10036. 212-840-5760. **Description:** Fiction and non-fiction. Does not accept unsolicited manuscripts. **Submissions:** Send query with SASE via regular mail. **Commission:** 15% domestic, 20% foreign. **Member:** AAR. **Contact:** Carl D. Brandt, Gail Hochman, Marianne Merola, Charles Schlessiger, Bill Contardi.

ANDREA BROWN LITERARY AGENCY, INC
1076 Eagle Dr., Salinas, CA 93905. 831-422-5925.
E-mail: ablit@redshift.com. **Description:** Children's and YA fiction and nonfiction only. Some adult fiction especially historical and Asian-related. **Submissions:** Query with outline, sample pages, bio/resumé, and SASE; no faxes. **Commission:** 15% domestic, 20% foreign. **Member:** SCBWI, WNBA. **Contact:** Andrea Brown, Laura Rennert, Caryn Wiseman.

CURTIS BROWN LTD.
10 Astor Place, New York, NY 10003. 212-473-5400.
Description: General trade fiction and nonfiction in a variety of categories. Also represents juvenile material, short stories, poetry, and screenplays. **Submissions:** Query first with SASE. Submit outline or sample chapters. No e-mail or fax queries. Responds in 3 weeks to queries, 5 weeks to manuscripts. **Member:** AAR. **Contact:** Timothy Knowlton, CEO; Peter L. Ginsberg, President.

KNOX BURGER ASSOCIATES LTD
Affiliate of Harold Ober Associates, Inc., 425 Madison Ave., New York, NY 10017. 212-759-8600. **Description:** Adult fiction and nonfiction. No science fiction, fantasy, or romance. Accepts unsolicited queries, but not manuscripts. **Submissions:** Query with SASE. No simultaneous, faxed, or electronic queries. **Commission:** 15%. **Member:** AAR. **Tips:** Highly selective in choosing clients. **Contact:** Knox Burger.

SHEREE BYKOFSKY ASSOCIATES, INC.
577 Second Ave., PMB 109, New York, NY 10016.
Website: www.shereebee.com. **Description:** Adult fiction (literary and commercial) and nonfiction (popular reference, business, self-help, humor, biography, memoir, women's interest, spiritual, health, fitness, multicultural, parenting, gay/lesbian, and cooking). **Submissions:** Query with outline, up to 3 sample pages or proposal, and SASE. Accepts simultaneous queries with notice. Responds in 1 week to queries, 1 month to manuscripts. **Commission:** 15% domestic, 15% foreign. **Member:** AAR, ASJA. **Tips:** No e-mails, phone calls, or unsolicited manuscripts. **Contact:** Sheree Bykofsky.

JULIE CASTIGLIA LITERARY AGENCY

1155 Camino del Mar, Suite 510, Del Mar, CA 92014. 858-755-8761.

Description: Fiction (ethnic, commercial, and literary) and nonfiction (science, biography, psychology, women's issues, business/finance, popular culture, health, and niche markets). **Submissions:** Accepts queries by referral only (editors, clients, or publishing professionals). Does not accept phone or fax queries. **Member:** AAR, PEN. **Contact:** Julie Castiglia, Winifred Golden.

DON CONGDON ASSOCIATES

156 Fifth Ave., Suite 625, New York, NY 10010. 212-645-1229.

E-mail: dca@doncongdon.com. **Description:** Trade books, both fiction and nonfiction, by professional writers. **Submissions:** Query with SASE. Responds in 1-2 weeks to queries, 1 month to manuscripts. **Commission:** 15% domestic, 19% foreign. **Member:** AAR. **Contact:** Don Congdon, Susan Ramer, Michael Congdon, Cristina Concepcion.

DOE COOVER AGENCY

P.O. Box 668, Winchester, MA 01890. 781-721-6000.

Website: www.doecooveragency.com. **Description:** Literary fiction and a broad range of nonfiction (biography/memoir, business, social science, cooking, gardening). Receives 500 queries/submissions per year. Accepts 2% of unsolicited material. Considers unsolicited queries, but not manuscripts. Unpublished writers considered. **Submissions:** Query with outline, sample pages, bio/resumé, and SASE. Accepts simultaneous queries, but not e-queries. Responds in 2 weeks. **Commission:** 15%. **Contact:** Frances Kennedy.

RICHARD CURTIS ASSOCIATES, INC.

171 E 74th St., New York, NY 10021.

Website: www.curtisagency.com. **Description:** Commercial adult nonfiction and commercial fiction by published authors. Receives 3,000 submissions/queries per year. Accepts less than 1% of unsolicited material. No unsolicited manuscripts. Considers unpublished writers in nonfiction only. **Submissions:** Query with 1-2 sample chapters, bio/resumé, and SASE. No simultaneous, fax, or e-queries. Responds in 4-6 weeks. **Commission:** 15% domestic, 25% foreign. **Member:** RWA, MWA, WWA, SFWA. **Tips:** Guidelines available on website. **Contact:** Pamela Valvera.

THE CYPHER AGENCY

816 Wolcott Ave., Beacon, NY 12508-4261. 845-831-5677.

E-mail: jimcypher@prodigy.net. Website: http://pages.prodigy.net/jimcypher.

Description: Represents nonfiction in the areas of biography/autobiography, current affairs, pop culture, gay/lesbian, government/politics/law, health/medicine, history, how-to, psychology, science/technology, sports, true crime, self-help, and women's studies. Receives 1,500 queries/yr; 200 submissions/yr. Accepts 10% of unsolicited material. Considers unpublished writers. Accepts unsolicited queries and manuscripts. **Submissions:** Submit book proposal with 2 sample chapters and SASE.

Accepts simultaneous and electronic queries. Responds in 1 week to queries, 1 month to proposals and manuscripts. **Commission:** 15% domestic, 20% foreign. **Member:** AAR. **Contact:** Jim Cypher.

JONATHAN DOLGER AGENCY

49 E 96th St., 9B, New York, NY 10128. 212-427-1853.
Description: Adult fiction, nonfiction, and illustrated books. Does not accept unsolicited manuscripts. **Submissions:** Query with SASE. **Member:** AAR. **Contact:** Herbert Erinmore.

DOUGLAS & KOPELMAN ARTISTS, INC.

393 W 49th St., Suite 5G, New York, NY 10019.
Description: Represents stage plays only. Does not accept unsolicited scripts. **Member:** AAR.

DUNHAM LITERARY, INC.

156 Fifth Ave., Suite 625, New York, NY 10010.
Website: www.dunhamlit.com. **Description:** Adult literary fiction/nonfiction and children's books. Receives 10,000+ queries/yr; 300+ submissions/yr. Accepts less than 1% of unsolicited material. Does not accept unsolicited manuscripts. Unpublished writers considered. **Submissions:** Query with SASE. Accepts mulitple queries, but no phone, fax, or e-queries. Responds in 2 weeks to queries. **Commission:** 15% domestic, 20% foreign. **Member:** AAR. **Tips:** "We highly recommend that writers review our website before submitting." **Contact:** Jennie Dunham.

DYSTEL & GODERICH LITERARY MANAGEMENT

One Union Square W, Suite 904, New York, NY 10003. 212-627-9100.
Website: www.dystel.com. **Description:** Adult fiction and nonfiction. Receives 15,000 queries/submission per year. Accepts 10% of unsolicited material. Considers unsolicited queries, but not manuscripts. Unpublished writers considered. **Submissions:** Query with bio/resumé. Accepts brief e-queries, but not simultaneous queries. Respond in 3-5 weeks to queries, 2 months to submissions. **Commission:** 15% domestic, 19% foreign. **Member:** AAR. **Contact:** Jane Dystel, Miriam Goderich, Stacey Kendall Glick, Michael Bourret, James McCarthy, Jessica Papin.

EDUCATIONAL DESIGN SERVICES, INC.

P.O. Box 253, Wantaugh, NY 11793-0253.
Description: Educational texts (K-12 only). Receives 300 queries/submissions per year; accepts 3% of unsolicited material. Considers unsolicited queries and manuscripts. Unpublished writers considered. **Submissions:** Query with outline, sample pages or complete manuscript, bio/resumé, and SASE. Accepts simultaneous queries, but not e-queries. Responds in 4-6 weeks. **Commission:** 15% domestic, 25% foreign. **Contact:** Bertram L. Linder.

ETHAN ELLENBERG LITERARY AGENCY

548 Broadway, Suite #5E, New York, NY 10012. 212-431-4554.
E-mail: agent@ethanellenberg.com. Website: www.ethanellenberg.com.
Description: All types of commercial fiction (thrillers, mysteries, children's, romance, women's fiction, ethnic, science fiction, fantasy, general fiction); literary fiction with strong narrative; and nonfiction (current affairs, health, science, psychology, cookbooks, New Age, spirituality, pop science, pop culture, adventure, true crime, biography and memoir). No poetry or short stories. Receives 10,000 queries/submission per year. Accepts 5% of unsolicited material. Accepts unsolicited queries and manuscripts. **Submissions:** For fiction, query with first 3 chapters, synopsis, and SASE. For nonfiction, send proposal with sample material, if available, and SASE. Accepts simultaneous and electronic queries (no attachments). No phone calls. Responds in 4-6 weeks to requested submissions. Responds to e-mail submissions if interested. **Commission:** 15% domestic, 20% foreign. **Member:** AAR. **Tips:** "We seek established and new writers in wide range of genres." **Contact:** Ethan Ellenberg, Michael Psaltis.

ANN ELMO AGENCY, INC.

60 E 42nd St., New York, NY 10165. 212-661-2880.
Description: Fiction (literary, contemporary, mystery, romance, thriller) and nonfiction (business, cooking, biography/memoir, self-help, pop culture, science, technology). **Submissions:** Query with SASE. Responds in 3 months. **Member:** AAR, MWA, Author's Guild. **Contact:** Lettie Lee, Andree Abecassis, Mari Cronin.

FELICIA ETH LITERARY REPRESENTATION

555 Bryant St., Suite 350, Palo Alto, CA 94301-1700. 650-375-1276.
Description: Selective mainstream literary fiction and diverse nonfiction in the areas of psychology, health, popular science, women's issues, investigative journalism, and biography. Does not accept unsolicited manuscripts. **Submissions:** Send query for fiction, proposal for nonfiction. **Commission:** 15% domestic, 20% foreign. **Member:** AAR. **Contact:** Felicia Eth.

FARBER LITERARY AGENCY, INC.

14 E 75th St., New York, NY 10021. 212-861-7075.
E-mail: farberlit@aol.com. Website: www.donaldfarber.com. **Description:** Adult fiction and nonfiction, YA and children's literature, and plays. Receives 4,000 queries/submissions per year. Accepts unsolicited queries and manuscripts. Unpublished writers considered. **Submissions:** Query with outline, 3 sample chapters, and SASE. Accepts simultaneous queries, but not e-queries. Responds in 2 weeks to queries, 3-10 weeks to submissions. **Commission:** 15%, includes legal services of Donald C. Farber. **Contact:** Ann Farber, Seth Farber, Donald Farber.

FLANNERY LITERARY

1140 Wickfield Ct., Naperville, IL 60563-3300. 630-428-2682.
E-mail: flanlit@aol.com. **Description:** Fiction and nonfiction for children and young adults, all genres, infant to college age. Accepts unsolicited queries/manuscripts. Unpublished writers considered. **Submissions:** Query by letter only (no phone, fax, or e-queries), include SASE. Accepts simultaneous queries. Responds in 2 weeks to queries, 3-4 weeks to submissions. **Commission:** 15% domestic, 20% foreign. **Contact:** Jennifer Flannery.

THE FOGELMAN LITERARY AGENCY

7515 Greenville Ave., Suite 712, Dallas, TX 75231. 214-361-9956.
E-mail: info@fogelman.com. Website: www.fogelman.com. **Description:** Women's fiction, romance, mystery, suspense, and thrillers. Nonfiction that targets a female audience, or has commercial/pop-culture appeal. **Submissions:** Published authors may call, unpublished authors are invited to submit a query (1-2 pages) with SASE. Responds in 3 days. **Commission:** 15% domestic, 10% foreign. **Member:** AAR, RWA. **Contact:** Evan M. Fogelman, Linda Kruger, Helen Brown.

ROBERT A. FREEDMAN DRAMATIC AGENCY, INC.

1501 Broadway, Suite 2310, New York, NY 10036. 212-840-5760.
Description: Screenplays, teleplays, and stage plays. Does not accept unsolicited manuscripts. **Submissions:** Send query with SASE. Accepts simultaneous queries. **Commission:** 10% domestic. **Member:** AAR. **Contact:** Robert A. Freedman, Selma Luttinger, or Marta Praeger for stage plays; Robin Kaver for screenplays or teleplays.

GELFMAN SCHNEIDER LITERARY AGENTS, INC.

250 W 57th St., Suite 2515, New York, NY 10107. 212-245-1993.
E-mail: mail@gelfmanschneider.com. **Description:** Contemporary women's commercial fiction, literary and commercial fiction, mystery and suspense, and some nonfiction. Receives 2,000 queries/submissions per year. Considers unsolicited queries, but not unsolicited manuscripts. Unpublished writers considered. **Submissions:** Query with outline, sample pages, bio, and SASE. Does not consider fax or e-mail queries. Responds in 4-6 weeks. **Commission:** 15% domestic, 20% foreign, 15% film/dramatic. **Member:** AAR. **Contact:** Jane Gelfman, Deborah Schneider.

GOODMAN ASSOCIATES

500 West End Ave., New York, NY 10024-4317. 212-873-4806.
Description: Adult book-length fiction and nonfiction. No plays, screenplays, poetry, textbooks, science fiction, or children's books. Does not accept unsolicited manuscripts. **Submissions:** Query with SASE. **Commission:** 15% domestic, 20% foreign. **Member:** AAR. **Tips:** Accepts new clients by recommendation only. **Contact:** Arnold P. Goodman, Elise Simon Goodman.

GRAYBILL & ENGLISH LLC

1875 Connecticut Ave. NW, Suite 712, Washington, DC 20009. 202-558-9798. Website: www.graybillandenglish.com. **Description:** 20% adult fiction, 80% adult nonfiction. Nina Graybill: serious nonfiction, literary fiction. Elaine English: commercial women's fiction, including romance (single titles). Kristen Auclair: nonfiction, women's issues, literary fiction. Jeff Kleinman: creative nonfiction, especially historical; prescriptive nonfiction, especially health; literary/commercial fiction. Lynn Whittaker: nonfiction, literary fiction, mystery. Receives 3,000 queries/submissions per year; accepts less than 10% of unsolicited material. Does not accept unsolicited manuscripts. Considers unpublished writers. **Submissions:** Send query letter with bio, proposal or up to 3 sample chapters, and SASE. Mutliple queries accepted. Responds in 2-3 weeks to queries, up to 8 weeks for requested submissions. **Commission:** 15% domestic, 20% foreign and dramatic. **Member:** AAR.

SANFORD J. GREENBURGER ASSOCIATES, INC.

55 Fifth Ave., Fl. 15, New York, NY 10003. 212-206-5600. Website: www.greenburger.com. **Description:** All types of fiction and nonfiction (sports, health, business, psychology, parenting, science, biography, gay/lesbian) and juvenile books. Considers unsolicited queries and manuscripts. Unpublished writers with strong credentials considered. **Submissions:** Query with proposal, including 3 sample chapters, bio/resume, and SASE. Accepts simultaneous queries, but not e-queries. Responds in 6-8 weeks. **Commission:** 15% domestic, 20% foreign. **Contact:** Heide Lange, Faith Hamlin, Matt Bialer, Elyse Cheney, Theresa Park, Daniel Mandel, Peter McGuigan, Julie Barber.

CHARLOTTE GUSAY LITERARY AGENCY

10532 Blythe Ave., Los Angeles, CA 90064. 310-559-0831. E-mail: gusay1@aol.com (queries only). Website: www.mediastudio.com/gusay. **Description:** Fiction, nonfiction (humor, travel, gardening, gender issues, biography/memoir, parenting, pyschology), children's/YA material, and screenplays. Receives 2,000 queries/submissions per year. Accepts unsolicited queries, but not manuscripts. Unpublished writers considered. **Submissions:** Submit 1-page query only, with bio/resume and SASE (preferably by regular mail). Simultaneous queries discouraged. Responds in 3-6 weeks to queries, 6-8 weeks to submissions. **Commission:** 15%. **Member:** Author's Guild, PEN/West, WGA. **Contact:** Charlotte Gusay.

REECE HALSEY NORTH

98 Main St., Suite 704, Tiburon, CA 94920. 415-789-9191. E-mail: info@reece-halseynorth.com. Website: www.kimberleycameron.com. **Description:** Represents adult fiction and nonfiction. Receives 1,000+ queries/submissions per month. Accepts 10% of unsolicited material. Unpublished writers considered. **Submissions:** Query with SASE. Accepts simultaneous queries and e-queries. **Commission:** 15% domestic, 20% foreign. **Member:** AAR, MWA, Sisters in Crime. **Tips:** "We take this writing life very seriously. We don't get paid by the hour—please be patient and polite!" **Contact:** Kimberley Cameron.

THE JOY HARRIS LITERARY AGENCY

156 Fifth Ave., Suite 617, New York, NY 10010. 212-924-6269.
E-mail: gen.office@jhlitagent.com. **Description:** Adult fiction and nonfiction.
Submissions: Query first with SASE. Submit outline or sample chapters. Responds
in 2 months. **Member:** AAR. **Contact:** Joy Harris.

JEFF HERMAN LITERARY AGENCY LLC

P.O. Box 1522, Stockbridge, MA 01262. 413-298-0077.
E-mail: jeff@jeffherman.com. Website: www.jeffherman.com. **Description:** General
adult nonfiction in the categories of business, reference, self-help, computers, recov-
ery/healing, and spirituality. Also represents a growing list of fiction titles. Receives
5,000 queries/submissions per year. Accepts less than 1% of unsolicited material.
Accepts unsolicited queries and manuscripts. Unpublished writers considered.
Submissions: Query with SASE. Accepts simultaneous queries and e-queries.
Commission: 15% domestic, 10% foreign. **Contact:** Jeff Herman, Deborah Levine.

THE BARBARA HOGENSON AGENCY, INC.

165 West End Ave., Suite 19-C, New York, NY 10023. 212-874-8084.
Description: Adult fiction, nonfiction, and stage plays. **Submissions:** Send query
with bio, synopsis, and SASE. Accepts simultaneous queries. **Commission:** 15%
plays, 15% books. **Member:** AAR, WGA, Author's Guild, Society of Stage Directors
& Choreographers. **Tips:** Client recommendations preferred.

IMG LITERARY

825 Seventh Ave., New York, NY 10019. 212-774-6900.
Website: www.imgworld.com. **Description: Submissions:** Query with SASE.
Contact: Lisa Queen.

JCA LITERARY AGENCY

27 W 20th St., Suite 1103, New York, NY 10011. 212-807-0888.
Website: www.jcalit.com. **Description:** Adult fiction (literary, thrillers, mysteries,
commercial) and nonfiction (narrative, history, science, pop culture, true crime). No
children's books, romance, or screenplays. Unpublished writers considered.
Submissions: Query with 50 sample pages, synopsis, and SASE. Accepts simultaneous queries. **Commission:** 15% domestic, 20% foreign. **Member:** AAR. **Tips:** "Be
straightforward, to-the-point. Don't try to hype us or bury us in detail." **Contact:** Jeff
Gerecke, Peter Steinberg.

NATASHA KERN LITERARY AGENCY

P.O. Box 2908, Portland, OR 97208-2908. 503-297-6190.
E-mail: nkern@natashakern.com. Website: www.natashakern.com.
Description: Commercial adult fiction (thrillers, mysteries, women's fiction, historical, romance) and nonfiction (health, natural science, investigative journalism, inspirational, New Age, psychology, self-help, parenting, gardening, business, current
affairs, and women's issues). No horror, true crime, children's/YA, short stories, poetry,

scripts, software, sports, photography, cookbooks, gift books, or scholarly works. Receives 10,000 queries/submissions per year; 1% of unsolicited material accepted. Considers unsolicited queries, but not manuscripts. Considers unpublished writers. **Submissions:** Query via regular mail with SASE and synopsis or query via e-mail (with no attachements). "We will respond if we are interested. Please see our submission guidelines on our website." Responds in 3-4 to mail queries, 8 weeks to manuscripts. **Commission:** 15% domestic, 20% foreign. **Contact:** Natasha Kern.

KIDDE, HOYT & PICARD

335 E 51st St., New York, NY 10022. 212-755-9465.
E-mail: khp@worldnet.att.net. **Description:** Mainstream fiction, literary fiction, romance, mysteries, and general nonfiction. Receives 10,000 queries/submissions per year. Will consider authors who have published short stories, articles, essays, or other short works. Consideration is also given to participants of writing workshops and related degree programs. Unsolicited queries considered, but not unsolicited manuscripts. **Submissions:** Send query with short synopsis, list of previous publishing experience, and SASE. Accepts simultaneous queries. Responds in 2 weeks to queries, 1-2 months to submissions. Do not fax queries. **Commission:** 15% domestic, 20% foreign. **Tips:** "Looking for exciting, witty, compelling characters, in psychologically suspenseful plot (fiction), and the counterpart of that in nonfiction." **Contact:** Katharine Kidde, Kristen Fuhs.

HARVEY KLINGER, INC.

301 W 53rd St., New York, NY 10019. 212-581-7068.
E-mail: queries@harveyklinger.com. Website: www.harveyklinger.com.
Description: Mainstream adult fiction and nonfiction, literary and commercial. Unpublished writers considered. Receives 5,000 queries/year; 1% of unsolicited material accepted. Does not accept unsolicited manuscripts. **Submissions:** Query with outline, sample pages, bio/resumé, and SASE. No simultaneous queries, phone calls, or faxes. Responds in 4-6 weeks to queries, 2-3 months to submissions. **Commission:** 15% domestic, 25% foreign. **Tips:** "We critique clients' work carefully to get manuscript in best possible form before submitting to publishers." **Contact:** David Dunton, Wendy Silbert.

LINDA KONNER LITERARY AGENCY

10 W 15th St., Suite 1918, New York, NY 10011. 212-691-3419.
E-mail: ldkonner@cs.com. **Description:** Adult nonfiction in the areas of self-help, health, fitness/nutrition, relationships, parenting, pets, personal finance, celebrities, pop culture. Writers must be experts in their field. Receives 1,500 queries/yr. Does not accept unsolicited manuscripts. **Submissions:** Query with SASE. Accepts simultaneous submissions and e-queries. Responds in 1-2 weeks. **Commission:** 15% domestic, 25% foreign. **Member:** AAR, ASJA, signatory of WGA. **Tips:** "The vast majority of projects I take on come from authors with a national profile, media experience and contacts, and appropriate academic credentials." **Contact:** Linda Konner.

ELAINE KOSTER LITERARY AGENCY LLC

55 Central Park W, Suite 6, New York, NY 10023. 212-362-9488.

Description: Fiction (commercial and literary), narrative nonfiction, self-help, and memoir. Receives 1,000+ queries/yr. Accepts 10% of unsolicited material. Accepts unsolicited queries, but not manuscripts. Rarely considers unpublished writers. **Submissions:** Query with SASE. Accepts simultaneous queries, but not e-queries. Responds in 2 weeks. **Commission:** 15% domestic, 20% foreign. **Member:** AAR.

BARBARA S. KOUTS LITERARY AGENCY LLC

P.O. Box 560, Bellport, NY 11713. 631-286-1278.

Description: Children's fiction and nonfiction. Receives 1,500 queries per year. Accepts 10% of unsolicited material. Accepts unsolicited queries, but not manuscripts. Unpublished writers considered. **Submissions:** Query with bio/resumé and SASE. Accepts simultaneous queries, but not e-queries. Responds in 1 week to queries, 6-8 weeks to submissions. **Commission:** 15% domestic, 20% foreign. **Member:** AAR. **Contact:** Barbara Kouts.

OTTO R. KOZAK LITERARY & MOTION PICTURE AGENCY

P.O. Box 152, Long Beach, NY 11561.

Description: Represents novice and professional scriptwriters for TV and film. Seeks docudramas, true stories, and scripts that are family-oriented or appeal to female audiences. No novels. Receives 800 queries/submission per year. Accepts 3% of unsolicited material. Considers unsolicited queries (with outline) and simultaneous queries. Does not accept e-queries or complete manuscripts. **Submissions:** Query with SASE. Responds in 2 weeks to queries, 6 weeks to submissions. **Commission:** 10%. **Contact:** Rob Kozak.

EDITE KROLL LITERARY AGENCY, INC

12 Grayhurst Park, Portland, ME 04102. 207-773-4922.

Description: Feminist and issue-oriented nonfiction, humor, children's fiction, and picture books written and illustrated by artists. No genre fiction. Unpublished writers considered. **Submissions:** Query with outline and sample chapter (dummy for picture books), a brief note about the author, and SASE. Accepts simultaneous queries. Keep queries brief; no phone, fax, or e-queries. **Commission:** 15% domestic, 20% foreign. **Contact:** Edite Kroll.

THE LA LITERARY AGENCY

P.O. Box 46370, Los Angeles, CA 90046. 323-654-5288. E-mail: laliteraryag@aol.com.

Description: Adult fiction and nonfiction. **Submissions:** Send query with outline, 50 sample pages, bio/resume, and SASE. Does not accept electronic submissions. **Contact:** Ann Cashman.

PETER LAMPACK AGENCY, INC.

551 Fifth Ave., Suite 1613, New York, NY 10176-0187. 212-687-9106.
E-mail: alampack@verizon.net. **Description:** Commercial and literary fiction and nonfiction by experts in a given field (especially autobiography, biography, law, finance, politics, history). No horror, sci-fi, westerns, or romance. No original screenplays. Receives 3,000 queries/submissions per year. Accepts less than 1% of unsolicited material. Considers unsolicited queries, but not manuscripts. Unpublished writers considered. **Submissions:** Send query with synopsis, sample chapter, credentials, and SASE. Include e-mail address if available. Simultaneous queries accepted, but *not* e-queries. **Commission:** 15% domestic, 20% foreign. **Contact:** Andrew Lampack.

MICHAEL LARSEN/ELIZABETH POMADA
LITERARY AGENCY

1029 Jones St., San Francisco, CA 94109-5023. 415-673-0939.
E-mail: larsenpoma@aol.com. Website: www.larsen-pomada.com. **Description:** Seeks new voices and fresh ideas in literary/commercial fiction and general nonfiction for adults. Receives 5,000 queries/submissions per year. Accepts 1% of unsolicited material. Considers unpublished writers and unsolicited queries. **Submissions:** For fiction, send query with 2-page synopsis, first 10 pages, complete contact info, and SASE. Accepts simultaneous queries with notice; does not accept e-queries. Responds in 6-8 weeks to queries, 4-6 weeks to submissions. **Commission:** 15% domestic, 20-30% foreign. **Member:** AAR, ASJA, Author's Guild. **Tips:** "For nonfiction, follow Michael Larsen's book *How To Write A Book Proposal*, then send by mail or e-mail the title or promotion plan." Michael and Elizabeth are co-founders of the San Francisco Writer's Conference: www.sanfranciscowritersconference.com. **Contact:** Elizabeth Pomada (fiction), Michael Larsen (nonfiction).

THE LESCHER AGENCY

47 East 19th St., New York, NY 10003. 212-529-1790. E-mail: susanlescher@aol.com; mc@lescherltd.com. **Description:** Fiction, including mysteries (no science fiction). Nonfiction, including travel literature, cookbooks, biography/memoir, psychology, and spiritual. **Submissions:** No unsolicited manuscripts. Query first via e-mail or regular mail (include SASE). Submit author bio and double-spaced synopsis describing project at length. **Member:** AAR. **Contact:** Susan Lescher, Mickey Choate.

LESCHER & LESCHER, LTD.

47 E 19th St., New York, NY 10003. 212-529-1790. E-mail: rl@lescherltd.com or mc@lescherltd.com. **Description:** A broad range of serious nonfiction, including current affairs, history, biography, memoir, politics, law, sociology, psychology, pop culture, and food/wine. Also represents literary and commercial fiction, including mysteries/thrillers, and some children's books. **Submissions:** Query with SASE. Accepts simultaneous queries and e-queries. Responds in 1-2 weeks to queries, 2-4 weeks to submissions. **Commission:** 15% domestic, 20% foreign. **Member:** AAR. **Contact:** Robert Lescher, Mickey Choate.

LEWIS & COMPANY

P.O. Box 741623, Dallas, TX 75374. 972-772-5260. E-mail: basha00@aol.com.
Description: Fiction (mystery/suspense/thriller, commercial/mainstream, romance, some literary) and nonfiction (self-help, how-to, metaphysical, gay/lesbian, memoir, psychology, ethnic). Accepts 5% of unsolicited material. Accepts unsolicited queries, but not manuscripts. Unpublished writers considered. **Submissions:** Query with SASE. Accepts simultaneous and electronic queries. Responds in 4-6 weeks to queries, 6-8 weeks to submissions. **Commission:** 15% domestic, 20% foreign. **Tips:** "Write a clear letter succinctly describing your book. Be sure to include an SASE. If you receive rejection notices, don't despair. Keep writing! A good book always will always find a home." **Contact:** Karen Lewis, Tracy Bisere.

LINDSEY'S LITERARY SERVICES

7502 Greenville Ave., Suite 500, Dallas, TX 75231. 214-890-9262.
Description: Quality fiction (mystery/suspense/thriller, mainstream, romance, women as strong heroines) and nonfiction (self-help, psychology, women's issues, some metaphysical). Accepts 5% of unsolicited material. Considers unsolicited queries and unpublished writers. Rarely considers unsolicited manuscripts. **Submissions:** Fiction: query with synopsis, first 3 chapters, and brief bio. Nonfiction: query with proposal, writing sample, brief bio detailing credentials and platform. Include SASE with all materials. Responds in 2-4 weeks to queries, 6-12 weeks to manuscripts. **Commission:** 15% domestic, 20% foreign. **Tips:** "As a small agency, we will aggressively represent our clients. Getting published in today's market is difficult. We look for quality work, and writers who are willing to go the extra mile." **Contact:** Emily Armenta, Bonnie James.

NANCY LOVE LITERARY AGENCY

250 E 65th St., Suite 4A, New York, NY 10021. 212-980-3499. **Description:** Adult nonfiction in the areas of health, self-help, parenting, medical, psychology, women's issues, biography, current affairs, pop science. Popular reference if by an authority with a fresh slant. Also represents adult fiction (mysteries/thrillers only). Receives 2,000 queries/submissions per year; 1% unsolicited material accepted. Considers unsolicited queries, but not manuscripts. **Submissions:** Query with SASE. Accepts simultaneous queries, but not e-queries. Responds in 4 weeks to queries. **Commission:** 15% domestic, 20% foreign. **Tips:** "Looking for brands, authorities with a track record." **Contact:** Miriam Tager.

DONALD MAASS LITERARY AGENCY

160 W 95th St., Suite 1B, New York, NY 10025. 212-866-8200.
Website: www.maassagency.com. **Description:** Represents fiction only. Does not accept unsolicited manuscripts. **Submissions:** Query first with 1-page letter, first 5 pages, and SASE. Responds in 2 weeks to queries, 3 months to manuscripts. **Member:** AAR, SFWA, MWA, RWA. **Contact:** Donald Maass, Jennifer Jackson, Rachel Vater.

GINA MACCOBY LITERARY AGENCY

P.O. Box 60, Chappaqua, NY 10514. 914-238-5630. **Description:** Fiction and nonfiction for adults and children. Does not accept unsolicited manuscripts. **Submissions:** Query with SASE. Responds in 2 months to queries.

CAROL MANN LITERARY AGENCY

55 Fifth Ave., New York, NY 10003. 212-206-5635.
E-mail: emily@carolmannagency.com. **Description:** General nonfiction and literary fiction. Spealizes in current affiars, self-help, popular culture, psychology, parenting, history. No genre fiction. Unpublished writers considered. **Submissions:** Query with outline and SASE. Does not accept queries via fax or e-mail. Responds in 3 weeks to queries. **Commission:** 15% domestic, 20% foreign. **Member:** AAR. **Contact:** Carol Mann, Emily Nurkin, Leylha Ahuile.

MANUS & ASSOCIATES LITERARY AGENCY, INC.

425 Sherman Ave., Suite 200, Palo Alto, CA 94306. 650-470-5151.
E-mail: manuslit@manuslit.com. Website: www.manuslit.com. **Description:** General fiction and dramatic nonfiction. No poetry, children's books, science fiction/fantasy, romance, screenplays, or magazine articles. Does not accept unsolicited manuscripts. **Submissions:** For nonfiction, send query, formal proposal, sample chapters, bio, and SASE. For fiction, send query, first 30 pages, bio, and SASE. Responds in 8 weeks. **Commission:** 15% domestic. **Member:** AAR. **Tips:** See website for more information regarding genres, writing proposals, and deal points. Also has office in NYC: 445 Park Ave., Fl. 10, New York, NY 10022. 212-644-8020. NYC office does not accept unsolicited material. **Contact:** Jillian Manus, Janet Manus, Jandy Nelson, Stephanie Lee, Donna Levin.

DENISE MARCIL LITERARY AGENCY, INC.

685 West End Ave., Suite 9C, New York, NY 10025. 212-932-3110.
Description: Seeking commercial fiction, especially thrillers, suspense, contemporary mainstream women's fiction, and chick lit. Nonfiction in the areas of self-help, how-to, reference, business, parenting/relationships, health, popular psychology, and books that help people's lives. Receives 3,000+ queries/submissions per year. Accepts less than 1% of unsolicited material. Unpublished writers considered. **Submissions:** Send 1-page query with SASE. Accepts simultaneous queries with notice. Responds in 4 weeks. **Commission:** 15% domestic, 20% foreign. **Member:** AAR. **Contact:** Denise Marcil.

JED MATTES, INC.

2095 Broadway, Suite 302, New York, NY 10023-2895. 212-595-5228. E-mail: general@jedmattes.com. **Description:** Fiction and nonfiction. Does not accept unsolicited manuscripts. **Submissions:** Query with SASE. **Member:** AAR. **Contact:** Fred Morris, Tejas Desai.

MARGRET MCBRIDE LITERARY AGENCY

7744 Fay Ave., Suite 201, La Jolla, CA 92037. 858-454-1550.
Website: www.mcbrideliterary.com. **Description:** Specializes in nonfiction (business, leadership, management) and fiction (legal, historical). No poetry, romance, children's, or screenplays. Query only, no unsolicited manuscripts. Unpublished writers considered. **Submissions:** Query with 1-2 page synopsis, bio/speaking schedule (nonfiction only), and SASE. No reply without SASE. Response time 6-8 weeks. Simultaneous submissions ok, but no e-mail or fax queries accepted. Do not phone, e-mail, or fax. **Member:** AAR. **Contact:** Michael J. Daley.

DORIS S. MICHAELS LITERARY AGENCY, INC.

1841 Broadway, Suite 903, New York, NY 10023.
Website: www.dsmagency.com. **Description:** High quality literary fiction; women's literary fiction; and nonfiction in the areas of current affairs, biography/memoirs, self-help, business, history, health, classical music, sports, women's issues, computers, and pop culture. Receives 5,000 queries/yr. Accepts .5% of unsolicited material. **Submissions:** Send query with short bio and credentials via e-mail (no attachments). Does not accept queries via mail, phone, or fax. See website for specific guidelines. **Commission:** 15% domestic, 20% foreign. **Member:** AAR, Women's National Book Association, Women in Publishing.

WILLIAM MORRIS AGENCY, INC.

1325 Avenue of the Americas, New York, NY 10019. 212-586-5100.
Website: www.wma.com. **Description:** Fiction and nonfiction. No screenplays or poetry. Does not accept unsolicited manuscripts. **Submissions:** Send query with synopsis, publication history, and SASE. No fax or e-queries. **Commission:** 15% domestic, 20% foreign. **Contact:** Literary Department Coordinator.

HENRY MORRISON, INC.

P.O. Box 235, Bedford Hills, NY 10507-0235. 914-666-3500. **Description:** Fiction and nonfiction. **Submissions:** Send query, outline, and SASE. Responds in 2 weeks to queries, 3 months to manuscripts. **Commission:** 15% domestic, 25% foreign. **Contact:** Henry Morrison.

JEAN V. NAGGAR LITERARY AGENCY

216 E 75th St., Suite 1E, New York, NY 10021. 212-794-1082.
Description: "Strong adult mainstream fiction and nonfiction, from literary to commercial, with a good story told in a distinctive voice." Receives 6,000 queries/submissions per year. Considers unsolicited queries, but not unsolicited manuscripts. Unpublished writers considered. **Submissions:** Query with outline, bio/resumé, and SASE. No electronic or simultaneous queries. Responds in 48 hours to queries, several weeks to requested submissions. **Commission:** 15% domestic, 20% foreign. **Contact:** Jean Naggar, Alice Tasman, Jennifer Weltz (children's/YA only).

NEW ENGLAND PUBLISHING ASSOCIATES

P.O. Box 5, Chester, CT 06412. 860-345-7323.
E-mail: nepa@nepa.com. Website: www.nepa.com. **Description:** General interest nonfiction for adult markets particularly in the areas of biography/memoir, business, true crime, science, law, nature, parenting, women's issues, current events, history, and politics. Receives 5,000 submissions/yr. **Submissions:** Send book proposal with 1-2 page summary, description of intended audience and competing titles, chapter outline, one sample chapter, bio/resume, list of previous publications, and SASE. See website for complete guidelines. Accepts simultaneous queries with notice. Responds in 3-4 weeks. **Commission:** 15% domestic, 20% foreign. **Member:** AAR, ASJA, Authors Guild. **Tips:** "We provide editorial guidance, representation, and manuscript development for book projects." **Contact:** Elizabeth Frost-Knappman, Edward W. Knappman, Ron Formica, Kris Schiavi, Vicki Harlow.

BETSY NOLAN LITERARY AGENCY

224 W 29th St., Fl. 15, New York, NY 10001. 212-967-8200.
E-mail: dblehr@cs.com. **Description:** Adult nonfiction, especially popular psychology, child care, cookbooks, African-American and Jewish issues. Does not accept unsolicited manuscripts. **Submissions:** Submit outline, no more than 3 sample chapters, author bio/resume, and SASE. **Commission:** 15% domestic, 20% foreign. **Contact:** Donald Lehr, Carla Glasser.

HAROLD OBER ASSOCIATES, INC.

425 Madison Ave., New York, NY 10017. 212-759-8600.
Description: General fiction and nonfiction. Does not handle scripts. **Submissions:** Query with SASE. No simultaneous, fax, or e-queries. Responds as quickly as possible to submissions. **Commission:** 15% domestic. **Member:** AAR. **Contact:** Phyllis Westberg, Emma Sweeney, Alexander C. Smithline.

THE RICHARD PARKS AGENCY

P.O. Box 693, Salem, NY 12865. 212-254-9067.
Website: www.richardparksagency.com. **Description:** General trade adult nonfiction with special emphasis on narrative nonfiction. Accepts fiction by referral only. Unpublished writers considered. Accepts unsolicited queries, but not manuscripts. **Submissions:** Query with SASE. Accepts multiple queries with notice. No phone calls, faxes, or e-mails. Responds in 2-4 weeks to queries, 4-6 weeks to requested submissions. **Commission:** 15% domestic, 20% foreign. **Member:** AAR.

JAMES PETER ASSOCIATES, INC.

P.O. Box 358, New Canaan, CT 06840. 203-972-1070.
E-mail: gene_brissie@msn.com. **Description:** Adult nonfiction, all subject areas. Considers unsolicited queries, but not manuscripts. Unpublished writers considered. **Submissions:** Query with outline, sample pages, bio/resumé, and SASE. Accepts simultaneous queries, but not e-queries. Responds in 2-3 weeks. **Commission:** 15% domestic, 20% foreign. **Contact:** Gene Brissie.

ALISON PICARD, LITERARY AGENT

P.O. Box 2000, Cotuit, MA 02635. 508-477-7192.
E-mail: ajpicard@aol.com. **Description:** Adult fiction, nonfiction, and children's/YA. No poetry, short stories or plays. Receives 5,000 queries/submissions per year. Accepts 5% of unsolicited material. Considers unsolicited queries, but not manuscripts. Unpublished writers considered. **Submissions:** Send query via mail or e-mail. Accepts simultaneous queries, but no phone or fax queries. Responds in 1 week to queries, 3 months to submissions. **Commission:** 15% domestic, 20% foreign. **Contact:** Alison Picard.

SUSAN ANN PROTTER LITERARY AGENT

110 W 40th St., Suite 1408, New York, NY 10018. 212-840-0480.
Description: Fiction (mysteries, thrillers, science fiction, and fantasy) and nonfiction (health/medicine, how-to, science, psychology, biography, reference, self-help). No children's/YA material. Does not accept unsolicited manuscripts. **Submissions:** Query first by letter with SASE. Does not accept queries by phone, fax, or e-mail. **Member:** AAR, Authors Guild. **Contact:** Susan Ann Protter.

HELEN REES LITERARY AGENCY

376 North St., Boston, MA 02113. 617-227-9014.
E-mail: reesliterary@aol.com. **Description:** Literary fiction and nonfiction (business, biography, health). No short stories, science fiction, children's, YA, or poetry. Unpublished writers considered. **Submissions:** Query via regular mail; include outline, bio/resumé, sample of work (to 50 pages), and SASE. No simultaneous queries or e-mail submissions. **Commission:** 15%. **Member:** AAR. **Contact:** Joan Mazmanian, Ann Collette.

JODY REIN BOOKS, INC.

7741 S Ash Ct., Centennial, CO 80122.
Website: www.jodyreinbooks.com. **Description:** Commercial and narrative nonfiction, by writers with media contacts, experience and expertise in their fields. Also, select outstanding works of literary/commercial fiction. Receives 2,000 queries/submissions per year. Accepts less than 1% of unsolicited material. Considers unsolicited queries, but not manuscripts. **Submissions:** Query with SASE. Accepts simultaneous queries, but not e-queries, faxes, or phone queries. Responds in 2-4 weeks to queries, 4-6 weeks to submissions. **Commission:** 15% domestic, 25% foreign. **Member:** AAR, Author's Guild. **Contact:** Johnna Hietala.

JODIE RHODES LITERARY AGENCY

8840 Villa La Jolla Dr., Suite 315, La Jolla, CA 92037. 858-625-0544.
E-mail: jrhodes1@san.rr.com. **Description:** Fiction (multicultural, African American, literary, mystery, suspense, thrillers), nonfiction (parenting, fitness/health, science, medicine, pop culture, politics, military, memoirs), and YA literature. Receives 9,000 queries/submissions per year. Accepts 1-2% of unsolicited material. Considers unpublished writers. **Submissions:** Send query with up to first 50 pages

and SASE. Accepts simultaneous queries, but not e-queries. Responds in 1-2 weeks. **Commission:** 15% domestic, 20% foreign. **Member:** AAR. **Tips:** "I seek writers who care passionately about their books and have something worth saying about the human condition. I have no interest in romance novels, erotica, horror, science fiction, or children's books."

ANGELA RINALDI LITERARY AGENCY

P.O. Box 7877, Beverly Hills, CA 90212-7877. 310-842-7665.
E-mail: amr@rinaldiliterary.com. **Description:** Adult fiction (commercial and literary) and nonfiction (narrative and practical/proactive). No cookbooks, screenplays, poetry, science fiction, romance, western, fantasy, or children's literature. Receives 6,000 queries/submissions per year. Accepts 1-2% of unsolicited material. Considers unpublished writers. Accepts unsolicited queries and manuscripts. **Submissions:** Send first 3 chapters with short synopsis and SASE. Accepts simultaneous queries (with notice) and e-queries (no attachments). Responds in 6-8 weeks. **Commission:** 15% domestic, 20% foreign. **Member:** AAR. **Contact:** Angela Rinaldi.

ANN RITTENBERG LITERARY AGENCY, INC

1201 Broadway, Suite 708, New York, NY 10001. 212-684-6936.
E-mail: info@rittlit.com. Website: www.rittlit.com. **Description:** Upmarket contemporary fiction and serious narrative nonfiction. Receives 1,000 queries/yr; 200 submissions/yr. Accepts 2% of unsolicited material. Accepts unsolicited queries, but not manuscripts. Unpublished writers considered. **Submissions:** Query with first chapter and SASE. Accepts simultaneous queries, but not e-queries. Responds in 4 weeks to queries; 8 weeks to submissions. **Commission:** 15% domestic, 20% foreign. **Member:** AAR. **Contact:** Ann Rittenberg, Ted Gideonse.

B.J. ROBBINS LITERARY AGENCY

5130 Bellaire Ave., North Hollywood, CA 91607. 818-760-6602.
E-mail: robbinsliterary@aol.com. **Description:** Represents literary fiction, women's fiction, narrative nonfiction, and trade nonfiction in the areas of parenting, health, medicine, and self-help. Receives thousands of queries/submissions per year. Accepts 1% of unsolicited material. Accepts unsolicited queries, but not manuscripts. Unpublished writers considered. **Submissions:** Send query with 3 sample chapters for fiction, proposal for nonfiction; SASE required. No e-queries. Considers simultaneous submissions. Responds in 2-4 weeks to queries, 8-12 weeks to manuscripts. **Commission:** 15% domestic, 20% foreign. **Member:** AAR. **Contact:** B.J. Robbins, Regina Su Mangum.

RITA ROSENKRANZ LITERARY AGENCY

440 West End Ave., Suite 15D, New York, NY 10024-5358.
Description: General nonfiction in the areas of biography, business, parenting, cooking, current affairs, health, history, how-to, military/war, theatre, nature, pop culture, religious/inspirational, science/technology, women's issues, humor, and decorative arts. Accepts 2% of unsolicited material. Accepts unsolicited queries and manuscripts.

Submissions: Submit outline, sample chapter, and SASE. No e-queries. Considers simultaneous submissions. Responds in 2 weeks. **Commission:** 15% domestic, 20% foreign. **Member:** AAR, Authors Guild, IWWG. **Contact:** Rita Rosenkranz.

ROSENSTONE/WENDER

38 E 29th St., Fl. 10, New York, NY 10016. 212-725-9445.
Description: Represents adult fiction and nonfiction, juvenile fiction and nonfiction, and stage plays. Accepts unsolicited queries, but not manuscripts. Unpublished writers considered. **Submissions:** Send query with SASE. **Member:** AAR. **Contact:** Phyllis Wender, Susan Cohen, Sonia Pabley.

GAIL ROSS LITERARY AGENCY, LLC

1666 Connecticut Ave. NW, Suite 500, Washington, DC 20009.
Website: www.gailross.com. **Description:** Adult nonfiction. Unpublished writers considered. **Submissions:** Query with outline, sample pages, resumé, and SASE. Accepts simultaneous queries. **Commission:** 15%. **Member:** AAR. **Contact:** Gail Ross, Jennifer Manguera.

PETER RUBIE LITERARY AGENCY

240 W 35 St., Suite 500, New York, NY 10001. 212-279-1776.
Website: www.prlit.com. **Description:** Peter Rubie (crime, science fiction, fantasy, literary fiction, thrillers, narrative/serious nonfiction, business, self-help, how-to, popular, food/wine, history, commercial science, music, education, parenting); June Clark (nonfiction in the areas of celebrity biographies, health, parenting, pets, women's issues, teen nonfiction, how-to, self-help, offbeat business, food/wine, commercial New Age, pop culture, and entertainment). **Submissions:** Query with SASE. Accepts e-queries. Responds in 2-3 months. New clients accepted through recommendations only. **Commission:** 15% domestic, 20% foreign. **Member:** AAR. **Tips:** "We look for professional writers and writers who are experts, have a strong platform and reputation in their field, and have an outstanding prose style." **Contact:** Peter Rubie (peterrubie@prlit.com) or June Clark (pralit@aol.com).

RUSSELL & VOLKENING, INC.

50 W 29th St., Suite 7E, New York, NY 10001. 212-684-6050.
Description: General fiction and nonfiction. No screenplays, romance, or science fiction. **Submissions:** Query with outline. **Member:** AAR.

VICTORIA SANDERS & ASSOCIATES

241 Avenue of the Americas, Suite 11H, New York, NY 10014. 212-633-8811.
E-mail: queriesvsa@hotmail.com. Website: www.victoriasanders.com. **Description:** Fiction, both literary and commercial, and nonfiction in the areas of biography, history, autobiography, psychology, gay studies, politics, and African-American, Asian, Latin, and women's studies. Receives 5,000 queries/yr; 300 submissions/yr. Accepts 10% of unsolicited material. Accepts unsolicited queries and manuscripts. Unpublished writers considered. **Submissions:** Submit outline, 2 sample chapters,

and SASE. Responds in 4 weeks. **Commission:** 15% domestic, 20% foreign. **Member:** AAR. **Contact:** Victoria Sanders, Benee Knauer.

SANDUM & ASSOCIATES

144 E 84th St., New York, NY 10028. 212-737-2011.
Description: Primarily nonfiction and literary fiction. **Submissions:** Query with sample pages, bio/resumé, and SASE. Accepts simultaneous queries. **Commission:** 15% domestic, 20% foreign. **Tips:** Accepts new clients by referral only. **Contact:** Howard E. Sandum.

WENDY SCHMALZ AGENCY

P.O. Box 831, Hudson, NY 12534-0831.
E-mail: wschmalz@earthlink.net. **Description:** Adult fiction, adult nonfiction, and children's books. Receives 1,250 queries/yr. Accepts unsolicited queries, but not manuscripts. Unpublished writers considered. **Submissions:** Send query letter. SASE required for all materials. Responds in 2 weeks to queries, 6 weeks to submissions. **Commission:** 15% domestic, 20% foreign. **Member:** AAR. **Tips:** Currently not accepting picture book submissions. **Contact:** Wendy Schmalz.

THE SEYMOUR AGENCY

475 Miner Street Rd., Canton, NY 13617-3256.
E-mail: marysue@slic.com. Website: www.theseymouragency.com.
Description: Represents nonfiction, literary fiction, and genre fiction in the areas of romance and westerns. Considers unsolicited manuscripts, unpublished writers, and unsolicited material. **Submissions:** For nonfiction, send proposal and first chapter. For fiction, send synopsis and first 50 pages. SASE required. Accepts e-queries and simultaneous submissions. **Commission:** 15% domestic (12.5% for published authors). **Member:** AAR, Author's Guild, RWA. **Contact:** Mary Sue Seymour.

ZACHARY SHUSTER HARMSWORTH LITERARY AGENCY

1776 Broadway, Suite 1405, New York, NY 10019. 212-765-6900. Website: www.zsh-literary.com. **Description:** Adult fiction (commercial and literary) and nonfiction (biography/memoir, business, psychology, and medicine). Receives 2,000 queries/submissions per year. Accepts less than 1% of unsolicited material. Unpublished writers considered. **Submissions:** Query with sample pages (up to 30) and SASE. Accepts simultaneous queries, but not fax or e-queries. Responds in 1-2 months to queries, 2-4 months to submissions. **Commission:** 15% domestic, 20% foreign.

BOBBE SIEGEL, LITERARY AGENT

41 W 83rd St., New York, NY 10024. 212-877-4985.
Description: Adult fiction and nonfiction. No plays (dramatic or screen), romances, juvenile, cookbooks, humor, or short stories. Considers unsolicited queries, but not manuscripts. Unpublished writers considered. **Submissions:** Query with SASE. Accepts simultaneous queries, but not e-queries. Responds in 2-3 weeks to queries, 2-3 months to submissions. **Commission:** 15% domestic, 20% foreign.

JACQUELINE SIMENAUER LITERARY AGENCY

P.O. Box A.G., Mantoloking, NJ 08738. 732-262-0783.
Description: Both fiction (literary and mainstream commercial) and nonfiction (health/medicine, popular psychology, how-to/self-help, women's issues, alternative health, spirituality, New Age, fitness/nutrition, current issues, true crime, business, celebrities, reference, social issues). Unpublished writers considered. **Submissions:** For fiction: query with first 3 chapters, synopsis, bio, and SASE. For nonfiction: query with SASE. Accepts simultaneous queries and e-queries. **Commission:** 15% domestic, 20% foreign. **Contact:** Jacqueline Simenauer (nonfiction), Fran Pardi (fiction).

PHILIP G. SPITZER LITERARY AGENCY

50 Talmage Farm Ln., East Hampton, NY 11937. 631-329-3650.
E-mail: spitzer516@aol.com. **Description:** Adult fiction (literary and suspense/mystery) and nonfiction. No unsolicited manuscripts. **Submissions:** Query with outline and sample chapters. **Member:** AAR. **Contact:** Philip Spitzer.

STIMOLA LITERARY STUDIO

308 Chase Ct., Edgewater, NJ 07020. 201-945-9353.
E-mail: LtryStudio@aol.com. **Description:** Preschool through YA fiction/nonfiction. Receives 500 queries/yr; 80 submissions/yr. Accepts 5% of unsolicited material. Considers unsolicited queries and manuscripts. **Submissions:** Query with SASE. Accepts e-queries. No simultaneous submissions. Responds in 2-3 weeks to queries, 3-4 weeks to submissions. **Commission:** 15%. **Member:** AAR. **Contact:** Rosemary B. Stimola.

PATRICIA TEAL LITERARY AGENCY

2036 Vista del Rosa, Fullerton, CA 92831-1336. 714-738-8333.
Description: Represents women's fiction and commercial nonfiction. Accepts unsolicited queries, but not manuscripts. **Submissions:** Send query with SASE via regular mail. Accepts simultaneous queries, but not e-queries. Responds in 1 week to queries, 60 days to submissions. **Commission:** 15% domestic, 20% foreign. **Member:** AAR. **Tips:** Not accepting new clients at this time. **Contact:** Patricia Teal.

SCOTT TREIMEL NY

434 Lafayette St., New York, NY 10003. 212-505-8353.
E-mail: st.ny@verizon.net. **Description:** Represents juvenile/YA fiction and nonfiction. Receives 3,000 queries/submissions per year. Published writers preferred. **Submissions:** Send query for works 50+ pages; send complete manuscript for picture books and works fewer than 50 pages. No simultaneous queries or e-queries. Responds in 90 days; SASE required. **Commission:** 15% domestic, 20% foreign. **Member:** AAR. **Tips:** No unicorns, fairies, or rainbows. **Contact:** Scott Treimel.

TRIDENT MEDIA GROUP, LLC

41 Madison Ave., Fl. 36, New York, NY 10010. 212-889-0620.
E-mail: mvaisman@tridentmediagroup.com. Website: www.tridentmediagroup.com.
Description: General fiction and nonfiction. Handles film and TV rights for clients only. Does not accept unsolicited manuscripts. **Submissions:** Query with SASE first. If requested, send outline and sample chapters. Responds in 2-6 weeks. **Member:** AAR. **Contact:** Ellen Levine, Sara Crowe, Melissa Flashman.

THE VINES AGENCY, INC.

648 Broadway, Suite 901, New York, NY 10012. 212-777-5522.
E-mail: jv@vinesagency.com. Website: www.vinesagency.com.
Description: Women's fiction, romantic suspense, thrillers, historical, supernatural thrillers, mainstream fiction, literary, political thrillers, legal thrillers. Also commercial nonfiction, both prescriptive and narrative. Receives 25,000 queries/yr; 1,000 submissions per year. Represents 11-12 submissions per year. Accepts unsolicited queries, but not manuscipts. Unpublished writers considered. **Submissions:** Submit outline, sample chapters, and SASE. Accepts e-queries. Simultaneous submissions accepted. Responds in 6 weeks. **Commission:** 15% domestic, 25% foreign. **Member:** Authors Guild, WGA. **Tips:** "We represent authors whose work we feel passionate about." **Contact:** James C. Vines, Alexis Caldwell.

WALES LITERARY AGENCY, INC.

P.O. Box 9428, Seattle, WA 98109-0428. 206-284-7114.
E-mail: waleslit@waleslit.com. **Description:** Mainstream and literary fiction and narrative nonfiction. Does not accept unsolicited manuscripts. **Submissions:** Query with brief description, outline, and writing sample(s). **Commission:** 15%. **Member:** AAR. **Contact:** Elizabeth Wales, Adrienne Reed, Josie Di Bernardo.

JOHN A. WARE LITERARY AGENCY

392 Central Park W, New York, NY 10025. 212-866-4733. **Description:** Adult fiction (non-category, thrillers, mysteries) and nonfiction (biography, history, current affairs, investigative journalism, social criticism, nature, Americana, folklore, "bird's eye views" of phenomena, science, medicine, and sports). No personal memoirs. Receives 2,000 queries/yr. Accepts 1-2% of unsolicited material. Accepts unsolicited queries, but not manuscripts. Unpublished writers considered. **Submissions:** Send query letter with SASE. Do not call or fax. Accepts simultaneous queries. Responds in 2 weeks to queries. **Commission:** 15% domestic, 20% foreign. **Contact:** John Ware.

WATKINS/LOOMIS AGENCY, INC.

133 E 35th St., Suite 1, New York, NY 10016. 212-532-0080.
Description: Adult literary fiction and nonfiction. Considers unsolicited queries and manuscripts. Considers unpublished writers. **Submissions:** Send query letter with first 3 chapters for fiction, and a query letter plus synopsis for nonfiction; SASE required. No simultaneous or electronic queries. Responds in 2-6 weeks. **Tips:** No romance, self-help, or novelty books. **Contact:** Katherine Fausset.

WIESER & ELWELL, INC.

80 Fifth Ave., Suite 1101, New York, NY 10011. 212-260-0860.
Description: Specializes in trade and mass market adult fiction and nonfiction. Unpublished writers considered. **Submissions:** Query with outline, 25 sample pages, bio/resumé, and SASE. **Commission:** 15%. **Contact:** Jake Elwell.

WITHERSPOON ASSOCIATES, INC.

235 E 31st St., New York, NY 10016. 212-889-8626.
Description: Adult fiction and nonfiction. Unpublished writers considered. **Submissions:** Query with sample pages and SASE. Does not accept simultaneous queries. Responds in 6 weeks. **Commission:** 15% domestic, 20% foreign. **Contact:** Kimberly Witherspoon, Maria Massie, David Forrer, Alexis Hurley.

ANN WRIGHT REPRESENTATIVES

165 W 46th St., Suite 1105, New York, NY 10036-2501. 212-764-6770.
E-mail: danwrightlit@aol.com. **Description:** Fiction and screenplays, varied subjects. Considers only queries or referrals, with SASE. Accepts .5% of unsolicited material. Considers unsolicited queries, but not manuscripts. Unpublished writers considered. **Submissions:** Accepts simultaneous queries, but not e-queries. Responds in 1-2 weeks to queries, 4-8 weeks to submissions. **Commission:** 10% film/tv, 10-20% literary. **Tips:** "Always open to new writers of screen material and to new authors of fiction with strong film potential." **Contact:** Dan Wright.

WRITERS HOUSE

21 W 26th St., New York, NY 10010. 212-685-2400.
Description: Represents trade books of all types, fiction and nonfiction, including all rights. No plays, screenplays, teleplays, or software. **Submissions:** Send 1-page query with SASE. Do not send manuscript unless requested. **Member:** AAR. **Tips:** "State in your query letter what's terrific about your book, what it is about, and why you are the most qualified one to write it." **Contact:** Submissions Dept.

THE ZACK COMPANY, INC.

243 W 70th St., Suite 8-D, New York, NY 10023-4366.
Website: www.zackcompany.com. **Description:** Adult fiction (commercial, thrillers, action, science fiction/fantasy, horror, historical fiction—*no women's fiction*) and nonfiction (narrative, military/history, politics, current affairs, science/technology, biography/memoir by political figures and celebrities, personal finance, parenting/relationships, health/medicine). Authors of nonfiction must be recognized experts in their field and have prior publishing credits. Receives 25,000 queries/yr; 500-750 submissions/yr. Accepts 1% of unsolicited material. Unpublished writers considered. **Submissions:** Query with SASE. **Member:** AAR, Author's Guild. **Tips:** "Before submitting, you should visit our website and read our submission guidelines. Send all material via regular mail; we do not accept e-queries." **Contact:** Andrew Zack.

SUSAN ZECKENDORF ASSOCIATES INC.

171 W 57th St., Suite 11B, New York, NY 10019. 212-245-2928.

Description: Commercial fiction (mysteries, thrillers, literary) and nonfiction (science, biography, health, parenting, social history, and classical music). Considers unsolicited queries, but not manuscripts. Unpublished writers considered. **Submissions:** Query with outline, bio/resumé and SASE. Accepts simultaneous queries, but not e-queries. Responds in 1 week to queries, 2 weeks to submissions. **Commission:** 15% domestic, 20% foreign. **Member:** AAR. **Tips:** "We're a small agency providing individual attention." **Contact:** Susan Zeckendorf.

ARTS COUNCILS

State arts councils are a resource frequently overlooked by writers, but they offer useful services that can boost a writer's career. First of all, many offer cash awards of various sorts. One type of award is a "project" grant; that is, a specific award to complete a specified piece of work. These are awarded based on details of a proposal the individual author or a sponsoring arts group submits. The criteria for project grants are the quality of writing (based on sample poems or pages of fiction or nonfiction submitted), the clarity of the project, and some indication of community support, such as a letter of support from a community group. For instance, a project to publish an anthology of multicultural writers from your state might qualify for a grant. Other projects can be as diverse and creative as printing poems on placards to place in public transit vehicles, or on billboards or in other nontraditional venues.

The other type of cash support is a fellowship award. Many states offer awards for writers based on the general quality of their work. There is no "project" requirement; the money awarded is simply to further the author's career and is "unrestricted"; that is, it may be used for any purpose at all.

The review process involves peer groups of writers, creative artists, and arts administrators from around the state. The important thing to know is that these panels constantly rotate their membership. Review is somewhat subjective; a panel that hated your work one year may love it the next. Don't give up applying for fellowships in particular, as these are the easiest to apply for. Keep sending in your 1-page form and 10 best poems (or whatever is requested) each year. You may be pleasantly surprised one year to be selected for a writing fellowship award.

For project grants, after you get a rough idea of your desired project, you may wish to call the arts council to talk briefly with a grants officer. This person may be able to help you think through some key elements of your project that will need to be covered in a proposal. Many arts councils also offer regional grants-writing workshops and sometimes fund local agencies that in turn offer awards to authors.

Finally, arts councils have a variety of other services, such as newsletters which publish information on regional and national competitions, requests for submissions for regional collections of writing, and so on.

All writers should contact their state agencies and get on their mailing list, to keep abreast of these valuable services.

ALABAMA STATE COUNCIL ON THE ARTS

201 Monroe St., Suite 110, Montgomery, AL 36130-1800. 334-242-4076, ext. 224. randy@arts.state.al.us. www.arts.state.al.us. **Description:** Newsletter, workshops, conferences, grants, and fellowships. **Contact:** Randy Shoults.

ALASKA STATE COUNCIL ON THE ARTS

411 W 4th Ave., Suite 1E, Anchorage, AK 99501-2343. 907-269-6610. aksca_info@eed.state.ak.us. www.eed.state.ak.us/aksca. **Description:** Offers grants to Alaska artists and arts organizations: Percent for Art Program; Contemporary Art Bank; Literary, Visual, and Community Native Arts Programs; Artists in the Schools.

ALBERTA FOUNDATION FOR THE ARTS

901 Standard Life Centre, 10405 Jasper Avenue NW, Edmonton, Alberta T5J 4R7 Canada. 780-427-2921. www.affta.ab.ca. **Description:** Grant programs and competitions. **Contact:** Paul Pearson.

ARIZONA COMMISSION ON THE ARTS

417 W Roosevelt, Phoenix, AZ 85003-1226. 602-255-5882. general@arizonaarts.org. www.arizonaarts.org. **Description:** Newsletter, workshops, conference, grants, and fellowships for Arizona writers. **Contact:** Paul Morris, Literature Director & Public Information Officer.

ARKANSAS ARTS COUNCIL

1500 Tower Bldg., 323 Center St., Little Rock, AR 72201. 501-324-9766. info@arkansasarts.com. www.arkansasarts.com. **Description:** Supports programs and services for arts organizations, schools, and individual artists. Also offers individual artists fellowships and grants. **Contact:** James E. Mitchell, Executive Director.

CALIFORNIA ARTS COUNCIL

1300 I St., Suite 930, Sacramento, CA 95814. 916-322-6395. www.cac.ca.gov. **Description:** Seeks to advance California through the arts and community. **Tips:** Does not offer grants to writers to finish or publish books. **Contact:** Ray Tatar, Literature Coordinator.

COLORADO COUNCIL ON THE ARTS

1380 Lawrence St., Suite 1200, Denver, CO 80204. 303-866-2732. coloarts@state.co.us. www.coloarts.state.co.us. **Description:** Newsletter and grants. **Contact:** Renée Bouée, Executive Director.

COMPAS: WRITERS & ARTISTS IN THE SCHOOLS

304 Landmark Center, 75 W Fifth St., St. Paul, MN 55102-1414. 651-292-3249. dei@compas.org. www.compas.org. **Description:** Nonprofit organization that collaborates with a wide of variety of arts, education, government, business, and philanthropic partners to employ professional artists, provide technical assistance, and offer grants to artists and agencies. **Contact:** Daniel Gabriel, Director.

CONNECTICUT COMMISSION ON THE ARTS

c/o The Arts Office of the Commission on Arts, Tourism, Culture, History, & Film (CATCHF), 755 Main St., One Financial Plaza, Hartford, CT 06103. 860-566-4770. artsinfo@ctarts.org. www.ctarts.org. **Description:** Dedicated to developing and strengthening Connecticut's cultural resources. Offers fellowships to Connecticut creative writers biannually. The next opportunity for writers will be in 2004. Awards are $5,000 and $2,500. **Contact:** Linda Dente, Fellowship Program Manager.

DELAWARE DIVISION OF THE ARTS

Carvel State Bldg., 820 N French St., Wilmington, DE 19801. 302-577-8278. www.artsdel.org. **Description:** Offers fellowships and grants to individual artists from Delaware. **Contact:** Kristin Pleasanton, Art/Artist Services Coordinator.

FLORIDA DIVISION OF CULTURAL AFFAIRS

1001 De Soto Park Dr., Tallahassee, FL 32301. 858-245-6470. culturalaffairs@dos.state.fl.us. www.florida-arts.org. **Description:** Encourages the development of culture and the arts statewide and provides cultural grant funding. **Contact:** Linda B. Downey, Director.

GEORGIA COUNCIL FOR THE ARTS

260 14th St. NW, Suite 401, Atlanta, GA 30318. 404-685-2787. www.gaarts.org. **Description:** Offers funding, programs, and services to both support and encourage excellence in the arts. **Contact:** Susan S. Weiner, Executive Director.

HAWAII STATE FOUNDATION ON CULTURE AND THE ARTS

250 S Hotel St., Fl. 2, Honolulu, HI 96813. 808-586-0307. sfca@sfca.state.hi.us. www.hawaii.gov/sfca. **Description:** Programs include Art in Public Places, Arts in Education, Community Outreach, Foundation Grants, Folk Arts, Individual Artists Fellowships, and History and Humanities. **Contact:** Ken Hamilton, Public Information Officer.

IDAHO COMMISSION ON THE ARTS

2410 North Old Penitentiary Rd., Boise, ID 83712. 208-334-2119. cconley@ica.state.id.us. www2.state.id.us/arts. **Description:** The state's principal cultural agency supports Idaho writers through annual grants and awards, readings and workshops. Grants are possible every year, but awards are given every three years (fellowships and writer-in-residence). **Contact:** Cort Conley, Director.

ILLINOIS ARTS COUNCIL

James R. Thompson Center, 100 W Randolph, Suite 10-500, Chicago, IL 60601. 312-814-6750. susan@arts.state.il.us; info@arts.state.il.us. www.state.il.us/agency/iac. **Description:** Biannual fellowships in poetry (odd-numbered fiscal years) and prose (even-numbered fiscal years). Deadline: September 1. Literary Arts Award for authors published in nonprofit Illinois literary publications. Deadline: March 1. Also offers a newsletter, workshops, grants, and prizes to Illinois organizations and writers.

INDIANA ARTS COMMISSION

402 W Washington St., Indianapolis, IN 46204-2741. 317-232-1268. **Description:** Promotes and encourages the arts throughout Indiana. Goals are to support the Regional Partnership Initiative, increase public awareness of the arts, and support arts education and individual artists.

INSTITUTO DE CULTURA PUERTORRIQUENA

P.O. Box 9024184, San Juan, PR 00902-4184. 787-724-3210. www.icp.gobierno.pr.
Description: Newsletter, workshops, conferences, grants, and prizes.

IOWA ARTS COUNCIL

Iowa Dept. of Cultural Affairs, State Historical Building, 600 E Locust, Des Moines,
IA 50319-0290. 515-281-6412. www.culturalaffairs.org/iac. **Description:** Seeks to
make the arts available to individuals living in Iowa. Offers grants for artists in arts
education, technical assistance and professional development, community development, and support for arts organizations. **Contact:** Sarah Oltrogge, Public Relations
Specialist.

KANSAS ARTS COMMISSION

700 SW Jackson, Suite 1004, Topeka, KS 66603-3761. 785-296-3335.
kac@arts.state.ks.us. http://arts.state.ks.us. **Description:** Offers programs, services,
and grants to the citizens of Kansas and works to encourage and promote the celebration of the arts statewide. **Contact:** Robert T. Burtch, Editor.

KENTUCKY ARTS COUNCIL

Old Capitol Annex, 300 W Broadway, Frankfort, KY 40601-1980. 502-564-3757.
kyarts@ky.gov. www.artscouncil.ky.gov. **Description:** Offers programs, grants, virtual
exhibits, and arts education. **Contact:** Gerri Combs, Executive Director.

LOUISIANA DIVISION OF THE ARTS

P.O. Box 44247, Baton Rouge, LA 70804-4247. 225-342-8180.
jborders@crt.state.la.us; arts@crt.state.la.us. www.crt.state.la.us. **Description:**
Workshops, conference, grants, and newsletter. **Contact:** James Borders, Executive
Director.

MAINE ARTS COMMISSION

25 State House Station, 193 State St., Augusta, ME 04333-0025. 207-287-2724.
kathy.shaw@maine.gov. www.mainearts.com. **Description:** Newsletter, workshops,
and grants. **Contact:** Alden C. Wilson, Director.

MANITOBA ARTS COUNCIL

525-93 Lombard Ave., Winnipeg, Manitoba R3B 3B1 Canada. 204-945-0422.
jthomas@artscouncil.mb.ca. www.artscouncil.mb.ca. **Description:** Provides grants
to professional writers working in poetry, fiction, creative nonfiction, theatre, and film
scripts. Manitoba residency required. Program guidelines available on website.
Contact: Joan Thomas, Program Consultant: Literary, Film and Video.

MARYLAND STATE ARTS COUNCIL

Literature Program, 175 W Ostend St., Suite E, Baltimore, MD 21230. 410-767-
6555. pdunne@mdbusiness.state.md.us. www.msac.org. **Description:** Grants and
awards. **Contact:** Pamela Dunne, Literature Program Director.

MASSACHUSETTS CULTURAL COUNCIL
10 St. James Ave., Fl. 3, Boston, MA 02116. 617-727-3668. mcc@art.state.ma.us. www.massculturalcouncil.org. **Description:** Newsletter and grants. **Contact:** Charles Coe, Literature Coordinator.

MICHIGAN COUNCIL FOR ARTS AND CULTURAL AFFAIRS
P.O. Box 30705, Lansing, MI 48909-8205. 517-241-4011. artsinfo@michigan.gov. www.cis.state.mi.us/arts. **Description:** Strives to increase public awareness of the arts, strengthen the arts and culture statewide, and support art education, communities, and artists. **Contact:** Betty Boone, Executive Director.

MINNESOTA STATE ARTS BOARD
Park Square Court, Suite 200, 400 Sibley St., St. Paul, MN 55101-1928. 651-215-1600, 800- 8MN-ARTS. msab@arts.state.mn.us. www.arts.state.mn.us. **Description:** Offers newsletter, workshops, and grants. **Contact:** Amy Frimpong, Artist Assistance Program Officer.

MISSISSIPPI ARTS COMMISSION
239 N Lamar St., Suite 207, Jackson, MS 39201. 601-359-6030. www.arts.state.ms.us. **Description:** Supports and encourages participation in, appreciation of, and education in the arts to meet the legitimate needs and aspirations of persons in all parts of the state of Mississippi. **Contact:** Diane Williams, Arts Industry Director-ADA Coordinator.

MISSOURI ARTS COUNCIL
Wainwright Office Complex, 111 N 7th St., Suite 105, St. Louis, MO 63101. 314-340-6845. bev.strohmeyer@ded.mo.gov. www.missouriartscouncil.org. **Description:** Offers a newsletter, conferences, and grants. **Contact:** Beverly Strohmeyer.

MONTANA ARTS COUNCIL
P.O. Box 202201, Helena, MT 59620-2201. 406-444-6430. mac@state.mt.us. www.art.state.mt.us. **Description:** Strives to promote and expand the Montana culture and the arts by offering support to individuals, organizations, schools, and communities in Montana. Only Montana residents are eligible for most programs. **Contact:** Kristin Han Burgoyne, Grants & Database Director.

NEBRASKA ARTS COUNCIL
Joslyn Castle Carriage House, 3838 Davenport St., Omaha, NE 68131-2329. 402-595-2122. www.nebraskaartscouncil.org. **Description:** Offers grants and other opportunities, and provides access to numerous resources.

NEVADA ARTS COUNCIL
716 N Carson St., Suite A, Carson City, NV 89701. 775-687-6680. www.nevadaculture.org. **Description:** Offers workshops, conferences, newsletter, and grants for Nevada residents.

NEW BRUNSWICK ARTS BOARD

634 Queen St., Suite 300, Fredericton, New Brunswick E3B 1C2 Canada. 506-444-4444. www.artsnb.ca. **Description:** Programs, scholarships, and artist-in-residence programs.

NEW HAMPSHIRE STATE COUNCIL ON THE ARTS

2 1/2 Beacon St., Concord, NH 03301. 603-271-2789. ystahr@nharts.state.nh.us. www.nh.gov/nharts. **Description:** Newsletter, e-news service, workshops, conferences, and grants. **Contact:** Yvonne Stahr, Programs Information Officer.

NEW JERSEY STATE COUNCIL ON THE ARTS

Artist Services, P.O. Box 306, Trenton, NJ 08625. 609-292-6130. don@arts.sos.state.nj.us. www.njartscouncil.org. **Description:** Workshops, newsletter, conferences, grants. **Contact:** Don Ehman, Program Associate.

NEW MEXICO ARTS

P.O. Box 1450, Santa Fe, NM 87504-1450. 505-827-6490. aweisman@oca.state.nm.us. www.nmarts.org. **Description:** State arts agency that provides grants to New Mexico nonprofit organizations to implement arts and cultural programs in their communities. **Tips:** Does not fund individuals.

NEW YORK STATE COUNCIL ON THE ARTS

175 Varick St., New York, NY 10014. 212-387-7000. kmasterson@nysca.org. www.nysca.org. **Description:** Offers support to a wide range of literary and multidisciplinary writing or literary organizations in the state of New York through the Literature Program (LIT). Program's objective is to develop and support public literary activity around the state. New applicants are encouraged to apply. Applicants must provide completed NYSCA application forms and specific additional narrative for the category in which they are applying. Application deadline: March 1. **Tips:** Offers translation grants, but does not offer funding for individual writers or a separate writer-in-residence. See guidelines on website. **Contact:** Kathleen Masterson, Director, Literature Program.

NEWFOUNDLAND & LABRADOR ARTS COUNCIL

P.O. Box 98, St. John's, Newfoundland A1C 5H5 Canada. 709-726-2212. nlacmail@nfld.net. www.nlac.nf.ca. **Description:** Supports the arts by providing financial assistance programs, services, resources, and grants to individuals and groups with an interest in the arts.

NORTH CAROLINA ARTS COUNCIL

Dept. of Cultural Resources, Raleigh, NC 27699-4632. 919-715-1519. debbie.mcgill@ncmail.net. www.ncarts.org. **Description:** Online newsletter, grants. **Contact:** Deborah McGill, Literature Director.

NORTH DAKOTA COUNCIL ON THE ARTS

1600 E Century Ave., Suite 6, Bismarck, ND 58503. 701-328-7590.
comserv@state.nd.us. www.discovernd.com/arts. **Description:** Newsletter and
grants. **Contact:** Janine Webb, Director.

NORTHWEST TERRITORIES ARTS COUNCIL

Dept. of Education, Culture and Employment, P.O. Box 1320, Yellowknife,
Northwest Territories X1A 2L9 Canada. 867-920-6370. www.pwnhc.ca/artscouncil.
Description: Financial assistance to NWT residents and organizations involved in
creative projects in the arts (music, writing, visual art, performing art).

OHIO ARTS COUNCIL

727 E Main St., Columbus, OH 43205-1796. 614-466-2613. bob.fox@oac.state.oh.us.
www.oac.state.oh.us. **Description:** Dedicated to encouraging the development of
the arts and to preserving Ohio's cultural heritage. Offers grants to organizations, fellowships to individuals, and service programs. **Contact:** Bob Fox, Literature Program
Coordinator.

OKLAHOMA ARTS COUNCIL

P.O. Box 52001-2001, Oklahoma City, OK 73152-2001. 405-521-2931.
okarts@arts.state.ok.us. www.state.ok.us/~arts. **Description:** Workshops, conferences, newsletters, grants.

ONTARIO ARTS COUNCIL

151 Bloor St. W, Fl. 5, Toronto, Ontario M5S 1T6 Canada. 416-961-1660.
info@arts.on.ca. www.arts.on.ca. **Description:** An agency of the provincial Ministry
of Culture, OAC provides support for artists and not-for-profit arts organizations in
Ontario through grants, awards, and services. **Contact:** Janice Lambrakos,
Information Services Coordinator.

OREGON ARTS COMMISSION

775 Summer St. NE, Suite 200, Salem, OR 97301-1284. 503-986-0086.
oregon.artscomm@state.or.us. www.oregonartscommission.org. **Description:**
Dedicated to fostering the arts in Oregon. Offers grants and programs. **Contact:**
Susan Hanf, Assistant Director.

PENNSYLVANIA COUNCIL ON THE ARTS

Room 216, Finance Bldg., Harrisburg, PA 17120. 717-787-6883. www.pacouncilont-
hearts.org. **Description:** Strives to foster the excellence and appreciation of the arts
in Pennsylvania. Offers grants, awards, and services. **Contact:** Lori Frush, Fellowship
Program.

PRINCE EDWARD ISLAND COUNCIL OF THE ARTS

115 Richmond St., Charlottetown, Prince Edward Island C1A 1A7 Canada. 902-368-
4410. www.peiartscouncil.com. **Description:** Contests and grants.

RHODE ISLAND STATE COUNCIL ON THE ARTS
83 Park St., Fl. 6, Providence, RI 02903-1037. 401-222-3880.
info@arts.ri.gov. www.arts.ri.gov. **Description:** Workshops and grants to Rhode
Island residents. **Contact:** Arts Council staff.

SASKATCHEWAN ARTS BOARD
2135 Broad St., Regina, Saskatchewan S4P 3V7 Canada. 306-787-4056.
sab@artsboard.sk.ca. www.artsboard.sk.ca. **Description:** Provides programs, services, consultation, and grants to assist artists and arts organizations in the province.

SOUTH CAROLINA ARTS COMMISSION
1800 Gervais St., Columbia, SC 29201. 803-734-8696. goldstsa@arts.state.sc.us.
www.southcarolinaarts.com. **Description:** Offers grants, programs, and resources to
South Carolina art organizations and South Carolina artists. **Contact:** Sara June
Goldstein, Program Director for Literary Arts.

SOUTH DAKOTA ARTS COUNCIL
800 Governors Dr., Pierre, SD 57501-2294. 605-773-3131. sdac@state.sd.us.
www.sdarts.org. **Description:** Offers grants to South Dakota writers. Also offers
workshops, conferences, and a newsletter. **Contact:** Dennis Holub, Executive
Director.

TENNESSEE ARTS COMMISSION
401 Charlotte Ave., Nashville, TN 37243-0780. 615-741-1701. www.arts.state.tn.us.
Description: Provides access to the arts in Tennessee. Various grants available.
Contact: Literary Arts Director.

TEXAS COMMISSION ON THE ARTS
P.O. Box 13406, Austin, TX 78711-3406. 512-463-5535. front.desk@arts.state.tx.us.
www.arts.state.tx.us. **Description:** Online newsletter, workshops, conferences,
grants. **Contact:** Gaye Greever McElwain, Director of Marketing.

UTAH ARTS COUNCIL
617 E South Temple, Salt Lake City , UT 84102-1177. 801-236-7555.
www.dced.state.ut.us/arts. **Description:** Fosters creativity and diversity in the arts in
Utah. Provides funding, training and development services, and educational programs in the arts. **Contact:** Guy Lebeda, Literature Coordinator.

VERMONT ARTS COUNCIL
136 State St., Drawer 33, Montpelier, VT 05633-6001. 802-828-3294.
mbailey@vermontartscouncil.org. www.vermontartscouncil.org.
Description: Workshops, newsletter, conferences, grants. **Contact:** Michele Bailey,
Director of Creation & Presentation Programs.

VIRGINIA COMMISSION FOR THE ARTS

223 Governor St., Lewis House, Fl. 2, Richmond, VA 23219-2010. 804-225-3132. pbaggett.arts@state.va.us. www.arts.virginia.gov. **Description:** Workshops, conferences, and grants. **Contact:** Peggy J. Baggett, Executive Director.

WASHINGTON STATE ARTS COMMISSION

P.O. Box 42675, Olympia, WA 98504-2675. 360-586-2421. bitsyb@wsac.wa.gov. www.arts.wa.gov. **Description:** Newsletter, workshops, grants (for nonprofit organizations only, no individuals). **Contact:** Bitsy Bidwell, Community Arts Development Manager.

WEST VIRGINIA COMMISSION ON THE ARTS

Arts Section/Division of Culture & History, The Cultural Center, 1900 Kanawha Blvd. E, Charleston, WV 25305. 304-558-0240, ext. 717. gordon.simmons@ wvculture.org. www.wvculture.org. **Description:** Promotion and preservation of West Virginia's arts and culture. Annual Fellowship competition for West Virginia writers; annual Professional Development for Artists grants, state residency required. **Contact:** Gordon Simmons, Individual Artist Services.

WISCONSIN ARTS BOARD

101 E Wilson St., Fl. 1, Madison, WI 53702. 608-266-0190. artsboard@arts.state.wi.us. www.arts.state.wi.us. **Description:** Provides funds, services, and information to artists, arts organizations, educational institutions, communities, and all other interested citizens of the state.

WYOMING ARTS COUNCIL

2320 Capitol Ave., Cheyenne, WY 82002. 307-777-7742. mshay@state.wy.us. www.wyomingartscouncil.org. **Description:** Offers three literary contests to writers from Wyoming: The Literary Fellowship Awards, the Warren Alder Fiction Award, and the Neltje Blanchan/Frank Nelson Doubleday Memorial Awards. **Contact:** Michael Shay, Literature Program Manager.

COLONIES

Writers' colonies offer solitude and freedom from everyday distractions so that writers can concentrate on their work. Though some colonies are quite small, with space for just three or four writers at a time, others can provide accommodations for as many as 30 or 40. The length of a residency may vary, too, from a couple of weeks to five or six months. These programs have strict admissions policies, and writers must submit a formal application or letter of intent, a resumé, writing samples, and letters of recommendation. As an alternative to the traditional writers' colony, a few of the organizations listed offer writing rooms for writers who live nearby. Write for application information first, enclosing a stamped, self-addressed envelope. Residency fees are subject to change.

EDWARD F. ALBEE FOUNDATION

14 Harrison St., New York, NY 10013. 212-226-2020. **Description:** On Long Island, "The Barn" (William Flanagan Memorial Creative Persons Center), offers 1-month residencies to 12 writers each season, from June 1-October 1. Applicants are chosen based on artistic talent and need. Applications (writing samples, project description, and resumé) are accepted January 1-April 1. No fees, but residents are responsible for food/travel expenses. **Contact:** Jakob Holder, Secretary.

ALTOS DE CHAVÓN

66 Fifth Ave., Room 604A, New York, NY 10011. 212-229-5370. **Description:** Nonprofit center for the arts in the Dominican Republic, for design innovation, international creative exchange, and the promotion of Dominican culture. Residencies average 12 weeks, offering emerging or established artists a chance to live and work in a setting of architectural and natural beauty. Selects 2-3 writers each year. Send letter of interest, writing sample, and resumé by July 15. Fees: $400/month. **Contact:** Carmen Lorente, Program Coordinator.

MARY ANDERSON CENTER

101 St. Francis Dr., Mount St. Francis, IN 47146. 812-923-8602. maca@iglou.com. www.maryandersoncenter.org. **Description:** Residencies (1-8 weeks) and retreats on the grounds of a Franciscan friary with 400 acres of rolling hills and woods. Private bedrooms for up to six writers, musicians, and visual artists. Includes working space and a visual artist's studio. Applicants selected based on project proposal and artists' body of work. Apply year-round (with $15 application fee). Fees: $60/day. Work exchange program available. **Contact:** Debra Carmody, Executive Director.

ATLANTIC CENTER FOR THE ARTS

1414 Art Center Ave., New Smyrna Beach, FL 32168. 386-427-6975; 800-393-6975. program@atlanticcenterforthearts.org. www.atlanticcenterforthearts.org. **Description:** Since 1982, Atlantic Center's residency program has provided artists from all artistic disciplines with spaces to live, work, and collaborate during three week residencies. Located just four miles from the east coast beaches of central

Florida, the pine- and palmette-wooded environment contains award-winning studios that include a resource library, painting studio, sculpture studio, music studio, dance studio, black box theater, and digital computer lab. Each residency session includes three master artists of different disciplines. The master artists each personally select a group of associates—talented, emerging artists—through an application process administered by ACA. During the residency, artists participate in informal sessions with their group, collaborate on projects, and work independently on their own projects. The relaxed atmosphere and unstructured program provide considerable time for artistic regeneration and creation. Atlantic Center for the Arts provides housing (private room/bath with work desk), weekday meals (provided by ACA chef) and shared studio space. Deadline: ongoing. Fees: $850 (financial aid available). **Contact:** Jim Frost, Program and Marketing Manager.

BLUE MOUNTAIN CENTER

P.O. Box 109, Blue Mountain Lake, NY 12812. bmc1@telenet.net. www.bluemountaincenter.org. **Description:** Residencies (4 weeks) for writers, artists, composers, and activists from mid-June through late October. Send brief biographical sketch, a plan for work at BMC, 5-10 slides or writing sample (approx. 30 pages, designate 10 pages for preliminary reading), and $20 application fee. Fees: none, contributions encouraged. **Tips:** "The admissions committee is particularly interested in applicants whose work demonstrates social or ecological concern. Students are discouraged from applying." **Contact:** Ben Strader.

BYRDCLIFFE ARTS COLONY

Artists' Residency Program, The Woodstock Guild, 34 Tinker St., Woodstock, NY 12498. 845-679-2079. wguild@ulster.net. www.woodstockguild.org. **Description:** The Villetta Inn, at a 400-acre arts colony, offers 1-month residencies (June-September) to fiction writers, poets, playwrights, and visual artists. Private studios, separate bedrooms, communal kitchen, and a peaceful environment. Submit application, resumé, writing sample, two letters of recommendation, and $5 application fee by April 1. Fees: $600/month. **Contact:** Carla T. Smith, Director.

CAMARGO FOUNDATION

125 Park Square Ct., 400 Sibley St., St. Paul, MN 55101-1982. 651-238-8805. camargo@jeromefdn.org. www.camargofoundation.org. **Description:** Maintains a center of studies in France for nine scholars and grad students each semester to pursue projects in humanities and social sciences on France and Francophone culture. Also, one artist, one composer, and one writer accepted each semester. Research should be at advanced stage. Send application form, curriculum vitae, three letters of recommendation, and project description by February 1. Writers, artists, and composers must send work samples. **Contact:** Michael Pritina, Director.

CENTRUM

P.O. Box 1158, Port Townsend, WA 98368. 360-385-3102. sally@centrum.org. www.centrum.org. **Description:** Residencies (1-4 weeks) for writers and other creative artists, September-May. Selected applicants receive free housing. Send application package (see website) and $20 application fee by August 1. **Contact:** Sally Rodgers, Coordinator.

DJERASSI RESIDENT ARTISTS PROGRAM

2325 Bear Gulch Rd., Woodside, CA 94062. 650-747-1250. drap@djerassi.org. www.djerassi.org. **Description:** Residencies (4 weeks) for artists in literature (prose, poetry, playwrights/screenwriters), choreography, music composition, visual arts, and media arts/new genres. Located in rural setting in Santa Cruz Mountains. Submit application (send SASE or see website) and $25 application fee by February 15 (for residency the following year). Fees: None. **Contact:** Judy Freeland, Residency Coordinator.

DORLAND MOUNTAIN ARTS COLONY

P.O. Box 6, Temecula, CA 92593. 909-302-3837. dorland@ez2.net. www.ez2.net/dorland. **Description:** Located on a Palomar Mountain foothill in Southern California, Dorland offers residencies (1-2 months) for novelists, playwrights, poets, nonfiction writers, composers, and visual artists. Submit application (send SASE or see website) by March 1 or September 1. Fees: $450/month (includes cottage, fuel, and firewood). **Tips:** "Without electricity, residents find a new, natural rhythm for their work." **Contact:** Karen Parrott, Director.

DORSET COLONY HOUSE

P.O. Box 510, Dorset, VT 05251. 802-867-2223. theatre@sover.net. www.dorset-colony.org. **Description:** Residencies (2-3 weeks) for writers and playwrights (up to nine at at a time) in the fall and spring. Low-cost rooms with kitchen facilities at historic Colony House. Applications accepted year-round. Fees: $150/week. Send SASE for details. **Contact:** Barbara Ax; John Nassivera, Director.

ALDEN B. DOW CREATIVITY CENTER

Northwood University, 4000 Whiting Dr., Midland, MI 48640-2398. 989-837-4478. creativity@northwood.edu. www.northwood.edu/abd. **Description:** Four 10-week residencies (early-June to mid-August) awarded yearly to individuals who wish to pursue project ideas without interruption. A project idea should be innovative, creative, and have potential to impact its field. A $750 stipend plus room/board are provided. No spouses or families. Submit application materials and $10 fee by December 31.

FINE ARTS WORK CENTER IN PROVINCETOWN

24 Pearl St., Provincetown, MA 02657. 508-487-9960. www.fawc.org. **Description:** Offers fellowships to ten writers and ten visual artists to work independently from October 1-May 1. Includes studio apartment, studio space for visual artists, and monthly stipends. Writer's deadline: December 1. Visual artists deadline: February 1.

GLENESSENCE WRITERS COLONY

1447 W Ward Ave., Ridgecrest, CA 93555. 760-446-5894. **Description:** Luxury villa in the Upper Mojave Desert (private rooms with bath, pool, spa, courtyard, shared kitchen, fitness center, and library). No children, pets, smoking. Seasonal (January through May). Reservations on a first-come basis. Fees: $565/month, meals not provided. **Contact:** Allison Swift, Director.

TYRONE GUTHRIE CENTRE

Annaghmakerrig, Newbliss, County Monaghan, Ireland. 353-47-54003. thetgc@indigo.ie. www.tyroneguthrie.ie. **Description:** Residencies (1-3 months) on a 450-acre forested estate, offering peace and seclusion to writers and other artists. Writers chosen based on CV, samples of published work, and outline of intended project. Fees:£2,550/month. Some longer-term residencies in old farmyard are available at £380/week. **Contact:** Sheila Pratschke, Director.

THE HAMBIDGE CENTER

P.O. Box 339, Rabun Gap, GA 30568. 706-746-5718. center@hambidge.org. www.hambidge.org. **Description:** Residencies (2-8 weeks) for artists in all disciplines. The center is on 600 pristine acres of quiet woods in the north Georgia mountains. Eight private cottages available. All fellowships partially underwritten, residents contribute $125/week. Download application from website or send SASE. Deadlines: October 1 for February to August; May 1 for September to December. **Contact:** Fran Lanier, Artists in Residence.

HEADLANDS CENTER FOR THE ARTS

944 Fort Barry, Sausalito, CA 94965. 415-331-2787. staff@headlands.org. www.headlands.org. **Description:** On 13,000 acres of open coastal space, residencies are available to current residents of Ohio, New Jersey, North Carolina, and California. Application requirements vary by state. Deadline: June. Decisions announced October for residencies beginning in March. Processing fee $10. Send SASE or visit website for details. **Contact:** Emma-Louise Anderson, Public Relations Manager.

HEDGEBROOK

2197 Millman Rd., Langley, WA 98260. 360-321-4786. hedgebrk@whidbey.com. www.hedgebrook.org. **Description:** Residencies (1-8 weeks) on 48 acres of farmland/woods on Whidbey Island in Washington State. Provides women writers (published or not) of all ages and from all cultural backgrounds with a natural place to work. Stipend program available for low income, without college degree, or age 55 and over. See website for more information or to download application. Fees: None. **Contact:** Beth Bradley, Executive Director.

KALANI OCEANSIDE RETREAT CENTER

Artist-in-Residence Program, RR2, Box 4500 Beach Rd., Pahoa, HI 96778. 808-965-7828, 800-800-6886. kalani@kalani.com. www.kalani.com. **Description:** Residencies (2-8 weeks) in rural coastal setting of 113 botanical acres. Hosts and sponsors educational programs to bring together creative people from around the world in culturally and artistically stimulating environment. Offers housing, various studio spaces. Applications accepted year-round. Fees: $50-$150/day, meals extra. **Contact:** Richard Koob, Director.

THE MACDOWELL COLONY

100 High St., Peterborough, NH 03458. 603-924-3886. info@macdowellcolony.org. www.macdowellcolony.org. **Description:** Residencies (up to 8 weeks) for 80-90 writers each year. Stipend available, up to $1,000 depending on financial need. Selection is competitive. Apply by January 15 for May-August; by April 15 for September-December; by September 15 for January-April. Travel grant of up to $1,000 also available. Send SASE for application or e-mail for details. **Contact:** Courtney Bethel.

THE MILLAY COLONY FOR THE ARTS

454 East Hill Rd., P.O. Box 3, Austerlitz, NY 12017-0003. 518-392-3103. director@millaycolony.org; nikkihayes@millaycolony.org. www.millaycolony.org. **Description:** Residencies (1 month), April-November at Steepletop (former home of Edna St. Vincent Millay). Provides studios, living quarters, and meals at no cost. Applications reviewed by independent jurors, selection based on talent. Send SASE or e-mail for application. Submit by November 1 for the coming season. **Contact:** Nikki Hayes, Executive Assistant.

MILLETT FARM: AN ART COLONY FOR WOMEN

295 Bowery, New York, NY 10003. **Description:** Summer residencies for women writers and visual artists at picturesque tree farm in rural New York. For housing, all residents contribute 5 hours of work each weekday morning and $300/month for meals. Preference given to writers who can stay all summer or at least 6 weeks. Also, 1-week master class ($500) available with Kate Millett. Send SASE for details. **Contact:** Kate Millett, Director.

MOLASSES POND WRITERS' RETREAT AND WORKSHOP

15 Granite Shore, Milbridge, ME 04658. 207-546-2506. **Description:** One-week workshop in June led by published authors who teach writing at UNH. Up to 10 writers stay in colonial farmhouse with private bed/work rooms. Applicants must be serious about their work. No children's literature or poetry. Submit statement of purpose and 15-20 pages of fiction or nonfiction between February 1-March 1. Fees: $480 (lodging, meals, tuition). **Contact:** Martha Barron Barrett, Coordinator.

MONTANA ARTISTS REFUGE

P.O. Box 8, Basin, MT 59631. 406-225-3500. mar@mt.net. www.montanaartistsrefuge.org. **Description:** Living and studio space in rural environment to artists in all disciplines. Writers can work with other artists or in solitude. Length of residency may be 1 month-1 year. Fees: $450-$550/month. Financial aid available, but limited. **Tips:** Download application from website or call for more information. **Contact:** Joy Lewis, Residency Coordinator.

NEW YORK MILLS ARTS RETREAT
AND REGIONAL CULTURAL CENTER

24 N Main Ave., Box 246, New York Mills, MN 56567. 218-385-3339. nymills@kulcher.org. www.kulcher.org. **Description:** A small house and studio are provided to 6-8 selected professional, emerging artists in all disciplines. Applicants may be eligible for Jerome Foundation Fellowships, which provide stipends of $750-$1,500. Special emphasis is given to providing opportunities for artists of color. Each fellowship artist returns a minimum of 8 hours of community service, usually teaching in area schools. Deadlines: April 1 and October 1. **Contact:** Heather Price.

OX-BOW

37 S Wabash Ave., Chicago, IL 60603. 312-899-7408. ox-bow@artic.edu. www.ox-bow.org. **Description:** Residencies (1-2 weeks in mid-June to mid-August) for writers to reside and work in a secluded, natural environment in Michigan. "Primarily for the visual arts, Ox-Bow nutures the creative process through instruction, example, and community." Resident writers are encouraged to present a reading of their work and to participate in the community life. Submit application by mid-February. Fees: $425/week.

RAGDALE

1260 N Green Bay Rd., Lake Forest, IL 60045. 847-234-1063, ext. 206. mosher@ragdale.org. www.ragdale.org. **Description:** Nonprofit artists' community that provides residencies for emerging and established artists, writers, and composers from all over the world. Postmark deadlines for applications are January 15 and June 1 annually. Ragdale is located in Lake Forest, IL, 30 miles north of Chicago and is open year-round except for May and brief periods in October and December. **Contact:** Melissa Mosher, Director of Admissions.

SASKATCHEWAN WRITERS/ARTISTS
COLONIES AND INDIVIDUAL RETREATS

P.O. Box 3986, Regina, Saskatchewan S4P 3R9 Canada. 306-565-8785. skcolony@attglobal.net. www.skwriter.com/colonies.html. **Description:** Offers a 6-week summer colony (July-August), a 2-week northern colony (August-September), and a 2-week winter colony (February). 1-4 weeks per calendar year are available to applicants. Also offers individual retreats (for Saskatchewan residents only) year-round, up to 3 residents at a time. Submit application by December 1 for winter, May 1 for summer, and June 25 for northern. Fees: $200-$225/week ($250-$275 for non-members). **Contact:** Shelley Sopher, Colony Coordinator.

JOHN STEINBECK ROOM

Long Island University, Southampton College Library, Southampton, NY 11968. 631-287-8382. library@southampton.liu.edu. **Description:** Provides a basic research facility to writers with either a current book contract or a confirmed magazine assignment. The room is available for a period of 6 months with one 6-month renewal permissible. Send SASE for application. **Contact:** Robert Gerbereux.

UCROSS FOUNDATION

Residency Program, 30 Big Red Ln., Clearmont, WY 82835. 307-737-2291.
ucross@wyoming.com. ucrossfoundation.org. **Description:** Residencies (2-8 weeks)
in the foothills of Big Horn Mountains for writers, artists, and scholars. Residency sessions offered in fall (August-December) and spring (February-June). Send application and $20 fee by March 1 for fall, October 1 for spring. Send SASE for details.
Fees: None. **Contact:** Sharon Dynak, Executive Director.

VERMONT STUDIO CENTER

P.O. Box 613, Johnson, VT 05656. 802-635-2727. info@vscvt.org. www.vermontstudiocenter.org. **Description:** Independent residencies (4-12 weeks) offered year-round, for 12-15 writers of fiction, nonfiction, and poetry. Includes studio space, room, meals, and community interaction. Also optional readings and private conferences with prominent visiting writers. Full fellowships, grants, and work-exchange aid are available. Send application and $25 fee by February 15, June 15, or September 30. Fees: $3,500/month.

VIRGINIA CENTER FOR THE CREATIVE ARTS

154 San Angelo Dr., Amherst, VA 24521. 434-946-7236. vcca@vcca.com.
www.vcca.com. **Description:** Residencies (2-8 weeks) available year-round for writers, composers, and visual artists at this working retreat in Virginia's Blue Ridge Mountains. About 300 residents accepted each year, 22 at any one time. Submit application by January 15, May 15, or September 15. Send SASE or visit website for details. **Contact:** Sheila Pleasants, Artists' Services Director.

THE WRITERS ROOM

740 Broadway, Fl. 12, New York, NY 10003. 212-254-6995. writersroom@writersroom.org. www.writersroom.org. **Description:** In the East Village, the Writers Room offers a quiet work space for all types of writers, at all stages of their careers. Holds 43 desks separated by partitions, a typing room, kitchen, and library. Open 24 hours/day, 365 days/year. See website for application guidelines and fees. Currently a 1-year wait for fulltime membership.

THE WRITERS STUDIO

Mercantile Library Assn., 17 E 47th St., New York, NY 10017. 212-755-6710.
info@mercantilelibrary.org. www.mercantilelibrary.org/studio.html. **Description:** Space available for writers to work in a quiet setting conducive to serious work. Offers writers a "carrel" on which to work, a locker, reference materials, and electrical outlets for laptop computers. The cost is $200 for three months. To apply, writers must have one or more of the following: proof of previously published work, a current contract with a publisher, a partially completed manuscript, or rejection slips and other correspondence with a publisher. Applications are available on website and are considered year-round. **Contact:** Harold Augenbraum, Director.

HELENE WURLITZER FOUNDATION OF NEW MEXICO

P.O. Box 1891, Taos, NM 87571. 505-758-2413. hwf@taosnet.com. **Description:** Rent-free, fully furnished houses, with free utilities, in Taos on 18-acre campus, offered to writers and artists in creative (not performing) media. Residency is usually 3 months, April 1-September 30, and on a limited basis October-March. Send SASE for application and guidelines. **Contact:** Michael A. Knight, Director.

YADDO

P.O. Box 395, Saratoga Springs, NY 12866-0395. 518-584-0746. chwait@yaddo.org. www.yaddo.org. **Description:** A 400-acre estate, with private bedrooms and studios for each visiting artist. All meals provided. Visual artists, writers, choreographers, film/video artists, performance artists, composers, and collaborators, working at a professional level, are invited for stays of 2-8 weeks. Submit application and $20 fee by January 15 or August 1. Fees: None. **Contact:** Candace Wait, Program Coordinator.

CONFERENCES & WORKSHOPS

Each year, hundreds of writers' conferences and workshops are held across the country. The following list, arranged by category, represents a sampling of some of these events; each listing includes the location, the month or season during which it is usually held, and the name/address of the person from whom specific information may be received. Writers are advised to write (always enclose an SASE), e-mail directly for full details, or check the websites. Additional events are listed annually in the April issue of *The Writer* magazine (Kalmbach Publishing Co.).

Writers' conferences are a great opportunity not only to develop writing skills in specific areas but also to hear presentations by leading professionals in your field. It's also a chance to meet and develop lasting friendships with other writers, as well as with agents and editors.

Writer workshops are smaller gatherings, focused on a specific topic; often these are sponsored by individual writing instructors or site-specific organizations.

MAJOR CONFERENCES

AMERICAN CHRISTIAN WRITERS CONFERENCE

Details: Varied dates/locations. Offers instruction, networking opportunites and one-on-one time with editors and professional freelance writers. **Contact:** Reg A. Forder, P.O. Box 110390, Nashville, TN 37222. 800-219-7483. E-mail: acwriters@aol.com. Website: www.acwriters.com.

ANNUAL CONFERENCE ON WRITING AND ILLUSTRATING FOR CHILDREN

Details: Held August 5-8, 2005 in Los Angeles, CA. Gathering of children's authors and illustrators. Attendees can participate in manuscript/portfolio consultations, and break-out sessions with separate tracks for illustrators, beginning writers, and professional writers or illustrators. **Contact:** SCBWI, 8271 Beverly Blvd., Los Angeles, CA 90048. 323-782-1010. E-mail: conference@scbwi.com. Website: www.scbwi.com.

ANNUAL PROFESSIONAL CONFERENCE

Details: 2005 dates TBA. Professional conference focusing on current topics in communications disciplines. Includes annual Clarion Awards. **Contact:** Patricia H. Troy, Executive Director, Association for Women in Communications, 780 Ritchie Hwy, Suite S-28, Severna Park, MD 21146. 410-544-7442. E-mail: pat@womcom.org. Website: www.womcom.org.

ANNUAL WINTER CONFERENCE

Details: Held in February 2005 in New York, NY. This conference uses New York's location as the center of the publishing industry to focus on the business of writing and illustrating for children. **Contact:** SCBWI, 8271 Beverly Blvd., Los Angeles, CA 90048. 323-782-1010. E-mail: conference@scbwi.org. Website: www.scbwi.org.

ASJA WRITERS CONFERENCE

Details: Held April 16-17, 2005 in New York, NY. For freelance nonfiction writers; includes panels and workshops. **Contact:** Brett Harvey, American Society of Journalists and Authors, 1501 Broadway, Suite 302, New York, NY 10036. 212-997-0947. E-mail: execdir@asja.org. Website: www.asja.org.

CAT WRITERS' ASSOCIATION ANNUAL CONFERENCE

Details: Held annually in November, seminar topics are of interest to all writers and include contract advice, media training, creating and selling a nonfiction project, manuscript critiques, and more. **Contact:** CWA Registration Chairperson, 4753 Deans Hwy, Vernon, NY 13476. Website: www.catwriters.org.

INSTITUTE FOR TRAVEL & GUIDEBOOK
WRITING AND PHOTOGRAPHY

Details: Held annually in Orlando, FL. 2005 dates TBA. For writers, experienced travelers, and others considering careers in article and guidebook work. Topics include a survey of travel and guidebook writing, article queries and book proposals, contracts/negotiations, editor/publisher relations, how the work gets done, Webzines and e-guidebooks, self-publishing, marketing, and photography. **Contact:** Herb Hiller, Society of American Travel Writers, 1500 Sunday Dr., Suite 102, Raleigh, NC 27607. 919-861-5586. E-mail: hiller@funport.net. Website: www.satw.org.

MAUI WRITERS CONFERENCE

Details: Held annually in August/September in Maui, HI. More than 125 agents, editors, bestselling authors, and renowned writing teachers on faculty. One hundred seminars and workshops in fiction, nonfiction, screenwriting, children's books, cookbooks, playwriting, magazine writing, poetry, and more. **Contact:** Shannon Tullius, P.O. Box 1118, Kihei, HI 96753. 808-879-0061. E-mail: writers@maui.net. Website: www.mauiwriters.com.

MAUI WRITERS RETREAT

Details: Held annually in August in Maui, HI. Learn from the masters during this six-day intensive program. Teaching in small, intimate, hands-on groups, the emphasis will be on how to shape and present a saleable manuscript. **Contact:** Shannon Tullius, P.O. Box 1118 Kihei, HI 96753. 808-879-0061. E-mail: writers@maui.net. Website: www.mauiwriters.com.

MYSTERY WRITERS CONFERENCE

Details: Held July 14-17, 2005 in Corte Madera, CA. Features authors, teachers, and panelists from around the country, creating an atmosphere where mystery writers learn all the clues to a successful writing career. Featured authors include Martin Cruz Smith, Harlan Coben, Ridley Pearson, Jan Burke, Lee Child, and Carl Hiaasen. **Contact:** Karen West, 51 Tamal Vista Blvd. Corte Madera, CA 94925. 415-927-0960, ext. 229. E-mail: conferences@bookpassage.com. Website: www.bookpassage.com.

NATIONAL WRITERS ASSOCIATION
FOUNDATION CONFERENCE

Details: 2005 dates TBA. Features major film producers, authors, editors, agents, publishers, and marketing specialists. Addresses both beginning and professional writers' needs by providing workshops taught by professionals in the business. **Contact:** Anita Whelchel, 3140 S Peoria St., #295 PMB, Aurora, CO 80014. 303-841-0246. E-mail: conference@nationalwriters.com. Website: www.nationalwriters.com.

NAWW ANNUAL CONFERENCE

Details: Held on April 16, 2005 in Arlington, TX. Experienced and emerging women writers unite to write. Offers workshops and keynote presentations. **Contact:** Sheri' McConnell, Founder/President, National Association of Women Writers, P.O. Box 183812, Arlington, TX 76096. 866-821-5829. E-mail: naww@onebox.com. Website: www.naww.org.

RWA ANNUAL CONFERENCE

Details: Held July 27-30, 2005 in Reno, NV. Offers workshops, author autographs, Golden Heart and RITA awards, and more. **Contact:** Romance Writers of America, 16000 Stuebner Airline, Suite 140, Spring, TX 77379. 832-717-5200. E-mail: info@rwanational.org. Website: www.rwanational.org.

LOCAL CONFERENCES/RETREATS

ANNUAL AGENTS CONFERENCE

Details: 2005 dates TBA. Provides writers an opportunity to exchange ideas and network with agents, editors, and authors. Panel and workshop discussions led by a wide range of published professional writers. **Contact:** Helen Ginger, Writers' League of Texas, 1501 W Fifth St., #E2, Austin TX 78703. 512-499-8914. E-mail: helen@writersleague.org. Website: www.writersleague.org.

ANNUAL NEW ENGLAND WRITERS CONFERENCE

Details: 2005 dates TBA. Includes a distinguished panel, seminars in all genres, poetry and fiction awards, book sales, and open reading. **Contact:** Dr. Frank Anthony and Susan Anthony, P.O. Box 5 Windsor, VT 05089. 802-674-2315. E-mail: newvtpoet@aol.com. Website: www.newenglandwriters.org.

ANNUAL WRITER'S WEEK AT UNCW

Details: Held March 21-25, 2005 at the UNCW campus in Wilmington, NC. UNCW's creative writing department hosts the Writer's Week Symposium for one week in the spring semester. Activities include workshops, panels, readings, and manuscript conferences. Previous visiting writers include Galway Kinnell, Andrea Barrett, and Tracy Kidder. **Contact:** Creative Writing Department, Univ. of North Carolina at Wilmington, 601 S College Rd. Wilmington, NC 28403. 910-962-7063.

ANNUAL WRITERS' CONFERENCE

Details: Held June 24-26, 2005 in the ancient city of Winchester, England. Offers participants the opportunity to develop creative ideas and gain technical/marketing skills under the guidance of 64 published authors, poets, playwrights, producers, and literary agents. Ten mini-courses, 20 workshops, 60 lectures/seminars and 300 one-to-one appointments. **Contact:** Barbara Large, Chinook, Southdown Rd. Shawford, Hampshire, SO21 2BY England. 44 (0)1962 712307. E-mail: writerconf@aol.com. Website: www.gmp.co.uk/writers/conference.

ANTIOCH WRITERS' WORKSHOP

Details: Held July 9-15, 2005 in Yellow Springs, OH. Small and intimate, yet professional and intense, this program offers talented faculty, morning lectures, afternoon intensive sessions, and panel discussions focusing on fiction, nonfiction, poetry, memoir, and mystery. **Contact:** Laura Carlson, Director, P.O. Box 494, Yellow Springs, OH 45387. 937-475-7357. E-mail: info@antiochwritersworkshop.com. Website: www.AntiochWritersWorkshop.com.

ARIZONA STATE POETRY SOCIETY
ANNUAL FALL CONFERENCE

Details: Held annually on a Saturday in November, locations vary. Programs vary but usually includes guest speakers/readers, workshops, etc. Winners of the ASPS annual contests are announced. Also, open readings. **Contact:** Genevieve Sargent, 1707 N Sunset Dr., Tempe, AZ 85281-1551. 480-990-7300. E-mail: aibopoet@myway.com. Website: www.azpoetry.org.

ARIZONA STATE POETRY SOCIETY
SPRING POETRY FESTIVAL

Details: Held annually on a Saturday in April, locations vary. Local poetry festival open to the public. Programs vary but usually include guest speakers/reader and/or workshops. Also, open readings. **Contact:** Genevieve Sargent, 1707 N Sunset Dr., Tempe, AZ 85281-1551. 480-990-7300. E-mail: aibopoet@myway.com. Website: www.azpoetry.org.

ASPEN SUMMER WORDS
WRITING RETREAT & LITERARY FESTIVAL

Details: 2005 dates TBA. An intensive writing retreat featuring hands-on 4-day workshops and a 2-day symposia in fiction, creative nonfiction, poetry, magazine writing, nature writing, and children's literature. The conference is complemented by a literary festival with readings, industry panels, agent meetings and social gatherings. **Contact:** Jamie Abbott, Aspen Writers' Foundation, 110 E Hallam St., Suite 116 Aspen, CO 81611. 970-925-3122. E-mail: info@aspenwriters.org. Website: www.aspenwriters.org.

BLUE HILLS WRITING INSTITUTE

Details: 2005 dates TBA. Experiment with various genres (personal essays, memoirs, autobiographies, family histories, spiritual explorations, journal writing, theraputic writing). **Contact:** Lauren Judge, Director, Curry College, 1071 Blue Hill Ave., Milton, MA 02186. 888-260-7325.

BLUE RIDGE MOUNTAIN
CHRISTIAN WRITERS CONFERENCE

Details: Held May 15-19, 2005 in Ridgecrest, NC. Designed to train, encourage, equip, and inspire Christian writers. **Contact:** Ron Pratt, One LifeWay Plaza, Nashville, TN 37234-0106. 615-251-2065. E-mail: ron.pratt@lifeway.com. Website: www.lifeway.com/christianwriters.

BOOK PASSAGE TRAVEL WRITERS
& PHOTOGRAPHERS CONFERENCE

Details: Annual conference for travel writers and photographers held August 11-14, 2005 in Corte Madera, CA. Featured authors include Isabel Allende, Bill Bryson, Tim Cahill, Don George, and Simon Winchester. **Contact:** Karen West, 51 Tamal Vista Blvd., Corte Madera, CA 94925. 415-927-0960, ext. 229. E-mail: conferences@book-passage.com. Website: www.bookpassage.com.

BUTLER UNIVERSITY CHILDREN'S
LITERATURE CONFERENCE

Details: Held January 29, 2005 at the Butler University campus in Indianapolis, IN. Opportunity to meet award-winning children's book authors and illustrators and attend sessions on topics of interest to teachers, librarians, writers, and illustrators. Also offers publisher materials/magazines and manuscript evaluations. **Contact:** R. Mullin, Kids Ink Children's Bookstore, 199 N Madison Ave., Greenwood, IN 83335. 317-882-1090. E-mail: kidsink@indy.net. Website: www.butler.edu/childlit.

CALLED TO WRITE CONFERENCE

Details: Held April 1-2, 2005 in Girard, KS. Hands-on workshops, presentations, writing exercises, panel discussions, and contests. **Contact:** Carol Russell, 894 165th St., Fort Scott, KS 66701. 620-547-2472. E-mail: rlrussell@ckt.net.

CANYONLANDS WRITERS RIVER TRIP

Details: 2005 dates TBA. Participants explore nature writing on a rafting adventure down the San Juan River. The retreat begins with an evening session in Bluff, UT followed by 4 days on the San Juan River rafting mild rapids (Class I-II). **Contact:** Canyonlands Field Institute Office Manager, P.O. Box 68, Moab, UT 84532. 800-860-5262. E-mail: info@canyonlandsfieldinst.org. Website: www.canyonlandsfieldinst.org.

CENTRUM'S PORT TOWNSEND WRITERS' CONFERENCE

Details: Held July 14-24, 2005 in Port Townsend, WA. Seaside retreat community exploring diverse opinions, styles, and genres. Critique and open-enrollment workshops available. **Contact:** Carla Vander Ven, P.O. Box 1158, Port Townsend, WA 98368. 360-385-3102. E-mail: info@centrum.org. Website: www.centrum.org.

CAPE COD WRITERS CONFERENCE PLACE IN THE SUN

Details: Held annually in Cape Cod, MA. 2005 dates TBA. Courses include fiction, memoir, journalism, historical biography, poetry, songwriting, and two manuscript preparation courses. The week includes an agent- and editor-in-residence, manuscript evaluations and personal conferences, and evening speakers and a Master Class. Scholarships available. **Contact:** Jacqueline M. Loring, Executive Director, P.O. Box 408, Osterville, MA 02655. 508-420-0200. E-mail: ccwc@capecod.net. Website: www.capecodwriterscenter.com.

COLORADO CHRISTIAN WRITERS CONFERENCE

Details: Held May 11-14, 2005 in Estes Park, CO. Christian writers conference with a faculty of 40-45 authors, editors, and agents. Five general sessions, seven continuing sessions, 42 workshops, panels, one-on-one appointments, Fiction Clinics, optional 30-minute critiques and more. **Contact:** Marlene Bagnull, Director, 316 Blanchard Rd., Drexel Hill, PA 19026. 888-760-9041. E-mail: mbagnull@aol.com. Website: www.writehisanswer.com/Colorado.

CREATIVE WRITING AT SACRED SITES

Details: Held in March 2005 in Yelapa, Mexico and July 2005 in St. Davids, Wales. Weekends at Patchwork Farm in Westhampton, MA (2005 dates TBA). **Contact:** Patricia Lee Lewis, Patchwork Farm Retreat, 292 Chesterfield Rd., Westhampton, MA 01027. 413-527-5819. E-mail: patricia@writingretreats.org. Website: www.writingretreats.org.

DESERT WRITERS WORKSHOP

Details: Held in October every year. Attendees explore inspirational and creative writing about the natural world. Also, the chance to work with noted faculty in small groups and enjoy free time to write, read, and learn about the area. CFI staff lead short field trips to natural and cultural historic sites. **Contact:** Canyonlands Field Institute Office Manager, P.O. Box 68, Moab, UT 84532. 800-860-5262. E-mail: info@canyonlandsfieldinst.org. Website: www.canyonlandsfieldinst.org.

DOLCE VITA WRITERS' HOLIDAY

Details: Seven-day holiday in Italy, March & October; includes five sessions of writing and marketing instructions, three cooking classes with an Italian chef, and sightseeing. **Contact:** Michael Sedge, The Sedge Group, Via Venezia 14/b80021, Afragola (NA) Italy. (39) 081-851-2208. E-mail: msedge@thesedgegroup.com. Website: www.absolutewrite.com/dolcevita.

DULUTH WRITERS' WORKSHOP

Details: Held in June, 2005 on the UMN Duluth campus. Six days of creative writing sessions in poetry, fiction, and personal essay. Workshop sessions, special events, panel discussions, and presentations. **Contact:** Linda Blustin, UMD Continuing Education, 403 Darland Admin. Bldg., 1049 University Dr., Duluth, MN 55812. 218-726-6111. E-mail: lblustin@d.umn.edu. Website: www.d.umn.edu/ce/.

FLORIDA SUNCOAST WRITERS' CONFERENCE

Details: Held in February, 2005 in Tampa, FL. Offers over 45 workshops on the novel, the short story, nonfiction books and articles, poetry, memoir, mystery/suspense, fantasy, travel writing, children's and YA literature, and various other subjects relating to today's markets and opportunities for writers. Also offers a manuscript reading and consultation service, special programs, and social events. **Contact:** Renee Warmack, USF Continuing Education, 4202 E Fowler Ave. MHH-116 Tampa, FL 33620. 813-974-5731. E-mail: dcistaff@admin.usf.edu. Website: http://english.cas.usf.edu/fswc.

FWA ANNUAL CONFERENCE

Details: 2005 dates TBA. Workshops, panels, manuscript critiques, and social events. **Contact:** Marcia Rankin, Conference Chair, Florida Writer's Association, 10615 Limewood Dr., Jacksonville, FL 32257. 904-343-4188. E-mail: annmar11@msn.com. Website: www.floridawriters.net.

GIG HARBOR WRITERS' CONFERENCE

Details: Held April 29-May 1, 2005 in Gig Harbor, WA. Three days of workshops, lectures, and readings focusing on the craft of writing. Keynote speaker for 2005 is Tad Bartimus. **Contact:** Kathleen O'Brien, Key Peninsula Cultural Arts Comm., P.O. Box 826, Gig Harbor, WA 98335. 253-265-1904. E-mail: director@peninsulawritersassociation.org. Website: www.peninsulawritersassociation.org.

GREATER PHILADELPHIA CHRISTIAN WRITERS CONFERENCE

Details: Held August 11-13, 2005 in Langhorne, PA. Christian writers conference with a faculty of 35-40 authors, editors, and agents. Four general sessions, six continuing sessions, 36 workshops, panels, one-on-one appointments, optional 30-minute paid critiques, and more. **Contact:** Marlene Bagnull, Founder & Director, 316 Blanchard Rd., Drexel Hill, PA 19026. 888-760-9041. E-mail: mbagnull@aol.com. Website: www.writehisanswer.com/Philadelphia.

GLORIETA CHRISTIAN WRITERS CONFERENCE

Details: Held October 26-30, 2005 in Glorieta, NM. Offers classes, sessions, roundtables, and individual interviews with a faculty of nearly 80 editors, agents, professional writers, and other experts. **Contact:** Linda Jewell, CLASServices Inc., P.O. Box 66810, Albuquerque, NM 87193. 800-433-6633. E-mail: anna@classervices.com or linda@classervices.com. Website: www.classervices.com.

GREEN RIVER SUMMER RETREAT

Details: 2005 dates TBA. Eclectic writers' retreat with activities generated by participants: sharing, critiquing, free writing. **Contact:** Mary O'Dell, 703 Eastbridge Ct., Louisville, KY 40223. 502-245-4902. E-mail: maryodell@netzero.net. Website: www.greenriverwriters.org.

GREEN RIVER WINTER RETREAT

Details: 2005 dates TBA. Eclectic writers' retreat with activities generated by participants: sharing, critiquing, freewriting. **Contact:** Mary O'Dell, 703 Eastbridge Ct., Louisville, KY 40223. 502-245-4902. E-mail: maryodell@netzero.net. Website: www.greenriverwriters.org.

HIGHLIGHTS FOUNDATION WRITERS WORKSHOP

Details: Held July 16-23, 2005 in Chautauqua, NY. Annual retreat in western New York State for individuals interested in writing for children. Opportunity to work in individual and small-group sessions with some of the most accomplished and prominent authors, illustrators, editors, and publishers in the world of children's literature. **Contact:** Kent L. Brown Jr., 814 Court St., Honesdale, PA 18431. 570-253-1192. E-mail: contact@highlightsfoundation.org. Website: www.highlightsfoundation.org.

HIGHLIGHTS FOUNDERS WORKSHOPS

Details: Workshops offered throughout spring and fall in Honesdale, PA. Includes Picture Books A-Z; Writing from the Heart; Life in the Spotlight; Real People, Real Stories; Science and Nature Writing for Kids; and more. **Contact:** Kent L. Brown Jr., 814 Court St., Honesdale, PA 18431. 570-253-1192. E-mail: contact@highlightsfoundation.org. Website: www.highlightsfoundation.org.

JACKSON HOLE WRITERS CONFERENCE

Details: 2005 dates TBA. Directed toward fiction, screenwriting, and creative nonfiction, offering programs relevant to all three disciplines: story structure, narrative thrust, character development, work habits and business techniques. In addition, separate sessions deal with skills particular to each specialty. Agent and editor roundtable discussions are geared specifically to teach attendees how their writing can be crafted, shaped, and packaged for sale. **Contact:** Jerimiah Rieman, Univ. of Wyoming, Dept. 3972, 1000 E University Ave., Laramie, WY 82070. 877-733-3618, ext. 1. E-mail: jrieman@uwyo.edu. Website: www.jacksonholewriters.org.

KEY WEST WRITERS' WORKSHOP

Details: Five weekend workshops held in Key West, FL. Limited to a maximum of 10 participants chosen by workshop leader from sample writing submitted with application. January 14-16, 2005—Sharon Olds; January 21-23, 2005—Allan Gurganus; February 11-13, 2005—Roxana Robinson; February 18-20, 2005—Robert Stone; February 25-27, 2005—Carolyn Forché. **Contact:** Irving Weinman, Florida Keys Community College, 5901 College Rd., Key West, FL 33040. 305-296-9081, ext. 302. E-mail: weinman_i@firn.edu. Website: www.fkcc.edu/kwww.htm.

LEAGUE OF UTAH WRITERS ROUNDUP

Details: Includes speakers, workshops, and one-on-one sessions with an agent or editor. This year's theme is "Write Like an Egyptian." **Contact:** Becky Crum, 801-255-4034. E-mail: bcrum10@comcast.net. Website: www.luwrite.com.

MAYHEM IN THE MIDLANDS

Details: Held May 26-29, 2005 in Omaha, NE. Conference for the mystery genre. Panel discussions, book signings, mystery dinner. Guest of Honor: Peter Robinson. Toastmaster: Donna Andrews. **Contact:** Maggie Tarelli-Falcon, Willa Cather Branch Library, 1905 S 44th St., Omaha, NE 68105-2807. 402-444-5496. E-mail: mtarelli-falcon@omaha.lib.ne.us. Website: www.omaha.lib.ne.us/mayhem/index.htm.

MENDOCINO COAST WRITERS CONFERENCE

Details: Held June 9-11, 2005 in Fort Bragg, CA. Workshops, lecture sessions, agent/editor panels, readings, private consultations. Top presenters are all dedicated teachers as well. Limited to 100 attendees. **Contact:** Stephen Garber, College of the Redwoods, 211 Del Mar Dr., Fort Bragg, CA 95437. 707-964-7735. E-mail: mcwc@direcway.com. Website: www.mcwc.org.

MID-ATLANTIC CREATIVE NONFICTION SUMMER WRITERS' CONFERENCE

Details: Held August 9-14, 2005 in Baltimore, MD. Offers intensive workshops devoted to creative nonfiction; special concentration on marketing. **Contact:** Megan Cornett, Goucher College, 1021 Dulaney Valley Rd., Baltimore, MD 21204. 800-697-4646. E-mail: mcornett@goucher.edu. Website: www.goucher.edu/cnf.

MIDLAND WRITERS CONFERENCE

Details: 2005 dates TBA. Annual event providing a forum for beginning and established writers to exchange ideas with professionals. **Contact:** Ann C. Jarvis, 1710 W St. Andrews, Midland, MI 48640. 989-837-3435. E-mail: ajarvis@midland-mi.org. Website: www.midland-mi.org/gracedowlibrary/writers.html.

MIDWEST WRITERS WORKSHOP

Details: Held July 28-30, 2005 in Muncie, IN. Annual workshop for aspiring and published writers. Sessions (genre, marketing, etc.) and manuscript evaluations. **Contact:** Jama Bigger, Dept. of Journalism, Ball State University, Muncie, IN 47306. 765-282-1055. E-mail: info@midwestwriters.org. Website: www.midwestwriters.org.

MOLASSES POND WRITERS' RETREAT & WORKSHOP

Details: Held June 19-25, 2005 in Wakefield, NH (Lake District). Led by published writers who teach at UNH. Open to 10 writers who stay in colonial farmhouses with private bed/work areas. Submit 15-20 pages of fiction or nonfiction between February 1-March 1. No children's literature or poetry. **Contact:** Martha Barron Barrett, 15 Granite Shore, Milbridge, ME 04658. 207-546-2506. E-mail: mbbarrett@surf-global.net.

MONTROSE CHRISTIAN WRITERS CONFERENCE

Details: Held July 24-29, 2005 in Montrose, PA. Classes and workshops for all writers, beginner through experienced, published writers. **Contact:** Patti Souder, MCWC Director, Montrose Bible Conference, 5 Locust St., Montrose, PA 18801. 570-278-1001 or 800-598-5030. E-mail: mbc@montrosebible.org. Website: www.montrosebible.org/writers.htm.

NEBRASKA SUMMER WRITERS' CONFERENCE

Details: Held June 18-24, 2005 in Lincoln, NE. Features workshops and panels in novel, short story, poetry, travel, nature writing, mystery, memoir, screenwriting, publishing, and manuscript consultation. **Contact:** Jonis Agee, Dept. of English, P.O. Box 880333, University of Nebraska, Lincoln, NE 68588. 402-472-1834. E-mail: nswc@unl.edu. Website: www.nswc.org.

ODYSSEY FANTASY WRITING WORKSHOP

Details: Held June 13-July 22, 2005 in Manchester, NH. Intensive six-week workshop for writers of fantasy, science fiction, and horror, run by Jeanne Cavelos, former senior editor at Bantam Doubleday Dell and winner of the World Fantasy Award. Writers-in-residence Melanie Tem and Steve Rasnic Tem will be present. **Contact:** Jeanne Cavelos, 20 Levesque Lane, Mont Vernon, NH 03057. 603-673-6234. E-mail: jcavelos@sff.net. Website: www.sff.net/odyssey.

OKLAHOMA WRITERS FEDERATION (OWFI) CONFERENCE

Details: Held April 29-April 30, 2005 in Oklahoma City, OK. Writers, editors, and agents meet for informative programs that teach authors skills to write well and get published. **Contact:** Deborah Bouziden, 8416 Huckleberry Rd., Edmond, OK 73034. 405-282-7230. E-mail: dbouziden@cox.net. Website: www.owfi.org.

OZARK CREATIVE WRITERS CONFERENCE

Details: Held October 6-8, 2005 in Eureka Springs, AR. For writers who seriously want to become published; includes well-known authors, agents and editors in several fields. **Contact:** Marcia Camp, 1818 N Taylor St., PMB #348, Little Rock, AR 72207. 501-603-0290. E-mail: ozarkcreativewriters@earthlink.net. Website: www.ozarkcreativewriters.org.

PACIFIC NORTHWEST WRITERS ASSOCIATION SUMMER CONFERENCE

Details: Held July 7-9, 2005 in Seattle, WA. Offers workshops, seminars, and master classes that are geared for every experience level, genre, and style. Writers may also schedule appointments with agents and editors. **Contact:** Pacific Northwest Writers Assoc., P.O. Box 2016, Edmonds, WA 98020. 425-673-2665. E-mail: pnwa@pnwa.org. Website: www.pnwa.org.

PACIFIC NORTHWEST CHILDREN'S BOOK CONFERENCE FOR WRITERS AND ILLUSTRATORS

Details: 2005 dates TBA. Held on the Lewis & Clark College campus in Portland, OR. Focus is on the craft of writing and illustrating for children/young people and acquiring specific information on enhancing possibilities for publication. Contact: Elizabeth Snyder, P.O. Box 1491, Portland, OR 97207. 503-725-4186. E-mail: snydere@pdx.edu. Website: www.haystack.pdx.edu/children.

REVWRITERS WRITERS CONFERENCE

Details: Held October 8, 2005 in Sellersville, PA. For those writing for their local congregation and/or the larger Christian market. **Contact:** Rev. Sue M. Lang, P.O. Box 81, Perkasie, PA 18944. 215-453-5066. E-mail: sue@revwriter.com. Website: www.revwriter.com.

ROPEWALK WRITERS RETREAT

Details: Held February 25-27, 2005 (Winter Weekend) and June 12-18, 2005 (Summer Program) in New Harmony, IN. Gives participants an opportunity to attend workshops and to confer privately with one of six prominent writers. **Contact:** Linda Cleek, USI Extended Services, 8600 University Blvd., Evansville, IN 47712. 812-464-1863. E-mail: ropewalk@usi.edu. Website: www.ropewalk.org.

SANDHILLS WRITERS CONFERENCE

Details: Held March 17-19, 2005 on the Augusta State Univ. campus in Augusta, GA. Three-day conference for intermediate writers featuring workshops, craft sessions, lectures, manuscript critiques, and readings by fiction, poetry, nonfiction, songwriting, and children's authors. Opportunities to meet agents and editors. **Contact:** Prof. Anthony Kellman, Augusta State University, 2500 Walton Way, Augusta, GA 30904. 706-737-1500. E-mail: akellman@aug.edu. Website: www.sandhills.aug.edu.

SANTA BARBARA WRITER'S CONFERENCE

Details: Held annually the last week in June in Santa Barbara, CA. Covers all genres of writing, for a maximum of 350 students. Distinguished speakers, such as Sue Grafton, Ray Bradbury, Fannie Flagg, and Christopher Buckley are among those in attendance. **Contact:** Mary or Barnaby Conrad, P.O. Box 304, Carpinteria, CA 93014. 805-684-2250.

SEWANEE WRITERS' CONFERENCE

Details: Held July 19-31, 2005 in Sewanee, TN. Features workshops in poetry, fiction, and playwriting. Over 100 contributors, scholars, and fellows meet with renowned faculty members and visitors to discuss their work and aspects of their craft. **Contact:** Cheri B. Peters, 310 St. Luke's Hall, The University of the South, 735 University Ave., Sewanee, TN 37383. 931-598-1141. E-mail: cpeters@sewanee.edu. Website: www.sewaneewriters.org.

SOUTH CAROLINA WRITERS WORKSHOP CONFERENCE
Details: 2005 dates TBA. A three-day, writer-friendly conference featuring hands-on and lecture-style sessions and approachable faculty in a relaxed setting. Enjoy true Southern hospitality in one of the nation's top vacation areas. **Contact:** Steve Vassey, SCWW, P.O. Box 7104, Columbia, SC 29202. 803-794-0832. E-mail: vasseyws@hotmail.com. Website: www.scwriters.com.

SOUTHAMPTON COLLEGE WRITERS CONFERENCE
Details: Held July 13-24, 2005 in Southampton, NY. Provides a forum for authors of all genres to study and discuss writing. Offers inspiration and guidance through workshops, lectures, readings, small-group discussions. **Contact:** Carla Caglioti, Summer Programs, Southampton College of Long Island University, 239 Montauk Highway, Southampton, NY 11968. 631-287-8175. E-mail: writers@southampton.liu.edu. Website: www.southampton.liu.edu/summmer.

SOUTHWEST WRITERS CONFERENCE SERIES
Details: A series of one-day conferences in Albuquerque, NM, each with a genre focus. Open to writers of varying experience levels. Lectures by authors, editors, agents, and publicists. November 04—Screenwriting; February 05—SciFi/Fantasy; May 05—Romance; August 05—Children's Lit. **Contact:** Lisa Polisar, SWW 3721 Morris St. NE, Suite A, Albuquerque, NM, 87111-3611. 505-265-9485. E-mail: swriters@aol.com. Website: www.southwestwriters.org.

SPOLETO WRITERS' WORKSHOP
Details: 2005 dates TBA. Workshop for serious writers in poetry, fiction, and creative nonfiction. Includes writing exercises and focuses on new directions and fresh approaches to revision. **Contact:** CJ Everett, Director, Spoleto Arts Symposia, P.O. Box 24287, St. Croix, US Virgin Islands 00824. 212-663-4440. E-mail: clintoneve@aol.com. Website: www.spoletoarts.com.

SPRINGMINGLE
Details: 2005 dates TBA. Writers and illustrators of children's books from AL, MS, and GA gather to learn and network. Speakers typically include editors and/or authors, illustrators, art directors. Attendees can participate in critiques. **Contact:** Jo S. Kittinger, Southern Breeze/SCBWISCBWI, P.O. Box 26282, Birmingham, AL 35260. E-mail: jskittinger@bellsouth.net. Website: www.southern-breeze.org.

SQUAW VALLEY WRITERS WORKSHOP
Details: 2005 dates TBA. Assists serious writers by exploring the art and craft as well as the business of writing. Offers regular morning workshops, craft lectures, panel discussions on editing and publishing, staff readings, and brief individual conferences. Morning workshops are divided between fiction, narrative nonfiction and memoir, and will be limited to 12-13 participants. **Contact:** Brett Hall Jones, P.O. Box 1416, Nevada City, CA 95959. 530-470-8440. E-mail: brett@squawvalleywriters.org. Website: www.squawvalleywriters.org.

STEAMBOAT SPRINGS WRITERS CONFERENCE
Details: Held July 16, 2005 in Steamboat Springs, CO. Sponsored by the Steamboat Springs Arts Council. Limited registration; two instructors; four seminars. Optional pre-conference activities. Both novices and professionals are welcome. **Contact:** H. Freiberger, P.O. Box 774284, Steamboat Springs, CO 80477. 970-879-9008. E-mail: sswriters@cs.com. Website: www.steamboatwriters.com.

SUMMER SEMINAR FOR WRITERS
Details: 2005 dates TBA. Intensive week of workshops, conferences, and readings with nationally-known writers and Sarah Lawrence faculty members. **Contact:** Grant Grastorf, Sarah Lawrence College, 1 Mead Way Bronxville, NY 10708. 914-395-2412. E-mail: grantg@sarahlawrence.edu. Website: www.sarahlawrence.edu.

TEXAS CHRISTIAN WRITERS CONFERENCE
Details: Held August 6, 2005 in Houston, TX. One-day conference featuring 3-4 authors or editors plus a large group session and 2-3 workshops. Attendees will have the opportunity for one-on-one conferences with faculty. **Contact:** Martha Rogers, 6038 Greenmont, Houston, TX 77092. 713-686-7209. E-mail: marthalrogers@sbc-global.net.

TMCC WRITERS' CONFERENCE
Details: Held April 7-10, 2005 in Reno, NV. Offers small critique sessions (9 fiction writers or 12 poets), lectures on craft and marketing, and networking opportunities with speakers. Writing submission (up to six poems or no more than 5,000 words of fiction) is required to apply. Call, e-mail, or see website for more information. **Contact:** Kathy Berry, Marketing Coordinator, Truckee Meadows Community Services, 5270 Neil Rd., #216, Reno, NV 89502. 775-824-8626. E-mail: kberry@tmcc.edu. Website: http://commserv.tmcc.edu.

WALLOON WRITERS' RETREAT
Details: 2005 dates TBA. Writers and poets, new and established, attend workshops, readings, and panel discussions. Past faculty include Jacquelyn Mitchard, Joyce Maynard, Thomas Lux, Christopher Castellani, Craig Holden, and Clare Rossini. **Contact:** John D. Lamb, Springfed Arts, P.O. Box 304 Royal Oak, MI 48068. 248-589-3913. E-mail: johndlamb@ameritech.net. Website: www.springfed.org.

WASHINGTON WRITERS CONFERENCE
Details: 2005 dates TBA. Offers panels and workshops on a broad array of writing-related topics, meetings with agents, and manuscript critiques. See website for more details. **Contact:** Joe Barbato, 733 15th St. NW, Suite 220, Washington, DC 20005. 202-737-9500. E-mail: info@washwriter.org. Website: www.washwriter.org.

WESLEYAN WRITERS CONFERENCE

Details: Held third week in June 2005 in Middletown, CT. Covers the novel, short story, fiction techniques, poetry, memoir, and literary journalism. The program includes seminars, lectures, readings, manuscript consultations, and publishing advice. Welcomes established writers, new writers, and anyone seeking a fuller understanding of the writer's craft. **Contact:** Anne Greene, Director, Wesleyan Univ., 279 Court St., Middletown, CT 06459. 860-685-3604. E-mail: agreene@wesleyan.edu. Website: www.wesleyan.edu/writers.

WEST CHESTER UNIVERSITY POETRY CONFERENCE

Details: Held June 8-11, 2005 in West Chester, PA. Combines a writers conference with a scholarly conference. Focuses on the traditional craft of poetry. **Contact:** Amy Brubaker, Dept. of English, Main Hall West Chester University, West Chester, PA 19382. 610-436-3235. E-mail: poetry@wcupa.edu. Website: www.wcupa.edu/_academics/sch_cas/poetry/.

WHITE COUNTY CREATIVE WRITERS CONFERENCE

Details: Held annually on Labor Day Weekend. Featured speakers, contests, social events for fiction writers. "In 2005 we will be celebrating our 10th anniversary, so we are planning to do something special." **Contact:** Christine Henderson, V.P., White County Creative Writers, P.O.Box 9122, Searcy, AR 72145. E-mail: wcwriters@hotmail.com. Website: www.whitecountycreativewriters.org.

WILLAMETTE WRITERS CONFERENCE

Details: Held August 5-7, 2005 in Portland, OR. Offers workshops in a variety of genres. **Contact:** Bill Johnson, 9045 SW Barbur Blvd., #5A, Portland, OR 97219. 503-452-1592. E-mail: wilwrite@teleport.com. Website: www.willamettewriters.com.

WRITE ON THE SOUND WRITERS CONFERENCE

Details: Held October 1-2, 2005 in Edmonds, WA. Over 20 individual workshops are presented by noted authors, educators and trade professionals who share their secrets, talents, and literary visions. A variety of workshops are offered, designed to appeal to beginning as well as seasoned writers. Also offers a contest, book signings and manuscript critiques. **Contact:** Frances Chapin or Kris Gillespie, 700 Main St., Edmonds, Washington 98020. 425-771-0228. E-mail: wots@ci.edmonds.wa.us. Website: www.ci.edmonds.wa.us/ArtsCommission/index.stm.

WRITE-BY-THE-LAKE WRITER'S WORKSHOP & RETREAT

Details: 2005 dates TBA. Workshops on poetry, fiction, screenwriting, mystery, children's writing and freelancing. Each section limited to 15 participants. **Contact:** Christine DeSmet, 610 Langdon St., Rm. 621, Madison, WI 53703. 608-262-3447. E-mail: cdesmet@dcs.wisc.edu. Website: www.dcs.wisc.edu/lsa/writing.

WRITE-TO-PUBLISH CONFERENCE

Details: Held June 8-11, 2005 in Wheaton, IL. Conference with classes/workshops for beginners through professionals with interest in the Christian book market. Also offers appointments with editors/agents, editor panels, and manuscript evaluations. College credit offered. **Contact:** Lin Johnson, 9731 N Fox Glen Dr., #6F, Niles, IL 60714. 847-296-3964. E-mail: brochure@writetopublish.com. Website: www.write-topublish.com.

WRITERS AT WORK

Details: Held June 20-25, 2005 at Westminster College in Salt Lake City, UT. Workshops in which students discuss writing techniques with nationally renowned instructors and writers, and participate in lectures, panels, readings, and one-on-one manuscript consultations with professional editors/agents. **Contact:** Lisa Peterson, P.O. Box 540370, North Salt Lake, UT 84054. 801-292-9285. E-mail: lisa@writersat-work.org. Website: www.writersatwork.org.

WRITERS INSTITUTE

Details: Held July 21-22, 2005 in Madison, WI. Sessions focus on fiction and non-fiction topics, as well as marketing and career issues. Sessions for beginners and advanced. Agents and editors also attend. **Contact:** Christine DeSmet, 610 Langdon St., Rm. 621, Madison, WI 53703. 608-262-3447. E-mail: cdesmet@dcs.wisc.edu. Website: www.dcs.wisc.edu.

WRITERS STUDIO AT UCLA

Details: Held February 3-6, 2005 at the UCLA Extension campus in Los Angeles, CA. Intensive four days of instruction and writing. Participants choose one of 10 workshops in which they work closely with a professional writer in classes limited to no more than 20 people. Focus on creative writing and screenwriting. **Contact:** Jennifer Danylyshyn, Program Assistant, UCLA Extension, Writers' Program Rm. 44010995, Le Conte Ave., Los Angeles, CA 90024. 310-825-0107. E-mail: writers@uclaextension.edu. Website: www.uclaextension.edu/writers.

WRITING AND ILLUSTRATING FOR KIDS

Details: Held in October, 2005 in Birmingham, AL. An all-day conference focused on the business of writing and illustrating for the children's market. Attendees will enjoy a keynote address and the opportunity to chose from approximately 30 workshops in four sessions. Faculty typically includes editors, an agent, authors, illustrators and sometimes an art director. Attendees may sign up for individual critiques or participate in informal critique groups. **Contact:** Brenda Posey, Southern Breeze, SCBWI, P.O. Box 26282 Birmingham, AL 35360. E-mail: b_posey@bellsouth.net. Website: www.southern-breeze.org.

YOUNG PLAYWRIGHTS URBAN RETREAT

Details: 2005 dates TBA. Weeklong intensive playwriting program for writers ages 14-21. Writers attend workshops, develop new material, and collaborate with professional directors, dramaturges, and actors on short plays created during the retreat. Young Playwrights, Inc., 306 W 38th St., Suite 300, New York, NY 10018. 212-594-5440. E-mail: writeaplay@aol.com. Website: www.youngplaywrights.org.

CLASSES/WORKSHOPS

APPALACHIAN WRITERS WORKSHOP
Details: Held July 31-August 5, 2005 in Hindman, KY. Well-known authors who are from and/or write about Appalachia teach workshops in several genres. Includes seminars, conferences with staff, nightly readings and book signings, readings by participants, sharing and learning. **Contact:** Mike Mullins, Hindman Settlement School, P.O. Box 844, Hindman, KY 41822. 606-785-5475. E-mail: mlm@tgtel.com. Website: www.hindmansettlement.org.

AUTOBIOGRAPHY OF THE SOUL
Details: 2005 dates TBA. Ten-day workshop with Sharon Doubiago. Designed for those desiring to look further inside their souls to connect with and write from their true voices. This class is appropriate for writers of all skill levels and experience, whether you publish poetry, write prose, or simply enjoy journaling. **Contact:** Liza Fourre, Director, Art Workshops in Guatemala, 4758 Lyndale Ave. S, Minneapolis, MN 55409. 612-825-0747. E-mail: info@artguat.org. Website: www.artguat.org.

BLOODY WORDS
Details: Held June 10-12, 2005 in Toronto, ON. Covers the mystery genre. Panels, discussions, readings, workshops, and banquet. Guests of honor: Anne Perry and Maureen Jennings. **Contact:** Cheryl Freedman, 17 Wales Ave., Toronto, Ontario M5T 1J2 Canada. 613-238-2583. E-mail: info@bloodywords.com. Website: www.bloodywords.com.

BLUEGRASS WRITERS SEMINAR
Details: Held October 14-16, 2005 in Louisville, KY. Workshops teaching how to create strong article leads, successful marketing query letters, captivating photo illustration captions, as well as how to conduct compassionate interviews, research, etc. **Contact:** Bill Thomas, P.O. Box 59, Glendale, KY 42740. 270-769-1823. Website: www.touchofsuccess.com.

CHILDREN'S BOOK WRITING AND ILLUSTRATING WORKSHOPS
Details: Held July 11-14, 2005 in New York, NY. Four-day intensive focusing on writing and illustrating children's picture books. Master class limited to 10 participants and is geared for the beginning and advanced author and/or artist. **Contact:** Robert Quackenbush, 460 E 79th St., New York, NY 10021. 212-744-3822. E-mail: rqstudios@aol.com. Website: www.rquackenbush.com.

CLASSEMINAR

Details: 2005 dates TBA. CLASS (Christian Leaders, Authors & Speakers Services) offers intensive three-day seminar with training in communication skills for both the spoken and written word. **Contact:** Anna Jones or Linda Jewell, CLASServices Inc., P.O. Box 66810, Albuquerque, NM 87193. 800-433-6633. E-mail: anna@classervices.com or linda@classervices.com. Website: www.classervices.com.

THE CLEARING WRITING WORKSHOPS

Details: Ongoing series of writing workshops in Ellison Bay, WI. Weekly classes range from Writing Your Life to poetry workshops, beginning and advanced writing classes. Past instructors include Norbert Blei, Judy Bridges, Jerry Apps, and John Lehman. **Contact:** The Clearing, P.O. Box 65, Ellison Bay, WI 54210. 920-854-5584. E-mail: clearing@theclearing.org. Website: www.theclearing.org.

HARVARD SUMMER SCHOOL WRITING PROGRAM

Details: Held June-August at the Harvard campus in Cambridge, MA. For writers at all levels, this program offers small classes, college credit, student-faculty readings, a published journal of student work, and workshops on special topics. **Contact:** Patricia Bellanca, Harvard Summer School Writing Program, 51 Brattle St. Cambridge, MA 02138. 617-496-8674. E-mail: summer@hudce.harvard.edu. Website: www.summer.harvard.edu.

TONY HILLERMAN WRITERS CONFERENCE

Details: 2005 dates TBA. Sessions on the art of the mystery with Tony Hillerman and others, as well as law enforcement professionals. **Contact:** Anne Hillerman, Santa Fe Workshops and Tours, 304 Calle Oso, Santa Fe, NM 87501. 505-471-1565. E-mail: wordharvest@yahoo.com. Website: www.sfworkshops.com.

HOW TO BE PUBLISHED WORKSHOPS

Details: Ongoing workshops throughout the year in various locations. Topics include marketing tips, query letters, manuscript structure, components of an effective novel, viewpoint, etc. **Contact:** Michael Garrett, P.O. Box 100031, Birmingham, AL 35210. 205-907-0140. E-mail: bookdoctor@bham.rr.com. Website: www.writing2sell.com.

IOWA SUMMER WRITING FESTIVAL

Details: 2005 dates TBA. Short-term, noncredit writing programs for adults, offered by The University of Iowa. 137 week-long and weekend workshops across the genres, including novel, short fiction, poetry, essay, memoir, humor, playwriting, writing for children and more. **Contact:** Amy Margolis, 100 Oakdale Campus, W310, University of Iowa, Iowa City, IA 52242. 319-335-4160. E-mail: iswfestival@uiowa.edu. Website: www.uiowa.edu/~iswfest.

METAPHOR & MYTH: A POETRY WORKSHOP

Details: Held October 2-3, 2004 (2005 dates TBA) in Madison, WI. Weekend workshop exploring poetry, sharing optional critique, and developing strategies for writing and publishing poetry. **Contact:** Laurel Yourke, 620 Lowell Center, 610 Langdon St., Madison, WI 53703-1195. 608-265-3972. E-mail: lyourke@dcs.wis.edu. Website: www.dcs.wisc.edu/classes.

NAWW AUTUMN WORKSHOP IN FLORIDA

Details: Held October 16, 2005 in Tampa, FL. Experienced and emerging writers will meet in Florida to unite to write. Workshops and networking. **Contact:** Sheri' McConnell, Founder/President, National Association of Women Writers, P.O. Box 183812, Arlington, TX 76096. 866-821-5829. E-mail: naww@onebox.com. Website: www.naww.org.

NAWW SUMMER WORKSHOP IN CALIFORNIA

Details: 2005 dates TBA. Experienced and emerging women writers meet in California to unite to write. Workshops and networking. **Contact:** Sheri' McConnell, Founder/President, National Association of Women Writers, P.O. Box 183812, Arlington, TX 76096. 866-821-5829. E-mail: naww@onebox.com. Website: www.naww.org.

NEW DIRECTIONS IN TRAVEL WRITING

Details: 2005 dates TBA. Ten-day workshop with Richard Harris. Practical writing exercises will hone your ability to capture places on paper-challenging you to observe and describe the people and places of Guatemala. Richard will spend one-on-one time with each student so he/she receives a personalized critique of their travel writing and ideas. **Contact:** Liza Fourre, Director, Art Workshops in Guatemala, 4758 Lyndale Ave. S, Minneapolis, MN 55409. 612-825-0747. E-mail: info@artguat.org. Website: www.artguat.org.

NOVELS-IN-PROGRESS WORKSHOP

Details: Held March 13-20, 2005 in Louisville, KY. Daily seminars and personal instruction, small group critique, one-on-one meetings with agents and editors. **Contact:** Jeff Yocom, Chairman, Green River Writers, Inc., 2011 Lauderdale Rd., Louisville, KY 40205. 502-417-5514. E-mail: novelsinprogress@bellsouth.net. Website: www.greenriverwriters.org/nipw.html.

POETRY SNAPSHOTS IN WORDS

Details: 2005 dates TBA. Ten-day workshop with Roseann Lloyd. Observing. Recording. Describing. With paper and pencil, participants observe their surroundings with the same nonjudgmental eye as a camera. **Contact:** Liza Fourre, Director, Art Workshops in Guatemala, 4758 Lyndale Ave. S, Minneapolis, MN 55409. 612-825-0747. E-mail: info@artguat.org. Website: www.artguat.org.

PORTLAND STATE UNIVERSITY
HAYSTACK SUMMER PROGRAM IN THE ARTS

Details: Held July 11-August 5, 2005 in Cannon Beach, OR. Weekend and week-long creative arts workshops on the north Oregon coast. Covers fiction, poetry, nonfiction, screenwriting, book publishing, dangerous writing and essay. Instructors include Diana Abu-Jaber, Judith Barrington, Gary Ferguson, Molly Gloss, Karen Karbo and Tom Spanbauer. **Contact:** Elizabeth Snyder, P.O. Box 1491, Portland, OR 97207. 503-725-4186. E-mail: snydere@pdx.edu. Website: www.haystack.pdx.edu.

PRAGUE SUMMER PROGRAM

Details: 2005 dates TBA. Study abroad program for writers and photographers. Partcipants have the opportunity to be mentored by some of the biggest names in world photography or contemporary English-language literature. **Contact:** Richard Katrovas, Academic Director, Western Michigan University, 1903 W Michigan Ave., Kalamazoo, MI 49008. 269-387-2594. E-mail: prague@wmich.edu. Website: www.wmich.edu/studyabroad/prague.

PUBLISHING INSTITUTE

Details: 2005 dates TBA. Intensive, full-time, 4-week graduate level course on all aspects of book publishing. Workshops and teaching sessions in editing, marketing, and production. Also, career counseling sessions and job fair during final week. **Contact:** Jill Smith, Associate Director, 2075 S University Blvd., D-114, Denver, CO 80210. 303-871-2570. E-mail: jsmith7@du.edu. Website: www.du.edu/pi.

RETREAT FROM HARSH REALITY

Details: Held April 22-24, 2005 in Stanwood, MI. Sponsored by the Mid-Michigan chapter of Romance Writers of America. Offers a casual atmosphere with a chance for learning, sharing and one-on-one conversations about writing. Keynote speaker: Elizabeth Grayson. **Contact:** Pam Trombley, Retreat Chair, 6845 Forest Way, Harbor Springs, MI 49740. 231-526-2153. E-mail: ptrombley@voyager.net. Website: www.midmichiganrwa.com.

SMOKIES IN THE SPRINGTIME WRITERS SEMINAR

Details: Held April 7-10, 2005 in Townsend, TN. Explicit instructions on how to break into writing nonfiction for national magazines, leading newspapers, captivating photo illustration captions, and how to create irresistable query letters and book proposals for the adult and children's markets. Also, information on how to conduct interviews and do research. **Contact:** Bill Thomas, Touch of Success Writing Seminars, Box 1436, Dunnellon, FL 34430. 352-867-0463. Website: www.touchofsuccess.com.

SPLIT ROCK ARTS PROGRAM

Details: Held July 3-August 13, 2005 in Minneapolis/St. Paul, MN. Workshops in a variety of genres (poetry, short story, novel, memoir, personal and travel essay, and more) taught by renowned writers from around the world. Graduate/undergraduate credit, scholarships, and high-amenity on-campus housing available. **Contact:** Andrea Gilats, Program Director, Split Rock Arts Program, University of Minnesota, 360 Coffey Hall, 1420 Eckles Ave., St. Paul, MN 55108. 612-625-8100. E-mail: srap@cce.umn.edu. Website: www.cce.umn.edu/splitrockarts.

SPRING WRITERS FESTIVAL

Details: Held April 15-17, 2005 at the Univ. of Wisconsin campus in Milwaukee, WI. Features nationally and regionally known authors sharing insights on the craft and business of writing and leading workshops and discussions. Participants have the opportunity to meet with professionals for individual critiques of writing samples. **Contact:** Anne O'Meara, UWM School of Continuing Education, 161 W Wisconsin Ave., Suite 7000, Milwaukee, WI 53203. 414-227-3311. E-mail: aomeara@uwm.edu. Website: www.sce-arts.uwm.edu.

STANZAS AND SECRETS: A POETRY WORKSHOP

Details: Held March 12-13, 2005 in Madison, WI. Weekend workshop exploring poetry, sharing optional critiques, and developing strategies for both writing and publishing poetry. **Contact:** Laurel Yourke, 620 Lowell Center, 610 Langdon St., Madison, WI 53703-1195. 608-265-3972. E-mail: lyourke@dcs.wisc.edu. Website: www.dcs.wisc.edu/classes.

SUMMER WRITING PROGRAM

Details: Held June 13-July 10, 2005 in Boulder, CO. Four-week long conference and workshop for students, poets, fiction writers, translators, performance artists, activists, Buddhist teachers, musicians, printers, editors, and others working in small press publishing. **Contact:** Lisa Birman, Co-Director, Naropa University, Summer Writing Program, 2130 Arapahoe Ave., Boulder, CO 80302. 303-546-5296. E-mail: lisab@naropa.edu. Website: www.naropa.edu.

TIN HOUSE SUMMER WRITERS WORKSHOP

Details: 2005 dates TBA. Eight-day writing intensive in Portland, OR consisting of morning workshops, afternoon craft seminars and publishing panels, and evening readings. Topics include fiction, nonfiction, poetry, film. **Contact:** Lee Montgomery, Director, *Tin House Magazine*, P.O. Box 10500 Portland, OR 97210. 503-219-0622. E-mail: summerworkshop@tinhouse.com. Website: www.tinhouse.com.

WILDBRANCH WORKSHOP IN OUTDOOR, NATURAL HISTORY AND ENVIRONMENTAL WRITING

Details: Held annually the second week in June in Craftsbury Common, VT. Week-long workshop of classes, lectures, discussion groups, and readings in the craft and techniques of fine writing about the world outdoors. Limited to 30 participants. **Contact:** David Brown, Sterling College, P.O. Box 72, Craftsbury Common, VT 05827. 800-648-3591. E-mail: wldbrnch@sterlingcollege.edu. Website: www.sterlingcollege.edu/wildbranch.htm.

WRITERS WORKSHOP IN SCIENCE FICTION

Details: Held June 26-July 10, 2005 in Lawrence, KS. Intensive workshop involving critiquing of three stories each, aimed at preparing writers to publish regularly. Culminates with the Campbell Conference (July 8-10) and Sturgeon Awards for the best science fiction novel and best short science fiction of the year. **Contact:** James

Gunn, English Dept., Univ. of Kansas, Lawrence, KS 66045. 785-864-3380. E-mail: jgunn@ku.edu. Website: www.ku.edu/~sfcenter.

WRITING A SUCCESSFUL SCREENPLAY

Details: Held February 26, 2005 in Madison, WI. Offers writing programs relevant to fiction, screenwriting, and creative nonfiction. Topics include story structure, narrative thrust, character development, work habits, and business techniques. **Contact:** Univ. of Wisconsin-Madison Liberal Studies & the Arts, 610 Langdon St., Rm. 616, Lowell Center, Madison, WI 53703. 608-262-3447. E-mail: cdesmet@dcs.wisc.edu. Website: www.dcs.wisc.edu/lsa/writing.

WRITING FROM THE WELL,
A WRITING WORKSHOP FOR WOMEN

Details: 2005 dates TBA. An intensive one-day creative writing workshop for women, utilizing the Amherst Writers & Artists method, held in Menlo Park, CA. Exercises are designed to inspire and tap into the well of life stories. **Contact:** Sharon A. Bray, 858 Arbor Rd., Menlo Park, CA 94025. 650-575-8372. E-mail: sharon@wellspringwriters.org. Website: www.wellspringwriters.org.

WRITING THE REGION:
MARJORIE KINNAN RAWLINGS WRITERS WORKSHOP

Details: Held July 20-24, 2005 in Gainesville, FL. Five-day workshop featuring fiction, nonfiction, poetry, and memoir. **Contact:** Norma M. Homan, P.O. Box 12246, Gainesville, FL 32604. 888-917-7001. E-mail: shakes@ufl.edu. Website: www.writingtheregion.com.

WRITING WITH STYLE

Details: 2005 dates TBA. Week-long workshop for writers of all levels. Writers are given the opportunity to edit and shape a manuscript under the guidance of an experienced writer or editor. **Contact:** Office of the Registrar, The Banff Centre, Box 1020, 107 Tunnel Mountain Rd., Banff, AB, T1L 1H5 Canada. 800-565-9989. E-mail: arts_info@banffcentre.ca. Website: www.banffcentre.ca.

YALE SUMMER PROGRAMS

Details: 2005 dates TBA. College-level creative writing courses in journalism, playwriting, poetry, fiction, and nonfiction. **Contact:** Yale University, P.O. Box 208733, New Haven, CT 06520. 203-432-2430. E-mail: summer.programs@yale.edu. Website: www.yale.edu/summer.

CONTESTS & AWARDS

Writers seeking the thrill of competition should review this list of literary prize offers, many designed to promote the as-yet-unpublished author. Most of the competitions listed here are for unpublished manuscripts and usually offer publication in addition to a cash prize. The prestige that comes with winning one of the more established awards can do much to further a writer's career, as editors, publishers, and agents are likely to consider the future work of the prize winner more closely.

There are hundreds of literary contests open to writers in all genres, and the following list covers a representative number of them. The summaries given below are intended merely as guides; since submission requirements are more detailed than space allows, writers should send an SASE for complete guidelines before entering any contest. Writers are also advised to check the monthly "Prize Offerings" column of *The Writer* magazine (Kalmbach Publishing Co., 21027 Crossroads Circle, P.O. Box 1612, Waukesha, WI 53187-1612) for additional contest listings and up-to-date contest requirements. Deadlines are annual unless otherwise noted.

POETRY

AKRON POETRY PRIZE

University of Akron Press, 374B Bierce Library, Akron, OH 44325-1703. 330-972-6896. uapress@uakron.edu. www.uakron.edu/uapress/poetryprize. **Details:** Offered annually for a collection of poems, 60-100 pages. Include list of previously published poems. **Submission Period:** May 15-June 30. **Entry Fee:** $25/submission. **Prizes:** $1,000 and publication.

ANHINGA PRIZE FOR POETRY

Anhinga Press, P.O. Box 10595, Tallahassee, FL 32302-0595. 850-442-1408. info@anhinga.org. www.anhinga.org. **Details:** Offered annually for an unpublished full-length collection of poetry, 48-72 pages, by a poet who has published no more than one full-length collection. **Submission Period:** February 15-May 1. **Entry Fee:** $20. **Prizes:** $2,000 and publication.

ANNUAL TENNESSEE CHAPBOOK PRIZE

Poems & Plays, Middle Tennessee State University, English Dept., Murfreesboro, TN 37132. gbrewer@mtsu.edu. **Details:** Poems and/or short plays eligible. Send 20-24 page manuscript, include acknowledgements and SASE. Winning entry published as interior chapbook in *Poems & Plays*. **Deadline:** December 31. **Entry Fee:** $10 (entrants receive copy of issue). **Prizes:** Publication and 50 copies. **Contact:** Gaylord Brewer, Editor.

TUPELO PRESS POETRY PRIZE FOR A FIRST BOOK

Tupelo Press, P.O. Box 539, Dorset, VT 05251. 802-366-8185. editors@tupelopress.org. www.tupelopress.org. **Details:** Accepts submissions of unpublished, full-length collections of poetry by poets who have not yet published a full collection. Submit full-length poetry manuscript between 50-80 pages. **Submission Period:** January 1-April 15 (postmarked). **Entry Fee:** $25. **Prizes:** Judge's prize of $3,000 and Editors' prize of $1,000, publication and distribution to the trade by Consortium Book Sales & Distribution. **Tips:** Send SASE or visit website for complete guidelines. **Contact:** Margaret Donovan, Managing Editor.

MURIEL CRAFT BAILEY MEMORIAL AWARD

Comstock Review, Attn: TW, Contests 2004, 4956 St. John Dr., Syracuse, NY 13215. poetry@comstockreview.org. www.comstockreview.org. **Details:** Submit original, unpublished poetry, no more than 40 lines/poem. No simultaneous submissions. Include SASE for notification. **Deadline:** July 1. **Entry Fee:** $3/poem. **Prizes:** $1,000, $250, $100. **Tips:** See website for complete rules. **Contact:** Peggy Flanders, Managing Editor.

BARNARD WOMEN POETS PRIZE

Barnard College, Dept. of English, 3009 Broadway, New York, NY 10027-6598. iwd2002@columbia.edu. www.barnard.columbia.edu/english/wpprize.html. **Details:** Prize given for a second book of poetry by a woman poet who has already published one book of poetry. Include SASE for notification. **Deadline:** October 15. **Entry Fee:** $20. **Prizes:** Honorarium of $1,500 and publication by W.W. Norton & Co. **Contact:** Ian Douglas.

BARROW STREET PRESS BOOK CONTEST

Barrow Street Press, Murray Hill Station, P.O. Box 1831, New York, NY 10156. info@barrowstreet.org. www.barrowstreet.org. **Details:** Given for the best previously unpublished manuscript of poetry (50-70 pages) in English. **Deadline:** June 30. **Entry Fee:** $25. **Prizes:** $1,000 and publication by Barrow Street Press.

BATTLE OF THE BARDS POETRY CONTEST

WriteLink, The Competition Secretary, 7 Melbourne Rd., Newbold, Coleorton, Leicestershire LE67 8JH, UK. sue@writelink.co.uk. www.writelink.co.uk. **Details:** Online poetry contest designed to put an end to procrastination: theme and word count are provided with 24 hours to complete the entry. Limited to 100; e-mail entries only. **Entry Fee:** £4.50 or $8. **Prizes:** £50 for winner and £25 each for two runners-up. **Tips:** See website for detailed guidelines.

ELINOR BENEDICT POETRY PRIZE

Passages North, Northern Michigan University, 1401 Presque Isle Ave., Marquette, MI 49855. 906-227-1203. passages@nmu.edu. http:myweb.nmu.edu/~passages. **Details:** Offered every other year. **Deadline:** December 31. **Entry Fee:** $8 for 1-5 poems. **Prizes:** $1,000. **Contact:** Deanna Fleischmann, Managing Editor.

THE BLUESTEM POETRY AWARD

Emporia State University, English Dept., Emporia, KS 66801-5087. 620-341-5216. bluestem@emporia.edu. www.emporia.edu/bluestem/. **Details:** Open to U.S. authors. Submit a previously unpublished book of poems at least 48 pages, written in English. **Deadline:** March 1. **Entry Fee:** $20. **Prizes:** $1,000 and publication. **Tips:** Send SASE or visit website for guidelines. **Contact:** Philip Heldrich, Director.

JOY BALE BOONE POETRY AWARD

Wind: A Journal of Writing & Community, P.O. Box 24548, Lexington, KY 40524. erik@uky.edu. www.wind.wind.org. **Details:** Submit any number of unpublished poems of 100 lines or less. **Deadline:** March 1 (postmark). **Entry Fee:** $3/poem. **Prizes:** Finalists: 1 year subscription; Winner: $500 and publication in *Wind*. **Contact:** Erik Brandon Tuttle, Co-Contest Coordinator.

BARBARA BRADLEY AWARD

New England Poetry Club, 16 Cornell St., Arlington, MA 02476-7710. info@nepoetryclub.org. www.nepoetryclub.org. **Details:** Open to female poets; submit an unpublished lyric poem under 21 lines. **Submission Period:** April 1-June 30. **Entry Fee:** Free for members; $10 for non-members. **Prizes:** $200. **Tips:** Entrants may submit up to 3 entries total out of all the contests sponsored by NEPC, but no more than 1 poem per contest. Send SASE or see website for specific guidelines and fees. **Contact:** Elizabeth Crowell, Contest Co-ordinator.

JOSEPH E. BRODINE/BRODINSKY POETRY CONTEST

Connecticut Poetry Society, P.O. Box 4053, Waterbury, CT 06704-0053. 203-753-7815. **Details:** Original, unpublished poetry up to 40 lines. Maximum 5 poems per contest. **Submission Period:** May 1-July 31. **Entry Fee:** $2/poem. **Prizes:** Cash prizes ($150, $100, $50) and Honorable Mentions. **Tips:** Identify each submission as Brodine/Brodinsky Contest. No simultaneous submissions.

HAYDEN CARRUTH AWARD FOR EMERGING POETS

Copper Canyon Press, P.O. Box 271, Port Townsend, WA 98368. 360-385-4925. poetry@coppercanyonpress.org. www.coppercanyonpress.org. **Details:** Open to new and emerging poets only. Send manuscript for first, second, or third book of poetry. **Submission Period:** November 1-November 30. **Entry Fee:** $25. **Prizes:** $1,000, publication by Copper Canyon Press, and 1-month residency at the Vermont Studio Center. **Tips:** See website for complete details and entry form.

COLORADO PRIZE FOR POETRY

Colorado Review, Colorado State University, Dept. of English, Fort Collins, CO 80523. 970-491-5449. creview@colostate.edu. www.coloradoreview.com. **Details:** A prize of $1,500, plus publication, for a book-length collection of original poems. **Submission Period:** October 1-January 15. **Entry Fee:** $25 (includes subscription to *Colorado Review*). **Tips:** See website or send SASE for guidelines.

CONNECTICUT RIVER REVIEW POETRY CONTEST

Connecticut Poetry Society, P.O. Box 4053, Waterbury, CT 06704-0053.
203-753-7815. editorcrr@yahoo.com (for queries only). **Details:** Submit up to 3
poems, 40 lines max. Include 2 copies (only 1 with contact info) and SASE for results.
No e-mail submissions. **Submission Period:** December 1-March 1. **Entry Fee:**
$10. **Prizes:** Cash prizes ($25, $50, $100) and publication in *Connecticut River
Review*.

THE CONTEMPORARY POETRY SERIES

University of Georgia Press, 330 Research Dr., Athens, GA 30602-4901. 706-369-
6130. books@ugapress.uga.edu. www.ugapress.org. **Details:** Four books of poetry
are selected each year for publication by both emerging and established poets.
Manuscripts must be at least 50 pages. **Submission Period:** Poets who have not
published a full-length collection must submit during the month of September. Poets
who have published at least 1 full-length collection must submit during the month of
January. **Entry Fee:** $20. **Prizes:** Publication by the University of Georgia Press.

DIANA DER-HOVANESSIAN PRIZE

New England Poetry Club, 16 Cornell St., Arlington, MA 02476-7710.
info@nepoetryclub.org. www.nepoetryclub.org. **Details:** Open to unpublished translations from any language. Send copy of original with submission. **Submission
Period:** April 1-June 30. **Entry Fee:** Free to members; $10 for non-members.
Prizes: $100. **Tips:** Entrants may submit up to 3 entries total out of all the contests
sponsored by NEPC, but no more than 1 poem/contest. Send SASE or see website
for specific guidelines and fees. **Contact:** Elizabeth Crowell, Contest Co-ordinator.

SUE SANIEL ELKIND POETRY CONTEST

Kalliope: a journal of women's literature & art
Florida Community College at Jacksonville, 11901 Beach Blvd., Jacksonville, FL
32245. 904-646-2081. www.fccj.org/kalliope. **Details:** Submit poetry in any style on
any subject, no more than 50 lines/poem. No limit on number of entries submitted.
Poems that have been previously published or have received monetary awards are not
eligible. **Deadline:** November 1. **Entry Fee:** $4/poem or $10/3 poems. **Prizes:**
$1,000 and publication in *Kalliope*. **Contact:** Mary Sue Koeppel, Editor.

FIELD POETRY PRIZE

FIELD: Contemporary Poetry and Poetics
Oberlin College Press, 10 N Professor St., Oberlin, OH 44074. 440-775-8408.
oc.press@oberlin.edu. www.oberlin.edu/ocpress. **Details:** Open to unpublished
poetry manuscripts, 50-80 pages. **Submission Period:** Must be postmarked in May.
Entry Fee: $22; includes one-year subscription to *FIELD*. **Prizes:** $1,000 and publication. **Tips:** See website for specific details.

FOUR WAY BOOKS INTRO PRIZE IN POETRY

Four Way Books, 225 Lincoln Place #5C, Brooklyn, NY 11217. 212-334-5430. four_way_editors@yahoo.com. www.fourwaybooks.com. **Details:** Open to all U.S. poets who have not published a book-length collection of poetry. **Deadline:** March 31. **Entry Fee:** $25/manuscript. **Prizes:** $1,000 honorarium, book publication, and a reading at Readings on the Bowery in New York City. **Tips:** Electronic submissions strongly encouraged; see website for details. **Contact:** C. Lowen, Coordinator.

ALLEN GINSBERG POETRY AWARDS

Poetry Center at Passaic County Community College, 1 College Blvd., Paterson, NJ 07505. 973-684-6555. www.pccc.edu/poetry. **Details:** Up to five previously unpublished poems, up to two pages each. Send four copies of each entry. Do not submit poems that imitate Allen Ginsberg's work. **Deadline:** April 1. **Entry Fee:** $13. **Prizes:** $1,000, $200, $100. **Contact:** Maria Mazziotti Gillan.

THE GREAT BLUE BEACON POETRY CONTEST

1425 Patriot Dr., Melbourne, FL 32940. ajircc@juno.com. **Details:** Poetry, any style, up to 24 lines. Submit no more than 5 entries. **Deadline:** TBA. **Entry Fee:** $2 for subscribers, $3 for non-subscribers. **Prizes:** $25, $15, $10. **Tips:** Send SASE or e-mail to request specific guidelines. **Contact:** Andy J. Byers.

GREG GRUMMER POETRY AWARD

Phoebe: A Journal of Literature and Art, George Mason University/MSN 2D6, 4400 University Dr., Fairfax, VA 22030-4444. phoebe@gmu.edu. **Details:** Open to outstanding, previously unpublished poetry. **Deadline:** December 1. **Entry Fee:** $12. **Prizes:** $1,000 and publication in *Phoebe*.

VIOLET REED HAAS POETRY CONTEST

Snake Nation Press, 110 W Force St., Valdosta, GA 31601. 229-244-0752. jeana@snakenationpress.org. www.snakenationpress.org. **Details:** $500 plus publication for a poetry manuscript of 50-75 pages. **Deadline:** June 15. **Entry Fee:** $10.

BEATRICE HAWLEY AWARD

Alice James Books, University of Maine at Farmington, 238 Main St., Farmington, ME 04938. 207-778-7071. ajb@umf.maine.edu. www.alicejamesbooks.org. **Details:** Open to poets who reside in the United States. Submit poetry manuscript (50-70 pages) with TOC and list of acknowledgements for previously unpublished poems. **Deadline:** December 1. **Entry Fee:** $20. **Prizes:** $2,000 and publication by Alice James Books. **Tips:** In addition to the winning manuscript, one or more additional manuscripts may be chosen for publication.

JAMES HEARST POETRY PRIZE

North American Review, University of Northern Iowa, 1222 W 27th St., Cedar Falls, IA 50614-0516. nar@uni.edu. webdelsol.com/NorthAmReview/NAR/. **Details:** Submit up to 5 previously unpublished poems. No simultaneous submissions. SASE not required. **Deadline:** October 31. **Entry Fee:** $18 (includes 1-year subscription). **Prizes:** Cash prizes ($1000, $100, $50) and publication in *North American Review*.

JOHN HOLMES AWARD

New England Poetry Club, 16 Cornell St., Arlington, MA 02476-7710. info@nepoetryclub.org. www.nepoetryclub.org. **Details:** Open to an unpublished poem written by a New England college student. **Submission Period:** April 1-June 30. **Entry Fee:** Free to New England college students. **Prizes:** $100. **Tips:** Entrants may submit one entry only. See website for specific guidelines. **Contact:** Elizabeth Crowell, Contest Co-ordinator.

FIRMAN HOUGHTON AWARD

New England Poetry Club, 16 Cornell St., Arlington, MA 02476-7710. info@nepoetryclub.org. www.nepoetryclub.org. **Details:** Open to an unpublished lyric poem in honor of the former NEPC president. **Submission Period:** April 1-June 30. **Entry Fee:** Free to members; $10 for non-members. **Prizes:** $250. **Tips:** Entrants may submit up to 3 entries total out of all the contests sponsored by NEPC, but no more than 1 poem per contest. Send SASE or see website for specific guidelines and fees. **Contact:** Elizabeth Crowell, Contest Co-ordinator.

QUENTIN R. HOWARD POETRY PRIZE

P.O. Box 24548, Lexington, KY 40524. erik@uky.edu. www.wind.wind.org. **Details:** Submit 24-28 page poetry chapbook. **Deadline:** October 31 (postmark). **Entry Fee:** $15. **Prizes:** Finalists: copy of winning chapbook; Runner-Up: publication and 15 copies; Winner: publication, $100, and 25 copies. **Contact:** Erik Brandon Tuttle, Co-Contest Coordinator.

INTERNATIONAL HAIKU CONTEST

NLAPW Palomar Branch, 11929 Caminito Corriente, San Diego, CA 92128. helensherry1@aol.com. **Details:** Contest open to previously unpublished haiku. Any style is acceptable; syllable count can be less than 17. Submit two copies of each haiku (1 per 3x5 card). Any number of haiku may be entered. **Deadline:** March 1. **Entry Fee:** $5/2 haiku. **Prizes:** Cash prizes ($100, $50, $25) and publication. **Tips:** All proceeds from this contest provide a scholarship for a student entering college. **Contact:** Helen J. Sherry.

IOWA POETRY PRIZES

University of Iowa Press, 119 W Park Rd., 100 Kuhl House, Iowa City, IA 52242. 319-335-2000. holly-carver@uiowa.edu. www.uiowapress.org. **Details:** Open to new as well as established poets of book-length collections of poetry. Poems must be written originally in English and be 50-150 manuscript pages. **Submission Period:** Must be postmarked in April. **Entry Fee:** $20. **Prizes:** Publication by the University of Iowa Press. **Contact:** Holly Carver, Director.

BARBARA MANDIGO KELLY PEACE POETRY AWARDS

Nuclear Age Peace Foundation, PMB 121, 1187 Coast Village Rd., Suite 1, Santa Barbara, CA 93108-2794. 805-965-3443. wagingpeace@napf.org. www.wagingpeace.org. **Details:** Submit original, unpublished poetry written in English. Open to all writers. Encourages poets to explore and illuminate positive visions of peace and the human spirit. Send up to 3 poems, no more than 40 lines/poem. **Deadline:** July 1. **Entry Fee:** $15 for up to 3 poems; no fee for youth entries. **Prizes:** $1,000 for adults; $200 for ages 13-18; $200 for under age 12. Awards Honorable Mentions in each category. **Tips:** Write for specific contest guidelines.

THE LEDGE ANNUAL POETRY AWARDS CONTEST

The Ledge, 40 Maple Ave., Bellport, NY 11713. **Details:** Submit unpublished poetry. **Deadline:** April 30. **Entry Fee:** $10 (or $15 subscription) for first 3 poems; $3 for each additional poem. **Prizes:** Cash prizes ($1,000, $250, $100) and publication in *The Ledge*. **Tips:** Accepts simultaneous submissions. Include SASE with submission. **Contact:** Timothy Monaghan, Editor.

THE LEDGE ANNUAL POETRY CHAPBOOK CONTEST

The Ledge, 40 Maple Ave., Bellport, NY 11713. **Details:** Authors may submit 16-28 pages of poetry with title page, bio, and acknowledgements. No restrictions on form or content. Include SASE. **Deadline:** October 31. **Entry Fee:** $15. **Prizes:** $1,000. **Tips:** Accepts simultaneous submissions. **Contact:** Timothy Monaghan, Editor.

LEVIS POETRY PRIZE

Four Way Books, P.O. Box 535, Village Station, New York, NY 10014. 212-334-5430. four_way_editors@yahoo.com. www.fourwaybooks.com. **Details:** Open to all U.S. poets. **Deadline:** March 31. **Entry Fee:** $25/manuscript. **Prizes:** $1,000 honorarium, book publication, a reading at Readings on the Bowery in New York City, and residency at The Fine Arts Work Center in Provincetown, MA (sponsored by FWB). **Tips:** Electronic submissions strongly encouraged; see website for details. **Contact:** Martha Rhodes, Contest Coordinator.

LIMERICK CONTEST

NLAPW Santa Clara Branch, 15724 Adams Ridge, Los Gatos, CA 95033. 408-353-1769. ralph_susan@juno.com. **Details:** Open to National League of American Pen Women members only. All entries must be original and previously unpublished. **Deadline:** March 17. **Entry Fee:** $4/limerick; 3 for $10. **Prizes:** Cash prizes for 1st, 2nd, and 3rd place; Honorable Mentions. **Contact:** Susan Zerweck, Contest Chair.

NAOMI LONG MADGETT POETRY AWARD

Lotus Press, Inc., P.O. Box 21607, Detroit, MI 48221. 313-861-1280. lotuspress@aol.com. **Details:** Open to African American poets. Submit manuscripts approximately 60-90 pages. **Submission Period:** April 1-June 30. **Entry Fee:** None. **Prizes:** $500 and publication by Lotus Press. **Tips:** E-mail or send SASE for complete guidelines.

MISSISSIPPI VALLEY POETRY CONTEST

Midwest Writing Center, P.O. Box 3188, Rock Island, IL 61204. 563-359-1057. mwc@midwestwritingcenter.org. www.midwestwritingcenter.org. **Details:** Send up to 5 unpublished poems, any length. Eight categories. **Deadline:** April 1. **Entry Fee:** $5 (students), $8 (adults). **Prizes:** $1,500 (total). **Tips:** K-12 poets encouraged to submit. **Contact:** Max Molleston, Chairman.

KATHRYN A. MORTON PRIZE IN POETRY

2234 Dundee Rd., Suite 200, Louisville, KY 40205. 502-458-4028. sarabandeb@aol.com. www.sarabandebooks.org. **Details:** Open to any U.S. citizen writing in English. Submit poetry manuscript of at least 48 pages. Individual poems may have been previously published, but the collection as a whole must be unpublished. Translations and previously self-published books are not eligible. **Submission Period:** January 2-February 15. **Entry Fee:** $20. **Prizes:** $2,000 and publication under standard royalty contract.

SHEILA MARGARET MOTTON PRIZE

New England Poetry Club, 16 Cornell St., Arlington, MA 02476-7710. info@nepoetryclub.org. www.nepoetryclub.org. **Details:** Open to a book of poetry published in the last two years. Send 2 copies of book with $5 handling fee for non-members. **Submission Period:** April 1-June 30. **Entry Fee:** Free to members. **Prizes:** $500. **Tips:** Entrants may submit up to 3 entries total out of all the contests sponsored by NEPC, but no more than 1 poem per contest. Send SASE or see website for specific guidelines and fees. **Contact:** Elizabeth Crowell, Contest Co-ordinator.

MUDFISH POETRY PRIZE

Box Turtle Press, 184 Franklin St., New York, NY 10013. 212-219-9278. **Details:** Submit any number of poems. All entries will be considered for publication. **Deadline:** June 29. **Entry Fee:** $15 for first 3 poems; $3 for each additional poem. **Prizes:** $1,000 and publication in *Mudfish*.

ERIKA MUMFORD PRIZE

New England Poetry Club, 16 Cornell St., Arlington, MA 02476-7710. info@nepoetryclub.org. www.nepoetryclub.org. **Details:** Open to an unpublished poem in any form on the subject of travel or foreign cultures. **Submission Period:** April 1-June 30. **Entry Fee:** Free to members; $10 for 3 entries to NEPC contests. **Prizes:** $250. **Tips:** Entrants may submit up to 3 entries total out of all the contests sponsored by NEPC, but no more than 1 poem/contest. Send SASE or see website for specific guidelines and fees. **Contact:** Elizabeth Crowell, Contest Co-ordinator.

HOWARD NEMEROV SONNET AWARD

The Formalist, 320 Hunter Dr., Evansville, IN 47711. **Details:** Open to original and unpublished sonnets. No translations. Place name, address, and phone number on the back of each entry, include SASE for contest results by September. **Deadline:** June 15. **Entry Fee:** $3/sonnet. **Prizes:** $1,000 and publication.

THE NEW ENGLAND/NEW YORK AWARD

Alice James Books, University of Maine at Farmington, 238 Main St., Farmington, ME 04938. 207-778-7071. ajb@umf.maine.edu. www.alicejamesbooks.org. **Details:** Open to poets who reside in New England or New York State, beginning no later than December 1, 2004. Submit poetry manuscript (50-70 pages) with TOC and list of acknowledgements for previously published work. Winners serve 3-year term on the Alice James Books Editorial Board. **Deadline:** October 1. **Entry Fee:** $20. **Prizes:** $2,000 and publication.

NEW LETTERS POETRY PRIZE

New Letters, University of Missouri-Kansas City, 5101 Rockhill Rd., Kansas City, MO 64110. 816-235-1168. newletters@umkc.edu. www.newletters.org/awardswriter.asp. **Details:** Offers $1,000 and publication to the best collection of 3-6 poems. All entries recieve consideration for publication in a future issue of *New Letters*. **Deadline:** May 19. **Entry Fee:** $15 (includes subscription). **Prizes:** $1,000 and publication.

GUY OWEN PRIZE

Southern Poetry Review, Armstrong Atlantic State University, Dept. of Language, Literature, & Philosophy, 11935 Abercorn St., Savannah, GA 31419-1997. 912-927-5289. www.spr.armstrong.edu. **Details:** Send 3-5 previously unpublished poems (10 pages maximum). Considers poems published online or posted there to be "previously published" work. Accepts simultaneous submissions with notice. Winning poem selected by a nationally-ranking poet. **Submission Period:** March 1-June 15. **Entry Fee:** $15 (includes subscription). **Prizes:** $1,000 and publication in *Southern Poetry Review*. **Tips:** Send hard copy only and include SASE for reply only; manuscripts will not be returned. **Contact:** Robert Parham, Editor.

PARALLEL AWARD FOR POETRY

Bellingham Review, Mail Stop 9053, Western Washington University, Bellingham, WA 98225. www.wwu.edu/~bhreview. **Details:** Submit previously unpublished poems of any length. **Submission Period:** December 1-March 15. **Entry Fee:** $15 for first entry of 3 poems; $10 for each additional poem. **Prizes:** $1,000 and publication in *Bellingham Review*. **Tips:** See website for complete contest guidelines.

PAVEMENT SAW CHAPBOOK CONTEST

Pavement Saw Press, P.O. Box 6291, Columbus, OH 43206. editor@pavementsaw.org. www.pavementsaw.org. **Details:** Open to collections of poetry of no more than 32 pages. **Deadline:** December 15. **Entry Fee:** $10. **Prizes:** $500 and 25 copies of winning chapbook. **Tips:** All U.S. entrants receive 2 recent chapbooks. **Contact:** David Baratier, Editor.

PAVEMENT SAW PRESS
TRANSCONTINENTAL POETRY AWARD

Pavement Saw Press, P.O. Box 6291, Columbus, OH 43206. editor@pavementsaw.org. www.pavementsaw.org. **Details:** Open to previously unpublished, full-length books of poetry. **Deadline:** August 15. **Entry Fee:** $15. **Prizes:** $1,000 and publication by Pavement Saw Press. **Tips:** Send SASE or e-mail for guidelines. **Contact:** David Baratier, Editor.

PEARL POETRY PRIZE

Pearl Editions, 3030 E Second St., Long Beach, CA 90803. www.pearlmag.com. **Details:** Open to all poets, with or without previous book publication. Submit poetry manuscript of 48-64 pages. **Submission Period:** May 1-July 15. **Entry Fee:** $20. **Prizes:** $1,000 and publication in *Pearl Editions*.

PERUGIA PRESS INTRO AWARD

Perugia Press, P.O. Box 60364, Florence, MA 01062. info@perugiapress.com. www.perugiapress.com. **Details:** Annual contest for a first or second book of poetry. Open to female poets only. Individual poems may be previously published, but not the collection as a whole. Send 48-72 page manuscript via regular mail. Include SASE for notification. **Submission Period:** August 1-November 15. **Entry Fee:** $20/submission. **Prizes:** $1,000 and publication. **Tips:** See website or send SASE or e-mail, for complete guidelines. **Contact:** Susan Kan, Director.

PHILBRICK POETRY AWARD

251 Benefit St., Providence, RI 02903. www.providenceathenaeum.org. **Details:** Open to residents of New England (CT, ME, MA, NH, RI, VT) who have not had a book of poetry published. One manuscript/entrant. **Submission Period:** June 15-October 15. **Entry Fee:** $8. **Prizes:** $500 and publication of chapbook.

POETRY IN PRINT

P.O. Box 30981, Albuquerque, NM 87190-0981. 505-888-3937. **Details:** Open to poetry of any topic, up to 60 lines. No limit to number of entries submitted. Include SASE with submission. **Deadline:** August 1. **Entry Fee:** $10. **Prizes:** $1,000. **Contact:** Robert G. English.

POETS OUT LOUD

Fordham University at Lincoln Center, 113 W 60th St., Room 924-I, New York, NY 10023. 212-636-6792. pol@fordham.edu. www.poetsoutloud.com. **Details:** Open to unpublished, full-length poetry manuscripts, 50-80 pages. **Deadline:** October 31. **Entry Fee:** $25. **Prizes:** $1,000 and publication by Fordham University Press.

RIVER OAK REVIEW POETRY CONTEST

Elmhurst College, 190 Prospect Ave., Elmhurst, IL 60126. 630-617-6483. annfw@elmhurst.edu. www.riveroakarts.org. **Details:** Poets may submit up to 4 previously unpublished poems. No "light verse" or erotica/porn. **Deadline:** September 1 (no contest in 2004 only). **Entry Fee:** $15/entry (includes subscription). **Prizes:** $500 and publication in *River Oak Review*.

BENJAMIN SALTMAN POETRY AWARD

Red Hen Press, P.O. Box 3537, Granada Hills, CA 91394. 818-831-0649. editors@redhen.org. www.redhen.org. **Details:** For best poetry collection, 48-90 pages. **Deadline:** October 31. **Entry Fee:** $20. **Prizes:** $1,000.

SLIPSTREAM ANNUAL POETRY CHAPBOOK COMPETITION

Slipstream Press, P.O. Box 2071, Niagara Falls, NY 14301. www.slipstreampress.org. **Details:** Send up to 40 pages of poetry with any style, format, or theme. Accepts previously published material and simultaneous submissions with notice. All entrants receive a free copy of winning chapbook. **Deadline:** December 1. **Entry Fee:** $15. **Prizes:** $1,000 and 50 copies. **Tips:** Include SASE for return of manuscript.

SOW'S EAR CHAPBOOK COMPETITION

Sow's Ear Poetry Review, 355 Mt. Lebanon Rd., Donalds, SC 29638-9115. 276-628-2651. errol@kitenet.net. **Details:** Send 22-26 pages of poetry, any length (no more than 1 poem/page). Accepts simultaneous submissions and previously published poems if writer holds publication rights. Include SASE or e-mail address for notification. **Deadline:** May 1. **Entry Fee:** $15 (includes option to receive copy of winning chapbook). **Prizes:** Publication, $1,000, 25 copies, distribution to subscribers. **Tips:** Write for specific guidelines. **Contact:** Errol Hess, Managing Editor.

SOW'S EAR POETRY COMPETITION

Sow's Ear Poetry Review, 355 Mt. Lebanon Rd., Donalds, SC 29638-9115. 276-628-2651. errol@kitenet.net. **Details:** Open to adults. No length limit. Accepts simultaneous submissions. Poets who submit 5+ poems receive free subscription. Include SASE or e-mail address for notification. **Deadline:** November 1 (send poems in Sept./Oct.). **Entry Fee:** $3/poem. **Prizes:** $1,000 and option of publication for approx. 20 finalists. **Contact:** Errol Hess, Managing Editor.

THE SPOON RIVER POETRY REVIEW EDITORS' PRIZE

4241 Dept. of English, Publications Unit, Illinois State University, Normal, IL 61790-4241. www.litline.org/spoon. **Details:** Submit 2 copies (one with name and address, the other without) of 3 unpublished poems, up to 10 pages total. **Deadline:** April 15. **Entry Fee:** $16. **Prizes:** $1,000 and publication in *The Spoon River Poetry Review*. **Tips:** Include SASE for notification. Does not accept submission via e-mail or fax.

SPRING POETRY CONTEST

Montgomery Chapter NLAPW, 91 Cloverfield Rd., Hope Hull, AL 36043. **Details:** Submit poetry up to 50 lines. Poems may have been previously published, but may not be joint authorship. No limit on number of entries. **Submission Period:** May 1-June 12. **Entry Fee:** $5/first two poems; $2 for each additional. **Prizes:** Cash prizes for 1st, 2nd, 3rd, and 4th places; also five Honorable Mentions. **Contact:** Mary Halliburton, Contest Chair.

ANN STANFORD POETRY PRIZE

Professional Writing Program, University of Southern California, WPH 404, Los Angeles, CA 90089. 213-740-3252. mpw@usc.edu. **Details:** Send up to five unpublished poems with SASE. All entrants receive free issue of the anthology. **Deadline:** April 15. **Entry Fee:** $10. **Prizes:** Cash prizes ($1,000, $200, $100) and publication in Southern California Anthology. **Contact:** James Ragan, Director.

AGNES LYNCH STARRETT POETRY PRIZE

University of Pittsburgh Press, 3400 Forbes Ave., Eureka Bldg., Fl. 5, Pittsburgh, PA 15260. 412-383-2456. www.pitt.edu/~press. **Details:** Annual award given to an unpublished, first book of poetry. **Submission Period:** March 1-April 30. **Entry Fee:** $20. **Prizes:** $5,000 and publication by The University of Pittsburgh Press. **Tips:** See website for specific guidelines.

HOLLIS SUMMERS POETRY PRIZE COMPETITION

Ohio University Press, Scott Quadrangle, Athens, OH 45701. 740-593-1155. www.ohiou.edu/oupress/. **Details:** Submit 60-95 manuscript pages of original, unpublished poetry. Open to both those who have published a collection and those who have not. **Deadline:** October 31. **Entry Fee:** $15. **Prizes:** $500 and publication by Ohio University Press. **Tips:** See guidelines at website.

KATE TUFTS DISCOVERY AWARD

Poetic Gallery for the Tufts Poetry Awards, Claremont Graduate University 160 E 10th St., Harper East B7, Claremont, CA 91711-6165. 909-621-8974. www.cgu.edu/tufts. **Details:** Awarded annually to an emerging poet whose work shows extraordinary promise. Submissions must be a first book of poetry. **Deadline:** September 1. **Entry Fee:** None. **Prizes:** $10,000. **Tips:** See website for detailed guidelines. **Contact:** Betty Terrell, Awards Coordinator.

KINGSLEY TUFTS POETRY AWARD

Poetic Gallery for the Tufts Poetry Awards, Claremont Graduate University 160 E 10th St., Harper East B7, Claremont, CA 91711-6165. 909-621-8974. www.cgu.edu/tufts. **Details:** Awarded annually for "a work by an emerging poet, one who is past the very beginning but has not yet reached the acknowledged pinnacle of his or her career." Send five copies of book. **Deadline:** September 1. **Entry Fee:** None. **Prizes:** $100,000. **Tips:** See website for detailed guidelines. **Contact:** Betty Terrell, Awards Coordinator.

TUPELO PRESS DORSET PRIZE

Tupelo Press, P.O. Box 539, Dorset, VT 05251. 802-366-8185. editors@tupelopress.org. www.tupelopress.org. **Details:** Open competition for all poets writing in English. Submit a previously unpublished, full-length poetry manuscript, 50-80 pages. **Submission Period:** September 1-November 15. **Entry Fee:** $25. **Prizes:** $3,000, publication, and 2-week stay at Dorset Writers Colony. **Contact:** Margaret Donovan, Managing Editor.

DANIEL VAROUJAN AWARD

New England Poetry Club, 16 Cornell St., Arlington, MA 02476-7710. info@nepoetryclub.org. www.nepoetryclub.org. **Details:** Open to unpublished poems (no translations) echoing the work and/or memory of Daniel Varoujan, a poet killed by Turks in 1915. **Submission Period:** April 1-June 30. **Entry Fee:** Free to members; $10 for non-members. **Prizes:** $1,000. **Tips:** Entrants may submit up to 3 entries total out of all the contests sponsored by NEPC, but no more than 1 poem per contest. Send SASE or see website for specific guidelines and fees. **Contact:** Elizabeth Crowell, Contest Co-ordinator.

WASHINGTON PRIZE

The Word Works, P.O. Box 42164, Washington, DC 20015. editor@wordworksdc.com. www.wordworksdc.com. **Details:** Open to original poetry by a living American writer. Send 48-64 page manuscript with name, address, phone number, e-mail address, and signature on title page only. Include table of contents, acknowledgments page, and a brief bio. **Deadline:** March 1. **Entry Fee:** $20. **Prizes:** $1,500 award for the winner and publication. **Tips:** See website for complete submission guidelines.

WALT WHITMAN AWARD

The Academy of American Poets, 588 Broadway, Suite 1203, New York, NY 10012-3250. 212-274-0343. mtyrell@poets.org. www.poets.org. **Details:** Open to American poets who have never before published a book of poetry. Manuscripts should be 50-100 pages of original poems, one poem/page. **Submission Period:** September 15-November 30. **Entry Fee:** $25. **Prizes:** $5,000, publication of manuscript by Louisiana State University Press, and 1-month residency at Vermont Studio Center. **Tips:** See website or write for guidelines.

WALLACE W. WINCHELL POETRY CONTEST

Connecticut Poetry Society, P.O. Box 4053, Waterbury, CT 06704-0053. 203-753-7815. editorcrr@yahoo.com (for queries only). **Details:** Submit original, unpublished poetry on any subject. 40-line limit; 5 poems maximum. No simultaneous submissions. Include SASE for notification. **Submission Period:** October 1-December 31. **Entry Fee:** $2/poem. **Prizes:** Cash prizes ($150, $100, $50) plus Honorable Mentions. **Tips:** For publication in *Connecticut River Review*, winning poems must be submitted by e-mail or on disc following notification.

FICTION

NELSON ALGREN AWARDS FOR SHORT FICTION

Chicago Tribune Literary Prizes, 435 N Michigan Ave., LL2, Chicago, IL 60611. **Details:** In memory of Chicago author Nelson Algren. Submit no more than two unpublished short stories, 2,500-10,000 words. Open to American writers only. **Submission Period:** November 1-February 28. **Entry Fee:** None. **Prizes:** First prize of $5,000 and 3 runner-up prizes of $1,500.

ALEXANDER PATTERSON CAPPON FICTION PRIZE

New Letters, University of Missouri-Kansas City, 5101 Rockhill Rd., Kansas City, MO 64110. 816-235-1168. newletters@umkc.edu. www.newletters.org/awardswriter.asp. **Details:** Offers $1,000 and publication for the best short story. All entries receive consideration for publication in a future issue of *New Letters*. **Deadline:** May 19. **Entry Fee:** $15 (includes subscription).

DAVID DORNSTEIN MEMORIAL CREATIVE WRITING CONTEST FOR YOUNG ADULT WRITERS

Coalition for the Advancement of Jewish Education, 261 W 35th St., Fl. 12A, New York, NY 10001. 212-268-4210. cajeny@caje.org. www.caje.org. **Details:** Offered annually to authors ages 18-35. Submit original, previously unpublished short stories, no more than 5,000 words, on a Jewish theme or topic. **Deadline:** December 31. **Entry Fee:** None. **Prizes:** Cash prizes ($700, $200, $100) and publication in the *CAJE Jewish Education News*.

THE EUREKA! FELLOWSHIP FOR SHORT STORY WRITING

The Writers' Colony at Dairy Hollow, 515 Spring St., Eureka Springs, AR 72632. director@writerscolony.org. www.writerscolony.org. **Details:** Awarded annually to a writer whose work demonstrates ability. **Deadline:** October 15. **Entry Fee:** $35. **Prizes:** One-month expense-paid residency at The Writers' Colony at Dairy Hollow.

FICTION OPEN

Glimmer Train Press, Inc., 1211 NW Glisan St., Suite 207, Portland, OR 97209. 503-221-0836. info@glimmertrain.com. www.glimmertrain.com. **Details:** Contest for short fiction on any theme, up to 20,000 words. **Submission Period:** May 1-June 30; November 1-January 15. **Entry Fee:** $15/story. **Prizes:** 1st place wins $2,000, publication in *Glimmer Train Stories*, and 20 copies. 2nd place wins $1,000; 3rd place wins $600. **Tips:** All stories must be submitted online; see website for specific guidelines.

FLASH FICTION CONTEST

NLAPW Pikes Peak Branch, 1015 Valley Rd., Colorado Springs, CO 80904. warnerwrit@aol.com. **Details:** Submit a complete story of 100 words or less. All genres welcome, including contemporary, historical, romance, mystery, sci-fi, horror, Western, adventure, and inspirational. **Deadline:** Mid-March. **Entry Fee:** $6. **Prizes:** Cash prizes ($60, $25, $15). **Contact:** Marylin Warner.

GLIMMER TRAIN PRESS SHORT-STORY AWARD

Glimmer Train Press, Inc., 1211 NW Glisan St., Suite 207, Portland, OR 97209. 503-221-0836. info@glimmertrain.com. www.glimmertrain.com. **Details:** Literary short stories by emerging writers. Stories should not exceed 12,000 words. Open only to writers whose fiction has not appeared in any publication with a circulation over 5,000. (Entries must be entirely unpublished.) **Submission Period:** February 1-March 31 for spring; August 1-September 30 for fall. **Entry Fee:** $12 per story. **Prizes:** $1,200 and publication; $500; $300. **Tips:** All stories must be submitted online; see website for specific submission guidelines.

THE GREAT BLUE BEACON
SHORT-SHORT STORY CONTEST

1425 Patriot Dr., Melbourne, FL 32940. ajircc@juno.com. **Details:** Submit short fiction, up to 1,000 words. Send no more than 5 entries. **Deadline:** TBA. **Entry Fee:** $4 for subscribers, $5 for non-subscribers. **Prizes:** $50, $25, $10. **Tips:** Send SASE or e-mail to request specific guidelines. **Contact:** Andy J. Byers.

DRUE HEINZ LITERATURE PRIZE

University of Pittsburgh Press, Eureka Building, Fl. 5, 3400 Forbes Ave., Pittsburgh, PA 15260. 412-383-2456. www.pitt.edu/~press. **Details:** Short fiction contest open to writers who have published a book-length collection of short fiction or at least 3 short stories or novellas in a literary or national magazine. Submit manuscripts of 150-300 pages. **Submission Period:** May 1-June 30. **Prizes:** $15,000 and publication by University of Pittsburgh Press. **Tips:** See website for specific guidelines.

HIDDEN TALENTS SHORT STORY CONTEST

Tall Tales Press Book Publishing Inc., 20 Tuscany Valley Park NW, Calgary, AB, Canada T3L 2B6. 403-874-4293. talltalespress@shaw.ca. www.talltalespress.com. **Details:** For fiction and non-fiction short stories up to 5,000 words. Also offers a contest for junior writers. **Deadline:** May 31. **Entry Fee:** $10 CDN or U.S.. **Prizes:** $500; $250; $100; $75. **Tips:** Follow all guidelines and proofread story before submitting. **Contact:** Steve Van Bakel.

IOWA SHORT FICTION AWARD

University of Iowa Press, Iowa Writers' Workshop
102 Dey House, 507 N Clinton St., Iowa City, IA 52242-1000. 319-335-2000. holly-carver@uiowa.edu. www.uiowa.edu/~uipress. **Details:** Open to writers who have not previously published a volume of prose fiction. Submit a collection of short stories totalling at least 150 pages. **Submission Period:** August 1-September 30. **Prizes:** Publication by the University of Iowa Press. **Contact:** Holly Carver.

JAMES JONES FIRST NOVEL FELLOWSHIP

c/o Wilkes University, English Dept., Wilkes-Barre, PA 18766. 570-408-4530. english@wilkes.edu. www.wilkes.edu/humanities/jones. **Details:** Award honors the spirit of unblinking honesty, determination and insight into modern culture exemplified by the late James Jones, author of *From Here to Eternity*. Open to all U.S. citizens who have not published a novel. Submit 2-page (maximum) outline and first 50 pages. **Deadline:** March 1. **Entry Fee:** $20. **Prizes:** $6,000 first prize and attendance at the society's annual conference to accept the award; $250 honorarium for runner-up. **Contact:** Francesca Amico, Coordinator.

SERENA MCDONALD KENNEDY AWARD

Snake Nation Press, 110 W Force St., Valdosta, GA 31601. 229-244-0752. jeana@snakenationpress.org. www.snakenationpress.org. **Details:** Open to well-written manuscripts on any topic. Submit no more than a 50,000-word novella or a 200-page manuscript of short stories. Accepts previously published works. **Deadline:** September 1. **Entry Fee:** $20. **Prizes:** $1,000 and publication.

E.M. KOEPPEL SHORT FICTION AWARD

Write Corner Press, P.O. Box 16369, Jacksonville, FL 32245. www.writecorner.com. **Details:** Open to unpublished short stories, any style, of no more than 3,000 words. Entrants may submit any number of stories. **Submission Period:** October 1-April 30 (postmarked). **Entry Fee:** $15/story or $25/2 stories. **Prizes:** Cash prizes (first place, $1,100; Editors' Choices, $100 each), publication by Write Corner Press, and P.L. Titus $500 scholarship. **Contact:** Mary Sue Koeppel, Editor.

MIGUEL MÁRMOL PRIZE FOR LATINA/O FIRST FICTION

Curbstone Press, 321 Jackson St., Willimantic, CT 06226. **Details:** Open to a first work of fiction in English by a Latina/o writer that reflects a respect for intercultural understanding and fosters an appreciation for human rights and civil liberties. Entrants who have previously had poetry or nonfiction published in book form are eligible. Send submissions of book-length novels or collections of stories. Include SASE for return of manuscript. **Deadline:** December 15. **Entry Fee:** $15. **Prizes:** Publication by Curbstone Press and $1,000 advance against royalties.

MARY MCCARTHY PRIZE IN SHORT FICTION

2234 Dundee Rd., Suite 200, Louisville, KY 40205. 502-458-4028. sarabandeb@aol.com. www.sarabandebooks.org. **Details:** Submit manuscript (collections of short stories, novellas, or short novel), 150-300 pages. Material that has previously appeared in magazines or anthologies is eligible. Translations and self-published collections are not eligible. **Submission Period:** January 1-February 15. **Entry Fee:** $20. **Prizes:** $2,000, publication, and standard royalty contract.

NELLIGAN PRIZE FOR SHORT FICTION

Colorado Review, Colorado State University, Dept. of English, Fort Collins, CO 80523. 970-491-5449. creview@colostate.edu. www.coloradoreview.com. **Details:** Annual contest awarded to the best short story. No length/theme restrictions and no limit on number of entries submitted. Stories must be previously unpublished. **Submission Period:** January 15-April 5. **Entry Fee:** $10/entry. **Prizes:** Publication in *Colorado Review*.

NEW YORK STORIES FICTION PRIZE

New York Stories, LaGuardia Community College/CUNY,
English Dept., E-103, 31-10 Thomson Ave., Long Island City, NY 11101.
nystories@lagcc.cuny.edu. www.newyorkstories.org. **Details:** Open to previously
unpublished stories up to 6,500 words. No simultaneous submissions. Include SASE
for contest results. **Deadline:** September 15. **Entry Fee:** $15/submission. **Prizes:**
First prize: $500 and publication; Second prize: $250 and possible publication.
Contact: Daniel Caplice Lynch.

THE NOTORIOUS FELLOWSHIP FOR LITERARY FICTION

The Writers' Colony at Dairy Hollow, 515 Spring St., Eureka Springs, AR 72632.
director@writerscolony.org. www.writerscolony.org. **Details:** Offers recognition to an
overlooked but gifted writer. Awarded annually to a writer of fiction (novels, short stories, poetry, or plays) whose work shows demonstrated ability and gift, but has never
achieved the success it deserves, either because the writer is early in his or her career
and still unpublished, or because the work is more "literary" than commercial.
Deadline: October 15. **Entry Fee:** $35. **Prizes:** One-month expense-paid residency
at The Writers' Colony at Dairy Hollow.

FLANNERY O'CONNOR AWARD FOR SHORT FICTION

University of Georgia Press, 330 Research Dr., Athens, GA 30602-4901.
706-369-6130. books@ugapress.uga.edu. www.ugapress.org. **Details:** Open to collections of short fiction written in English, 200-275 pages. Collections that include
long stories or novellas accepted, however no novels or single novellas. Accepts pieces
that have appeared in magazines or anthologies, but not those which have been published in a full-length collection by the author. **Submission Period:** April 1-May 31.
Entry Fee: $20. **Prizes:** $1,000 and publication by the University of Georgia Press.

PEARL SHORT STORY PRIZE

Pearl Magazine, 3030 E Second St., Long Beach, CA 90803. www.pearlmag.com.
Details: Submit previously unpublished short stories, no longer than 4,000 words.
Accepts simultaneous submissions with notice. All submissions considered for publication. **Submission Period:** April 1-May 31. **Entry Fee:** $10/story. **Prizes:** $250
and publication in *Pearl*.

POCKETS FICTION-WRITING CONTEST

Pockets Magazine, 1908 Grand Ave., P.O. Box 340004, Nashville, TN 37203-0004.
pockets@upperroom.org. **Details:** Open to unpublished short stories, 1,000-1,600
words (disqualified if longer or shorter; note word count on cover sheet). No historical fiction. **Submission Period:** March 1-August 15. **Prizes:** $1,000 and publication
in *Pockets*. **Tips:** Submissions returned only if accompanied by an SASE with sufficient first-class postage.

PRISM INTERNATIONAL'S SHORT FICTION CONTEST

University of British Columbia, Dept. of Creative Writing,
Buch E462-1866 Main Mall, Vancouver, British Columbia V6T 1Z1 Canada.
604-822-2514. prism@interchange.ubc.ca. http://prism.arts.ubc.ca. **Details:** Fiction
contest open to original, unpublished short stories. Entries must be no longer than 25
pages. Translations eligible. **Deadline:** February 6. **Entry Fee:** $25 plus $7 for each
additional entry. **Prizes:** Cash prizes (winner receives $2,000; 5 prizes of $200).

RIVER OAK REVIEW SHORT STORY CONTEST

Elmhurst College, 190 Prospect Ave., Elmhurst, IL 60126. 630-617-6483.
ronw@elmhurst.edu. **Details:** Open to unpublished short stories of no more than
5,000 words. No genre fiction (i.e. mystery, romance, western) or erotica/porn.
Deadline: September 1. **Entry Fee:** $15 (includes subscription). **Prizes:** $500 and
publication in *River Oak Review.*

SHORT STORY AWARD FOR NEW WRITERS

Glimmer Train Press, Inc., 1211 NW Glisan St., Suite 207, Portland, OR 97209.
503-221-0836. info@glimmertrain.com. www.glimmertrain.com. **Details:** Open to
original, unpublished stories, up to 12,000 words. **Submission Period:** (Spring)
February 1-March 31; (Fall) August 1-September 30. **Entry Fee:** $12. **Prizes:**
$1,200 and publication; $500; $300. **Tips:** All stories must be submitted online; see
website for specific submission guidelines.

JOHN SIMMONS SHORT FICTION AWARD

University of Iowa Press, Iowa Writers' Workshop,
102 Dey House, 507 N Clinton St., Iowa City, IA 52242-1000. 319-335-2000.
holly-carver@uiowa.edu. www.uiowa.edu/~uipress. **Details:** Submit a book-length
collection of short fiction. Limited to authors who have not yet published a book of
prose. **Submission Period:** August 1-September 30. **Prizes:** Publication by the
University of Iowa Press. **Contact:** Holly Carver, Director.

SOUTH CAROLINA FICTION PROJECT

South Carolina Arts Commission, 1800 Gervais St., Columbia, SC 29201.
803-734-8696. goldstsa@arts.state.sc.us. www.southcarolinaarts.com. **Details:** Short
story competition open to South Carolina writers. Up to 12 previously unpublished
stories of 2,500 words or less. Stories are not required to have Southern theme or to
be set in South Carolina. **Deadline:** January 15. **Entry Fee:** None. **Prizes:** $500 and
publication in *The Post and Courier.* **Tips:** See website for guidelines and application. **Contact:** Sara June Goldstein, Program Director for Literary Arts.

JAMES STILL SHORT FICTION AWARD

P.O. Box 24548, Lexington, KY 40524. erik@uky.edu. www.wind.wind.org.
Details: Submit any number of short stories, any subject matter, no more than 4,000
words. **Deadline:** July 30 (postmark). **Entry Fee:** $10/story. **Prizes:** Finalists: 1-year
subscription to *Wind*; Winner: $500 and publication in *Wind.*

SYDNEY TAYLOR MANUSCRIPT COMPETITION

Assn. of Jewish Libraries, 315 Maitland Ave., Teaneck, NJ 07666. 201-862-0312. rkglasser@aol.com. www.jewishlibraries.org. **Details:** Open to writers who have no previously published fiction works. Submit book-length manuscript of 64-200 pages. Stories must have a positive Jewish focus, universal appeal, and be appropriate for readers ages 8-11. **Deadline:** December 31. **Entry Fee:** None. **Prizes:** $1,000. **Contact:** Rachel Glasser, Coordinator.

PETER TAYLOR PRIZE FOR THE NOVEL

Knoxville Writers' Guild, P.O. Box 2565, Knoxville, TN 37901-2565. www.knoxvillewritersguild.org. **Details:** Open to U.S. residents writing in English. Submit unpublished novel manuscripts 40,000 words or more. **Submission Period:** February 1-April 30. **Entry Fee:** $20. **Prizes:** $1,000 and publication by the University of Tennessee Press. **Tips:** See website for details. **Contact:** Brian Griffin, Director.

VERY SHORT FICTION AWARD

Glimmer Train Press, Inc., 1211 NW Glisan St., Suite 207, Portland, OR 97209. 503-221-0836. info@glimmertrain.com. www.glimmertrain.com. **Details:** Short stories up to 2,000 words. **Submission Period:** (Summer) June 1-July 31; (Winter) November 1-January 31. **Entry Fee:** $10/story. **Prizes:** 1st place wins $1,200, publication in *Glimmer Train Stories*, and 20 copies; 2nd place wins $500; 3rd place wins $300. **Tips:** All stories must be submitted online; see website for specific submission guidelines.

THE WEEKENDER CHALLENGE

WriteLink, The Competition Secretary, 7 Melbourne Road, Newbold, Coleorton, Leicestershire LE67 8JH, UK. sue@writelink.co.uk. www.writelink.co.uk. **Details:** Online short story contest designed to put an end to procrastination: theme and word count are provided with 36 hours to complete the entry. E-mail entries only. **Entry Fee:** £4. **Prizes:** £50 for winner and £25 each for two runners up. **Tips:** See website for detailed guidelines.

PHOEBE WINTER FICTION PRIZE

Phoebe: A Journal of Literature and Art, George Mason University/MSN 2D6, 4400 University Dr., Fairfax, VA 22030-4444. **Details:** Open to unpublished short stories, no longer than 25 pages. **Deadline:** December 1. **Entry Fee:** $12. **Prizes:** $1,000 and publication in *Phoebe*. **Tips:** Send SASE or e-mail for guidelines.

TOBIAS WOLFF AWARD FOR FICTION

Bellingham Review, Mail Stop 9053, Western Washington University, Bellingham, WA 98225. www.wwu.edu/~bhreview. **Details:** Submit a previously unpublished short story or novel excerpt up to 9,000 words. **Submission Period:** December 1-March 15. **Entry Fee:** $15 for first entry, $10 for each additional entry. **Prizes:** $1,000 and publication in *Bellingham Review*.

ZOETROPE SHORT FICTION CONTEST

Zoetrope: All Story, 916 Kearny St., San Francisco, CA 94133. contests@all-story.com. www.all-story.com. **Details:** Awards 3 monetary prizes for an unpublished short story no longer than 5,000 words. **Submission Period:** June 1-October 1. **Entry Fee:** $15. **Prizes:** $1,000, $500, $250. **Tips:** Do not submit material via e-mail or fax.

NONFICTION

DOROTHY CHURCHILL CAPPON
CREATIVE NONFICTION PRIZE

New Letters, University of Missouri-Kansas City, 5101 Rockhill Rd., Kansas City, MO 64110. 816-235-1168. newletters@umkc.edu. www.newletters.org/awardswriter.asp. **Details:** Offers $1,000 and publication for the best expository nonfiction. All entries receive consideration for publication in a future issue of *New Letters*. **Deadline:** May 19. **Entry Fee:** $15 (includes subscription). **Prizes:** $1,000 and publication.

JANE CUNNINGHAM CROLY/GFWC
PRINT JOURNALISM CONTEST

General Federation of Women's Clubs, 1734 N St. NW, Washington, DC 20036. 202-347-3168. skranz@gfwc.org. www.gfwc.org. **Details:** Award offered for excellence in covering issues of concern to women. Submit three pieces published in the previous year that demonstrate a concern for the rights and advancement of women, an awareness of women's sensitivity and strength, and/or an attempt to counteract sexism. **Deadline:** March 5. **Entry Fee:** $50. **Prizes:** $1,000. **Contact:** Sally Kranz.

ANNIE DILLARD AWARD FOR NONFICTION

Bellingham Review, Mail Stop 9053, Western Washington University, Bellingham, WA 98225. www.wwu.edu/~bhreview. **Details:** Open to previously unpublished nonfiction essays on any topic and in any style, up to 9,000 words. **Submission Period:** December 1-March 15. **Entry Fee:** $15 for first entry; $10 for each additional entry. **Prizes:** $1,000 and publication in *Bellingham Review*. **Tips:** See website for complete contest guidelines.

EVENT CREATIVE NONFICTION CONTEST

The Douglas College Review, P.O. Box 2503, New Westminister, British Columbia V3L 5B2 Canada. 604-527-5293. event@douglas.bc.ca. http://event.douglas.bc.ca. **Details:** Previously unpublished creative nonfiction up to 5,000 words. **Deadline:** April 15. **Entry Fee:** $25 (includes subscription to *Event* magazine). **Prizes:** Three $500 prizes and publication.

EXCELLENCE IN URBAN JOURNALISM AWARD

The Enterprise Foundation, 10227 Wincopin Cir., Suite 500, Columbia, MD 21044. 410-772-2737. www.enterprisefoundation.org. **Details:** Broadcasts, articles or series written by one reporter or a team can qualify. Topics may include, but are not limited to, housing, community safety, community development, welfare-to-work, and child care. The piece should discuss how a city or community has been affected by the situation. Ideally, the entry should include reporting on the outcome or resolution of the situation, or show responses through editorials, letters to the editor, etc. Submissions must have been printed, broadcast or transmitted during the 2003 calendar year. **Deadline:** June 1. **Entry Fee:** None. **Prizes:** $5,000. **Contact:** Karen Burley.

THE ROGERS COMMUNICATION LITERARY NONFICTION CONTEST

PRISM international, Creative Writing Program, UBC, Buch E462-1866 Main Mall, Vancouver, British Columbia V6T 1Z1 Canada. 604-822-2514. http://prism.arts.ubc.ca. **Details:** Open to original, unpublished material. Translations are eligible. No simultaneous submissions. **Deadline:** September 30. **Entry Fee:** $25 for first manuscript, $7 for each additional. **Prizes:** Publication in winter issue of *PRISM*.

TINY LIGHTS ANNUAL PERSONAL ESSAY CONTEST

Tiny Lights: A Journal of Personal Essay, P.O. Box 928, Petaluma, CA 94953. 707-762-3208. www.tiny-lights.com. **Details:** Submit personal essay/memoir, up to 2,000 words. **Deadline:** February 17. **Entry Fee:** $15 for first essay; $10 for each additional essay. **Prizes:** Cash prizes ($300, $200, $150, $100) and publication. **Tips:** See website for contest guidelines.

LAMAR YORK PRIZE FOR NONFICTION

The Chattahoochee Review, Georgia Perimeter College, 2101 Womack Rd., Dunwoody, GA 30338-4497. gpccr@gpc.edu. www.chattahoochee-review.org. **Details:** Submit an essay no more than 5,000 words. Does not accept essays with scholarly/theoretical slant; all other approaches and subjects are welcome. **Submission Period:** October 1-January 31. **Entry Fee:** $10. **Prizes:** $1,000 and publication in *The Chattahoochee Review*. **Contact:** Lawrence Hetrick.

YOUNG WRITERS' AWARD

Turning Wheel, Journal of Socially Engaged Buddhism, P.O. Box 3470, Berkeley, CA 94703. 510-655-6169. sue@bpf.org. www.bpf.org. **Details:** Contest for best essay on the theme of an issue. Open to writers who are 30 years of age or younger and who have not been previously published in *Turning Wheel*. **Entry Fee:** None. **Prizes:** $500. **Tips:** See website for guidelines and deadlines. Do not submit material by fax. **Contact:** Sue Moon, Editor.

DRAMA

DRURY UNIVERSITY PLAYWRITING CONTEST

900 N Benton Ave., Springfield, MO 65802. 417-873-6821. msokol@drury.edu.
Details: Prizes of $300 and two $150 honorable mentions, plus possible production (Open Eye Theatre), for original, previously unproduced one-act plays. **Deadline:** December 1. **Contact:** Mick Sokol, Assistant Professor of Theatre.

DUBUQUE FINE ARTS PLAYERS
ONE-ACT PLAYWRITING CONTEST

1686 Lawndale Dr., Dubuque, IA 52001. 563-582-5502. garms@clarke.edu. **Details:** Open to original one-act plays up to 40 minutes. Submit two copies. **Deadline:** January 31. **Entry Fee:** $10. **Prizes:** Cash prizes ($600, $300, $200) and full production of all winning scripts. **Tips:** Send SASE for application and guidelines.

JOHN GASSNER MEMORIAL PLAYWRITING AWARD

The New England Theatre Conference, Inc., PMB 502, 198 Tremont St., Boston, MA 02116-4750. 617-851-8535. mail@netconline.org. www.netconline.org. **Details:** New, unpublished full-length plays that have not been produced by a professional or Equity company. Open to New England residents and NETC members. **Deadline:** April 15. **Entry Fee:** $10. **Prizes:** Cash prizes ($1,000 and $500). **Tips:** See website for guidelines and application.

MARILYN HALL AWARDS

Beverly Hills Theatre Guild, P.O. Box 39729, Los Angeles, CA 90039-0729.
Details: Annual award for plays for young and adolescent audiences, 45-90 minutes. Entrants may submit up to 2 English-written scripts that have not been previously submitted or published. Plays must be original or adaptations or translations; no musicals. Plays may have had one non-professional or educational theatre production. Open to U.S. citizens and legal residents. **Submission Period:** January 15-last day of February. **Prizes:** $200, $300, $500. **Tips:** Authors will be notified in June. Materials will not be returned. Send SASE for guidelines and entry form.

AURAND HARRIS MEMORIAL PLAYWRITING AWARD

The New England Theatre Conference, Inc., PMB 502, 198 Tremont St., Boston, MA 02116-4750. 617-851-8535. mail@netconline.org. www.netconline.org. **Details:** New, unpublished full-length plays for young audiences. Open to New England residents and NETC members. **Deadline:** May 1. **Entry Fee:** $20. **Prizes:** $1,000 and $500. **Tips:** Guidelines and applications available on website.

JULIE HARRIS PLAYWRIGHT AWARDS

Beverly Hills Theatre Guild, P.O. Box 39729, Los Angeles, CA 90039-0729. **Details:** Annual award for original, full-length plays 75-80 minutes. Scripts must be written in English and may not have been previously submitted, published, or produced. Open to U.S. citizens and legal residents. **Submission Period:** August 1-November 1.

Tips: Authors will be notified in June. Materials will not be returned. Send SASE for specific guidelines and entry form.

MARC A. KLEIN PLAYWRITING AWARD

Case Western Reserve University, Dept. of Theater and Dance, 10900 Euclid Ave., Cleveland, OH 44106-7077. 216-368-4868. ksg@case.edu. **Details:** Open to original, previously unproduced full-length plays by students currently enrolled at a U.S. college or university. **Deadline:** December 1. **Prizes:** $1,000 and production.

NATIONAL CHILDREN'S THEATRE FESTIVAL

Actors' Playhouse at the Miracle Theatre, 280 Miracle Mile, Coral Gables, FL 33134. 305-444-9293, ext. 615. maulding@actorsplayhouse.org. www.actorsplayhouse.org. **Details:** Annual playwriting prize offering $500, full production of winning musical, and author's transportation and lodging to the Festival based upon availability. **Deadline:** June 1. **Entry Fee:** $10. **Tips:** See website for complete rules, guidelines, and entry form. **Contact:** Earl Maulding, Festival Director.

PLAYHOUSE ON THE SQUARE NEW PLAY COMPETITION

51 S. Cooper in Overton Square, Memphis, TN 38104. 901-725-0776. info@playhouseonthesquare.org. www.playhouseonthesquare.org. **Details:** Previously unproduced full-length comedies and dramas; cast up to 15. **Deadline:** April 1. **Prizes:** $500 and production.

RICHARD RODGERS AWARDS

American Academy of Arts and Letters, 633 W 155th St., New York, NY 10032. **Details:** Offers subsidized productions or staged readings in New York City by a nonprofit theater for a musical. **Deadline:** November 1. **Entry Fee:** None. **Tips:** Send SASE for application and guidelines.

THE TEN-MINUTE MUSICALS PROJECT

Box 461194, West Hollywood, CA 90046. www.tenminutemusicals.org. **Details:** Submit complete original stage musicals (any musical style) which run 7-20 minutes. Accepts previously produced material as well as excerpts from full-length shows. Cast limited to 10 members: five men and five women. See website for complete guidelines. **Deadline:** August 31. **Prizes:** $250 royalty advance. **Tips:** Also holds occasional workshops and readings. "Start with a strong story, even it if means postponing work on music and lyrics until dramatic foundation is complete." **Contact:** Michael Koppy, Producer.

SCREENWRITING

THE AUSTIN FILM FESTIVAL
SCREENWRITERS COMPETITION

Austin Film Festival, 1604 Nueces St., Austin, TX 78701-1106. 512-478-4795. info@austinfimfestival.com. www.austinfilmfestival.com. **Details:** Offers two first prizes for unpublished screenplays in the Adult/Family category and the Comedy category. **Deadline:** May 7 (postmark). **Entry Fee:** $40. **Prizes:** $5,000, reimbursement of travel expenses, the AFF Bronze Typewriter award, and admission to the Film Festival and Heart of Film Screenwriters Conference.

"HOLLYWOOD CONNECTION"
SCREENWRITING COMPETITION

Monterey County Film Commission, P.O. Box 111, Monterey, CA 93942. 831-646-0910. filmmonterey@redshift.com. www.filmmonterey.org. **Details:** Screenwriting contest open to all genres. **Deadline:** April 1. **Entry Fee:** $45. **Prizes:** Top three winners get the opportunity to meet with agents and producers in Hollywood to discuss their screenplays. Other awards for artistic talent and screenplays with Monterey County locations. **Tips:** See website for contest guidelines prior to submitting. **Contact:** Ann Quamen.

THE HOLLYWOOD SCREENPLAY AWARDS

CCS Entertainment Group, 433 N Camden Dr., Suite 600, Beverly Hills, CA 90210. 310-288-1881. awards@hollywoodawards.com. www.hollywoodawards.com. **Details:** Open to non-produced, non-optioned screenplays. Selects one screenplay each month. All selected screenplays become finalists in the annual contest where first, second, and third place winners are chosen. **Deadline:** August 18. **Entry Fee:** $55/script. **Prizes:** Cash prizes and opportunity to meet with industry professionals.

HUMANITAS PRIZE

17575 Pacific Coast Hwy, P.O. Box 861, Pacific Palisades, CA 90272. humanitasmail@aol.com. www.humanitasprize.org. **Details:** Awards screenplays and teleplays that emphasize human values. Awards are given in the categories of 30-minute program; 60-minute program; 90-minute program; PBS/cable; feature film; Sundance feature; children's live action; and children's animation. **Deadline:** April 1. **Entry Fee:** None. **Prizes:** Cash prizes ranging from $10,000-$25,000.

MOONDANCE INTERNATIONAL
FILM FESTIVAL SCREENWRITING CONTEST

970 Ninth St., Boulder, CO 80302. moondanceff@aol.com. www.moondancefilmfestival.com. **Details:** Open to films, screenplays, short screenplays, feature and short screenplays for children, short stories, and stageplays. **Deadline:** March 15. **Entry Fee:** $25-$75. **Tips:** E-mail for additional information.

DON AND GEE NICHOLL SCREENWRITING FELLOWSHIPS

Academy of Motion Picture Arts & Sciences, 1313 N Vine St., Los Angeles, CA 90028. 310-247-3010. nicholl@oscars.org. www.oscars.org/nicholl. **Details:** Accepts original feature film scripts by writers who do not make their living writing screenplays. No translations. **Deadline:** May 1. **Entry Fee:** $30. **Prizes:** Up to 5 fellowships of $30,000 each.

"SET IN PHILADELPHIA" SCREENWRITING COMPETITION

Greater Philadelphia Film Office, 100 S Broad St., Suite 600, Philadelphia, PA 19110. 215-686-2668. sip@film.org. www.film.org. **Details:** Open to all screenwriters who submit an original feature-length screenplay set primarily in Philadelphia. **Deadline:** First Monday in December. **Entry Fee:** $45. **Prizes:** Grand Prize: $10,000, opportunity to meet with industry professionals, critique from judges, and free admission to Philadelphia Film Festival. Regional Award: Best screenplay written by a Philadelphia resident, $2,500, critique from judges, and admission to Philadelphia Film Festival. Irene I. Parisi Award: Best screenplay by a screenwriter 25 years or younger, $1,000 and admission to Philadelphia Film Festival. **Contact:** Joan Bressler.

THUNDERBIRD FILMS
ANNUAL SCREENPLAY COMPETITION

Thunderbird Films, 214 Riverside Dr., #112, New York, NY 10025. 212-352-4498. estannard@dekker.com. **Details:** Open to feature-length screenplays that have not been sold or optioned. **Deadline:** October 1. **Entry Fee:** $40. **Prizes:** $2,000 and possible option by Thunderbird Films. **Contact:** Eric Stannard, Coordinator.

CHILDREN'S/YA

MARGUERITE DE ANGELI CONTEST

Delacorte Press/Random House, Inc., 1745 Broadway, New York, NY 10019. www.randomhouse.com/kids. **Details:** Contemporary or historical fiction manuscripts, 80-144 pages for readers ages 7-10. Open to U.S. and Canadian writers who have not previously published a novel for middle-grade readers. **Submission Period:** April 1-June 30. **Prizes:** $1,500 cash, book contract for hardcover and paperback edition, and $7,500 advance.

DELACORTE PRESS CONTEST
FOR A FIRST YOUNG ADULT NOVEL

Delacorte Press/Random House, Inc., 1745 Broadway, Fl. 9, New York, NY 10019. 212-354-6500. www.randomhouse.com/kids. **Details:** Open to writers who have not previously published a YA novel. Submit a book-length manuscript with a contemporary setting, for readers ages 12-18. **Deadline:** December 31. **Prizes:** $1,500, book contract for hardcover and paperback edition, and $7,500 advance.

HIGHLIGHTS FOR CHILDREN FICTION CONTEST

Highlights for Children, 803 Church St., Honesdale, PA 18431-1824. 570-253-1080. eds@highlights-corp.com. www.highlights.com. **Details:** Annual contest with a different theme each year. Open to stories for beginning readers up to 500 words, for more advanced readers up to 800 words. No stories that glorify war, crime, or violence. **Submission Period:** January 1-February 28. **Entry Fee:** None. **Prizes:** Three prizes of $1,000 each and publication in *Highlights*. **Tips:** Send SASE or e-mail for guidelines. **Contact:** Marileta Robinson, Senior Editor.

CULINARY

THE AMERICAN EGG BOARD
FELLOWSHIP FOR CULINARY WRITING

The Writers' Colony at Dairy Hollow, 515 Spring St., Eureka Springs, AR 72632. director@writerscolony.org. www.writerscolony.org. **Details:** Awarded annually to a culinary writer of demonstrated ability whose work involves the creative use of eggs in cooking and/or baking. **Deadline:** October 15. **Entry Fee:** $35. **Prizes:** One-month expense-paid residency at The Writer's Colony at Dairy Hollow.

CORDON D'OR–GOLD RIBBON CUISINE AWARDS

Cordon d'Or Gold Ribbon Cuisine, P.O. Box 13908, St. Petersburg, FL 33733. 727-867-2813. nmekinney@aol.com. www.cordondorcuisine.com. **Details:** Prizes awarded in several categories including Literary Cookbook, Illustrated Cookbook, Culinary Arts Article of the Year. **Deadline:** April 2, 2005. **Contact:** Noreen Kinney.

THE TYSON FELLOWSHIP FOR CULINARY WRITING

The Writers' Colony at Dairy Hollow, 515 Spring St., Eureka Springs, AR 72632. director@writerscolony.org. www.writerscolony.org. **Details:** Awarded annually to a culinary writer whose work pertains to traditional American home or regional cooking, and embodies the Tyson mandate of "feeding the world like family." **Deadline:** October 15. **Entry Fee:** $35. **Prizes:** One-month expense-paid residency at The Writers' Colony at Dairy Hollow.

THE WEBER OUTDOOR COOKING FELLOWSHIP

The Writers' Colony at Dairy Hollow, 515 Spring St., Eureka Springs, AR 72632. director@writerscolony.org. www.writerscolony.org. **Details:** Awarded annually to a culinary writer of demonstrated ability whose work pertains to the history and practice of outdoor cooking (including grilling and barbecue). Cookbooks, scholarly or historical works, and culinary memoir are all eligible. The outdoor cooking investigated may be of any nationality, any course or courses in the meal, any method, and may date from any period in history. Writing which explores marinades, sauces, rubs, brines, and other pre- or post-outdoor grilling enhancements is also eligible. **Deadline:** October 15. **Entry Fee:** $35. **Prizes:** One-month expense-paid residency at The Writers' Colony at Dairy Hollow.

INSPIRATIONAL

A CUP OF COMFORT FOR FAITH

Adams Media Corp., 57 Littlefield St., Avon, MA 02322. 800-872-5627. cupofcomfort@adamsmedia.com. www.cupofcomfort.com. **Details:** Submit creative nonfiction anecdotal stories; 1,000-2,000 words. Inspirational true stories and testimonials of the power of faith, such as answers to prayers; evidence of God's holy grace; miracles; divine intervention; affirmation of religious teachings/scriptures in daily life; finding or reclaiming one's faith. Traditional religions only. **Deadline:** July 1. **Prizes:** Publication; $500; $100; complimentary copy of book.

A CUP OF COMFORT FOR LOVE

Adams Media Corp., 57 Littlefield St., Avon, MA 02322. 800-872-5672. cupofcomfort@adamsmedia.com. www.cupofcomfort.com. **Details:** Submit creative nonfiction anecdotal stories; 1,000-2,000 words. Real-life romantic "love stories" for/about couples, lovers, soul mates—including puppy love; true love; new love; enduring love; first love; unrequited love; the love of one's life; mature love; rekindled love; friends become lovers; unique engagement, wedding, anniversary experiences; turning points and milestones in a marriage/partnership; defining moments and "aha" moments that spark, shape, or strengthen a love relationship. **Deadline:** August 1. **Prizes:** Publication; $500; $100; complimentary copy of book.

A CUP OF COMFORT FOR SPIRITUALITY

Adams Media Corp., 57 Littlefield St., Avon, MA 02322. 800-872-5627. cupofcomfort@adamsmedia.com. www.cupofcomfort.com. **Details:** Submit creative nonfiction anecdotal stories; 1,000-2,000 words. Soulful true stories about positive spiritual experiences and relationships—such as gifts or lessons of spiritual teachers/mentors; discovering a spiritual path, divine truth, or kindred spirit; receiving and actualizing (putting into positive action) a spiritual lession; miracles; epiphanies; divine intervention and direction; evidence of a higher spirit; awakening or deepening one's inner spirit; enlightening, life-defining, life-changing spiritual experiences. All benevolent spiritual paths and religions welcome. **Deadline:** December 31. **Prizes:** Publication; $500; $100; complimentary copy of book.

THE ROCKING CHAIR READER

Adams Media Corp., 57 Littlefield St., Avon, MA 02322. 800-872-5627. rockingchairreader@adamsmedia.com. www.rockingchairreader.com. **Details:** Submit creative nonfiction anecdotal stories; 500-1,000 words. Artfully woven, slice-of-life tales of Americana. True, heartwarming, humorous or inspiring, nostalgic stories capturing the heart and soul of a kindler, gentler, simpler way of American life; the charms of small-town and rural America; the joys of close-knit families and tight-knit communities; or the "good old days" of bygone eras. **Deadline:** November 1. **Prizes:** Publication; $50; $250; complimentary copy of book.

MULTIPLE

ALLIGATOR JUNIPER'S NATIONAL WRITING CONTEST

Alligator Juniper, Prescott College, 301 Grove Ave., Prescott, AZ 86301. 928-778-2090. aj@prescott.edu. www.prescott.edu/highlights/aj.html. **Details:** Open to previously unpublished short fiction, creative nonfiction, and poetry. Stories and essays can be up to 30 pages; poetry up to 5 poems or 5 pages. **Submission Period:** May 1-October 1. **Entry Fee:** $10/entry. **Prizes:** $500 and publication. **Tips:** See website for specific guidelines. Entrants are required to agree to all submission guidelines in order for work to be considered. **Contact:** Miles Waggener.

AMERICAN MARKETS NEWSLETTER COMPETITION

American Markets Newsletters, 1974 46th Ave., San Francisco, CA 94116. **Details:** Fiction and nonfiction to 2,000 words, both published and unpublished. All entries will be considered for worldwide syndication. **Deadline:** July 31 and December 31. **Entry Fee:** AMN subscribers, $12 for 1 entry, $22 for 2 entries, $30 for 3 entries. **Prizes:** Cash prizes ($250, $50, $30) plus syndication. **Tips:** Authors receive the standard 50% of everything received from publication fees.

ANNUAL TAMPA WRITERS ALLIANCE CONTEST

10028 Strafford Oak Ct., #706, Tampa, FL 33624. 813-908-3095. the1lark@hotmail.com. www.tampawriters.org. **Details:** Awards for submissions of unpublished fiction, nonfiction, play/script writing, poetry, and "excellence in Florida writing." Open to writers 18+ years of age. Entrants may submit one entry/category. **Deadline:** October 1. **Entry Fee:** $10/entry (non-members). **Prizes:** Cash prizes ($50, $25, $15) and publication in *The Wordsmith* (TWA's annual anthology). **Tips:** See website for forms, rules, and FAQs. **Contact:** M. Lark Underwood, Coordinator.

ARTS AWARDS

National Foundation for Advancement in the Arts, 444 Brickell Ave., P-14, Miami, FL 33131. 1-800-970-2787. info@nfaa.org. www.artsawards.org. **Details:** Identifies young artists (high school seniors or 17-18 years of age) in the disciplines of dance, film and video, classical, pop and jazz music, photography, theater, visual arts, voice and writing, for scholarships and financial support toward their continued arts education. **Deadline:** Applications due October 1; submissions due November 1. **Entry Fee:** Before June 2: $25 online, $30 by mail; after June 2: $35 online, $40 by mail. **Prizes:** $10,000, $3,000, $1,500, $1,000, $500, $100. **Tips:** See website for details.

ASF TRANSLATION PRIZE

American-Scandinavian Foundation, 58 Park Ave., New York, NY 10016. 212-879-9779. ahenkin@amscan.org. www.amscan.org. **Details:** Translations of literary prose (50+ pages) or poetry (25+ pages) originally written after 1800 in Danish, Finnish, Icelandic, Norwegian, or Swedish. Send SASE or e-mail for guidelines. **Deadline:** June 1. **Entry Fee:** None. **Prizes:** $2,000, publication in *Scandinavian Review*, and bronze medallion. **Contact:** Andrey Henkin, Fellowships and Grants.

CHELSEA AWARDS

Chelsea, P.O. Box 773, Cooper Station, New York, NY 10276-0773. **Details:** Awards for fiction and poetry. Traditional and experimental fiction, previously unpublished, up to 30 typed pages or 7,500 words. Collection of 4-6 poems, not to exceed 500 lines. Focus is on quality and fresh, original use of language. **Deadline:** June 15 (fiction), December 15 (poetry). **Entry Fee:** $10; entrants receive subscription to *Chelsea*. **Prizes:** $1,000 each and publication in Chelsea. **Tips:** Send SASE for guidelines.

CNW/FFWA FLORIDA STATE WRITING COMPETITION

Florida Freelance Writers Assn., P.O. Box A, North Stratford, NH 03590. 603-922-8338. www.writers-editors.com. **Details:** Contest open to all writers. Categories include fiction, nonfiction, children's and poetry. **Deadline:** March 15. **Entry Fee:** $5-$20. **Prizes:** $50-$100. **Tips:** Send SASE for guidelines and entry form, or visit website. **Contact:** Dana K. Cassell.

DOROTHY DANIELS HONORARY WRITING AWARDS

National League of American Pen Women, P.O. Box 1485, Simi Valley, CA 93062. 805-493-1081. cdoering@adelphia.net. **Details:** Original, unpublished poetry to 50 lines, fiction to 2,000 words and nonfiction to 1,500 words. **Deadline:** July 31. **Entry Fee:** $5/poem; $5/fiction or nonfiction entry. **Prizes:** $100 in 3 categories.

WILLIAM FAULKNER WISDOM WRITING COMPETITION

Pirate's Alley Faulkner Society, Faulkner House, 624 Pirate's Alley, New Orleans, LA 70116. 504-586-1609. faulkhouse@aol.com. www.wordsandmusic.org. **Details:** Unpublished works of fiction, nonfiction, or poetry. **Deadline:** April 30. **Entry Fee:** $10-$35. **Prizes:** $250-$7,500. **Tips:** Send SASE or see website for guidelines and entry form. **Contact:** Rosemary James, Director.

FELLOWSHIPS FOR HISTORICAL RESEARCH
BY CREATIVE AND PERFORMING ARTISTS AND WRITERS

American Antiquarian Society, 185 Salisbury St., Worcester, MA 01609-1634. 508-471-2131. jmoran@mwa.org. www.americanantiquarian.org. **Details:** At least three fellowships, for creative and performing artists, writers, filmmakers, and journalists, for research on pre-20th century American history. Residencies 4-8 weeks; travel expenses and stipends of $1,200 per month. Write for guidelines. **Deadline:** October 5. **Contact:** James David Moran.

THE FLORIDA REVIEW EDITOR'S AWARDS

University of Central Florida, Dept. of English, Orlando, FL 32816. 407-823-2038. flreview@mail.ucf.edu. www.flreview.com. **Details:** Open to unpublished fiction and nonfiction to 10,000 words and poetry to 40 lines. **Deadline:** April 1. **Entry Fee:** $15. **Prizes:** Three $1,000 awards.

DEANN LUBELL PROFESSIONAL WRITERS' COMPETITION

NLAPW Palm Springs Branch, P.O. Box 1166, 45300 Portola Ave., Palm Desert, CA 92261-9998. **Details:** Open only to published/produced writers in the following categories: magazine articles, essays, and editorials; poetry; short stories; web-based articles; and screenwriting/playwriting. **Entry Fee:** $15. **Prizes:** $100, $75 and $50 in each category. **Tips:** Send SASE for complete guidelines and contest dates. **Contact:** Kristin Johnson.

MID-LIST PRESS FIRST SERIES
AWARDS FOR POETRY AND THE NOVEL

Mid-List Press, 4324 12th Ave. S, Minneapolis, MN 55407-3218. guide@midlist.org. www.midlist.org. **Details:** Unpublished poetry collections and novels by writers who have not previously published in the category under submission. Poetry manuscripts must be at least 60 pages; novels must be at least 50,000 words. **Deadline:** February 1. **Entry Fee:** $30. **Prizes:** Publication and advance against royalties. **Tips:** All submissions must follow guidelines exactly and include entry form. See website for detailed guidelines.

MID-LIST PRESS FIRST SERIES
AWARDS FOR SHORT FICTION AND CREATIVE NONFICTION

Mid-List Press, 4324 12th Ave. S, Minneapolis, MN 55407-3218. guide@midlist.org. www.midlist.org. **Details:** Unpublished short fiction collections and creative nonfiction by writers who have not published collections in the category under submission. Manuscripts must be at least 50,000 words. **Deadline:** July 1. **Entry Fee:** $30. **Prizes:** Publication and advance against royalty. **Tips:** See website for detailed guidelines. All submissions must follow guidelines exactly and include entry form.

PRAIRIE SCHOONER PRIZE BOOK SERIES

University of Nebraska, 201 Andrews Hall, P.O. Box 880334, Lincoln, NE 68588-0334. 402-472-0911. kgrey2@unl.edu. www.unl.edu/schooner/psmain.htm. **Details:** Annual contest for a collection of poetry and a collection of short fiction. Open to all writers (both published and unpublished), including non-U.S. citizens writing in English. Stories and poems previously published in periodicals are eligible. Novels will not be considered. Simultaneous submissions accepted with notice. **Submission Period:** January 15-March 15. **Entry Fee:** $25. **Prizes:** $3,000 and publication by the University of Nebraska Press. **Contact:** Kelly Grey Carlisle, Managing Editor.

PHILIP ROTH RESIDENCE IN CREATIVE WRITING

Bucknell University, Stadler Center for Poetry, Lewisburg, PA 17837. **Details:** Awards fall residency (studio, lodging, meals) and $2,000 stipend, for a writer, over 21, not currently enrolled in a university, to work on a first or second book. Awarded alternately to a fiction writer and a poet. **Deadline:** March 15.

MONA SCHREIBER PRIZE FOR HUMOROUS FICTION AND NONFICTION

11362 Homedale St., Los Angeles, CA 90049. www.brashcyber.com. **Details:** Writers of comedic essays, articles, short stories, poetry, shopping lists, and other forms are invited to submit. Send unpublished works up to 750 words. Include e-mail address for notification; do not send SASE. **Deadline:** December 1. **Entry Fee:** $5/entry. **Prizes:** Cash prizes ($500, $250, $100). **Tips:** "Humor is subjective. Uniqueness is suggested. Weirdness is encouraged."

LEIF AND INGER SJÖBERG PRIZE

American-Scandinavian Foundation, 58 Park Ave., New York, NY 10016. 212-879-9779. ahenkin@amscan.org. www.amscan.org. **Details:** Translations of literary prose (50+ pages) or poetry (25+ pages) originally written after 1800 in Danish, Finnish, Icelandic, Norwegian, or Swedish. Send SASE or e-mail for guidelines. **Deadline:** June 1. **Entry Fee:** None. **Prizes:** $1,000, publication in *Scandinavian Review*, and bronze medallion. **Contact:** Andrey Henkin, Fellowships and Grants.

SOUL-MAKING LITERARY COMPETITION

NLAPW Nob Hill Branch, Webhallow, 1544 Sweetwood Dr., Colma, CA 94015. www.soulmakingcontest.us. **Details:** Categories are the Janice Farrel Poetry Prize, Sheila K. Smith Short Story Prize, Rosalie Fleming Memorial Essay and Creative Nonfiction Prize, Joanna Catherine Scott Novel Excerpt Prize, Kathryn Handley Prose Poem Prize, Carolyn A. Clark Short-Short Story/Flash Fiction Prize, and Clarence Douglas Wright Song/Lyric Prize. **Deadline:** November 30. **Entry Fee:** $5. **Prizes:** $100, $50 and $25 in each category.

SOUTHWEST WRITERS ANNUAL CONTEST

SouthWest Writers, 3721 Morris NE, Suite A, Dept. TW, Albuquerque, NM 87111. 505-265-9485. swriters@aol.com. www.southwestwriters.org. **Details:** Contest open to novels (first 10 pages, mainstream/genre/YA); short stories (up to 2,400 words, mainstream/literary/genre/YA); short nonfiction (800-2,400 words, any topic); book-length nonfiction (first 10 pages); children's material (fiction, nonfiction, picture books); screenplays (first 20 pages); and poetry (up to 50 lines). **Deadline:** June 1. **Prizes:** Cash prizes in each category ($150, $100, $75), plus $1,000 Storyteller Award selected from first-place winners. **Tips:** See website or write for guidelines and entry fees. **Contact:** Judy Ducharme and Sandy Schairer, Contest Co-Chairs.

OTHER

THE BRIDGE FUND FELLOWSHIP FOR THE CREATION OF ORIGINAL MATERIALS FOR TEACHING ARKANSAS HISTORY

The Writers' Colony at Dairy Hollow, 515 Spring St., Eureka Springs, AR 72632. director@writerscolony.org. www.writerscolony.org. **Details:** Awarded annually to a writer, librarian, teacher, or dramatist for the creation of original, innovative material which brings the teaching of Arkansas history alive. The material may be educational (lesson plans, workbooks, coursework), or dramatic (scripts for videos, plays for children, historically-based character development for living history enactments or interactive school visits, imagined diaries). Work may include historically-based fiction, nonfiction, or memoir; it may be wholly original, or it may use existing primary materials in an original manner. **Deadline:** October 15. **Entry Fee:** $35. **Prizes:** One-month expense-paid residency at The Writers' Colony at Dairy Hollow.

THE MOONDANCER FELLOWSHIP
FOR NATURE AND OUTDOOR WRITING

The Writers' Colony at Dairy Hollow, 515 Spring St., Eureka Springs, AR 72632. director@writerscolony.org. www.writerscolony.org. **Details:** Awarded annually to a nature and/or outdoor writer of demonstrated ability. Acceptable projects include books and magazine articles. **Deadline:** October 15. **Entry Fee:** $35. **Prizes:** One-month expense-paid residency at The Writers' Colony at Dairy Hollow.

FRED STARR FELLOWSHIP FOR HISTORICALLY
BASED WRITING ON THE FOLKLORE AND CUSTOMS
OF THE SOUTHERN HIGHLANDS

The Writers' Colony at Dairy Hollow, 515 Spring St., Eureka Springs, AR 72632. director@writerscolony.org. www.writerscolony.org. **Details:** Awarded annually to a writer of gift whose work is set in or otherwise pertains to the folklore, customs, and history of America's Southern Highlands (the Appalachians, Ozarks, Ouachitas, or Great Smokey Mountains). **Deadline:** October 15. **Entry Fee:** $35. **Prizes:** One-month expense-paid residency at The Writers' Colony at Dairy Hollow.

GREETING CARD PUBLISHERS

Companies selling greeting cards and novelty items (T-shirts, coffee mugs, buttons, etc.) often have their own specific requirements for the submission of ideas, verse, and artwork. In general, however, each verse or message should be typed double-spaced on a 3x5 or 4x6 card. Use only one side of the card, and be sure to put your name and address in the upper left-hand corner. Keep a copy of every verse or idea you send. (It's also advisable to keep a record of what you've submitted to each publisher.) Always enclose an SASE, and do not send out more than ten verses or ideas in a group to any one publisher. Never send original artwork unless a publisher indicates a definite interest in using your work.

AMBERLEY GREETING CARD COMPANY

11510 Goldcoast Dr., Cincinnati, OH 45249-1695. 513-489-2775. www.amberleygreeting.com. **Description:** Humorous ideas for cards: birthday, illness, friendship, anniversary, congratulations, "miss you," etc. Short, humorous verse ok. Send SASE for writer's guidelines. Pays $150/idea.

BLUE MOUNTAIN ARTS

P.O. Box 1007, Boulder, CO 80306. 303-449-0536. editorial@spsstudios.com. www.sps.com. **Description:** Poetry and writings suitable for publication on greeting cards and in books. Looking for original, heartfelt poetry and prose on love, friendship, family, special occasions, positive living, aspirations, self-help, and other similar topics. Submit seasonal material (Christmas, Valentine's Day, Mother's Day, etc.) 5 months in advance. Full book manuscripts also accepted. Pays $300 for the first work chosen for publication on a card (payment scale escalates after that) and $50 if poem is used only in a book anthology. Pays on publication. Card and/or book guidelines available on request. **Tips:** "Definitely get a feel for what we publish by trying to find our cards and books in stores, but don't study them too closely, as we're looking for fresh, new ideas—not rewrites of existing cards."

BRILLIANT ENTERPRISES

117 W Valerio St., Santa Barbara, CA 93101-2927. www.ashleighbrilliant.com. **Description:** Illustrated epigrams emphasizing truth, wit, universality, and originality. This line of greeting cards is very unusual and should be studied carefully before material is submitted. Payment is $60. Send $2 for catalog and samples. **Tips:** "Writers will be wasting their time and ours unless they first study our very unusual line. We supply a catalogue for $2." **Contact:** Ashleigh Brilliant.

COMSTOCK CARDS

600 S Rock, Suite 15, Reno, NV 89502-4115. 775-856-9400. www.comstockcards.com. **Description:** Adult humor, outrageous or sexual content, for greeting cards, invitations, and notepads. SASE required. Payment varies, on publication. Guidelines on website. **Contact:** Production Department.

DAYSPRING GREETING CARDS

P.O. Box 1010, Siloam Springs, AR 72761. info@dayspring.com.
Description: Inspirational material for everyday occasions and most holidays. Currently only accepting freelance copy submissions from published greeting card authors. Qualified writers should print "Previously Published" on lower left corner of mailing envelope containing the submissions. No more than 10 submissions at a time. Payment is $60 on acceptance. Send SASE or e-mail for guidelines. **Tips:** Type the word "Write" in the subject line of e-mail to receive submission guidelines.

DESIGN DESIGN, INC.

P.O. Box 2266, Grand Rapids, MI 49501-2266. **Description:** Short verses for both humorous and sentimental concepts for greeting cards. Everyday (birthday, get well, just for fun, etc.) and seasonal (Christmas, Valentine's Day, Easter, Mother's Day, Father's Day, graduation, Halloween, Thanksgiving) material. Flat fee payment on publication. Include SASE with submission.

DUCK & COVER

P.O. Box 21640, Oakland, CA 94620. duckcover@aol.com. **Description:** Does not produce any greeting cards. However, makes buttons, magnets, and stickers with fresh, original, and outrageous slogans. Send SASE for writer's guidelines.

EPHEMERA, INC.

P.O. Box 490, Phoenix, OR 97535. 541-535-4195. mail@ephemera-inc.com. www.ephemera-inc.com. **Description:** Provocative, irreverent, and outrageously funny slogans for novelty buttons, magnets, and stickers. Submit a typed list of slogans. SASE. Pays $50/slogan, on acceptance. **Tips:** "We're looking for satirical slogans about pop culture, free speech, work attitudes, women's and men's issues, coffee, booze, pot, drugs, food, politics, aging boomers, teens, gays and lesbians. Surprise us! Make us laugh out loud!"

FRAVESSI GREETINGS, INC.

P.O. Box 1800, Enfield, CT 06082. 800-223-0963. info@fravessi.com. www.fravessi.com. **Description:** Short verse, mostly humorous or sentimental; cards with witty prose. Christmas and everyday material. Pays varying rates, on acceptance.

FREEDOM GREETING CARDS

Plesh Creative Group, Inc., 38 A Park St., Medfield, MA 02052. 508-359-6400. www.freedomgreetings.com. **Description:** Traditional and humorous messages for everyday occasions and all major seasons. Pays negotiable rates, on acceptance. Query with SASE.

GALLANT GREETINGS CORPORATION

P.O. Box 308, Franklin Park, IL 60131. 847-671-6500. info@gallantgreetings.com. www.gallantgreetings.com. **Description:** Seeks ideas for seasonal, humorous and traditional greeting cards.

KATE HARPER DESIGNS

kateharp@aol.com. **Description:** Edgy humor about everyday life. Young writers encouraged to submit. Also needs submissions by kids for "Kid Quote" line. Pays $25 and sample cards. Contact via e-mail only. For standard guidelines, type "guidelines/adult" in subject line; for "Kid Quote" guidelines, type "guidelines/kids." Buys 100% freelance work several times/year.

OATMEAL STUDIOS GREETING CARD COMPANY

Box 138 TW, Rochester, VT 05767. 802-767-3171. www.oatmealstudios.com. **Description:** Humorous ideas for all occasions. Pays $75/idea purchased. **Tips:** "Your ideas must be original! We look forward to seeing your work!"

P.S. GREETINGS

5730 North Tripp, Chicago, IL 60646. www.psgreetings.com. **Description:** Manufacturer of everyday and Christmas greeting cards. Seeks material for all major holidays, particular interest in Christmas. Writers should send verses or poems applicable to product line. Payment is one-time, flat fee; buys exclusive rights for all greeting and/or stationery products for indefinite use. Only submissions accompanied by an SASE will be returned. Responds within 30 days. **Contact:** Design Director.

PARAMOUNT CARDS, INC.

P.O. Box 6546, Providence, RI 02940-6546. **Description:** Light humor, traditional, and inspirational sentiments for everyday occasions, Christmas, Valentine's Day, Easter, Mother's Day, Father's Day, graduation and Thanksgiving. Submit each idea (10-15 per submission) on a 3x5 card with name and address on each; include SASE. Payment varies, on acceptance. **Contact:** Editorial Freelance Coordinator.

RECYCLED PAPER GREETINGS, INC.

3636 N Broadway, Chicago, IL 60613-4488. www.recycled.com. **Description:** Seeks original copy that is hip, flip, and concise. Risqué material considered. Send up to 10 pieces; mock-up ideas complete with artwork required. Will not consider ideas without appropriate artwork included with submission. Allow 12 weeks for response. Payment made if design tests well and is picked up for distribution. SASE for guidelines. **Tips:** "Freelance guidelines can be found on our website. We don't accept online submissions." **Contact:** Gretchen Hoffman, John LeMoine.

ROCKSHOTS, INC.

20 Vandam St., Fl. 4, New York, NY 10013. 212-243-9661. www.rockshots.com. **Description:** Humorous, sexy line of greeting cards. Combination of sexy and humorous come-on type greeting and "cute" insult cards. Card gag can adopt a sentimental style, then take an ironic twist and end on an offbeat note. No sentimental or conventional material. Put gag lines on 8x11 paper with name, address, phone, and social security numbers in right corner, or individually on 3x5 cards. Submit 10 ideas/batch. Pays $50 per copy upon acceptance. Send SASE for guidelines.

MARCEL SCHURMAN COMPANY

101 New Montgomery, Fl. 6, San Francisco, CA 94105. 415-284-0133. www.schurmanfinepapers.com. **Description:** Seeking sincere, positive, and clever text ideas for traditional and humorous greeting cards. Seeking text that goes beyond the standard generic verse. Poetry and off-color humor are not appropriate for this line. Flat fee per text purchase. Send SASE or see website for submission guidelines. **Contact:** Text Editor.

VAGABOND CREATIONS, INC.

2560 Lance Dr., Dayton, OH 45409. 937-298-1124. vagabond@siscom.net. www.vagabondcreations.com. **Description:** Greeting cards with graphics only on cover (no copy) and short punch line inside: birthday, everyday, Valentine's Day, Christmas, and graduation. Mildly risqué humor with double entendre acceptable. Ideas for illustrated theme stationery. Pays $20, on acceptance.

ORGANIZATIONS

AMERICAN SOCIETY OF JOURNALISTS AND AUTHORS

1501 Broadway, Suite 302, New York, NY 10036. 212-997-0947. execdir@asja.org. www.asja.org. **Mission:** A national organization for independent writers of nonfiction. Promotes high standards of writing. **Membership Requirements:** Membership is open to professional freelance writers of nonfiction; qualifications are judged by the membership committee. Call or write for application details. **Member Benefits:** Referral services, many discount services, and ways to explore professional issues and concerns with other writers; also produces a free electronic bulletin board for freelancers on contract issues in the new-media age. Members receive a monthly newsletter with confidential market information. Also hosts annual writers conference with buying editors, publishers, and agents. **Contact:** Brett Harvey, Executive Director.

ASSITEJ/USA-INTERNATIONAL ASSOCIATION OF THEATRE FOR CHILDREN AND YOUNG PEOPLE

724 Second Ave. S, Nashville, TN 37210. 615-254-5719. usassitej@aol.com. **Mission:** National service organization promoting the power of professional theatre for young audiences through excellence, collaboration, and innovation across cultural and international boundaries. **Member Benefits:** Sponsors festivals and forums for interchange among theatres and theatre artists. Also produces publications related to the field. **Dues:** $65 (individual), $35, (retiree), $30 (student).

ASSOCIATION OF AMERICAN PUBLISHERS

71 Fifth Ave., Fl. 2, New York, NY 10003-3004. 212-255-0200. kblough@publishers.org. www.publishers.org. **Mission:** National trade organization for the U.S. publishing industry. **Contact:** Patricia Schroeder, President; Kathryn Blough, Vice President.

ASSOCIATION OF WRITERS AND WRITING PROGRAMS

George Mason University, Mail Stop 1E3, Fairfax, VA 22030. 703-993-4301. www.awpwriter.org. **Mission:** Nonprofit organization of teachers, writers, writing programs, and others who love literature. **Member Benefits:** Annual contests for poetry, short fiction, creative nonfiction, and novels. Prague Summer Seminars Fellowship Competition. Annual conferences. **Dues:** $59 ($37 for students), $20 for subscription to *AWP Chronicle* only.

THE AUTHORS GUILD

31 E 28th St., Fl. 10, New York, NY 10016. 212-563-5904. staff@authorsguild.org. www.authorsguild.org or www.authorsguild.net. **Mission:** Largest organization of published writers in the U.S. **Membership Requirements:** Open to writers who have published a book in the last seven years with an established publisher, or who have published three articles in general-circulation periodicals in the prior 18 months, are eligible for active membership. An unpublished writer with a contract offer may

be eligible for associate membership. **Member Benefits:** Access to website-building software for writers with discounted site-hosting fees, free reviews of publishing and agency contracts, access to group health insurance, quarterly news bulletin, and seminars on subjects of concern. Also lobbies on behalf of authors on issues such as copyright, taxation, freedom of expression. **Dues:** $90 for first year. **Contact:** Paul Aiken, Executive Director.

THE AUTHORS LEAGUE OF AMERICA

31 E 28th St., Fl. 10, New York, NY 10016. 212-564-8350. staff@authorsguild.com. www.authorsguild.com. **Mission:** National organization representing 14,000 authors and dramatists on matters of joint concern, such as copyright, taxes, freedom of expression, etc. **Membership Requirements:** Restricted to authors and dramatists who are members of the Authors Guild and the Dramatists Guild.

DRAMATISTS GUILD OF AMERICA

1501 Broadway, Suite 701, New York, NY 10036-3909. 212-398-9366, ext. 11. membership@dramaguild.com. www.dramatistsguild.com. **Mission:** A professional association of playwrights, composers, and lyricists who work to protect author rights and to improve working conditions. **Membership Requirements:** Open to all playwrights, produced or not. **Member Benefits:** Use of guild contracts; a toll-free number for members in need of business advice; discount tickets; access to health insurance programs and group term-life insurance plan; many seminars. Frederick Loewe room is available to members for readings and rehearsals at a nominal fee. Publishes *Dramatists Guild Resource Directory* and *The Dramatist Magazine*. **Dues:** $150 (active), $95 (associate), $35 (student). **Contact:** Christopher C. Wilson, Executive Director; Tom Epstein, Director of Membership Services.

INTERNATIONAL ASSOCIATION OF CRIME WRITERS
NORTH AMERICAN BRANCH

P.O. Box 8674, New York, NY 10116-8674. 212-243-8966. mfrisque@igc.org. **Mission:** Promotes communication among crime writers worldwide, encourages translation of crime writing into other languages, and defends authors against censorship. **Membership Requirements:** Membership open to published authors of crime fiction, nonfiction, and screenplays. Agents, editors, critics, and booksellers are also eligible to apply. **Member Benefits:** Sponsors conferences, publishes quarterly newsletter, *Border Patrol*, and awards annual Hammett Prize for Literary Excellence in Crime Writing (fiction or nonfiction) to a U.S. or Canadian author. **Dues:** $60/year. **Contact:** Mary A. Frisque, Executive Director.

INTERNATIONAL WOMEN'S WRITING GUILD

Box 810, Gracie Station, New York, NY 10028-0082. 212-737-7536. iwwg@iwwg-com. www.iwwg.com. **Mission:** A network for personal and professional empowerment of women through writing. **Membership Requirements:** Any woman may join regardless of portfolio. **Member Benefits:** Six issues of a 32-page newsletter, a list of literary agents, independent small presses, and publishing services, access to group health insurance plan, reduced rates at writing conferences, referral services, and events, including an annual summer conference at Skidmore College in Saratoga Springs, NY, regional writing clusters, and year-round supportive networking. **Dues:** $45/year. **Contact:** Hannelore Hahn, Executive Director.

MYSTERY WRITERS OF AMERICA

17 E 47th St., Fl. 6, New York, NY 10017. 212-888-8171. www.mysterywriters.org. **Mission:** Works to raise the prestige of mystery and detective writing, to encourage the reading of mysteries, and to defend the rights and increase the income of all writers in mystery, detective, and fact-crime writing. **Membership Requirements:** Membership categories: Active (open to any writer who is traditionally published and has earned a minimum of $100 in mystery, suspense, or crime writing); Associate (professionals in allied fields); Corresponding (writers living outside the U.S.); and Affiliate (general members). **Member Benefits:** Presents the annual Edgar Allan Poe Awards for the best mystery writing in a variety of fields. **Dues:** $95. **Contact:** Margery Flax, Office Manager.

NATIONAL ASSOCIATION OF SCIENCE WRITERS

P.O. Box 890, Hedgesville, WV 25427. 304-754-5077. diane@nasw.org. www.nasw.org. **Mission:** Promotes and helps to improve the flow of accurate information about science through all media. **Membership Requirements:** Anyone actively engaged in the dissemination of science information is eligible to apply. Members must be principally involved in reporting on science through newspapers, magazines, TV, or other media that reach the public directly. **Dues:** $75/year (students $25/year). **Contact:** Diane McGurgan, Executive Director.

NATIONAL ASSOCIATION OF WOMEN WRITERS

P.O. Box 183812, Arlington, TX 76096. 866-821-5829. naww@onebox.com. www.naww.org. **Mission:** "NAWW is where women unite to write. We strive to support, encourage, and teach women writers of all levels." **Member Benefits:** Access to writing resources, participation in workshops and conferences, and access to online writing forums. See website for current listing of member benefits. **Dues:** $55 (US) and $65 (outside the US). **Contact:** Sheri' McConnell, Founder/President.

NATIONAL CONFERENCE OF EDITORIAL WRITERS

3899 N Front St., Harrisburg, PA 17110. 717-703-3015. ncew@pa-news.org. www.ncew.org. **Mission:** Nonprofit organization working to improve the quality of editorial pages and broadcast editorials, and to promote high standards among opinion writers and editors. **Membership Requirements:** Open to opinion writers and editors for general-circulation newspapers, radio or television stations, and syndicated columnists; teachers and students of journalism; and others who determine editorial policy. **Member Benefits:** Networking opportunities, regional meetings, page exchanges, foreign tours, educational opportunities and seminars, annual convention, and a subscription to quarterly journal, *The Masthead*. **Dues:** Based on circulation or broadcast audience: $90-$200; $100 for journalism educators; $25 for students.

THE NATIONAL LEAGUE OF AMERICAN PEN WOMEN

National Headquarters-Pen Arts Building, 1300 17th St. NW, Washington, DC 20036-1973. 202-785-1997. nlapwi@juno.com. www.americanpenwomen.org. **Mission:** Promotes development of creative talents of professional women in the arts. **Membership Requirements:** Membership is through local branches, in categories of Art, Letters, and Music. **Contact:** Wanda A. Rider, National President.

NATIONAL WRITERS ASSOCIATION

3140 S Peoria, Suite 295, Aurora, CO 80014. 303-841-0246. sandywrter@aol.com. www.nationalwriters.com. **Mission:** Full-service organization assisting writers, from formatting a manuscript to assistance finding agents and publishers. **Member Benefits:** Awards cash prizes in 5 contests each year. Published book contest, David R. Raffelock Award for Publishing Excellence. Also referral services, conferences, and financial assistance. **Dues:** $65 Individual, $35 Student, $85 Professional. **Contact:** Sandy Whelchel, Executive Director.

NATIONAL WRITERS UNION

113 University Place, Fl. 6, New York, NY 10003. 212-254-0279. nwu@nwu.org. www.nwu.org. **Mission:** Works for equitable payment and fair treatment for freelance writers through collective action. Over 6,000 members in 17 chapters nationwide including authors, poets, cartoonists, journalists, and technical writers. The NWU is affiliated with the United Auto Workers (UAW), and through the UAW, the AFL-CIO. **Membership Requirements:** Open to writers who have published a book, play, 3 articles, 5 poems, a short story, or an equivalent amount of newsletter, publicity, technical, commercial, government, or institutional copy, or have written unpublished material and are actively seeking publication. **Member Benefits:** Offers contract advice and grievance assistance, job hotline, agent information, press credentials for working journalists, support for book tour promotions, a quarterly magazine, e-mail networking lists (for journalists, book authors, poets, writers, etc.), sample contracts, and resource materials. Also sponsors workshops and seminars. **Dues:** $160/year. **Contact:** Dian Killian, Senior Organizer.

NEW DRAMATISTS

424 W 44th St., New York, NY 10036. www.newdramatists.org. **Mission:** Service organization for playwrights, providing time, space, and other resources to develop their craft. **Membership Requirements:** Seven-year residencies are open to residents of New York City and surrounding tri-state area. National memberships for those outside the area who spend time in NYC. Apply between July 15-September 15. **Member Benefits:** Resources for playwrights; readings and workshops; a director-in-residence program; national script distribution for company members; artist work spaces; international playwright exchange programs; script copying facilities; and a free ticket program. **Dues:** None. **Tips:** See website for more information.

NORTHWEST PLAYWRIGHTS GUILD

318 SW Palatine Hill Rd., Portland, OR 97219. 503-452-4778. bjscript@teleport.com. www.nwpg.org. **Mission:** Chapters in Portland, OR and Seattle, WA. Encourages the creation and production of new plays. **Member Benefits:** Support through play development, staged readings, and networking for play competitions and production opportunities. Oregon chapter offers Page to Stage and Living Room Theater to help playwrights develop new work. Monthly and quarterly newsletters. **Dues:** $25/year. **Contact:** Tonya Derrickson, Director; Bill Johnson, Office Manager.

OUTDOOR WRITERS ASSOCIATION OF AMERICA

121 Hickory St., Suite 1, Missoula, MT 59801. 406-728-7434. owaa@montana.com. www.owaa.org. **Mission:** A nonprofit organization of outdoor communicators. **Member Benefits:** Annual awards: Ham Brown Award, Jade of Chiefs, Excellence in Craft, Mountain of Jade Award, Jackie Pfeiffer Memorial Award. Also online search and referral services; annual conference. **Dues:** $125 individual, $30 student, $325 supporting. **Contact:** William H. Geer, Executive Director.

PEN AMERICAN CENTER

568 Broadway, New York, NY 10012. 212-334-1660. pen@pen.org. www.pen.org. **Mission:** One of over 130 centers worldwide of International PEN. Members are poets, playwrights, essayists, editors, and novelists, also literary translators and agents who have made a substantial contribution to the literary community. Main office in New York City; branches in Boston, Chicago, New Orleans, Portland, Oregon, and San Francisco. **Membership Requirements:** Membership open to writers who have published 2 books of literary merit, also editors, agents, playwrights, and translators who meet specific standards. Apply to membership committee. **Member Benefits:** Literary events and awards, outreach projects, assistance to writers in financial need, and international and domestic human-rights campaigns on behalf of literary figures imprisoned because of their writing. **Dues:** $75/year. **Contact:** Michael Roberts, Executive Director.

THE PLAYWRIGHTS' CENTER

2301 Franklin Ave. E, Minneapolis, MN 55406-1099. 612-332-7481. info@pwcenter.org. www.pwcenter.org. **Mission:** Provides services to support playwrights and playwriting, nurtures artistic excellence and new visions, fosters initiative and leadership, practices cultural pluralism, discovers emerging artists, and connects playwrights with audiences. **Member Benefits:** Offer annual awards: McKnight Residency and Commission, McKnight Advancement Grant, Jerome fellowships, Many Voices residencies, McKnight Theater Artist Grants. Members may apply for all programs and participate in special activities, including classes, outreach programs, and PlayLabs. **Dues:** $75 local individual, $30 student/senior, $40 low-income member, $40 member over 100 miles. **Contact:** Polly Carl, Executive Director; Kristen Gandrow, Director of New Play Development.

POETRY SOCIETY OF AMERICA
15 Gramercy Park, New York, NY 10003. 212-254-9628. www.poetrysociety.org.
Mission: Seeks to raise awareness of poetry, to deepen understanding of it, and to
encourage more people to read, listen to, and write poetry. **Member Benefits:**
Presents more than 40 readings and events across the country each year, and places
posters on buses and subways through "Poetry in Motion®." Also offers annual contests for poetry, Chapbook Fellowship Programs, poetry festivals, and publishes a
biannual journal. **Dues:** $45 ($25 for students). **Contact:** Alice Quinn, Executive
Director; Brett Lauer, Poetry in Motion Director & Programs Associate.

POETS & WRITERS
72 Spring St., New York, NY 10012. 212-226-3586. www.pw.org. **Mission:** Fosters
the professional development of poets and fiction writers and promotes communication throughout the literary community. Also publishes *Poets & Writers* magazine
(which contains information on markets for writers) and A *Directory of American
Poets and Fiction Writers*, and supports readings and writing workshops at varied
venues. **Contact:** Elliot Figman, Executive Director.

PUBLICATION RIGHTS CLEARINGHOUSE
National Writers Union, 113 University Pl., Fl. 6, New York, NY 10003. 212-254-
0279. prc@nwu.org. www.nwu.org. **Mission:** The collective-licensing agency of the
National Writers Union created in 1996 to help writers license and collect royalties
for the reuse of their published works in electronic databases and other media.
Modeled after similar organizations in the music industry. Writers license non-exclusive secondary rights to the PRC; the PRC licenses those rights to secondary users
and distributes payment to writers. **Membership Requirements:** Enrollment is
free and is open to both NWU members and non-members. **Contact:** Dian Killian,
Director.

ROMANCE WRITERS OF AMERICA
16000 Stuebner Airline, Suite 140, Spring, TX 77379. 832-717-5200. info@rwana-
tional.org. www.rwanational.org. **Mission:** Nonprofit organization for published or
unpublished writers interested in the field of romantic fiction. **Member Benefits:**
Offers conferences, and awards: RITA (for published romance novels), Golden Heart
(for unpublished manuscripts). **Dues:** $75/year. **Contact:** Charis Calhoon,
Commmunications Manager.

SCIENCE FICTION AND FANTASY WRITERS OF AMERICA
P.O. Box 877, Chestertown, MD 21620. execdir@sfwa.org. www.sfwa.org. **Mission:**
Promotes the professional interests of science fiction and fantasy writers.
Membership Requirements: Open to any writer who has sold a work of science
fiction or fantasy. Write for application. **Member Benefits:** Presents annual Nebula
Award for excellence in the field; publishes the "Bulletin" and "SFWA Handbook" for
members (also available to non-members). **Dues:** $50 (active), $35 ("affiliate"), plus
$10 installation fee. **Contact:** Jane Jewell, Executive Director.

SISTERS IN CRIME

P.O. Box 442124, Lawrence, KS 66044-8933. sistersincrime@juno.com. www.sistersincrime.org. **Mission:** Fights discrimination against women in the mystery field, educates publishers and the public about inequalities in the treatment of female authors, and increases awareness of their contribution to the field. **Membership Requirements:** Open (writers, editors, booksellers, librarians, etc.). **Member Benefits:** Quarterly newsletter and *Books in Print* membership directory. **Dues:** $35 (U.S.), $40 (foreign). **Contact:** Beth Wasson, Executive Secretary.

SOCIETY OF AMERICAN TRAVEL WRITERS

1500 Sunday Dr., Suite 102, Raleigh, NC 27607. 919-861-5586. nshore@satw.org. www.satw.org. **Mission:** Represents writers and other professionals who strive to provide travelers with accurate reports on destinations, facilities, and services. **Membership Requirements:** Active membership limited to travel writers and freelancers with a steady volume of published or distributed work about travel. **Dues:** $130/yr (active), $250/yr (associate). Application fees: $250 (active), $500 (associate). **Contact:** Nicole Shore, Membership Director.

SOCIETY OF CHILDREN'S BOOK WRITERS & ILLUSTRATORS

8271 Beverly Blvd., Los Angeles, CA 90048. 323-782-1010. scbwi@scbwi.org. www.scbwi.org. **Mission:** National organization of authors, editors, publishers, illustrators, librarians, and educators; for beginners and established professionals alike. **Membership Requirements:** Full memberships open to anyone who has had at least one children's book or story published. Associate memberships open to all interested in children's literature. **Member Benefits:** Referrals, conferences, grants program. Also annual awards: Golden Kite Book Award, Magazine Merit Award. **Dues:** $60/year. **Contact:** Lin Oliver, Executive Director.

SOCIETY OF ENVIRONMENTAL JOURNALISTS

P.O. Box 2492, Jenkintown, PA 19046. 215-884-8174. sej@sej.org. www.sej.org. **Mission:** Dedicated to improving the quality, accuracy, and visibility of environmental reporting. **Member Benefits:** Serves 1,300 members and the journalism community with quarterly *SEJournal*, annual and regional conferences, EJToday news digest service, TipSheet, Watchdog TipSheet, comprehensive website, journalism awards, mentor programs, and online membership directory. **Dues:** $40, $30 (student). **Contact:** Beth Parke, Executive Director.

SOCIETY OF PROFESSIONAL JOURNALISTS

3909 N Meridian St., Indianapolis, IN 46208. 317-927-8000. spj@spj.org. www.spj.org. **Mission:** Serves the interests of print, broadcast, and wire journalists (10,000+ members and 300 chapters). Also promotes ethical reporting. **Member Benefits:** Journalists' legal defense fund, freedom of information resources, professional development seminars, and awards. Members receive *Quill*, a magazine on current issues in the field. **Dues:** $72 (professional), $36 (student). **Contact:** Terrence G. Harper, Executive Director.

THE SONGWRITERS GUILD OF AMERICA

1560 Broadway, Suite 1306, New York, NY 10036. songnews@aol.com. www.song-writersguild.com. **Member Benefits:** Provides published and unpublished songwriters with sample contracts, contract review, and a service that collects royalties from publishers. Additionally, SGA offers group health and life insurance plans, conducts workshops and critique sessions, and provides newsletters. **Dues:** $70 (associate membership), $85 and up (full membership).

THEATRE COMMUNICATIONS GROUP

520 Eighth Ave., Fl. 24, New York, NY 10018-4156. 212-609-5900. tcg@tcg.org. www.tcg.org. **Mission:** National organization seeking to increase organizational efficiency of member theatres, encourage artistic talent and achievement, and promote greater public appreciation for the theatre field. **Member Benefits:** Offers a wide array of services to strengthen, nurture, and promote the not-for-profit American theatre (artistic and management programs, advocacy activities, International programs and publications). Individual members receive *American Theatre* magazine. **Dues:** $35 (individual). **Contact:** Terence Nemeth, Vice President.

WESTERN WRITERS OF AMERICA

1012 Fair St., Franklin, TN 37064. 615-791-1444. tncrutch@aol.com. www.western-writers.org. **Mission:** Promotes distribution, readership, and appreciation of the West and its literature. **Membership Requirements:** Open to professional writers of fiction and nonfiction on the history and literature of the American West. **Member Benefits:** Annual convention last week of June. Sponsors annual Spur Awards and Owen Wister Award for published work and produced screenplays. **Dues:** $75/year. **Contact:** James A. Crutchfield, Secretary/Treasurer/Managing Editor.

WRITERS GUILD OF AMERICA (WGA), EAST

555 W 57th St., Suite 1230, New York, NY 10019-2967. 212-767-7806. www.wgaeast.org. **Mission:** Represents writers in motion pictures, broadcast, cable and new media industries, including news and entertainment. **Membership Requirements:** To qualify for membership, a writer must meet requirements for employment or sale of material. **Dues:** $25/quarter + 1.5% of earnings. Also, quarterly dues based on percentage of the member's earnings in any of the fields over which the guild has jurisdiction. Initiation fee: $1,500 for WGAE (writers living east of the Mississippi), $2,500 for WGAW (for those west of the Mississippi). **Contact:** Mona Mangan, Executive Director.

WRITERS GUILD OF AMERICA (WGA), WEST

7000 W 3rd St., Los Angeles, CA 90048. 323-951-4000. www.wga.org. **Mission:** Represents writers in motion pictures, broadcast, cable and new media industries, including news and entertainment. **Membership Requirements:** To qualify for membership, a writer must meet requirements for employment or sale of material. **Member Benefits:** Publishes *Written By*, an official publication for screen and television writers. **Dues:** $25/quarter + 1.5% of earnings. Also, quarterly dues based on percentage of the member's earnings in any of the fields over which the guild has jurisdiction. Initiation fee: $1,500 for WGAE (writers living east of the Mississippi), $2,500 for WGAW (for those west of the Mississippi). **Contact:** Victoria Risken, President.

WRITERS INFORMATION NETWORK (WIN)

Professional Assn. for Christian Writers, P.O. Box 11337, Bainbridge Island, WA 98110. 206-842-9103. writersinfonetwork@juno.com. www.christianwritersinfo.net. **Mission:** Provides a link between Christian writers and the religious publishing industry. **Membership Requirements:** Submit resumé or biographical sketch with application. Go to website to download membership application. **Member Benefits:** Offers professional development in writing, marketing, and speaking. Also publishes the *WIN-INFORMER*, a magazine reporting on CBA industry news and trends. **Dues:** $40/year. **Contact:** Elaine Wright Colvin, Founder/Director.

SYNDICATES

Syndicates buy material from writers and artists to sell to newspapers all over the country and the world. Authors are paid either a percentage of the gross proceeds or an outright fee. Of course, features by people well known in their fields have the best chance of being syndicated. In general, syndicates want columns that have been popular in a local newspaper or magazine. Since most syndicated fiction has been published previously in magazines or books, beginning fiction writers should try to sell their stories to magazines before submitting them to syndicates.

Always query syndicates before sending manuscripts, since their needs change frequently, and be sure to enclose SASEs with queries and manuscripts.

AGEVENTURE NEWS SERVICE

Demko Publishing, 19432 Preserve Dr., Boca Raton, FL 33498. 561-482-6271. editor@demko.com. www.demko.com. **Description:** AgeVenture presents work to international audience of 3 million readers in 29 countries. Topics must address baby-boomer and retiree concerns. Submissions should be between 250-500 words; specify costs for use at time of submission. 25% freelance written. Submit manuscripts, 200-500 words, as e-mail text (no attached files).

AMERICAN PRESS SERVICE

P.O. Box 917, Van Nuys, CA 91408. 818-997-6497. iscs1assoc@aol.com. **Description:** Features on all subjects especially arts, entertainment, hobbies, and books. Query with SASE. **Contact:** Israel I. Bick, VP/Senior Editor.

AMPERSAND COMMUNICATIONS

2311 S Bayshore Dr., Miami, FL 33133-4728. 305-285-2200. amprsnd@aol.com. www.ampersandcom.com. **Description:** Feature material for online use, and for newspapers, magazines, and special-interest publications. Sells content to end-users directly and through marketing agreements with other online syndication services. Topics include: book reviews, business, medicine and health, business travel, pets, cooking, food/wine, senior lifestyles, environmental issues, timesharing and vacation ownership, home improvement, travel. 5% freelance written. Query or send manuscript, 800-1,000 words. **Tips:** "We are most interested in receiving freelance submissions for our business travel column."

ASK THE BUILDER

3166 N Farmcrest Dr., Cincinnati, OH 45213-1112. 513-531-9229. tim@askthebuilder.com. www.askthebuilder.com. **Description:** Features articles on residential building and remodeling. Submit electronic press-release or product information via e-mail; lead with a 100-word (max.) summary of the press release. Color images for the *Ask the Builder* e-zine should be in GIF or JPEG format (width: 250 pixels; height: proportional; resolution: 72 dpi; send as email attachment). **Tips:** Only submit news and information if it is relevant to home building and remodeling. **Contact:** Tim Carter.

BUDDY BASCH FEATURE SYNDICATE

720 West End Avenue, No. 1216, New York, NY 10025-6299. 212-666-2300. **Description:** Pieces on entertainment, travel, human interest, science and medical, food. Accepts little·freelance. Query or send complete manuscript; include SASE.

CONTINENTAL FEATURES/CONTINENTAL NEWS SERVICE

501 W Broadway, Plaza A, P.M.B. #265, San Diego, CA 92101. 858-492-8696. continentalnewstime@lycos.com. www.continentalnewsservice.com. **Description:** Seeks economic/political/social summary analysis articles on foreign nation(s). Also, columns on U.S. business and finance news/issues. Writer should query or submit photocopy samples of writing if speciality is different from topics listed above. Include three references or three letters of recommendation with clips. 700-800 word maximum. Payment is 70% of gross newspaper/feature sales proceeds. **Tips:** No horoscope/astrology pieces. **Contact:** Gary P. Salamone.

COPLEY NEWS SERVICE

Box 120190, San Diego, CA 92112. 619-293-1818. infofax@copleynews.com. www.copleynews.com. **Description:** Features columns on music, books, cars, fashion, films, sports, gardening, home improvement, and other special interests. 1,500 subscribers. Query with clips. 75% freelance written. **Tips:** "The market is tight at the moment and we are buying very little. Still, we like to know what is available in case there is a change in our lineup." **Contact:** Glenda Winders, Editorial Director.

HISPANIC LINK NEWS SERVICE

1420 N St. NW, Washington, DC 20005. 202-234-0280. charles@hispaniclink.org. **Description:** Trend articles, opinion and personal experience pieces, and general features with Hispanic focus, 650-700 words; editorial cartoons. Pays $25 for op-ed columns and cartoons, on acceptance. **Tips:** Send SASE for guidelines.

HOLLYWOOD INSIDE SYNDICATE

P.O. Box 49957, Los Angeles, CA 90049. 818-509-7840. holywood@ez2.net. www.ez2.net/hollywood. **Description:** Short pieces on world-class celebrities, or column-type items for internationally syndicated "Hollywood Inside" column.

KING FEATURES SYNDICATE

888 Seventh Ave., New York, NY 10019. 212-455-4000. kfscartoonists@hearst.com. www.kingfeatures.com. **Description:** Columns, comics. Does not buy individual articles; looking for ideas for nationally syndicated columns. Submit cover letter, 6 sample columns of 650 words each, bio sheet and any additional clips, and SASE. No simultaneous submissions. Send SASE for guidelines. **Contact:** Glenn Mott, Managing Editor.

MOTOR NEWS MEDIA CORP.

7177 Hickman Rd., Suite 11D, P.O. Box 7543, Urbandale, IA 50322-7543. 515-270-6782. mnmedia@qwest.net. www.motornewsmedia.com. **Description:** New or unique automotive stories and features. Automotive reviews not needed. 30% free-lance written. Please contact prior to sending manuscript; unsolicited manuscripts are not encouraged. If requested, send manuscript (650-800 words) by mail with sample, print references, and SASE. Pays $125/feature.

NATIONAL GAY LESBIAN
BISEXUAL TRANSGENDER TRAVEL DESK

2790 Wrondel Way, PMB #444, Reno, NV 89502. 775-348-7990. nglbtraveldesk@aol.com. **Description:** Looking for "rookie" travel writers to write only about cities in their state. Also looking for stringers for national gay/lesbian guidebook to North America. Send e-mail to editors with author bio. Articles run 1,200-2,400 words. 80% freelance. Pays $25/story. **Tips:** "You must get a local gay/lesbian newspaper in your area to accept stories and then we will give you assignments. We prefer people who travel rather than those who have experience."

NATIONAL NEWS BUREAU

P.O. Box 43039, Philadelphia, PA 19129. 215-849-9016. nnbfeature@aol.com. www.nationalnewsbureau.com. **Description:** Articles, 500-1,500 words, celebrity interviews, consumer news, how-tos, travel pieces, reviews, entertainment pieces, features, etc. Include resumé and SASE with submission. 60% freelance written. Pays on publication.

NEW DIMENSIONS WORLD BROADCASTING NETWORK

P.O. Box 569, Ukiah, CA 95482. 707-468-5215. info@newdimensions.org. www.newdimensions.org. **Description:** Programming presents a diversity of views from many different traditions and cultures, and strives to provide listeners with prac-tical knowledge and perennial wisdom. New Dimensions fosters living a more healthy life of mind, body and spirit while deepening connections to self, family, community, the natural world and the planet. No unsolicited manuscripts; query first. **Tips:** "We're a social profit, public benefit, tax-exempt, educational organization."

NEW YORK TIMES SYNDICATION SALES

122 E 42nd St., Fl. 14, New York, NY 10168. 212-499-3300/800-972-3550. nytsf@nytimes.com. www.nytimes.com/syndicate. **Description:** Articles on interna-tional, seasonal, health, lifestyle, and entertainment topics, to 1,500 words (previously published or unpublished). Query with published article or tear sheet and SASE. No calls please. Pays 50% royalty on collected sales.

NEWSPAPER ENTERPRISE ASSOCIATION/
UNITED FEATURE SYNDICATE

200 Madison Ave., Fl. 4, New York, NY 10016. 212-293-8500/800-221-4816. www.unitedfeatures.com. **Description:** National features and columns on news, pol-itics, sports, business, entertainment, and lifestyles, for over 600 daily newspapers. Payment varies. **Tips:** Send submissions c/o Submissions Editor. See website for guidelines.

TRIBUNE MEDIA SERVICES

435 N Michigan Ave., Suite 1400, Chicago, IL 60611. tms@tribune.com. www.tmsfeatures.com. **Description:** Continuing columns, comic strips, features, editorial cartoons, puzzles, and word games. Query with clips. Responds in 6-8 weeks. Guidelines available at www.comicspage.com. **Contact:** Submissions Editor.

TRIBUNE MEDIA SERVICES INTERNATIONAL

202 W First St., Fl. 10, Los Angeles, CA 90012. www.tmsinternational.com. **Description:** Commentary, features, columns, editorial cartoons, comics, puzzles and games; news services and online products. See website for submission guidelines.

WHITEGATE FEATURES SYNDICATE

71 Faunce Dr., Providence, RI 02906. 401-274-2149. 102404.574@compuserve.com. www.whitegatefeatures.com. **Description:** Newspaper syndicate serving newspapers and magazines across the country and around the world. Send photocopies only and do not include SASE; editor will contact if interested. Include bio along with list of ideas. **Tips:** "Always looking for good writing, great drawings, and new, fresh material." **Contact:** Eve Green or Mari Howard.

WRITING PROGRAMS

BOSTON UNIVERSITY

Master of Arts Program, 236 Bay State Road, Boston, MA 02215. 617-252-2510. Website: www.bu.edu/writing/. **Description:** One-year intensive program, with competitive admission; small, quality workshops, and a widely recognized faculty and alumni. **Admission requirements:** Manuscript (writing sample) and GRE scores. **Application Deadline:** March 1. **Sample coursework:** Courses available in four major fields of concentration: fiction, creative nonfiction, cinema/TV/drama, and poetry. **Scholarships and Fellowships:** Full-tuition scholarships and teaching fellowships are available. **Additional information:** Graduates of this program have received numerous awards, fellowships, and teaching positions, and many have spent time on best-seller lists. Faculty and alumni include Nobel Laureates and Poet Laureates. **Program director/coordinator:** Leslie Epstein.

CHAPMAN UNIVERSITY

MFA Program, One University Dr., Orange, CA 92866. 716-997-6711. E-mail: engdept@chapman.edu. Website: www.chapman.edu. **Description:** 60 unit, 3-year program with classes evenly divided between writing and literature. Students choose emphasis in fiction, poetry, or scriptwriting, and will write a thesis project and defend it before a committee. **Admission requirements:** A cumulative GPA of 3.0 or better in the final 60 units of undergraduate study, or GRE scores of 470 (Verbal section) and 4.5 (Analytical Writing section) with a cumulative GPA of 2.5 or better. Students must submit a portfolio of written work, preferably including prose fiction and letters of recommendation. **Application Deadline:** Rolling deadline, but advised to apply as early as possible. **Sample coursework:** Coursework varies, but typically involves a wide scope of reading material and writing/revising new material. Work is assessed and discussed against a common background of illustrative literature and commonly held knowledge of the craft. Some teachers assign specific topics for writing assignments, but in workshop classes students are generally encouraged to write as they choose. **Scholarships and Fellowships:** All prospective students are automatically considered for graduate fellowships, but encourgaged to apply early for timely consideration. Fellowships are essentially tuition remission fellowships that continue for a period of 3 years. **Additional information:** See website or contact the Office of Graduate Admissions. Applications are considered on the basis of students' entire admission portfolio. **Program director/coordinator:** Jim Blaylock.

EASTERN WASHINGTON UNIVERSITY

Creative Writing Program, 705 W First Ave., Spokane, WA 99201. 509-623-4221. Website: www.creativewriting.ewu.edu. **Description:** The MFA program is an intensive, 2-year, pre-professional course of study with an emphasis on the practice of literature as a fine art. Students concentrate on poetry, fiction, or literary nonfiction. The MFA is a terminal degree program. **Admission requirements:** GRE scores, writing sample of 10-20 pages of poetry and/or 15-25 pages of prose, application form,

800-word letter stating the applicant's reasons for pursuing the MFA, and two letters of reference. Applicants for teaching assistantships must write an additional letter in which they describe their interest in and prior experience in teaching. **Application Deadline:** March 1 for teaching assistantship. **Sample coursework:** Coursework in the study of literature from the vantage point of its composition and history, but the students' principle work is done in advanced workshops and in the writing of a book-length thesis of publishable quality in fiction, creative nonfiction, or poetry. **Scholarships and Fellowships:** Teaching assistantships and non-resident tuition waivers available. **Additional information:** Minimum total credits for MFA is 72 credits. Students expected to take coursework in areas outside their concentration. **Program director/coordinator:** Lynn Ellis

EMERSON COLLEGE

Master of Arts in Publishing and Writing, 120 Boylston Street, Boston, MA 02116. 617-824-8750. Website: http://www.emerson.edu/writing_lit_publishing/ **Description:** Program is designed to meet the needs of students who are interested in pursuing careers in publishing or as writers or professionals in a writing-related field. Courses in book, magazine and electronic publishing, fiction and nonfiction writing, and in literature and criticism. Internship and apprenticeship opportunities are available through the program in Boston publishing and production firms and advertising agencies. **Admission requirements:** Bachelor's degree from an accredited institution, a GPA of 3.0 or better, GRE scores, creative or nonfiction writing sample, personal statement. **Application Deadline:** January 5 for fall admission. **Sample coursework:** Offers courses in magazine and book publishing, ethics, editing, design and production, desktop publishing, and writing. **Scholarships and Fellowships:** One Presidential Fellowship is awarded to an incoming student. Some merit aid is available in the form of teaching assistantships. A Bookbuilder's Scholarship is awarded to students currently in the program. **Additional information:** While professional experience in publishing is not required, such experience adds favorably to an applicant's potential admission. A display of interest or involvement in publishing on some level—whether professional or on campus—is desirable. **Program director/coordinator:** Jeffrey L. Seglin

MANHATTANVILLE COLLEGE

Master of Arts in Writing Program, 2900 Purchase Street, Purchase, NY 10577. 914-694-3425. E-mail: dowdr@mville.edu. Website: www.mville.edu. **Description:** The 32-credit program is intended for experienced and aspiring writers seeking to explore the craft of writing and improve their skills in fiction, nonfiction and poetry while also deepening their knowledge of the humanities. Program may be completed in as little as two years and is ideal for working professionals and adult students. **Admission requirements:** Bachelor's degree from an accredited college or university, writing sample, and demonstrated potential in writing and critical thinking. **Application Deadline:** Rolling admission. **Sample coursework:** The core courses are offered in fiction, poetry, and creative nonfiction. Elective topics include the contemporary novel, writing for children, and screenwriting. **Scholarships and Fellowships:** A

Graduate Fellowship is awarded to an advanced student selected to be the editor of *Inkwell*, Manhattanville's literary journal. **Additional information:** Courses are scheduled in the evenings and during the day. There are also week-long and weekend workshops offered during the summer and fall and a calendar of inspiring lectures and readings throughout the year. Manhattanville College has a thriving literary community of published and aspiring writers. Courses and workshops are taught by distinguished authors and editors. **Program director/coordinator:** Ruth Dowd.

MINNESOTA STATE UNIVERSITY

MFA Creative Writing Program, 230 Armstrong Hall, Mankato, MN 56001. 507-389-2117. Website: www.english.mnsu.edu. **Description:** Combines a studio/workshop and academic program of study that prepares students for a variety of careers. **Admission requirements:** Applicants must have the equivalent of an English minor. **Application Deadline:** Rolling deadline. Apply by February 1 for teaching assistantships. **Sample coursework:** Writing workshops, form and technique courses, contemporary genre courses, career-related courses, and literature courses, in addition to writing a thesis. **Scholarships and Fellowships:** The Robert Wright scholarship offers modest support for tuition and books to three winners. Teaching assistantships also available. **Additional information:** "The MFA program in creative writing meets the needs of students who want to strike a balance between the development of individual creative talent and the close study of literature and language. Candidates in the program will find it appropriate training for careers in freelancing, college-level teaching, editing and publishing, arts administration, and several other areas." (quoted from website) **Program director/coordinator:** Richard Robbins.

NEW YORK UNIVERSITY

Graduate Program in Creative Writing, 19 University Place, Rm. 219, New York, NY 10003. 212-998-8816. Website: http://cwp.fas.nyu.edu/page/home. **Description:** Students have option of MA in English with creative writing focus or MFA in creative writing. Both programs are designed to be completed in two years and require successful completion of 32 credits as well as a creative thesis in either fiction or poetry. **Admission requirements:** Writing sample (25 pages for fiction applicants, 10 pages for poetry applicants), three letters of recommendation, statement of purpose, current resumé, two official copies of transcripts from previous institutions attended, GRE scores, and $75 application fee. **Application Deadline:** It is recommended that students apply by December 15; final deadline of January 4. No extensions for any portion of the application. **Sample coursework:** Workshops/seminars in poetry and fiction. Coursework encompasses both examination/anaylsis of these forms of writing as well as drafting original material. **Scholarships and Fellowships:** Full or partial departmental fellowships consisting of tuition remission and/or stipend support. Some fellowship support is available through outreach programs and teaching opportunities. All students are also considered for several *New York Times* fellowships. **Program director/coordinator:** Russell Carmony.

SPALDING UNIVERSITY

Brief Residency MFA in Writing Program
851 S Fourth St., Louisville, KY 40203. 502-585-9911.
Website: www.spalding.edu/mfa. **Description:** The program consists of 4 semesters and 5 residencies. Students attend intensive 10-day residencies in the spring/fall and correspond with faculty mentors for the rest of the semester. Areas of concentration: fiction, poetry, creative nonfiction, writing for children, screenwriting, playwriting. Students have the opportunity to minor in a second area. **Admission requirements:** Writing sample, personal essay, letters of recommendation, and application form and fee. **Application Deadline:** February 15 for spring and July 15 for fall. **Sample Coursework:** During the residency students participate in workshops, panel discussions, and faculty/student/guest readings. Workshops focus on specific genres, but there is the opportunity to experiment with other modes of writing. During the home phase, students send instructors packets of mostly original creative writing, questions about the craft of writing, and short essays commenting on the individualized reading list. The mentor responds with constructive criticism, comments, and suggestions for revision or further reading. Students also exchange ideas with other students. **Scholarships and Fellowships:** Scholarships, graduate assistantships, and financial aid available. **Additional information:** See website or call for more information. **Program director/coordinator:** Sena Jeter Naslund.

UNIVERSITY OF NEW MEXICO

Creative Writing Program and Professional Writing Program.
MSC 03 2170, Albuquerque, NM 87131. 505-277-6248.
Website: www.unm.edu/~english. **Description:** These programs foster the creation of literary art by requiring students to develop a critical understanding of the literary tradition and to engage in an intensive study of the art and craft of writing publishable works of fiction, poetry, and creative nonfiction. The coursework also offers pre-professional preparation for employment in a variety of fields (writing, secondary and post-secondary teaching, corporate communications). **Admission requirements:** Letter of intent, transcripts from all post-secondary schools attended, writing sample, three letters of recommendation, and GRE scores. **Application Deadline:** February 1. **Sample coursework:** A minimum of 34 hours of coursework and submission of a book-length thesis of original poems, fiction, creative nonfiction, or the equivalent for technical or professional writing. The thesis will be defended in an oral examination conducted by the program's thesis committee. **Scholarships and Fellowships:** Teaching Assistantships, Poets & Writers Assistantship, Blue Mesa Review Editorial Assistantship, Taos Conference Assistantship. **Additional information:** Applications for teaching assistantships accepted for fall semester only. Creative writing candidates applying for teaching assistantships must also submit a sample of their critical writing. **Program director/coordinator:** Sharon Oard Warner.

UNIVERSITY OF NORTH CAROLINA

MFA Program, 134 McIver Building, UNCG, P.O. Box 26170, Greensboro, NC 27402-6170. Website: www.uncg.edu/eng/mfa. **Description:** Two-year residency program providing students with studio time in which to study the writing of poetry or fiction. The program's flexibility permits students to develop their particular talents through small classes in writing, literature, and the arts. Students read and comment on each other's work under the guidance of resident and visiting faculty, who also meet with students in one-on-one tutorials. **Admission requirements:** Applicants must meet requirements of The Graduate School, including a satisfactory score on the GRE. Admission is competitive and based primarily on the applicant's ability and potential as a writer. The writing sample (8-10 pages of poetry or 30 pages of fiction) must be sent in addition to the formal application. **Application Deadline:** February 1. **Sample coursework:** Courses are designed for full-time residential students and require 36 hours of coursework. 12-18 credits in writing courses required, including workshop courses. At least four courses must be taken in a related academic field. Editing and teaching courses are also available. Students also complete a thesis. **Scholarships and Fellowships:** Research and teaching assistantships, fellowhips, and out-of-state tuition waivers are available. **Additional information:** The MFA Writing Program publishes *The Greensboro Review*, and hosts a number of visiting writers. **Program directory/coordinator:** Jim Clark.

UNIVERSITY OF SOUTHERN CALIFORNIA

Master of Professional Writing Program, WPH 404, Los Angeles, CA 90089-4034. 213-740-3252. E-mail: mpw@usc.edu. Web site: http://www.usc.edu/dept/LAS/mpw/. **Description:** 30-unit, multi-disciplinary program that prepares students for careers in writing in all genres (fiction, nonfiction, poetry, playwriting, screenwriting). The program focuses on theory, techniques, structures, disciplines, and markets. Each class is taught in an intimate workshop (8-12 students). **Admission requirements:** Bachelor's degree from an accredited college or university with a minimum GPA of 3.0, GRE scores, 10-page writing sample, and three letters of recommendation. **Application Deadline:** Rolling admission. **Sample coursework:** Courses available in four major fields of concentration: fiction, creative nonfiction, cinema/TV/drama, and poetry. **Scholarships and Fellowships:** Variety of merit scholarshsips available. Applications are competitive and are based upon previous academic, publishing, and professional performance. **Additional information:** One of the oldest and most distinguished writing programs in the nation, the USC professional writing program has a celebrated faculty and curriculum in novel, film, TV, drama, poetry, and nonfiction. **Program director/coordinator:** James Ragan.

WESTERN MICHIGAN UNIVERSITY

Creative Writing Program, 1903 Michigan Avenue, Kalamazoo, MI 49008. 269-387-2572. Website: www.wmich.edu/english. **Description:** MFA program for students who wish to become professional writers of fiction, poetry, drama, creative nonfiction. Completion of program qualifies students to teach at the college/university level. **Admission requirements:** Applications (Graduate College and departmental), 34-hour undergraduate major with a GPA of at least 3.0 (with at least 20 hours of literature courses), GRE scores, writing sample, creative portfolio, statement of purpose, and three letters of recommendation. **Application Deadline:** February 1. **Sample coursework:** The program requires 42 s/hours of courses in writing, literature, and literary theory, and an MFA project of 6 s/hrs (an original book-length work of fiction, poetry, drama, or nonfiction). Workshops provide for much independent work, individual instruction and practical experience in criticism and rewriting, and well as the challenge and inspiration of work with and for one's peers. **Scholarships and Fellowships:** Teaching assistantships and fellowships. Teaching Assistants teach two or three sections of introductory composition each year and receive tuition remission, a salary/stipend, and health insurance. **Additional information:** Western Michigan University also offers a Ph.D. in English with Creative Writing emphasis. **Program director/coordinator:** Jil Larson.

WEST VIRGINIA UNIVERSITY

Creative Writing Program, P.O. Box 6296, Morgantown, WV 26506-6296. 304-293-3107. Website: www.as.wvu.edu/english/. **Description:** 45-hour program including creative writing workshops, graduate level English courses, and a thesis. **Admission requirements:** Admission is based primarily on writing sample, but applicants must also submit GRE scores, letters of recommendation, and a personal statement. **Application Deadline:** February 1. **Sample coursework:** Students take writing workshops, literature course, and courses on theory and cultural studies. **Scholarships and Fellowships:** All admitted students receive graduate teaching assistantships. **Program director/coordinator:** James Harms.

MAIN INDEX

CONTEST INDEX